COLD WAR AMERICA
1946 to 1990

COLD WAR AMERICA
1946 to 1990

Ross Gregory

Richard Balkin
General Editor

Facts On File
An imprint of Infobase Publishing

Cold War America, 1946 to 1990

Facts On File, Inc.
An imprint of Infobase Publishing
132 West 31st Street
New York NY 10001

ISBN-13: 978-0-8160-3868-8
ISBN-10: 0-8160-3868-6

Library of Congress Cataloging-in-Publication Data
Gregory, Ross.
    Cold War America, 1946 to 1990/Ross Gregory.
        p. cm.—(Almanacs of American life)
    ISBN 0-8160-3868-6 (hardcover)
    1. United States—History—1945. 2. United States—Social conditions—1945. 3. Cold War—Social aspects—United States. I. Title. II. Series.
    E741 .G76 2002
    973.92—dc21   2001051136

Facts On File books are available at special discounts when purchased in bulk quantities for businesses, associations, institutions, or sales promotions. Please call our Special Sales Department in New York at (212) 967-8800 or (800) 322-8755.

You can find Facts On File on the World Wide Web at http://www.factsonfile.com

Text design by Fred Pusterla
Cover design by Cathy Rincon
Maps and graphs by Dale Williams, Jeremy Eagle, and Sholto Ainslie

Printed in the United States of America

VB Hermitage 10 9 8 7 6 5 4

This book is printed on acid-free paper.

For

Shirley, Theresa, Graham, Darren, and Danielle

Note on Photos

Many of the illustrations and photographs used in this book are old, historical images. The quality of the prints is not always up to modern standards, as in some cases the originals are damaged. The content of the illustrations, however, made their inclusion important despite problems in reproduction.

Contents

List of Maps

Preface

The title, *Cold War America,* is not intended to suggest that the volume contains a history of the cold war, with focus on international relations and military considerations. The purpose, instead, is to examine aspects of life in the United States during the years of the cold war—which one can reasonably identify as the 45 (really 46) years following the Second World War. The timeline carries a conclusion that a genuine fissure developed between the United States and the Soviet Union almost immediately following the end of the world conflict and, on the other end, that virtually all the forces proclaiming an end to the cold war, except for dismantlement of the USSR, were in place by the year 1990. To be sure, diplomatic and military affairs were exceptionally important during these years. They constituted a life-and-death proposition for millions of military people (and for many thousands, the outcome was death). The nation, and indeed the world as a whole, faced the prospect of utter destruction. The fact that the world survived more or less intact should not suggest that the danger had not existed. For whatever reason, perhaps it was the weapons themselves, the nation and the world was spared a nuclear holocaust and life went on, influenced—sometimes blatantly, sometimes subtly—by the continuing tension but also following the needs, wishes, and aspirations of an ever-changing American populace. It is the purpose of this volume to describe the course of society and its constituent parts, at least the major ones—to measure direction and change during the years 1946 to 1990.

Such an understanding of course must be multifaceted, requiring attention to themes and subthemes too numerous for a short introduction. The reach and dimension, however, can be suggested in a few broad categories. American society in the post–Second World War period was striking in sheer size and scope. The population grew by 100 million people and the economy came to be measured not in billions but trillions of dollars. The knowledge of humankind truly expanded at remarkable speed and the country experienced scientific and technological change that only a few years earlier had been the subject of fantasy: Placing a person on the moon and the emerging computer revolution were two examples. The American population and culture, diverse at the start of the period, underwent a continuously evolving diversification that affected politics, government—virtually all aspects of society. The changes called into question some of the most accepted and honored standards, principles, and institutions in the land.

Needless to say, the information in this study is unique to the period, but organization and structure remains consistent with other volumes in this series. The volume is designed to convey information basic to the period and also material that would be meaningful from the perspective of a few years or even decades later. There is some room for choice in the selection of topics but—hopefully—not in the presentation of data. The numbers must be allowed to fall where they will. The volume offers a multidimensional approach that is concerned with both breadth in the selection of topics and depth in the extent of coverage. It seeks to intermingle tabular arrangements of statistics with introductions, essays, personal profiles, and other forms of discussion, but the basic information is within the data. One cannot acquire a full picture of a subject from a recitation of statistics, but one cannot get an accurate picture without them. Behind every persuasive argument or statement of fact there is, or needs to be, numbers.

People from libraries, museums, government agencies, and my classes who helped me in various ways probably numbered in the dozens. I will not mention names, but I offer them warmest gratitude. There is a small number of people, the closest to me or to the project, whom I do want to mention. Jessica (Grace) Baby gave invaluable help one summer in finding materials on the Internet. Diether H. Haenicke, former president of Western Michigan University, provided a grant that was useful in many ways, especially with illustrations. My daughter, Theresa, helped with computer searches for photographs; my sons, Graham and Darren, helped lead me through the thicket of popular music after the 1960s. At Facts On File Nicole Bowen and Gene Springs were the most cordial and cooperative editors. Two people deserve special thanks: Shirley, my wife, offered more support and patience than I had a right to ask for; free with information about a period she remembers, Shirley remained a wise adviser. Richard Balkin, the series editor, always was on top of things. Continuously generous with ideas and encouragement, Rick helped keep me going.

Ross Gregory
Kalamazoo, Michigan

CHAPTER 1 The Americans: Population and Immigration

The American Population

The fact that first catches one's attention in surveying the American population in the 44 years between 1946 and 1990 is the great growth in numbers: from 141 million to 253 million. In passing the 250 million mark by 1990, the nation had reached these milestones: It had increased its population by 100 million in 40 years (it had taken approximately 140 years to reach the first 100 million); national population had doubled in 60 years and trebled in 90—since the start of the 20th century. Reasons for growth continued to be the two standard ones—birthrate and immigration—and they served to complement each other. The United States experienced a remarkable surge in the birthrate during the first 18 years of the period, the era of the "baby boom," and when the surge halted and a sharp decline set in during the late 1960s, immigration, which had begun to pick up, increased markedly in the 1970s and 1980s. The rate of population growth did slow at the end of the period, but because it was calculated on a large population base, the numbers in absolute terms increased considerably in the 1980s.

Population trends underwent some changes in the era and in other cases extended patterns long under way. After struggling for decades to catch up, the number of females passed males for the first time in 1946. More males continued to be born each year, but a longer life expectancy allowed females to sustain their lead and in most years to add to it. People continued a trend of moving from countryside to city, although the pace of change slowed in the 1970s and 1980s. Directional shifts were to the South and, more strikingly, to the West. California passed New York in the 1960s as the most populous state; it so rapidly extended its lead that by 1990 California stood—in the fashion that New York for decades had done—as clearly the giant of the states. Between 1950 and 1990 California's population increased by more than 19 million, a number larger than the total population of any other state. Two other warm-

TABLE 1.1 ESTIMATED POPULATION (IN THOUSANDS) OF THE UNITED STATES BY SEX AND BY COLOR, 1946–1990

Year	Total	Sex		Color			Males per 100 Females
		Male	Female	White	Nonwhite		
1946	141,389	70,631	70,757	126,565	14,824		. . .
1947	144,126	71,946	72,180	129,059	15,067		. . .
1948	146,631	73,130	73,502	131,308	15,323		. . .
1949	149,188	74,335	74,853	133,598	15,590		. . .
1950	151,684	75,539	76,146	135,814	15,865		98.6
1951	154,287	76,792	77,496	138,049	16,241		. . .
1952	156,954	78,061	78,893	140,344	16,616		. . .
1953	159,565	79,295	80,270	142,073	17,003		. . .
1954	162,391	80,647	81,744	144,891	17,423		. . .
1955	165,275	82,030	83,246	147,428	17,848		. . .
1956	168,221	83,434	84,786	149,923	18,297		. . .
1957	171,274	84,892	86,382	152,512	18,766		. . .
1958	174,141	86,236	87,905	154,922	19,220		. . .
1959	177,830	87,995	89,834	157,655	20,175		. . .
					Black	Other	
1960	180,671	89,320	91,352	160,023	19,066	1,642	97.1
1961	183,691	90,740	92,952	162,533	19,437	1,721	. . .
1962	186,538	92,066	94,472	164,885	19,852	1,801	. . .
1963	189,242	93,303	95,939	167,104	20,255	1,882	. . .
1964	191,889	94,518	97,371	169,257	20,672	1,960	. . .
1965	194,303	95,609	98,694	171,205	21,064	2,034	. . .
1966	196,560	96,620	99,941	172,998	21,434	2,129	. . .
1967	198,712	97,564	101,148	174,695	21,780	2,237	. . .
1968	200,706	98,426	102,280	176,246	22,117	2,343	. . .
1969	202,677	99,287	103,390	177,782	22,431	2,464	. . .
1970	204,879	100,266	104,613	179,491	22,787	2,600	94.8
1971	206,230	100,439	105,791	180,411	23,084	2,725	. . .
1972	208,232	101,450	106,782	181,894	23,465	2,875	. . .
1973	209,851	102,229	107,622	183,032	23,796	3,031	. . .
1974	211,391	102,945	108,446	184,083	24,113	3,193	. . .
1975	213,051	103,723	109,328	185,158	24,436	3,457	. . .
1976	214,669	104,477	110,192	186,227	24,772	3,670	. . .
1977	216,432	105,240	111,092	187,365	25,112	3,865	. . .
1978	218,228	106,120	112,108	188,657	25,487	4,083	. . .
1979	220,099	107,006	113,093	189,968	25,863	4,268	. . .

(continued)

TABLE 1.1   (continued)

Year	Total	Sex		Color			Males per 100 Females
		Male	Female	White	Nonwhite		
					Black	Other	
1980	227,061	110,528	116,533	195,185	26,771	5,150	94.5
1981	229,307	111,423	117,884	196,635	27,133	5,657	...
1982	231,821	112,644	119,177	198,037	27,508	6,039	...
1983	234,023	113,721	120,302	199,420	27,867	6,505	...
1984	236,158	114,765	121,393	200,708	28,212	6,757	...
1985	238,740	116,161	122,579	202,031	28,569	7,324	...
1986	241,078	117,360	123,718	203,430	28,942	7,506	...
1987	243,419	118,539	124,880	204,770	29,325	7,872	...
1988	245,807	119,738	126,069	206,129	29,723	8,256	...
1989	248,240	120,982	127,258	207,540	30,143	8,618	...
1990	252,688	122,431	127,875	209,150	30,620	9,523	95.1

Note: Population estimates vary in accordance with time of year the estimates were made (usually April or July), with revisions that the Census Bureau will make over the years with acquisition of new information, and with differences in the population that is being counted. For the most part the estimates in this table came in July. The categories of Total, Male, and Female during the years 1946–90 and the categories White, Black, and Other during the years 1946–70 included armed forces overseas. For the years 1971–90 the categories White, Black, and Other included armed forces at home but not abroad. After the year 1960 the classification of Other came to mean largely American Indians and Alaska Natives and Asians and Pacific Islanders. Hispanics of course were counted but not given a separate category in this table. Hispanics, so noted the Census Bureau, could belong to any race.

Source: Ben J. Wattenberg, *The Statistical History of the United States, From Colonial Times to the Present* (New York, 1976), 8—a reproduction of the Census Bureau's *Historical Statistics of the United States, Colonial Times to 1970*; Bureau of the Census, *Statistical Abstract of the United States: 1978* (Washington, D.C., 1978), 28; *Statistical Abstract of the United States: 1980* (Washington, D.C., 1980), 28; *Statistical Abstract of the United States: 1987* (Washington, D.C., 1987), 17; *Statistical Abstract of the United States: 1993* (Washington, D.C., 1993), 16–18.

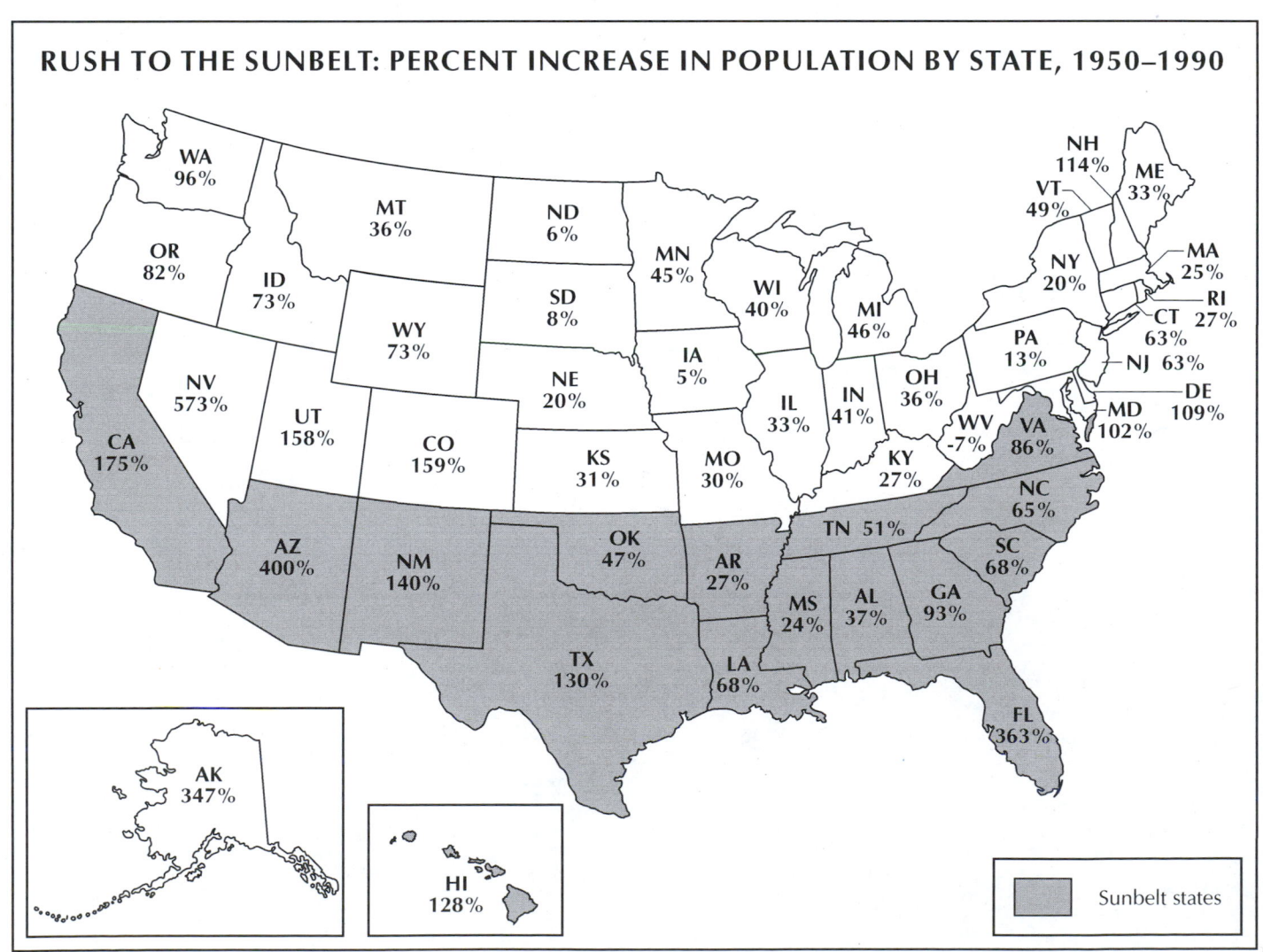

RUSH TO THE SUNBELT: PERCENT INCREASE IN POPULATION BY STATE, 1950–1990

Levittown, Pennsylvania, offered affordable, look-alike suburban mass-produced housing, popular in the immediate postwar period. Pioneer communities built by the Wm. Levitt Company were called Levittowns. (National Archives)

TABLE 1.2 POPULATION DENSITY AND AREA OF RESIDENCEᵃ, 1940–1990

Year	Total Population	Percent Increase	Population per Square Mile	Percent Urban	Percent Rural
1940	131,669,275	7.2	44.2	56.5	43.5
1950	150,697,361	14.5	50.7	64.0	36.0
1960	179,323,175	18.5	50.6	69.9	30.1
1970	203,302,031	13.4	57.4	73.5	26.5
1980	226,545,805	11.4	64.0	73.7	26.3
1990	248,709,873	9.8	70.3	75.2	24.8

ᵃ Resident population only, as of April 1.
Source: John W. Wright, ed., *The New York Times 1998 Almanac* (New York, 1997), 267.

weather states, Florida and Texas, came next in absolute growth. In proportionate terms, Nevada, which increased its population nearly eight times, ranked first, although the numbers remained small. Population of states of the East and Midwest grew slowly, and in the upper Great Plains it grew hardly at all during more than 40 years. One state, West Virginia, lost population between 1946 and 1990.

While the United States continued to be a predominantly white nation at the start of the 1990s, with more than 80 percent of the people identified as Caucasian, trends of the era—especially the 1970s and 1980s—revealed steady and rapid growth in the proportion of people placed in other racial or ethnic classifications. Projections suggested that these trends would accelerate in years to come. If the face of America was changing, so also were its faces.

TABLE 1.3   U.S. RESIDENT POPULATION, BY REGION AND DIVISION, 1960–1990[a]

Region and Division	Population (millions)					Percent Distribution				
	1960	1970	1980	1985	1990	1960	1970	1980	1985	1990
United States	179.3	203.3	226.5	237.9	248.7	100.0	100.0	100.0	100.0	100.0
Northeast	44.7	49.1	49.1	49.9	50.8	24.9	24.1	21.7	21.0	20.4
New England	10.5	11.8	12.3	12.7	13.2	5.9	5.8	5.5	5.4	5.3
Middle Atlantic	34.2	37.2	36.8	37.1	37.6	19.1	18.3	16.2	15.6	15.1
Midwest	51.6	56.6	58.9	58.8	59.7	28.8	27.8	26.0	24.7	24.0
East North Central	36.2	40.3	41.7	41.4	42.0	20.2	19.8	18.4	17.4	16.9
West North Central	15.4	16.3	17.2	17.4	17.7	8.6	8.0	7.6	7.3	7.1
South	55.0	62.8	75.4	81.4	85.4	30.7	30.9	33.3	34.2	34.4
South Atlantic	26.0	30.7	37.0	40.2	43.6	14.5	15.1	16.3	16.9	17.5
East South Central	12.1	12.8	14.7	15.0	15.2	6.7	6.3	6.5	6.3	6.1
West South Central	17.0	19.3	23.7	26.3	26.7	9.5	9.5	10.5	11.0	10.7
West	28.1	34.8	43.2	47.8	52.8	15.6	17.1	19.1	20.1	21.2
Mountain	6.9	8.3	11.4	12.7	13.7	3.8	4.1	5.0	5.4	5.5
Pacific	21.2	26.5	31.8	35.1	39.1	11.8	13.1	14.0	14.7	15.7

[a] Resident population only, as of April 1, except in 1985.
Source: Bureau of Census, *Statistical Abstract 1993,* 23.

TABLE 1.4   UNITED STATES POPULATION BY STATE, 1940–1990

State	1940	1950	1960	1970	1980	1990
Total U.S.	132,164,569	151,325,798	179,323,175	203,302,031	226,542,203	248,709,873
Ala.	2,832,961	3,061,743	3,266,740	3,444,354	3,894,025	4,040,587
Alaska	72,524	128,643	226,167	302,583	401,851	550,043
Ariz.	499,261	749,587	1,302,161	1,775,399	2,716,546	3,665,228
Ark.	1,949,387	1,909,511	1,786,272	1,923,322	2,286,357	2,350,725
Calif.	6,907,387	10,586,223	15,717,204	19,971,069	23,667,764	29,760,021
Colo.	1,123,296	1,325,089	1,753,947	2,209,596	2,889,735	3,294,394
Conn.	1,709,242	2,007,280	2,535,234	3,032,217	3,107,564	3,287,116
Del.	266,505	318,085	446,292	548,104	594,338	666,168
D.C.	663,091	802,178	763,956	756,668	638,432	606,900
Fla.	1,897,414	2,771,305	4,951,560	6,791,418	9,746,961	12,937,926
Ga.	3,123,723	3,444,578	3,943,116	4,587,930	5,462,982	6,478,216
Hawaii	422,770	499,794	632,772	769,913	964,691	1,108,229
Idaho	524,873	588,637	667,191	713,015	944,127	1,006,749
Ill.	7,897,241	8,712,176	10,081,158	11,110,285	11,427,409	11,430,602
Ind.	3,427,796	3,934,224	4,662,498	5,195,392	5,490,214	5,544,159
Iowa	2,538,268	2,621,073	2,757,537	2,825,368	2,913,808	2,776,755
Kans.	1,801,028	1,905,299	2,178,611	2,249,071	2,364,236	2,477,574
Ky.	2,845,627	2,944,806	3,038,156	3,220,711	3,660,324	3,685,296
La.	2,363,880	2,683,516	3,257,022	3,644,637	4,206,116	4,219,973
Maine	847,226	913,774	969,265	993,722	1,125,043	1,227,928
Md.	1,821,244	2,343,001	3,100,689	3,923,897	4,216,933	4,781,468
Mass.	4,316,721	4,690,514	5,148,578	5,689,170	5,737,093	6,016,425
Mich.	5,256,106	6,371,766	7,823,194	8,881,826	9,262,044	9,295,297
Minn.	2,792,300	2,982,483	3,413,864	3,806,103	4,075,970	4,375,099
Miss.	2,183,796	2,178,914	2,178,141	2,216,994	2,520,770	2,573,216
Mo.	3,784,664	3,954,653	4,319,813	4,677,623	4,916,762	5,117,073
Mont.	559,456	591,024	674,767	694,409	786,690	799,065
Nebr.	1,315,834	1,325,510	1,411,330	1,485,333	1,569,825	1,578,385
Nev.	110,247	160,083	285,278	488,738	800,508	1,201,833
N.H.	491,524	533,242	606,921	737,681	920,610	1,109,252
N.J.	4,160,165	4,835,329	6,066,782	7,171,112	7,365,011	7,730,188
N.Mex.	531,818	681,187	951,023	1,017,055	1,303,302	1,515,069
N.Y.	13,479,142	14,830,192	16,782,304	18,241,391	17,558,165	17,990,455
N.C.	3,571,623	4,061,929	4,556,155	5,084,411	5,880,095	6,628,637
N.Dak.	641,935	619,636	632,446	617,792	652,717	638,800
Ohio	6,907,612	7,946,627	9,706,397	10,657,423	10,797,603	10,847,115
Okla.	2,336,434	2,233,351	2,328,284	2,559,463	3,025,487	3,145,585
Oreg.	1,089,684	1,521,341	1,768,687	2,091,533	2,633,156	2,842,321
Pa.	9,900,180	10,498,012	11,319,366	11,800,766	11,864,720	11,881,643
R.I.	713,346	791,896	859,488	949,723	947,154	1,003,464
S.C.	1,899,804	2,117,027	2,382,594	2,590,713	3,120,729	3,486,703

State	1940	1950	1960	1970	1980	1990
S.Dak.	642,961	652,740	680,514	666,257	690,768	696,004
Tenn.	2,915,841	3,291,718	3,567,089	3,926,018	4,591,023	4,877,185
Tex.	6,414,824	7,711,194	9,579,677	11,198,655	14,225,513	16,986,510
Utah	550,310	688,862	890,627	1,059,273	1,461,037	1,722,850
Vt.	359,231	377,747	389,881	444,732	511,456	562,758
Va.	2,677,773	3,318,680	3,966,949	4,651,448	5,346,797	6,187,358
Wash.	1,736,191	2,378,963	2,853,214	3,413,244	4,132,353	4,866,692
W.Va.	1,901,974	2,005,552	1,860,421	1,744,237	1,950,186	1,793,477
Wis.	3,137,587	3,434,575	3,951,777	4,417,821	4,705,642	4,891,769
Wyo.	250,742	290,529	330,066	332,416	469,557	453,588

Note: Excludes military and overseas population.
Source: John W. Wright, *The Universal Almanac, 1995* (New York, 1994), 291.

Once-thriving small towns, such as Welch, West Virginia, shown here in 1946, experienced decline and abandonment in ensuing decades. (National Archives)

TABLE 1.5 U.S. POPULATION ABROAD, BY SELECTED COUNTRY, 1989

Country	Total[a]	Resident U.S. Citizens	U.S. Tourists
Total[b]	4,244.4	2,241.7	1,164.5
Australia	84.2	67.0	13.9
Belgium	19.5	12.8	4.5
Brazil	53.8	41.5	11.6
Canada	650.7	259.7	388.9
Colombia	23.5	20.8	2.1
Costa Rica	27.7	23.7	3.6
Dominican Republic	65.7	48.8	15.6
Egypt	26.2	17.8	2.7
France	134.3	44.6	88.5
Greece	67.5	54.0	9.6
Hong Kong	25.0	17.3	6.6
Ireland	36.5	31.8	4.4
Israel	93.7	77.2	15.9
Italy	157.7	83.4	49.4
Japan	94.6	34.9	8.6
Jerusalem	35.3	30.0	5.8
Mexico	690.2	425.4	262.0
Netherlands	32.5	22.5	3.9
Panama	27.1	7.5	0.3
Philippines	197.6	120.6	3.4
Portugal	32.1	20.8	8.6
Saudi Arabia	25.1	20.1	1.2
South Korea	54.9	11.7	15.5
Spain	106.1	61.4	26.0
Switzerland	36.5	24.1	11.4
Turkey	23.0	11.2	2.8
United Kingdom	256.9	170.1	42.5
Venezuela	24.0	20.3	3.3
West Germany	627.8	152.3	12.3

a Includes Dept. of Defense noncombatant employees, other U.S. government employees, and dependents of U.S. military and civilian employees, not shown separately.

b Includes other countries not shown separately.
Note: Population figures are in thousands, as of May 1.
Source: Mark Hoffman, ed., *The World Almanac and Book of Facts 1992* (New York, 1991), 76.

Racial and Ethnic Diversity in the American Population

The following tables, all based on information supplied by the Bureau of the Census, indicate that the government's methods of classifying the population, and the terminology as well, have changed to correspond with the change in the volume of diversity in the people of the United States. For much of American history the population consisted largely of two groups: a huge majority of whites and a small but conspicuous minority group of African Americans, numbering much of the time in the neighborhood of 10 percent of the population. The rest of the people frequently were combined in a catchall category of *Others* or *All Others*. The Census Bureau at times might distinguish between the two or three largest groups, but the category as a whole represented a tiny minority—in 1940 about one-half of 1 percent—of the total population. Terminology reflected popular usage at a given time. *Negro* usually identified black people until the 1960s; after that point *black* came to be used interchangeably with *Afro* or *African American*. In the 1960s the numbers of the nonwhite, or perhaps more accurately the non–Anglo, groups began to increase markedly, with sharp growth in the movement from specified parts of Latin America and impressive growth in the numbers of the American Indian population. The 1970s and, even more remarkable, the 1980s produced still larger increases in the numbers of people of various minority groups but notably from Latin America and East Asia. The Census Bureau moved to establish new forms of identification for general groups and subclassifications within the group. *Asian* and *Pacific Islander* became generic labels. *Native American* often replaced *Indian*, although both terms continued to be used. *Hispanics* replaced *Spanish-origin* as a label for people from Latin America, and the bureau hastened to explain that Hispanics did not constitute a race but could belong to any race. In 1980 Hispanics received their own category, with an understanding that they might be counted twice—as Hispanics and as members of another racial category.

The most striking population trend in the last quarter of the 20th century, a change expected to continue into the 21st, was the steady proportional decline in the category of whites, the people who had controlled and in large measure defined the United States since its inception. This trend corresponded with and was enhanced by a modest but steady increase in the proportion of black Americans and a much more dramatic surge in numbers of people with roots in Latin America (the Hispanics) and East Asia. Encouraged by self-appointed spokespeople for the subgroups and by politicians who curried their support, an emphasis on ethnicity or race as opposed to national identity or even individualism produced ramifications in politics, economics, and virtually every area of American society. *Diversity* and *multiculuralism* had become buzzwords, taken at face value as virtuous, as the nation entered the final decade of the century.

TABLE 1.6 RESIDENT POPULATION BY RACE, 1940–1970

Year	White	Nonwhite					
		Black	Indian	Japanese	Chinese	All Other	Total Nonwhite
1940	118,214,870	12,865,518	333,969	126,947	77,504	50,467	13,454,405
1950	134,942,028	15,042,286	343,410	141,768	117,629	110,240	15,755,333
1960	158,831,732	18,871,831	523,591	464,332	237,292	394,397	20,491,443
1970	177,748,975	22,580,289	792,730	591,290	435,062	1,063,580	25,462,951

Source: Dan Golenpaul, ed., *Information Please Almanac, Atlas and Yearbook, 1974* (New York, 1973), 708.

TABLE 1.7 RESIDENT POPULATION BY RACE AND HISPANIC ORIGIN, 1980–1990

Race/Hispanic Origin[a]	1980		1990		Change	
	Number	Percent	Number	Percent	Number	Percent
Total Population	226,545,805	100.0	248,709,873	100.0	22,164,068	9.8
White	188,371,622	83.1	199,686,070	80.3	11,314,448	6.0
Black	26,495,025	11.7	29,986,060	12.1	3,491,035	13.2
American Indian, Eskimo, or Aleut	1,420,400	0.6	1,959,234	0.8	538,834	37.9
Asian or Pacific Islander	3,500,439	1.5	7,273,662	2.9	3,773,223	107.8
Other Race	6,758,319	3.0	9,804,847	3.9	3,046,528	45.1
Hispanic origin	14,608,673	6.4	22,354,059	9.0	7,745,386	53.0

[a] Persons of Hispanic origin may be of any race.
Source: Wright, *New York Times Almanac 1998,* 268.

TABLE 1.8 RESIDENT POPULATION OF THE STATES BY RACE AND HISPANIC ORIGIN, 1990

State	Total	White	Black	American Indian, Eskimo, or Aleut	Asian or Pacific Islander	Other	Hispanic Origin[a]
United States	248,709,873	199,586,070	29,986,050	1,959,234	7,273,662	9,804,847	22,354,059
Ala.	4,040,587	2,975,797	1,020,705	16,506	21,797	5,782	24,629
Alaska	550,043	415,492	22,451	85,698	19,728	6,674	17,803
Ariz.	3,665,228	2,963,186	110,524	203,527	55,206	332,785	688,338
Ark.	2,350,725	1,944,744	373,912	12,773	12,530	6,766	19,876
Calif.	29,760,021	20,524,327	2,208,801	242,164	2,845,659	3,939,070	7,687,938
Colo.	3,294,394	2,905,474	133,146	27,776	59,862	168,136	424,302
Conn.	3,287,116	2,859,353	274,269	6,654	50,698	96,142	213,116
Del.	666,168	535,094	112,460	2,019	9,057	7,538	15,820
D.C.	606,900	179,667	399,604	1,466	11,214	14,949	32,710
Fla.	12,937,926	10,749,285	1,759,534	36,355	154,302	238,470	1,574,143
Ga.	6,478,216	4,600,148	1,746,565	13,348	75,781	42,374	108,922
Hawaii	1,108,229	369,616	27,195	5,099	685,236	21,083	81,390
Idaho	1,006,749	950,451	3,370	13,780	9,365	29,783	52,927
Ill.	11,430,602	8,952,978	1,694,273	21,836	285,311	476,204	904,446
Ind.	5,544,159	5,020,700	432,092	12,720	37,617	41,030	98,788
Iowa	2,776,755	2,683,090	48,090	7,349	25,476	12,750	32,647
Kans.	2,477,574	2,231,986	143,076	21,965	31,750	48,797	93,670
Ky.	3,685,296	3,391,832	262,907	5,769	17,812	6,976	21,984
La.	4,219,973	2,839,138	1,299,281	18,541	41,099	21,914	93,044
Maine	1,227,928	1,208,360	5,138	5,998	6,683	1,749	6,829
Md.	4,781,468	3,393,964	1,189,899	12,972	139,719	44,914	125,102
Mass.	6,016,425	5,405,374	300,130	12,241	143,392	155,288	287,549
Mich.	9,295,297	7,756,086	1,291,706	55,638	104,983	86,884	201,596
Minn.	4,375,099	4,130,395	94,944	49,909	77,886	21,965	53,884
Miss.	2,573,216	1,633,461	915,057	8,525	13,016	3,157	15,931
Mo.	5,117,073	4,486,228	548,208	19,835	41,277	21,525	61,702
Mont.	799,065	741,111	2,381	47,679	4,259	3,635	12,174
Nebr.	1,578,385	1,480,558	57,404	12,410	12,422	15,591	36,969
Nev.	1,201,833	1,012,695	78,771	19,637	38,127	52,603	124,419
N.H.	1,109,252	1,087,433	7,198	2,134	9,343	3,144	11,333
N.J.	7,730,188	6,130,465	1,036,825	14,970	272,521	275,407	739,861
N.Mex.	1,515,069	1,146,028	30,210	134,355	14,124	190,352	579,224
N.Y.	17,990,455	13,385,255	2,859,055	62,651	693,760	989,734	2,214,026
N.C.	6,628,637	5,008,491	1,456,323	80,155	52,166	31,502	76,726
N.Dak.	638,800	604,142	3,524	25,917	3,462	1,755	4,665
Ohio.	10,847,115	9,521,756	1,154,826	20,358	91,179	58,996	139,696
Okla	3,145,585	2,583,512	233,801	252,240	33,563	42,289	86,160
Oreg.	2,842,321	2,636,787	46,178	38,496	69,269	51,591	112,707
Pa.	11,881,643	10,520,201	1,089,795	14,733	137,438	119,476	232,262
R.I.	1,003,464	917,375	38,861	4,071	18,325	24,832	45,752

(continued)

TABLE 1.8 (continued)

State	Total	White	Black	American Indian, Eskimo, or Aleut	Asian or Pacific Islander	Other	Hispanic Origin[a]
S.C.	3,486,703	2,406,974	1,039,884	8,246	22,382	9,217	30,551
S.Dak.	696,004	637,515	3,258	50,575	3,123	1,533	5,252
Tenn.	4,877,185	4,048,068	778,035	10,039	31,839	9,204	32,741
Tex.	16,986,510	12,774,762	2,021,632	65,877	319,459	1,804,780	4,339,905
Utah	1,722,850	1,615,845	11,576	24,283	33,371	37,775	84,597
Vt.	562,758	555,088	1,951	1,696	3,215	808	3,661
Va.	6,187,358	4,791,739	1,162,994	15,282	159,053	58,290	160,288
Wash.	4,866,692	4,308,937	149,801	81,483	210,958	115,513	214,570
W.Va.	1,793,477	1,725,523	56,295	2,458	7,459	1,742	8,489
Wis.	4,891,769	4,512,523	244,539	39,387	53,583	41,737	93,194
Wyo.	453,588	427,061	3,606	9,479	2,806	10,636	25,751

[a]Persons of Hispanic origin may be of any race.
Source: Wright, *Universal Almanac 1995,* 294.

TABLE 1.9 MINORITY POPULATION OF THE 50 LARGEST METROPOLITAN AREAS BY RACE AND HISPANIC ORIGIN, 1990

Metropolitan Area[a]	Total Population (1,000)	Percent of Total Metropolitan Population			
		Black	American Indian, Eskimo, Aleut	Asian and Pacific Islander	Hispanic Origin[b]
New York–Northern N.J.–Long Island, N.Y.–N.J.–Conn.–Pa. CMSA	19,342	17.8	0.2	4.6	14.7
Los Angeles–Riverside–Orange County, Calif. CMSA	14,532	8.5	0.6	9.2	32.9
Chicago–Gary–Kenosha, Ill.–Ind.–Wis. CMSA	8,240	19.0	0.2	3.1	10.9
Washington, D.C.–Baltimore, Md.–Va.–W.Va. CMSA	6,727	25.2	0.3	3.7	3.9
San Francisco–Oakland–San Jose, Calif. CMSA	6,253	8.6	0.7	14.8	15.5
Philadelphia–Wilmington–Atlantic City, Pa.–N.J.–Del.–Md. CMSA	5,893	18.4	0.2	2.0	3.8
Boston–Brockton–Nashua, Mass.–N.H.–Me.–Conn. CMSA	5,455	4.8	0.2	2.5	4.4
Detroit–Ann Arbor–Flint, Mich. CMSA	5,187	20.5	0.4	1.4	2.0
Dallas–Fort Worth, Tex. CMSA	4,037	14.0	0.5	2.4	13.0
Houston–Galveston–Brazonia, Tex. CMSA	3,731	17.9	0.3	3.5	20.7
Miami–Fort Lauderdale, Fla. CMSA	3,193	18.5	0.2	1.4	33.3
Seattle–Tacoma–Bremerton, Wash. CMSA	2,970	4.5	1.3	6.1	3.0
Atlanta, Ga. MSA	2,960	25.2	0.2	1.8	2.0
Cleveland–Akron, Ohio CMSA	2,860	15.6	0.2	1.0	1.9
Minneapolis–St. Paul, Minn.–Wis. MSA	2,539	3.5	1.0	2.6	1.5
San Diego, Calif. MSA	2,498	6.4	0.8	7.9	20.4
St. Louis, Mo.–Ill. MSA	2,493	17.0	0.2	1.0	1.1
Pittsburgh, Pa. MSA	2,395	7.5	0.1	0.7	0.6
Phoenix–Mesa, Ariz. MSA	2,238	3.5	2.2	1.6	17.0
Tampa–St. Petersburg–Clearwater, Fla. MSA	2,068	9.0	0.3	1.1	6.7
Denver–Boulder–Greeley, Colo. CMSA	1,980	5.0	0.7	2.2	12.8
Cincinnati–Hamilton, Ohio–Ky.–Ind. CMSA	1,818	11.2	0.1	0.8	0.5
Portland–Salem, Oreg.–Wash. CMSA	1,793	2.5	1.0	3.2	4.0
Milwaukee–Racine, Wis. CMSA	1,607	13.3	0.5	1.2	3.8
Kansas City, Mo.–Kans. MSA	1,583	12.7	0.5	1.1	2.9
Sacramento–Yolo, Calif. CMSA	1,481	6.9	1.1	7.7	11.6
Norfolk–Virginia Beach–Newport News, Va.–N.C. MSA	1,443	28.3	0.3	2.4	2.3
Indianapolis, Ind. MSA	1,380	13.2	0.2	0.8	0.9
Columbus, Ohio MSA	1,345	12.1	0.2	1.6	0.8
San Antonio, Tex. MSA	1,325	6.7	0.4	1.2	47.4
New Orleans, La. MSA	1,285	34.8	0.3	1.7	4.2
Orlando, Fla. MSA	1,225	12.0	0.3	1.7	8.2
Buffalo–Niagara Falls, N.Y. MSA	1,189	10.3	0.6	0.9	2.0
Charlotte–Gastonia–Rock Hill, N.C.–S.C. MSA	1,162	19.9	0.4	1.0	0.9
Hartford, Conn. MSA	1,158	8.3	0.2	1.5	6.9

Metropolitan Area[a]	Total Population (1,000)	Percent of Total Metropolitan Population			
		Black	American Indian, Eskimo, Aleut	Asian and Pacific Islander	Hispanic Origin[b]
Providence–Fall River–Warwick, R.I.–Mass. MSA	1,134	3.3	0.3	1.8	4.2
Salt Lake City–Ogden, Utah MSA	1,072	1.0	0.8	2.4	5.8
Rochester, N.Y. MSA	1,062	8.9	0.3	1.3	3.0
Greensboro—Winston-Salem—High Point, N.C. MSA	1,050	19.3	0.3	0.7	0.7
Memphis, Tenn.–Ark.–Miss. MSA	1,007	40.7	0.2	0.8	0.8
Nashville, Tenn. MSA	985	15.5	0.2	1.0	0.8
Oklahoma City, Okla. MSA	959	10.5	4.8	1.9	3.6
Dayton–Springfield, Ohio MSA	951	13.3	0.2	1.0	0.8
Louisville, Ky.–Ind. MSA	949	12.9	0.2	0.6	0.6
Grand Rapids–Muskegon–Holland, Mich. MSA	938	6.9	0.6	0.9	3.1
Jacksonville, Fla. MSA	907	20.0	0.3	1.7	2.5
Richmond–Petersburg, Va. MSA	866	29.2	0.3	1.4	1.1
West Palm Beach–Boca Raton, Fla. MSA	864	12.5	0.1	1.0	7.7
Albany–Schenectady–Troy, N.Y. MSA	861	4.6	0.2	1.2	1.7
Raleigh–Durham–Chapel Hill, N.C. MSA	856	24.2	0.3	1.6	1.3

[a] Metropolitan areas are shown in rank order of total population of consolidated metropolitan statistical areas (CMSA) and metropolitan statistical areas (MSA).
[b] Persons of Hispanic origin may be of any race.
Source: Bureau of the Census, Statistical Abstract:1993, 41.

TABLE 1.10 NEW YORK CITY—POPULATION DISTRIBUTION, BY RACE/ETHNICITY, 1980 AND 1987

Race/Ethnicity	Percent Distribution	
	1980	1987
Hispanic	19.9	22.9
White	52.6	46.4
Black	24.0	25.3
Asian	3.5	5.5

Source: Reddy, Record of Hispanic Americans, 181.

TABLE 1.11 MIAMI/DADE COUNTY—HISPANIC POPULATION DISTRIBUTION, 1988

Total Population	Hispanic Population	Percent Hispanic
1,900,000	861,000	45.3
Hispanic Ethnicity	Population Percent	
Cubans	67.0	
Nicaraguans	9.5	
Puerto Ricans	6.0	
Columbians	5.0	
Mexicans	2.0	
Other Hispanics	10.0	

Source: Reddy, Record of Hispanic Americans, 180–181.

TABLE 1.12 LOS ANGELES—POPULATION DISTRIBU- TION, BY RACE/ETHNICITY, 1990

Race/Ethnicity	L.A. Region Percent Distribution		
	South Central	Koreatown	City as a Whole
Hispanic	45.1	67.9	39.9
Black	55.5	5.0	14.0
White	10.5	25.4	52.8
Asian	1.1	26.5	9.8

Source: Reddy, Record of Hispanic Americans, 179.

Black Americans

The black population underwent numerous changes in the United States during the last half of the 20th century. The number nearly doubled in the 40 years after 1950, a rate of growth substantially larger than the national average. In the 1980s the rate more than doubled the growth rate of white Americans. By 1990 black people made up more than 12 percent of all Americans. Increase in the black population in large measure stemmed from a high birthrate and steady lengthening of life expectancy. Although a modest black immigration to the United States persisted in these years, it did not begin to keep pace with inward movement of other minority groups, and immigration was the reason why other groups showed a higher growth rate than African Americans. Black people continued to move from the South to the North and West, but at no point did fewer than 50 percent live in the southern states. The pace of departure virtually came to a halt after 1970, and the start of the 1990s gave signs of a reverse migration back to the South. Movement from countryside to town continued at a higher rate than for whites.

The most profound change in the status of black people came not because of numbers or movement, although both of these factors would affect developments that took place. The postwar period had little more than begun when the nation had to confront the contradiction between its avowed principles and the reality of the black experience in the United States. It was, as Swedish sociologist Gunnar Myrdal gently put it, "an American dilemma." Resolving that dilemma, or even defining it, began the Civil Rights movement, which shook the nation to its foundations. Solving the problems having to do with its black citizens was one of the largest, if not the largest, domestic issues in the 45 years that followed the Second World War. And as the nation moved into the 1990s, it still was.

At the start of the postwar era, most African Americans lived in the South, where many still were sharecroppers. (Library of Congress)

TABLE 1.13   AFRICAN-AMERICAN POPULATION TOTALS

Year	Total Population	Black Population	Percentage
1940	131,669,275	12,865,518	9.8
1950	151,325,798	15,044,937	9.9
1960	179,323,175	18,871,831	10.5
1970	203,211,926	22,580,289	11.1
1980	226,545,805	26,495,025	11.7
1990	248,709,873	29,986,060	12.1

Source: Mypho Mabunda, ed., *The African-American Almanac* (Detroit, 1997), 536.

TABLE 1.14   REGIONAL DISTRIBUTION OF THE BLACK POPULATION, 1940–1990

Year	Percentage of Blacks Living in			
	Northeast	North Central	South	West
1940	10.6	11.0	77.0	1.3
1950	13.4	14.8	68.0	3.8
1960	16.0	18.3	59.9	5.8
1970	19.2	20.2	53.0	7.5
1980	18.3	20.1	53.0	8.5
1990	18.7	19.1	52.8	9.4

Source: Mabunda, *African-American Almanac,* 534.

TABLE 1.15   PERCENTAGE OF POPULATION LIVING IN URBAN TERRITORY, 1940–1990

Year	Total Population	Blacks	Whites
1940	56.5	48.6	57.5
1950	64.0	62.4	64.3
1960[a]	69.9	73.2	69.5
1970	73.5	81.3	72.4
1980	73.7	85.3	71.3
1990	75.2	87.2	71.9

[a] Denotes first year for which figures include Alaska and Hawaii.
Source: Mabunda, *African-American Almanac,* 535.

TABLE 1.16 BLACK POPULATION CHANGE IN 14 CENTRAL CITIES AND THEIR SUBURBS, 1960–1980

Area	Black Population 1980	Percent Black 1960	Percent Black 1970	Percent Black 1980	Percent Change in Black Population 1960–70	Percent Change in Black Population 1970–80
Central Cities						
New York City	1,784,000	14.0	21.2	25.2	53.3	7.0
Chicago	1,197,000	22.9	32.7	39.8	35.7	8.6
Detroit	759,000	28.9	43.7	63.1	37.0	14.9
Philadelphia	639,000	26.4	33.6	37.8	23.5	−2.3
Los Angeles	505,000	13.5	17.9	17.0	50.4	0.3
Washington, D.C.	448,000	53.9	71.1	70.3	30.6	−16.6
Houston	440,000	22.9	25.7	27.6	47.2	39.1
Baltimore	431,000	34.7	46.4	54.8	29.1	2.6
New Orleans	308,000	37.2	45.0	55.3	14.5	15.3
Memphis	308,000	37.0	38.9	47.6	31.6	26.9
Atlanta	283,000	38.3	51.3	66.6	36.8	12.1
Dallas	266,000	19.0	24.9	29.4	62.7	26.3
Cleveland	251,000	28.6	38.3	43.8	14.8	−12.7
St. Louis	206,000	28.6	40.9	47.4	18.6	−18.8
Suburbs (1970 definition)						
New York City	285,000	4.8	5.9	7.6	55.5	31.4
Chicago	231,000	2.9	3.6	5.6	65.5	79.9
Detroit	128,000	3.7	3.6	4.5	26.1	32.5
Philadelphia	245,000	6.1	6.6	8.1	34.1	28.9
Los Angeles	398,000	3.6	6.2	9.6	105.0	65.7
Washington, D.C.	390,000	6.4	7.9	16.6	98.3	134.9
Houston	36,000	12.9	8.8	6.2	6.2	21.4
Baltimore	126,000	7.0	7.0	9.1	25.6	54.9
New Orleans	79,000	15.9	12.5	12.6	26.9	40.4
Memphis	37,000	40.2	31.7	21.0	−34.8	−18.4
Atlanta	179,000	8.5	6.2	14.2	23.5	222.4
Dallas	50,000	8.3	5.2	4.7	1.1	35.4
Cleveland	94,000	0.8	3.4	7.1	452.8	110.6
St. Louis	201,000	6.0	7.7	10.9	65.0	50.4

Source: Harry A. Ploski and James Williams, *The Negro Almanac: A Reference Work on the African Americans* (Detroit, 1989), 493.

TABLE 1.17 THIRTY CITIES WITH LARGEST PROPORTION OF BLACK POPULATION, 1980

City Rank	City	Percentage of Total
1.	East St. Louis, Ill.	95.6
2.	East Cleveland, Ohio	86.5
3.	East Orange, N.J.	83.5
4.	Compton, Calif.	74.8
5.	Prichard, Ala.	73.7
6.	Gary, Ind.	70.8
7.	Washington, D.C.	70.3
8.	Atlanta, Ga.	66.6
9.	Detroit, Mich.	63.1
10.	Newark, N.J.	58.2
11.	Inglewood, Calif.	57.3
12.	Birmingham, Ala.	55.6
13.	New Orleans, La.	55.3
14.	Baltimore, Md.	54.8
15.	Camden, N.J.	53.0
16.	Richmond, Va.	51.3
17.	Wilmington, Del.	51.1
18.	Savannah, Ga.	49.0
19.	Mount Vernon, N.Y.	48.7
20.	Richmond, Calif.	47.9
21.	Memphis, Tenn.	47.6
22.	Albany, Ga.	47.6
23.	Durham, N.C.	47.1
24.	Jackson, Miss.	47.0
25.	Oakland, Calif.	46.9
26.	Charleston, S.C.	46.5
27.	St. Louis, Mo.	45.6
28.	Trenton, N.J.	45.4
29.	Portsmouth, Va.	45.1
30.	Macon, Ga.	44.5

Source: Ploski and Williams, *Negro Almanac*, 502.

TABLE 1.18 TWENTY U.S. CITIES WITH LARGEST BLACK POPULATIONS, 1990

Black Rank	Overall Rank	City	Total Population ('000s)	Black Population ('000s)	Percent Black
1.	1	New York, N.Y.	7,322.6	2,102.5	29
2.	3	Chicago, Ill.	2,783.7	1,087.7	39
3.	7	Detroit, Mich.	1,028.0	777.9	76
4.	5	Philadelphia, Pa.	1,585.6	631.9	40
5.	2	Los Angeles, Calif.	3,485.4	487.7	14
6.	4	Houston, Tex.	1,630.6	458.0	28
7.	13	Baltimore, Md.	736.0	435.8	59
8.	19	Washington, D.C.	606.9	399.6	66
9.	18	Memphis, Tenn.	610.3	334.7	55
10.	25	New Orleans, La.	496.9	307.7	62
11.	8	Dallas, Tex.	1,006.9	297.0	30
12.	36	Atlanta, Ga.	394.0	264.3	67
13.	24	Cleveland, Ohio	505.6	235.4	47
14.	17	Milwaukee, Wis.	628.1	191.3	31
15.	34	St. Louis, Mo.	396.7	188.4	48
16.	60	Birmingham, Ala.	266.0	168.3	63
17.	12	Indianapolis, Ind.	742.0	165.6	22
18.	15	Jacksonville, Fla.	673.0	163.9	24
19.	39	Oakland, Calif.	372.2	163.3	44
20.	56	Newark, N.J.	275.2	160.9	59

Source: Wright, *Universal Almanac 1995*, 296.

TABLE 1.19   TEN STATES WITH THE LARGEST BLACK POPULATION, 1990

Rank	State	Black Population	Percent of Total Population
1.	N.Y.	2,859,055	15.9
2.	Calif.	2,208,801	7.4
3.	Tex.	2,021,632	11.9
4.	Fla.	1,759,534	13.6
5.	Ga.	1,746,565	27.0
6.	Ill.	1,694,273	14.8
7.	N.C.	1,456,323	22.0
8.	La.	1,299,281	30.8
9.	Mich.	1,291,706	13.9
10.	Md.	1,189,899	24.9

Source: Wright, *Universal Almanac 1995*, 296.

TABLE 1.20   TEN STATES WITH HIGHEST PERCENTAGE OF BLACK POPULATION, 1990

Rank	State	Total Population	Black Population	Percent Black
1.	Miss.	2,573,216	915,057	35.6
2.	La.	4,219,973	1,299,281	30.8
3.	S.C.	3,486,703	1,039,884	29.8
4.	Ga.	6,478,216	1,746,565	27.0
5.	Ala.	4,040,587	1,020,705	25.3
6.	Md.	4,781,468	1,189,899	24.9
7.	N.C.	6,628,637	1,456,323	22.0
8.	Va.	6,187,358	1,162,994	18.8
9.	Del.	666,168	112,460	16.9
10.	Tenn.	4,877,185	778,035	16.0

Source: Wright, *Universal Almanac 1995*, 296.

Some African Americans established enclaves in sections of large northern cities, as exemplified by this bar in the South Side of Chicago. (Library of Congress)

TABLE 1.21   BLACK POPULATION OF METROPOLITAN AREAS, 1980–1990

Rank	Metropolitan Area	1980	1990	Number Change	Percent Change
1.	New York–Northern New Jersey–Long Island, N.Y.–N.J.–Conn. CMSA	2,825,102	3,289,465	464,363	16.4
2.	Chicago–Gary–Lake County, Ill.–Ind.–Wis. CMSA	1,557,287	1,547,725	−9,562	−0.6
3.	Los Angeles–Anaheim–Riverside, Calif. CMSA	1,059,124	1,229,809	170,685	16.1
4.	Philadelphia–Wilmington–Trenton, Pa.–N.J.–Del.–Md. CMSA	1,032,882	1,100,347	67,465	6.5
5.	Washington, D.C.–Md.–Va. MSA	870,657	1,041,934	171,277	19.7
6.	Detroit–Ann Arbor, Mich. CMSA	921,168	975,199	54,031	5.9
7.	Atlanta, Ga. MSA	525,676	736,153	210,477	40.0
8.	Houston–Galveston–Brazoria, Tex. CMSA	564,838	665,378	100,540	17.8
9.	Baltimore, Md. MSA	560,952	616,065	55,113	9.8
10.	Miami–Fort Lauderdale, Fla. CMSA	394,042	591,440	197,398	50.1
11.	Dallas–Fort Worth, Tex. CMSA	419,030	554,616	135,586	32.4
12.	San Francisco–Oakland, San Jose, Calif. CMSA	468,477	537,753	69,276	14.8
13.	Cleveland–Akron–Lorain, Ohio CMSA	425,861	441,940	16,079	3.8
14.	New Orleans, La. MSA	409,076	430,470	21,394	5.2
15.	St. Louis, Mo.–Ill. MSA	407,918	423,182	15,264	3.7
16.	Memphis, Tenn.–Ark.–Miss. MSA	364,253	399,011	34,758	9.5
17.	Norfolk–Virginia Beach–Newport News, Va. MSA	326,102	398,093	71,991	22.1
18.	Richmond–Petersburg, Va. MSA	221,456	252,340	30,884	13.9
19.	Birmingham, Ala. MSA	240,271	245,726	5,455	2.3
20.	Boston–Lawrence–Salem, Mass.–N.H. MSA	176,265	239,059	62,794	35.6
21.	Charlotte–Gastonia–Rock Hill, N.C.–S.C. MSA	194,056	231,654	37,598	19.4
22.	Milwaukee–Racine, Wis. CMSA	164,571	214,182	49,611	30.1
23.	Cincinnati–Hamilton, Ohio–Ky.–Ind. CMSA	185,728	203,607	17,879	9.6
24.	Kansas City, Mo.–Kans. MSA	180,161	200,508	20,347	11.3
25.	Tampa–St. Petersburg–Clearwater, Fla. MSA	148,465	185,503	37,038	24.9
26.	Raleigh-Durham, N.C. MSA	146,624	183,447	36,823	25.1
27.	Greensboro–Winston-Salem–High Point, N.C. MSA	162,134	182,284	20,150	12.4
28.	Jacksonville, Fla. MSA	156,025	181,265	25,240	16.2
29.	Pittsburgh–Beaver Valley, Pa. CMSA	181,644	178,857	−2,787	−1.5
30.	Indianapolis, Ind. MSA	157,254	172,326	15,072	9.6
31.	Jackson, Miss. MSA	149,457	167,899	18,442	12.3
32.	Columbus, Ohio MSA	137,287	164,602	27,315	19.9
33.	San Diego, Calif. MSA	104,452	159,306	54,854	52.5
34.	Baton Rouge, La. MSA	137,581	156,509	18,928	13.8
35.	Charleston, S.C. MSA	133,478	153,227	19,749	14.8
36.	Nashville, Tenn. MSA	137,348	152,349	15,001	10.9
37.	Columbia, S.C. MSA	117,906	137,906	20,000	17.0
38.	Orlando, Fla. MSA	90,595	133,308	42,713	47.1
39.	Mobile, Ala. MSA	126,835	130,512	3,677	2.9
40.	Dayton–Springfield, Ohio MSA	118,294	126,238	7,944	6.7
41.	Louisville, Ky.–Ind. MSA	120,610	124,761	4,151	3.4
42.	Augusta, Ga.–S.C. MSA	106,729	123,482	16,753	15.7
43.	Seattle–Tacoma, Wash. CMSA	87,976	123,266	35,290	40.1
44.	Buffalo–Niagara Falls, N.Y. CMSA	113,975	121,956	7,981	7.0
45.	Shreveport, La. MSA	110,478	116,892	6,414	5.8
46.	Greenville–Spartanburg, S.C. MSA	97,561	111,334	13,773	14.1
47.	West Palm Beach–Boca Raton–Delray Beach, Fla. MSA	77,576	107,705	30,129	38.8
48.	Montgomery, Ala. MSA	94,494	105,196	10,702	11.3
49.	Sacramento, Calif. MSA	61,594	101,940	40,346	65.5
50.	Little Rock–North Little Rock, Ark. MSA	90,783	101,862	11,079	12.2

Source: Wright, *Universal Almanac 1995*, 295.

American Indians

The post–Second World War period answered one question with respect to Native Americans: Indians would survive as a distinct racial/ethnic group. The issue had seemed somewhat in doubt early in the century. The Indian population had dropped below a quarter million in 1910, and in 1950 there were barely 350,000. But after that point the numbers showed impressive growth: Aided, perhaps, by a more effective or liberal standard for counting Native Americans, the total reached the million mark in the 1970s and the second million (or close to it) came by 1990. The largest numbers resided in four southwestern states: California, Oklahoma, Arizona, and New Mexico. The government still recognized some 300 reservations, but only 25 percent of the Indians lived on them (another 10 percent lived in special Indian areas in Oklahoma). Whether the people lived on reservations or within the general populace, virtually all faced markedly substandard living conditions (although they were higher off the reservation than on them). Many Indians were determined to preserve their identity even though the traditional lifestyle no longer seemed conducive to maintaining an acceptable standard of living. Near the end of the period there emerged some propensity toward creative economic ventures, such as specialized manufacturing projects or the opening of gambling casinos on tribal lands. If these activities offered jobs and a measure of self-sufficiency for the tribes involved, they did not seem to provide much in support of traditional Indian culture during this time.

TABLE 1.22 POPULATION OF AMERICAN INDIANS AND THE TOTAL UNITED STATES POPULATION, 1940–1980

	American Indian		Total United States	
Date	Size	% Change from Previous Decade	Size	% Change from Previous Decade
1940	345,252	0.6	131,669,275	7.2
1950	357,499	3.5	151,325,798	14.5
1960	523,591	46.5	179,323,175	18.5
1970	792,730	51.4	203,302,031	13.4
1980	1,366,676	72.4	226,545,805	11.4
1990	1,959,234	37.9	248,709,873	9.8

Source: Marlita A. Reddy, *Statistical Record of Native North Americans* (Detroit, 1995), 344.

TABLE 1.23 AMERICAN INDIAN POPULATION, BY STATE, 1940–1980

State	1940	1950	1960	1970	1980
Ala.	464	928	1,276	2,443	7,502
Alaska	11,283	14,089	14,444	16,276	21,869
Ariz.	55,076	65,761	83,387	95,812	152,498
Ark.	278	533	580	2,014	9,364
Calif.	18,675	19,947	39,014	91,018	198,275
Colo.	1,360	1,567	4,238	8,336	17,734
Conn.	201	333	923	2,222	4,431
Del.	14	?	597	656	1,307
D.C.	190	330	587	956	996
Fla.	690	1,011	2,504	6,677	19,134
Ga.	106	333	749	2,347	7,442
Hawaii	?	?	472	1,126	2,655
Idaho	3,537	3,800	5,231	6,687	10,418
Ill.	624	1,443	4,704	11,413	15,846
Ind.	223	438	948	3,887	7,682
Iowa	733	1,084	1,708	2,992	5,369
Kans.	1,165?	2,381	5,069	8,672	15,256
Ky.	44	234	391	1,531	3,518
La.	1,801	409?	3,587	5,294	11,969
Maine	1,251	1,522	1,879	2,195	4,057
Md.	73	314	1,538	4,239	7,823
Mass.	769	1,201	2,118	4,475	7,483
Mich.	6,282	7,000	9,701	16,854	39,734
Minn.	12,528	12,533	15,496	23,128	34,831
Miss.	2,134	2,502	3,442	4,113	6,131
Mo.	330	547	1,723	5,405	12,129
Mont.	16,841	16,606	21,181	27,130	37,598
Nebr.	3,401	3,954	5,545	6,624	9,145
Nev.	4,747	5,025	6,681	7,933	13,306
N.H.	50	74	135	361	1,297
N.J.	211	621	1,699	4,706	8,176
N.Mex.	34,510	41,901	56,255	72,788	107,338
N.Y.	8,651	10,640	16,491	28,355	38,967
N.C.	22,546	3,742?	38,129	44,406	64,536
N.Dak.	10,114	10,766	11,736	14,369	20,120
Ohio	338	1,146	1,910	6,654	11,985
Okla.	63,125	53,769	64,689	98,468	169,292
Oreg.	4,594	5,820	8,026	13,510	26,591
Pa.	441	1,141	2,122	5,533	9,179
R.I.	196	385	932	1,390	2,872
S.C.	1,234	554	1,098	2,241	5,665
S.Dak.	23,347	23,344	25,794	32,365	44,948
Tenn.	114	339	638	2,276	5,013
Tex.	1,103	2,736	5,750	17,957	39,740
Utah	3,611	4,201	6,961	11,273	19,158

State	1940	1950	1960	1970	1980
Vt.	16	30	57	229	968
Va.	198	1,056	2,155	4,853	9,211
Wash.	11,394	13,816	21,076	33,386	58,186
W.Va.	25	160	181	751	1,555
Wis.	12,265	12,196	14,297	18,924	29,320
Wyo.	2,349	3,237	4,020	4,980	7,057

Source: Reddy, *Record of Native Americans,* 344–346.

TABLE 1.24 PERCENTAGE OF THE AMERICAN INDIAN POPULATION IN THE UNITED STATES WHO ARE URBAN, 1940–1980

Year	Percent
1940	7.2
1950	13.4
1960	27.9
1970	44.5
1980	49.0

Source: Reddy, *Record of Native Americans,* 347.

TABLE 1.25 AMERICAN INDIAN POPULATION, 1990

State	American Indian Population
United States	1,959,234
Ala.	16,506
Alaska	85,698
Ariz.	203,527
Ark.	12,773
Calif.	242,164
Colo.	27,776
Conn.	6,654
Del.	2,019
D.C.	1,466
Fla.	36,335
Ga.	13,348
Hawaii	5,099
Idaho	13,780
Ill.	21,836
Ind.	12,720
Iowa	7,349
Kans.	21,965
Ky.	5,769
La.	18,541
Maine	5,998
Md.	12,972
Mass.	12,241
Mich.	55,638
Minn.	49,909
Miss.	8,525
Mo.	19,835
Mont.	47,679
Nebr.	12,410
Nev.	19,637
N.H.	2,134
N.J.	14,970
N.Mex.	134,355
N.Y.	62,651
N.C.	80,155
N.Dak.	25,917

State	American Indian Population
Ohio	20,358
Okla.	252,420
Oreg.	38,496
Pa.	14,733
R.I.	4,071
S.C.	8,246
S.Dak.	50,575
Tenn.	10,039
Tex.	65,877
Utah	24,283
Vt.	1,696
Va.	15,282
Wash.	81,483
W.Va	2,458
Wis.	39,387
Wyo.	9,479

Source: Mark T. Mattson, *Atlas of the 1990 Census* (New York, 1992), 125.

TABLE 1.26 AMERICAN INDIAN POPULATION GROWTH COMPARED WITH OTHER GROUPS, 1980–1990

Race/Ethnicity	% Population Increase
Asian	107.8
Hispanic	53.0
Native American	37.9
Black	13.2
White	6.0

Source: Reddy, *Record of Native Americans,* 346.

Asian and Pacific Islanders

One of the most striking and least expected changes in the American population after 1945 was the extent of growth, especially in the 1970s and 1980s, in the number of people with antecedents in East Asia. At the start of the period only American Indians had smaller numbers in the Census Bureau's catchall grouping of "others." Half of the Asian Americans then were Japanese and the remainder mostly Chinese and Filipino. Immigration restrictions helped keep the total small, at least until the 1960s. Thereafter the numbers began to pick up. Immigration policy changed beginning in 1965. In some measure the growth followed the foreign policy of the United States. The closer American involvement with an Asian nation—for either friendly or hostile purposes—the more likely people from that nation would end up in the United States. The process probably began with the Philippine Islands and extended to Japan and Korea in the 1950s, and afterward the nations of Southeast Asia beginning in the 1970s. In the 1980s the traffic came as almost a torrent. This surge grew out of several factors: continued fallout from social and political upheaval, especially in the Indochinese peninsula, an opening of the Peoples Republic of China to the world, and a general globalization of social and economic change—forces that sharpened the appeal of the nation that still symbolized modernization and opportunity and which had perhaps the world's most liberal immigration laws. The largest rate of population growth after 1980 came by far in people classified as Asian/Pacific Islander. Half of these people lived in four states: California, Hawaii, New York, and Texas, with California easily leading the way. Overwhelmingly, the Asian Americans were city dwellers.

Daniel K. Inouye, U.S. senator from Hawaii, symbolized the resilience of Japanese Americans in recovering from a harsh wartime experience. (Courtesy Senator Daniel K. Inouye)

TABLE 1.27 POPULATION OF THE UNITED STATES BY ASIAN ETHNICITY, BY DECADE, 1940–1990

Year	Total, U.S.	Total Asian	Chinese	Filipino	Asian Indian	Japanese	Korean	Vietnamese
1940	132,165,129	489,984	106,334	98,535	. . .	285,115	8,568	. . .
1950	151,325,798	599,091	150,005	122,707	. . .	326,379	7,030	. . .
1960	179,323,175	877,934	237,292	176,310	. . .	464,332	. . .	. . .
1970	203,211,926	1,429,562	436,062	343,060	. . .	591,290	69,150	. . .
1980	226,545,805	3,466,421	812,178	781,894	387,223	716,331	357,393	245,025
1990	248,709,873	7,273,662	1,645,472	1,406,770	815,447	847,562	798,849	614,547

Source: Susan B. Gall and Timothy L. Gall, eds., *Statistical Record of Asian Americans* (Detroit, 1993), 572.

TABLE 1.28   ASIAN/PACIFIC ISLANDER POPULATION INCREASE, 1980–1990

Race/Ethnicity	U.S. Population, Total		Increase, 1980–1990	
	1990	1980	Number	Percent
Total U.S. Population	248,709,873	226,545,805	22,164,068	9.8
Asian/Pacific Islander American	7,273,662	3,726,440	3,547,222	95.2
Chinese	1,645,472	812,178	833,294	102.6
Filipino	1,406,770	781,894	624,876	79.9
Japanese	847,562	716,331	131,231	18.3
Asian Indian	815,447	387,223	428,224	110.6
Korean	798,849	357,393	441,456	123.5
Vietnamese	614,547	245,025	369,522	150.8
Cambodian	147,411	16,044	131,367	818.8
Hmong	90,082	5,204	84,878	1,631.0
Laotian	149,014	47,683	101,331	212.5
Thai	91,275	45,279	45,996	101.6
Hawaiian	211,014	172,346	38,668	22.4
Guamanian	62,964	39,520	23,444	59.3
Samoan	49,345	30,695	18,650	60.8
Other Asian/Pacific Islander	343,910	69,625	274,285	393.9

Source: Gall and Gall, *Record of Asian Americans,* 569.

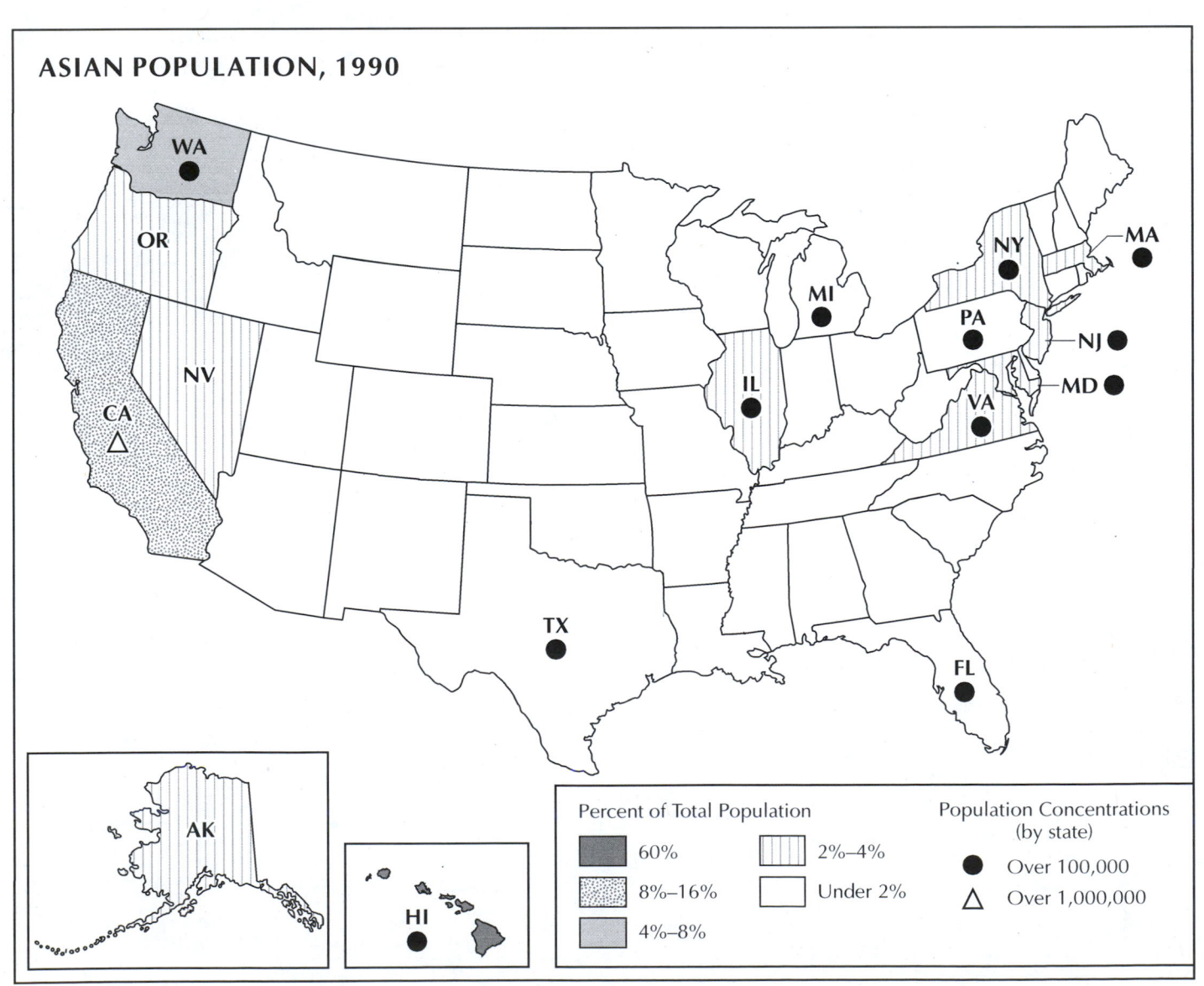

ASIAN POPULATION, 1990

Percent of Total Population
- 60%
- 8%–16%
- 4%–8%
- 2%–4%
- Under 2%

Population Concentrations (by state)
- ● Over 100,000
- △ Over 1,000,000

TABLE 1.29 ASIAN AND PACIFIC ISLANDER POPULATION OF METROPOLITAN AREAS, 1980–1990

Rank	Metropolitan Areas	1980	1990	Population Change, 1980–1990	
				Number	Percent
1.	Los Angeles–Anaheim–Riverside, Calif. CMSA	561,876	1,339,048	777,172	138.3
2.	San Francisco–Oakland–San Jose, Calif. CMSA	454,647	926,961	472,314	103.9
3.	New York–Northern N.J.–Long Island, N.Y.–N.J.–Conn. CMSA	370,731	873,213	502,482	135.5
4.	Honolulu, Hawaii MSA	456,465	526,459	69,994	15.3
5.	Chicago–Gary–Lake County, Ill.–Ind.–Wis. CMSA	144,626	256,050	111,424	77.0
6.	Washington, D.C.–Md.–Va. MSA	83,008	202,437	119,429	143.9
7.	San Diego, Calif. MSA	89,861	198,311	108,450	120.7
8.	Seattle–Tacoma, Wash. CMSA	78,255	164,286	86,031	109.9
9.	Houston–Galveston–Brazoria, Tex. CMSA	53,056	132,131	79,075	149.0
10.	Philadelphia–Wilmington–Trenton, Penn.–N.J.–Del.–Md. CMSA	53,291	123,458	70,167	131.7

Source: Wright, *New York Times Almanac 1998,* 274.

TABLE 1.30 CALIFORNIA AND HAWAII CITIES AND PLACES RANKED BY ASIAN/PACIFIC ISLANDER POPULATION, 1990

City or Place: California	Total Population	Asian/Pacific Islander	
		Population	Percent of Total
Los Angeles	3,485,398	341,807	9.8
San Francisco	723,959	210,876	29.1
San Jose	782,248	152,815	19.5
San Diego	1,110,549	130,945	11.8
Long Beach	429,433	58,266	13.6
Sacramento	369,365	55,426	15.0
Oakland	372,242	54,931	14.8
Stockton	210,943	48,087	22.8
Fresno	354,202	44,358	12.5
Daly City	92,311	40,466	43.8
Monterey Park	60,738	34,898	57.5

City or Place: Hawaii	Total Population	Asian/Pacific Islander	
		Population	Percent of Total
Honolulu	365,272	257,552	70.5
Hilo	37,808	26,533	70.2
Waipahu	31,435	26,340	83.8
Kaneohe	35,448	23,261	65.6
Pearl City	30,993	22,968	74.1
Waimalu	29,967	20,317	67.8
Mililani	29,359	17,973	61.2
Kailua	36,818	14,395	39.1
Kahului	16,889	13,809	81.8
Wahiawa	17,386	12,013	69.1

Source: Gall and Gall, *Record of Asian Americans,* 605, 609.

Hispanics

The term *Hispanics* or generally *Latino/as* refers to people whose origins are in part the former Spanish American empire. The territory includes Mexico, Central and South America (except for Brazil, which belonged to a Portuguese empire), and the Caribbean islands (except Haiti). Hispanic Americans have their roots in all the countries of this area, although people of different national origin congregated in different parts of the United States. Large numbers of Mexican Americans, who constituted more than half of all Hispanics, lived in California and Texas, where by 1990 they made up one-fourth of the population of each state. Many Puerto Ricans lived in New York City. Cuban Americans resided in large numbers in Florida, notably Miami, a legacy of the revolution of Fidel Castro and his troubles with the United States.

Before 1970 the number of Hispanics, most of them from Mexico, was small and probably undercounted by the Census Bureau. Hispanics then did not merit a separate category, and the Census Bureau failed to count third- or fourth-generation people or individuals who did not present a Spanish surname. Since 1970 and especially since 1980, the number has grown in dramatic fashion, the change traceable partly to different methods of counting but more to a higher birthrate and immigration from Hispanic countries, notably Mexico. If recent patterns continued, it was anticipated that Hispanics would become the largest minority group, surpassing African Americans in the first decade of the 21st century, if not earlier. Numbers allowed Hispanics to speak with a louder voice and be noticed. Descendant from a different culture or cultures, speaking a different language (at least in the first generation), Hispanics became an important part in the many controversies about multiculturalism in the 1980s and 1990s. As with groups from the outside in the past, the extent to which they would change the dominant culture, be absorbed by it, or persist as distinct subcultures remained to be seen.

TABLE 1.31 HISPANIC POPULATION, BY STATE AND ETHNICITY, 1990

State	Total Population	Hispanic Population					
		Total		Mexicans	Puerto Ricans	Cubans	Other Ethnicities
		Number	Percent				
Total U.S.	248,709,873	22,354,059	9.00	13,495,938	2,727,754	1,043,932	5,086,435
Ala.	4,040,587	24,629	0.60	9,509	3,553	1,463	10,104
Alaska	550,043	17,803	3.20	9,321	1,938	277	6,267
Ariz.	3,665,228	688,338	18.80	616,195	8,256	2,079	61,808
Ark.	2,350,725	19,876	0.80	12,496	1,176	494	5,710
Calif.	29,760,021	7,687,938	25.80	6,118,996	126,417	71,977	1,370,548
Colo.	3,294,394	424,302	12.90	282,478	7,225	2,058	132,541
Conn.	3,287,116	213,116	6.50	8,393	146,842	6,386	51,495
Del.	666,168	15,820	2.40	3,083	8,257	728	3,752
D.C.	606,900	32,710	5.40	2,981	2,204	1,241	26,284
Fla.	12,937,926	1,574,143	12.20	161,499	247,010	674,052	491,582
Ga.	6,478,216	108,922	1.70	49,182	17,443	7,818	34,479
Hawaii	1,108,229	81,390	7.30	14,367	25,778	558	40,687
Idaho	1,006,749	52,927	5.30	43,213	665	164	8,885
Ill.	11,430,602	904,446	7.90	623,688	146,059	18,204	116,495
Ind.	5,544,159	98,788	1.80	66,736	14,021	1,853	16,178
Iowa	2,776,755	32,647	1.20	24,386	1,270	488	6,503
Kans.	2,477,574	93,670	3.80	75,798	3,570	1,403	12,899
Ky.	3,685,296	21,984	0.60	8,692	3,682	1,075	8,535
La.	4,219,973	93,044	2.20	23,452	6,180	8,569	54,843
Maine	1,227,928	6,829	0.60	2,153	1,250	350	3,076
Md.	4,781,468	125,102	2.60	18,434	17,528	6,367	82,773
Mass.	6,016,425	287,549	4.80	12,703	151,193	8,106	115,547
Mich.	9,295,297	201,596	2.20	138,312	18,538	5,157	39,589
Minn.	4,375,099	53,884	1.20	34,691	3,286	1,539	14,368
Miss.	2,573,216	15,931	0.60	6,718	1,304	497	7,412
Mo.	5,117,073	61,702	1.20	38,274	3,959	2,108	17,361
Mont.	799,065	12,174	1.50	8,362	437	124	3,251
Nebr.	1,578,385	36,969	2.30	29,665	1,159	480	5,665
Nev.	1,201,833	124,419	10.40	85,287	4,272	5,988	28,872
N.H.	1,109,252	11,333	1.00	2,362	3,299	578	5,094
N.J.	7,730,188	739,861	9.60	28,759	320,133	85,378	305,591
N.Mex.	1,515,069	579,224	38.20	328,836	2,635	903	246,850
N.Y.	17,990,455	2,214,026	12.30	93,244	1,086,601	74,345	959,836
N.C.	6,628,637	76,726	1.20	32,670	14,620	3,723	25,713
N.Dak.	638,800	4,665	0.70	2,878	386	63	1,338
Ohio	10,847,115	139,696	1.30	57,815	45,853	3,559	32,469
Okla.	3,145,585	86,160	2.70	63,226	4,693	1,043	17,198
Oreg.	2,842,321	112,707	4.00	85,632	2,764	1,333	22,978
Pa.	11,881,643	232,262	2.00	24,220	148,988	7,485	51,569
R.I.	1,003,464	45,752	4.60	2,437	13,016	840	29,459
S.C.	3,486,703	30,551	0.90	11,028	6,423	1,652	11,448
S.Dak.	696,004	5,252	0.80	3,438	377	44	1,393
Tenn.	4,877,185	32,741	0.70	13,879	4,292	2,012	12,558
Tex.	16,986,510	4,339,905	25.50	3,890,820	42,981	18,195	387,909
Utah	1,722,850	84,597	4.90	56,842	2,181	456	25,118
Vt.	562,758	3,661	0.70	725	659	168	2,109
Va.	6,187,358	160,288	2.60	33,044	23,698	6,268	97,278
Wash.	4,866,692	214,570	4.40	155,864	9,345	2,281	47,080
W.Va.	1,793,477	8,489	0.50	2,810	897	261	4,521
Wis.	4,891,769	93,194	1.90	57,615	19,116	1,679	14,784
Wyo.	453,588	25,751	5.70	18,730	325	63	6,633

Source: Marlita A. Reddy, *Statistical Record of Hispanic Americans* (Detroit, 1993), 162–163.

These Hispanic migrant workers labor near Salinas, California. (U.S. Department of Agriculture)

TABLE 1.32 METROPOLITAN AREAS WITH LARGE NUMBERS OF HISPANIC ORIGIN POPULATION, 1990

Metropolitan Area	Number of Those with Hispanic Origin (1,000)	Percent of Total Metro Area
Hispanic Origin		
Los Angeles–Riverside–Orange County, Calif. CMSA	4,779	32.9
New York–Northern N.J.–Long Island, N.Y.–N.J.–Conn.–Pa. CMSA	2,843	14.7
Miami–Fort Lauderdale, Fla. CMSA	1,062	33.3
San Francisco–Oakland–San Jose, Calif. CMSA	970	15.5
Chicago–Gary–Kenosha, Ill.–Ind.–Wis. CMSA	898	10.9
Houston–Galveston–Brazoria, Tex. CMSA	773	20.7
San Antonio, Tex. MSA	628	47.4
Dallas–Fort Worth, Tex. CMSA	526	13.0
San Diego, Calif. MSA	511	20.4
El Paso, Tex. MSA	412	69.6
Phoenix–Mesa, Ariz. MSA	380	17.0
McAllen–Edinburg–Mission, Tex. MSA	327	85.2
Fresno, Calif. MSA	267	35.3
Washington, D.C.–Baltimore, Md.–Va.–W.Va. CMSA	259	3.9
Denver–Boulder–Greeley, Colo. CMSA	254	12.8
Boston–Brockton–Nashua, Mass.–N.H.–Me.–Conn. CMSA	239	4.4

Metropolitan Area	Number of Those with Hispanic Origin (1,000)	Percent of Total Metro Area
Hispanic Origin		
Philadelphia–Wilmington–Atlantic City, Pa.–N.J.–Del.–Md. CMSA	224	3.8
Albuquerque, N.Mex. MSA	218	37.1
Brownsville–Harlingen–San Benito, Tex. MSA	213	81.9
Corpus Christi, Tex. MSA	182	52.0
Austin–San Marcos, Tex. MSA	177	20.9
Sacramento–Yolo, Calif. CMSA	172	11.6
Tucson, Ariz. MSA	163	24.5
Bakersfield, Calif. MSA	152	28.0
Tampa–St. Petersburg–Clearwater, Fla. MSA	139	6.7
Laredo, Tex. MSA	125	93.9
Visalia–Tulare–Porterville, Calif. MSA	121	38.8
Salinas, Calif. MSA	120	33.6
Stockton–Lodi, Calif. MSA	113	23.4
Detroit–Ann Arbor–Flint, Mich. CMSA	105	2.0
Orlando, Fla. MSA	101	8.2

Source: Statistical Abstract, 1993, 40.

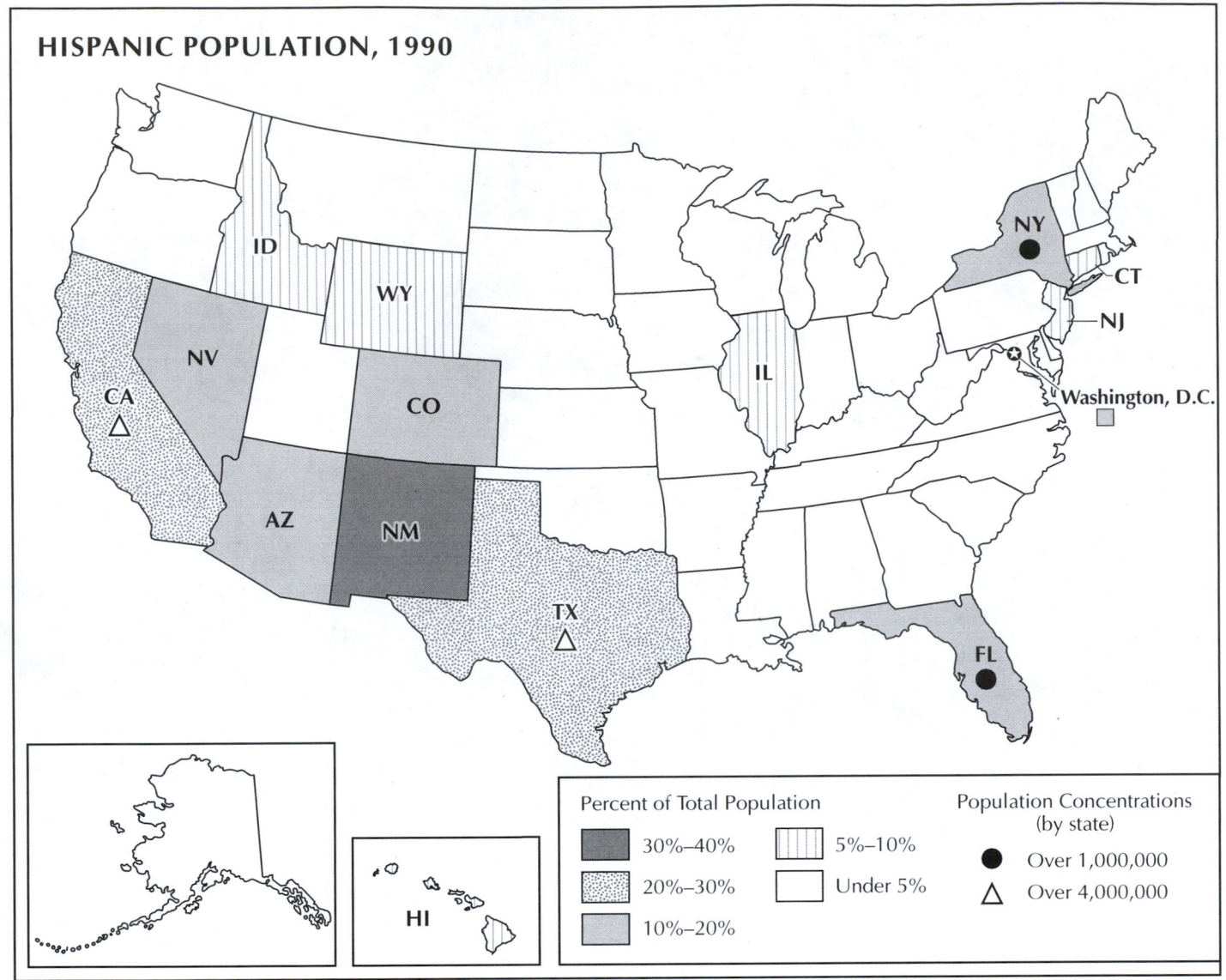

HISPANIC POPULATION, 1990

Percent of Total Population
- 30%–40%
- 20%–30%
- 10%–20%
- 5%–10%
- Under 5%

Population Concentrations (by state)
- ● Over 1,000,000
- △ Over 4,000,000

Immigration

Always a major force in the history of the United States and the life of its people, immigration underwent new changes and sparked new controversies in the last half of the 20th century. The period began as an extension of themes in effect for approximately two decades. Regular immigration, controlled by tight and discriminatory legislation, was not large. As had been the case during the entire history of the United States, most of it was white and of European origin. Even though previous subjective limitations were reconfirmed, with slight modifications, in new legislation in 1952, the numbers started to pick up, due largely to special measures designed to address exceptional social and international circumstances. A "war brides" provision, designed to cover foreign spouses of American service personnel abroad—a product of the war or immediate postwar period—alone authorized some 125,000 new entrants. The troubled aftermath of the war and start of the cold war in Europe moved Congress to pass other special refugee and displaced persons laws that circumvented regular immigration policy. In the 1950s Europeans continued to make up more than 50 percent of the people coming to the United States.

The era of the 1960s, however, produced major changes and the beginning of large new themes. In the first place, Congress in 1965 replaced the previous racially based quota system with a new law that increased absolute maximum immigration, treated each nation (and presumably races and other groups) equally, and established an elaborate program of preferences for gaining entry into the United States. The law of 1965 and amendments that followed provided a foundation for substantive changes in the racial and ethnic mix of immigration, but political and economic upheaval in many parts of the world continued to be important factors. After the 1960s the absolute number of immigrants increased markedly. Legislation limited normal immigration to 270,000 per year (with no more than 20,000 from a single country), but there were so many exceptions to the law that the average in the 1980s was more than 700,000 per year, the second highest decade in U.S. history. A law passed in 1990 envisioned a maximum of 675,000 per year, but virtually no one believed that immigration would be held to that number in any year, and signals suggested that the 1990s well could bring the largest immigration ever recorded.

The period also produced a dramatic shift in the origin—and thus the racial or ethnic characteristics—of the immigrants. Europeans (most of whom were white people), who historically had dominated the lists, made up less than 20 percent of the total in the 1970s and fewer than 10 percent in the 1980s. Since the start of the 1960s the origin of the largest number of immigrants has been Latin America. Hispanics made up more than 50 percent of legal immigrants in the 1960s and nearly 50 percent in the two decades that followed. Starting in the 1970s, second largest has been immigration from Asia. Asians and Hispanics together composed at least 80 percent of immigration in the 1970s and nearly 90 percent in the 1980s, and they were changing the face of America—its politics, its economics, and almost every aspect of society.

Feeling continued to grow that the United States, perhaps alone among nations of the world, had lost control of its borders, if not immigration policy in general; that such huge numbers were a financial burden and (considering the attitudes, racial and ethnic content of the immigrants) were divisive and were a threat to the basic fabric of the nation. Most pressure for controls came from affected states—California, for example—and especially at a time when Republicans, who did not expect much support from racial and ethnic minority groups, were in power. Purists pointed to Emma Lazarus's noble inscription on the Statue of Liberty, and they received support from some politicians, mostly Democrats, accustomed to receiving immigrant or family-of-immigrant votes. Hispanics opposed virtually all restriction on immigration or on immigrants already living in the United States. Some demographers insisted that because of falling birthrates in the general populace, only immigration would allow the nation to maintain its population.

TABLE 1.33   IMMIGRATION BY REGION OF LAST RESIDENCE, 1941–1990

Intercensal Decade	Total	Europe[a]		Asia[b]		Africa		Americas[c]	
		Percent	Number	Percent	Number	Percent	Number	Percent	Number
1941–1950	1,035,039	60.0	621,023	3.1	32,086	0.7	7,245	34.3	355,019
1951–1960	2,515,479	52.7	1,325,657	6.1	153,444	0.6	15,093	39.6	996.130
1961–1970	3,321,677	33.8	1,122,727	12.9	428,496	0.9	29,895	51.7	1,717,307
1971–1980	4,493,314	17.8	799,810	35.3	1,586,140	1.8	80.880	44.1	1,981,551
1981–1990	7,338,062	9.6	705,630	38.3	2,817,391	2.6	192,212	48.7	3,580,928

[a] Includes all of former USSR except 1941–1950 when the country was divided into European and Asian USSR.
[b] Includes Southwest Asia, e.g., Iraq, Israel, Syria, Turkey.
[c] Includes Canada, Mexico, the Caribbean, Central America, and South America.
Source: Gall and Gall, *Record of Asian Americans,* 442–443.

TABLE 1.34   IMMIGRATION RATE BY DECADE, 1941–1990

Period	Total Number ('000s)	Rate per 1,000 U.S. Population
1941–50	1,035	0.7
1951–60	2,515	1.5
1961–70	3,322	1.7
1971–80	4,493	2.1
1981–90	7,338	2.9
Highest Rate		
1901–10	8,795	10.4

Source: Wright, *Universal Almanac 1995,* 315.

TABLE 1.35   IMMIGRATION AS PERCENT OF POPULATION GROWTH, 1945–1990

Period	Percent
1945–49	10.2
1950–54	10.6
1955–59	10.7
1960–64	12.5
1965–69	19.7
1971–80	19.4
1981–90	32.8
Highest Percent	
1901–10	39.6

Source: Wright, *Universal Almanac 1995,* 315.

TABLE 1.36 IMMIGRATION BY REGION AND LAST COUNTRY OF RESIDENCE, 1940–1980

Region and Country of Last Residence[a]	1941–1950	1951–1960	1961–1970	1971–1980
All Countries	1,035,039	2,515,479	3,321,677	4,493,314
Europe	621,147	1,325,727	1,123,492	800,368
Austria-Hungary	28,329	103,743	26,022	16,028
Austria	24,860	67,106	20,621	9,478
Hungary	3,469	36,637	5,401	6,550
Belgium	12,189	18,575	9,192	5,329
Czechoslovakia	8,347	918	3,273	6,023
Denmark	5,393	10,984	9,201	4,429
France	38,809	51,121	45,237	25,069
Germany	226,578	477,765	190,796	74,414
Greece	8,973	47,608	85,969	92,369
Ireland	19,789	48,362	32,966	11,490
Italy	57,661	185,491	214,111	129,368
Netherlands	14,860	52,277	30,606	10,492
Norway-Sweden	20,765	44,632	32,600	10,472
Norway	10,100	22,935	15,484	3,941
Sweden	10,665	21,697	17,116	6,531
Poland	7,571	9,985	53,539	37,234
Portugal	7,423	19,588	76,065	101,710
Romania	1,076	1,039	2,531	12,393
Soviet Union	571	671	2,465	38,961
Spain	2,898	7,894	44,659	39,141
Switzerland	10,547	17,675	18,453	8,235
United Kingdom	139,306	202,824	213,822	137,374
Yugoslavia	1,576	8,225	20,381	30,540
Other Europe	8,486	16,350	11,604	9,282
Asia	37,028	153,249	427,642	1,588,178
China[b]	16,709	9,657	34,764	124,326
Hong Kong[c]	...	15,541	75,007	113,467
India	1,761	1,973	27,189	164,134
Iran	1,380	3,388	10,339	45,136
Israel[d]	476	25,476	29,602	37,713
Japan	1,555	46,250	39,988	49,775
Korea[e]	107	6,231	34,526	267,638
Philippines	4,691	19,307	98,376	354,987
Turkey	798	3,519	10,142	13,399
Vietnam	...	335	4,340	172,820
Other Asia	9,551	21,572	63,369	244,783
North America	354,804	996,944	1,716,374	1,982,735
Canada & Newfoundland	171,718	377,952	413,310	169,939
Mexico	60,589	299,811	453,937	640,294
Caribbean	49,725	123,091	470,213	741,126
Cuba	26,313	78,948	208,536	264,863
Dominican Republic	5,627	9,897	93,292	148,135
Haiti	911	4,442	34,499	56,335
Jamaica	...	8,869	74,906	137,577
Other Caribbean	16,874	20,935	58,980	134,216
Central America	21,665	44,751	101,330	134,640
El Salvador	5,132	5,895	14,992	34,436
Other Central America	16,533	38,856	86,338	100,204
South America	21,831	91,628	257,954	295,741
Argentina	3,338	19,486	49,721	29,897
Colombia	3,858	18,048	72,028	77,347
Ecuador	2,417	9,841	36,780	50,077
Other South America	12,218	44,253	99,425	138,420
Other America	29,276	59,711	19,630	995
Africa	7,367	14,092	28,954	80,779
Oceania	14,551	12,976	25,122	41,242
Not specified	142	12,491	93	12

[a] Data for 1940–79 refers to country of last residence and data for 1980 refers to country of birth.
[b] Beginning in 1957 includes Taiwan.
[c] Data not reported separately until 1952.
[d] Data not reported separately until 1949.
[e] Data not reported separately until 1948.
Source: Reddy, Record of Hispanic Americans, 34–35.

TABLE 1.37 IMMIGRATION BY REGION AND SELECTED COUNTRY OF LAST RESIDENCE, 1981–1990

Region and Country of Last Residence	1981–1990	1985	1986	1987	1988	1989	1990
All Countries	7,338,062	570,009	601,708	601,516	643,025	1,090,924	1,536,483
Europe	761,550	69,526	69,224	67,967	71,854	94,338	124,026
Austria-Hungary	24,885	2,521	2,604	2,401	3,200	3,586	4,733
Austria	18,340	1,930	2,039	1,769	2,493	2,845	3,774
Hungary	6,545	591	565	632	707	741	959
Belgium	7,066	775	843	859	706	705	827
Czechoslovakia	7,227	684	588	715	744	526	578
Denmark	5,370	465	544	515	561	617	674
France	32,353	3,530	3,876	3,809	3,637	4,101	4,265
Germany	91,961	10,028	9,853	9,923	9,748	10,419	12,152
Greece	38,377	3,487	3,497	4,087	4,690	4,588	3,887
Ireland	31,969	1,288	1,757	3,032	5,121	6,983	9,740
Italy	67,254	6,351	5,711	4,666	5,332	11,089	16,246
Netherlands	12,238	1,235	1,263	1,303	1,152	1,253	1,515
Norway-Sweden	15,182	1,557	1,564	1,540	1,669	1,809	1,930
Norway	4,164	386	367	372	446	556	552
Sweden	11,018	1,171	1,197	1,168	1,223	1,253	1,378
Poland	83,252	7,409	6,540	5,818	7,298	13,279	18,364
Portugal	40,431	3,811	3,804	4,009	3,290	3,861	4,066
Romania	30,857	3,764	3,809	2,741	2,915	3,535	3,496
Soviet Union	57,677	1,532	1,001	1,139	1,408	4,570	14,779

Region and Country of Last Residence	1981–1990	1985	1986	1987	1988	1989	1990
Spain	20,433	2,278	2,232	2,056	1,972	2,179	2,744
Switzerland	8,849	980	923	964	920	1,072	1,288
United Kingdom	159,173	15,591	16,129	15,889	14,667	16,961	19,054
Yugoslavia	18,762	1,521	1,915	1,793	2,039	2,464	2,778
Other Europe	8,234	719	771	708	785	741	910
Asia	2,738,157	255,164	258,546	248,293	254,745	296,420	321,879
China	346,747	33,095	32,389	32,669	34,300	39,284	40,639
Hong Kong	98,215	10,795	9,930	8,785	11,817	15,257	14,367
India	250,786	24,536	24,808	26,394	25,312	28,599	28,809
Iran	116,172	12,327	12,031	10,323	9,846	13,027	14,905
Israel	44,273	4,279	5,124	4,753	4,444	5,494	5,906
Japan	47,085	4,552	4,444	4,711	5,085	5,454	6,431
Korea	333,746	34,791	35,164	35,397	34,151	33,016	30,964
Philippines	548,764	53,137	61,492	58,315	61,017	66,119	71,279
Turkey	23,233	1,690	1,975	2,080	2,200	2,538	3,205
Vietnam	280,782	20,367	15,010	13,073	12,856	13,174	14,755
Other Asia	648,354	55,595	56,179	51,793	53,717	74,458	90,619
North America	3,615,225	225,519	254,078	265,026	294,906	672,639	1,050,527
Canada & Newfoundland	156,938	16,354	16,060	16,741	15,821	18,294	24,642
Mexico	1,655,843	61,290	66,753	72,511	95,170	405,660	680,186
Caribbean	872,051	79,374	98,527	100,615	110,949	87,597	112,635
Cuba	144,578	17,115	30,787	27,363	16,610	9,523	9,436
Dominican Republic	252,035	23,861	26,216	24,947	27,195	26,744	42,136
Haiti	138,379	9,872	12,356	14,643	34,858	13,341	19,869
Jamaica	208,148	18,277	18,916	22,430	20,474	23,572	23,667
Other Caribbean	128,911	10,249	10,252	11,232	11,812	14,417	17,527
Central America	468,088	28,447	30,086	30,366	31,311	101,273	146,243
El Salvador	213,539	10,093	10,881	10,627	12,043	57,628	79,601
Other Central America	254,549	18,354	19,205	19,739	19,268	43,645	66,642
South America	461,847	40,052	42,650	44,782	41,646	59,812	86,821
Argentina	27,327	1,925	2,318	2,192	2,556	3,766	5,953
Colombia	122,849	11,802	11,213	11,482	10,153	14,918	23,783
Ecuador	56,315	4,601	4,518	4,656	4,736	7,587	12,474
Other South America	255,356	21,724	24,601	26,452	24,201	33,541	44,611
Other America	458	2	2	11	9	3	. . .
Africa	176,893	15,236	15,500	15,730	17,124	22,485	32,797
Oceania	45,205	4,552	4,352	4,437	4,324	4,956	6,804
Not specified	1,032	12	8	63	72	86	450

Source: Reddy, *Record of Hispanic Americans*, 34–35.

TABLE 1.38   ASIAN IMMIGRATION BY COUNTRY OF ORIGIN, 1941–1990

Decade	Chinese	Japanese	Asian Indian	Korean	Filipino	Vietnamese
1941–1950	16,709	1,555	1,761	. . .	4,691	. . .
1951–1960	9,657[a]	46,250	1,973	6,231	19,307	. . .
1961–1970	34,764	39,988	27,189	34,526	98,376	3,788
1971–1980	12,326	49,775	164,134	271,956	360,216	179,681
1981–1990	366,622[b]	43,248	261,841	338,824	495,271	401,419

[a] Beginning in 1957, Chinese total includes immigration from Taiwan.
[b] Beginning in 1982, Taiwan was no longer included in the Chinese total. From 1982 to 1990 immigration from Taiwan was 118,105. These immigrants were not included in the total for China.
Source: Gall and Gall, *Record of Asian Americans*, 451.

Preference System Immigration Act of 1965

Exempt from preference requirements and numerical quotas: spouses, unmarried minor children, and parents of U.S. citizens.

1. Unmarried adult children of U.S. citizens. 20 percent.
2. Spouses and unmarried adult children of permanent resident aliens. 20 percent (26 percent after 1980).
3. Members of the professions and scientists and artists of exceptional ability. 10 percent: requires certification from U.S. Department of Labor.
4. Married children of U.S. citizens. 10 percent.
5. Brothers and sisters of U.S. citizens over 21. 24 percent.
6. Skilled and unskilled workers in occupations for which labor is in short supply in the U.S. 10 percent: requires certification from U.S. Department of Labor.
7. Refugees from communist or communist-dominated countries, or the Middle East. 6 percent.
8. Nonpreference: applicants not entitled to any of the above. (Since there are more preference applicants than can be accommodated, this has not been used.)

Source: Roger Daniels, *Coming to America: A History of Immigration and Ethnicity in American Life* (New York, 1990), 342.

TABLE 1.39 IMMIGRATION FROM MEXICO, CENTRAL AMERICA, AND CARIBBEAN, 1941–1990

Year	Mexico	Total Caribbean	Central America
1941–50	60,589	49,725	21,665
1951–60	299,811	123,091	44,751
1961–70	453,994	470,213	101,330
1971–80	640,294	741,126	134,640
1981–90	1,655,843	872,051	468,088
1985	61,290	79,374	28,447
1986	66,753	98,527	30,086
1987	72,511	100,615	30,366
1988	95,170	110,949	31,311
1989	405,660	87,597	101,273
1990	680,186	112,635	146,243

Source: Reddy, Record of Hispanic Americans, 34–35.

Exemptions to Visa Limitations and Number Admitted, 1989

The major categories of immigrants exempt from the 270,000 limit are:

- Immediate relatives of U.S. citizens (spouses, children, parents of children over 21): 217,514.
- Refugees and asylee adjustments: 84,288.
- Special immigrants (including certain ministers of religion, certain former employees of the U.S. government abroad): 4,986.
- Amerasians born in Vietnam: 8,589.
- Babies born abroad to legal permanent residents (number not available).
- Aliens who have unlawfully resided in the U.S. since Jan. 1, 1982 (a provision of the Immigration Reform and Control Act, 1986): 478,814.

Source: Wright, Universal Almanac 1991, 202.

Refugees and Asylum

A major reason why immigration totals vastly exceeded the maximum specified in regular legislation was because of special provisions, usually produced in piecemeal fashion, for refugees and individuals seeking asylum. A refugee was defined as a person living outside his/her country who for specific reasons, usually some form of persecution or impending threat, could not or would not return. That individual sought refuge in the United States. The refugee issue as a rule pertained to groups, often measured in thousands, if not hundreds of thousands. The problem of asylum applied to a refugee already present in the United States, legally or illegally, who applied to have the residence legitimized. An appeal for asylum at times involved a single individual, and it could affect relations with the nation from which the asylee departed. Beginning shortly after the end of the Second World War, the United States adopted several refugee measures in response to crises, political upheaval, or simply the existence of oppressive regimes. The largest groups of refugees came in waves, each of which could be traced to a well-known incident or set of circumstances abroad. First came a response to large numbers of "displaced persons" in Europe, a product of the Second World War, followed by people fleeing communist control of Eastern Europe, including brutal Soviet suppression of the Hungarian Rebellion of 1956. Hundreds of thousands of people fled Cuba shortly after seizure of control by Fidel Castro in 1959–60, most of them taking residence in Florida; a smaller, but still substantial, flight from Cuba came in 1980 in what became known as the Mariel Boatlift. An end to the wars in Indochina in the mid-1970s, culminating in communist victories in three countries, produced some of the largest waves of immigration since the Second World War.

The United States generally has been liberal and generous in its response to oppression in foreign lands. Even so, the existence of so much upheaval and so many refugees in the last half of the 20th century necessitated some selectivity in identifying situations worthy of a new act of Congress. These decisions and the absense of others has led to charges of discrimination, perhaps based on racial prejudice, as in the case of Haitians fleeing their country in the 1980s. The problem partly stemmed from the fact that refugee status represented a reaction to persecution, usually but not always political, of some sort. It did not apply to poor economic conditions in a country. Escape from economic depravity returned one to the familiar issue of illegal immigrants.

TABLE 1.40 REFUGEE STATUS GRANTED BY COUNTRY OF ORIGIN, 1980–1990

Country	1980–1988	1989	1990
Afghanistan	23,840	1,770	1,593
Albania	421	47	98
Angola	501	19	60
Benin	0	0	4
Bulgaria	1,140	110	327
Cambodia	116,191	2,114	260
Cameroon	0	0	3
China	1,156	2	6
Cuba	8,597	2,517	1,318
Czechoslovakia	8,896	925	341
Egypt	120	0	0
El Salvador	107	8	15
Ethiopia	19,663	1,697	3,061
Ghana	0	0	7
Greece	421	0	0
Hong Kong	1,777	102	208
Hungary	4,916	1,075	274
Iran	24,015	5,132	3,312
Iraq	6,654	111	47
Laos	120,544	10,780	9,060
Lebanon	448	1	0
Lesotho	28	2	2
Liberia	0	0	4
Libya	17	1	0
Macau	81	0	1
Malawi	49	6	0
Mozambique	91	4	3
Namibia	89	0	0
Nicaragua	200	323	527
Peru	0	0	3
Philippines	96	0	0
Poland	32,735	3,585	1,483
Romania	29,087	3,173	3,561
Somalia	9	14	33
South Africa	188	21	34
Sudan	32	1	7
Syria	745	1	0
Tanzania	1	0	0
Turkey	721	0	0
Uganda	69	40	27
USSR	48,191	39,704	52,866
Vietnam	258,922	22,198	21,078
Yugoslavia	74	1	6
Zaire	127	18	70
All Others	341	0	0
Totals	711,303	95,505	99,697

Source: Gall and Gall, Record of Asian Americans, 442–443.

TABLE 1.41   PERSONS ADMITTED AS REFUGEES, 1948–1980

Admitted Under Parole Authority		
Years	Classification	Number
1948–52	Displaced Persons	about 450,000
1953–56	Refugee Relief Act	about 205,000
1956	East European orphans	925
1956–57	Hungarians	38,045
1958–62	Portuguese (victims of earthquakes in the Azores)	4,811
1960–65	East European escapees (Fair Share Refugee Law)	19,745
1962	Chinese from Hong Kong and Macao	14,741
1962–79	Cubans	692,219
1963	Russian Old Believers from Turkey	200
1972–73	Ugandan Asians	1,500
1973–79	Soviet Union	35,758
1975–79	Indochinese (10 separate programs)	about 400,000
1975–77	Chileans	1,400
1976–77	Chileans, Bolivians, Uruguayans	343
1978–79	Lebanese	1,000
1979	Cuban prisoners	15,000
1980	Refugees, all sources	110,000
Admitted Under 1965 Immigration Act		
1968–80	Seventh preference[a]	about 130,000
Admitted Without Authority		
1980	Cuban-Haitian "special entrants" (boat people from Mariel, etc.)	140,000
Total[b]		about 2,261,564

[a] Refers to that provision in act of 1965 that applied to refugees from communist countries or Middle East.
[b] Because legal immigration in 1945–80 was recorded at 10,900,000, refugees made up slightly more than 20 percent of the total.
Source: Daniels, *Coming to America,* 337.

TABLE 1.42   SOUTHEAST ASIAN REFUGEE ARRIVALS BY NATIONALITY, 1975–1990

Fiscal Year	Country or Nationality			
	Cambodia	Laos	Vietnam	Total
1975	4,600	800	125,000	130,394
1976	1,100	10,200	3,200	14,466
1977	300	400	1,900	2,563
1978	1,300	8,000	11,100	20,397
1979	6,000	30,200	44,500	80,678
1980	16,000	55,500	95,200	166,727
1981	27,100	19,300	86,10	132,454
1982	20,100	9,400	42,600	72,155
1983	13,191	2,946	23,030	39,167
1984	19,849	7,224	24,927	52,000
1985	19,237	5,233	25,383	49,853
1986	10,054	12,894	22,443	45,391
1987	1,949	15,604	22,611	40,164
1988	2,900	14,589	17,958	35,447
1989	2,220	12,762	30,805	45,787
1990	2,325	8,712	41,021	52,065

Source: Gall and Gall, *Record of Asian Americans,* 451.

TABLE 1.43   ASYLUM GRANTEES, 1984–1990

Nationality	1984	1985	1986	1987	1988	1989	1990
All Nationalities	11,627	6,514	4,284	5,093	7,340	9,229	5,672
Afghanistan	268	92	91	24	50	23	24
Bulgaria	19	11	13	4	14	17	26
China, Mainland	16	74	22	27	90	150	679
Cuba	18	65	17	73	36	107	229
El Salvador	503	129	90	39	149	443	260
Ethiopia	361	210	217	205	570	517	382
Guatemala	6	11	7	7	42	102	65
Hungary	82	65	26	14	40	33	20
Iran	7,442	4,087	1,568	1,346	1,107	723	256
Laos	8	1	2	2	4	7	38
Lebanon	19	27	4	48	73	76	86
Libya	17	88	55	115	79	39	23
Nicaragua	1,153	557	1,284	2,213	3,725	5,092	2,277
Panama	. . .	. . .	. . .	. . .	47	318	251
Peru	1	. . .	. . .	1	1	24	27
Poland	953	549	456	558	488	329	39
Romania	192	113	152	137	398	650	204
Somalia	35	22	16	14	79	128	204
Soviet Union	70	35	44	33	47	127	264
Syria	36	41	57	67	36	28	63
Other	428	337	163	166	265	296	255

Source: Reddy, *Record of Hispanic Americans,* 114.

Illegal Immigration

Illegal immigrants, identified under such various names as undocumented aliens or simply illegals, continued to be an issue of mystery and much controversy. The number of people remained unknown, of course, and estimates placed the number at between 3 million and 12 million living illegally in the United States during this period. The bulk of them came from Latin America, and within Latin America mostly from Mexico, although efforts to smuggle people in from other countries, especially from Asia, became conspicuous in the 1980s. Focus remained on the traffic across the 2,000-mile U.S.–Mexican border, as the United States searched for ways to keep the illegals out. A border police, established in 1924 for that purpose, was by the 1980s intercepting more than 1 million per year, most of them unemployed or underemployed working- or peasant-class people who sought a higher income north of the border. Proposals for dealing with the problem included substantially increasing the border police, of course, as well as fencing off all or much of the southwest border with Mexico. A Reform and Control Act of 1986 (also called the Simpson Act) struck at the economic incentive for the traffic by imposing stiff penalties on employers who knowingly hired illegal immigrants, but the measure also made provision for temporary agricultural workers, and it offered to legitimize certain classes of illegal aliens—perhaps several million people—already living in the country. The measure provoked contrasting charges (before passage and afterward) of being harsh and inhumane on the one hand, and permissive, loosely administered, and ineffective on the other. Perhaps the only clear conclusion was that illegal immigration continued and that it would remain an important issue for the 1990s.

TABLE 1.44 TOTAL POPULATION AND ESTIMATED ILLEGAL POPULATION FOR THE 10 STATES WITH THE GREATEST NUMBER OF ILLEGALS, 1987

State	Total Population	Illegals	Percent Illegals
California	27,663,000	1,742,343	6.3
New York	17,825,000	398,153	2.2
Texas	16,789,000	316,480	1.9
Illinois	11,582,000	229,703	2.0
Florida	12,023,000	136,121	1.1
New Jersey	7,672,000	62,956	0.8
Virginia	5,904,000	57,851	1.0
Maryland	4,535,000	54,448	1.2
Arizona	3,386,000	42,538	1.3
Washington	4,538,000	37,433	0.8
Total U.S. Population	243,399,000	3,500,000	1.4

Note: Only about 1 percent of U.S. residents are illegal aliens, but 6 percent are illegal in California.
Source: American Demographics, September, 1988, 43.

TABLE 1.45 ALIENS EXPELLED, 1946–1990

Year	Total	Deported	Required to Depart
1946	116,320	14,375	101,945
1950	579,105	6,628	572,477
1955	247,797	15,028	232,769
1960	59,625	6,829	52,796
1965	105,406	10,143	95,263
1970	320,241	16,893	303,348
1975	679,000	23,000	656,000
1980	737,000	17,000	719,000
1985	1,062,000	21,000	1,041,000
1990	1,045,000	26,000	1,019,000

Source: George T. Kurian, Datapedia of the United States, 1790–2000: America Year-by-Year (Lanham, Md., 1994), 68.

TABLE 1.46 BORDER-PATROL ACTIVITIES, 1984–1990

Activities	1984	1985	1986	1987	1988	1989	1990
Persons Apprehended	1,149,847	1,272,435	1,705,278	1,168,861	980,522	906,535	1,123,223
Deportable Aliens Located	1,140,466	1,262,435	1,692,544	1,158,030	969,214	891,147	1,103,353
Mexican aliens	1,104,429	1,218,695	1,635,702	1,123,725	928,278	830,985	1,054,849
Working in agriculture	83,706	76,054	80,922	15,862	3,333	2,592	4,661
Working in trades, crafts industry, and service	24,854	26,674	44,971	25,386	13,362	8,078	7,544
Welfare/seeking employment	925,653	1,054,073	1,419,542	986,584	836,065	725,008	865,739
Canadian aliens	5,805	5,868	6,235	4,814	4,237	5,297	5,746
All others	30,232	37,872	50,607	29,491	36,699	54,865	42,758
Smugglers of Aliens Located	13,435	14,666	19,275	11,560	10,373	13,794	21,901
Aliens Located Who Were Smuggled into the United States	91,722	95,741	114,665	59,268	50,122	50,638	71,049
Seizures (conveyances)	6,456	7,327	10,512	7,512	6,643	10,789	17,275
Value of Seizures (dollars)	44,505,793	122,007,498	165,106,668	590,638,336	721,213,999	1,212,724,497	830,734,350
Narcotics	42,939,946	119,822,206	161,736,752	582,395,375	700,523,810	1,191,505,137	797,768,179
Other	1,565,847	2,185,292	3,369,916	8,242,961	20,690,189	21,219,360	32,966,171

Source: Reddy, Record of Hispanic Americans, 135.

TABLE 1.47 FOREIGN-BORN POPULATION, BY PLACE OF BIRTH, 1980 AND 1990

(as of April 1)

Place of Birth	1980 (1,000)	1990 Number (1,000)	1990 Percent Distribution
Total	14,080	19,767	100.0
Europe	4,743	4,017	20.3
Austria	146	88	0.4
Belgium	36	34	0.2
Czechoslovakia	113	87	0.4
Denmark	43	35	0.2
Finland	29	22	0.1
France	120	119	0.6
Germany	849	712	3.6
Greece	211	177	0.9
Hungary	144	110	0.6
Ireland	198	170	0.9
Italy	832	581	2.9
Latvia	34	26	0.1
Lithuania	48	30	0.2
Netherlands	103	96	0.5
Norway	63	42	0.2
Poland	418	388	2.0
Portugal	212	210	1.1
Romania	67	91	0.5
Spain	74	76	0.4
Sweden	77	54	0.3
Switzerland	43	39	0.2
United Kingdom	669	640	3.2
Yugoslavia	153	142	0.7
Soviet Union	406	334	1.7
Asia	2,540	4,979	25.2
Afghanistan	4	28	0.1
Burma	11	20	0.1
Cambodia	20	119	0.6
China	286	530	2.7
Hong Kong	80	147	0.7
India	206	450	2.3
Indonesia	30	48	0.2
Iran	122	211	1.1
Iraq	32	45	0.2
Israel	67	86	0.4
Japan	222	290	1.5
Jordan	22	32	0.2
Korea	290	568	2.9
Laos	55	172	0.9
Lebanon	53	86	0.4
Malaysia	10	34	0.2
Pakistan	31	92	0.5
Philippines	501	913	4.6
Saudi Arabia	17	13	0.1
Syria	22	37	0.2
Taiwan	75	244	1.2
Thailand	55	107	0.5
Turkey	52	55	0.3
Vietnam	231	543	2.7
Canada	843	745	3.8
Mexico	2,199	4,298	21.7
Caribbean	1,258	1,938	9.8
Antigua-Barbuda	4	12	0.1
Bahamas	14	22	0.1
Barbados	27	43	0.2
Cuba	608	737	3.7
Dominican Republic	169	348	1.8
Grenada	7	18	0.1
Haiti	92	225	1.1
Jamaica	197	334	1.7
Trinidad and Tobago	66	116	0.6
Central America	354	1,134	5.7
Belize	14	30	0.2
Costa Rica	30	44	0.2
El Salvador	94	465	2.4
Guatemala	63	226	1.1
Honduras	39	109	0.6
Nicaragua	44	169	0.9
Panama	61	86	0.4
South America	561	1,037	5.2
Argentina	69	93	0.5
Bolivia	14	31	0.2
Brazil	41	82	0.4
Chile	35	56	0.3
Colombia	144	286	1.4
Ecuador	86	143	0.7
Guyana	49	121	0.6
Peru	55	144	0.7
Uruguay	13	21	0.1
Venezuela	33	42	0.2
Africa	200	364	1.8
Cape Verde	10	14	0.1
Egypt	43	66	0.3
Ethiopia	8	35	0.2
Ghana	8	21	0.1
Kenya	6	14	0.1
Morocco	10	16	0.1
Nigeria	26	55	0.3
South Africa	16	35	0.2
Oceania	78	104	0.5
Australia	36	42	0.2
Fiji	8	16	0.1
New Zealand	11	15	0.1
Tonga	6	11	0.1
Western Samoa	13	11	0.1

Source: Bureau of Census, *Statistical Abstract, 1993*, 50.

TABLE 1.48 FIVE STATES WITH HIGHEST PERCENTAGE OF FOREIGN-BORN POPULATION, 1990

State	Foreign-Born Population	Foreign-Born Population as a Percentage of Total Population	Percent of Total Population Entering U.S., 1980–90
California	6,458,825	21.7	10.9
New York	2,851,861	15.8	6.6
Hawaii	162,704	14.7	6.0
Florida	1,662,601	12.8	5.1
New Jersey	966,610	12.5	5.0

Source: Wright, *Universal Almanac 1995,* 315.

Naturalization: How to Become an American Citizen

A person who desires to be naturalized as a citizen of the United States may obtain the necessary application form as well as detailed information from the nearest office of the Immigration and Naturalization Service or from the clerk of a court handling naturalization cases.

An applicant must be at least 18 years old. He must have been a lawful resident of the United States continuously for five years. For husbands and wives of U.S. citizens the period is three years in most instances. Special provisions apply to certain veterans of the Armed Forces.

An applicant must have been physically present in this country for at least half of the required five years' residence.

Every applicant for naturalization must:

(1) demonstrate an understanding of the English language, including an ability to read, write, and speak words in ordinary usage in the English language (persons physically unable to do so, and persons who, on the date of their examinations, are over 50 years of age and have been lawful permanent residents of the United States for 20 years or more are exempt).

(2) have been a person of good moral character, attached to the principles of the Constitution, and well disposed to the good order and happiness of the United States for five years just before filing the petition or for whatever other period of residence is required in his case and continue to be such a person until admitted to citizenship; and

(3) demonstrate a knowledge and understanding of the fundamentals of the history, and the principles and form of government, of the U.S.

When the applicant files his petition he pays the court clerk $50. At the preliminary hearing he may be represented by a lawyer or social service agency. There is a 30-day wait. If action is favorable, there is a final hearing before a judge, who administers the following oath of allegiance:

I hereby declare, on oath, that I absolutely and entirely renounce and abjure all allegiance and fidelity to any foreign prince, potentate, state or sovereignty, to whom or which I have heretofore been a subject or citizen; that I will support and defend the Constitution and laws of the United States of America against all enemies, foreign and domestic; that I will bear true faith and allegiance to the same; that I will bear arms on behalf of the United States when required by the law; that I will perform noncombatant service in the armed forces of the United States when required by the law; that I will perform work of national importance under civilian direction when required by the law; and that I take this obligation freely without any mental reservation or purpose of evasion; so help me God.

Source: As summarized in Hoffman, ed., *World Almanac and Book of Facts, 1992,* 825.

CHAPTER 2 Weather and Climate

The addition of Alaska and Hawaii as states in the 1950s meant that the United States, more than ever, experienced virtually every known climate and aspect of weather. Although the bulk of the nation rested in the temperate zone, it was on the fringes of other zones and in the path of atmospheric and oceanic forces that could produce abrupt and powerful change in the weather. Some individuals—meteorologists, for example, and dedicated weather watchers—heralded this grand diversity, although they did not acclaim some of the destructive turns of nature. Others who preferred more steadiness or comfort from the climate moved to the southern states, to Florida or Arizona if they could manage it, or retired there when work was done. Most Americans, it seemed, took the weather as it came, frequently complaining but assuming that it was what fate had handed them.

The last half of the 20th century did produce forces that were either new or newly discovered. Scientists could show that national and world climate had been slowly warming for many years, and they blamed the problem on human behavior, notably deforestation and burning of fossil fuels for industry and industrialized society. The experts could not agree on the long-range impact of this force, although they inclined toward pessimism. Some warned of impending catastrophe. Americans became acquainted with something called acid rain, another consequence of industrial society that involved precipitation—rain or even snow—picking up chemicals placed in the air by automobiles and coal-fueled power plants and bringing them down to spoil plants, trees, and lakes. In the late 1980s a new—in truth, newly discovered—weather phenomenon called El Niño, which began with mysterious warming of normally cold specified Pacific waters every few years, attracted attention as a weather maker of unappreciated dimension. Evidently there had been eight El Niños between the 1940s and 1980s, and they had produced huge changes in weather. Unfortunately it was difficult to determine what the changes would be. If El Niño of 1976–77 had produced drought in California and bitter cold in the East, El Niño in 1982–83 had brought huge storms that broke off pieces of the coast in California and a mild winter along the Atlantic coast. Worldwide this Pacific current of the 1980s had caused perhaps as many as 2,000 deaths and damage measured in billions of dollars. These new manifestations of weather and others as well remained issues to be reckoned with in the 1990s, although the government did begin in 1990 with a law designed to address problems related to acid rain and global warming.

Some of the most concrete weather-related changes after 1945 had to do with forecasting and reporting. The most useful aides before that time had been weather balloons and buoys, airplanes that flew above weather systems, and forms of communication—such as radio—that relayed information on to other weather stations. Helpful as these devices had been—and they would continue to be used—forecasting remained as much an art as a science, and one with justification could speak of "weather prediction."

After 1945, technology developed for other purposes found its way into learning about weather. By the 1950s radar, originally a tool of military forces, was regularly detecting weather phenomena over short distances. A more sophisticated Doppler Radar, adopted by the National Storm Center in 1971, could track movement and even wind velocity of a storm. Radar could identify thunderstorms or snowstorms on the way and could warn of possible tornadoes. In 1960 the U.S. government launched its first weather satellite, *Tiros 1*. Although regarded as experimental, it became a meteorologist's dream and the precursor of a network of satellites to come. Most useful in tracking tropical storms, satellites also could detect forest fires, snowpacks, ice jams, and possibly emerging tornadoes. The computer, introduced into

weather forecasting, provided the same sort of service it supplied to other areas: storing and analysis of data, doing in almost an instant what previously had taken many people and many hours. Placing the data in context of established models, the computer allowed its operator to forecast what was likely to happen, at least in the two or three days ahead. Professionalism went beyond equipment. By the end of the 1970s most media weather forecasters were trained meteorologists. Most television stations had or had access to radar units including, by the end of the 1980s, Doppler Radar. Technology in communication satellites and in emerging television cable systems came together in May 1982 with introduction of a national weather channel, based in Atlanta, which reported national, international, and customized local weather continuously around the clock.

Modern methods of detection, analysis, and reporting did not mean that weather had become fully predictable. Systems did not always follow a model—hurricanes could turn, tornadoes emerged and died in seconds, thunderstorms developed on the spot. Nature persisted in guarding an element of mystery.

The U.S. government launched its first weather satellite in 1960. Here, a scientist works on a geostationary operational environmental satellite (GOES) prior to launch, 1980. (National Oceanic and Atmospheric Administration/Department of Commerce)

Methods of Measuring Comfort or Discomfort

Meteorologists developed systems for explaining and measuring sensations of hot and cold. Sensation of cold (wind chill) varied in accordance with changing mixtures of wind speed and temperature. Degrees of feeling hot (heat index) combined relative humidity and temperature.

TABLE 2.1   WIND-CHILL TABLE[a]

Wind Speed (mph)	Actual Temperature (in degrees Fahrenheit)																
	35	30	25	20	15	10	5	0	−5	−10	−15	−20	−25	−30	−35	−40	−45
5	33	27	21	16	12	7	0	−5	−10	−15	−21	−26	−31	−36	−42	−47	−52
10	22	16	10	3	−3	−9	−15	−22	−27	−34	−40	−46	−52	−58	−64	−71	−77
15	16	9	2	−5	−11	−18	−25	−31	−38	−45	−51	−58	−65	−72	−78	−85	−92
20	12	4	−3	−10	−17	−24	−31	−39	−46	−53	−60	−67	−74	−81	−88	−95	−103
25	8	1	−7	−15	−22	−29	−36	−44	−51	−59	−66	−74	−81	−88	−96	−103	−110
30	6	−2	−10	−18	−25	−33	−41	−49	−56	−64	−71	−79	−86	−93	−101	−109	−116
35	4	−4	−12	−20	−27	−35	−43	−52	−58	−67	−74	−82	−89	−97	−105	−113	−120
40	3	−5	−13	−21	−29	−37	−45	−53	−60	−69	−76	−84	−92	−100	−107	−115	−123
45	2	−6	−14	−22	−30	−38	−46	−54	−62	−70	−78	−85	−93	−102	−109	−117	−125

[a]Both temperature and wind cause heat loss from body surfaces. A combination of cold and wind makes a body feel colder than the actual temperature. The table shows, for example, that a temperature of 20 degrees Fahrenheit, plus a wind of 20 miles per hour, causes a body heat loss equal to that in minus 10 degrees with no wind. In other words, the wind makes 20 degrees feel like minus 10.
Source: National Weather Service, cited in Robert Famighetti, ed., *The World Almanac and Book of Facts 1996* (New York, 1995), 186.

TABLE 2.2   HEAT INDEX[a]

Relative Humidity	Air Temperature[b]										
	70	75	80	85	90	95	100	105	110	115	120
	Apparent Temperature										
0%	64	69	73	78	83	87	91	95	99	103	107
10%	65	70	75	80	85	90	95	100	105	111	116
20%	66	72	77	82	87	93	99	105	112	120	130
30%	67	73	78	84	90	96	104	113	123	135	148
40%	68	74	79	86	93	101	110	123	137	151	. . .
50%	69	75	81	88	96	107	120	135	150	. . .	. . .
60%	70	76	82	90	100	114	132	149	. . .	. . .	. . .
70%	70	77	85	93	106	124	144	. . .	. . .	. . .	. . .
80%	71	78	86	97	113	136	. . .	. . .	. . .	. . .	. . .
90%	71	79	88	102	122	. . .	. . .	. . .	. . .	. . .	. . .
100%	72	80	91	108	. . .	. . .	. . .	. . .	. . .	. . .	. . .

[a]The heat index is a measure of the contribution that high humidity makes with abnormally high temperatures in reducing the body's ability to cool itself. For example, the index shows that for an actual air temperature of 100 degrees Fahrenheit and a relative humidity of 50 percent, the effect on the human body would be the same as 120 degrees. Sunstroke and heat exhaustion are likely when the heat index reaches 105. This index is a measure of what hot weather "feels like" to the average person for various temperatures and relative humidities.
[b]Degrees Fahrenheit.
Source: National Weather Service, cited in Famighetti, ed., *World Almanac and Book of Facts 1996* (New York, 1995), 186.

TABLE 2.3   NORMAL DAILY MEAN TEMPERATURE[a]—SELECTED CITIES

State	Station	Jan.	Feb.	Mar.	Apr.	May	Jun.	Jul.	Aug.	Sep.	Oct.	Nov.	Dec.	Annual Avg.
Ala.	Mobile	49.9	53.2	60.5	67.8	74.5	80.4	82.3	81.8	77.9	68.4	59.8	53.0	67.5
Alaska	Juneau	24.2	28.4	32.7	39.7	47.0	53.0	56.0	55.0	49.4	42.2	32.0	27.1	40.6
Ariz.	Phoenix	53.6	57.7	62.2	69.9	78.8	88.2	93.5	91.5	85.6	74.5	61.9	54.1	72.6
Ark.	Little Rock	39.1	43.6	53.1	62.1	70.2	78.4	81.9	80.6	74.1	63.0	52.1	42.8	61.8
Calif.	Los Angeles	56.8	57.6	58.0	60.1	62.7	65.7	69.1	70.5	69.9	66.8	61.6	56.9	63.0
Calif.	Sacramento	45.2	50.7	53.6	58.3	65.3	71.6	75.7	75.1	71.5	64.2	53.3	45.3	60.8
Calif.	San Diego	57.4	58.6	59.6	62.0	64.1	66.8	71.0	72.6	71.4	67.7	62.0	57.4	64.2
Calif.	San Francisco	48.7	52.2	53.3	55.6	58.1	61.5	62.7	63.7	64.5	61.0	54.8	49.4	57.1
Colo.	Denver	29.7	33.4	39.0	48.2	57.2	66.9	73.5	71.4	62.3	51.4	39.0	31.0	50.3
Conn.	Hartford	24.6	27.5	37.5	48.7	59.6	68.5	73.7	71.6	63.3	52.2	41.9	29.5	49.9

State	Station	Jan.	Feb.	Mar.	Apr.	May	Jun.	Jul.	Aug.	Sep.	Oct.	Nov.	Dec.	Annual Avg.
Del.	Wilmington	30.6	33.4	42.7	52.2	62.5	71.5	76.4	75.0	68.0	56.2	46.3	35.8	54.2
D.C.	Washington	34.6	37.5	47.2	56.5	66.4	75.6	80.0	78.5	71.3	59.7	49.8	39.4	58.0
Fla.	Jacksonville	52.4	55.2	61.1	67.0	73.4	79.1	81.6	81.2	78.1	69.8	61.9	55.1	68.0
Fla.	Miami	67.2	68.5	71.7	75.2	78.7	81.4	82.6	82.8	81.9	78.3	73.6	69.1	75.9
Ga.	Atlanta	41.0	44.8	53.5	61.5	69.2	76.0	78.8	78.1	72.7	62.3	53.1	44.5	61.3
Hawaii	Honolulu	72.9	73.0	74.4	75.8	77.5	79.4	80.5	81.4	81.0	79.6	77.2	74.1	77.2
Idaho	Boise	29.0	35.9	42.4	49.1	57.5	66.5	74.0	72.5	62.6	51.8	39.9	30.1	50.9
Ill.	Chicago	21.0	25.4	37.2	48.6	58.9	68.6	73.2	71.7	64.4	52.8	40.0	26.6	49.0
Ill.	Peoria	21.6	26.3	39.0	51.4	61.9	71.5	75.5	73.1	66.1	54.0	41.2	27.0	50.7
Ind.	Indianapolis	25.5	29.6	41.4	52.4	62.8	71.9	75.4	73.2	66.6	54.7	43.0	30.9	52.3
Iowa	Des Moines	19.4	24.7	37.3	50.9	62.3	71.8	76.6	73.9	65.1	53.5	39.0	24.4	49.9
Kans.	Wichita	29.5	34.8	45.4	56.4	65.6	75.7	81.4	79.3	70.3	58.6	44.7	33.0	56.2
Ky.	Louisville	31.7	35.7	46.3	56.3	65.3	73.2	77.2	75.8	69.5	57.6	47.1	36.9	56.1
La.	New Orleans	51.3	54.3	61.6	68.5	74.8	80.0	81.9	81.5	78.1	69.1	61.1	54.5	68.1
Maine	Portland	20.8	23.3	33.0	43.3	53.3	62.4	68.6	67.3	59.1	48.5	38.7	26.5	45.4
Md.	Baltimore	31.8	34.8	44.1	53.4	63.4	72.5	77.0	75.6	68.5	56.6	46.8	36.7	55.1
Mass.	Boston	28.6	30.3	38.6	48.1	58.2	67.7	73.5	71.9	64.8	54.8	45.3	33.6	51.3
Mich.	Detroit	22.9	25.4	35.7	47.3	58.4	67.6	72.3	70.5	63.2	51.2	40.2	28.3	48.6
Mich.	Sault Ste. Marie	12.9	14.0	24.0	38.2	50.5	58.0	63.8	62.6	55.1	45.3	33.0	19.0	39.7
Minn.	Duluth	7.0	12.3	24.4	38.6	50.8	59.8	66.1	63.7	54.2	43.7	28.4	12.8	38.5
Minn.	Minneapolis– St. Paul	11.8	17.9	31.0	46.4	58.5	68.2	73.6	70.5	60.5	48.8	33.2	17.9	44.9
Miss.	Jackson	44.1	47.9	56.7	64.6	72.0	78.8	81.5	80.9	75.9	64.7	55.8	47.8	64.2
Mo.	Kansas City	25.7	31.2	42.7	54.5	64.1	73.2	78.5	76.1	67.5	56.6	43.1	30.4	53.6
Mo.	St. Louis	29.3	33.9	45.1	56.7	66.1	75.4	79.8	77.6	70.2	58.4	46.2	33.9	56.1
Mont.	Great Falls	21.2	27.4	33.3	43.6	53.1	61.6	68.2	66.9	56.6	47.5	33.9	23.9	44.8
Nebr.	Omaha	21.1	26.9	38.6	51.9	62.4	72.1	76.9	74.1	65.1	53.4	39.0	25.1	50.6
Nev.	Reno	32.9	38.0	42.8	48.6	56.5	65.1	71.6	69.6	60.4	50.8	40.3	32.7	50.8
N.H.	Concord	18.6	21.8	32.4	43.9	55.2	64.2	69.5	67.3	58.8	47.8	37.1	24.3	45.1
N.J.	Atlantic City	30.9	33.0	41.5	50.0	60.4	69.4	74.7	73.4	68.1	54.9	45.8	35.8	53.0
N.Mex.	Albuquerque	34.2	40.0	46.9	55.2	64.2	74.2	78.5	75.9	68.6	57.0	44.3	35.3	56.2
N.Y.	Albany	20.6	23.5	34.3	46.4	57.6	66.9	71.8	69.6	61.3	50.2	39.7	26.5	47.4
N.Y.	Buffalo	23.6	24.5	33.8	45.2	56.6	65.9	71.1	69.0	61.9	51.1	40.5	29.1	47.7
N.Y.	New York[b]	31.5	33.6	42.4	52.5	62.7	71.6	76.8	75.5	68.2	57.5	47.6	36.6	54.7
N.C.	Charlotte	39.3	42.5	50.9	59.4	67.4	75.7	79.3	78.3	72.4	61.3	52.1	42.6	60.1
N.C.	Raleigh	38.9	42.0	50.4	59.0	67.0	74.3	78.1	77.1	71.1	60.1	51.2	42.6	59.3
N.Dak.	Bismarck	9.2	15.7	28.2	43.0	55.0	64.4	70.4	68.3	57.0	45.7	28.6	14.0	41.6
Ohio	Cincinnati	28.1	31.8	43.0	53.2	62.9	71.0	75.1	73.5	67.3	55.1	44.3	33.5	53.2
Ohio	Cleveland	24.8	27.2	37.3	47.6	58.0	67.6	71.9	70.4	63.9	52.8	42.6	30.9	49.6
Ohio	Columbus	26.4	29.6	40.9	51.0	61.2	69.2	73.2	71.5	65.5	53.7	42.9	31.9	51.4
Okla.	Oklahoma City	35.9	40.9	50.3	60.4	68.4	76.7	82.0	81.1	73.0	62.0	49.6	39.3	60.0
Oreg.	Portland	39.6	43.6	47.3	51.0	57.1	63.5	68.2	68.6	63.3	54.5	46.1	40.2	53.6
Pa.	Philadelphia	30.4	33.0	42.4	52.4	62.9	71.8	76.7	75.5	68.2	56.4	46.4	35.8	54.3
Pa.	Pittsburgh	26.1	28.7	39.4	49.6	59.5	67.9	72.1	70.5	63.9	52.4	42.3	31.5	50.3
R.I.	Providence	27.9	29.7	37.4	47.4	57.3	66.9	72.7	71.3	64.1	53.6	44.0	32.8	50.4
S.C.	Columbia	43.8	46.8	55.2	63.0	70.9	77.4	80.8	79.7	74.2	63.3	54.6	46.9	63.1
S.Dak.	Sioux Falls	13.8	19.7	32.5	46.9	58.4	68.3	74.3	71.4	60.9	48.6	33.0	18.3	45.5
Tenn.	Memphis	39.7	44.2	53.1	62.9	71.2	79.1	82.6	81.0	74.2	63.1	52.5	43.7	62.3
Tenn.	Nashville	36.2	40.4	50.2	59.2	67.7	75.6	79.3	78.1	71.8	60.4	50.0	40.5	59.1
Tex.	Dallas– Fort Worth	43.4	47.9	56.7	65.5	72.8	81.0	85.3	84.9	77.4	67.2	56.2	46.9	65.4
Tex.	El Paso	42.8	48.1	55.1	63.4	71.8	80.4	82.3	80.1	74.4	64.0	52.4	44.1	63.2
Tex.	Houston	50.4	53.9	60.6	68.3	74.5	80.4	82.6	82.3	78.2	69.6	61.0	53.5	67.9
Utah	Salt Lake City	27.9	34.1	41.8	49.7	58.8	69.1	77.9	75.6	65.2	53.2	40.8	29.7	52.0
Vt.	Burlington	16.3	18.2	30.7	43.9	56.3	65.2	70.5	67.9	58.9	47.8	36.8	23.0	44.6
Va.	Norfolk	39.1	41.0	48.6	57.0	66.1	74.1	78.2	77.2	71.9	61.2	52.5	43.8	59.2
Va.	Richmond	35.7	38.7	48.0	57.3	66.0	73.9	78.0	76.8	70.0	58.6	49.6	40.1	57.7
Wash.	Seattle-Tacoma	40.1	43.5	45.6	49.2	55.1	60.9	65.2	65.5	60.6	52.8	45.3	40.5	52.0
Wash.	Spokane	27.1	33.3	38.7	45.9	53.9	62.0	68.8	68.4	58.9	47.3	35.1	27.8	47.3
W.Va.	Charleston	32.1	35.5	45.9	54.8	63.5	71.4	75.1	73.9	67.7	56.2	46.8	37.0	55.0
Wis.	Milwaukee	18.9	23.0	33.3	44.4	54.6	65.0	70.9	69.3	61.7	50.3	37.7	24.4	46.1
Wyo.	Cheyenne	26.5	29.3	33.6	42.5	52.0	61.3	68.4	66.4	57.4	47.0	35.2	27.8	45.6
P.R.	San Juan	77.0	77.1	78.0	79.4	80.9	82.3	82.6	82.7	82.5	81.9	80.0	78.1	80.2

[a] In Fahrenheit degrees. Airport data except as noted. Based on standard 30-year period, 1961 through 1990.
[b] City office data.

Source: Bureau of the Census, *Statistical Abstract of the United States 1993* (Washington, D.C., 1994), 231.

TABLE 2.4 SUNSHINE, AVERAGE WIND SPEED, MEAN NUMBER OF DAYS MINIMUM WITH TEMPERATURE BELOW 32 DEGREES FAHRENHEIT, AND AVERAGE RELATIVE HUMIDITY—SELECTED CITIES[a]

State	Station	Average Percentage of Possible Sunshine — Length of Record (yr.)	Annual	Average Wind Speed (mph) — Length of Record (yr.)	Annual	Jan.	Jul.	Minimum Temperature 32 Degrees or Less — Length of Records (yr.)	Mean Number (days)	Average Relative Humidity (percent) — Length of Record (yr.)	Annual M	Annual A	Jan. M	Jan. A	Jul. M	Jul. A
Ala.	Mobile	[b]40	[b]59	42	9.0	10.4	7.0	28	23	28	86	57	81	61	89	60
Alaska	Juneau	33	30	45	8.3	8.3	7.5	46	142	24	84	73	80	77	83	70
Ariz.	Phoenix	95	86	45	6.3	5.3	7.2	30	8	30	51	23	66	32	45	20
Ark.	Little Rock	32	62	48	7.8	8.6	6.7	30	60	30	84	57	80	61	88	56
Calif.	Los Angeles	32	73	42	7.5	6.7	7.8	31	(Z)	31	79	64	69	59	86	68
Calif.	Sacramento	42	78	41	7.9	7.2	9.0	40	17	30	82	46	90	70	76	28
Calif.	San Diego	50	68	50	6.9	5.9	7.4	30	(Z)	30	76	62	70	56	82	66
Calif.	San Francisco	38	66	63	10.6	7.2	13.6	31	2	31	84	61	86	66	86	59
Colo.	Denver	41	70	42	8.7	8.7	8.3	30	157	30	67	40	63	49	68	34
Conn.	Hartford	36	57	36	8.5	9.0	7.5	31	135	31	76	52	71	56	78	51
Del.	Wilmington	. . .	. . .	42	9.1	9.8	7.8	43	100	43	78	55	75	60	79	54
D.C.	Washington	42	56	42	9.4	10.0	8.2	30	71	30	74	53	69	55	76	53
Fla.	Jacksonville	39	63	41	8.0	8.2	7.1	49	15	54	88	56	87	57	88	58
Fla.	Miami	14	73	41	9.3	9.5	7.9	26	(Z)	26	84	61	84	59	84	63
Ga.	Atlanta	55	61	52	9.1	10.5	7.6	30	54	30	82	56	78	59	88	60
Hawaii	Honolulu	38	69	41	11.4	9.7	13.3	21	—	21	72	56	81	62	67	51
Idaho	Boise	48	64	51	8.8	8.0	8.4	51	124	51	69	43	80	70	54	22
Ill.	Chicago	10	55	32	10.3	11.6	8.2	32	133	32	80	60	76	67	82	57
Ill.	Peoria	47	57	47	10.0	11.2	7.8	31	129	31	83	61	79	68	86	59
Ind.	Indianapolis	46	55	42	9.6	10.9	7.4	31	118	31	83	62	80	70	87	60
Iowa	Des Moines	40	59	41	10.9	11.7	9.0	29	135	29	79	60	75	67	82	57
Kans.	Wichita	37	65	37	12.3	12.2	11.3	37	111	37	80	55	79	62	78	48
Ky.	Louisville	43	56	43	8.4	9.7	6.7	30	89	30	81	58	76	64	85	58
La.	New Orleans	17	60	42	8.2	9.4	6.1	44	13	42	87	63	85	66	91	66
Maine	Portland	50	57	50	8.8	9.2	7.6	50	157	50	79	59	76	61	80	59
Md.	Baltimore	40	57	40	9.2	9.7	8.0	40	97	37	77	54	71	57	81	53
Mass.	Boston	55	58	33	12.5	13.9	11.0	26	98	26	72	58	67	57	74	57
Mich.	Detroit	25	53	32	10.4	12.0	8.5	32	136	32	81	60	80	69	82	53
Mich.	Sault Ste. Marie	49	47	49	9.3	9.8	7.8	49	181	49	85	67	81	75	89	61
Minn.	Duluth	40	52	41	11.1	11.6	9.4	29	185	29	81	63	76	70	85	59
Minn.	Minneapolis–St. Paul	52	58	52	10.6	10.5	9.4	31	156	31	78	59	74	67	80	54
Miss.	Jackson	26	60	27	7.4	8.6	5.9	27	50	27	91	58	87	64	93	59
Mo.	Kansas City	18	62	18	10.8	11.5	9.4	18	110	18	81	60	76	63	84	57
Mo.	St. Louis	31	57	41	9.7	10.6	8.0	30	100	30	83	59	81	65	85	56
Mont.	Great Falls	46	61	49	12.8	15.3	10.1	29	157	29	66	45	66	60	65	29
Nebr.	Omaha	54	60	54	10.6	10.9	8.9	26	141	26	81	59	78	65	84	57
Nev.	Reno	42	79	48	6.6	5.6	7.0	27	174	27	70	32	79	51	63	18
N.H.	Concord	49	54	48	6.7	7.2	5.7	25	173	25	81	54	75	58	84	52
N.J.	Atlantic City	30	56	32	10.1	11.0	8.5	26	110	26	81	56	77	58	83	57
N.Mex.	Albuquerque	51	76	3	11.8	11.7	10.6	30	119	30	60	29	70	40	60	27
N.Y.	Albany	52	52	52	8.9	9.8	7.4	25	149	25	80	57	77	63	81	55
N.Y.	Buffalo	47	49	51	12.0	14.3	10.3	30	133	30	80	63	79	72	78	55
N.Y.	New York[c]	104	58	58	9.4	10.7	7.6	77	80	61	72	56	68	60	75	55
N.C.	Charlotte	40	63	41	7.5	7.9	6.6	30	67	30	83	54	78	55	87	57
N.C.	Raleigh	36	59	41	7.8	8.5	6.7	26	78	26	85	54	78	55	89	58
N.Dak.	Bismarck	51	59	51	10.2	10.0	9.2	31	186	31	80	56	74	68	83	47
Ohio	Cincinnati	7	52	43	9.1	10.7	7.1	28	108	28	28	81	59	78	67	85
Ohio	Cleveland	47	49	49	10.6	12.3	8.6	30	124	30	79	62	77	69	81	57
Ohio	Columbus	39	49	41	8.5	10.1	6.6	31	119	31	80	59	76	67	84	56
Okla.	Oklahoma City	36	68	42	12.4	12.8	10.9	25	77	25	79	54	77	59	80	49
Oreg.	Portland	41	48	42	7.9	9.9	7.6	50	43	50	86	60	86	76	82	45
Pa.	Philadelphia	48	56	50	9.5	10.3	8.1	31	97	31	76	55	73	59	79	54
Pa.	Pittsburgh	38	46	38	9.1	10.7	7.2	31	123	30	78	57	75	65	83	54
R.I.	Providence	37	58	37	10.6	11.2	9.5	27	119	27	75	55	70	56	77	56
S.C.	Columbia	37	64	42	6.9	7.2	6.3	24	61	24	87	51	82	54	89	54
S.Dak.	Sioux Falls	[d]48	[d]63	42	11.1	11.1	9.8	27	168	27	81	60	76	67	82	53
Tenn.	Memphis	35	64	42	8.9	10.1	7.5	49	57	51	81	57	78	63	84	57
Tenn.	Nashville	48	56	49	8.0	9.2	6.5	25	76	25	84	57	79	63	89	57
Tex.	Dallas–Fort Worth	12	64	37	10.8	11.2	9.6	27	40	27	82	56	79	59	80	48
Tex.	El Paso	48	83	48	8.9	8.4	8.3	30	65	30	57	27	65	34	62	29

State	Station	Average Percentage of Possible Sunshine		Average Wind Speed (mph)				Minimum Temperature 32 Degrees or Less		Average Relative Humidity (percent)						
		Length of Record (yr.)	Annual	Length of Record (yr.)	Annual	Jan.	Jul.	Length of Records (yr.)	Mean Number (days)	Length of Record (yr.)	Annual M	Annual A	Jan. M	Jan. A	Jul. M	Jul. A
Tex.	Houston	21	56	21	7.9	8.3	7.0	21	21	21	90	59	85	63	92	58
Utah	Salt Lake City	52	66	61	8.9	7.7	9.6	31	125	31	67	43	79	69	52	22
Vt.	Burlington	47	49	47	8.9	9.7	7.9	26	156	25	77	59	71	63	78	53
Va.	Norfolk	26	61	42	10.7	11.5	9.0	42	54	42	78	57	74	58	82	59
Va.	Richmood	40	62	42	7.7	8.1	6.8	61	85	56	83	53	80	57	85	56
Wash.	Seattle-Tacoma	24	46	42	9.0	9.8	8.3	31	31	31	83	62	81	74	82	49
Wash.	Spokane	42	54	43	8.9	8.8	8.6	31	139	31	77	52	85	78	64	27
W.Va.	Charleston	e7	e40	43	6.3	7.5	5.0	43	100	43	83	56	77	62	90	60
Wis.	Milwaukee	50	54	50	11.6	12.7	9.7	30	141	30	81	64	76	68	82	61
Wyo.	Cheyenne	51	65	33	13.0	15.4	10.3	31	171	31	65	44	57	50	70	38
P.R.	San Juan	35	66	35	8.4	8.5	9.6	35	. . .	35	79	65	81	64	79	66

– Represents zero. Z Less than one-half a day. . . . Not available. [a] [Airport data, except as noted. For period of record through 1990, except as noted. M = morning. A = afternoon] [b] Recording site is in Montgomery, Ala. [c] City office data. [d] Recording site is in Rapid City, S. Dak. [e] Recording site is Elkins, W.Va.

Source: Bureau of the Census, *Statistical Abstract of the United States 1992* (Washington, D.C., 1993), 227.

TABLE 2.5 NORMAL MONTHLY AND ANNUAL PRECIPITATION—SELECTED CITIES[a]

State	Station	Jan.	Feb.	Mar.	Apr.	May	Jun.	Jul.	Aug.	Sep.	Oct.	Nov.	Dec.	Annual
Ala.	Mobile	4.76	5.46	6.41	4.48	5.74	5.04	6.85	6.96	5.91	2.94	4.10	5.31	63.96
Alaska	Juneau	4.54	3.75	3.28	2.77	3.42	3.15	4.16	5.32	6.73	7.84	4.91	4.44	54.31
Ariz.	Phoenix	0.67	0.68	0.88	0.22	0.12	0.13	0.83	0.96	0.86	0.65	0.66	1.00	7.66
Ark.	Little Rock	3.42	3.61	4.91	5.49	5.17	3.57	3.60	3.26	4.05	3.75	5.20	4.83	50.86
Calif.	Los Angeles	2.40	2.51	1.98	0.72	0.14	0.03	0.01	0.15	0.31	0.34	1.76	1.66	12.01
Calif.	Sacramento	3.73	2.87	2.57	1.16	0.27	0.12	0.05	0.07	0.37	1.08	2.72	2.51	17.52
Calif.	San Diego	1.80	1.53	1.77	0.79	0.19	0.07	0.02	0.10	0.24	0.37	1.45	1.57	9.90
Calif.	San Francisco	4.35	3.17	3.06	1.37	0.19	0.11	0.03	0.05	0.20	1.22	2.86	3.09	19.70
Colo.	Denver	0.50	0.57	1.28	1.71	2.40	1.79	1.91	1.51	1.24	0.98	0.87	0.64	15.40
Conn.	Hartford	3.41	3.23	3.63	3.85	4.12	3.75	3.19	3.65	3.79	3.57	4.04	3.91	44.14
Del.	Wilmington	3.03	2.91	3.43	3.39	3.84	3.55	4.23	3.40	3.43	2.88	3.27	3.48	40.84
D.C.	Washington	2.72	2.71	3.17	2.71	3.66	3.38	3.80	3.91	3.31	3.02	3.12	3.12	38.63
Fla.	Jacksonville	3.31	3.93	3.68	2.77	3.55	5.69	5.60	7.93	7.05	2.90	2.19	2.72	51.32
Fla.	Miami	2.01	2.08	2.39	2.85	6.21	9.33	5.70	7.58	7.63	5.64	2.66	1.83	55.91
Ga.	Atlanta	4.75	4.81	5.77	4.26	4.29	3.56	5.01	3.66	3.42	3.05	3.86	4.33	50.77
Hawaii	Honolulu	3.55	2.21	2.20	1.54	1.13	0.50	0.59	0.44	0.78	2.28	3.00	3.80	22.02
Idaho	Boise	1.45	1.07	1.29	1.24	1.08	0.81	0.35	0.43	0.80	0.75	1.48	1.36	12.11
Ill.	Chicago	1.53	1.36	2.69	3.64	3.32	3.78	3.66	4.22	3.82	2.41	2.92	2.47	35.82
Ill.	Peoria	1.51	1.42	2.91	3.77	3.70	3.99	4.20	3.10	3.87	2.65	2.69	2.44	36.25
Ind.	Indianapolis	2.32	2.46	3.79	3.70	4.00	3.49	4.47	3.64	2.87	2.63	3.23	3.34	39.94
Iowa	Des Moines	0.96	1.11	2.33	3.36	3.66	4.46	3.78	4.20	3.53	2.62	1.79	1.32	33.12
Kans.	Wichita	0.79	0.96	2.43	2.38	3.81	4.31	3.13	3.02	3.49	2.22	1.59	1.20	29.33
Ky.	Louisville	2.86	3.30	4.66	4.23	4.62	3.46	4.51	3.54	3.16	2.71	3.70	3.64	44.39
La.	New Orleans	5.05	6.01	4.90	4.50	4.56	5.84	6.12	6.17	5.51	3.05	4.42	5.75	61.88
Maine	Portland	3.53	3.33	3.67	4.08	3.62	3.44	3.09	2.87	3.09	3.90	5.17	4.55	44.34
Md.	Baltimore	3.05	3.12	3.38	3.09	3.72	3.67	3.69	3.92	3.41	2.98	3.32	3.41	40.76
Mass.	Boston	3.59	3.62	3.69	3.60	3.25	3.09	2.84	3.24	3.06	3.30	4.22	4.01	41.51
Mich.	Detroit	1.76	1.74	2.55	2.95	2.92	3.61	3.18	3.43	2.89	2.10	2.67	2.82	32.62
Mich.	Sault Ste. Marie	2.42	1.74	2.30	2.35	2.71	3.14	2.71	3.61	3.69	3.23	3.45	2.88	34.23
Minn.	Duluth	1.22	0.80	1.91	2.25	3.03	3.82	3.61	3.99	3.84	2.49	1.80	1.24	30.00
Minn.	Minneapolis– St. Paul	0.95	0.88	1.94	2.42	3.39	4.05	3.53	3.62	2.72	2.19	1.55	1.08	28.32
Miss.	Jackson	5.24	4.70	5.82	5.57	5.05	3.18	4.51	3.77	3.55	3.26	4.81	5.91	55.37
Mo.	Kansas City	1.09	1.10	2.51	3.12	5.04	4.72	4.38	4.01	4.86	3.29	1.92	1.58	37.62
Mo.	St. Louis	1.81	2.12	3.58	3.50	3.97	3.72	3.85	2.85	3.12	2.68	3.28	3.03	37.51
Mont.	Great Falls	0.91	0.57	1.10	1.41	2.52	2.39	1.24	1.54	1.24	0.78	0.66	0.85	15.21
Nebr.	Omaha	0.74	0.77	2.04	2.66	4.52	3.87	3.51	3.24	3.72	2.28	1.49	1.02	29.86
Nev.	Reno	1.07	0.99	0.71	0.38	0.69	0.46	0.28	0.32	0.39	0.38	0.87	0.99	7.53
N.H.	Concord	2.51	2.53	2.72	2.91	3.14	3.15	3.23	3.32	2.81	3.23	3.66	3.16	36.37
N.J.	Atlantic City	3.46	3.06	3.62	3.56	3.33	2.64	3.83	4.14	2.93	2.82	3.58	3.32	40.29
N.Mex.	Albuquerque	0.44	0.46	0.54	0.52	0.50	0.59	1.37	1.64	1.00	0.89	0.43	0.50	8.88
N.Y.	Albany	2.36	2.27	2.93	2.99	3.41	3.62	3.18	3.47	2.95	2.83	3.23	2.93	36.17
N.Y.	Buffalo	2.70	2.31	2.68	2.87	3.14	3.55	3.08	4.17	3.49	3.09	3.83	3.67	38.58
N.Y.	New York	3.42	3.27	4.08	4.20	4.42	3.67	4.35	4.01	3.89	3.56	4.47	3.91	47.25
N.C.	Charlotte	3.71	3.84	4.43	2.68	3.82	3.39	3.92	3.73	3.50	3.36	3.23	3.48	43.09
N.C.	Raleigh	3.48	3.69	3.77	2.59	3.92	3.68	4.01	4.02	3.19	2.86	2.98	3.24	41.43
N.Dak.	Bismarck	0.45	0.43	0.77	1.67	2.18	2.72	2.14	1.72	1.49	0.90	0.49	0.51	15.47
Ohio	Cincinnati	2.59	2.69	4.24	3.75	4.28	3.84	4.24	3.35	2.88	2.86	3.46	3.15	41.33
Ohio	Cleveland	2.04	2.19	2.91	3.14	3.49	3.70	3.52	3.40	3.44	2.54	3.17	3.09	36.63
Ohio	Columbus	2.18	2.24	3.27	3.21	3.93	4.04	4.31	3.72	2.96	2.15	3.22	2.86	38.09
Okla.	Oklahoma City	1.13	1.56	2.71	2.77	5.22	4.31	2.61	2.60	3.84	3.23	1.98	1.40	33.36

(continued)

TABLE 2.5 (continued)

State	Station	Jan.	Feb.	Mar.	Apr.	May	Jun.	Jul.	Aug.	Sep.	Oct.	Nov.	Dec.	Annual
Oreg.	Portland	5.35	3.85	3.56	2.39	2.06	1.48	0.63	1.09	1.75	2.67	5.34	6.13	36.30
Pa.	Philadelphia	3.21	2.79	3.46	3.62	3.75	3.74	4.28	3.80	3.42	2.62	3.34	3.38	41.41
Pa.	Pittsburgh	2.54	2.39	3.41	3.15	3.59	3.71	3.75	3.21	2.97	2.36	2.85	2.92	36.85
R.I.	Providence	3.88	3.61	4.05	4.11	3.76	3.33	3.18	3.63	3.48	3.69	4.43	4.38	45.53
S.C.	Columbia	4.42	4.12	4.82	3.28	3.68	4.80	5.50	6.09	3.67	3.04	2.90	3.59	49.91
S.Dak.	Sioux Falls	0.51	0.64	1.64	2.52	3.03	3.40	2.68	2.85	3.02	1.78	1.09	0.70	23.86
Tenn.	Memphis	3.73	4.35	5.41	5.46	4.98	3.57	3.79	3.43	3.53	3.01	5.10	5.74	52.10
Tenn.	Nashville	3.58	3.81	4.85	4.37	4.88	3.57	3.97	3.46	3.46	2.62	4.12	4.61	47.30
Tex.	Dallas–Fort Worth	1.83	2.18	2.77	3.50	4.88	2.98	2.31	2.21	3.39	3.52	2.29	1.84	33.70
Tex.	El Paso	0.40	0.41	0.29	0.20	0.25	0.67	1.54	1.58	1.70	0.76	0.44	0.57	8.81
Tex.	Houston	3.29	2.96	2.92	3.21	5.24	4.96	3.60	3.49	4.89	4.27	3.79	3.45	46.07
Utah	Salt Lake City	1.11	1.23	1.91	2.12	1.80	0.93	0.81	0.86	1.28	1.44	1.29	1.40	16.18
Vt.	Burlington	1.82	1.63	2.23	2.76	3.12	3.47	3.65	4.06	3.30	2.88	3.13	2.42	34.47
Va.	Norfolk	3.78	3.43	3.70	3.06	3.81	3.82	5.06	4.81	3.90	3.15	2.85	3.23	44.64
Va.	Richmond	3.24	3.16	3.61	2.96	3.84	3.62	5.03	4.40	3.34	3.53	3.17	3.26	43.16
Wash.	Seattle-Tacoma	5.38	3.99	3.54	2.33	1.70	1.50	0.76	1.14	1.88	3.23	5.83	5.91	37.19
Wash.	Spokane	1.98	1.49	1.49	1.18	1.41	1.26	0.67	0.72	0.73	0.99	2.15	2.42	16.49
W.Va.	Charleston	2.91	3.04	3.63	3.31	3.94	3.59	4.99	4.01	3.24	2.89	3.59	3.39	42.53
Wis.	Milwaukee	1.60	1.45	2.67	3.50	2.84	3.24	3.47	3.53	3.38	2.41	2.51	2.33	32.93
Wyo.	Cheyenne	0.40	0.39	1.03	1.37	2.39	2.08	2.09	1.69	1.27	0.74	0.53	0.42	14.40
P.R.	San Juan	2.81	2.15	2.35	3.76	5.93	4.00	4.37	5.32	5.28	5.71	5.94	4.72	52.34

a In inches. Airport data, except as noted. Based on standard 30-year period, 1961 through 1990.
Source: Bureau of Census, *Statistical Abstract 1992*, 224.

TABLE 2.6 SNOW AND ICE PELLETS—SELECTED CITIES[a]

State	Station	Length of Record Yr.	Jan.	Feb.	Mar.	Apr.	May	Jun.	Jul.	Aug.	Sep.	Oct.	Nov.	Dec.	Annual
Ala.	Mobile	49	0.1	0.2	...	T	...	...	T	...	...	...	T	0.1	0.4
Alaska	Juneau	46	25.9	18.8	15.5	3.7	...	T	...	...	T	1	12.3	22.2	99.4
Ariz.	Phoenix	53	T	...	T	T	...	...	...	...	...	...	...	...	T
Ark.	Little Rock	48	2.5	1.5	0.5	T	...	...	...	...	...	...	0.2	0.7	5.4
Calif.	Los Angeles	55	T	T	T	...	...	...	...	...	...	...	...	T	T
Calif.	Sacramento	42	T	...	T	...	...	...	...	...	...	...	...	T	T
Calif.	San Diego	50	T	...	T	...	...	...	...	...	...	...	T	T	T
Calif.	San Francisco	63	...	T	T	...	...	...	...	...	...	...	...	...	T
Colo.	Denver	56	7.9	7.5	12.8	9.0	1.7	...	T	T	1.6	3.7	8.2	7.4	59.8
Conn.	Hartford	36	12.3	11.6	9.5	1.6	...	...	...	...	...	0.1	2.1	10.6	47.8
Del.	Wilmington	43	6.8	6.2	3.2	0.2	T	...	T	...	...	0.1	1	3.5	21.0
D.C.	Washington	47	5.5	5.4	2.1	...	T	...	T	...	...	...	0.9	3.2	17.1
Fla.	Jacksonville	49	T	...	...	...	...	...	T	...	...	...	...	...	T
Fla.	Miami	48	...	...	...	...	...	...	...	...	...	...	...	...	...
Ga.	Atlanta	56	0.9	0.5	0.4	T	...	...	...	...	...	...	...	0.2	2
Hawaii	Honolulu	44	...	...	...	...	...	...	...	...	...	...	...	...	...
Idaho	Boise	51	6.8	3.6	1.8	0.7	0.1	T	T	T	...	0.1	2.2	6	21.3
Ill.	Chicago	32	10.7	8.5	6.6	1.7	0.1	...	...	T	T	0.5	2.0	8.6	38.7
Ill.	Peoria	47	6.5	5.5	4.1	0.9	...	...	T	...	...	0.1	2.0	6.0	25.1
Ind.	Indianapolis	59	6.1	5.8	3.5	0.5	...	...	...	T	...	0.2	1.8	5.0	22.9
Iowa	Des Moines	51	8.1	7.3	6.5	2	...	...	...	...	T	0.2	2.7	6.9	33.7
Kans.	Wichita	37	4.7	4.4	2.6	0.3	T	T	...	...	...	...	1.2	3.4	16.6
Ky.	Louisville	43	5.4	4.4	3.3	0.1	T	...	...	...	...	...	1.1	2.2	16.5
La.	New Orleans	44	...	0.1	T	T	T	...	...	...	...	...	T	0.1	0.2
Maine	Portland	50	19.4	17.5	12.4	2.9	0.2	...	...	...	T	0.2	3.1	14.7	70.4
Md.	Baltimore	40	6.1	6.7	3.7	0.1	T	...	...	...	...	...	1.1	3.6	21.3
Mass.	Boston	55	12.2	11.4	7.4	0.9	...	...	...	...	...	...	1.4	7.4	40.7
Mich.	Detroit	32	10.0	9.1	6.8	1.7	T	...	...	...	T	0.2	3.1	10.6	41.5
Mich.	Sault Ste. Marie	49	28.6	19.3	15.2	5.5	0.5	T	...	T	0.1	2.3	15.3	30	116.8
Minn.	Duluth	47	16.9	11.3	13.8	6.4	0.7	...	...	T	...	1.3	11	15.5	76.9
Minn.	Minneapolis–St. Paul	52	9.9	8.4	10.9	3	0.1	T	...	...	...	0.4	7.1	9.4	49.2
Miss.	Jackson	27	0.6	0.2	0.2	...	...	...	...	...	...	...	...	...	1
Mo.	Kansas City	56	5.7	4.4	3.7	0.7	T	T	...	...	...	...	1	4.5	20
Mo.	St. Louis	54	5.3	4.5	4.3	0.4	T	T	...	...	...	T	1.4	4	19.9
Mont.	Great Falls	53	9.9	8.5	10.4	7.3	1.8	0.3	T	T	1.6	3.1	7.5	8.9	59.3

State	Station	Length of Record Yr.	Jan.	Feb.	Mar.	Apr.	May	Jun.	Jul.	Aug.	Sep.	Oct.	Nov.	Dec.	Annual
Nebr.	Omaha	55	7.3	6.8	6.6	0.8	0.1	T	...	...	T	0.3	2.5	5.7	30.1
Nev.	Reno	48	5.8	5.2	4.6	1.3	0.9	...	...	...	...	0.4	2.2	4.3	24.7
N.H.	Concord	49	18.1	14.7	10.6	2.3	0.1	...	...	...	...	0.1	4.0	13.7	63.6
N.J.	Atlantic City	46	5.3	5.5	2.7	0.4	T	...	...	...	...	T	0.4	2.3	16.6
N.Mex.	Albuquerque	51	2.5	2.2	1.9	0.6	...	T	T	...	T	0.1	1.1	2.6	11.0
N.Y.	Albany	44	16.5	14.3	10.9	2.8	0.1	...	T	...	T	0.2	4.3	15.2	64.3
N.Y.	Buffalo	47	23.8	18.5	11.1	3.2	0.3	T	...	...	T	0.2	11.4	22.8	91.3
N.Y.	New York	122	7.6	8.5	5.0	0.9	T	...	T	...	...	...	0.9	5.5	28.4
N.C.	Charlotte	51	2.1	1.8	1.3	...	...	...	...	...	...	...	0.1	0.5	5.8
N.C.	Raleigh	46	2.4	2.7	1.4	...	...	...	...	...	...	...	0.1	0.8	7.4
N.Dak.	Bismarck	51	7.2	6.7	8.3	3.8	0.8	T	T	T	0.3	1.3	5.8	6.9	41.1
Ohio	Cincinnati	43	7.0	5.4	4.3	0.5	...	...	...	...	...	0.2	2.1	4.0	23.5
Ohio	Cleveland	49	12.3	11.7	10.3	2.4	0.1	...	...	...	T	0.6	5.0	11.9	54.3
Ohio	Columbus	43	8.3	6.2	4.5	1	...	T	...	...	T	...	2.3	5.7	28.0
Okla.	Oklahoma City	51	3.1	2.6	1.4	...	T	...	...	...	...	T	0.5	1.8	9.4
Oreg.	Portland	50	3.4	0.9	0.5	T	...	T	...	T	T	...	0.5	1.4	6.7
Pa.	Philadelphia	48	6.6	6.5	3.6	0.3	T	...	...	...	...	...	0.7	3.6	21.3
Pa.	Pittsburgh	38	11.6	9.4	8.1	1.8	0.1	T	...	...	T	0.2	3.4	8.2	42.8
R.I.	Providence	37	9.8	9.8	7.4	0.7	0.2	...	...	...	...	0.1	1.1	7.1	36.2
S.C.	Columbia	43	0.5	0.9	0.2	T	...	...	...	...	...	...	T	0.2	1.8
S.Dak.	Sioux Falls	45	6.5	8.0	9.7	2.3	...	T	...	...	...	0.5	5.2	7.4	39.6
Tenn.	Memphis	40	2.5	1.4	0.9	T	T	...	...	...	...	T	0.1	0.7	5.6
Tenn.	Nashville	49	4.0	3.1	1.4	...	...	...	...	T	...	T	0.5	1.6	10.6
Tex.	Dallas–Fort Worth	37	1.3	1.0	0.2	T	T	...	...	...	...	...	0.1	0.3	2.9
Tex.	El Paso	51	1.3	0.9	0.4	0.4	T	...	T	...	...	...	1.0	1.7	5.7
Tex.	Houston	56	0.2	0.2	...	...	...	T	...	...	...	...	T	...	0.4
Utah	Salt Lake City	62	13.0	9.5	9.9	5.0	0.6	T	...	...	0.1	1.3	6.4	12	57.8
Vt.	Burlington	47	18.8	16.5	12	3.6	0.2	...	T	...	T	0.2	6.8	18.7	76.8
Va.	Norfolk	42	2.8	3.0	1.1	...	...	T	...	...	...	...	...	0.9	7.8
Va.	Richmond	53	5.1	4.2	2.5	0.1	T	...	...	...	...	T	0.4	2.0	14.3
Wash.	Seattle-Tacoma	46	5.3	1.7	1.4	0.1	T	...	T	...	T	...	1.3	2.5	12.3
Wash.	Spokane	43	16.3	7.8	4.1	0.7	0.1	T	...	...	...	0.4	6.2	15.0	50.6
W.Va.	Charleston	43	10.6	8.8	4.6	0.9	...	...	T	T	T	0.1	2.2	5.0	32.2
Wis.	Milwaukee	50	12.9	9.8	8.7	1.8	0.1	...	T	T	T	0.2	3.0	10.5	47.0
Wyo.	Cheyenne	55	6.2	5.9	12.4	9.0	3.5	0.2	T	T	0.8	3.6	6.8	6.2	54.6
P.R.	San Juan	35	...	...	...	...	...	...	...	...	T	...	...	...	T

... Represents zero or rounds to zero. T denotes trace.
[a] In inches. Airport data, except as noted. For period of record through 1990.
Source: Bureau of Census, *Statistical Abstract 1992*, 226.

Weather as a Destructive Force

Hurricanes

Besides being a supplier of elements necessary to life, a determinant of schedules and setter of human moods, weather can become a destroyer of property, hopes, and life itself. The most powerful and destructive manifestations of weather have taken on the generic label of *storms,* and storms, of course, can take many forms. Among the most threatening and spectacular are the tropical storms that threaten the Atlantic and Gulf coasts of the United States in late summer and early autumn of virtually every year. The most intense tropical storms received the designation of *hurricane*. Although the character and frequency of hurricanes has not changed over the broad scope of years, methods of detecting and observing them have undergone major transformation. Slow to form and slow moving, these storms lend themselves to the various tracking and measuring devices developed since the 1950s, provide areas in their path time for preparation, and add drama to the life and death of each storm and of course to the destruction left behind.

A better warning system did not mean a reduction in the absolute amount of destruction. Because the targeted areas all had become more fully settled and developed over the years, the most costly hurricanes, with rare exceptions, were the recent ones. If the passage of time produced advance warning technology, it also placed more expensive property in the path of destructive storms. The most obvious saving came in lives lost. Probably the most intense hurricane to strike the United States in the 20th century was Camille in 1969. It left 256 dead, second-highest number in the postwar era. But in a list of killer hurricanes of the century, Camille ranked only 11th and was a far cry from the less-powerful storm that arrived virtually unannounced at Galveston in 1900 and took more than 6,000 lives.

The process of tracking hurricanes became professionalized and systematized at the National Hurricane Center in Florida. In the 1970s the government adopted the Saffir/Simpson Scale, devised by two officials at the center, for classifying hurricanes. In the 1950s the National Weather Service concluded that naming hurricanes would make them easier to identify and study. The practice of using women's names, which began in 1953, evolved from a practice of referring to storms as "she," possibly in the way that the feminine pronoun was used to identify ships and nations. In a move consistent with the gender-neutral or at least gender-equal emphasis in that period, the Weather Service began in 1979 to use men's names as well. Since that time male names alternate with female alphabetically in formation of each year's list.

TABLE 2.7 SAFFIR/SIMPSON HURRICANE SCALE RANGES

Name	Winds (in mph)	Barometric Pressure (at storm's center, in inches)	Storm Surge (in feet)	Damage
Tropical Depression	Less than 39 mph	Above 29 inches	None	Little
Tropical Storm	39 to 74 mph	Above 29 inches	Very minor	Minor flooding
Category 1 Hurricane	75 to 95 mph	Above 28.94 inches	4 to 5 feet	Damage to shrubbery, trees, mobile homes; low-lying roads inundated; small craft torn from moorings.
Category 2 Hurricane	96 to 110 mph	28.50 to 28.91 inches	6 to 8 feet	Some trees blown down; some windows and roofs damaged; evacuation of some shoreline residencies required.
Category 3 Hurricane	111 to 130 mph	27.91 to 28.47 inches	9 to 12 feet	Large trees blown down; mobile homes destroyed; serious flooding on coast; low-lying escape routes cut off three to five hours before storm center.
Category 4 Hurricane	131 to 155 mph	27.17 to 27.88 inches	13 to 18 feet	Trees blown down; complete destruction of mobile homes; major erosion of beaches; massive evacuation of all residencies within two miles of shore required.
Category 5 Hurricane	Above 155 mph	Less than 27.17 inches	More than 18 feet	Very severe and extensive damage to all buildings; roofs blown away; small buildings overturned or blown away; massive evacuation of all residents five to ten miles inland required.

Source: Ti Sanders, *Weather: A User's Guide to the Atmosphere* (South Bend, 1985), 92.

TABLE 2.8 MOST INTENSE ATLANTIC COAST HURRICANES, 1946–1990
(measured at time of landfall)

Rank	Hurricane	Year	Category	Millibars[a]	Inches[a]
1.	Camille (Mississippi/Southeast, Louisiana/Virginia)	1969	5	909	26.35
2.	Donna (Florida/Eastern U.S.)	1960	4	930	27.46
3.	Carla (North of Central Texas)	1961	4	931	27.49
4.	Hugo (South Carolina)	1989	4	934	27.58
5.	Hazel	1954	4	938	27.70
6.	Unnamed (Southeastern Florida/Southeastern Louisiana, Mississippi)	1947	4	940	27.76
7.	Gloria (Eastern U.S.)	1985	3[b]	942	27.82
8.	Audrey (Southwestern Texas/Northern Texas)	1957	4	945	27.91
9.	Celia (Southern Texas)	1970	3	945	27.91
10.	Allen (Southern Texas)	1980	3[c]	945	27.91
11.	Frederic (Alabama/Mississippi)	1979	3	946	27.94
12.	Betsy (Southeastern Florida/Southeastern Louisiana)	1965	3	948	27.99
13.	Diana (North Carolina)	1984	3	949	28.02
14.	Beulah (Southern Texas)	1967	3	950	28.05
15.	Hilda (Central Louisiana)	1964	3	950	28.05
16.	Gracie (South Carolina)	1959	3	950	28.05
17.	Carmen (Central Louisiana)	1974	3	952	28.11
18.	Edna (New England)	1954	3[d]	954	28.17
19.	Unnamed (Southeastern Florida)	1949	3	954	28.17
20.	Eloise (Northwestern Florida)	1975	3	955	28.20

[a] Both millibars and inches are instruments for measuring barometric pressure. The lower the number, in either case, the more intense the storm.
[b] Winds and tides did not justify 4; moving at more than 30 mph.
[c] Reached category 5 three times over water.
[d] Moving more than 30 mph.
Source: Richard A. Wood, *The Weather Almanac* (Detroit, 1996), 64.

Hurricane Elena in the Gulf of Mexico, heading for the United States in September 1985, as seen from the Space Shuttle *Discovery* (NASA)

TABLE 2.9   MOST DESTRUCTIVE NORTH ATLANTIC HURRICANES, 1946–1990

Date	Areas Hardest Hit	Land Stations with Highest Wind Speed	Deaths (U.S. only)	Est. Damage (millions)	Remarks
Sep. 4–21, 1947	Florida and Mid-Gulf Coast	Hillsboro Light, Fla. (155 mph)	51	110	Wind damage especially heavy along Gulf Coast and Florida east coast.
Aug. 25–31, 1954	North Carolina to New England	Block Island, R.I. (135 mph)	60	461	"Carol"—more damage than any other single storm to this date. Water and high waves flooded low-lying areas; 1,000 injuries in Long Island–New England area.
Sep. 2–14, 1954	New Jersey to New England	Block Island, R.I. (87 mph)	21	40	"Edna"—New England again heavily hit. Gusts of 120 mph at Martha's Vineyard, Mass.
Oct. 5–18, 1954	South Carolina to New York	New York, N.Y. (113 mph) (See Remarks)	95	252	"Hazel"—several N.C. localities had winds of 130–150 mph with unusually heavy wave damage resulting. Est. 400–1,000 casualties in Haiti. In Canada there were 78 deaths, mostly due to flooding.
Aug. 7–21, 1955	North Carolina to New England	Wilmington, N.C. (83 mph)	184	832	"Diane"—worst floods in history in Southern New England. 16 in. of rain in Hartford area.
Jun. 25–28, 1957	Texas to Alabama	Sabine/Pass, Tex. (100 mph)	390	150	"Audrey"—gave an early start to the hurricane season and wiped out Cameron, La. Two weeks later "Bertha" struck same area.

(continued)

TABLE 2.9 (continued)

Date	Areas Hardest Hit	Land Stations with Highest Wind Speed	Deaths (U.S. only)	Est. Damage (millions)	Remarks
Aug. 29–Sep. 13, 1960	Florida to New England	Ft. Myers, Fla. (92 mph) Block Island, R.I. (130 mph) (See Remarks)	50	500	"Donna"—hurricane winds from a single storm swept the entire Atlantic seaboard from Florida to New England for the first time in a 75-year record. Winds estimated near 140 mph with gusts 175–180 mph on Central Keys and lower southwest Florida coast. 115 deaths in Antilles, most from flash floods in Puerto Rico.
Sep. 3–15, 1961	Texas coast	Port Lavaca, Tex. (145 mph)	46	408	"Carla"—devastated Texas Gulf Coast cities with 15-foot tides and 15-inch rains. Gusts to 175 mph at Port Lavaca.
Aug. 20–Sep. 5, 1964	Southern Florida, Eastern Virginia	Miami, Fla. (110 mph)	3	129	"Cleo"—first hurricane in Miami area since 1950. Killed 214 in Caribbean Islands.
Aug. 28–Sep. 16, 1964	Northeastern Florida, Southern Georgia	St. Augustine, Fla. (125 mph)	5	250	"Dora"—first storm of full hurricane force on record to move inland from east over northeastern Florida.
Aug. 27–Sep. 12, 1965	Southern Florida and Louisiana	Port Sulphur, La. (136 mph)	75	1,420	"Betsy"—Damage in Louisiana, $1.2 billion, 27,000 homes destroyed, 17,500 injured or ill, 300,000 evacuated. Gusts of 165 mph at Pine Key, Fla.
Sep. 5–22, 1967	Southern Texas	Brownsville, Texas (109 mph gust)	15	200	"Beulah"—main damage was caused by torrential rains.
Aug. 14–22, 1969	Mississippi, Louisiana, Alabama, Virginia, W. Virginia	Oil drilling rig east of Boothville, La. (172 mph)	256	1,420	"Camille"—68 additional persons missing. One of most destructive killer storms ever to hit U.S.
Jul. 23–Aug. 5, 1970	Texas coast	Corpus Christi, Tex. (130 mph)	11	453.8	"Celia"—Gusts of 161 mph recorded.
Jun. 14–23, 1972	Florida to New York	Key West, Fla. (43 mph)	117	2,100	"Agnes"—Devastating floods with many record-breaking river crests. Pa. hardest hit, with 50 deaths.
Sep. 13–24, 1975	Florida and Southern Alabama	Ozark, Ala. (104 mph)	21	490	"Eloise"—Structures destroyed from Panama City Beach, Fla., to Ft. Walton Beach, Fla. Major flooding from rainfall.
Aug. 6–10, 1976	New York, New Jersey, and Southern New England	Bridgeport, Conn. (77 mph gust)	5	100	"Belle"—Crop damage in the Northeast. Considerable inland stream and road flooding.
Aug. 25–Sep. 7, 1979	Florida to New England	Fort Pierce, Fla. (95 mph gust)	5	320	"David"—1200 deaths in the Dominican Republic. Homes 80 percent destroyed in Dominica.
Aug. 29–Sep. 14, 1979	Alabama and Mississippi	Dauphin Island, Alabama (145 mph gust)	5	2300	"Frederic"—highest dollar damage ever in the United States.
Aug. 3–10, 1980	Caribbean Islands to Texas Gulf Coast	Port Mansfield, Texas (120 mph gust)	28	300	"Allen"—Highest tides in 61 years. More than 200 killed in Caribbean Islands. Extensive crop damage in Caribbean.
Aug. 15–21, 1983	Texas Coast	Hobby Airport (94 mph)	21	2000	"Alicia"—Extensive damage in Galveston/Houston area.
Aug. 28–Sep. 4, 1985	Florida to Mississippi	Dauphin Island, Ala. (96 mph)	4	1,000	"Elena"—1 million persons evacuated.
Sep. 16–27, 1985	North Carolina Outer Banks and Long Island, N.Y.	Chesapeake Bay Bridge (92 mph)	8	1,000	"Gloria"—downed trees and power outages across southern New England.
Oct. 26–Nov. 1, 1985	Louisiana	Pensacola, Fla. (63 mph gust)	12	1,500	"Juan"—Serious damage to offshore oil rigs. Sustained flooding over SE Louisiana.
Sep. 10–22, 1989	Caribbean Islands from Guadeloupe to Puerto Rico; South Carolina and North Carolina	Roosevelt Roads, P.R. (104 mph) Charleston, S.C. (87 mph)	49	7,000	"Hugo"—Storm surge flood waters reached 20 feet above normal along portions of S.C. Coast. New record-high dollar damage.

Source: Otto Johnson, ed., *The 1991 Information Please Almanac, Atlas & Yearbook* (Boston, 1991), 667–669.

Tornadoes

Tornadoes in several ways represent a reverse of the activity of hurricanes. Originating over land, not water, the tornadoes' winds turn counterclockwise around a hollow core. The storm develops when a convergence of warm and cold air masses creates an atmospheric vacuum, and air rushing in to fill the void starts to rotate. The tornado season shifts with passage of the warm months but generally is most intense from April through June and is for the most part over at the time the hurricane season begins. Tornadoes cover a much smaller area than hurricanes and have a much shorter life, but the winds can be substantially more intense and are devastating in the area they strike. Because tornadoes have been so numerous and short lived, there has been no systematic effort to give them names. A Japanese scientist did devise a system for measuring strength of the whirling winds, but the character of these storms—their unpredictability, short life, and enormous danger—has made it nearly impossible to apply the scale with precision to given situations. The large increase in the number of tornadoes since 1946 probably better reflects methods of detection and reporting than proliferation of activity. The same factors do much to explain a general reduction in yearly number of deaths, although the numbers indicate that the suddenness of these storms, their hit-and-miss behavior, and great intensity kept them a continuing threat to life and property.

Tornado Characteristics

Time of day during which tornadoes are most likely to occur is midafternoon, generally between 3 and 7 P.M., but they have occurred at all times of day.

Direction of movement is usually from southwest to northeast. (Note: Tornadoes associated with hurricanes may move from an easterly direction.)

Length of path averages 4 miles (6 km), but may reach 300 miles (483 km). A tornado traveled 293 miles (472 km) across Illinois and Indiana on May 26, 1917, and lasted 7 hours and 20 minutes.

Width of path averages about 300–400 yards (273–364 m) but tornadoes have cut paths a mile and more in width.

Speed of travel averages from 25 to 40 miles (40.25–64.4 km) per hour, but speeds ranging from stationary to 68 miles (109.5 km) per hour have been reported.

The cloud directly associated with a tornado is a dark, heavy cumulonimbus (the familiar thunderstorm cloud) from which a whirling funnel-shaped pendant extends to the ground.

Precipitation associated with the tornado usually occurs first as rain just preceding the storm, frequently with hail, and as a heavy downpour immediately to the side of the tornado's path.

Louisville, Kentucky, after tornado of April 3, 1974: One of scores of tornadoes that struck the central United States, this twister had 250-mph winds and destroyed 900 homes. (*Louisville Courier-Journal*)

Sound occurring during a tornado has been described as a roaring, rushing noise, closely approximating that made by a train speeding through a tunnel or over a trestle, or the roar of many airplanes.

Source: Wood, *Weather Almanac,* 82.

Tornado-Intensity Rating System

The intensity of tornadoes is defined according to the Fujita Scale (or F scale), which ranges from F0 to F6 as outlined below.

F0: 40–72 mph (64–116 km/hr) winds. Damage is light and might include damage to tree branches, chimneys, and billboards. Shallow-rooted trees may be pushed over.

F1: 73–112 mph (118–180 km/hr) winds. Damage is moderate; mobile homes may be pushed off foundations and moving autos pushed off the road.

F2: 113–157 mph (182–253 km/hr) winds. Damage is considerable. Roofs can be torn off houses, mobile homes demolished, and large trees uprooted.

F3: 158–206 mph (254–334 km/hr) winds. Damage is severe. Even well-constructed houses may be torn apart, trees uprooted, and cars lifted off the ground.

F4: 207–260 mph (333–419 km/hr) winds. Damage is devastating. Houses can be leveled and cars thrown; objects become deadly missiles.

F5: 261–318 mph (420–512 km/hr) winds. Damage is incredible. Structures are lifted off foundations and carried away; cars become missiles. Less than 2% of all tornadoes reach an intensity of this magnitude.

F6: The maximum tornado wind speeds are not expected to exceed 318 mph (512 km/hr)

Source: Wood, *Weather Almanac,* 82.

TABLE 2.10   TORNADOES THAT CAUSED OUTSTANDING DAMAGE, 1947–1989

Date	Number of Tornadoes	Deaths	Property Losses (in $)	States in Which Storms Occurred
Apr. 9–10, 1947	8	167	10,030,750	Texas, Okla., Kans.
Mar. 21–22, 1952	31	343	15,327,100	Ark., Tenn., Mo., Miss., Ala., Ky.
Jun. 7–9, 1953	12	234	93,230,840	Mich., Ohio, and New England states
May 11, 1953	1	114	39,500,000	Tex.
May 25, 1955	13	102	11,747,500	Okla. and Kans.
Apr. 11–12, 1965	47	257	200,000,000	Iowa, Ill., Wis., Mich., Ind., Ohio
May 15, 1968	7	63	65,000,000	Ark., Iowa, Ill.
May 11, 1970	1	26	135,000,000	Texas
Feb. 21, 1971	(1)	117	17,000,000	La., Miss.
Mar. 31, 1973	2	9	115,000,000	Ga., S.C.
May 26–28, 1973	96	22	. . .ᵃ	Hawaii and 18 states in South, Southwest, Midwest, and East
Apr. 3–4, 1974	144	307	500,000,000+	13 states in East, South, and Midwest
May 6, 1975	3	3	400,000,000+	Nebr.
Apr. 4, 1977	7	22	15,000,000	Ala.
Dec. 3, 1978	13	4	100,000,000+	La. and Ark.
Apr. 10, 1979	10	54	. . .ᵃ	Texas and Okla.
Oct. 3, 1979	1	3	200,000,000	Conn.
May 13, 1980	1	5	40,000,000	Mich.
Aug. 9–11, 1980	29	0	50,000,000+	Tex.
Apr. 4, 1981	1	3	12,900,000	Wis.
Jul. 3, 1983	22	0	11,000,000+	Wis.
Apr. 26–27, 1984	47	16	. . .	Iowa, Ill., Kans., La., Mich., Minn., Mo., Okla., S.Dak., Wis.
May 31, 1985	30	76	102,500,000+	Ohio, Pa., N.Y.
Feb. 5, 1986	1	2	50,000,000	Tex.
Feb. 27, 1987	1	6	28,000,000	Laurel, Miss.
May 22, 1987	1	30	1,300,000	Saragosa, Tex.
Nov. 15–16, 1987	49	11	70,000,000+	La., Miss., Okla., Tex.
Nov. 15–16, 1988	44	7	35,000,000+	Ark., Ill., Iowa, Kans., Mo., Okla., Tex.
Nov. 28, 1988	1	2	77,500,000	Raleigh, N.C.
May 5, 1989	17	7	64,000,000+	Ga., S.C., N.C.
Nov. 15, 1989	1	21	100,000,000	Huntsville, Ala.
Nov. 15–16, 1989	39	30	100,000,000+	Ala., Ark., Ga., Tenn., N.J., Pa., N.Y.

ᵃ Not definitely known; believed to be large.
Source: Johnson, *1991 Information Please Almanac,* 669.

TABLE 2.11 NATIONAL TORNADOES, TORNADO DAYS, DEATHS, AND RESULTING LOSSES, BY YEAR, 1946–1990

Year	Number Tornadoes	Tornado Days	Total Deaths	Most Deaths in Single Tornado	Total Property Losses[s]	Property Loss Frequency*		
						Category 5	Category 6	Category 7 and Over
1946	106	65	78	15	7	29	7	0
1947	165	78	313	169	7	46	7	1
1948	183	68	139	33	7	62	11	2
1949	249	80	211	58	7	54	13	0
1950	200	88	70	18	7	47	9	0
1951	262	113	34	6	7	35	11	2
1952	240	98	229	57	7	53	19	0
1953	421	136	515	116	8	63	18	7
1954	550	160	36	6	7	63	8	1
1955	593	152	126	80	7	74	13	1
1956	504	155	83	25	7	83	24	1
1957	856	154	192	44	8	129	26	3
1958	564	166	66	19	7	70	8	1
1959	604	156	58	21	7	70	4	1
1960	616	172	46	16	7	65	11	1
1961	697	169	51	16	7	103	21	1
1962	657	152	28	17	7	51	10	0
1963	464	141	31	5	7	77	15	1
1964	704	156	73	22	7	113	17	5
1965	906	181	299	44	8	126	30	11
1966	585	150	98	58	8	79	13	4
1967	926	173	114	33	8	125	33	8
1968	660	171	131	34	8	82	26	6
1969	608	155	66	32	8	98	16	3
1970	653	171	72	26	8	97	24	6
1971	888	192	156	58	8	71	30	5
1972	741	194	27	6	8	100	28	1
1973	1102	206	87	7	9	219	67	9
1974	947	184	361	34	9	166	82	25
1975	920	204	60	9	9	189	31	11
1976	835	169	44	5	8	145	41	5
1977	852	189	43	22	8	173	40	6
1978	788	173	53	16	9	153	53	6
1979	852	186	84	42	9	169	62	11
1980	866	176	28	5	9	201	79	13
1981	783	175	24	5	9	144	43	12
1982	1046	182	64	10	9	254	79	13
1983	931	190	34	3	9	211	85	10
1984	907	166	122	16	9	193	90	35
1985	684	168	94	18	9	114	55	14
1986	764	168	15	3	9	157	66	9
1987	656	151	59	30	8	112	32	6
1988	702	156	32	5	9	148	48	17
1989	856	160	50	21	9	133	60	18
1990	1133	181	53	29	8	215	91	18

Note: The above estimated losses are based on values at time of occurrence.
[s] Storm damages in categories:
  5. $50,000 to $500,000
  6. $500,000 to $5 million
  7. $5 million to $50 million
  8. $50 million to $500 million
  9. $500 million and more
* Number of Times Property Losses reported in *Storm Data* in categories 5, 6, 7, and more.
Source: Wood, *Weather Almanac*, 97.

Other Storms

The United States continued to be subject to other weather phenomena that lacked the drama of hurricanes and tornadoes but still had the capacity to threaten life and property and affect areas for years to come. Dust storms remained an issue on the Great Plains. Partly a product of another element of weather—absence of rainfall—dust storms after 1946 did not equal the intensity or impact of the great black blizzards of the 1930s. Dust clouds nonetheless darkened the sky for miles around in many years, and the storms fed off periods of drought, notably in 1952–56 and 1988. Conditions otherwise had changed since the era of the dust bowl. Government subsidies eased the blow caused by a failed crop. Utilization of underground aquifers and other techniques facilitated irrigation. Growth of metropolitan areas meant that most people's living did not depend on the weather.

People in large parts of the country accepted snow as a regular part of life. In most areas snowfall came from movement of weather systems. The right combination of moisture, cold air, and wind could produce a blizzard or at least heavy snow. In the East snowstorms often were called northeasters (or nor' easters) from direction of the winds. Improved weather forecasting and better snow-removal equipment (in places that had it) eased and shortened the distress but by no means ended it. Blizzards nearly always shut down cities, isolated the countryside, and caused hardship and death. Areas that regularly experienced heaviest snowfall lived under different weather conditions. Cold air moving over warm water produced "lake-effect" snow, especially on the eastern side of Lake Michigan in Michigan and the eastern end of Lake Erie in western New York. One lake-effect blizzard brought 40 inches and drifts much higher to Buffalo, New York, in January 1977. The largest snowfalls came as a result of "upslope" movement of air, forced to rise when it bumped into mountains. Snowfalls could reach 10 feet on the western side of mountains near the Pacific Coast. The record of 189 inches fell at Mount Shasta, California, during a storm in February 1959.

The most common form of weather disturbance, the thunderstorm, produced the most diverse consequences. By bringing rain for a parched earth, water for emptied reservoirs and rivers, relief from a hot spell, it could be essential to life itself. It could delay or cancel sporting events, picnics, reunions, summer concerts, or any outdoor activity. Thunderstorms carried potential for serious trouble. While weaker than in hurricanes and tornadoes, their winds could cause huge damage. If frequent and persistent enough, the storms can produce flooding on a general scale; if intense and concentrated enough, they can produce deadly flash floods. Thunderstorms provided spawning conditions for tornadoes. They often brought lightning, thereby creating a different set of problems. Lightning struck buildings, airplanes, and livestock. It sparked fires that could grow rapidly in dry and undeveloped areas. Largely because it took its victims one at a time, it received far less attention than it deserved as a killer. Causing death of approximately 150 Americans each year (and injury to another 250), lightning was on average a more persistent threat to life than either hurricanes or tornadoes.

TABLE 2.12 THE BEAUFORT SCALE FOR MEASURING WIND STRENGTH

Wind Force (the Beaufort numbers)	Description	Wind Speed	
		km/h	mph
0	Calm	less than 1	less than 1
1	Light air	1–5	1–3
2	Light breeze	6–11	4–7
3	Gentle breeze	12–19	8–12
4	Moderate breeze	20–29	13–18
5	Fresh breeze	30–39	19–24
6	Strong breeze	40–50	25–31
7	Near gale	51–61	32–38
8	Gale	62–74	39–46
9	Strong gale	75–87	47–54
10	Storm	88–101	55–63
11	Violent storm	102–117	64–73
12	Hurricane	118+	74+

Note: The scale has unofficially been extended to Force 17 to describe tropical storms.
Source: Clive Carpenter, The Changing World of Weather (New York, 1991), 31.

TABLE 2.13 RECORD U.S. BLIZZARDS AND SNOWSTORMS, 1946–1983

Date	Location	Depth	Remarks
Jan. 1946	Stampede Pass, Wash.	192.2 in.	Record snowfall for one month
Nov. 2–8, 1946	New Mexico	36 in.	Unprecedented for area
Mar. 2–5, 1947	Readsboro, Vt.	50 in.	Record snow for state
Mar. 2–5, 1947	Peru, Mass.	47 in.	Record snow for state
Jan. 1–6, 1949	Colo. to Dak.	7–30 in.	70 mph wind, 39 deaths
Mar. 25–27, 1950	Dumont, S.Dak.	60 in.	Record snow for state
Nov. 22–28, 1950	Ohio, Pa., W.Va.	33–57 in.	Record snow each state
Mar. 10–14, 1951	Iowa City, Iowa	27.2 in.	Record snow for state
Apr. 2–5, 1955	Colo. to Dak.	30–52 in.	Heavy late spring storm
Mar. 16–17, 1956	New England, N.Y., Pa.	20 in.	Severe wind and snow
Feb. 13–19, 1958	N.C. to N.Y.	36 in.	43 dead, $500 million damage
Mar. 19–22, 1958	Va. to New England	17–30 in.	49 dead, severe storm
Feb. 18–20, 1960	Md. to New England	20–36 in.	Millions $ in damage
Jan. 19–20, 1961	N.C. to N.Y.	10–30 in.	37 dead, cities halted
Feb. 3–5, 1961	N.C. to New England	10–36 in.	73 dead, 15-ft. drifts
Feb. 2–5, 1964	N.Mex., Tex., Okla.	18–36 in.	2nd largest area storm
Jan. 29–31, 1966	Va. to New England	12–36 in.	50 dead, 20-ft. drifts
Mar. 2–5, 1966	Nebr. to Dakotas	12–36 in.	15 persons, 100,000 cattle dead; 30-ft. drifts
Jan. 26–27, 1967	Chicago, Midwest	23 in.	Record snow and ice
Feb. 9–10, 1969	N.Y., New England	15 in.	New York City hit badly

Date	Location	Depth	Remarks
Feb. 1969	Mt. Wash. Vt.	172.8 in.	Month state record
Feb. 10–11, 1973	Ga. to Carolinas	15–21 in.	South's worst storm in 20th century thus far
Dec. 1–2, 1974	Mich., Ohio	17–20 in.	Record snow in Detroit
Jan. 10–12, 1975	North Great Plains area	8–15 in.	60 dead, 20-ft. drifts, 80 mph winds
Jan. 3–31, 1977	W. Va.	104 in.	W. Va. one month record
Jan. 26–Feb. 1, 1977	Ill., Ind., Ohio, N.Y., Pa.	12–71 in.	75 dead, 69 mph winds
Jan. 26–28, 1978	East and Midwest	12–34 in.	100 dead, 100 mph winds, drifts to 25 ft.
Feb. 6–7, 1978	Northeast	18–38 in.	100 mph winds
Jan. 13–14, 1979	Chicago, Midwest	20.7 in.	Chicago paralyzed
Mar. 2, 1980	South & Mid-Atlantic	10–28 in.	36 dead, Fla. crops damaged
Jan. 10–23, 1982	N. Minn.	38 in.	Paralyzing blizzard
Jan. 31, 1982	St. Louis & Midwest	18–22 in.	Paralyzing blizzard
Jan. 1982	Muskegon, Mich.	89 in.	Record month snow
Dec. 24–25, 1982	Denver, Colo.	24 in.	Travelers stranded
Feb. 11–12, 1983	Northeast	17–35 in.	Record snow in Philadelphia
Nov. 27–28, 1983	Rockies and Central Plains	15–22 in.	50 dead, blizzards

Source: David C. Whitney, ed., *Reader's Digest 1986 Almanac and Yearbook* (Pleasantville, N.Y., 1985), 152.

TABLE 2.14 CASUALTIES FROM LIGHTNING

National Total Deaths by Year for Period 1959–1990

Year	Jan.	Feb.	Mar.	Apr.	May	Jun.	Jul.	Aug.	Sep.	Oct.	Nov.	Dec.	Annual
1959	1	0	1	4	18	25	50	39	13	7	0	0	158
1960	0	0	1	5	7	33	25	17	9	0	0	0	97
1961	0	0	1	2	9	23	47	20	10	1	0	0	113
1962	0	0	3	6	27	20	26	28	9	1	0	0	120
1963	0	0	4	3	11	37	42	20	10	2	0	81[a]	210
1964	0	0	9	6	15	21	29	19	7	1	1	0	108
1965	0	0	2	4	12	34	39	28	4	2	0	0	125
1966	0	0	1	1	8	15	21	16	11	3	0	0	76
1967	1	0	1	2	3	26	21	14	1	2	1	1	73
1968	0	0	0	1	5	24	30	29	9	3	1	1	103
1969	0	0	1	5	13	17	27	13	14	3	0	0	93
1970	0	0	0	1	17	25	27	19	21	1	0	0	111
1971	0	0	2	1	12	27	33	19	19	0	0	0	113
1972	0	0	1	1	5	21	31	28	3	1	0	0	91
1973	0	1	2	3	10	24	31	18	13	2	1	0	105
1974	0	2	0	7	12	21	28	24	6	0	2	0	102
1975	0	1	3	3	11	19	28	18	6	2	0	0	91
1976	0	0	0	1	9	19	19	19	3	2	0	0	72
1977	0	0	0	4	9	19	16	35	14	1	0	0	98
1978	0	0	1	1	9	26	24	22	3	1	0	1	88
1979	0	0	0	3	11	4	20	16	4	3	2	0	63
1980	0	0	0	0	7	16	27	20	5	1	0	0	76
1981	0	0	0	4	5	13	19	19	5	0	2	0	67
1982	1	0	0	3	5	14	29	18	4	3	0	0	77
1983	0	0	1	2	4	8	28	23	8	1	2	0	77
1984	0	0	1	3	10	14	20	10	7	1	1	0	67
1985	0	0	0	5	12	12	26	8	8	1	1	0	73
1986	0	0	0	2	9	13	21	17	5	1	0	0	68
1987	0	0	0	2	14	18	28	15	7	2	0	0	86
1988	0	0	0	3	9	17	21	14	2	1	2	0	69
1989	0	0	1	1	9	14	19	18	4	1	0	0	67
1990	1	0	3	1	3	18	22	15	10	0	0	1	74

National Total Injuries by Year for Period 1959–1990

Year	Jan.	Feb.	Mar.	Apr.	May	Jun.	Jul.	Aug.	Sep.	Oct.	Nov.	Dec.	Annual
1959	0	0	0	5	27	52	110	103	23	3	1	1	325
1960	0	0	2	11	12	70	28	50	16	9	4	0	202
1961	0	0	7	14	15	49	83	50	31	5	1	1	256
1962	0	0	3	5	39	38	90	49	12	6	0	0	242
1963	7	0	0	6	14	64	55	44	18	1	0	0	209
1964	0	0	10	15	14	38	99	53	8	1	1	0	239
1965	3	2	2	4	26	42	59	59	19	1	0	0	217

(continued)

TABLE 2.14   (continued)

Year	Jan.	Feb.	Mar.	Apr.	May	Jun.	Jul.	Aug.	Sep.	Oct.	Nov.	Dec.	Annual
1966	0	2	1	2	37	39	42	44	15	1	0	0	183
1967	0	0	0	4	7	35	59	33	4	2	0	1	145
1968	0	0	4	2	16	52	117	155	14	9	1	0	370
1969	0	0	0	4	19	75	39	23	12	0	0	1	173
1970	0	0	1	5	40	40	82	43	43	4	1	0	259
1971	0	1	0	1	24	71	79	54	22	1	1	0	254
1972	0	0	8	6	12	24	72	54	24	2	1	0	203
1973	0	0	10	2	20	23	74	59	29	9	2	0	228
1974	1	9	1	3	12	27	56	51	12	1	0	0	173
1975	0	3	0	1	30	60	107	154	42	1	0	1	399
1976	0	1	0	7	16	39	73	68	13	1	0	1	219
1977	0	0	0	3	35	58	58	67	62	4	4	0	291
1978	0	0	5	3	19	100	73	54	42	5	0	0	301
1979	0	2	4	26	32	73	55	49	9	2	2	0	254
1980	0	1	2	11	11	49	50	134	16	1	0	0	275
1981	1	0	2	9	34	60	108	52	9	3	13	0	291
1982	1	0	2	6	38	20	54	32	11	4	* 4	2	174
1983	0	0	24	3	25	24	87	113	30	31	0	0	337
1984	0	0	7	5	13	43	80	53	44	7	1	0	253
1985	0	0	29	4	42	48	61	33	27	4	0	0	248
1986	0	2	4	2	15	68	112	43	22	3	0	0	271
1987	0	0	2	8	66	49	121	70	43	3	1	1	364
1988	0	0	1	14	22	53	133	63	19	5	1	0	311
1989	1	0	8	16	23	70	135	51	12	4	2	0	322
1990	12	0	4	6	10	43	88	62	25	1	0	1	252

a On December 8, 1963, the crash of a jetliner killing 81 people near Elkton, Maryland, was attributed to lightning by the Civil Aeronautics Board investigators.
Source: Wood, *Weather Almanac*, 113.

TABLE 2.15   THE ODDS OF A WHITE CHRISTMAS

If you want a white Christmas, head for Fairbanks, Alaska, or International Falls, Minnesota, where there is a 100 percent chance of snow on the ground on December 25. Here are the chances, by percentage, of at least an inch of snow being on the ground on Christmas Day. These odds are based on snowfall records at National Weather Service offices for the places listed. States not listed here have zero odds throughout the state (though under extremely unusual conditions snow may come to some places where the official odds are zero).

City	Percent Chance
Alabama	
Birmingham	0
Huntsville	9
Mobile	0
Montgomery	0
Alaska	
Anchorage	87
Barrow	93
Bethel	80
Cold Bay	37
Cordova	46
Fairbanks	100
Juneau	50
King Salmon	79
Kotzebue	87
McGrath	90
Nome	73
St. Paul	43

City	Percent Chance
Arizona	
Flagstaff	50
Phoenix	0
Prescott	0
Tucson	0
Winslow	16
Yuma	0
Arkansas	
Fort Smith	0
Little Rock	3
Texarkana	0
California	
Bakersfield	0
Bishop	4
Burbank	0
Eureka	0
Fresno	0
Long Beach	0
Los Angeles	0
Oakland	0
Red Bluff	0
Sacramento	0
San Diego	0
San Francisco	0
Santa Maria	0
Colorado	
Alamosa	47
Colo. Springs	20
Denver	23
Grand Junction	27
Pueblo	27

City	Percent Chance
Connecticut	
Bridgeport	33
Hartford	43
New Haven	43
Delaware	
Wilmington	26
District of Columbia	
Washington	17
Idaho	
Boise	16
Idaho Falls	30
Lewiston	3
Pocatello	43
Illinois	
Cairo	6
Chicago	43
Moline	33
Peoria	30
Rockford	36
Springfield	26
Indiana	
Evansville	10
Fort Wayne	43
Indianapolis	26
South Bend	56
Iowa	
Burlington	33
Des Moines	46
Dubuque	60
Sioux City	43
Waterloo	50
Kansas	
Concordia	36
Dodge City	23
Goodland	26
Topeka	23
Wichita	17
Kentucky	
Lexington	12
Louisville	16
Maine	
Caribou	97
Portland	63
Maryland	
Baltimore	20
Frederick	27
Massachusetts	
Boston	30
Nantucket	10
Pittsfield	44
Worcester	75
Michigan	
Alpena	73
Detroit	40
Escanaba	62
Flint	54
Grand Rapids	60
Lansing	50
Marquette	90
Muskegon	53
St. Ste. Marie	93

City	Percent Chance
Minnesota	
Duluth	90
Int'l Falls	100
Minneapolis	73
Rochester	71
St. Cloud	59
Missouri	
Columbia	27
Kansas City	20
St. Joseph	30
St. Louis	13
Springfield	7
Montana	
Billings	53
Glasgow	52
Great Falls	43
Havre	43
Helena	57
Kalispell	60
Missoula	57
Nebraska	
Grand Island	33
Lincoln	37
Norfolk	40
North Platte	33
Omaha	40
Scottsbluff	29
Valentine	40
Nevada	
Elko	47
Ely	30
Las Vegas	0
Reno	7
Winnemucca	23
New Hampshire	
Concord	67
New Jersey	
Atlantic City	7
Newark	27
Trenton	23
New Mexico	
Albuquerque	7
Clayton	12
Raton	13
Roswell	3
New York	
Albany	43
Binghamton	70
Buffalo	50
New York	23
Rochester	60
Schenectady	64
Syracuse	67
North Carolina	
Asheville	7
Cape Hatteras	0
Charlotte	3
Greensboro	13
Raleigh	3
Wilmington	0
Winston-Salem	15

(continued)

TABLE 2.15 (continued)

City	Percent Chance
North Dakota	
Bismarck	60
Devils Lake	79
Fargo	77
Williston	53
Ohio	
Akron-Canton	43
Cincinnati	17
Cleveland	37
Columbus	23
Dayton	30
Mansfield	60
Sandusky	38
Toledo	40
Youngstown	43
Oklahoma	
Oklahoma City	0
Tulsa	3
Oregon	
Astoria	0
Eugene	0
Medford	3
Pendleton	0
Portland	0
Roseburg	7
Salem	0
Pennsylvania	
Allentown	33
Erie	47
Harrisburg	33
Philadelphia	23
Pittsburgh	30
Reading	33
Scranton	53
Williamsport	43
Rhode Island	
Block Island	17
Providence	33
South Carolina	
Charleston	0
Columbia	0
Florence	0
Greenville	7
South Dakota	
Huron	37
Rapid City	30
Sioux Falls	43
Tennessee	
Bristol	18
Chattanooga	3
Knoxville	10
Memphis	0
Nashville	10
Oak Ridge	12
Utah	
Milford	29
Salt Lake City	43
Wendover	3

City	Percent Chance
Vermont	
Burlington	77
Virginia	
Lynchburg	17
Norfolk	10
Richmond	10
Roanoke	27
Washington	
Olympia	0
Seattle	7
Spokane	33
Walla Walla	3
Yakima	20
West Virginia	
Charleston	26
Elkins	19
Huntington	24
Parkersburg	23
Wisconsin	
Green Bay	60
LaCrosse	63
Madison	57
Milwaukee	40
Wyoming	
Casper	40
Cheyenne	23
Lander	63
Sheridan	67

Source: Jack Williams, *The USA Today Weather Almanac 1995* (New York, 1994), 367–368.

Floods and Flash Floods

Drawing on their experience from before the Second World War, governments on all levels from national to local took measures to protect against floods. They dammed up rivers to hold back the water; they built walls around cities situated along the rivers that were designed to push the water downstream. But floods continued to come—partly because nature did not yield gracefully to being mastered, partly because Americans insisted on living where the rivers wanted to go and persisted with practices that fostered rapid runoff of precipitation. In some cases flooding developed from rainfall that lasted for a prolonged period; in many cases floods grew out of hurricanes that brought tidal surges and massive downpours after the strongest winds had subsided. The years that produced the most floods—1969 (445) and 1972 (555)—corresponded with the landfall of hurricanes Camille and Agnes; the year with the fewest—31 in 1988—encountered no major Atlantic hurricane. Some of the heaviest flooding during this period in the eastern states followed arrival of Agnes in 1972. As with hurricanes generally, flooding in the period after 1945 produced fewer deaths than in previous years but frequently an increase in the value of damage.

The most deadly floods were those that came virtually without warning and affected a small area. The greatest danger of a flash flood came from a situation in which massive rainfall for a short period (two or three hours might be enough) trapped water in a small place and then directed it along a single path of departure. The danger had expanded with the propensity of people to settle near banks and on the floodplain of rivers and streams and with growing popularity of narrow canyon areas as recreation sites. Two examples from the 1970s exemplified the problem. In June 1972 heavy thunderstorm cells stalled over the floodplain near Rapid City, South Dakota, pouring 15 inches of rainfall into Rapid Creek in five hours. Debris floating downstream clogged the spillway of Canyon Lake Dam, causing the reservoir to back up and the dam to break under the increased pressure. A torrent of water swept both sides of the creek, flooded downtown Rapid City, and killed 237. A similar situation occurred in July 1976 in a portion of Rocky Mountain National Park in Colorado. Four hours of localized torrential rainfall flooded the Big Thompson River and sent a wave 20 feet high down the canyon, destroying more than 500 homes, 52 businesses, and the highway in the canyon, killing 139 people.

TABLE 2.16　SOME MAJOR FLOODS IN THE UNITED STATES, 1947–1980

Period	Rivers or Basins	Damage in Millions	Deaths
May–July 1947	Missouri and Mississippi	235	29
May–June 1948	Columbia	101	75
June–July 1951	Kansas and Missouri	923	60
April 1952	Red River of north and upper Mississippi	198	11
August 1955	Northeast states	714	186
December 1955	Pacific Coast states	154	61
April–June 1957	Texas, Arkansas, Kansas, Louisiana, Missouri, and Oklahoma	105	18
December 1964	California and Oregon	415	40
March–May 1965	Upper Mississippi, Missouri, and Red North	181	16
June 1965	South Platte	416	16
May 1968	North New Jersey	166	. . .
January–February 1969	California	399	60
March–April 1969	Upper Midwest	151	. . .
August 1969	James	116	153
August 1971	New Jersey and Pennsylvania	138	. . .
June 1972	Black Hills, South Dakota	164	237
June 1972	Eastern States	4019	105
May 1973	South Platte	120	. . .
Spring 1973	Mississippi	1154	33
May 1975	Mississippi	. . .	. . .
July 1975	Red River of north	273	4
September 1975	New York and Pennsylvania	296	9
July 1976	Thompson Canyon, Colorado	. . .	139
September–October 1976	Southern California and Arizona	160	. . .
April 1977	Kentucky rivers	424	22
July 1977	Johnstown, Pennsylvania	200	76
September 1977	Kansas City creeks	5	23
November 1977	Taccoa, Georgia	. . .	38
February–March 1978	Los Angeles area	100	20
August 1978	Southeast Texas	100	33
April 1978	Pearl River in Louisiana and Mississippi	1,000	15
April 1979	Southeast Texas	500	1
May 1979	Red River of the North	. . .	. . .
July 1979	East Texas	750	1
February 1980	Arizona and Southern California	500	36
April 1980	Mississippi and Louisiana	. . .	. . .

Source: David M. Ludlum, *The American Weather Book* (Boston, 1982), 81–82.

Eruption of Mount St. Helens in Washington on May 18, 1980. (David E. Wiesprecht, U.S. Geological Survey, Cascades Observatory, Vancouver, Washington)

Mount St. Helens: Weather Impostor

Eruption of a volcano normally was not considered a feature of weather, but a major one could seriously affect atmospheric conditions. The eruption on May 18, 1980, of Mount St. Helens, a peak of the Cascades range in Washington, was an act of nature that took on features of a terrible storm. It produced ash-laden clouds that darkened the sky as at nightfall and inhibited breathing; momentary wind gusts devastated 250 square miles of surrounding recreation, timber, and private lands and left in its wake 57 people dead or missing.

CHAPTER 3 Chronology, 1946–1990

The Postwar Period and Start of the Cold War, 1946–1960

January 21, 1946   The United States Steel Workers Union closes the steel mills in a crippling strike over wages.

March 5, 1946   Former British prime minister Winston Churchill, with President Harry Truman present, makes his "iron curtain" speech at Fulton, Missouri.

March 13, 1946   The United Auto Workers Union ends a 113-day strike at General Motors in a victory.

April 1, 1946   Some 400,000 United Mine Workers go on strike for better wages and medical benefits—another blow to economic recovery.

A huge tidal wave, a tsunami, kills 179 in Hawaii.

May 23, 1946   The Railway Trainmen and Engineers strike, shutting down the railroads.

June 21, 1946   President Truman names Fred Vinson chief justice of the Supreme Court.

July 1, 1946   The United States begins atomic tests at tiny Bikini Atoll in the Marshall Islands.

July 4, 1946   In fulfillment of an American pledge made much earlier, the Philippine Islands receives its independence.

July 30, 1946   The United States joins UNESCO: United Nations Educational, Scientific, and Cultural Organization.

September 20, 1946   Secretary of Commerce (and former vice president) Henry A. Wallace resigns his post amidst furor about his criticism of foreign policy.

October 23, 1946   The General Assembly of the United Nations meets in New York City and accepts $8.5 million from John D. Rockefeller, Jr., to build a permanent site for the new organization.

November 5, 1946   Republicans sweep the off-year elections, gaining clear control of both houses of Congress.

December 7, 1946   In the nation's worst hotel fire, 127 die at the Winecoff Hotel in Atlanta.

Other events of 1946   The trials of Nazi leaders begin in August in Nuremburg, Germany.

A symposium in Buffalo suggests that lung cancer might be linked to smoking.

It's a Wonderful Life opens on the screen, *Annie Get Your Gun* on stage. Procter & Gamble introduces Tide soap powder.

The short-waisted Eisenhower jacket becomes fashionable.

A skimpy female bathing suit makes an appearance in Paris and is called a bikini.

March 12, 1947   President Truman announces a program, directed at Greece and Turkey, that will be called the Truman Doctrine—a far-reaching shot in the cold war.

April 11, 1947   Infielder Jackie Robinson joins the Brooklyn Dodgers, breaking a color line (a ban on blacks) that had been in effect in major league baseball for more than 50 years.

April 16, 1947   A ship explosion nearly destroys the town of Texas City, Texas, killing 500, injuring 2,000.

June 5, 1947   Speaking at the commencement at Harvard, Secretary of State George C. Marshall proposes a massive program of economic aid for Europe that will become known as the Marshall Plan.

June 23, 1947   The Republican 80th Congress overrides a presidential veto and passes the Taft-Hartley Act, which imposed major restrictions on labor unions.

July 7, 1947   Congress passed a new law of presidential succession, making the speaker of the house (not the secretary of state) next in line after the president and vice president.

July 26, 1947   Truman signs the National Security Act, reorganizing military forces under what will become a Department of Defense.

October 5, 1947   Truman becomes the first president to address the nation via televison.

October 14, 1947   Air Force Captain Chuck Yeager is the first to break the sound barrier in an experimental Bell X-1 aircraft.

December 23, 1947   President Truman pardons 1,523 men who evaded the draft during the Second World War.

December 27, 1947   New York City experiences the largest snowfall on record: Nearly 26 inches causes 80 deaths and shuts down the city.

Other events of 1947   The first Levittown (practical, mass-produced postwar housing) opens on Long Island—all buyers had to be white.

Buses replace the last trolley cars in New York City, ending an era.

Polaroid introduces its instant "Land" camera, Goodyear a tubeless tire.

Peter Paul produces a candy bar called Almond Joy.

Epoxy glue makes an appearance.

Deaths include Al Capone and Henry Ford.

January 5, 1948   An art show featuring 17 huge paintings by little-known artist Jackson Pollock opens in New York. Many viewers wonder what all the swirls were about, but the art world is dazzled.

February 7, 1948   General Dwight Eisenhower retires from the army to become president of Columbia University.

March 8, 1948   The Supreme Court rules that religious instruction in public schools is unconstitutional.

May 10, 1948   Faced with a national rail strike, Truman orders the army to take over the railroads.

May 14, 1948   Israel declares its independence, coming out of an area called Palestine; Truman quickly extends recognition.

May 25, 1948   General Motors and the U.A.W. sign a landmark contract that tied wage increases to the cost of living.

June 26, 1948   Faced with a Soviet blockade of the western sectors of occupied Berlin, the United States begins to supply the city by air.

The Berlin Airlift—another round in a fledgling cold war—will last more than a year.

July 15, 1948   Democrats meet and nominate Harry Truman for the presidency and Senator Alben Barkley for the vice presidency.

A strong (for that day) civil rights platform will cause southern Democrats to bolt the party.

July 17, 1948   Southern Democrats meet separately, form the States' Rights (Dixiecrat) Party, and nominate Governor J. Strom Thurmond of South Carolina for the presidency.

July 22, 1948   Liberal defectors from the Democrat Party form the Progressive Party, with Henry Wallace as its presidential nominee.

July 26, 1948   President Truman issues an executive order that prohibits segregation in the armed forces and calls for an end to discrimination in the national government.

July 31, 1948   Truman dedicates Idlewild Airport in New York; it later will be renamed the John F. Kennedy Airport.

August 3, 1948   Testifying before a congressional committee, Whittaker Chambers, a former communist, names Alger Hiss as a communist spy and in so doing instigated the Hiss case that helped fuel the Red Scare and give publicity to obscure freshman congressman Richard Nixon.

October 24, 1948   In a speech before a congressional committee, elder statesman Bernard Baruch described mounting trouble with the Soviet Union as a cold war, thus giving a name to an era.

November 2, 1948   After a vigorous "whistle stop" campaign that targeted the "do-nothing" Republican 80th Congress, Truman scored a major upset victory over Thomas E. Dewey. Defecting Democrats do poorly.

Other events of 1948   The first self-serve McDonald's restaurant opens in California.

The long-playing (33 rpm) record appears on the market, as does a new word game called Scrabble.

Bell Laboratories introduces a tiny transistor to replace bulky and expendable vacuum tubes.

A 200-inch reflecting telescope, largest in the world, goes into operation at Mount Palomar, California.

The Voice of America begins radio broadcasts abroad.

Alfred Kinsey, professor of zoology at Indiana University, publishes *Sexual Behavior in the Human Male,* a dispassionate, but nonetheless sensational, study of a topic heretofore virtually forbidden from public discussion.

January 21, 1949   Dean Acheson becomes secretary of state, replacing George Marshall, at start of Truman's new term.

March 2, 1949   The first nonstop flight around the world is completed. The airplane, an American B-50 bomber, was refueled four times in the air.

June 28, 1949   The United States returns home the final combat troops in Korea, leaving some 500 advisers.

July 21, 1949   The Senate by a vote of 82–13 ratifies the North Atlantic Treaty Organization (NATO), committing the United States to the first entangling alliance in 150 years.

August 3, 1949   Congress declares June 14 to be Flag Day.

September 23, 1949   President Truman announces that the Soviet Union has exploded an atomic bomb, much earlier than expected.

October 1, 1949   Mao Zedong announces the formation of the People's Republic of China (communist, or "Red" China), in effect claiming victory in China's three-year civil war, an event that was—and would continue to be—deemed a substantial defeat for the United States.

October 14, 1949   Eleven high-ranking American communists are convicted of conspiring overthrow of the U.S. government.

October 26, 1949   Congress raises the minimum wage from 40 to 75 cents an hour.

December 26, 1949   Albert Einstein, a naturalized citizen, announces his theory of relativity.

Other events of 1949   The small, "unbreakable" 45 rpm phonograph record is introduced by RCA.

Northwest Airlines is the first to serve alcoholic drinks in flight.

Actress Ingrid Bergman scandalizes public opinion (and at least stuns the film world) by leaving her husband for Italian film director Roberto Rossellini.

William Faulkner wins the Nobel Prize for literature.

The Catholic Church threatens to excommunicate communists.

New popular songs include "Rudolph the Red-Nosed Reindeer."

January 17, 1950   Bandits rob Brink's, Inc., in Boston of $2.8 million; the case will not be solved until 1956.

January 31, 1950   Truman gives the order to proceed on development of the "Super," a hydrogen bomb vastly more powerful than the previous atomic bomb.

February 9, 1950   Speaking in Wheeling, West Virginia, Senator Joseph McCarthy of Wisconsin claims to have a list of 205 communists working in the Department of State, thus firing the first shot in an upheaval that will become known as McCarthyism.

February 15, 1950   The United States learns that the Soviet Union and the People's Republic of China have signed an alliance, the Sino-Soviet Pact, seemingly confirming suspicion of a growing world communist conspiracy.

March 1, 1950   Arrested in Britain, scientist Klaus Fuchs is sentenced to 14 years of imprisonment for passing atomic secrets to the Soviet Union. Fuchs confessed.

May 11, 1950   Truman dedicates the Grand Coulee Dam in the state of Washington.

June 25, 1950   War begins when North Korean troops cross the 38th parallel in an invasion of South Korea.

June 30, 1950   Truman orders U.S. ground forces to assist the South Koreans, bringing America into the Korean War.

August 8, 1950   An American, Florence Chadwick, swims the English Channel in 13 hours, 23 minutes, breaking the woman's record.

October 7, 1950   United States and United Nations forces cross the 38th parallel, invading North Korea and starting a new phase in the Korean War.

November 2, 1950   CBS television begins to broadcast in color.

November 26, 1950   Chinese troops open a massive counteroffensive in North Korea, pushing back UN forces, trapping many Americans and causing others to retreat.

Other events of 1950   New York opens the Port Authority Bus Terminal.

Charles Schulz, a young man who began to cartoon in a correspondence course, starts a strip called *Peanuts*.

A young Baptist minister, Billy Graham, begins a radio show called *Hour of Decision*.

Diner's Club introduces a credit card.

Nat "King" Cole's "Mona Lisa" is a popular song; "Frosty the Snowman" is another.

Minute Rice is a successful new product; Silly Putty is another.

February 26, 1951   The Twenty-second Amendment, which generally limits a president to two terms, is ratified and becomes part of the U.S. Constitution. The amendment represents a Republican reaction to Franklin Roosevelt's being elected to four terms.

April 4, 1951   Dwight Eisenhower ends retirement to become commander of the NATO alliance in Europe.

April 11, 1951   President Truman fires General Douglas MacArthur, hero of the Second World War and commander of United States and United Nations forces in the Korean War, for insubordination in his criticism of American policy in the Korean War.

June 4, 1951   In *Dennis v. United States* the Supreme Court, in upholding an earlier conviction of communist leaders, virtually (but not explicitly) rules that it is illegal in the United States to be a communist.

June 14, 1951   The first commercial electronic digital computer (UNIVAC), weighing eight tons, begins operation in Philadelphia.

July 11, 1951   The Missouri River begins a flooding that will devastate Kansas City and cause more than $1 billion in damage.

September 8, 1951   Forty-nine nations sign the American-sponsored peace treaty with Japan, ending the Second World War and the American occupation of Japan, although the troops stayed under different arrangements.

Other events of 1951   *Dennis the Menace* appears as a comic strip.

Power steering becomes available in automobiles, introduced by Chrysler.

The first section of the New Jersey Turnpike opens to traffic.

Alan Freed, a disc jockey in Cleveland, first uses a term *rock and roll* to identify catchy new music.

Super Glue appears, as does *Jet* magazine.

Bobby Thomson hits a miracle home run to allow the New York Giants to defeat the Brooklyn Dodgers in a National League baseball playoff.

The Yankee Clipper, Joe DiMaggio, announces retirement.

February 29, 1952   New York City installs in Times Square four signs instructing pedestrians, "don't walk," the first of their kind.

A weary Korean girl carries her brother past an American tank near Haengju during the Korean War. (National Archives)

March 30, 1952   President Truman announces that he will not seek reelection, even though the Twenty-second Amendment does not forbid it.

June 14, 1952   Truman presides over laying of the keel for the first atomic-powered submarine, the *Nautilus*.

June 25, 1952   Truman vetoes the McCarran-Walter immigration bill on grounds that the measure, which retained a quota system, is discriminatory. Within the next two days, Congress overrides the veto.

July 7, 1952   On its first trip to Europe, the SS *United States* established a new transatlantic speed record of 3 days, 10 hours, 40 minutes.

July 11, 1952   At the end of a heated convention, the Republicans nominate General Eisenhower for the presidency and Senator Richard Nixon of California for the vice presidency.

July 26, 1952   In a long convention the Democrats nominate Governor Adlai E. Stevenson of Illinois for the presidency and Senator John Sparkman of Alabama for the vice presidency—a familiar north-south, liberal-conservative ticket balance.

September 23, 1952   Faced with charge of corrupt financial dealings and possible removal from the ticket, Nixon defends himself in an emotional radio and television address that will become known as the "Checkers" speech—the name of his dog.

November 4, 1952   Eisenhower and Nixon win substantially, obtaining votes of all but nine states; Congress is split; controversial Senator Joseph McCarthy is reelected.

November 16, 1952   The government announces that testing of the hydrogen bomb has been completed at Eniwetok Atoll in the Marshall Islands.

November 29, 1952   Fulfilling a campaign promise, President-Elect Eisenhower begins a three-day visit of the battlefront in Korea; the war is in a stalemate as are negotiations for a truce.

Other events of 1952   The *Today Show* debuts on NBC, as does a new kind of magazine comic book: *Mad*.

Sony produces a tiny transistor radio.

No-calorie ginger ale becomes the first sugar-free soft drink.

Holiday Inn opens in Memphis its first motel.

3-D movies appear in theaters.

An ABC station in Philadelphia premieres a new show called *Bandstand*.

An American named George undergoes a "sex-change" operation in Denmark and presents himself/herself to the world as Christine Jorgensen.

March 5, 1953   Soviet Premier Joseph Stalin dies; his death has far-reaching consequences for the continuing cold war.

April 1, 1953 Congress creates a new Department of Health, Education, and Welfare; the first head will be Oveta Culp Hobby of Texas.

June 1, 1953 American mountain climbers (and perhaps Americans in general) are thrilled to learn that British Edmund Hillary and his guide Tenzing Norgay are the first to reach the summit of Mount Everest.

June 19, 1953 Convicted spies, Ethel and Julius Rosenberg, are executed at Sing Sing prison, after failure of numerous appeals—the only individuals executed for treason in peacetime.

July 27, 1953 The Korean War ends with an armistice signed at Panmunjom by UN and communist delegates.

July 31, 1953 Senator Robert A. Taft of Ohio dies at age 63. Known as Mr. Republican and leading spokesman for a conservative ideology, he made several unsuccessful tries for the presidential nomination.

August 19, 1953 With aid from the C.I.A., opposition forces overthrow the prime minister of Iran, and the shah (the king), who is returned to power, is grateful to the United States.

October 5, 1953 Earl Warren of California becomes chief justice of the Supreme Court, succeeding Fred Vinson, who has died.

December 9, 1953 General Electric Corporation announces that it will dismiss all employees who are communist.

Other events of 1953 *TV Guide* begins publication.

Swanson introduces the TV dinner.

Radial tires appear on the market.

Maureen Connolly, an American, is the first woman to win the Grand Slam of tennis.

CinemaScope, a wide-screen movie process, is introduced in *The Robe.*

A new magazine, *Playboy,* hits the stands, the creation of Hugh Hefner; the first centerfold is Marilyn Monroe, who had posed for the photo in 1949.

March 1, 1954 Puerto Rican nationalists open fire in the U.S. Capitol building, wounding five members of Congress.

April 1, 1954 The president announces establishment of a new Air Force Academy at Colorado Springs, Colorado; it will be the equivalent of West Point (army) and Annapolis (navy).

April 7, 1954 President Eisenhower pronounces his "domino theory" in the context of a conflict in French Indochina. If the area fell to the communists, so Eisenhower warned, a chain of communist victories would follow in southeast Asia.

April 22, 1954 Senate hearings begin over a dispute between Senator Joseph McCarthy and the U.S. Army; McCarthy charges that the army coddled communists. The hearings will receive widespread television coverage.

U.S. Air Force B-47—first long-range jet bomber of the cold war; it was superseded by the B-52. (author's photograph)

May 7, 1954 After a seven-month siege, the final French fortress in Vietnam (Indochina) falls to the forces of Ho Chi Minh's Vietminh; the communists have won, at least in the northern part of the territory.

May 17, 1954 The Supreme Court under Chief Justice Warren hands down its epochal decision in *Brown v. Board of Education*, ruling that segregation in the public schools is unconstitutional.

June 18, 1954 A coup engineered by the C.I.A. begins in Guatemala; it will oust Jacobo Arbenz Guzmán, the reformist, popularly elected president.

September 9, 1954 The United States and seven other nations join in a collective security pact for the Pacific area called the Southeast Asia Treaty Organization (SEATO); Secretary of State John Foster Dulles is the author.

December 2, 1954 Senate colleagues condemn (officially censure) Joseph McCarthy for his behavior in recent Army-McCarthy hearings; the move marks beginning of the end of McCarthyism.

Other events of 1954 The publishing empire of Henry Luce (*Time, Life*) introduces a new member, *Sports Illustrated*.

RCA offers color television sets at $1,000 each.

The *Tonight Show* begins on NBC.

Rising screen personality Marilyn Monroe weds baseball player Joe DiMaggio.

Elvis Presley, age 19, cuts his first record, in Memphis: "I'm All Right, Mamma."

Powerful Hurricane Hazel strikes the Atlantic coast.

January 8, 1955 Researchers announce the effectiveness of new drugs, thorazine and resperine, in treatment of mental disorder.

January 20, 1955 Military technology advances as the first atomic-powered American submarine, *Nautilus*, engages in sea trials.

April 12, 1955 After lengthy testing, the Salk polio vaccine is proclaimed safe and effective.

April 18, 1955 Naturalized American Albert Einstein dies at age 76 in Princeton, New Jersey.

May 27, 1955 An outbreak of tornadoes kills 121 in the Midwest and Southwest.

May 31, 1955 In a decision that some people called Brown II, the Supreme Court rules that desegregation could proceed gradually, with "all deliberate speed."

June 13, 1955 The Legion of Decency of the Catholic Church forces theaters to remove a poster of Marilyn Monroe holding down her dress (or trying to) for the movie *The Seven Year Itch*.

July 18, 1955 Eisenhower and Dulles meet with leaders of France, Britain, and the Soviet Union in what will be called a summit conference in Geneva, Switzerland. No agreements result, but an emerging "spirit of Geneva" suggests possible better times ahead for east-west relations.

USS *Nautilus*, first atomic-powered submarine, undergoes sea trials, January 20, 1955. (National Archives)

September 24, 1955 Eisenhower experiences a heart attack in Denver; he will be hospitalized three weeks.

September 26, 1955 The New York Stock Exchange undergoes its largest dollar loss in a single day in history—some $44 billion.

September 30, 1955 Rising actor James Dean, age 24, dies in a high-speed crash of his Porsche Spyder in California.

October 26, 1955 With the support of the United States, Ngo Dinh Diem becomes president of a new nation, the Republic of South Vietnam.

December 1, 1955 Seamstress Rosa Parks refuses to give up her bus seat to a white man in Montgomery, Alabama, thus challenging the city's, and the South's, policy of segregation. The move touches off a boycott of the bus company, viewed by many as the first step in the Civil Rights movement.

Other events of 1955 Disneyland opens its gate in Anaheim, California.

Ray Kroc opens his first franchise for a fledgling McDonald's organization in Des Plaines, Illinois.

Colonel Harlan Sanders introduces Kentucky Fried Chicken, and Kenner toys introduces Play Doh.

Captain Kangaroo, a children's show, begins on television.

A student at the University of Maryland, Jim Henson, locally performs an act with puppets—he calls them muppets.

The movie *The Blackboard Jungle* popularizes a song, "Rock Around the Clock," the band of Bill Haley and his Comets, and a musical form called rock and roll.

Allen Ginsberg, leader of a group of artistic intellectuals known as the Beats, reads his signature poem, "Howl," for which he will be arrested for obscenity.

March 12, 1956 More than 100 southern members of Congress sign a manifesto urging resistance to court desegregation rulings.

April 19, 1956 Charming and sophisticated actress Grace Kelly, winner of an Oscar in 1954, becomes a genuine princess when she marries Prince Rainier of Monaco. Nearly everyone agrees that the prince has the better of the bargain.

June 29, 1956 Wheels for a national interstate highway system were set in motion with signing of the Highway Act.

June 30, 1956 A devastating airplane accident occurs when a TWA Constellation and a United DC-7 collide over the Grand Canyon, killing 128.

July 25, 1956 The Italian luxury liner *Andrea Doria,* like the *Titanic,* another said-to-be unsinkable ship, is rammed by the Swedish liner *Stockholm* off the coast of Nantucket, killing 52. After floundering for 12 hours, the *Doria* slips beneath the waves.

August 11, 1956 Jackson Pollock, leader of a new wave of American and world artists, dies in an automobile crash.

October 31, 1956 Eisenhower condemns British-French-Israeli action against Egypt in what will be called the Suez War. American denunciation was encouraged by its criticism, at generally the same time, of Soviet action in the Hungarian uprising. The Suez crisis will strain the western alliance and facilitate Soviet influence in the Middle East.

November 6, 1956 The Republican ticket of Eisenhower and Nixon defeats the Democrats' Stevenson and Senator Estes Kefauver by a larger margin than in 1952. But the Democrats keep control of Congess.

Other events of 1956 New products that appear include Comet Cleanser, Pampers disposable diapers, nonstick cookware by Teflon, a revolutionary toothpaste with fluoride called Crest from Procter and Gamble.

The Huntley-Brinkley Report (national news) premieres, as does *As the World Turns* and *Edge of Night,* on television, *My Fair Lady* on Broadway, and *The Ten Commandments* on film.

The publishing sensation was the novel *Peyton Place* by Grace Metalious.

Don Larsen of the New York Yankees pitched a perfect game in the World Series.

Demonstrating spectacular appeal to youthful music followers and record buyers, Elvis Presley hits his stride with numerous hit records, including "Hound Dog."

Deceased for the year included literary curmudgeon H. L. Mencken, giant of radio comedy Fred Allen, and band leader Tommy Dorsey.

March 7, 1957 Congress approves the Eisenhower Doctrine, designed to resist communism in the Middle East. The move represents a U.S. response to a perceived power vacuum in aftermath of the Suez crisis.

March 29, 1957 Jimmy Hoffa, aggressive vice president of the Teamsters Union, is indicted for bribery.

April 9, 1957 Fiat, an Italian small-car producer, seeks to compete in the American market—unsuccessfully, as it turns out.

May 2, 1957 Powerless, Senator Joseph McCarthy dies in virtual obscurity in Bethesda, Maryland.

June 27–28, 1957 Hurricane Audrey strikes the Texas and Louisiana coasts, leaving 531 dead or missing.

September 4, 1957 Governor Orville Faubus of Arkansas calls out the National Guard to prevent black children from entering Central High School in Little Rock.

September 25, 1957 With some reluctance Eisenhower nationalizes the Arkansas National Guard and orders further army troops to enforce desegregation of Central High School.

October 4, 1957 The Soviet Union's launching of the first earth satellite (called *Sputnik*) stuns the United States and provokes a hurried movement to catch up, especially in the area of rocketry.

November 25, 1957 President Eisenhower suffers a minor stroke but is not disabled.

December 15, 1957 The air force tests its first Atlas intercontinental ballistic missile (ICBM).

Other events of 1957 Theodore Geisel, who will become known as Dr. Seuss, produces his first colorful childrens' book, *The Cat in the Hat;* later in the year comes *How the Grinch Stole Christmas!*.

New products include: a portable electric typewriter by Smith Corona; a sack dress; Fortran computer language; Darvon, a powerful painkiller; Edsel, a midsized car by Ford that will be a lemon.

Whamo Corporation in California produces a plastic disc that spins in the air—they called it a Frisbee.

Deaths included Humphrey Bogart and Oliver Hardy—the large one in the Laurel and Hardy team.

Another death of sorts, or worse, occurs when the Brooklyn Dodgers pack up and go to Los Angeles; crosstown rivals, the Giants, follow them to California, settling in San Francisco.

February 28, 1958 The postal service increases cost of first-class mail from three to four cents per ounce—the normal cost of sending a letter. Airmail goes from six to seven cents.

March 24, 1958 In perhaps a fitting reflection of an era, and to the dismay of millions of fans, Elvis Presley is drafted; he will spend most of his roughly two-year stint in Germany.

April 11, 1958 Texan pianist Van Cliburn, 23, wins the International Tchaikovsky Piano Contest in Moscow.

May 12, 1958 The United States forms a defense arrangement with Canada called NORAD—the North American Air Defense Command.

June 28, 1958 Big Mac, world's longest suspension bridge, opens over the Straits of Mackinac and connects the lower and upper peninsulas of Michigan.

August 5, 1958 The atomic submarine *Nautilus* makes the first underwater crossing of the North Pole. The trip takes four days.

July 15, 1958 Eisenhower dispatches marines from the sixth Fleet to Lebanon on request of the beleaguered Lebanese president—a move ostensibly legitimized by the Eisenhower Doctrine. The troops remain only a few weeks.

September 2, 1958 The National Defense Education Act, a rare case of the national government supporting education, becomes law. Prompted by launching of *Sputnik,* the measure stresses science.

September 12, 1958 Texas Instruments develops a computer microchip.

September 22, 1958 Presidential Chief of Staff Sherman Adams resigns under fire for a charge of corrupt finances.

October 26, 1958 Pan American Airlines begins jet passenger service to Europe in the new Boeing 707; British Airways started three weeks earlier.

November 4, 1958 Democrats win off-year elections, gaining 15 seats in the Senate, 48 in the House.

November 8, 1958 Harry Winston, a jeweler, donates the Hope Diamond, measured at 44.5 carats, to the Smithsonian Institution.

Other events of 1958 Bank Americard and American Express issue instruments of business called credit cards.

A sugar substitute, Sweet-N-Low, comes on the market.

Recording star Eddie Fisher leaves his wife, Debbie Reynolds, for Elizabeth Taylor.

Mimi Jordan, age 10, is national Hula Hoop champion, and Bobby Fisher is world chess champion at 15.

The recording industry awards for the first time its prizes, called Grammys.

January 3, 1959 Alaska becomes the 49th state, supplanting Texas as the largest in territory.

January 7, 1959 The United States recognizes the new regime of Fidel Castro—a revolutionary leader who has deposed dictator Fulgencio Batista—in Cuba.

April 6, 1959 The City Council of New York supports study of the prospect of New York City becoming the 51st state.

April 25, 1959 The St. Lawrence Seaway begins operation, opening the interior of the United States to the Atlantic Ocean, making Chicago an international port.

May 20, 1959 Some 5,000 Japanese Americans who had renounced American citizenship during the Second World War now get it back.

June 11, 1959 The postmaster general bans the novel *Lady Chatterley's Lover* from the mails, labeling the work "smutty," "obscene," "filthy."

July 23, 1959 Vice President Richard Nixon begins a visit to the Soviet Union, opening a cultural exhibit and perhaps signaling an easing of cold war tensions. In Moscow he will engage Premier Nikita Khrushchev in what becomes known as the "kitchen debate."

August 21, 1959 Hawaii officially becomes the 50th state—a fact that, of course, requires a rearrangement of the U.S. flag.

September 15, 1959 Soviet Premier Khrushchev arrives in the United States for a personal visit.

October 21, 1959 The Guggenheim Museum, designed—not without controversy—by Frank Lloyd Wright, opens in New York City.

Other events of 1959 Barbie Doll makes its appearance, courtesy of Mattel Corporation.

Heart treatment devices, electrocardiography and internal pacemaker, are developed.

In a referendum Oklahomans end 51 years of prohibition; liquor now can be purchased.

The Sound of Music appears on Broadway, and *Ben-Hur* appears on film.

Rock singer Buddy Holly and members of his group, the Crickets, die in a plane crash; other deaths include singer Billie Holliday,

diplomat John Foster Dulles, filmmaker Cecil B. DeMille, actress Ethel Barrymore, architect Frank Lloyd Wright.

January 19, 1960 Demonstrations in Tokyo against renewal of a defense pact with the United States cause Eisenhower to cancel a visit to Japan.

February 1, 1960 Four black college students are denied service at the lunch counter of Woolworth's in Greensboro, North Carolina. Their refusal to depart the premises becomes a "sit-in," a new device of passive resistance in the Civil Rights movement.

February 23, 1960 Work begins on demolition of Ebbets Field in Brooklyn, former home of the Dodgers. Mourners are numerous.

April 2, 1960 NASA launches its first weather satellite.

April 27, 1960 A congressional committee begins investigation of possible payment by record companies to disc jockeys; this form of bribery to gain exposure for their records will be called payola.

May 1, 1960 An American U-2 spy plane is shot down over the Soviet Union; the pilot, Gary Francis Powers, is captured and he confesses his mission. The U-2 incident torpedoes a summit conference planned for Paris, cancels a presidential visit to the Soviet Union, and sends the off-again, on-again Soviet-American relations back to off.

June 4, 1960 The United States, which earlier had protested Cuban confiscation of American property, now charges the Castro regime with a "campaign of slander" against the United States.

July 11, 1960 Effective organization and financial backing help Senator John F. Kennedy of Massachusetts win the Democrat presidential nomination, despite concerns about his youth and Catholic religion. Making Senator Lyndon B. Johnson of Texas the vice presidential nominee balances the ticket.

July 27, 1960 Not unexpectedly, the Republicans pick Vice President Nixon as the presidential nominee; Ambassador (at the UN) Henry Cabot Lodge, Jr., will be his running mate.

October 12, 1960 Unconventional Premier Khrushchev bangs his shoe on a table in protest of a speech heard at the UN in New York.

November 8, 1960 After a campaign highlighted by the first direct presidential "debates," Kennedy and Johnson defeat Nixon and Lodge in a genuine cliff-hanger in popular vote; Congress remains modestly Democrat.

Other events of 1960 A revolutionary oral contraceptive for women, precursor of a sexual revolution, the pill, goes on the market.

Other new products include aluminum cans for drinks and felt-tip pens.

Chubby Checker takes a song, "The Twist," to the top of the charts and in so doing popularized a new dance and a new style: dancing alone.

Wilma Rudolph wins three gold medals at the Olympic games.

The run of *Camelot* on Broadway provides more dash for a new Kennedy administration.

The "king" of Hollywood, Clark Gable, succumbs to heart trouble at 59.

The Era of the Sixties, 1961–1970

January 3, 1961 In response to various moves by the new Cuban leader, notably seizure of American property, the Eisenhower administration breaks relations with Cuba. They will not be restored in the 20th century.

January 20, 1961 New president Kennedy gives a challenging and inspiring inaugural address, with several memorable passages.

April 12, 1961 The Soviet Union sends the first human into space, Yuri Gagarin, who orbits the Earth in 89 minutes.

March 1, 1961 By executive order Kennedy creates the Peace Corps, a new form of foreign policy that is pitched to the idealism of youth; Congress will ratify the step.

March 13, 1961 Kennedy proposes a new program for Latin America that will be called Alliance for Progress, which essentially involved economic development, at some expense to the United States.

April 17, 1961 A plot of the CIA to depose the Castro administration, approved by Eisenhower and later by Kennedy, is launched and fails in short order. Called the Bay of Pigs project, it will add to the hostility between the United States and Castro, now associated with the USSR.

May 5, 1961 The United States takes a step in the space race, albeit a modest one. Not yet prepared to go into space, Alan Shepard makes a 300-mile suborbital flight in a Mercury capsule.

June 4, 1961 Kennedy meets with Khrushchev in Vienna in what will be a contentious session. Khrushchev insists on supporting revolutionary movements; Kennedy leaves, convinced that he must be tough.

August 13, 1961 As an extension of a third crisis over the divided city of Berlin, the communists construct a concrete wall between the east and west sectors. As in two previous crises, Kennedy insists on holding fast to the western zones of the city.

October 6, 1961 Kennedy advises that a "prudent family" would take steps to build or obtain a fallout shelter as protection from nuclear war.

Other events of 1961 The first electric toothbrush hits the market.

IBM produces a "Selectric" typewriter.

The Civil Rights movement in the South moves to "freedom riders," who seek to dramatize continued segregation; the riders often faced violent resistance.

Roger Maris of the Yankees hits 61 home runs, breaking Babe Ruth's 1927 record.

Former speaker of the house and Democrat power broker, Sam Rayburn, dies, as do painter Grandma Moses and Ernest Hemingway, perhaps America's most famous novelist.

February 4, 1962 Kennedy bans all trade with Cuba.

February 10, 1962 Gary Francis Powers, pilot of the ill-fated U-2 aircraft, is released by the Soviets in exchange for American release of a Soviet spy.

February 28, 1962 Lt. Colonel John Glenn is the first American to orbit Earth; he circles three times in a Mercury capsule.

April 10, 1962 Kennedy denounces an increase in steel prices, thus touching off a battle with the steel industry and in a general way with big business; two weeks later the companies will rescind the increase.

June 25, 1962 In a case involving New York, the Supreme Court rules that prayer in the public schools is unconstitutional, a violation of separation of church and state.

August 5, 1962 Many people are stunned and saddened to hear that screen star Marilyn Monroe, age 36, has died, apparently from an overdose of sleeping pills.

September 30, 1962 Having previously been denied admission to the University of Mississippi by state officials, a black student, James Meredith, now is escorted into the school by federal marshalls. An ensuing riot will lead to two deaths, many injuries, and intervention by 3,000 troops.

October 22, 1962 President Kennedy appears on national television to announce that the Soviet Union was installing medium-range offensive missiles in Cuba, setting in motion what will be the Cuban missile crisis. The crisis will end after six days, with withdrawal of the missiles, but not before Kennedy has blockaded Cuba, prepares to attack the island, and threatens to launch nuclear-armed missiles on the Soviet Union. It is brinksmanship of the highest order.

December 23, 1962 The Cuban government begins to release 1,179 prisoners captured in the Bay of Pigs fiasco; the United States agrees in effect to pay ransom: some $50 million in food and medical supplies.

Other events of 1962 Johnny Carson becomes host of the popular *Tonight Show* on NBC.

K-Mart and Wal-Mart open as discount stores.

Dulles Airport opens outside Washington in Virginia—the first civilian airport designed for jet aircraft.

The environmental movement in a sense begins with publication of Rachel Carson's deftly named *Silent Spring,* which warned of the effect of chemical pesticides on wildlife.

Eleanor Roosevelt, the beloved (but also often ridiculed) former first lady and elder stateswoman, dies on November 7.

March 18, 1963 In the case of *Gideon v. Wainwright* the Supreme Court rules that defendants in state courts are to be supplied with an attorney, if they can not afford one.

April 10, 1963 The atomic submarine *Thresher* sinks in the North Atlantic, killing the crew of 129.

May 6, 1963 In an ongoing civil rights confrontation, some 1,000 demonstrators are arrested by police in Birmingham, Alabama.

June 11, 1963 Determined to prevent desegregation of his state's schools, Governor George Wallace of Alabama nonetheless yields to pressure from the national government and allows two black students to enroll in the University of Alabama.

June 17, 1963 Adding to the "school prayer" series of decisions, the Court declares reading of the Bible (as a religious observance) in the public schools to be unconstitutional.

June 20, 1963 Perhaps sobered by events of the previous year, the governments of the United States and the Soviet Union agree to establish a "hot line" for highest-level, rapid communication between each other.

July 25, 1963 In a first sign of progress in negotiation over nuclear weaponry, a limited test-ban treaty is signed by the United States, Soviet Union, and Great Britain. It prohibits virtually all nuclear testing other than underground.

August 28, 1963 At the end of the civil rights march on Washington, some 200,000 gather at the Lincoln Memorial to hear Martin Luther King, Jr., who reaches a new oratorical peak with his "I Have a Dream" speech.

September 15, 1963 Reflective of continuing racial violence in the South, a black church is bombed; four girls are killed.

November 2, 1963 As part of a coup against the government of South Vietnam, President Ngo Dinh Diem and his brother are assassinated; U.S. leaders have advance knowledge of the coup but not of the assassination.

November 22, 1963 President Kennedy is mortally wounded while riding in a motorcade in Dallas, Texas; his wife, Jackie, sitting beside him, is not injured; Governor John Connally of Texas, in the front seat, is wounded; Vice President Johnson, also in Dallas, is sworn in as president.

November 24, 1963 Lee Harvey Oswald, arrested for Kennedy's murder, is shot dead by a local nightclub owner, Jack Ruby, as Oswald is being moved by the Dallas police. The killing is captured on live network television.

Other events of 1963 Popular new products include: the soft drink Tab, perma-press clothing, touch-tone telephones, cassette tape recorders, an effective measles vaccine, a metal tennis racket, and Weight Watchers International Incorporated.

Stevie Wonder, age 12, releases his first album on Motown Records.

Betty Friedan publishes *The Feminine Mystique.*

Eddie Fisher, having abandoned Debbie Reynolds for Elizabeth Taylor, now finds himself abandoned by Taylor in favor of Richard Burton, her Welsh costar in the spectacular film production *Cleopatra.*

On the day of John F. Kennedy's assassination, November 22, 1963, aboard *Air Force One,* Lyndon B. Johnson takes the presidential oath of office. (The John Fitzgerald Kennedy Library)

January 11, 1964 A surgeon general's report finds cigarette smoking harmful to health; two days later the FTC announces that it will require warnings on all cigarette packages.

January 23, 1964 The Twenty-fourth Amendment, forbidding a poll tax for national elections, receives ratification.

February 25, 1964 Cassius Marcellus Clay, loud-mouthed young boxer from Louisville, wins the heavyweight championship by knocking out Sonny Liston; converted in 1967 to Islam, Clay will become Muhammad Ali.

March 14, 1964 Jack Ruby is sentenced to death for murder of Lee Harvey Oswald; he will die in prison in 1967, awaiting a new trial.

July 2, 1964 President Johnson signs into law the epochal Civil Rights Act, a measure passed after lengthy debate, dramatic national attention, and racial upheaval in the deep South; broadly put, it is designed to prevent discrimination based on race (but sex also is mentioned) and to foster social and educational integration.

August 2, 1964 Naval officials report that American warships were attacked off the coast of North Vietnam; the facts seemed unclear, but Johnson treated the episode as a provocation to which he replied with military strikes and an appeal for broad congressional support; he receives it on August 7 in the Gulf of Tonkin Resolution, a major document of the Vietnam War.

August 4, 1964 Three civil rights workers (two white, one black) reported missing near Philadelphia, Mississippi, on June 22, are found buried under an earthen dam. Several local white men will be acquitted in a state court; seven later will be convicted of lesser federal offenses (e.g., a violation of a person's civil rights); the episode is part of the sensational Mississippi Freedom Summer of 1964.

August 7, 1964 Congress passes the "War on Poverty" bill—Johnson's omnibus measure that includes VISTA and a job corps.

September 24, 1964 After lengthy investigation, a blue-ribbon commission chaired by Chief Justice Earl Warren (the Warren Commission) reports that Lee Harvey Oswald acted alone in the assassination of John Kennedy. In spite of numerous future detractors and alternative theories, the Warren Report will stand the test of time.

October 14, 1964 Martin Luther King, Jr., is awarded the Nobel Peace Prize.

November 3, 1964 The Democrat ticket of President Lyndon Johnson and Senator Hubert Humphrey of Minnesota defeats the Republican ticket of Senator Barry Goldwater of Arizona and Congressman William Miller of New York. It is a Democrat landslide both in the presidential race and in both houses of Congress.

Other events of 1964 Ford introduces the Mustang.

The G.I. Joe doll appears.

The first disco, called "Whiskey-a-Go-Go," opens on Sunset Strip in Los Angeles.

Sidney Poitier is the first African American to receive the best actor award (in *Lilies of the Field*).

The Broadway musical holds on with Carol Channing in *Hello, Dolly,* and Barbra Streisand in *Funny Girl*.

Race riots erupt in New York and New Jersey.

February 6, 1965   In response to enemy (Vietcong) attack on an American airbase at Pleiku, Johnson orders bombing of North Vietnam, a considerable escalation of the war.

February 21, 1965   Malcolm X, charismatic black leader, is assassinated in Harlem at age 39; the murder evidently grew out of a division within the Nation of Islam.

March 7, 1965   Alabama state police attack demonstrators for voting rights in Selma, Alabama; these events will inspire a larger march two weeks later, protected by military forces.

March 8, 1965   Two battalions of American marines arrive to protect an airbase at Danang; these troops represent the first outright combat forces sent to Vietnam.

April 6, 1965   NASA launches the first commercial satellite, named *Early Bird*.

April 28, 1965   American marines land in the Dominican Republic, the first direct military intervention in Latin America in many years; the troops reportedly are there to prevent communist control of the island nation.

July 14, 1965   Adlai E. Stevenson, twice Democrat nominee for president, now ambassador to the United Nations, dies of heart attack on a London street; he was 65.

July 25, 1965   The crowd at the Newport Jazz Festival boos singer Bob Dylan off stage because he uses electric instruments.

July 30, 1965   Johnson signs into law the Medicare bill, a measure that is to provide limited medical care for the aged under the Social Security System—another part of Kennedy's New Frontier Program that Johnson incorporates into his Great Society.

August 6, 1965   Johnson signs into law another civil rights measure, the Voting Rights Act, which is designed to facilitate suffrage for blacks in the South.

August 11, 1965   Watts, a black neighborhood of Los Angeles, experiences a race riot that will last five days and cause 34 deaths, damage of approximately $40 million, and the arrest of thousands.

October 3, 1965   Congress passes a law that provides the first substantive change in immigration policy in 40 years; the measure abolishes the discriminatory quota system.

Other events of 1965   Miniskirts, with hemlines several inches above the knees, become fashionable.

Skateboarding is a new sport, Nutrasweet an improved sugar-substitute.

The Gateway Arch is completed in St. Louis.

The Astrodome opens in Houston, thus pioneering the massive enclosed, air-conditioned stadium, large enough to accommodate any sport, even baseball.

In this year after the warning about cigarettes, it was striking to note that singer Nat "King" Cole, only 45, died of lung cancer, as did groundbreaking newscaster of radio and television Edward R. Murrow, often filmed with a cigarette in his hand or mouth.

Stan Laurel, the skinny one of Laurel and Hardy, dies.

April 21, 1966   Michael DeBakey implants the first artificial heart in a human at a hospital in Houston.

May 11, 1966   Joseph Hirshhorn gives his modern art collection, valued at $35 million, to the United States.

June 13, 1966   In the case of *Miranda v. Arizona,* the Supreme Court rules that defendants in state proceedings must be apprised of their rights, including the right to remain silent and the right to an attorney.

June 29, 1966   The government announces that increased bombing in North Vietnam includes the cities of Hanoi and Haiphong and that recent deployment raises United States forces in Vietnam to nearly 300,000.

July 12, 1966   Rioting takes place on Chicago's west side; racial disturbances will follow in several cities during the summer.

July 19, 1966   Richard Speck is charged with murdering eight nurses in Chicago.

August 1, 1966   Shooting from a 27-story tower on the campus of the University of Texas at Austin, Charles Whitman, an Eagle Scout, kills 12 and wounds 33.

November 8, 1966   In the off-year elections, Republicans gain three seats in the Senate and a striking 47 in the House—results that will place in jeopardy further "Great Society" legislation; among the Republicans elected was Edward R. Brooke of Massachusetts, the first black United States senator in 85 years.

Other events of 1966   Catholics now are allowed to eat meat on Fridays, except during Lent.

Bill Russell of the Boston Celtics becomes the first black coach (and at $125,000 the highest paid coach) in the NBA.

Frank Sinatra, 50, marries Mia Farrow, 21, in Las Vegas.

Paul Simon and Arthur Garfunkel release "Feelin' Groovy" (The 59th Street Bridge Song).

New shows on television include *Family Affair, Hollywood Squares,* and *Star Trek*.

Pennsylvania Station in New York City falls to a wrecker.

January 27, 1967   Fire breaks out in *Apollo I* Spacecraft during testing at Cape Kennedy, Florida; caused by a defective wire, the fire kills astronauts Virgil Grissom, Edward White, and Roger Chafee.

March 1, 1967   The House of Representatives votes to deny seating to Adam Clayton Powell, Jr., black congressman from Harlem, for fraudulent use of government funds.

March 9, 1967   Svetlana Alliluyeva, daughter of Joseph Stalin, defects to the United States.

May 1, 1967   Elvis Presley marries Priscilla Beaulieu, an old girlfriend.

June 12, 1967   In the case of *Loving v. Virginia,* the Supreme Court strikes down a Virginia law forbidding interracial marriage; by implication, laws in 15 other states become invalid.

June 18, 1967   Some 500,000 attend a pop festival at Monterey, California—largest gathering yet for a rock concert.

June 23 and 25, 1967   President Johnson meets briefly with Premier Aleksei Kosygin of the Soviet Union in New Jersey.

July 23, 1967   Rioting that begins in Detroit will continue until July 30, when it is suppressed by the army; in its wake the riot will leave 41 dead, 2,000 injured, destruction of 5,000 homes, and a cost of $400 million.

July 29, 1967   Fuel leaking from a damaged Skyhawk airplane causes a fire aboard the aircraft-carrier *Forrestal* that kills 134 in the Gulf of Tonkin.

October 2, 1967   Thurgood Marshall, former attorney for the NAACP and great-grandson of a slave, is sworn in as the first African-American justice of the Supreme Court.

October 21, 1967   Large antiwar riots in Washington, D.C., lead to arrest of some 650.

November 7, 1967   Local elections produce landmark victories for black candidates; Carl Stokes in Cleveland and Richard Hatcher in Gary, Indiana, are the first black mayors of major American cities; three black men are elected to state legislatures in three southern states—the first in the 20th century.

December 8, 1967   Antiwar demonstrations lead to the arrest of nearly 600 in New York City, among them baby doctor Benjamin Spock and beat-poet Allen Ginsberg.

Other events of 1967   The Corporation for Public Broadcasting begins operation.

Rolling Stone magazine first hits the market, as does a compact microwave oven (produced by Amana) and quartz-powered watches.

U.S. Navy patrol craft plows waters of Cai Ngay Canal, Vietnam. (National Archives)

William Styron's *Confessions of Nat Turner* is published.

The Carol Burnett Show debuts on television.

Deaths include Vivien Leigh, star of *Gone With the Wind,* folk singer Woody Guthrie, and Che Guevara, hero of the Cuban revolution, killed in the jungles of Bolivia.

January 22, 1968   A B-52 bomber of the Strategic Air Command crashes off the coast of Greenland. The bomber carries four unarmed hydrogen bombs, and although there is leakage of radioactive material, no nuclear explosion takes place.

January 23, 1968   North Korea seizes the U.S. navy intelligence ship *Pueblo* and holds the crew of 83 men; release will be negotiated but not for nearly a year.

January 30, 1968   Enemy forces in Vietnam use the lunar New Year holiday to launch attacks on 35 centers, mostly provincial capitals; Saigon, and the U.S. embassy, are hit; Viet Cong forces are badly mauled in this so-called Tet Offensive, but they score a huge psychological victory in the United States.

February 29, 1968   A presidential committee (the Kerner Commission) investigating racial relations reports existence of, and condemns, a condition of two "separate and unequal" nations, black and white.

March 12, 1968   In a stunning result Senator Eugene McCarthy of Minnesota receives nearly as many votes as the president in the Democrat presidential primary in New Hampshire.

March 16, 1968   Senator Robert Kennedy of New York enters the race for the Democrat presidential nomination.

March 31, 1968   Sobered, perhaps, by growing challenge within his own party, doubtless burdened by weight of office and the war in Vietnam, Johnson stuns the nation with an announcement that he will not seek reelection.

April 4, 1968   Martin Luther King, Jr., is assassinated at a motel in Memphis; James Earl Ray will be convicted of the crime, although he later will renounce his confession.

April 22–23, 1968   Student protesters, many of them members of Students for a Democratic Society (SDS), seize buildings of Columbia University and bring operations to a halt. The school will close for the semester.

June 5, 1968   Celebrating an important victory in the California primary in his quest for the Democrat nomination, Robert Kennedy is assassinated in Los Angeles; a Jordanian immigrant, Sirhan Sirhan, will be convicted of the crime.

August 8, 1968   In winning the Republican presidential nomination, Richard Nixon records a remarkable political comeback; he picks Governor Spiro Agnew of Maryland for the vice presidency.

August 29, 1968   During a tumultuous Democrat convention, and with tumultuous events outside in the streets of Chicago, Vice President Hubert Humphrey receives the presidential nomination; his choice for running mate, Senator Edmund Muskie of Maine, is a good one, but the party seems hopelessly split on the war.

October 3, 1968   George Wallace of Alabama receives the Independent Party nomination for the presidency; former air force chief Curtis LeMay is his running mate.

October 19, 1968   The former president's widow, Jackie Kennedy, marries multimillionaire Greek shipping magnate Aristotle Onassis.

November 6, 1968   Nixon and Agnew defeat Humphrey and Muskie in a close race, doubtless made closer by candidacy of Wallace, who received 10 million votes.

December 27, 1968   *Apollo 8* and its crew—Frank Borman, James Lovell, and William Anders—reach the Moon, make 10 orbits, speak to the people on Earth, and send back startling pictures.

Other events of 1968   Blacks continue to score firsts: Arthur Ashe, victor in the U.S. open, is first African American to win a major tennis title; Shirley Chisholm of New York is the first black congresswoman; Diahann Carroll is first black woman to have a television series—*Julia.*

New products and developments include waterbeds, jacuzzis, a movie rating system, Nehru jackets, Cunard's *Queen Elizabeth II, 60 Minutes* and *Laugh-In* on television, *Hair* (and nudity) on Broadway, "Hey Jude" from the Beatles.

March 28, 1969   Former military hero and president Dwight Eisenhower dies of heart failure at age 78.

April 9, 1969   Student demonstrators seize the administration building at Harvard University, only one of numerous cases of activism and disruption in this continuing time of student unrest.

June 22, 1969   Actress and musical icon Judy Garland is found dead in London, age 47.

July 18, 1969   Senator Edward Kennedy of Massachusetts, the sole remaining Kennedy son, drives off a bridge at Chappaquiddick, Massachusetts, killing Mary Jo Kopechne; the event profoundly affects Kennedy's appeal as a future president, but it by no means ends his political career.

July 20, 1969   Astronaut Neil Armstrong becomes the first person to set foot on the Moon; Edwin Aldrin joins him on the surface, and the third member of the *Apollo 11* mission, Michael Collins, remains aboard the command module.

August 9, 1969   Charles Manson and members of his cult brutally kill seven people, including actress Sharon Tate, in Beverly Hills, California.

August 15–18, 1969   The Woodstock music festival near Bethel, New York, attracts approximately 400,000 people.

August 17, 1969   Hurricane Camille, the century's most powerful, strikes the Gulf coast, killing 300.

October 3, 1969   President Nixon formalizes his plan for ending U.S. involvement in the Vietnam War; it is called "Vietnamization," the idea being to equip the Vietnamese to handle the conflict on their own.

November 15, 1969   The Second Vietnam Moratorium Day draws 250,000 demonstrators in Washington, D.C.

November 20, 1969   Militant American Indians seize Alcatraz Island in San Francisco Bay, demanding it be given to Native Americans.

Other events of 1969   Yale University admits female undergraduates.

Penthouse magazine begins publication.

Rubella vaccination starts.

The Brady Bunch, Sesame Street, and Hee Haw appear on television.

Star Trek ends its original run.

The Saturday Evening Post stops production after 148 years.

Julie Nixon, daughter of the president, marries David Eisenhower, grandson of a former president.

February 18, 1970   A jury finds the "Chicago 7" innocent of conspiring to incite riots at the Democrat convention; five are convicted of lesser charges.

March 28, 1969   A townhouse in New York used by radical group, the Weathermen, explodes, killing three; others barely escape.

April 18, 1970   Apollo 13 comes down in the Pacific after a harrowing, aborted mission to the Moon, caused by power failure in the command module.

April 20, 1970   In line with Vietnamization, Nixon promises withdrawal of more Americans from Vietnam; by year's end the number will be down to 340,000, 200,000 fewer than the previous year.

April 30, 1970   American and South Vietnamese troops pursue the enemy into Cambodia, touching off major antiwar protest.

May 4, 1970   The Ohio National Guard fires on antiwar demonstrators, killing four, wounding nine at Kent State University.

May 12, 1970   The Senate unanimously approves Harry Blackmun for the Supreme Court.

July 1, 1970   New York adopts the nation's most liberal abortion law—abortion on demand in first 24 weeks of pregnancy.

September 28, 1970   Egyptian president Gamel A. Nasser dies suddenly, and he is succeeded by Anwar Sadat—an event of much greater importance to the United States than anyone expected at that time.

Other events of 1970   A powerful antidepressant drug, Lithium, is approved by FDA.

The World Trade Center is completed in New York.

New York holds its first marathon.

Childproof safety caps appear on medicine bottles.

Monday night football begins on ABC.

Doonesbury, a "comic strip" of satire and political commentary appears, authored by former Yale student Gary Trudeau.

To the dismay of millions of American (and other) rockers, Paul McCartney leaves the Beatles, marking the group's breakup.

Legislation drops the voting age to 18 for national elections.

Soldiers await a helicopter that will evacuate the body of a fallen comrade, Long Khanh Province, Vietnam. (National Archives)

The Era of the Seventies, 1971–1980

February 9, 1971 *Apollo 14* ends a journey of nine days in space, including a day and a half on the Moon.

March 23, 1971 The Senate refuses to fund an American SST, supersonic transport aircraft, leaving the field to the Europeans.

March 29, 1971 Army Lt. William Calley is convicted of murder of 22 South Vietnamese civilians at My Lai on March 16, 1968 (even though perhaps 300 Vietnamese died that day); Calley's original life sentence will be reduced to house arrest and then to a pardon by Nixon.

April 10, 1971 Chinese leaders welcome an American table-tennis team, seemingly a signal that China, estranged more than 20 years, wants to talk.

April 30, 1971 The Supreme Court upholds busing as a method of attacking segregation in the public schools.

June 13, 1971 The *New York Times* begins publication of the "Pentagon Papers," a classified study in the Defense Department about Vietnam that was stolen and released by Daniel Ellsberg.

June 20, 1971 The Twenty-sixth Amendment, lowering the voting age to 18, receives ratification.

June 28, 1971 The Supreme Court upholds the draft resistance (as a conscientious objector) of former heavyweight champion Muhammad Ali.

August 15, 1971 President Nixon announces several economic moves, including a 90-day freeze on prices, wages, and rents.

September 8, 1971 The Kennedy Center for artistic performances opens in Washington, D.C.

Other events of 1971 Scientists at Intel in California develop a tiny silicon chip called a microprocessor—Intel 4004.

Look magazine stops publication after 34 years.

The FTC bans cigarette ads on television.

Amtrak, the government-sponsored rail passenger service, begins operation.

Walt Disney World opens in Orlando, Florida.

Smilies, the little yellow smiley faces, appear all over the place.

The environmental group Greenpeace begins to operate.

February 21, 1972 President Nixon arrives in Beijing to start a historic visit to the People's Republic of China. The visit marks a beginning to the end of 20 years of Sino-American hostility. Official relations, however, are not restored.

March 22, 1972 The Senate approves an Equal Rights Amendment (ERA); it goes to the states, where the ratification effort will fail.

May 2, 1972 J. Edgar Hoover, the only head of the FBI since its start 48 years earlier, powerful player in Washington's inner political circles, dies at age 77.

May 15, 1872 Arthur Bremer shoots George Wallace as he campaigns for the Democrat presidential nomination; Wallace is left paralyzed and in pain for the rest of his life.

May 22, 1972 Nixon begins a week's visit to the Soviet Union (the first president to do so), where he will sign an arms limitation agreement called SALT.

June 14, 1972 The EPA bans the chemical pesticide DDT.

June 17, 1972 Five men are arrested for breaking into Democrat National Committee Headquarters at the Watergate Hotel complex in Washington, D.C., setting in motion a devastating presidential scandal that will consume more than two years.

June 29, 1972 Calling the death penalty "cruel and unusual punishment," the Supreme Court, voting 5–4, declares it unconstitutional.

July 10, 1972 The Democrats nominate an honest, unexciting antiwar senator, George McGovern, for the presidency; the vice presidential nominee, Senator Thomas Eagleton of Missouri, will withdraw from the ticket three weeks later on disclosure that he had been treated for emotional disorder.

President and Pat Nixon tour the Great Wall of China during their epochal visit of February 1972. (National Archives)

September 3, 1972 American Bobby Fischer defeats Soviet Boris Spassky in the world championship in chess.

September 11, 1972 American swimmer Mark Spitz of Indiana University wins seven gold medals at Munich Olympic games that are marked with terrorist murder of 11 Israeli athletes.

November 3, 1972 The ticket of Nixon and Agnew wins reelection in a landslide: nearly 61 percent of popular vote, all but 13 of the electoral vote; but Congress remains Democrat.

November 14, 1972 For the first time the Dow Jones industrial average closed above the lofty mark of 1,000.

Other events of 1972 Hsing-hsing and Ling-ling, the giant pandas sent as a gift from the People's Republic of China, arrive for a long residency at the Washington zoo.

Life magazine ends publication.

Home Box Office starts operation, as does Federal Express and *Ms.* magazine, edited by feminist leader Gloria Steinem.

The Best and the Brightest by David Halberstam is popular nonfiction.

The Godfather, with Marlon Brando, is a hit movie.

January 5, 1973 Air terrorism causes airports in the United States to begin to inspect luggage and passengers.

January 22, 1973 Former president Lyndon Johnson dies of a heart attack, age 64.

In the case of *Roe v. Wade,* the Supreme Court rules that abortion cannot be banned during the first two trimesters of pregnancy, although there could be some regulation in the second trimester.

January 27, 1973   An armistice is signed that officially ends the Vietnam War for the United States; all American troops are to be withdrawn; all enemy-held American prisoners are to be freed.

The government announces that the military draft will end.

February 14, 1973   The first American prisoners return home from North Vietnam.

February 27, 1973   Members of the American Indian Movement (AIM), seize a compound at Wounded Knee, South Dakota, and begin a siege that will last 71 days.

April 30, 1973   Amid charges of a White House obstruction of justice, presidential aides John Erlichman, H. R. Haldeman, and John Dean resign in what has become the Watergate scandal.

May 17–November 15, 1973   Senator Sam Ervin chairs a special Senate investigation into the Watergate episode; John Dean will be the star witness, but there are several important ones.

July 16, 1973   Appearing before the Irvin Committee, Alexander Butterfield, a lesser presidential aide, reveals almost in passing that all conversations in the Oval Office were taped.

October 6, 1973   Start of a fourth Arab-Israeli war will lead to an Arab oil embargo on the United States and an American energy crisis.

October 10, 1973   Vice President Agnew pleads no contest to charges of accepting bribes and income tax evasion; he is fined but serves no prison time; he resigns his office.

In accordance with the Twenty-fifth Amendment, Nixon selects a successor—Congressman Gerald Ford—and Congress approves the selection.

October 20, 1973   The Saturday Night Massacre in the Watergate crisis: Three high-ranking administration officials resign or are fired; at issue is access to the presidential tapes.

November 7, 1973   Congress overrides a presidential veto, and the War Powers Act—designed to restrict presidential war-making without congressional approval—becomes law.

Other events of 1973   The American League in baseball adopts a designated-hitter rule.

The University of Miami is the first school to award athletic scholarships to women.

In a tennis match somewhat curiously deemed "battle of the sexes," Billie Jean King, age 29, defeats Bobby Riggs, age 55.

A once-in-a-lifetime thoroughbred, Secretariat, is first horse to win the triple crown of racing in 25 years, winning one of the races by 31 lengths.

Sears Tower in Chicago becomes world's tallest building.

The American Psychiatric Association declassifies homosexuality as a mental illness.

February 4, 1974   Newspaper heiress Patricia Hearst is captured by members of the Symbionese Liberation Army; later, in a bizarre turn of events, Patty Hearst, taking the name Tanya, joins her captors, even helping them in a bank robbery; she will be arrested in 1975.

March 18, 1974   Arab states finally agree to end the oil embargo imposed in October 1973.

April 3, 1974   In the greatest outbreak of tornadoes in a single day—perhaps 130 in an 18-hour period—storms ravage an area from Georgia to Canada; 320 die; hardest hit: Zenia, Ohio.

Nixon announces he will pay back taxes of more than $300,000; he had claimed improper deductions.

April 8, 1974   Hank Aaron of the Atlanta Braves hit the 715th home run of his baseball career, thus breaking the record held by Babe Ruth.

June 30, 1974   Russian ballet performer Mikhail Baryshnikov defects in Canada en route to the United States.

July 14, 1974   In an ongoing contest over the Watergate episode, the Supreme Court rules that Nixon must turn 64 specified tapes over to a special prosecutor; the tapes will contain the "smoking gun": evidence that Nixon lied and was involved in a cover-up.

July 27–30, 1974   The House Judiciary Committee votes three articles of impeachment of the president.

August 8, 1974   Nixon announces his resignation, to take effect the next day; admitting no guilt, he says he lacked the power base to continue.

August 9, 1974   Gerald R. Ford is sworn in as president.

August 21, 1974   President Ford nominates Nelson Rockefeller of New York as the new vice president; Congress approves the choice.

September 8, 1974   President Ford pardons Nixon for any possible crimes associated with the Watergate scandal.

Other events of 1974   The Heimlich maneuver, to clear blocked breathing passage, is introduced.

Streaking—young men and/or women dashing about naked—is a momentary fad.

First supermarket scanner goes into operation in Troy, Ohio, scanning its first item, a pack of chewing gum.

Moses Malone is the first basketball player to go directly from high school to the NBA.

A list of the deceased includes Cass Elliott (the Mamas and the Papas), Samuel Goldwyn (the G in MGM), Chet Huntley *(Huntley-Brinkley Report)*, Walter Lippmann, Ed Sullivan, former chief justice Earl Warren.

January 1, 1975   H. R. Haldeman, John Erlichman, John Mitchell, and Robert Mardian, all former high-ranking officials of the Nixon administration, are convicted of obstruction of justice.

April 30, 1975   The U.S.-supported government in Saigon surrenders to the enemy, marking end to the Vietnam War and a defeat for the United States. Remaining Americans and close South Vietnamese associates scramble to evacuate.

May 14, 1975   President Ford orders seizure of U.S. ship *Mayaguez*, captured by communists in Cambodia.

July 17, 1975   American spacecraft *Apollo* links up with Soviet vessel *Soyuz;* they remain linked in orbit for two days.

August 18, 1975   Former Teamster president James Hoffa disappears under suspicious circumstances; he never will be found.

September 5, 1975   Manson cult member Lynette "Squeaky" Fromme attempts to assassinate President Ford; the gun jams.

September 12, 1975   Justice William O. Douglas, appointed by Roosevelt, resigns after a record 36 years on the high court.

September 22, 1975   Sara Jane Moore attempts to assassinate the president; a bystander deflects the weapon; the shot misses.

September 28, 1975   Congress votes to admit women to the military service academies.

October 1, 1975   In the "Thrilla in Manila," heavyweight champion Muhammad Ali defeats Joe Frazier in 14 rounds in the Philippines.

November 20, 1975   A Senate committee chaired by Frank Church gives first reports of the CIA using assassination as policy.

November 26, 1975   After first refusing to do so, Ford approves $2 billion in loans to a bankrupt New York City.

Other events of 1975   *Saturday Night Live,* featuring such performers as John Belushi, Gilda Radner, Dan Ackroyd, and Chevy Chase, makes its television debut.

Lyme disease, caused by a tick, is first diagnosed in Lyme, Connecticut.

Customized vans appear on the market, as do plastic soft-drink bottles.

Auto producers offer first rebates.

New cars now have catalytic converters.

Popular movies include *One Flew Over the Cuckoo's Nest* and *Jaws.*

Television hits include *Barney Miller* and *Welcome Back, Kotter.*

February 17, 1976 Influenced by recent Senate hearings, Ford announces reform of intelligence services, the FBI and the CIA.

March 29, 1976 The Supreme Court rules 6–3 that states can disallow certain homosexual acts.

March 31, 1976 The Supreme Court of New Jersey upholds the right of the parents to remove their comatose daughter Karen Anne Quinlan from life support; the decision will prompt other right-to-die cases.

July 2, 1976 The Supreme Court rules that the death penalty is not unconstitutional, thus providing for its reinstatement.

July 4, 1976 Celebrations abound as the United States observes its bicentennial birthday; largest ceremonies take place in New York and Philadelphia.

July 17, 1976 Memories of Vietnam and Watergate much alive, the Democrats nominate a virtual unknown for the presidency, Jimmy Carter, former governor of Georgia, who stresses his honesty and modesty.

July 20, 1976 *Viking I* (soon to be followed by *Viking II*) lands on Mars and begins to send pictures back to Earth.

August 26, 1976 A mysterious illness—to be dubbed "Legionaires' disease"—kills 28 at American Legion Convention in Philadelphia.

September 16, 1976 The Episcopal Church approves ordination of women for the clergy.

November 3, 1976 The Democrat ticket of Carter and Senator Walter Mondale narrowly defeats Republican ticket of Ford and Senator Robert Dole; Democrats control Congress.

December 9, 1976 A federal judge punishes school officials in Boston for not following plan of busing for desegregation.

Other events of 1976 The VCR appears on the market.

Citizens band radio (CB) becomes popular, especially with truckers.

Scientists at M.I.T. produce the first synthetic gene.

Women become eligible for Rhodes Scholarships.

Barbara Walters becomes the first female news anchor on a national network (ABC).

Famous people who die include eccentric, reclusive multimillionaire Howard Hughes and longtime "boss" of Chicago Richard Daley.

January 17, 1977 A firing squad in Utah carries out the first death sentence in 10 years: convicted murderer Gary Mark Gilmore.

January 21, 1977 President Carter grants unconditional pardon to nearly all draft resisters during the Vietnam War.

January 28–29, 1977 The Midwest and the Northeast suffer from a major blizzard.

March 27, 1977 Two 747 jumbo jets collide on a runway in the Canary Islands, killing 574—the worst accident in aviation history.

April 18, 1977 President Carter calls the continuing problem of an energy supply, dramatized by proven unreliability of foreign sources of petroleum, the "moral equivalent of war."

July 13–14, 1977 A power failure and blackout of 25 hours in New York City produces a crime spree and evidently a miniature baby boom some nine months later.

July 29, 1977 The first oil carried by the Alaska pipeline arrives at Valdez after a journey of 800 miles.

August 4, 1977 Congress creates a new Department of Energy, the 12th executive body of cabinet rank.

August 10, 1977 Terror in New York from a serial killer who called himself "Son of Sam" ends with arrest of 24-year-old David Berkowitz, who had killed seven and injured others.

August 16, 1977 Elvis Presley dies at age 42 of mysterious, probably drug-related causes.

September 7, 1977 The Carter administration signs a new treaty with Panama, the major condition of which is that the United States will relinquish control of the canal in December 1999; the Senate still has to approve.

September 21, 1977 Bert Lance, friend of the president and director of the Office of Management and Budget, resigns under fire for his financial operations.

Other events of 1977 Demonstrating his simplicity and openness, Carter wears a business suit (no top hat and tails) and walks in the parade at his inaugural.

Clogs become fashionable footwear for both sexes.

Medical diagnosis advances with introduction of the MRI, magnetic resonance imaging.

NASA tests its first space shuttle.

Generic goods begin to produce competition for brand-name products.

Television sensation of the year is small-screen adaptation of Alex Haley's novel, *Roots*.

February 15, 1978 An obscure boxer named Leon Spinks defeats heavyweight champion Muhammad Ali.

March 19, 1978 Another hazard of the issue of energy appears when the supertanker *Amoco Cadiz* runs aground off coast of France, spilling 68 million gallons of oil that will bespoil a wide area.

June 6, 1978 Voters in California pass Proposition 13, heralded as the first major shot in a broadening revolt against taxation.

June 28, 1978 The Supreme Court recognizes the principle of reverse discrimination in the Bakke case, which rejects quotas as a tool of affirmative action.

August 8, 1978 Carter approves a measure to guarantee loans of $1.6 billion to stave off bankruptcy of New York City.

September 17, 1978 Carter's mediation of talks between President Anwar Sadat of Egypt and Premier Menachem Begin of Israel leads to signing of the Camp David Accords—the foundation for a landmark Israeli-Egyptian peace treaty.

November 18, 1978 Nearly 1,000 American followers of cult leader Jim Jones commit mass suicide in Jonestown, Guyana, after members murder a U.S. congressman.

Other events of 1978 Large popularity of film *Saturday Night Fever* with John Travolta marks perhaps peak popularity of a dance style called disco.

Volkswagen begins to produce cars in the United States.

Ultrasound appears as a supplement to X ray.

China adopts Pinyin as a new method of translating Chinese characters into English; the name of Chinese leader Teng Hsiao-ping, for example, now will be rendered Deng Xiaoping.

Coca-Cola reaches an agreement to start to sell Coke in China.

Garfield (a cat) appears in comic strip.

Dallas starts on CBS.

Evita comes to the Broadway stage.

January 1, 1979 As part of an agreement reached earlier, the United States grants recognition to the People's Republic of China and breaks diplomatic relations with Taiwan.

January 16, 1979 Faced with mounting popular opposition, Muhammad Reza Pahlavi, shah of Iran, friend and ally of the United States, departs the country, never to return; the new Iranian regime will be a theocracy of fundamentalist Muslims, headed by the Ayatollah Ruhollah Khomeini.

February 26, 1979 To deal with a second energy crisis provoked partly by conditions in Iran, Carter asks for power to order gas rationing and other measures of conservation.

March 28, 1979 The worst nuclear accident in U.S. history takes place at Three-Mile-Island plant near Harrisburg, Pennsylvania, which releases large clouds of radioactive steam.

April 4, 1979 Bill Rodgers of the United States runs the Boston Marathon in a record 2 hours, 9 minutes, 27 seconds.

May 25, 1979 A DC-10 of American Airlines crashes shortly after leaving O'Hare Airport in Chicago, killing 272.

Jimmy Carter helped negotiate the signing of the Camp David Accords by Anwar Sadat of Egypt (left) and Menachem Begin of Israel (right). (Courtesy Jimmy Carter Library)

June 11, 1979   Actor John Wayne dies of cancer at age 72.

June 18, 1979   Carter and Soviet Leader Leonid Brezhnev sign SALT II, designed to allow each power approximate parity in strategic weaponry; each side is limited to 2,250 delivery systems; the Senate, of course, needs to approve the treaty.

August 5, 1979   Patricia Harris becomes the first black female member of the cabinet as secretary of Housing and Urban Development (HUD).

October 1, 1979   Pope John Paul II begins a week's visit to the United States, which includes stops at six eastern and midwestern cities.

November 4, 1979   Iranian militants seize the U.S. embassy in Tehran and capture 66 hostages; 13, blacks and women, will be released but the remainder are held in a hostage crisis with Iran that will last nearly 15 months.

December 27, 1979   The government participates in the "bail-out" of the beleaguered Chrysler Corporation, guaranteeing $1.75 billion in loans; Chrysler will pay off the debt by 1984.

Other events of 1979   Jerry Falwell, Baptist minister from Virginia, forms the Moral Majority, to move the church into political activity.

The Treasury begins to produce the Susan B. Anthony silver dollar.

Sony produces the Walkman.

A board game, Trivial Pursuit, becomes popular as home and party entertainment.

The courts begin to hear "palimony" suits—financial claims from romantic relationships outside of marriage.

Larry Bird and Earvin Johnson compete in a college basketball game, preparatory to both entering the NBA.

January 4, 1980   Carter announces major economic sanctions against the USSR in retaliation for Soviet invasion of Afghanistan.

January 29, 1980   Canadian officials help six Americans escape from Iran.

March 10, 1980   Jean Harris, head of an eastern girls school, kills Dr. Herman Tarnower, founder of the Scarsdale Diet, after he drops her as a lover.

April–August 1980   The Freedom Flotilla takes place as 125,000 Cubans flee to the United States; unexpectedly, the Castro regime allowed them to depart.

April 12, 1980   The U.S. Olympic Committee grants Carter's request (demand?) that the United States not participate in the Olympic games in Moscow this year.

April 24, 1980   Eight American servicemen die in an unsuccessful attempt at rescue of the hostages in Iran.

May 17, 1980   A race riot breaks out in Miami in protest of charges of police brutality; 18 die, 400 are injured.

May 18, 1980   Mount St. Helens in Washington explodes in violent volcanic eruption, killing 26 and destroying terrain for miles around.

June 1, 1980   Ted Turner begins CNN, the nation's first 24-hour news channel; from a base in Atlanta, the station feeds into the cable system.

September 19, 1980   Iraq invades Iran, bringing a new dimension to the continuing hostage crisis.

November 4, 1980   The Republican ticket of Ronald Reagan and George H.W. Bush defeat a weakened President Carter and Vice President Mondale by 52 percent of popular vote to 41.6 percent (Independent candidate John Anderson received most of the remainder); Reagan and Bush had all but 49 of the electoral votes. Republicans control the Senate.

December 8, 1980   Former Beatle John Lennon is murdered by a deranged fan near his home in New York City.

Other events of 1980   The 3-M Corporation introduces Post-it notes.

In-line rollerblade skates start to catch on.

An ABC late-night television show, *Night-Line* with Ted Koppel, designed to follow the hostage crisis, becomes permanent.

A French firm introduces a new abortion pill called RU-486 (mifepristone).

The United States boycotts the summer Olympics in Moscow in protest of Soviet action in Afghanistan; Japan and West Germany follow suit.

The Museum of Modern Art in New York exhibits 1,000 paintings of Pablo Picasso.

In a major sports feat of the modern era, the U.S. hockey team, made up of college and low-level professional players, defeats a heavily favored Soviet team and wins the gold medal in winter games at Lake Placid, New York.

The Eighties, 1981–1990

January 20, 1981   The Carter administration negotiates a deal through which the hostages in Iran will be released after 444 days of captivity. Timing of the deal, inauguration day, leaves a false impression that Reagan's people were responsible.

February 17, 1981   Chrysler Corporation announces losses of $1.71 billion, largest in history of U.S. business; losses of Ford and General Motors verify that Americans are turning to smaller, more efficient foreign cars.

March 2, 1981   Reagan announces an intent to send advisers and funds to support President José Duarte, at war with leftist rebels in El Salvador.

March 30, 1981   President Reagan is wounded by an assassin outside the Hilton Hotel in Washington; three others, including Press Secretary James Brady, are injured; the young man who fires the shots, John Hinckley, Jr., later will be found innocent on grounds of insanity.

April 12, 1981   NASA launches *Columbia*, a shuttle and first reusable space vehicle; *Columbia* will return after two days and 36 orbits.

June 12, 1981   Major league baseball players strike, largely over the issue of free agency; the stoppage will last seven weeks, until August 9.

June 21, 1981   A long reign of terror ends in Atlanta with arrest of Wayne Williams, a 28-year-old black man who will be implicated in the murder of 28, many of them black children.

July 18, 1981   Two aerial walkways collapse at the packed Hyatt Hotel in Kansas City, killing 113 and injuring 190.

July 29, 1981   Congress passes Reagan's tax-reduction legislation, designed to reduce taxes by $750 billion over five years.

August 6, 1981   Reagan fires 12,000 air-traffic controllers who have gone on strike.

September 21, 1981   Sandra Day O'Connor, appointed by Reagan, becomes the first female member of the Supreme Court.

October 6, 1981   Anwar Sadat, courageous president of Egypt, close friend of the United States, and pathmaker for settlement in the Middle East, is assassinated by fundamentalist soldiers in Cairo.

Other events of 1981   Pac-Man video games appear.

The FDA approves aspartame for use as a sweetener.

MTV debuts on television.

Walter Cronkite retires as anchor of the popular CBS evening news show.

Actress Natalie Wood drowns in waters off California.

A deadly new disease that seems to affect mostly homosexual men and intravenous drug users receives a name: AIDS, acronym for acquired immune deficiency syndrome.

January 5, 1982   A federal judge strikes down a law in Arkansas that requires teaching creation as well as evolution in public schools.

January 13, 1982   A Boeing 737 airliner crashes in an icy Potomac River in Washington, D.C., killing 78.

February 28, 1982   The United Auto Workers conclude an agreement with Ford that trades wage and benefit gains for job security.

June 6, 1982   The Israeli army invades southern Lebanon, to drive away Palestinian warriors, creating new problems for the United States.

June 15, 1982   The Supreme Court rules that all children are entitled to public education, challenging a law in Texas that denies public schooling for aliens.

June 30, 1982   The ERA (Equal Rights Amendment) is defeated when it falls three states short of the 38 needed for ratification.

July 9, 1982   A Pan American jet liner crashes near airport in New Orleans, killing 154.

July 16, 1982   The Reverend Sun Myung Moon marries 4,150 followers in a massive ceremony at Madison Square Garden, New York.

July 28, 1982   San Francisco becomes the first city to ban sale of handguns; few cities follow.

August 26, 1982   Plagued by lawsuits alleging medical problems from asbestos, the Manville Corporation files for bankruptcy.

October 26, 1982   The Reagan administration reports a record budget deficit of $110 billion for fiscal 1982.

November 10, 1982   Leonid Brezhnev, Soviet leader since 1964, dies at age 75; Yuri Andropov succeeds him.

November 13, 1982   The Vietnam Veterans Memorial, a black granite wall inscribed with names of nearly 60,000 killed in Vietnam, is dedicated in Washington, D.C.

December 2, 1982   Barney Clark, 61, receives the first artificial heart, in Salt Lake City; he will live 112 days.

Other events of 1982   Halcion, a sleep medication by Upjohn, comes on the market.

USA Today hits the newsstands.

Plastic surgeons begin a procedure called liposuction.

National Football League players strike for 57 days.

Braniff International Airlines files for bankruptcy.

Honda begins to produce cars in Ohio.

Gandhi is a successful movie; *Cats,* a musical by Andrew Lloyd Webber, debuts on Broadway.

Jimmy Connors defeats John McEnroe in the longest singles final at Wimbledon: 4 hours, 14 minutes.

John Belushi dies of drug overdose.

Princess Grace (Grace Kelly) dies at 52 in an auto crash in Monaco.

January 31, 1983   Reagan declares Times Beach, Missouri, a disaster area caused by dioxin, a chemical used to control dust on roads; the town will be virtually abandoned.

March 23, 1983   Reagan announces plans for a spectacular missile defense system, Strategic Defense Initiative (SDI), better known as Star Wars; after costing some $30 billion, the program will be canceled in 1993.

April 4, 1983   The space shuttle *Challenger* makes its first flight into space; two astronauts will make a space walk.

April 12, 1983   Harold Washington is elected first black mayor of Chicago.

June 18, 1983   Sally Ride becomes the first American female astronaut in space, aboard shuttle *Challenger*.

September 1, 1983   A Soviet fighter plane shoots down a South Korean 747 airliner over Sakhalin Island, killing 269, including 61 Americans, one of whom was a congressman.

Reagan sends 2,000 marines into Lebanon as peacekeepers, seeking to bring order to that divided and beleaguered land.

September 26, 1983   Australian yacht *Australia II* defeats America's *Liberty* to win the America's Cup, breaking a U.S. win streak of 132 years.

October 23, 1983   A large truck bomb explodes near the American marine compound in Lebanon, killing 241 American armed-services members.

October 25–30, 1983   United States forces invade tiny island of Grenada, near South America, to oust a Cuban-oriented regime and to evacuate some 700 U.S. citizens.

November 2, 1983   Reagan signs into law a measure proclaiming the third Monday in January as Martin Luther King, Jr., Day and a national holiday.

Other events of 1983   The compact disc makes a debut.

Apple Computers introduces a new device called a mouse.

Drivers in Chicago are the first to use cellular phones.

Vanessa Williams becomes the first black Miss America; she will lose the title the next year after publication of nude pictures in *Penthouse*.

Guion Bluford, aboard *Challenger* on August 30, is the first black astronaut in space.

A Bible produced by the National Council of Churches addresses God in a gender-neutral fashion.

Long-running television series *M*A*S*H* shows its last episode, watched by a record 125 million viewers.

Crack cocaine hits the streets, a devastating development because of the drug's strength, addictive qualities, and low cost.

January 10, 1984   The United States and the Vatican establish diplomatic relations, after 116 years of not doing so.

February 1, 1984   Reagan orders marines withdrawn from Lebanon.

February 3, 1984   On its fourth mission *Challenger* features two astronauts flying free of the spacecraft, propelled by jet backpacks.

February 9, 1984   Soviet leader Andropov dies after a brief tenure; he will be replaced by Konstantin Chernenko, also in poor health.

April 26, 1984   Reagan makes his first visit to China.

July 12, 1984   For the first time, a presidential nominee, Democrat Walter Mondale, chooses a woman as his vice presidential running mate, Congresswoman Geraldine Ferraro of New York.

July 28–August 12, 1984   The summer Olympic games are held in Los Angeles; in an obvious payback gesture the Soviet Union boycotts the games and 13 other communist states do the same.

October 12, 1984   Reagan signs the Boland II amendment that prohibits government agencies from supporting military activity in Nicaragua; Congess also outlaws aid to the Contras.

November 6, 1984   The Republican ticket of Reagan and Bush scores a landslide victory: 59 percent of the vote; electoral vote of all states but one, Mondale's home, Minnesota.

December 3, 1984   A gas leak at a chemical factory of Union Carbide in Bophal, India, kills 3,000; after five years of legal maneuver, the American company will pay damages of $470 million.

December 22, 1984   Bernard Goetz, a modern vigilante, shoots four black youth (none fatally) who prepared to rob him in a New York subway; Goetz, who was white, was viewed variously by blacks as a hero and as an agent of oppression.

Other events of 1984   Jim Fixx, fitness guru and author of works about running, dies of heart attack at 52—while running.

The Cosby Show begins on television.

Madonna, brazen and daring singer and entertainment personality, turns underwear into outerwear.

Film *The Killing Fields* reminds viewers of the horrors of Cambodia in the previous decade.

The film industry adds PG 13 to its rating system.

The year 1984 is proclaimed to be the year of the yuppie—young urban (or upwardly mobile) professional, said to be an insatiable consumer.

February 21, 1985   Reagan reiterates that he opposes the leftist Sandinista regime in Nicaragua and its new president, Daniel Ortega. He wants to aid a counterrevolutionary force called the Contras, aid to whom was outlawed by Congress on October 12, 1984.

March 11, 1985   In a move, the significance of which could not have been known, Soviet communists pick Mikhail Gorbachev as leader, replacing Chernenko, who died the previous day.

April 23, 1985   The Coca-Cola Corporation announces that it is changing the formula for its beverage; in July the company announced that because of numerous complaints, it would resume production of the original recipe, calling it Coke Classic.

May 5, 1985   Reagan creates a stir, when after laying a wreath at Bergen-Belsen concentration camp in Germany (where Anne Frank died), he visits a cemetery at nearby Bitburg that contains graves of SS soldiers.

May 15, 1985   Police in Philadelphia end a siege by bombing headquarters of a black radical group, killing 11 and causing a fire that destroys 61 homes.

May 28, 1985   The FBI arrests retired naval officer John Walker and his son Michael for espionage.

June 14, 1985   A TWA plane is seized by terrorists over skies of Athens; plane, crew, and 153 passengers are held 17 days then released, except for one American serviceman, who is killed.

September 1, 1985   A team of French and U.S. scientists locate the wreck of *Titanic,* more than two miles down; the sighting will be the first since April 14, 1912, when the great liner sank, taking 1,522 lives.

October 11, 1985   American fighter planes force down an Egyptian plane carrying hijackers of an Italian cruise ship *Achille Lauro;* hijackers kill one American.

November 19, 1985   Reagan meets for the first time with Gorbachev in Geneva; they accomplish nothing but agree to meet again.

December 12, 1985   Crash of a chartered airliner off the coast of Newfoundland kills all 256 aboard; most are members of the 101st Airborne Division, American soldiers returning home after duty in the Sinai peninsula.

Other events of 1985   Nintendo video games become popular.

The Disney Channel and Home Shopping Network come to cable TV.

Montgomery Ward halts catalog sales.

ABC television network is sold to Capital City Communications for $3.5 billion.

General Electric acquires NBC network and RCA for $6.3 billion.

Libby Riddle becomes the first woman to win the difficult Iditarod dogsled race in Alaska.

A mother who had taken fertility medication gives birth to six in Orange, California.

Actor Rock Hudson, age 59, dies of AIDS, casting huge attention on this startling new disease.

January 28, 1986   Space shuttle *Challenger* explodes a minute after takeoff, killing all seven aboard, including Christa McAuliffe, a teacher from New Hampshire.

April 14, 1986   Reagan blames Libya and its leader Muammar Qaddafi for a bombing in West Berlin that killed an American and orders an air strike on Libyan targets.

June 4, 1986   Jonathan Ray Pollard is found guilty of spying for Israel and is sentenced to prison.

July 3–6, 1986   Americans celebrate the 100th birthday of the Statue of Liberty.

July 17, 1986   LTV Corporation, second largest steel company in the United States, files for bankruptcy.

September 17, 1986   The Senate confirms William Rehnquist, whom Reagan has elevated to chief justice of the Supreme Court; Antonin Scalia, Reagan's appointee, will be confirmed as a new justice.

October 2, 1986   The Senate overrides Reagan's veto of a bill imposing sanctions on the segregationist government of South Africa.

October 10, 1986   Federal officials seize 4,620 pounds of cocaine in West Palm Beach, Florida, a record haul.

October 17, 1986   The Senate passes an immigration bill that by fining employers is designed to reduce illegal immigration.

October 22, 1986   Reagan signs a measure that provides major revision of tax policy, reducing brackets from 14 to 3.

November 3–6, 1986   American newspapers publish a story that the Reagan administration secretly sold arms to Iran in exchange for release of American hostages held in the Middle East.

November 4, 1986   Democrats retain a majority in the House and win eight Senate seats, placing them in control of Congress for the first time in six years.

November 14, 1986   In a development that perhaps symbolized a motif of the 1980s, stock broker Ivan Boesky pleads guilty to insider trading; his sentence is reduced because he leads the government to an even larger fish, junk bond manipulator Michael Milken.

December 10, 1986   Elie Wiesel, famed author and concentration camp survivor, receives the Nobel Peace Prize.

Other events of 1986   Robert Penn Warren becomes the first poet laureate of the United States.

Rhode Island is the first state to establish a recycling policy.

Halley's comet makes the first appearance in 75 years, but the sighting is disappointing;

Actor Clint Eastwood, famous for roles as a tough cowboy and cop, is elected mayor of Carmel, California.

Len Bias, basketball star from the University of Maryland, top draft choice of the Boston Celtics, dies of drug overdose.

Singer Corporation, long a symbol of American enterprise abroad, stops selling sewing machines.

President and Nancy Reagan aboard a battleship, July 4, 1986 (Courtesy Ronald Reagan Library)

January 5, 1987 Reagan presents Congress with the nation's first trillion-dollar budget ($1,024.3 billion), which includes a deficit of $107.8 billion.

January 8, 1987 The Dow Jones average closes at 2002.25—the first time over 2,000.

March 10, 1987 Television evangelist Jim Bakker, cohost of the PTL program, confesses an adulterous affair with secretary Jessica Hahn in 1980. The scandal will end his career.

April 7, 1987 Mayor Harold Washington of Chicago is reelected by 54 percent to 43 percent. He receives 97 percent of the black vote; 15 percent of whites.

May 4, 1987 Former senator Gary Hart, front-runner for the Democrat presidential nomination in 1988, is discovered in an affair with model Donna Rice; he drops from the race on May 8.

May 17, 1987 Iraqi missiles strike the American frigate *Stark* in the Persian Gulf, killing 37. Iraq apologizes to the United States, which had started to tilt toward Iraq in the long war with Iran.

July 7, 1987 Lt. Colonel Oliver North (of the National Security Council) will begin testimony before Congress about the growing Iran-Contra scandal, in which he played a major part; National Security Adviser John Poindexter will begin testimony on July 15, as will Secretary of State George Shultz on July 23. North insists that his superiors approved all the dealings; Reagan (and Vice President Bush) deny any knowledge that money from selling arms to Iran was being diverted to the Contras in Nicaragua; questions and inconsistencies abound, but no one will be punished.

August 7, 1987 Alan Greenspan replaces Paul Volcker as chairman of the Federal Reserve Board; under Volcker, inflation during the years 1979–87 dropped from 13.3 percent to 1.1 percent.

September 10, 1987 Pope John Paul II begins a 10-day visit to the United States.

September 17, 1987 Reagan and other officials commemorate the 200th aniversary of the Constitution.

October 4, 1987 Canada and the United States agree to a free-trade pact.

October 19, 1987 Stock prices dropped 508 points, 22.6 percent of the total, nearly doubling the crash of 1929. Referred to at the time as Black Monday, it was the worst day in the history of Wall Street to that time.

October 23, 1987 By a vote of 58–42 the Senate fails to confirm Robert Bork for the Supreme Court.

November 28, 1987 Twana Brawley, a 15-year-old black girl in Wappinger Falls, New York, claims that she was kidnapped and raped by six white men; a grand jury will find the charge to be fraudulent.

December 8, 1987 In their third meeting, Reagan and Gorbachev agree to an INF Treaty—a pact that eliminates all intermediate range (300–3400 miles) missiles.

Other events of 1987 Andy Warhol, pop art entrepreneur, dies after gall bladder surgery.

A court orders Rotary Clubs to admit women.

The National Museum of Women in the Arts opens in Washington.

Influenced by the spread of AIDS, televison stations begin to carry advertisements for condoms; the first station to act is KRON in San Francisco.

The FDA approves a new drug, AZT, as treatment for AIDS, and an anticholesterol "statin" drug called Lovastatin, marketed by Merck under the brand name Mevacor.

Texaco Petroleum Corporation files for protection under the bankruptcy laws, the largest firm to do so.

February 3, 1988 The Senate approves appointment of Anthony Kennedy as justice of the Supreme Court; Kennedy is Reagan's third choice after rejection of Robert Bork and Douglas Ginsburg.

February 21, 1988 In the wake of the fall of Jim Bakker, popular televangelist Jimmy Swaggart admits reports of his consorting with a prostitute; Swaggart eventually will be renounced as a minister of the Assemblies of God.

April 18, 1988 U.S. warships in the Persian Gulf, protecting Kuwaiti tankers from Iran, clash with Iranian forces.

May 4, 1988 Nearly 1.4 million aliens meet the deadline for applying for amnesty under new legislation.

July 3, 1988 American cruiser *Vincennes* mistakenly shoots down an Iranian passenger liner over the Persian Gulf, killing all 290 aboard.

July 20, 1988 The Democrats select little-known Governor Michael Dukakis of Massachusetts for the presidential nomination and Senator Lloyd Bentsen of Texas for the vice presidency.

July–August 1988 Summer drought feeds fires that consume millions of acres in the West, including thousands of acres of forestland in Yellowstone National Park.

August 10, 1988 Reagan signs a bill that supplies an apology and $20,000 per person to Japanese Americans interned during the Second World War.

October 3, 1988 Space shuttle *Discovery* completes the first mission after the disaster of *Challenger.*

November 8, 1988 The Republican ticket of Vice President Bush and Senator Dan Quayle of Indiana soundly trounces the Democrats with 54 percent of popular vote; 40 out of 50 states; but the Democrats hold on to Congress.

December 21, 1988 Pan American flight 103, a Boeing 747, is blown from the sky by a terrorist bomb over Lockerbie, Scotland; all 259 on the plane and 11 on the ground are killed.

December 21, 1988 Drexel Burnham Lambert agrees to pay a $650 million penalty for securities fraud.

Other events of 1988 Prozac, an antidepressant produced by Eli Lilly, makes a debut; it will be enormously successful.

America's worst drought in 50 years causes the nation, for the first time in its history, to import grain.

Beaches in New York and New Jersey are bespoiled by washed-up medical waste.

Roseanne begins as a series on ABC; *Rain Man,* featuring Dustin Hoffman and Tom Cruise, is a popular new movie.

Songwriter Irving Berlin observes his 100th birthday.

Venerable and charming Wrigley Field in Chicago, home of the Cubs, yields to the advance of civilization; the Cubs permit installation of lights and Wrigley's first night baseball game.

Further meetings between Reagan and Gorbachev and a new emerging Soviet attitude suggest that exceptional developments are underway in international affairs.

January 4, 1989 Navy F-14 jets shoot down two Libyan fighters off the coast of Libya.

January 6, 1989 The Labor Department reports that unemployment has dropped to 5.3 percent, lowest in 14 years.

February 10, 1989 As chair of the Democrat National Committee, Ronald Brown of Washington, D.C., becomes the first African American to head a major national party.

March 24, 1989 Supertanker *Exxon Valdez* runs aground and spills 11 million gallons of crude oil into pristine Prince William Sound, Alaska; the worst oil spill in U.S. history, it caused enormous financial and environmental damage.

April 10, 1989 An explosion inside a 16-inch gun turret on the battleship *Iowa* killed 47 sailors as the recommissioned ship was on maneuvers.

April 19, 1989 Young black and Hispanic boys "wilding" in New York rape and beat nearly to death a female jogger in Central Park. They will be identified and punished.

May 4, 1989 Lt. Colonel Oliver North is convicted of charges related to the Iran-Contra scandal, but conviction later will be overturned.

June 21, 1989   In a 5–4 vote, the Supreme Court rules that burning the American flag constitutes freedom of expression, a right that must be preserved.

August 10, 1989   President Bush appoints General Colin Powell to be chairman of the Joint Chiefs of Staff—the first African American to hold that post.

August 30, 1989   Wealthy Manhattan property owner Leona Helmsley, nicknamed the "Queen of Mean," is convicted of fraud and tax evasion, fined, and sentenced to prison.

September 21, 1989   Hurricane Hugo slams ashore near Charleston, South Carolina, taking 24 lives and devastating the affected area.

October 17, 1989   As the nation watches a World Series game at Candlestick Park, San Francisco, the city is struck by an earthquake that measures 6.9 on the Richter Scale; 60 die, 3,000 are injured, damage is huge.

November 7, 1989   Results of local elections produce the first black mayor of New York City, David Dinkins, and the first black governor of Virginia since Reconstruction, Douglas Wilder.

November 9, 1989   The Berlin Wall is opened to Berliners, and its total destruction begins, without any opposition. It is the most convincing evidence to that point that the cold war is indeed ending.

December 20, 1989   The United States invades Panama to depose its dictator, Manuel Noriega, who is charged with involvement in the drug traffic in the United States; Noriega will be captured and transported to the United States for trial.

Other events of 1989   The Teenage Mutant Ninja Turtles become popular with youngsters.

Bristol-Myers and Squibb merge to form a pharmaceutical giant.

The Los Angeles *Herald Examiner* ceases publication after 86 years.

Pete Rose, record-setting baseball player and manager of the Cincinnati Reds, is banned from professional baseball for life by Commissioner Bart Giamatti, for gambling on games.

Ford buys prestigious Jaguar Motor Company of Great Britain.

Kareem Abdul Jabbar retires from the Los Angeles Lakers and from professional basketball.

January 18, 1990   In a sting operation, Mayor Marion Barry of Washington, D.C., is arrested for smoking crack cocaine.

February 26, 1990   Election of Violeta Chamorro as president of Nicaragua, ousting incumbent Daniel Ortega, accomplishes what President Reagan had tried for nearly eight years to do.

March 11, 1990   Lithuania declares itself independent of the USSR and gets away with it.

March 18, 1990   A dozen works of art by the Old Masters are stolen from Isabella Stewart Gardner Museum in Boston. The works are worth $100 million and represent the largest art heist on record.

March 25, 1990   Fire in the crowded Happy Land social club kills 87 in the Bronx.

May 29, 1990   Russian politician Boris Yeltsin, no longer a communist, is elected chairman of the Russian Supreme Soviet.

July 26, 1990   President Bush signs the Americans with Disabilities Act, designed to prevent discrimination against, and provide assistance for, disabled people.

August 2, 1990   Iraqi troops invade and overrun Kuwait, a tiny Arab state on the Persian Gulf that possesses large oil reserves. President Bush denounces the move.

August 7, 1990   Bush sends the first contingent of U.S. forces to the Persian Gulf area. They are to constitute part of an operation, code-named Desert Shield, to protect Saudi Arabia from an invasion by Iraq.

September 27, 1990   The Senate confirms nomination of David Souter, appointed to the Supreme Court by Bush to replace William Brennan, who retires.

October 3, 1990   In a move that virtually no one would have dared to predict, East and West Germany reunify, and the Gorbachev regime stands by and watches—further indication of a new Soviet attitude and an end to the cold war.

October 20, 1990   Bush vetoes a civil rights bill on grounds that it would promote quotas in hiring; the Senate fails by one vote to override.

Other events of 1990   *Seinfeld* begins a long run on NBC.

Dr. Jack Kevorkian of Detroit introduces his suicide machine.

All U.S. airlines ban smoking on domestic flights.

General Motors introduces a new car, Saturn.

The FDA approves Norplant, a birth control insert.

NASA sends the costly and sophisticated Hubble telescope into space aboard shuttle *Discovery,* only to learn that its ability to peer into space, the chief mission, was limited by improper operation of its mirrors.

Deceased of the year include Jim Henson, creator of the Muppets, actress Ava Gardner, actress Greta Garbo, composer Aaron Copland; conductor and composer Leonard Bernstein dies five days after announcing his retirement.

By the end of the year a coalition of forces put together by President Bush has exceeded 500,000 in the Persian Gulf area; a good portion of them are American; Desert Shield has become Desert Storm, and its objectives are to drive Iraqi forces from Kuwait, to assure the security of Saudi Arabia, and perhaps to provoke a change in the government of Iraq. The United Nations has given Iraqi leader Saddam Hussein a deadline of January 15, 1991, to withdraw from Kuwait. Desert Storm is about to begin.

CHAPTER 4 The American Economy

A discussion of the American economy in the 50 or so years after the Second World War quickly becomes a litany of superlative terminology. In the broad scope of national and international economics it was an account of enormous growth. Measured in current dollars, the gross national product increased 250 percent between 1945 and 1960. It doubled again in the 1960s, nearly trebled in the 1970s (albeit a time of very high inflation, which of course inflated the numbers); it came reasonably close to doubling another time in the 1980s. Beneath the veneer of broad economic statistics one could find categories of remarkable growth and material betterment for large groups of people. Many millions of middle-class people in the 1970s and 1980s had more in the way of comfort and convenience than the richest individuals had had at a time when their grandparents, or even their parents, were of comparable age.

Looking beneath the national numbers one also could find less appealing segments of the economic system. It was essentially a capitalist economy, and capitalism continued to show itself subject to periods of growth and recession, good times and bad—of different degrees, of course, depending on the times. The economy remained responsive to various national pressures, and as the era moved along, the impact of international economic development became markedly greater. Within broad periods of expansion, one could find shorter times of little growth and even an occasional year of economic loss, especially if one took inflation into account. During the decade of the 1980s, when expansion generally continued, the unemployment rate at one point reached nearly depression-era proportion.

As a rule, however, American capitalism was at its best when it came to production. Problems more commonly came in the area of distribution. Some of the richest people in the world long had been Americans; the United States had been known for the large size—and after 1946 the striking growth—in its middle class, but the nation continued to have a substantial number of people left out, loosely and commonly referred to as poor. In the 1960s the government devised a method for classifying the poor by specifying an income designation as the poverty line. Poverty in the first instance thus was an expression of class. People beneath the poverty line were the impoverished class, and because most people were white, the bulk of poor people were white. Probing deeper and giving close attention to proportion and ratio quickly revealed that poverty, and economic representation all along the line, was also a matter of race and ethnicity. The largest proportion of people left out were nonwhite: African Americans and Native Americans being most conspicuous—one because the numbers of people were so large, the other because the economic numbers were so low.

Poverty related to ethnicity lost much of its force or at least underwent change in the postwar era. The world war and the postwar boom did much to move white ethnic groups—Polish, Italians, Irish, various Slavic nationalities—into the middle class. What essentially was left were the Hispanics, a classification so poorly understood and defined that it did not have a name (Mexicans was most commonly used), and the government did not count it separately until the 1970s. As Hispanics began—because of a high birthrate and high immigration, legal or otherwise—to appear in growing numbers, they became rivals to black Americans, overrepresented in a major way below the poverty line.

For much of the period one did not think of women being rich or poor in terms of a separate identity. The economic status of a female probably was determined by class if she was white and by race and ethnicity if she was nonwhite or Hispanic. In the 1970s women began to receive more separate identity—partly because of the women's movement, which demanded it, and partly because of major changes in social and cultural practices and attitudes. A new emphasis on gender had mixed consequences: Some women, acting on their own and demanding their rights, moved up the economic ladder; a more common direction, because of social changes, was downward, often below the poverty line.

At the start of the postwar era, it seemed that everything had been arranged to enhance the economy of the United States. The nation was intact, undamaged by war, and a massive wartime economy was in place, in need only of retooling. The population had a demand for goods that were pent up by scarcities of war; it had money saved up and offered anew in various government programs for returning veterans. Benefits in a G.I. Bill of Rights, for example, produced an enormous rush to build and sell new houses. Competitors to the United States had been weakened, drained financially, damaged or—as in the case of Germany and Japan—virtually destroyed. The Korean War and the cold war assured continuing major government participation in the economy. The world was open to American capitalism, and the United States made the most of it. New York became, or remained, the world's capital of finance; the dollar became the world's currency.

In the 1960s the economy slowed somewhat at the start. President John F. Kennedy endorsed a tax reduction calculated to "get America moving again." The Vietnam War poured increasing amounts of money into the economy, and it raised questions as to the ultimate consequences for economic stability. By the 1960s Europe and Japan essentially had recovered from the Second World War (albeit with much American assistance) and were placing themselves in a position to challenge economic domination of the United States. Developing nations (then known as the Third World), seeking to modernize, urged American companies to locate in their lands, offering numerous enticements, not the least of which was very low labor costs.

Although national numbers continued to climb during the 1970s, with many economic segments it appeared that everything that could go wrong did; the Vietnam War caused government deficits to increase; deficits helped fuel inflation, which reached 10 percent in 1973, the last official year of the war for the United States; modern economies in Europe and Japan competed with an older American economy in selling goods abroad and in the United States. Less expensive, and in some cases better quality, foreign goods caused some American firms to close down or leave the country.

A first energy crisis in 1973–74 created a shortage and caused the price of oil to quadruple. The second crisis of 1978–80 produced new rounds of price increases. At a time when Americans wanted energy-efficient four-cylinder cars, United States firms were tooled to produce six-cylinder and V-8 engines. Japan, by contrast, was ready to go with its little Toyotas, Datsuns, and Hondas. By the end of the 1970s the economic numbers almost defied credibility: Gasoline sold at $1.40 per gallon; inflation ran at 13 percent, the prime interest rate 20 percent; unemployment stood at 7 percent and was still rising. President Jimmy Carter said there was a national crisis of confidence; the people thought there was a crisis of Jimmy Carter.

Under the new leadership of Ronald Reagan, the 1980s heralded a purported new era of American economics. Influenced by the theories of economist Arthur Laffler, the Reagan administration sought to institute an approach termed "supply-side" economics, a strategy that stressed sharply lower taxes, lower government spending, and fewer controls, a system designed to promote private savings, investment, and initiative. One consequence would be a balanced national budget; the ultimate objective of course was more economic growth. The keynote was a massive tax reduction measure, passed in 1981.

The results varied: The economy worsened substantially until 1983, a consequence that the new administration blamed on Jimmy Carter. Unemployment passed 10 percent; companies continued to shut down; foreign goods flooded the market.

In 1983 the economy began not to reverse itself but at least to improve. Automobile companies improved their product lines and, stung by criticism, worked to improve quality. A glut of oil production brought the price down sharply. Unemployment dropped, interest rates receded. Reagan's people would trumpet several years of growth. But it did not go as Arthur Laffler had planned. Congress did not want to reduce domestic spending; Reagan wanted to—and did—provide huge new sums of money for the military forces. Reduced taxes and increased spending could lead to only one result: record budget deficits. Continuing American propensity to buy cheaper and presumably better foreign products led to another troubling development, record deficits in trade, most conspicuously with Japan. As meaningful numbers about the effects of the new economics began to appear later in the 1980s, they confirmed what critics had feared. Reaganomics had produced a significant shift in income from the poor to the rich. The economic contradictions and potential problems seemed to faze the president not at all; he turned the presidency over to his successor, George H. W. Bush, in 1989 and headed into retirement, convinced that he had placed the country on sound economic footing.

Reagan had another reason for believing that his basic economic instincts had been right. Capitalism was riding high at the end of the 1980s. Socialist economies, which had seemed promising—some had said that it was the wave of the future—40 years earlier, were floundering or failing altogether. The People's Republic of China, at one

TABLE 4.1 GROSS NATIONAL PRODUCTa, 1946–1990
(in billions of dollars)

Year	Actual Dollars		1987 Dollars	
	Total	Percent Change	Total	Percent Change
1946	212.6	−0.4	1,276.0	−20.5
1947	235.5	10.8	1,258.5	−1.4
1948	261.8	11.2	1,307.0	3.9
1949	260.7	−0.4	1,311.8	0.4
1950	288.5	10.7	1,425.6	8.7
1951	333.6	15.6	1,567.4	9.9
1952	351.8	5.5	1,634.3	4.3
1953	372.0	5.7	1,694.2	3.7
1954	373.1	0.3	1,683.3	−0.6
1955	406.8	9.0	1,779.0	5.7
1956	429.1	5.5	1,815.5	2.1
1957	451.8	5.3	1,850.9	1.9
1958	457.5	1.3	1,839.7	−0.6
1959	497.0	8.6	1,939.6	5.4
1960	516.6	3.9	1,982.8	2.2
1961	535.4	3.6	2,037.1	2.7
1962	575.8	7.5	2,143.3	5.2
1963	607.7	5.5	2,231.8	4.1
1964	653.0	7.5	2,358.1	5.7
1965	708.1	8.4	2,488.9	5.5
1966	774.9	9.4	2,633.2	5.8
1967	819.8	5.8	2,702.6	2.6
1968	895.5	9.2	2,815.6	4.2
1969	965.6	7.8	2,890.9	2.7
1970	1,017.1	5.3	2,891.5	0.0
1971	1,104.9	8.6	2,975.9	2.9
1972	1,215.7	10.0	3,128.8	5.1
1973	1,362.3	12.1	3,298.6	5.4
1974	1,474.3	8.2	3,282.4	−0.5
1975	1,599.1	8.5	3,247.6	−1.1
1976	1,785.5	11.7	3,412.2	5.1
1977	1,994.6	11.7	3,569.0	4.6
1978	2,254.5	13.0	3,739.0	4.8
1979	2,520.8	11.8	3,845.3	2.8
1980	2,742.1	8.8	3,823.4	−0.6
1981	3,063.8	11.7	3,884.4	1.6
1982	3,179.8	3.8	3,796.1	−2.3
1983	3,434.4	8.0	3,939.6	3.8
1984	3,801.5	10.7	4,174.5	6.0
1985	4,053.6	6.6	4,295.0	2.9
1986	4,277.7	5.5	4,413.5	2.8
1987	4,544.5	6.2	4,544.5	3.0
1988	4,908.2	8.0	4,726.3	4.0
1989	5,266.8	7.3	4,852.7	2.7
1990	5,567.8	5.7	4,916.5	1.3

a GNP measures goods and services from labor and property of U.S. residents, wherever they are produced.
Source: Arnsey J. Darnay, Economic Indicators Handbook (Detroit, 1994), 7–8.

TABLE 4.2 GROSS DOMESTIC PRODUCTa, 1946–1990
(in billions of dollars)

Year	Actual Dollars		1987 Dollars	
	Total	Percent Change	Total	Percent Change
1946	211.9	−0.6	1,272.1	−20.6
1947	234.3	10.6	1,252.8	−1.5
1948	260.3	11.1	1,300.0	3.8
1949	259.3	−0.4	1,305.5	0.4
1950	287.0	10.7	1,418.5	8.7
1951	331.6	15.5	1,558.4	9.9
1952	349.7	5.5	1,624.9	4.3
1953	370.0	5.8	1,685.5	3.7
1954	370.9	0.2	1,673.8	−0.7
1955	404.3	9.0	1,768.3	5.6
1956	426.2	5.4	1,803.6	2.0
1957	448.6	5.3	1,838.2	1.9
1958	454.7	1.4	1,829.1	−0.5
1959	494.2	8.7	1,928.8	5.5
1960	513.3	3.9	1,970.8	2.2
1961	531.8	3.6	2,023.8	2.7
1962	571.6	7.5	2,128.1	5.2
1963	603.1	5.5	2,215.6	4.1
1964	648.0	7.4	2,340.6	5.6
1965	702.7	8.4	2,470.5	5.5
1966	769.8	9.5	2,616.2	5.9
1967	814.3	5.8	2,685.2	2.6
1968	889.3	9.2	2,796.9	4.2
1969	959.5	7.9	2,873.0	2.7
1970	1,010.7	5.3	2,873.9	0.0
1971	1,097.2	8.6	2,955.9	2.9
1972	1,207.0	10.0	3,107.1	5.1
1973	1,349.6	11.8	3,268.6	5.2
1974	1,458.6	8.1	3,248.1	−0.6
1975	1,585.9	8.7	3,221.7	−0.8
1976	1,768.4	11.5	3,380.8	4.9
1977	1,974.1	11.6	3,533.3	4.5
1978	2,232.7	13.1	3,703.5	4.8
1979	2,488.6	11.5	3,796.8	2.5
1980	2,708.0	8.8	3,776.3	−0.5
1981	3,030.6	11.9	3,843.1	1.8
1982	3,149.6	3.9	3,760.3	−2.2
1983	3,405.0	8.1	3,906.6	3.9
1984	3,777.2	10.9	4,148.5	6.2
1985	4,038.7	6.9	4,279.8	3.2
1986	4,268.6	5.7	4,404.5	2.9
1987	4,539.9	6.4	4,539.9	3.1
1988	4,900.4	7.9	4,718.6	3.9
1989	5,250.8	7.2	4,838.0	2.5
1990	5,546.1	5.6	4,897.3	1.2

a GDP measures goods and services produced in the United States, regardless of the nationality of who is supplying the labor and property.
Source: Darnay, Economic Indicators Handbook, 14–15.

time the symbol of social revolution, had been moving toward a market economy for more than 10 years. A new Soviet leader admitted economic failures and called for major restructuring of the original communist system. Every loosening of controls in Eastern Europe sent those countries dashing toward capitalism. Nations in all parts of the world were begging for American private investment; workers' groups and local governments were trying to keep the companies at home. Conservatives interpreted these events as the ultimate and inevitable triumph of private enterprise. If somewhat sobered by these developments, liberals doubted that they should be accepted as eternal economic truth. Skeptics preferred to see the victories of capitalism as a response to economic stimuli at a specific time. They argued that Reaganomics confirmed that evils of capitalism that had produced leftist economics in the first place had not vanished.

TABLE 4.3   GROSS NATIONAL PRODUCT—
A NATIONAL COMPARISON, 1986

Rank	Country	Aggregate GNP ($ million)
	Top 10	
1.	United States	4,221,750
2.	Japan	1,559,720
3.	Germany, West	735,940
4.	France	595,180
5.	United Kingdom	504,850
6.	Italy	489,880
7.	Canada	361,720
8.	China	314,800
9.	Brazil	250,520
10.	India	213,440

Source: William T. Kurian, *The New Book of World Rankings* (New York, 1991), 68.

TABLE 4.4   GROSS NATIONAL PRODUCT PER CAPITA—
A NATIONAL COMPARISON, 1986

Rank	Country	GNP per Capita ($ million)
	Top 10	
1.	Bermuda	20,420
2.	Switzerland	17,840
3.	United States	17,500
4.	Luxembourg	15,920
5.	Norway	15,480
6.	Brunei	15,400
7.	United Arab Emirates	14,410
8.	Canada	14,100
9.	Kuwait	13,890
10.	Iceland	13,370

Source: Kurian, *New Book of Rankings*, 70.

TABLE 4.5   NEW HOUSING STARTS AND MOBILE
HOMES SHIPPED, 1945–1990

(in thousands)

Year	Number of Units Started	Year	Mobile Homes Shipped
1945	326	1965	216
1950	1,952	1970	401
1955	1,646	1975	213
1960	1,296	1980	222
1965	1,510	1983	296
1970	1,469	1984	295
1975	1,171	1985	284
1980	1,313	1986	244
1982	1,072	1987	233
1983	1,712	1988	218
1984	1,756	1989	198
1985	1,745	1990	188
1986	1,807	. . .	. . .
1987	1,623	. . .	. . .
1988	1,488	. . .	. . .
1989	1,376	. . .	. . .
1990	1,193	. . .	. . .

Source: Otto Johnson, *Information Please Almanac, Atlas and Yearbook, 1992* (Boston, 1991), 46.

TABLE 4.6   EXPENDITURES FOR NEW PLANTS AND
EQUIPMENT[a], 1950–1990

(in billions of dollars)

Year	Manufacturing	Transportation[b]	Total Nonmanufacturing	Total
1950	7.73	2.87	18.08	25.81
1955	12.50	3.10	24.58	37.08
1960	16.36	3.54	32.63	48.99
1965	25.41	5.66	45.39	70.79
1970	36.99	7.17	69.16	106.15
1975	53.66	9.95	108.95	162.60
1980	112.60	13.56	205.48	318.08
1984	139.61	13.44	278.77	418.38
1985	152.88	14.57	302.05	454.93
1986	137.95	15.05	309.16	447.11
1987	141.06	15.07	320.45	461.51
1988	163.45	16.63	344.77	508.22
1989	183.80	18.84	380.13	563.93
1990	192.78	21.59	399.52	592.31

[a] Data exclude agriculture. [b] Transportation is included in total nonmanufacturing.
Source: Information Please Almanac, 1992, 46.

TABLE 4.7 BUSINESS FORMATIONS AND FAILURES, 1950–1990

Year or Month	Index of Net Business Formation (1967 = 100)	New Business Incorporations (number)	Business Failure Rate[a]	Business Failures — Number of Failures			Business Failures — Amount of Current Liabilities (millions of dollars)		
				Total	Under $100,000	$100,000 and Over	Total	Under $100,000	$100,000 and Over
1950	87.7	93,092	34.3	9,162	8,746	416	248.3	151.2	97.1
1951	86.7	83,778	30.7	8,058	7,626	432	259.5	131.6	128.0
1952	90.8	92,946	28.7	7,611	7,081	530	283.3	131.9	151.4
1953	89.7	102,706	33.2	8,862	8,075	787	394.2	167.5	226.6
1954	88.8	117,411	42.0	11,086	10,226	860	462.6	211.4	251.2
1955	96.6	139,915	41.6	10,969	10,113	856	449.4	206.4	243.0
1956	94.6	141,163	48.0	12,686	11,615	1,071	562.7	239.8	322.9
1957	90.3	137,112	51.7	13,739	12,547	1,192	615.3	267.1	348.2
1958	90.2	150,781	55.9	14,964	13,499	1,465	728.3	297.6	430.7
1959	97.9	193,067	51.8	14,053	12,707	1,346	692.8	278.9	413.9
1960	94.5	182,713	57.0	15,445	13,650	1,795	938.6	327.2	611.4
1961	90.8	181,535	64.4	17,075	15,006	2,069	1,090.1	370.1	720.0
1962	92.6	182,057	60.8	15,782	13,772	2,010	1,213.6	346.5	867.1
1963	94.4	186,404	56.3	14,374	12,192	2,182	1,352.6	321.0	1,031.6
1964	98.2	197,724	53.2	13,501	11,346	2,155	1,329.2	313.6	1,015.6
1965	99.8	203,897	53.3	13,514	11,340	2,174	1,321.7	321.7	1,000.0
1966	99.3	200,010	51.6	13,061	10,833	2,228	1,385.7	321.5	1,064.1
1967	100.0	206,569	49.0	12,364	10,144	2,220	1,265.2	297.9	967.3
1968	108.3	233,635	38.6	9,636	7,829	1,807	941.0	241.1	699.9
1969	115.8	274,267	37.3	9,154	7,192	1,962	1,142.1	231.3	910.8
1970	108.8	264,209	43.8	10,748	8,019	2,729	1,887.8	269.3	1,618.4
1971	111.1	287,577	41.7	10,326	7,611	2,715	1,916.9	271.3	1,645.6
1972	119.3	316,601	38.3	9,566	7,040	2,526	2,000.2	258.8	1,741.5
1973	119.1	329,358	36.4	9,345	6,627	2,718	2,298.6	235.6	2,063.0
1974	113.2	319,149	38.4	9,915	6,733	3,182	3,053.1	256.9	2,796.3
1975	109.9	326,345	42.6	11,432	7,504	3,928	4,380.2	298.6	4,081.6
1976	120.4	375,766	34.8	9,628	6,176	3,452	3,011.3	257.8	2,753.4
1977	130.8	436,170	28.4	7,919	4,861	3,058	3,095.3	208.3	2,887.0
1978	138.1	478,019	23.9	6,619	3,712	2,907	2,656.0	164.7	2,491.3
1979	138.3	524,565	27.8	7,564	3,930	3,634	2,667.4	179.9	2,487.5
1980	129.9	533,520	42.1	11,742	5,682	6,060	4,635.1	272.5	4,362.6
1981	124.8	581,242	61.3	16,794	8,233	8,561	6,955.2	405.8	6,549.3
1982	116.4	566,942	89.0	24,908	11,509	13,399	15,610.8	541.7	15,069.1
1983	117.5	600,400	110.0	31,334	15,509	15,825	16,072.9	635.1	15,437.8
1984	121.3	634,991	107.0	52,078	19,618	32,460	29,268.6	409.8	28,858.8
1985	120.9	662,047	115.0	57,253	36,539	20,714	36,937.4	423.9	36,513.5
1986	120.4	702,738	120.0	61,616	38,908	22,708	44,724.0	838.3	43,885.7
1987	121.2	685,572	102.0	61,111	38,949	22,162	34,723.8	746.0	33,977.8
1988	124.1	685,095	98.0	57,097	38,300	18,797	39,573.0	686.9	38,886.1
1989	124.8	676,565	65.0	50,361	33,312	17,049	42,328.8	670.5	41,658.2
1990	120.7	646,107	75.0	60,508	40,530	19,978	59,836.5	730.0	59,106.5

[a] Failure per 10,000 listed enterprises.
Source: Council of Economic Advisers, *Economic Report of the President 1992* (Washington, D.C., 1992), 404.

TABLE 4.8 BUSINESS CYCLE EXPANSIONS AND CONTRACTIONS

Business Cycle Reference Dates		Duration in Months			
Trough	Peak	Contraction (trough from previous peak)	Expansion (trough to peak)	Cycle — Trough from Previous Trough	Cycle — Peak from Previous Peak
October 1945	November 1948	8	37	88	45
October 1949	July 1953	11	**45**	48	**56**
May 1954	August 1957	**10**	39	**55**	49
April 1958	April 1960	8	24	47	32
February 1961	December 1969	10	**106**	34	**116**
November 1970	November 1973	**11**	36	**117**	47
March 1975	January 1980	16	58	52	74
July 1980	July 1981	6	12	64	18
November 1982	July 1990	16	92	28	108

Note: Figures printed in bold are the wartime expansions (World War II, Korean War, and Vietnam War), the postwar contractions, and the full cycles that include the wartime expansions.
Source: Ronald Alsop, ed., *The Wall Street Journal Almanac, 1998* (New York, 1997), 156.

TABLE 4.9 CORPORATE PROFITS AND CAPITAL ADJUSTMENTS, 1959–1990

(billions of dollars; quarterly data at seasonally adjusted annual rates)

Year or Quarter	Corporate Profits with Inventory Valuation and Capital Consumption Adjustments	Corporate Profits Tax Liability	Corporate Profits After Tax with Inventory Valuation and Capital Consumption Adjustments		Undistributed Profits with Inventory Valuation and Capital Consumption Adjustments
			Total	Dividends	
1959	52.3	23.6	28.6	12.7	15.9
1960	50.7	22.7	28.0	13.4	14.6
1961	51.6	22.8	28.8	14.0	14.8
1962	59.6	24.0	35.6	15.0	20.6
1963	65.1	26.2	38.9	16.1	22.8
1964	72.1	28.0	44.1	18.0	26.1
1965	82.9	30.9	52.0	20.2	31.8
1966	88.6	33.7	54.9	20.9	34.0
1967	86.0	32.7	53.3	22.1	31.2
1968	92.6	39.4	53.2	24.6	28.6
1969	89.6	39.7	49.9	25.2	24.7
1970	77.5	34.4	43.1	23.7	19.4
1971	90.3	37.7	52.6	23.7	28.8
1972	103.2	41.9	61.3	25.8	35.5
1973	116.4	49.3	67.1	28.1	39.0
1974	104.5	51.8	52.7	30.4	22.3
1975	121.9	50.9	71.0	30.1	40.9
1976	147.1	64.2	82.8	35.6	47.2
1977	175.7	73.0	102.6	40.7	61.9
1978	199.7	83.5	116.2	45.9	70.3
1979	202.5	88.0	114.5	52.4	62.1
1980	177.7	84.8	92.9	59.0	33.9
1981	182.0	81.1	100.9	69.2	31.7
1982	151.5	63.1	88.4	70.0	18.4
1983	212.7	77.2	135.4	81.2	54.2
1984	264.2	94.0	170.2	82.7	87.5
1985	280.8	96.5	184.2	92.4	91.9
1986	271.6	106.5	165.1	109.8	55.4
1987	319.8	127.1	192.8	106.2	86.5
1988	365.0	137.0	228.0	115.3	112.6
1989	351.7	138.0	213.7	127.9	85.8
1990	319.0	135.3	183.6	133.7	49.9

Source: Council of Advisors, *Economic Report of the President, 1992,* 397.

TABLE 4.10 RECORDED MERGERS IN MANUFACTURING AND MINING, 1946–1990

Year	Mergers
1946	419
1948	223
1950	219
1953	295
1955	683
1958	589
1960	844
1963	861
1965	1,008
1968	2,407
1970	1,315
1973	1,919
1976	1,081
1978	1,279
1980	1,889
1983	2,533
1985	3,489
1986	4,463
1987	4,024
1988	4,233
1989	4,167
1990	4,168

Source: George T. Kurian, *Datapedia of the United States 1790–2000* (Lanham, Md., 1994), 371.

TABLE 4.11 LARGEST CORPORATE MERGERS OR ACQUISITIONS IN THE UNITED STATES

Company	Acquirer	Dollars (in billions)	Year
RJR Nabisco	Kohlberg Kravis Roberts	24.9	1988
Warner Communications	Time	13.9	1989
Gulf Oil	Chevron	13.3	1984
Kraft	Philip Morris	11.5	1988
Squibb	Bristol-Myers	11.5	1989
Getty Oil	Texaco	10.1	1984
Conoco	DuPont	8.0	1981
Standard Oil	British Petroleum	7.9[a]	1987
Federated Dept. Stores	Campeau	7.4	1988
MCA	Matsushita	6.5	1990
Marathon Oil	U.S. Steel	6.5	1981
Contel	GTE	6.2	1990
Beatrice	Kohlberg Kravis Roberts	6.2	1986
RCA	General Electric	6.2	1986
Superior Oil	Mobil Oil	5.7	1984
Pillsbury	Grand Metropolitan	5.7	1988
General Foods	Philip Morris	5.6	1986
Safeway Stores	Kohlberg Kravis Roberts	5.3	1986
Farmers Group	B.A.T. Industries	5.2	1988
Southern Pacific	Santa Fe Railroad	5.2	1983
Southland	J.T. Acquisition	5.1	1987
Hughes Aircraft	General Motors	5.0	1985
Nabisco	R.J. Reynolds	4.9	1985
Signal Cos.	Allied Corp.	4.9	1986
Sperry	Burroughs	4.8	1986
Connecticut General	INA	4.3	1981
Borg-Warner	AV Holdings	4.2	1987
Texasgulf	Elf Aquitaine	4.2	1981
Cities Service	Occidental Petroleum	4.0	1982
Dome Petroleum	Amoco	3.8	1987
R.H. Macy	various investors	3.7	1986
American Hospital	Baxter Travenol	3.7	1986
Owens-Illinois	Kohlberg Kravis Roberts	3.6	1987
Belridge Oil	Shell Oil	3.6	1979
NWA	Checchi Group	3.6	1988
Allied Stores	Campeau	3.5	1986

(continued)

TABLE 4.11 (continued)

Company	Acquirer	Dollars (in billions)	Year
Fort Howard Paper	Morgan Stanley Group	3.5	1988
ABC Broadcasting	Capital Cities Comm.	3.5	1985
Columbia Pictures	Sony	3.4	1989
Viacom	National Amusements	3.4	1987
McCaw Cellular	LIN Broadcasting	3.3	1989
Panhandle Eastern	Texas Eastern	3.2	1989
Chesebrough-Pond's	Unilever N.V.	3.1	1987
MidCon	Occidental Petroleum	3.0	1986
American Medical Intl.	IMA Holdings	3.0	1989
Texas Oil and Gas	USX Corp.	3.0	1986
Ernhart	Black & Decker	2.8	1989
Camation	Nestle	2.8	1984
Celanese	American Hoechst	2.7	1987
Esmark	Beatrice Foods	2.7	1984
G.D. Searie	Monsanto	2.7	1986
Continental Group	Kiewit-Murdock	2.7	1984
St. Joe Minerals	Fluor	2.6	1981
Electronic Data Systems	General Motors	2.6	1984
Firestone Tire	Bridgestone	2.6	1988
Macmillan	Maxwell Comm.	2.6	1988
Associated-Dry Goods	May Dept. Stores	2.5	1986

a For the 45% of Standard Oil that British Petroleum did not already own.
Source: Mark S. Hoffman, ed., *The World Almanac and Book of Facts 1992* (New York, 1991), 148.

TABLE 4.12   LARGEST AMERICAN BUSINESSES, 1990

(in millions of dollars)

50 Largest Industrial Corporations		
	Sales	Assets
General Motors	126,017.0	180,236.5
Exxon	105,885.0	87,707.0
Ford Motor	98,274.7	173,662.7
Int'l Business Machines	69,018.0	87,568.0
Mobil	58,770.0	41,665.0
General Electric	58,414.0	153,884.0
Philip Morris	44,323.0	46,569.0
Texaco	41,235.0	25,975.0
E.I. Du Pont De Nemours	39,839.0	38,128.0
Chevron	39,262.0	35,089.0
Chrysler	30,868.0	46,374.0
Amoco	28,277.0	32,209.0
Boeing	27,595.0	14,591.0
Shell Oil	24,423.0	28,496.0
Procter & Gamble	24,376.0	18,487.0
Occidental Petroleum	21,947.0	19,743.0
United Technologies	21,783.2	15,918.3
Dow Chemical	20,005.0	23,953.0
USX	19,462.0	17,268.0
Eastman Kodak	19,075.0	24,125.0
Atlantic Richfield	18,819.0	23,864.0
Xerox	18,382.0	31,495.0
Pepsico	17,802.7	17,143.4
McDonnell Douglas	16,351.0	14,965.0
Conagra	15,517.7	4,804.2
Tenneco	14,893.0	19,034.0
Phillips Petroleum	14,032.0	12,130.0
RJR Nabisco Holdings	13,879.0	32,915.0
Hewlett-Packard	13,233.0	11,395.0
Digital Equipment	13,084.5	11,654.8
Minnesota Mining & Mfg.	13,021.0	11,079.0
International Paper	12,960.0	13,669.0
Westinghouse Electric	12,915.0	22,033.0
Georgia-Pacific	12,665.0	12,060.0
Rockwell International	12,442.5	9,738.1
Allied-Signal	12,396.0	10,456.0
Sun	11,909.0	9,000.0
Sara Lee	11,652.0	7,636.4
Caterpillar	11,540.0	11,951.0
Goodyear Tire & Rubber	11,453.1	8,963.6
Johnson & Johnson	11,232.0	9,506.0
Motorola	10,885.0	8,742.0
Aluminum Co. of America	10,865.1	11,413.2
Anheuser-Busch	10,750.6	9,634.3
Unocal	10,740.0	9,762.0
Bristol-Myers Squibb	10,509.0	9,215.0
Coca-Cola	10,406.3	9,278.2
General Dynamics	10,182.0	6,573.0
Unisys	10,111.3	10,288.6
Lockheed	9,977.0	6,860.0

25 Largest Retailing Companies		
	Sales	Assets
Sears Roebuck	55,971.7	96,252.8
Wal-Mart Stores	32,601.6	11,388.9
Kmart	32,080.0	13,899.0
American Stores	22,155.5	7,244.7
Kroger	20,261.0	4,118.5
J.C. Penney	17,410.0	12,325.0
Safeway	14,873.6	4,739.1
Dayton Hudson	14,739.0	8,524.0
Great Atlantic & Pacific Tea	11,164.2	2,831.6
May Department Stores	11,027.0	8,295.0
Woolworth	9,789.0	4,305.0
Winn-Dixie	9,744.5	1,732.7
Melville	8,686.8	3,662.2
Albertson's	8,218.6	2,013.5
Southland	8,037.1	2,799.0
R.H. Macy	7,266.8	6,483.3
McDonald's	6,639.6	10,667.5
Supermarkets General Holdings	6,126.0	2,438.8
Walgreen	6,063.0	1,913.6
Publix Super Markets	5,820.7	1,475.7
Food Lion	5,584.5	1,559.5
Toys "R" Us	5,521.2	3,582.4
Price	5,428.8	1,210.1
Vons	5,333.9	1,712.8
The Limited	5,253.5	2,871.9

Source: Fortune Magazine, reproduced in Johnson, *Information Please Almanac, 1992,* 48–49.

Automobiles led the charge into the postwar economy and consumer culture. Shown here is the 1950 Studebaker. (From the Collection of Studebaker National Museum, South Bend, Indiana)

TABLE 4.13   TOP 50 FRANCHISES, 1989

Rank	Franchise	Business	Franchise Fees (in dollars)	Number of Franchises
1.	McDonald's	Fast food restaurants	22,500	8,101
2.	Century 21 Real Estate	Real estate brokers	11,000–25,000	7,133
3.	Kentucky Fried Chicken	Fast food restaurants	20,000	5,707
4.	Dairy Queen	Ice cream stores	30,000	5,181
5.	Burger King, Inc.	Fast food restaurants	40,000	5,083
6.	H & R Block	Tax preparation	600–1,200	4,892
7.	Jazzercise	Dance fitness centers	500	4,100
8.	Servicemaster	Commercial cleaning services	6,000–17,000	3,893
9.	Domino's Pizza	Pizza delivery and takeout	1,320–3,250	3,654
10.	Subway Sandwiches & Salads	Fast food restaurants	7,500	3,586
11.	Baskin-Robbins Ice Cream	Ice cream stores	N.A.	3,398
12.	Budget Rent A Car	Car rental	15,000	3,171
13.	7-Eleven Store	Convenience stores	varies	3,103
14.	Electronic Realty Associates	Real estate brokers	16,900	3,001
15.	Wendy's	Fast food restaurants	25,000	2,560
16.	Radio Shack	Electronics retailers	15,000–40,000	2,246
17.	Diet Center	Weight loss centers	30,000	2,236
18.	Chem-Dry	Carpet and upholstery cleaning	7,600–7,900	2,134
19.	Hardee's Food Systems	Fast food restaurants	15,000	2,106
20.	Arby's	Fast food restaurants	25,000–37,500	1,931
21.	Little Caesars Pizza	Pizza takeout	15,000	1,880
22.	Dunkin' Donuts	Donut shops	30,000–40,000	1,841
23.	Realty World	Real estate brokers	13,000–15,000	1,826
24.	RE/MAX	Real estate brokers	10,000–20,000	1,617
25.	Dollar Rent A Car	Car rental	N.A.	1,600+
26.	Midas Muffler & Brake Shops	Auto maintenance centers	10,000	1,590
27.	Rainbow International	Carpet dyeing and cleaning	15,000	1,559
28.	Jani-King International	Janitorial services	6,500+	1,509
29.	Holiday Inns	Hotel/motel	varies	1,410
30.	Fantastic Sam's	Discount hair cutters	25,000	1,321
31.	TCBY Yogurt	Frozen yogurt stores	20,000	1,321
32.	American Intl. Rent-a-Car	Car rentals and leasing	25,000+	1,304
33.	Packy the Shipper	Packaging/shipping centers	395	1,300
34.	Western Auto	Auto supplies, bicycles, lawn and garden	0	1,253
35.	PIP Printing	Business printing	40,000	1,152

(continued)

TABLE 4.13   (continued)

Rank	Franchise	Business	Franchise Fees (in dollars)	Number of Franchises
36.	Ben Franklin Stores, Inc.	Variety/craft stores	24,000	1,104
37.	Jiffy Lube	Auto maintenance	35,000	1,057
38.	Quality Inns International	Hotel/motel	35,000	1,040
39.	Taco Bell	Mexican fast food restaurants	35,000	1,035
40.	Kwik-Kopy Printing Centers	Printing services	22,000	1,005
41.	Coast to Coast Total Hardware	Hardware retailers	5,000	933
42.	Decorating Den	Home decorating services	7,000–19,000	925
43.	Minuteman Press International	Printing centers	27,500	909
44.	Sonic Drive In Restaurants	Fast food drive-in restaurants	15,000	908
45.	European Body Wrap	Body wrapping	1,000	903
46.	Nutri-System	Weight loss centers	13,000	890
47.	Mail Boxes Etc.	Postal services	19,500	867
48.	One Hour Martinizing	Dry cleaners	20,000	856
49.	Days Inn of America Franchising, Inc.	Hotel/motel	varies	853
50.	The Medicine Shoppe	Drug stores	18,000	822

Source: John W. Wright, *The Universal Almanac 1991* (New York, 1990), 231.

TABLE 4.14   TEN FASTEST-GROWING INDUSTRIES, 1990
(billions of constant 1987 dollars)

Industry	Change in Value of Shipments
Computers and peripherals	3.0
Radio communication equipment	2.2
Misc. plastics products, except bottles	1.9
Commercial printing	1.5
Aircraft engines and engine parts	1.3
Pharmaceutical preparations	1.2
Poultry slaughtering and processing	1.1
Aircraft	1.1
Surgical appliances and supplies	0.9
Surgical and medical instruments	0.9

Source: Wright, *Universal Almanac, 1991,* 228.

The Stock Market

While the form and volume of the stock market changed drastically in the last quarter of the 20th century, its original objectives remained in force. The market was a place for financing trade and business expansion through the issuance and sale of stocks and bonds. Purchase of a stock made the holder part owner of a business and entitled to a share of whatever profit, if any, that company produced. It probably was inevitable that the buying and selling of securities would become a special skill and business of its own, as opposed to an investor's simply wishing to become part owner of a profitable company. The stock market became synonymous with speculation, creative buying and selling; the trade itself became the end product. The focus of American investment activity was New York City, and in New York all paths led to Wall Street, center of the exchange system. The oldest and largest such establishment was the New York Stock Exchange.

Methods for measuring stock market activity also became important instruments for evaluating economic health of the nation. Established in 1957, the Standard & Poor's 500 was a market-weighted index containing 500 stocks chosen for various features: market size, liquidity, representation of a group. Standard & Poor's multiplied stock price by the number of shares to determine that weight in the index corresponded with its market value. A far more familiar measurement of the market came in the Dow Jones Industrial Average. Dating to the 1890s, this index was composed of 30 blue-chip stocks (issued by sound, prestigious firms) selected by editors of the *Wall Street Journal* newspaper. During this period, a day's or year's performance of the stock market usually depended on whether the Dow was up or down and by what numbers.

The Dow certainly had a tradition of going either way. Fluctuation long had marked market behavior, but beginning with a low point in the great crash of 1929–33, the general trend of the Dow Industrial Average was upward. The incline was gradual and unsteady until the 1980s. It took the Dow some 75 years to reach 1,000. The market reached that point in 1972. It then fell back, hovered and stagnated and did not reach 1,000 as a yearly average until 1983. The second thousand came quickly. The Dow reached 2,000 in 1987 and seemed poised to go to 3,000 before year's end. Then, investors panicked. Troubled by high interest rates, a cheapened dollar, and a soaring trade deficit, they rushed into a sell-off more substantial than the great crash of 1929. The market lost more than 22 percent of its value in one day—October, 19, 1987. Recovery, however, began almost immediately. By 1989 the market had regained its losses; in October 1990 the Dow came within one quarter-point of reaching 3,000. In the decade between 1981 and 1990, the Dow Jones Industrial Average (and generally the New York Stock Market) gained more than 1,700 points, a larger increase in current dollars than in the entire previous history—nearly 100 years—of the Dow index. Although the stock market continued to stand as one barometer of the power and health of the economy, the lack of a devastating fallout from the crash of 1987 suggested that size, complexity, and built-in safeguards had equipped the economic system with resiliency to withstand the sort of sudden shock that the market could produce.

TABLE 4.15   SIGNIFICANT HISTORICAL DATES, NEW YORK STOCK EXCHANGE, 1952–1990

Date	Year	Event
Sep. 29	1952	Trading hours changed. Weekdays, 10 A.M.–3:30 P.M. No Saturdays.
Jun. 4	1953	First member corporation—Woodcock, Hess & Co.
Jul. 14	1966	New NYSE Composite Index inaugurated.
Dec. 20	1966	Transmission of trade and quote data from Floor fully automated.
Mar. 26	1970	Public ownership of member firms approved.
Feb. 18	1971	New York Stock Exchange incorporated.
Jul. 27	1971	First member organization listed—Merrill Lynch.
Jul. 13	1972	Board of Directors, with 10 public members, replaced Board of Governors.
May 11	1973	Depository Trust Company succeeded Central Certificate Service.
Oct. 1	1974	Trading hours extended to 4 P.M.
Apr. 30	1975	Fixed commission system abolished.
Jun. 16	1975	Full consolidated tape introduced.
Jan. 19	1976	New high-speed data line began to transmit market data at up to 36,000 characters a minute.
Mar. 1	1976	Designated Order Turnaround (Dot) System inaugurated.
Mar. 4	1976	Alternative listing standards adopted to facilitate listing of major foreign corporations.
May 24	1976	Specialists began handling odd lots in their stocks.
Feb. 3	1977	Foreign broker/dealers permitted to obtain membership.
Apr. 17	1978	Intermarket Trading System (ITS) inaugurated.
Aug. 7	1980	New York Futures Exchange (NYFE) opened.
May 17	1982	Trading started through experimental linkage between the NASD and Intermarket Trading System (ITS) operated by NYSE and six other exchanges.
Aug. 18	1982	First 100 million share day (132,681,120 shares).
Sep. 23	1983	Trading started in options on NYSE Composite Index.
Nov. 6	1984	NYSE opened on presidential election day for first time ever.
Nov. 16	1984	NYSE launched SuperDot 250.
Mar. 28	1985	Ronald Reagan became first U.S. president to visit the NYSE while in office.
Jun. 3	1985	NYSE began to trade in options on three OTC stocks.
Sep. 30	1985	Trading hours changed to 9:30 A.M.–4 P.M.
Oct. 21	1985	NYSE began to trade in options on two listed stocks.
Jun. 5	1986	Board of Directors expanded to 24 outside directors: 12 public members, and 12 industry members.
Sep. 21	1987	Highest price paid for a membership ($1,150,000).
Oct. 19	1987	Largest point drop in Dow Jones Industrial Average: 508 points.
Oct. 20	1987	Highest volume day: 608,148,710 shares.
Oct. 19	1988	The SEC approved a series of initiatives by the NYSE and the Chicago Mercantile Exchange to coordinate procedures between the equities and futures markets, including coordinated circuit breakers; a joint effort against front-running; interexchange communications; and shared audit trail and surveillance information.
Nov. 7	1988	The NYSE opened an office in London to assist European companies in gaining access to the U.S. capital markets and listing on the NYSE.
Jun. 12	1990	The NYSE's Market Volatility and Investor Confidence Panel released the results of a six-month study recommending initiatives aimed at reducing market volatility and enhancing investor confidence.
Aug. 6	1990	The NYSE implemented a new rule requiring Trade Date + 1 (T+1) completion of transactions effected on the NYSE.

Source: New York Stock Exchange, *Fact Book for the Year 1993* (New York, 1994), 98–99.

TABLE 4.16   NEW YORK STOCK EXCHANGE SHARES TRADED, 1946–1990

Year	Total Volume (millions)	Percent Turnover	Daily Average (thousands)	High (thousands)	Low (thousands)
1946	363.7	22	1,370	3,624	487
1950	524.8	23	1,980	4,859	1,061
1955	649.6	19	2,578	7,717	1,230
1960	766.7	12	3,042	5,303	1,894
1965	1,556.3	16	6,179	11,434	3,028
1970	2,937.4	19	11,564	21,345	6,660
1975	4,693.4	21	18,551	35,158	8,670
1980	11,352.3	36	44,871	84,297	16,132
1985	27,510.7	54	109,169	181,027	62,055
1986	35,680.0	64	141,028	244,293	48,865
1987	47,801.3	73	188,938	608,149	86,366
1988	40,849.3	55	161,461	343,949	72,088
1989	41,698.5	52	165,470	416,396	68,869
1990	39,664.5	46	156,777	292,364	56,853

Source: NYSE, *Fact Book, 1993,* 100–101.

TABLE 4.17   DOW JONES INDUSTRIAL AVERAGE— HIGHS AND LOWS, 1961–1990

High			Low	
Date	DJIA	Year	Date	DJIA
Dec. 13	734.91	1961	Jan. 3	610.25
Jan. 3	726.01	1962	Jun. 26	535.76
Dec. 18	767.21	1963	Jan. 2	646.79
Nov. 18	891.71	1964	Jan. 2	766.08
Dec. 31	969.26	1965	Jun. 28	840.59
Feb. 9	995.15	1966	Oct. 7	744.32
Sep. 25	943.08	1967	Jan. 3	786.41
Dec. 3	985.21	1968	Mar. 21	825.13
May 14	968.85	1969	Dec. 17	769.93
Dec. 29	842.00	1970	May 6	631.16
Apr. 28	950.82	1971	Nov. 23	797.97
Dec. 11	1036.27	1972	Jan. 26	889.15
Jan. 11	1051.70	1973	Dec. 5	788.31
Mar. 13	891.66	1974	Dec. 6	577.60
Jul. 15	881.81	1975	Jan. 2	632.04
Sep. 21	1014.79	1976	Jan. 2	858.71
Jan. 3	999.75	1977	Nov. 2	800.85
Sep. 8	907.74	1978	Feb. 28	742.12
Oct. 5	897.61	1979	Nov. 7	796.67
Nov. 20	1000.17	1980	Apr. 21	759.13
Apr. 27	1024.05	1981	Sep. 25	824.01
Dec. 27	1070.55	1982	Aug. 12	776.92
Nov. 29	1287.20	1983	Jan. 3	1027.04
Jan. 6	1286.64	1984	Jul. 24	1086.57
Dec. 16	1553.10	1985	Jan. 4	1184.96
Dec. 2	1955.57	1986	Jan. 22	1502.29
Aug. 25	2722.42	1987	Oct. 19	1738.74
Oct. 21	2183.50	1988	Jan. 20	1879.14
Oct. 9	2791.41	1989	Jan. 3	2144.64
Jul. 16	2999.75	1990	Oct. 11	2365.10

Source: World Almanac, 1992, 143.

TABLE 4.18 COMMON STOCK PRICES AND YIELDS, 1952–1990

| Year or Month | Common Stock Prices | | | | | | | Common Stock Yields (percent) | |
| | New York Stock Exchange Indexes (Dec. 31, 1965 = 50) | | | | | Dow Jones Industrial Average | Standard & Poor's Composite Index (1941–43 = 10) | Dividend-Price Ratio | Earnings-Price Ratio |
	Composite	Industrial	Transportation	Utility	Finance				
1952	13.81	. . .	. . .	. . .	. . .	270.76	24.50	5.80	9.47
1953	13.67	. . .	. . .	. . .	. . .	275.97	24.73	5.80	10.26
1954	16.19	. . .	. . .	. . .	. . .	333.94	29.69	4.95	8.57
1955	21.54	. . .	. . .	. . .	. . .	442.72	40.49	4.08	7.95
1956	24.40	. . .	. . .	. . .	. . .	493.01	46.62	4.09	7.55
1957	23.67	. . .	. . .	. . .	. . .	475.71	44.38	4.35	7.89
1958	24.56	. . .	. . .	. . .	. . .	491.66	46.24	3.97	6.23
1959	30.73	. . .	. . .	. . .	. . .	632.12	57.38	3.23	5.78
1960	30.01	. . .	. . .	. . .	. . .	618.04	55.85	3.47	5.90
1961	35.37	. . .	. . .	. . .	. . .	691.55	66.27	2.98	4.62
1962	33.49	. . .	. . .	. . .	. . .	639.76	62.38	3.37	5.82
1963	37.51	. . .	. . .	. . .	. . .	714.81	69.87	3.17	5.50
1964	43.76	. . .	. . .	. . .	. . .	834.05	81.37	3.01	5.32
1965	47.39	. . .	. . .	. . .	. . .	910.88	88.17	3.00	5.59
1966	46.15	46.18	50.26	45.41	44.45	873.60	85.26	3.40	6.63
1967	50.77	51.97	53.51	45.43	49.82	879.12	91.93	3.20	5.73
1968	55.37	58.00	50.58	44.19	65.85	906.00	98.70	3.07	5.67
1969	54.67	57.44	46.96	42.80	70.49	876.72	97.84	3.24	6.08
1970	45.72	48.03	32.14	37.24	60.00	753.19	83.22	3.83	6.45
1971	54.22	57.92	44.35	39.53	70.38	884.76	98.29	3.14	5.41
1972	60.29	65.73	50.17	38.48	78.35	950.71	109.20	2.84	5.50
1973	57.42	63.08	37.74	37.69	70.12	923.88	107.43	3.06	7.12
1974	43.84	48.08	31.89	29.79	49.67	759.37	82.85	4.47	11.59
1975	45.73	50.52	31.10	31.50	47.14	802.49	86.16	4.31	9.15
1976	54.46	60.44	39.57	36.97	52.94	974.92	102.01	3.77	8.90
1977	53.69	57.86	41.09	40.92	55.25	894.63	98.20	4.62	10.79
1978	53.70	58.23	43.50	39.22	56.65	820.23	96.02	5.28	12.03
1979	58.32	64.76	47.34	38.20	61.42	844.40	103.01	5.47	13.46
1980	68.10	78.70	60.61	37.35	64.25	891.41	118.78	5.26	12.66
1981	74.02	85.44	72.61	38.91	73.52	932.92	128.05	5.20	11.96
1982	68.93	78.18	60.41	39.75	71.99	884.36	119.71	5.81	11.60
1983	92.63	107.45	89.36	47.00	95.34	1,190.34	160.41	4.40	8.03
1984	92.46	108.01	85.63	46.44	89.28	1,178.48	160.46	4.64	10.02
1985	108.09	123.79	104.11	56.75	114.21	1,328.23	186.84	4.25	8.12
1986	136.00	155.85	119.87	71.36	147.20	1,792.76	236.34	3.49	6.09
1987	161.70	195.31	140.39	74.30	146.48	2,275.99	286.83	3.08	5.48
1988	149.91	180.95	134.12	71.77	127.26	2,060.82	265.79	3.64	8.01
1989	180.02	216.23	175.28	87.43	151.88	2,508.91	322.84	3.45	7.41
1990	183.46	225.78	158.62	90.60	133.26	2,678.94	334.59	3.61	6.47

Source: Council of Advisors, *Economic Report of the President, 1992,* 403.

TABLE 4.19 NEW YORK STOCK EXCHANGE MEMBERSHIP PRICES, 1945–1990

Year	High ($)	Low ($)
1945	95,000	49,000
1950	54,000	46,000
1955	90,000	80,000
1960	162,000	135,000
1965	250,000	190,000
1970	320,000	130,000
1971	300,000	145,000
1972	250,000	150,000
1973	190,000	72,000
1974	105,000	65,000
1975	138,000	55,000
1976	104,000	40,000
1977	95,000	35,000
1978	105,000	46,000
1979	210,000	82,000
1980	275,000	175,000
1981	285,000	220,000
1982	340,000	190,000
1983	425,000	310,000
1984	400,000	290,000
1985	480,000	310,000
1986	600,000	455,000
1987	1,150,000	605,000
1988	820,000	580,000
1989	675,000	420,000
1990	430,000	250,000

Source: NYSE, *Fact Book 1991* (New York, 1991), 88.

TABLE 4.20 FIFTY LEADING STOCKS IN MARKET VALUE, 1990

Stock	Market Value (millions of $)	Listed Shares (millions of $)
Exxon Corp.	93,808	1,812.7
International Business Machines	64,591	571.6
General Electric	53,272	926.5
Morris (Philip)	48,403	935.3
Merck & Co.	40,940	455.5
Coca-Cola Co.	38,947	839.8
Bristol-Myers Squibb	35,769	531.9
Wal-Mart Stores	34,578	1,143.1
American Telephone & Telegraph	32,815	1,089.3
Procter & Gamble	31,444	363.0
Johnson & Johnson	27,529	383.7
BellSouth Corporation	26,703	486.6
Amoco Corp.	26,468	505.3
Mobil Corporation	25,401	438.0
Chevron Corp.	24,846	342.1
du Pont de Nemours	24,750	673.5
PepsiCo., Inc.	22,643	862.6
General Motors	21,740	630.2
Bell Atlantic	21,423	399.5
Eli Lilly	20,721	282.9
Atlantic Richfield	20,705	167.7
GTE Corp.	20,600	704.3
Minnesota Mining & Manufacturing	20,238	236.0
Abbott Laboratories	19,692	437.6
American Information Technologies (Ameritech)	19,612	293.8
Pacific Telesis	19,585	432.8
American Home Products	18,695	355.2
Schlumberger Ltd.	17,610	304.3
American International Group	17,284	224.8
Waste Management	16,990	482.0
Southwestern Bell	16,850	300.9
Texaco Inc.	16,595	274.3
Boeing Co.	15,935	349.3
US WEST	15,649	402.6
Eastman Kodak	15,552	373.6
Dow Chemical	15,538	327.1
Royal Dutch Petroleum	15,283	194.1
NYNEX Corp.	14,678	206.4
Anheuser-Busch	14,460	335.3
Disney (Walt)	13,894	136.7
Pfizer Inc.	13,401	165.4
McDonald's Corp.	12,164	417.7
Ford Motor	11,893	444.6
Ralston Purina	11,749	114.6
Kellogg Co.	11,719	154.5
Schering-Plough Corporation	11,598	261.4
Warner-Lambert Company	10,822	160.3
Westinghouse Electric	10,544	370.0
Pacific Gas & Electric	10,537	419.4
BCE Inc.	10,386	304.4
Total	**$1,177,048**	**23,023.9**

Source: *Information Please Almanac, 1992,* 50.

Market Talk: Bulls and Bears

A Bull market is an optimistic, rising market marked with buying based on expectation that prices will increase. To be official the Bull requires a 30 percent increase in the Dow Jones Average after 50 calendar days or a 13 percent increase after 155. The Bear market is pessimistic, a selling market based on expectation of further decline. To be a Bear the Dow must drop 30 percent in 50 calendar days or 13 percent after 145 calendar days.

TABLE 4.21   DEFINED BULL MARKETS, 1947–1990

Beginning		Ending			
Date	DJIA	Date	DJIA	% Gain	Days
5/17/47	163.21	6/15/48	193.16	18.4	395
6/13/49	161.60	1/05/53	293.79	81.8	1,302
9/14/53	255.49	4/06/56	521.05	103.9	935
10/22/57	419.79	1/05/60	685.47	63.3	805
10/25/60	566.05	12/13/61	734.91	29.8	414
6/26/62	535.76	2/09/66	995.15	85.7	1,324
10/07/66	744.32	12/03/68	985.21	32.4	788
5/26/70	631.16	4/28/71	950.82	50.6	337
11/23/71	797.97	1/11/73	1051.70	31.8	415
12/06/74	577.60	9/21/76	1014.79	75.7	655
2/28/78	742.12	9/08/78	907.74	22.3	192
4/21/80	759.13	4/27/81	1024.05	34.9	371
8/12/82	776.92	11/29/83	1287.20	65.7	474
7/24/84	1086.57	8/25/87	2722.42	150.6	1,127
10/19/87	1738.74	7/16/90	2999.75	72.5	1,001
10/11/90	2365.10	. . .	. . .	. . .	. . .

Source: Wall Street Journal Almanac, 1998, 347.

TABLE 4.22   DEFINED BEAR MARKETS, 1946–1990

Beginning		Ending			
Date	DJIA	Date	DJIA	% Decline	Days
5/29/46	212.50	5/17/47	163.21	−23.2	353
6/15/48	193.16	6/13/49	161.60	−16.3	363
1/05/53	293.79	9/14/53	255.49	−13.0	252
4/06/56	521.05	10/22/57	419.79	−19.4	564
1/05/60	685.47	10/25/60	566.05	−17.4	294
12/13/61	734.91	6/26/62	535.76	−27.1	195
2/09/66	995.15	10/07/66	744.32	−25.2	240
12/03/68	985.21	5/26/70	631.16	−35.9	539
4/28/71	950.82	11/23/71	797.97	−16.1	209
1/11/73	1051.70	12/06/74	577.60	−45.1	694
9/21/76	1014.79	2/28/78	742.12	−26.9	525
9/08/78	907.74	4/21/80	759.13	−16.4	591
4/27/81	1024.05	8/12/82	776.92	−24.1	472
11/29/83	1287.20	7/24/84	1086.57	−15.6	238
8/25/87	2722.42	10/19/87	1738.74	−36.1	55
7/16/90	2999.75	10/11/90	2365.10	−21.2	87

Source: Wall Street Journal Almanac, 1998, 348.

Energy

The economy ran on energy, and the more reliable and efficient the energy supply the better the economy ran. The purposes of energy in American society have been to supply heat, generate electricity for numerous activities, and fuel the various kinds of machines necessary for society to function. In the postwar period a new function that appeared—the cooling of buildings, which came to be regarded as important as heating—was in fact an extension of the electrical component. For many years the energy supply had rested largely on three fossil fuels: coal, natural gas, and petroleum. In the 1950s a new source of energy, nuclear power, appeared on the scene and at one point gave signs of bringing an absolute revolution to the system. Concerns about safety and other considerations prevented a major transformation from taking place, but nuclear power did establish its niche, producing a fairly steady 20 percent of electricity each year and powering some of the navy's most modern warships.

With postwar retirement of the steam locomotive and a shift away from coal in modern residential heating, the emphasis in energy usage shifted from coal to natural gas and petroleum. Such a change carried risks that were detectable but not fully appreciated by a consumer society that enjoyed the availability of inexpensive fuel. Although the United States was more than self-sufficient in coal and able to produce most of its needs in natural gas, the domestic oil industry could not nearly keep pace with growing needs of the gluttonous motor-vehicle culture of the 1950s and 1960s. Petroleum, of course, is not a renewable energy; when a supply is extinguished one must find another source or do without. Faced with dwindling domestic reserves, American companies had begun to purchase oil from abroad. Economic and political ramifications of U.S. dependency on foreign petroleum sources did not appear until the 1970s when the Arab-Israeli War of 1973 produced an Arab oil embargo placed on the United States during 1973–74 (angered at American support of Israel, Arab nations refused to sell petroleum to the United States). Later in that same decade the Iranian revolution of 1978–79 halted what had been substantial Iranian oil production, creating a worldwide shortage. These developments provoked two energy crises in the United States, each of which produced a scary but far from devastating shortage of petroleum products; the scarcity was accompanied in both cases by a sharp increase in price.

The nation responded to the crises with various energy-saving activities, including a national speed limit of 55 miles per hour and an industrywide movement to produce smaller, more energy-efficient automobiles. Many power plants shifted back to burning coal, making that fuel again the leading producer of energy in the nation. These efforts and more creative and challenging ventures in quest of energy supplies other than fossil fuel began to lose momentum in the 1980s as the world came to experience an oversupply of petroleum; the price came down—but not nearly to the pre-1973 level—and the Ronald Reagan administration seemed interested only in finding more oil. Even though the nation continued to purchase some 40 percent of its petroleum from foreign sources that, as recent experience had revealed, were less than reliable, there was little mention of an energy problem as the 1990s began and no sense of urgency in taking steps to stave off the next energy crisis.

TABLE 4.23 ENERGY PRODUCTION BY SOURCE, 1949–1990

(in quadrillion Btu[a])

Year	Coal	Natural Gas	Crude Oil	Natural Gas Plant Liquids	Nuclear Electric Power	Hydroelectric Power	Total
1949	11.97	5.38	10.68	0.71	. . .	1.42	30.18
1950	14.06	6.23	11.45	0.82	. . .	1.42	33.98
1951	14.42	7.42	13.04	0.92	. . .	1.42	37.22
1952	12.73	7.96	13.28	1.00	. . .	1.47	36.45
1953	12.28	8.34	13.67	1.06	. . .	1.41	36.77
1954	10.54	8.68	13.43	1.11	. . .	1.36	35.13
1955	12.37	9.34	14.41	1.24	. . .	1.36	38.73
1956	13.31	10.00	15.18	1.28	. . .	1.43	41.21
1957	13.06	10.61	15.18	1.29	. . .	1.52	41.65
1958	10.78	10.94	14.20	1.29	. . .	1.59	38.81
1959	10.78	11.95	14.93	1.38	. . .	1.55	40.60
1960	10.82	12.66	14.93	1.46	0.01	1.61	41.49
1961	10.45	13.10	15.21	1.55	0.02	1.66	41.99
1962	10.90	13.72	15.52	1.59	0.03	1.82	43.58
1963	11.85	14.51	15.97	1.71	0.04	1.77	45.85
1964	12.52	15.30	16.16	1.80	0.04	1.89	47.72
1965	13.06	15.78	16.52	1.88	0.04	2.06	49.34
1966	13.47	17.01	17.56	2.00	0.06	2.06	52.17
1967	13.83	17.94	18.65	2.18	0.09	2.35	55.04
1968	13.61	19.07	19.31	2.32	0.14	2.35	56.81
1969	13.86	20.45	19.56	2.42	0.15	2.65	59.10
1970	14.61	21.67	20.40	2.51	0.24	2.63	62.07
1971	13.19	22.28	20.03	2.54	0.41	2.82	61.29
1972	14.09	22.21	20.04	2.60	0.58	2.86	62.42
1973	13.99	22.19	19.49	2.57	0.91	2.86	62.06
1974	14.07	21.21	18.57	2.47	1.27	3.18	60.84
1975	14.99	19.64	17.73	2.37	1.90	3.15	59.86
1976	15.65	19.48	17.26	2.33	2.11	2.98	59.89
1977	15.76	19.57	17.45	2.33	2.70	2.33	60.22
1978	14.91	19.49	18.43	2.25	3.02	2.94	61.10
1979	17.54	20.08	18.10	2.29	2.78	2.93	63.80
1980	18.60	19.91	18.25	2.25	2.74	2.90	64.76
1981	18.38	19.70	18.15	2.31	3.01	2.76	64.42
1982	18.64	18.32	18.31	2.19	3.13	3.27	63.96
1983	17.25	16.59	18.39	2.18	3.20	3.53	61.28
1984	19.72	18.01	18.85	2.27	3.55	3.35	65.92
1985	19.33	16.98	18.99	2.24	4.15	2.94	64.84
1986	19.51	16.54	18.38	2.15	4.47	3.02	64.30
1987	20.14	17.14	17.67	2.22	4.91	2.59	64.91
1988	20.74	17.60	17.28	2.26	5.66	2.31	66.08
1989	21.35	17.85	16.12	2.16	5.68	2.77	66.13
1990	22.46	18.36	15.57	2.17	6.16	2.93	67.85

[a] *Btu* means "British thermal units," the accepted instrument for measuring energy. One Btu is roughly the energy released in burning one wooden match. The term thus is meaningful only in showing comparisons.
Source: U.S. Department of Energy, *Annual Energy Review,* 1991 (Washington, D.C., 1992), 9.

TABLE 4.24 ENERGY CONSUMPTION BY SOURCE, 1949–1990

(in quadrillion Btu)

Year	Coal	Natural Gas	Petroleum	Nuclear Electric Power	Hydroelectric Power	Total
1949	11.98	5.15	11.88	0	1.45	30.46
1950	12.35	5.97	13.32	0	1.44	33.08
1951	12.55	7.05	14.43	0	1.45	35.47
1952	11.31	7.55	14.96	0	1.50	35.30
1953	11.37	7.91	15.56	0	1.44	36.27
1954	9.71	8.33	15.84	0	1.39	35.27
1955	11.17	9.00	17.25	0	1.41	38.82
1956	11.35	9.61	17.94	0	1.49	40.38
1957	10.82	10.19	17.93	0	1.56	40.48
1958	9.53	10.66	18.53	. . .	1.63	40.35
1959	9.52	11.72	19.32	. . .	1.59	42.14
1960	9.84	12.39	19.92	0.01	1.66	43.80

TABLE 4.24 (continued)

Year	Coal	Natural Gas	Petroleum	Nuclear Electric Power	Hydroelectric Power	Total
1961	9.62	12.93	20.22	0.02	1.68	44.46
1962	9.91	13.73	21.05	0.03	1.82	46.53
1963	10.41	14.40	21.70	0.04	1.77	48.32
1964	10.96	15.29	22.30	0.04	1.91	50.50
1965	11.58	15.77	23.25	0.04	2.06	52.68
1966	12.14	17.00	24.40	0.06	2.07	55.66
1967	11.91	17.94	25.28	0.09	2.34	57.57
1968	12.33	19.21	26.98	0.14	2.34	61.00
1969	12.38	20.68	28.34	0.15	2.66	64.19
1970	12.26	21.79	29.52	0.24	2.65	66.43
1971	11.60	22.47	30.56	0.41	2.86	67.89
1972	12.08	22.70	32.95	0.58	2.94	71.26
1973	12.97	22.51	34.84	0.91	3.01	74.28
1974	12.66	21.73	33.45	1.27	3.31	72.54
1975	12.66	19.95	32.73	1.90	3.22	70.55
1976	13.58	20.35	35.17	2.11	3.07	74.36
1977	13.92	19.93	37.12	2.70	2.51	76.29
1978	13.77	20.00	37.97	3.02	3.14	78.09
1979	15.04	20.67	37.12	2.78	3.14	78.90
1980	15.42	20.39	34.20	2.74	3.12	75.96
1981	15.91	19.93	31.93	3.01	3.11	73.99
1982	15.32	18.51	30.23	3.13	3.57	70.85
1983	15.89	17.36	30.05	3.20	3.90	70.52
1984	17.07	18.51	31.05	3.55	3.76	74.10
1985	17.48	17.83	30.92	4.15	3.36	73.95
1986	17.26	16.71	32.20	4.47	3.39	74.24
1987	18.01	17.74	32.87	4.91	3.07	76.84
1988	18.85	18.55	34.22	5.66	2.64	80.20
1989	18.94	19.38	34.21	5.68	2.88	81.35
1990	19.12	19.30	33.55	6.16	2.95	81.29

Source: Dept. of Energy, *Annual Energy Review, 1991*, 11.

TABLE 4.25 TYPE OF HEATING IN OCCUPIED HEATING UNITS, 1950–1989

(in percent)

Year	Coal	Natural Gas	Liquefied Gas	Distillate Fuel Oil	Kerosene	Electricity	Wood
1950	33.8	26.0	2.3	22.1	. . .	0.6	9.7
1960	12.2	43.1	5.1	32.4	. . .	1.8	4.2
1970	2.9	55.2	6.0	26.0	. . .	7.7	1.3
1973	1.2	55.5	6.4	24.9	. . .	10.4	0.9
1974	1.0	55.7	5.8	23.8	. . .	11.9	0.9
1975	0.8	56.4	5.7	22.5	. . .	12.6	1.2
1976	0.7	55.7	5.7	22.2	. . .	13.7	1.2
1977	0.6	55.2	5.6	20.7	0.6	14.8	1.6
1978	0.5	55.1	5.4	20.3	0.5	15.9	1.4
1979	0.5	55.1	5.3	19.5	0.5	16.9	1.4
1980	0.4	55.4	5.2	18.1	0.5	17.7	1.7
1981	0.4	55.4	5.0	17.0	0.4	18.6	2.3
1983	0.5	55.2	4.6	14.9	0.5	18.5	4.8
1985	0.5	51.3	4.1	14.1	1.2	20.8	7.1
1987	0.4	50.6	4.0	14.0	1.2	22.7	6.0
1989	0.4	50.6	3.9	13.3	1.1	24.6	4.9

Source: Dept. of Energy, *Annual Energy Review, 1991*, 49.

TABLE 4.26   UNITED STATES COAL PRODUCTION AND CONSUMPTION, 1950–1990
(in millions of short tons)

| Year | Production | Consumption | Consumption by Sector | | | | |
			Commercial, Residential	Coke Plants	Transportation	Electric Utilities	Misc.
1950	560.4	494.1	114.6	104.0	63.0	91.9	120.6
1955	490.8	447.0	68.4	107.7	17.0	143.8	110.1
1960	434.3	398.1	40.9	81.4	3.0	176.7	96.0
1965	527.0	472.0	25.7	95.3	0.7	244.8	105.6
1970	612.7	523.2	16.1	96.5	0.3	320.2	90.2
1975	654.6	562.6	9.4	83.6	0.0	406.0	63.6
1980	829.7	702.7	6.5	66.7	0.0	569.3	60.3
1985	883.6	818.0	7.8	41.1	0.0	693.8	75.4
1990	1,029.1	896.4	6.7	39.8	0.0	773.5	76.3

Source: Dept. of Energy, *Annual Energy Review 1991,* 189, 193.

Devastation in the cause of energy: "Strip-mining, or "open-pit" coal mining, in western Pennsylvania (Special Collections, Indiana University of Pennsylvania)

TABLE 4.27   UNITED STATES NATURAL GAS PRODUCTION AND CONSUMPTION, 1950–1990

(in trillions of cubic feet per year)

Year	Production	Consumption	Consumption by Sector			
			Residential, Commercial	Industrial	Transportation	Electric Utilities
1950	6.02	5.77	1.59	3.43	0.13	0.63
1955	9.03	8.69	2.75	4.54	0.25	1.15
1960	12.23	11.97	4.12	5.77	0.35	1.72
1965	15.29	15.28	5.34	7.11	0.50	2.32
1970	21.01	21.14	7.24	9.25	0.72	3.93
1975	19.24	19.54	7.43	8.36	0.58	3.16
1980	19.40	19.88	7.36	8.20	0.63	3.68
1985	16.45	17.28	6.86	6.87	0.50	3.04
1990	17.81	18.72	7.01	8.25	0.66	2.79

Source: Dept. of Energy, *Annual Energy Review 1991*, 167.

TABLE 4.28   U.S. NUCLEAR GENERATION OF ELECTRICITY, 1957–1990

Year	Operable Units	Net Generation of Electricity	
		Billion Net Kilowatt-Hours	Percent of Total U.S. Generation
1957	1	a	a
1960	3	0.5	0.1
1965	6	3.7	0.3
1970	18	21.8	1.4
1975	54	172.5	9.0
1980	70	251.1	11.0
1985	95	383.7	15.5
1986	100	414.0	16.6
1987	107	455.3	17.7
1988	108	527.0	19.5
1989	110	529.4	19.0
1990	111	576.9	20.5

a Negligible.
Source: Annual Energy Review 1991, 237.

TABLE 4.29   NUCLEAR REACTORS— LEADING COUNTRIES, 1986

Rank	Country	Number of Nuclear Reactors Operable
1.	United States	95
2.	Soviet Union	48
3.	France	43
4.	United Kingdom	38
5.	Japan	33
6.	Canada	17
7.	Germany, West	17
8.	Sweden	12
9.	Spain	8
10.	Belgium	7

Source: George T. Kurian, *The New Book of World Rankings* (New York, 1991), 166.

TABLE 4.30   COAL RESERVES— LEADING COUNTRIES, 1990

Rank	Country	Million Metric Tons
1.	China	737,100
2.	United States	263,843
3.	United Arab Emirates	244,700
4.	Australia	65,702
5.	Germany, West	59,069
6.	South Africa	58,404
7.	Poland	42,700
8.	Mongolia	24,000
9.	Indonesia	23,232
10.	Germany, East	21,000

Source: Kurian, *New World Rankings*, 167.

TABLE 4.31   PETROLEUM PRODUCTS— AMOUNT AND SOURCES, 1949–1990

(million barrels per day)

Year	Total Production	Total Imports	Petroleum Products Supplied
1949	5.48	0.65	5.76
1950	5.91	0.85	6.46
1951	6.72	0.84	7.02
1952	6.87	0.95	7.27
1953	7.11	1.03	7.60
1954	7.03	1.05	7.76
1955	7.58	1.25	8.46
1956	7.95	1.44	8.78
1957	7.98	1.57	8.81
1958	7.52	1.70	9.12
1959	7.93	1.78	9.53
1960	7.96	1.81	9.80
1961	8.17	1.92	9.98
1962	8.35	2.08	10.40
1963	8.64	2.12	10.74
1964	8.77	2.26	11.02
1965	9.01	2.47	11.51
1966	9.58	2.57	12.08
1967	10.22	2.54	12.56
1968	10.60	2.84	13.39
1969	10.83	3.17	14.14
1970	11.30	3.42	14.70
1971	11.16	3.93	15.21
1972	11.18	4.74	16.37
1973	10.95	6.26	17.31
1974	10.46	6.11	16.65
1975	10.01	6.06	16.32
1976	9.74	7.31	17.46
1977	9.86	8.81	18.43
1978	10.27	8.36	18.85
1979	10.14	8.46	18.51
1980	10.17	6.91	17.06
1981	10.18	6.00	16.06
1982	10.20	5.11	15.30
1983	10.25	5.05	15.23
1984	10.51	5.44	15.73
1985	10.58	5.07	15.73
1986	10.23	6.22	16.28
1987	9.94	6.68	16.67
1988	9.76	7.40	17.28
1989	9.16	8.06	17.33
1990	8.91	8.02	16.99

Source: Annual Energy Review 1991, 119.

TABLE 4.32 PETROLEUM PRODUCTS SUPPLIED, BY TYPE, 1949–1990

(million barrels per day)

Year	Motor Gasoline	Jet Fuel	Distillate Fuel Oil	Residual Fuel Oil	Liquefied Petroleum Gases	Other Products	Total Products
1949	2.50	NA	0.90	1.36	0.19	0.81	5.76
1950	2.72	NA	1.08	1.52	0.23	0.90	6.46
1951	2.99	NA	1.23	1.55	0.28	0.98	7.02
1952	3.12	0.05	1.30	1.52	0.30	0.98	7.27
1953	3.30	0.09	1.34	1.54	0.33	1.00	7.60
1954	3.37	0.13	1.44	1.43	0.35	1.03	7.76
1955	3.66	0.15	1.59	1.53	0.40	1.12	8.46
1956	3.75	0.20	1.68	1.54	0.44	1.16	8.78
1957	3.82	0.20	1.69	1.50	0.45	1.15	8.81
1958	3.93	0.26	1.79	1.45	0.49	1.19	9.12
1959	4.07	0.29	1.81	1.54	0.58	1.24	9.53
1960	4.13	0.28	1.87	1.53	0.62	1.36	9.80
1961	4.20	0.29	1.90	1.50	0.64	1.44	9.98
1962	4.34	0.31	2.01	1.50	0.70	1.55	10.40
1963	4.47	0.32	2.05	1.48	0.76	1.68	10.74
1964	4.40	0.32	2.05	1.52	0.81	1.92	11.02
1965	4.59	0.60	2.13	1.61	0.84	1.74	11.51
1966	4.81	0.67	2.18	1.72	0.89	1.82	12.08
1967	4.96	0.82	2.24	1.79	0.94	1.81	12.56
1968	5.26	0.95	2.39	1.83	1.05	1.91	13.39
1969	5.53	0.99	2.47	1.98	1.22	1.95	14.14
1970	5.78	0.97	2.54	2.20	1.22	1.98	14.70
1971	6.01	1.01	2.66	2.30	1.25	1.98	15.21
1972	6.38	1.05	2.91	2.53	1.42	2.08	16.37
1973	6.67	1.06	3.09	2.82	1.45	2.21	17.31
1974	6.54	0.99	2.95	2.64	1.41	2.13	16.65
1975	6.67	1.00	2.85	2.46	1.33	2.00	16.32
1976	6.98	0.99	3.13	2.80	1.40	2.16	17.46
1977	7.18	1.04	3.35	3.07	1.42	2.37	18.43
1978	7.41	1.06	3.43	3.02	1.41	2.51	18.85
1979	7.03	1.08	3.31	2.83	1.59	2.67	18.51
1980	6.58	1.07	2.87	2.51	1.47	2.57	17.06
1981	6.59	1.01	2.83	2.09	1.47	2.08	16.06
1982	6.54	1.01	2.67	1.72	1.50	1.86	15.30
1983	6.62	1.05	2.69	1.42	1.51	1.94	15.23
1984	6.69	1.18	2.84	1.37	1.57	2.07	15.73
1985	6.83	1.22	2.87	1.20	1.60	2.01	15.73
1986	7.03	1.31	2.91	1.42	1.51	2.09	16.28
1987	7.21	1.38	2.98	1.26	1.61	2.22	16.67
1988	7.34	1.45	3.12	1.38	1.66	2.34	17.28
1989	7.33	1.49	3.16	1.37	1.67	2.31	17.33
1990	7.23	1.52	3.02	1.23	1.56	2.43	16.99

Source: Annual Energy Review 1991, 125.

TABLE 4.33 LEADING EXPORTERS OF PETROLEUM TO THE UNITED STATES, 1960–1990

(in thousands of barrels per day)

Year	OPEC[a] Algeria	Indonesia	Nigeria	Saudi Arabia	Venezuela	Arab OPEC[b]	Total	Non-OPEC Canada	Mexico	United Kingdom	Virgin Islands and Puerto Rico	Total
1960	1	77	0	84	911	292	1,314	120	16	. . .	36	1,815
1961	0	62	0	73	879	284	1,286	190	40	1	44	1,917
1962	0	69	0	74	906	241	1,265	250	49	2	41	2,082
1963	1	63	0	108	900	258	1,283	265	48	3	44	2,123
1964	6	68	0	131	933	293	1,361	299	47	. . .	47	2,259
1965	9	63	15	158	994	324	1,476	323	48	. . .	47	2,468
1966	4	53	11	147	1,018	300	1,471	384	45	6	61	2,573
1967	5	66	5	92	938	177	1,259	450	49	11	96	2,537
1968	6	73	9	74	886	272	1,302	506	45	28	145	2,840
1969	2	88	49	65	875	276	1,336	608	43	20	189	3,166
1970	8	70	50	30	989	196	1,343	766	42	11	271	3,419
1971	15	111	102	128	1,020	327	1,673	857	27	10	368	3,926
1972	92	164	251	190	959	530	2,063	1,108	21	9	432	4,741
1973	136	213	459	486	1,135	915	2,993	1,325	16	15	429	6,256
1974	190	300	713	461	979	752	3,280	1,070	8	8	481	6,112
1975	282	390	762	715	702	1,383	3,601	846	71	14	496	6,056
1976	432	539	1,025	1,230	700	2,424	5,066	599	87	31	510	7,313
1977	559	541	1,143	1,380	690	3,185	6,193	517	179	126	571	8,807
1978	649	573	919	1,144	646	2,963	5,751	467	318	180	522	8,363
1979	636	420	1,080	1,356	690	3,058	5,637	538	439	202	523	8,456
1980	488	348	857	1,261	481	2,551	4,300	455	533	176	476	6,909
1981	311	366	620	1,129	406	1,848	3,323	447	522	375	389	5,996
1982	170	248	514	552	412	854	2,146	482	685	456	366	5,113
1983	240	338	302	337	422	632	1,862	547	826	382	322	5,051
1984	323	343	216	325	548	819	2,049	630	748	402	336	5,437
1985	187	314	293	168	605	472	1,830	770	816	310	275	5,067
1986	271	318	440	685	793	1,162	2,837	807	699	350	265	6,224
1987	295	285	535	751	804	1,274	3,060	848	655	352	294	6,678
1988	300	205	618	1,073	794	1,839	3,520	999	747	315	264	7,402
1989	269	183	815	1,224	873	2,130	4,140	931	767	215	353	8,061
1990	280	114	800	1,339	1,025	2,244	4,296	934	755	189	315	8,018

[a] Organization of Petroleum Exporting Countries.
[b] Includes Algeria, Iraq, Kuwait, Libya, Qatar, Saudi Arabia, and United Arab Emirates.
Source: Dept. of Energy, Annual Energy Review 1991, 125.

TABLE 4.34 AVERAGE WELLHEAD PRICE OF U.S. CRUDE OIL, 1946–1990

(current dollars per barrel of 42 gallons)

Year	Price
1946	1.41
1950	2.51
1955	2.77
1960	2.88
1965	2.86
1970	3.18
1973	3.89
1974	6.74
1976	8.14
1978	8.96
1979	12.51
1980	21.59
1981	31.77
1983	26.19
1985	24.09
1986	12.51
1987	15.40
1988	12.58
1989	15.86
1990	20.03

Source: Ben J. Wattenberg, *The Statistical History of the United States* (New York, 1976), 593; W. Willard Miller, Ruby M. Miller, *Energy and American Society* (Santa Barbara, 1993), 84–85.

TABLE 4.35 ESTIMATED PROVED CRUDE OIL RESERVES, BY AREA, 1950–1990

(in millions of barrels)

Year	Africa	Australasia	Canada	Latin America	Middle East	Western Europe	Soviet Union	United States	Total World
1950	202.5	1,557.0	1,200.0	11,400.8	32,413.0	289.0	4,741.0	24,649.5	76,452.7
1955	112.0	2,708.0	2,207.6	14,356.0	97,459.0	1,049.2	10,047.0	29,560.7	159,499.6
1960	7,273.5	10,175.5	3,497.1	24,435.6	181,436.0	1,496.0	30,002.0	31,719.3	290,035.1
1965	19,395.0	11,613.7	6,177.5	25,525.0	212,180.0	2,035.6	30,750.0	30,990.5	338,668.0
1970	54,679.5	13,138.2	8,619.8	29,179.8	333,506.0	1,779.0	60,000.0	29,631.9	530,534.1
1975	68,299.5	21,047.7	7,171.2	40,578.0	403,858.2	25,814.0	111,400.0	34,250.0	712,418.5
1980	57,072.1	19,355.2	6,800.0	56,472.5	361,947.3	23,476.4	90,000.0	29,810.0	644,933.0
1985	55,540.6	18,529.9	7,075.0	83,315.7	398,380.8	24,425.5	84,100.0	28,466.0	699,813.4
1990	58,836.6	22,545.4	6,133.5	125,026.9	660,247.2	18,822.1	84,100.0	26,501.0	1,002,212.7

Source: Miller & Miller, *Energy and American Society,* 77.

Energy and the Environment

It was inevitable that the issue of energy would come to clash with the issue of the environment. Because virtually all energy came from utilization of the earth's resources, any manner of acquisition or transport of the materials or chemical change in the production process could modify and perhaps contaminate the land, water, or air in the areas involved. The possibilities were numerous.

Mining coal amounted to nothing less than seizing part of the earth, and it affected the landscape regardless of the method used. Consequences of traditional underground mining mostly were hidden, but abandoned, forgotten shafts possessed a potential for various kinds of future accidents. Ugly scars and barren hills stood as testimony to increasingly popular and efficient open-pit, or strip, mining that destroyed everything in its path and left areas looking like war zones, at least in the stages of extraction. Law required the companies to fill the holes, smooth over the hills, and return some measure of topsoil. Assurances that fertility also had been restored were unconvincing.

Burning coal produced smoke, soot, and a new term, *smog,* which had been an urban plague and health hazard for many years. Small wonder that coal fell into disuse at the end of the 1950s. A return to coal after the oil crises of the 1970s would not have been possible without the desulfurization controls on power plants built after 1980. The smoke billowing from smokestacks that seemed to reach to the sky might contain fewer chemicals, but it still was black and bountiful.

Nuclear energy was clean and silent; there was almost nothing to see around the power plant, but this exotic and little-understood power source carried special hazards for health and atmosphere. The problem of spent but still radioactive waste appeared immediately. Packed in allegedly leakproof containers, the stuff for 25 years was simply dumped into the ocean. Dumping stopped in 1970, allowing the issue to resurface and become seemingly perpetual. The most common solution—some form of elaborate burial procedure—was far from satisfactory to everyone, and there persisted opposition in affected areas to transport of the goods to a final resting place. It was impossible to forget that nuclear power belonged to an activity that produced the most destructive of superweapons. Fear of an accident seemed to materialize in an alarming but largely contained incident at the Three-Mile-Island plant in Pennsylvania in 1979 and the far more destructive meltdown at Chernobyl in the Soviet Union in 1986. By that time environmentalists had produced so many challenges, delays, and expensive lawsuits that the Atomic Energy Commission had given up on the construction of new plants.

Perhaps the most familiar environmental hazards came from the world of petroleum. Burned gasoline and other petroleum by-products produced such gases as carbon monoxide, which could be exceptionally harmful to health (in closed quarters it could be fatal) and to the atmosphere. Mandated new emission controls on motor vehicles, especially during the years 1968–71, and an end to the use of leaded gasoline reduced pollution markedly. It so happened that much of the petroleum came from one part of the world, and the people who used it lived great distances away. Environmental risks from the transport of petroleum grew in proportion to the distances involved and the massive amounts being moved. Kept within its designated usage, petroleum worked like magic; outside its element crude oil bespoiled everything and killed much of the wildlife that it touched. Construction of an Alaskan pipeline, merely the first leg of a long transportation process, was delayed by worry that it might leak and that the simple presence of this huge, aboveground tube would endanger wildlife in the area. The pipeline began operations in 1977. Behemoths that dwarfed the largest warships or anything ever seen in the ocean were built specially to carry petroleum; there were only a few ocean oil spills, but each became international news. The major spillage in American waters—the incident of the *Exxon Valdez* in 1989—was by comparison small, but because it took place within a confined area (Prince William Sound in Alaska), the effects were devastating. Double-bottomed ships, a hull within a hull, surely helped, but transporting petroleum continued to be risky, and the conflict between producing the people's energy and protecting the well-being of Earth remained unending.

Ecological disaster in American waters: A tanker pumps oil from the punctured *Exxon Valdez*, Prince William Sound, Alaska, 1989. (National Marine Fisheries Service)

TABLE 4.36   OIL SPILLS

Major Oil Spills				
Name	Place	Date	Cause	Tons
Ixtoc I oil well	southern Gulf of Mexico	Jun. 3, 1979	Blowout	600,000
Nowruz oil field	Persian Gulf	Feb., 1983	Blowout	600,000 (est.)
Atlantic Empress & Aegean Captain	off Trinidad & Tobago	Jul. 19, 1979	Collision	300,000
Castillo de Bellver	off Cape Town, South Africa	Aug. 6, 1983	Fire	250,000
Amoco Cadiz	near Portsall, France	Mar. 16, 1978	Grounding	223,000
Torrey Canyon	off Land's End, England	Mar. 18, 1967	Grounding	119,000
Sea Star	Gulf of Oman	Dec. 19, 1972	Collision	115,000
Urquiola	La Coruna, Spain	May 12, 1976	Grounding	100,000
Hawaiian Patriot	northern Pacific	Feb. 25, 1977	Fire	99,000
Othello	Tralhavet Bay, Sweden	Mar. 20, 1970	Collision	60,000–100,000
Other Notable Oil Spills (in gallons[a])				
World Glory	off South Africa	Jun. 13, 1968	Hull failure	13,524,000
Burmah Agate	Galveston Bay, Tex	Nov. 1, 1979	Collision	10,700,000
Exxon Valdez	Prince William Sound, Alaska	Mar. 24, 1989	Grounding	10,080,000
Keo	off Massachusetts	Nov. 5, 1969	Hull failure	8,820,000
Storage tank	Sewaren, N.J.	Nov. 4, 1969	Tank rupture	8,400,000
Ekofisk oil field	North Sea	Apr. 22, 1977	Well blowout	8,200,000
Argo Merchant	Nantucket, Mass.	Dec. 15, 1976	Grounding	7,700,000
Pipeline	West Delta, La.	Oct. 15, 1967	Dragging anchor	6,720,000
Tanker	off Japan	Nov. 30, 1971	Ship broke in half	6,258,000
Storage tank	Monongahela River	Jan. 2, 1988	Tank rupture	3,800,000

[a] It took 269 gallons or 6.4 barrels to equal one ton. The *Exxon Valdez* spilled some 35,000 tons.
Source: Hoffman, *World Almanac 1992,* 545.

Banking and Finance

Changes in the U.S. banking system predictably included an expansion designed to at least keep pace with the nation's economic growth. There were in fact fewer banks in the United States in 1990 than in 1946, but the number of branches, offices, and of course deposits, assets, and all phases of banking activity increased markedly. No less than in economic activity generally, banking became global, an international enterprise. Banks of one nation did business in other nations and with banks of other nations. The United States share in international banking shrank gradually but significantly. Of the 50 largest banks in the world in 1990, only one was American; the six largest were Japanese.

Banking legislation of the 1960s was pointed toward promoting truth and openness in business practices; laws in the 1970s often focused on preventing racial, sexual, or other kind of discrimination, mostly in the awarding of loans. The late 1970s and 1980s were marked with removal of many regulations on banking practices, measures that fostered an overlapping of activity of the various kinds of financial institutions. The functions of commercial banks, savings and loan institutions, and money-market funds became blurred. All seemingly were competing in the attraction of capital, acceptance of checking accounts, and awarding of loans. Financial institutions floated many loans that could not be repaid. Bank failures, which had averaged approximately six per year since the end of the Second World War, increased to more than 200 during some years of the 1980s.

Much of the attention came to be placed on the savings and loan institutions, the so-called thrifts, which because of deregulation legislation of 1980 faced new opportunities (or challenges, depending on one's point of view). To compensate for being locked in to long-term, low fixed-rate loans granted earlier, the thrifts took chances on loans that offered a much higher rate of interest. Many of the loans failed, especially in the Southwest, an area that suffered from a slowdown in the oil business. Property that had supported the loans and that was subject to foreclosure declined in value. More than 500 thrifts went under between 1980 and 1988. The underwriting government agency, the Federal Savings and Loan Insurance Corporation (FSLIC) ran out of money. Congress in 1989 turned the problem over to the Federal Deposit Insurance Corporation (FDIC). As the 1990s began, estimates put the cost to the government (and thus the taxpayers) to "bail out" the savings and loan industry at beyond $400 billion.

TABLE 4.37   BANKS IN THE UNITED STATES, BY NUMBER AND DEPOSITS, 1945–1990

| | Total Number of Banks | | | | | | Total Deposits (millions of dollars) | | | |
| | Commercial Banks | | | | | | Commercial Banks | | | |
Year	All Banks	National	State	Nonmembers[a]	All Savings	All Deposits	National	State	Nonmembers[a]	All Savings
1945	15,969	5,017	1,864	6,421	2,667	151,524	77,778	41,865	16,307	15,574
1950	16,500	4,958	1,912	6,576	3,054	171,963	84,941	41,602	19,726	25,694
1955	17,001	4,692	1,847	6,698	3,764	235,211	102,796	55,739	26,198	50,478
1960	17,549	4,530	1,641	6,955	4,423	310,262	120,242	65,487	34,369	90,164
1965	18,384	4,815	1,405	7,327	4,837	467,633	185,334	78,327	51,982	151,990
1970	18,205	4,621	1,147	7,743	4,694	686,901	285,436	101,512	95,566	204,367
1975	18,792	4,744	1,046	8,595	4,407	1,157,648	450,308	143,409	187,031	376,900
1980	18,763	4,425	997	9,013	4,328	1,832,716	656,752	191,183	344,311	640,470
1985	18,033	4,959	1,070	8,378	3,626	3,140,827	1,241,875	354,585	521,628	1,022,739
1990	15,158	3,979	1,009	7,355	2,815	3,637,292	1,558,915	397,797	693,438	987,142

[a] Nonmembers are banks that do not belong to the Federal Reserve System. National and State banks are members.
Note: Comprises all FDIC-insured commercial and savings banks, including savings and loan institutions (S&Ls).
Source: Federal Deposit Insurance Corp. (as of Dec. 31, 1997) in Robert Farmighetti, ed., *The World Almanac and Book of Facts, 1999* (Mahwah, N.J., 1998), 116.

TABLE 4.38   BRANCH BANKING—COMMERCIAL BANKS AND TRUST COMPANIES, 1946–1990

Year	Banks	Branches	Offices	Assets (millions of dollars)
1946	13,359	3,928	17,287	147,365
1950	13,446	4,832	18,278	166,792
1955	13,237	6,965	20,202	209,145
1960	13,126	10,556	23,682	256,322
1965	13,544	15,872	29,416	375,394
1970	13,511	21,839	35,350	570,158
1975	14,384	30,205	44,589	1,086,674
1980	14,434	38,738	53,172	1,855,687
1985	14,417	43,293	57,710	2,730,672
1990	12,347	50,406	62,753	3,389,470

Source: Federal Deposit Insurance Corporation, *Statistics on Banking: Historical, 1934–1994* (Washington, D.C., 1995), A–1, A–48–49.

TABLE 4.39 MONEY MARKET INTEREST RATES AND MORTGAGE RATES, 1950–1990

Type	1950	1955	1960	1965	1970	1975	1980	1981	1985	1990
Prime rate charged by banks	1.45	2.18	3.85	4.38	7.72	7.86	15.26	18.87	9.93	10.01
Financial Commercial Paper (3 months)	1.41	1.97	3.54	4.27	7.23	6.15	11.49	14.08	7.77	7.87
Prime Bankers Accept. (90 days)	1.15	1.71	3.51	4.22	7.31	6.29	12.87	15.34	7.91	7.93
Eurodollar deposits	. . .	. . .	. . .	. . .	8.52	7.03	14.00	16.79	8.27	8.16
Taxable Money Market Funds	. . .	. . .	. . .	. . .	. . .	6.36	12.68	16.82	7.71	7.82
Certificates of Deposit (CD)										
6 months	. . .	. . .	. . .	. . .	. . .	. . .	. . .	. . .	7.83	7.35
12 months	. . .	. . .	. . .	. . .	. . .	. . .	. . .	. . .	8.29	7.42
2.5 years	. . .	. . .	. . .	. . .	. . .	. . .	. . .	. . .	9.00	7.52
U.S. Gov't Security (3 months)	1.22	1.75	2.87	3.95	6.39	5.78	11.39	14.04	7.47	7.50
Federal Reserve (NY) Discount Rate	1.50 — 1.75	1.50 — 2.50	3.00 — 4.00	4.00 — 4.50	5.5 — 6.0	6.25 — 7.25	10. — 13.0	12. — 13.0	7.50	6.50
Home Mortgages										
FHA Insured, secondary market	4.15	4.65	6.16	5.47	9.05	9.19	13.44	16.31	12.24	10.2
Conventional new home	. . .	. . .	. . .	5.83	8.52	9.10	13.95	16.52	12.29	10.1
Conventional, existing home	. . .	. . .	. . .	5.87	8.56	9.14	13.95	16.55	12.29	10.1

Source: Bureau of the Budget, *Statistical Abstract of the United States, 1972* (Washington, D.C., 1972), 455; *Statistical Abstract, 1993,* 520.

TABLE 4.40 BANK FAILURES, 1947–1990

Year	Closed or Assisted
1947	1
1949	4
1950	1
1952	3
1954	3
1956	3
1958	8
1960	2
1962	2
1964	8
1966	8
1969	9
1970	8
1972	3
1975	14
1976	17
1978	7
1980	10
1981	10
1982	42
1983	48
1984	72
1985	120
1986	145
1987	184
1988	221
1989	207
1990	169

Source: Luman Long, ed., *The World Almanac and Book of Facts, 1969 Edition* (New York, 1968), 144; *World Almanac, 1992,* 156.

TABLE 4.41 MONEY IN CIRCULATION, 1945–1990

Date	Dollars (in millions)	Per Capita
Jun. 30, 1945	26,746.4	191.1
Jun. 30, 1950	27,156.3	179.0
Jun. 30, 1955	30,229.3	182.9
Jun. 30, 1960	32.064.6	177.5
Jun. 30, 1965	39,719.8	204.1
Jun. 30, 1970	54,351.0	265.4
Jun. 30, 1975	81,196.4	380.1
Jun. 30, 1980	127,097.2	558.3
Jun. 30, 1985	185,890.7	778.6
Jun. 30, 1987	215,158.6	883.5
Jun. 30, 1988	235,415.9	956.6
Jun. 30, 1989	249,182.7	1,002.5
Mar. 31, 1990	257,664.4	1,028.4

Source: World Almanac, 1992, 158.

TABLE 4.42 GOLD RESERVES OF CENTRAL BANKS AND GOVERNMENTS, 1973–1990
(million fine troy ounces)

Year End	All Countries	United States	Canada	Japan	Belgium	France	Germany	Italy	Netherlands	Switzerland	United Kingdom
1973	1,022.24	275.97	21.95	21.11	42.17	100.91	117.61	82.48	54.33	83.20	21.01
1974	1,020.24	275.97	21.95	21.11	42.17	100.93	117.61	82.48	54.33	83.20	21.03
1975	1,018.71	274.71	21.95	21.11	42.17	100.93	117.61	82.48	54.33	83.20	21.03
1976	1,014.23	274.68	21.62	21.11	42.17	101.02	117.61	82.48	54.33	83.28	21.03
1977	1,029.19	277.55	22.01	21.62	42.45	101.67	118.30	82.91	54.63	83.28	22.23
1978	1,036.82	276.41	22.13	23.97	42.59	101.99	118.64	83.12	54.78	83.28	22.83
1979	944.44	264.60	22.18	24.23	34.21	81.92	95.25	66.71	43.97	83.28	18.25
1980	952.99	264.32	20.98	24.23	34.18	81.85	95.18	66.67	43.94	83.28	18.84
1981	953.72	264.11	20.46	24.23	34.18	81.85	95.18	66.67	43.94	83.28	19.03
1982	949.16	264.03	20.26	24.23	34.18	81.85	95.18	66.67	43.94	83.28	19.01
1983	947.84	263.39	20.17	24.23	34.18	81.85	95.18	66.67	43.94	83.28	19.01
1984	946.79	262.79	20.14	24.23	34.18	81.85	95.18	66.67	43.94	83.28	19.03
1985	949.39	262.65	20.11	24.33	34.18	81.85	95.18	66.67	43.94	83.28	19.03
1986	949.11	262.04	19.72	24.23	34.18	81.85	95.18	66.67	43.94	83.28	19.01
1987	944.49	262.38	18.52	24.23	33.63	81.85	95.18	66.67	43.94	83.28	19.01
1988	944.92	261.87	17.14	24.23	33.67	81.85	95.18	66.67	43.94	83.28	19.00
1989	938.95	261.93	16.10	24.23	30.23	81.85	95.18	66.67	43.94	83.28	18.99
1990	940.29	261.91	14.76	24.23	30.23	81.85	95.18	66.67	43.94	83.28	18.94

Source: World Almanac, 1992, 158.

International Business

No topic of economics was more difficult to understand than the intricacies of international finance and the business transactions that developed between the United States and other nations. Emerging trends in American operations on the world market were easy enough to detect, starting with the most familiar international activity: trade. At the end of the Second World War, the United States stood alone as the world's economic giant. Controlling 60 percent of world industrial capacity, it virtually had foreign markets to itself. The country exported not only agricultural products, as had been its practice, but also manufactured goods, including large amounts of consumer products. This honeymoon period did not last long. The huge American advantage in trade soon began to erode as the war-weakened nations of Europe and Asia gradually recovered. Through various aid programs to both former allies and former enemies, the United States assisted in the emergence of its competitors.

In a broader scope perhaps the most striking aspect of international economics was its size. The export trade of the United States continued to increase at a remarkable rate as the nation blended in with a vast global economy. Exports of some $12 billion in 1946 had grown to more than $40 billion in 1970. By 1980 it had passed $200 billion, and in 1990 it was nearly $400 billion worth of goods sold abroad. Unfortunately, perhaps, imports of the United States increased at an ever greater rate. The ever-changing but generally diminishing value of the dollar was a factor. The nation faced a need to import supplies no longer abundant nationally, the best-known example of which was petroleum. It simply developed that other countries were able to produce some goods more efficiently and, at least in popular perception, to produce better goods. The first trade deficit appeared in 1971; by the late 1970s it had become a standard fact of life, and the question was not "if" but "how much?" If a huge trade deficit became a considerable political issue, attitudes about

its significance differed. Imported goods probably allowed Americans to purchase better products at lower prices. Some economists argued that it represented nothing more than the normal operation of global economics. What many Americans saw, however, was that goods purchased in the United States were no longer being made in the United States. Not only were foreign producers exploiting the American market, but American firms were moving abroad to produce the goods, expecting to ship them back to the United States.

International trade became vastly more complex due to the increasing propensity of individuals or firms in one country to invest in the securities, property, or activities of another. The United States led the way in foreign investment, starting in the capital-starved countries of Europe and Asia in the aftermath of the Second World War. By 1980 nearly one-sixth of assets of nonfinancial United States firms were invested abroad. Foreign investors started later, but they caught up fast. The United States offered financial and political stability and by far the world's largest market, which perhaps could be better exploited from within than from outside. Foreign investment in the United States roughly equaled American investment abroad by the mid-1980s, and it continued to soar. Between 1985 and 1990 it more than doubled. The age of the multinational corporation had arrived, with implications that no one fully understood. Some activities, to be sure, were easy to observe. Movement of an American factory to South Korea or Mexico produced sorrow, and probably anger, in the area being abandoned. Opening of a foreign factory on an American site was exciting news. States and municipalities competed with one another to bring them in. But the patriotic citizen wishing to "buy American" was totally confused. Was a Chevrolet made in Canada or a Ford from Mexico an American car, or was it a Toyota produced in Tennessee or a Mazda (a company largely owned by Ford) made in Michigan? The multinational carried a national name and had its headquarters in a single country, but its loyalty seemed to be to itself.

TABLE 4.43 U.S. INTERNATIONAL TRANSACTIONS, 1946–1990

(millions of dollars; quarterly data seasonally adjusted, except as noted. Credits [+], debits [−])

| Year or Quarter | Merchandise[a] | | | Services | | | Investment Income | | | Balance on Goods, Services, and Income | Unilateral Transfers, Net | Balance on Current Account |
	Exports	Imports	Net	Net Military Transac-tions	Net Travel and Transpor-tation Receipts	Other Services, Net	Receipts on U.S. Assets Abroad	Payments on Foreign Assets in U.S.	Net			
1946	11,764	−5,067	6,697	−424	733	310	772	−212	560	7,876	−2,991	4,885
1947	16,097	−5,973	10,124	−358	946	145	1,102	−245	857	11,714	−2,722	8,992
1948	13,265	−7,557	5,708	−351	374	175	1,921	−437	1,484	7,390	−4,973	2,417
1949	12,213	−6,874	5,339	−410	230	208	1,831	−476	1,355	6,722	−5,849	873
1950	10,203	−9,081	1,122	−56	−120	242	2,068	−559	1,509	2,697	−4,537	−1,840
1951	14,243	−11,176	3,067	169	298	254	2,633	−583	2,050	5,838	−4,954	884
1952	13,449	−10,838	2,611	528	83	309	2,751	−555	2,196	5,727	−5,113	614
1953	12,412	−10,975	1,437	1,753	−238	307	2,736	−624	2,112	5,371	−6,657	−1,286
1954	12,929	−10,353	2,576	902	−269	305	2,929	−582	2,347	5,861	−5,642	219
1955	14,424	−11,527	2,897	−113	−297	299	3,406	−676	2,730	5,516	−5,086	430
1956	17,556	−12,803	4,753	−221	−361	447	3,837	−735	3,102	7,720	−4,990	2,730
1957	19,562	−13,291	6,271	−423	−189	482	4,180	−796	3,384	9,525	−4,763	4,762
1958	16,414	−12,952	3,462	−849	−633	486	3,790	−825	2,965	5,431	−4,647	784
1959	16,458	−15,310	1,148	−831	−821	573	4,132	−1,061	3,071	3,140	−4,422	−1,282
1960	19,650	−14,758	4,892	−1,057	−964	639	4,616	−1,238	3,379	6,886	−4,062	2,824
1961	20,108	−14,537	5,571	−1,131	−978	732	4,999	−1,245	3,755	7,949	−4,127	3,822
1962	20,781	−16,260	4,521	−912	−1,152	912	5,618	−1,324	4,294	7,664	−4,277	3,387
1963	22,272	−17,048	5,224	−742	−1,309	1,036	6,157	−1,560	4,596	8,806	−4,392	4,414
1964	25,501	−18,700	6,801	−794	−1,146	1,161	6,824	−1,783	5,041	11,063	−4,240	6,823
1965	26,461	−21,510	4,951	−487	−1,280	1,480	7,437	−2,088	5,350	10,014	−4,583	5,431
1966	29,310	−25,493	3,817	−1,043	−1,331	1,497	7,528	−2,481	5,047	7,987	−4,955	3,031
1967	30,666	−26,866	3,800	−1,187	−1,750	1,742	8,021	−2,747	5,274	7,878	−5,294	2,583
1968	33,626	−32,991	635	−596	−1,548	1,759	9,367	−3,378	5,990	6,240	−5,629	611
1969	36,414	−35,807	607	−718	−1,763	1,964	10,913	−4,869	6,044	6,135	−5,735	399
1970	42,469	−39,866	2,603	−641	−2,038	2,330	11,748	−5,515	6,233	8,486	−6,156	2,331
1971	43,319	−45,579	−2,260	653	−2,345	2,649	12,707	−5,435	7,272	5,969	−7,402	−1,433
1972	49,381	−55,797	−6,416	1,072	−3,063	2,965	14,765	−6,572	8,192	2,749	−8,544	−5,795
1973	71,410	−70,499	911	740	−3,158	3,406	21,808	−9,655	12,153	14,053	−6,913	7,140
1974	98,306	−103,811	−5,505	165	−3,184	4,231	27,587	−12,084	15,503	11,210	−9,249	1,962
1975	107,088	−98,185	8,903	1,461	−2,812	4,854	25,351	−12,564	12,787	25,191	−7,075	18,116
1976	114,745	−124,228	−9,483	931	−2,558	5,027	29,286	−13,311	15,975	9,894	−5,686	4,207
1977	120,816	−151,907	−31,091	1,731	−3,565	5,680	32,178	−14,217	17,961	−9,285	−5,226	−14,511
1978	142,054	−176,001	−33,947	857	−3,573	6,879	41,824	−21,680	20,144	−9,639	−5,788	−15,427
1979	184,473	−212,009	−27,536	−1,313	−2,935	7,251	63,096	−32,961	30,136	5,603	−6,593	−991
1980	224,269	−249,750	−25,481	−1,822	−997	8,912	71,388	−42,532	28,856	9,467	−8,349	1,119
1981	237,085	−265,063	−27,978	−844	144	12,552	84,975	−53,626	31,349	15,223	−8,331	6,892
1982	211,198	−247,642	−36,444	112	−992	12,981	85,346	−57,097	28,250	3,907	−9,775	−5,868
1983	201,820	−268,900	−67,080	−163	−4,227	13,859	81,972	−54,549	27,423	−30,188	−9,956	−40,143
1984	219,900	−332,422	−112,522	−2,147	−9,153	14,042	92,935	−69,542	23,394	−86,385	−12,621	−99,006
1985	215,935	−338,083	−122,148	−4,096	−10,788	14,008	82,282	−66,115	16,166	−106,859	−15,473	−122,332
1986	223,367	−368,425	−145,058	−4,907	−8,939	18,551	80,982	−70,013	10,969	−129,384	−16,009	−145,393
1987	250,266	−409,766	−159,500	−3,662	−8,006	18,012	90,536	−82,908	7,629	−145,527	−14,674	−160,201
1988	320,337	−447,323	−126,986	−5,743	−3,844	19,925	110,669	−105,317	5,353	−111,294	−14,943	−126,236
1989	361,451	−477,368	−115,917	−6,204	2,621	25,998	128,651	−125,963	2,688	−90,814	−15,491	−106,305
1990	389,550	−497,665	−108,115	−7,220	4,140	29,456	130,091	−118,146	11,945	−69,794	−22,329	−92,123

[a] Excludes military.

Source: Council of Economic Advisors, *Economic Report of the President, 1992* (Washington, D.C., 1992), 412.

TABLE 4.44 FOREIGN EXCHANGE RATES, 1967–1990

(currency units per U.S. dollar, except as noted)

Period	Belgium (franc)	Canada (dollar)	France (franc)	Germany (mark)	Italy (lira)	Japan (yen)
March 1973	39.408	0.9967	4.5156	2.8132	568.17	261.90
1967	49.689	1.0789	4.9206	3.9865	624.09	362.13
1968	49.936	1.0776	4.9529	3.9920	623.38	360.55
1969	50.142	1.0769	5.1999	3.9251	627.32	358.36
1970	49.656	1.0444	5.5288	3.6465	627.12	358.16
1971	48.598	1.0099	5.5100	3.4830	618.34	347.79
1972	44.020	.9907	5.0444	3.1886	583.70	303.13
1973	38.955	1.0002	4.4535	2.6715	582.41	271.31
1974	38.959	.9780	4.8107	2.5868	650.81	291.84
1975	36.800	1.0175	4.2877	2.4614	653.10	296.78
1976	38.609	.9863	4.7825	2.5185	833.58	296.45
1977	35.849	1.0633	4.9161	2.3236	882.78	268.62
1978	31.495	1.1405	4.5091	2.0097	849.13	210.39
1979	29.342	1.1713	4.2567	1.8343	831.11	219.02
1980	29.238	1.1693	4.2251	1.8175	856.21	226.63
1981	37.195	1.1990	5.4397	2.2632	1138.58	220.63
1982	45.781	1.2344	6.5794	2.4281	1354.00	249.06
1983	51.123	1.2325	7.6204	2.5539	1519.32	237.55
1984	57.752	1.2952	8.7356	2.8455	1756.11	237.46
1985	59.337	1.3659	8.9800	2.9420	1908.88	238.47
1986	44.664	1.3896	6.9257	2.1705	1491.16	168.35
1987	37.358	1.3259	6.0122	1.7981	1297.03	144.60
1988	36.785	1.2306	5.9595	1.7570	1302.39	128.17
1989	39.409	1.1842	6.3802	1.8808	1372.28	138.07
1990	33.424	1.1668	5.4467	1.6166	1198.27	145.00

Period	Netherlands (guilder)	Sweden (krona)	Switzerland (franc)	United Kingdom (pound)	Multilateral Trade-Weighted Value of the U.S. Dollar (March 1973 = 100)	
					Nominal	Real
March 1973	2.8714	4.4294	3.2171	247.24	100.0	100.0
1967	3.6024	5.1621	4.3283	275.04	120.0	. . .
1968	3.6198	5.1683	4.3163	239.35	122.1	. . .
1969	3.6240	5.1701	4.3131	239.01	122.4	. . .
1970	3.6166	5.1862	4.3106	239.59	121.1	. . .
1971	3.4953	5.1051	4.1171	244.42	117.8	. . .
1972	3.2098	4.7571	3.8186	250.34	109.1	. . .
1973	2.7946	4.3619	3.1688	245.25	99.1	98.9
1974	2.6879	4.4387	2.9805	234.03	101.4	99.4
1975	2.5293	4.1531	2.5839	222.17	98.5	94.1
1976	2.6449	4.3580	2.5002	180.48	105.7	97.6
1977	2.4548	4.4802	2.4065	174.49	103.4	93.3
1978	2.1643	4.5207	1.7907	191.84	92.4	84.4
1979	2.0073	4.2893	1.6644	212.24	88.1	83.2
1980	1.9875	4.2310	1.6772	232.46	87.4	84.9
1981	2.4999	5.0660	1.9675	202.43	103.4	100.9
1982	2.6719	6.2839	2.0327	174.80	116.6	111.8
1983	2.8544	7.6718	2.1007	151.59	125.3	117.3
1984	3.2085	8.2708	2.3500	133.68	138.2	128.8
1985	3.3185	8.6032	2.4552	129.74	143.0	132.4
1986	2.4485	7.1273	1.7979	146.77	112.2	103.6
1987	2.0264	6.3469	1.4918	163.98	96.9	90.9
1988	1.9778	6.1370	1.4643	178.13	92.7	88.2
1989	2.1219	6.4559	1.6369	163.82	98.6	94.4
1990	1.8215	5.9231	1.3901	178.41	89.1	86.0

Source: Economic Advisors, *Economic Report of the President, 1992,* 420.

TABLE 4.45 EXCHANGE RATES—INDEXES OF VALUE OF FOREIGN CURRENCY RELATIVE TO U.S. DOLLAR, 1970–1990

(1982=100)

Year	United States	Belgium	Canada	Denmark	France	Germany[a]	Italy	Japan	Netherlands	Norway	Sweden	United Kingdom
1970	100.0	92.2	118.3	111.3	119.0	66.6	215.9	69.5	73.9	90.3	121.2	137.1
1980	100.0	156.8	105.6	148.2	155.9	133.8	158.3	110.4	134.6	130.8	148.6	133.1
1981	100.0	123.7	103.0	116.9	121.0	107.7	118.9	112.9	107.4	112.4	124.0	115.8
1982	100.0	100.0	100.0	100.0	100.0	100.0	100.0	100.0	100.0	100.0	100.0	100.0
1983	100.0	89.6	100.2	91.2	86.3	95.1	89.1	104.8	93.6	88.4	81.9	86.7
1984	100.0	79.3	95.3	80.6	75.3	85.3	77.1	104.9	83.3	79.1	76.0	76.5
1985	100.0	77.2	90.4	78.7	73.3	82.5	70.9	104.4	80.5	75.1	73.0	74.2
1986	100.0	102.5	88.8	103.1	95.0	111.9	90.8	147.9	109.1	87.3	88.2	84.0
1987	100.0	122.6	93.1	121.9	109.4	135.0	104.4	172.2	131.9	95.8	99.0	93.8
1988	100.0	124.5	100.3	123.8	110.4	138.2	104.0	194.3	135.1	99.0	102.4	101.9
1989	100.0	116.2	104.2	114.0	103.1	129.1	98.7	180.4	125.9	93.4	97.3	93.7
1990	100.0	137.0	105.8	134.8	120.8	150.2	113.0	171.8	146.7	103.2	106.1	102.1

[a] Designates West Germany, before unification.
Source: Bureau of the Census, *Statistical Abstract, 1992,* 850.

TABLE 4.46 VALUE OF EXPORTS AND IMPORTS, BY AREA, 1946–1983

(in millions of dollars)

Year	Europe Exports to	Europe Imports from	UK Exports to	UK Imports from	Germany Exports to	Germany Imports from	The Americas (not including United States) Exports to	The Americas (not including United States) Imports from	Asia Exports to	Asia Imports from	Japan Exports to	Japan Imports from
1946	4,122	804	855	158	83	3	3,684	2,762	1,327	887	102	81
1947	5,670	817	1,103	205	128	6	6,199	3,401	2,330	1,055	415	35
1948	4,279	1,121	644	290	863	32	5,307	4,100	2,130	1,346	325	63
1949	4,118	925	700	228	822	46	4,861	3,995	2,256	1,240	468	82
1950	3,306	1,449	548	335	440	104	4,902	5,064	1,540	1,638	418	182
1951	5,121	2,119	1,000	466	521	233	6,607	5,826	2,410	1,983	601	205
1952	5,089	2,029	787	485	450	212	6,682	6,025	2,541	1,813	633	229
1953	5,711	2,335	826	546	363	277	6,514	6,117	2,783	1,626	686	262
1954	5,118	2,083	808	501	505	278	6,521	5,896	2,577	1,467	693	279
1955	5,126	2,453	1,006	616	607	366	6,903	6,262	2,581	1,876	683	432
1956	6,437	2,963	985	726	943	494	8,243	6,856	3,418	1,996	998	558
1957	6,844	3,147	1,164	766	1,330	607	9,001	7,048	3,961	1,985	1,319	601
1958	5,570	3,341	905	864	888	629	7,999	6,703	3,411	1,984	987	667
1959	5,559	4,607	1,097	1,137	880	920	7,692	7,071	3,284	2,603	1,079	1,029
1960	7,406	4,268	1,487	993	1,275	897	7,684	6,864	4,186	2,722	1,447	1,149
1961	7,371	4,141	1,206	898	1,343	856	7,673	6,995	4,653	2,583	1,837	1,055
1962	7,758	4,621	1,128	1,005	1,581	962	7,724	7,591	4,676	2,960	1,574	1,358
1963	8,738	4,811	1,213	1,079	1,582	1,003	7,944	7,850	5,448	3,192	1,844	1,498
1964	9,436	5,307	1,532	1,143	1,606	1,171	9,207	8,390	5,802	3,620	2,009	1,768
1965	9,364	6,292	1,615	1,405	1,650	1,341	9,917	9,212	6,012	4,528	2,080	2,414
1966	10,003	7,857	1,737	1,786	1,674	1,796	11,429	10,829	6,733	5,276	2,364	2,963
1967	10,298	8,227	1,960	1,710	1,706	1,955	11,883	11,741	7,146	5,348	2,695	2,999
1968	11,347	10,337	2,289	2,058	1,709	2,721	13,411	14,148	7,582	6,911	2,954	4,054
1969	12,642	10,334	2,335	2,120	2,142	2,603	14,713	15,547	8,261	8,275	3,490	4,888
1970	14,817	11,395	2,536	2,194	2,741	3,127	15,612	16,928	10,023	9,621	4,652	5,875
1971	14,562	12,881	2,369	2,499	2,831	3,651	16,850	18,730	9,855	11,780	4,055	7,259
1972	16,181	15,744	2,658	2,987	2,808	4,250	19,690	21,930	11,297	15,117	4,963	9,064
1973	23,161	19,812	3,564	3,657	3,756	5,345	25,033	27,322	18,419	18,157	8,313	9,676
1974	30,070	24,625	4,574	4,061	4,985	6,324	35,745	40,325	25,785	27,345	10,679	12,338
1975	32,732	21,623	4,527	3,784	5,194	5,381	38,843	37,796	28,223	27,055	9,563	11,268
1976	35,901	23,640	4,801	4,254	5,731	5,592	41,074	43,356	29,729	39,367	10,145	15,504
1977	37,304	28,802	5,951	5,141	5,989	7,238	43,751	50,697	31,436	49,312	10,529	18,550
1978	43,608	36,483	7,116	6,514	6,957	9,962	50,394	56,473	39,630	58,264	12,885	24,458
1979	54,342	41,681	10,635	8,028	8,478	10,955	61,555	68,509	48,771	66,739	17,581	26,248
1980	67,512	46,602	12,694	9,842	10,960	11,693	74,114	78,687	60,168	80,299	20,790	30,714
1981	69,715	53,410	12,439	12,835	10,277	11,379	81,667	85,436	63,849	92,033	21,823	37,612
1982	63,664	53,413	10,645	13,095	9,291	11,975	67,312	84,467	64,822	85,170	20,966	37,744
1983	58,871	55,243	10,621	12,470	8,737	12,695	63,970	96,873	63,813	91,464	21,894	41,183

Source: Thelma Liesner, *Economic Statistics, 1900–1983* (New York, 1985), 59.

TABLE 4.47 TOP 20 PARTNERS IN TOTAL U.S. TRADE, 1984–1990

(domestic and foreign merchandise, F.a.s.; general imports, customs; millions of dollars)

Country	1984	1985	1986	1987	1988	1989	1990
Canada	118,255	122,293	123,764	130,899	153,020	166,762	175,238
Japan	80,710	91,414	108,793	112,824	127,244	138,046	138,240
Mexico	30,012	32,767	29,693	34,853	43,888	52,144	58,548
Germany	26,365	29,453	35,839	38,956	40,929	41,927	46,946
United Kingdom	26,701	26,210	26,814	31,455	36,341	39,156	43,772
Taiwan	19,771	21,096	25,315	32,034	36,843	35,647	34,149
Korea, South	15,335	15,969	19,084	25,086	31,337	33,195	32,892
France	14,150	15,578	17,344	18,673	22,478	24,593	26,776
Italy	12,309	14,299	15,446	16,569	18,351	19,148	20,711
China	6,069	7,717	7,877	9,791	13,532	17,745	20,031
Netherlands	11,623	11,350	11,913	12,180	14,675	16,174	17,988
Singapore	7,654	7,735	8,105	10,254	13,741	16,347	17,859
Hong Kong	11,329	11,182	11,921	13,837	15,925	16,014	16,328
Belgium/ Luxembourg	8,440	8,305	9,405	10,360	11,904	13,077	15,027
Saudi Arabia	9,305	6,381	7,061	7,806	9,396	10,731	14,009
Brazil	10,261	10,666	10,698	11,905	13,561	13,214	13,038
Australia	7,468	8,277	8,179	8,500	10,514	12,204	12,967
Venezuela	9,920	9,936	8,238	9,165	9,769	9,796	12,554
Switzerland	5,679	5,764	8,229	7,400	8,808	9,626	10,396
Malaysia	4,576	3,839	4,150	4,818	5,833	7,614	8,697

Source: Department of Commerce, *Trade Highlights, 1990* (Washington, D.C., 1991), 23.

TABLE 4.48 FOREIGN INVESTMENT IN THE UNITED STATES AND U.S. INVESTMENT ABROAD, 1950–1989

(in millions of dollars)

Year	All Areas	Canada	Europe	Japan
Foreign Direct Investment in the United States				
1950	3,391	1,029	2,228	. . .
1960	6,910	1,934	4,707	88
1970	13,270	3,117	9,554	229
1980	83,046	12,162	54,688	4,723
1981	108,714	12,116	72,377	7,697
1982	124,677	11,708	83,193	9,677
1983	137,061	11,434	92,936	11,336
1984	164,583	15,286	108,211	16,044
1985	184,615	17,131	121,413	19,313
1986	220,414	20,318	144,181	26,824
1987	271,788	24,013	186,076	35,151
1988	328,850	27,361	216,418	53,354
1989	400,817	31,538	262,011	69,699
U.S. Investment Abroad				
1950	11,788	3,579	1,733	19
1960	32,778	11,198	6,681	254
1970	78,178	22,790	24,516	1,483
1980	215,578	44,978	96,539	6,243
1981	227,342	46,957	101,318	6,807
1982	221,343	44,509	99,877	6,872
1983	207,203	44,339	92,178	7,661
1984	211,480	46,730	91,589	7,936
1985	230,250	46,909	105,171	9,235
1986	259,562	49,994	122,165	11,332
1987	314,307	57,783	150,439	15,684
1988	333,501	62,610	156,932	17,927
1989	373,436	66,856	176,736	19,341

Source: Harold W. Stanley and Richard G. Niemi, *Vital Statistics on American Politics,* (Washington, D.C., 1992), 364.

TABLE 4.49 DIRECT FOREIGN INVESTMENT IN THE UNITED STATES, BY AREA AND COUNTRY, 1980–1990

(in millions of dollars)

Area and Industry	1980	1983	1984	1985	1986	1987	1988	1989	1990
All areas	**83,046**	**137,061**	**164,583**	**184,615**	**220,414**	**263,394**	**314,754**	**368,924**	**396,702**
Petroleum	12,200	18,209	25,400	28,270	29,094	37,815	36,006	40,345	42,165
Manufacturing	32,993	47,665	51,802	59,584	71,963	93,865	122,582	150,949	157,431
Finance and insurance	12,027	10,934	24,881	27,429	34,978	39,455	44,010	59,597	53,782
Trade, wholesale and retail	15,210	26,513	31,219	35,873	42,920	45,399	53,590	54,005	59,627
Canada	**12,162**	**11,434**	**15,286**	**17,131**	**20,318**	**24,684**	**26,566**	**30,370**	**30,037**
Petroleum	1,817	1,391	1,544	1,589	1,432	1,088	1,181	1,141	1,394
Manufacturing	5,227	3,313	4,115	4,607	6,108	8,085	9,730	9,766	9,652
Finance and insurance	1,612	1,061	3,245	4,008	4,283	5,797	5,769	7,356	7,779
Europe	**54,688**	**92,936**	**108,211**	**121,413**	**144,181**	**181,006**	**208,942**	**239,190**	**250,973**
Petroleum	10,137	16,326	23,142	25,636	26,139	35,700	33,499	32,649	33,608
Manufacturing	21,953	36,866	39,083	45,841	56,016	74,300	95,641	118,129	121,292
Finance and insurance	8,673	8,450	15,945	17,022	21,787	26,336	27,121	33,157	29,400
United Kingdom	14,105	32,152	38,387	43,555	55,935	75,519	95,698	103,458	102,790
Petroleum	−257	5,955	10,991	12,155	11,758	17,950	19,522	16,666	15,841
Manufacturing	6,159	9,221	9,179	11,687	16,500	30,372	41,708	50,166	47,304
Finance and insurance	3,350	3,777	5,485	6,483	10,163	9,801	11,256	12,790	12,577
Netherlands	19,140	29,182	33,728	37,056	40,717	46,636	48,128	56,734	63,938
Petroleum	9,265	8,646	9,981	11,481	. . .	. . .	9,045	10,061	12,686
Manufacturing	4,777	11,222	12,497	13,351	13,293	15,615	17,843	23,090	24,717
Switzerland	5,070	7,464	8,146	10,568	12,058	13,772	14,372	18,746	17,745
Manufacturing	3,116	4,165	4,774	6,881	7,520	6,921	7,613	11,798	10,393
Finance and insurance	1,033	1,830	. . .	5,425	2,517	3,211	3,506	4,492	4,796
Germany	7,596	10,845	12,330	14,816	17,250	21,905	25,250	28,386	28,309
Manufacturing	3,875	4,487	4,389	6,015	7,426	10,298	13,980	15,560	15,695
Finance and insurance	1,248	1,416	1,902	. . .	1,962	3,442	2,683	3,139	2,484
Other Europe	8,777	13,293	15,620	15,417	18,221	23,174	25,494	31,866	38,191
Petroleum	991	1,679	2,080	. . .	. . .	. . .	4,580	4,786	4,806
Manufacturing	4,026	7,771	7,704	7,907	11,277	11,094	14,497	17,515	23,183
Finance and insurance	1,193	−908	. . .	. . .	. . .	2,189	406	2,519	1,408
Japan	**4,723**	**11,336**	**16,044**	**19,313**	**26,824**	**34,421**	**51,126**	**67,268**	**81,775**
Other areas	**11,472**	**21,356**	**25,043**	**26,758**	**29,091**	**23,283**	**28,120**	**32,096**	**33,917**

Source: Bureau of the Census, *Statistical Abstract, 1993,* 798.

TABLE 4.50 U.S. MERCHANDISE EXPORTS AND IMPORTS BY PRINCIPAL END-USE CATEGORY, 1965–1990
(billions of dollars; quarterly data seasonally adjusted)

Year or Quarter	Exports							Imports						
			Nonagricultural Products							Nonpetroleum Products				
	Total	Agricultural Products	Total	Industrial Supplies and Materials	Capital Goods Except Automotive	Automotive	Other	Total	Petroleum and Products	Total	Industrial Supplies and Materials	Capital Goods Except Automotive	Automotive	Other
1965	26.5	6.3	20.2	7.6	8.1	1.9	2.6	21.5	2.0	1.5	19.5	9.1	0.9	8.0
1966	29.3	6.9	22.4	8.2	8.9	2.4	2.9	25.5	2.1	2.2	23.4	10.2	1.8	9.2
1967	30.7	6.5	24.2	8.5	9.9	2.8	3.0	26.9	2.1	2.5	24.8	10.0	2.4	9.9
1968	33.6	6.3	27.3	9.6	11.1	3.5	3.2	33.0	2.4	2.8	30.6	12.0	4.0	11.8
1969	36.4	6.1	30.3	10.3	12.4	3.9	3.7	35.8	2.6	3.4	33.2	11.8	4.9	13.0
1970	42.5	7.4	35.1	12.3	14.7	3.9	4.3	39.9	2.9	4.0	36.9	12.4	5.5	15.0
1971	43.3	7.8	35.5	10.9	15.4	4.7	4.5	45.6	3.7	4.3	41.9	13.8	7.4	16.4
1972	49.4	9.5	39.9	11.9	16.9	5.5	5.6	55.8	4.7	5.9	51.1	16.3	8.7	20.2
1973	71.4	18.0	53.4	17.0	22.0	6.9	7.6	70.5	8.4	8.3	62.1	19.6	10.3	23.9
1974	98.3	22.4	75.9	26.3	30.9	8.6	10.0	103.8	26.6	9.8	77.2	27.8	12.0	27.5
1975	107.1	22.2	84.8	26.8	36.6	10.6	10.8	98.2	27.0	10.2	71.2	24.0	11.7	25.3
1976	114.7	23.4	91.4	28.4	39.1	12.1	11.7	124.2	34.6	12.3	89.7	29.8	16.2	31.4
1977	120.8	24.3	96.5	29.8	39.8	13.4	13.5	151.9	45.0	14.0	106.9	35.7	18.6	38.6
1978	142.1	29.9	112.2	34.0	47.3	15.7	15.2	176.0	42.6	19.4	133.4	40.6	25.0	48.4
1979	184.5	35.6	148.9	52.1	60.0	18.3	18.5	212.0	61.0	24.5	151.1	47.5	26.5	52.6
1980	224.3	42.2	182.1	65.3	76.3	17.4	23.2	249.8	79.4	31.4	170.4	52.9	28.1	58.0
1981	237.1	44.0	193.0	63.8	83.9	19.7	25.6	265.1	78.6	36.9	186.5	56.4	30.9	62.3
1982	211.2	37.2	174.0	58.0	76.0	17.4	22.5	247.6	62.0	38.4	185.6	48.9	34.0	64.3
1983	201.8	37.1	164.7	52.9	71.3	18.6	21.8	268.9	55.3	43.2	213.6	53.9	43.2	73.3
1984	219.9	38.4	181.5	56.8	77.0	22.6	25.1	332.4	58.0	60.5	274.4	66.0	56.6	91.4
1985	215.9	29.6	186.4	54.8	79.6	25.1	26.8	338.1	51.3	61.4	286.8	62.4	65.1	97.9
1986	223.4	27.4	196.0	59.4	82.9	25.3	28.3	368.4	34.4	72.1	334.0	69.9	78.1	113.9
1987	250.3	29.5	220.7	63.6	92.4	28.1	36.6	409.8	42.9	85.1	366.8	70.8	85.2	125.7
1988	320.3	38.2	282.1	82.6	119.0	33.9	46.6	447.3	39.6	102.2	407.7	83.1	87.9	134.5
1989	361.5	42.2	319.3	91.9	139.3	34.9	53.1	477.4	50.9	112.5	426.4	84.2	87.4	142.4
1990	389.6	40.2	349.3	96.7	153.8	37.4	61.4	497.7	62.1	116.4	435.6	82.5	87.3	149.3

Source: Economic Advisors, *Economic Report of the President, 1992*, 414.

TABLE 4.51 U.S. RELIANCE ON FOREIGN SUPPLIES OF MINERALS

Mineral	Percent Imported in 1990	Major Sources (1986–1989)	Major Uses
Columbium	100	Brazil, Canada, Thailand, Germany	Steelmaking and aerospace alloys
Graphite	100	Mexico, China, Brazil, Madagascar	Metallurgical processes
Manganese	100	Gabon, South Africa	Steelmaking
Mica (sheet)	100	India, Belgium, France, Brazil	Electronic and electrical equipment
Strontium (Celestite)	100	Mexico, Spain, Germany	Television picture tubes, pyrotechnics
Bauxite and alumina	98	Australia, Guinea, Jamaica, Suriname	Aluminum production
Diamonds (industrial)	92	South Africa, Britain, Ireland, Zaire	Machinery for grinding and cutting
Fluorspar	90	Mexico, South Africa	Raw material for metallurgical and chemical industries
Platinum group	88	South Africa, Britain, USSR	Catalytic converters for autos, electrical and electronic equipment
Cobalt	86	Zaire, Zambia, Canada, Norway	Aerospace alloys
Tantalum	85	Thailand, Brazil, Australia, Germany	Electronic components
Nickel	83	Canada, Australia, Norway	Stainless steel and other alloys
Chromium	79	South Africa, Zimbabwe, Turkey, Yugoslavia	Stainless steel
Tin	76	Brazil, Indonesia, China	Cans, electrical construction
Tungsten	73	China, Bolivia, Germany, Peru	Lamp filaments
Barite	69	China, Morocco, India	Oil drilling fluids
Potash	68	Canada, Israel, USSR	Fertilizer
Cadmium	54	Canada, Australia, Mexico, Germany	Batteries, plating and coating of metals
Silver	NA	Canada, Mexico, Britain, Peru	Photography, electrical and electronic products

Source: U.S. Bureau of Mines information, cited in *World Almanac, 1992*, 685.

TABLE 4.52 **JAPANESE-OWNED MANUFACTURING PLANTS IN THE UNITED STATES, BY STATE, 1989**

State	Manufacturing Plants	By Number of Plants
Ala.	17	1. Calif.
Alaska	26	2. Ohio
Ariz.	10	3. Ill.
Ark.	13	4. Ga.
Calif.	235	5. Mich.
Colo.	10	6. Ind.
Conn.	9	7. Ky.
Del.	2	8. Tex.
D.C.	0	9. N.J.
Fla.	14	10. N.C.
Ga.	65	11. Tenn.
Hawaii	14	12. Wash.
Idaho	1	13. Pa.
Ill.	86	14. N.Y.
Ind.	53	15. Alaska
Iowa	6	16. Mass.
Kans.	6	17. S.C.
Ky.	49	18. Oreg.
La.	4	19. N.H.
Maine	9	20. Ala
Md.	12	Va.
Mass.	24	22. Mo.
Mich.	61	23. Fla.
Minn.	5	Hawaii

State	Manufacturing Plants	By Number of Plants
Miss.	7	25. Ark.
Mo.	15	26. Md.
Mont.	0	27. Okla.
Nebr.	9	28. Ariz.
Nev.	9	Colo.
N.H.	20	30. Conn.
N.J.	47	Maine
N.Mex.	2	Nebr.
N.Y.	35	Nev.
N.C.	43	34. Miss.
N.Dak.	0	Wis.
Ohio	100	36. Iowa
Okla.	11	Kans.
Oreg.	22	38. Minn.
Pa.	36	39. La.
R.I.	1	Utah
S.C.	23	Vt.
S.Dak.	1	42. Del.
Tenn.	41	N.Mex.
Tex.	48	W.Va.
Utah	4	45. Idaho
Vt.	4	R.I.
Va.	17	S.Dak.
Wash.	40	48. D.C.
W.Va.	2	Mont.
Wis.	7	N.Dak.
Wyo.	0	Wyo.
U.S.	1,275	

Source: Congressional Quarterly, Inc., *CQ's State Fact Finder: Ranking Across America* (Washington, D.C., 1993), 32.

TABLE 4.53   U.S. INVESTMENT ABROAD BY COUNTRY, 1980–1990
(in millions of dollars)

Country	1980	1985	1987	1988	1989	1990 Total	1990 Manufacturing	1990 Petroleum	1990 Finance
All countries	215,375	230,250	314,307	335,893	370,091	421,494	168,220	59,736	98,889
Developed countries	158,214	172,058	237,508	252,649	274,564	312,186	134,658	41,551	67,917
Canada	45,119	46,909	57,783	62,656	65,548	68,431	33,231	10,691	12,025
Europe	96,287	105,171	150,439	157,077	175,213	204,204	83,992	24,356	52,227
Austria	524	493	691	669	588	767	63	. . .	. . .
Belgium	6,259	5,038	7,267	7,501	7,941	9,462	4,331	327	2,059
Denmark	1,266	1,281	1,070	1,161	1,234	1,633	286	. . .	295
France	9,347	7,643	11,868	13,041	14,069	17,134	11,051	. . .	960
Greece	347	210	132	195	264	300	84	37	. . .
Ireland	2,319	3,693	5,425	5,886	5,522	6,776	4,885	−41	1,549
Italy	5,397	5,906	9,264	9,496	10,294	12,971	8,535	605	1,005
Luxembourg	652	690	660	841	1,127	1,119	539	22	238
Netherlands	8,039	7,129	14,842	16,145	18,133	22,778	8,144	1,636	8,642
Norway	1,679	3,215	3,843	4,371	3,547	3,633	121	2,954	. . .
Portugal	257	237	495	546	488	590	285	. . .	. . .
Spain	2,678	2,281	4,076	4,966	6,096	7,480	4,998	116	3
Sweden	1,474	933	1,139	1,119	1,129	1,526	1,060	16	36
Switzerland	11,280	15,766	19,665	18,734	19,209	23,733	1,177	. . .	11,049
Turkey	207	234	207	246	310	507	117	173	. . .
United Kingdom	28,460	33,024	44,512	49,459	59,827	64,983	20,636	11,331	23,071
West Germany	15,415	16,764	24,388	21,832	24,550	27,715	17,489	3,136	2,863
Japan	6,225	9,235	15,684	18,009	18,488	20,994	10,623	3,419	2,240
Australia	7,654	8,772	11,363	12,823	13,331	14,529	6,060	2,615	1,116
New Zealand	579	576	743	833	1,140	3,139	341	. . .	257
South Africa	2,350	1,394	1,497	1,252	843	889	411	. . .	54

Country	1980	1985	1987	1988	1989	1990			
						Total	Manu-facturing	Petro-leum	Finance
Developing countries	**53,206**	**52,764**	**73,017**	**80,060**	**92,098**	**105,721**	**33,562**	**15,658**	**30,972**
Latin America	38,761	28,261	47,551	53,506	62,727	72,467	23,802	5,275	27,250
South America	16,342	17,623	21,227	21,815	23,612	24,920	15,242	2,038	2,065
Argentina	2,540	2,705	2,744	2,597	2,684	2,889	1,566	437	164
Brazil	7,704	8,893	10,951	12,609	14,522	15,416	11,286	650	1,351
Chile	536	88	348	672	1,069	1,341	275	. . .	418
Colombia	1,012	2,148	3,104	2,248	1,977	2,043	799	. . .	30
Ecuador	322	361	466	431	393	389	174	121	. . .
Peru	1,665	1,243	1,022	976	939	600	78	−2	. . .
Venezuela	1,908	1,588	2,095	1,903	1,503	1,581	963	278	74
Central America	10,193	9,658	12,218	13,380	16,050	18,911	8,171	2,269	5,647
Mexico	5,986	5,088	4,913	5,712	7,280	9,360	7,314	80	314
Panama	3,170	3,959	6,622	6,874	7,889	8,521	363	1,927	5,312
Other	1,037	611	683	794	881	1,029	494	263	21
Costa Rica	303	113	141	169	163	193	. . .	. . .	. . .
El Salvador	105	73	51	56	57	66	. . .	. . .	. . .
Guatemala	229	213	174	201	215	245	. . .	. . .	. . .
Honduras	288	171	185	240	317	315	. . .	. . .	. . .
Other W. Hemisphere	12,226	980	14,106	18,311	23,065	28,636	389	967	19,539
Bahamas	2,712	3,795	3,814	4,112	4,257	4,301	60	235	841
Bermuda	11,045	13,116	19,215	19,022	17,717	18,972	. . .	−60	18,185
Dominican Republic	316	212	156	138	361	478	. . .	. . .	. . .
Jamaica	407	122	103	134	223	276	152	. . .	3
Netherlands Antilles	−4,336	−20,499	−14,235	−9,983	−5,956	−1,401	38	. . .	−1,689
Trinidad and Tobago	951	484	400	447	503	413	9	. . .	6
Other Africa	3,778	4,497	4,372	4,219	3,993	3,780	416	2,716	265
Egypt	1,038	1,926	1,669	1,637	1,744	1,451	45	1,117	−4
Libya	575	325	310	315	252	246	. . .	228	. . .
Nigeria	18	44	894	660	406	210	67	163	. . .
Middle East	2,163	4,606	4,084	3,806	4,166	4,755	911	2,033	884
Israel	379	717	635	701	756	818	311	. . .	. . .
Saudi Arabia	1,037	2,442	2,092	1,782	1,955	2,523	576	558	. . .
United Arab Emirates	384	792	694	672	652	584	13	. . .	. . .
Bahrain	−16	440	−340	−311	−28	−100	. . .	. . .	. . .
Other Asia and Pacific	8,505	15,400	17,010	18,528	21,212	24,719	8,433	5,635	2,573
China: Taiwan	498	750	1,372	1,621	1,921	2,273	1,449	−9	127
Hong Kong	2,078	3,295	4,389	5,240	5,948	6,537	775	188	2,007
India	398	383	439	436	527	639	511	11	−1
Indonesia	1,314	4,475	3,070	2,921	3,770	3,827	135	3,209	. . .
Malaysia	632	1,140	952	1,135	1,174	1,425	861	379	47
Philippines	1,259	1,032	1,396	1,513	1,657	1,655	818	149	95
Singapore	1,204	1,874	2,384	2,311	2,318	3,971	2,361	775	126
South Korea	575	743	1,178	1,501	1,855	2,096	920	7	98
Thailand	361	1,074	1,274	1,132	1,271	1,515	461	719	23
Other	186	635	556	719	772	782	141	207	. . .
China: Mainland	−6	311	207	307	371	289	. . .	. . .	. . .
International	**3,955**	**5,428**	**3,782**	**3,184**	**3,430**	**3,586**	**−**	**2,527**	**−**
Addendum—OPEC	*6,090*	*10,383*	*9,899*	*8,827*	*9,046*	*9,828*	*1,930*	*5,516*	*941*

Source: Bureau of Census, *Statistical Abstract, 1992,* 789.

Employment

Working and the workforce changed in many ways during the years 1946 to 1990. The labor force and the number of people employed roughly doubled. People employed on farms shrank from some 10 million to fewer than 3 million, and the displaced farmers needed to be absorbed into the nonagricultural workforce. More people were working, and the people who worked represented a larger portion of the general population. The unemployment rate continued to be one of the two or three most important economic indicators. The rate fluctuated fairly broadly—from a low of 2.9 percent in 1953 to a high of nearly 10 percent in 1982. Lowest rates corresponded with the period after the Second World War and during the Vietnam War era; highest rates began with the end of the war in Indochina and reached almost to the end of the 1980s.

The most important shifts in employment practices involved a stagnation (and eventually a decline) in traditional manufacturing work that set in in the 1960s and became persistent and seemingly permanent. Despite a huge growth in population, there were fewer manufacturing jobs in 1990 than there had been in 1966. The great growth came in service work—a nearly sixfold increase between 1947 and 1990 and more than threefold growth in all service-related areas. By the 1980s appealing and rewarding opportunities had broadened in various highly skilled technological industries. In spite of constant conservative complaints about centralization of power and the bloated Washington bureacracy, employment in the national government increased slowly; the largest growth came in state and local government, if only because there were so many more units.

An element receiving increased attention in the workplace was the intersection between race, ethnicity, gender, and employment practices. The starting point had been the scarcity of opportunities open to members of minority groups—the "last hired, first fired" adage applied to blacks, their high unemployment rate and concentration in low-paying menial jobs. Employment had been a part of the Civil Rights movement, and the Civil Rights Act of 1964 carried specific antidiscrimination provisions. That measure also had introduced a new term: *affirmative action,* which by the 1980s had been redefined to mean preferential employment treatment for members of designated underrepresented groups. The unemployment rate for blacks in 1990 was approximately double that of the white rate.

Perhaps the most striking change in the composition of the workforce was the increase in the number of women. If approximately 33 percent of women had been working in 1950, by 1990 it had grown to nearly 60 percent, and women were making up nearly half of the workforce. More than half of married women worked; more than 80 percent of black women with children 6–13 worked. Women were having fewer children, having them later, or returning to work after childbirth. Many women still worked in such traditionally female jobs as nursing, clerical, and elementary school teaching, but women in growing numbers had broken into previously male-dominated professions. Better educated and trained for specific careers, women also could claim the offerings of affirmative-action programs. Perhaps the largest changes produced from affirmative action came in the area of gender.

TABLE 4.54 EMPLOYMENT STATUS OF THE CIVILIAN NONINSTITUTIONAL POPULATION, 1947–1990[a]

(thousands of persons)

| | | Civilian Labor Force | | | | | | | | Not in Labor Force |
| | Civilian Noninstitutional Population | | | Employed | | | | Unemployed | | |
Year		Total	Percent of Population	Total	Percent of Population	Agriculture	Non-agricultural Industries	Number	Percent of Labor Force	
1947	101,827	59,350	58.3	57,038	56.0	7,890	49,148	2,311	3.9	42,477
1948	103,068	60,621	58.8	58,343	56.6	7,629	50,714	2,276	3.8	42,447
1949	103,994	61,286	58.9	57,651	55.4	7,658	49,993	3,637	5.9	42,708
1950	104,995	62,208	59.2	58,918	56.1	7,160	51,758	3,288	5.3	42,787
1951	104,621	62,017	59.2	59,961	57.3	6,726	53,235	2,055	3.3	42,604
1952	105,231	62,138	59.0	60,250	57.3	6,500	53,749	1,883	3.0	43,093
1953	107,056	63,015	58.9	61,179	57.1	6,260	54,919	1,834	2.9	44,041
1954	108,321	63,643	58.8	60,109	55.5	6,205	53,904	3,532	5.5	44,678
1955	109,683	65,023	59.3	62,170	56.7	6,450	55,722	2,852	4.4	44,660
1956	110,954	66,552	60.0	63,799	57.5	6,283	57,514	2,750	4.1	44,402
1957	112,265	66,929	59.6	64,071	57.1	5,947	58,123	2,859	4.3	45,336
1958	113,727	67,639	59.5	63,036	55.4	5,586	57,450	4,602	6.8	46,088
1959	115,329	68,369	59.3	64,630	56.0	5,565	59,065	3,740	5.5	46,960
1960	117,245	69,628	59.4	65,778	56.1	5,458	60,318	3,852	5.5	47,617
1961	118,771	70,459	59.3	65,746	55.4	5,200	60,546	4,714	6.7	48,312
1962	120,153	70,614	58.8	66,702	55.5	4,944	61,759	3,911	5.5	49,539
1963	122,416	71,833	58.7	67,762	55.4	4,687	63,076	4,070	5.7	50,583
1964	124,485	73,091	58.7	69,305	55.7	4,523	64,782	3,786	5.2	51,394
1965	126,513	74,455	58.9	71,088	56.2	4,361	66,726	3,366	4.5	52,058
1966	128,058	75,770	59.2	72,895	56.9	3,979	68,915	2,875	3.8	52,288
1967	129,874	77,347	59.6	74,372	57.3	3,844	70,527	2,975	3.8	52,527
1968	132,028	78,737	59.6	75,920	57.5	3,817	72,103	2,817	3.6	53,291
1969	134,335	80,734	60.1	77,902	58.0	3,606	74,296	2,832	3.5	53,602
1970	137,085	82,771	60.4	78,678	57.4	3,463	75,215	4,093	4.9	54,315
1971	140,216	84,382	60.2	79,367	56.6	3,394	75,972	5,016	5.9	55,834
1972	144,126	87,034	60.4	82,153	57.0	3,484	78,669	4,882	5.6	57,091
1973	147,096	89,429	60.8	85,064	57.8	3,470	81,594	4,365	4.9	57,667
1974	150,120	91,949	61.3	86,794	57.8	3,515	83,279	5,156	5.6	58,171
1975	153,153	93,775	61.2	85,846	56.1	3,408	82,438	7,929	8.5	59,377
1976	156,150	96,158	61.6	88,752	56.8	3,331	85,421	7,406	7.7	59,991
1977	159,033	99,009	62.3	92,017	57.9	3,283	88,734	6,991	7.1	60,025
1978	161,910	102,251	63.2	96,048	59.3	3,387	92,661	6,202	6.1	59,659
1979	164,863	104,962	63.7	98,824	59.9	3,347	95,477	6,137	5.8	59,900
1980	167,745	106,940	63.8	99,303	59.2	3,364	95,938	7,637	7.1	60,806
1981	170,130	108,670	63.9	100,397	59.0	3,368	97,030	8,273	7.6	61,460
1982	172,271	110,204	64.0	99,526	57.8	3,401	96,125	10,678	9.7	62,067
1983	174,215	111,550	64.0	100,834	57.9	3,383	97,450	10,717	9.6	62,665
1984	176,383	113,544	64.4	105,005	59.5	3,321	101,685	8,539	7.5	62,839
1985	178,206	115,461	64.8	107,150	60.1	3,179	103,971	8,312	7.2	62,744
1986	180,587	117,834	65.3	109,597	60.7	3,163	106,434	8,237	7.0	62,752
1987	182,753	119,865	65.6	112,440	61.5	3,208	109,232	7,425	6.2	62,888
1988	184,613	121,669	65.9	114,968	62.3	3,169	111,800	6,701	5.5	62,944
1989	186,393	123,869	66.5	117,342	63.0	3,199	114,142	6,528	5.3	62,523
1990	189,164	125,840	66.5	118,793	62.8	3,223	115,570	7,047	5.6	63,324

[a] Applies to persons more than 16 years old who were not institutionalized, as in correctional facilities, nursing homes, or juvenile detention centers.
Source: Eva E. Jacobs, ed., *Handbook of Labor Statistics* (Lanham, Md., 1997), 11.

(thousands of persons; monthly data seasonally adjusted)

| | Goods-Producing Industries | | | | Manufacturing | | | | Service-Producing Industries | | | | | | Government | | |
Year	Total	Total	Min-ing	Con-struc-tion	Total	Durable Goods	Non-dura-ble Goods	Year	Total	Trans-porta-tion and Public Utilities	Whole-sale Trade	Retail Trade	Finance, Insur-ance, and Real Estate	Ser-vices	Total	Federal	State and Local
1946	41,652	17,248	862	1,683	14,703	7,785	6,918	1946	24,404	4,061	2,298	6,077	1,675	4,697	5,595	2,254	3,341
1947	43,857	18,509	955	2,009	15,545	8,358	7,187	1947	25,348	4,166	2,478	6,477	1,728	5,025	5,474	1,892	3,582
1948	44,866	18,774	994	2,198	15,582	8,298	7,285	1948	26,092	4,189	2,612	6,659	1,800	5,181	5,650	1,863	3,787
1949	43,754	17,565	930	2,194	14,441	7,462	6,979	1949	26,189	4,001	2,610	6,654	1,828	5,239	5,856	1,908	3,948
1950	45,197	18,506	901	2,364	15,241	8,066	7,175	1950	26,691	4,034	2,643	6,743	1,888	5,356	6,026	1,928	4,098
1951	47,819	19,959	929	2,637	16,393	9,059	7,334	1951	27,860	4,226	2,735	7,007	1,956	5,547	6,389	2,302	4,087
1952	48,793	20,198	898	2,668	16,632	9,320	7,313	1952	28,595	4,248	2,821	7,184	2,035	5,699	6,609	2,420	4,188
1953	50,202	21,074	866	2,659	17,549	10,080	7,468	1953	29,128	4,290	2,862	7,385	2,111	5,835	6,645	2,305	4,340
1954	48,990	19,751	791	2,646	16,314	9,101	7,213	1954	29,239	4,084	2,875	7,360	2,200	5,969	6,751	2,188	4,563
1955	50,641	20,513	792	2,839	16,882	9,511	7,370	1955	30,128	4,141	2,934	7,601	2,298	6,240	6,914	2,187	4,727
1956	52,369	21,104	822	3,039	17,243	9,802	7,442	1956	31,266	4,244	3,027	7,831	2,389	6,497	7,278	2,209	5,069
1957	52,853	20,964	828	2,962	17,174	9,825	7,351	1957	31,889	4,241	3,037	7,848	2,438	6,708	7,616	2,217	5,399
1958	51,324	19,513	751	2,817	15,945	8,801	7,144	1958	31,811	3,976	2,989	7,761	2,481	6,765	7,839	2,191	5,648
1959	53,268	20,411	732	3,004	16,675	9,342	7,333	1959	32,857	4,011	3,092	8,035	2,549	7,087	8,083	2,233	5,850
1960	54,189	20,434	712	2,926	16,796	9,429	7,367	1960	33,755	4,004	3,153	8,238	2,628	7,378	8,353	2,270	6,083
1961	53,999	19,857	672	2,859	16,326	9,041	7,285	1961	34,142	3,903	3,142	8,195	2,688	7,619	8,594	2,279	6,315
1962	55,549	20,451	650	2,948	16,853	9,450	7,403	1962	35,098	3,906	3,207	8,359	2,754	7,982	8,890	2,340	6,550
1963	56,653	20,640	635	3,010	16,995	9,586	7,410	1963	36,013	3,903	3,258	8,520	2,830	8,277	9,225	2,358	6,868
1964	58,283	21,005	634	3,097	17,274	9,785	7,489	1964	37,278	3,951	3,347	8,812	2,911	8,660	9,596	2,348	7,248
1965	60,765	21,926	632	3,232	18,062	10,374	7,688	1965	38,839	4,036	3,477	9,239	2,977	9,036	10,074	2,378	7,696
1966	63,901	23,158	627	3,317	19,214	11,250	7,963	1966	40,743	4,158	3,608	9,637	3,058	9,498	10,784	2,564	8,220
1967	65,803	23,308	613	3,248	19,447	11,408	8,039	1967	42,495	4,268	3,700	9,906	3,185	10,045	11,391	2,719	8,672
1968	67,897	23,737	606	3,350	19,781	11,594	8,187	1968	44,160	4,318	3,791	10,308	3,337	10,567	11,839	2,737	9,102
1969	70,384	24,361	619	3,575	20,167	11,862	8,304	1969	46,023	4,442	3,919	10,785	3,512	11,169	12,195	2,758	9,437
1970	70,880	23,578	623	3,588	19,367	11,176	8,190	1970	47,302	4,515	4,006	11,034	3,645	11,548	12,554	2,731	9,823
1971	71,214	22,935	609	3,704	18,623	10,604	8,019	1971	48,278	4,476	4,014	11,338	3,772	11,797	12,881	2,696	10,185
1972	73,675	23,668	628	3,889	19,151	11,022	8,129	1972	50,007	4,541	4,127	11,822	3,908	12,276	13,334	2,684	10,649
1973	76,790	24,893	642	4,097	20,154	11,863	8,291	1973	51,897	4,656	4,291	12,315	4,046	12,857	13,732	2,663	11,068
1974	78,265	24,794	697	4,020	20,077	11,897	8,181	1974	53,471	4,725	4,447	12,539	4,148	13,441	14,170	2,724	11,446
1975	76,945	22,600	752	3,525	18,323	10,662	7,661	1975	54,345	4,542	4,430	12,630	4,165	13,892	14,686	2,748	11,937
1976	79,382	23,352	779	3,576	18,997	11,051	7,946	1976	56,030	4,582	4,562	13,193	4,271	14,551	14,871	2,733	12,138
1977	82,471	24,346	813	3,851	19,682	11,570	8,112	1977	58,125	4,713	4,723	13,792	4,467	15,302	15,127	2,727	12,399
1978	86,697	25,585	851	4,229	20,505	12,245	8,259	1978	61,113	4,923	4,985	14,556	4,724	16,252	15,672	2,753	12,919
1979	89,823	26,461	958	4,463	21,040	12,730	8,310	1979	63,363	5,136	5,221	14,972	4,975	17,112	15,947	2,773	13,174
1980	90,406	25,658	1,027	4,346	20,285	12,159	8,127	1980	64,748	5,146	5,292	15,018	5,160	17,890	16,241	2,866	13,375
1981	91,156	25,497	1,139	4,188	20,170	12,082	8,089	1981	65,659	5,165	5,376	15,172	5,298	18,619	16,031	2,772	13,259
1982	89,566	23,813	1,128	3,905	18,781	11,014	7,767	1982	65,753	5,082	5,296	15,161	5,341	19,036	15,837	2,739	13,098
1983	90,200	23,334	952	3,948	18,434	10,707	7,726	1983	66,866	4,954	5,286	15,595	5,468	19,694	15,869	2,774	13,096
1984	94,496	24,727	966	4,383	19,378	11,479	7,899	1984	69,769	5,159	5,574	16,526	5,689	20,797	16,024	2,807	13,216
1985	97,519	24,859	927	4,673	19,260	11,464	7,796	1985	72,660	5,238	5,736	17,336	5,955	21,999	16,394	2,875	13,519
1986	99,525	24,558	777	4,816	18,965	11,203	7,761	1986	74,967	5,255	5,774	17,909	6,283	23,053	16,693	2,899	13,794
1987	102,200	24,708	717	4,967	19,024	11,167	7,858	1987	77,492	5,372	5,865	18,462	6,547	24,235	17,010	2,943	14,067
1988	105,536	25,173	713	5,110	19,350	11,381	7,969	1988	80,363	5,527	6,055	19,077	6,649	25,669	17,386	2,971	14,415
1989	108,329	25,322	693	5,187	19,442	11,420	8,022	1989	83,007	5,644	6,221	19,549	6,695	27,120	17,779	2,988	14,791
1990	109,971	24,958	711	5,136	19,111	11,115	7,995	1990	85,014	5,826	6,205	19,683	6,739	28,240	18,322	3,085	15,237

Source: Council of Advisors, *Economic Report of the President, 1992,* 344–345.

Weary and grimy, underground miners finish a shift at Kopperston, West Virginia, August, 22 1946. (National Archives)

Gender and Professions: An Opinion Poll, 1950

Interviewing Date 6/4–9/50
Survey #456-K   Question #14

Suppose a young man came to you and asked your advice about taking up a profession. Assuming that he was qualified to enter any of these professions, which one of them would you first recommend to him? (on card)

Doctor of medicine	29%	Professor, teacher	5%
Engineer, builder	16%	Banker	4%
Business executive	8%	Dentist	4%
Clergyman	8%	Veterinarian	3%
Lawyer	8%	None, don't know	9%
Government worker	6%		

Interviewing Date 6/4–9/50
Survey #456-K   Question #15

Suppose a young girl came to you and asked your advice about taking up a profession. Assuming that she was qualified to enter any of these professions, which one of them would you first recommend?

Nurse	33%	Actress	3%
Teacher	15%	Journalist	2%
Secretary	8%	Musician	2%
Social service worker	8%	Model	2%
Dietician	7%	Librarian	2%
Dressmaker	4%	Medical, dental technician	1%
Beautician	4%	Others	2%
Airline stewardess	3%	Don't know	4%

The views of men on this subject were nearly identical with those of women.

Source: (Both Questions) American Institute of Public Opinion, *The Gallup Poll: Public Opinion, 1935–1971* (New York, 1972), 925.

TABLE 4.56 WOMEN IN THE LABOR FORCE, 1940–1990

Year	Number (thousands)	% Female Population Age 16 and Older	% of Labor Force Population Age 16 and Older
1940	12,845	25.4	24.3
1950	18,408	33.9	29.0
1960	23,268	37.8	32.5
1970	31,580	43.4	37.2
1980	45,611	51.6	42.0
1988	54,904	56.6	44.5
1989	56,198	57.5	44.8
1990	56,554	57.5	45.3

Source: Information Please Almanac, 1992, 54.

TABLE 4.57 MOTHERS PARTICIPATING IN THE LABOR FORCE, 1955–1990

(figures in percentage)

Year	Mothers with Children		
	Under 18 Years	6 to 17 Years	Under 6 Years
1955	27.0	38.4	18.2
1965	35.0	45.7	25.3
1975	47.4	54.8	38.9
1980	56.6	64.4	46.6
1981	58.1	65.5	48.9
1982	58.5	65.8	49.9
1983	58.9	66.3	50.5
1984	60.5	68.2	52.1
1985	62.1	69.9	53.5
1986	62.8	70.4	54.4
1987	64.7	72.0	56.7
1988	65.0	73.3	56.1
1989	. . .	. . .	. . .
1990	66.7	74.7	58.2

Source: Information Please Almanac, 1992, 54.

TABLE 4.58 MARITAL STATUS OF WOMEN IN THE CIVILIAN LABOR FORCE, 1960–1990

Year	Female Labor Force (1,000)				Percent Distribution, Female Labor Force			Female Labor Force as Percent of Female Population			
	Total	Single	Married	Other	Single	Married	Other	Total	Single	Married	Other
1960	23,240	5,410	12,893	4,937	23.3	55.5	21.2	37.7	58.6	31.9	41.6
1965	26,200	5,976	14,829	5,396	22.8	56.6	20.6	39.3	54.5	34.9	40.7
1970	31,543	7,265	18,475	5,804	23.0	58.6	18.4	43.3	56.8	40.5	40.3
1975	37,475	9,125	21,484	6,866	24.3	57.3	18.3	46.3	59.8	44.3	40.1
1976	38,983	9,689	22,139	7,156	24.9	56.8	18.4	47.3	61.0	45.3	40.5
1977	40,613	10,311	22,776	7,526	25.4	56.1	18.5	48.4	62.1	46.4	41.5
1978	42,631	11,067	23,539	8,025	26.0	55.2	18.8	50.0	63.7	47.8	42.8
1979	44,235	11,597	24,378	8,260	26.2	55.1	18.7	50.9	64.6	49.0	43.1
1980	45,487	11,865	24,980	8,643	26.1	54.9	19.0	51.5	64.4	49.9	43.6
1981	46,696	12,124	25,428	9,144	26.0	54.5	19.6	52.1	64.5	50.5	44.6
1982	47,755	12,460	25,971	9,324	26.1	54.4	19.5	52.6	65.1	51.1	44.8
1983	48,503	12,659	26,468	9,376	26.1	54.6	19.3	52.9	65.0	51.8	44.4
1984	49,709	12,867	27,199	9,644	25.9	54.7	19.4	53.6	65.6	52.8	44.7
1985	51,050	13,163	27,894	9,993	25.8	54.6	19.6	54.5	66.6	53.8	45.1
1986	52,413	13,512	28,623	10,277	25.8	54.6	19.6	55.3	67.2	54.9	45.6
1987	53,658	13,885	29,381	10,393	25.9	54.8	19.4	56.0	67.4	55.9	45.7
1988	54,742	14,194	29,921	10,627	25.9	54.7	19.4	56.6	67.7	56.7	46.2
1989	56,030	14,377	30,548	11,104	25.7	54.5	19.8	57.4	68.0	57.8	47.0
1990	56,554	14,229	30,970	11,354	25.2	54.8	20.1	57.5	66.9	58.4	47.2

Source: Statistical Abstract, 1993, 399.

TABLE 4.59 PERCENT OF FEMALE WORKERS IN SELECTED OCCUPATIONS, 1975–1990

Occupation	Percentage of Women Employed Within Occupation		
	1975	1985	1990
Airline pilot	—	2.6	5.1
Auto mechanic	0.5	0.6	0.8
Bartender	35.2	47.9	55.6
Bus driver	37.7	49.2	51.6
Cab driver, chauffeur	8.7	10.9	9.5
Carpenter	0.6	1.2	1.3
Child care worker	98.4	96.1	97.0
Computer programmer	25.6	34.3	36.0
Computer systems analyst	14.8	28.0	34.5
Data entry keyer	92.8	90.7	87.2
Data-processing equipment repairer	1.8	10.4	11.4
Dental assistant	100.0	99.0	98.7
Dentist	1.8	6.5	9.5
Economist	13.1	34.5	43.8
Editor, reporter	44.6	51.7	52.0
Garage gas station attendant	4.7	6.8	4.7
Lawyer, judge	7.1	18.2	20.8
Librarian	81.1	87.0	83.3
Mail carrier	8.7	17.2	24.9
Office machine repairer	1.7	5.7	5.4
Physician	13.0	17.2	19.3
Registered nurse	97.0	95.1	94.5
Social worker	60.8	66.7	68.2
Teacher, college/university	31.1	35.2	37.7
Teacher, elementary school	85.4	84.0	85.2
Telephone installer/repairer	4.8	12.8	11.3
Telephone operator	93.3	88.8	89.0
Waiter	91.1	84.0	80.8
Welder	4.4	4.8	4.0

Source: John Wright, *Universal Almanac, 1991* (New York, 1990), 224.

TABLE 4.60 WOMEN AS A PERCENTAGE OF ALL CIVILIAN EMPLOYEES IN SELECTED OCCUPATIONS, BY RACE AND HISPANIC ORIGIN, 1990

Occupation	Percent Female All Races	Percent White Female	Percent Black Female	Percent Hispanic Origin[a] Female
Secretary	99.0	89.5	7.5	5.1
Textile sewing machine operator	89.2	66.5	14.6	18.0
Health aide, except nursing	84.8	65.6	17.0	4.7
Waiter	80.8	74.2	3.3	4.3
Production inspector, checker, or examiner	52.2	42.4	7.9	4.5
Bus driver	51.5	42.4	8.6	2.3
Financial manager	44.3	41.3	1.8	1.0
Assembler	43.5	34.1	7.3	5.6
Computer programmer	36.0	30.6	2.4	1.0
Precision food	32.7	25.3	6.7	3.1
Insurance sales	32.6	29.3	2.6	1.3
Stock handler and bagger	25.0	21.9	2.2	2.3
Farm worker	21.0	19.0	1.3	4.2
Physician	19.3	16.2	0.5	0.5
Laborer, except construction	18.7	14.4	3.7	1.9
Police and detective force	13.9	9.8	3.9	0.8
Electrical and electronic equipment repairer	8.7	6.5	1.8	0.3
Engineer	8.0	7.0	0.1	0.3
Construction trades	1.9	1.7	0.1	0.1
Total, all occupations	45.4	38.7	5.0	3.0

[a] Persons of Hispanic origin may be of any race.
Source: Paula Ries and Ann J. Stone, *The American Woman 1992–93: A Status Report* (New York, 1992), 340.

TABLE 4.61   ANNUAL INDEXES OF MANUFACTURING PRODUCTIVITY AND RELATED MEASURES, 12 COUNTRIES

(1982 = 100)

Country	1960	1970	1973	1979	1980	1981	1982	1983	1984	1985	1986	1987	1988	1989	1990
						Output per Hour									
United States	58.4	77.2	89.4	97.3	96.6	97.9	100.0	105.0	110.0	114.8	120.0	126.4	132.1	133.3	136.6
Canada	51.6	76.9	91.9	103.8	99.9	104.8	100.0	107.3	116.3	119.8	117.9	119.0	119.6	120.2	121.8
Japan	18.6	52.0	66.1	88.8	92.1	95.5	100.0	101.9	106.1	112.0	110.3	119.4	126.6	133.1	138.0
Belgium	24.2	44.3	57.8	82.2	87.5	94.2	100.0	110.2	114.6	116.4	117.8	123.0	129.8	134.9	140.5
Denmark	32.4	57.2	72.7	92.9	98.0	99.6	100.0	104.9	104.3	105.0	98.9	98.4	100.4	103.1	105.5
France	30.7	58.5	68.7	89.9	90.6	93.4	100.0	102.5	104.5	108.8	110.8	113.0	120.6	126.4	127.7
Germany	38.6	67.0	78.5	100.2	98.4	100.5	100.0	105.3	108.9	112.9	113.4	111.5	115.4	120.7	126.2
Italy	29.1	54.6	65.2	91.1	95.5	97.8	100.0	105.2	115.7	122.3	123.7	127.2	130.5	134.5	138.8
Netherlands	26.5	52.9	67.3	92.9	93.9	97.5	100.0	106.6	115.0	118.7	119.1	118.7	123.4	126.9	129.4
Norway	47.8	74.5	86.4	97.7	96.3	96.5	100.0	105.2	112.6	116.0	114.6	120.4	119.7	124.2	127.1
Sweden	36.2	69.1	81.2	94.9	96.4	95.8	100.0	106.5	111.9	112.6	114.3	115.7	117.3	117.6	118.2
United Kingdom	49.4	70.8	84.1	90.2	89.9	94.5	100.0	108.4	114.0	117.8	122.6	130.1	137.2	143.8	145.0
						Unit Labor Costs (U.S. dollar basis)									
United States	38.3	46.3	48.0	76.9	86.7	93.8	100.0	97.7	96.3	96.8	96.8	94.0	93.0	95.8	96.5
Canada	40.6	44.1	48.2	72.1	83.1	88.9	100.0	99.0	91.0	88.2	91.4	97.8	109.1	120.0	128.7
Japan	24.4	33.4	56.6	107.6	106.7	112.6	100.0	105.7	104.6	102.7	155.2	170.8	185.3	173.4	167.5
Belgium	34.6	48.2	72.3	148.0	154.8	125.8	100.0	86.1	79.4	80.8	110.2	128.9	126.6	119.6	144.4
Denmark	28.8	43.4	65.7	129.1	126.2	107.8	100.0	92.9	87.3	90.4	128.3	166.7	170.2	160.2	194.6
France	32.2	36.2	55.0	108.2	125.2	109.2	100.0	92.9	86.5	87.8	116.7	136.9	132.4	122.9	148.0
Germany	20.4	34.2	56.4	108.9	121.2	101.7	100.0	94.8	86.2	85.0	119.5	153.7	157.8	147.7	175.8
Italy	29.5	46.0	63.1	106.9	116.3	103.2	100.0	99.1	89.5	87.5	115.4	136.3	137.9	138.9	171.0
Netherlands	23.7	38.9	62.0	120.4	126.8	103.0	100.0	91.8	77.2	75.6	104.4	129.8	130.8	119.7	141.2
Norway	18.7	29.8	46.0	97.5	110.2	105.2	100.0	92.6	85.0	85.7	110.4	131.8	145.2	137.7	157.6
Sweden	31.3	42.8	61.0	117.4	130.2	120.4	100.0	84.4	81.0	84.9	109.3	129.6	140.9	145.7	172.5
United Kingdom	23.4	28.7	37.7	88.3	118.1	112.1	100.0	85.5	76.7	77.2	91.0	102.2	111.1	106.7	128.7

Source: Bureau of Labor Statistics, *Monthly Labor Review,* March 1992, 91.

TABLE 4.62   CIVILIAN UNEMPLOYMENT RATE BY DEMOGRAPHIC CHARACTERISTIC, 1948–1990

(percent: monthly data seasonally adjusted)

Year	All Civilian Workers	White							Black and Other or Black						
		Total	Males			Females			Total	Males			Females		
			Total	16–19 Years	20 Years and Older	Total	16–19 Years	20 Years and Older		Total	16–19 Years	20 Years and Older	Total	16–19 Years	20 Years and Older
									Black and Other						
1948	3.8	3.5	3.4	...	...	3.8	...	...	5.9	5.8	...	...	6.1	...	...
1949	5.9	5.6	5.6	...	...	5.7	...	...	8.9	9.6	...	...	7.9	...	...
1950	5.3	4.9	4.7	...	...	5.3	...	...	9.0	9.4	...	...	8.4	...	...
1951	3.3	3.1	2.6	...	...	4.2	...	...	5.3	4.9	...	...	6.1	...	...
1952	3.0	2.8	2.5	...	...	3.3	...	...	5.4	5.2	...	...	5.7	...	...
1953	2.9	2.7	2.5	...	...	3.1	...	...	4.5	4.8	...	...	4.1	...	...
1954	5.5	5.0	4.8	13.4	4.4	5.5	10.4	5.1	9.9	10.3	14.4	9.9	9.2	20.6	8.4
1955	4.4	3.9	3.7	11.3	3.3	4.3	9.1	3.9	8.7	8.8	13.4	8.4	8.5	19.2	7.7
1956	4.1	3.6	3.4	10.5	3.0	4.2	9.7	3.7	8.3	7.9	15.0	7.4	8.9	22.8	7.8
1957	4.3	3.8	3.6	11.5	3.2	4.3	9.5	3.8	7.9	8.3	18.4	7.6	7.3	20.2	6.4
1958	6.8	6.1	6.1	15.7	5.5	6.2	12.7	5.6	12.6	13.7	26.8	12.7	10.8	28.4	9.5
1959	5.5	4.8	4.6	14.0	4.1	5.3	12.0	4.7	10.7	11.5	25.2	10.5	9.4	27.7	8.3
1960	5.5	5.0	4.8	14.0	4.2	5.3	12.7	4.6	10.2	10.7	24.0	9.6	9.4	24.8	8.3
1961	6.7	6.0	5.7	15.7	5.1	6.5	14.8	5.7	12.4	12.8	26.8	11.7	11.9	29.2	10.6
1962	5.5	4.9	4.6	13.7	4.0	5.5	12.8	4.7	10.9	10.9	22.0	10.0	11.0	30.2	9.6
1963	5.7	5.0	4.7	15.9	3.9	5.8	15.1	4.8	10.8	10.5	27.3	9.2	11.2	34.7	9.4
1964	5.2	4.6	4.1	14.7	3.4	5.5	14.9	4.6	9.6	8.9	24.3	7.7	10.7	31.6	9.0
1965	4.5	4.1	3.6	12.9	2.9	5.0	14.0	4.0	8.1	7.4	23.3	6.0	9.2	31.7	7.5
1966	3.8	3.4	2.8	10.5	2.2	4.3	12.1	3.3	7.3	6.3	21.3	4.9	8.7	31.3	6.6
1967	3.8	3.4	2.7	10.7	2.1	4.6	11.5	3.8	7.4	6.0	23.9	4.3	9.1	29.6	7.1
1968	3.6	3.2	2.6	10.1	2.0	4.3	12.1	3.4	6.7	5.6	22.1	3.9	8.3	28.7	6.3
1969	3.5	3.1	2.5	10.0	1.9	4.2	11.5	3.4	6.4	5.3	21.4	3.7	7.8	27.6	5.8
1970	4.9	4.5	4.0	13.7	3.2	5.4	13.4	4.4	8.2	7.3	25.0	5.6	9.3	34.5	6.9
1971	5.9	5.4	4.9	15.1	4.0	6.3	15.1	5.3	9.9	9.1	28.8	7.3	10.9	35.4	8.7
1972	5.6	5.1	4.5	14.2	3.6	5.9	14.2	4.9	10.0	8.9	29.7	6.9	11.4	38.4	8.8

(continued)

TABLE 4.62   (continued)

Year	All Civilian Workers	White							Black and Other or Black						
		Total	Males			Females			Total	Males			Females		
			Total	16–19 Years	20 Years and Older	Total	16–19 Years	20 Years and Older		Total	16–19 Years	20 Years and Older	Total	16–19 Years	20 Years and Older
											Black				
1972	5.6	5.1	4.5	14.2	3.6	5.9	14.2	4.9	10.4	9.3	31.7	7.0	11.8	40.5	9.0
1973	4.9	4.3	3.8	12.3	3.0	5.3	13.0	4.3	9.4	8.0	27.8	6.0	11.1	36.1	8.6
1974	5.6	5.0	4.4	13.5	3.5	6.1	14.5	5.1	10.5	9.8	33.1	7.4	11.3	37.4	8.8
1975	8.5	7.8	7.2	18.3	6.2	8.6	17.4	7.5	14.8	14.8	38.1	12.5	14.8	41.0	12.2
1976	7.7	7.0	6.4	17.3	5.4	7.9	16.4	6.8	14.0	13.7	37.5	11.4	14.3	41.6	11.7
1977	7.1	6.2	5.5	15.0	4.7	7.3	15.9	6.2	14.0	13.3	39.2	10.7	14.9	43.4	12.3
1978	6.1	5.2	4.6	13.5	3.7	6.2	14.4	5.2	12.8	11.8	36.7	9.3	13.8	40.8	11.2
1979	5.8	5.1	4.5	13.9	3.6	5.9	14.0	5.0	12.3	11.4	34.2	9.3	13.3	39.1	10.9
1980	7.1	6.3	6.1	16.2	5.3	6.5	14.8	5.6	14.3	14.5	37.5	12.4	14.0	39.8	11.9
1981	7.6	6.7	6.5	17.9	5.6	6.9	16.6	5.9	15.6	15.7	40.7	13.5	15.6	42.2	13.4
1982	9.7	8.6	8.8	21.7	7.8	8.3	19.0	7.3	18.9	20.1	48.9	17.8	17.6	47.1	15.4
1983	9.6	8.4	8.8	20.2	7.9	7.9	18.3	6.9	19.5	20.3	48.8	18.1	18.6	48.2	16.5
1984	7.5	6.5	6.4	16.8	5.7	6.5	15.2	5.8	15.9	16.4	42.7	14.3	15.4	42.6	13.5
1985	7.2	6.2	6.1	16.5	5.4	6.4	14.8	5.7	15.1	15.3	41.0	13.2	14.9	39.2	13.1
1986	7.0	6.0	6.0	16.3	5.3	6.1	14.9	5.4	14.5	14.8	39.3	12.9	14.2	39.2	12.4
1987	6.2	5.3	5.4	15.5	4.8	5.2	13.4	4.6	13.0	12.7	34.4	11.1	13.2	34.9	11.6
1988	5.5	4.7	4.7	13.9	4.1	4.7	12.3	4.1	11.7	11.7	32.7	10.1	11.7	32.0	10.4
1989	5.3	4.5	4.5	13.7	3.9	4.5	11.5	4.0	11.4	11.5	31.9	10.0	11.4	33.0	9.8
1990	5.5	4.7	4.8	14.2	4.3	4.6	12.6	4.1	11.3	11.8	32.1	10.4	10.8	30.0	9.6

Source: Council of Advisors, *Economic Report of the President, 1992,* 341.

TABLE 4.63   U.S. UNEMPLOYMENT RATES COMPARED WITH EIGHT INDUSTRIAL COUNTRIES, 1975–1990

Year	U.S.	Canada	Australia	Japan	France	West Germany	Italy	Sweden	United Kingdom
1975	8.5	6.9	4.9	1.9	4.2	3.4	3.4	1.6	4.6
1976	7.7	7.2	4.8	2.0	4.6	3.4	3.9	1.6	5.9
1977	7.1	8.1	5.6	2.0	5.2	3.4	4.1	1.8	6.4
1978	6.1	8.4	6.3	2.3	5.4	3.3	4.1	2.2	6.3
1979	5.8	7.5	6.3	2.1	6.1	2.9	4.4	2.1	5.4
1980	7.1	7.5	6.1	2.0	6.5	2.8	4.4	2.0	7.0
1981	7.6	7.6	5.8	2.2	7.6	4.0	4.9	2.5	10.5
1982	9.7	11.0	7.2	2.4	8.3	5.6	5.4	3.1	11.3
1983	9.6	11.9	10.0	2.7	8.6	6.9	5.9	3.5	11.8
1984	7.5	11.3	9.0	2.8	10.0	7.1	5.9	3.1	11.7
1985	7.2	10.5	8.3	2.6	10.5	7.2	6.0	2.8	11.2
1986	7.0	9.6	8.1	2.8	10.6	6.6	7.5	2.6	11.2
1987	6.2	8.9	8.1	2.9	10.8	6.3	7.9	2.2	10.3
1988	5.5	7.8	7.2	2.5	10.3	6.3	7.9	1.9	8.6
1989	5.3	7.5	6.2	2.3	9.6	5.7	7.8	1.6	7.2
1990	5.6	8.1	6.9	2.1	9.1	5.0	7.0	1.8	6.9

Source: Mark S. Littmann, *A Statistical Portrait of the U.S., Social Conditions and Trends* (Lanham, Maryland, 1998), 272.

Labor Unions

The union movement began the post–Second World War period with strength but faced with major challenges. Successes of the previous decade and activities within some unions (charges of corruption and communist affiliation) had sparked an antiunion backlash that found expression in passage of the Taft-Hartley Act of 1947, a measure designed to restrain the union movement. In addition to other restrictions, the law contained a provision that authorized the states to legitimize the so-called open shop, in which employees could choose not to join a union. Such measures, termed *right-to-work laws,* passed in few, mostly southern, states. Hostility to the Taft-Hartley Act pro-moted a measure of unity in the movement, which culminated in the merger in 1955 of the two major general unions, the AFL and the CIO—organizations that a few years earlier had been involved in bitter fratricidal conflict.

From that point, however, the union movement seemed to go downhill. Most blue-collar jobs in manufacturing, mining, and construction had been unionized, and other categories of workers—women, white-collar, and professional people—showed little inclination toward organization. Companies increasingly turned to automation or moved to more business-friendly southern states. The 1960s brought the beginning of decline in manufacturing work, as companies moved work or moved themselves out of the country. More and more goods on the American market were being produced abroad. The 1980s added to these problems a presidential administration with little sympathy for the union movement, as was exemplified in 1981 in President Ronald Reagan's firing of air traffic controllers on strike. Long strikes at Greyhound bus line (1983) and Hormel Meatpacking (1985–86) showed management's willingness to hire replacement workers—the hated scabs. Faced with company threats to shut down or move out, unions had to consider "give-back" demands, calling for low or no wage increases and reductions in fringe benefits, notably medical insurance. The internationalization of business and expansion in the American market of cheaper, foreign-produced goods further eroded local standards of labor.

The unions nonetheless scored some victories. President John F. Kennedy in an executive order in 1962 authorized unionization of federal workers, and the most successful recruitment campaigns came with public employees on all levels. Many teachers, also on several levels (including college professors), become dues-paying members of unions. By contrast, most people involved in the highly technical specialties of the global economy showed little inclination toward unionism, and many in the low-wage service work were, for one reason or another, not organized. Unionism seemed to be holding its own and gave no indication of dying out at the start of the 1990s. But it was a holding action on a lower scale. At the peak in the late 1940s, unions claimed 35 percent of the workforce as members. In 1990 they had to be content with 16–17 percent.

TABLE 4.64   TRADE-UNION MEMBERSHIP, 1945–1990

Year	Members ('000s)	Percent of Labor Force
1945	14,322	35.5
1950	14,267	31.5
1955	16,802	33.2
1960	17,049	31.4
1965	17,299	28.4
1970	19,381	27.3
1975	19,611	25.5
1980	19,843	21.9
1985	16,996	18.0
1990	16,740	16.1

Source: Bureau of Labor Statistics, cited in Chris Cook, David Waller, *The Longman Handbook of Modern American History, 1763–1996* (New York, 1998), 199.

TABLE 4.65   STATES WITH RIGHT-TO-WORK LAWS, 1953–1982

State	1953	1960	1975	1980	1982
Ala.	yes	yes	yes	yes	yes
Ariz.	yes	yes	yes	yes	yes
Ark.	yes	yes	yes	yes	yes
Fla.	no	no	yes	yes	yes
Ga.	yes	yes	yes	yes	yes
Iowa	yes	yes	yes	yes	yes
Kans.	yes	yes	yes	yes	no
La.	no	no	no	yes	yes
Miss.	no	yes	yes	yes	yes
Nebr.	yes	yes	yes	yes	yes
Nev.	yes	yes	yes	yes	yes
N.C.	yes	yes	yes	yes	yes
N.Dak.	yes	yes	yes	yes	yes
S.C.	no	yes	yes	yes	yes
S.Dak.	yes	yes	yes	yes	yes
Tenn.	yes	yes	yes	yes	yes
Tex.	yes	yes	yes	yes	yes
Utah	no	yes	yes	yes	yes
Va.	yes	yes	yes	yes	yes
Wyo.	no	no	yes	yes	yes

Source: Leo Troy, Neil Sheflin, *Union Sourcebook: Membership, Structure, Finance Directory* (West Orange, N.J., 1985), 3–10.

TABLE 4.66   MEMBERSHIP IN MAJOR AFL-CIO UNIONS, 1955–1989
(in thousands)

Organizations	1955	1965	1975	1985	1989
Actors and Artists	34	61	76	100	97
Automobiles, Aerospace and Agriculture (UAW)	1,260	1,150	a	974	917
Boilermakers, Shipbuilders	151	108	123	110	75
Bricklayers	120	120	143	95	84
Carpenters	750	700	700	609	613
Clothing & Textile workers	. . .	. . .	. . .	228	180
Communications workers	249	288	476	524	492
Electronic workers	. . .	. . .	. . .	198	171
Electrical workers	460	616	856	791	744
Operating Engineers	200	270	300	330	330
Firefighters	72	87	123	142	142
Food & commercial workers	. . .	. . .	. . .	989	999
Garment workers	383	363	363	210	153
Government employees	47	132	255	199	156
Graphic communications	. . .	. . .	. . .	141	124
Hotel & Restaurant workers	300	300	421	327	278
Laborers	. . .	403	475	383	406
Letter Carriers Assn.	100	130	151	186	201

(continued)

TABLE 4.66 (continued)

Organizations	1955	1965	1975	1985	1989
Machinists & Aerospace	627	663	780	520	517
Musicians	250	225	215	671	54
Oil, Chemical, Atomic	160	140	145	108	71
Painters	182	160	160	133	128
Paperworkers	. . .	. . .	275	232	210
Plumbing and Pipe fitting	200	217	228	226	220
Postal workers	. . .	. . .	249	232	213
Retail, wholesale, department store	97	114	118	106	137
Service employees	. . .	. . .	480	688	762
Sheet metal workers	50	100	120	108	108
State, county, municipal workers	99	237	647	997	1,090
Steelworkers	980	876	1,062	572	481
Teachers	40	97	396	470	544
Teamsters	. . .	. . .	. . .	. . .	1,161
Transit union	. . .	98	90	94	96
Totals, AFL-CIO unions	12,622	12,919	14,070	13,109	13,556

[a] Disaffiliated 7/1/68; reaffiliated 7/1/81.
Source: C. D. Gifford, ed., *Directory of U.S. Labor Unions* (Washington, D.C., 1996), 83–85.

TABLE 4.67 WORK STOPPAGES OF 1,000 WORKERS OR MORE, 1947–1990

(workers and days idle in thousands)

Year	Stoppages Beginning in Year		Days Idle	
	Number	Workers Involved	Number	Percent of Working Time
1947	270	1,629	25,720	. . .
1949	262	2,537	43,420	0.22
1950	424	1,698	30,390	.26
1952	470	2,746	48,820	.38
1954	265	1,075	16,630	.13
1956	287	1,370	26,840	.20
1958	332	1,587	17,900	.13
1960	222	896	13,260	.09
1962	211	793	11,760	.08
1964	246	1,183	16,850	.11
1966	321	1,300	31,320	.10
1968	392	1,855	35,567	.20
1970	381	2,468	52,761	.29
1972	250	975	16,764	.09
1974	434	1,796	31,809	.16
1976	231	1,519	23,962	.12
1978	219	1,006	23,774	.11
1980	187	795	20,844	.09
1982	96	656	9,061	.04
1984	62	376	8,499	.04
1986	69	533	11,861	.05
1988	40	118	4,381	.02
1990	44	185	5,926	.02

Source: Bureau of Labor Statistics, *Handbook of Labor Statistics, 1989*, 543; *Statistical Abstract, 1993*, 434.

TABLE 4.68 WORKERS KILLED OR DISABLED ON THE JOB, 1960–1990, AND BY INDUSTRY GROUP, 1990

	Deaths						Disabling Injuries (1,000)
	Total		Manufacturing		Nonmanufacturing		
Year	Number (1,000)	Rate[a]	Number (1,000)	Rate[a]	Number (1,000)	Rate[a]	
1960	13.8	21	1.7	10	12.1	25	1,950
1965	14.1	20	1.8	10	12.3	24	2,100
1970	13.8	18	1.7	9	12.1	21	2,200
1975	13.0	15	1.6	9	11.4	17	2,200
1980	13.2	13	1.7	8	11.5	15	2,200
1984	11.5	11	1.1	6	10.4	12	1,900
1985	11.5	11	1.2	6	10.3	12	2,200
1986	11.1	10	1.0	5	10.1	11	1,800
1987	11.3	10	1.0	5	10.3	11	1,800
1988	11.0	10	1.1	6	9.9	10	1,800
1989	10.7	9	1.1	6	9.6	10	1,700
1990	10.5	9	1.1	6	9.4	10	1,800

Industry Group, 1990	Deaths		Disabling Injuries (1,000)
	Number (1,000)	Rate[a]	
Total	**10.5**	**9**	**1,800**
Agriculture	1.3	42	120
Mining and quarrying	0.3	43	30
Construction	2.1	33	210
Manufacturing	1.1	6	360
Transportation and utilities	1.3	22	120
Trade	1.2	4	330
Services	1.6	4	340
Government	1.6	9	290

[a] Per 100,000 workers.
Source: Statistical Abstract, 1992, 419.

Earnings and Income

Wage earners appeared on the surface to have made considerable gains during this period. As measured in current dollars, hourly and weekly wages increased in all categories between the years 1946 and 1990. The record became much less impressive when it recorded earnings in constant dollars, which allowed for inflation, and when one took into account the changing size of the groups being measured. The areas of employment with highest wages and largest increase—manufacturing, construction, and mining—were areas that experienced little, if any, growth in the number of the people involved. Mining experienced an absolute loss. Areas of employment that contained the largest increase in numbers—notably service work and retail trade—also produced the lowest wages.

There were marked differences in earnings and income relating to race, ethnicity, and gender that changed slowly, if at all, over the passage of years. In places with union-scale rates, race and ethnicity did not openly make a difference; the differences probably stemmed from job classification and promotion, which began to moderate at the end of the period, if only because affirmative-action mandates began to kick in. But in terms of general earnings and income, whether one measured money income or per capita or household income, whites had more than blacks by substantial amounts that had lessened only slightly by 1990. Hispanics, late-comers to the comparison tables, lagged behind black people in per capita income, but they surpassed African Americans in household income.

Earning differences stemming from gender were understandably huge at the beginning of the postwar period when the bulk of society recognized and generally accepted a sharp division of labor based on sex. On average, women made about 60 percent of what men earned for the same kind of work in 1960, and nearly all the high-paying jobs went to men. Even though challenges to employment practices and principles began to surface with some regularity in the 1960s, genuine change would take time to filter through the system and would involve educational choices and opportunities, legislation, lawsuits, court trials, and of course a considerable change in attitudes. Women's earn-

TABLE 4.69   AVERAGE HOURLY EARNINGS OF PRODUCTION OR NONSUPERVISORY WORKERS ON PRIVATE NONAGRICULTURAL PAYROLLS, BY INDUSTRY, 1946–1990

(dollars)

Year	Total Private	Mining	Construction	Manufacturing Total	Durable Goods	Nondurable Goods	Transportation and Public Utilities	Wholesale Trade	Retail Trade	Finance Insurance and Real Estate	Services
1946	...	...	...	1.08	1.14	1.00	...	...	...	...	...
1947	...	1.47	1.54	1.22	1.28	1.15	...	1.22	0.84	1.14	...
1948	...	1.66	1.71	1.33	1.39	1.25	...	1.31	0.90	1.20	...
1949	...	1.72	1.79	1.38	1.45	1.30	...	1.36	0.95	1.26	...
1950	1.34	1.77	1.86	1.44	1.45	1.30	...	1.36	0.98	1.26	...
1951	1.45	1.93	2.02	1.56	1.65	1.45	...	1.52	1.06	1.45	...
1952	1.52	2.01	2.13	1.64	1.74	1.51	...	1.61	1.09	1.51	...
1953	1.61	2.14	2.28	1.74	1.85	1.58	...	1.69	1.16	1.58	...
1954	1.65	2.14	2.38	1.78	1.89	1.62	...	1.76	1.20	1.65	...
1955	1.71	2.20	2.45	1.85	1.98	1.68	...	1.83	1.25	1.70	...
1956	1.80	2.33	2.57	1.95	2.08	1.77	...	1.93	1.30	1.78	...
1957	1.89	2.45	2.71	2.04	2.18	1.85	...	2.02	1.37	1.84	...
1958	1.95	2.47	2.82	2.10	2.25	1.92	...	2.09	1.42	1.89	...
1959	2.02	2.56	2.93	2.19	2.35	1.98	...	2.18	1.47	1.95	...
1960	2.09	2.60	3.07	2.26	2.42	2.05	...	2.24	1.52	2.02	...
1961	2.14	2.64	3.20	2.32	2.48	2.11	...	2.31	1.56	2.09	...
1962	2.22	2.70	3.31	2.39	2.55	2.17	...	2.37	1.63	2.17	...
1963	2.28	2.75	3.41	2.45	2.63	2.22	...	2.45	1.68	2.25	...
1964	2.36	2.81	3.55	2.53	2.70	2.29	2.89	2.52	1.75	2.30	1.94
1965	2.46	2.92	3.70	2.61	2.78	2.36	3.03	2.60	1.82	2.39	2.05
1966	2.56	3.05	3.89	2.71	2.89	2.45	3.11	2.73	1.91	2.47	2.17
1967	2.68	3.19	4.11	2.82	2.99	2.57	3.23	2.87	2.01	2.58	2.29
1968	2.85	3.35	4.41	3.01	3.18	2.74	3.42	3.04	2.16	2.75	2.42
1969	3.04	3.60	4.79	3.19	3.38	2.91	3.63	3.23	2.30	2.93	2.61
1970	3.23	3.85	5.24	3.35	3.55	3.08	3.85	3.43	2.44	3.07	2.81
1971	3.45	4.06	5.69	3.57	3.79	3.27	4.21	3.64	2.60	3.22	3.04
1972	3.70	4.44	6.06	3.82	4.07	3.48	4.65	3.85	2.75	3.36	3.27
1973	3.94	4.75	6.41	4.09	4.35	3.70	5.02	4.07	2.91	3.53	3.47
1974	4.24	5.23	6.81	4.42	4.70	4.01	5.41	4.38	3.14	3.77	3.75
1975	4.53	5.95	7.31	4.83	5.15	4.37	5.88	4.72	3.36	4.06	4.02
1976	4.86	6.46	7.71	5.22	5.57	4.71	6.45	5.02	3.57	4.27	4.31
1977	5.25	6.94	8.10	5.68	6.06	5.11	6.99	5.39	3.85	4.54	4.65
1978	5.69	7.67	8.66	6.17	6.58	5.54	7.57	5.88	4.20	4.89	4.99
1979	6.16	8.49	9.27	6.70	7.12	6.01	8.16	6.39	4.53	5.27	5.36
1980	6.66	9.17	9.94	7.27	7.75	6.56	8.87	6.95	4.88	5.79	5.85
1981	7.25	10.04	10.82	7.99	8.53	7.19	9.70	7.55	5.25	6.31	6.41
1982	7.68	10.77	11.63	8.49	9.03	7.75	10.32	8.08	5.48	6.78	6.92
1983	8.02	11.28	11.94	8.83	9.38	8.09	10.79	8.54	5.74	7.29	7.31
1984	8.32	11.63	12.13	9.19	9.73	8.39	11.12	8.88	5.85	7.63	7.59
1985	8.57	11.98	12.32	9.54	10.09	8.72	11.40	9.15	5.94	7.94	7.90
1986	8.76	12.46	12.48	9.73	10.28	8.95	11.70	9.34	6.03	8.36	8.18
1987	8.98	12.54	12.71	9.91	10.43	9.19	12.03	9.59	6.12	8.73	8.49
1988	9.28	12.80	13.08	10.19	10.71	9.45	12.26	9.98	6.31	9.06	8.88
1989	9.66	13.26	13.54	10.48	11.01	9.75	12.60	10.39	6.53	9.53	9.38
1990	10.01	13.68	13.77	10.83	11.35	10.12	12.97	10.79	6.75	9.97	9.83

Source: Jacobs, *Handbook of Labor Statistics, 1997,* 132.

ings of 72 percent of men's in 1990 might seem to be a gross injustice, but it represented a 12 percent gain in 10 years. In the 20 years before 1980, there had been no change at all.

In the broad scope of general earning and accumulation of wealth, two trends appeared in the postwar era. The lower reaches of wage earners held their own, even scored small fractional gains in the 35 years after 1945. Losses by the highest quintile (one-fifth) income group were at least proportionate to the lowest quintile's gain. These trends reversed themselves fairly abruptly at the start of the 1980s. The lowest levels of income lost in their share of national earnings, and in 10 years the highest 5 percent increased their share of national wealth by two full percentage points, which was, needless to say, a gain considerably larger than if it had been simply a 2 percent increase in previous earnings. It would appear that the proverb "the rich get richer and the poor get poorer" was in full swing as the last half of the 20th century was approaching an end.

TABLE 4.70   AVERAGE WEEKLY EARNINGS IN CURRENT DOLLARS, BY GROUP, 1947–1990

Industry Group	1947	1950	1955	1960	1965	1970	1975	1980	1985	1990
Average weekly earning	46	53	68	81	95	120	164	235	299	345
Manufacturing	49	58	75	90	108	133	191	289	386	442
Mining	60	68	90	105	124	164	249	397	520	603
Construction	59	70	91	113	138	195	266	368	454	526
Trans., public utility	. . .	. . .	. . .	. . .	125	156	233	351	450	505
Wholesale trade	50	58	74	91	106	137	183	267	352	411
Retail trade	34	40	49	58	67	82	109	147	175	194
Finance, insurance, realty	43	51	64	75	89	113	148	210	289	357
Services	. . .	. . .	. . .	. . .	74	97	135	191	257	319

Source: Bureau of Labor Statistics, *Handbook of Statistics, 1989*, 320–322.

TABLE 4.71   AVERAGE WEEKLY EARNINGS IN CONSTANT (1977) DOLLARS, BY GROUP, 1947–1990

Industry Group	1947	1950	1955	1960	1965	1970	1975	1980	1985	1990[a]
Average weekly earning	123	134	153	165	183	187	184	173	170	259
Manufacturing	133	147	170	183	206	208	215	212	220	332
Mining	162	169	203	215	237	256	280	292	296	453
Construction	159	176	206	230	266	304	300	270	265	395
Trans., public utility	. . .	. . .	. . .	. . .	240	243	262	250	257	379
Wholesale trade	136	146	169	186	204	214	206	197	200	309
Retail trade	92	100	110	118	128	128	123	108	100	146
Finance, insurance, realty	117	127	145	154	171	176	167	154	165	268
Services	. . .	. . .	. . .	. . .	141	151	152	140	146	240

[a] Statistics for 1990 are in 1982 dollars.
Source: Bureau of Labor Statistics, *Handbook of Statistics, 1989*, 320–322.

TABLE 4.72 MANUFACTURING PRODUCTION WORKER STATISTICS, 1955–1990

Year	All Employees	Production Workers	Average Weekly Earnings	Average Hourly Earnings	Average Hours per Week
1955	16,882,000	13,288,000	$75.30	$1.85	40.7
1960	16,796,000	12,586,000	89.72	2.26	39.7
1965	18,062,000	13,434,000	107.53	2.61	41.2
1970	19,367,000	14,044,000	133.33	3.35	39.8
1975	18,323,000	13,043,000	190.79	4.83	39.5
1980	20,285,000	14,214,000	288.62	7.27	39.7
1985	19,260,000	13,092,000	386.37	9.54	40.5
1987	19,024,000	12,970,000	406.31	9.91	41.0
1988	19,403,000	13,254,000	418.40	10.18	41.1
1989	19,612,000	13,375,000	429.27	10.47	41.0
1990	19,111,000	12,974,000	441.86	10.83	40.8

Source: *World Almanac, 1992*, 684.

TABLE 4.73 COMPARISON OF MEDIAN EARNINGS OF YEAR-ROUND, FULL-TIME WORKERS 15 YEARS AND OVER, BY SEX, 1960–1990

Year	Median Earnings		Earnings Gap in Current Dollars	Women's Earnings as a Percent of Men's	Percent Men's Earnings Exceeded Women's	Earnings Gap in Constant 1990 Dollars
	Women's	Men				
1960	$3,257	$5,368	2,111	60.7	64.8	8,569
1970	5,323	8,966	3,643	59.4	68.4	11,529
1980	11,197	18,612	7,415	60.2	66.2	11,776
1981	12,001	20,260	8,259	59.2	68.8	11,981
1982	13,014	21,077	8,063	61.7	62.0	11,023
1983	13,915	21,881	7,966	63.6	57.2	10,453
1984	14,780	23,218	8,438	63.7	57.1	10,614
1985	15,624	24,195	8,571	64.7	54.9	10,411
1986	16,232	25,256	9,024	64.3	55.6	10,761
1987	16,911	25,946	9,035	65.2	53.4	10,395
1988	17,606	26,656	9,050	66.0	51.4	9,999
1989	18,778	27,430	8,652	68.5	46.1	9,119
1990	19,822	27,678	7,856	71.6	39.6	7,856

Source: Otto Johnson, ed., *Information Please Almanac, 1993* (Boston, 1992), 59.

TABLE 4.74 EFFECTIVE FEDERAL MINIMUM HOURLY WAGE RATES, 1950–1990

In Effect	Minimum Rate for Nonfarm Workers	Percent of Average Earnings[a]	Minimum Rate for Farm Workers (in dollars)
1950–55	$0.75	54	. . .
1956–60	1.00	52	. . .
1961–62	1.15	50	. . .
1963–66	1.25	51	. . .
1967	1.40	50	1.00
1968–73	1.60	54	1.15
1974	2.00	46	1.60
1975	2.10	45	1.80
1976–77	2.30	46	2.00
1978	2.65	44	2.65
1979	2.90	45	2.90
1980	3.10	44	3.10
1981–88	3.35	43	3.35
1989–90	3.35	32	3.35

[a] Percent of average hourly earnings in manufacturing.
Source: *Statistical Abstract, 1991*, 418.

TABLE 4.75 MEDIAN EARNINGS BY WOMEN AND MEN WHO WORK FULL-TIME, YEAR-ROUND, BY RACE AND HISPANIC ORIGIN, 1960–1990

(income in 1991 dollars)

Year	Total Women	White	Black	Hispanic	Total Men	White	Black	Hispanic
1960	13,777	. . .	. . .	. . .	22,706	. . .	. . .	. . .
1962	14,168	. . .	. . .	. . .	23,893	. . .	. . .	. . .
1964	14,828	. . .	. . .	. . .	25,070	. . .	. . .	. . .
1966	15,268	. . .	. . .	. . .	26,528	. . .	. . .	. . .
1968	16,102	16,546	12,589	. . .	27,688	28,432	19,198	. . .
1970	17,554	17,848	14,665	. . .	29,568	30,416	21,001	. . .
1972	18,108	18,399	15,789	. . .	31,295	32,495	22,396	. . .
1974	18,291	18,422	17,223	15,549	31,132	31,801	22,878	23,319
1976	18,570	18,697	17,541	16,000	30,851	31,672	23,186	23,542
1978	18,866	19,018	17,799	16,294	31,740	32,274	24,907	23,679
1980	18,530	18,663	17,661	16,018	30,801	31,703	22,419	22,437
1982	18,541	18,749	17,284	15,831	30,028	30,776	22,087	21,915
1984	19,375	19,537	17,985	16,445	30,436	31,411	21,808	22,206
1986	20,172	20,408	18,310	17,194	31,386	32,219	22,790	20,896
1988	20,270	20,515	19,040	17,091	30,689	31,348	23,453	20,552
1990	20,656	20,892	18,799	16,331	28,843	30,096	22,002	19,941

Source: Cheryl Russell and Margaret Ambry, *The Official Guide to American Incomes* (Ithaca, N.Y., 1993), 51–52.

TABLE 4.76   PER CAPITA INCOME AND PERSONAL CONSUMPTION EXPENDITURES, 1950–1990

(in current dollars)

Year	Gross National Product	Personal Income	Disposable Personal Income	Personal Consumption Expenditures			
				Durable Goods	Nondurable Goods	Services	Total
1950	1,900	1,504	1,368	203	648	416	1,267
1955	2,456	1,901	1,687	235	755	570	1,560
1960	2,851	2,265	1,986	240	847	741	1,829
1965	3,268	2,840	2,505	327	987	954	2,268
1970	4,951	4,056	3,489	418	1,318	1,385	3,121
1975	7,401	6,081	5,291	627	1,927	2,135	4,689
1980	11,985	9,916	8,421	963	2,992	3,653	7,607
1985	16,776	13,895	11,861	1,555	3,807	5,622	10,985
1990	21,737	18,477	15,695	1,910	4,748	7,888	14,547

Source: Otto Johnson, ed., *Information Please Almanac, Atlas and Yearbook, 1997* (Boston, 1996), 137.

TABLE 4.77   PER CAPITA MONEY INCOME IN CURRENT AND CONSTANT (1990) DOLLARS, BY RACE AND HISPANIC ORIGIN, 1970–1990

(in dollars)

Year	Current Dollars				Constant (1990) Dollars			
	All Races	White	Black	Hispanic	All Races	White	Black	Hispanic
1970	3,177	3,354	1,869	. . .	10,702	11,298	6,296	. . .
1975	4,818	5,072	2,972	2,847	11,705	12,322	7,220	6,916
1980	7,787	8,233	4,804	4,865	12,351	13,059	7,620	7,717
1981	8,476	8,979	5,129	5,349	12,187	12,910	7,375	7,691
1982	8,980	9,527	5,360	5,448	12,163	12,903	7,260	7,379
1983	9,548	10,125	5,755	5,852	12,529	13,287	7,552	7,679
1984	10,328	10,939	6,277	6,401	12,992	13,761	7,896	8,052
1985	11,013	11,671	6,840	6,613	13,377	14,177	8,308	8,033
1986	11,670	12,352	7,207	7,000	13,917	14,730	8,594	8,348
1987	12,391	13,143	7,645	7,653	14,256	15,121	8,796	8,805
1988	13,123	13,896	8,271	7,956	14,499	15,353	9,138	8,790
1989	14,056	14,896	8,747	8,390	14,815	15,701	9,220	8,843
1990	14,387	15,265	9,017	8,424	14,387	15,265	9,017	8,424

Source: *Statistical Abstract, 1992*, 454.

TABLE 4.78   MONEY INCOME OF HOUSEHOLDS—MEDIAN HOUSEHOLD INCOME IN CURRENT AND CONSTANT (1990) DOLLARS, BY RACE AND HISPANIC ORIGIN OF HOUSEHOLDER, 1970–1990

Year	Median Income in Current Dollars				Median Income in Constant (1990) Dollars				Annual Percent Change of Median Income of All Households	
	All Households	White	Black	Hispanic	All Households	White	Black	Hispanic	Current Dollars	Constant (1990) Dollars
1970	8,734	9,097	5,537	(NA)	29,421	30,644	18,652	(NA)	7	2
1975	11,800	12,340	7,408	8,865	28,667	29,978	17,997	21,536	6	-1
1977	13,572	14,272	8,422	10,647	29,272	30,781	18,164	22,963	7	1
1978	15,064	15,660	9,411	11,803	30,197	31,392	18,865	23,660	11	3
1979	16,461	17,259	10,133	13,042	29,634	31,071	18,242	23,479	9	-2
1980	17,710	18,684	10,764	13,651	28,091	29,636	17,073	21,653	8	-5
1981	19,074	20,153	11,309	15,300	27,425	28,977	16,261	21,999	8	-2
1982	20,171	21,117	11,968	15,178	27,320	28,601	16,210	20,557	6	. . .
1983	21,018	22,035	12,473	15,794	27,581	28,915	16,368	20,726	4	1
1984	22,415	23,647	13,471	16,992	28,197	29,747	16,946	21,375	7	2
1985	23,618	24,908	14,819	17,465	28,688	30,255	18,000	21,214	5	2
1986	24,897	26,175	15,080	18,352	29,690	31,214	17,983	21,885	5	4
1987	26,061	27,458	15,672	19,336	29,984	31,591	18,031	22,247	5	1
1988	27,225	28,781	16,407	20,359	30,079	31,798	18,127	22,493	5	. . .
1989	28,906	30,406	18,083	21,921	30,468	32,049	19,060	23,105	6	1
1990	29,943	31,231	18,676	22,330	29,943	31,231	18,676	22,330	4	-2

Source: *Statistical Abstract, 1992*, 445.

TABLE 4.79   PERSONAL INCOME PER CAPITA IN CURRENT AND CONSTANT (1982) DOLLARS, BY STATE, 1980–1989

Region, Division, and State	Current Dollars					Constant (1982) Dollars					Income Rank	
	1980	1985	1987	1988	1989	1980	1985	1987	1988	1989	1980	1989
United States	**9,919**	**13,896**	**15,423**	**16,513**	**17,596**	**11,427**	**12,452**	**12,895**	**13,295**	**13,546**	(X)	(X)
Northeast	**10,603**	**15,570**	**17,792**	**19,373**	**20,694**	**12,216**	**13,952**	**14,876**	**15,599**	**15,931**	(X)	(X)
New England	**10,542**	**15,950**	**18,633**	**20,249**	**21,504**	**12,145**	**14,292**	**15,579**	**16,304**	**16,554**	(X)	(X)
Maine	8,218	11,903	13,985	15,045	16,248	9,468	10,666	11,693	12,114	12,508	39	26
N.H.	9,788	15,367	18,032	19,410	20,267	11,276	13,770	15,077	15,628	15,602	23	7
Vt.	8,577	12,373	14,256	15,268	16,371	9,881	11,087	11,920	12,293	12,603	35	24
Mass.	10,612	16,305	19,140	20,898	22,174	12,226	14,610	16,003	16,826	17,070	12	3
R.I.	9,518	13,779	15,644	16,870	17,950	10,965	12,347	13,080	13,583	13,818	27	14
Conn.	12,112	18,227	21,288	23,190	24,683	13,954	16,332	17,799	18,671	19,002	2	1
Middle Atlantic	**10,624**	**15,441**	**17,503**	**19,072**	**20,414**	**12,240**	**13,836**	**14,635**	**15,356**	**15,715**	(X)	(X)
N.Y.	10,721	15,773	17,906	19,663	21,073	12,351	14,134	14,972	15,832	16,222	10	5
N.J.	11,573	17,618	20,303	22,265	23,778	13,333	15,787	16,976	17,927	18,305	4	2
Pa.	9,891	13,554	15,103	16,135	17,269	11,395	12,145	12,628	12,991	13,294	18	20
Midwest	**9,919**	**13,569**	**14,997**	**15,856**	**16,926**	**11,427**	**12,159**	**12,539**	**12,766**	**13,030**	(X)	(X)
East North Central	**10,077**	**13,694**	**15,174**	**16,130**	**17,214**	**11,609**	**12,271**	**12,687**	**12,987**	**13,252**	(X)	(X)
Ohio	9,723	13,176	14,529	15,427	16,373	11,202	11,806	12,148	12,421	12,604	25	23
Ind.	9,245	12,424	13,894	14,721	15,779	10,651	11,133	11,617	11,853	12,147	31	30
Ill.	10,837	14,730	16,366	17,567	18,824	12,485	13,199	13,684	14,144	14,491	7	11
Mich.	10,165	14,001	15,473	16,391	17,444	11,711	12,546	12,937	13,197	13,429	15	19
Wis.	9,845	13,234	14,652	15,378	16,449	11,342	11,858	12,251	12,382	12,663	20	22
West North Central	**9,534**	**13,273**	**14,575**	**15,205**	**16,244**	**10,984**	**11,893**	**12,186**	**12,242**	**12,505**	(X)	(X)
Minn.	10,062	14,144	15,716	16,472	17,657	11,592	12,674	13,140	13,262	13,593	16	15
Iowa	9,537	12,619	13,859	14,316	15,487	10,987	11,037	11,588	11,527	11,922	26	32
Mo.	9,298	13,250	14,582	15,331	16,292	10,712	11,873	12,192	12,344	12,542	29	25
N.Dak.	8,538	11,951	12,641	12,342	13,563	9,836	10,709	10,569	9,937	10,441	37	44
S.Dak.	8,217	11,029	12,370	12,599	13,685	9,467	9,883	10,343	10,144	10,535	40	41
Nebr.	9,274	12,967	13,976	14,569	15,446	10,684	11,619	11,686	11,730	11,891	30	33
Kans.	9,941	13,812	14,962	15,688	16,498	11,453	12,376	12,510	12,631	12,701	17	21
South	**8,944**	**12,608**	**13,817**	**14,810**	**15,773**	**10,305**	**11,297**	**11,552**	**11,924**	**12,143**	(X)	(X)
South Atlantic	**9,171**	**13,301**	**15,022**	**16,073**	**17,123**	**10,566**	**11,918**	**12,560**	**12,941**	**13,182**	(X)	(X)
Del.	10,249	14,547	16,319	17,347	18,483	11,808	13,035	13,645	13,967	14,229	14	12
Md.	10,790	15,970	18,231	19,639	21,013	12,431	14,310	15,243	15,812	16,176	8	6
D.C.	12,322	17,811	19,579	22,063	23,491	14,196	15,960	16,370	17,764	18,084	(X)	(X)
Va.	9,827	14,468	16,531	17,712	18,927	11,321	12,964	13,822	14,261	14,570	21	10
W.Va.	7,915	10,073	10,959	11,578	12,345	9,119	9,026	9,163	9,322	9,503	46	49
N.C.	7,999	11,662	13,284	14,243	15,198	9,215	10,450	11,107	11,468	11,700	44	34
S.C.	7,589	10,729	12,070	12,907	13,634	8,743	9,614	10,092	10,392	10,496	48	42
Ga.	8,348	12,616	14,316	15,280	16,053	9,618	11,305	11,970	12,303	12,358	38	27
Fla.	9,764	13,935	15,538	16,515	17,647	11,249	12,487	12,992	13,297	13,585	24	17
East South Central	**7,752**	**10,640**	**11,976**	**12,853**	**13,673**	**8,931**	**9,534**	**10,013**	**10,349**	**10,526**	(X)	(X)
Ky.	8,022	10,768	11,963	12,792	13,743	9,242	9,649	10,003	10,300	10,580	43	39
Tenn.	8,030	11,252	12,913	13,895	14,694	9,251	10,082	10,797	11,188	11,312	42	35
Ala.	7,704	10,698	11,982	12,814	13,625	8,876	9,586	10,018	10,317	10,489	47	43
Miss.	6,926	9,249	10,250	11,055	11,724	7,979	8,288	8,570	8,901	9,025	50	50
West South Central	**9,326**	**12,679**	**12,993**	**13,933**	**14,817**	**10,744**	**11,361**	**10,864**	**11,218**	**11,406**	(X)	(X)
Ark.	7,465	10,525	11,385	12,141	12,901	8,600	9,431	9,519	9,775	9,931	49	48
La.	8,682	11,302	11,439	12,238	12,921	10,002	10,127	9,564	9,853	9,497	34	47
Okla.	9,393	12,139	12,481	13,306	14,154	10,821	10,877	10,436	10,713	10,896	28	37
Tex.	9,798	13,476	13,734	14,753	15,702	11,288	12,075	11,483	11,878	12,088	22	31
West	**10,843**	**14,763**	**16,247**	**17,278**	**18,349**	**12,492**	**13,229**	**13,585**	**13,912**	**14,125**	(X)	(X)
Mountain	**9,445**	**12,730**	**13,813**	**14,590**	**15,566**	**10,881**	**11,407**	**11,549**	**11,747**	**11,983**	(X)	(X)
Mont.	8,924	11,015	12,331	12,870	14,078	10,281	9,870	10,310	10,362	10,838	33	38
Idaho	8,569	10,817	11,838	12,652	13,707	9,872	9,693	9,898	10,187	10,552	36	40
Wyo.	11,339	12,834	12,819	13,720	14,508	13,063	11,500	10,718	11,047	11,169	6	36
Colo.	10,598	14,699	15,624	16,471	17,553	12,210	13,171	13,064	13,262	13,513	13	18
N.Mex.	8,169	11,197	11,872	12,401	13,140	9,411	10,033	9,926	9,985	10,115	41	45
Ariz.	9,172	12,957	14,355	14,995	15,802	10,567	11,610	12,003	12,073	12,165	32	29
Utah	7,952	10,653	11,532	12,225	13,079	9,161	9,546	9,642	9,843	10,069	45	46
Nev.	11,421	14,693	16,381	17,849	19,269	13,158	13,166	13,696	14,371	14,834	5	9
Pacific	**11,343**	**15,504**	**17,125**	**18,237**	**19,331**	**13,068**	**13,892**	**14,319**	**14,684**	**14,881**	(X)	(X)
Wash.	10,725	14,076	15,535	16,364	17,647	12,356	12,613	12,989	13,176	13,585	9	16
Oreg.	9,866	12,628	13,850	14,811	15,919	11,366	11,315	11,580	11,925	12,255	19	28
Calif.	11,603	16,035	17,749	18,915	19,929	13,368	14,368	14,840	15,229	15,342	3	8
Alaska	13,835	18,785	18,282	19,237	21,656	15,939	16,832	15,286	15,489	16,671	1	4
Hawaii	10,617	13,900	15,540	16,840	18,472	12,232	12,455	12,993	13,559	14,220	11	13

Source: Statistical Abstract, 1991, 442.

TABLE 4.80 ECONOMIC GAIN IN 1980s

All Families (by income group)	Shares of Pretax Adjusted Family Income (AFI) (%)				
	1977	1980	1985	1988	1989
Lowest quintile	4.7	4.3	3.7	3.5	3.6
Second quintile	10.8	10.5	9.5	9.1	9.2
Middle quintile	16.3	16.0	15.1	14.6	14.7
Fourth quintile	22.9	22.9	22.2	21.7	21.7
81 to 90 percent	15.6	15.7	15.7	15.3	15.4
91 to 95 percent	10.1	10.1	10.4	10.1	10.3
96 to 99 percent	11.6	11.7	12.4	12.6	12.7
Top 1 percent	8.3	9.2	11.6	13.4	13.0
Overall	100.0	100.0	100.0	100.0	100.0
Highest quintile	45.6	46.7	50.1	51.4	51.4
Top 10 percent	30.0	31.0	34.4	36.1	36.0
Top 5 percent	19.9	20.9	24.0	26.0	25.7

Source: Kevin Phillips, *Boiling Point: Republicans, Democrats and the Decline of Middle-Class Prosperity* (New York, 1993), 279.

TABLE 4.81 SHARE OF AGGREGATE INCOME RECEIVED BY HIGH- AND LOW-INCOME HOUSEHOLDS, 1967–1990

Year	Number (1,000)	Income at Selected Positions (Dollars) Upper Limit of Each Fifth ($)					Percent Distribution of Income	
		Lowest Fifth	Second	Third	Fourth	Highest Fifth	Lowest Fifth	Top 5 Percent
1967	60,446	12,248	23,883	33,910	48,343	77,570	4.0	17.5
1968	61,805	13,063	24,766	35,497	49,877	78,031	4.2	16.6
1970	64,374	13,230	25,348	36,874	52,609	83,171	4.1	16.6
1972	68,251	13,518	26,035	38,485	55,074	88,653	4.1	17.0
1973	69,859	13,872	26,353	39,091	56,470	89,513	4.2	16.6
1974	71,163	13,878	25,742	38,038	55,205	87,378	4.3	16.5
1975	72,867	13,185	24,746	37,393	53,690	84,725	4.3	16.6
1980	82,368	13,466	25,253	38,716	56,687	91,227	4.2	16.5
1982	83,918	13,022	24,766	37,841	56,428	93,146	4.0	17.0
1984	86,789	13,551	25,361	39,073	59,023	97,706	4.0	17.1
1985	88,458	13,692	25,761	39,908	60,021	99,173	3.9	17.6
1986	89,479	13,856	26,503	41,132	62,176	104,262	3.8	18.0
1988	92,830	14,259	26,934	41,975	63,380	107,285	3.8	18.3
1990	94,312	14,174	26,830	41,047	62,597	107,434	3.9	18.6

Source: Johnson, *Information Please Almanac, 1997,* 53.

TABLE 4.82 APPROXIMATE NUMBERS OF MILLIONAIRES, DECAMILLIONAIRES, CENTIMILLIONAIRES, AND BILLIONAIRES IN THE UNITED STATES, 1953–1988

Year	Millionaires	Deca-millionaires	Centi-millionaires	Billionaires
1953	27,000	800	. . .	. . .
1957	. . .	. . .	44	1
1961/1962	80,000	2,500	. . .	1
1965	90,000	. . .	. . .	. . .
1968/1969	121,000	. . .	153	2
1972–1973	180,000	. . .	. . .	4
1976	250,000	. . .	. . .	2
1978	450,000	. . .	. . .	1
1979	519,000	. . .	. . .	
1980	574,000	. . .	. . .	?
1981	638,000	. . .	. . .	?
1982	. . .	38,885	400	13
1983	. . .	. . .	500	15
1984		. . .	600	12
1985	832,000	. . .	700	13
1986	. . .	. . .	900	26
1987	1,239,000	81,816	1,200	49
1988	1,500,000	100,000	1,200	51

Source: Kevin Phillips, *The Politics of the Rich and Poor* (New York, 1990), 239.

Poverty

There always had been poverty in the United States—before, as Lyndon Johnson had put it, "it even had a name" and before there was a system for identifying impoverishment. In 1964 the Social Security System estimated the income needed to obtain a minimally acceptable standard of living and deemed it to be the poverty level. The largest number of impoverished people, before 1964 or afterward, always had been white only because the largest number of people had been white. The largest proportion by far had been nonwhites, of whom African Americans were most numerous. As Hispanics became more prominent in society and the Census Bureau began to classify them separately, they consistently produced poverty percentages substantially higher than non-Hispanic whites, frequently approaching the more-than-30-percent attributed to black people.

Democrat politicians frequently bemoaned the number of people in need, and now and then some gave them concrete attention. John Kennedy became acquainted with the "other America" but had time before his death to obtain only piecemeal legislation. Lyndon Johnson's major legislative objective was the War on Poverty, a multifaceted program (with no shortage of critics) that produced genuine but, of course, limited results. The poverty rate dropped more than 7 points between 1964 and 1969, and it would go lower in years to come. A poverty rate of 11 percent–12 percent that remained throughout the 1970s constituted a marked improvement from the 22 percent in 1960, but it still amounted to 25,000,000 people. The rates of poverty increased significantly in the 1980s, and they included familiar faces. The African-American rate passed one-third of the black people, and the Hispanic rate, while high, remained a few points behind blacks.

The new feature was the feminization of poverty, a phenomenon that grew out of several factors, including the "new morality" and women's "liberation." Women—black women, especially—had children out of wedlock in record numbers: now shamelessly, perhaps, but with no means to support them. Divorce came easily, but it scarcely was free; the mother got the kids and also the need to reenter the workforce with little preparation for doing anything. The fashionable "no-fault" settlements usually called for splitting assets down the middle, which on the surface seemed fully equitable, but it was a far cry from another time when the wife got (or, from the male point of view, seemed to get) everything. By the 1980s, 66 percent of adults classified as poor were women. There might have been a Reagan revolution, but it did not reach the nation's impoverished classes, an increasing number of whom were female.

TABLE 4.83   PERSONS BELOW THE POVERTY LEVEL, CALENDAR YEARS 1960–1990
(in thousands)

| Year | All Persons | Persons in Families | | | | Persons 65 Years and Older |
		Total	Householders	Children under 18 Years	Other Family Members	
1960	39,851	34,925	8,243	17,288	9,394	. . .
1961	39,628	34,509	8,391	16,577	9,541	. . .
1962	38,625	33,623	8,077	16,630	8,916	. . .
1963	36,436	31,498	7,554	15,691	8,253	. . .
1964	36,055	30,912	7,160	15,736	8,016	. . .
1965	33,185	28,358	6,721	14,388	7,249	. . .
1966	28,510	23,809	5,784	12,146	5,879	5,114
1967	27,769	22,771	5,667	11,427	5,677	5,388
1968	25,389	20,695	5,047	10,739	4,909	4,632
1969	24,147	19,175	5,008	9,501	4,667	4,787
1970	25,420	20,330	5,260	10,235	4,835	4,793
1971	25,559	20,405	5,303	10,344	4,757	4,273
1972	24,460	19,577	5,075	10,082	4,420	3,738
1973	22,973	18,299	4,828	9,453	4,018	3,354
1974	23,370	18,817	4,922	9,967	3,928	3,085
1975	25,877	20,789	5,450	10,882	4,457	3,317
1976	24,975	19,632	5,311	10,081	4,240	3,313
1977	24,720	19,505	5,311	10,028	4,165	3,177
1978	24,497	19,062	5,280	9,722	4,059	3,233
1979	26,072	19,964	5,461	9,993	4,509	3,682
1980	29,272	22,601	6,217	11,114	5,270	3,871
1981	31,822	24,850	6,851	12,068	5,931	3,853
1982	34,398	27,349	7,512	13,139	6,698	3,751
1983	35,303	27,933	7,647	13,427	6,859	3,625
1984	33,700	26,458	7,277	12,929	6,251	3,330
1985	33,064	25,729	7,223	12,483	6,032	3,456
1986	32,370	24,754	7,023	12,257	5,475	3,477
1987	32,221	24,725	7,005	12,275	5,445	3,563
1988	31,745	24,048	6,874	11,935	5,238	3,481
1989	32,415	24,882	6,895	12,541	5,446	3,312
1990	33,585	25,232	7,098	12,715	5,419	3,658

Source: Moody, Facts & Figures on Finance, 48.

TABLE 4.84 PERSONS BELOW THE POVERTY LEVEL, BY RACE AND HISPANIC ORIGIN, 1959–1990

(percent)

Year	White	Black	Hispanic Origin	Total
1959	18.1	55.1	. . .	22.4
1960	17.8	. . .	. . .	22.2
1961	17.4	. . .	. . .	21.9
1962	16.4	. . .	. . .	21.0
1963	15.3	. . .	. . .	19.5
1964	14.9	. . .	. . .	19.0
1965	13.3	. . .	. . .	17.3
1966	11.3	41.8	. . .	14.7
1967	11.0	39.3	. . .	14.2
1968	10.0	34.7	. . .	12.8
1969	9.5	32.2	. . .	12.1
1970	9.9	33.5	. . .	12.6
1971	9.9	32.5	. . .	12.5
1972	9.0	33.3	. . .	11.9
1973	8.4	31.4	21.9	11.1
1974	8.6	30.3	23.0	11.2
1975	9.7	31.3	26.9	12.3
1976	9.1	31.1	24.7	11.8
1977	8.9	31.3	22.4	11.6
1978	8.7	30.6	21.6	11.4
1979	9.0	31.0	21.8	11.7
1980	10.2	32.5	25.7	13.0
1981	11.1	34.2	26.5	14.0
1982	12.0	35.6	29.9	15.0
1983	12.1	35.7	28.0	15.2
1984	11.5	33.8	28.4	14.4
1985	11.4	31.3	29.0	14.0
1986	11.0	31.1	27.3	13.6
1987	10.4	32.4	28.0	13.4
1988	10.1	31.3	26.7	13.0
1989	10.0	30.7	26.2	12.8
1990	10.7	31.9	26.2	13.5

Source: Stanley and Niemi, *Statistics on Politics,* 375.

TABLE 4.85 AVERAGE INCOME CUTOFFS FOR A NONFARM FAMILY OF FOUR, 1960–1990

Year	At Poverty Level	At 125 Percent of Poverty Level
1960	3,022	3,778
1970	3,968	4,960
1975	5,500	6,875
1976	5,815	7,269
1977	6,191	7,739
1978	6,662	8,328
1979	7,412	9,265
1980	8,414	10,518
1981	9,287	11,609
1982	9,862	12,328
1983	10,178	12,723
1984	10,609	13,261
1985	10,989	13,736
1986	11,203	14,004
1987	11,611	14,514
1988	12,092	15,115
1989	12,674	15,843
1990	13,359	16,699

Source: Chadwick & Heaten, *Handbook,* 251.

TABLE 4.86 FAMILIES BELOW POVERTY LEVEL AND BELOW 125 PERCENT OF POVERTY LEVEL, BY RACE AND HISPANIC ORIGIN, 1960–1990

Year	Number Below Poverty Level (1,000) All Races	White	Black	Hispanic	Percent Below Poverty Level All Races	White	Black	Hispanic	Below 125 Percent of Poverty Level Number (1,000)	Percent
1960	8,243	6,115	. . .	. . .	18.1	14.9	. . .	. . .	11,525	25.4
1970	5,260	3,708	1,481	. . .	10.1	8.0	29.5	. . .	7,516	14.4
1971	5,303	3,751	1,484	. . .	10.0	7.9	28.8	. . .	. . .	. . .
1972	5,075	3,441	1,529	477	9.3	7.1	29.0	20.6	7,347	13.5
1973	4,828	3,219	1,527	468	8.8	6.6	28.1	19.8	7,044	12.8
1974	4,922	3,352	1,479	526	8.8	6.8	26.9	21.2	7,195	12.9
1975	5,450	3,838	1,513	627	9.7	7.7	27.1	25.1	7,974	14.2
1976	5,311	3,560	1,617	598	9.4	7.1	27.9	23.1	7,647	13.5
1977	5,311	3,540	1,637	591	9.3	7.0	28.2	21.4	7,713	13.5
1978	5,280	3,523	1,622	559	9.1	6.9	27.5	20.4	7,417	12.8
1979	5,461	3,581	1,722	614	9.2	6.9	27.8	20.3	7,784	13.1
1980	6,217	4,195	1,826	751	10.3	8.0	28.9	23.2	8,764	14.5
1981	6,851	4,670	1,972	792	11.2	8.8	30.8	24.0	9,568	15.7
1982	7,512	5,118	2,158	916	12.2	9.6	33.0	27.2	10,279	16.7
1983	7,647	5,220	2,161	981	12.3	9.7	32.3	25.9	10,358	16.7
1984	7,277	4,925	2,094	991	11.6	9.1	30.9	25.2	9,901	15.8
1985	7,223	4,983	1,983	1,074	11.4	9.1	28.7	25.5	9,753	15.3
1986	7,023	4,811	1,987	1,085	10.9	8.6	28.0	24.7	9,476	14.7
1987	7,005	4,567	2,117	1,168	10.7	8.1	29.4	25.5	9,338	14.3
1988	6,874	4,471	2,089	1,141	10.4	7.9	28.2	23.7	9,284	14.1
1989	6,784	4,409	2,077	1,133	10.3	7.8	27.8	23.4	9,267	14.0
1990	7,098	4,622	2,193	1,244	10.7	8.1	29.3	25.0	9,564	14.4

Note: Table measures income below which a family was (1.) at the poverty level and (2.) only 25 percent above the poverty level.
Source: Bruce A. Chadwick and Tim B. Heaton, *Statistical Handbook on the American Family* (Phoenix, 1999), 255.

TABLE 4.87 POVERTY RATE AND FAMILIES WITH FEMALE HOUSEHOLDERS, 1959–1990

(in percent)

Year	Poverty Rate for Families	Poverty Rate for Families with Female Householder	Families with Female Householder as a Percent of All Families	Poor Families with Female Householder as a Percent of All Poor Families
1959	18.5	42.6	9.8	23.0
1962	17.2	42.9	10.0	25.2
1966	11.8	33.1	10.5	29.8
1970	10.1	32.5	11.5	37.1
1974	8.8	32.1	13.0	47.2
1978	9.1	31.4	14.6	50.3
1982	12.2	36.3	15.4	45.7
1986	10.9	34.6	16.2	51.4
1987	10.7	34.2	16.4	52.2
1988	10.4	33.4	16.5	53.0
1989	10.3	32.2	16.5	51.7
1990	10.7	33.4	17.0	53.1

Source: Littman, *Statistical Portrait of the U.S.*, 305.

TABLE 4.88 RECIPIENTS OF SOCIAL INSURANCE PROGRAMS, 1987

Program	Number of Recipients (thousands)	Percentage of U.S. Population
Nonmeans-tested		
Social Security (OASDI)	37,973.0	15.6
Medicare (hospital insurance)	31,853.0	13.1
Veterans programs	3,829.0	1.6
Railroad retirement	935.3	0.4
State unemployment insurance	2,032.0	0.8
State temporary disability	151.6	0.1
Means-tested[a]		
Medicaid	23,109.0	9.5
Supplemental Security Income	4,457.8	1.8
Aid to Families with Dependent Children	11,027.0	4.5
Food stamps	19,113.0	7.8
General assistance	1,168.0	0.5

[a] Means-tested pertains to a requirement to demonstrate financial need based on assets and income.
Source: Stanley and Niemi, *Statistics on Politics*, 386.

TABLE 4.89 AID TO FAMILIES WITH DEPENDENT CHILDREN VERSUS THE POVERTY LINE, 1945–1990

Year	Average Monthly Benefit per Family	Yearly Benefit	Average Poverty Threshold[a]
1945	48.18	578.16	. . .
1950	71.33	855.96	. . .
1955	84.17	1,010.04	. . .
1960	105.75	1,269.00	3,022
1961	110.97	1,331.64	3,054
1962	116.30	1,395.60	3,089
1963	120.19	1,442.28	3,128
1964	126.88	1,522.56	3,169
1965	133.20	1,598.40	3,223
1966	142.83	1,713.96	3,335
1967	155.19	1,862.28	3,410
1968	168.41	2,020.92	3,553
1969	174.89	2,098.68	3,743
1970	183.13	2,197.56	3,968
1971	187.16	2,245.92	4,137
1972	188.87	2,266.44	4,275
1973	190.91	2,290.92	4,540
1974	204.27	2,451.24	5,038
1975	219.44	2,633.28	5,500
1976	236.10	2,833.20	5,815
1977	246.27	2,955.24	6,191
1978	253.89	3,046.68	6,662
1979	262.86	3,154.32	7,412
1980	280.03	3,360.36	8,414
1981	282.04	3,384.48	9,287
1982	303.02	3,636.24	9,862
1983	312.82	3,753.84	10,178
1984	325.44	3,905.28	10,609
1985	342.15	4,105.80	10,989
1986	355.04	4,260.48	11,203
1987	361.37	4,336.44	11,611
1988	374.07	4,488.84	12,092
1989	. . .	. . .	12,675
1990 (prelim.)	. . .	. . .	13,360

[a] Poverty threshold is for a family of four.
Source: Stanley and Niemi, *Statistics on Politics*, 387.

Agriculture

American agriculture underwent many sharp turns and experienced numerous radical changes in the last half of the 20th century. Between 1946 and 1990 the number of farms declined from roughly six million to barely more than two million. The average size of farms more than doubled. The farm population decreased fivefold, from approximately 25 million to fewer than 5 million. Farm production nonetheless more than doubled and one suspects that farmers could have produced a great deal more had market conditions suggested that it would be wise to do so. The increase in efficiency, as measured in yield per acre of certain crops, was astonishing.

After the Second World War, American farmers behaved as they always had: utilizing the most up-to-date equipment and most advanced scientific knowledge about every stage of the production process to raise more and better goods. New types of growing aids—fertilizers, herbicides, pesticides—appeared with remarkable frequency. A shrinking number of draft animals remained on the job for a few years after the Second World War, and then, except for the Budweiser Clydesdales and pulling contests at state and county fairs, the horses and mules disappeared, their existence not even appearing as a farm statistic. Large machines replaced small ones, and new devices came on line to perform nearly every farm function. Science was even putting the bull of the cattle herd out of business.

The agricultural transformation, however, did not unfold as an account of uninterrupted triumph. The ability to produce carried the ability to overproduce; too many goods meant low prices. Agricultural advance in other countries—the "green revolution"—placed frequent pressure on the world price of many items. Government price supports remained a constant, if controversial, feature of American agriculture. Weather—too little rain, too much rain, a storm or a flood—could destroy crops and the year's income. Large machines and the technological miracle makers, even the fertilizers and chemicals, cost considerable money. Strange as it sounded, becoming efficient was becoming expensive. All the forces of agriculture, it would appear, seemed arranged in favor of the large farm and the agricultural corporation and against the traditional independent farmer. Some farmers, the numbers suggest a good many of them, quit because they were deeply in debt or at least could not make a profit. Some were foreclosed on or simply lost their farms. Others sold out because they found an opportunity to make a huge sum in a very short time. Here one aspect of postwar America intersected with another. If the farm population was shrinking, the urban population and the cities themselves were expanding, stretching out into the countryside. Building the first Levittown created a scenario that would be repeated many thousand times in many years to come. Surely the most tragic feature of the post-1945 transformation was not the shrinkage of the number of farms, for farms could be absorbed into larger organizations, but the amount of precious farmland lost, for once topsoil was dug up, it could no more than Humpty-Dumpty be returned to its former state. Many millions of people in 1990 lived on land that in 1946 had been producing crops.

TABLE 4.90 BASIC FARM CHARACTERISTICS, 1945–1990

Year	Farm Population (thousands)	Percentage of Total Population	Number of Farms (thousands)	Acres in Farms (thousands)	Average Size Farm (acres)
1945	24,420	17.5	5,859	1,141,615	195
1950	23,048	15.3	5,388	1,161,420	216
1955	19,078	11.6	4,654	1,201,900	258
1960	15,635	8.7	3,962	1,175,646	297
1965	12,363	6.4	3,356	1,139,597	340
1970	9,712	4.8	2,954	1,102,769	373
1975	8,864	4.1	2,521	1,059,420	420
1980	6,051	2.7	2,439	1,038,885	426
1985	5,355	2.2	2,292	1,012,073	441
1990	4,591	1.9	2,140	987,420	461

Source: R. Douglas Hurt, *American Agriculture: A Brief History* (Ames, Iowa, 1994), 395.

TABLE 4.91 FARMS—NUMBER AND ACREAGE, BY STATE, 1980 AND 1990

State	Farms (1,000) 1980	Farms (1,000) 1990	Acreage (mil.) 1980	Acreage (mil.) 1990	Acreage per Farm 1980	Acreage per Farm 1990
U.S.	2,440	2,143	1,039	988	426	461
Ala.	59	47	12	10	207	219
Alaska	a	a	2	1	3,378	1,724
Ariz.	8	8	38	36	5,080	4,615
Ark.	59	47	17	16	280	330
Calif.	81	85	34	31	417	362
Colo.	27	27	36	33	1,358	1,249
Conn.	4	4	a	a	117	108
Del.	4	3	1	1	186	197
Fla.	39	41	13	11	344	266
Ga.	59	49	15	13	254	255
Hawaii	4	5	2	2	458	372
Idaho	24	22	15	14	623	628
Ill.	107	83	29	29	269	343
Ind.	87	68	17	16	193	240
Iowa	119	104	34	34	284	322
Kans.	75	69	48	48	644	694
Ky.	102	93	15	14	143	152
La.	37	34	10	9	273	265
Maine	8	7	2	1	195	199
Md.	18	15	3	2	157	148
Mass.	6	7	1	1	116	99
Mich.	65	54	11	11	175	200
Minn.	104	89	30	30	291	337
Miss.	55	40	15	13	265	325

State	Farms (1,000) 1980	Farms (1,000) 1990	Acreage (mil.) 1980	Acreage (mil.) 1990	Acreage per Farm 1980	Acreage per Farm 1990
Mo.	120	108	31	30	261	281
Mont.	24	25	62	61	2,601	2,449
Nebr.	65	57	48	47	734	826
Nev.	3	3	9	9	3,100	3,560
N.H.	3	3	1	a	160	163
N.J.	9	8	1	1	109	107
N.Mex.	14	14	47	45	3,467	3,296
N.Y.	47	39	9	8	200	218
N.C.	93	62	12	10	126	156
N.Dak.	40	34	42	41	1,043	1,191
Ohio	95	84	16	16	171	187
Okla.	72	70	35	33	481	471
Oreg.	35	37	18	18	517	488
Pa.	62	53	9	8	145	153
R.I.	1	1	a	a	87	92
S.C.	34	25	6	5	188	212
S.Dak.	39	35	45	44	1,169	1,266
Tenn.	96	89	14	12	142	139
Tex.	196	186	138	132	705	710
Utah	14	13	12	11	919	856
Vt.	8	7	2	2	226	216
Va.	58	46	10	9	169	193
Wash.	38	37	16	16	429	432
W.Va.	22	21	4	4	191	180
Wis.	93	80	19	18	200	220
Wyo.	9	9	35	35	3,846	3,910

a Less than 500 farms or 500,000 acres.
Source: *Statistical Abstract, 1991*, 645.

TABLE 4.92 U.S. FARMS—CLASSIFICATION BY TENURE OF OPERATOR, 1945–1987

Year	Farms (number)	Tenure of Operator (percent) Full Owners	Part Owners	Managers	All Tenants
1945	5,859,169	56.4	11.3	.7	31.7
1950	5,388,437	57.4	15.3	.4	26.9
1954	4,783,021	57.4	18.2	.4	24.0
1959	3,710,503	57.1	21.9	.6	20.5
1964	3,157,857	57.6	24.8	.6	17.1
1969	2,730,250	62.5	24.6	. . .	12.9
1974	2,314,013	61.5	27.2	. . .	11.3
1978	2,257,775	57.5	30.2	. . .	12.3
1982	2,240,976	59.2	29.3	. . .	11.6
1987	2,087,759	59.3	29.2	. . .	11.5

Source: Department of Agriculture, *Agricultural Statistics, 1991* (Washington, D.C., 1991), 356.

TABLE 4.93 LAND IN U.S. FARMS—CLASSIFICATION BY TENURE OF OPERATOR, 1945–1987

Year	Land in Farms (acres)	Tenure of Operator (percent) Full Owners	Part Owners	Managers	All Tenants
1945	1,141,615,364	36.1	32.5	9.3	22.0
1950	1,161,419,720	36.1	36.4	9.2	18.3
1954	1,158,191,511	34.2	40.7	8.6	16.5
1959	1,123,507,574	31.0	44.0	9.8	14.8
1964	1,110,187.000	28.7	48.0	10.2	13.1
1969	1,062,892.501	35.3	51.8	. . .	13.0
1974	1,017,030.357	35.3	52.6	. . .	12.0
1978	1,014,777,234	32.7	55.3	. . .	12.0
1982	986,796,579	34.7	53.8	. . .	11.5
1987	964,470,625	32.9	53.9	. . .	13.2

Source: *Agricultural Statistics, 1991*, 356.

TABLE 4.94   FARMS—NUMBER, 1974–1987, AND ACREAGE, 1978–1987, BY SIZE OF FARM

Size of Farm	Number of Farms (1,000)				Land in Farms (mil. acres)			Cropland Harvested (mil. acres)			Percent Distribution, 1987		
	1974	1978	1982	1987	1978	1982	1987	1978	1982	1987	Number of Farms	All Land in Farms	Cropland Harvested
Total	2,314	2,258	2,241	2,088	1,014.8	986.8	964.5	317.1	326.3	282.2	100.0	100.0	100.0
Under 10 acres	128	151	188	183	0.6	0.7	0.7	0.2	0.3	0.2	8.8	0.1	0.1
10 to 49 acres	380	392	449	412	10.9	12.1	11.1	4.5	4.5	3.9	19.8	1.2	1.4
50 to 99 acres	385	356	344	311	25.9	24.8	22.5	10.2	9.5	7.9	14.9	2.3	2.8
100 to 179 acres	443	403	368	334	55.0	49.9	45.3	23.3	21.2	17.1	16.0	4.7	6.1
180 to 259 acres	253	234	211	192	50.6	45.7	41.5	23.7	21.7	17.2	9.2	4.3	6.1
260 to 499 acres	363	348	315	286	124.6	113.0	103.0	64.5	60.5	47.3	13.7	10.7	16.8
500 to 999 acres	207	213	204	200	146.7	140.5	138.5	75.2	77.6	67.4	9.6	14.4	23.9
1,000 to 1,999 acres	93	98	97	102	133.0	132.4	138.8	58.2	64.5	61.1	4.9	14.4	21.7
2,000 acres and over	62	63	65	67	467.4	467.5	463.2	57.3	66.6	60.2	3.2	48.0	21.3

Source: Statistical Abstract, 1992, 645.

Farming on a massive scale. Parallel terraces are planted in cotton with windstrips in wheat. (U.S. Department of Agriculture)

TABLE 4.95   FARM INPUT USE, SELECTED INPUTS, 1947–1990

Year	Farm Population, April — Number (thousands)	As Percent of Total Population	Farm Employment (thousands) — Total	Family Workers	Hired Workers	Crops Harvested (millions of acres)	Selected Indexes of Input Use (1977 = 100) — Total	Farm Labor	Farm Real Estate	Mechanical Power and Machinery	Agricultural Chemicals	Feed, Seed, and Livestock Purchases
1947	25,829	17.9	10,382	8,115	2,267	355	104	297	106	54	15	51
1948	24,383	16.6	10,363	8,026	2,337	356	104	285	107	62	16	52
1949	24,194	16.2	9,964	7,712	2,252	360	108	285	108	68	18	56
1950	23,048	15.2	9,926	7,597	2,329	345	106	265	109	72	19	58
1951	21,890	14.2	9,546	7,310	2,236	344	106	251	109	77	21	62
1952	21,748	13.9	9,149	7,005	2,144	349	105	237	108	81	23	63
1953	19,874	12.5	8,864	6,775	2,089	348	103	220	108	82	24	63
1954	19,019	11.7	8,651	6,570	2,081	346	102	214	108	82	24	65
1955	19,078	11.5	8,381	6,345	2,036	340	104	220	108	83	26	66
1956	18,712	11.1	7,852	5,900	1,952	324	103	212	106	84	27	69
1957	17,656	10.3	7,600	5,660	1,940	324	100	196	105	83	27	68
1958	17,128	9.8	7,503	5,521	1,982	324	98	182	104	83	28	73
1959	16,592	9.3	7,342	5,390	1,952	324	101	183	105	84	32	77
1960	15,635	8.7	7,057	5,172	1,885	324	99	177	103	83	32	77
1961	14,803	8.1	6,919	5,029	1,890	302	98	167	103	80	35	81
1962	14,313	7.7	6,700	4,873	1,827	295	98	163	104	80	38	83
1963	13,367	7.1	6,518	4,738	1,780	298	98	155	104	79	43	83
1964	12,954	6.7	6,110	4,506	1,604	298	98	148	104	80	46	85
1965	12,363	6.4	5,610	4,128	1,482	298	97	144	103	80	49	86
1966	11,595	5.9	5,214	3,854	1,360	294	96	132	102	82	56	89
1967	10,875	5.5	4,903	3,650	1,253	306	98	128	104	85	66	92
1968	10,454	5.2	4,749	3,535	1,213	300	97	124	102	86	69	89
1969	10,307	5.1	4,596	3,419	1,176	290	96	118	102	86	73	93
1970	9,712	4.7	4,523	3,348	1,175	293	96	112	105	85	75	96
1971	9,425	4.5	4,436	3,275	1,161	305	97	108	103	87	81	102
1972	9,610	4.6	4,373	3,228	1,146	294	97	110	102	86	86	104
1973	9,472	4.5	4,337	3,169	1,168	321	98	109	100	90	90	107
1974	9,264	4.3	4,389	3,075	1,314	328	98	109	99	92	92	99
1975	8,864	4.1	4,342	3,026	1,317	336	97	106	97	96	83	93
1976	8,253	3.8	4,374	2,997	1,377	337	98	100	98	98	96	101
1977	6,194	2.8	4,155	2,859	1,296	345	100	100	100	100	100	100
1978	6,501	2.9	3,957	2,689	1,268	338	102	100	100	104	107	108
1979	6,241	2.8	3,774	2,501	1,273	348	105	99	103	104	123	115
1980	6,051	2.7	3,705	2,402	1,303	352	103	96	103	101	123	114
1981	5,850	2.5	3,552	2,267	1,285	366	102	96	104	98	129	108
1982	5,628	2.4	3,400	2,136	1,264	362	98	93	102	89	118	107
1983	5,787	2.5	3,247	2,007	1,240	306	96	97	101	86	102	103
1984	5,754	2.4	3,094	1,976	1,118	348	95	92	99	85	120	103
1985	5,355	2.2	2,941	1,904	1,037	342	91	85	97	80	115	102
1986	5,226	2.2	2,749	1,768	981	325	89	80	96	77	109	109
1987	4,986	2.1	2,734	1,743	992	302	89	78	95	74	111	116
1988	4,951	2.0	2,789	1,810	979	297	87	75	94	74	112	111
1989	4,801	1.9	2,873	1,926	947	318	87	76	93	73	119	113
1990	4,591	1.8	2,869	1,965	904	322	88	80	93	71	122	113

Source: Council of Advisers, *Economic Report of the President, 1992,* 407.

TABLE 4.96 FARM OUTPUT AND PRODUCTIVITY INDEXES, 1947–1990

(1977 = 100)

Year	Farm Output Total	Crops Total	Feed Grains	Food Grains	Oil Crops	Livestock and Products	Per Unit of Total Input	Per Hour of Farm Work	Crop Production per Acre
1947	58	56	39	64	22	65	55	18	57
1948	63	64	57	62	27	64	60	21	64
1949	62	61	50	53	26	67	57	20	60
1950	61	59	51	49	26	70	58	22	59
1951	63	60	47	49	26	73	60	24	59
1952	66	62	50	63	26	74	62	26	62
1953	66	62	49	57	26	74	64	28	62
1954	66	61	51	51	28	77	65	29	61
1955	69	63	54	48	30	79	66	30	63
1956	69	63	54	50	34	79	67	31	64
1957	67	62	58	47	33	78	67	33	65
1958	73	69	64	69	39	79	74	39	73
1959	74	68	66	55	36	83	73	39	72
1960	76	72	69	66	38	82	76	42	77
1961	76	70	62	60	43	86	78	44	78
1962	77	71	62	56	44	86	78	46	81
1963	80	74	68	59	46	89	82	51	83
1964	79	72	59	65	46	91	81	52	81
1965	82	76	70	67	53	89	84	56	85
1966	79	73	70	67	55	91	83	59	83
1967	83	77	79	76	56	94	85	64	86
1968	85	79	75	80	64	94	87	68	89
1969	85	80	78	74	65	95	88	72	91
1970	84	77	71	69	66	99	87	74	88
1971	92	86	92	81	68	100	95	85	96
1972	91	87	88	77	74	101	94	83	99
1973	93	92	91	86	87	99	95	86	99
1974	88	84	74	91	71	100	90	81	88
1975	95	93	91	108	86	95	99	90	96
1976	97	92	96	107	74	99	98	97	94
1977	100	100	100	100	100	100	100	100	100
1978	104	102	108	93	105	101	101	104	105
1979	111	113	116	108	129	104	105	113	113
1980	104	101	97	121	99	108	101	109	100
1981	118	117	121	144	114	109	116	123	115
1982	116	117	122	138	121	107	119	125	116
1983	96	88	67	117	91	109	100	100	100
1984	112	111	116	129	106	107	118	121	112
1985	118	118	134	121	117	110	129	139	120
1986	111	109	123	107	110	110	124	139	116
1987	110	108	106	107	108	113	124	142	123
1988	102	92	73	98	89	116	116	135	106
1989	114	107	108	107	106	116	130	147	119
1990	119	114	112	136	107	118	135	142	127

Source: Council of Advisers, *Economic Report of the President, 1992,* 406.

TABLE 4.97 LIVESTOCK ON FARMS

(in thousands)

Type	1950	1960	1965	1970	1975	1980	1985	1990
Cattle	77,963	96,236	109,000	112,369	132,028	111,242	109,582	98,162
Dairy cows	23,853	19,527	16,981	13,303	11,220	10,758	10,311	10,153
Sheep	29,826	33,170	25,127	20,423	14,515	12,699	10,716	11,363
Swine	58,937	59,026	56,106	57,046	54,693	67,318	54,073	51,150
Chickens	535,266	1,976,737	2,535,141	3,220,085	3,173,820	4,201,706	4,689,973	3,236,993
Turkeys	44,134	84,458	105,914	116,139	124,165	165,243	185,427	304,863

Source: *Information Please Almanac, 1992,* 61.

Large farms require large, expensive equipment. (U.S. Department of Agriculture)

TABLE 4.98   AGRICULTURAL OUTPUT BY STATES, 1990 CROPS

State	Corn (1,000 bu)	Wheat (1,000 bu)	Cotton (1,000 ba)	Potatoes (1,000 cwt)	Tobacco (1,000 lb)	Cattle (1,000 head)	Swine (1,000 head)
Ala.	13,920	6,650	400.0	1,943	. . .	1,750	. . .
Alaska	. . .	. . .	. . .	. . .	. . .	8.2	. . .
Ariz.	1,120	9,266	1,015.0	1,794	. . .	830	. . .
Ark.	6,935	49,000	1,100.0	. . .	. . .	1,700	. . .
Calif.	25,600	47,906	2,805.8	17,783	. . .	4,800	. . .
Colo.	128,650	86,950	. . .	24,032	. . .	2,900	. . .
Conn.	. . .	. . .	. . .	. . .	3,000	76	. . .
Del.	19,780	3,060	. . .	2,009	. . .	31	. . .
Fla.	5,325	1,815	45.0	9,792	19,040	1,925	. . .
Ga.	37,400	20,650	410.0	. . .	103,200	1,400	1,100
Hawaii	. . .	. . .	. . .	. . .	. . .	205	. . .
Idaho	3,900	99,600	. . .	112,340	. . .	1,660	. . .
Ill.	1,320,800	91,200	. . .	837	. . .	1,950	5,700
Ind.	703,050	50,440	. . .	858	13,440	1,250	4,300
Iowa	1,562,400	3,375	. . .	160	. . .	4,500	13,800
Kans.	188,500	472,000	1.1	. . .	. . .	5,700	1,500
Ky.	120,000	20,000	. . .	. . .	437,153	2,420	920
La.	21,576	12,870	1,180.0	. . .	. . .	1,050	. . .
Maine	. . .	. . .	. . .	20,520	. . .	116	. . .
Md.	53,100	9,880	. . .	324	9,443	315	. . .
Mass.	. . .	. . .	. . .	650	. . .	71	. . .
Mich.	238,050	41,250	. . .	12,115	. . .	1,225	1,250
Minn.	762,600	138,620	. . .	16,110	. . .	2,600	4,500
Miss.	11,200	15,600	1,851.1	. . .	. . .	1,370	. . .
Mo.	205,800	76,000	305.0	957	5,625	4,400	2,800

State	Corn (1,000 bu)	Wheat (1,000 bu)	Cotton (1,000 ba)	Potatoes (1,000 cwt)	Tobacco (1,000 lb)	Cattle (1,000 head)	Swine (1,000 head)
Mont.	855	145,865	. . .	2,492	. . .	2,300	4,300
Nebr.	934,400	85,500	. . .	3,539	. . .	5,800	. . .
Nev.	. . .	980	. . .	2,345	. . .	570	. . .
N.H.	. . .	. . .	. . .	. . .	. . .	46	. . .
N.J.	8,850	1,247	. . .	1,012	. . .	70	. . .
N.Mex.	7,975	8,125	126.0	3,400	. . .	1,360	. . .
N.Y.	60,760	7,105	. . .	7,890	. . .	1,540	. . .
N.C.	72,760	22,550	271.0	3,380	639,620	900	2,800
N.Dak.	36,800	385,220	. . .	16,675	. . .	1,700	. . .
Ohio	417,450	79,650	. . .	1,911	20,500	1,650	2,000
Okla.	10,032	201,600	380.0	. . .	. . .	5,250	. . .
Oreg.	2,700	57,616	. . .	23,014	. . .	1,400	. . .
Pa.	109,610	10,500	. . .	5,400	19,780	1,860	920
R.I.	. . .	. . .	. . .	294	. . .	7.0	. . .
S.C.	14,400	14,440	145.0	. . .	109,905	590	. . .
S.Dak.	234,000	128,004	. . .	1,980	. . .	3,380	1,770
Tenn.	43,860	17,640	490.0	. . .	99,416	2,300	620
Tex.	130,500	130,200	5,085.0	3,072	. . .	13,200	. . .
Utah	2,660	7,170	. . .	1,643	. . .	780	. . .
Vt.	. . .	. . .	. . .	. . .	. . .	297	. . .
Va.	36,500	12,220	6.6	1,980	109,498	1,700	. . .
Wash.	14,000	150,080	. . .	67,980	. . .	1,330	. . .
W.Va	5,250	552	. . .	. . .	2,880	490	. . .
Wis.	354,000	10,085	. . .	23,075	13,575	4,170	1,200
Wyo.	6,000	6,113	. . .	561	. . .	1,220	. . .
U.S. Total	**7,933,068**	**2,738,594**	**15,616.6**	**393,867**	**1,606,851**	**98,162**	**54,362[a]**

[a] Includes states not listed individually. The 16 listed states accounted for roughly 91 percent of the total.
Source: Information Please Almanac, 1992, 61.

Corporation farming is specialized farming. Professional grain harvesters at work (U.S. Department of Agriculture)

TABLE 4.99 PRODUCTION EFFICIENCY—CORN AND WHEAT, 1946–1990

Year	Corn Acres Harvested (1,000)	Corn Yield per Acre (bushels)	Wheat Acres Harvested (1,000)	Wheat Yield per Acre (bushels)
1946	87,600	36.7	67,100	17.2
1950	81,800	37.6	61,600	16.5
1955	79,500	40.6	47,300	19.8
1960	71,400	54.7	51,900	26.1
1965	55,300	73.8	49,600	26.5
1969	54,600	83.9	47,600	30.7
1976	71,500	88.0	70,900	30.3
1978	71,900	101.0	56,500	31.4
1980	73,000	91.0	71,100	33.5
1982	72,700	113.2	78,000	35.5
1984	71,900	106.7	67,000	38.8
1986	69,000	119.4	60,700	34.4
1988	58,300	84.6	53,200	34.1
1989	64,700	116.3	62,200	32.7
1990	67,000	118.5	69,400	39.5

Source: Department of Agriculture, *Agricultural Statistics, 1961* (Washington, D.C., 1961), 1, 29; Department of Agriculture, *Agricultural Statistics, 1970* (Washington, D.C., 1970), 1, 28; Department of Agriculture, *Agricultural Statistics, 1991* (Washington, D.C., 1991), 1, 31.

TABLE 4.100 AVERAGE PRICES RECEIVED BY U.S. FARMERS, 1940–1990

Year	Hogs	Cattle (beef)	Calves (veal)	Sheep	Lambs	Milk Cows	Milk	Chickens (excl. broilers)	Broilers	Turkeys	Eggs	Wool
1940	5.39	7.56	8.83	3.95	8.10	61	1.82	13.0	17.3	15.2	18.0	28.4
1950	18.00	23.30	26.30	11.60	25.10	198	3.89	22.2	27.4	32.8	36.3	62.1
1960	15.30	20.40	22.90	5.61	17.90	223	4.21	12.2	16.9	25.4	36.1	42.0
1970	22.70	27.10	34.50	7.51	26.40	332	5.71	9.1	13.6	22.6	39.1	35.4
1975	46.10	32.20	27.20	11.30	42.10	412	8.75	9.9	26.3	34.8	54.5	44.8
1980	38.00	62.40	76.80	21.30	63.60	1,190	13.05	11.0	27.7	41.3	56.3	88.1
1984	47.10	57.30	59.90	16.40	60.10	895	13.46	15.9	33.7	48.9	72.3	79.5
1985	44.00	53.70	62.10	23.90	67.70	860	12.76	14.8	30.1	49.1	57.1	63.3
1986	49.30	52.60	61.10	25.60	69.00	820	12.51	12.5	34.5	47.1	61.6	66.8
1987	51.20	61.10	78.50	29.50	77.60	920	12.54	11.0	28.7	34.8	54.9	91.7
1988	42.30	66.60	89.20	25.60	69.10	990	12.26	9.2	33.1	38.6	52.8	138.0
1989	42.50	69.50	90.80	24.40	66.10	1,030	13.56	14.9	36.6	40.9	68.9	124.0
1990	53.70	74.60	95.60	23.20	55.50	1,160	13.74	9.3	32.6	39.4	70.9	80.0

Figures represent dollars per 100 lb. for hogs, beef cattle, veal calves, sheep, lamb, and milk (wholesale); dollars per head for milk cows; cents per lb. for chickens, broilers, turkeys, and wool; cents per dozen for eggs; weighted calendar year prices for livestock and livestock products other than wool. For 1943–63, wool prices are weighted on marketing year basis. The marketing year was changed in 1964 from a calendar year to a Dec.–Nov. basis for hogs, chickens, broilers, and eggs.

Year	Corn	Wheat	Upland cotton	Oats	Barley	Rice	Soy-beans	Sorghum	Peanuts	Cotton-seed	Hay	Potatoes	Apples
1940	0.62	0.67	9.8	0.30	0.39	1.80	0.89	0.87	3.7	21.70	9.78	0.85	NA
1950	1.52	2.00	39.9	0.79	1.19	5.09	2.47	1.88	10.9	86.60	21.10	1.50	NA
1960	1.00	1.74	30.1	0.60	0.84	4.55	2.13	1.49	10.0	42.50	21.70	2.00	2.7
1970	1.33	1.33	21.9	0.62	0.97	5.17	2.85	2.04	12.8	56.40	26.10	2.21	6.5
1975	2.54	3.55	51.1	1.45	2.42	8.35	4.92	4.21	19.0	97.00	52.10	4.48	8.8
1980	3.11	3.91	74.4	1.79	2.86	12.80	7.57	5.25	25.1	129.00	71.00	6.55	12.1
1984	2.63	3.39	58.7	1.67	2.29	8.04	5.84	4.15	27.9	99.50	72.70	5.69	15.5
1985	2.23	3.08	56.8	1.23	1.98	6.53	5.05	3.45	24.4	66.00	67.60	3.92	17.3
1986	1.50	2.42	51.5	1.21	1.61	3.75	4.78	2.45	29.2	80.00	59.70	5.03	19.1
1987	1.94	2.57	63.7	1.56	1.81	7.27	5.88	3.04	28.0	82.50	65.00	4.38	12.7
1988	2.54	3.72	55.6	2.61	2.80	6.83	7.42	4.05	28.0	118.00	85.20	6.02	17.4
1989	2.36	3.72	63.6	1.49	2.42	7.35	5.69	3.75	28.0	105.00	85.40	7.36	13.9
1990	2.28	2.61	67.1	1.14	2.14	6.68	5.74	3.79	34.7	121.00	80.60	6.08	20.9

Figures represent cents per lb. for cotton, apples, and peanuts; dollars per bushel for oats, wheat, corn, barley, and soybeans; dollars per 100 lb. for rice, sorghum, and potatoes; dollars per ton for cottonseed and baled hay; weighted crop year prices. The marketing year is described as follows: apples, June–May; wheat, oats, barley, hay, and potatoes, Jul.–Jun.; cotton, rice, peanuts, and cottonseed, Aug.–Jul.; soybeans, Sep.–Aug.; and corn and sorghum grain, Oct.–Sep.
Source: World Almanac, 1999, 142.

TABLE 4.101 FARM INCOME, 1946–1990

(billions of dollars; quarterly data at seasonally adjusted annual rates)

	Income of Farm Operators from Farming						
	Gross Farm Income						
		Cash Marketing Receipts					
Year	Total[a]	Total	Livestock and Products	Crops	Value of Inventory Changes	Production Expenses	Net Farm Income
1946	29.6	24.8	13.8	11.0	.0	14.5	15.1
1947	32.4	29.6	16.5	13.1	−1.8	17.0	15.4
1948	36.5	30.2	17.1	13.1	1.7	18.8	17.7
1949	30.8	27.8	15.4	12.4	−.9	18.0	12.8
1950	33.1	28.5	16.1	12.4	.8	19.5	13.6
1951	38.3	32.9	19.6	13.2	1.2	22.3	15.9
1952	37.8	32.5	18.2	14.3	.9	22.8	15.0
1953	34.4	31.0	16.9	14.1	−.6	21.5	13.0
1954	34.2	29.8	16.3	13.6	.5	21.8	12.4
1955	33.5	29.5	16.0	13.5	.2	22.2	11.3
1956	34.0	30.4	16.4	14.0	−.5	22.7	11.3
1957	34.8	29.7	17.4	12.3	.6	23.7	11.1
1958	39.0	33.5	19.2	14.2	.8	25.8	13.2
1959	37.9	33.6	18.9	14.7	.0	27.2	10.7
1960	38.6	34.0	19.0	15.0	.4	27.4	11.2
1961	40.5	35.2	19.5	15.7	.3	28.6	12.0
1962	42.3	36.5	20.2	16.3	.6	30.3	12.1
1963	43.4	37.5	20.0	17.4	.6	31.6	11.8
1964	42.3	37.3	19.9	17.4	−.8	31.8	10.5
1965	46.5	39.4	21.9	17.5	1.0	33.6	12.9
1966	50.5	43.4	25.0	18.4	−.1	36.5	14.0
1967	50.5	42.8	24.4	18.4	.7	38.2	12.3
1968	51.8	44.2	25.5	18.7	.1	39.5	12.3
1969	56.4	48.2	28.6	19.6	.1	42.1	14.3
1970	58.8	50.5	29.5	21.0	.0	44.5	14.4
1971	62.1	52.7	30.5	22.3	1.4	47.1	15.0
1972	71.1	61.1	35.6	25.5	.9	51.7	19.5
1973	98.9	86.9	45.8	41.1	3.4	64.6	34.4
1974	98.2	92.4	41.3	51.1	−1.6	71.0	27.3
1975	100.6	88.9	43.1	45.8	3.4	75.0	25.5
1976	102.9	95.4	46.3	49.0	−1.5	82.7	20.2
1977	108.8	96.2	47.6	48.6	1.1	88.9	19.9
1978	128.4	112.4	59.2	53.2	1.9	103.2	25.2
1979	150.7	131.5	69.2	62.3	5.0	123.3	27.4
1980	149.3	139.7	68.0	71.7	−6.3	133.1	16.1
1981	166.3	141.6	69.2	72.5	6.5	139.4	26.9
1982	164.1	142.6	70.3	72.3	−1.4	140.3	23.8
1983	153.9	136.8	69.6	67.2	−10.9	139.6	14.2
1984	168.0	142.8	72.9	69.9	6.0	142.0	26.0
1985	161.2	144.1	69.8	74.3	−2.3	132.6	28.6
1986	156.1	135.4	71.6	63.8	−2.2	125.2	30.9
1987	168.4	141.8	76.0	65.8	−2.3	131.0	37.4
1988	177.9	151.2	79.6	71.6	−4.1	139.9	38.0
1989	191.9	160.8	83.9	76.9	3.8	146.7	45.3
1990	198.1	169.5	89.2	80.3	3.3	153.3	44.8

[a] Cash marketing receipts and inventory changes plus Government payments, other farm cash income, and nonmoney income.
Source: Council of Economic Advisers, *Economic Report of the President, 1998* (Washington, D.C., 1998), 393.

TABLE 4.102 **FARM INCOME—MARKETINGS AND GOVERNMENT PAYMENTS, BY STATE, 1989 AND 1990**

(thousands of dollars)

| State | 1989 Farm Marketings | | | 1990 Farm Marketings | | | |
	Total	Crops	Livestock and Products	Total	Crops	Livestock and Products	Government Payments
Ala.	2,670,904	696,322	1,974,582	2,737,422	654.909	2,082,513	82,226
Alaska	28,631	19,771	8,860	26,539	18,977	7,562	1,117
Ariz.	1,926,022	1,181,836	744,186	1,865,492	1,046,246	819,246	43,349
Ark.	4,156,869	1,496,114	2,660,755	4,259,205	1,552,776	2,706,429	312,696
Calif.	18,050,380	12,857,370	5,193,010	18,858,873	13,343,714	5,515,159	252,333
Colo.	3,969,206	1,320,629	2,648,577	4,213,419	1,184,074	3,029,345	236,723
Conn.	426,259	239,892	186,367	445,901	250,068	195,833	2,123
Del.	661,640	159,032	502,608	643,661	183,829	459,832	3,213
Fla.	6,246,284	5,030,897	1,215,387	5,708,300	4,448,019	1,260,281	37,155
Ga.	3,907,761	1,626,283	2,281,478	3,842,186	1,574,081	2,268,105	130,593
Hawaii	585,002	493,215	91,787	587,689	499,245	88,444	519
Idaho	2,745,336	1,661,606	1,083,730	2,934,519	1,780,841	1,153,678	133,431
Ill.	6,978,820	4,727,437	2,251,383	7,937,793	5,460,821	2,476,972	506,603
Ind.	4,281,440	2,455,574	1,825,866	4,930,668	2,871,067	2,059,601	244,170
Iowa	9,048,625	3,755,249	5,293,376	10,319,173	4,437,024	5,882,149	753,733
Kans.	6,548,317	2,132,274	4,416,043	6,994,864	2,098,649	4,896,215	834,746
Ky.	2,924,151	1,266,117	1,658,034	3,098,398	1,400,075	1,698,323	81,610
La.	1,707,682	1,093,656	614,026	1,921,224	1,284,157	637,067	154,631
Maine	444,038	227,953	216,085	460,387	240,492	219,895	6,982
Md.	1,336,215	477,149	859,066	1,345,165	516,701	828,464	17,386
Mass.	433,955	321,032	112,923	418,462	302,525	115,937	3,023
Mich.	2,922,761	1,611,462	1,311,299	3,183,356	1,785,034	1,398,322	168,831
Minn.	6,513,260	2,819,850	3,693,410	7,011,173	3,253,477	3,757,696	511,759
Miss.	2,275,837	981,002	1,294,835	2,432,964	1,111,288	1,321,676	185,969
Mo.	3,920,049	1,751,019	2,169,030	3,938,589	1,667,974	2,270,615	299,065
Mont.	1,553,782	624,526	929,256	1,605,731	742,052	863,679	299,599
Nebr.	8,725,832	3,079,816	5,646,016	8,845,164	2,807,674	6,037,490	624,646
Nev.	243,589	101,556	142,033	333,435	115,085	218,350	5,347
N.H.	138,824	73,429	65,395	133,892	70,720	63,172	1,856
N.J.	661,691	464,363	197,328	647,383	451,510	195,873	15,744
N.Mex.	1,458,917	484,706	974,211	1,528,793	482,814	1,045,979	63,840
N.Y.	2,853,916	917,270	1,936,646	3,006,046	1,022,887	1,983,159	59,304
N.C.	4,592,584	2,082,348	2,510,236	4,866,512	2,213,714	2,652,798	73,255
N.Dak.	2,151,510	1,482,514	668,996	2,537,350	1,723,899	813,451	545,378
Ohio	3,786,524	2,088,064	1,698,460	4,171,818	2,335,424	1,836,394	197,006
Okla.	3,514,760	1,137,297	2,377,463	3,554,437	1,191,312	2,363,125	319,040
Oreg.	2,284,656	1,546,451	738,205	2,311,783	1,557,088	754,695	89,137
Pa.	3,602,210	991,513	2,610,697	3,767,174	1,053,407	2,713,767	41,414
R.I.	78,317	65,461	12,856	70,793	58,269	12,524	191
S.C.	1,234,700	680,310	554,390	1,175,560	599,038	576,522	62,637
S.Dak.	2,982,194	950,887	2,031,307	3,348,717	1,036,068	2,312,649	332,851
Tenn.	1,945,725	863,290	1,082,435	2,038,610	928,009	1,110,601	91,029
Tex.	10,923,494	4,062,624	6,860,870	11,980,527	4,268,378	7,712,149	974,702
Utah	755,279	188,181	567,098	754,826	178,686	576,140	34,897
Vt.	429,318	50,247	379,071	446,722	48,951	397,771	5,793
Va.	2,039,137	694,323	1,344,814	2,119,633	740,881	1,378,752	32,378
Wash.	3,689,120	2,456,532	1,232,588	3,815,779	2,420,139	1,395,640	205,425
W.Va.	310,275	60,316	249,959	338,132	69,517	268,615	6,049
Wis.	5,399,559	1,049,982	4,349,577	5,706,149	1,124,923	4,581,226	181,243
Wyo.	827,171	162,735	664,436	766,767	157,193	609,574	31,283
U.S.	**$160,892,528**	**$76,761,482**	**$84,131,046**	**$169,987,155**	**$80,363,701**	**$89,623,454**	**$9,298,030**

Source: World Almanac, 1992, 160.

Earnings and Expenses and a Parity Price

When the government began during the Depression of the 1930s to seek to improve the income of farmers, there logically appeared the need to find some standard of measuring the desired improvement. Officials concluded that farm prices should be elevated to a position commensurate with farm, or simply living, expenses. Research produced a calculation that during the years 1909–14 the relationship between prices and cost had been reasonable and equitable and that reestablishment of that ratio would be the objective of government policy. When prices received attained a level equitable with prices paid, they were said to have reached a state of parity. Farmers hoped to receive prices that were at or above the parity level. Prices beneath 100 percent of parity signaled that agriculture was not receiving a fair share of income, and the lower the parity number, the greater the hardship that farmers were having to bear. The two tables of commodity prices, which utilized the original parity ratio, revealed that farmers received good prices—above parity—for seven years after the Second World War; then prices began a slide that continued, except for a brief period in the 1970s, to the 1990s. By 1986 prices reached 51, barely half of the established objective. A following table that utilized a different index told a slightly different story. Prices received exceeded prices paid until 1980, at which time the negative ratio continued to broaden. Small wonder that the farmer's share of the market price also declined. Between 1950 and 1990 the producer's share of the market price of food went from nearly 50 percent to only 30 percent.

TABLE 4.103 INDEXES OF PRICES RECEIVED AND PRICES PAID BY FARMERS, 1950–1990
(1975 = 100)

Year or Month	Prices Received by Farmers			Prices Paid by Farmers						Addendum: Average Farm Real Estate Value per Acre
	All Farm Products	Crops	Livestock and Products	All Commodities, Services, Interest, Taxes, and Wage Rates	Production Items					
					Total	Tractors and Self-propelled Machinery	Fertilizer	Fuels and Energy	Wage Rates	
1950	56	54	58	37	42	. . .	54	. . .	22	14
1951	66	61	70	41	47	. . .	57	. . .	25	16
1952	63	62	64	42	47	. . .	59	. . .	26	18
1953	56	55	56	40	44	. . .	59	. . .	27	18
1954	54	56	52	40	44	. . .	59	. . .	27	18
1955	51	53	49	40	43	. . .	58	. . .	27	19
1956	50	54	47	40	43	. . .	57	. . .	28	19
1957	51	52	51	42	44	. . .	58	. . .	29	21
1958	55	52	57	43	46	. . .	58	. . .	30	22
1959	53	51	53	43	46	. . .	57	. . .	32	23
1960	52	51	53	44	46	. . .	57	. . .	33	24
1961	53	52	52	44	46	. . .	58	. . .	33	25
1962	53	54	53	45	47	. . .	58	. . .	34	26
1963	53	55	51	45	47	. . .	57	. . .	35	27
1964	52	55	49	45	47	. . .	57	. . .	36	29
1965	54	53	54	47	48	39	57	49	38	31
1966	58	55	60	49	50	40	56	49	41	33
1967	55	52	57	49	50	42	55	50	44	35
1968	56	52	60	51	50	44	52	50	48	38
1969	59	50	67	53	52	47	48	51	53	40
1970	60	52	67	55	54	49	48	52	57	42
1971	62	56	67	58	57	51	50	53	59	43
1972	69	60	77	62	61	54	52	54	63	47
1973	98	91	104	71	73	58	56	57	69	53
1974	105	117	94	81	83	68	92	79	79	66
1975	101	105	98	89	91	82	120	88	85	75
1976	102	102	101	95	97	91	102	93	93	86
1977	100	100	100	100	100	100	100	100	100	100
1978	115	105	124	108	108	109	100	105	107	109
1979	132	116	147	123	125	122	108	137	117	125
1980	134	125	144	138	138	136	134	188	127	145
1981	139	134	143	150	148	152	144	213	138	158
1982	133	121	145	159	153	165	144	210	144	157
1983	135	128	141	161	152	174	137	202	148	148
1984	142	138	146	164	155	181	143	201	151	146
1985	128	120	136	162	151	178	135	201	154	128
1986	123	107	138	159	144	174	124	162	159	112
1987	127	106	146	162	148	174	118	164	166	103
1988	138	126	150	170	157	181	130	167	171	106
1989	148	134	160	178	165	193	137	180	185	111
1990	149	127	170	184	171	202	131	204	191	112

Source: Council of Advisers, *Economic Report of the President, 1992,* 408.

TABLE 4.104 FARM-TO-RETAIL PRICE SPREADS, 1951–1975

Year	Market Basket of Farm Food Products			
	Retail Cost (dollars)	Farm Value (dollars)	Farm—Retail Spread (dollars)	Farmer's Share of Retail Cost (percent)
1951	1,024.04	496.77	527.27	49
1952	1,034.04	481.73	552.31	47
1953	1,003.31	445.48	557.83	44
1954	985.79	421.37	564.42	43
1955	969.35	394.78	574.57	41
1956	972.21	389.88	582.33	40
1957	1,007.41	401.46	605.95	40
1958	1,064.16	429.55	634.61	40
1959	1,040.20	398.27	641.93	38
1960	1,051.70	408.12	643.58	39
1963	1,006.94	377.94	629.00	38
1964	1,008.92	377.13	631.79	37
1965	1,037.15	415.82	621.33	40
1966	1,092.49	445.41	647.08	41
1967	1,080.64	419.07	661.57	39
1968	1,119.62	441.42	678.20	39
1969	1,178.98	481.24	697.74	41
1970	1,228.43	477.99	750.44	39
1971	1,250.47	479.61	770.86	38
1972	1,310.82	524.14	786.68	40
1973	1,537.30	700.78	836.52	46
1974	1,749.56	747.64	1,001.92	43
1975	1,876.07	784.12	1,091.95	42

Source: *Agricultural Statistics, 1961*, 467; *Agricultural Statistics, 1976* (Washington, D.C., 1976), 448.

TABLE 4.105 INDEX OF FARM-TO-MARKET PRICE SPREADS, 1976–1990

Year	Market Basket of Food Products			
	Retail Cost	Farm Value	Farm to Retail Spread	Farm Value Share of Retail Cost (%)
	Index 1982–84 = 100	*Index 1982–84 = 100*	*Index 1982–84 = 100*	
1976	65	72	61	38
1977	66	72	63	37
1978	74	83	68	38
1979	82	92	77	38
1980	88	97	83	37
1981	95	99	92	36
1982	98	99	98	35
1983	99	97	100	34
1984	103	104	103	35
1985	104	96	108	32
1986	106	95	112	31
1987	112	97	119	30
1988	117	100	125	30
1989	125	107	134	30
1990	134	112	145	30

Source: *Agricultural Statistics, 1991*, 378.

Prices and Inflation

A dollar is a dollar, and at any given time a dollar will buy a dollar's worth of goods. Change in the value of a dollar over a period of time represents a mark of change in what the dollar will buy. That quantity is of course affected by change in price, which theoretically could involve a reduction, called deflation, but the recent history of the United States more commonly has been characterized by price increases, or inflation. Efforts to measure price changes and the changing value of the dollar are called price indexes, in which a year or a small number of years is arbitrarily chosen as a standard with which other years will be compared. Identification of the selected year will not change the amount of inflation or deflation, but it will affect the numbers that appear in the index. The first table in this unit, which surveyed a broad scope of American history, established the year 1860 (the time of the Civil War) as the base. The survey revealed some fluctuation in price, of course,

TABLE 4.106 THE VALUE OF A DOLLAR, 1860–1990
(composite Consumer Price Index; 1860 = $1)

Year	Value
1860	1.00
1885	1.00
1903	.96
1921	2.22
1930	1.90
1944	1.92
1946	2.00
1947	2.17
1948	2.48
1949	2.68
1950	2.65
1951	2.68
1952	2.89
1953	2.95
1954	2.98
1955	2.99
1956	2.98
1957	3.02
1958	3.13
1959	3.22
1960	3.24
1961	3.29
1962	3.33
1963	3.36
1964	3.40
1965	3.45
1966	3.51
1967	3.61
1968	3.71
1969	3.87
1970	4.08
1971	4.32
1972	4.50
1973	4.65
1974	4.94
1975	5.48
1976	5.98
1977	6.33
1978	6.74
1979	7.25
1980	8.09
1981	9.18
1982	10.13
1983	10.75
1984	11.10
1985	11.58
1986	11.99
1987	12.22
1988	12.66
1989	13.18
1990	13.81

Source: Scot Derks, *The Value of a Dollar: Prices and Incomes in the United States 1860–1999* (Lakeville, Conn., 1999), 2.

but it also pointed to a remarkable price stability for 50 years. A dollar in 1910 would buy the same amount of goods as it did in 1860. The First World War and its immediate aftermath drove prices upward, and within approximately 10 years—by the early 1920s—the dollar had lost half of its value. Through a period of basic stability in the 1920s and a time of modest deflation in the 1930s, the dollar (albeit an inflated dollar) essentially retained its value for a quarter century. In 1946 the currency would buy as much as it had purchased in 1920.

The history of the post–Second World War period, however, left a legacy of inflation, as one would expect in a time of an expanding population and booming economy. Prices began to move upward—slowly at first, but except for a single year, the direction was unrelenting. Between 1946 and 1970, roughly 25 years, the value of the dollar again was cut in half. In terms of price stability, the 1970s was a time of disaster. Influenced by the final phase of the Vietnam War and by two stunning energy crises, the dollar was halved again in 10 years. The pace of inflation slowed in the 1980s, but it still continued. A different base (other tables in this unity utilized the years 1982–84) produced different numbers, but the theme was the same. Prices went up, and the relative value of the dollar went down. To prosper or even to survive in such a setting, it was necessary to experience an increase in earnings that at least kept pace with the increase in price.

TABLE 4.107 CONSUMER PRICE INDEXES, SELECTED GROUPS, AND PURCHASING POWER OF THE CONSUMER DOLLAR, 1946–1990

(1982–1984 = 100, except as noted)

	All Urban Consumers					Urban Wage Earners and Clerical Workers				
Year	All Items	Food	Renters' Costs	Apparel and Upkeep	Purchasing Power of Consumer Dollar	All Items	Food	Renters' Costs	Apparel and Upkeep	Purchasing Power of Consumer Dollar
1946	19.5	19.8	. . .	34.4	511.5	19.6	19.8	. . .	34.6	508.8
1947	22.3	24.1	. . .	39.9	447.4	22.5	24.1	. . .	40.1	445.1
1948	24.1	26.1	. . .	42.5	415.1	24.2	26.1	. . .	42.7	412.9
1949	23.8	25.0	. . .	40.8	419.3	24.0	25.0	. . .	41.0	417.1
1950	24.1	25.4	. . .	40.3	415.1	24.2	25.4	. . .	40.5	412.9
1951	26.0	28.2	. . .	43.9	384.6	26.1	28.2	. . .	44.1	382.5
1952	26.5	28.7	. . .	43.5	376.5	26.7	28.7	. . .	43.7	374.5
1953	26.7	28.3	. . .	43.1	373.5	26.9	28.3	. . .	43.3	371.5
1954	26.9	28.2	. . .	43.1	371.7	27.0	28.2	. . .	43.3	369.7
1955	26.8	27.8	. . .	42.9	373.2	26.9	27.8	. . .	43.1	371.2
1956	27.2	28.0	. . .	43.7	367.8	27.3	28.0	. . .	44.0	365.9
1957	28.1	28.9	. . .	44.5	354.9	28.3	28.9	. . .	44.7	353.1
1958	28.9	30.2	. . .	44.6	345.7	29.1	30.2	. . .	44.8	343.8
1959	29.1	29.7	. . .	45.0	342.7	29.3	29.7	. . .	45.2	340.9
1960	29.6	30.0	. . .	45.7	337.3	29.8	30.0	. . .	45.9	335.5
1961	29.9	30.4	. . .	46.1	334.0	30.1	30.4	. . .	46.3	332.2
1962	30.2	30.6	. . .	46.3	330.4	30.4	30.6	. . .	46.6	328.7
1963	30.6	31.1	. . .	46.9	326.5	30.8	31.1	. . .	47.1	324.8
1964	31.0	31.5	. . .	47.3	322.0	31.2	31.5	. . .	47.5	320.3
1965	31.5	32.2	. . .	47.8	316.6	31.7	32.2	. . .	48.0	315.0
1966	32.4	33.8	. . .	49.0	308.0	32.6	33.8	. . .	49.2	306.3
1967	33.4	34.1	. . .	51.0	299.3	33.6	34.1	. . .	51.2	297.7
1968	34.8	35.3	. . .	53.7	287.3	35.0	35.3	. . .	54.0	285.8
1969	36.7	37.1	. . .	56.8	272.6	36.9	37.1	. . .	57.1	271.2
1970	38.8	39.2	. . .	59.2	257.4	39.0	39.2	. . .	59.5	256.0
1971	40.5	40.4	. . .	61.1	246.6	40.7	40.3	. . .	61.4	245.3
1972	41.8	42.1	. . .	62.3	239.1	42.1	42.1	. . .	62.7	237.9
1973	44.4	48.2	. . .	64.6	225.1	44.7	48.2	. . .	65.0	223.9
1974	49.3	55.1	. . .	69.4	202.9	49.6	55.1	. . .	69.8	201.8
1975	53.8	59.8	. . .	72.5	185.9	54.1	59.8	. . .	72.9	184.9
1976	56.9	61.6	. . .	75.2	175.7	57.2	61.6	. . .	75.6	174.7
1977	60.6	65.5	. . .	78.6	164.9	60.9	65.5	. . .	79.0	164.0
1978	65.2	72.0	. . .	81.4	153.2	65.6	72.0	. . .	81.7	152.4
1979	72.6	79.9	. . .	84.9	138.0	73.1	80.0	. . .	85.2	136.9
1980	82.4	86.8	. . .	90.9	121.5	82.9	87.0	. . .	90.9	120.6
1981	90.9	93.6	. . .	95.3	109.8	91.4	93.7	. . .	95.6	109.6
1982	96.5	97.4	. . .	97.8	103.5	96.9	97.4	. . .	97.8	103.3
1983	99.6	99.4	103.0	100.2	100.3	99.8	99.4	. . .	100.2	100.0
1984	103.9	103.2	108.6	102.1	96.1	103.3	103.2	. . .	102.0	96.8
1985	107.6	105.6	115.4	105.0	92.8	106.9	105.4	103.6	105.0	93.5
1986	109.6	109.0	121.9	105.9	91.3	108.6	108.8	109.5	105.8	92.0
1987	113.6	113.5	128.1	110.6	88.0	112.5	113.3	114.6	110.4	89.0
1988	118.3	118.2	133.6	115.4	84.6	117.0	117.9	119.2	114.9	85.5
1989	124.0	125.1	138.9	118.6	80.7	122.6	124.8	123.9	117.9	81.6
1990	130.7	132.4	146.7	124.1	76.6	129.0	132.1	130.1	123.1	77.5

Source: Jacobs, Handbook of Labor Statistics, 1997, 256–257.

TABLE 4.108 CONSUMER PRICE INDEXES, BY MAJOR GROUPS, 1960–1990

(1982–84=100; represents annual averages of monthly figures; reflects buying patterns of all urban consumers)

Year	All Items	Energy	Food	Shelter	Apparel and Upkeep	Trans-portation	Medical Care	Fuel Oil	Electri-city	Utility (piped gas)	Telephone Ser-vices	All Com-modities
1960	29.6	22.4	30.0	25.2	45.7	29.8	22.3	13.5	29.9	17.6	58.3	33.6
1961	29.9	22.5	30.4	25.4	46.1	30.1	22.9	14.0	29.9	17.9	58.5	33.8
1962	30.2	22.6	30.6	25.8	46.3	30.8	23.5	14.0	29.9	17.9	58.5	34.1
1963	30.6	22.6	31.1	26.1	46.9	30.9	24.1	14.3	29.9	17.9	58.6	34.4
1964	31.0	22.5	31.5	26.5	47.3	31.4	24.6	14.0	29.8	17.9	58.6	34.8
1965	31.5	22.9	32.2	27.0	47.8	31.9	25.2	14.3	29.7	18.0	57.7	35.2
1966	32.4	23.3	33.8	27.8	49.0	32.3	26.3	14.7	29.7	18.1	56.5	36.1
1967	33.4	23.8	34.1	28.8	51.0	33.3	28.2	15.1	29.9	18.1	57.3	36.8
1968	34.8	24.2	35.3	30.1	53.7	34.3	29.9	15.6	30.2	18.2	57.3	38.1
1969	36.7	24.8	37.1	32.6	56.8	35.7	31.9	15.9	30.8	18.6	58.0	39.9
1970	38.8	25.5	39.2	35.5	59.2	37.5	34.0	16.5	31.8	19.6	58.7	41.7
1971	40.5	26.5	40.4	37.0	61.1	39.5	36.1	17.6	33.9	21.0	61.6	43.2
1972	41.8	27.2	42.1	38.7	62.3	39.9	37.3	17.6	35.6	22.1	65.0	44.5
1973	44.4	29.4	48.2	40.5	64.6	41.2	38.8	20.4	37.4	23.1	66.7	47.8
1974	49.3	38.1	55.1	44.4	69.4	45.8	42.4	32.2	44.1	26.0	69.5	53.5
1975	53.8	42.1	59.8	48.8	72.5	50.1	47.5	34.9	50.0	31.1	71.7	58.2
1976	56.9	45.1	61.6	51.5	75.2	55.1	52.0	37.4	53.1	36.3	74.3	60.7
1977	60.6	49.4	65.5	54.9	78.6	59.0	57.0	42.4	56.6	43.2	75.2	64.2
1978	65.2	52.5	72.0	60.5	81.4	61.7	61.8	44.9	60.9	47.5	76.0	68.8
1979	72.6	65.7	79.9	68.9	84.9	70.5	67.5	63.1	65.6	55.1	75.8	76.6
1980	82.4	86.0	86.8	81.0	90.9	83.1	74.9	87.7	75.8	65.7	77.7	86.0
1981	90.9	97.7	93.6	90.5	95.3	93.2	82.9	107.3	87.2	74.9	84.6	93.2
1982	96.5	99.2	97.4	96.9	97.8	97.0	92.5	105.0	95.8	89.8	93.2	97.0
1983	99.6	99.9	99.4	99.1	100.2	99.3	100.6	96.5	98.9	104.7	99.2	99.8
1984	103.9	100.9	103.2	104.0	102.1	103.7	106.8	98.5	105.3	105.5	107.5	103.2
1985	107.6	101.6	105.6	109.8	105.0	106.4	113.5	94.6	108.9	104.8	111.7	105.4
1986	109.6	88.2	109.0	115.8	105.9	102.3	122.0	74.1	110.4	99.7	117.2	104.4
1987	113.6	88.6	113.5	121.3	110.6	105.4	130.1	75.8	110.0	95.1	116.5	107.7
1988	118.3	89.3	118.2	127.1	115.4	108.7	138.6	75.8	111.5	94.5	116.0	111.5
1989	124.0	94.3	125.1	132.8	118.6	114.1	149.3	80.3	114.7	97.1	117.2	116.7
1990	130.7	102.1	132.4	140.0	124.1	120.5	162.8	98.6	117.4	97.3	117.7	122.8

Source: Statistical Abstract, 1993, 482.

TABLE 4.109 CONSUMER PRICE INDEXES—PERCENT CHANGE IN MAJOR GROUPS, 1960–1990

(in percent; minus sign indicates decrease)

Year	All Items	Energy	Food	Shelter	Apparel and Upkeep	Trans-portation	Medical Care	Fuel Oil	Electri-city	Utility (piped gas)	Tele-phone Services	All Com-modities
1960	1.7	2.3	1.0	2.0	1.6	. . .	3.7	−1.5	1.4	6.7	1.6	0.9
1961	1.0	0.4	1.3	0.8	0.9	1.0	2.7	3.7	. . .	1.7	0.3	0.6
1962	1.0	0.4	0.7	1.6	0.4	2.3	2.6	. . .	. . .	. . .	. . .	0.9
1963	1.3	. . .	1.6	1.2	1.3	0.3	2.6	2.1	. . .	. . .	0.2	0.9
1964	1.3	−0.4	1.3	1.5	0.9	1.6	2.1	−2.1	−0.3	. . .	. . .	1.2
1965	1.6	1.8	2.2	1.9	1.1	1.6	2.4	2.1	−0.3	0.6	−1.5	1.1
1966	2.9	1.7	5.0	3.0	2.5	1.3	4.4	2.8	. . .	0.6	−2.1	2.6
1967	3.1	2.1	0.9	3.6	4.1	3.1	7.2	2.7	0.7	. . .	1.4	1.9
1968	4.2	1.7	3.5	4.5	5.3	3.0	6.0	3.3	1.0	0.6	. . .	3.5
1969	5.5	2.5	5.1	8.3	5.8	4.1	6.7	1.9	2.0	2.2	1.2	4.7
1970	5.7	2.8	5.7	8.9	4.2	5.0	6.6	3.8	3.2	5.4	1.2	4.5
1971	4.4	3.9	3.1	4.2	3.2	5.3	6.2	6.7	6.6	7.1	4.9	3.6
1972	3.2	2.6	4.2	4.6	2.0	1.0	3.3	. . .	5.0	5.2	5.5	3.0
1973	6.2	8.1	14.5	4.7	3.7	3.3	4.0	15.9	5.1	4.5	2.6	7.4
1974	11.0	29.6	14.3	9.6	7.4	11.2	9.3	57.8	17.9	12.6	4.2	11.9
1975	9.1	10.5	8.5	9.9	4.5	9.4	12.0	8.4	13.4	19.6	3.2	8.8
1976	5.8	7.1	3.0	5.5	3.7	10.0	9.5	7.2	6.2	16.7	3.6	4.3
1977	6.5	9.5	6.3	6.6	4.5	7.1	9.6	13.4	6.6	19.0	1.2	5.8
1978	7.6	6.3	9.9	10.2	3.6	4.6	8.4	5.9	7.6	10.0	1.1	7.2
1979	11.3	25.1	11.0	13.9	4.3	14.3	9.2	40.5	7.7	16.0	−0.3	11.3
1980	13.5	30.9	8.6	17.6	7.1	17.9	11.0	39.0	15.5	19.2	2.5	12.3
1981	10.3	13.6	7.8	11.7	4.8	12.2	10.7	22.3	15.0	14.0	8.9	8.4
1982	6.2	1.5	4.1	7.1	2.6	4.1	11.6	−2.1	9.9	19.9	10.2	4.1
1983	3.2	0.7	2.1	2.3	2.5	2.4	8.8	−8.1	3.2	16.6	6.4	2.9
1984	4.3	1.0	3.8	4.9	1.9	4.4	6.2	2.1	6.5	0.8	8.4	3.4
1985	3.6	0.7	2.3	5.6	2.8	2.6	6.3	−4.0	3.4	−0.7	3.9	2.1
1986	1.9	−13.2	3.2	5.5	0.9	−3.9	7.5	−21.7	1.4	−4.9	4.9	−0.9
1987	3.6	0.5	4.1	4.7	4.4	3.0	6.6	2.3	−0.4	−4.6	−0.6	3.2
1988	4.1	0.8	4.1	4.8	4.3	3.1	6.5	. . .	1.4	−0.6	−0.4	3.5
1989	4.8	5.6	5.8	4.5	2.8	5.0	7.7	5.9	2.9	2.8	1.0	4.7
1990	5.4	8.3	5.8	5.4	4.6	5.6	9.0	22.8	2.4	0.2	0.4	5.2

Note: . . . Represents zero.
Source: Statistical Abstract, 1993, 482.

TABLE 4.110 CONSUMER PRICE INDEX—CHANGE BY YEAR IN PERCENT, 1946–1990

Year	% Change
1946	18.1
1947	8.8
1948	3.0
1949	−2.1
1950	5.9
1951	6.0
1952	0.8
1953	0.7
1954	−0.7
1955	0.4
1956	3.0
1957	2.9
1958	1.8
1959	1.7
1960	1.4
1961	0.7
1962	1.3
1963	1.6
1964	1.0
1965	1.9
1966	3.5
1967	3.0
1968	4.7
1969	6.2

Year	% Change
1970	5.6
1971	3.3
1972	3.4
1973	8.7
1974	12.3
1975	6.9
1976	4.9
1977	6.7
1978	9.0
1979	13.3
1980	12.5
1981	8.9
1982	3.8
1983	3.8
1984	3.9
1985	3.8
1986	1.1
1987	4.4
1988	4.4
1989	4.6
1990	6.1

Source: Wall Street Journal Almanac, 1998, 160.

TABLE 4.111 ANNUAL PERCENT CHANGES IN CONSUMER PRICES, UNITED STATES AND OECD COUNTRIES, 1970–1990

(covers member countries of Organization for Economic Cooperation and Development [OECD])

Country	1970	1975	1979	1980	1981	1982	1983	1984	1985	1986	1987	1988	1989	1990
United States	5.8	9.1	11.3	13.5	10.3	6.1	3.2	4.3	3.5	1.9	3.7	4.1	4.8	5.4
OECD, total	6.0	11.8	10.7	14.2	10.9	8.1	5.7	5.8	5.1	3.2	3.9	4.8	5.8	6.3
OECD, Europe	6.1	14.4	12.7	17.7	13.4	11.5	9.5	9.0	7.9	5.3	5.1	7.1	8.3	8.6
Australia	3.9	15.1	9.1	10.2	9.7	11.1	10.1	3.9	6.8	9.1	8.5	7.2	7.6	7.3
Canada	3.3	10.7	9.1	10.2	12.4	10.8	5.8	4.3	4.0	4.2	4.4	4.0	5.0	4.8
Japan	7.7	11.8	3.7	7.8	4.9	2.7	1.9	2.2	2.0	0.6	−0.1	0.7	2.3	3.1
New Zealand	6.5	14.7	13.7	17.2	15.4	16.2	7.3	6.2	15.4	13.2	15.8	6.4	5.7	6.1
Austria	4.4	8.4	3.7	6.4	6.8	5.4	3.3	5.6	3.2	1.7	1.4	2.0	2.5	3.3
Belgium	3.9	12.8	4.5	6.6	7.1	8.7	7.7	6.3	4.9	1.3	1.6	1.2	3.1	3.4
Denmark	5.8	9.6	9.6	12.3	11.7	10.1	6.9	6.3	4.7	3.6	4.0	4.6	4.8	2.7
Finland	2.8	17.9	7.5	11.6	12.0	9.6	8.3	7.1	5.9	2.9	4.1	5.1	6.6	6.1
France	5.2	11.8	10.8	13.6	13.4	11.8	9.6	7.4	5.8	2.7	3.1	2.7	3.6	3.4
Greece	3.2	13.4	19.0	24.9	24.5	21.0	20.2	18.4	19.3	23.0	16.4	13.5	13.7	20.4
Ireland	8.2	20.9	13.3	18.2	20.4	17.1	10.5	8.6	5.4	3.8	3.1	2.1	4.1	3.3
Italy	5.1	17.2	15.7	21.1	18.7	16.3	15.0	10.6	8.6	6.1	4.6	5.0	6.6	6.1
Luxembourg	4.6	10.7	4.5	6.3	8.1	9.4	8.7	5.6	4.1	0.3	−0.1	1.4	3.4	3.7
Netherlands	3.6	10.2	4.2	6.5	6.7	5.9	2.7	3.3	2.3	0.1	−0.7	0.7	1.1	2.5
Norway	10.6	11.7	4.8	10.9	13.7	11.3	8.4	6.3	5.7	7.2	8.7	6.7	4.6	4.1
Portugal	6.3	20.4	23.9	16.6	20.0	22.4	25.5	28.8	19.6	11.8	9.4	9.7	12.6	13.4
Spain	5.9	16.9	15.6	15.6	14.5	14.4	12.2	11.3	8.8	8.8	5.2	4.8	6.8	6.7
Sweden	7.0	9.8	7.2	13.7	12.1	8.6	8.9	8.0	7.4	4.3	4.2	5.8	6.4	10.5
Switzerland	3.6	6.7	3.6	4.0	6.5	5.6	3.0	2.9	3.4	0.8	1.4	1.9	3.2	5.4
Turkey	28.7	19.5	58.7	110.2	36.6	29.7	31.4	48.4	45.0	34.6	38.9	75.4	63.3	60.3
United Kingdom	6.4	24.2	13.4	18.0	11.9	8.6	4.6	5.0	6.1	3.4	4.1	4.9	7.8	9.5
Germany	3.4	6.0	4.1	5.5	6.3	5.3	3.3	2.4	2.2	−0.1	0.2	1.3	2.8	2.7

Source: Statistical Abstract, 1992, 473.

Sample Prices in Current Dollars 1946–1990

TABLE 4.112 TUITION AND FEES FOR ACADEMIC YEAR AT PUBLIC FOUR-YEAR COLLEGES AND UNIVERSITIES, 1959–1990

Year	Cost
1959	$198
1960	198
1962	265
1964	281
1966	298
1968	366
1970	427
1972	527
1974	552
1976	656
1978	732
1980	836
1982	1,042
1984	1,284
1986	1,536
1988	1,726
1990	2,035

Source: Derks, *Value of a Dollar*, 483.

TABLE 4.113 MEDIAN SALES PRICE FOR NEW HOMES, 1950–1990

Year	Price
1950	$9,422
1960	15,200
1966	21,400
1968	24,700
1970	23,400
1972	27,600
1974	35,900
1976	44,200
1978	55,700
1980	64,600
1982	69,300
1984	79,900
1986	92,000
1988	112,500
1990	122,900

Source: Derks, *Value of a Dollar*, 490.

TABLE 4.114 AVERAGE PRICE OF RESIDENTIAL ELECTRICITY, 1946–1990

(per kWh, in dollars)

Year	Price
1946	0.032
1950	0.029
1954	0.027
1958	0.025
1962	0.024
1966	0.022
1970	0.022
1974	0.031
1978	0.043
1982	0.069
1986	0.074
1990	0.076

Source: Derks, *Value of a Dollar*, 482.

TABLE 4.115 WHOLESALE PRICE OF SUGAR, 1946–1990

(per pound, in dollars)

Year	Price
1946	0.064
1950	0.078
1954	0.086
1958	0.086
1962	0.089
1966	0.096
1970	0.112
1974	0.321
1978	0.167
1982	0.270
1986	0.234
1990	0.300

Source: Derks, *Value of a Dollar*, 489.

TABLE 4.116 ADVERTISED NEW-CAR PRICES, 1946–1990

Year	Car	Price ($)
1946	DeSoto Custom Suburban, 8 pass. sedan	2,093–2,631
1947	Chevrolet Fleetmaster, 4-door sedan	1,212–2,013
1949	Buick Roadmaster Riviera, hardtop	3,203
1949	Packard Super 8 DeLuxe	2,894–2,919
1956	Plymouth Fury, hardtop	2,866
1959	Chevrolet Corvette convertible	3,631–3,934
1961	Chevrolet Corvair Monza	2,850
1964	Pontiac Grand Prix	2,895
1968	Volkswagen Station Wagon (bus)	2,602
1976	Volkswagen Rabbit	3,500
1980	Pontiac Firebird	6,132
1981	Cadillac Eldorado	19,700
1987	Mazda RX-7 Roadster	22,000
1988	Dodge Medallion, 4-door	8,995
1990	Ford Escort	5,999
1990	Ford Taurus, 4-door	9,999

Source: Derks, *Value of a Dollar*, 267, 310, 334, 335, 357, 400, 417, 432, 451.

TABLE 4.117 COST OF MISCELLANEOUS GOODS, 1946–1989

Item	1946	1950	1954	1959	1964	1968	1975	1982	1986	1989
Baseball	$1.67	2.45	2.79	2.77	2.37	2.75	2.39	. . .	. . .	. . .
Bicycle	41.50	44.95	51.50	49.95	45.95	46.95	74.99	99.99	119.99	89.99
Camera film	.32	.38	.43	.45	2.89	6.69	5.33	. . .	. . .	. . .
Coca-Cola	.05	.05	.05	.05	. . .	. . .	. . .	. . .	. . .	. . .
Electric iron	7.60	6.45	6.95	6.45	13.66	14.75	22.79	29.99	39.99	39.99
Washing machine	79.95	64.95	69.95	79.95	244.95	239.95	249.95	. . .	399.99	. . .
Flashlight battery	.10	.09	.11	.18	.21	. . .	.35	1.15	1.35	. . .
Diapers	2.98	2.65	2.74	2.72	2.54	2.45	3.77	38.99	16.49	. . .
Power mower	. . .	87.50	104.50	86.50	99.95	96.50	79.00	249.99	. . .	249.99
Toothpaste	.37	.43	.63	. . .	. . .	. . .	. . .	. . .	. . .	. . .
Wedding ring (man's)	7.95	6.75	6.45	6.46	7.00	8.50	. . .	. . .	. . .	. . .

Source: Derks, Value of a Dollar, 272, 293, 314, 338, 363, 403, 419, 434.

Taxes

For government to function it needs money, and the most common form of raising revenue has been to require the citizenry, and groups emerging therefrom, to pay taxes. All levels of U.S. government imposed taxation of some form. The national government in the 20th century largely relied on personal and corporation income taxes; the states utilized both income and sales taxes, and local agencies preferred property taxes. The agency responsible for collecting national taxes has been the Internal Revenue Service, and although the payment of taxes has been said to be voluntary, the revenue service has numerous devices for supervising compliance with tax laws, and, indeed, most citizens pay the income tax before they even see the money—through compulsory deduction at the workplace.

Beginning at least with the American Revolution, payment of taxes—or the amount the citizen was required to pay—has sparked controversy based both on principle and simple financial fact. Taxes are said to be one of the two (death being the other one) inevitable aspects of life, and the tax collector came to be thought of as one of the great proverbial villains of history. Since the 1930s the Democrats have generally been associated with higher taxation because they favored more government programs, which of course cost money. Many Democrats did not object to using the tax power to bring a measure of social and economic leveling to society. Opposed to many government programs, commonly identified with propertied groups, the Republicans persistently clamored for lower taxes. During the brief period in the post–Second World War era that the Republicans controlled Congress (1947–48), they predictably began by selectively cutting taxes—over three vetoes by Democrat President Harry S. Truman. From the 1950s to the 1980s the Democrats controlled the legislature, and taxation remained, if not—as compared with other nations—strikingly high, it at least was sharply graduated and enormously complicated.

TABLE 4.118 FEDERAL INDIVIDUAL INCOME TAX RATES AND EXEMPTIONS, 1946–1990

Years	Personal Exemptions Single ($)	Personal Exemptions Married— Joint Return ($)	Personal Exemptions Dependents ($)	Rates (range in percent)	Taxable Income Brackets[a] Lowest: Amount Under ($)	Taxable Income Brackets[a] Highest: Amount Over ($)
1946–47	500	1,000	500	19.0–86.45[b]	2,000	200,000
1948–49	600	1,200	600	16.6–82.13[b]	2,000	200,000
1950	600	1,200	600	17.4–84.36[b]	2,000	200,000
1952–53	600	1,200	600	20.4–91.0[b]	2,000	200,000
1954–63	600	1,200	600	20.0–91.0[b]	2,000	200,000
1964	600	1,200	600	16.0–77.0	500	100,000
1965–67	600	1,200	600	14.0–70.0	500	100,000
1968	600	1,200	600	14.0–75.25	500	100,000
1969	600	1,200	600	14.0–77.0	500	100,000
1970	625	1,250	625	14.0–71.75	500	100,000
1971	675	1,350	675	14.0–70.0	500	100,000
1972–76	750	1,500	750	14.0–70.0	500	100,000
1977–78	750	1,500	750	0.–70.0	3,200	203,200
1979–81	1,000	2,000	1,000	0.0–70.0	3,400	215,400
1982	1,000	2,000	1,000	0.0–50.0	3,400	85,600
1983	1,000	2,000	1,000	0.0–50.0	3,400	109,400
1984	1,000	2,000	1,000	0.0–50.0	3,400	162,400
1985	1,040	2,080	1,040	0.0–50.0	3,540	169,020
1986	1,080	2,160	1,080	0.0–50.0	3,670	175,250
1987	1,900	3,800	1,900	11.0–38.5	3,000	90,000
1988	1,950	3,900	1,950	15.0–28.0	29.750	171,090
1989	2,000	4,000	2,000	15.0–28.0	30,950	149,250
1990	2,050	4,100	2,050	15.0–28.0	32,450	78,400

[a] Married filing joint return.
[b] Subject to maximum effective rate limitation: 85.5% for 1946–47, 80% for 1950, 87.2% for 1951, 88% for 1952–53, 87% for 1954–57.
Source: Advisory Commission on Intergovernmental Relations, Significant Features of Fiscal Federalism Vol. I (Washington, D.C., 1995), 21.

In the 1980s the Republicans got even. With a doctrinaire conservative, Ronald Reagan, in the presidency, with a few fellow-traveling Reagan Democrats (or boll-weevil Democrats) willing to support the Republicans, Congress in 1981 passed the largest tax-cut measure in history, a $750 billion reduction over six years. With Reagan administration approval and both parties supporting the measure, Congress also passed a tax reform law in 1986 that vastly simplified the system by reducing income tax brackets, setting the top rate at 28 percent in most cases, and eliminating many deductions. As revealed in the substance of the tax cut and in the recipients of general economic gain in the decade, most of the benefits of tax policy in the 1980s went to people with the highest incomes—as, indeed, supply-side economics was designed to do. Of course, the national income tax was only the first deduction from an employee's take-home pay. By the 1980s the worker also faced a separate deduction for Social Security; many states had their own income tax, and numerous cities or local entities had one as well.

TABLE 4.119 TAX-RATE SCHEDULES, 1989

Taxable Income	What One Pays
Married Individuals Filing Joint Returns, and Surviving Spouses	
$0.00–$30,950	15% of sum over $0.00
$30.950–$74,850	$4,642.50 + 28% of sum over $30,950
$74,850–$155,320	$16,934.50 + 33% of sum over $74,850
$155,320 and over	$43,489.60 + 28% of sum over $155,320
Heads of Households	
$0.00–$24,850	15% of sum over $0.00
$24,850–$64,200	$3,727.50 + 28% of sum over $24,850
$64,200–$128,810	$14,745.50 + 33% of sum over $64,200
$128,810 and over	$36,066.80 + 28% of sum over $128,810
Single Individuals	
$0.00–$18,550	15% of sum over $0.00
$18,550–$44,900	$2,782.50 + 28% of sum over $18,550
$44,900–$93,130	10,160.50 + 33% of sum over $44,900
$93,130 and over	26,076.40 + 28% of sum over $93,130
Filing Separate Returns	
$0.00–$15,475	15% of sum over $0.00
$15,475–$37,425	$2,321.25 + 28% of sum over $15,475
$37,425–$117,895	$8,467.25 + 33% of sum over $37,425
$117,895 and over	$35,022.35 + 28% of sum over $117,895

Source: Wright, Universal Almanac, 1991, 121.

TABLE 4.120 FEDERAL, STATE, AND LOCAL TAX RECEIPTS, PER CAPITA AND PERCENT DISTRIBUTION
(selected fiscal years 1946–1990)

Year	Per Capita				Percentage Distribution			
	Total	Federal	State	Local	Total	Federal	State	Local
1946	357	276	44	38	100.0	77.3	12.2	10.5
1948	377	277	54	46	100.0	73.6	14.3	12.1
1950	365	252	60	53	100.0	69.1	16.3	14.6
1952	548	414	73	61	100.0	75.5	13.3	11.2
1953	571	429	76	66	100.0	75.2	13.3	11.5
1954	569	423	77	69	100.0	74.3	13.6	12.1
1955	539	388	78	73	100.0	72.0	14.5	13.5
1956	602	436	88	78	100.0	72.3	14.7	13.0
1957	637	457	95	85	100.0	71.8	14.9	13.3
1958	631	446	95	90	100.0	70.6	15.1	14.2
1959	630	435	100	94	100.0	69.1	15.9	15.0
1960	709	495	113	101	100.0	69.8	15.9	14.3
1961	724	497	118	109	100.0	68.7	16.3	15.1
1962	756	516	126	114	100.0	68.3	16.6	15.1
1963	794	543	134	117	100.0	68.4	16.9	14.7
1964	834	567	144	124	100.0	67.9	17.2	14.9
1965	859	578	151	130	100.0	67.2	17.6	15.2
1966	949	642	167	141	100.0	67.6	17.5	14.8
1967	1,056	731	177	148	100.0	69.2	16.8	14.0
1968	1,096	743	196	157	100.0	67.8	17.9	14.3
1969	1,297	901	222	174	100.0	69.5	17.1	13.4
1970	1,357	916	249	192	100.0	67.5	18.4	14.1
1971	1,352	877	263	211	100.0	64.9	19.4	15.6
1972	1,513	971	303	239	100.0	64.2	20.0	15.8
1973	1,654	1,057	345	252	100.0	63.9	20.8	15.2
1974	1,825	1,185	373	266	100.0	65.0	20.5	14.6

	Per Capita				Percentage Distribution			
Year	Total	Federal	State	Local	Total	Federal	State	Local
1975	1,942	1,247	409	286	100.0	64.2	21.1	14.7
1976	2,063	1,310	441	312	100.0	63.5	21.4	15.1
1977	2,392	1,549	501	342	100.0	64.7	20.0	14.3
1978	2,646	1,725	557	364	100.0	65.2	21.1	13.8
1979	2,952	1,979	612	361	100.0	67.0	20.7	12.2
1980	3,222	2,181	658	383	100.0	67.6	20.5	11.9
1981	3,653	2,505	732	415	100.0	68.6	20.0	11.4
1982	3,779	2,557	773	449	100.0	67.7	20.4	11.9
1983	3,765	2,455	824	485	100.0	65.2	21.9	12.9
1984	4,114	2,687	904	524	100.0	65.3	22.0	12.7
1985	4,466	2,925	975	566	100.0	65.5	21.8	12.7
1986	4,681	3,057	1,020	605	100.0	65.3	21.8	12.9
1987	5,110	3,368	1,092	650	100.0	66.0	21.3	12.7
1988	5,409	3,587	1,120	702	100.0	66.3	20.7	13.0
1989	5,832	3,889	1,195	748	100.0	66.7	20.5	12.8
1990	6,033	4,015	1,208	809	100.0	66.6	20.0	13.4

Source: Tax Foundation, *Facts & Figures on Government Finance, 1993* (Washington, D.C., 1993), 17.

TABLE 4.121   TOTAL TAXES AS A PERCENTAGE OF TOTAL INCOME

(selected calendar years 1945–1990)

Year	Total Taxes as a Percentage of Income
1945	25.7
1946	25.8
1947	25.9
1948	24.1
1949	22.9
1950	25.5
1951	27.3
1952	27.3
1953	27.1
1954	25.7
1955	26.5
1956	27.3
1957	27.5
1958	26.9
1959	27.9
1960	28.9
1961	29.0
1962	29.0
1963	29.5
1964	28.2
1965	28.1
1966	28.9
1967	29.4
1968	31.0
1969	32.5
1970	31.5
1971	30.9
1972	32.1
1973	32.0
1974	32.9
1975	31.6
1976	32.3
1977	32.6
1978	32.4
1979	32.6
1980	32.9
1981	33.7
1982	33.3
1983	32.3
1984	32.1
1985	32.5
1986	32.6
1987	33.5
1988	33.1
1989	33.2
1990	32.9

Source: Moody, *Facts & Figures on Finance,* 16.

TABLE 4.122 SOCIAL SECURITY TAX RATES[a]
(calendar years 1937–1990)

Year	Maximum Taxable Base (dollars)	Tax Rate (percent)			Maximum Tax (dollars)		
		Combined Employer & Employee	Employer or Employee Alone	Self-Employed	Combined Employer & Employee	Employer or Employee Alone	Self-Employed
1937–1949	3,000	2	1	[b]	60	30	[b]
1950	3,000	3	1.5	[b]	90	45	[b]
1951–1953	3,600	3	1.5	2.25	108	54	81
1954	3,600	4	2	3	144	72	108
1955–1956	4,200	4	2	3	168	84	126
1957–1958	4,200	4.5	2.25	3.375	189	95	142
1959	4,800	5	2.5	3.75	240	120	180
1960–1961	4,800	6	3	4.5	288	144	216
1962	4,800	6.25	3.125	4.7	300	150	226
1963–1965	4,800	7.25	3.625	5.4	348	174	259
1966	6,600	8.4	4.2	6.15	554	277	406
1967	6,600	8.8	4.4	6.4	581	290	422
1968	7,800	8.8	4.4	6.4	686	343	499
1969–1970	7,800	9.6	4.8	6.9	749	374	538
1971	7,800	10.4	5.2	7.5	811	406	585
1972	9,000	10.4	5.2	7.5	936	468	675
1973	10,800	11.7	5.85	8	1,264	632	864
1974	13,200	11.7	5.85	7.9	1,544	772	1,043
1975	14,100	11.7	5.85	7.9	1,650	825	1,114
1976	15,300	11.7	5.85	7.9	1,790	895	1,209
1977	16,500	11.7	5.85	7.9	1,931	965	1,304
1978	17,700	12.1	6.05	8.1	2,142	1,071	1,434
1979	22,900	12.3	6.13	8.1	2,808	1,404	1,855
1980	25,900	12.3	6.13	8.1	3,175	1,588	2,098
1981	29,700	13.3	6.65	9.3	3,950	1,975	2,762
1982	32,400	13.4	6.7	9.35	4,342	2,171	3,029
1983	35,700	13.4	6.7	9.35	4,784	2,392	3,338
1984	37,800	14	7.0	14.0	5,292	2,646	5,292
1985	39,600	14.1	7.05	14.1	5,584	2,792	5,584
1986	42,000	14.3	7.15	14.3	6,006	3,003	6,006
1987	43,800	14.3	7.15	14.3	6,263	3,132	6,263
1988	45,000	15.02	7.51	15.02	6,759	3,380	6,759
1989	48,000	15.02	7.51	15.02	7,210	3,605	7,210
1990	51,300	15.3	7.65	15.3	7,849	3,924	7,849

[a] Includes old-age, survivors, disability, and hospital insurance (DI since 1956 and HI since 1966).
[b] Not covered until January 1, 1951.
Source: Moody, *Facts & Figures on Finance,* 118.

TABLE 4.123 BENEFACTORS OF TAX CHANGES IN 1980s
(total federal effective tax rates for all families)

All Families (by income group)	1977	1980	1985	1988	1989	Percent Change 1977–1989
Lowest quintile	9.3	8.1	10.3	9.3	9.3	0.1
Second quintile	15.4	15.6	15.8	15.9	15.7	1.4
Middle quintile	19.5	19.8	19.1	19.8	19.4	−.4
Fourth quintile	21.8	22.9	21.7	22.4	22.0	.7
81 to 90 percent	24.0	25.3	23.4	24.6	24.2	.9
91 to 95 percent	25.2	26.3	24.2	26.0	25.6	1.5
96 to 99 percent	27.0	27.9	24.3	26.5	26.2	−2.9
Top 1 percent	35.5	31.7	24.9	26.9	26.7	−24.7
Overall	22.8	23.3	21.7	22.9	22.6	−.7
Highest quintile	27.2	27.5	24.1	26.0	25.6	−5.8
Top 10 percent	28.8	28.6	24.5	26.5	26.2	−9.0
Top 5 percent	30.6	29.6	24.6	26.7	26.5	−13.5

Source: Phillips, *Boiling Point,* 282.

TABLE 4.124 DECLINING IMPORTANCE OF PERSONAL EXEMPTION—FEDERAL INCOME TAX PERSONAL EXEMPTION AS A PERCENT OF INDIVIDUAL INCOME, 1948–1990

Year	1948	1954	1960	1966	1972	1978	1984	1990
Personal exemption	$600	$600	$600	$600	$750	$750	$1,000	$2,050[a]
Exemption as percent of individual income	42%	33%	27%	20%	16%	9%	8%	16%

[a] If exemption was equal to percent of income applied in 1948, it would be $7,781 in 1990.
Source: Phillips, *Boiling Point,* 281.

TABLE 4.125 "TAX FREEDOM DAY" AND "TAX BITE IN EIGHT-HOUR DAY"
(calendar years 1946–1990)

Year	Tax Freedom Day[a]	Tax Bite in the Eight-Hour Day[b] (hours:minutes)		
		Total	Federal	State and Local
1946	March 31	1:57	1:30	:27
1947	April 3	2:01	1:33	:28
1948	March 28	1:55	1:26	:29
1949	March 24	1:48	1:16	:32
1950	April 3	2:02	1:30	:32
1951	April 10	2:11	1:40	:31
1952	April 10	2:12	1:40	:32
1953	April 10	2:12	1:40	:32
1954	April 6	2:05	1:30	:35
1955	April 9	2:09	1:34	:35
1956	April 11	2:13	1:37	:36
1957	April 13	2:14	1:37	:37
1958	April 10	2:12	1:32	:40
1959	April 14	2:16	1:36	:40
1960	April 17	2:22	1:40	:42
1961	April 18	2:22	1:38	:44
1962	April 18	2:21	1:38	:43
1963	April 19	2:23	1:39	:44
1964	April 15	2:18	1:33	:45
1965	April 15	2:17	1:33	:44
1966	April 18	2:21	1:36	:45
1967	April 20	2:24	1:37	:47
1968	April 25	2:32	1:39	:53
1969	May 1	2:38	1:48	:50
1970	April 28	2:34	1:40	:54
1971	April 25	2:31	1:36	:55
1972	April 29	2:36	1:39	:57
1973	April 29	2:36	1:41	:55
1974	May 3	2:41	1:45	:56
1975	April 28	2:35	1:38	:57
1976	May 1	2:40	1:42	:58
1977	May 3	2:41	1:43	:58
1978	May 3	2:41	1:45	:56
1979	May 3	2:41	1:48	:53
1980	May 1	2:39	1:48	:51
1981	May 4	2:43	1:52	:51
1982	May 3	2:41	1:48	:53
1983	April 30	2:38	1:43	:55
1984	April 28	2:36	1:42	:54
1985	May 1	2:38	1:44	:54
1986	May 1	2:38	1:43	:55
1987	May 4	2:42	1:47	:55
1988	May 3	2:42	1:46	:56
1989	May 4	2:43	1:47	:56
1990	May 5	2:45	1:47	:58

[a] "Tax Freedom Day" represents the date on which the average person would finish paying Federal, state, and local taxes if all earnings since January 1 were turned over to the governments to fulfill annual tax obligations.
[b] The "Tax Bite in the Eight-Hour Day" reflects the amount of time out of each workday that the average person spends earning enough money to pay tax obligations.
Source: Tax Foundation, *Facts & Figures on Government Finance, 1991* (Washington, D.C., 1991), 17.

CHAPTER 5 Transportation

General Trends

The transportation system of the United States was a major contributor to and a major benefactor of many of the economic, technological, political, and cultural changes that affected the nation, if not the world, in the decades following the Second World War. The system grew in accordance with economic and population growth; it shifted in accordance with demographic shifts. It responded to international changes on many fronts, notably to political crises, which placed the energy supply (especially petroleum products) in jeopardy. The transportation establishment, and the system in general, was affected by the emergence of foreign nations as consumers of automobiles, airplanes, and other items, making them potential customers of the United States. Some of these same countries, in Europe and Asia but also Latin America, became producers of these items, making them competitors of American transportation companies. All sectors of American transportation did not change in the same ways. The largest growth came in segments related to cars, trucks, and other motor vehicles and airplanes. The sharpest decline in activity involved railroads, especially in the carrying of passengers, and in water-borne passenger service.

Technological changes in the decades following the Second World War largely involved an extension of—new forms in—processes already begun in transportation. Cars became better, airplanes faster, safer, with much longer range. Perhaps most significant is that nearly all methods of transport came within the reach of all. Virtually any adult who wanted one had a car, and by the 1980s most families and many individuals had more than one. It was a rare American who by the 1980s had not traveled on a jet liner; for most of the few who had not, it was a matter of choice, not opportunity. The most striking innovation, a means for humans to travel beyond the planet, became a startling reality in the 1960s. The mission to the Moon foreshadowed more such activity in the decades to come and surely into the next century.

Globalization was a compelling theme of the last half of the 20th century, and transportation provided the fuel on which it moved. Advances in air travel made it possible for Americans as a matter of course to travel from country to country and continent to continent. Competition in many areas of enterprise became global, and transportation felt the effects profoundly. Globalization opened new markets for American industries, but it also brought new competitors into the contest. Boeing Aircraft came to face a more formidable challenge from a European consortium than from such traditional rivals as Douglas or Lockheed. American automobile companies, which had been laggard in exploiting a slowly developing foreign market, discovered that by the time those markets began to expand, producers from other areas—notably Europe and Japan—were in a position to move in and squeeze the Americans out.

For American consumers and for producers, the story of transporation in the decades following 1945 was a continuing account of growth (in several areas), change, and adjustment. For consumers the keystones were the automobile and the airplane. Although both were more readily available than ever before, they came at considerable financial cost and remained subject to abrupt shocks, as in the energy crises of the 1970s. U.S. producers went from a position of absolute domination of important areas of enterprise—such as automobiles and airplanes—to a brief period of weeding out weaker competitors in the United States. The three major automobile firms and the three or four aircraft companies that survived by the 1960s largely had the U.S. market to themselves.

The two decades after 1970 were much different. Competition from foreign companies jolted American manufacturers and forced them to change and to seek ways to control their own market. The struggle still went on in 1990, and by that time the process of globalization had taken new turns. Some Japanese cars were built in the United States; some American cars—the parts or the assembled vehicles—were being built in Mexico and other countries. American firms collaborated with foreign companies; sometimes they owned part of each other. The terms *American made* and *import* had begun to lose meaning.

Motor Vehicles

American automobile manufacturers faced an almost ideal situation at the end of the Second World War. Nearly everyone, it seemed, wanted a new car, and increased income and savings during the war made it possible for millions of them to afford one. The companies could sell everything they made, and in addition to the multidimensional "Big Three" companies of General Motors, Ford, and Chrysler, several older independents and even a new firm—Kaiser-Fraser—competed on the market. By 1960 more than three-quarters of families owned a car, many had more than one, and related industries such as road construction, restaurants, motels, and suburban shopping centers expanded accordingly—as did movement of people to the suburbs.

It did not take many years, however, for supply to catch up with demand, causing tighter competition among sellers and greater selectivity with buyers. In this setting bigness mattered. One by one the independents began to falter; some dropped out altogether, others tried merger. Studebaker joined with Packard in 1954, but the union produced little benefit. Packard, so stylish and prestigious in the prewar years, vanished from the market in 1958, and Studebaker held on only a few years longer. By the end of the 1970s there remained only four firms: the Big Three (and one of them, Chrysler, was fighting off bankruptcy) and tiny American Motors, product of a merger of Nash and Hudson, which struggled to survive by marketing a small car called Rambler. By that time competition for the Big Three, almost a Big Two, came from a different source.

Many changes came to the automobile during these years, all within the basic framework of a carriage propelled by an internal combustion engine. Some were refinements designed to increase comfort and ease of operation; others represented a response to pressures brought on by customer taste or changes in the national or international marketplace. In selecting "optional" equipment customers responded most quickly to automatic transmission and slowest to air conditioning. Otherwise, fuel injection replaced carburetors, steel-belted radial tires became standard, front-wheel drive became more popular than rear-wheel-drive vehicles. Several changes had to do with air pollution and safety. In the 1970s new emission controls removed most hydrocarbons and carbon monoxide and in the mid-1980s use of leaded gasoline came to an end. Changes in safety devices, inspired partly by Ralph Nader's *Unsafe at Any Speed,* a volume about the Chevrolet Corvair, included various kinds of locks and different bumpers and roofs. The most familiar safety device took the form of seat belts required on all vehicles, followed by introduction of air bags for first the driver's side and then both sides of the front seat of motor vehicles.

The American love affair with the motor vehicle in no way had diminished by the end of the 1980s, but it had found new forms of expression. In the 1960s station wagons had caught on as a means of hauling children of the baby-boom era, and in the 1980s pickup trucks, vans, and minivans began to capture a growing share of the market. Many Americans preferred foreign to domestic makes. People wishing to apply a principle—to "buy American," for example, or "punish General Motors"—found themselves bewildered. Foreign

Introduction of the spirited 1949 "Rocket 88" Oldsmobile was a major step in the auto industry's (and society's) rush to the horsepower race via the V-8 engine. (Oldsmobile History Center, Lansing, Michigan)

TABLE 5.1 WORLD MOTOR VEHICLE PRODUCTION
(in thousands)

Year	U.S.	Canada	Europe	Japan	Other	Total	U.S. % of World Total
1950	8,006	388	1.991	32	160	10,577	75.7
1955	9,204	452	3,738	68	166	13,628	67.5
1960	7,905	398	6,830	482	873	16,488	50.4
1965	11,138	847	9,571	1,876	835	24,267	49.4
1970	8,284	1,160	13,243	5,289	1,427	29,403	32.1
1975	8,987	1,424	13,473	6,942	2,172	32,998	27.2
1976	11,489	1,640	15,202	7,841	2,155	38,341	30.0
1977	12,703	1,775	15,885	8,515	2,069	40,947	31.0
1978	12,899	1,818	16,118	9,269	2,195	42,299	30.5
1979	11,480	1,632	16,293	9,636	2,478	41,519	27.7
1980	8,010	1,374	15,446	11,043	2,641	38,514	20.8
1981	7,943	1,323	14,440	11,180	2,344	37,230	21.3
1982	6,986	1,276	14,808	10,732	2,311	36,113	19.3
1983	9,205	1,524	15,708	11,112	2,206	39,755	23.2
1984	10,939	1,829	15,293	11,465	2,532	42,058	26.0
1985	11,653	1,933	15,959	12,271	2,995	44,811	26.0
1986	11,335	1,854	16,701	12,260	3,147	45,297	25.0
1987	10,925	1,635	17,518	12,249	3,576	45,903	23.8
1988	11,214	1,949	18,213	12,700	4,134	48,210	23.3
1989	10,874	1,934	18,946	13,026	4,216	48,996	22.2
1990	9,780	1,896	18,614	13,487	4,336	48,113	20.3

Source: MVMA (Motor Vehicle Manufacturers Association), *Motor Vehicle Facts and Figures '91* (Detroit, 1991), 30.

brands were being made in the United States; American cars were being made abroad. As for the companies, they only wanted to make money. Automobiles remained vital to American culture, and the automobile industry a bellwether of the economy if not the United States in general. The most striking change between the years 1946 and 1990 had been the United States's loss of its position as king of the automobile world, marked among other ways by a drastic reduction in the nation's share of world vehicle production.

TABLE 5.2   MOTOR-VEHICLE RETAIL SALES IN UNITED STATES, 1949–1990

(in thousands)

Year	New Passenger Cars			New Trucks		
	Domestic	Import	Total	Domestic	Import	Total
1949	5,119	a	. . .	1,134	a	. . .
1950	6,665	a	. . .	1,337	a	. . .
1951	5,143	21	5,164	1,111	a	1,111
1952	4,228	29	4,257	864	a	864
1953	5,775	33	5,808	965	a	965
1954	5,474	32	5,506	857	1	858
1955	7,408	58	7,466	1,012	3	1,015
1956	5,844	98	5,942	903	7	910
1957	5,826	207	6,033	876	16	894
1958	4,289	379	4,668	731	29	760
1959	5,468	614	6,100	928	37	966
1960	6,142	499	6,641	926	37	963
1961	5,556	379	5,935	908	29	937
1962	6,753	339	7,092	1,068	32	1,100
1963	7,334	386	7,720	1,230	40	1,270
1964	7,617	484	8,101	1,351	42	1,393
1965	8,763	569	9,332	1,539	14	1,553
1966	8,377	651	9,028	1,619	17	1,636
1967	7,568	769	8,337	1,524	21	1,545
1968	8,625	1,031	9,656	1,807	24	1,831
1969	8,464	1,118	9,582	1,936	34	1,970
1970	7,119	1,280	8,400	1,746	65	1,811
1971	8,681	1,561	10,242	2,011	85	2,096
1972	9,327	1,614	10,940	2,486	143	2,629
1973	9,676	1,748	11,424	2,916	232	3,148
1974	7,454	1,399	8,853	2,512	176	2,688
1975	7,053	1,571	8,624	2,249	229	2,478
1976	8,611	1,499	10,110	2,944	237	3,181
1977	9,109	2,074	11,183	3,352	323	3,675
1978	9,312	2,002	11,314	3,773	336	4,109
1979	8,341	2,332	10,673	3,010	470	3,480
1980	6,581	2,398	8,979	2,001	487	2,487
1981	6,209	2,327	8,536	1,809	451	2,260
1982	5,759	2,224	7,982	2,146	414	2,560
1983	6,795	2,387	9,182	2,658	471	3,129
1984	7,592	2,439	10,390	3,475	618	4,093
1985	8,205	2,838	11,042	3,902	779	4,682
1986	8,215	3,245	11,460	3,921	941	4,863
1987	7,081	3,196	10,277	4,055	858	4,912
1988	7,526	3,004	10,530	4,508	641	5,149
1989	7,073	2,699	9,772	4,403	538	4,941
1990	6,897	2,404	9,301	4,215	631	4,846

a Negligible.

Source: MVMA, *Moter Vehicle Facts and Figures* '76 (Detroit, 1976), 15; MVMA, *Facts and Figures* '91, 7.

TABLE 5.3   YEARLY U.S. MOTOR-VEHICLE REGISTRATIONS AND PASSENGER-CAR SCRAPPAGE, 1946–1990

Year	Automobiles	Buses	Trucks	Total	New Cars Registered During Year	Cars Scrapped During Year
1946	28,213,336	173,585	5,986,081	34,373,002	1,815,196	478,038
1947	30,845,350	187,457	6,808,691	37,841,498	3,167,231	855,517
1948	33,350,894	196,726	7,537,911	41,085,531	3,490,952	1,220,041
1949	36,453,351	208,929	8,028,016	44,690,296	4,838,342	2,315,110
1950	40,333,591	223,652	8,604,448	49,161,691	6,326,438	3,711,820
1951	42,682,591	230,461	9,009,913	51,922,965	5,060,903	3,137,989
1952	43,817,580	240,485	9,207,341	53,265,406	4,158,394	2,465,936
1953	46,422,443	244,251	9,554,395	56,221,089	5,738,989	3,491,000
1954	48,461,219	248,346	9,800,688	58,510,253	5,535,464	3,247,436
1955	52,135,583	255,249	10,302,987	62,693,819	7,169,908	4,312,759
1956	54,200,784	258,764	10,694,262	65,153,810	5,955,248	4,309,153
1957	55,906,195	264,062	10,960,814	67,131,071	5,281,656	4,221,607
1958	56,870,684	270,163	11,158,561	68,299,408	5,575,893	2,981,641
1959	59,561,726	265,114	11,670,559	71,497,399	6,364,634	4,348,719
1960	61,558,847	272,129	11,937,589	73,768,565	6,045,822	4,294,118
1961	63,275,499	279,668	12,291,365	75,846,582	6,425,973	4,360,774
1962	65,928,547	285,219	12,809,150	79,022,916	7,314,715	4,741,017
1963	68,978,589	297,401	13,416,324	82,692,314	7,877,424	5,319,286
1964	71,950,198	305,490	14,041,445	86,297,133	8,592,728	5,704,373
1965	75,252,040	314,271	14,790,437	90,356,748	9,197,480	6,173,512
1966	78,331,488	323,197	15,522,114	94,176,799	8,688,162	6,984,214
1967	80,458,317	337,197	16,193,618	96,989,132	8,590,365	6,200,017
1968	83,698,100	351,804	16,998,546	101,048,450	9,485,392	6,348,488
1969	87,153,381	364,340	17,885,836	105,403,557	9,414,509	7,460,984
1970	89,309,101	379,021	18,747,781	108,435,903	8,709,902	6,021,041
1971	92,752,515	397,627	19,772,212	112,922,354	10,178,662	7,058,029
1972	96,948,813	407,706	21,261,643	118,618,102	11,353,586	7,987,384
1973	101,578,539	425,313	23,153,024	125,156,876	9,996,071	7,193,679
1974	104,898,256	446,547	24,598,284	129,943,087	8,301,759	5,668,708
1975	106,712,551	462,144	25,775,710	132,950,405	9,406,522	6,828,903
1976	110,351,327	478,339	27,719,597	138,549,263	10,319,298	8,233,925
1977	113,696,111	491,674	29,562,485	143,750,270	10,960,194	7,907,075
1978	116,574,999	500,362	31,702,604	148,777,965	11,032,068	9,312,274
1979	120,247,990	520,367	33,349,742	154,118,099	9,603,185	8,404,993
1980	121,723,650	528,801	33,637,241	155,889,692	8,817,281	7,542,480
1981	123,461,507	543,894	34,451,110	158,456,511	7,949,799	6,921,273
1982	123,697,863	559,197	35,252,765	159,509,825	8,336,651	6,242,544
1983	126,727,873	565,515	36,547,781	163,841,169	9,732,353	6,674,928
1984	127,866,900	583,671	38,047,099	166,497,670	10,372,287	7,728,594
1985	132,108,164	593,527	38,989,042	171,690,733	11,048,203	8,442,465
1986	135,431,112	593,720	40,166,499	176,191,331	10,684,054	8,103,356
1987	137,323,632	602,055	41,118,762	179,044,449	10,424,490	8,754,185
1988	141,251,695	612,611	42,529,368	184,393,674	10,220,604	8,981,300
1989	143,081,443	625,040	43,554,084	187,260,567	9,414,552	8,896,662
1990	143,549,627	626,987	44,478,848	188,655,462	8,616,179	8,565,401

Source: Ward's Communications, *1970 Automotive Yearbook* (Detroit, 1970), 100; Ward's Communications, *Ward's Automotive Yearbook 1992* (Detroit, 1992), 240, 250.

TABLE 5.4   NEW-CAR PRICES AND CONSUMER EXPENDITURES PER NEW CAR, 1950–1990

Year	Consumer Expenditure Per New Car[a]			Median Annual Family Earnings	Weeks of Earnings to Equal Car Cost
	Domestic	Import	Average		
1950	$2,211	$1,775	$2,210	$3,319	34.6
1955	2,508	2,206	2,506	4,418	29.5
1960	2,918	2,063	2,853	5,620	26.4
1965	3,074	2,120	3,014	6,957	22.5
1971	3,919	2,769	3,742	10,285	18.9
1975	5,084	4,384	4,950	13,719	18.8
1980	7,609	7,482	7,574	21,023	18.7
1982	9,865	9,957	9,890	23,433	21.9
1985	11,733	12,875	12,022	27,144	23.0
1987	13,239	14,602	13,657	29,744	23.9
1989	14,957	16,127	15,292	32,448	24.5
1990	15,641	17,010	16,012	33,960	24.5

[a] Average price per new car, U.S. Department of Commerce.
Source: MVMA, *Motor Vehicle Facts and Figures '82* (Detroit, 1982), 42; MVMA, *Facts and Figures '91*, 40.

TABLE 5.5 OPTIONAL EQUIPMENT PURCHASED, 1957

Equipment	Percent of Cars
Heater	97.4%
Radio	83.9
Automatic Transmission	81.8
White Wall Tires	67.5
Windshield Washer	56.4
Power Steering	40.5
Power Brakes	34.9
Power Seats	11.1
Power Windows	9.1
Seat Belts	3.9

Source: MVMA, *Automotive Facts and Figures 1958* (Detroit, 1958), 35.

TABLE 5.6   FACTORY-INSTALLED EQUIPMENT IN U.S. CARS, 1949–1990

(percentage of cars equipped with specified equipment)

Model Year	% Auto Trans.	% Air Cond.	% Disc Brakes	% Power Steer.	% Radial Tires
1949	43.1	a	a	a	a
1950	33.1	a	a	a	a
1951	44.8	a	a	a	a
1952	47.4	a	a	4.6	a
1953	49.4	a	a	11.7	a
1954	58.3	a	a	18.0	a
1955	70.3	1.5	a	23.2	a
1956	74.8	2.8	a	27.7	a
1957	79.9	3.7	a	38.1	a
1958	76.8	4.6	a	42.8	a
1959	71.5	6.2	a	40.0	a
1960	71.4	6.9	a	38.0	a
1961	74.1	8.1	a	40.0	a
1962	74.4	11.3	a	43.6	a
1963	76.3	14.1	a	50.1	a
1964	77.7	17.9	a	53.8	a
1965	80.6	23.3	a	59.6	a
1966	83.5	29.3	4.0	66.6	a
1967	86.7	38.0	6.1	74.3	a
1968	89.0	44.3	12.7	80.0	a
1969	90.2	55.3	27.8	84.6	a
1970	91.3	60.1	41.0	85.0	a
1971	91.1	63.4	63.1	82.5	a
1972	90.5	67.5	73.6	85.7	a
1973	93.4	72.6	85.7	87.7	13.3
1974	89.8	67.9	84.1	83.4	33.3
1975	91.6	72.6	85.7	89.9	82.3
1976	91.4	74.0	98.8	89.9	77.3
1977	95.2	81.7	100.0	92.0	83.8
1978	93.1	80.8	100.0	92.7	84.4
1979	89.7	79.8	100.0	88.7	92.8
1980	82.7	73.0	100.0	83.7	95.4
1981	81.7	76.4	100.0	83.5	99.9
1982	84.5	80.7	100.0	88.1	99.9
1983	86.6	83.5	100.0	90.5	99.9
1984	85.2	84.0	100.0	89.9	100.0
1985	86.2	87.2	100.0	92.3	100.0
1986	85.9	88.5	100.0	92.3	100.0
1987	88.0	85.2	100.0	93.9	100.0
1988	86.2	90.3	100.0	97.1	100.0
1989	87.5	91.0	100.0	98.0	100.0
1990	88.4	91.9	100.0	97.3	100.0

a None or negligible.
Source: *Ward's Automotive Yearbook 1980* (Detroit, 1980), 115; *Ward's Yearbook 1991*, 276.

TABLE 5.7 TOP-SELLING U.S. CARS, TRUCKS, AND SPORTS UTILITY VEHICLES, 1990

Cars		
Brand	Units	Market Share
Honda Accord	417,179	4.5%
Ford Taurus	313,274	3.4%
Chevy Cavalier	295,123	3.2%
Ford Escort	288,727	3.1%
Toyota Camry	284,595	3.0%
Chevy Corsica/Beretta	277,176	3.0%
Toyota Corolla	228,211	2.5%
Honda Civic	220,852	2.4%
Chevy Lumina	218,288	2.3%
Ford Tempo	215,200	2.3%

Trucks and Sports Utility Vehicles

Small Pickup	
Brand	Units
Ford Ranger	280,610
Chevy S-10	210,318
Toyota	181,719

Sports Utility Vehicles	
Brand	Units
Ford Explorer/Bronco II	181,748
Chevy Blazer S	146,989
Jeep Cherokee	124,864

Vans	
Brand	Units
Dodge Caravan	205,956
Ford Aerostar	177,860
Plymouth Voyager	171,527

Source: 1991 Ward's Automotive Yearbook, 202.

Gas-guzzlers, Beetles, and the Japanese Invasion

In the postwar era American companies preferred to produce large cars with large engines, and a survey of the prevailing forces—an apparent abundance of inexpensive energy, rapidly improving highways, and customer response—offered little reason why they should not do so. Distinguishing characteristics of the era were the gaudy tail fins, which began with Cadillac in 1948, and the horsepower race. The contest for power and speed, which came to involve improvement and increased use of the V-8 engine, received a major boost in 1949 when General Motors placed a large V-8 in a fairly small Oldsmobile 88. The "Rocket 88," with its speed and acceleration, had such immediate success that it even inspired a song to proclaim its glories. It set the stage for things to come. Chrysler introduced its powerful hemi V-8 shortly thereafter and even began to put it in its low-classed Plymouths. Chevrolet, leader of the low-priced three (Ford and Plymouth were the others) and best-selling car in the country, long had depended on a reliable but sluggish "straight" six-cylinder engine. In 1955 Chevrolet introduced its first V-8, thereby joining the horsepower race and the movement to glitz. Tail fins on the 1957 Chevy would become the most time-honored of them all. Production of large, powerful machines, as manifested in the V-8 engine, dominated the American automotive industry for at least a quarter-century, to the end of the

1970s. The gas-guzzlers might not produce even 15 miles per gallon on the highway or 10 in the city, but with fuel prices at 30–35 cents per gallon, less if there happened to be a price war under way; drivers did not seem to care.

One vehicle, however, managed to buck the trend. The Volkswagen came to the United States from a storied past in Germany. Designed by Ferdinand Porsche in the 1930s, favored by Adolf Hitler as the "people's car" (*Volkswagen*) in his new society, the bug or beetle did not go into full production because of the War. The concept of Porche's vehicle was revived by a British occupation officer and then by German managers who believed that inexpensive basic transportation would be suitable to cash-strapped postwar Germany and to people in many countries. The beetle appeared in the United States as a novelty, a virtual antidote to the trend of automobile marketing. It was tiny, cramped, slow, almost ugly. Nonetheless it had appeal. Everyone seemed to know something about its origin, and hundreds of thousands of American soldiers encountered the car during their occupation service in Germany. And it was a reliable car. Top speed was around 60, less going up a hill, but the air-cooled engine needed no water or antifreeze, could produce 30 miles per gallon, and was virtually indestructable. One could drive it "wide-open" (as fast as it would go) without damage to the engine. Placing the engine over the pulling wheels in the rear gave exceptional traction: in winter the Volkswagen could move when American cars sat and spun their wheels. Choice of a car always had been an expression of image, and in the atmosphere of the 1950s and 1960s ownership of a VW could give off signals of individuality, creativity, and simple good common sense. The Volkswagen so completely dominated foreign competition in the United States that during a period of 15 or so years, it not only outsold all foreign brands but in several years outsold all foreign brands combined. The Volkswagen introduced Americans to the merits of the small car. It legitimized the idea that someone besides Americans could manufacture effective and efficient automobiles. The domination ended partly because the Beetle and its successors—notably the Rabbit—fell victim to a condition it had helped create.

Popularity of the Volkswagen existed as a type of automotive subculture in the United States. Growth of the market for foreign brands that began in the mid-1970s by contrast represented an entirely new trend for automobile production and consumption. The emphasis on size and horsepower never had been universally popular. Critics long had pointed to the wastefulness of big cars, to the damage that they produced in speed and attitudes. Growing concerns about air and noise pollution and highway safety further suggested a need for a different philosophy to encompass the motor vehicle. The decisive push came from international events in the 1970s. Events in the Middle East—the war of 1973 and Iranian revolution of 1978–79—produced two energy crises in the United States marked by shortage of petroleum products (which included gasoline) and two rounds of major increases in price. By 1980–81 a gallon of gasoline fetched nearly $1.40. It began to sink in that the time of inexpensive gas had gone and that the future of energy supplies, not to mention the price, would be highly unpredictable. Perceptions rapidly changed. The revered V-8 now took on the appearance of a dinosaur, or part of one. Small, energy-efficient automobiles, probably powered by four-cylinder engines, became the item of the era. Ill prepared to meet these pressures, American manufacturers could only begin to design new cars and new engines. Japanese producers, who had done their homework, had the machines ready to go. By the time Detroit had adjusted to the new reality, Japanese car manufacturers had established themselves in the American market and broken old company loyalty. Such names as Toyota, Datsun, and Honda, once the object of derision, now earned a vote of confidence, even a measure of prestige, from the American automobile buyer. One can follow the story in the tables pertaining to gasoline prices and gasoline mileage, changing emphasis in engine production and automobile registration,

TABLE 5.8 DOMESTIC CAR ENGINE PRODUCTION, 1956–1990

Model Year	%—4 cyl.	%—6 cyl.	%—8 cyl.	Total Units
1956	. . .	18.6	81.4	6,295,000
1960	. . .	43.3	56.7	6,012,000
1962	2.5	41.4	56.1	6,687,000
1963	1.2	36.5	62.3	7,340,000
1964	. . .	31.1	68.9	7,891,000
1965	. . .	26.6	73.4	8,842,500
1966	0.1	21.5	78.4	8,605,700
1967	. . .	16.4	83.6	7,658,600
1968	. . .	13.7	86.3	8,399,000
1969	0.1	11.0	88.9	8,476,700
1970	0.1	12.8	87.1	7,586,700
1971	7.2	12.3	80.5	7,181,000
1972	9.4	10.8	79.8	9,022,900
1973	8.6	9.9	81.5	10,310,300
1974	12.7	18.7	68.6	8,336,700
1975	8.5	18.9	72.6	6,647,682
1976	10.3	20.9	68.8	8,445,360
1977	6.3	17.9	75.8	9,524,063
1978	10.1	23.9	66.0	9,260,732
1979	17.4	23.6	59.0	9,568,263
1980	31.4	36.5	32.1	7,349,729
1981	39.9	33.2	26.9	7,094,858
1982	41.4	30.3	28.3	5,710,121
1983	38.7	29.1	32.2	6,158,514
1984	45.0	26.9	28.1	8,709,676
1985	46.4	26.2	27.4	8,384,738
1986	51.0	28.6	20.4	8,621,092
1987	54.1	27.4	18.5	7,669,871
1988	48.9	33.8	17.3	7,668,153
1989	47.0	38.0	15.0	7,688,215
1990	46.6	38.1	15.3	6,925,229

Source: Bureau of the Census, *Statistical Abstract of the United States, 1971* (Washington, D.C., 1971), 536; *1991 Ward's Automotive Yearbook*, 59.

TABLE 5.9 VOLKSWAGEN SALES IN THE UNITED STATES, 1949–1990

Year	Sales	% of All Imports
1949	2	. . .
1950	157	0.9
1952	601	2.0
1954	6,343	19.5
1956	50,011	50.9
1958	78,588	20.8
1960	159,995	32.1
1962	192,570	56.8
1964	307,173	63.4
1965	383,978	67.4
1966	420,018	63.8
1968	563,522	57.0
1970	569,182	46.0
1972	480,689	31.0
1974	327,488	24.0
1976	199,062	14.0
1978[a]	239,612	12.0
1980	255,127	10.0
1982	149,422	7.0
1984	155,322	6.0
1986	201,165	6.0
1988	166,372	4.0
1990	125,906	4.0

[a] Between 1978 and 1988 sales included cars manufactured in the United States as well as imported automobiles.
Source: *Ward's Automotive Yearbook for 1967* (Detroit, 1967), 170, *Ward's Automotive Yearbook, 1970*, (Detroit, 1970), 137, *Ward's Automotive Yearbook, 1972*, 119, *Ward's Automotive Yearbook, 1976*, (Detroit, 1976), 133, *Ward's Automotive Yearbook, 1980*, (Detroit, 1980), 152, *Ward's Automotive Yearbook, 1984* (Detroit, 1984), 110, *1988 Ward's Automotive Yearbook*, (Detroit, 1988), 170, *1991 Ward's Automotive Yearbook*, 243.

domestic and foreign, especially in 1974–75 and 1980–82. American carmakers blamed Japanese success on lower production costs, especially for labor, and barriers erected over the Japanese market. Statistics, however, revealed that while Japanese auto workers at one time had earned considerably less than their American counterparts, by the end of the 1980s the gap had narrowed considerably. While charges of a closed Japanese market might have merit, it failed to account for Japan's remarkable success in competing in the United States. Whether or not Japanese cars were better than American makes at the start of the 1990s, many Americans thought they were.

TABLE 5.10 U.S. NEW-CAR REGISTRATIONS, FOREIGN AND DOMESTIC[a], 1955–1990

Year	Total	Domestic	Foreign	Foreign Share
1955	7,169,908	7,111,443	58,465	0.8
1956	5,955,248	5,857,061	98,187	1.7
1957	5,982,342	5,775,515	206,827	3.4
1958	4,654,515	4,275,998	378,517	8.1
1959	6,041,275	5,427,144	614,131	10.2
1960	6,576,650	6,077,865	498,785	7.6
1961	5,854,747	5,476,125	378,622	6.5
1962	6,938,863	6,599,703	339,160	4.9
1963	7,556,717	7,171,093	385,624	5.1
1964	8,065,150	7,581,019	484,131	6.0
1965	9,313,912	8,744,497	569,415	6.1
1966	9,008,488	8,350,365	658,123	7.3
1967	8,357,421	7,678,201	779,220	9.3
1968	9,403,862	8,418,095	985,767	10.5
1969	9,446,524	8,384,907	1,061,617	11.2
1970	8,388,204	7,157,243	1,230,961	14.7
1971	9,838,626	8,343,013	1,487,613	15.1
1972	10,487,794	8,958,392	1,529,402	14.6
1973	11,350,995	9,631,082	1,719,913	15.1
1974	8,701,094	7,331,946	1,369,148	15.7
1975	8,261,840	6,760,912	1,500,928	18.2
1976	9,751,485	8,304,848	1,446,637	14.8
1977	10,826,234	8,849,722	1,976,512	18.3
1978	10,946,094	9,000,000	1,946,094	17.8
1979	10,356,705	8,005,652	2,351,053	22.7
1980	8,760,937	6,291,757	2,469,180	28.2
1981	8,443,919	6,012,239	2,431,680	28.8
1982	7,754,342	5,485,711	2,268,631	29.3
1983	8,924,186	6,466,829	2,457,357	27.5
1984	10,128,729	7,604,755	2,523,974	24.9
1985	10,888,608	7,877,476	3,011,132	27.6
1986	11,139,842	7,695,652	3,444,190	30.9
1987	10,122,154	6,497,618	3,624,536	35.8
1988	10,479,931	6,770,053	3,709,878	35.4
1989	9,852,617	6,313,174	3,539,443	35.9
1990	9,159,629	6,018,097	3,141,532	34.3

[a]Foreign cars includes imports as well as foreign makes manufactured in the United States, which began in 1978. Domestic makes includes cars imported by U.S. firms.
Source: *Ward's Automotive Yearbook, 1972,* 119, *1988,* 170, *1991,* 237.

TABLE 5.11 MILES PER GALLON AND GASOLINE PRICES, 1945–1990

Year	Average Passenger Car[a]	Miles per Gallon			New Car			Gasoline Prices (cents per gallon, inc. tax)	
		All Motor Vehicles[b]	Domestic		Import	Average		Leaded Regular	Unleaded Regular
1945	14.9	13.1	. . .		. . .	. . .		. . .	. . .
1950	14.9	12.9	16.0		. . .	. . .		26.8	. . .
1955	14.5	12.7	16.0		. . .	16.1		29.1	. . .
1960	14.3	12.4	15.5		. . .	16.1		31.1	. . .
1965	14.3	12.5	15.4		. . .	15.9		31.2	. . .
1970	13.5	12.0	14.1		. . .	15.2		35.7	. . .
1975	13.5	12.2	15.1		23.3	15.8		56.7	. . .
1976	13.5	12.1	16.6		25.4	17.5		59.0	. . .
1977	13.8	12.3	17.2		27.7	18.3		62.2	65.6
1978	14.0	12.3	18.7		27.3	19.9		62.6	67.0
1979	14.4	12.5	19.3		26.1	20.3		85.7	80.3
1980	15.5	13.3	22.6		29.6	24.3		119.1	124.5
1981	15.9	13.6	24.2		31.5	25.9		131.1	137.8
1982	16.7	14.1	25.0		31.1	26.6		122.2	129.6
1983	17.1	14.2	24.6		32.4	26.4		115.7	124.1
1984	17.8	14.5	25.6		32.0	26.9		112.9	121.2
1985	18.2	14.6	26.3		31.5	27.6		111.5	120.2
1986	18.3	14.7	26.6		31.6	28.2		85.7	92.7
1987	19.2	15.1	27.0		31.2	28.5		89.7	94.8
1988	19.9	15.6	27.4		31.5	28.8		89.9	94.6
1989	20.3	15.9	27.1		30.6	28.3		99.8	102.1
1990	20.9	16.3	26.9		29.9	28.1		114.9	116.4

[a] From 1960–65 passenger cars included motorcycles.
[b] Includes passenger cars, motorcycles, buses, and trucks.
Source: Bureau of the Census, *Historical Statistics of the United States, Colonial Times to 1970, Part I,* (Washington, D.C., 1975), 716, U.S. Department of Transportation, *Annual Energy Review, 1991* (Washington, D.C., 1992), 53, 161; MVMA, *Automobile Facts & Figures, 1991,* 74.

TABLE 5.12 TOP 10 FOREIGN CAR REGISTRATION—1966, 1978, 1990[a]

1966			1978			1990		
Rank	Make	Total	Rank	Make	Total	Rank	Make	Total
1.	Volkswagen	420,018	1.	Toyota	427,465	1.	Honda	719,189
2.	Opel	31,555	2.	Datsun	337,523	2.	Toyota	709,246
3.	Volvo	25,126	3.	Honda	258,151	3.	Nissan	421,648
4.	Datsun	21,726	4.	Volkswagen	239,612	4.	Mazda	222,561
5.	MG	21,709	5.	Subaru	79,015	5.	Mitsubishi	139,827
6.	Standard Triumph	17,184	6.	Fiesta	76,001	6.	Acura	138,340
7.	Mercedes Benz	16,081	7.	Mazda	71,921	7.	Hyundai	134,704
8.	Toyota	15,814	8.	Fiat	57,946	8.	Volkswagen	125,906
9.	Simca	12,596	9.	Volvo	48,494	9.	Subaru	108,238
10.	Renault	11,500	10.	Colt	45,126	10.	Volvo	91,256
Total All Others		**64,814**	**Total All Others**		**304,840**	**Total All Others**		**674,751**
Grand Total		**658,123**	**Grand Total**		**1,946,094**	**Grand Total**		**3,485,666**

[a] Includes North American–built and imported cars.
Source: Ward's Automotive Yearbook, 1970, 137, Ward's Automotive Yearbook, 1980, 152, 1991 Ward's Automotive Yearbook, 243.

TABLE 5.13 JAPANESE TRANSPLANT CAR PRODUCTION IN THE UNITED STATES, 1982–1990

Make	1990	1989	1988	1987	1986	1985	1984	1983	1982
Honda	435,437	361,670	366,355	324,064	234,159	145,337	138,572	55,337	1,500
Nissan	95,844	115,584	109,897	117,334	65,147	43,810	. . .	. . .	. . .
Toyota	218,195	151,150	18,527	. . .	. . .	. . .	. . .	. . .	. . .
Mazda	184,428	216,200	167,205	4,200	. . .	. . .	. . .	. . .	. . .
Diamond-Star	148,379	90,741	2,409	. . .	. . .	. . .	. . .	. . .	. . .
NUMMI	205,287	192,235	129,978	187,378	205,795	64,601	. . .	. . .	. . .
Subaru-Isuzu	32,461	2,600	. . .	. . .	. . .	. . .	. . .	. . .	. . .
Total	1,320,031	1,130,180	794,371	632,976	509,101	253,751	138,572	55,337	1,500
Big 3 Prod.	4,757,854	5,693,778	6,307,028	6,400,157	7,186,316	7,724,689	7,367,789	6,423,410	4,877,722

Source: 1991 Ward's Automotive Handbook, 19.

Some Volkswagen owners look down on other Volkswagen owners.

The "Bus" and the "Beetle," 1963. Volkswagen produced not only popular cars but also witty advertisements. (Volkswagen of America)

TABLE 5.14   IMPORT NEW-CAR MARKET PENETRATION[a]
(state registrations % total)

10 Highest States	1987	1986
Hawaii	62.8	63.5
California	56.6	51.9
Oregon	52.2	48.8
Washington	52.1	48.2
Colorado	48.7	45.1
Washington DC	48.6	46.9
Alaska	47.5	41.3
Utah	45.7	44.0
Connecticut	43.0	37.7
Rhode Island	42.6	33.5
10 Lowest States	**1987**	**1986**
Michigan	14.9	11.4
Iowa	18.5	15.8
South Dakota	18.9	15.8
Indiana	19.6	15.9
Minnesota	21.1	19.1
North Dakota	21.5	19.1
Wisconsin	21.7	18.2
Nebraska	23.1	20.1
Ohio	23.7	19.5
Missouri	26.2	21.7

[a] Includes U.S.-built cars of foreign manufacturers.
Source: 1991 Ward's Automotive Handbook, 170.

TABLE 5.15   HOURLY COMPENSATION FOR MOTOR VEHICLE PRODUCTION WORKERS, 1975 AND 1980–1990
(in U.S. dollars)

Country or Area	1975	1980	1981	1982	1983	1984	1985	1986	1987	1988	1989	1990
United States	9.53	15.88	16.94	17.99	18.23	18.92	19.63	19.97	20.51	21.11	21.51	21.93
Canada	7.25	10.63	11.58	12.30	12.65	13.05	12.99	13.38	14.56	16.56	17.74	19.23
Mexico	2.94	4.38	5.27	3.56	2.61	2.55	2.66	2.03	2.45	. . .	3.12	2.75
Brazil	1.29	2.01	2.53	2.47	1.79	1.59	1.64	. . .	. . .	. . .	. . .	. . .
Australia	5.83	8.61	9.45	9.92	9.45	10.07	8.35	8.77	9.74	11.42	12.20	12.96
Japan	3.56	6.97	7.61	7.21	7.83	7.90	8.09	11.80	13.83	16.36	15.65	15.77
Korea	0.48	1.33	1.40	1.55	1.68	1.87	1.92	2.00	2.32	3.41	4.92	5.73
Taiwan	0.64	1.68	1.99	1.86	1.66	2.09	1.85	2.23	2.83	3.50	4.16	4.76
Belgium	7.16	14.27	12.33	10.34	9.99	9.64	9.91	13.61	16.98	17.44	17.04	20.94
Denmark	5.78	10.10	8.70	8.25	7.94	7.49	7.52	10.52	13.85	14.90	14.04	16.88
France	5.10	9.98	9.11	8.85	8.79	8.20	8.38	11.24	13.41	14.02	13.75	15.94
Germany	7.89	15.56	13.34	13.03	13.16	11.92	12.09	16.83	21.44	23.00	22.29	27.12
Ireland	3.77	7.31	6.63	6.77	6.47	6.05	6.21	8.32	10.15	11.14	10.31	14.14
Italy	5.16	8.13	7.64	7.67	7.81	7.69	7.72	10.38	12.79	13.54	14.00	17.17
Netherlands	6.72	11.64	9.51	9.32	8.95	8.13	8.35	11.29	14.06	14.65	13.89	16.44
Portugal	. . .	2.87	2.79	2.65	2.53	2.22	2.26	3.09	3.65	3.92	. . .	. . .
Spain	. . .	7.11	7.03	6.69	5.69	5.35	5.54	7.74	9.54	10.85	. . .	. . .
Sweden	7.44	12.70	11.95	10.36	9.18	9.64	10.14	12.75	15.43	17.13	17.75	21.13
United Kingdom	4.01	6.50	7.87	7.62	7.11	6.66	7.05	8.70	10.63	12.28	12.30	14.04
Global Average	**4.45**	**8.30**	**8.09**	**7.81**	**7.55**	**7.42**	**7.49**	**9.19**	**10.96**	**11.85**	**11.30**	**13.00**

Source: Ward's Communications, *1992 Ward's Automotive Yearbook,* 64.

TABLE 5.16   MOTOR-VEHICLE DEATHS AND DEATH RATES, 1946–1990

Year	No. of Deaths	Estimated No. of Vehicles (millions)	Death Rates Per 10,000 Motor Vehicles	Death Rates Per 100,000,000 Vehicle Miles	Death Rates Per 100,000 Population
1946	33,411	34.4	9.72	9.80	23.9
1947	32,697	37.8	8.64	8.82	22.8
1948	32,259	41.1	7.85	8.11	22.1
1949	31,701	44.7	7.09	7.47	21.3
1950	34,763	49.2	7.07	7.59	23.0
1951	36,996	51.9	7.13	7.53	24.1
1952	37,794	53.3	7.10	7.36	24.3
1953	37,956	56.3	6.74	6.97	24.0
1954	35,586	58.6	6.07	6.33	22.1
1955	38,426	62.8	6.12	6.34	23.4
1956	39,628	65.2	6.07	6.28	23.7
1957	38,702	67.6	5.73	5.98	22.7
1958	36,981	68.8	5.37	5.56	21.3
1959	37,910	72.1	5.26	5.41	21.5
1960	38,137	74.5	5.12	5.31	21.2
1961	38,091	76.4	4.98	5.16	20.8
1962	40,804	79.7	5.12	5.32	22.0
1963	43,564	83.5	5.22	5.41	23.1
1964	47,700	87.3	5.46	5.63	25.0
1965	49,163	91.8	5.36	5.54	25.4
1966	53,041	95.9	5.53	5.70	27.1
1967	52,924	98.9	5.35	5.50	26.8
1968	54,862	103.1	5.32	5.40	27.5
1969	55,791	107.4	5.19	5.21	27.7
1970	54,633	111.2	4.92	4.88	26.8
1971	54,381	116.3	4.68	4.57	26.3
1972	56,278	122.3	4.60	4.43	26.9
1973	55,511	129.8	4.28	4.24	26.3
1974	46,402	134.9	3.44	3.59	21.8
1975	45,853	137.9	3.33	3.45	21.3
1976	47,038	143.5	3.28	3.33	21.6
1977	49,510	148.8	3.33	3.35	22.5
1978	52,411	153.6	3.41	3.39	23.6
1979	53,524	159.6	3.35	3.50	23.8
1980	53,172	161.6	3.29	3.50	23.4
1981	51,385	164.1	3.13	3.30	22.4
1982	45,779	165.2	2.77	2.88	19.8
1983	44,452	169.4	2.62	2.68	19.0
1984	46,263	171.8	2.69	2.69	19.6
1985	45,901	177.1	2.59	2.59	19.3
1986	47,865	181.4	2.63	2.60	19.9
1987	48,290	183.9	2.63	2.51	19.9
1988	49,078	189.0	2.60	2.42	20.1
1989	47,575	191.7	2.48	2.26	19.3
1990	46,814	192.9	2.43	2.18	18.8

Source: National Safety Council, *Accident Facts, 1998 Edition* (Itasca, Ill., 1998), 104–05.

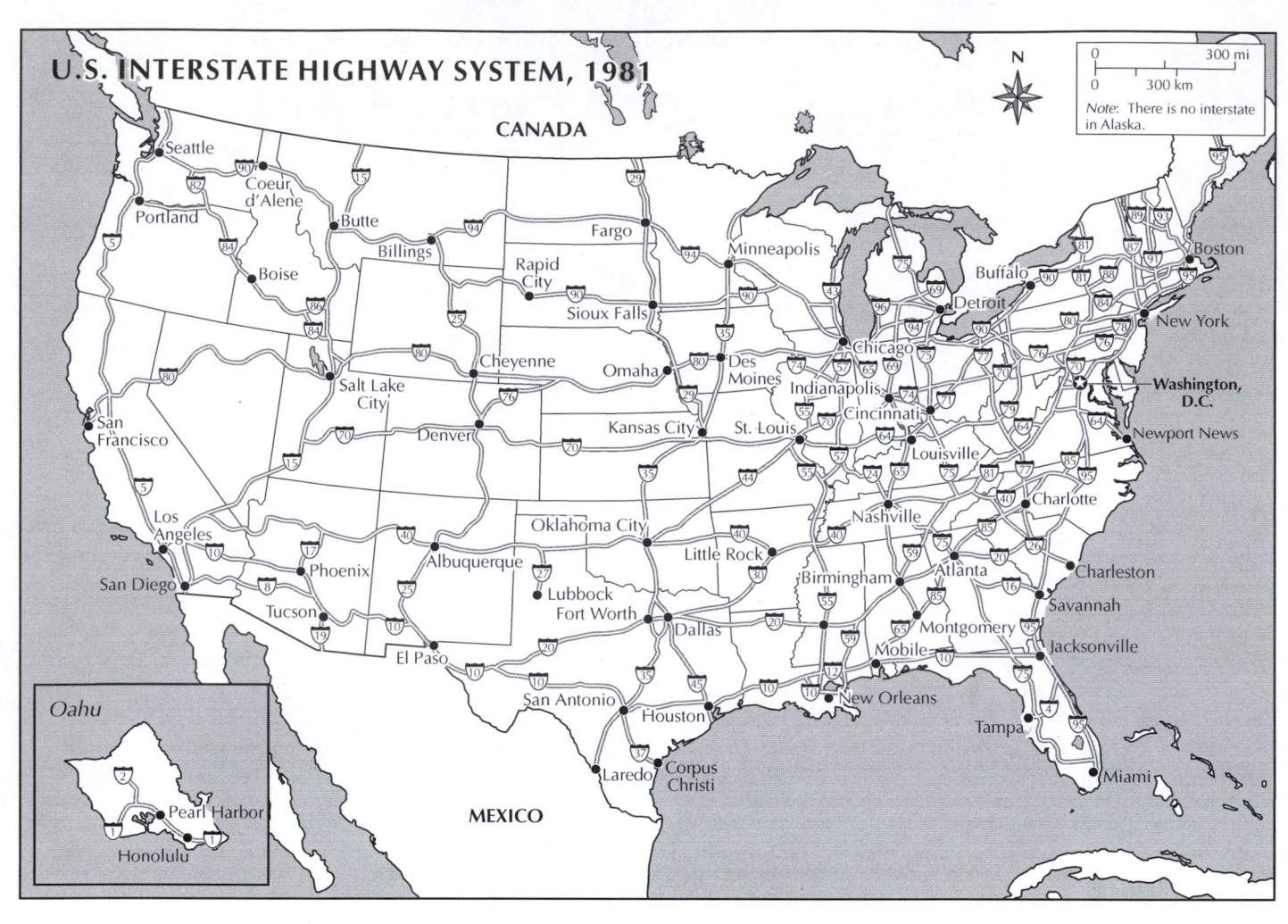

U.S. INTERSTATE HIGHWAY SYSTEM, 1981

Note: There is no interstate in Alaska.

CANADA

Seattle, Coeur d'Alene, Portland, Boise, Butte, Billings, Fargo, Rapid City, Sioux Falls, Cheyenne, Salt Lake City, San Francisco, Denver, Omaha, Des Moines, Minneapolis, Chicago, Kansas City, St. Louis, Indianapolis, Cincinnati, Louisville, Detroit, Buffalo, Boston, New York, Washington, D.C., Newport News, Los Angeles, San Diego, Phoenix, Tucson, Albuquerque, Lubbock, Fort Worth, Dallas, El Paso, Oklahoma City, Little Rock, Nashville, Birmingham, Montgomery, Mobile, New Orleans, Atlanta, Charlotte, Charleston, Savannah, Jacksonville, Tampa, Miami, San Antonio, Houston, Laredo, Corpus Christi

Oahu — Pearl Harbor, Honolulu

MEXICO

TABLE 5.17   ROADS, STREETS, AND HIGHWAYS, 1945–1990

Year	Surfaced Mileage ('000s)			Total Mileage ('000s)			
	State Control	County and Local Control	Total	State Control	County and Local Control	Total	Percent Surfaced
1945	482	1,239	1,721	574	2,745	3,319	51.9
1950	542	1,397	1,939	609	2,704	3,313	58.5
1955	610	1,663	2,273	651	2,767	3,418	66.5
1960	660	1,897	2,557	694	2,852	3,546	72.1
1965	701	2,075	2,776	728	2,962	3,690	75.2
1970	748	2,198	2,946	781	2,949	3,730	79.0
1975	763	2,338	3,101	796	3,042	3,838	80.8
1980	753	2,605	3,358	781	3,174	3,955	84.9
1985	612	2,868	3,480	613	3,249	3,862	90.1
1988	618	2,873	3,491	619	3,252	3,871	90.2
1989	619	2,888	3,507	620	3,257	3,877	90.5
1990	619	2,899	3,518	620	3,260	3,880	90.7

Source: MVMA, *Motor Vehicle Facts & Figures* (Washington, D.C., 1996), 69.

Aerial view of Long Island highways leading to New York City in the 1950s—an increasingly familiar sight throughout the nation. (National Archives)

TABLE 5.18 RURAL AND URBAN ROAD MILEAGE, BY STATE, 1989

State	Rural Mileage	Urban Mileage	Total Mileage
Ala.	73,691	16,844	90,535
Alaska	10,462	1,810	12,272
Ariz.	43,919	13,479	57,398
Ark.	69,466	7,656	77,122
Calif.	91,578	72,720	164,298
Colo.	66,132	11,229	77,361
Conn.	9,045	10,869	19,914
Del.	3,828	1,589	5,417
Fla.	59,305	48,650	107,955
Ga.	87,345	20,665	108,010
Hawaii	2,663	1,419	4,082
Idaho	58,911	2,406	61,317
Ill.	103,957	31,921	135,878
Ind.	73,941	17,803	91,744
Iowa	103,778	8,773	112,551
Kans.	124,169	8,987	133,156
Ky.	62,098	7,613	69,711
La.	46,277	12,244	58,521
Maine	19,781	2,459	22,240
Md.	16,333	12,162	28,495
Mass.	13,201	20,606	33,807
Mich.	90,968	27,028	117,996
Minn.	115,458	14,095	129,553
Miss.	64,988	7,324	72,312
Mo.	104,230	15,847	120,077
Mont.	69,092	2,268	71,360
Nebr.	87,509	4,950	92,459
Nev.	41,780	3,076	44,856
N.H.	12,387	2,416	14,803
N.J.	11,791	22,455	34,246
N.Mex.	49,367	5,440	54,807
N.Y.	73,263	37,701	110,964
N.C.	75,165	19,063	94,228
N.Dak.	84,579	1,805	86,384
Ohio	82,126	31,313	113,439
Okla.	99,578	12,091	111,669
Oreg.	86,325	9,105	95,430
Pa.	88,447	27,830	116,277
R.I.	1,484	4,400	5,884
S.C.	54,699	9,405	64,104
S.Dak.	71,622	1,756	73,378
Tenn.	68,854	15,227	84,081
Tex.	217,044	88,648	305,692
Utah	37,430	5,541	42,971
Vt.	12,923	1,170	14,093
Va.	52,228	15,054	67,282
Wash.	65,011	16,428	81,439
W.Va.	31,425	3,052	34,477
Wis.	95,447	14,366	109,813
Wyo.	37,624	1,917	39,541
District of Columbia	. . .	1,102	1,102
TOTAL	**3,122,724**	**753,777**	**3,876,501**

Source: MVMA, *Motor Vehicle Facts & Figures 1991,* 84.

Like highway construction, bridge building increased in the postwar era. One of the largest, the Mackinac Bridge (Big Mac), here under construction in the 1950s, connected the two peninsulas of Michigan. (Michigan Department of Transportation)

Air Transport

The most striking aspect of air transportation after 1946 was an explosion in the number of customers. Passengers trebled in the first eight years; they had multiplied 13 times by 1970, and by the end of the 1980s the number approached a half-billion per year. Reasons for expansion included an increase in disposable individual wealth (more people could afford to fly), greater confidence in the safety of the enterprise, and the development of new aircraft that enhanced comfort, safety, efficiency, and especially speed of flying. The matching of jet engines with passenger aircraft beginning in the late 1950s changed flying in almost every respect, but especially in speed and efficiency. Thereafter the aircraft companies—led by Boeing—developed jet planes to fit almost every condition: the DC 9 for short distances, Boeing's 727 and 737 for medium-length trips, and the "jumbo" Boeing 747, DC 10 (Douglas) and L1011 (Lockheed) for coast-to-coast and intercontinental travel. Other companies specialized in smaller jets for private and company use; still others produced conventional propellor-driven craft of many types and sizes for the public market. Small airlines usually purchased aircraft with two piston-type engines to feed traffic from small cities into the large metropolitan airports.

Explosion of flying did not come without bumps, bruises, and outright tragedy. More traffic meant congestion in the skies and on the ground; the need for larger and better airports, for more sophisticated guidance systems in the tower and cockpit never ended. Airliner crashes, rare as they might be, continued to attract national media coverage. In 1958 Congress created two agencies: the Federal Aviation Agency to oversee safety standards and the Civil Aeronautics Board to supervise routes and rates. In the 1970s and beyond international problems spilled over to the business with a wave of forceable seizure of aircraft in flight (thus creating a new word: *skyjacking*) and other acts of terrorism that involved planes or airports. International politics in the 1980s led to violent destruction of three jumbo jets and death of everyone aboard: a Korean 747 shot down by the Soviets; an Iranian Airbus destroyed by an American ship; a Pan-Am 747 blown out of the air over Scotland by a bomb placed aboard. The first energy crisis of 1973–74 roughly doubled fuel costs, and the second crisis of 1978–80 doubled them again.

Consistent with a trend of the era, Congress deregulated the airline industry in 1978, a move that raised concerns about safety (as did

President Ronald Reagan's firing of striking air-traffic controllers in 1982) and set off a bewildering state of affairs in the 1980s. New airlines popped up suddenly and many expired just as fast. Rate wars provoked intense competition and need to cut costs, which caused labor troubles and more worry about safety. Merger and corporate takeover affected virtually aspect of the industry as well as most of the companies. By the end of the 1980s some of the most prestigious air-lines, including three of the traditional big four—Eastern, Pan American, and TWA—stood on the verge of collapse. The end of the era seemed to foretell an industry dominated by a small number of large firms, although it was nearly impossible to tell how the situation would play out. Perhaps the most that one could predict was that the passengers would continue to come.

TABLE 5.19 SCHEDULED AIR TRANSPORTATION, DOMESTIC AND INTERNATIONAL, 1946–1990

							Ton-miles flown				
Year	Number of Operators[a]	Aircraft in Service	Persons Employed	Revenue Passengers Carried (1,000)	Revenue Passenger-miles Flown (millions)	Average Passenger-mile Rate (dollars)	Express and Freight (1,000)	Mail (1,000)	Fuel Consumed Gasoline (million gal.)	Average Available Seats	Average Speed (mpn)
Domestic											
1946	23	674	69,182	12,213	5,945	.0463	15,096	32,969	236	25.3	160
1950	52	960	61,903	17,345	8,007	.0554	60,588	47,740	418	37.5	180
1955	42	1212	95,548	38,025	18,852	.0536	96,378	88,751	912	51.2	208
1960	42	1594	133,717	56,352	30,567	.0609	191,585	135,923	922	65.5	235
1965	40	1896	169,952	92,073	51,887	.0606	597,324	225,992	448	89.2	314
1970	33	2437	242,206	153,408	104,156	.0587	1,229,000	705,711	. . .	110.4	350
1975	33	2260	290,000	205,000	162,800	.0770	2,049,000	1,109,000	9,507	130.4	403
1978	34	2345	329,000	275,000	226,800	.0850	2,313,000	1,181,000	10,534	140	409
1980	72	2505	371,000	297,000	255,200	.1130	2,465,000	1,342,000	11,311	143.1	405
1985	86	2860	355,000	382,000	336,400	.1230	2,887,000	1,659,000	12,603	152.5	409
1988	88	4439	481,000	455,000	423,300	.1230	4,789,000	1,837,000	15,094	153.1	409
1989	62	4477	507,000	454,000	432,700	.1310	5,359,000	1,911,000	15,624	152.1	406
1990	60	4665	545,000	466,000	457,900	.1340	5,524,000	2,004,000	16,252	151.9	408
International											
1946	5	147	27,372	1,041	1,104	.0831	38,590	8,165	60	27.2	166
1950	6	160	20,883	1,675	2,214	.0728	152,228	26,228	154	41	218
1955	9	147	26,655	3,416	4,499	.0666	229,966	61,233	258	56.4	244
1960	13	. . .	29,054	5,904	8,306	.0635	386,933	103,335	205	89.9	307
1965	10	. . .	36,882	10,847	16,789	.0529	943,128	254,093	41	129.1	451
1970	6	. . .	48,520	16,260	27,563	.0500	1,966,009	548,845	2,241	154.9	482
1975	2	. . .	. . .	16,000	31,100	.0720	4,796,000	426,000	1,949	224.8	482
1978	2	. . .	. . .	21,000	44,100	.0750	5,818,000	374,000	1,913	244.1	489
1980	. . .	. . .	. . .	24,000	54,400	.0750	5,742,000	393,000	2,093	274.5	494
1985	. . .	. . .	. . .	25,000	65,800	.0980	6,020,000	445,000	2,488	296.6	497
1988	. . .	. . .	. . .	35,000	94,000	.1040	9,632,000	470,000	3,192	281.3	488
1989	. . .	. . .	. . .	37,000	102,700	.1040	10,275,000	496,000	3,537	277.1	486
1990	. . .	. . .	. . .	42,000	117,700	.1080	10,600,000	513,000	3,791	275.7	489

[a]The Airline Deregulation Act of 1978 produced changes that left no clear distinction between domestic and international operators.
Source: Ben J. Wattenberg, ed., *The Statistical History of the United States* (New York, 1976), 769, *Statistical Abstract of the United States, 1992,* 625.

TABLE 5.20 AIRPORTS, AIRCRAFT, AND PILOTS, 1946–1990

	Airports and Landing Fields		Total Civil Aircraft	Total	Certified Airplane Pilots			
Year	Total	Lighted			Airline Transport	Commercial	Private	Percent Female
1946	4,490	1,019	81,002	400,061	7,654	203,251	189,156	. . .
1950	6,403	1,670	92,809	. . .	. . .	. . .	. . .	. . .
1955	6,839	1,247	85,320	643,201	13,700	211,142	418,359	. . .
1960	6,881	2,133	111,580	783,232	20,985	262,437	499,810	2.9
1965	9,566	2,878	142,078	497,770	22,440	116,665	196,393	3.7
1970	11,261	3,554	154,450	732,729	34,430	186,821	303,779	4.0
1975	13,251	4,171	196,300	728,000	43,000	189,000	306,000	5.2
1980	15,161	4,738	259,400	827,000	70,000	183,000	357,000	6.4
1985	16,318	4,941	274,900	710,000	83,000	152,000	311,000	6.1
1987	17,015	4,922	275,100	700,000	91,000	144,000	301,000	6.1
1989	17,446	4,443	274,800	700,000	102,000	145,000	293,000	6.1
1990	17,490	4,822	275,900	703,000	108,000	149,000	299,000	5.8

Source: Wattenberg, *Statistical History,* 733; *Statistical Abstract, 1960,* 579; *Statistical Abstract, 1970,* 563; *Statistical Abstract, 1982–83,* 633; *Statistical Abstract, 1993,* 639.

TABLE 5.21   MAJOR AIRCRAFT IN EVOLUTION OF COMMERCIAL AIR TRAVEL, 1946–1990[a]

Model	Manufacturer	Passengers	Engines (no. & type)	Cruising Speed	Year Introduced
DC 3	Douglas	35	2 piston	217	1935
DC 4	Douglas	86	4 piston	250	1942
202	Martin	53	2 piston	255	1946
377 (Stratocruiser)	Boeing	93	4 piston	312	1947
LO949 (Constellation)	Lockheed	96	4 piston	300	1947
240	Convair	51	2 piston	270	1948
DC 6	Douglas	87	4 piston	300	1951
L1049 (Super Constellation)	Lockheed	102	4 piston	300	1954
DC 7	Douglas	99	4 piston	310	1955
707	Boeing	100/181	4 jet	615	1957
L188 (Electra)	Lockheed	64/104	4 turboprop	405	1958
DC 8	Douglas	116/259	4 jet	580	1958
990	Convair	103	4 jet	600	1961
DC 9	McDonnell-Douglas	90/172	2 jet	593	1965
727	Boeing	70/145	3 jet	620	1967
737	Boeing	105/149	2 jet	577	1967
747	Boeing	331/452	4 jet	565	1969
Concorde	British Airways/Aerospatiale	144	4 jet	1,350	1969
DC 10	McDonnell-Douglas	250/380	3 jet	615	1972
A 300 (Airbus)	Airbus Industries	220/345	2 jet	460	1974
L1011 (Tristar)	Lockheed	250/400	3 jet	615	1976
767	Boeing	211/290	2 jet	550	1981
757	Boeing	178/290	2 jet	494	1982

[a] Specification for aircraft of the same model will change with modification over the years.
Source: Dan Golenpaul, ed., *Information Please Almanac 1957* (New York, 1956), 485, Otto Johnson, ed., *Information Please Almanac 1988* (New York, 1987), 358–59, Enzo Angelucci, *World Encyclopedia of Civil Aircraft* (New York), 1982, 286–90.

Pacemaker of the age of jet flight, the Boeing 707 came on line in the late 1950s. (The Boeing Company Archives)

TABLE 5.22   AIR TRANSPORTATION ACCIDENTS ON DOMESTIC SCHEDULED AIR CARRIERS, 1946–1990

Year	Total Accidents	Fatal Accidents	Passenger Fatalities
1946	33	9	75
1947	44	8	199
1948	56	5	83
1949	35	8	96
1950	39	4	96
1951	45	11	142
1952	44	6	46
1953	37	5	86
1954	49	4	16
1955	45	8	156
1956	55	4	143
1957	44	4	32
1958	42	4	114
1959	61	9	209
1960	62	10	326
1961	56	5	124
1962	35	5	158
1963	39	4	48
1964	45	6	106
1965	55	6	205
1966	50	4	59
1967	43	8	226
1968	44	11	258
1969	37	7	132
1970	31	1	0

Year	Total Accidents	Fatal Accidents	Passenger Fatalities
1971	39	6	194
1972	43	7	186
1973	32	6	217
1974	43	7	460
1975	29	2	122
1976	21	2	36
1977	18	2	75
1978	19	4	16
1979	18	5	352
1980	15	. . .	38
1981	25	4	4
1982	15	3	233
1983	23	4	15
1984	14	1	197
1985	17	4	197
1986	21	2	5
1987	32	4	231
1988	28	3	285
1989	25	8	131
1990	24	6	39

Source: Wattenberg, *Statistical History of the U.S.* 744; George Thomas Kurian, *Datapedia of the United States 1789–2000, America Year by Year* (Lanham, Md., 1994), 293.

Major Airplane Accidents Involving Americans, 1952–1990

January 22, 1952, Elizabeth, New Jersey   29 killed, including former Secretary of War Robert P. Patterson, when airliner hit apartments; seven of dead were on ground.

June 18, 1953, near Tokyo, Japan   Crash of U.S. Air Force "Globemaster" killed 129 servicemen.

December 16, 1960, New York City   United and Trans World planes collided in fog, crashed in two boroughs, killing 134 in air and on ground.

February 15, 1961, near Brussels, Belgium   72 on board and farmer on ground killed in crash of Sabena plane: U.S. figure-skating team wiped out.

December 24, 1966, Binh Thai, South Vietnam   Crash of military-chartered plane into village killed 129.

November 14, 1970, Huntington, West Virginia   Chartered plane carrying 43 players and coaches of Marshall University football team crashed; 75 dead.

July 30, 1971, Morioka, Japan   Japanese Boeing 727 and F-86 fighter collided in midair; toll was 162.

September 4, 1971, near Juneau, Alaska   Alaska Airlines Boeing 727 crashed into Chilkoot Mountains; 111 killed.

December 30, 1972, Miami, Florida   Eastern Airlines Lockheed 1011 TriStar Jumbo jet crashed into Everglades; 101 killed, 75 survived.

April 4, 1975, near Saigon, Vietnam   Air Force Galaxy C-5A crashed after takeoff, killing 172, mostly Vietnamese children.

March 27, 1977, Santa Cruz de Tenerife, Canary Islands   Pan American and KLM Boeing 747s collided on runway. All 249 on KLM plane and 333 of 394 aboard Pan Am jet killed. Total of 582 is highest for any type of aviation disaster.

September 25, 1978, San Diego, California   Pacific Southwest plane collided in midair with Cessna. All 135 on airliner, two in Cessna, and seven on ground killed for total of 144.

May 25, 1979, Chicago   American Airlines DC-10 lost left engine upon takeoff and crashed seconds later, killing all 272 persons aboard and three on the ground in worst U.S. air disaster.

March 14, 1980, Warsaw, Poland   LOT Polish Airlines Ilyushin 62 crashed while attempting landing; 22 boxers and officials of a U.S. amateur boxing team killed along with 65 others.

August 30, 1983, near Siberia   Near island of Sakhalin off Siberia South Korean civilian jetliner shot down by Soviet fighter after it strayed off course into Soviet airspace. All 269 people aboard killed.

December 12, 1985   A chartered Arrow Air DC-8, bringing American soldiers home for Christmas, crashed on takeoff from Gander, Newfoundland. All 256 aboard died.

May 9, 1987, Poland   Polish airliner, Ilyushin 62M on charter flight to New York, crashes after takeoff from Warsaw, killing 183.

August 16, 1987, Detroit   Northwest Airlines McDonnell Douglas MD-30 plunges to heavily traveled boulevard, killing 156. Girl, four, only survivor.

July 3, 1988, Persian Gulf   U.S. Navy cruiser *Vincennes* shot down Iran Air A300 Airbus, killing 290 persons, after mistaking it for an attacking jet fighter.

August 28, 1988, Ramstein Air Force Base, West Germany   Three jets from Italian air force acrobatic team collided in midair during air show and crashed, killing 70 persons, including the pilots and spectators on the ground. It is worst air-show disaster in history.

December 21, 1988, Lockerbie, Scotland   A New-York-bound Pan-Am Boeing 747 exploded in flight from a terrorist bomb and crashed into a Scottish village, killing all 259 aboard and 11 persons on the ground. Passengers included 38 Syracuse University students and many U.S. military personnel.

February 24, 1989, UAL 811, near Hawaii   About 100 miles southwest of Hawaii, a 10- × 40-ft hole blew open in the fuselage of a United Airline Boeing 747. Nine passengers were sucked out of the jet liner to their deaths 20,000 ft over the Pacific: 27 other passengers were injured.

Source: Otto Johnson, ed., *Information Please Almanac 1992* (1991), 388.

TABLE 5.23   BUSIEST U.S. AIRPORTS, ENPLANING (BOARDING) ONLY, 1988

Rank	Airport	Total Enplaned Passengers
1.	Chicago (O'Hare), Ill.	26,596,800
2.	Atlanta, Ga.	21,824,125
3.	Dallas/Ft. Worth (Regional), Tex.	21,014,158
4.	Los Angeles, Calif.	18,643,319
5.	Denver, Colo.	14,441,817
6.	San Francisco, Calif.	13,347,979
7.	New York (La Guardia), N.Y.	11,321,800
8.	Newark, N.J.	10,837,963
9.	New York (John F. Kennedy), N.Y.	10,660,421
10.	Boston, Mass.	10,141,298
11.	St. Louis, Mo.	9,554,454
12.	Miami, Fla.	9,461,760
13.	Phoenix, Ariz.	9,455,324
14.	Detroit, Mich.	9,213,713
15.	Honolulu, Oahu, Hawaii	8,396,313
16.	Pittsburgh, Pa.	8,378,639
17.	Minneapolis St. Paul, Minn.	8,170,952
18.	Orlando, Fla.	7,473,086
19.	Washington (National), D.C.	7,259,448
20.	Houston (Intercontinental), Tex.	6,871,886
21.	Las Vegas, Nev.	6,864,803
22.	Seattle-Tacoma, Wash.	6,825,513
23.	Philadelphia, Pa.	6,633,677
24.	Charlotte, N.C.	6,619,780
25.	San Diego, Calif.	5,180,587

Source: U.S. Department of Transportation, *FAA Statistical Handbook of Aviation 1988* (Washington, D.C., 1990), 82.

TABLE 5.24   BUSIEST U.S. AIRPORTS, ALL OPERATIONS, 1988

Tower	Air Carrier Rank	Air Carrier Operations	Air Taxi	General Aviation	Military	Total Rank	Total Operations
Chicago O'Hare Int'l	1.	631,073	129,981	31,208	3,487	1	795,749
Atlanta International	2.	562,698	191,203	27,449	1,336	2	782,686
Dallas Ft. Worth Reg'l	3.	490,327	149,880	22,554	1,507	3	664,268
Los Angeles Int'l	4.	435,751	135,728	55,548	4,871	4	631,898
Denver Stapleton Int'l	5.	374,614	94,171	40,205	2,336	6	511,326
San Francisco	6.	321,420	104,884	32,378	2,531	7	461,213
St. Louis Int'l	7.	285,710	89,098	43,364	11,198	12	429,370
Newark	8.	282,488	67,775	25,971	588	22	376,822
LaGuardia	9.	269,643	66,403	27,608	533	26	364,187
Phoenix Sky Harbor Int'l	10.	268,236	65,697	114,529	6,880	9	455,342
Pittsburgh Greater Int'l	11.	256,627	97,706	25,937	6,675	18	386,945
Miami International	12.	254,597	56,417	45,718	1,688	28	358,420
Detroit Metro Wayne County	13.	250,445	69,470	59,939	307	19	380,161
Boston Logan	14.	246,423	146,793	51,683	274	10	445,173
John F. Kennedy Int'l	15.	221,615	81,318	25,012	681	30	328,626
Minneapolis–St. Paul Int'l	16.	214,025	87,442	73,146	5,193	20	379,806
Charlotte Douglas	17.	213,291	104,298	83,895	3,743	16	405,227
Memphis International	18.	211,732	63,570	76,906	6,590	27	358,798
Houston Intercontinental	19.	205,969	40,103	50,098	1,108	34	297,278
Philadelphia Int'l	20.	195,506	161,685	57,199	1,214	14	415,604
Washington National	21.	190,609	60,213	76,494	321	31	327,637
Orlando Int'l Airport	22.	188,024	60,396	37,843	4,072	37	290,335
Honolulu	23.	187,445	57,366	86,418	35,912	25	367,141
Las Vegas McCarren	24.	177,700	80,766	105,340	8,801	23	372,607
Seattle Tacoma	25.	175,746	119,656	15,614	467	32	311,483

Source: FAA Handbook 1988, 15.

TABLE 5.25   TOP 25 U.S. AIRLINES, 1988

Airline	Passengers ('000s)	Rank	Revenue Passenger Miles[a] ('000s)	Rank
American	64,296	1.	64,752,866	2.
Delta	59,969	2.	51,652,125	3.
United	56,326	3.	69,024,633	1.
Continental	37,636	4.	40,498,243	4.
Northwest	35,784	5.	40,148,340	5.
Eastern	35,621	6.	28,793,436	8.
USAir	32,466	7.	17,315,319	9.
Piedmont	27,117	8.	13,051,317	10.
Trans World	25,124	9.	34,699,818	6.
Southwest	16,842	10.	7,711,064	11.
Pan American	16,755	11.	29,308,089	7.
America West	12,651	12.	6,949,731	12.
Hawaiian	5,497	13.	3,008,063	15.
Alaska	4,772	14.	3,559,508	14.
Braniff	4,322	15.	4,047,099	13.
Midway	4,258	16.	2,990,582	16.
Aloha	3,426	17.	450,472	21.
Air Wisconsin	2,420	18.	421,328	22.
PSA	2,365	19.	915,641	18.
Horizon Air	1,397	20.	285,176	24.
Westair	1,218	21.	231,273	26.
Florida Express	1,166	22.	564,218	20.
Aspen	878	23.	157,716	27.
Presidential	844	24.	325,654	23.
Midwest Express	402	25.	261,098	25.

[a] One paying passenger traveling one mile generates one revenue passenger mile.
Source: John W. Wright, ed., *The Universal Almanac 1991* (New York, 1990), 279.

TABLE 5.26   TOP 15 U.S. CARGO AIRLINES, 1988

Rank	Airline	Freight Ton-miles[a] ('000s)
1.	Flying Tiger	2,792,107
2.	Northwest	1,476,061
3.	Federal Express	1,228,207
4.	United	942,167
5.	Pan American	714,534
6.	American	489,755
7.	Continental	487,782
8.	Delta	476,429
9.	Trans World	447,027
10.	Eastern	164,484
11.	Challenge Air Cargo	74,196
12.	Piedmont	67,519
13.	Zantop	62,909
14.	Rosenbalm	51,563
15.	Alaska	40,605

[a] One ton of freight traveling one mile equals one freight ton mile.
Source: Wright, *Universal Almanac 1991*, 280.

Railroads

Long the dominant force in travel across country, railroad passenger service had been in decline since the 1920s, the system as a whole running annual deficits. The Second World War reversed the trend for passenger and freight service as well and perhaps created an illusion of good times to come. It was not to be in the years after 1945. Even though railroad companies upgraded equipment (diesel engines and air-conditioned cars became commonplace) and brightened and speeded up the trains, they could not keep pace with competitors in any dimension, save possibly travel safety. Automobiles offered privacy, individualized movement, and a way of moving about a destination after one had arrived. Airplanes far surpassed trains in speed over long distances. By 1970 trains carried less than 1 percent of intercity travel and only 6 percent of commercial traffic; airplanes had most of the rest. Even the mail and express service, which had accompanied the passenger trains, shifted to trucks and airplanes. The intercity trains all lost money and one by one were dropped from service, even the most prestigious ones. In many small and middle-sized towns the depots along the tracks closed, were leveled, or given a new function, perhaps as a bus station or a museum. The grandiose train stations in the large cities evolved into small ghost towns, awaiting destruction, preservation as a historical structure, or modernization and reduction in size to meet the needs of a specialized clientele. Passenger trains that survived carried commuter traffic into the cities in morning and away from town in the evening.

Even so, the railroad companies, the national government, and considerable segments of the population hesitated to have intercity train travel pass into oblivion. Highway traffic produced noise, air pollution, and appalling casualties. Travel by bus was tedious and confining, especially over long distances. A segment of the populace remained unwilling to fly. Such considerations and emerging concerns over energy supplies produced a compromise in the form of national legislation passed in October 1970 that created the National Railroad Passenger Corporation, better known as Amtrak. This special corporation was to provide specified intercity passenger service on tracks owned by 19 railroad companies. Given time to acquire modern equipment and to identify the most effective routing, Amtrak stopped the decline of train travel, produced a slight increase that leveled out at 20 million to 21 million passengers per year. The system nonetheless lost money annually and existed largely through subsidies from Congress. Having survived efforts to drastically pare down operations or end them altogether, Amtrak stood as a safe, comfortable, speedy (faster than cars, slower than planes) alternative to conventional travel and as a possible safety valve for transportation crises—suspected or unanticipated—of the future.

As a carrier of freight, railroads experienced decline that was more proportionate than absolute; although trains suffered losses to other transport competitors, the record remained far less dismal than in passenger service. Railroads carried more freight in 1990 than 1946, but their share of all freight was cut approximately in half. To protect their domain and hopefully to add to it, railroad companies produced numerous changes. Steam engines gave way to diesels; automation and computerization came to switching and terminal operations; the "piggyback" innovation placed truck trailers and then standardized compartments on flatbeds; special bilevel and trilevel cars allowed railroads to transport approximately half the new automobiles to their destination. Major competition came from trucks (in many kinds of goods), pipelines (oil and other fluids), and river barges (coal and grain). The railroads survived this competition reasonably well, and in the 1980s they continued to be the largest transporter of freight, but they had lost a long-held position as the only powerhouse contributor to that enterprise.

Still pulled by a massive, hooded Hudson steam locomotive on its New York–Chicago run, the Twentieth Century Limited remained in 1948 the nation's, if not the world's, most famous train. (National New York Central RR Museum)

TABLE 5.27   RAILROAD FREIGHT AND PASSENGER TRAFFIC, 1946–1990

Year	Revenue Freight[a]: 2,000-pound Tons (1,000)	Passengers (1,000)
1946	1,367,000	794,800
1948	1,507,000	646,500
1950	1,355,000	488.000
1952	1,382,600	471,000
1954	1,224,000	440,800
1956	1,447,400	430,000
1958	1,190,400	381,600
1960	1,240,800	327,200
1962	1,193,700	313,100
1964	1,354,600	314,400
1966	1,448,900	307,500
1968	1,431,300	301,400
1970	1,484,900	289,500
1972	1,448,900	. . .
1974	1,530,000	274,000
1976	1,370,700	268,000
1978	1,390,400	281,000
1980	1,492,400	300,000
1982	1,268,600	. . .
1984	1,429,400	. . .
1986	1,306,000	. . .
1988	1,429,000	. . .
1990	1,425,000	. . .

[a] Class I railroads; a Class I railroad was one that grossed more than $50 million a year.
Source: Wattenberg, *Historical Statistics*, 727–29; Kurian, *Datapedia*, 275–76; *Statistical Abstract*, 626.

TABLE 5.28   ANNUAL RAILROAD CARLOADINGS[a], 1945–1990

Year	Total
1945	41,918,000
1950	38,903,000
1955	32,761,707
1960	27,886,950
1965	28,344,381
1970	27,015,020
1975	22,929,843
1980	22,223,000
1981	21,342,987
1982	18,584,760
1983	19,013,250
1984	20,945,536
1985	19,501,242
1986	19,588,666
1987	20,602,204
1988	22,599,993
1989	21,226,015
1990	21,884,649

[a] Only Class 1 railroads, except for 1945 and 1950.
Source: Johnson, *Information Please Almanac 1992*, 65.

TABLE 5.29 RAILROAD MILEAGE AND EQUIPMENT, 1946–1990

Year	Miles of Track	Locomotives in Service	Pass. Cars in Service	Freight Cars Number	Freight Cars Average Capacity[a]
1946	398,000	45,511	38,697	1,768,400	51.3
1950	396,000	42,951	37,359	1,745,800	52.6
1955	391,000	33,533	32,118	1,723,700	53.7
1960	382,000	31,178	25,746	1,690,400	55.4
1965	371,000	30,061	20,022	1,515,200	59.8
1970	360,000	29,122	11,378	1,453,700	67.1
1975	324,000	28,210	6,471	1,359,000	72.9
1980	290,000	28,094	4,347	1,168,000	78.5
1985	257,000	22,932	2,502	867,000	83.2
1990	239,000	18,835	. . .	659,000	87.5

[a] In tons.
Source: Wattenberg, *Historical Statistics*, 727–29, 732–33; Kurian, *Datapedia*, 275–76.

TABLE 5.30 AMTRAK OPERATIONS, 1974–1990

Year	Revenue Passengers Carried (1,000)	Revenue (mil. $)	Expenses (mil. $)	Profit or Loss (mil. $)
1974	18,000	. . .	. . .	. . .
1975	18,000	. . .	. . .	. . .
1976	19,000	. . .	. . .	. . .
1977	19,000	. . .	. . .	. . .
1978	19,000	. . .	. . .	. . .
1979	21,000	. . .	. . .	. . .
1980	21,000	. . .	. . .	. . .
1981	20,000	. . .	. . .	. . .
1982	19,000	. . .	. . .	. . .
1983	19,000	. . .	. . .	. . .
1984	20,000	. . .	. . .	. . .
1985	21,000	825	1,600	−865
1986	20,000	861	1,563	−702
1987	21,000	973	1,672	−699
1988	21,000	1,106	1,757	−651
1989	21,000	1,269	1,934	−665
1990	22,000	1,308	2,012	−704

Source: Statistical Abstract, 1992, 619, Wright, *Universal Almanac, 1991,* 280.

TABLE 5.31 U.S. RAILROADS AND TRAIN-MILES OPERATED, 1987

Rank	Railroad	Train-miles Operated
	CLASS I RAILROADS, TOTAL	532,861,687
1.	Burlington Northern Inc.	88,753,970
2.	CSX Transportation	70,699,184
3.	Union Pacific Railroad Co.	70,109,027
4.	Norfolk Southern Corp.	50,630,032
5.	Consolidated Rail Corp. (Conrail)	49,705,075
6.	Atchison, Topeka and Santa Fe Railway Co.	49,677,394
7.	Southern Pacific Transportation Co.	35,531,871
8.	Amtrak (National Railroad Passenger Corp.)	34,972,173
9.	Chicago and North Western	17,535,636
10.	Kansas City Southern Railway Co.	10,711,722
11.	Soo Line Railroad Co.	9,173,719
12.	Illinois Central Gulf Railroad Co.	8,506,155
13.	St. Louis Southwestern Railway Co.	8,152,286
14.	Denver and Rio Grande Western Railroad Co.	6,575,793
15.	Grand Trunk Western Railroad Co.	5,394,661
16.	Louisiana and Arkansas Railway Co.	4,722,051
17.	Missouri-Kansas Texas Railroad Co.	4,114,217
18.	Florida East Coast Railway Co.	3,342,822
19.	Elgin, Joliet and Eastern Railway Co.	1,814,914
20.	Delaware and Hudson Railway	1,553,838
21.	Springfield Terminal Railway Co.	1,185,147
	CLASS II RAILROADS	7,256,814
	CLASS III RAILROADS	69,215,928
	Total, all railroads	**609,334,429**

Note: Railroads are classified according to total annual gross operating revenue (in 1978 dollars): class I, more than $50 million; class II, $10–$50 million; class III, less than $10 million.
Source: Wright, *Universal Almanac 1991,* 280.

TABLE 5.32 COMMUTER RAIL SYSTEMS IN THE UNITED STATES, 1988

System	Passenger Trips ('000s)	Passenger Miles ('000s)	Station	Route Miles	Vehicles Operated
New York—LIRR[1]	96,101.9	2,107,010.4	136	623.3	1,049
New York—Metro-North	55,887.9	1,359,925.7	106	535.3	673
Newark—NJT Corp.[2]	43,396.0	1,025,597.0	151	755.2	722
Chicago Commuter Rail Bd.	29,395.6	600,215.7	121	417.0	383
Chicago—Burlington Northern	12,882.0	255,753.8	26	74.4	161
Chicago & NW, Trans. Co.	22,610.7	499,765.5	62	309.4	328
Philadelphia—SEPTA	25,450.1	335,941.1	181	375.6	283
San Francisco—CALTRANS	5,591.5	130,359.9	26	93.8	67
Staten Island (New York) Rapid Transit	6,227.6	42,970.6	22	28.6	36

[1] Long Island Railroad [2] New Jersey Transit.
Source: Wright, *Universal Almanac 1991,* 280.

TABLE 5.33   INTERCITY PASSENGER MILES BY MODE, 1945–1990

(in billions)

Year	Auto/Truck Miles	Auto/Truck Percent	Bus Miles	Bus Percent	Railroad Miles	Railroad Percent	Air Miles	Air Percent	Total
1945	220.3	63.8	27.4	7.9	93.5	27.1	4.3	1.2	345.5
1950	438.3	87.0	22.7	4.5	32.5	6.5	10.1	2.0	503.6
1955	637.4	89.7	21.9	3.1	28.7	4.0	22.9	3.2	710.8
1960	706.1	90.4	19.3	2.5	21.6	2.8	34.0	4.4	781.0
1965	817.7	89.2	23.8	2.6	17.6	1.9	58.1	6.3	917.2
1970	1,026.0	86.9	25.3	2.1	10.9	0.9	118.6	10.0	1,180.8
1975	1,170.7	86.4	25.4	1.9	10.1	0.7	148.3	11.0	1,354.5
1980	1,210.3	82.5	27.4	1.9	11.0	0.7	219.1	14.9	1,467.8
1982	1,226.0	82.3	26.9	1.8	10.2	0.7	226.7	15.2	1,498.8
1984	1,277.4	81.0	24.6	1.6	10.8	0.7	263.7	16.7	1,576.5
1986	1,367.8	79.4	23.7	1.4	11.7	0.7	320.3	18.6	1,723.5
1988	1,494.7	79.6	23.1	1.2	12.6	0.7	346.9	18.5	1,877.3
1990	1,638.8	80.6	23.0	1.1	13.2	0.6	358.9	18.0	2,033.9

Source: AAMA, *Motor Vehicle Facts & Figures, 1997,* 66.

TABLE 5.34   DOMESTIC FREIGHT TRAFFIC BY MAJOR CARRIERS, 1945–1990

(in millions of ton-miles)[a]

Year	Railroads Ton-miles	Railroads Percent of Total	Inland Waterways Ton-miles	Inland Waterways Percent of Total	Motor Trucks Ton-miles	Motor Trucks Percent of Total	Oil Pipelines Ton-miles	Oil Pipelines Percent of Total	Air Carriers Ton-miles	Air Carriers Percent of Total
1945	690,809	67.3	142,737	13.9	66,948	6.5	126,530	12.3	91	. . .
1950	596,940	56.2	163,344	15.4	172,860	16.3	129,175	12.1	318	. . .
1955	631,385	49.5	216,508	17.0	223,254	17.5	203,244	16.0	481	. . .
1960	579,130	44.1	220,253	16.8	285,483	21.7	228,626	17.4	778	. . .
1965	708,700	43.3	262,421	16.0	359,218	21.9	306,393	18.7	1,910	0.1
1970	771,168	39.8	318,560	16.4	412,000	21.3	431,000	22.3	3,274	0.2
1975	759,000	36.7	342,210	16.5	454,000	22.0	507,300	24.6	3,732	0.2
1980	932,000	37.2	420,000	16.9	567,000	22.6	588,000	23.1	4,528	0.2
1983	841,000	36.0	359,000	15.4	575,000	24.6	556,000	23.8	5,870	0.3
1985	895,000	36.4	382,000	15.6	610,000	24.9	564,000	22.9	6,080	0.2
1986	889,000	35.5	393,000	15.7	634,000	25.4	578,000	23.1	7,100	0.3
1987	972,000	36.8	411,000	15.6	661,000	25.1	587,000	22.2	8,670	0.3
1988	1,028,000	37.0	438,000	15.8	699,000	25.1	605,000	21.8	9,300	0.3
1989	1,048,000	37.3	448,000	15.9	716,000	25.4	591,000	21.0	10,210	0.36
1990	1,080,000	37.6	461,000	16.0	735,000	25.6	585,000	20.4	10,480	0.37

[a] Mail and express included, except railroads for 1970.
Source: Johnson, *Information Please Almanac 1992,* 65.

TABLE 5.35   PASSENGER DEATHS AND DEATH RATES, 1950–1990

Year	Passenger Cars & Taxis Number	Passenger Cars & Taxis Rate[a]	Buses Number	Buses Rate[a]	Railroad Passenger trains Number	Railroad Passenger trains Rate[a]	Scheduled Domestic Air Transport Planes Number	Scheduled Domestic Air Transport Planes Rate[a]
1950	22,200	2.90	100	.18	184	.58	96	1.15
1955	25,100	2.70	100	.18	19	.07	156	.76
1960	24,800	2.20	70	.13	33	.16	297	.93
1965	32,500	2.40	100	.16	12	.07	205	.38
1970	34,800	2.10	130	.19	10	.09	0	.00
1975	27,200	1.40	110	.15	8	.08	113	.08
1980	27,339	1.29	42	.05	4	.04	28	.01
1985	22,974	.96	47	.04	3	.03	202	.07
1990	23,924	1.05	24	.02	3	.02	11	.003

[a] Rate based on 100 million passenger miles.
Source: National Safety Council, *Accident Facts 1970 Edition,* 76; *1980 Edition,* 75; *1992 Edition,* 90.

Urban Transport

During the years 1946 to 1990 public urban transportation declined markedly but still continued to provide an important community service. Even with the increasing problems of traffic congestion and shortage of parking places, urban workers and shoppers preferred to come to town by car. In many towns and small cities, public transport vanished or maintained only a token presence. In the metropolitian areas, however, there remained a need for ways other than the private car to get about the city. Taxis, while probably indispensable to the urban transportation scheme, were too expensive for regular use. Thus mass transit or urban transit remained a persisting problem in all large cities, if only because of sharply escalating costs amid a prospect of reduced ridership. Methods of transport maintained trends established in the 1930s and 1940s. The traditional streetcar or trolley—electric-powered coaches that ran on tracks in the center of the street—vanished altogether (except in San Francisco). Something called a trolley bus or coach, which was powered by electricity but ran on tires not tracks, claimed a small but not insignificant share of the market. Electric railway systems ran either underground (subway), above ground (elevated), or at ground level and remained steady contributors to city travel, although many of the busiest ones were lodged between urban and interurban classification. The dominant force of public transport within the city itself in terms of passengers and even more conspicuously in numbers of vehicles continued to be the motor bus, but the bus did not escape the trend of the time. If there were more buses on the streets in 1990 than in 1946, only half as many people rode them.

Century leaves the scene: A victim of the airplane and automobile, the Twentieth Century Limited stopped operation in 1967. (National New York Central RR Museum)

TABLE 5.36   PUBLIC-TRANSIT EQUIPMENT AND PASSENGERS, 1946–1990

	Equipment				Passengers Carried (millions)		
Year	Railway Cars	Trolley Coaches	Motor Buses	Total Passengers (millions)	Railway Cars	Trolley Coaches	Motor Buses
1946	33,479	3,916	52,450	23,372	11,862	1,311	10,199
1950	22,986	6,504	56,820	17,246	6,168	1,658	9,420
1955	14,532	6,157	52,400	11,529	3,077	1,202	7,250
1960	11,866	3,826	49,600	9,395	2,313	657	6,425
1965	10,664	1,453	49,600	8,253	2,134	305	5,814
1970	10,600	1,050	49,700	7,332	2,116	182	5,034
1975	9,608	703	50,811	6,972	1,810	. . .	5,084
1980	9,641	823	59,411	8,567	2,256	142	5,837
1985	9,326	676	64,285	8,636	2,432	142	5,675
1990	10,419	832	59,753	8,873	2,749	126	5,677

Source: Wattenberg, Historical Statistics, 721; Statistical Abstract, 1982–83, 623; Statistical Abstract, 1988, 584; Statistical Abstract, 1993, 626.

Water Transport

Travel by water remained an indispensable part of the transportation system of the United States. With respect to the movement of domestic freight, vessels on the inland waterways, of which the Great Lakes and Mississippi River systems were most important, continued to carry a consistent 16 to 17 percent each year. Transport by ship dominated freight commerce abroad. Airlines took a meaningful portion of specialized international cargo, such as mail and goods for which speed of delivery was vital, but the bulk of foreign trade remained the burden of the trudging but steady oceangoing merchant ships. In the second half of the 20th century the United States continued a trend begun earlier—

reversed briefly during the Second World War—of relying on foreign ships. The portion of foreign trade carried in United States bottoms dwindled from more than 50 percent in the late 1940s to a mere 7 percent in 1990. Few vessels came from American shipyards, and few flew the American flag. Shipowners could register vessels under any flag they chose, and as a rule they sought out nations, such as Liberia and Panama, that had legislation most favorable to their interests. Major innovations in merchant shipping included the container ship that facilitated loading and unloading and the supertankers, vessels that dwarfed the largest warships of any era. Built as a response to the world's growing demand for oil, these behemoths carried a potential for disaster proportionate to their size if one happened to flounder and spill its cargo.

TABLE 5.37   EXPORTS AND IMPORTS, BY METHOD OF TRANSPORT, 1950–1968

Item	1950	1955	1960	1965	1967	1968
Exports						
Value, all methods of transportation	10,275	15,547	20,575	27,478	31,526	34,413
Vessel	...	9,227	13,142	16,926	18,772	19,511
Percent of total	...	59.4	63.9	61.6	59.5	58.6
Air	...	...	...	2,289	3,233	3,789
Shipping weight:						
Vessel	...	225,169	248,456	343,461	375,198	389,336
Air	...	...	...	457	540	654
Imports						
Value, all methods of transportation	8,852	11,384	14,654	21,366	26,812	33,114
Vessel	...	8,073	11,106	14,943	17,492	21,234
Percent of total	...	70.9	75.8	69.9	65.2	64.1
Air	...	...	...	1,316	1,947	2,548
Shipping weight:						
Vessel	...	283,069	398,085	511,509	512,686	566,222
Air	...	...	...	192	305	431

Exports and Imports, by Method of Transport, 1970–1990

Item	Unit	Exports						Imports					
		1970	1980	1985	1988	1989	1990	1970	1980	1985	1988	1989	1990
All methods	Bil. dol.	43.2	220.7	213.1	320.4	363.8	393.0	40.0	240.8	345.3	441.3	473.4	495.3
Vessel	Bil. dol.	24.6	120.9	91.7	126.0	146.3	150.8	24.8	165.1	208.4	255.8	269.9	283.4
Air	Bil. dol.	6.1	46.1	52.3	91.6	101.9	110.5	3.4	28.0	51.3	77.5	84.4	90.9
Shipping weight: Vessel	Bil. kg.	218.0	363.7	317.7	361.8	390.6	372.4	271.4	443.1	361.5	466.8	494.7	496.3
Air	Bil. kg.	0.4	1.0	0.8	1.4	1.6	1.5	0.3	0.6	1.3	1.5	4.3	1.7

[a] Value in millions of dollars, except percent; shipping weight in millions of pounds. Export data include both domestic and foreign; import data for general imports only.
Source: Statistical Abstract, 1969, 574, Statistical Abstract, 1993, 642.

TABLE 5.38   VESSELS ENTERED AND CLEARED IN FOREIGN TRADE—NET REGISTERED TONNAGE, BY FLAG OF CARRIER VESSEL, 1946–1990

Yearly Average or Year	Number of Vessels	All Ports				Seaports					
		Tonnage, all Vessels				Tonnage, all Vessels			Tonnage, with Cargo		
		Total	Percent U.S.	U.S.	Foreign	Total	U.S.	Foreign	Total	U.S.	Foreign
Entered:											
1946–1950	48,813	87	46	52.8	41	75	42	32	50	26	23
1951–1955	48,082	114	39	34.3	75	100	35	65	78	26	51
1956–1960	51,874	155	31	20.0	124	139	26	112	110	21	88
1961–1965	49,670	187	33	17.9	154	166	29	136	127	18	108
1966–70	53,459	232	29	12.5	203	206	27	180	157	18	139
1971–75	53,760	319	30	9.5	290	292	28	264	220	24	196
1976–80	53,700	458	40	8.7	418	425	38	387	316	30	286
1981–85	50,124	452	57	12.4	395	424	55	369	277	36	241
1986–90	61,978	548	46	8.4	502	521	45	476	346	30	315
1970	53,293	254	26	10.3	226	227	24	202	171	19	152
1975	51,443	355	32	9.9	323	326	30	297	240	26	215
1980	53,645	492	52	10.6	440	460	50	410	310	34	276
1985	53,531	451	53	11.7	398	426	52	374	283	34	249
1986	56,859	489	49	10.0	439	463	48	415	310	32	278
1987	59,563	518	48	9.3	470	492	47	445	333	29	304
1988	62,097	556	47	8.5	509	527	46	481	352	30	322
1989	64,946	587	44	7.4	543	558	42	516	367	31	335
1990	66,424	589	41	7.0	548	564	40	524	367	30	337
Cleared:											
1946–1950	45,135	87	44	51.5	42	74	40	33	54	29	25
1951–1955	45,324	115	39	34.2	75	101	35	65	68	25	42
1956–1960	49,079	156	31	19.9	125	140	27	113	85	19	65
1961–1965	48,098	189	33	17.9	155	167	30	137	95	20	75
1966–70	52,415	232	30	12.8	202	206	27	179	122	23	99
1971–75	53,039	324	31	9.9	293	296	29	267	149	21	127
1976–80	52,931	453	41	9.1	412	420	38	382	203	26	177
1981–85	50,291	460	57	12.4	403	432	55	377	251	34	217
1986–90	60,249	551	47	8.6	504	524	46	478	284	31	253

Yearly Average or Year	Number of Vessels	All Ports Tonnage, all Vessels Total	Percent U.S.	U.S.	Foreign	Seaports Tonnage, all Vessels Total	U.S.	Foreign	Tonnage, with Cargo Total	U.S.	Foreign
1970	52,195	253	27	10.6	226	226	25	201	132	20	112
1975	51,017	363	34	10.3	329	334	31	303	168	23	144
1980	52,928	487	54	11.1	433	456	51	405	246	33	213
1985	53,095	461	55	11.9	406	435	53	382	253	36	217
1986	55,710	491	51	10.4	441	466	49	417	246	33	212
1987	58,307	521	49	9.4	472	495	48	447	269	31	238
1988	60,540	561	49	8.7	512	531	47	484	295	31	264
1989	63,042	590	45	7.6	545	561	44	517	304	30	274
1990	63,648	592	43	7.3	550	566	41	525	304	29	275

[In millions of net tons, except as indicated. Includes Puerto Rico and Virgin Islands. Seaports comprise all ports except Great Lakes ports.
Sources: Statistical Abstract, 1971, 564, Statistical Abstract, 1992, 634.

TABLE 5.39 MERCHANT VESSELS LAUNCHED AND OWNED—WORLD AND UNITED STATES, 1950–1990[a]

Year	World Launched Number	Gross Tons (1,000)	World Owned Number	Gross Tons (1,000)	United States Launched Number	Gross Tons (1,000)	United States Owned Number	Gross Tons (1,000)
1950	990	3,489	27,922	83,996	51	437	4,531	27,404
1955	1,437	5,315	29,967	100,069	26	73	4,225	26,343
1960	2,005	8,382	36,311	129,770	49	379	4,059	24,837
1970	2,814	20,980	52,444	227,490	156	375	2,983	18,463
1980	2,412	13,101	73,832	419,911	205	555	5,579	18,464
1984	2,210	18,334	76,068	418,682	73	84	6,441	19,292
1985	1,964	18,157	76,395	416,269	66	180	6,447	19,518
1986	1,634	16,845	75,266	404,910	36	223	6,496	19,901
1987	1,528	12,259	75,240	403,498	29	164	6,427	20,178
1988	1,575	10,909	75,680	403,406	60	11	6,442	20,832
1989	1,593	13,236	76,100	410,481	10	4	6,375	20,588
1990	1,672	15,885	78,336	423,627	16	15	6,348	21,328

[a] Vessels of 100 gross tons and over. Excludes sailing ships, nonpropelled craft, and all ships built of wood.
Sources: Statistical Abstract, 1971, 568, Statistical Abstract, 1992, 636.

TABLE 5.40 COMMERCE AT MAJOR U.S. PORTS, 1988
(tonnage)

Rank	Port	Total	Domestic	Foreign
1.	New Orleans, La.	175,500,858	107,904,683	67,596,175
2.	New York, N.Y.	155,061,783	99,416,833	55,644,950
3.	Houston, Tex.	124,886,883	60,269,197	64,617,686
4.	Valdez Harbor, Ala.	107,144,515	107,137,158	7,357
5.	Baton Rouge, La.	78,857,473	50,862,340	27,995,133
6.	Corpus Christi, Tex.	57,931,945	23,719,730	34,212,215
7.	Tampa, Fla.	50,252,299	29,429,174	20,823,125
8.	Norfolk, Va.	46,872,002	10,707,123	36,164,879
9.	Long Beach, Calif.	46,559,885	25,063,239	21,496,646
10.	Los Angeles, Calif.	45,213,855	23,192,340	22,021,515
11.	Texas City, Tex.	42,746,698	19,719,829	23,026,869
12.	Baltimore, Md.	41,925,745	13,193,637	28,732,108
13.	Duluth Superior, Minn.	40,002,268	32,942,447	7,059,821
14.	Philadelphia, Pa.	37,826,999	14,505,234	23,321,765
15.	Lake Charles, La.	37,311,924	15,391,008	21,920,916
16.	Mobile, Ala.	36,476,377	19,694,707	16,781,760
17.	Pittsburgh, Pa.	34,373,364	34,373,364	0
18.	Portland, Oreg.	31,970,940	12,631,448	19,339,492
19.	Beaumont, Tex.	31,947,319	22,207,204	9,740,115
20.	Marcus Hook, Pa.	29,815,233	13,443,448	16,371,785
21.	St. Louis, Mo.	29,011,497	29,011,497	0
22.	Pascagoula, Miss.	28,527,726	11,654,688	16,873,038
23.	Port Arthur, Tex.	23,801,409	8,710,408	15,091,001
24.	Chicago, Ill.	22,893,740	19,914,938	2,978,802
25.	Paulsboro, N.J.	22,004,472	9,505,939	12,498,533
26.	Newport News, Va.	21,391,195	2,349,466	19,041,729
27.	Tacoma, Wash.	20,667,517	5,599,652	15,067,865
28.	Boston, Mass.	20,641,073	8,164,425	12,476,648
29.	Richmond, Calif.	18,912,900	14,111,103	4,801,797
30.	Seattle, Wash.	18,645,664	7,269,342	11,376,322
31.	Huntington, W. Va.	17,700,717	17,700,717	0
32.	Lorain Harbor, Ohio	17,475,549	17,443,727	31,822
33.	Indiana Harbor, Ind.	16,643,362	16,154,640	488,722
34.	Jacksonville, Fla.	15,805,551	8,650,231	7,155,320
35.	Detroit, Mich.	15,331,351	12,142,101	3,189,250
36.	Freeport, Tex.	15,137,891	8,822,971	6,314,920
37.	Toledo, Ohio	14,741,752	8,763,052	5,978,700
38.	Cleveland, Ohio	14,550,876	11,565,041	2,985,835
39.	Port Everglades, Fla.	14,207,239	9,507,320	4,699,919
40.	Savannah, Ga.	13,980,978	2,901,798	11,079,180
41.	Anacortes, Wash.	13,637,730	10,817,217	2,820,513
42.	San Juan, P.R.	13,503,267	7,942,552	5,560,715
43.	Galveston, Tex.	12,354,709	2,984,429	9,370,280
44.	Presque Isle, Mich.	11,433,323	7,462,283	3,971,040
45.	Cincinnati, Ohio	11,242,990	11,242,990	0
46.	Honolulu, Hawaii	10,654,845	8,942,733	1,712,112
47.	Ashtabula, Ohio	10,335,305	4,617,244	5,718,061
48.	Conneaut, Ohio	10,220,234	3,702,055	6,518,179
49.	Calcite, Mich.	10,205,105	8,608,127	1,596,978
50.	Memphis, Tenn.	10,200,387	10,200,387	0
51.	Oakland, Calif.	10,140,753	3,604,430	6,536,323

Source: Wright, Universal Almanac 1991, 278.

TABLE 5.41 MAJOR MERCHANT FLEETS OF THE WORLD, BY TONNAGE AND NUMBER OF SHIPS, 1988

Rank	Country	Deadweight Tons (000s)	Number of Ships[a]	Rank
1.	Liberia	93,537	1,465	3
2.	Panama	68,884	3,208	1
3.	Japan	44,819	1,265	4
4.	Greece	39,387	1,030	7
5.	Cyprus	30,318	1,168	6
6.	USSR	24,479	2,439	2
7.	British Colonies[b]	22,245	514	10
8.	United States[c]	21,200	444	11
9.	China	17,992	1,211	5
10.	Nassau Bahamas	15,203	337	17
11.	Philippines	13,749	530	8
12.	Singapore	11,634	432	12
13.	Italy	11,268	525	9
14.	Korea, South	10,548	423	13
15.	Brazil	9,763	325	20
	All others[d]	153,531	7,991	...
	Total	**588,557**	**23,307**	...

[a] Oceangoing merchant ships of 1,000 gross tons and over.
[b] Hong Kong and Gibraltar.
[c] Privately owned.
[d] Includes 265 U.S. government–owned ships of 4,545,000 deadweight tons.
Source: Wright, *Universal Almanac 1991,* 278.

End of an Era

Perhaps no theme better illustrates the idea that the post–Second World War period would not be an extension of the prewar era than the case of the transatlantic passenger liner. Heirs of a fabled operation stretching back many decades, ship owners anticipated enlarged business brought on by an increase in travel between the United States and Europe. Ship companies set to building new vessels or returning to service the best and largest of the older ones that had been commandeered for military operations during the war. Conspicuous for its absence was France's majestic *Normandie,* which had fallen victim to a war-related accident while interned in New York. Cunard's *Queens* were back at sea by 1947; America's most illustrious competitor, a new ship named *United States,* promptly broke the speed record across the Atlantic, thus capturing the Blue Ribband from the British. Even by that time, however—in July 1952—ship owners encountered signals ominous for their future. The ships were expensive to build and operate, given safety standards and expectations of employees and customers of that era. Competition stiffened with more countries entering the race. But any observer could see that the most serious challenge came from another source. Each year airplanes carried a larger share of passenger service to Europe, and almost each year the planes became better and faster. In 1956 airplanes passed ships in number of passengers carried, at which time, incidently, the airlines still used propellor-driven aircraft. The final blow came in the late 1950s with introduction of jet airliners, which substantially reduced time of travel even more. One by one the shipping lines left competition; their vessels sat idle, awaiting a new fate. A few were turned into museums or something similar, as in the case of Cunard's *Queen Elizabeth,* largest of the lot, which became a stationary floating university in East Asia. Many would be broken up for scrap, an unfitting end it would seem for an agent of such a distinguished enterprise. New ships, indeed, had arrived on the scene and more were to follow. These were the cruise ships and they were different. They sailed and broadcast destinations but did not seem to go anywhere. Not designed as a true means of transportation, they functioned as a floating resort and casino. They were colorful and glamorous, with a remarkable array of services. But one did not think of passage on a cruise ship as a dignified or prestigious experience, and except perhaps for some of the individuals who took a cruise, few people remembered their names.

TABLE 5.42 25 LARGEST TRANSATLANTIC LINERS FROM 1945

Rank	Ship	Tonnage	Company	Flag
1.	Queen Elizabeth	83,673	Cunard Line	British
2.	Queen Mary	81,237	Cunard Line	British
3.	Queen Elizabeth 2	67,107	Cunard Line	British
4.	France	66,348	French Line	French
5.	United States	53,329	US Lines	American
6.	Liberte;	51,839	French Line	French
7.	Raffaello	45,933	Italian Line	Italian
8.	Michelangelo	45,911	Italian Line	Italian
9.	Canberra	45,733	P&O-Orient	British
10.	Aquitania	45,647	Cunard Line	British
11.	Ile de France	44,356	French Line	French
12.	Oriana	41,923	P&O-Orient	British
13.	Rotterdam	38,645	Holland-America	Dutch
14.	Nieuw Amsterdam	36,667	Holland-America	Dutch
15.	Mauretania	35,655	Cunard Line	British
16.	Australis	34,449	Chandris Lines	Panamanian/Greek
	ex-America	(33,532)	US Lines	American
17.	Caronia	34,172	Cunard Line	British
18.	Leonardo da Vinci	33,340	Italian Line	Italian
19.	Bremen	32,336	North German Lloyd	West German
20.	Independence	30,293	American Export	American
21.	Constitution	30,293	American Export	American
22.	Hanseatic	30,029	Hamburg-Atlantic	West German
23.	Iberia	29,734	P&O-Orient	British
24.	Arcadia	29,614	P&O-Orient	British
25.	Cristoforo Colombo	29,191	Italian Line	Italian

Source: William H. Miller, *Transatlantic Liners 1945–1980* (New York, 1981), 219.

Sample Transatlantic Sailing from New York, July 11–18, 1959

Westerdam, Holland-America; Rotterdam	**Saturday, July 11, 1959**	Noon 5th Street, Hoboken
	Sunday, July 12 No sailings	
Constitution, American Export; Mediterranean	**Monday, July 13**	Noon 84 HR, West 44th St
Atlantic, American Banner; Amsterdam	**Tuesday, July 14**	11.59 pm 97 HR, West 57th St
Queen Mary, Cunard; Southampton *Statendam*, Holland-America; Rotterdam	**Wednesday, July 15**	1.30 pm 90 HR, West 50th St Noon 5th Street, Hoboken
Berlin, North German Lloyd; Bremerhaven *United States*, United States Lines; Bremerhaven *Guadalupe*, Spanish Line; Spain *Zion*, Zim Lines; Haifa	**Thursday, July 16**	11.00 am 88 HR, West 48th St Noon 86 HR, West 46th St Noon 15 ER, Maiden Lane 6.00 pm Kent St, Brooklyn
Nieuw Amsterdam, Holland-America Rotterdam *Andes*, Royal Mail Lines; Southampton *Parthia*, Cunard; Liverpool *America*, United States Lines; Bremerhaven	**Friday, July 17**	Noon 5th Street, Hoboken Noon 97 HR, West 57th St 3.30 pm 92 HR, West 52nd St 4.00 pm 86 HR, West 46th St
Liberté;, French Line; Le Havre *Kungsholm*, Swedish-American; Gothenburg	**Saturday, July 18**	11.30 am 88 HR, West 48th St 4.30 pm 97 HR, West 57th St

Source: William H. Miller, *The Last Atlantic Liners* (London, 1985), 183.

TABLE 5.43 MODE OF TRANSPORT BETWEEN THE UNITED STATES AND EUROPE—UNITED STATES AND FOREIGN CARRIERS COMBINED, 1949–1972

Year Ended June 30	Number of Passengers (thousands) U.S.-Flag Plus Foreign-Flag			Air as Percent of Air Plus Sea
	Total	Air	Sea	
1949	844	256	588	30.3
1950	1021	297	724	29.1
1951	981	318	663	32.4
1952	1140	372	768	32.6
1953	1249	497	752	39.8
1954	1364	573	791	42.0
1955	1514	692	822	45.7
1956	1734	878	856	50.6
1957	1861	1038	823	55.8
1958	2024	1220	804	60.3
1959	2231	1465	766	65.7
1960	2485	1748	737	70.3
1961	2804	2092	712	74.6
1962	2975	2275	700	76.5
1963	3351	2640	711	78.8
1964	3784	3084	700	81.5
1965	4323	3681	642	85.1
1966	4809	4243	566	88.2
1967	5323	4827	496	90.7
1968	5925	5539	386	93.5
1969	6689	6341	348	94.8
1970	7994	7695	299	96.3
1971	9071	8865	206	97.7
1972	10658	10480	178	98.3

Source: Civil Aeronautics Board, *Handbook of Airline Statistics 1973 Edition* (Washington, D. C., 1974), 610.

Chronology of Significant Transatlantic Liner Events

August 1945 First commercial transatlantic crossing since the war, made by Norwegian America *Stavangerfjord*.

June 1946 Holland-America Line resumes transatlantic passenger service with *Westerdam*.

September 1946 Swedish-American *Stockholm* launched; first new postwar liner for North Atlantic service.

October 1946 *Queen Elizabeth* commissioned following war duties.

November 1946 *America* recommissioned following war service.

January 1947 Italian Line resumes transatlantic liner service with *Saturnia*.

July 1947 *Queen Mary* recommissioned after war service.

August 1947 Cunard *Media* completed: first new transatlantic passenger ship to enter service.

October 1947 *Nieuw-Amsterdam* recommissioned following war service.

January 1949 Cunard *Caronia* commissioned; first large liner designed mostly for cruising.

May 1949 Home Lines begin North Atlantic passenger operations.

July 1949 *Ile De France* recommissioned after war duties.

December 1949 Cunard *Aquitania* retired; last four-stacker.

August 1950 French *Liberté* recommissioned.

January 1951 Polish *Batory* withdrawn from transatlantic service through political troubles in the United States.

July 1951 Holland America *Ryndam* introduces tourist class dominance of passenger accommodations.

July 1952 *United States* sweeps the North Atlantic and takes the Blue Ribband from *Queen Mary*; last record-breaker.

January 1955 North German Lloyd resumes transatlantic passenger service with *Berlin*.

July 1956 Italian *Andrea Doria* sinks off Nantucket after collision with Swedish *Stockholm*.

October 1958 First commercial jet aircraft service across the Atlantic.

November 1958 *Ile de France* retired.

September 1959 *Rotterdam* commissioned; first Atlantic liner to dispense with conventional funnel.

December 1960 Cunard's *Britannic* retired; last of the original White Star Line fleet.

January 1961 Portuguese *Santa Maria* hijacked by political rebels during transatlantic crossing.

November 1961 French *Liberté* retired.

February 1962 *France* commissioned; last of the purposely designed transatlantic superliners.

Put out of business by the airplane, the luxury liner *Queen Mary* rests at Long Beach, California, as hotel, restaurant, and tourist attraction. (Queen Mary Enterprises)

February 1963   *Queen Elizabeth* makes first cruise in the history of the Cunard *Queens.*

October 1963   Home Lines ceases transatlantic passenger services.

April 1966   Soviets resume North Atlantic passenger service (first since 1949) with *Alexandr Pushkin* to Montreal.

September 1967   *Queen Mary* retired from transtlantic service; last three-stacker.

October 1968   Cunard ends its Canadian passenger service.

November 1968   Zim Lines ceases Atlantic passenger operations.

September 1968   American Export Lines ceases Atlantic liner services.

October 1968   *Queen Elizabeth* retired from transatlantic service.

May 1969   *Queen Elizabeth 2* commissioned; last of the superliners.

November 1969   *United States* withdrawn; United States Lines ends transatlantic passenger service.

May 1971   *Queen Mary* opens as hotel and museum ship at Long Beach, California.

September 1971   Holland-America Line and North German Lloyd cease transatlantic operations.

November 1971   Canadian Pacific ends Atlantic liner service.

January 1972   Former *Queen Elizabeth,* as the *Seawise University,* destroyed by fire at Hong Kong.

March 1973   Spanish Line ceases North Atlantic passenger operations.

May 1973   Soviets open irregular Atlantic service to New York with *Mikhail Lermontov.*

September 1974   *France* withdrawn; French Line ends Atlantic liner runs.

January 1975   Greek Line ceases all passenger operations.

December 1975   Swedish-American Line ends passenger service.

June 1976   Italian Line ends transatlantic passenger service.

May 1980   *France* recommissioned as cruise ship *Norway.*

1981   Jugolinija ends transatlantic passenger operations; termination of all regular liner service to the Mediterranean area. Soviets withdraw from all Atlantic liner service.

Source: Miller, *Last Liners,* 181–82.

CHAPTER 6 Communications

The Course of the Communications System

One of the largest areas of American economic enterprise, the communications industry in the postwar world grew rapidly in size, technological advance, and diversity. Starting with well-defined components of telephone and telegraph, postal service, newspapers and books, and an elementary broadcast operation, the industry expanded into a gigantic maze of overlapping and interrelated entities, offering new technologies in telephone, radio, television, cable, film, video, e-mail, and other computer-based activities. While the more familiar postal service and print media remained important parts of the vast communication complex, much of the change and growth took place in electronic-driven operations, where technology and organizational tactics caused the constituent elements to become mixed in together. At some point after 1970, for example, it no longer became fashionable to speak merely of the telephone business; it now became telecommunications and its realm included, but went far beyond, the operations of Ma Bell.

Technological changes were manifold, of course, but a few of the major ones included launching of the communication satellites, beginning in the 1960s; a cable network, HBO, that began to rent space on an RCA satellite in 1975, making possible national distribution of its programming; and a demonstration by the Apple Computer company in the late 1970s that a computer could be a personal instrument, affordable for an individual to purchase, and possible for the nonspecialist (with a little instruction) to operate. In the 1980s came expansion of fiber-optic network systems that transmitted communication by digital technology, clarifying the transmission and producing mes-

sages readable by different types of equipment. By that time there had been, starting in the late 1960s, a linking together of computer systems, laying a foundation for direct communication between personal computers on an international basis, through a network called the Internet.

Connection between elements of the business appeared in the fact that email messages, read almost instantly by a computer, traveled over telephone lines. An emerging organizational structure was exemplified by the merger in 1989 of *Time,* originally a respected magazine publisher, with Warner Brothers, a film studio, producing a corporation that functioned in magazines and book publishing; worked in movie and television production; controlled cable stations, including HBO, and cable systems; and soon would join with a telephone company. Other multifaceted mergers took place or appeared on the corporate horizon. Americans as a whole surely marveled at the ease with which they could communicate and acquire massive amounts of information, but critics warned of the danger in having so much that the people saw and heard originate with a few massive organizations, each reaching like an octopus in many directions. Only the U.S. mail, it appeared, stood outside control of the private corporations, and one even could hear calls for privatization of the postal service.

Postal Service

The United States post office began the postwar period as part of the federal system; its leader, the postmaster general, was a member of the cabinet and in traditional practice the major dispenser of political patronage. The service maintained a virtual monopoly in the delivery of written communications. By the 1960s, charges of mismanagement, poor service, and repeated deficits led the Richard Nixon administration to seek reorganization of the system. What followed was the Postal Service Act of 1969, which created an independent, self-supporting postal corporation owned by the national government. The postmaster general remained the CEO but he or she lost cabinet rank and stood accountable to a board of directors.

In the 1970s and 1980s the Postal Service came to face competition from rapid delivery systems such as Federal Express (now FedEx), private package transport companies such as United Parcel Service (UPS), from a new method of message transmission called a fax, and from technologies—including a form of instant communication referred to as e-mail—emerging on an electronic internet. The service responded with changes. It produced an express system of its own, starting in 1977. A five-digit zip code system established in 1963—identifying regional and local postal zones—was expanded to nine digits in 1983. A new self-adhesive, peel and stick stamp, test-marketed in 1989, proved to be an immediate success. The extent of automation and computerization of postal operations could be seen in the fact that although the amount of mail handled multiplied nearly five times between 1946 and 1990, the number of postal workers did not even double. The service continued to face criticism on many fronts (many people referred to it as "snail mail"), but the nation continued to rely on it. In 1988 the U.S Postal Service still delivered 77 percent of all personal and business correspondence. Modernization of operations evidently had been effective, but expansion of the marketplace provided another explanation for durability of the postal service. The volume of mail had grown more than the competition from private carriers.

Space-race breakthrough and everyone can watch it. President John and Mrs. Kennedy, Vice President Lyndon Johnson, and aides follow on television the suborbital flight of astronaut Alan Shephard in May 1961. (John F. Kennedy Library)

Mail Service: Definitions and Charges, 1989

1. *First class mail.* The standard personal letter or communication. Rate: 1st ounce, $.25; each of next nine ounces, $.20; 11th ounce, $.10; for letters more than 11 ounces, use priority mail. Some 50–60 percent of all mail is first class.

2. *Second class mail.* Authorized newspapers and magazines, classroom and nonprofit publications. Rates are based on weight and content: $.092 to $.197 per pound for advertising part and $.069 for nonadvertising part of the publication. Normally not used by private senders.

3. *Third class mail.* Books, catalogues, circulars, also various merchandise (seeds, etc.) weighing less than 16 ounces. Rates: same as first class for first four ounces; $.15 for fifth and sixth ounces; $.10 for each two ounces between 6 and 16 ounces. Bulk rate for heavier mail: $.36 per pound.

4. *Fourth class mail.* Parcel post. Rates depend on weight and zone of destination. Maximum charge is $25.46 for a 70-pound parcel sent to zone 9. Personal written messages forbidden.

5. *Priority mail.* Two-day domestic delivery service between major business centers. Packages weighing up to 2 pounds cost $2.40 whatever the destination in the United States. Cost of parcels more than 2 pounds depends on weight and zone. Maximum charge is $72.24 for a 70-pound package sent to zone 7.

6. *Express mail.* Overnight delivery service for packages up to 70 pounds and 108 inches (length and width) in size. First 8 ounces cost $8.75; 8 ounces–2 pounds, $12.00; 2–5 pounds, $15.25; 5–70 pounds, consult postal service.

Source: John Wright, ed., *The Universal Almanac, 1991* (New York, 1990), 120; Bureau of Census, *Statistical Abstract, 1992*, 549.

TABLE 6.1   FIRST CLASS MAIL RATES, 1946–1990

Date of Rate Change	Each oz	First oz	Each Added oz	Post Card	Express Mail[a]
1946[b]	$.03	. . .	. . .	$.01	. . .
1952	$.03	. . .	. . .	$.02	. . .
1958	$.04	. . .	. . .	$.03	. . .
1963	$.05	. . .	. . .	$.04	. . .
1968	$.06	. . .	. . .	$.05	
1971	$.08	. . .	. . .	$.06	. . .
1974	$.10	. . .	. . .	$.08	. . .
1975 (Sep)	. . .	$.10	$.09	$.07	. . .
1975 (Dec)[c]	. . .	$.13	$.11	$.09	. . .
1978	. . .	$.15	$.13	$.10	. . .
1981 (Mar)	. . .	$.18	$.17	$.12	. . .
1981 (Nov)	. . .	$.20	$.17	$.13	$9.35
1985	. . .	$.22	$.17	$.14	$10.75
1988	. . .	$.25	$.20	$.15	$12.00[d]

[a] For weight up to 2 pounds, all zones.
[b] Rate established in 1932, still in force in 1946.
[c] In 1975, surface first class mail was upgraded to airmail.
[d] Over 8 ounces and up to 2 pounds.
Source: Bureau of the Census, *Statistical Abstract of the United States, 1993* (Washington, D.C., 1993), 560.

TABLE 6.2   OPERATIONS OF THE POSTAL SERVICE, 1946–1990

(in thousands, except for post offices)

Year	Post Offices	Pieces of Mail All Kinds	Employees	Revenues	Expenditures	Surplus or Deficit
1946	41,751	36,318,158	487	$1,224,572	$1,353,654	$ −148,083
1950	41,464	45,063,737	501	1,677,487	2,222,949	−545,462
1955	38,316	55,233,564	512	2,349,477	2,721,150	−362,673
1960	35,238	63,674,604	563	3,276,588	3,873,953	−634,534
1965	33,624	71,873,166	596	4,483,390	5,275,840	−792,450
1970	32,002	84,881,833	741	7,701,695	7,867,269	−165,574
1975	30,754	89,300,000	702	11,590,000	12,578,000	−988,000
1980	30,326	106,300,000	667	19,106,000	19,412,000	−312,000
1984	29,750	131,500,000	702	26,474,000	26,357,000	+117,000
1986	29,344	147,400,000	785	31,021,000	30,716,000	+305,000
1988	29,203	161,000,000	824	35,939,000	36,119,000	−140,000
1990	28,959	166,300,000	809	40,074,000	40,490,000	−416,000

Source: Ben J. Wattenberg, ed., *The Statistical History of the United States* (New York, 1976), 804, 806; Bureau of the Census, *Statistical Abstract of the United States, 1992* (Washington, D.C., 1992), 549–51.

TABLE 6.3   POSTAL TRAFFIC, BY CLASS OF MAIL, 1946–1990

(in millions of pieces)

Year	Airmail and First Class[a]	Second Class	Third Class	Fourth Class	Priority Mail	Franked and Free for Blind
1946	20,059	5,932	6,055	944	. . .	
1950	24,500	6,265	10,343	1,179	. . .	34
1955	28,713	6,740	15,050	1,136	. . .	51
1960	33,235	7,535	17,910	1,016	. . .	114
1965	38,068	8,600	19,454	1,045	. . .	129
1970	50,174	9,914	19,974	977	185	218
1975	52,482	9,713	21,867	801	207	336
1980	60,332	10,221	30,381	633	248	540
1985	72,517	10,380	52,170	576	308	710
1990	89,917	10,680	63,725	663	518	574

[a] Starting in 1980, includes express mail, established as a class in October 1977, and mailgrams.
Source: Wattenberg, *Statistical History of the U.S.*, 806; Bureau of Census, *Statistical Abstract, 1992*, 550.

TABLE 6.4 DOMESTIC AIRMAIL RATES, 1946–1975

(includes Alaska, Hawaii, Puerto Rico, all outlying areas except the Canal Zone)

Effective Date	Rate
1946	$.05 per oz
1949	$.06 per oz, $.04 per postcard
1958	$.07 per oz, $.05 per postcard
1963	$.08 per oz, $.06 per postcard
1968	$.10 per oz, $.08 per postcard
1971	$.11 per oz, $.09 per postcard
1974	$.13 per oz, $.11 per postcard
1975[a]	$.13 per oz, $.11 per postcard

[a] Beginning on October 11, 1975, domestic airmail merged with first class mail.
Source: Wattenberg, *Statistical History of the U.S.,* 807; Bureau of the Census, *Statistical Abstract of the United States, 1976* (Washington, D.C., 1976), 531.

TABLE 6.5 INTERNATIONAL AIR MAIL RATES FROM THE UNITED STATES, 1961–1990

(excludes Canada and Mexico)

Date of Rate Change	Zone 1[a]		Zone 1[b]		Zone 1[c]		Postal and Postcards	Aerograms
	Each 1/2 oz up to 2 oz	Each Added 1/2 oz	Each 1/2 oz up to 2 oz	Each Added 1/2 oz	Each 1/2 oz up to 2 oz	Each Added 1/2 oz		
1961 (July 1)	$0.13	$0.13	$0.15	$0.15	$0.25	$0.25	$0.11	$0.11
1967 (May 1)	$0.15	$0.15	$0.20	$0.20	$0.25	$0.25	$0.13	$0.13
1971 (July 1)	$0.17	$0.17	$0.21	$0.21	$0.21	$0.21	$0.13	$0.13
1974 (March 2)	$0.21	$0.17	$0.26	$0.21	$0.26	$0.21	$0.18	$0.18
1976 (January 3)	$0.25	$0.21	$0.31	$0.26	$0.31	$0.26	$0.21	$0.22
1981 (January 1)	$0.35	$0.30	$0.40	$0.35	$0.40	$0.35	$0.28	$0.30
1985 (February 17)	$0.39	$0.33	$0.44	$0.39	$0.44	$0.39	$0.33	$0.36
1988 (April 17)[d]	$0.45	$0.42	$0.45	$0.42	$0.45	$0.42	$0.36	$0.39
1989 (August)	$0.45	$0.42	$0.45	$0.42	$0.45	$0.42	$0.36	$0.39

[a] Caribbean, Central and South America.
[b] Europe and Mediterranean Africa.
[c] Rest of the world.
[d] Air letters collapsed to a single schedule except Canada and Mexico.
Source: Bureau of the Census, *Statistical Abstract of the United States, 1991* (Washington, D.C., 1991), 555.

TABLE 6.6 SOURCES OF POSTAL REVENUE, 1950–1990

(in millions of dollars)

Year	Operating Postal Revenue	Stamps, Cards, Etc.	2nd Class Cash Postage	Permit, Meter Postage	Box Rents	Misc.	Money Order Revenue	Gov't Approp.	% of Rev.
1950	1,606	862	40	678	14	11	63	. . .	. . .
1955	2,266	999	64	1,136	26	41	66	. . .	. . .
1960	3,198	1,245	86	1,699	29	130	81	634	. . .
1965	4,374	1,528	131	2,529	34	152	59	793	. . .
1970	6,290	1,936	192	3,883	44	235	57	1,509	. . .
1975	10,015	2,819	284	6,241	67	556	53	1,533	13.2
1980	17,143	4,287	881	10,828	160	892	95	1,610	8.4
1985	27,736	6,520	1,339	17,747	230	1,774	126	970	3.3
1987	31,528	7,246	1,326	20,280	273	2,255	148	650	2.0
1989	37,979	8,381	1,594	24,534	362	2,959	148	436	1.1
1990	39,201	8,638	1,580	25,311	394	3,124	154	453	1.1

Source: Bureau of Census, *Statistical Abstract, 1971,* 479; Bureau of Census, *Statistical Abstract, 1992,* 549.

Telephones

The telephone system underwent major change during the last half of the 20th century in three categories: new technology, restructuring of the entire system in the 1980s, and blending of the reorganized and fragmented telephone service with other means of communication.

At the start of the period standard telephone service involved use of the black, rotary-dialed telephone in major cities; other places had desk phones that required operator assistance in placing calls, and in the countryside one still could find the older box fastened on the wall, with speaker protruding, a listening device hanging from a cord, and a ringer crank on the side. In all cases long distance calls had to be completed by an operator. Aided by such developments as the communication satellite and efficient fiber-optic transmission, standard service by the end of the 1980s had advanced to direct dialing anywhere in the world; reception in a call from London to the United States was as clear as if it were from the next room; there were telephones that one could carry around—cordless phones at home and cellphones when leaving the premises; also available were answering services, voice-mail, conference calls, and even telephones that showed a picture of the caller.

At the start, telephone service remained in the hands of American Telephone and Telegraph Company (AT&T), also known as Bell Telephone. Virtually no one doubted that Bell possessed a monopoly, but because the Federal Communications Commission provided continuous supervision and regulation of the industry, and because the system generally worked, there were few complaints on philosophical grounds, other than from potential competitors, notably the MCI Corporation, which also wanted to supply long-distance service. In 1974—during the Richard Nixon administration—the Department of Justice filed an antitrust suit against AT&T, charging the firm with monopolistic practices. After a long legal struggle, the two sides reached an agreement in 1982 that went into effect in 1984. AT&T was allowed to keep its manufacturing element, Western Electric, its research element, Bell Laboratories, its retail sales, international operations, and long-distance services, although other companies could enter competition for the long-distance business. The penalty was called divestiture: AT&T had to divest itself of 22 companies that provided local telephone service throughout the nation. In the realm of local service, Ma Bell was broken up. Telephone service generally continued as in the past, but some changes soon could be detected. Customers of local service now had to deal with one of seven independent regional companies instead of AT&T. Competition with Bell telephone came to long-distance service. Perhaps the most significant effect of the change came in the seemingly constant pestering from competing long-distance firms to induce customers to switch their service.

Developments in Telephone Communication, 1946–1990

1947 The cellular telephone is developed by Bell Laboratories.

1950 The soon-to-be familiar black, rotary-dial desk telephone is introduced.

1951 Direct-dial long-distance service starts in the United States (as opposed to operator-assisted calls).

1956 The first transatlantic telephone cable is completed—between Britain and Canada and the United States.

1960 *Echo I,* the first communication satellite, is launched by NASA.

1962 Telstar, the first active communications satellite, is launched by AT&T.

1963 The first touch-tone, press-button telephone service becomes available in Pennsylvania.

1965 *Early Bird,* the first commercial communications satellite, is put in orbit.

1967 Regular transatlantic direct-dial telephone service begins between New York and London and New York and Paris.

1968 An emergency telephone system using the prefix 911 is inaugurated in Haleyville, Alabama, and New York City. Many other cities soon follow.

A court rules that people can buy their own telephone equipment—instead of being required to rent from the service supplier, probably AT&T.

1970 The first picturephone service opens in Pittsburgh.

1977 A new fiber-optic communication system is tested in Chicago.

1982 The court orders breakup of the AT&T telephone monopoly. Reorganization, complete by 1984, allows AT&T. to retain long-distance service and certain facilities but requires relinquishment of local and regional service.

1983 Motorists in Chicago are the first to use cellular phones on a regular basis. The cost: $3,000 for the phone; $150 per month for service.

1985 In a Bell Laboratories test, a single optical fiber was able to carry some 300,000 conversations at the same time.

1987 AT&T completes computerized "digitalization" of long-distance service, making transmission more efficient.

Source: The New York Public Library Desk Reference, (New York, 1993), 381–87; Thomas Streissguth, *Communications: Sending the Message* (Minneapolis, 1997), 130; Bruce Wetterau, *The New York Public Library Book of Chronologies* (New York, 1990), 215.

TABLE 6.7 **AMERICAN TELEPHONE SERVICE BEFORE DIVESTITURE OF AMERICAN TELEPHONE AND TELEGRAPH (BELL TELEPHONE), 1945–1980**

Year	Number of Telephones	Households with Telephones (in percent)	Portion Controlled by Bell (in percent)		
			Telephones	Local Calls	Long Distance Calls
1945	27,867,000	46.2	83.3	83.4	98.0
1950	43,004,000	61.8	84.8	84.5	98.6
1955	54,525,000	71.8	85.4	81.5	83.8
1960	74,342,000	78.3	84.7	78.8	83.5
1965	93,656,000	84.6	84.0	77.9	82.4
1970	120,218,000	90.5	83.1	77.7	84.0
1975	148,600,000	93.0	81.9	77.0	79.0
1980	180,200,000	96.0	80.7	75.0	79.0

Source: Leonard S. Hyman, Richard C. Toole, and Rosemary M. Avellis, *The New Telecommunications Industry: Evolution and Organization* (1987), 103, 108, 136–37, 174–77.

TABLE 6.8 **THE BABY BELLS (REGIONAL BELL OPERATING COMPANIES EMERGING FROM REORGANIZATION OF AT&T IN 1984)**

Company	Local Telephone Service Area	Headquarters
Ameritech	Illinois, Indiana, Michigan, Ohio, Wisconsin	Chicago, Ill.
BellAtlantic	Delaware, Maryland, New Jersey Pennsylvania, Virginia, Washington, D.C., West Virginia	Philadelphia, Pa.
BellSouth	Alabama, Florida, Georgia, Kentucky Louisiana, Mississippi, North Carolina, South Carolina, Tennessee	Atlanta, Ga.
NYNEX	Connecticut, Massachusetts, Maine, New York, New Hampshire, Vermont, Rhode Island	New York, N.Y.
Pacific Telesis Corp.	California, Nevada	San Francisco, Calif.
Southwestern Bell Corp.	Texas, Oklahoma, Missouri, Arkansas, Kansas	San Antonio, Tex.
U.S. WEST	Arizona, Colorado, Idaho, Iowa, Minnesota, Montana, Nebraska, New Mexico, North Dakota, Oregon, South Dakota, Utah, Washington, Wyoming	Englewood, Colo.

Source: Ronald J. Alsop, *The Wall Street Journal Almanac, 1998* (New York, 1997), 489.

TABLE 6.9 COMPETITION FOR LONG-DISTANCE MARKET—MARKET SHARE BY CORPORATION, 1984–1990

(all statistics based on fourth-quarter reports)

Year	AT&T	MCI	Sprint	Worldcom	Others
1984	87.7%	4.9%	3.0%	. . .	4.4%
1985	85.7	6.3	3.2	. . .	4.8
1986	81.5	7.9	5.1	. . .	5.6
1987	78.3	9.0	6.2	. . .	6.5
1988	73.9	11.7	7.2	0.1%	7.1
1989	69.0	13.7	8.9	0.2	8.2
1990	65.5	15.1	9.1	0.3	9.0

Source: Alsop, *Wall Street Journal Almanac, 1998,* 488.

TABLE 6.10 COST OF UNLIMITED LOCAL TELEPHONE SERVICE, 1946–1990

Year	Monthly Charge (in dollars)
1946	$3.84
1948	4.09
1950	4.47
1952	4.83
1954	5.18
1956	5.34
1958	5.44
1960	5.64
1962	5.71
1964	5.76
1966	5.77
1968	5.72
1970	5.87
1972	6.51
1974	7.14
1976	7.77
1978	8.16
1980	8.32
1982	9.73
1984	13.35
1986	16.13
1988	16.59
1990	19.79

Source: Barry Cole, *After the Breakup: Assessing the New Post AT&T Divestiture Era* (New York, 1991), 189.

TABLE 6.11 CELLULAR TELEPHONES, 1984–1990

Year	Systems	Subscribers	Annual Revenue (in dollars)	Average Monthly Bill (in dollars)
1984	32	92,000	178,000,000	. . .
1985	102	340,000	482,000,000	. . .
1986	. . .	682,000	823,000,000	. . .
1987	312	1,230,000	1,152,000,000	96.82
1988	517	2,069,000	1,960,000,000	98.02
1989	584	3,508,000	3,341,000,000	89.30
1990	751	5,283,000	4,549,000,000	80.90

Source: Bureau of Census, *Statistical Abstract, 1993,* 564.

TABLE 6.12 SALES OF SELECTED EQUIPMENT, 1983–1990

(in thousands)

Year	Answering Machines	Fax Machines	Modems[a]
1983	2,200	95.4	770
1984	3,000	115.5	960
1985	4,220	139.5	1,220
1986	6,450	218.5	1,380
1987	8,800	583.8	1,810
1988	11,100	1,260.9	2,020
1989	12,500	1,725.1	2,500
1990	13,500	. . .	. . .

[a] A modem is a device that transmits computer information through phone lines.
Source: Wright, *Universal Almanac, 1991,* 242.

Radio and Television

First there was radio and then came television. Each in its day swept the country as an exciting new medium of entertainment, and each from the time of introduction became an exceptional form of communication of news, information, and exposure to many facets of society and culture. Radio dominated the airwaves from the early 1920s to the mid-to-late 1950s. Television superseded radio as the primary source of entertainment and communications in the 1950s; an exact date is difficult to identify; the reign continued for the rest of the century.

As television assumed the sort of programming schedule once found in its predecessor, radio did not vanish but shifted its focus to such areas as music, sporting events, news, and public affairs. No longer burdened with a rigid and costly schedule, perhaps from a national network, radio could be more flexible and concerned with public concerns. No longer a central, even elegant piece of furniture in the living room, the radio still was around the house somewhere. At some point, probably in the 1960s, radio ceased being optional equipment on automobiles. Every new car had one. Well suited to remaining in the background, undemanding of its client's full attention, radio was alive and well in the 1990s.

In the beginning television functioned as an agent of communication in much the same fashion as radio had done. Entertainment was communication of sorts and now it had a visual effect. Movement to a new era of information in television corresponded with the technological and structural changes that began to appear in the 1960s and 1970s. Needless to say, the operation of a communication satellite became a turning point, which—among other changes—led to rapid growth in the number of cable systems. In creating an opportunity for a proliferation of channels and networks, cable also encouraged specialization in programming and/or in the targeted audience. Information could supersede entertainment in such circumstances, although there probably was some attempt to promote a blending of the two. A public affairs network (C-SPAN) began operation in 1979, an around-the-clock national weather channel in 1982. Ted Turner's Cable News Network (CNN), which went on cable in 1980, soon became a source for international news, and it attracted an international audience. In a broadening crisis in the Persian Gulf between Iraq and an American-led coalition in 1990, both sides received information from CNN. Among devices for the dissemination of information in 1990, nothing surpassed television.

New form of communication and politics. A family watches the presidential debate between John F. Kennedy and Richard M. Nixon, September 26, 1960. (National Archives)

TABLE 6.13   U.S. RADIO STATIONS , 1946–1990

Year	Radio Stations on Air
1946	961
1950	2,773
1955	3,211
1960	4,133
1965	5,249
1970	6,760
1975	7,744
1980	8,566
1981	9,361
1982	9,461
1983	9,678
1984	10,021
1985	10,359
1986	9,824
1987	10,074
1988	10,244
1989	10,674
1990	10,819

Source: Wright, *Universal Almanac, 1995,* 234.

TABLE 6.14 RADIO SALES BY CATEGORY, 1954–1990

(in thousands)

Year	Table	Clock	Portable	Sub-Total	Auto	Total
1954	2,759	1,922	1,438	6,119	4,124	10,243
1955	3,002	2,243	2,082	7,327	6,863	14,190
1956	3,360	2,475	3,116	8,951	5,057	14,008
1957	3,360	2,612	3,980	9,952	5,496	15,448
1958	3,230	2,462	5,105	10,797	3,715	14,512
1959	4,156	3,733	7,883	15,772	5,501	21,273
1960	4,511	3,780	9,740	18,031	6,432	24,463
1961	5,012	3,991	14,651	23,654	5,568	29,222
1962	4,333	4,488	15,960	24,781	7,249	32,030
1963	3,640	4,300	15,662	23,602	7,946	31,548
1964	3,820	4,253	15,485	23,558	8,313	31,871
1965	4,370	5,448	21,871	31,689	10,037	41,726
1966	6,229	5,141	23,409	34,779	9,394	44,173
1967	4,116	5,362	22,206	31,684	9,527	41,211
1968	6,383	5,376	22,563	34,322	12,510	46,832
1969	4,681	7,801	26,932	39,414	11,939	51,353
1970	5,714	4,874	23,461	34,049	10,378	44,427
1971	4,760	6,460	22,885	34,105	13,505	47,610
1972	4,926	7,474	29,749	42,149	13,162	55,311
1973	3,023	10,425	24,204	37,652	12,546	50,198
1974	2,764	9,174	21,292	33,230	10,762	43,992
1975	2,253	6,641	16,382	25,276	9,239	34,515
1976	2,876	7,353	21,427	31,656	12,445	44,101
1977	1,990	11,447	26,599	40,036	12,890	52,926
1978	1,805	11,488	22,074	35,367	12,668	48,035
1979	1,250	9,354	17,044	27,648	12,381	40,029
1980	896	9,932	17,234	28,062	11,470	39,532
1981	1,005	9,087	19,323	29,415	12,883	42,298
1982	808	8,210	23,645	32,663	12,306	44,969
1983	930	12,443	26,123	39,496	12,081	51,577
1984	1,354	16,316	28,783	46,453	15,630	62,083
1985	677	9,968	10,929	21,574	15,497	37,071
1986	337	11,330	13,696	25,363	15,783	41,146
1987	149	13,716	14,245	28,110	12,826	40,936
1988	170	12,425	11,028	23,623	13,808	37,431
1989	419	15,387	9,447	25,253	11,394	36,647
1990	357	11,497	9,731	21,585	12,251	33,836

Source: Warren Publishing, Inc., *Television & Cable Factbook, 1995* (New York, 1995), 1–18.

TABLE 6.15 TELEVISION STATIONS ON THE AIR, 1946–1990

Year	Stations	Year	Stations
1946	6	1970	862
1948	16	1972	906
1950	98	1974	938
1952	108	1976	960
1954	356	1978	982
1956	459	1980	1,011
1958	523	1982	1,065
1960	559	1984	1,138
1962	603	1986	1,235
1964	649	1988	1,362
1966	699	1990	1,442
1968	785	. . .	. . .

Source: *Television & Cable Factbook, 1995,* iv.

TABLE 6.16 HOUSEHOLDS WITH TELEVISION, 1950–1990

Year	Percent
1950	12
1955	67
1960	88
1965	92
1970	95
1975	97
1980	98
1985	98
1990	98

Source: Bureau of Census, *Statistical Abstract, 1971,* 487; *Statistical Abstract, 1992,* 551.

TABLE 6.17 TELEVISION SALES, 1959–1990

(in thousands)

Year	Total Sales	Color Sets
1959	6,368	90
1960	5,829	120
1962	7,134	438
1964	9,764	1,404
1966	12,714	5,012
1968	13,211	6,215
1970	12,220	5,320
1972	17,084	8,845
1974	15,279	8,411
1976	14,131	8,194
1978	17,407	10,674
1980	18,532	11,803
1982	16,406	11,484
1984	20,992	16,083
1986	22,163	18,204
1988	22,796	20,216
1990	21,795	20,384

Source: Television & Cable Factbook, 1995, 1–7.

TABLE 6.18 BASIC CABLE TV SYSTEMS AND SUBSCRIBERS, 1952–1990

Year	Number of Systems[a]	Subscribers ('000s)	Percent of U.S. Households with TV
1952	70	14	0.1%
1955	400	150	0.5
1960	640	650	1.4
1965	1,325	1,300	2.3
1970	2,490	3,900	6.7
1975	3,506	8,600	12.6
1980	4,225	15,200	19.9
1981	4,375	17,830	22.3
1982	4,825	24,290	29.8
1983	5,600	28,320	34.0
1984	6,200	32,930	39.3
1985	6,600	36,340	42.8
1986	7,500	39,160	45.6
1987	7,900	41,690	47.7
1988	8,500	43,790	49.4
1989	9,050	47,770	52.8
1990	9,575	51,900	56.4

[a] As of January 1.
Source: Wright, Universal Almanac, 1991, 241; Television and Cable Factbook, 1995, iv.

TABLE 6.19 VIDEOCASSETTE RECORDERS IN USE, 1975–1990

(in thousands)

Year	Households with VCR	Percent of Households with TV
1975	30	. . .
1978	200	0.3
1980	840	1.1
1982	2,530	3.1
1984	8,880	10.6
1986	30,290	36.0
1988	51,390	58.0
1990	76,000	71.9

Source: Wright, Universal Almanac, 1991, 242; Bureau of Census, Statistical Abstract, 1992, 551.

TABLE 6.20 TOP 10 CABLE NETWORKS, 1988

Rank	Network	Subscribers ('000s)	Number of Systems	Launch Date	Content
1.	Entertainment and Sports Programming Network (ESPN)	54,000	21,500	1979	Sports events, business news
2.	Cable News Network (CNN)	52,700	8,970	1980	24-hour news, special-interest reports
3.	Superstation TBS	51,000	12,930	1976	Movies, sports, original and syndicated shows
4.	USA Network	49,800	10,100	1980	Sports, family entertainment
5.	Nickelodeon/Nick at Nite	48,900	7,310	1979	Children's programming, young adults
6.	Music Television (MTV)	48,600	5,845	1981	Music videos, concerts, interviews
7.	The Nashville Network (TNN)	47,800	8,605	1983	Country music, talk shows, sports
8.	Cable Satellite Public Affairs Network (C-SPAN)	46,800	3,485	1979	Public affairs
9.	The Family Channel	46,800	8,600	1977	Movies, family entertainment, religious shows
10.	The Discovery Channel	46,100	6,500	1985	Nonfiction, nature, science, etc.

Source: Wright, Universal Almanac, 1991, 241.

TABLE 6.21   THE ELECTRONIC HOME, 1990

Percent of U.S. Homes	Facilities
99%	Have a radio
98	Have a TV set
96	Have a color TV set
92	Have an audio system
68	Have a VCR
64	Have two or more TV sets
55	Buy basic cable
52	Own prerecorded videocassettes
31	Have a telephone answering device
29	Buy one or more pay channels
25	Have a cordless telephone
23	Have a home computer
19	Have color TV with MTS
19	Have a compact disc player
13	Have a home alarm system
10	Have a camcorder
6	Have projection TV
3.5	Have LCD TV
3	Have satellite dishes

Source: Wright, *Universal Almanac, 1991*, 241.

A soldier "writes" home in the electronic age. War-weary President Johnson listens to a tape from his son-in-law, Capt. Charles Robb, from Vietnam. (LBJ Library photo by Jack Kightlinger)

The Next Generation: Enter the Internet

One would be hard-pressed to determine which electronic development in postwar communication was the most miraculous or most far-reaching. For several years it certainly seemed to be television, and then with more new technology and gradual awakening to its potentialities, the computer came to occupy center stage. At the start of the 1990s a rapidly growing group of converts was swearing that the future of communication belonged to the Internet. An extension of computer technology, the Internet consisted of a national and international network of interconnected computer systems. The Internet transmitted vast storehouses of information in possession of participating bodies that could become available—"accessed," in computer language—in an instant. The Internet also used a process to send what was called e-mail (electronic mail) through which messages could be transmitted over the same network of computer systems—to another state, another country, to another room in the same building, in a matter of seconds, and a reply could be had almost as fast.

The Internet grew out of the cold war, when, beginning in 1969 the Department of Defense set up a system called ARPAnet through which researchers at various sites could communicate with one another. Starting with four university locations, the number grew to some 200 in 1974. In the 1980s more and more computer systems came aboard. The National Science Foundation established its own network and invited everyone to join. It was not possible to determine the number of participating systems at the end of the 1980s or the

TABLE 6.22   U.S. UNIT SALES OF AND REVENUES FROM MICRO-, MINI- AND MAINFRAME COMPUTERS, 1960–1990

(in thousands)

Year	Microcomputers Units	Microcomputers Revenues (in dollars)	Minicomputers Units	Minicomputers Revenues (in dollars)	Mainframes Units	Mainframes Revenues (in dollars)
1960	. . .	. . .	. . .	. . .	1.79	590.0
1965	. . .	. . .	0.60	66.0	5.35	1,770.0
1970	. . .	. . .	6.06	485.0	5.70	3,600.0
1975	10.5	20.0	26.99	1,484.0	6.70	5,410.0
1980	796.0	1,550.0	95.87	5,752.0	9.90	8,840.0
1981	1,157.0	2,550.0	101.99	6,242.0	10.70	9,640.0
1982	1,950.0	4,390.0	108.50	6,410.0	10.60	10,300.0
1983	3,249.0	7,470.0	116.80	6,830.0	9.98	10,480.0
1984	5,190.0	11,940.0	170.40	9,887.0	11.33	11,890.0
1985	4,750.0	11,260.0	153.80	8,901.0	10.91	11,850.0
1986	5,060.0	11,740.0	143.70	8,148.0	10.99	12,090.0
1987	5,460.0	12,830.0	145.80	8,291.0	11.20	12,340.0
1988	5,990.0	14,380.0	160.00	9,040.0	11.24	12,550.0
1989	6,649.0	15,600.0	165.00	9,340.0	11.52	12,790.0
1990	6,915.0	16,600.0	157.30	8,856.0	11.64	12,860.0

Source: Wright, *Universal Almanac, 1991*, 527.

TABLE 6.23   E-MAIL COMMUNICATIONS, 1980–1990

(in millions of messages)

Year	Number of Messages
1980	.43
1981	.47
1982	.54
1983	.67
1984	1.0
1985	1.67
1986	4.1
1987	5.25
1988	6.96
1989	8.6
1990	12.43

Source: Bernard Johnston, ed., *Collier's Encyclopedia, 1995 Edition* (Vol. 21, New York, 1995), 116.

number of users (1 million might be a reasonable guess), but the number was growing in leaps and bounds. There was no World Wide Web in 1990; it was not yet an information superhighway, but the Internet was an explosion about to take place.

The Print Media

The print media continued to be an important aspect of the system of communication and dispersion of information. Newspapers and magazines retained a vital if ever-narrowing niche in reporting of news; books, publication of which had proliferated markedly in the 40 years after 1950, remained popular entertainment, the standard avenue of in-depth inquiry and most extensive depository of information of all sorts.

Faced with competition first from radio, then television and other electronic media in the 1980s, newspapers struggled to hold their own. The number declined slowly but steadily; a modest increase in circulation of the dailies did not nearly keep pace with growth in population or in television and other electronic forms of communication. Quality journalism continued to exist, and newspapers left their mark on national and local developments—the high point perhaps being reached during 1972–74, in the involvement of the Washington Post in exposure of the Watergate scandal and ultimately bringing down a president. But several newspapers either ceased publication or merged with a local competitor. Cities without multiple newspapers—and different points of view—became the standard. By 1990

fewer than 40 cities had more than a single daily paper. In 1982 the Gannett Company founded USA Today, an openly national daily (except for weekends) that used color and graphics and featured short stories and much popular culture. Although charged with lowering journalistic standards, USA Today soon became one of the two or three most popular newspapers in the country and established practices that competitors would find it difficult to avoid imitating. Many of the publications that survived belonged to one of such newspaper chains as Gannett, Hearst, Knight-Ridder, or Scripps-Howard—thus diminishing, if not destroying, their independence. By 1990 some 82 percent of dailies were chain-owned.

The American magazine market showed a great deal of fluidity over the years. Influenced by themes and moods of the time, new publications were born, others declined or ceased publication; a few showed remarkable durability. In the surveys listed below, the most stable periodicals included *Reader's Digest, National Geographic,* and *Better Homes and Gardens.* Such male-oriented publications as *Playboy* and *Penthouse,* daring and risque at the time of their introduction, showed a considerable reduction in popularity between the 1970s and 1990. Some traditional standards, such as *The Saturday Evening Post* and *Collier's,* dropped from the lists entirely. It also was noteworthy that the survey of 1953 classified "comic books," the cartoon-formated but increasingly violent and sexually oriented miniature tabloids, as magazines. Rapidly growing in popularity, they also sparked a great deal of controversy. New on the market in the 1950s, pathbreaking *Mad* magazine fit the physical characteristics of the comic book, but its thrust was social and political satire.

TABLE 6.24   NUMBER AND CIRCULATION OF DAILY AND SUNDAY NEWSPAPERS, 1946–1990
(circulation in thousands)

| | Total | | Daily | | | | Sunday | |
| | | | Morning | | Evening | | | |
Year	Number	Circ.	Number	Circ.	Number	Circ.	Number	Circ.
1946	1,763	50.928	334	20,546	1,429	30,382	497	43,665
1950	1,772	53,829	322	21,266	1,450	32,563	549	46,582
1955	1,760	56,147	316	22,183	1,454	33,964	541	46,448
1960	1,763	58,882	312	24,029	1,459	34,853	563	47,699
1965	1,751	60,358	320	24,107	1,444	36,251	562	48,600
1970	1,748	62,108	334	25,934	1,429	36,174	586	49,217
1975	1,756	60,700	339	25,500	1.436	35,200	639	51,100
1980	1,745	62,200	387	29,400	1,388	32,800	736	54,700
1985	1,676	62,800	482	36,400	1,220	26,400	798	58,800
1990	1,611	62,300	559	41,300	1,084	21,000	863	62,600

Source: Bureau of Census, *Statistical Abstract, 1971,* 490; Bureau of Census, *Statistical Abstract, 1992,* 557.

TABLE 6.25   NEWSPAPERS AND PERIODICALS, 1946–1990

Year	1946	1950	1955	1960	1970	1975	1980	1985	1990
Newspapers									
Total	12,804	12,115	11,415	11,315	11,383	11,400	9,620	9,134	11,471
Semiweekly	286	337	324	324	357	506	537	517	579
Weekly	10,424	9,794	9,126	8,979	8,903	8,824	7,159	6,811	8,420
Daily	2,020	1,894	1,860	1,854	1,838	1,819	1,744	1,701	1,788
Periodicals									
Total	6,693	6,960	7,648	8,422	9,573	9,657	10,236	11,090	11,092
Weekly	1,331	1,443	1,602	1,580	1,856	1,918	1,716	1,367	553
Semimonthly	253	416	503	527	589	537	645	801	435
Monthly	3,595	3,694	3,782	4,113	4,314	4,087	3,985	4,088	4,239
Bimonthly	345	436	608	743	957	1,009	1,114	1,361	2,087
Quarterly	595	604	674	895	1,108	1,093	1,444	1,759	2,758

Source: Bureau of the Census, *Statistical Abstract, 1971,* 491; Bureau of the Census, *Statistical Abstract, 1992,* 557.

TABLE 6.26 LARGEST DAILY NEWSPAPERS, 1974[a]

Newspaper	Circulation
New York (N.Y.) Daily News	2,028,522
Los Angeles (Calif.) Times	1,005,442
New York (N.Y.) Times	843,267
Detroit (Mich.) News	663,249
Chicago (Ill.) Tribune	660,826
Detroit (Mich.) Free Press	627,826
New York (N.Y.) Post	598,512
Philadelphia (Pa.) Bulletin	585,158
Chicago (Ill.) Sun-Times	550,893
Washington (D.C.) Post	521,114
Boston (Mass.) Globe	486,361
San Francisco (Calif.) Chronicle	465,012
Long Island (N.Y.) Newsday	452,586
Philadelphia (Pa.) Inquirer	427,251
Los Angeles (Calif.) Herald-Examiner	418,803
Cleveland (Ohio) Plain Dealer	408,377
Chicago (Ill.) Daily-News	402,004
Washington (D.C.) Star	379,599
Miami (Fla.) Herald	376,856
Baltimore (Md.) Sun	373,655
Cleveland (Ohio) Press	364,961
Newark (N.J.) Star-Ledger	361,006
Boston (Mass.) Herald-American	346,101
Milwaukee (Wis.) Journal	343,557
Long Island (N.Y.) Press	324,187
Kansas City (Mo.) Times	317,519
Houston (Tex.) Chronicle	299,921
Houston (Tex.) Post	296,292
Kansas City (Mo.) Star	296,256
St. Louis (Mo.) Post-Dispatch	289,009
Buffalo (N.Y.) News	277,812
Pittsburgh (Pa.) Press	273,669
St. Louis (Mo.) Globe-Democrat	271,815
Dallas (Tex.) News	264,750
Minneapolis (Minn.) Star	252,294
Denver (Colo.) Post	248,885
Philadelphia (Pa.) Daily News	247,720
Atlanta (Ga.) Journal	244,189
Des Moines (Ia.) Register	241,403
Dallas (Tex.) Times Herald	241,191
Portland (Ore.) Oregonian	238,414
Seattle (Wash.) Times	232,726
Minneapolis (Minn.) Tribune	228,291
Indianapolis (Ind.) Star	224,630
Louisville (Ky.) Courier-Journal	223,834
Fort Worth (Tex.) Star-Telegram	222,980

[a] Does not include *Wall Street Journal*, circulation 1,637,430.

Source: Laurence Urdang, ed., *The CBS News Almanac, 1976* (Maplewood, N.J., 1975), 767.

TABLE 6.27 TOP 100 DAILY NEWSPAPERS IN THE UNITED STATES, 1989

Rank	Newspaper	Average Daily Paid Circulation
1.	*Wall Street Journal*	1,835,713
2.	*USA Today*	1,325,507
3.	*New York Daily News*	1,194,237
4.	*Los Angeles Times*	1,107,623
5.	*New York Times*	1,068,217
6.	*Washington Post*	772,749
7.	*Chicago Tribune*	720,155
8.	*Long Island Newsday*	700,174
9.	*Detroit News*	690,422
10.	*Detroit Free Press*	626,434
11.	*San Francisco Chronicle*	560,640
12.	*Chicago Sun-Times*	535,864
13.	*Boston Globe*	516,031
14.	*New York Post*	507,568
15.	*Philadelphia Inquirer*	504,903
16.	*Newark Star-Ledger*	463,738
17.	*Houston Chronicle*	437,481
18.	*Cleveland Plain Dealer*	433,615
19.	*Miami Herald*	427,954
20.	*Minneapolis Star Tribune*	406,292
21.	*St. Louis Post-Dispatch*	376,888
22.	*Dallas Morning News*	371,537
23.	*Boston Herald*	358,218
24.	*St. Petersburg Times*	349,460
25.	*Denver Rocky Mountain News*	345,943
26.	*Orange County-Santa Ana Register*	343,899
27.	*Houston Post*	325,407
28.	*Phoenix Arizona Republic*	322,534
29.	*Buffalo News*	312,246
30.	*Portland Oregonian*	310,446
31.	*Atlanta Constitution*	284,015
32.	*New Orleans Times-Picayune*	276,195
33.	*Kansas City Times*	275,844
34.	*Milwaukee Journal*	275,632
35.	*San Jose Mercury News*	274,484
36.	*Tampa Tribune*	268,681
37.	*San Diego Union*	268,450
38.	*Orlando Sentinel*	266,549
39.	*Sacramento Bee*	259,497
40.	*Columbus Dispatch*	252,206
41.	*Denver Post*	240,162
42.	*Baltimore Sun*	238,533
43.	*Charlotte Observer*	236,496
44.	*Indianapolis Star*	234,888
45.	*Seattle Times*	233,106
46.	*Pittsburgh Press*	232,282
47.	*Philadelphia Daily News*	232,129
48.	*Louisville Courier-Journal*	231,042
49.	*Hartford Courant*	227,763
50.	*Dallas Times Herald*	225,691
51.	*Fort Lauderdale Sun-Sentinel*	224,208
52.	*Oklahoma City Daily Oklahoman*	220,183
53.	*Des Moines Register*	209,765
54.	*Memphis Commercial Appeal*	209,205
55.	*Providence Journal*	204,196
56.	*Seattle Post-Intelligencer*	203,560
57.	*St. Paul Pioneer Press Dispatch*	200,508
58.	*Cincinnati Enquirer*	196,290
59.	*Los Angeles Daily News*	185,736
60.	*Atlanta Journal*	181,440
61.	*San Antonio Express-News*	179,590
62.	*Dayton Daily News*	178,615
63.	*Milwaukee Sentinel*	178,364
64.	*Jacksonville Times-Union*	173,528
65.	*Austin American-Statesman*	172,518
66.	*Kansas City Star*	170,801
67.	*San Antonio Light*	170,800
68.	*Baltimore Evening Sun*	170,750
69.	*Birmingham News*	170,327
70.	*West Palm Beach Post*	169,360
71.	*Pittsburgh Post-Gazette*	164,309
72.	*Hackensack Record*	156,019
73.	*Toledo Blade*	155,579
74.	*Little Rock Gazette*	154,001
75.	*Akron Beacon Journal*	153,550
76.	*Norfolk Virginian Pilot*	150,958
77.	*Asbury Park Press*	150,590
78.	*Fort Worth Star-Telegram*	150,190
79.	*Riverside Press-Enterprise*	147,424
80.	*Fresno Bee*	146,723
81.	*Grand Rapids Press*	143,101
82.	*Richmond Times-Dispatch*	142,151
83.	*Raleigh News & Observer*	141,800
84.	*Columbia State*	141,742
85.	*San Francisco Examiner*	137,969

(continued)

TABLE 6.27 (continued)

Rank	Newspaper	Average Daily Paid Circulation
86.	*Allentown Morning Call*	137,228
87.	*Christian Science Monitor*	137,161
88.	*Oakland Tribune*	134,504
89.	*Las Vegas Review-Journal*	132,903
90.	*Rochester Democrat and Chronicle*	129,394
91.	*Nashville Tennessean*	126,092
92.	*Tulsa World*	123,510
93.	*Long Beach Press-Telegram*	123,371
94.	*Lexington Herald-Leader*	122,673
95.	*Omaha World-Herald*	121,985
96.	*San Diego Tribune*	121,835
97.	*Worcester Telegram & Gazette*	120,568
98.	*Wilmington News Journal*	120,143
99.	*Wichita Eagle*	119,013
100.	*Tacoma Morning News-Tribune*	118,807

Source: Wright, *Universal Almanac, 1991,* 237.

TABLE 6.28 TOP 100 MAGAZINES RANKED BY CIRCULATION, 1989

Rank	Publication	Total Paid Circulation	Percent Change 1988–89
1.	*Modern Maturity*	20,326,933	13.4%
2.	*NRTA/AARP News Bulletin*	20,001,538	13.5
3.	*Reader's Digest*	16,434,254	−3.1
4.	*TV Guide*	16,330,051	−3.5
5.	*National Geographic*	10,829,328	3.0
6.	*Better Homes & Gardens*	8,027,010	−1.5
7.	*Family Circle*	5,212,555	−11.7
8.	*McCall's*	5,150,814	0.1
9.	*Ladies' Home Journal*	5,117,712	2.1
10.	*Good Housekeeping*	5,114,774	1.7
11.	*Woman's Day*	4,401,746	−14.3
12.	*Time*	4,393,237	−7.3
13.	*Guideposts*	4,239,396	−3.0
14.	*National Enquirer*	4,222,755	−1.9
15.	*Redbook*	3,906,453	−2.5
16.	*Sports Illustrated*	3,771,389	9.7
17.	*Playboy*	3,657,904	7.4
18.	*Star*	3,562,367	−1.7
19.	*People Weekly*	3,346,535	2.1
20.	*Newsweek*	3,288,453	−0.8
21.	*Prevention*	3,161,788	6.3
22.	*The American Legion Magazine*	2,873,927	5.3
23.	*Cosmopolitan*	2,778,497	−7.8
24.	*Smithsonian*	2,324,112	1.9
25.	*Glamour*	2,321,942	9.0
26.	*U.S. News & World Report*	2,303,328	−2.6
27.	*Southern Living*	2,298,099	0.7
28.	*Penthouse*	2,088,445	1.7
29.	*Field & Stream*	2,020,624	−1.0
30.	*Motorland*	1,835,576	2.9
31.	*VFW Magazine*	1,827,861	1.5
32.	*Popular Science*	1,826,156	−0.3
33.	*Country Living*	1,825,191	6.9
34.	*Ebony*	1,819,042	4.2
35.	*Money*	1,816,298	0.3
36.	*Home & Away*	1,775,649	3.3
37.	*NEA Today*	1,757,557	−0.5
38.	*Seventeen*	1,753,064	−2.8
39.	*Life*	1,736,797	−6.9
40.	*Parents Magazine*	1,733,456	−1.0

Rank	Publication	Total Paid Circulation	Percent Change 1988–89
41.	*Popular Mechanics*	1,688,784	4.3
42.	*Discovery*	1,596,646	0.0
43.	*1,001 Home Ideas*	1,559,917	1.4
44.	*Woman's World*	1,529,503	9.1
45.	*Outdoor Life*	1,513,017	0.0
46.	*The Elks Magazine*	1,501,587	−1.4
47.	*The Family Handyman*	1,471,095	19.3
48.	*Boys' Life*	1,439,494	−1.7
49.	*The American Rifleman*	1,419,971	4.0
50.	*The American Hunter*	1,411,156	4.1
51.	*Globe*	1,402,944	−7.5%
52.	*Western Living*	1,398,674	−2.3
53.	*Bon Appetit*	1,349,396	3.2
54.	*Golf Digest*	1,343,536	1.0
55.	*US*	1,342,129	7.0
56.	*New Woman*	1,338,816	−3.9
57.	*The Workbasket*	1,306,275	−18.0
58.	*Vogue*	1,262,158	3.3
59.	*True Story*	1,240,252	−4.8
60.	*Home Mechanix*	1,221,150	0.0
61.	*Sesame Street Magazine*	1,215,811	−7.4
62.	*Soap Opera Digest*	1,206,009	13.8
63.	*Rolling Stone*	1,194,915	0.9
64.	*Self*	1,173,440	−4.2
65.	*Mademoiselle*	1,141,271	1.8
66.	*Travel & Leisure*	1,111,264	0.2
67.	*Changing Times*	1,065,032	−10.7
68.	*Organic Gardening*	1,053,736	1.8
69.	*American Health*	1,048,075	10.1
70.	*Weight Watchers Magazine*	1,037,284	6.4
71.	*Teen*	1,034,756	−14.0
72.	*Michigan Living*	1,028,746	1.5
73.	*Golf Magazine*	1,027,560	9.3
74.	*Discover*	1,027,089	2.0
75.	*National Examiner*	1,025,487	−9.7
76.	*Health*	1,005,453	−1.5
77.	*Yankee*	1,000,962	−0.2
78.	*Sport*	995,985	6.9
79.	*Country Home*	971,571	6.3
80.	*Scouting*	957,675	−2.8
81.	*Home*	942,779	2.7
82.	*Car and Driver*	927,957	−0.7
83.	*Weekly World News*	927,809	−9.2
84.	*Psychology Today*	927,652	−4.1
85.	*Working Woman*	903,704	1.8
86.	*Omni*	902,356	−3.8
87.	*House Beautiful*	902,002	6.1
88.	*Business Week*	900,989	1.0
89.	*YM*	900,351	6.5
90.	*Hot Rod*	897,792	0.7
91.	*Jet*	892,006	5.0
92.	*Workbench*	875,202	−3.1
93.	*Vista USA*	871,008	1.1
94.	*Nation's Business*	857,289	−0.8
95.	*Essence*	850,116	0.0
96.	*Consumers Digest*	844,659	10.8
97.	*Elle*	826,956	0.0
98.	*Food & Wine*	823,763	7.7
99.	*American Legion Aux. National News*	821,696	4.6
100.	*Victoria*	810,353	50.9
	Total	**260,477,673**	**1.6**

Source: Wright, *Universal Almanac, 1991,* 238.

TABLE 6.29 TOP 50 MAGAZINES RANKED BY REVENUES, 1989

Rank	Publication	Revenues	Percent Change 1988–89
1.	Time	$373,385,017	6.8%
2.	Sports Illustrated	336,671,529	4.0
3.	People Weekly	326,203,199	6.8
4.	TV Guide	322,985,623	−3.7
5.	Business Week	260,575,042	14.6
6.	Newsweek	255,918,694	5.9
7.	Fortune	167,284,538	21.7
8.	Forbes	157,696,946	22.5
9.	U.S. News & World Report	152,843,252	19.3
10.	Better Homes & Gardens	152,436,109	−0.2
11.	Family Circle	152,208,684	13.3
12.	Good Housekeeping	148,033,344	14.5
13.	Woman's Day	135,632,500	17.3
14.	Cosmopolitan	125,711,842	9.7
15.	Reader's Digest	113,644,537	−0.3
16.	Ladies' Home Journal	104,742,667	25.0
17.	Vogue	101,001,807	15.4
18.	Glamour	88,833,183	2.1
19.	Money	79,668,320	−0.1
20.	Redbook	75,031,696	9.4
21.	McCall's	74,798,588	19.5
22.	Rolling Stone	71,093,073	14.5
23.	Golf Digest	63,995,011	15.8
24.	Elle	62,648,418	13.0
25.	Southern Living	61,224,697	−0.7
26.	Parents	60,344,516	13.6
27.	Life	56,846,163	16.7
28.	Bride's	55,280,547	26.3
29.	Car and Driver	54,303,468	20.9
30.	The New Yorker	54,033,158	13.0
31.	Travel & Leisure	53,342,754	19.2
32.	Gentlemen's Quarterly	49,899,443	13.2
33.	Mademoiselle	48,697,898	0.1
34.	Modern Maturity	47,455,205	18.8
35.	New York Magazine	47,430,625	7.4
36.	Inc.	46,642,250	10.5
37.	Playboy	46,503,864	14.4
38.	Architectural Digest	46,049,915	9.2
39.	Sunset	44,372,483	−4.2
40.	Smithsonian	43,766,044	5.7
41.	Country Living	42,604,156	14.2
42.	Self	42,326,178	21.8
43.	Vanity Fair	41,616,840	51.1
44.	Field & Stream	39,941,583	8.3
45.	Seventeen	39,590,128	2.4
46.	Modern Bride	38,456,726	24.0
47.	Esquire	38,016,280	21.3
48.	Ebony	38,011,050	0.1
49.	Road & Track	37,654,712	14.3
50.	Town & Country	36,280,310	12.7

Source: Wright, *Universal Almanac, 1991*, 238.

TABLE 6.30 NEW BOOKS AND NEW EDITIONS PUBLISHED, BY SUBJECT, 1950–1990

Year	1950	1960	1970	1975	1980	1985	1988	1990
Total	**11,022**	**15,012**	**36,071**	**39,372**	**42,377**	**50,070**	**55,446**	**46,738**
Agriculture	111	121	200	456	461	536	666	514
Art	317	422	852	1,561	1,691	1,545	1,602	1,262
Biography	538	746	735	1,968	1,891	1,953	2,250	1,957
Business	190	240	658	820	1,185	1,518	1,647	1,191
Education	209	308	842	1,038	1,011	1,085	1,113	1,039
Fiction	1,211	1,642	1,998	3,805	2,835	5,105	5,564	5,764
General	262	233	568	1,113	1,643	2,905	2,475	1,760
History	456	695	1,010	1,823	2,220	2,327	3,260	2,243
Home econ.	150	155	235	728	879	1,228	1,057	758
Juvenile	907	1,628	2,472	2,292	2,659	3,801	4,954	5,172
Language	. . .	. . .	339	438	529	632	628	649
Law	228	303	355	915	1,102	1,349	1,343	896
Literature	510	560	1,349	1,904	1,686	1,964	2,272	2,049
Medicine	312	388	1,144	2,282	3,292	3,579	3,900	3,014
Music	88	82	217	305	357	364	329	289
Philosophy/Psych.	380	496	843	1,374	1,429	1,559	1,955	1,683
Poetry, Drama	453	404	973	1,501	1,179	1,166	1,270	874
Religion	626	983	1,315	1,778	2,055	2,564	2,746	2,285
Science	499	833	1,955	2,942	3,109	3,304	3,743	2,742
Sociology, Econ.	447	651	3,867	6,590	7,152	7,441	8,247	7,042
Sports, rec.	153	233	583	1,225	971	1,154	1,099	973
Technology	366	574	930	1,720	2,337	2,526	2,694	2,092
Travel	221	372	848	794	504	465	669	495

Source: George T. Kurian, *Datapedia of the United States, 1790–2000* (Lanham, Md., 1994), 307–08.

In the Beginning Was the Word

Communication originated with speech. Remarkable growth of the communication media, be it television, airmail, or e-mail, merely improved the means by which the spoken, or written, word could be spread. The standard instrument of communication in many areas of society was the speech or other form of extended public statement. With the objective of identifying the best speeches of the 20th century in mind, two professors of communication arts and sciences proceeded near the end of the century to survey 137 of their colleagues, compile the findings, and analyze the speeches from a perspective of presentation, style, and effect. The results—a ranked list of 100 most important speeches—suggested that significance of the statements were associated with the means by which they could be communicated. The speech ranked highest, for example, Martin Luther King, Jr.'s "I Have A Dream" Speech, was undeniably powerful, but it also benefited from being almost endlessly repeated in print, on radio, or television. Repetition of course was a testimony to impact, but one would wonder if the effect would have been as great had the speech been given in 1910. The list also was surely influenced by the age and orientation of the people participating in the survey. Approximately two-thirds of the speeches came in the years 1946–90; only six were delivered after 1990, the remainder came during 1900–45, six of them from Franklin D. Roosevelt. Listed below are the survey's top 25 speeches of the 20th century.

Best Speeches of the 20th Century: A Survey

1. Martin Luther King, Jr., "I Have a Dream," August 28, 1963. Washington, D.C.
2. John F. Kennedy, Inaugural Address, January 20, 1961, Washington, D.C.
3. Franklin D. Roosevelt, First Inaugural, March 4, 1933, Washington, D.C.
4. Franklin D. Roosevelt, War Message, December 8, 1941, Washington, D.C.
5. Barbara Jordan, Keynote Speech, Democrat National Convention, July 12, 1976, New York City.
6. Richard M. Nixon, "Checkers Speech," (Defending his behavior), September 23, 1952, Los Angeles.
7. Malcolm X, "The Ballot or the Bullet," April 3, 1964, Cleveland.
8. Ronald Reagan, Speech after *Challenger* disaster, January 28, 1986, Washington, D.C.
9. John F. Kennedy, Speech to Houston Ministers, September 12, 1960, Houston.

Martin Luther King, Jr., and other participants in the March on Washington, August 28, 1963 (National Archives)

10. Lyndon B. Johnson, Speech to Congress on Voting Rights Bill, March 15, 1965, Washington, D.C.
11. Mario Cuomo, "A Tale of Two Cities," (Keynote—Democrat Convention, 1984), July 16, 1984, San Francisco.
12. Jesse Jackson, "Rainbow Coalition," (Democrat Convention, 1964), July 17, 1964, San Francisco.
13. Barbara Jordan, On Impeachment of Nixon, July 25, 1974, Washington, D.C.
14. Douglas MacArthur, "Old Soldiers Never Die," (Farewell Speech), April 19, 1951, Washington, D.C.
15. Martin Luther King, Jr., "I've Been to the Mountaintop," April 3, 1968, Memphis.
16. Theodore Roosevelt, "The Man with the Muckrake," April 14, 1906, Washington, D.C.
17. Robert F. Kennedy, Remarks on assassination of Martin Luther King, Jr., April 4, 1968, Indianapolis.
18. Dwight D. Eisenhower, Farewell Address, Jan. 17, 1961, Washington, D.C.
19. Woodrow Wilson, War Message, April 2, 1917, Washington, D.C.
20. Douglas MacArthur, "Duty, Honor, Country," (Farewell to West Point), May 12, 1962, West Point, N.Y.
21. Richard M. Nixon, "Silent Majority," (On Vietnam War), November 3, 1969, Washington, D.C.
22. John F. Kennedy, *"Ich bin ein Berliner,"* June 26, 1963, West Berlin.
23. Clarence Darrow, Summation at Leopold and Loeb trial, July 31, 1924, Chicago.
24. Russell Conwell, "Acres of Diamonds," Delivered many times, many locations, 1900–25.
25. Ronald Reagan, "A Time for Choosing" (For presidential candidacy of Barry Goldwater), October 27, 1964, Los Angeles.

Source: USA Today, December 30, 1999.

CHAPTER 7 Vital Statistics and Health Care

One cannot understand the course of the United States during the years of the cold war without looking in some depth at vital statistics. Population data relates information about size and magnitude, an account of a society undergoing exceptional growth. In somewhat the same fashion, vital statistics measure and describe the dimensions of diversity in the nation. Population numbers identify size of groups, vital statistics tell about behavior: in childbearing and under what terms, for example, about divorce, marriage, and family. Not far beneath the surface were the values and attitudes about lifestyle that guided the statistics. Having fewer children, for example, suggested how people preferred to (or were willing to) live, as did statistics about marriage, differing definitions of families.

If statistics suggest changing values, the values point to emergence of new issues or of a willingness to deal with old ones. Availability of data—or the shortage of it—in itself suggested directions taken by society. Government agencies supplied plentiful and continuous information about the standard social topics—births, deaths, marriage, divorce, and others. But there were few, if any, reliable statistics about abortion before the 1970s and few polls to show how people approached the issue. One encountered few statistics about sexual behavior or contraception before the 1970s (Alfred Kinsey's studies notwithstanding), not because people had no interest in these subjects but because mores of the time identified them as essentially private matters. Neither academicians nor opinion pollsters gave much indication of considering such sensitive matters appropriate for study or public exposure. In preparing his studies about sexual behavior Alfred Kinsey so worried that he might be charged with seeking attention by selecting a racy, titillating topic that he picked an obscure publisher of medical books, filled the pages with tables and scholarly language and produced two volumes that would be considered dull if not for the subject matter. Beginning approximately with the 1970s, with some subjects it came earlier, there was little hesitation to deal with virtually all aspects of human behavior. The statistics suggested that society was changing.

Births

The postwar period began with a bang, or at least a boom. In fact, an increase in the birthrate had begun during the war, but it was the years immediately following the conflict that produced a remarkable demographic turn. The birthrate surged to more than 26 live births per 1,000 population in 1947, the highest since 1921. The year 1954 produced the first yield of 4 million babies. The birthrate remained above 20, and the annual number of births above 4 million, until 1964. Thus the period of the baby boom lasted from 1946 to 1964, and it constituted a genuine demographic bulge—a pig in a python, as the experts put it—of some 75 million new citizens. Sheer size alone preordained that the baby boomers would influence the national direction. But this generation also brought attitudes conditioned by timing and circumstances of its upbringing that would be considerably different from those of its parents, who had come of age in a time of depression and world war. As it passed through stages of life, the baby boom generation produced ripples that were felt in different forms through the rest of the 20th century and, as the boomers reached retirement age, into the new millennium. There was, for example, much doubt that the Social Security System would be able to endure the shock of so many new takers.

Suggestions that one baby boom would beget another, however, did not materialize. By the time the boomers reached the age of reproduction, starting roughly in the late 1960s, social standards had begun to change. The prospect of becoming parents or of remaining married because one was a parent had lost some of its appeal. Divorce became commonplace. Technology had produced new ways to prevent conception; shifts in legal and social attitudes legitimized ending pregnancies already in progress. The baby boom gave way to a "bust," a remarkably rapid decline in the birthrate. By 1976 the rate had dropped to 14.6, lower than the worst years of the Great Depression. A slight upturn in the 1980s (in 1990, 4 million babies were born for the first time since 1965) came only because there were so many people to reproduce. In each of 20 years after 1970 the birthrate was lower than any other year (before 1970) in American history, and as of 1990 there appeared no indication that the trend soon would come to an end.

Shifts within the birthrate were partly responsible for the continuing change in national racial and ethnic structure. African Americans and Hispanics had higher birthrates than the group classified as white. One of the most pronounced demographic themes was the steady increase in illegitimate births in virtually all racial and ethnic groups. Sharpest growth came in the 20 years after 1970. By 1990 nearly 30 percent of all babies were born to unmarried mothers. Whites experienced a slower rate of increase

TABLE 7.1   LIVE BIRTHS BY SEX, SEX RATIO, AND RACE, 1945–1990

Year	White		Black		All Races		Males per 1,000 Females
	Male	Female	Male	Female	Male	Female	
1945	1,232,972	1,162,591	163,721	160,543	1,404,587	1,330,869	1,055
1950	1,575,309	1,488,318	236,082	230,636	1,823,555	1,730,594	1,054
1955	1,776,355	1,682,093	281,846	276,405	2,073,719	1,973,576	1,055
1960	1,848,192	1,752,552	303,566	298,698	2,179,708	2,078,142	1,049
1965	1,604,422	1,519,438	294,272	286,854	1,927,054	1,833,304	1,051
1970	1,590,140	1,501,124	290,508	281,854	1,915,378	1,816,008	1,055
1975	1,312,308	1,239,688	259,610	251,971	1,613,135	1,531,063	1,054
1978	1,378,222	1,302,894	279,589	271,942	1,709,394	1,623,885	1,053
1980	1,490,140	1,408,592	299,033	290,583	1,582,616	1,759,642	1,053
1982	1,531,577	1,453,240	288,816	279,690	1,885,676	1,794,861	1,051
1985	1,560,342	1,477,571	295,100	286,724	1,927,983	1,832,578	1,052
1986	1,548,769	1,470,406	301,468	291,442	1,924,868	1,831,679	1,051
1988	1,591,061	1,511,022	324,495	314,067	2,002,424	1,907,086	1,050
1990	1,688,088	1,602,185	347,082	337,254	2,129,495	2,028,717	1,050

Source: Department of Health and Human Services, *Vital Statistics of the United States, 1992, Vol. I, Natality* (Hyattsville, Md., 1996), 68.

in illegitimate births than most groups (only certain Asian nationalities had lower rates), but the change nonetheless was considerable—from 5.5 percent of all white births in 1970 to 20.5 percent in 1990. The proportion of Hispanic Americans born illegitimate reached beyond one-third in 1990; for Native Americans it was more than 50 percent. In 1990 two-thirds of all black children were born to unmarried women. The statistics on the surface would indicate a connection between illegitimacy and lower social and economic classes—as traditionally had been the case—

but they also point to other forces at work. Once considered an expression of unrestrained passion by youngsters in their teens, illegitimacy by the 1980s came to be more commonly associated with older, probably more experienced, individuals. A review of the treatment of sexual issues by virtually all of the entertainment media, coupled with unblushing out-of-wedlock parentage by high profile couples of all colors, especially in entertainment, suggested that a broadly based shift in cultural attitudes had taken place in the quarter-century before the 1990s.

Top 10 First Names of Americans by Decade of Birth

Boys

1940–1949 James, Robert, John, William, Richard, David, Charles, Thomas, Michael, Ronald

1950–1959 Michael, Robert, James, John, David, William, Richard, Thomas, Mark, Steven

1960–1969 Michael, David, John, James, Robert, William, Mark, Richard, Thomas, Jeffrey

1970–1979 Michael, Christopher. David, Jason, James, John, Robert, Brian, Matthew, William

1980–1989 Michael, Christopher, Matthew, David, Joshua, Daniel, James, Jason, Robert, Andrew

Girls

1940–1949 Mary, Barbara, Patricia, Linda, Carol, Maria, Sandra, Nancy, Susan, Betty

1950–1959 Deborah, Mary, Linda, Susan, Patricia, Maria, Barbara, Karen, Nancy, Donna

1960–1969 Lisa, Maria, Mary, Susan, Karen, Kimberly, Deborah, Patricia, Michelle, Linda

1970–1979 Jennifer, Amy, Michelle, Melissa, Angela, Lisa, Heather, Kimberly, Jessica, Maria

1980–1989 Jessica, Jennifer, Amanda, Ashley, Sarah, Nicole, Stephanie, Melissa, Brittany, Elizabeth

Source: World Almanac Books, *The World Almanac and Book of Facts 1999* (Mahwah, N.J., 1998), 698.

TABLE 7.2 BIRTHRATES AND FERTILITY RATES BY RACE, 1946–1990

Year	Birthrate[a]				Fertility Rate[b]			
	All Races	White	All Other		All Races	White	All Other	
			Total	Black			Total	Black
1946	24.1	23.6	28.4	. . .	101.9	100.4	113.9	. . .
1947	26.6	26.1	31.2	. . .	113.3	111.8	125.9	. . .
1948	24.9	24.0	32.4	. . .	107.3	104.3	131.6	. . .
1950	24.1	23.0	33.3	. . .	106.2	102.3	137.3	. . .
1952	25.1	24.1	33.4	. . .	113.8	110.0	142.7	. . .
1954	25.3	24.2	34.7	. . .	117.9	113.5	152.2	. . .
1956	25.2	24.0	35.1	. . .	121.0	115.9	159.7	. . .
1958	24.5	23.3	33.9	. . .	120.0	114.8	159.1	. . .
1960	23.7	22.2	32.1	31.9	118.0	113.2	153.6	153.5
1962	22.4	21.4	30.5	. . .	112.0	107.5	147.8	. . .
1964	21.1	20.0	29.2	29.5	104.7	99.8	140.0	142.6
1966	18.4	17.4	26.1	26.2	90.8	86.2	123.5	124.7
1968	17.6	16.6	24.2	24.2	85.2	81.3	111.9	112.7
1970	18.4	17.4	25.1	25.3	87.9	84.1	113.0	115.4
1972	15.6	14.5	22.8	22.5	73.1	68.9	99.5	99.9
1974	14.8	13.9	21.2	20.8	67.8	64.2	89.8	89.7
1976	14.6	13.6	20.8	20.5	65.0	61.5	85.8	85.8
1978	15.0	14.0	21.6	21.3	65.5	61.7	87.0	86.7
1980	15.9	14.9	22.5	22.1	68.4	64.7	88.6	88.1
1982	15.9	14.9	22.0	21.5	67.3	63.9	85.3	84.3
1984	15.6	14.6	21.2	21.0	65.5	62.3	81.8	81.5
1986	15.6	14.6	21.4	21.5	65.4	62.1	81.9	82.6
1988	16.0	14.8	22.5	22.6	67.3	63.4	95.9	87.0
1990	16.7	15.5	23.3	23.8	70.9	66.9	89.4	91.9

[a] Birthrates per 1,000 population.
[b] Fertility rates pertain to the number of births 1,000 women age 15–44 will have in a given year.
Source: U.S. Department of Health and Human Services, *Vital Statistics of the United States, 1990, Vol. I, Natality* (Hyattsville, Md., 1994), 1.

TABLE 7.3 **FERTILITY RATES BY RACE AND HISPANIC ORIGIN, 1945–1990**

Year	All Races	White	Black	American Indian	Asian or Pacific Islander	Hispanic Origin
1945	85.9	83.4	. . .	. . .	. . .	. . .
1950	106.2	102.3	. . .	. . .	. . .	. . .
1955	118.3	113.7	. . .	. . .	. . .	. . .
1960	118.0	113.2	153.5	. . .	. . .	. . .
1965	96.3	91.3	133.2	. . .	. . .	. . .
1970	87.9	84.1	115.4	. . .	. . .	. . .
1975	66.0	62.5	87.9	. . .	. . .	. . .
1980	68.4	65.6	84.7	82.7	73.2	95.4
1981	67.3	64.8	82.0	79.6	73.7	97.5
1982	67.3	64.8	80.9	83.6	74.8	96.1
1983	65.7	63.4	78.7	81.8	71.7	91.8
1984	65.5	63.2	78.2	79.8	69.2	91.5
1985	66.3	64.1	78.8	78.6	68.4	94.0
1986	65.4	63.1	78.9	75.9	66.0	93.9
1987	65.8	63.3	80.1	75.6	67.1	93.0
1988	67.3	64.5	82.6	76.8	70.2	96.4
1989	69.2	66.4	86.2	79.0	68.2	104.9
1990	70.9	68.3	86.8	76.2	69.6	107.7

Source: Ronald J. Alsop, ed., *The Wall Street Journal Almanac 1998* (New York, 1997). 692.

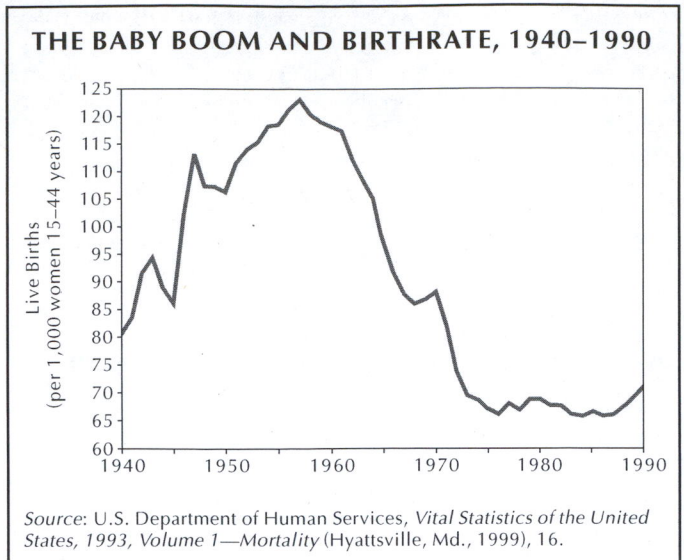

THE BABY BOOM AND BIRTHRATE, 1940–1990

Source: U.S. Department of Human Services, *Vital Statistics of the United States, 1993, Volume 1—Mortality* (Hyattsville, Md., 1999), 16.

TABLE 7.4 **ILLEGITIMATE LIVE BIRTHS AND BIRTHRATES, BY RACE, 1946–1990**

Year	Total Births (1,000)	Rate[a]	White Births (1,000)	White Rate[a]	Black Births (1,000)	Black Rate[a]
1946	125	10.9	. . .	. . .	. . .	. . .
1948	130	12.5	. . .	. . .	. . .	. . .
1950	142	14.1	54	6.1	88	71.2
1955	183	19.3	61	7.9	119	87.2
1956	194	20.4	68	8.3	126	92.1
1958	209	21.2	76	8.8	134	97.8
1960	224	21.6	83	9.2	142	98.3
1962	245	21.9	93	9.8	147	97.5
1964	276	23.0	114	11.0	161	97.2
1966	302	23.4	133	12.0	170	92.8
1968	339	24.4	155	13.2	184	86.6
1970	399	26.4	175	13.8	224	89.9
1972	403.2	24.9	160.5	12.0	242.7	86.9
1974	418.1	24.1	168.5	11.8	249.6	81.5
1976	488.1	24.7	197.1	12.6	271.0	76.4
1978	543.9	26.2	233.6	13.7	310.2	76.5
1980	665.7	29.4	320.1	17.6	345.7	77.2
1982	715.2	30.0	355.2	18.8	360.0	73.9
1984	770.4	31.0	391.9	20.1	378.4	71.4
1986	878.5	34.3	466.8	23.2	380.3	80.9
1988	1005.3	38.6	539.7	26.6	426.7	88.9
1990	1165.4	43.8	647.4	31.8	472.7	93.9

[a] Live births per 1,000 females age 15–44.
Source: Ben J. Wattenberg, *The Statistical History of the United States, Colonial Times to 1970* (New York, 1976), 52; George T. Kurian, *Datapedia of the United States 1790–2000* (Lanham, Md., 1994), 40; Bureau of Census, *Statistical Abstract of the United States, 1993* (Washington, D. C., 1993), 78.

TABLE 7.5 PERCENTAGE OF BIRTHS TO UNMARRIED WOMEN, 1940–1990

Year	All	White	Black
1940	3.8	. . .	. . .
1950	4.0	. . .	. . .
1955	4.5	. . .	. . .
1960	5.3	. . .	. . .
1965	7.7	. . .	. . .
1970	10.7	5.5	37.5
1975	14.3	7.1	49.5
1980	18.4	11.2	56.1
1985	22.0	14.7	61.2
1986	23.4	15.9	62.4
1987	24.5	16.9	63.4
1988	25.7	18.0	64.7
1989	27.1	19.2	65.7
1990	28.0	20.4	66.5

Source: Wall Street Journal Almanac, 1998, 711.

TABLE 7.6 BIRTHS TO UNMARRIED MOTHERS BY AGE—NUMBER AND PERCENT, 1940–1990

(number in thousands)

Year	All Ages	Number			Percent		
		Under 20	20–24	25 and Over	Under 20	20–24	25 and Over
1940	90	43	27	20	48	30	22
1950	142	59	43	39	42	30	29
1955	183	73	56	55	40	30	30
1960	224	92	68	65	41	30	29
1965	291	129	91	72	44	31	25
1970	399	200	127	72	50	32	18
1975	448	234	134	80	52	30	18
1980	666	272	237	157	41	36	24
1985	828	280	300	248	34	36	30
1990	1,165	361	404	401	31	35	34

Source: Department of Health and Human Services, Births to Unmarried Mothers: United States, 1980–92 (Hyattsville, Md., 1995), 17.

TABLE 7.7 ILLEGITIMATE BIRTHS AS PERCENT OF ALL BIRTHS, BY RACE AND HISPANIC ORIGIN, 1970–1990

Race and Origin of Mother	1970	1975	1980	1981	1982	1983	1984	1985	1986	1987	1988	1989	1990
All mothers	10.7	14.3	18.4	18.9	19.4	20.3	21.0	22.0	23.4	24.5	25.7	27.1	28.0
White	5.5	7.1	11.2	11.8	12.3	12.9	13.6	14.7	15.9	16.9	18.0	19.2	20.4
Black	37.5	49.5	56.1	56.9	57.7	59.2	60.3	61.2	62.4	63.4	64.7	65.7	66.5
American Indian or Alaskan Native	22.4	32.7	39.2	41.2	42.6	45.3	46.1	46.8	48.8	51.1	51.7	52.7	53.6
Asian or Pacific Islander	. . .	. . .	7.3	7.0	7.9	8.6	9.2	9.5	10.0	11.0	11.5	12.4	13.2
Chinese	3.0	1.6	2.7	2.4	2.5	3.3	3.4	3.0	3.5	4.5	3.9	4.2	5.0
Japanese	4.6	4.6	5.2	6.2	7.1	7.2	6.9	7.9	7.9	7.9	8.8	9.4	9.6
Filipino	9.1	6.9	8.6	9.1	9.9	10.3	10.8	11.4	12.0	12.7	13.6	14.8	15.9
Other Asian or Pacific Islander[a]	. . .	. . .	8.5	7.7	8.7	9.5	10.4	10.9	11.4	12.4	13.2	14.2	14.9
Hispanic origin (selected states)	. . .	. . .	23.6	24.5	25.6	27.5	28.3	29.5	31.6	32.6	34.0	35.5	36.7
Mexican American	. . .	. . .	20.3	20.7	21.9	23.7	24.2	25.7	27.9	28.9	30.6	31.7	33.3
Puerto Rican	. . .	. . .	46.3	48.0	49.0	49.5	50.8	51.1	52.6	53.0	53.3	55.2	55.9
Cuban	. . .	. . .	10.0	14.3	15.9	16.1	16.2	16.1	15.8	16.1	16.3	17.5	18.2
Central and South American	. . .	. . .	27.1	29.0	30.2	33.0	34.0	34.9	38.0	37.1	36.4	38.9	41.2
Other and unknown Hispanic	. . .	. . .	22.4	25.0	26.3	28.2	30.0	31.1	31.9	34.2	35.5	37.0	37.2
Non-Hispanic white (selected states)	. . .	. . .	9.6	10.0	10.5	11.0	11.5	12.4	13.5	14.3	15.2	16.1	16.9
Non-Hispanic black (selected states)	. . .	. . .	57.3	58.0	59.0	60.5	61.5	62.1	63.3	64.2	64.8	66.0	66.7

[a] Includes Hawaiians and part Hawaiians.
Source: U.S. Department of Health and Human Services, Health, United States, 1992 (Hyattsville, Md., 1993), 25.

The Birthing Process

Tables below suggest major changes in the method and safety of giving birth. The popularity of Cesarean section surged, increasing nearly fivefold, in the quarter-century before 1990. Although every age group showed marked increase in this procedure, the guiding principle seemed to be that the older the mother, the more likely she would choose or need a Caesarean section. The second table revealed an almost equal change—some fivefold—in the reduction of infant mortality since 1940. These welcome numbers surely were attributable to better medical facilities, greater social awareness, and expansion of government programs. There continued to be a conspicuous difference between the white rate and the black, but the decline in black infant mortality nonetheless was significant.

TABLE 7.8 BIRTHS BY CESAREAN SECTION BY AGE OF MOTHER, 1965–1990

(in percentage)

Year	All Ages	Under 20	20–24	25–29	30–34	35 and Older
1965	4.5	3.1	3.5	4.3	6.4	7.9
1970	5.5	3.9	4.9	5.9	7.5	8.3
1975	10.4	8.4	9.0	11.1	13.6	15.0
1980	16.5	14.5	15.8	16.7	18.0	20.6
1984	21.1	16.5	19.6	20.8	24.6	28.7
1990	23.5	16.6	21.0	23.3	27.8	31.4

Source: Bureau of Census, Statistical Abstract 1993, 77.

TABLE 7.9   INFANT MORTALITY RATE[a], 1940–1990

Year	All Races			White			All Other					
							Total			Black		
	Both Sexes	Male	Female	Both Sexes	Male	Female	Both Sexes	Male	Female	Both Sexes	Male	Female
1940	47.0	52.5	41.3	43.2	48.3	37.8	73.8	82.2	65.2	72.9	81.1	64.6
1950	29.2	32.8	25.5	26.8	30.2	23.1	44.5	48.9	39.9	43.9	48.3	39.4
1960	26.0	29.3	22.6	22.9	26.0	19.6	43.2	47.9	38.5	44.3	49.1	39.4
1970	20.0	22.4	17.5	17.8	20.0	15.4	30.9	34.2	27.5	32.6	36.2	29.0
1975	16.1	17.9	14.2	14.2	15.9	12.3	24.2	26.2	22.2	26.2	28.3	24.0
1980	12.6	13.9	11.2	10.9	12.1	9.5	20.2	21.9	18.4	22.2	24.2	20.2
1985	10.6	11.9	9.3	9.2	10.4	7.9	16.8	18.3	15.3	19.0	20.8	17.2
1986	10.4	11.5	9.1	8.8	9.9	7.7	16.7	18.5	14.9	18.9	20.9	16.8
1987	10.1	11.2	8.9	8.5	9.5	7.5	16.5	18.1	14.8	18.8	20.6	16.8
1988	10.0	11.0	8.9	8.4	9.4	7.3	16.1	17.3	14.8	18.5	20.0	17.0
1989	9.8	10.8	8.8	8.1	9.0	7.1	16.3	17.6	15.0	18.6	20.0	17.2
1990	9.2	10.3	8.1	7.6	8.5	6.6	15.5	17.0	14.0	18.0	19.6	16.2

[a] Rates are infant (under 1 year) deaths per 1,000 live births in specified group. Beginning in 1980, race for live births is tabulated according to race of mother.
Source: Alsop, *Wall Street Journal Almanac, 1998,* 695.

Birth Control

American women had several methods of birth control at their disposal as the postwar period began. It was not acceptable in those days to ask questions about such an intimate issue, and so systematic and continuing surveys were not available, but clues from various quarters suggested that more than 50 percent of women used some form of contraception. Reasons for not doing so varied, ranging from a desire to become pregnant (or not minding if it happened), to inconvenience, to religion.

The Roman Catholic Church continued to demand that its members not utilize "artificial" birth control, a rule that seemed to cover almost everything. Priests told Catholic women that they could employ the rhythm method, which identifies and exploits the so-called safe period in a woman's cycle. Referred to by some with disdain as "Vatican roulette" and in truth a form of abstinence, the rhythm method was the only way of preventing babies (other than abstinence itself) that the church would condone. The information that did exist (and perhaps the size of Catholic families) suggested that many Catholic women dutifully sought to use rhythm for some 15 or 20 years into the postwar period. But Catholics were subject to influence other than from the church; and as they, and the new generation, faced the temptations and challenges that began in the 1960s, aware that science had developed an easy and reliable form of contraception, they succumbed. By the 1970s, if not earlier, Catholics were using every method of birth control available and using it as often as the general population.

For many years the most popular forms of birth control had been a condom or a diaphragm that placed a physical barrier in the path to conception. Usually effective when used properly and consistently, some felt that these devices were imperfect because they placed a barrier to the most intimate contact and because logistics of their use could interfere with the spontanaety of the act. An effort to find a simple pill had long been a target of the country's most famous exponent of birth control, Margaret Sanger. In the 1950s Sanger joined forces with wealthy heiress Katherine McCormick and approached Gregory Pincus, a biologist who had done research in related areas. It was a combination of Sanger's drive, McCormick's money, and Pincus's work and professional connections that in 1954 made possible the first tests of a contraceptive medication that functioned by blocking female ovulation. Passing these tests and others that followed, surviving

condemnation and challenges from the Catholic Church, of course, and even from some feminists who viewed the exercise as a risky male conspiracy, the first "pill" received approval of the FDA and arrived on the market in 1960 under the brand name Enovid, produced by the Searle Pharmaceutical Corporation.

Introduction of the contraceptive pill encountered immediate customer approval. Its popularity continued to grow as new brands came on the market and as its reliabilty was confirmed and its safety increased. The pill was (and is) credited with supplying a scientific foundation for some of the social transformation that took shape beginning in the 1960s. The pill did not, however, come trouble-free. Individuals could forget to take it and in some cases it carried side effects. Unlike the condom, it permitted the most intimate physical contact, and, therefore, it provided no protection from any form of sexually transmitted disease. The problem struck with stunning force with identification of the AIDS (acquired immune deficiency syndrome) epidemic at the start of the 1980s and knowledge that HIV, the virus that caused the disease, traveled through transfer of certain body fluids into the bloodstream of another, which could happen through unprotected sex. And AIDS carried a prospect of death. More than ever before the term *protection* meant much more than avoidance of unwanted pregnancy, and what had been a major complaint about the condom or diaphram—that it disallowed direct contact—now became a virtue. The campaign for "safe sex" that began in the 1980s stressed condom use to present STDs, but did not suggest that those on the pill switch, only that they add condoms. The pill was much more effective in preventing pregnancy than were condoms. Even so, perhaps because many people felt confident about their health or that of their partners or because they simply were willing to take a risk, the contraceptive pill remained an important means of birth control, popular with unmarried women. The condom underwent a modest renewal of popularity in the 1980s, but the method of birth control that surpassed all others was female or male sterilization—an approach that, as with the pill, offered no protection against disease.

Birth Control: The Catholic View, 1959

Birth Control, Artificial—The prevention of conception and birth by the use of any means contrary to the law of nature. Such means include the use of drugs, medications, instruments, devices, cleansings and actions that prevent the normal performance and fulfillment of the act of sex—a serious and unnatural sin because it frustrates the very nature and purposes of the power of sex. The Church holds that artificial birth control is wrong for everyone, and not just Catholics, because it is against the law of nature.

The practice or use of rhythm by married couples is essentially different from the practice of artificial birth control, even though the two practices may have the same result, viz., failure to conceive. In artificial birth control the act is deliberately frustrated and conception is prevented by a positive human action; in rhythm the act is normally performed and fulfilled, and conception fails to occur because of an accident or condition of nature which is not humanly caused but simply exists.

For proportionately serious reasons and with mutual consent, married persons may practise rhythm for as long as the sufficient reasons obtain. Even when so doing, however, they are still morally bound to respect the marriage rights of each other at all times and to consent to the exercise of those rights at any time in response to need or a reasonable request. The practice of rhythm may never be so absolute as to admit of no exception; it is not intended to be an excuse or reason for sin outside of the so-called "safe" period. Married persons should seek the advice of a confessor regarding the use of rhythm.

Source: Felician A Foy, ed., *The 1960 Catholic Almanac* (Garden City, 1960), 290.

TABLE 7.10   METHODS OF CONTRACEPTION: MARRIED USERS BY RELIGION, 1955 AND 1960

Method	Total		Protestant		Catholic		Jewish	
	1955	1960	1955	1960	1955	1960	1955	1960
Number of users	1,901	1,948	1,362	1,347	453	466	64	101
Percentage reporting[a]								
Condom	43	50	48	56	25	28	72	74
Diaphragm	36	38	41	46	17	12	56	51
Rhythm	34	35	25	27	65	67	8	9
Douche	28	24	32	28	18	17	11	8
Withdrawal	15	17	17	18	13	17	6	4
Jelly alone	6	11	8	14	2	4	2	8
Suppositories	4	6	5	8	2	3	3	. . .
Abstinence	2	4	4	3	1	9	. . .	2
Other	2	1	3	1	1	. . .	. . .	. . .
Total[b]	170	186	183	201	144	157	158	156

[a] Percentage of users measured by wife's religion.
[b] The total exceeds 100 because many couples reported two or more methods.
Source: Pascal K. Whelpton et al., *Fertility and Family Planning in the United States* (Princeton, 1966), 278.

TABLE 7.11   CONTRACEPTION: MARRIED WHITE WOMEN, 15–44 YEARS, BY RELIGION—1965, 1973, AND 1976

(in percentage)

Year	1965	1973	1976
Women who use any contraception			
Catholic	56.8	66.4	67.5
Protestant	66.5	72.1	68.9
Contraceptors who use rhythm method			
Catholic	31.9	8.1	8.9
Protestant	4.5	2.6	3.7
Contraceptors who use birth control pill			
Catholic	17.9	34.1	33.1
Protestant	26.8	36.1	33.1

Source: National Center for Health Statistics, *Trends in Contraceptive Practice: United States, 1965–76* Hyattsville, Md., 1982), 10, 15.

TABLE 7.12   METHODS OF CONTRACEPTION: ALL USERS, AGE 15–44, 1988, AND MARRIED USERS—BY PERCENTAGE, 1973–1988

Method	All Users	Currently Married Users		
	1988	1973	1982	1988
Sterilization	39.2	23.5	42.4	48.7
Female	27.5	12.3	26.9	31.4
Male	11.7	11.2	15.5	17.3
Pill	30.7	36.1	19.3	20.4
IUD	2.0	9.6	6.9	2.0
Diaphragm	5.7	3.4	6.5	6.2
Condom	14.6	13.5	14.1	14.3
Foam	1.1	5.0	2.8	1.4
Per. abst.	2.3	4.0	4.6	2.8
Withdrawal	2.2	2.1	1.7	2.3
Other	2.1	2.7	1.7	1.9
Total	100.0	100.0	100.0	100.0

Source: Bruce A. Chadwick and Tim B. Wheaton, *Statistical Handbook on the American Family* (Phoenix, 1992), 163.

Abortion

Abortion, the deliberate, induced termination of a fetus, always has been a delicate issue in American life, and it increasingly became a controversial one as well. As the United States entered the post–Second World War era, abortion was illegal in all the states; most Americans regarded abortion as immoral and probably believed that it constituted killing of an unborn child. Supporters of a change in attitude had long argued that criminalization of abortion had promoted an illegal, often dangerous, underground industry and that at the very least the laws needed to take into account exceptional circumstances—such as rape, evidence of trouble in the fetus, or the danger that childbirth might present to the mother's health. Emergence, or reemergence, of a strong women's rights movement in the 1960s carried over to the fight for abortion rights, seeking to place emphasis on the woman instead of the unborn child. Acceptance of the interpretation that a fetus was not a person but a part of the woman's body and that the Constitution carried an implied, if undefined, right of individual privacy blended to produce the position that because women had the private right to control their bodies, they had the constitutional right to abortion.

In the late 1960s and early 1970s several states changed their laws to take into account exceptional circumstances that related to abortion. A very small number of states, notably New York, substantially broadened the area within which abortion was permissible. On January 23, 1973, the Supreme Court handed down its decision in the case of *Roe v. Wade*, which, along with a second decision, explicitly struck down abortion laws in Texas and Georgia and by implication invalidated measures in 44 other states. In this decision the court identified three classifications in the cycle of pregnancy: In the first trimester (three months) the states can pass no laws restricting abortion—women had the right of "abortion on demand"; in the second trimester the states could regulate procedure in certain reasonable ways; in the third trimester the states could legislate more rigorously, even prohibit abortion, but not in cases that affected the health and life of the mother. The right to abortion thus became the law of the land.

Needless to say, *Roe v. Wade* sparked a lengthy and intense debate that continued for the rest of the 20th century. Opponents of abortion, to whom January 23, 1973, was a "day of infamy," formed such organiza-

tions as the National Right to Life Committee. The largest antiabortion organization was the Roman Catholic Church, although evidence suggested that the church hierarchy felt more strongly about the issue than did its clientele. Shock troops of the movement came mostly from Protestant Evangelicals, including such organizations as the Moral Majority, founded in the 1970s by Baptist minister Jerry Falwell. The object was to halt abortion on demand, preferably through a different court decision or if necessary through a constitutional amendment. A small fringe faction that resorted to violent tactics did much to tarnish the antiabortion cause with the general populace.

Supporters of abortion rights—who deemed their cause "pro-choice"—supported such organizations as the National Abortion and Reproductive Action League, Planned Parenthood, and the National Organization for Women. Antiabortion groups had large influence within the Republican Party; pro-choice groups had at least as much influence with the Democrats.

Statistics from various quarters revealed much support for a middle ground between making all abortion legal and making all abortion illegal, but they also suggested why such a ground was difficult to find. The number of abortions (or at least the number reported) soared in the first years after the court's decision, reaching a peak rate of more than 29 (per 1,000 women) in 1980 and 1981. Thereafter the number leveled off and the rate (but not the number) declined slightly in the last half of the 1980s. Most women who had abortions were white, if only because there were many more white women. The ratio was much higher for nonwhites, especially blacks. In Washington, D.C., a city largely inhabited by African Americans, there were nearly two and one-half abortions for every live birth in 1975. Roman Catholic women were at least as willing as women of other religious groups to have abortions. Very few abortions (less than 5 percent) came because of rape, danger to women's health, or because of a malformed fetus. The most common reasons involved the effect a new child would have on the lifestyle of the mother or the family or because of financial considerations. In 1987 unmarried women had more than 80 percent of abortions; close to 60 percent of unmarried pregnancies were aborted. In sum, the reasons for most abortions were the same reasons that most people (and a majority of people being polled) found unacceptable justification for having an abortion. The debate went on.

TABLE 7.13   ABORTIONS: ESTIMATED NUMBER, RATE, AND RATIO, BY RACE—1972–1990

(refers to women 15 to 44 years old at time of abortion)

	All Races				White				Black and Other			
	Women 15–44 Years Old (1,000)	Abortions			Women 15–44 Years Old (1,000)	Abortions			Women 15–44 Years Old (1,000)	Abortions		
Year		Number (1,000)	Rate per 1,000 Women	Ratio per 1,000 Live Births		Number (1,000)	Rate per 1,000 Women	Ratio per 1,000 Live Births		Number (1,000)	Rate per 1,000 Women	Ratio per 1,000 Live Births
1972	44,588	586	13.2	184	38,532	455	11.8	175	6,056	131	21.7	223
1975	47,606	1,034	21.7	331	40,857	701	17.2	276	6,749	333	49.3	565
1978	50,920	1,410	27.7	413	43,427	969	22.3	356	7,493	440	58.7	665
1979	52,016	1,498	28.8	420	44,266	1,062	24.0	373	7,750	435	56.2	625
1980	53,048	1,554	29.3	428	44,942	1,094	24.3	376	8,106	460	56.5	642
1981	53,901	1,577	29.3	430	45,494	1,108	24.3	377	8,407	470	55.9	645
1982	54,679	1,574	28.8	428	46,049	1,095	23.8	373	8,630	479	55.5	646
1983	55,340	1,575	28.5	436	46,506	1,084	23.3	376	8,834	491	55.5	670
1984	56,061	1,577	28.1	423	47,023	1,087	23.1	366	9,038	491	54.3	646
1985	56,754	1,589	28.0	422	47,512	1,076	22.6	360	9,242	513	55.5	659
1986	57,483	1,574	27.4	416	48,010	1,045	21.8	350	9,473	529	55.9	661
1987	57,964	1,559	27.1	405	48,288	1,017	21.1	338	9,676	542	56.0	648
1988	58,192	1,591	27.3	401	48,325	1,026	21.2	333	9,867	565	57.3	638
1989	58,365	1,557	26.8	380	48,104	1,006	20.9	309	10,261	561	54.7	650
1990	58,700	1,609	27.4	389	48.224	1,039	21.5	318	10,476	570	54.4	655

Source: Bureau of the Census, *Statistical Abstract of the United States, 1993* (Washington, D.C., 1993), 83; Bureau of the Census, *Statistical Abstract of the United States, 1994* (Washington, D.C., 1994), 85.

TABLE 7.14   ABORTIONS BY SELECTED CHARACTERISTICS, 1973–1988

Characteristic	Number (1,000)				Percent Distribution				Abortion Ratio[a]			
	1973	1980	1985	1988	1973	1980	1985	1988	1973	1980	1985	1988
Total abortions	745	1,554	1,589	1,591	100	100	100	100	193	300	297	286
Age of women:												
Less than 15 years old	12	15	17	14	2	1	1	1	476	607	624	553
15 to 19 years old	232	445	399	393	31	29	25	25	280	451	462	444
20 to 24 years old	241	549	548	520	32	35	35	33	181	310	328	327
25 to 29 years old	130	304	336	347	17	20	21	22	128	213	219	218
30 to 34 years old	73	153	181	197	10	10	11	12	165	213	203	194
35 to 39 years old	41	67	87	96	6	4	5	6	246	317	280	254
40 years old and over	17	21	21	24	2	1	1	2	334	461	409	361
Race of woman:												
White	549	1,094	1,076	1,026	74	70	68	65	178	274	265	250
Black and other	196	460	513	565	26	30	32	36	252	392	397	389
Marital status of woman:												
Married	216	320	281	277	29	21	18	17	74	98	88	87
Unmarried	528	1,234	1,307	1,314	71	79	82	83	564	649	605	556
Number of prior live births:												
None	411	900	872	814	55	58	55	51	242	365	358	333
One	115	305	349	379	15	20	22	24	108	208	219	227
Two	104	216	240	262	14	14	15	17	190	283	288	288
Three	61	83	85	93	8	5	5	6	228	288	281	276
Four or more	55	51	43	43	7	3	3	3	196	251	230	213
Number of prior induced abortions:												
None	. . .	1,043	944	908	. . .	67	60	57	. . .	. . .	. . .	. . .
One	. . .	373	416	429	. . .	24	26	27	. . .	. . .	. . .	. . .
Two or more	. . .	138	228	254	. . .	9	14	16	. . .	. . .	. . .	. . .
Weeks of gestation:												
Less than 9 weeks	284	800	811	800	38	52	51	50	. . .	. . .	. . .	. . .
9 to 10 weeks	222	417	425	424	30	27	27	27	. . .	. . .	. . .	. . .
11 to 12 weeks	131	202	198	198	18	13	12	12	. . .	. . .	. . .	. . .
13 weeks or more	108	136	154	168	15	9	10	11	. . .	. . .	. . .	. . .

[a] Number of abortions per 1,000 abortions and live births.
Source: Statistical Abstract, 1993, 83.

TABLE 7.15   LEGAL ABORTIONS, A COUNTRY COMPARISON, 1988[a]

The Top Ten Countries		
Rank	Country	Legal Abortions per 1,000 Live Births
1.	Soviet Union	230.0
2.	Bulgaria	107.2
3.	Romania	99.0
4.	Yugoslavia	74.0
5.	Cuba	70.8
6.	Hungary	65.8
7.	Czechoslovakia	52.8
8.	Greenland	51.3
9.	Singapore	47.1
10.	United States	42.8

Selected Other Countries		
Rank	Country	Legal Abortions per 1,000 Live Births
12.	Denmark	40.0
14.	Japan	37.9
19.	France	23.9
21.	United Kingdom	20.7
22.	Israel	19.2
24.	Canada	16.5
26.	West Germany	14.8
35.	India	2.0
36.	Chile	1.0
37.	Greece	0.2

[a] This data is based on a ranking of 37 nations in which abortion was legal and was reported. The numbers do not take into account the many abortions that were performed illegally or were not reported. China, a nation in which abortions were encouraged, is not included in the table. It is clear that the nations with the highest rates were communist states where abortion was financed by government and where perhaps there was little objection based on religion. It also is clear that the United States ranked very high among the nations with which it has the most dealings.
Source: George T. Kurian, The New Book of World Rankings (New York, 1991), 38–39.

TABLE 7.16 PUBLIC OPINION AND ABORTION, 1965–1990

The National Opinion Research Center asked the following question: "Please tell me whether or not you think it should be possible for a pregnant woman to obtain a legal abortion . . .

1. If the woman's health is seriously endangered."

Year	1965 (%)	1972 (%)	1976 (%)	1980 (%)	1985 (%)	1988 (%)	1990 (%)
Yes	73	86	91	90	90	89	92
No	27	14	9	10	10	11	8

2. If she became pregnant as a result of rape."

Year	1965 (%)	1972 (%)	1976 (%)	1980 (%)	1985 (%)	1988 (%)	1990 (%)
Yes	59	79	84	83	81	81	85
No	41	21	16	17	19	19	15

3. If there is a strong chance of serious defect in the baby."

Year	1965 (%)	1972 (%)	1976 (%)	1980 (%)	1985 (%)	1988 (%)	1990 (%)
Yes	57	79	84	83	78	78	83
No	43	21	16	17	22	22	17

4. If the family has low income and cannot afford any more children."

Year	1965 (%)	1972 (%)	1976 (%)	1980 (%)	1985 (%)	1988 (%)	1990 (%)
Yes	22	49	53	52	43	42	48
No	78	51	47	48	57	58	52

5. If she is not married and does not want to marry the man."

Year	1965 (%)	1972 (%)	1976 (%)	1980 (%)	1985 (%)	1988 (%)	1990 (%)
Yes	18	44	50	48	41	40	45
No	82	56	50	52	59	60	55

6. If she is married and does not want any more children."

Year	1965 (%)	1972 (%)	1976 (%)	1980 (%)	1985 (%)	1988 (%)	1990 (%)
Yes	16	40	46	47	40	40	45
No	84	60	54	53	60	60	55

Source: Barbara Hinkson Craig and David M. O'Brien, *Abortion and American Politics* (Chatham, N.J., 1993), 250, 252, 254.

TABLE 7.17 PREGNANCIES BY OUTCOME, AGE OF WOMAN, AND RACE, 1988

Item	Total	Under 15 Years Old	15 to 19 Years Old	20 to 24 Years Old	25 to 29 Years Old	30 to 34 Years Old	35 to 39 Years Old	40 Years Old and Older
				Number (1,000)				
Total, all pregnancies	**6,341**	**27**	**988**	**1,774**	**1,821**	**1,195**	**456**	**79**
Live births	3,910	11	478	1,067	1,239	804	270	41
Induced abortions	1,591	14	393	520	347	197	96	24
Fetal losses	840	3	117	187	234	194	91	14
White, all pregnancies	4,698	11	673	1,270	1,406	927	350	59
Live births	3,046	4	315	805	1,011	661	218	32
Induced abortions	1,026	6	264	332	219	125	63	17
Fetal losses	626	2	94	133	177	141	69	10
Other races, all pregnancies	1,643	16	315	504	415	268	106	20
Live births	863	7	163	263	229	142	52	9
Induced abortions	565	8	129	187	129	72	33	7
Fetal losses	214	1	23	54	58	53	21	4
				Rate Per 1,000 Women				
Total, all pregnancies	**109.0**	**3.3**	**110.8**	**185.3**	**166.7**	**109.7**	**47.2**	**9.6**
Live births	67.2	1.3	53.6	111.5	113.4	73.7	27.9	5.0
Induced abortions	27.3	1.7	44.0	54.2	31.8	18.1	9.9	3.0
Fetal losses	14.4	0.3	13.2	19.6	21.5	17.8	9.4	1.7
White, all pregnancies	97.2	1.8	93.4	161.7	155.3	102.2	43.2	8.4
Live births	63.0	0.6	43.7	102.5	111.6	72.9	26.9	4.6
Induced abortions	21.2	0.9	36.6	42.3	24.1	13.8	7.8	2.4
Fetal losses	13.0	0.2	13.1	16.9	19.5	15.5	8.5	1.5
Other races, all pregnancies	166.5	9.7	184.3	292.3	221.9	146.5	68.1	16.6
Live births	87.5	4.0	95.3	152.3	122.3	77.8	33.4	7.3
Induced abortions	57.3	4.9	75.5	108.5	68.8	39.6	21.0	6.2
Fetal losses	21.7	0.7	13.6	31.5	30.8	29.1	13.8	3.0
				Percent Distribution				
Total, all pregnancies	100.0	100.0	100.0	100.0	100.0	100.0	100.0	100.0
Live births	61.7	39.2	48.4	60.2	68.1	67.2	59.1	51.6
Induced abortions	25.1	50.5	39.7	29.3	19.1	16.5	21.0	30.9
Fetal losses	13.3	10.3	11.9	10.6	12.9	16.2	19.9	17.4
White, all pregnancies	100.0	100.0	100.0	100.0	100.0	100.0	100.0	100.0
Live births	64.8	35.6	46.9	63.4	71.9	71.3	62.2	54.1
Induced abortions	21.8	50.2	39.2	26.2	15.6	13.5	18.1	28.7
Fetal losses	13.3	14.2	14.0	10.5	12.6	15.2	19.8	17.2
Other races, all pregnancies	100.0	100.0	100.0	100.0	100.0	100.0	100.0	100.0
Live births	52.6	41.8	51.7	52.1	55.1	53.1	49.0	44.2
Induced abortions	34.4	50.7	41.0	37.1	31.0	27.0	30.8	37.6
Fetal losses	13.1	7.5	7.4	10.8	13.9	19.9	20.2	18.2

Source: Statistical Abstract, 1993, 82.

TABLE 7.18   IDEAL NUMBER OF CHILDREN, 1945–1990

Year	Number of Children[a]			
	None	One	Two	Three or More
1945	1	1	22	76
1957	1	1	19	78
1970	0	1	39	60
1980	1	3	51	37
1990	3	3	57	29

[a] Percent saying number is ideal, for selected years.
Source: Margaret Ambry and Cheryl Russell, *The Official Guide to the American Marketplace* (Ithaca, N.Y., 1992), 420.

Sexual Behavior and Attitudes

Americans traditionally had found sexual activity a sensitive subject. Although there had always been free, lively, frequently coarse discussion among young men, open attention to sex was a different proposition. In many circles mention of such intimate matters was considered inappropriate and in poor taste; in other circles it was thought to be downright dirty. Not surprisingly, there had been virtually no effort to measure the boundaries of sexual behavior or to survey attitudes about it.

The principal exception in the postwar period had been the work of a stodgy, middle-aged scientist, a professor of biology at Indiana University, Alfred C. Kinsey, who almost by accident began taking "sex histories" of those of his students bold enough to participate. The project mushroomed. Kinsey established the Institute for Sex Research at Indiana, a move that brought him funds and staff to broaden his work. He eventually published his findings in two dry, scholarly but nonetheless sensational volumes, *Sexual Behavior of the Human Male* (1948) and *Sexual Behavior of the Human Female* (1953). Most stunning about Kinsey's work, aside from the fact that he broached the subject at all, was his revelation of the extent of sexual activity inside, outside, and as a supplement to marriage, the various and bizarre forms it took, that it could be and was for the pleasure of females as well as males. Such sensational material invited criticism, and it soon came. Clergymen attacked Kinsey's casual treatment of a sensitive subject (or for treating it at all); scholars raised questions, some of them legitimate, about aspects of his research. None of this criticism diminished the idea that Kinsey was a major pioneer in social science.

Kinsey's work revealed that Americans were doing a great deal more with sex than it would appear, and the effect was greater because of an impression that they were hardly doing anything at all, at least little that was considered inappropriate. Even allowing for Kinsey's corrections, the immediate postwar era was a time of social conservatism. Most people believed that sexual intercourse was something that should be saved for marriage—one heard it from the pulpit and from the parents. Childbirth before marriage did take place, of course, but the number was not large, and when it happened, it perhaps no longer was treated as a disgrace but still was the sort of behavior one tried to hide if at all possible. In a Gallup Poll of 1948 only 30 percent of women and 34 percent of men approved of women wearing slacks (long pants) in public. In another poll in 1955 73 percent of women and 55 percent of men disapproved of women wearing Bermuda shorts (a new style that was considerably longer than the so-called short shorts) "on the streets." As a rule in the movies a kiss was as far as one could go.

What followed in the early to mid-1960s probably could be better termed evolution—for it still was going on as the 1990s began—than a revolution in sexual behavior and even more markedly in public exposure to the subject. The change might have been encouraged by Kinsey's studies, but it was fed by several forces that grew out of the sixties. Development of the contraceptive pill, which was most popular with unmarried women, did much to remove a major detriment, the fear of pregnancy, to intercourse. The baby boom generation began to reach sexual maturity in the 1960s and with it came attitudes and expectations different from the generation that had preceded it. Many—by no means all—discovered that it was fun, fashionable, and even inspiring to challenge prevailing attitudes, whether they had to do with race, Vietnam, or sexual mores. Sexual restraint, in this thinking, was old stuff; one should do what one wanted. The late 1960s and early 1970s marked a major revival of a woman's movement, and although there soon would develop several factions, with different emphases, there was fairly broad agreement that equality for females, even if variously defined, was the ultimate goal. Equality, as it developed, often involved allowing women to do whatever men were doing. Carried over to sexual behavior, the idea had the effect of substantially (but not entirely) removing what had been a powerful and persistent restraint on premarital sexual activity: the girl's propensity—some would say her responsibility—to say no. Supreme Court rulings on censorship substantially broadened the territory into which the media could tread in dealing with sex. Now it was possible to see nudity on the screen and couples in bed, and sex acts, either implicit or explicit, became commonplace—a far cry from the Production Code of the film industry's Hays Committee in the 1940s and 1950s.

Change in sexual behavior and social attitudes that began in the 1960s became more pronounced in the 1970s and 1980s. By the 1980s women were twice as likely to have had intercourse before age 18 as in the late 1950s. By the 1980s some 70 percent of all married women had had premarital intercourse (In 1953, Kinsey had put the number at 50 percent, at the time a stunning statistic). An overwhelming majority of abortions had been performed on unmarried women. The large increase in the rate of illegitimate births after 1970 reflected both increased activity and greater acceptance of childbirth out of wedlock. The liberalization of attitudes did not carry over to extramarital activity. Polls through the 1970s and 1980s revealed a fairly consistent feeling that sex by a married person with anyone other than the spouse was wrong. More than 80 percent of both husbands and wives in 1988 reported having had relations with only one partner during the previous year.

Surveys and special studies since the 1970s have examined relations between males and females extensively; researchers have done less with homosexual behavior. They have failed to produce a reliable statistic on the number of people involved. Kinsey, who first probed the issue, reported in 1948 that 37 percent of males had had at least one homosexual contact and that some 10 percent of adults were practicing homosexuals. Recent scholars have challenged these numbers as too high, and although there was no agreement on a number, 2 or 3 percent often came up. Polls continued to show that a substantial majority of people disapproved of homosexuality but not to the extent of establishing policy discriminatory against gay people. Discovery of AIDS in the early 1980s and an initial belief that AIDS almost exclusively afflicted gay people produced a measure of nonchalance about the disease if not hostility directed at homosexuals. Better understanding of the disease and death of such prominent people as performers Rock Hudson and Liberace caused sentiment to turn into alarm and sympathy for the people affected. The shift corresponded with a growing movement to honor diversity in all its forms. Diversity was to manifest itself, among other ways, in an increased tolerance toward almost any point of view. Homosexuals would benefit, perhaps more than any group, from popular endorsement of this attitude.

TABLE 7.19   PERCENTAGE OF MEN AND WOMEN WHO HAVE HAD INTERCOURSE BY AGE 18, 1956–1988[a]

Year	1956–58	1959–64	1965–67	1968–70	1971–73	1974–79	1980–82	1983–85	1986–88
Men	. . .	. . .	. . .	55	61	64	63	64	73
Women	27	31	31	35	45	47	51	52	56

[a] Data obtained from tabulations of the National Surveys of Family Growth.
Source: The Allan Guttmacher Institute, *Sex and America's Teenagers* (New York, 1994), 20.

TABLE 7.20   WOMEN AGE 15–19 WHO HAVE EVER HAD INTERCOURSE, BY SELECTED CHARACTERISTICS, 1988

(in percentage)

Women	Percent
Black	61
Hispanic	49
White	52
Poor	60
Low income	53
Higher income	50
Roman Catholic	48
Fundamentalist Protestant	55
Other	54
Protestant	60
Urban	53
Rural	53

Source: Guttmacher Institute, *Sex and Teenagers,* 26.

TABLE 7.21   ADULTS REPORTING SEXUAL PARTNERS IN PAST 12 MONTHS, BY MARITAL STATUS, SEX, AND AGE, 1988[a]

Number of Sex Partners	Age of Respondents				
	18–29	30–44	45–60	61+	Total
All Men					
0	9.7%	8.2%	16.4%	30.3%	14.6%
1	46.1	71.0	64.6	60.6	61.3
2	9.1	5.6	6.4	0.8	5.6
3	9.7	3.9	1.8	2.3	4.7
4	6.1	2.6	0.9	2.3	3.1
5–10	8.5	1.3	0.9	. . .	2.8
10+	3.0	0.9	1.8	. . .	1.4
No answer	7.9	6.5	7.3	3.8	6.4

Number of Sex Partners	Age of Respondents				
	18–29	30–44	45–60	61+	Total
All Women					
0	7.3%	7.1%	28.5%	60.8%	26.7%
1	66.0	77.8	62.9	29.8	58.2
2	13.1	5.2	2.6	0.8	5.2
3	4.2	4.8	0.7	. . .	2.6
4	2.1	0.8	. . .	. . .	0.7
5–10	1.0	0.4	. . .	0.4	0.5
10+	. . .	0.4	0.7	. . .	0.2
No answer	6.3	3.6	4.6	8.2	5.9

Number of Sex Partners	Age of Respondents				
	18–29	30–44	45–60	61+	Total
Married Men, Spouse in Household					
0	0%	3.8%	8.9%	20.4%	8.5%
1	80.0	87.2	78.5	74.2	81.2
2	2.0	2.6	3.8	. . .	2.1
3	4.0	. . .	1.3	1.1	1.1
4	2.0	. . .	. . .	1.1	0.5
5–10	. . .	0.6	1.3	. . .	0.5
10+	. . .	. . .	1.3	. . .	0.3
No answer	12.0	5.8	5.1	3.2	5.8

Number of Sex Partners	Age of Respondents				
	18–29	30–44	45–60	61+	Total
Married Women, Spouse in Household					
0	0%	3.5%	7.3%	24.5%	8.8%
1	89.3	91.6	85.4	65.3	82.9
2	3.6	. . .	. . .	1.0	1.0
3	24	. . .	. . .	. . .	0.5
4	. . .	. . .	. . .	. . .	. . .
5–10	. . .	. . .	. . .	1.0	0.2
10+	. . .	. . .	1.2	. . .	0.2

[a] . . . indicates zero. Survey by National Opinion Research Center.
Source: Wright, *Universal Almanac, 1991,* 207.

TABLE 7.22   SEXUAL FREQUENCY BY SELECTED CHARACTERISTICS, 1988–1989

Question: *How often did you have sex during the last 12 months?*[a]
(row percentages)

Characteristics		Not at All	Once or Twice	About Once a Month	2–3 Times a Month	About Once a Week	2–3 Times a Week	More Than 3 Times a week	(n)
Male	Non-Hispanic/White	13.7	6.6	8.0	18.0	23.6	24.8	5.3	(512)
	Black	2.7	2.7	16.2	13.5	13.5	43.2	8.1	(37)
	Hispanic	5.0	10.0	10.0	. . .	35.0	30.0	10.0	(20)
	Other	26.7	6.7	20.0	6.7	20.0	20.0	. . .	(15)
Female	Non-Hispanic/White	29.4	6.3	7.9	15.3	16.8	19.9	4.4	(619)
	Black	26.3	13.7	7.4	15.8	11.6	22.1	3.2	(95)
	Hispanic	27.3	6.8	2.3	20.5	13.6	25.0	4.5	(44)
	Other	15.8	31.6	26.3	21.1	5.3	. . .	. . .	(19)
Male	Age 18–24	20.0	8.0	10.7	12.0	18.7	24.0	6.7	(75)
	25–34	7.4	8.1	5.4	12.1	21.5	35.6	10.1	(149)
	35–44	5.8	1.5	4.4	19.7	29.2	33.6	5.8	(137)
	45–64	7.4	5.2	9.6	24.4	27.4	23.0	3.0	(135)
	65+	36.4	12.5	19.3	12.5	14.8	4.5	. . .	(88)
Female	Age 18–24	16.5	8.9	7.6	15.2	15.2	24.1	12.7	(79)
	25–34	5.1	10.7	5.1	15.7	20.2	38.8	4.5	(178)
	35–44	11.0	7.6	6.2	22.1	21.4	26.9	4.8	(145)
	45–64	28.7	8.6	12.0	19.6	14.8	12.9	3.3	(209)
	65+	75.0	3.7	7.9	6.1	7.3	. . .	. . .	(164)
Male	Education								
	0–11	17.6	8.8	9.8	10.8	23.5	23.5	5.9	(102)
	12	13.1	5.7	8.0	17.7	21.1	28.0	6.3	(175)
	13–15	12.3	5.8	11.0	15.6	24.0	26.0	5.2	(154)
	16	11.8	7.4	7.4	22.1	22.1	23.5	5.9	(68)
	17+	9.5	6.0	6.0	20.2	27.4	27.4	3.6	(84)
Female	0–11	45.8	6.5	7.5	12.4	9.5	12.4	6.0	(201)
	12	27.5	6.1	8.8	12.6	19.5	21.8	3.8	(262)
	13–15	18.8	10.5	7.3	18.8	16.2	25.1	3.1	(191)
	16	21.4	2.9	4.3	24.3	15.7	27.1	4.3	(70)
	17+	13.7	19.6	13.7	21.6	17.6	11.8	2.0	(51)
Male	Married	5.8	4.2	9.2	20.3	27.5	28.6	4.4	(360)
	Widowed	72.2	. . .	5.6	5.6	11.1	. . .	5.6	(18)
	Divorced	10.4	6.3	6.3	14.6	25.0	22.9	14.6	(48)
	Separated	6.7	13.3	6.7	33.3	6.7	33.3	. . .	(15)
	Never Married	25.2	12.6	9.8	8.4	15.4	23.1	5.6	(143)
Female	Married	10.8	6.3	10.0	20.7	21.8	25.7	4.7	(381)
	Widowed	90.4	2.6	1.8	2.6	1.8	.9	. . .	(114)
	Divorced	31.8	10.0	7.3	16.4	14.5	18.2	1.8	(110)
	Separated	25.6	7.7	5.1	12.8	15.4	23.1	10.3	(39)
	Never Married	24.8	15.0	9.0	13.5	11.3	20.3	6.0	(133)

[a] General Social Surveys—National Opinion Research Center.
Source: Chadwick and Wheaton, *Handbook on the Family,* 141.

TABLE 7.23 ATTITUDES TOWARD SEXUAL ISSUES

1. If a man and a woman have sex relations before marriage, is it wrong? Percent saying "not wrong at all"[a]

Year	1972	1975	1977	1979	1982	1985	1987	1988	1989
	26	32	36	. . .	40	42	. . .	40	39

2. It is . . . a good idea for a couple to live together before getting married . . . to find out whether they . . . get along? Percent saying "agree"[b]

Year	1972	1975	1977	1979	1982	1985	1987	1988	1989
	. . .	35	39	37	42	46	53	51	. . .

3. If two people really like each other, it's all right for them to have sex even if they've known each other only a very short time. Percent saying "agree"[c]

Year	1972	1975	1977	1979	1982	1985	1987	1988	1989
	. . .	50	50	49	48	. . .	52	50	50

4. What is your opinion about a married person having sexual relations with someone other than the marriage partner? Percent saying "always wrong"[a]

Year	1972	1975	1977	1979	1982	1985	1987	1988	1989
	69[e]	73[e]	72	. . .	72	75	75	74	71

5. What about sexual relations between two adults of the same sex? Percent saying "always wrong"[a]

Year	1972	1975	1977	1979	1982	1985	1987	1988	1989
	70[e]	67[e]	69	. . .	70	75	75	74	71

6. Do you think homosexual relations between consenting adults should or should not be legal? Percent saying "not legal"[d]

Year	1972	1975	1977	1979	1982	1985	1987	1988	1989
	. . .	. . .	43	. . .	39	47	54	55	36

7. It is important to have laws prohibiting homosexual relations. Percent saying "agree"[c]

Year	1972	1975	1977	1979	1982	1985	1987	1988	1989
	. . .	. . .	49	47	47	48	53	. . .	. . .

[a] Survey conducted by National Opinion Research Center.
[b] Respondants were high school students. Survey by Survey Research Center, University of Michigan.
[c] Respondants were college students. Survey by Cooperative Research Program at U.C.L.A.
[d] Survey by Gallup Poll.
[e] Statistics are for years 1973 and 1974 instead of 1972 and 1975.
Source: Chadwick and Wheaton, *Handbook on the Family*, 145–46.

Marriage

On the whole the marriage rate remained reasonably steady in the 45 years after 1945. The sharpest shift came at the start, in the immediate postwar period, which experienced a momentary surge in marriages that can be explained as a rush into unions that the war had prevented or at least delayed and an effort to establish a "normal" life in the wake of the great upheaval of wartime. In 1946 the rate stood at a high—and for the general period, abnormal—point of 16.4 marriages per 1,000 population. Then the rate moved down, losing four points in two years, and reached the low point of 8.4 in 1958. By 1966 the rate had climbed back to slightly less than 10 and remained in that territory—a point or less below or a point or less above 10—through the 1980s. Perhaps more striking than the marriage rate was the change in age at (first) marriage and the fact that so many of those who wed did not remain married. The age of first marriage edged upward begining in the 1950s and by 1990 had increased more than three years for both men and women. Men still waited longer than women and the differ-

ence remained nearly the same in 1990 as it had been in the 1940s: approximately three years. Clearly, however, both sexes were taking longer to marry. In 1960, 90 percent of women married before they reached 30; in 1990 only 69 percent had done so. In 1970, 21 percent of men were not married at age 30; in 1990 46 percent were single.

Some of the more interesting statistics involved interracial marriage, especially between blacks and whites. Unions of this sort long had been a delicate, and in the former Confederate states, a risky, issue, especially if the coupling involved a black man and white woman. Interracial marriage remained illegal in 16 states well into the postwar era; not until June 1967 did the Supreme Court find such legislation unconstitutional. By striking down a law in Virginia, it also made measures in 15 other states inoperable. Thereafter the number of black-white marriages remained small as compared with all marriages, but the increase was enough to attract notice, and most of the growth came in unions between black men and white women. Also noticable, if less controversial, was growth of interracial marriage other than a black-white combination.

TABLE 7.24 MARRIAGES AND MARRIAGE RATES, 1945–1990

Year	Number	Rate per 1,000 Population		
		Total Population	Men 15 Years of Age and Older	Women 15 Years and Older
1945	1,612,992	12.2	35.8	30.5
1950	1,667,231	11.1	30.7	29.8
1955	1,531,000	9.3	27.2	25.8
1960	1,523,000	8.5	25.4	24.0
1965	1,800,000	9.3	27.9	26.0
1970	2,158,802	10.6	31.1	28.4
1975	2,152,662	10.0	27.9	25.6
1980	2,390,252	10.6	28.5	26.1
1985	2,412,625	10.1	27.0	24.9
1986	2,407,099	10.0	26.6	24.5
1987	2,403,378	9.9	26.3	24.3
1988	2,395,926	9.8	26.0	24.0
1989	2,403,268	9.7	25.8	23.9
1990	2,443,489	9.8	26.0	24.1

Source: Alsop, *Wall Street Journal Almanac, 1998*, 693.

TABLE 7.25 MEDIAN AGE AT FIRST MARRIAGE, BY SEX, 1947–1990

Year	Men	Women
1947	23.7	20.5
1950	22.8	20.3
1955	22.6	20.2
1960	22.8	20.3
1965	22.8	20.6
1970	23.2	20.8
1975	23.5	21.1
1980	24.7	22.0
1985	25.5	23.3
1990	26.1	23.9

Source: Bureau of the Census, *Marital Status and Living Arrangements: March 1990* (Washington, D.C., 1991), 1.

TABLE 7.26 INTERRACIAL MARRIED COUPLES, 1960–1990

(in thousands)

Year	1960	1970	1980	1990
All married couples	40,491	44,597	49,714	53,227
Interracial married couples	. . .	310	651	964
Black-white married couples	51	65	167	211
husband white, wife black	26	24	45	61
husband black, wife white	25	41	122	150
Other interracial married couples	. . .	245	484	753
husband black	. . .	8	20	24
wife black	. . .	4	14	9
husband white	. . .	139	287	436
wife white	. . .	94	163	284
Hispanic/Hispanic couples	. . .	. . .	1,906	3,857
Hispanic/non-Hispanic couples	. . .	. . .	891	1,434

Source: John W. Wright, *The New York Times 1998 Almanac* (New York, 1997), 281; Alsop, *Wall Street Journal Almanac 1998*, 710.

Divorce

Divorce rates began the postwar period at a high level. The first year after the war, 1946, produced 610,000 divorces with a rate of 4.3 per 1,000 population, both national records that probably were explanable in hasty wartime marriages or the failure of unions in which the members had grown apart during the experience of war. As the country moved into the cold war era, with couples concerned with economic betterment, buying a new house, and in generally being accepted by their peers, the number of divorces and the rate dropped sharply. One of the trademarks of the early anticommunist movement (promiscuity being associated with communism) was for couples to stay together (there were of course other reasons to do so). Those couples who produced the baby boom were expected, as they had been in the past, to cooperate in its rearing, at least in the early stages. The lowest number of divorces in the postwar era (368,000) and the lowest ratio (2:1) came in 1958. Marriages for the most part held together in the 1950s, either because they were working or because the partners felt that they should stick it out.

As the 1960s produced new attitudes and priorities, and as the baby boomers reached age of marriage, the divorce rate began to move slowly but steadily upward. Even though the 1970s theoretically brought another shift in emphasis, it did not reverse the trend in the breakup of marriages. The largest increase in divorce came in the 1970s, the highest ratio in national history (5.3) recorded in 1979, a number that would be repeated in 1981. If the end of the 1980s produced a slight decline, it was a reduction of a high starting point. The rate continued to stand very close to 5. High divorce rates affected virtually all groups, but some had higher numbers than others. With respect to age, the people most affected after 1970 were young: Half of the women and more than half of the men divorcing in 1988 were under age 25. With respect to race and ethnicity the effect was most profound with black couples.

The condition of marriage and divorce in the cold war era perhaps can best be summed up in a table that measured the maritial status of the population more than 15 years old in a given year. In the year 1950 more than 67 percent of males of all races were married, and the status of women was similar; white men ranked very close to the national average, black men, some 64 percent of whom were married, were only 3 percent below the average. By 1990 the national average had dropped nearly 7 percent, no mean decline in itself. White men ranked slightly above the national average—nearly 63 percent of males were married. Approximately 59 percent of white women were married—3 percent higher than the average, also 3 percent lower than the men, largely because, one must assume, husbands died earlier than wives. Between 1950 and 1990 the marriage rate dropped a remarkable 19.7 percent for black men and 22.2 percent for black women. Only 45 percent of black men and 40 percent of black women 15 years and older were married in 1990. If, as often has been the case, marriage has been taken as a mark of a stable society, it would appear that in the half-century since the Second World War, American society in general, and black society in particular, became substantially more unstable.

TABLE 7.27 DIVORCE AND ANNULMENTS AND RATES, 1946–1990

(rate per 1,000)

Year	Divorces and Annulments	Total Population	Married Women 15 Years and Older
1946	610,000	4.3	17.9
1947	483,000	3.4	13.6
1948	408,000	2.8	11.2
1950	385,000	2.6	10.3
1952	392,000	2.5	10.1
1954	379,000	2.4	9.5
1956	382,000	2.3	9.4
1958	368,000	2.1	8.9
1960	393,000	2.2	9.2
1962	413,000	2.2	9.4
1964	450,000	2.4	10.0
1966	499,000	2.5	10.9
1968	584,000	2.9	12.5
1970	708,000	3.5	14.9
1972	845,000	4.0	17.0
1974	977,000	4.6	19.3
1976	1,083,000	5.0	21.1
1978	1,130,000	5.1	21.9
1980	1,189,000	5.2	22.6
1982	1,170,000	5.1	21.7
1984	1,169,000	5.0	21.5
1986	1,178,000	4.9	21.2
1988	1,167,000	4.8	20.7
1990	1,182,000	4.7	20.9

Note: "Total population" includes people under 15 as well.
Source: Department of Health and Human Services, *Supplements to Vital Statistics Report, 1989 and 1990*, 9.

TABLE 7.28 DIVORCED PERSONS PER 1,000 MARRIED PERSONS, BY SEX AND RACE, 1960–1990

Race	1960	1970	1980	1990
Both Sexes				
All races	35	47	100	142
White	33	44	92	133
Black	62	83	203	282
Hispanic	. . .	61	98	129
Male				
All races	28	35	79	118
White	27	32	74	112
Black	45	62	149	208
Hispanic	. . .	40	64	103
Female				
All races	42	60	120	166
White	38	56	110	153
Black	78	104	258	358
Hispanic	. . .	81	132	155

Source: Bureau of Census, *Marital Status: March 1990*, 3.

TABLE 7.29 MARITAL STATUS OF THE POPULATION 15 YEARS AND OLDER BY SEX AND RACE, 1950–1990

(percent)

Year	Married	Unmarried Total	Never Married	Widowed	Divorced
Males					
All Races					
1950	67.5	32.5	26.4	4.1	2.0
1960	69.3	30.7	25.3	3.5	1.8
1970	66.8	33.2	28.1	2.9	2.2
1980	63.2	36.8	29.6	2.4	4.8
1990	60.7	39.3	29.9	2.5	7.6
White					
1950	67.8	32.1	26.1	4.0	2.0
1960	70.3	29.7	24.5	3.4	1.8
1970	68.0	32.0	27.2	2.7	2.1
1980	65.0	35.0	28.1	2.3	4.7
1990	62.8	37.2	28.0	2.4	6.8
Black					
1950	64.4	35.6	28.5	5.2	1.9
1960	60.9	39.1	32.4	4.8	2.0
1970	56.9	43.1	35.6	4.4	3.1
1980	48.9	51.1	41.1	3.7	6.3
1990	45.1	54.9	43.4	3.4	8.1
Females					
All Races					
1950	65.8	34.2	20.0	11.8	2.4
1960	65.9	34.1	19.0	12.5	2.6
1970	61.9	38.1	22.1	12.5	3.5
1980	58.9	41.1	22.5	12.0	6.6
1990	56.9	43.1	22.8	11.5	8.9
White					
1950	66.2	33.8	19.9	11.5	2.4
1960	66.6	33.4	18.7	12.3	2.5
1970	62.8	37.2	21.3	12.4	3.4
1980	60.7	39.3	21.0	11.9	6.4
1990	59.1	40.9	20.6	11.6	8.6
Black					
1950	62.0	38.0	20.7	14.6	2.7
1960	59.8	40.2	21.6	14.3	4.3
1970	54.1	45.9	27.7	13.8	4.4
1980	44.6	55.4	33.6	13.0	8.7
1990	40.2	59.8	36.9	11.6	11.2

Source: Mark S. Littman, *A Statistical Portrait of the U. S., Social Conditions and Trends* (Lanham, Md., 1998), 210.

Families and Households

As utilized by the Bureau of Census, virtually every American was (and is) part of a household and part of a family. The terms came to refer to living arrangements as opposed to related individuals who lived in different places. Having determined that every person, even one who lived alone, belonged to some form of household, the bureau established two principal categories: the family household made up of two or more persons related by birth, marriage, or adoption, and the nonfamily household made up of a person living alone or with other unrelated individuals.

Not unexpectedly, the number of households has increased sharply since the Second World War; the fact that only a small portion of the growth has come in family households was probably unanticipated.

Either because of divorce, slowness to marry, or the willingness of men and women to cohabit outside of marriage, the great increase has come in nonfamily households—a situation that also reflected changed social values and practices. The proportion of married-couple households decreased nearly 20 percent between 1950 and 1990, and the nonfamily households grew by approximately the same percentage. A major increase also came in single-parent households, which usually involved a divorced or never-married woman with children. Such conditions, which offered an open invitation to social problems, fell most heavily on black families. If 67 percent of black children lived with two parents in 1960, by 1990 the number had dropped to fewer than 40 percent. More than half of black children lived with only a mother.

Another conspicuous change has been the increase in unmarried heterosexual cohabitation, the bulk of the growth coming after 1970. If at the start of the 1970s some 11 percent of couples had lived together before marriage, by the mid-1980s the number approached 50 percent, and the younger the people involved the more likely they were willing to cohabit before (or as a substitute for) marriage. Because much of the increase in households came in breaking off from family households and because, beginning in the 1960s, the birthrate underwent a sharp decline, it logically followed that the average size of the family would decrease in a corresponding way.

TABLE 7.30   PERCENTAGE DISTRIBUTION OF HOUSEHOLDS, BY TYPE, 1947–1990

Year	Family Households				Nonfamily Households		
	Total	Married Couple	Other Family		Total	Male Householder	Female Householder
			Male Householder	Female Householder			
1947	89.4	78.3	2.8	8.2	10.6	3.5	7.0
1950	89.2	78.2	2.7	8.3	10.8	3.8	7.0
1955	87.2	75.7	2.8	8.7	12.8	4.3	8.5
1960	85.0	74.3	2.3	8.4	15.0	5.1	8.9
1965	83.3	72.6	2.0	8.7	16.7	5.7	11.0
1970	81.2	70.5	1.9	8.7	18.8	6.4	12.4
1975	78.1	66.0	2.1	10.0	21.9	8.3	13.6
1980	73.9	60.9	2.2	10.8	26.1	10.9	15.3
1985	72.3	58.0	2.6	11.7	27.7	11.7	16.1
1990	70.8	56.0	3.1	11.7	29.2	12.4	16.8

Source: Littman, *Statistical Portrait of the U.S.*, 213.

TABLE 7.31   FAMILIES MAINTAINED BY WOMEN, WITH NO HUSBAND PRESENT, 1960–1990
(numbers in thousands)

Women	1960		1970		1975		1980		1990	
	Number	Percent	Number	Percent	Number	Percent	Number	Percent	Number	Percent
Age of women:										
Under 35 years	796	17.7	1,364	24.4	2,356	32.5	3,015	34.6	3,699	34.0
35 to 44 years	940	20.9	1,074	19.2	1,510	20.9	1,916	22.0	2,929	26.9
45 to 64 years	1,731	38.5	2,021	36.1	2,266	31.3	2,514	28.9	2,790	25.6
65 years and over	1,027	22.9	1,131	20.2	1,108	15.3	1,260	14.5	1,471	13.5
Median age	50.1	...	48.5	...	43.4	...	41.7	...	40.7	...
Presence of children:										
No own children under 18 years	2,397	53.3	2,665	47.7	2,838	39.2	3,260	37.4	4,290	39.4
With own children under 18 years	2,097	46.7	2,926	52.3	4,404	60.8	5,445	62.6	6,599	60.6
Total own children under 18 years	4,674	...	6,694	...	9,227	...	10,204	...	11,378	...
Average per family	1.04	...	1.20	...	1.27	...	1.17	...	1.04	...
Average per family with children	2.24	...	2.29	...	2.10	...	1.87	...	1.72	...
Race:										
White	3,547	78.9	4,165	74.5	5,212	72.0	6,052	69.5	7,306	67.1
Black	947	21.1	1,382	24.7	1,940	26.8	2,495	28.7	3,275	30.1
Other	...	...	44	0.8	90	1.2	158	1.8	309	2.8
Marital status:										
Married, husband absent	1,099	24.5	1,326	23.7	1,647	22.7	1,769	20.3	1,947	17.9
Widowed	2,325	51.7	2,396	42.9	2,559	35.3	2,570	29.5	2,536	23.3
Divorced	694	15.4	1,259	22.5	2,110	29.1	3,008	34.6	3,949	36.3
Never married	376	8.4	610	10.9	926	12.8	1,359	15.6	2,457	22.6
Total families maintained by women	**4,494**	**100.0**	**5,591**	**100.0**	**7,242**	**100.0**	**8,705**	**100.0**	**10,890**	**100.0**

Source: Otto Johnson, ed., *The 1992 Information Please Almanac* (Boston, 1991), 808.

TABLE 7.32 FAMILY AND NONFAMILY HOUSEHOLDS, BY RACE, HISPANIC ORIGIN, AND TYPE, 1970–1990

Race, Hispanic Origin, and Type	Number (1,000)				Percent Distribution			
Family Households	1970	1980	1985	1990	1970	1980	1985	1990
White, total	**46,166**	**52,243**	**54,400**	**56,590**	**100**	**100**	**100**	**100**
Married couple	41,029	44,751	45,643	46,981	89	86	84	83
Male householder	1,038	1,441	1,816	2,303	2	3	3	4
Female householder	4,099	6,052	6,941	7,306	9	12	13	13
Black, total	**4,856**	**6,184**	**6,778**	**7,470**	**100**	**100**	**100**	**100**
Married couple	3,317	3,433	3,469	3,750	68	56	51	50
Male householder	181	256	344	446	4	4	5	6
Female householder	1,358	2,495	2,964	3,275	28	40	44	44
Asian or Pacific Islander, total	. . .	**818**	. . .	**1,531**	. . .	**100**	. . .	**100**
Married couple	. . .	691	. . .	1,256	. . .	84	. . .	82
Male householder	. . .	39	. . .	86	. . .	5	. . .	6
Female householder	. . .	88	. . .	188	. . .	11	. . .	12
Hispanic, total	**2,004**	**3,029**	**3,939**	**4,840**	**100**	**100**	**100**	**100**
Married couple	1,615	2,282	2,824	3,395	81	75	72	70
Male householder	82	138	210	329	4	5	5	7
Female householder	307	610	905	1,116	15	20	23	23
Nonfamily Households								
White, total	**10,436**	**18,522**	**20,928**	**23,573**	**100**	**100**	**100**	**100**
Male householder	3,406	7,499	8,608	9,951	33	40	41	42
Female householder	7,030	11,023	12,320	13,622	67	60	59	58
Black, total	**1,367**	**2,402**	**2,703**	**3,015**	**100**	**100**	**100**	**100**
Male householder	564	1,146	1,244	1,313	41	48	46	44
Female householder	803	1,256	1,459	1,702	59	52	54	56
Hispanic, total	**299**	**654**	**944**	**1,093**	**100**	**100**	**100**	**100**
Male householder	150	365	509	587	50	56	54	54
Female householder	148	289	435	506	49	44	46	46

Source: Bureau of Census, *Statistical Abstract, 1993*, 56.

TABLE 7.33 LIVING ARRANGEMENTS OF CHILDREN UNDER 18 YEARS, BY RACE AND HISPANIC ORIGIN, 1960–1990

Living Arrangement	Numbers in Thousands				Percent Distribution			
	1960	1970	1980	1990	1960	1970	1980	1990
All Races								
Children under 18 years	63,727	69,162	63,427	64,137	100.0	100.0	100.0	100.0
Living with—Two parents	55,877	58,939	48,624	46,503	87.7	85.2	76.7	72.5
One parent	5,829	8,199	12,466	15,867	9.1	11.9	19.7	24.7
Mother only	5,105	7,452	11,406	13,874	8.0	10.8	18.0	21.6
Father only	724	748	1,060	1,993	1.1	1.1	1.7	3.1
Other relatives	1,601	1,547	1,949	1,422	2.5	2.2	3.1	2.2
Nonrelatives only	420	477	388	346	0.7	0.7	0.6	0.5
White								
Children under 18 years	55,077	58,790	52,242	51,390	100.0	100.0	100.0	100.0
Living with—Two parents	50,082	52,624	43,200	40,593	90.9	89.5	82.7	79.0
One parent	3,932	5,109	7,901	9,870	7.1	8.7	15.1	19.2
Mother only	3,381	4,581	7,059	8,321	6.1	7.8	13.5	16.2
Father only	551	528	842	1,549	1.0	0.9	1.6	3.0
Other relatives	774	696	887	708	1.4	1.2	1.7	1.4
Nonrelatives only	288	362	254	220	0.5	0.6	0.5	0.4
Black								
Children under 18 years	8,650	9,422	9,375	10,018	100.0	100.0	100.0	100.0
Living with—Two parents	5,795	5,508	3,956	3,781	67.0	58.5	42.2	37.7
One parent	1,897	2,996	4,297	5,485	21.9	31.8	45.8	54.8
Mother only	1,723	2,783	4,117	5,132	19.9	29.5	43.9	51.2
Father only	173	213	180	353	2.0	2.3	1.9	3.5
Other relatives	827	820	999	654	9.6	8.7	10.7	6.5
Nonrelatives only	132	97	123	98	1.5	1.0	1.3	1.0
Hispanic								
Children under 18 years	. . .	4,006	5,459	7,174	. . .	100.0	100.0	100.0
Living with—Two parents	. . .	3,111	4,116	4,789	. . .	77.7	75.7	66.8
One parent	. . .	. . .	1,152	2,154	. . .	. . .	21.1	30.0
Mother only	. . .	. . .	1,069	1,943	. . .	. . .	19.6	27.1
Father only	. . .	. . .	83	211	. . .	. . .	1.5	2.9
Other relatives	. . .	. . .	183	177	. . .	. . .	3.4	2.5
Nonrelatives only	. . .	. . .	8	54	. . .	. . .	0.1	0.8

Source: Bureau of Census, *Marital Status: March 1990*, 5.

TABLE 7.34 UNMARRIED-COUPLE HOUSEHOLDS, BY PRESENCE OF CHILDREN, 1960–1990

(in thousands)

Year	Total	Without Children Under 15 Years	With Children Under 15 Years
1960	439	242	197
1970	523	327	196
1978	1,137	865	272
1980	1,589	1,159	431
1982	1,863	1,387	475
1984	1,988	1,373	614
1986	2,220	1,558	662
1988	2,558	1,786	802
1990	2,856	1,966	891

Source: Bureau of Census, *Marital Status: March 1990,* 14.

TABLE 7.35 BALANCE OF MALES AND FEMALES 85 YEARS AND OLDER, 1940–1990

Year	Sex Ratio	Excess of Females (thousands)
1940	75.0	52
1950	69.7	103
1960	63.9	205
1970	53.3	430
1980	43.7	877
1990	38.6	1,339

Sex ratio is males per 100 females 85 years old and older.
Source: Darnay, *Record of Older Americans,* 32.

TABLE 7.36 GROWTH OF OLDER POPULATION, 1940–1990

(in thousands)

	Year					
	1940	1950	1960	1970	1980	1990
Total number (all ages)	131,669	150,697	179,323	203,302	226,546	248,710
65 to 74 years						
Number	6,376	8,415	10,997	12,447	15,581	18,045
Percent	4.8	5.6	6.1	6.1	6.9	7.3
75 to 79 years						
Number	1,504	2,128	3,054	3,838	4,794	6,103
Percent	1.1	1.4	1.7	1.9	2.1	2.5
80 to 84 years						
Number	774	1,149	1,580	2,286	2,935	3,909
Percent	0.6	0.8	0.9	1.1	1.3	1.6
80 years and over						
Number	1,139	1,726	2,509	3,695	5,175	6,930
Percent	0.9	1.1	1.4	1.8	2.3	2.8
85 years and over						
Number	365	577	929	1,409	2,240	3,021
Percent	0.3	0.4	0.5	0.7	1.0	1.2
65 years and over						
Number	9,019	12,269	16,560	19,980	25,550	31,079
Percent	6.8	8.1	9.2	9.8	11.3	12.5

Source: Arsen J. Darnay, ed., *Statistical Record of Older Americans* (Detroit, 1994), 47–48.

TABLE 7.37 LIVING ARRANGEMENTS OF THE ELDERLY, 1980 AND 1990

(in thousands)

Living Arrangement and Age	1980			Percent Distribution		1990			Percent Distribution	
	Total	Men	Women	Men	Women	Total	Men	Women	Men	Women
65 years and older	24,157	9,889	14,268	100.0	100.0	29,566	12,334	17,232	100.0	100.0
Alone	7,067	1,447	5,620	14.6	39.4	9,176	1,942	7,233	15.7	42.0
With spouse	12,781	7,441	5,340	75.2	37.4	16,003	9,158	6,845	74.3	39.7
With other relatives	3,892	832	3,060	8.4	21.4	3,734	953	2,782	7.7	16.1
With nonrelatives only	417	169	248	1.7	1.7	653	281	372	2.3	2.2
65 to 74 years	15,302	6,621	8,681	100.0	100.0	17,979	8,013	9,966	100.0	100.0
Alone	3,750	797	2,953	12.0	34.0	4,350	1,042	3,309	13.0	33.2
With spouse	9,436	5,285	4,151	79.8	47.8	11,353	6,265	5,089	78.2	51.1
With other relatives	1,890	436	1,454	6.6	16.7	1,931	528	1,401	6.6	14.1
With nonrelatives only	226	103	123	1.6	1.4	345	178	167	2.2	1.7
75 to 84 years	7,172	2,708	4,464	100.0	100.0	9,354	3,562	5,792	100.0	100.0
Alone	2,664	505	2,159	18.6	48.4	3,774	688	3,086	19.3	53.3
With spouse	2,977	1,882	1,095	69.5	24.5	4,145	2,537	1,607	71.2	27.7
With other relatives	1,394	271	1,123	10.0	25.2	1,237	264	974	7.4	16.8
With nonrelatives only	137	50	87	1.8	1.9	198	73	125	2.0	2.2
85 years and older	1,683	560	1,123	100.0	100.0	2,233	758	1,475	100.0	100.0
Alone	653	145	508	25.9	45.2	1,051	213	838	28.1	56.8
With spouse	368	274	94	48.9	8.4	505	356	150	47.0	10.2
With other relatives	608	125	483	22.3	43.0	567	160	406	21.1	27.5
With nonrelatives only	54	16	38	2.9	3.4	110	29	81	3.8	5.5

Source: Bureau of Census, *Marital Status: March 1990,* 12.

TABLE 7.38   EXPECTATION OF LIFE, BY RACE AND SEX, 1946–1990

Year	All Races Both Sexes	All Races Male	All Races Female	White Both Sexes	White Male	White Female	All Other Both Sexes	All Other Male	All Other Female	Black Both Sexes	Black Male	Black Female
1946	66.7	64.4	69.4	67.5	65.1	70.3	59.1	57.5	61.0	. . .	. . .	. . .
1950	68.2	65.6	71.1	69.1	66.5	72.2	60.0	59.1	62.9	. . .	. . .	. . .
1955	69.6	66.7	72.8	70.5	67.4	73.7	63.7	61.4	66.1	. . .	. . .	. . .
1960	69.7	66.6	73.1	70.6	67.4	74.1	63.6	61.1	66.3	. . .	. . .	. . .
1965	70.2	66.8	73.7	71.0	67.6	74.7	64.1	61.1	67.4	. . .	. . .	. . .
1970	70.8	67.1	74.7	71.7	68.0	75.6	65.3	61.3	69.4	64.1	60.0	68.3
1975	72.6	68.8	76.6	73.4	69.5	77.3	68.0	63.7	72.4	66.8	62.4	71.3
1980	73.7	70.0	77.4	74.4	70.7	78.1	69.5	65.3	73.6	68.1	63.8	72.5
1985	74.7	71.1	78.2	75.3	71.8	78.7	71.0	67.0	74.8	69.3	65.0	73.4
1987	74.9	71.4	78.3	75.6	72.1	78.9	71.0	66.9	75.0	69.1	64.7	73.4
1989	75.1	71.7	78.5	75.9	72.5	79.2	70.9	66.7	74.9	68.8	64.3	73.3
1990	75.4	71.8	78.8	76.1	72.7	79.4	71.2	67.0	75.2	69.1	64.5	73.6

Source: U.S. Department of Health and Human Services, *Vital and Health Statistics, Supplements to the Monthly Vital Statistics Report: Advance Reports 1989 and 1990* (Hyattsville, Md., 1996), 16.

TABLE 7.39   LIFE EXPECTANCY AT BIRTH, ACCORDING TO SEX—SELECTED COUNTRIES, 1984 AND 1989

Male — At Birth — Country	1984	1989	Female — At Birth — Country	1984	1989
Japan	74.8	76.2	Japan	80.7	82.5
Hong Kong	75.1	74.3	France	80.1	81.5
Greece	73.8	74.3	Switzerland	80.8	81.3
Sweden	73.9	74.2	Netherlands	79.9	81.1
Switzerland	73.8	74.1	Canada	80.1	80.6
Israel	73.2	73.9	Spain	79.8	80.3
Netherlands	73.0	73.7	Sweden	80.1	80.1
Canada	73.0	73.7	Hong Kong	81.4	80.1
Spain	73.2	73.6	Norway	79.8	80.0
Italy	71.3	73.3	Italy	77.9	79.9
Norway	73.0	73.3	Australia	79.3	79.6
Australia	72.6	73.3	Greece	78.6	79.4
France	71.7	73.1	Federal Republic of Germany	78.1	79.2
England and Wales	71.9	72.9	Finland	79.0	79.0
Federal Republic of Germany	71.3	72.6	Austria	77.3	78.9
Kuwait	70.4	72.5	United States	78.2	78.6
Denmark	71.8	72.2	England and Wales	77.9	78.4
Cuba	72.2	72.2	Portugal	76.2	78.2
Austria	70.1	72.1	Belgium	77.8	78.2
Costa Rica	74.5	72.1	Denmark	77.8	77.9
United States	71.2	71.8	Israel	76.7	77.6
Ireland	70.8	71.7	New Zealand	77.8	77.3
Northern Ireland	70.3	71.4	Northern Ireland	76.5	77.3
New Zealand	71.2	71.4	Ireland	76.3	77.2
Singapore	70.2	71.4	Puerto Rico	78.3	77.2
Belgium	70.8	71.4	Costa Rica	78.4	76.9
Portugal	69.3	71.1	Singapore	75.6	76.7
Finland	70.5	70.9	German Democratic Republic	75.4	76.4
Scotland	69.9	70.6	Scotland	75.9	76.2
German Democratic Republic	69.6	70.1	Kuwait	74.5	75.8
Chile	67.4	70.0	Chile	74.8	75.7
Puerto Rico	71.6	69.1	Poland	75.0	75.5
Yugoslavia	67.1	69.0	Czechoslovakia	74.6	75.4
Bulgaria	68.5	68.3	Cuba	75.3	75.3
Czechoslovakia	67.1	67.7	Yugoslavia	73.0	74.8
Poland	66.8	66.7	Bulgaria	74.5	74.8
Romania	67.1	66.4	U.S.S.R	72.7	73.9
Hungary	65.1	65.5	Hungary	73.3	73.9
U.S.S.R.	62.9	64.2	Romania	72.7	72.3

Source: Department of Health and Human Services, *Health, United States, 1992* (Hyattsville, Md., 1993), 42–43.

TABLE 7.40 DEATH RATES BY SEX AND RACE, 1940–1990

(number of deaths per 1,000 population)

Year	1940	1950	1960	1970	1975	1978	1980	1985	1988	1990
All Races										
Both Sexes	10.8	9.6	9.5	9.5	8.8	8.7	8.8	8.8	8.9	8.6
Male	12.0	11.1	11.0	10.9	10.0	9.8	9.8	9.5	9.5	9.2
Female	9.5	8.2	8.1	8.1	7.6	7.6	7.9	8.1	8.3	8.1
White										
Both Sexes	10.4	9.5	9.5	9.5	8.9	8.8	8.9	9.0	9.1	8.9
Male	11.6	10.9	11.0	10.9	10.0	9.8	9.8	9.6	9.6	9.4
Female	9.2	8.0	8.0	8.1	7.8	7.8	8.1	8.4	8.7	8.5
Black										
Both Sexes	. . .	. . .	10.4	10.0	8.8	8.6	8.6	8.5	8.9	8.7
Male	. . .	. . .	11.8	11.9	10.6	10.2	10.3	9.9	10.3	10.0
Female	. . .	. . .	9.1	8.3	7.3	7.1	7.3	7.3	7.6	7.5
American Indian										
Both Sexes	. . .	. . .	. . .	. . .	. . .	. . .	4.9	4.2	4.1	4.0
Male	. . .	. . .	. . .	. . .	. . .	. . .	6.0	4.9	4.9	4.8
Female	. . .	. . .	. . .	. . .	. . .	. . .	3.8	3.4	3.4	3.3
Asian or Pacific Islander										
Both Sexes	. . .	. . .	. . .	. . .	. . .	. . .	3.0	2.8	2.8	2.8
Male	. . .	. . .	. . .	. . .	. . .	. . .	3.6	3.4	3.4	3.4
Female	. . .	. . .	. . .	. . .	. . .	. . .	2.2	2.2	2.3	2.3

Source: Littman, *Statistical Portrait of the U.S.*, 241.

TABLE 7.41 DEATH RATES FOR SELECTED CAUSES, BY SEX, 1950–1990

Sex and Cause of Death	1950	1960	1970	1980	1985	1990
All Persons	Deaths per 100,000 Resident Population					
All Causes	841.5	760.9	714.3	585.8	548.9	520.2
Natural causes	766.6	695.2	636.9	519.7	493.0	465.1
Diseases of heart	307.2	286.2	253.6	202.0	181.4	152.0
Ischemic heart disease	. . .	. . .	. . .	149.8	126.1	102.6
Cerebrovascular diseases	88.8	79.7	66.3	40.8	32.5	27.7
Malignant neoplasms	125.4	125.8	129.8	132.8	134.4	135.0
Respiratory system	12.8	19.2	28.4	36.4	39.1	41.4
Colorectal	. . .	17.7	16.8	15.5	14.9	13.6
Prostate[2]	13.4	13.1	13.3	14.4	14.7	16.7
Breast[3]	22.2	22.3	23.1	22.7	23.3	23.1
Chronic obstructive pulmonary diseases	4.4	8.2	13.2	15.9	18.8	19.7
Pneumonia and influenza	26.2	28.0	22.1	12.9	13.5	14.0
Chronic liver disease and cirrhosis	8.5	10.5	14.7	12.2	9.7	8.6
Diabetes mellitus	14.3	13.6	14.1	10.1	9.7	11.7
Human immunodeficiency virus infection	. . .	. . .	. . .	. . .	. . .	9.8
External causes	73.9	65.7	77.4	66.1	55.9	55.1
Unintentional injuries	57.5	49.9	53.7	42.3	34.8	32.5
Motor vehicle-related injuries	23.3	22.5	27.4	22.9	18.8	18.5
Suicide	11.0	10.6	11.8	11.4	11.5	11.5
Homicide and legal intervention	5.4	5.2	9.1	10.8	8.3	10.2
Male	Deaths per 100,000 Resident Population					
All causes	1,001.6	949.3	931.6	777.2	723.0	680.2
Natural causes	. . .	. . .	. . .	675.5	637.9	595.8
Diseases of heart	383.8	375.5	348.5	280.4	250.1	206.7
Ischemic heart disease	. . .	. . .	. . .	214.8	179.6	144.0
Cerebrovascular diseases	91.9	85.4	73.2	44.9	35.5	30.2
Malignant neoplasms	130.8	143.0	157.4	165.5	166.1	166.3
Respiratory system	21.3	34.8	50.6	59.7	60.7	61.0
Colorectal	. . .	18.6	18.7	18.3	17.9	16.8
Prostate	13.4	13.1	13.3	14.4	14.7	16.7
Chronic obstructive pulmonary diseases	6.0	13.7	23.4	26.1	28.1	27.2
Pneumonia and influenza	30.6	35.0	28.8	17.4	18.4	18.5
Chronic liver disease and cirrhosis	11.4	14.5	20.2	17.1	13.7	12.2
Diabetes mellitus	11.4	12.0	13.5	10.2	10.0	12.3
Human immunodeficiency virus infection	. . .	. . .	. . .	. . .	. . .	17.7
External causes	. . .	. . .	. . .	101.7	85.2	84.4
Unintentional injuries	83.7	73.9	80.7	64.0	51.8	47.7
Motor vehicle-related injuries	36.4	34.5	41.1	34.3	27.3	26.3
Suicide	17.3	16.6	17.3	18.0	18.8	19.0
Homicide and legal intervention	8.4	7.9	14.9	17.4	12.8	16.3

(continued)

TABLE 7.41 (continued)

Sex and Cause of Death	1950	1960	1970	1980	1985	1990
Female	Deaths per 100,000 Resident Population					
All causes	688.4	590.6	532.5	432.6	410.3	390.6
Natural causes	. . .	. . .	. . .	400.1	382.2	363.5
Diseases of heart	233.9	205.7	175.2	140.3	127.4	108.9
Ischemic heart disease	. . .	. . .	. . .	98.8	84.2	70.2
Cerebrovascular diseases	86.0	74.7	60.8	37.6	30.0	25.7
Malignant neoplasms	120.8	111.2	108.8	109.2	111.7	112.7
Respiratory system	4.6	5.2	10.1	18.3	22.5	26.2
Colorectal	. . .	16.9	15.4	13.4	12.6	11.3
Breast	22.2	22.3	23.1	22.7	23.3	23.1
Chronic obstructive pulmonary diseases	2.9	3.5	5.4	8.9	12.5	14.7
Pneumonia and influenza	22.0	21.8	16.7	9.8	10.1	11.0
Chronic liver disease and cirrhosis	5.8	.6.9	9.8	7.9	6.1	5.3
Diabetes mellitus	17.1	15.0	14.4	10.0	9.4	11.1
Human immunodeficiency virus infection	. . .	. . .	. . .	. . .	. . .	2.1
External causes	. . .	. . .	. . .	32.5	28.1	27.0
Unintentional injuries	31.7	26.8	28.2	21.8	18.7	17.9
Motor vehicle-related injuries	10.7	11.0	14.4	11.8	10.5	10.7
Suicide	4.9	5.0	6.8	5.4	4.9	4.5
Homicide and legal intervention	2.5	2.6	3.7	4.5	3.9	4.2

Source: Department of Health and Human Services, *Health, United States 1996–97* (Hyattsville, Md., 1997), 111.

TABLE 7.42   DEATH RATES FOR SUICIDE, BY RACE AND SEX, 1950–1990
(deaths per 100,000 population)

Race and Sex	1950	1960	1970	1975	1980	1985	1988	1989	1990
All races	11.0	10.6	11.8	. . .	11.4	11.5	11.5	11.3	11.5
White male	18.1	17.5	18.2	19.6	18.9	19.9	19.9	19.7	20.1
Black male	7.0	7.8	9.9	11.4	11.1	11.5	11.9	12.6	12.5
White female	5.3	5.3	7.2	7.3	5.7	5.3	5.1	4.8	4.8
Black female	1.7	1.9	2.9	2.9	2.4	2.1	2.5	2.4	2.4

Source: Health and Human Services, *Health, U.S., 1992*, 78–79.

TABLE 7.43   DEATH RATES FOR HOMICIDE AND LEGAL INTERVENTION, BY RACE AND SEX, 1950–1990
(deaths per 100,000 population)

Race and Sex	1950	1960	1970	1975	1980	1985	1988	1989	1990
All races	5.4	5.2	9.1	. . .	10.8	8.3	9.0	9.4	10.2
White male	3.9	3.9	7.3	9.3	10.9	8.1	7.8	8.1	9.4
Black male	51.1	44.9	82.1	79.8	71.9	50.2	58.6	61.9	68.7
White female	1.4	1.5	2.2	2.9	3.2	2.9	2.9	2.8	2.8
Black female	11.7	11.8	15.0	16.1	13.7	10.9	12.8	13.0	13.9

Note: Legal intervention pertains to death caused by public officials—execution, death by police action, etc.
Source: Health and Human Services, *Health, U. S., 1992*, 76–77.

TABLE 7.44 PRINCIPAL CLASSES OF ACCIDENTAL DEATHS, 1946–1990

Year	Total Deaths	Total Rate[a]	Motor-Vehicle Deaths	Motor-Vehicle Rate[a]	Work Deaths	Work Rate[a]	Home Deaths	Home Rate[a]	Public Nonmotor Vehicle Deaths	Public Nonmotor Vehicle Rate[a]
1946	98,033	70.0	33,411	23.9	16,500	11.8	33,000	23.6	17,500	12.5
1947	99,579	69.4	32,697	22.8	17,000	11.9	34,500	24.1	18,000	12.6
1948 (5th Revn.)[b]	98,001	67.1	32,259	22.1	16,000	11.0	35,000	24.0	17,000	11.6
1948 (6th Revn.)[b]	93,000	63.7	32,259	22.1	16,000	11.0	31,000	21.2	16,000	11.0
1949	90,106	60.6	31,701	21.3	15,000	10.1	31,000	20.9	15,000	10.1
1950	91,249	60.3	34,763	23.0	15,500	10.2	29,000	19.2	15,000	9.9
1951	95,871	62.5	36,996	24.1	16,000	10.4	30,000	19.6	16,000	10.4
1952	96,172	61.8	37,794	24.3	15,000	9.6	30,500	19.6	16,000	10.3
1953	95,032	60.1	37.955	24.0	15,000	9.5	29,000	18.3	16,500	10.4
1954	90,032	55.9	35,586	22.1	14,000	8.7	28,000	17.4	15,500	9.6
1955	93,443	56.9	38,426	23.4	14,200	8.6	28,500	17.3	15,500	9.4
1956	94,780	56.6	39,628	23.7	14,300	8.5	28,000	16.7	16,000	9.6
1957	95,307	55.9	38,702	22.7	14,200	8.3	28,000	16.4	17,500	10.3
1958	90,604	52.3	36,981	21.3	13,300	7.7	26,500	15.3	16,500	9.5
1959	92,080	52.2	37,910	21.5	13,800	7.8	27,000	15.3	16,500	9.3
1960	93,806	52.1	38,137	21.2	13,800	7.7	28,000	15.6	17,000	9.4
1961	92,249	50.4	38,091	20.8	13,500	7.4	27,000	14.8	16,500	9.0
1962	97,139	52.3	40,804	22.0	13,700	7.4	28,500	15.3	17,000	9.2
1963	100,669	53.4	43,564	23.1	14,200	7.5	28,500	15.1	17,500	9.3
1964	105,000	54.9	47,700	25.0	14,200	7.4	28,000	14.6	18,500	9.7
1965	108,004	55.8	49,163	25.4	14,100	7.3	28,500	14.7	19,500	10.1
1966	113,563	58.1	53,041	27.1	14,500	7.4	29,500	15.1	20,000	10.2
1967	113,169	57.3	52,924	26.8	14,200	7.2	29,000	14.7	20,500	10.4
1968	114,864	57.6	54,862	27.5	14,300	7.2	28,000	14.0	21,500	10.8
1969	116,385	57.8	55,791	27.7	14,300	7.1	27,500	13.7	22,500	11.2
1970	114,638	56.2	54,633	26.8	13,800	6.8	27,000	13.2	23,500	11.5
1971	113,439	54.8	54,381	26.3	13,700	6.6	26,500	12.8	23,500	11.4
1972	115,448	55.2	56,278	26.9	14,000	6.7	26,500	12.7	23,500	11.2
1973	115,821	54.8	55,511	26.3	14,300	6.8	26,500	12.5	24,500	11.6
1974	104,622	49.0	46,402	21.8	13,500	6.3	26,000	12.2	23,000	10.8
1975	103,030	47.8	45,853	21.3	13,000	6.0	25,000	11.6	23,000	10.6
1976	100,761	46.3	47,038	21.6	12,500	5.7	24,000	11.0	21,500	10.0
1977	103,202	47.0	49,510	22.5	12,900	5.9	23,200	10.6	22,200	10.1
1978	105,561	47.5	52,411	23.6	13,100	5.9	22,800	10.3	22,000	9.9
1979	105,312	46.9	53,524	23.8	13,000	5.8	22,500	10.0	21,000	9.4
1980	105,718	46.5	53,172	23.4	13,200	5.8	22,800	10.0	21,300	9.4
1981	100,704	43.9	51,385	22.4	12,500	5.4	21,700	9.4	19,800	8.6
1982	94,082	40.6	45,779	19.7	11,900	5.1	21,200	9.1	19,500	8.4
1983	92,488	39.5	44,452	19.0	11,700	5.0	21,200	9.0	19,400	8.3
1984	92,911	39.3	46,263	19.6	11,500	4.9	21,200	9.0	18,300	7.7
1985	93,457	39.1	45,901	19.2	11,500	4.8	21,600	9.0	18,800	7.9
1986	95,277	39.5	47,865	19.9	11,100	4.6	21,700	9.0	18,700	7.8
1987	95,020	39.0	48,290	19.8	11,300	4.6	21,400	8.8	18,400	7.6
1988	97,100	39.7	49,078	20.1	11,000	4.5	22,700	9.3	18,400	7.5
1989	95,027	38.3	47,575	19.2	10,900	4.4	22,500	9.1	18,200	7.3
1990	93,000	37.3	46,800	18.8	10,600	4.2	21,000	8.4	18,500	7.4

[a] Rates are deaths per 100,000 population.
[b] In 1948 a revision was made in the calculation of causes of death. The first figures for 1948 are comparable with those for earlier years, the second with those for later years.
Source: National Safety Council, *Accident Facts, 1992 Edition* (Chicago, 1992), 26–27.

TABLE 7.45 REPORTED CASES OF COMMON INFECTIOUS DISEASES, 1950–1990

Disease	1950	1960	1970	1980	1990
Aseptic meningitis	N.A.	1,593	6,480	8,028	11,852
Brucellosis (undulant fever)	3,510	751	213	183	85
Diphtheria	5,796	918	435	3	4
Encephalitis	1,135	2,341	1,950	1,402	1,446
Legionnellosis	N.A.	N.A.	N.A.	N.A.	1,370
Leprosy (Hansen disease)	44	54	129	223	198
Malaria	2,184	72	3,051	2,062	1,292
Meningococcal infections	3,788	2,259	2,505	2,840	2,451
Mumps	N.A.	N.A.	105,000	8,600	5,300
Pertussis (whooping cough)	120,700	14,800	4,200	1,700	4,600
Plague	N.A.	2	13	18	2
Poliomyelitis	33,300	3,190	33	9	7

Disease	1950	1960	1970	1980	1990
Rabies, in animals	7,901	3,567	3,224	6,421	4,826
Rabies, in humans	18	2	3	0	1
Rubella (German measles)	N.A.	N.A.	56,600	3,900	1,100
Tetanus	486	368	148	95	64
Trichinosis	327	160	109	131	129
Tuberculosis	N.A.	55,500	37,100	27,700	25,700
Tularemia	927	390	172	234	152
Typhoid fever	2,484	816	346	510	552
Typhus fever, tick-borne	464	204	380	1,163	654
Venereal disease					
Gonorrhea	286,700	258,900	600,100	1,004,000	690,200
Syphilis	217,600	122,500	91,400	68,800	134,300

Source: Wright, *Universal Almanac, 1995,* 216.

TABLE 7.46 TRENDS IN CANCER SURVIVAL, BY RACE AND SITE, 1960–1990

Site	White					Black				
	Relative 5-Year Survival Percent					Relative 5-Year Survival Percent				
	1960–63	1970–73	1974–76	1977–79	1983–90	1960–63	1970–73	1974–76	1977–79	1983–90
All sites	39	43	50	51	56	27	31	39	39	40
Oral cavity & pharynx	45	43	55	54	55	...	...	36	36	34
Esophagus	4	4	5	6	11	1	4	4	3	6
Stomach	11	13	14	16	18	8	13	16	15	19
Colon	43	49	50	53	61	34	37	46	48	50
Rectum	38	45	49	51	58	27	30	42	38	49
Liver	...	...	4	3	7	...	...	1	6	4
Pancreas	1	2	3	2	3	1	2	2	4	5
Larynx	53	62	66	68	69	...	...	59	55	53
Lung & bronchus	8	10	12	14	14	5	7	11	11	11
Melonoma of skin	60	68	80	82	85	...	...	66	51	70
Female breast	63	68	75	75	82	46	51	63	63	66
Cervix uteri	58	64	69	69	70	47	61	64	62	56
Corpus uteri	73	81	89	86	85	31	44	60	58	55
Ovary	32	36	36	38	42	32	32	40	40	38
Prostate	50	63	68	72	81	35	55	58	62	66
Testis	63	72	79	88	94	...	...	76	...	87
Urinary bladder	53	61	74	76	81	24	36	48	55	60
Kidney & renal pelvis	37	46	51	51	57	38	44	49	51	52
Brain & nervous system	18	20	22	24	27	19	19	27	28	31
Thyroid gland	83	86	92	92	95	...	...	88	91	90
Hodgkin's disease	40	67	72	73	79	...	...	68	73	74
Non-Hodgkin's lymphoma	31	41	48	48	53	...	...	48	50	45
Multiple myeloma	12	19	24	25	27	...	...	27	34	29
Leukemia	14	22	35	38	40	...	...	32	30	31

Source: Allan R. Cook, ed., *The New Cancer Sourcebook* (Detroit, 1996), 32.

TABLE 7.47 AIDS CASES REPORTED, BY PATIENT CHARACTERISTIC, 1981–1990

Characteristic	Number of Cases										Percent Distribution	
	Total	1981–1982	1983	1984	1985	1986	1987	1988	1989	1990[a]	1981–1982	1990[a]
Total	142,424	838	2,059	4,435	8,182	13,124	21,117	30,858	33,714	28,097	100.0	100.0
Age												
Under 5 years old	1,937	12	31	47	110	156	265	443	503	370	1.4	1.3
5 to 12 years old	442	1	1	3	18	28	56	126	102	107	0.1	0.4
13 to 29 years old	29,144	196	457	960	1,685	2,815	4,385	6,383	6,780	5,483	23.4	19.5
30 to 39 years old	65,581	396	929	2,108	3,838	6,093	9,634	14,199	15,553	12,831	47.3	45.7
40 to 49 years old	30,726	169	446	923	1,707	2,685	4,516	6,529	7,340	6,411	20.2	22.8
50 to 59 years old	10,330	58	166	312	626	968	1,553	2,163	2,431	2,053	6.9	7.3
60 years old and over	4,264	6	29	82	198	379	708	1,015	1,005	842	0.7	3.0
Sex												
Male	128,243	780	1,902	4,142	7,597	12,068	19,290	27,562	30,053	24,849	93.1	88.4
Female	14,173	58	157	293	585	1,056	1,826	3,294	3,658	3,246	6.9	11.6
Not reported	8	0	0	0	0	0	1	2	3	2	0	0
Race/ethnic group												
White, non-Hispanic	81,081	467	1,174	2,689	4,957	7,822	12,969	17,177	18,632	15,194	55.8	54.1
Black, non-Hispanic	41,119	251	565	1,119	2,080	3,392	5,382	9,107	10,321	8,902	30.0	31.7
Hispanic	18,785	117	311	605	1,085	1,785	2,554	4,274	4,352	3,702	14.0	13.2
Other/unknown	1,439	3	9	22	60	125	212	300	409	299	0.2	1.1

Characteristic	Total	1981–1982	1983	1984	1985	1986	1987	1988	1989	1990[a]	Percent Distribution 1981–1982	1990[a]
Leading States[b]												
New York	32,178	456	865	1,584	2,483	3,781	3,966	6,975	6,022	6,046	54.4	21.5
California	27,653	120	440	1,002	1,936	2,615	4,853	5,743	6,435	4,509	14.3	16.1
Florida	12,684	69	153	314	554	1,024	1,662	2,696	3,492	2,720	8.2	9.7
Texas	10,424	20	89	250	483	940	1,670	2,231	2,399	2,342	2.4	8.3
New Jersey	9,638	63	136	281	468	767	1,509	2,455	2,231	1,728	7.5	6.2
Illinois	4,298	18	39	100	188	347	629	993	1,139	845	2.2	3.0
Pennsylvania	4,086	19	37	91	202	310	657	852	1,075	843	2.3	3.0
Georgia	3,816	13	25	56	191	304	517	839	1,102	769	1.6	2.7
Massachusetts	3,062	13	34	87	165	281	452	711	756	563	1.6	2.0
Maryland	2,785	5	27	54	148	188	457	545	719	642	0.6	2.3
District of Columbia	2,493	3	19	90	178	226	466	501	498	512	0.4	1.8
Ohio	2,121	8	7	30	53	212	335	507	485	484	1.0	1.7
Louisiana	2,069	0	18	55	104	165	337	401	513	476	0	1.7
Washington	1,958	1	6	59	112	170	328	349	497	436	0.1	1.6
Virginia	1,859	0	27	40	108	160	242	348	392	542	0	1.9
Michigan	1,795	4	9	32	61	150	211	456	505	367	0.5	1.3
Connecticut	1,733	10	18	57	86	176	251	415	432	288	1.2	1.0
Missouri	1,624	1	7	27	50	74	238	411	441	375	0.1	1.3
North Carolina	1,512	0	9	15	66	81	210	278	447	406	0	1.4
Colorado	1,451	5	21	38	62	166	226	325	389	219	0.6	0.8
Percent of total	90.7	98.8	96.5	96.1	94.1	92.5	91.0	90.8	88.9	89.4	. . .	. . .

[a] January 1 through August.
[b] States with at least 1,400 total cases reported through August 1990.
Source: Bureau of Census, *Statistical Abstract, 1991,* 119.

Before the polio vaccine, there was the iron lung. This unit in 1949 was in the Riley Hospital, Indianapolis. (IUPUI University Library Special Collections and Archives)

TABLE 7.48 TRANSMISSION OF AIDS, 1981–1989

Transmission of AIDS in Adults and Adolescents, 1981–1989						
Characteristic	Males	Percent	Females	Percent	Both Sexes	Percent
Homosexual/bisexual males	70,093	67	. . .	. . .	70,093	61
Intravenous (IV) drug abusers	18,721	18	5,491	52	24,212	21
Homosexual male and IV drug abusers	8,117	8	. . .	. . .	8,117	7
Hemophilia/coagulation disorder	1,034	1	28	. . .	1,062	1
Heterosexuals	2,308	2	3,322	31	5,630	5
Blood transfusion	1,768	2	1,062	10	2,830	2
Undetermined	3,134	3	708	7	3,842	3
Total	**105,175**	**91**	**10,611**	**9**	**115,786**	**100**

Transmission of AIDS in Children, 1981–1989[a]		
Characteristic	Totals	Percent
Hemophilia/Coagulation Disorder	106	5
Mother with/at risk of AIDS	1,614	81
Blood transfusion	212	11
Undetermined	63	3
Total	**1,995**	**100**

[a] Provisional data includes all patients under 13 years of age at time of diagnosis.
Source: (both tables) Wright, *Universal Almanac, 1991*, 258.

TABLE 7.49 AIDS CASES AND DEATHS IN THE UNITED STATES, 1981–1993

Year	Cases Diagnosed	Cases Diagnosed to Date	Known Deaths	Known Deaths to Date
Pre-1981	92	92	31	31
1981	315	407	128	159
1982	1,156	1,563	461	620
1983	3,084	4,647	1,502	2,122
1984	6,198	10,845	3,478	5,600
1985	11,775	22,620	6,929	12,529
1986	19,042	41,662	12,021	24,550
1987	28,560	70,222	16,270	40,820
1988	35,267	105,489	20,903	61,723
1989	41,681	147,170	27,449	89,172
1990	46,075	193,245	30,649	119,821

Source: Wright, *Universal Almanac, 1995*, 218.

Medical Care and Medical Care Providers

The health care industry underwent major change in the period following the Second World War, as one would expect in a nation that experienced rapid population growth and new developments in the way the industry went about its business. The number of doctors increased, of course, although for several years the rate of growth was slow. The nation had only 142 doctors for each 100,000 people in 1950, and the ratio grew by only 19 in the 20 years that followed. That period produced much concern about a doctor shortage, a shortcoming that some people attributed to a conspiracy by the American Medical Association. The increase in the number of physicians picked up somewhat after 1970, and by 1990 the United States had 244 doctors per 100,000 population. The increase came partly from growth in the number of American medical schools and in the number of students admitted into the programs, but an important new factor after 1970 was entry into the United States of individuals of foreign extraction educated in foreign medical schools. By the 1980s more than 25 percent of new doctors came from abroad. The years after 1970 also produced an increase in female physicians that corresponded with a general change in attitude toward women in society. A total of 21,000 female doctors in 1970 grew to 93,000 20 years later, and by that time women made up a much larger proportion of medical student clientele than had been the case in 1950 or even 1970.

The medical profession showed a clear tendency toward specialization. The number of doctors engaged in general or family practice changed little after 1970. The growth came in nearly all the specialties but especially in pediatrics, obstetrics, and surgery. Physicians who offered themselves as specialists in internal medicine even surpassed the number in family practice and in some fashion perhaps became the general practitioners of the day.

It was a curious fact that the large increase in medical patients did not lead to a corresponding increase in hospitals. The number of hospitals grew slowly until the mid-1970s and then began to decline. By 1990 there were fewer hospitals—and more striking, hospital beds—than in 1950 despite an increase of nearly 100,000,000 in population. The explanation appeared in the great surge in outpatient activity; new medical knowledge, improved facilities and procedures made it possible for patients to have their treatment at a hospital or a doctor's clinic and go home.

The last half of the 20th century was a period of great advance in medicine and medical procedure, a time of open-heart surgery, organ transplants, new testing devices, medications of many kinds. With all its wealth, technology, and incentive, the United States remained a leader in world medical knowledge. Prominent foreign individuals often came to this country when they needed the most sophisticated treatment. Changes in medical science surely improved the quality of life for many people and eased or eliminated pain until the malady vanished or the end came. Records verify that changes in medicine, added to numerous other social, economic, and behavioral practices lengthened the time of life. In the 45 years after 1945 average life expectancy in the United States increased by 9.5 years, not an insignificant amount, but perhaps not as much as one might expect, given the large advance in medical science. In the 45 years before 1946, before many of the "miracle" treatments had become available, life expectancy had increased by 12.6 years, and this period included the life-shortening two world wars (substantially larger engagements, one might add, than the various conflicts in which the nation became involved after 1945).

The most striking change in the medical system—situation might be a better word, for there was no system—was in the cost. Here the numbers were truly remarkable. Total medical costs multiplied some 56 times between 1950 and 1990. The average cost of a day in a hospital increased 130-fold between 1946 and 1990. The health-care industry indeed became a business with many arms and branches, and some of the more important changes of the 1980s had to do with management aspects of the operation. Whatever American medicine was or was not as the century moved to a close, it stood as manifestation of the capitalist objective of profit.

The United States spent more money on health care, a larger portion of gross domestic product, more money per capita, than any other nation. Yet by 1990 millions of people could not claim inclusion in some medical program (they were "not covered," as one commonly put it), and other millions were not adequately covered. As the United States moved toward the new millennium, health care remained one of the largest, if not the largest, social and economic problems.

Some Major Developments in Health and Medicine, 1946–1990

1951 Antabuse, a drug designed to stop alcoholics from drinking, is introduced.

American surgeon John H. Gibbon, Jr., develops the heart-lung machine.

1952 Jonas Salk develops a killed-virus vaccine against polio.

1953 American James Watson and British Francis Crick determine the structure of DNA, the basis for heredity.

1954 Joseph Murray and other American surgeons perform the first successful kidney transplant.

1956 The kidney dialysis machine, developed in The Netherlands, comes into use in the United States.

1957 Polish-American Albert B. Sabin develops a live-virus vaccine against polio. It will supersede the Salk product.

The first antianxiety benzodiazepine, a tranquilizer to be marketed as Librium, is discovered.

1958 American Clarence W. Lillehei produces the first pacemaker for the heart.

A Scottish doctor first uses ultrasound to evaluate unborn babies.

1960 An oral contraceptive medication that blocks female ovulation, the "pill," comes on the market.

1962 Lasers are used for the first time in eye surgery.

1963 Valium, another antianxiety benzodiazepine, is introduced.

Americans Thomas Starzl and Francis Moore perform the first liver transplant.

1964 The surgeon general reports on the risk to health produced by smoking cigarettes. The Federal Trade Commission rules that beginning in 1965 cigarette packages must carry a warning that cigarette smoking can be harmful. James Hardy of the United States performs the first lung transplant.

1965 Medicare (a national program) and Medicaide (a shared national and state program) are established to help fund medical care for the aged and poor.

Helen Keller (center), spokesperson for the blind, with Polly Thompson, meets President Eisenhower, November 3, 1953. (National Archives)

1967 South African surgeon Christian Barnaard performs the first heart transplant. The recipient will live 18 days. Surgeon Rene Favaloro performs in Cleveland the first coronary bypass operation. Mammography is introduced to detect breast cancer.

1969 Dr. Denton Cooley of Texas implants the first temporary artificial heart in a human. The patient, Haskell Karp, will live short of three days.

1971 Raymond V. Damadian of New York applies for a patent for using magnetic resonance imaging, to be called an MRI, in finding internal malfunctions, such as tumors.

A British engineer combines X rays and computers to produce another method of internal detection, known as computerized axial tomography, or a CAT scan.

1975 Researchers at the Squibb Institute succeed in blocking human angiotensin-converting enzymes, thus producing the first ACE inhibitor of high blood pressure, known as Captopril.

1976 A strange new disease, which will be known as Legionnaire's disease, is discovered at an American Legion Convention in Philadelphia.

1977 A German surgeon invents balloon angioplasty, a method short of surgery, to remove blockage in an artery.

1978 The first "test-tube" baby, a girl named Louise Brown, is born in England.

1980 The Salk and Sabine vaccines have been so successful that it is possible to pronounce polio globally to be extinct.

Researchers in New York develop a successful vaccine against hepatitis B.

1981 Scientists identify and label a new disease that has signs of being devastating. They call it AIDS because it constitutes an acquired immune deficiency syndrome.

1982 A team of doctors led by William DeVries places an artificial heart (Jarvik 7) in a patient in Utah. The patient, Barney Clark, will live 112 days.

1986 Use of a blood test to detect prostate cancer, called a PSA, is approved in the United States.

1987 The Food and Drug Administration approves AZT, a drug marketed as Retrovir, for treatment of people with AIDS.

A new antidepressant drug, fluoxetine, with trade name of Prozac, is approved for use in the United States.

1988 The Food and Drug Administration approves alpha interferon for treatment of genital warts.

1990 The FDA approves use of Norplant, a birth control device implanted under the skin.

Source: Bryan Bunch, *Handbook of Health & Medicine* (Detroit, 1994), 291–92, 324–25, 476–77, 504–05, 525–26.

TABLE 7.50   HOSPITAL STATISTICS, 1946–1990

Year	Hospitals	Beds (in thousands)	Admissions (in thousands)	Average Daily Census (in thousands)	Outpatient Visits (in thousands)	FTE Personnel[a] Number (in thousands)	Payroll Amount (in millions of dollars)	Employee Benefits Amount (in millions of dollars)	Total Expenses Amount (in millions of dollars)
1946	6,125	1,436	15,675	1,142	. . .	830	1,103	. . .	1,963
1950	6,788	1,456	18,483	1,253	. . .	1,058	2,191	. . .	3,651
1955	6,956	1,604	21,073	1,363	. . .	1,301	3,582	. . .	5,594
1960	6,876	1,658	25,027	1,402	. . .	1,598	5,588	. . .	8,421
1965	7,123	1,704	28,812	1,403	125,793	1,952	8,551	. . .	12,948
1970	7,123	1,616	31,759	1,298	181,370	2,537	15,706	. . .	25,556
1971	7,097	1,556	32,664	1,237	199,725	2,589	17,635	$ 1,531	28,812
1972	7,061	1,550	33,265	1,209	219,182	2,671	19,530	1,925	32,667
1973	7,123	1,535	34,352	1,189	233,555	2,769	21,330	2,238	36,290
1974	7,174	1,513	35,506	1,167	250,481	2,919	23,821	2,611	41,406
1975	7,156	1,466	36,157	1,125	254,844	3,023	27,135	3,175	48,706
1976	7,082	1,434	36,776	1,090	270,951	3,108	30,438	3,848	56,005
1977	7,099	1,407	37,060	1,066	263,775	3,213	33,742	4,691	63,630
1979	6,988	1,372	37,802	1,043	262,009	3,382	41,464	6,155	79,796
1980	6,965	1,365	38,892	1,060	262,951	3,492	46,970	7,221	91,886
1981	6,933	1,362	39,169	1,061	265,332	3,661	54,516	8,738	107,146
1982	6,915	1,360	39,095	1,053	313,667	3,746	62,015	10,420	123,219
1983	6,888	1,350	38,887	1,028	273,168	3,707	67,742	12,036	136,315
1984	6,872	1,339	37,938	970	276,566	3,630	71,007	13,005	144,114
1985	6,872	1,318	36,304	910	282,140	3,625	74,387	13,875	153,327
1986	6,841	1,290	35,219	883	294,634	3,647	78,589	14,400	165,194
1987	6,821	1,267	34,439	873	310,707	3,742	83,778	15,318	178,662
1988	6,780	1,248	34,107	863	336,208	3,839	91,841	16,990	196,704
1989	6,720	1,226	33,742	853	352,248	3,937	99,256	19,375	214,886
1990	6,649	1,213	33,774	844	368,184	4,063	108,719	21,797	234,870

[a] Note: FTE—full-time employees
Source: American Hospital Association, *Hospital Statistics, 1994–95 Edition* (Chicago, 1994), 2.

TABLE 7.51 HOSPITAL EXPENSE PER DAY, 1946–1990[a]

Year	Amount
1946	5.21
1950	7.98
1955	11.24
1960	16.46
1965	25.29
1970	53.95
1975	134.00
1980	245.00
1985	460.00
1990	678.00

[a] In dollars. Average of hospitals registered by the American Hospital Association.
Source: Kurian, *Datapedia*, 54.

TABLE 7.52 PHYSICIANS IN THE UNITED STATES—SELECTED CHARACTERISTICS, 1950–1990

Year[a]	Total Physician[b]	Total Population ('000s)[c]	Total Physician per 100,000 Total Population	Total Population per One Physician	Total Patient Care Physician	Total Patient Care Physician per 100,000 Total Population	Total Population per Patient Care Physician
1950	219,997	154,668	142	703	. . .	. . .	. . .
1955	241,711	168,373	144	697	. . .	. . .	. . .
1960	260,484	183,236	142	703	. . .	. . .	. . .
1965	292,088	197,147	148	675	259,418	132	760
1970	334,028	208,066	161	623	278,535	134	747
1975	393,742	219,272	180	557	311,937	142	703
1980	467,679	231,266	202	494	376,512	163	614
1981	485,123	233,459	208	481	389,369	167	600
1982	501,958	235,691	213	458	408,663	173	577
1983	519,546	238,139	218	458	423,361	178	563
1984	536,986	240,543	223	448	437,089	182	550
1985	552,716	242,946	228	440	448,820	185	541
1986	569,160	245,163	232	431	462,126	188	531
1987	585,597	247,488	237	423	478,511	193	517
1989	600,789	249,876	240	416	493,159	197	507
1990	615,421	252,164	244	410	503,870	200	500

[a] Data for 1989 and 1990 are as of January 1. Data prior to 1989 are as of December 31.
[b] Includes all federal and nonfederal physicians in the United States and Possessions, inactive physicians, and those with unknown addresses as of December 31 each year. Excluded are nonfederal physicians with temporary foreign addresses. (Note: Possessions include Canal Zone prior to 1980, Pacific Islands, Puerto Rico, and Virgin Islands).
[c] Includes U.S. residents, Armed Forces overseas, and civilians in U.S. Possessions as of July 1 each year.
Source: American Medical Association, *Physician Characteristics and Distribution in the U.S. 1992 Edition*, (Chicago, 1992), 35.

TABLE 7.53 PHYSICIANS BY SEX, EDUCATION, AND SPECIALTY, 1970–1990

(in thousands)

Activity	1970	1975	1980	1985	1986	1988	1989	1990
Doctors of medicine, total	**334.0**	**393.7**	**467.7**	**552.7**	**569.2**	**585.6**	**600.8**	**615.4**
Professionally active	310.8	340.3	414.9	497.1	505.8	521.3	536.8	547.3
Place of medical education:								
U.S. medical graduates	256.4	. . .	333.3	392.0	398.3	410.3	423.2	432.9
Foreign medical graduates	54.4	. . .	81.6	105.1	107.4	111.0	113.6	114.4
Sex: Male	289.5	313.1	370.2	425.3	429.0	. . .	. . .	454.0
Female	21.4	27.2	44.7	71.9	76.8	. . .	. . .	93.3
Active Non-Federal	281.3	312.1	397.1	475.6	483.8	499.6	516.4	526.8
Patient care	255.0	287.8	361.9	431.5	436.9	453.2	468.9	479.5
Office-based practice	188.9	213.3	271.3	329.0	325.8	337.5	350.1	359.9
General and family practice	50.8	46.3	47.8	53.9	53.6	55.1	56.3	57.6
Cardiovascular diseases	3.9	5.0	6.7	9.1	9.4	9.9	10.2	10.7
Dermatology	2.9	3.4	4.4	5.3	5.4	5.5	5.7	6.0
Gastroenterology	1.1	1.7	2.7	4.1	4.4	4.8	4.9	5.2
Internal medicine	23.0	28.2	40.5	52.7	52.3	55.5	56.9	57.8
Pediatrics	10.3	12.7	17.4	22.4	22.5	23.4	24.7	26.5
Pulmonary diseases	0.8	1.2	2.0	3.0	3.2	3.5	3.6	3.7
General surgery	18.1	19.7	22.4	24.7	23.5	23.7	24.7	24.5
Obstetrics and gynecology	13.8	15.6	19.5	23.5	23.6	24.3	25.2	25.5
Ophthalmology	7.6	8.8	10.6	12.2	12.1	12.5	12.8	13.1
Orthopedic surgery	6.5	8.1	10.7	13.0	13.1	13.5	14.1	14.2
Otolaryngology	3.9	4.3	5.3	5.8	5.8	6.0	6.2	6.4

(continued)

TABLE 7.53   (continued)

Activity	1970	1975	1980	1985	1986	1988	1989	1990
Plastic surgery	1.2	1.7	2.4	3.3	3.4	3.5	3.6	3.8
Urological surgery	4.3	5.0	6.2	7.1	7.0	7.2	7.3	7.4
Anesthesiology	7.4	9.0	11.3	15.3	15.3	16.0	16.7	17.8
Diagnostic radiology	0.9	2.0	4.2	7.7	8.1	8.6	9.0	9.8
Emergency medicine	. . .	. . .	. . .	. . .	7.3	7.6	8.0	8.4
Neurology	1.2	1.9	3.2	4.7	4.8	5.1	5.4	5.6
Pathology, anatomical/clinical	3.0	4.2	6.0	6.9	6.5	6.7	7.0	7.3
Psychiatry	10.1	12.2	15.9	18.5	18.2	18.7	19.6	20.0
Radiology	5.8	7.0	7.8	7.4	6.1	6.1	6.2	6.1
Other specialty	12.4	15.3	24.1	28.5	20.2	20.3	21.7	22.8
Hospital-based practice	66.1	74.5	90.6	102.5	111.1	115.7	118.8	119.6
Residents and interns	45.8	53.5	59.6	72.2	77.6	79.5	80.0	81.7
Full-time hospital staff	20.3	21.0	31.0	30.3	33.5	36.2	38.8	38.0
Other professional activity	26.3	24.3	35.2	44.0	46.9	46.4	47.5	47.3
Federal	29.5	28.2	17.8	21.6	21.9	21.7	20.4	20.5
Patient care	23.5	24.1	14.6	17.3	17.0	16.9	15.6	15.6
Office-based practice	3.5	2.1	0.7	1.2	1.2	1.1	1.1	1.1
Hospital-based practice	20.0	22.0	13.9	16.1	15.8	15.8	14.4	14.6
Residents and interns	5.4	4.3	2.4	3.3	2.9	2.7	2.1	1.7
Full-time hospital staff	14.6	17.7	11.4	12.9	12.9	13.0	12.4	12.8
Other professional activity	6.0	4.1	3.2	4.3	5.0	4.8	4.8	4.8
Inactive	19.6	21.4	25.7	38.6	46.8	48.0	48.8	52.7
Not classified	0.4	26.1	20.6	14.0	13.7	13.4	12.4	12.7
Unknown address	3.2	5.9	6.4	3.0	2.9	2.9	2.8	2.8
Doctors of osteopathy	**14.3**	**15.4**	**18.8**	**24.0**	**25.5**	**28.3**	**29.6**	**30.9**
Medical and osteopathic schools	110	123	141	142	142	142	142	141
Students	42.6	59.3	70.1	73.2	72.8	71.9	71.6	72.0
Graduates	8.8	13.9	16.2	17.8	17.7	17.5	17.2	16.9

Source: *Statistical Abstract, 1993,* 118.

TABLE 7.54   DENTISTS AND NURSES, 1946–1990

People	1946	1950	1955	1960	1965	1970	1975	1980	1985	1990
Dentists (1,000)	. . .	89	98	102	109	118	127	141	156	186
Rate (per 100,000 pop.)	. . .	59	59	56	56	58	50	60	60	63
Dental Schools	39	41	43	47	49	53	59	60	60	58
Students (1,000)	7.3	11.5	12.6	13.6	13.9	16.0	20.8	22.8	19.6	15.8
Graduates (1,000)	2.7	2.6	3.1	3.3	3.2	3.7	5.0	5.3	5.4	4.2
Nurses, active registered (1,000)	. . .	375	430	504	613	700	961	1,273	1,538	1,715
Rate (per 100,000 pop.)	. . .	249	259	282	319	368	446	560	644	690
Nursing programs	1,271	1,203	1,139	1,119	1,153	1,328	1,360	1,385	1,473	1,470
Students (1,000)	129	99	108	115	130	165	250	231	218	221
Graduates (1,000)	36	26	29	30	25	44	75	76	82	66

Source: Ben J. Wattenberg, *The Statistical History of the United States: From Colonial Times to the Present* (New York, 1976), 75–76; *Statistical Abstract, 1993,* 118.

TABLE 7.55   ORGAN TRANSPLANTS AND GRAFTS, 1981–1990

Procedure	Heart	Liver	Kidney	Heart-Lung	Pancreas	Cornea (Grafts)
1981	62	26	4,883	5	. . .	15,500
1985	719	602	7,695	30	130	26,300
1986	1,368	924	976	45	140	28,000
1987	1,512	1,199	8,967	41	180	35,930
1988	1,647	1,680	9,123	74	243	36,900
1989	1,673	2,160	8,890	67	413	38,464
1990	1,998	2,534	9,433	52	529	40,631
Number of Centers						
1981	8	1	157	. . .	. . .	. . .
1990	148	85	232	79	83	107
Number of People Waiting						
1990	1,769	1,248	17,955	226	474	. . .
One-Year Survival Rate (percent)[a]						
1989	82	65	92	55	45	95
Average Cost						
1988	$57,000–110,000	$135,000–238,000	$30,000–40,000	$130,000–200,000	$30,000–40,000	$3,500–4,000

[a] Denotes success rate.
Source: Bureau of Census, *Statistical Abstract, 1992,* 117; Wright, *Universal Almanac, 1991,* 254.

TABLE 7.56   MEDICAL DEVICE IMPLANTS, BY AGE, SEX, AND RACE, 1988

(in thousands, except percent. Based in the National Health Interview Survey)

Device	Total	Percent Distribution							
		Age				Sex		Race	
		Under 18 Years Old	18–44 Years Old	45–64 Years Old	65 Years Old and Older	Male	Female	White	Black
Artificial joints	1,625	0.6	13.0	24.6	61.7	39.9	60.1	92.3	6.2
Hip joints	816	0.5	6.5	26.3	66.7	37.5	62.4	93.5	5.5
Knee joints	521	. . .	10.9	20.5	68.5	41.8	58.2	88.1	10.0
Fixation devices	4,890	3.9	44.3	28.4	23.4	57.2	42.8	91.7	6.6
Head	351	4.3	67.8	22.8	5.4	57.3	42.7	93.2	4.8
Torso	563	5.3	49.6	31.8	13.3	62.7	37.5	92.2	6.9
Upper extremities	646	3.7	55.9	25.4	15.0	70.4	29.7	91.6	5.6
Lower extremities	2,690	3.0	39.6	27.9	29.4	52.8	47.2	91.1	7.7
Other	622	6.4	34.4	34.1	25.1	57.9	42.1	93.6	3.7
Other devices:									
Ear vent tubes	1,494	25.8	27.0	34.6	12.6	39.9	61.1	92.3	6.2
Silicone implants	620	0.5	73.1	23.7	2.9	8.2	91.8	97.6	0.8
Breast implants	544	0.6	73.0	24.1	2.6	2.0	98.0	98.5	. . .
Shunt or catheter	321	24.3	24.3	22.1	29.3	50.5	49.2	85.7	12.5
Dental implants	275	2.2	57.8	27.3	12.7	56.4	43.6	93.8	4.0
Heart valve	279	(NA)	14.7	35.5	49.8	52.3	47.8	89.2	10.0
Pacemaker	460	(NA)	(NA)	13.5	86.7	50.4	49.6	93.7	6.2
Eye lens	3,765	(NA)	(NA)	18.7	81.3	37.6	62.4	95.6	3.5

Source: Statistical Abstract, 1993, 140.

Medical Costs

Medical costs soared after the 1940s, although the great surge came after 1970. From a national cost of $11 billion in 1950, the total ballooned to $660 billion in 1990. Hospital care, traditionally the largest part of the bill, which took 30 percent of the costs in 1950, grew to 47 percent in the early 1980s before it leveled off. The price of a day in a hospital, $8 in 1950, increased slowly and stood at no more than $54 20 years later. Then the sky fell in; within another 20 years the price increased 13 times to an average of $678 a day, and in 1990 one could find $1,000-a-day hospitals in many places.

Reasons for the changes are familiar and in some cases fully understandable; the cost of everything has grown since the 1940s. But the price of medical care moved far ahead of inflation or the general cost of living. The health-care industry developed newer, more sophisticated equipment, which was expensive to purchase and maintain and which probably required skilled technicians to operate. Various procedures not available in the 1940s now could be had, but at great cost. Doctors ordered many more tests if only because the means for doing so existed. Many of them were unnecessary, but they at least did provide the physician with some protection against a malpractice claim. Malpractice premiums were high. The existence of insurance protection, which most patients had, placed the physician one step removed from inflicting financial pain on the person he or she was serving. Insurance probably drove up the price of tests, and there were problems if the patient had no insurance and still needed the test. The United States increasingly had a larger elderly population, and elderly people needed more health care. Finally there was the vague area of waste, overcharging and outright fraud—doubtless a major cause of cost inflation but difficult to prove in some cases because the subject was technical and somewhat subjective; in other cases the mistake, or theft, could be documented, but the process took time and skilled personnel.

Availability of medical care has always been an issue in this nation that largely left medicine up to principles of supply and demand, closely connected to capitalist economics. The concept of a medical program of any sort was slow to catch on in the United States. In 1947 fewer than one-third of the population had private insurance, and there were virtually no public programs to speak of. The idea of a national medical program was one of the important political issues for several years after the Second World War, if only because President Harry S. Truman proposed such a plan in virtually every program he sent to Congress. Truman's intention was honorable, his proposal deserving of more favorable attention than it received, but the timing might be called to question. In that seedtime of the cold war, with the nation rising on all fronts to combat "Godless communism," Truman's program had no chance. Labeling the plan "socialized medicine," opponents—mostly political conservatives and health-care providers—conveyed the message that a national program was not only bad policy but also constituted the taking up of the worst features of the enemy's system. There would be no comparable proposal, neither from Democrat nor Republican, for many years to come. Government, on both the state and national levels, did find incentive and ways to move slowly in increments, providing support for some people in need of medical treatment. Medicine in the United States thus remained overwhelmingly in private hands, and the care providers fought tooth and nail to keep it so, but government (national and state) increasingly paid a larger portion of the costs. Medical costs continued to cause vibrations that could be felt throughout the economy; they affected the national budget and the national debt, the balance sheet of corporations, the ability of small companies to succeed or fail; medical provisions often occupied center stage in union-management negotiations. A fully paid, comprehensive medical program was often a more-sought-after condition of employment than a high salary.

TABLE 7.57 COST OF BRAND NAMES COMPARED WITH GENERIC EQUIVALENT, 1990

Generic/(Brand Name)	Brand Name Price	Generic Price	Percentage of Savings
Allopurinol (Zyloprim) 300 mg	$47.00	$18.55	60%
Amitriptyline HCL (Elavil) 25 mg	$33.55	$5.55	83
Chlorpropamide (Diabinese) 250 mg	$59.20	$6.35	89
Clonidine HCL (Catapres) 0.1 mg	$40.15	$12.20	70
Doxycycline hyclate (Vibramycin) 100 mg	$46.05	$14.65	68
Imipramine HCL (Tofranil) 25 mg	$43.90	$10.15	77
Indomethacin (Indocin) 25 mg	$49.80	$16.20	67
Hydroxyzine HCL (Atarax) 25 mg	$65.20	$14.30	78
Methyldopa (Aldomet) 250 mg	$27.30	$17.05	38
Propranolol HCL (Inderal) 20 mg	$27.60	$10.55	62

Source: Prevention Magazine, Prevention's Giant Book of Facts, (Emmans, Pa., 1991) 415.

TABLE 7.58 PERSONAL HEALTH-CARE EXPENDITURES AND PERCENT DISTRIBUTION, BY SOURCE OF FUNDS, 1940–1990

Year	Total in Billions[a]	Per Capita	All Sources	Out-of-Pocket Payments	Private Health Insurance	Other Private Funds	Government Total	Government Federal	Government State and Local
			Percent Distribution						
1940	3.5	26	100.0	[a]81.3	[b]	2.6	16.1	4.1	12.0
1950	10.9	70	100.0	65.5	9.1	2.9	22.4	10.4	12.0
1955	15.7	93	100.0	58.1	16.1	2.8	23.0	10.5	12.5
1960	23.6	124	100.0	55.3	21.2	1.8	21.7	9.0	12.6
1965	35.2	172	100.0	52.7	24.7	2.0	20.6	8.4	12.2
1970	63.8	297	100.0	39.0	23.2	2.6	35.3	23.0	12.2
1971	70.1	323	100.0	37.7	23.5	2.6	36.2	24.1	12.1
1972	78.0	356	100.0	37.1	23.4	2.7	36.8	24.4	12.4
1973	87.1	394	100.0	36.7	23.7	2.5	37.1	24.3	12.8
1974	99.9	448	100.0	34.9	24.2	2.5	38.5	26.0	12.5
1975	114.5	510	100.0	33.3	24.8	2.4	39.6	27.0	12.5
1976	130.5	576	100.0	32.1	25.7	2.9	39.3	28.1	11.2
1977	147.7	647	100.0	31.4	26.4	2.8	39.3	27.9	11.4
1978	164.8	715	100.0	30.2	27.1	3.0	39.7	28.4	11.3
1979	187.5	805	100.0	29.0	28.1	3.1	39.8	28.7	11.2
1980	217.0	923	100.0	27.8	28.6	3.6	40.1	29.2	10.9
1981	252.0	1,061	100.0	27.2	28.9	3.7	40.2	29.6	10.6
1982	283.3	1,181	100.0	26.6	29.6	3.8	40.0	29.6	10.4
1983	311.5	1,286	100.0	26.4	29.7	3.7	40.1	30.0	10.2
1984	341.5	1,397	100.0	26.6	29.9	3.6	40.0	30.0	10.0
1985	376.4	1,525	100.0	26.7	30.2	3.7	39.3	29.6	9.7
1986	410.5	1,647	100.0	26.3	30.3	3.8	39.5	29.3	10.2
1987	449.7	1,787	100.0	25.8	31.1	3.8	39.3	28.8	10.4
1988	499.3	1,964	100.0	25.9	31.7	3.9	38.5	28.3	10.1
1989	550.1	2,142	100.0	24.8	32.6	3.7	38.9	28.8	10.1
1990	614.7	2,369	100.0	24.1	32.8	3.5	39.5	29.0	10.6

[a] Includes all expenditures for health services and supplies other than expenses for program administration and net cost of private health insurance and government public-health activities.
[b] Out-of-pocket payments and private health insurance are combined for these years.
Source: Health and Human Services, Health, U.S., 1995, 249.

TABLE 7.59 U.S. HEALTH EXPENDITURES BY TYPE OF SERVICE, 1960–1990

(in billions of dollars)

Type of Expenditure	1960	1970	1980	1985	1986	1987	1988	1989	1990
National health expenditures	27.1	74.4	250.1	422.6	454.8	494.1	546.0	602.8	666.2
Health services & supplies	25.4	69.1	238.9	407.2	438.9	476.8	526.2	582.1	643.4
Personal health care	23.9	64.9	219.4	369.7	400.8	439.3	482.8	529.9	585.3
Hospital care	9.3	27.9	102.4	168.3	179.8	194.2	212.0	232.6	256.0
Physician services	5.3	13.6	41.9	74.0	82.1	93.0	105.1	113.6	125.7
Dental services	2.0	4.7	14.4	23.3	24.7	27.1	29.4	31.6	34.0
Other professional services	0.6	1.5	8.7	16.6	18.6	21.1	23.8	27.1	31.6
Home health care	0.0	0.1	1.3	3.8	4.0	4.1	4.5	5.6	6.9
Drugs & other medical nondurables	4.2	8.8	21.6	36.2	39.7	43.2	46.3	50.6	54.6
Vision products & other medical durables	0.8	2.0	4.6	7.1	8.1	9.1	10.1	11.4	12.1
Nursing home care	1.0	4.9	20.0	34.1	36.7	39.7	42.8	47.7	53.1
Other personal health care	0.7	1.4	4.6	6.4	7.1	7.8	8.7	9.7	11.3
Program administration & net cost of private health insurance	1.2	2.8	12.2	25.2	24.6	22.9	26.8	33.9	38.7
Government public-health activities	0.4	1.4	7.2	12.3	13.5	14.6	16.6	18.3	19.3
Research & construction	1.7	5.3	11.3	15.4	16.0	17.3	19.8	20.7	22.8
Research	0.7	2.0	5.4	7.8	8.5	9.0	10.3	11.0	12.4
Construction	1.0	3.4	5.8	7.6	7.4	8.2	9.5	9.6	10.4
Average Annual % Change from Previous Year Shown									
National health expenditures	. . .	10.6	12.9	11.1	7.6	8.6	10.5	10.4	10.5
Health services & supplies	. . .	10.5	13.2	11.3	7.8	8.7	10.3	10.6	10.5
Personal health care	. . .	10.5	13.0	11.0	8.4	9.6	9.9	9.8	10.5
Hospital care	. . .	11.7	13.9	10.4	6.8	8.0	9.2	9.7	10.1
Physician services	. . .	9.9	11.9	12.1	10.9	13.3	13.1	8.0	10.7
Dental services	. . .	9.1	11.9	10.1	6.4	9.6	8.5	7.3	7.6
Other professional services	. . .	9.6	19.1	13.8	12.0	13.6	12.4	14.0	16.6
Home health care	. . .	14.5	25.2	23.3	3.6	3.6	9.6	24.8	22.5
Drugs & other medical nondurables	. . .	7.6	9.4	10.8	9.9	8.6	7.2	9.3	7.9
Vision products & other medical durables	. . .	9.6	8.5	9.4	13.0	12.3	11.8	12.9	6.1
Nursing home care	. . .	17.4	15.2	11.3	7.6	8.0	7.8	11.5	11.4
Other personal health care	. . .	7.1	12.8	6.9	11.1	10.0	12.1	11.2	16.4
Program administration & net cost of private health insurance	. . .	9.0	16.0	15.5	−2.5	−6.6	16.9	26.6	14.1
Government public-health activities	. . .	13.9	18.0	11.3	9.6	8.3	13.5	10.4	5.6
Research & construction	. . .	12.1	7.8	6.4	3.7	8.2	14.9	4.3	10.2
Research	. . .	10.9	10.8	7.4	9.5	5.7	14.5	6.8	11.9
Construction	. . .	12.8	5.6	5.4	−2.4	11.1	15.3	1.5	8.3

Source: World Almanac and Book of Facts, 1992, 949.

TABLE 7.60 NATIONAL HEALTH EXPENDITURES AS A PORTION OF GROSS NATIONAL PRODUCT AND FEDERAL GOVERNMENT EXPENDITURES, 1940–1990

Year	Gross National Product in Billions	National Health Expenditures			Federal Government Expenditures		
		Amount in Billions	Percent of Gross National Product	Amount per Capita	Total in Billions	Health in Billions	Health as a Percent of Total
1940	99.7	4.0	4.0	29	10.0	. . .	. . .
1950	284.8	12.7	4.5	80	41.2	$1.6	3.9
1955	398.0	17.7	4.4	101	68.6	2.0	2.9
1960	515.3	27.1	5.3	143	93.9	2.9	3.1
1965	705.1	41.6	5.9	204	125.3	4.8	3.8
1966	772.0	45.9	5.9	222	145.3	7.5	5.2
1967	816.4	51.7	6.3	248	165.8	12.2	7.4
1968	892.6	58.5	6.6	278	182.9	14.1	7.7
1969	963.9	65.7	6.8	309	191.3	16.1	8.4
1970	1,015.5	74.4	7.3	346	207.8	17.7	8.5
1971	1,102.7	82.3	7.5	379	224.8	20.4	9.1
1972	1,212.8	92.3	7.6	421	249.0	22.9	9.2
1973	1,359.3	102.5	7.5	464	269.3	25.2	9.4
1974	1,472.8	116.1	7.9	521	305.5	30.5	10.0
1975	1,598.4	132.9	8.3	592	364.2	36.4	10.0
1976	1,782.8	152.2	8.5	672	393.7	42.9	10.9
1977	1,990.5	172.0	8.6	753	430.1	47.6	11.1
1978	2,249.7	193.7	8.6	839	470.7	54.3	11.5
1979	2,508.2	217.2	8.7	932	521.1	61.4	11.8

(continued)

TABLE 7.60 (continued)

Year	Gross National Product in Billions	National Health Expenditures			Federal Government Expenditures		
		Amount in Billions	Percent of Gross National Product	Amount per Capita	Total in Billions	Health in Billions	Health as a Percent of Total
1980	2,731.9	250.1	9.2	1,063	615.1	72.0	11.7
1981	3,052.6	290.2	9.5	1,221	703.3	84.0	11.9
1982	3,166.0	326.1	10.3	1,358	781.2	93.3	11.9
1983	3,405.7	358.6	10.5	1,479	835.9	103.2	12.3
1984	3,772.2	389.6	10.3	1,592	895.6	112.6	12.6
1985	4,014.9	422.6	10.5	1,710	985.6	123.6	12.5
1986	4,231.6	454.8	10.7	1,822	1,034.8	133.1	12.9
1987	4,515.6	494.1	10.9	1,961	1,071.9	144.0	13.4
1988	4,873.7	546.0	11.2	2,146	1,114.2	156.7	14.1
1989	5,200.8	602.8	11.6	2,346	1,187.2	175.0	14.7
1990	5,465.1	666.2	12.2	2,566	1,275.7	195.4	15.3

Source: Health and Human Services, *Health, U.S., 1991*, 266.

TABLE 7.61   U.S. HEALTH EXPENDITURES COMPARED WITH OTHER COUNTRIES IN PERCENT OF GROSS DOMESTIC PRODUCT AND PER CAPITA EXPENDITURE,[a] 1960–1990

Country	1960		1970		1980		1990	
	% GDP	Per Capita	% GDP	Per Capita	% GDP	Per Capita	% GDP	Per Capita
Australia	4.9	$98	5.7	$212	7.3	$669	8.2	$1,316
Austria	4.4	67	5.4	166	7.9	697	7.1	1,160
Belgium	3.4	53	4.1	131	6.6	588	7.6	1,247
Canada	5.5	105	7.1	255	7.3	729	9.2	1,691
Denmark	3.6	67	6.1	215	6.8	595	6.5	1,069
Finland	3.9	55	5.7	165	6.5	521	8.0	1,292
France	4.2	73	5.8	208	7.6	716	8.9	1,539
West Germany	4.3	91	5.7	230	8.1	860	8.2	1,642
Greece	2.4	16	3.3	60	3.6	190	4.2	389
Iceland	3.3	50	5.0	139	6.2	637	8.0	1,375
Ireland	3.8	37	5.3	98	8.8	468	6.6	748
Italy	3.6	50	5.2	157	7.0	591	8.1	1,322
Japan	. . .	27	4.4	132	6.4	535	6.0	1,082
Luxembourg	. . .	. . .	3.7	150	6.2	617	6.6	1,499
Netherlands	3.8	68	5.9	205	7.9	693	8.3	1,325
New Zealand	4.3	92	5.2	177	6.0	463	7.0	937
Norway	3.0	47	4.6	135	7.0	639	7.8	1,365
Portugal	. . .	. . .	2.8	45	5.8	264	6.5	616
Spain	1.5	14	3.7	83	5.7	332	6.9	813
Sweden	4.7	90	7.1	274	9.4	867	8.8	1,492
Switzerland	3.3	93	5.2	270	7.3	850	8.4	1,782
Turkey	. . .	. . .	2.4	23	3.3	77	2.5	119
United Kingdom	3.9	77	4.5	149	5.6	453	6.0	957
United States	5.1	141	7.1	341	8.9	1,052	12.1	2,683

[a] Per capita health expenditures adjusted to U.S. dollars using GDP purchasing power parities for each year.
Source: Wall Street Journal Almanac 1998, 732.

Medicare

A principal reason why after 1970 a high percentage of Americans could claim medical insurance was the program called Medicare. A project of the national government, thus making it qualify as a form of socialized medicine, Medicare was designed to provide assistance to some of the nation's most vulnerable citizens: older people with small incomes and high medical costs who could not afford medical insurance if indeed the companies were willing to insure such high-risk clients. Proposed by the John F. Kennedy administration in 1961 and passed in 1965 as a part of the Great Society of Lyndon B. Johnson, the program provided limited medical support for people older than age 65 and for nonelderly who received Social Security disability payments or who had permanent kidney failure.

The program had two parts: Part A, hospital insurance and limited other patient benefits, and Part B, supplemental medical insurance, to cover physicians' charges, various tests, and medical procedures. In a time of soaring medical costs, Medicare doubtless became a lifesaver for millions of people who otherwise might have had no outside source of funding. The program, however, was not without weaknesses. It contained deductables, required a monthly contribution from all participants, and a copayment for many charges. Some procedures, such as yearly mammograms and cancer screening tests, were not covered. Most conspicuous was failure to cover outpatient prescription drugs—which for elderly people could be enormous—and the virtually all-consuming expenses of long-term care, such as a nursing home.

TABLE 7.62 SELECTED NATIONS AND DATE THEY ADOPTED UNIVERSAL HEALTH-CARE SYSTEMS, 1883–1986

Nation	Year
Germany	1883
Switzerland	1911
New Zealand	1938
Belgium	1945
United Kingdom	1946
Sweden	1947
Greece	1961
Japan	1961
Canada	1966
Denmark	1973
Australia	1974
Italy	1978
Portugal	1979
Spain	1986

Source: USA Today, November 20, 1998.

Not surprisingly, the number of enrollees increased as the program unfolded, and costs jumped in proportion to the number of participants and sharp growth in medical charges. Bolstered by a large body of employed baby boomers who could pay into the system, the program remained financially solvent for approximately the first quarter-century. But problems loomed ahead. Administrators dreaded the time when baby boomers would reach retirement age and individuals responsible for paying into the system would come from the baby bust, the low birthrate that began in the late 1960s. Specialists calculated that the Hospital Insurance Fund would begin to lose money in 1995 and that by 2001, having used up its reserves, the fund would be in the red. The picture was not as dismal for Part B, the Supplemental Insurance Program, which drew on contributions from the Treasury and from premiums from participants that could be increased as costs increased.

As a first experiment with limited socialized medicine, Medicare revealed some of the benefits and difficulties with a massive government effort to solve a massive social problem. While probably indispensable for millions of people, the program did not cover needed services; it was expensive (as indeed any medical system would be), and it carried an invitation for exploitation by the caregivers, either through overcharging, unnecessary procedures, or outright fraud. Also, of course, Medicare was designed to assist only a portion of the population. The United States continued to stand virtually alone among the democratic and/or industrialized states in its failure to establish a national medical program.

TABLE 7.63 MEDICARE ENROLLMENT AND EXPENDITURES, 1967–1990

Type of Service	1967	1970	1975	1980	1985	1989	1990
Enrollees	Number in Millions						
Total	19.5	20.5	25.0	28.5	31.1	33.6	34.2
Hospital insurance	19.5	20.4	24.6	28.1	30.6	33.0	33.7
Supplementary medical insurance	17.9	19.6	23.9	27.4	30.0	32.1	32.6
Expenditures	Amount in Millions						
Total	$4,737	$7,493	$16,316	$36,822	$72,294	$100,586	$110,984
Total hospital insurance	3,430	5,281	11,581	25,577	48,414	60,803	66,997
Inpatient hospital	3,034	4,827	10,877	24,082	44,680	53,822	59,301
Skilled nursing facility	282	246	278	401	577	2,978	2,876
Home health agency	29	51	160	568	2,144	2,765	3,517
Hospice	. . .	. . .	. . .	. . .	43	238	356
Administrative expenses	77	157	266	512	834	792	758
Peer review activity	. . .	. . .	. . .	14	136	208	189
Total supplementary medical insurance	1,307	2,212	4,735	11,245	23,880	39,783	43,987
Physician	1,128	1,790	3,415	8,188	17,311	27,057	29,628
Outpatient hospital	33	114	652	1,935	4,304	7,662	8,475
Home health agency	10	34	87	195	54	73	81
Group practice prepayment	19	26	80	203	720	2,308	2,827
Independent laboratory	7	11	39	114	558	1,194	1,457
Administrative expenses	110	237	462	610	933	1,489	1,519
	Percent Distribution of Expenditures						
Total hospital insurance	100.0	100.0	100.0	100.0	100.0	100.0	100.0
Inpatient hospital	88.5	91.4	93.9	94.2	92.3	88.5	88.5
Skilled nursing facility	8.2	4.7	2.4	1.6	1.2	4.9	4.3
Home health agency	0.8	1.0	1.4	2.2	4.4	4.5	5.2
Hospice	. . .	. . .	. . .	. . .	0.1	0.4	0.5
Administrative expenses	2.2	3.0	2.3	2.0	1.7	1.3	1.1
Peer review activity	. . .	. . .	. . .	0.1	0.3	0.3	0.3
Total supplementary medical insurance	100.0	100.0	100.0	100.0	100.0	100.0	100.0
Physician	86.3	80.9	72.1	72.8	72.5	68.0	67.4
Outpatient hospital	2.5	5.2	13.8	17.2	18.0	19.3	19.3
Home health agency	0.8	1.5	1.8	1.7	0.2	0.2	0.2
Group practice prepayment	1.5	1.2	1.7	1.8	3.0	5.8	6.4
Independent laboratory	0.5	0.5	0.8	1.0	2.3	3.0	3.3
Administrative expenses	8.4	10.7	9.8	5.4	3.9	3.7	3.5

Source: Health and Human Services, Health, U.S., 1993, 243.

TABLE 7.64   MEDICARE SPENDING PER BENEFICIARY, 1975–1990

Year	Total	Admin. Costs	Inpatient Hospital Care	Nursing Homes	Home Health Agencies and Hospices	Outpatient Hospital Services	Doctors' Services and Laboratories
1975	$1,355	$61	$904	$25	$19	$50	$296
1976	1,481	71	970	25	26	63	326
1977	1,637	59	1,074	26	31	77	369
1978	1,744	66	1,146	24	34	87	387
1979	1,811	63	1,176	22	37	95	418
1980	1,954	61	1,266	21	40	105	460
1981	2,117	62	1,373	21	45	114	501
1982	2,300	59	1,482	21	53	135	550
1983	2,449	58	1,542	22	66	146	616
1984	2,554	63	1,588	22	76	146	659
1985	2,775	68	1,744	22	84	154	703
1986	2,817	64	1,703	21	84	185	760
1987	2,886	62	1,648	22	84	207	864
1988	2,960	67	1,636	24	80	221	931
1989	3,071	69	1,655	69	85	237	955
1990	3,326	69	1,767	102	110	260	1,018

a 1990 subtotals are estimates.
Source: *World Almanac and Book of Facts, 1992*, 951.

TABLE 7.65   OPERATIONS OF MEDICARE HOSPITAL INSURANCE TRUST FUND, 1970–1990

(in millions)

Fiscal Year	Income							
	Payroll Taxes	Income from Taxation of Benefits	Railroad Retirement Account Transfers	Reimbursement for Uninsured Persons	Premiums from Voluntary Enrollees	Payments for Military Wage Credits	Interest and Other Income	Total Income
1970	$4,785	...	$64	$617	—	$11	$137	$5,614
1975	11,291	...	132	481	$6	48	609	12,568
1980	23,244	...	244	697	17	141	1,072	25,415
1985	46,490	...	371	766	38	86	3,182	50,933
1986	53,020	...	364	566	40	−714	3,167	56,442
1987	57,820	...	368	447	40	94	3,982	62,751
1988	61,901	...	364	475	42	80	5,148	68,010
1989	67,527	...	379	515	42	86	6,567	75,116
1990	70,655	...	367	413	113	107	7,908	79,563
Projections for Future								
2000	127,825	4,975	399	155	1,655	63	4,774	139,846
2001	134,092	5,368	398	150	1,807	63	1,846	143,724
2002	141,081	5,802	409	141	1,974	63	−1,484	147,986
2003	148,298	6,271	421	137	2,150	63	−5,400	151,940
2004	155,719	6,784	435	146	2,343	63	−9,991	155,499
2005	165,585	7,343	451	150	2,538	63	−15,287	160,843
2006	173,464	7,943	468	147	2,752	63	−21,254	163,582

Fiscal Year	Disbursements			Trust Fund	
	Benefits Payments	Administrative Expenses	Total Disbursements	Net Increase in Fund	Fund at End of Year
1970	$4,804	$149	$4,953	$661	$2,677
1975	10,353	259	10,612	1,956	9,870
1980	23,790	497	24,288	1,127	14,490
1985	47,841	813	48,654	4,103	21,277
1986	49,018	667	49,685	17,370	38,648
1987	49,967	836	50,803	11,949	50,596
1988	52,022	707	52,730	15,281	65,877
1989	57,433	805	58,238	16,878	82,755
1990	65,912	774	66,687	12,876	95,631
Projections for Future					
2000	172,650	1,518	174,168	−34,322	37,457
2001	187,328	1,605	188,933	−45,209	−7,752
2002	203,021	1,696	204,717	−56,731	−64,483
2003	219,751	1,794	221,545	−69,605	−134,088
2004	237,542	1,896	239,438	−83,939	−218,027
2005	256,139	2,003	258,142	−97,299	−315,326
2006	275,934	2,117	278,051	−114,469	−429,795

Source: *Wall Street Journal Almanac, 1998*, 137–38.

TABLE 7.66 OPERATIONS OF MEDICARE SUPPLEMENTARY MEDICAL INSURANCE FUND, 1970–1990
(in millions)

Fiscal Year	Income				Disbursements			Balance at End of Year
	Premium from Enrollees	Government Contributions	Interest And Other Income	Total Income	Benefit Payments	Administrative Expenses	Total Disbursements	
1970	$936	$928	$12	$1,876	$1,979	$217	$2,196	$57
1975	1,887	2,330	105	4,322	3,765	405	4,170	1,424
1980	2,928	6,932	415	10,275	10,144	593	10,737	4,532
1985	5,524	17,898	1,155	24,577	21,808	922	22,730	10,646
1986	5,699	18,076	1,228	25,003	25,169	1,049	26,218	9,432
1987	6,480	20,299	1,018	27,797	29,937	900	30,837	6,392
1988	8,756	25,418	828	35,002	33,682	1,265	34,947	6,447
1989	11,548	30,712	1,022	43,282	36,867	1,450	38,317	11,412
1990	11,494	33,210	1,434	46,138	41,498	1,524	43,022	14,527
Projections for Future								
2000	22,057	76,619	1,990	100,666	98,017	2,078	100,095	34,482
2001	23,037	85,374	2,017	110,428	107,500	2,164	109,664	35,246
2002	24,070	95,367	2,052	121,489	118,384	2,255	120,639	36,096
2003	25,183	106,572	2,077	133,832	130,582	2,351	132,933	36,995
2004	26,382	119,057	2,099	147,538	144,040	2,454	146,494	38,039
2005	27,671	134,274	2,141	164,086	159,200	2,562	161,762	40,363
2006	29,028	151,738	2,276	183,042	176,201	2,675	178,876	44,529

Source: Wall Street Journal Almanac, 1998, 138–39.

TABLE 7.67 PERSONS WITHOUT HEALTH INSURANCE COVERAGE, BY SELECTED CHARACTERISTIC, 1989
(in percent, except as indicated)

Characteristic	Total	Under 65 Years Old					65 Years and Older
		Total	Under 18 Years	18 to 24 Years	25 to 44 Years	45 to 64 Years	
All persons (1,000)	243,532	214,313	64,003	25,401	78,795	46,114	29,219
Persons not covered	13.9	15.7	14.9	27.4	15.5	10.5	1.2
Sex							
Male	15.1	16.7	15.1	31.3	17.6	9.6	1.3
Female	12.7	14.6	14.7	23.7	13.6	11.2	1.2
Race							
White	12.8	14.5	14.0	26.3	14.4	9.4	1.0
Black	20.2	21.9	18.9	34.3	22.5	17.5	2.5
Other	19.7	20.4	18.9	27.8	20.7	17.5	8.4
Education							
Less than 12 years	20.8	30.1	. . .	42.1	35.5	19.9	1.5
12 years	14.4	16.6	. . .	29.8	16.8	8.5	0.7
More than 12 years	8.4	9.2	. . .	16.0	9.0	5.8	1.3
Employment Status							
Currently employed	13.9	14.3	. . .	26.6	13.6	9.0	1.5
Unemployed	38.3	39.2	. . .	44.5	40.8	26.5	. . .
Not in labor force	10.8	18.5	. . .	26.0	21.2	12.8	1.2
Family Income							
Less than $5,000	27.1	31.3	25.5	27.3	42.4	35.5	1.5
$5,000 to $9,999	27.7	36.9	31.6	43.5	43.5	32.2	1.6
$10,000 to $19,999	24.3	30.1	30.2	37.5	32.0	21.3	1.1
$20,000 to $34,999	10.6	11.6	10.9	22.1	11.8	6.8	1.0
$35,000 to $49,999	5.8	6.0	4.0	18.4	5.8	3.9	0.8
$50,000 or more	3.6	3.7	2.3	12.9	3.7	1.9	1.6

Source: Statistical Abstract, 1993, 116.

Substance Use and Abuse

Tobacco

The postwar period began as an extension of the 1940s. Use of tobacco in all forms remained acceptable, even popular. Many people certainly considered chewing tobacco a nasty practice, but it was accepted as a part of life in some circles. Farmers' wives reluctantly acquiesced if they believed a "chaw" helped their man get through a day in the fields; old-timers insisted that one was not fully equipped to play baseball unless he carried a wad that caused the cheek to bulge out. Youngsters soon got the message. The smell of cigars probably provoked the largest protest, but some men, mostly older ones, used them, perhaps convinced that they carried a mark of distinction and success. Many women agreed that there was something special about a man who smoked a pipe.

Domination of the smokers' world of course remained with cigarettes. Small, inexpensive, easy to carry and utilize, cigarettes had been established as a mark of fashion and personality, said to be capable of enhancing any mood or self-image, be it masculinity, femininity, sophistication, or intellectualism. Fueled by effective advertising and an apparent alliance between the tobacco industry and the stars of radio, movies, and professional sports, the industry had its most successful decade in the 1940s and while the rate of growth slowed somewhat in the following decade, the 1950s also showed marked increase in the sale of cigarettes. The craggy Marlboro Man, who appeared in 1955, helped legitimize use of filter cigarettes by "masculine" smokers. In 1955 approximately half the adult population used tobacco products; the bulk of them smoked cigarettes.

But trouble was not far away. An article in *Reader's Digest* in 1954 gave broad publicity to a lingering suspicion that tobacco, especially cigarettes, carried health risks in several forms and was particularly harmful to the respiratory system. Later studies turned up more alarming information about the relationship between cigarettes and various forms of cancer, emphysema, and other pulmonary disorders, heart attack, stroke, and vascular disease. Smoking by expectant mothers could cause miscarriage and underweight and sickly babies. In 1964 the government began what would be a succession of antismoking steps. The surgeon general confirmed a link between smoking and lung cancer. In 1965 Congress required that a warning label be placed on cigarette packages; in 1970 the warning was made more concrete and threatening. Faced with harsh new legislation, tobacco companies removed cigarette ads from radio and television.

A changing national mood revealed itself in statistics. Tobacco companies continued to show an increase in absolute sales in the two decades after 1960, but each decade produced a reduction in consumption per capita. By 1990 there was a decline in both categories. The portion of adults who smoked cigarettes underwent a corresponding, and steady, decline—from 42.4 percent in 1965 to 25.6 percent in 1990. Saddled with restrictive legislation and threatened by more, faced with grisly health details and smoke-free movements in a growing list of places, terrified of that first court decision that found cigarette companies responsible for someone's death, the tobacco industry clearly was on the defensive.

The public mood had shifted sharply during the 35 years before 1990, but the industry had not folded. It continued to do well in the courts and to sell cigarettes at home and abroad. There had been a considerable reduction in the percentage of smokers, but the shrinkage was not the same in all categories. Women who had been slower to start smoking (in 1955 there had been a 26-percent differential with

men), were slower to give it up. By 1990 the differential was barely 5 percent. Many young people remained perplexingly oblivious to the facts about smoking. The proportion of adult Americans who smoked had been roughly cut in half, down to some 25 percent, in the 35 years before 1990. But that 25 percent left some 45 million American smokers, and there still was the foreign market.

TABLE 7.68   U.S. CIGARETTE CONSUMPTION, 1940–1990

(persons 18 years and older)

Year	Consumption	
	Billions	Per Capita
1940	181.9	1,976
1950	369.8	3,552
1960	484.4	4,171
1970	536.5	3,985
1980	631.5	3,849
1990	525.0	2,817

Source: New York Times Almanac, 1998, 400.

Some Prominent People Who Died from Lung Cancer, Emphysema, or Smoking-related Illness

Desi Arnaz, actor, 1986
Lucille Ball, actress, 1972
Tallulah Bankhead, actress, 1968
Jack Benny, comedian, 1974
Humphrey Bogart, actor, 1957
Yul Brynner, actor, 1985
Nat ("King") Cole, singer, 1965
Gary Cooper, actor, 1961
Sammy Davis, Jr., singer, 1990
Walt Disney, producer, 1966
Jimmy Dorsey, band leader, 1957
Duke Ellington, band leader, 1974
Bob Fosse, choreographer, 1987
Jackie Gleason, actor, 1987
Arthur Godfrey, entertainer, 1959
Betty Grable, actress, 1973
Susan Hayward, actress, 1975
Lillian Hellman, author, 1984
Judy Holiday, actress, 1965
Chet Huntley, news anchor, 1974
Moe Howard, comic, 1975
Spike Jones, musician, 1965
Buster Keaton, actor, 1966
Alan Jay Lerner, playwright, lyricist, 1986
Steve McQueen, actor, 1980
Edward R. Murrow, broadcasting pioneer, 1965
Dick Powell, actor, 1963
Ayn Rand, author, 1982
Rod Serling, director, 1975
Ed Sullivan, television host, 1974
Franchot Tone, actor, 1968
Ernest Tubb, singer, 1984

Source: National Anti-tobacco Institute.

TABLE 7.69 TOBACCO SMOKING BY RACE, AGE, RESIDENCE, AND SEX, 1955

(in thousands of persons 18 years and older)

Color, Residence, and Age (in Years)	Male								Female			
	Total Persons	Nonsmoker of Cigarettes	Cigarette Smoker		Cigar Smoker		Pipe Smoker		Total Persons	Nonsmoker of Cigarettes	Cigarette Smoker	
			Occasional	Regular	Occasional	Regular	Occasional	Regular			Occasional	Regular
Total	**49,581**	**20,219**	**2,005**	**24,667**	**7,391**	**2,636**	**4,630**	**3,645**	**55,096**	**38,048**	**2,086**	**12,986**
By race:												
White	44,870	18,452	1,691	22,387	6,772	2,343	4,310	3,370	49,645	34,393	1,793	11,737
Nonwhite	4,711	1,767	314	2,280	619	293	320	275	5,451	3,655	293	1,249
By residence:												
Urban	32,572	12,616	1,312	16,791	4,886	1,975	3,086	2,191	37,453	24,542	1,601	9,858
Rural nonfarm	10,456	4,339	403	5,187	1,593	469	1,040	822	11,473	8,210	369	2,542
Rural farm	6,553	3,264	290	2,689	912	192	504	632	6,170	5,296	116	586
By age:												
18 to 24	5,405	2,202	262	2,605	481	70	408	174	7,400	4,651	369	2,118
25 to 34	11,065	3,404	377	6,655	1,841	326	1,206	483	12,196	6,950	589	4,192
35 to 44	10,755	3,437	398	6,286	1,727	456	1,200	622	11,484	7,020	466	3,596
45 to 54	9,100	3,325	379	4,899	1,415	619	938	635	9,399	6,674	353	2,067
55 to 64	6,934	3,392	312	2,865	1,024	625	540	672	7,296	6,080	212	767
65 and older	6,322	4,459	277	1,357	903	540	338	1,059	7,261	6,673	97	246
Percent	100.0	40.8	4.0	49.8	14.9	5.3	9.3	7.4	100.0	69.1	3.8	23.6
By race:												
White	100.0	41.1	3.8	49.9	15.1	5.2	9.6	7.5	100.0	69.3	3.6	23.6
Nonwhite	100.0	37.5	6.7	48.4	13.1	6.2	6.8	5.8	100.0	67.1	5.4	22.9
By residence:												
Urban	100.0	38.7	4.0	51.5	15.0	6.1	9.5	6.7	100.0	65.5	4.3	26.3
Rural nonfarm	100.0	41.5	3.9	49.6	15.2	4.5	9.9	7.9	100.0	71.6	3.2	22.2
Rural farm	100.0	49.8	4.4	41.0	13.9	2.9	7.7	9.6	100.0	85.8	1.9	9.5
By age:												
18 to 24	100.0	40.7	4.8	48.2	8.9	1.3	7.5	3.2	100.0	62.3	4.9	28.4
25 to 34	100.0	30.8	3.4	60.1	16.6	2.9	10.9	4.4	100.0	57.0	4.8	34.4
35 to 44	100.0	32.0	3.7	58.4	16.1	4.2	11.2	5.8	100.0	61.1	4.1	31.3
45 to 54	100.0	36.5	4.2	53.8	15.5	6.8	10.3	7.0	100.0	71.0	3.8	22.0
55 to 64	100.0	48.9	4.5	41.3	14.8	9.0	7.8	9.7	100.0	83.3	2.9	10.5
65 and older	100.0	70.5	4.4	21.5	14.3	8.5	5.3	16.8	100.0	91.9	1.3	3.4

Source: Bureau of the Census, *Statistical Abstract of the United States, 1961* (Washington, D.C., 1961), 802.

TABLE 7.70 CURRENT CIGARETTE SMOKING, BY SEX, AGE, AND RACE, 1965–1990[a]

(in percent)

Sex, Age, and Race	1965	1974	1979	1983	1985	1987	1988	1990
Total smokers, 18 years old and older	**42.4**	**37.1**	**33.5**	**32.1**	**30.1**	**28.8**	**28.1**	**25.5**
Male, total	51.9	43.1	37.5	35.1	32.6	31.2	30.8	28.4
18 to 24 years	54.1	42.1	35.0	32.9	28.0	28.2	25.5	26.6
25 to 34 years	60.7	50.5	43.9	38.8	38.2	34.8	36.2	31.6
35 to 44 years	58.2	51.0	41.8	41.0	37.6	36.6	36.5	34.5
45 to 64 years	51.9	42.6	39.3	35.9	33.4	33.5	31.3	29.3
65 years and older	28.5	24.8	20.9	22.0	19.6	17.2	18.0	14.6
White, total	51.1	41.9	36.8	34.5	31.7	30.5	30.1	28.0
18 to 24 years	53.0	40.8	34.3	32.5	28.4	29.2	26.7	27.4
25 to 34 years	60.1	49.5	43.6	38.6	37.3	33.8	35.4	31.6
35 to 44 years	57.3	50.1	41.3	40.8	36.6	36.2	35.8	33.5
45 to 64 years	51.3	41.2	38.3	35.0	32.1	32.4	30.0	28.7
65 years and older	27.7	24.3	20.5	20.6	18.9	16.0	16.9	13.7
Black, total	60.4	54.3	44.1	40.6	39.9	39.0	36.5	32.5
18 to 24 years	62.8	54.9	40.2	34.2	27.2	24.9	18.6	21.3
25 to 34 years	68.4	58.5	47.5	39.9	45.6	44.9	41.6	33.8
35 to 44 years	67.3	61.5	48.6	45.5	45.0	44.0	42.5	42.0
45 to 64 years	57.9	57.8	50.0	44.8	46.1	44.3	43.2	36.7
65 years and older	36.4	29.7	26.2	38.9	27.7	30.3	29.8	21.5

(continued)

TABLE 7.70   (continued)

Sex, Age, and Race	1965	1974	1979	1983	1985	1987	1988	1990
Female, total	33.9	32.1	29.9	29.5	27.9	26.5	25.7	22.8
18 to 24 years	38.1	34.1	33.8	35.5	30.4	26.1	26.3	22.5
25 to 34 years	43.7	38.8	33.7	32.6	32.0	31.8	31.3	28.2
35 to 44 years	43.7	39.8	37.0	33.8	31.5	29.6	27.8	24.8
45 to 64 years	32.0	33.4	30.7	31.0	29.9	28.6	27.7	24.8
65 years and older	9.6	12.0	13.2	13.1	13.5	13.7	12.8	11.5
White, total	34.0	31.7	30.1	29.4	27.7	26.7	25.7	23.4
18 to 24 years	38.4	34.0	34.5	36.5	31.8	27.8	27.5	25.4
25 to 34 years	43.4	38.6	34.1	32.2	32.0	31.9	31.0	28.5
35 to 44 years	43.9	39.3	37.2	34.8	31.0	29.2	28.3	25.0
45 to 64 years	32.7	33.0	30.6	30.6	29.7	29.0	27.7	25.4
65 years and older	9.8	12.3	13.8	13.2	13.3	13.9	12.6	11.5
Black, total	33.7	36.4	31.1	32.2	31.0	28.0	27.8	21.2
18 to 24 years	37.1	35.6	31.8	32.0	23.7	20.4	21.8	10.0
25 to 34 years	47.8	42.2	35.2	38.0	36.2	35.8	37.2	29.1
35 to 44 years	42.8	46.4	37.7	32.7	40.2	35.3	27.6	25.5
45 to 64 years	25.7	38.9	34.2	36.3	33.4	28.4	29.5	22.6
65 years and older	7.1	8.9	8.5	13.1	14.5	11.7	14.8	11.1

[a] A current smoker is a person who has smoked at at least 100 cigarettes and still smokes; includes occasional smokers.
Source: Statistical Abstract, 1993, 138.

Illegal Drugs

With respect to illicit drugs, including the nonalcoholic narcotics, the postwar period produced a situation much different from trends in the status of tobacco. In the 1940s and 1950s such substances as marijuana, opium, and cocaine—all of them illegal—belonged to a small drug underworld, normally associated with racial and ethnic ghettoes in large cities and with such select clientele as entertainers, especially jazz musicians. Information came mostly from rumor; marijuana, for example, was not a narcotic but in popular usage was placed in the category with drugs that were. Use of any of them was considered tantamount to addiction; partakers of such a substance often were referred to as "dope fiends," and in some circles people still called marijuana, probably the mildest of the substances, the killer drug—a position supported not many years earlier by the American Medical Association. Before the 1960s narcotics, with few exceptions, belonged to the underclasses, a forbidden world that carried prospect of danger, if not death.

The change that came in the 1960s was more gradual than appeared on the surface. It probably began with illicit drug use by the Beats, or Beatniks, in the 1950s and Hippies in the 1960s and spread within a few years to a broader spectrum of people willing to challenge social convention and anxious to do whatever they wished. By the late 1960s a different attitude about drugs stood at the core of a youth-driven counterculture and had begun to extend into the more conventional middle class. Explanation for the shift ranged from critics who passed it off as another manifestation of spoiled-brat baby boomers seeking self-satisfaction of any kind, to defenders who insisted that their behavior exposed the failures and hypocrisies of their elders. Whatever the reason, the generation that came of age in the late 1960s and early 1970s popularized and legitimized use of drugs; some individuals defended the activity as an instrument of positive individual growth.

Such arguments convinced neither large portions of the population nor the governing bodies. The drugs remained illegal. Harmful effects became evident almost from the start. Bad trips and overdose became part of the lexicon; an entire vocabulary grew up. Some drugs produced bizarre, destructive behavior. Drug abuse caused the death of several prominent entertainers. Studies continued on long-term effects of this or that drug, but immediate effects could be seen in cases brought to hospital emergency rooms, in institutions or parts of institutions given over to short-term or long-term care of drug abusers. Mothers hooked on cocaine brought babies into the world already suffering from addiction.

The era of the counterculture and Vietnam War passed, but the status of drugs did not revert to what it had been in the 1940s. The genie had been let out of the bottle, so to speak, and a new area of huge financial gain had opened up. The peak year of activity came in 1979 when estimates put the number of illegal drug users at 24 million. After that point, drug use underwent a reduction with virtually all age groups, although there continued to be a considerable drug traffic in every year. By far the most common drug was marijuana, a smoked substance, somewhat similar to tobacco, that was classified as a depressant or tranquilizer. Pot was a "downer." Cocaine, a fairly costly short-term stimulant, something of an elitist drug, took on new life with introduction in 1986 of an inexpensive smoked version called crack, which produced an immediate, intense but only momentary high. Crack was highly addictive. Dealing with illegal drugs remained at the end of the 1980s an issue with mounting medical, social, legal, and in all cases financial, consequences. Efforts at solving the problem had ranged from Richard Nixon's declaration of war on drugs, to admonition of another president's wife, Nancy Reagan, that young people "just say no," to spending larger sums of money to reduce both supply and consumption. The supply side, stopping the traffic and arresting the dealers, seemed to receive the most attention. A movement that attracted support at the start of the 1990s was for legalized use of marijuana in specified medical situations, such as an antidote to side effects of chemotherapy.

TABLE 7.71 DRUG USE AMONG YOUNG PEOPLE, 12–17 AND 18–25, 1974–1990

(percent of persons aged 12 to 17 and aged 18 to 25 reporting drug use in the past year, 1974 to 1990)

Persons Age 12 to 17	1974	1976	1979	1982	1985	1988	1990
Any illicit drug use	. . .	. . .	26.0	22.0	23.7	16.8	15.9
Marijuana/hashish	18.5	22.3	24.1	20.6	19.7	12.6	11.3
Cocaine	2.7	2.6	4.2	4.1	4.0	2.9	2.2
Inhalants	2.4	2.2	4.6	. . .	5.1	3.9	4.0
Hallucinogens	4.3	3.1	4.7	3.6	2.7	2.8	2.4
Heroin	. . .	0.6	. . .	. . .	. . .	0.4	0.6
Nonmedical use of psychotherapeutics	. . .	. . .	5.6	8.3	8.5	5.4	7.0
Stimulants	3.0	3.7	2.9	5.6	4.3	2.8	3.0
Sedatives	2.0	2.0	2.2	3.7	2.9	1.7	2.2
Tranquilizers	2.0	2.9	2.7	3.3	3.4	1.5	1.5
Analgesics	. . .	. . .	2.2	3.7	3.8	3.0	4.8
Alcohol	51.0	47.5	53.6	52.4	51.7	44.6	41.0
Persons Age 18 to 25	**1974**	**1976**	**1979**	**1982**	**1985**	**1988**	**1990**
Any illicit drug use	. . .	. . .	49.4	43.4	42.6	32.0	28.7
Marijuana/hashish	34.2	35.0	46.9	40.4	36.9	27.9	24.6
Cocaine	8.1	7.0	19.6	18.8	16.3	12.1	7.5
Inhalants	1.2	1.4	3.8	. . .	2.1	4.1	3.0
Hallucinogens	6.1	6.0	9.9	6.9	4.0	5.6	3.9
Heroin	0.8	0.6	0.8	. . .	0.6	0.3	0.5
Nonmedical use of psychotherapeutics	. . .	. . .	16.3	16.1	15.6	11.3	7.0
Stimulants	8.0	8.8	10.1	10.8	9.9	6.4	3.4
Sedatives	4.2	5.7	7.3	8.7	5.0	3.3	2.0
Tranquilizers	4.6	6.2	7.1	5.9	6.4	4.6	2.4
Analgesics	. . .	. . .	5.2	4.4	6.6	5.5	4.1
Alcohol	77.1	77.9	86.6	87.1	87.2	81.7	80.2

Source: Ambry and Russell, *Guide to American Marketplace,* 356.

TABLE 7.72 DRUG USE AMONG ADULTS, 1974–1990

(percent of persons aged 26 or older reporting drug use in the past year and in the lifetime, 1974 to 1990)

Reported Drug Use in Past Year	1974	1976	1979	1982	1985	1988	1990
Any illicit drug use	. . .	. . .	10.0	11.8	13.3	10.2	10.1
Marijuana/hashish	3.8	5.4	9.0	10.6	9.5	6.9	7.3
Cocaine	. . .	0.6	2.0	3.8	4.2	2.7	2.4
Inhalants	. . .	. . .	1.0	. . .	0.8	0.4	0.5
Hallucinogens	. . .	. . .	0.5	0.8	1.0	0.6	0.4
Heroin	. . .	. . .	. . .	. . .	. . .	0.2	0.1
Nonmedical use of psychotherapeutics	. . .	. . .	2.3	3.1	6.2	4.7	3.4
Stimulants	. . .	0.8	1.3	1.7	2.6	1.7	1.0
Sedatives	. . .	0.6	0.8	1.4	2.0	1.2	0.8
Tranquilizers	. . .	1.2	0.9	1.1	2.8	1.8	1.0
Analgesics	. . .	. . .	0.5	1.0	2.9	2.1	1.9
Alcohol	62.7	64.2	72.4	72.0	73.6	68.6	66.6
Reported Drug Use in Lifetime	**1974**	**1976**	**1979**	**1982**	**1985**	**1988**	**1990**
Illicit drug use	. . .	. . .	23.0	24.7	31.5	33.7	35.3
Marijuana/hashish	9.9	12.9	19.6	23.0	27.2	30.7	31.8
Cocaine	0.9	1.6	4.3	8.5	9.5	9.9	10.9
Inhalants	1.2	1.9	3.9	. . .	5.0	3.9	3.8
Hallucinogens	1.3	1.6	4.5	6.4	6.2	6.6	7.4
Heroin	0.5	0.5	1.0	1.1	1.1	1.1	0.9
Nonmedical use of psychotherapeutics	. . .	. . .	9.2	8.8	13.8	11.3	11.5
Stimulants	3.0	5.6	5.8	6.2	7.9	6.6	6.9
Sedatives	2.0	2.4	3.5	4.8	5.2	3.3	3.7
Tranquilizers	2.0	2.7	3.1	3.6	7.2	4.5	4.2
Analgesics	. . .	. . .	2.7	3.2	5.6	4.5	5.1
Alcohol	73.2	74.7	91.5	88.2	89.4	88.6	86.8

Source: Ambry and Russell, *Guide to American Marketplace,* 357.

TABLE 7.73   COMMONLY ABUSED DRUGS[a]

Drug	Primary Effect	Popular Names
Alcohol	Depressant	Drink, booze
Amphetamines	Stimulant	Pep pills, uppers: *methamphetamines:* speed, meth
Barbituates	Depressant	Sleeping pills, dolls
Cocaine	Stimulant	Coke, snow, lady; *smokable form:* crack
Heroin	Depressant	Snow, smack; *synthetic heroin:* China white, Persian heroin, gasoline dope; *combined heroin and cocaine:* speedball
D-lysergic acid diethylamide	Hallucinogen	LSD, acid
Marijuana	Hallucinogen/ depressant	Pot, grass, joint, cannabis, dope, reefer
MDMA (combination of synthetic mescaline and an amphetamine)	Stimulant/ hallucinogen	Ecstasy
Mescaline	Hallucinogen	Peyote, cactus
Morphine	Depressant	
PCP (phencyclidine)	Hallucinogen	Angel dust
Tranquilizers	Depressants	Downers; *brand names:* Valium, Librium, Darvon, etc.

[a] Many of these drugs were available throughout the period 1946–90 if one knew where to look. Popular prescription tranquilizers, such as Valium, did not begin to appear until the 1950s; LSD did not come on the market until the 1960s; smokeable cocaine, crack, did not appear until 1986. Various combinations were developed at various times. Most significant by the end of the 1980s was the widespread availability of them all.
Source: Wright, *Universal Almanac, 1995,* 224.

TABLE 7.74   DRUGS MENTIONED MOST FREQUENTLY IN EMERGENCY-ROOM SITUATIONS—ESTIMATES OF SELECTED HOSPITALS, 1972–1988[a]

Rank	Drug Name	Number of Mentions	Percent of Total Episodes
1.	Alcohol-in-combination	123,758	30.93
2.	Cocaine	102,727	25.68
3.	Heroin/morphine	36.576	9.14
4.	Acetaminophen	30,885	7.72
5.	Aspirin	21,982	5.49
6.	Marijuana/hashish	16,492	4.12
7.	Alprazolam	16,465	4.12
8.	Ibuprofen	15.628	3.91
9.	Diazepam	14,852	3.71
10.	Amitriptyline	8,785	2.20

[a] Estimates came from the Drug Abuse Warning Network (DAWN), established in 1972 by the Drug Enforcement Administration. Changes in the number of reporting hospitals prevented a claim that these numbers constituted a representative sample, but they did suggest trends.
Source: Jerome H. Jaffe, *Encyclopedia of Drugs and Alcohol* (New York, 1995), 397.

Alcohol

Alcohol was the American drug of choice in 1946, and it remained so in 1990. In each of these years, alcohol continued to be the product most associated with substance abuse. Unlike marijuana and cocaine, alcohol was legal. Unlike users of illegal drugs, the higher the level of education, the more likely a person would be to partake of alcohol, although lesser-educated people certainly drank as well. People in many circles perceived drinking alcohol as the truly American way of relaxing. "We don't smoke marijuana in Muskogee," boasted singer Merle Haggard in his patriotic, "Okie from Muskogee." Real Okies, he claimed, relaxed by drinking "white lightnin'," a homemade alcoholic beverage.

TABLE 7.75   MINIMUM AGE FOR PURCHASE OF ALCOHOLIC BEVERAGES—1965, 1975, AND 1989

State	1965	1975	1989
Alabama	21	21	21
Alaska	21	19	21
Arizona	21	19	21
Arkansas	21	21	21
California	21	21	21
Colorado	21[a]	21[a]	21
Connecticut	21	18	21
Delaware	21	20	21
D.C.	21[b]	21[b,g]	21
Florida	21	18	21
Georgia	21	18	21
Hawaii	20	18	21
Idaho	21[c]	19	21
Illinois	21	19[h]	21
Indiana	21	21	21
Iowa	21	18	21
Kansas	21[a]	21[a]	21
Kentucky	21	21	21
Louisiana	18	18	21
Maine	21	18	21
Maryland	21	18[h]	21
Massachusetts	21	18	21
Michigan	21	18	21
Minnesota	21	18	21
Mississippi	none	21[g]	21
Missouri	21	21	21
Montana	21	18	21
Nebraska	21	19	21
Nevada	21	21	21
New Hampshire	21	18	21
New Jersey	21	18	21
New Mexico	21	21	21
New York	18	18	21
North Carolina	21[b]	21[b]	21
North Dakota	21	21	21
Ohio	21[a]	21[a]	21
Oklahoma	21[d]	21	21
Oregon	21	21[g]	21
Pennsylvania	21	21	21
Rhode Island	21	18	21
South Carolina	21[e]	18	21
South Dakota	21[f]	21[a]	21
Tennessee	21	18	21
Texas	21	18	21
Utah	21	21	21
Vermont	21	18	21
Virginia	21[a]	21[a]	21
Washington	21	21	21
West Virginia	21[a]	18	21
Wisconsin	21[g]	18	21
Wyoming	21	19	21

[a] 3.2 beer: 18.
[b] light wine: 18.
[c] beer: 20.
[d] 3.2 beer (female): 18.
[e] beer and wine: 18.
[f] 3.2 beer: 19.
[g] beer: 18.
[h] hard liquor: 21.
Source: Luman H. Long, ed., *The World Almanac and Book of Facts 1966* (New York, 1966), 779; Ann Golenpaul, ed., *Information Please Almanac, Atlas and Yearbook 1976* (New York, 1975), 734; Otto Johnson, ed., *Information Please Almanac, Atlas and Yearbook 1990* (Boston, 1989), 826.

Not surprisingly, consumption of alcoholic drink increased in both absolute terms and in the more meaningful per capita usage. A slow increase in the 1950s preceded a surge in the tumultuous 1960s, followed by a 9 percent growth in the 1970s. Although the 1980s produced a meaningful reduction in drinking (some 12 percent), the decade ended with more than 100 millions drinking alcohol, approximately 15 million of them to the extent of dependency or some form of abuse. For a part of the period, governments made it easier for people to drink. Jolted by demands from rebellious siblings, impressed by apparent logic in their insistence that if you are old enough to fight (at age 18, in Vietnam) and you are old enough to vote, you should be old enough to drink—legislators beginning in the late 1960s lowered the drinking age (usually set at 21) in state after state. By 1975 only 13 states had failed to make some concession on the drinking age. The most common change was across-the-board reduction to 18 for all kinds of alcohol. A reaction did not take long to set in. The mood of the era passed, of course, partly because the Vietnam War ended and many movements associated with the period petered out. Alcohol-related automobile accidents increased markedly, and teenage drinking was accepted as a major cause. In the 1980s one state after another rescinded (or modified) its earlier legislation, and by the end of the decade the grand experiment in egalitarianism had ended. All states set the drinking age at 21.

The more people that drank, and the more that they drank, the more problems of the practice became apparent. Drinking could cause fatal liver disease, damage to the nervous system, psychological problems of many kinds. Unborn children could be affected by the mother's drinking. Alcohol frequently played a part in suicide, spousal abuse, criminal activity, and of course automobile accidents. The message of "demon rum" came from old organizations, even the Women's Christian Temperance Union (founded in 1874), and from new ones. Mothers Against Drunk Driving (MADD), established in 1980, was followed by Students Against Driving Drunk (SADD) in 1981. Public policy that followed usually took the form of identifying alcoholic content in a driver's system (a practice begun in 1951) and lowering the amount necessary for criminal action. Americans seemed to be united in assailing alcohol abuse, but there appeared almost no support for another movement of absolute prohibition and little evidence of the sort of firestorm that was building against the tobacco companies.

TABLE 7.76   U.S. ALCOHOL CONSUMPTION, 1940–1990[a]

Year	Beer	Wine	Spirits	All Beverages
1940	0.73	0.16	0.67	1.56
1950	1.04	0.23	0.77	2.04
1960	0.99	0.22	0.86	2.07
1970	1.14	0.27	1.11	2.52
1980	1.38	0.34	1.04	2.76
1990	1.34	0.33	0.78	2.46

[a] Gallons of ethanol per capita, based on population age 15 and older to 1970 and age 14 and older to 1990.
Source: New York Times Almanac, 1998, 399.

TABLE 7.77   U.S. CONSUMPTION OF ALCOHOL, COMPARED WITH OTHER COUNTRIES, 1990

(adult consumption per capita)

Rank Order	Absolute Alcohol	Liters
1.	France	16.5
2.	Luxembourg	16.4
3.	Germany	15.0
4.	Austria	14.0
5.	Hungary	13.5
6.	Spain	13.0
7.	Switzerland	12.9
8.	Portugal	12.6
9.	Belgium	12.0
10.	Denmark	11.7
11.	Bulgaria	11.6
12.	Czechoslovakia	11.5
13.	Australia	10.7
14.	Netherlands	10.3
15.	Italy	10.3
16.	New Zealand	10.1
17.	Ireland	10.0
18.	Romania	9.9
19.	Finland	9.6
20.	United Kingdom	9.4
21.	United States	9.2

Source: Dwight B. Heath, *International Handbook on Alcohol and Culture* (Westport, Conn., 1995), 364–65.

TABLE 7.78   DEATHS AND DEATH RATES FOR ALCOHOL-INDUCED CAUSES, BY RACE AND SEX, 1980–1990

(age-adjusted rates per 100,000)

Year	All Races Both Sexes	All Races Male	All Races Female	White Both Sexes	White Male	White Female	All Other Total Both Sexes	All Other Total Male	All Other Total Female	All Other Black Both Sexes	All Other Black Male	All Other Black Female
Number												
1980	19,765	14,447	5,318	14,815	10,936	3,879	4,950	3,511	1,439	4,451	3,170	1,281
1985	17,741	13,216	4,525	13,216	9,922	3,294	4,525	3,294	1,231	4,114	3,030	1,084
1990	19,757	14,842	4,915	14,904	11,334	3,570	4,853	3,508	1,345	4,337	3,172	1,165
Rate												
1980	8.4	13.0	4.3	6.9	10.8	3.5	18.8	29.5	10.0	20.4	32.4	10.6
1985	7.0	11.0	3.4	5.8	9.2	2.8	14.6	23.5	7.2	16.8	27.7	8.0
1990	7.2	11.4	3.4	6.2	9.9	2.8	13.6	22.0	6.8	16.1	26.6	7.7

Source: Bureau of the Census, *Statistical Abstract of the United States, 1995* (Washington, D.C., 1995), 101.

TABLE 7.79 **ALCOHOLISM DEATHS AND MORTALITY RATES—AMERICAN INDIANS AND ALL RACES, 1969–1986[a]**

(deaths per 100,000 resident population)

Year	Indian & Alaska Native Number	Indian & Alaska Native Rate	All U.S. Races Number	All U.S. Races Rate	Ratio Indian to All U.S. Races
1969	267	56.6	15,138	7.7	7.4
1971	334	62.9	16,891	8.4	7.5
1973	399	66.1	17,791	8.6	7.7
1975	403	62.2	18,190	8.6	7.2
1977	429	55.5	18,437	8.3	6.7
1979	398	45.1	17,064	7.4	6.1
1981	338	35.8	16,745	7.0	5.2
1983	293	28.9	15,424	6.1	4.7
1985	281	26.1	15,844	6.2	4.2
1986	272	24.6	15,525	6.4	3.8

[a] For 1969–78, numbers include deaths due to alcoholism, alcoholic psychosis, and cirrhosis of the liver; for 1979 and after, numbers include deaths due to alcohol dependence syndrome, alcoholic psychosis, and chronic liver disease and cirrhosis.
Source: Robert O'Brien & Morris Chafetz, *The Encyclopedia of Alcoholism* (New York, 1991), 31.

TABLE 7.80 **ALCOHOL-RELATED TRAFFIC CRASH FATALITIES AS A PORTION OF ALL TRAFFIC CRASH FATALITIES, 1977–1987**

Year	Traffic Crash Crashes	Traffic Crash Fatalities	Alcohol-Related Traffic Crash Fatalities	Percent of All Traffic Crash Fatalities
1977	42,064	47,715	17,414	36.5
1978	44,433	50,327	18,362	36.5
1979	45,212	51,084	20,245	39.6
1980	45,271	51,077	21,114	41.3
1981	43,979	49,268	20,662	41.9
1982	38,899	43,721	18,622	42.6
1983	37,971	42,584	17,847	41.9
1984	39,622	44,241	18,523	41.9
1985	39,196	43,825	18,040	41.2
1986	41,090	46,082	20,038	43.5
1987	41,435	46,386	19,918	42.9

Source: O'Brien & Chafetz, *Encyclopedia of Alcoholism*, 273.

TABLE 7.81 **ALCOHOL-RELATED FATALITIES, BY AGE, 1977–1987**

(in percent)

Year	Under 16	16–24	25–44	45–64	Older than 64	Unknown
1977	5.5	43.2	32.4	14.2	4.3	0.4
1978	5.0	42.9	34.3	13.2	4.2	0.4
1979	4.8	42.6	35.4	12.8	4.1	0.4
1980	4.5	42.4	36.2	12.7	4.0	0.3
1981	4.1	40.1	38.4	12.9	4.3	0.3
1982	4.3	41.0	38.3	12.1	4.1	0.3
1983	4.1	39.6	40.0	12.0	4.2	0.2
1984	3.9	39.6	40.0	11.7	4.5	0.3
1985	4.1	37.8	41.2	11.9	4.6	0.4
1986	4.2	38.4	41.8	11.0	4.3	0.4
1987	4.2	35.3	44.0	11.6	4.7	0.2

Source: O'Brien & Chafetz, *Encyclopedia of Alcoholism*, 276.

TABLE 7.82 **TRENDS IN SELECTED BEHAVIOR AND PERCEPTIONS AMONG U.S. HIGH SCHOOL SENIORS, 1975–1990**

Year	"Ever" Tried in Lifetime — Any Illicit Drugs[a]	"Ever" Tried in Lifetime — Cigarettes	"Ever" Tried in Lifetime — Alcohol	"Great Risk" if Smoke 1 or More Packs of Cigarettes Every Day	"Great Risk" if Take 1 or 2 Drinks Nearly Every Day	"Great Risk" if Take 5 or More Drinks Once, Twice Weekend	"Most" or "All" of Best Friends Drink Alcohol	"Most" or "All" of Best Friends Get Drunk At Least Once a Week
1975	36.2	73.6	90.4	51.3	21.5	37.8	68.4	30.1
1976	35.4	75.4	91.9	56.4	21.2	37.0	64.7	26.6
1977	35.8	75.7	92.5	58.4	18.5	34.7	66.2	27.6
1978	36.5	75.3	93.1	59.0	19.6	34.5	68.9	30.2
1979	37.4	74.0	93.0	63.0	22.6	34.9	68.5	32.0
1980	38.7	71.0	93.2	63.7	20.3	35.9	68.9	30.1
1981	42.8	71.0	93.2	63.3	21.6	36.3	67.7	29.4
1982	41.1	70.1	92.8	60.5	21.6	36.0	69.0	29.9
1983	40.4	70.6	92.6	61.2	21.6	38.6	69.0	31.0
1984	40.3	69.7	92.6	63.8	23.0	41.7	66.6	29.6
1985	39.7	68.8	92.2	66.5	24.4	43.0	66.0	29.0
1986	37.7	67.6	91.3	66.0	25.1	39.1	68.0	31.8
1987	35.8	67.2	92.2	68.6	26.2	41.9	71.8	31.3
1988	32.5	66.4	92.0	68.0	27.3	42.6	68.1	29.6
1989	31.4	65.7	90.7	67.2	28.5	44.0	67.1	31.1
1990	29.4	64.4	89.5	68.2	31.3	47.1	60.5	27.5

[a] Other than marijuana.
Source: Metlife, *Statistical Bulletin*, January–March, 1993, 21.

TABLE 7.83 **CURRENT USERS OF CIGARETTES, ALCOHOL, MARIJUANA, AND/OR COCAINE, 1988**
(in percent)

Substance and Age Group	Total	Sex		Race/Ethnicity			Region			
		Male	Female	White[b]	Black[b]	Hispanic	Northeast	Midwest	South	West
Cigarettes: Total	28.8	32.2	25.6	28.7	30.3	26.3	29.3	29.6	31.1	22.9
12 to 17 years old	11.8	12.4	11.2	13.9	5.1	7.5	11.4	12.9	12.4	9.1
18 to 25 years old	35.2	35.6	34.8	36.9	29.5	28.2	33.8	45.0	34.0	27.8
26 to 34 years old	37.1	40.7	33.6	37.2	36.1	33.6	35.7	45.8	34.0	33.8
35 years old and older	27.3	32.2	23.0	26.3	35.5	27.6	29.1	23.3	33.0	19.5
Alcohol: Total	53.4	60.6	46.7	55.1	44.3	49.2	59.2	55.7	45.1	60.3
12 to 17 years old	25.2	26.8	23.5	27.4	15.9	25.4	30.2	27.9	21.2	24.7
18 to 25 years old	65.3	74.5	56.6	68.8	50.0	61.4	70.8	73.0	53.2	74.7
26 to 34 years old	64.2	73.9	54.8	66.2	57.0	58.8	68.8	72.8	55.9	65.4
35 years old and older	51.5	58.6	45.4	52.7	44.9	46.0	58.1	50.9	43.7	59.7
Marijuana: Total	5.9	7.9	4.0	5.6	6.3	6.0	5.5	6.7	4.8	7.3
12 to 17 years old	6.4	6.1	6.7	6.8	4.4	5.2	6.5	6.7	5.9	7.0
18 to 25 years old	15.5	20.0	11.2	15.7	15.0	13.8	18.4	17.9	12.2	16.3
26 to 34 years old	10.8	14.8	7.0	11.2	9.3	9.1	9.6	14.2	8.8	11.9
35 years old and older	1.4	2.2	0.7	1.1	2.2	a	1.1	1.1	0.9	3.1
Cocaine: Total	1.5	2.0	1.0	1.3	2.0	2.6	2.1	1.5	1.0	1.7
12 to 17 years old	1.1	0.9	1.4	1.3	a	1.3	0.9	1.7	a	2.5
18 to 25 years old	4.5	6.0	3.0	4.2	4.3	6.7	7.0	4.8	2.9	4.7
26 to 34 years old	2.6	3.6	1.6	2.3	3.0	3.9	2.6	3.3	1.8	3.1
35 years old and older	0.4	0.5	a	0.3	1.1	a	1.0	a	a	a

a Base too small to meet statistical standard of a reliable figure.
b Non-Hispanic.
Source: Statistical Abstract, 1991, 122.

CHAPTER 8 Religion

The Course of Religion, 1946–1990

As would benefit a nation of such growing population and cultural and ethnic diversity where popular attitudes and constitutional principles tolerated almost any point of view, religion in the United States underwent numerous turns in the last half of the 20th century. In the face of so many new pressures and forces, it was remarkable that the country experienced as much continuity as it did. The explanation probably rested in a basic foundation in Judeo-Christian heritage, the fact that the bulk of the population maintained an association with Christianity, albeit in vastly differing ways, and the fact that the United States remained rich and powerful—a force that tended to discourage large upheaval of any sort.

Statistics suggested an upsurge in religious activity, at least in church membership, in the immediate postwar period. Religious organizations experienced an increase of more than 20 million members in the 1940s and a remarkable growth of nearly 28 million in the 1950s. By 1960, 65 percent of the populace claimed religious affiliation of some sort (as compared with 49 percent in 1940). Explanations of the surge often placed more emphasis on social and economic than religious factors. The cold war battle against "godless communism" placed religion in league with patriotism and individual self-interest. Postwar culture stressed commonality, fitting in, and church membership in the 1950s carried an automatic mark of respectability. Popular music fed the theme with such songs as "I Believe," "The Man Upstairs," and "Vaya Con Dios." Most Christian churches experienced growth; some of the most impressive gains came in the respectable and relatively undemanding mainline denominations, such as Methodist and Lutheran. The Roman Catholic Church showed steady growth throughout the period, if only because of the Catholic practice of registering virtually every Catholic baby at birth. The spirit of commonality carried over to religion in formation of the National Council of Churches in 1950, merger of various Protestant denominations, and aspects of the Second Vatican Council of 1962–65.

Although affiliation with religious organizations remained generally high—more than 60 percent—throughout the 1960s, other signals suggested that a weakening of faith had set in. Statistics on attendance at worship service, which never had kept pace with membership, pointed to sharper decline beginning in the mid-1960s. By the early 1970s only 40 percent went to church. In 1970, 75 percent of the people polled believed that religion was losing its influence. Mainline Protestant churches that had reached peak membership between 1965 and 1970 began a slide that would reach well into the 1980s. Between 1965 and 1989 the Presbyterian Church lost 25 percent of its membership; the Episcopal lost 28 percent, and the Methodist (United Methodist) lost 18 percent. The Catholic Church continued to put up large numbers, but evidence pointed to a substantial difference between membership and commitment.

By the mid-1970s a shift clearly was taking place within the ranks of American Christianity. The participants in that shift in politics would take the form of the Religious Right. In denominational circles it meant growth in the popularity of churches peopled by Bible-believing, "born-again" constituents who took their religion seriously and with considerable vigor. In large measure they reacted to social and legal changes underway for several years: changing attitudes toward sex, pornography, and marriage; new policies with respect to affirmative action, prayer in schools, and, above all, abortion. To the extent that there was a catalyst for the political aspect of the movement it would be the Supreme Court decision in 1973 that legalized abortion. Denominational benefactors included "fringe" churches that could be called evangelical, fundamentalist, and perhaps pentecostal. The Assemblies of God was such a sect, although certain branches of the more familiar Baptist Church also joined up. The most prominent leaders, Jerry Falwell and Pat Robertson, were Baptist ministers.

A considerable force in political and religious circles though most of the 1980s, conservative Protestantism could claim victories in national and local elections, restrictions on various public policies, and growth of certain denominations. In its politics and its tactics—not to mention its image—the movement provoked hostility—often taking the form of ridicule—from groups whose interests were being threatened. Embarrassed by hypocrisy and exploitive behavior within its most conspicuous leadership, wounded by excessive activity from radical members, the Religious Right, if not conservative Christianity in general, by the late 1980s was placed on the defensive.

Religion in the United States thus has been, and continued to be, erratic and diverse. A study in 1977 revealed approximately 800 separate Christian groups and more than 200 that were non-Christian. The non-Christian or quasi-Christian groups lent themselves to no single generalization other, perhaps, than there had been a lot of them and they differed considerably.

It was standard practice to identify the three great religions in the United States as Protestantism, Catholicism, and Judaism. There continued to be a lack of popular understanding about the relationship between the Jewish people and the faith. How many Jews practiced Judaism on a regular basis? The Census Bureau did not try to determine. In counting adherents to Judaism the bureau simply included everyone who was ethnically Jewish. Judaism continued to ride on the three branches of Orthodox, Reform, and Conservative; the postwar years produced a surge in the construction of synagogues. Many American Jews nonetheless observed the faith only nominally if at all. The holocaust of the Second World War and the creation in 1948 of the state of Israel provided powerful reasons for stressing one's Jewishness. Seeming perpetual vulnerability of Israel regularly reinforced the attitude, but the terrible slaughter of the holocaust led many Jews to question the workings, if not the existence, of a supreme being. If a decline in postwar anti-Semitism and acceptance of Jews into greater American society were regarded as positive trends, they did not do much for the faith. Orthodox Judaism no less than orthodox Christianity carried demands on behavior and attitude. Assimilation, however, was a part of acceptance in American culture. Marriage to non-Jews rose from 6 percent in 1950 to 30 percent in 1990. Judaism held its own, but it would appear that the enormous influence of Jewish people in American arts and sciences, education, entertainment, and other areas did not extend to religion.

If the numbers of other groups never were known exactly, most were small and attracted attention only because of some exceptional circumstance. Most Americans knew little about Buddhism except what they might have learned in college, and they encountered the faith only when the Dalai Lama visited the United States or on learning that actors Richard Gere and Harrison Ford were Buddhist. Many people doubted that the Church of Scientology, which claimed 3 million members, was really a church, but they paid it more attention on learning that another actor, John Travolta, was a member. Such terms as *Unification Church, the New Age, Branch Davidians* and others provoked an emotional reaction or none at all. Islam, to be sure, was different—a bonafide, powerful world religion that was destined to grow in the United States. Even so, the surge in the number of Muslims remained an item for the near future, and up to the year 1990, the major influence of Islam came in the pressure of its representative governments on policy of the United States. Protestantism, long the dominant religious force, still could claim a majority of people who expressed a preference, but in the course of recent history two other groups—the Catholics and Jews—had reached a position of social equality. If the pattern of recent immigration continued, especially the large increase from East Asia, one could expect continued growth in the number and size of nontraditional religions. If indicators foretold a predominantly Christian United States as far as one could see, they also foretold even more diversity, inside the faith and out.

Surveys Conducted by the Princeton Religion Research Center—The Gallup Organization

TABLE 8.1 PERCENT OF AMERICANS WHO BELIEVE IN GOD OR A UNIVERSAL SPIRIT, 1944–1986

Year	Percent
1944	96
1947	94
1952	99
1953	98
1954	96
1959	97
1965	97
1967	97
1969	98
1975	94
1976	94
1981	95
1986	94

Source: The Princeton Religion Research Center, Religion in America 1990 (Princeton, 1990), 16.

TABLE 8.2 PERCENT OF AMERICANS WHO BELIEVE IN LIFE AFTER DEATH, 1944–1988

Year	Percent
1944	76
1948	68
1952	77
1957	74
1961	74
1965	75
1968	73
1975	69
1978	71
1980	67
1981	71
1988	71

Source: Princeton Research Center, Religion in America 1990, 25.

TABLE 8.3 THE LAST JUDGMENT
Question: *How much do you agree with the statement: "We will all be called before God at the judgment day to answer for our sins." (1988)*

Those Asked	Completely Agree (%)	Mostly Agree (%)	Mostly Disagree (%)	Completely Disagree (%)
National	52	28	8	6
Men	45	31	10	7
Women	59	25	7	5
Under 30	45	35	8	6
30–45	50	26	9	9
50 and older	60	24	8	4
Protestants	60	26	7	3
White	58	26	7	4
Black	66	27	4	1
Evangelicals	78	17	2	2
Non-Evangelicals	45	33	10	5
Catholics	49	35	9	2

Source: Princeton Research Center, Religion in America 1990, 21.

TABLE 8.4 OPINION POLLS OF RELIGIOUS PREFERENCE—MAJOR FAITHS, 1947–1989[a]

Year	Protestant	Catholic	Jewish	Other	None
1947	69%	20%	5%	1%	6%
1952	67%	25%	4%	1%	2%
1957	66%	26%	3%	1%	3%
1962	70%	23%	3%	2%	2%
1967	67%	25%	3%	3%	2%
1972	63%	26%	2%	4%	5%
1974	60%	27%	2%	5%	6%
1976	61%	27%	2%	4%	6%
1977–78	60%	29%	2%	1%	8%
1980	61%	28%	2%	2%	7%
1982	57%	29%	2%	4%	8%
1984	57%	28%	2%	4%	9%
1986	58%	27%	2%	4%	9%
1988–89	56%	28%	2%	4%	10%

[a] Gallup Organization surveys of nearly 18,000 persons 18 and older.
Source: Princeton Research Center, Religion in America 1990, 29.

TABLE 8.5 RELIGIOUS POPULATION OF THE UNITED STATES, 1940–1990
(in thousands, except as indicated)

Religious Body	1940	1950	1960	1970	1975	1980	1990
Total	64,502	86,830	114,449	131,045	131,013	134,817	156,336
Members as % of population	49	57	64	63	61	59	63
Buddhists	. . .	. . .	20	100	60	60	19
Eastern churches	. . .	1,859	2,699	3,850	3,696	3,823	3,976
Jews	. . .	5,000	5,367	5,870	6,115	5,920	5,981
Old Catholic, Polish National, Armenian churches	. . .	337	590	848	846	924	950
Roman Catholics	21,284	28,635	42,105	48,125	48,882	50,450	58,568
Protestants[a]	37,815	51,080	63,669	71,173	71,043	73,479	86,684
Miscellaneous[b]	. . .	. . .	. . .	449	372	161	1,166

[a] Includes such non-Protestants as Latter-Day Saints and Jehovah's Witnesses.
[b] Officially non-Christian groups—Spiritualists, Ethical Culture, etc.
Source: Bureau of Census, Statistical Abstract of the United States, 1970 (Washington, D.C., 1970), 42; Statistical Abstract, 1993 (Washington, D.C., 1993), 67.

TABLE 8.6   CHURCH MEMBERSHIP STATISTICS, 1940–1989

(for selected U.S. denominations)

Denomination	1940	1947	1950	1955	1960	1965	1970	1975	1980	1985	1989
Assemblies of God[b]	198,834	241,782	318,478	400,047	508,602	572,123	625,027	785,348	1,064,490	2,082,878	2,137,890
Baptist General Conference	...	...	48,647[c]	54,000	72,056	86,719	103,955	115,340	133,385	132,546	133,742
Christian and Missionary Alliance	22,832[d]	...	58,347	57,109[e]	59,657	64,586	112,519	145,833	189,710	227,846	265,863
Christian Church (Disciples of Christ)	1,658,966	1,889,066	1,767,964	1,897,736	1,801,821	1,918,471	1,424,479	1,302,164	1,177,984	1,116,326	1,052,271
Church of God (Anderson, Ind)	74,497	95,325	107,094	123,523	170,261	143,231	150,198	166,257	176,429	185,593	199,786
Church of God (Cleveland, Tenn.)	63,216		121,706[f]	142,668	170,261	205,465	272,278	343,249	435,012		582,203
Church of Jesus Christ of Latter-day Saints	724,401[d]	911,279	1,111,314	1,230,021	1,486,887	1,789,175	2,073,146	2,336,715	2,811,000	3,860,000	4,175,400
Church of the Brethren	176,908	182,497	186,201	195,609	199,947	194,815	182,614	179,336	170,839	159,184	149,681
Church of the Nazarene	165,532	201,487[g]	226,684	270,576	307,629	343,380	383,284	441,093	484,276	522,082	561,253
Cumberland Presbyterian Church	73,357	75,427	81,806	84,990	88,452	78,917	92,095	94,050	96,553	98,037	90,906
Episcopal Church	1,996,434	2,155,514	2,417,464	2,852,965[h]	3,269,325	3,429,153[a]	3,285,826	2,857,513	2,786,004	2,739,422	2,433,413
Evangelical Covenant Church of America	45,634	51,850	55,311	60,090	65,780	67,441	71,808	77,737	84,150	89,014	
Evangelical Lutheran Church in America		(3,117,626)	(3,982,508)	(4,672,083)	(5,295,502)	(5,684,298)	(5,650,137)	(5,401,765)	(5,384,271)	(5,341,452)	5,238,798
Free Methodist Church of North America	45,890	46,783[g]	48,574	51,437	55,338	59,415	64,901	67,043	68,477	72,223	75,869
Jehovah's Witnesses	...	...	...	187,120	250,000	330,358	388,920	560,897	565,309	730,441	825,570
Lutheran Church—Missouri Synod	1,277,097	1,422,513	1,674,901	2,004,110	2,391,195	2,692,889	2,788,536	2,763,545	2,625,650	2,628,164	2,609,025
Mennonite Church	51,304	52,596	56,480	70,283	73,125	80,087	88,522	94,209	99,511	91,167	92,517
North American Baptist Conference			41,560	47,319	50,646	53,711	55,080	42,629[j]	43,041	42,863	42,629
Presbyterian Church (U.S.A.)	(2,690,969)	(2,969,382)	(3,210,635)	(3,701,635)	(4,161,860)	(4,254,460)	(4,045,408)	(3,535,825)	(3,362,086)	3,048,235	2,886,482
Reformed Church in America	255,107	274,455	284,504	319,593	354,621	385,754	367,606	355,052	345,532	342,375	330,650
Reorganized Church of Jesus Christ of Latter Day Saints	106,554	116,888	124,925	137,856	155,291	168,355	152,670	157,762	190,087	192,082	190,183
Roman Catholic Church	21,284,455	24,402,124	28,634,878	33,396,647	42,104,900	46,246,175	48,214,729	48,881,872	50,449,842	52,654,908	57,019,948
Salvation Army	238,357	205,881	209,341	249,641	254,141	287,991	326,934	384,817	417,359	427,825	445,566
Seventh-day Adventist Church	176,218	208,030	237,168	277,162	317,852	364,666	420,419	495,699	571,141	651,954	701,781
Southern Baptist Convention	4,949,174	6,079,305	7,079,889	8,467,439	9,731,591	10,770,573	11,628,032	12,733,124	13,600,126	14,477,364	14,907,826
United Church of Christ	(1,708,146)	(1,835,853)	(1,977,418)	(2,116,322)	(2,241,134)	2,070,413	1,960,608	1,818,762	1,736,244	1,683,777	1,625,969
United Methodist Church	(8,043,454)	(9,135,248)	(9,653,178)	(10,029,535)	(10,641,310)	(11,067,497)	10,509,198	9,861,028	9,519,407	9,192,172	8,979,139
Wisconsin Evangelical Lutheran Synod	256,007[d]	259,097	307,216	328,969	348,184[i]	358,466	381,321	395,440	407,043	415,389	419,312

a Data for 1966
b Assemblies of God statistics for 1971 and later are full-membership statistics
c Data for 1952
d Data for 1939
e Data for 1954
f Data for 1951
g Data for 1945
h Data for 1956
i Data for 1961
j Adjusted downward to eliminate Canadian membership previously reported.

Source: National Council of the Churches of Christ, *Yearbook of American and Canadian Churches, 1990* (Nashville, 1990), 272–73.

TABLE 8.7 MAJOR RELIGIOUS AFFILIATIONS, 1985–1990[a]

Family/Denomination	Local Congregations	Total Clergy	Total Membership	% of Total Affiliated
All Religiously Affiliated	350,337	547,064	147,607,394	100.0
Roman Catholic Church	23,500	53,111	57,019,948	38.6
Baptist Churches	**97,994**	**147,356**	**28,463,978**	**19.3**
Southern Baptist Convention	37,739	64,100	14,907,826	
National Baptist Convention, USA, Inc.	26,000	27,500	5,500,000	
National Baptist Convention of America	11,398	28,574	2,668,799	
American Baptist Churches in the USA	5,833	8,242	1,548,573	
Baptist Bible Fellowship International	3,449	4,500	1,405,900	
Progressive National Baptist Convention Inc.	655	863	521,692	
American Baptist Association	1,705	1,760	250,000	
National Primitive Baptist Convention Inc.	616	636	250,000	
Baptist Missionary Association of America	1,339	2,648	229,315	
General Association of Regular Baptist Churches	1,582	N.A.	216,468	
Conservative Baptist Association of America	1,126	1,324	210,000	
Free Will Baptists, National Association of	2,517	2,900	204,489	
Liberty Baptist Fellowship	510	N.A.	200,000	
Baptist General Conference	792	1,700	133,742	
Other (10 denominations)	2,733	2,619	217,174	
Methodist Churches	**53,737**	**56,697**	**13,229,155**	**9.0**
United Methodist Church	37,514	38,303	8,979,139	
African Methodist Episcopal Church	6,200	6,550	2,210,000	
African Methodist Episcopal Zion Church	6,060	6,698	1,220,260	
Christian Methodist Episcopal Church	2,340	2,650	718,922	
Other (8 denominations)	1,623	2,496	100,834	
Lutheran Churches	**18,988**	**27,859**	**8,374,898**	**5.7**
Evangelical Lutheran Church in America	11,067	17,246	5,238,798	
Lutheran Church—Missouri Synod	5,990	8,271	2,609,025	
Wisconsin Evangelical Lutheran Synod	1,198	1,573	419,312	
Others (10 denominations)	733	769	107,763	
Pentecostal Churches	**40,280**	**78,596**	**7,931,294**	**5.4**
Church of God in Christ	9,982	10,426	3,709,661	
Assemblies of God	11,192	30,471	2,137,890	
Church of God (Cleveland, Tenn.)	5,763	7,544	582,203	
United Pentecostal Church International	3,592	7,447	500,000	
International Church of the Foursquare Gospel	1,404	5,179	203,060	
Church of God in Christ, International	300	1,600	200,000	
Pentecostal Holiness Church International	1,475	2,095	119,073	
Others (21 denominations)	6,572	13,834	479,407	
Orthodox (Eastern) Churches	**2,070**	**2,720**	**4,659,939**	**3.2**
Greek Orthodox Archdiocese of North and South America	535	655	1,950,000	
Orthodox Church in America	440	531	1,000,000	
Armenian Church of America, Diocese of the	66	61	450,000	
Antiochian Orthodox Christian Archdiocese of North America	160	325	350,000	
American Apostolic Church of America	30	29	180,000	
Coptic Orthodox Church	42	49	165,000	
Apostolic Catholic Assyrian Church of the East	22	109	120,000	
Others (13 denominations)	775	961	444,939	
Latter-day Saints Churches	**18,192**	**48,322**	**4,370,690**	**3.0**
Church of Jesus Christ of Latter-day Saints	9,049	30,960	4,175,400	
Reorganized Church of Jesus Christ of Latter Day Saints	1,048	16,912	190,183	
Others (2 denominations)	95	450	5,107	
Churches of Christ	**23,067**	**13,493**	**3,748,887**	**2.5**
Churches of Christ	13,375	N.A.	1,626,000	
Christian Churches and Churches of Christ	5,579	6,596	1,070,616	
Christian Church (Disciples of Christ)	4,113	6,897	1,052,271	
Presbyterian Churches	**14,211**	**24,080**	**3,366,411**	**2.3**
Presbyterian Church (USA)	11,469	20,078	2,886,482	
Presbyterian Church in America	1,100	1,949	217,374	
Other (7 denominations)	1,642	2,053	256,555	
Episcopal Church	**7,372**	**14,831**	**2,433,413**	**1.6**
Reformed Churches	**8,125**	**12,799**	**2,205,589**	**1.5**
United Church of Christ	6,388	9,870	1,625,969	
Reformed Church in America	928	1,727	330,650	
Christian Reformed Church in North America	712	1,099	225,699	
Others (4 denominations)	97	103	23,271	

(continued)

TABLE 8.7 (continued)

Family/Denomination	Local Congregations	Total Clergy	Total Membership	% of Total Affliated
Holiness Churches	**12,429**	**19,451**	**1,245,810**	**0.8**
Church of the Nazarene	5,158	9,138	561,253	
Christian and Missionary Alliance	1,829	2,370	265,863	
Church of God (Anderson, Ind.)	2,338	3,410	199,786	
Wesleyan Church	1,650	3,076	110,027	
Christian Congregation	1,454	1,457	108,881	
Jehovah's Witnesses	**9,141**	**0**	**825,570**	**0.5**
Adventist Churches	**4,636**	**5,068**	**733,249**	**0.5**
Seventh-Day Adventists	4,193	4,493	701,781	
Others (3 denominations)	443	575	31,468	
Church of Christ, Scientist	**N.A.**	**N.A.**	**700,000**	**0.4**
Salvation Army	**1,122**	**5,184**	**445,566**	**0.3**
Roman Rite Churches	**295**	**291**	**345,022**	**0.2**
Polish National Catholic Church of America	162	141	282,411	
North American Old Roman Catholic Church	133	150	62,611	
Mennonite Churches	**2,501**	**6,573**	**250,645**	**0.2**
Mennonite Church	1,034	2,545	92,517	
Old Order Amish Church	785	3,140	70,650	
Others (9 denominations)	682	888	87,478	
International Confederation of Community Churches	**210**	**350**	**250,000**	**0.2**
Brethren Churches	**1,804**	**3,754**	**225,842**	**0.2**
Church of the Brethren	1,102	2,436	149,681	
Others (5 denominations)	702	1,318	76,161	
Unitarian Universalist Association	**1,010**	**1,252**	**182,211**	**0.1**
Evangelical Free Church of America	**1,040**	**1,795**	**165,000**	**0.1**
Friends (Quaker) Churches (5 denominations)	**1,405**	**1,082**	**118,070**	**0.1**
Total Christian Churches	**345,686**	**N.A.**	**141,443,624**	**95.8**
Jews	**3,416**	**6,500**	**5,944,000**	**4.0**
Muslims	**N.A.**	**N.A.**	**3,000,000**[b]	**N.A.**
Buddhist Churches of America	**67**	**107**	**19,441**	**0.1**
Other Religions	**1,168**	**N.A.**	**200,329**	**0.1**

[a] A year was not always indicated in these yearly surveys, but in this report of 1991, it usually was between 1988 and 1990. A few churches used an earlier year.
[b] There were no reliable statistics on the number of Muslims in the United States. The number 3,000,000 was equal to number of Muslim immigrants in the United States.
Source: Reports to the *Yearbook of American and Canadian Churches, 1991* as arranged in John Wright, ed., *The Universal Almanac 1994* (Kansas City, 1994), 232.

TABLE 8.8 ATTENDANCE AT WORSHIP SERVICE, 1947–1990

(participation by adults in percent)

Year	Percent
1947	45
1950	39
1954	46
1956	46
1958	49
1960	47
1962	46
1964	45
1966	44
1968	43
1970	40
1972	40
1974	40
1976	42
1978	41
1980	40
1982	41
1984	40
1986	40
1988	42
1989	43
1990	40

Source: National Council of the Churches of Christ, *Yearbook of American Churches, 1970* (New York, 1970), 337; *Yearbook of American and Canadian Churches, 1990,* 292; *Yearbook of American Churches, 1991,* 302.

TABLE 8.9 WOMEN MEMBERS OF THE CLERGY, 1940–1986

(number and % of all clergy)

Year	Number	Percent
1940	3,148	2.3
1950	6,777	4.1
1960	4,727	2.3
1970	6,314	2.0
1977	10,470	4.0
1986	20,730	7.9

Source: Churches of Christ, *Yearbook of American and Canadian Churches, 1978* (Nashville, 1978), 259; *Yearbook of American Churches, 1989,* 261–62.

TABLE 8.10 DENOMINATIONS WITH LARGEST NUMBER OF FEMALE CLERGY, 1986

Rank	Denomination	Number of Female Clergy
1.	Assemblies of God	3,718
2.	Salvation Army	3,220
3.	United Methodist Church	1,891
4.	Presbyterian Church	1,519
5.	United Church of Christ	1,460
6.	Episcopal Church	796
7.	Christian Church (Disciples of Christ)	743
8.	International Church of the Foursquare Gospel	666
9.	Lutheran Church in America	484
10.	American Baptist Churches	429

Source: Churches of Christ, *Yearbook of American Churches, 1989,* 262.

Women and the Priesthood: A Catholic View

Report of National Conference of Catholic Bishops (1972)

The constant tradition and practice of the Catholic Church against the ordination of women, interpreted . . . as of divine law, is of such a nature as to constitute a clear teaching . . . of the Church . . ., this is Catholic doctrine.

Archbishop Joseph L. Bernardin (1975):

It is not correct to say that the fact . . . that women have not been ordained up to now can be explained simply by culturally conditioned notions of male superiority. This is a serious theological issue. Throughout its history the Catholic Church has not called women to the priesthood.

Source: Felician A. Foy, ed., *1976 Catholic Almanac* (Huntington, Ind., 1975), 121–22.

Catholicism in the United States

The Roman Catholic Church of the immediate post–Second World War period remained essentially what it had been for many decades. Aloof, tightly structured, seemingly preoccupied with protecting its institutional self, it faced an American clientele that was undergoing change. Historically immigrants or children of immigrants, working-class, defensive, semi-isolated, and subjected to discrimination of various levels, Catholics in the 1940s and 1950s were beginning to break free. The Second World War had been a major force for amalgamation, whether one served in the armed forces or the home front, and the prosperity of the postwar era reached many groups that previously had been left behind. Some of the largest proportionate gains had been scored by members of white minority groups, many of whom had been Catholic. If there had been doubts about heightened acceptability of Catholics into greater American society, they largely had been put to rest by election to the presidency of John F. Kennedy in 1960.

It therefore was appropriate, even mandatory, that the American Catholic Church move to keep pace with changes in its constituency. To many people's surprise the initiative for change came from the international church. On the death in 1958 of Pope Pius XII, whom many had considered conservative, if not reactionary—Hitler's pope, the harshest critics called him—the College of Cardinals selected the man who, nearly 77 years old, would become Pope John XXIII. The new pope's age provided perhaps an explanation for the surprise many Catholics felt on hearing in 1959 that he planned to call an ecumenical council, the first in nearly a century, to consider changes in the church and its position within the world.

The Second Vatican Council of 1962–65—Vatican II, as American Catholics would call it—produced several decisions that loosened discipline within church hierarchy and between the clergy and the populace and sought to place the church within the diverse world of the 20th century. American Catholics first felt effects of the changes in liturgy and church discipline. Now masses were heard in English (not Latin); the priest faced the congregation; the people were encouraged to sing and in other ways participate in the ceremony. Other traditional practices, such as fast and abstinence, confession directly to a priest, were eliminated or made optional. The new era, to be sure, produced awkward moments: Some Catholics, to whom mass was a ritual of prescribed motions, did not want to sing, and to see the music led by someone with a guitar and tambourine bordered on sacrilege. To other people the changes were refreshing, liberating, consistent with popular movements of the 1960s and early 1970s. For others the church had taken away the distinctions that made them Catholic.

Although it would be a mistake to hold reforms of Vatican II solely responsible for what followed, the ensuing years produced some difficult times for the established American church. The popular injunction

This Cathedral in New Ulm, Minnesota, is pictured during a folk guitar mass—very popular with the young people. (National Archives)

to "do your own thing" was engaging, even compelling, to young people. Attendance at mass dropped sharply; few people asked a priest to hear confession. Many priests and members of other religious orders left their vocation; fewer people entered seminaries, and there were fewer seminaries to enter. Between 1965 and 1985 female religious orders (the nuns) lost nearly 65,000 of their personnel.

The 1970s and 1980s produced pressure for even further change. Critics blamed shortage of priests on the rule of celibacy; to get married or have a romantic relationship, one had to leave the priesthood and many men did. The feminist movement, which contained many Catholics and several nuns, found no logical reason why women could not become members of the clergy. Revelations about priestly molestation of children—and of the church's handling of such matters—raised many questions, including about the sexual climate in which the leadership functioned. The issues that affected the general populace most directly were birth control (the church still condemned all "artificial" methods) and the ban on remarriage after divorce. Many Catholics cynically viewed annulment, often called the church's substitute for divorce, as an option open only for the rich and powerful. Abortion remained for Catholics, as with other people, a delicate and painful issue. Although most probably supported the church's opposition to abortion, the proportion of Catholic women who had chosen such a procedure was comparable to other white groups.

A large number of individuals, perhaps a majority, resolved the dilemma faced in their catholicism with selectivity: They obeyed the commandments they chose and ignored the others. These "cafeteria" or "a la carte" Catholics found such an approach imperfect but workable. The demand of conservatives for a return to traditional church discipline seemed out of the question.

As the 1980s came to an end the Catholic Church continued to record steady gains in membership and in its share of the world of American Christendom. But the numbers failed to measure either a level of commitment or of the diversity within the membership. The course of immigration what it was (large numbers from Catholic countries of Latin America) could mean only that the diversity would increase. One almost could say that the Catholic Church was not catholic any more.

Holy Days of Obligation: Roman Catholic Church

Every Catholic who had attained age of reason, was not prevented by sickness or other sufficient cause, was obliged to rest from servile work and attend Holy Mass on the following days:

Before Vatican Council II (1960)

All Sundays of the year.
Circumcision of Our Lord (January 1)
Ascension (40 days after Easter)
Assumption of Blessed Virgin (August 15)
All Saints Day (November 1)
Immaculate Conception (December 8)
Christmas (December 25)

After Vatican Council II
All days are the same except that January 1 was changed to Solemnity of Mary the Mother of God.

Days of Fast

Days of fasting bound everyone between 21 and 59, except when health or ability to work became an issue. The individual could have one full meal and two small meatless meals. No eating in between.

Before Vatican Council II (1960)

1. All weekdays of Lent.
2. Ember days—1960: March 9–11, June 8–11, September 21–24, December 14–17.
3. Pentecost (June 4)
4. Immaculate Conception
5. Christmas (December 24) (20 days in all)

After Vatican Council II (1974)

1. Ash Wednesday
2. Good Friday (2 days)

Days of Abstinence

Days of Abstinence required everyone seven and older (in 1960) to refrain from eating meat on the designated days.

Before Vatican Council II (1960)

1. All Fridays of the year.
2. Ash Wednesday
3. Holy Saturday
4. Immaculate Conception
5. Christmas (December 24)

Partial: (meat once per day)

1. Ember Wednesdays
2. Ember Saturdays
3. Pentecost

After Vatican Council II (1974)

1. Ash Wednesday
2. Good Friday
3. All Fridays of Lent (Minimum age raised to 14)

Source: Felician A. Foy, ed., *The 1960 National Catholic Almanac* (New York, 1960), 128; Foy, *1976 Catholic Almanac*, 287.

TABLE 8.11   ROMAN CATHOLIC CLERGY, DEACONS, AND MEMBERS OF RELIGIOUS ORDERS, 1950–1990

Year	Priests	Deacons	Brothers	Sisters
1950	42,970	...	7,377	147,310
1955	46,970	...	8,752	158,069
1960	53,796	...	10,473	168,527
1965	58,432	...	12,271	179,954
1970	59,192	...	11,623	160,931
1975	58,909	...	8,625	135,204
1980	58,621	4,093	7,941	126,517
1985	57,317	7,204	7,544	115,396
1990	52,547	9,639	6,722	102,519

Source: National Council of the Churches of Christ, *Yearbook of American and Canadian Churches, 1986* (Nashville, 1989), 267; *Yearbook of American Churches, 1991*, 290.

Brief Glossary Associated with Conservative, usually Protestant, Christianity

born again   Originated in John 3:3–7 in which Jesus told Nicodemus that he had to be "born again" to see the Kingdom of God. Thus it was necessary to undergo a complete spiritual rebirth, after which the individual would be changed, a new person.

charismatic movement   A fairly recent energetic, joyous worship marked with emphasis on faith healing and speaking in tongues. Popularity grew with both Protestants and Catholics in late 1960s and 1970s.

evangelical   The term means "good news," and it refers to responsibility of born-again, "Bible-believing" Christians to share their beliefs and spiritual joy with other people, through "witnessing" or other means.

fundamentalism   The term has a fairly lengthy historical background, but in "fundamental" essentials it entailed belief in certain basic truths, all of which were contained in the Bible, which represented the inspired word of God. Practice of these truths have taken different forms.

glossolalia   The word given to identify the practice of "speaking in tongues," or strange unknown languages—a power given to the Apostles (and others present) on the day of Pentecost. Not all Protestants, not even all fundamentalists, and only charismatic Catholics approve of this form of worship.

pentecostal   As with glossolalia, pentecostal pertains to the day of Pentecost, at which time the people present were granted supernatural powers, such as speaking in tongues, healing, and prophecy. People who accept such "gifts of the spirit" are called Pentecostals. The Assemblies of God is the largest such body.

rapture   That moment when Christ will return to resurrect the righteous who have died and remove the "saved" who are still alive. Those left behind will face the "tribulation," seven years during which evil forces control the earth.

revival   Dating to at least the 18th century, revival pertains to emotional Protestant gatherings, often held in large tents, designed to reinvigorate believers and to convert as many as possible of those persons who were not.

secular humanism   A belief that human beings, relying on their own devices, are capable of managing affairs of the world, with no need of God. Bible-believing Christians insisted that this human-centered (as opposed to being God-centered) society, was (and is) doomed to destruction. They believe that God is in charge.

Source: (In part) Glenn H. Utter and John W. Storey, *The Religious Right* (Santa Barbara, 1995), 269–75.

Television Evangelists and Emergence of the Religious Right

Christianity and mass communication media made a good mix almost from the start. Most denominations maintained a desire, many considered it a duty, to spread the word, the good news, to as many people as possible. Aimee Semple McPherson and other evangelists had used radio shortly after it had been developed in the 1920s, and the number of radio preachers proliferated in the 1940s and 1950s, many of them reaching local or regional audiences. By the end of the 1950s all three major radio networks had lifted a ban on sale of radio airtime to religious broadcasters. The shift to television was as logical as it had been for normal programming, and for a while, the government facilitated the transfer. The FCC ruled that local stations must allot time for religious broadcasting, and at first networks forbade accepting payment for these programs. A reversal of that policy, allowing stations to sell airtime, did nothing to discourage preachers from taking their message to the small screen.

By the 1970s ministers controlled, not only programs but also stations and even networks. The messengers and the message had moved some distance from the programs of Bishop Sheen, Walter Maier, or even Billy Graham's crusades. No less than other types of programs, shows on religion lent themselves to showmanship and extravagant claims and behavior. The spiritual message, it often appeared, became subordinate to or a vehicle for the interests and antics of such messengers as Oral Roberts, the spellbinding Jimmy Swaggart, Jim and Tammy-Faye Bakker, whose *P.T.L.* program was patterned after the *Tonight Show* of Johnny Carson. Network television provided a lucrative platform for soliciting donations and other devices for accumulating funds that could be used for various purposes, including supporting the lifestyle of the recipients or construction of multifaceted empires that in the case of Swaggart and Roberts included colleges.

The movement of televangelism into politics must have seemed to the people involved entirely logical and proper. Many of the issues emerging in the 1970s—prayer or any religious observance in public schools, sexuality, sexual orientation, aspects of the feminist movement, and, of course, abortion—did involve moral and often spiritual questions; most had become objects of public policy and thus connected to qualifications of political leaders. The television preachers most prominent on a national level of the politicization of religion were Jerry Falwell and Pat Robertson, both southern Baptists. The means by which an emerging Religious Right—many of which membership had been former Democrats—took up nearly the entire program of the Republican Party was a complex proposition. It partly had to do with the fact that many liberal leaders endorsed social positions that evangelicals found reprehensible; seizing the opportunity, conservative Republicans fashioned their programs to appeal to various religious groups. The marriage became strongest at the start of the 1980s with Falwell's Moral Majority effectively targeting several Democrat senators and with the two presidential administrations of Ronald Reagan, surely the favorite politician of the Religious Right.

Televangelism suffered deep wounds in the late 1980s. The humiliation of Oral Roberts, Jimmy Swaggart, and the Bakkers destroyed two of the largest and most aggressive broadcasting establishments and exposed the ease with which hypocrisy could infiltrate their brand of emotional Christianity. Even some of the most devout followers wearied of the spectacle of preachers begging for money, calling it "a love offering," perhaps suggesting that earthly prosperity or even prospect for an eternal life hinged on an individual's generosity to the cause. Religious broadcasting by no means ended, but the theatrics lessened, and some of the worst offenders spoke to a considerably reduced audience, if they were able to continue at all. The Religious Right lived to fight another day, but it too had been affected by the preachers' scandals and by extremist tactics of a few zealots in the battle against abortion. Robertson's campaign for the Republican nomination in 1988 fizzled; the Moral Majority disbanded, and Ronald Reagan, the movement's political hero, retired in 1989.

TABLE 8.12 PERCENTAGE OF AMERICANS WHO REGARD THEMSELVES "BORN-AGAIN," 1988

Question: *Would you describe yourself as a "born-again" or evangelical Christian, or not?*

National	Five Surveys during 1988 (Telephone and Personal)			
	Yes 33%	No 63%	Not Sure 4%	Number of Interviews 5,045
Sex				
Men	29	67	4	2,514
Women	37	59	4	2,531
Age				
18–29 years	30	66	4	1,137
30–49 years	31	66	3	2,031
50 & older	39	57	4	1,836
Region				
East	21	75	4	1,208
Midwest	32	64	4	1,338
South	49	47	4	1,527
West	26	70	4	971
Race				
Whites	31	65	4	4,420
Non-whites	49	47	4	606
Blacks	57	40	3	431
Hispanics	24	68	8	311
Education				
College graduates	22	76	2	1,384
College incomplete	30	66	4	1,240
High school graduates	35	61	4	1,700
Not high school graduates	45	49	6	690
Household Income				
$40,000 and over	25	73	2	984
$25,000–$39,999	33	64	3	940
$15,000–$24,999	35	60	5	687
Under $15,000	40	55	5	842
Religion				
Protestants	49	48	3	2,883
Catholics	12	83	5	1,345

Source: Princeton Research Center, *Religion in America, 1990*, 41.

Milestones in Religious Broadcasting

1948 *The Lutheran Hour,* a radio show hosted by Walter Maier, becomes on January 1 the first regularly scheduled television broadcast of a religious program.

1950 Evangelist Billy Graham begins broadcasting his crusade over local radio stations. He calls the program *Hour of Decision.*

1952 Fulton J. Sheen, a Catholic bishop, starts a televison program called *Life Is Worth Living.*

1955 Tent-revivalist Oral Roberts begins regular television broadcasting of his program.

1956 Jerry Falwell begins radio and television coverage of Sunday services from Thomas Road Baptist Church in Lynchburg, Virginia.

1957 NBC and CBS joins ABC in lifting a ban on sale of radio airtime to independent religious broadcasters.

1957 For the first time Billy Graham's crusade (in New York) is carried on television.

1966 Evangelist Pat Robertson, who in 1961 had formed the Christian Broadcast Network, introduces the talk-show format in *The 700 Club.*

1970 California-based minister Robert Schuller (who had held services at a drive-in theater) begins to broadcast the *Hour of Power.*

1973 Jimmy Swaggart brings his high-energy revivalism to television in *The Jimmy Swaggart Telecast.*

1974 Jim Bakker takes over a religious television talk show that, joined by his wife, Tammy Faye, he calls *The PTL Club—Praise the Lord* or *People That Love.*

1977 James Dobson (a psychologist, not a preacher) brings *Focus on the Family* to radio in Los Angeles.

1979 The Moral Majority, started by Jerry Falwell, and the Freedom Forum, headed by Pat Robertson, take religious programming into national politics.

1987 Oral Roberts informs viewers of a message from God that unless he raised $8 million he would be "taken home" (would die). Roberts was ridiculed as an embarrassment to the faith if not mentally defective, but he got the money.

TABLE 8.13   INFLUENCE OF RELIGION—OPINION POLLS, 1957–1989

Answer to question: *"Do you think religion . . . is increasing its influence on American life . . . or losing its influence?"*

Year	Increasing %	Losing %
1957	69	14
1962	45	31
1965	33	45
1967	23	57
1968	18	67
1970	14	75
1974	31	56
1976	44	45
1978	37	48
1980	35	46
1983	44	42
1985	49	39
1986	48	39
1988	36	49
1989	33	49

Source: Princeton Research Center, *Religion in America, 1990,* 60.

1987 Jim Bakker resigns leadership of the PTL Club over evidence of sexual improprieties with a secretary. He later will be imprisoned for fraud.

1988 In a tearful performance Jimmy Swaggart admits—what already had been established—that he engaged in "perverted" sexual behavior (recently, with a prostitute). The Assemblies of God defrock Swaggart, and his religious empire disintegrates, but he continues to preach on television.

1988 Pat Robertson's campaign for the Republican presidential nomination fails badly. Robertson returns to The 700 Club.

1989 Jerry Falwell disbands the Moral Majority.

Source: J. Gordon Melton, Phillip C. Lucas, and Jon R. Stone, *Prime-Time Religion: An Encyclopedia of Religious Broadcasting* (Phoenix, 1997), 393–95.

CHAPTER 9 Politics and Government

The political system of the United States encountered many tests and challenges in the half-century that followed the Second World War. The cold war produced a complex and persistent set of circumstances that made new demands on the government and its leadership, raised questions that went to the core of national political philosophy, and created a temptation to sacrifice values and principles for the sake of survival and security. The most immediate internal threat came, it would appear, at the beginning of the period, when the nation's acknowledged adversary, the USSR, emerged as a dangerous enemy and at the same time the possessor of an alternate political and economic program that carried considerable appeal. After a brief experiment in the 1950s with using suppression as a counterforce to the perceived threat—during the era of Joseph McCarthy when government itself sponsored serious restrictions on civil liberties—the nation returned to its senses, confident that the collective will would take it in the right direction. The idea of communism as a meaningful, even preferable, alternative took care of itself, although not before considerable passage of time and great expense to the United States.

If most Americans generally rejected extremism on the right in the 1950s, they also refused to yield to the most drastic thrusts from the left in the 1960s. The rejection partly represented a reaction to the tactics and demeanor of the so-called New Left and cultural fellow travelers from within the counterculture; partly it came from the reformers' failure to formulate a concrete and effective program. A favorite slogan, "Power to the People," lacked specificity, to put it mildly. The problem was not a shortage of issues. Although Vietnam, racism, excesses of capitalism, and a general maldistribution of wealth were genuine issues, they did not lend themselves to easy resolution, whatever the political system. Large and complex as it was, the war in Vietnam might have been open to the simplest—but still not simple —solution. The general populace rejected the most radical symbols of a new politics, certainly the bombings and rampages, as well as the bizarre and unblushing social behavior that seemed to be part of the package. The election of Richard Nixon in 1968 and his overwhelming reelection in 1972 stood as undeniable evidence that the center— perhaps a little to right of center—had held.

So America was left with, and for the most part content with, the broad and flexible mainstream, and its generous boundaries left much room for movement and political combat. The continuing reach of the coalition of Franklin D. Roosevelt put the Democrats in charge of the government at the start, and they would continue to dominate Congress throughout the period. Control of the presidency during 1946–90 was fairly even, although most of the presidents after 1970 were Republican. It almost appeared that the people had come to prefer divided government: the Democrats to attend to major social problems, the Republicans to keep a lid on things. Americans evidently did not want to leave either party fully in charge.

A distinctly nonrevolutionary political environment nonetheless left much room for change. And one of the changes was revolutionary: For the only time in its history, the Americans, in effect, kicked out a president, Richard Nixon, in 1974. Nixon's vice president, Spiro Agnew, had also been forced to resign, from a totally different issue. The resignation of Agnew and Nixon allowed the nation to experience application (twice) of a new Twenty-fifth Amendment that addressed the issue of vacancy in one of the two top offices. Preparation of this amendment had been set in motion by perhaps the most tragic event in politics of the era, the assassination of John F. Kennedy on November 22, 1963. Striking down a young leader—he was 46—at the time he seemed to be hitting his stride, Kennedy's killing earned a place in the memory of everyone old enough to remember it—a national mourning fostered for the first time by relentless media (notably television) coverage. Assassination of a president was exceptional but by no means unheard of; attempts to do so were not unusual. Three other presidents would face assassination efforts between 1946 and 1990, one (Ford) was threatened twice and one (Reagan) was seriously wounded.

Reduction of the voting age from 21 to 18, which came in ratification of the Twenty-sixth Amendment in 1971, added millions of new voters to the rolls. The civil rights revolution in the southern states in the 1950s and 1960s produced several political consequences. The first and most important, of course, was that black people in the South at last obtained the suffrage, a right theoretically granted some 100 years earlier. Not only did southern blacks begin to vote, especially after 1965, but they also began to hold office. Starting with election of Maynard Jackson in 1973, Atlanta would become accustomed to having a black mayor. The new politics of race brought about another change. A South that had remained solidly Democratic more or less from the 1880s to the 1940s had changed by 1972 to the solid Republican South, at least in presidential elections. The white people switched parties, mostly because of the national Democratic Party's identification with civil rights. The size of the shift was be lessened by the fact that black people now voted, most of them Democratic, and it was be interrupted in 1976 when Jimmy Carter—a native son southerner— ran for the presidency, but as a rule the Republicans could count on the southern states in presidential elections, and an increasing number of state and local contests produced the same result.

Although a women's movement took longer than the race-oriented crusade to get underway, it had effects that were nearly as profound and perhaps more far-reaching. Women became more politically active, beginning approximately in the mid-1960s; issues increasingly had to be framed with gender in mind. More women voted and voted independently (as opposed to mimicking their husbands—one of the older sexist, but sometimes valid, slanders). Women were elected to, and/or appointed to, political office in increasing numbers. They became members of congress and state legislatures, senators, cabinet members, mayors, and governors. The appointment of Sandra Day O'Connor to the Supreme Court in 1981 meant that females had attained every level of office in the land, save the two highest. As the running mate of Walter Mondale in 1984, Geraldine Ferraro had grabbed for the second highest ring, and by that time virtually no one doubted that the presidency would be in some woman's future at some point. The emergence of the American female in government surely was one of the most important political changes of the post–Second World War era, if not the 20th century, and unlike the politicization of black people, it had little grounding in legislation. The change came largely in attitude.

The debate over policy began the postwar period as an extension of the familiar liberal-conservative contest, muddled by the fact that the liberal side, the Democrats, contained some of the most conservative politicians in the land, the southerners, and the conservative side, the Republicans, included downright reactionaries and others more liberal than many Democrats. These left-of-center individuals were called liberal or moderate Republicans, and an example was Nelson Rockefeller of New York. In general the Democratic leadership favored using the national government as an instrument of "social justice," helping people in need, and the Republicans warned about the dangers of too much spending and the growing encroachment of the national government on state authority and rights of private individuals. The debate in large measure centered on economics as

Geraldine Ferraro (right), pictured with Rosalynn Carter, was the first woman to run for the vice presidency (in 1984) on a major party ticket. (Courtesy Jimmy Carter Library)

exemplified in policy with respect to taxes, labor unions, regulation of business, and welfare programs. Both parties endorsed Americanism and the need to promote freedom, but they differed in priority. The Democrats championed so-called First Amendment freedoms (freedom of speech and expression, and so on), and the Republicans worried more about government encroachment on economic activity.

Contests over economic policy never vanished from the scene, and in basic philosophy the position of the parties remained essentially unchanged into the 1990s. But other issues emerged. The cold war and its ramifications at home and abroad demanded attention and supplied politicians with new issues and arguments. From 1947 until its end at the start of the 1990s, the cold war helped to define virtually everything the United States did in world affairs and many issues within the nation.

The liberals' quest for social justice reached high tide in Lyndon Johnson's program of the Great Society in 1964–65, and then it was weakened by the Vietnam War on one side and race riots and student upheaval on the other. Starting in the 1960s, race, ethnicity, and gender became important components for the political agenda. Starting in the 1970s social issues, notably abortion, began to reshape politics and the parties. It was no longer a simple case of haves against have-nots, although these themes remained a part of the political debate. There

seemed to emerge a pattern of alternating administrations profiting from the failures of their predecessors, but it was interesting to note that the only presidents elected more than once (there were three) all were Republican. If the parties seemed much the same as they had been in 1946 when it came to economics, they had changed with respect to appeal and constituency. The center continued to hold, if only because it stretched.

Religious Affiliation of the Presidents

Harry S. Truman	Baptist
Dwight D. Eisenhower	Presbyterian
John F. Kennedy	Roman Catholic
Lyndon B. Johnson	Disciples of Christ
Richard Nixon	Society of Friends (Quaker)
Gerald R. Ford	Episcopalian
Jimmy Carter	Baptist
Ronald Reagan	Episcopalian
George Bush	Episcopalian

Source: Congressional Quarterly, *American Leaders 1789–1991* (Washington, D.C., 1991), 7.

TABLE 9.1   AMERICAN PRESIDENTIAL ELECTIONS, 1944–1988

Year	Presidential Candidate	Party	Votes Electoral	Votes Popular
1944	Franklin D. Roosevelt	Democratic	432	25,611,936
	Thomas E. Dewey	Republican	99	22,013,372
1948	Harry S. Truman	Democratic	303	24,105,587
	Thomas E. Dewey	Republican	189	21,970,017
	J. Strom Thurmond	States' Rights	39	1,169,134
1952	Dwight D. Eisenhower	Republican	442	33,936,137
	Adlai E. Stevenson	Democratic	89	27,314,649
1956	Dwight D. Eisenhower	Republican	457	35,585,245
	Adlai E. Stevenson	Democratic	73	26,030,172
1960	John F. Kennedy	Democratic	303	34,221,344
	Richard M. Nixon	Republican	219	34,106,671
1964	Lyndon B. Johnson	Democratic	486	43,126,584
	Barry Goldwater	Republican	52	27,177,838
1968	Richard M. Nixon	Republican	301	31,785,148
	Hubert H. Humphrey	Democratic	191	31,274,503
	George Wallace	Am. Indep.	46	9,901,151
1972	Richard M. Nixon	Republican	520	47,170,179
	George M. McGovern	Democratic	17	29,171,791
1976	Jimmy Carter	Democratic	297	40,830,763
	Gerald R. Ford	Republican	240	39,147,793
1980	Ronald Reagan	Republican	489	43,904,153
	Jimmy Carter	Democratic	49	35,483,883
1984	Ronald Reagan	Republican	525	54,455,074
	Walter F. Mondale	Democratic	13	37,577,137
1988	George Bush	Republican	426	48,886,097
	Michael S. Dukakis	Democratic	111	41,809,074

Source: Thomas L. Connelly and Michael D. Senecal, *Almanac of American Presidents: From 1789 to the Present* (New York, 1991), 439–40.

Honoring a campaign pledge, president-elect Eisenhower (center) visits the Korean War, sharing "chow" with soldiers of the Third Infantry Division, December 1952. (Courtesy Dwight D. Eisenhower Library)

TABLE 9.2   THE PRESIDENTS AND THEIR CABINETS, 1945–1993

The Truman Administration

Title	Office Holder	Dates
President	Harry S. Truman	1945–1953
Vice President	Alben W. Barkley	1949–1953
Secretary of State	Edward R. Stettinius, Jr. James F. Byrnes George C. Marshall Dean G. Acheson	1945 1945–1947 1947–1949 1949–1953
Secretary of Treasury	Fred M. Vinson John W. Snyder	1945–1946 1946–1953
Secretary of War Attorney General	Robert P. Patterson Kenneth C. Royall Tom C. Clark J. Howard McGrath James P. McGranery	1945–1947 1947 1945–1949 1949–1952 1952–1953
Postmaster General	Frank C. Walker Robert E. Hannegan Jesse M. Donaldson	1945 1945–1947 1947–1953
Secretary of Navy	James V. Forrestal	1945–1947
Secretary of Interior	Harold L. Ickes Julius A. Krug Oscar L. Chapman	1945–1946 1946–1949 1949–1953
Secretary of Agriculture	Clinton P. Anderson Charles F. Brannan	1945–1948 1948–1953
Secretary of Commerce	Henry A. Wallace W. Averell Harriman Charles W. Sawyer	1945–1946 1946–1948 1948–1953
Secretary of Labor	Lewis B. Schwellenbach Maurice J. Tobin	1945–1948 1948–1953
Secretary of Defense	James V. Forrestal Louis A. Johnson George C. Marshall Robert A. Lovett	1947–1949 1949–1950 1950–1951 1951–1953

The Eisenhower Administration

Title	Office Holder	Dates
President	Dwight D. Eisenhower	1953–1961
Vice President	Richard M. Nixon	1953–1961
Secretary of State	John Foster Dulles Christian A. Herter	1953–1959 1959–1961
Secretary of Treasury	George M. Humphrey Robert B. Anderson	1953–1957 1957–1961
Attorney General	Herbert Brownell, Jr. William P. Rogers	1953–1958 1958–1961
Postmaster General	Arthur E. Summerfield	1953–1961
Secretary of Interior	Douglas McKay Fred A. Seaton	1953–1956 1956–1961
Secretary of Agriculture	Ezra T. Benson	1953–1961
Secretary of Commerce	Sinclair Weeks Lewis L. Strauss Frederick H. Mueller	1953–1958 1958–1959 1959–1961
Secretary of Labor	Martin P. Durkin James P. Mitchell	1953 1953–1961
Secretary of Defense	Charles E. Wilson Neil H. McElroy Thomas S. Gates, Jr.	1953–1957 1957–1959 1959–1961
Secretary of Health, Education, and Welfare	Oveta Culp Hobby Marion B. Folsom Arthur S. Flemming	1953–1955 1955–1958 1958–1961

The Kennedy Administration

Title	Office Holder	Dates
President	John F. Kennedy	1961–1963
Vice President	Lyndon B. Johnson	1961–1963
Secretary of State	Dean Rusk	1961–1963
Secretary of Treasury	C. Douglas Dillon	1961–1963
Attorney General	Robert F. Kennedy	1961–1963
Postmaster General	J. Edward Day John A. Gronouski	1961–1963 1963
Secretary of Interior	Stewart L. Udall	1961–1963
Secretary of Agriculture	Orville L. Freeman	1961–1963
Secretary of Commerce	Luther H. Hodges	1961–1963
Secretary of Labor	Arthur J. Goldberg W. Willard Wirtz	1961–1962 1962–1963
Secretary of Defense	Robert S. McNamara	1961–1963
Secretary of Health, Education, and Welfare	Abraham A. Ribicoff Anthony J. Celebrezze	1961–1962 1962–1963

The Johnson Administration

Title	Office Holder	Dates
President	Lyndon B. Johnson	1963–1969
Vice President	Hubert H. Humphrey	1965–1969
Secretary of State	Dean Rusk	1963–1969
Secretary of Treasury	C. Douglas Dillon Henry H. Fowler	1963–1965 1965–1969
Attorney General	Robert F. Kennedy Nicholas Katzenbach Ramsey Clark	1963–1964 1965–1966 1967–1969
Postmaster General	John A. Gronouski Lawrence F. O'Brien Marvin Watson	1963–1965 1965–1968 1968–1969
Secretary of Interior	Stewart L. Udall	1963–1969
Secretary of Agriculture	Orville L. Freeman	1963–1969
Secretary of Commerce	Luther H. Hodges John T. Connor Alexander B. Trowbridge Cyrus R. Smith	1963–1964 1964–1967 1967–1968 1968–1969
Secretary of Labor	W. Willard Wirtz	1963–1969
Secretary of Defense	Robert S. McNamara Clark Clifford	1963–1968 1968–1969
Secretary of Health, Education, and Welfare	Anthony J. Celebrezze John W. Gardner Wilbur J. Cohen	1963–1965 1965–1968 1968–1969
Secretary of Housing and Urban Development	Robert C. Weaver Robert C. Wood	1966–1969 1969
Secretary of Transportation	Alan S. Boyd	1967–1969

The Nixon Administration

Title	Office Holder	Dates
President	Richard M. Nixon	1969–1974
Vice President	Spiro T. Agnew Gerald R. Ford	1969–1973 1973–1974
Secretary of State	William P. Rogers Henry A. Kissinger	1969–1973 1973–1974
Secretary of Treasury	David M. Kennedy John B. Connally George P. Shultz William E. Simon	1969–1970 1971–1972 1972–1974 1974
Attorney General	John N. Mitchell Richard G. Kleindienst Elliot L. Richardson William B. Saxbe	1969–1972 1972–1973 1973 1973–1974
Postmaster General	Winton M. Blount	1969–1971
Secretary of Interior	Walter J. Hickel Rogers Morton	1969–1970 1971–1974
Secretary of Agriculture	Clifford M. Hardin Earl L. Butz	1969–1971 1971–1974
Secretary of Commerce	Maurice H. Stans Peter G. Peterson Frederick B. Dent	1969–1972 1972–1973 1973–1974
Secretary of Labor	George P. Shultz James D. Hodgson Peter J. Brennan	1969–1970 1970–1973 1973–1974

Secretary of Defense	Melvin R. Laird	1969–1973
	Elliot L. Richardson	1973
	James R. Schlesinger	1973–1974
Secretary of Health, Education, and Welfare	Robert H. Finch	1969–1970
	Elliot L. Richardson	1970–1973
	Casper W. Weinberger	1973–1974
Secretary of Housing and Urban Development	George Romney	1969–1973
	James T. Lynn	1973–1974
Secretary of Transportation	John A. Volpe	1969–1973
	Claude S. Brinegar	1973–1974

The Ford Administration

Title	Office Holder	Dates
President	Gerald R. Ford	1974–1977
Vice President	Nelson A. Rockefeller	1974–1977
Secretary of State	Henry A. Kissinger	1974–1977
Secretary of Treasury	William E. Simon	1974–1977
Attorney General	William Saxbe	1974–1975
	Edward Levi	1975–1977
Secretary of Interior	Rogers Morton	1974–1975
	Stanley K. Hathaway	1975
	Thomas Kleppe	1975–1977
Secretary of Agriculture	Earl L. Butz	1974–1976
	John A. Knebel	1976–1977
Secretary of Commerce	Frederick B. Dent	1974–1975
	Rogers Morton	1975–1976
	Elliot L. Richardson	1976–1977
Secretary of Labor	Peter J. Brennan	1974–1975
	John T. Dunlop	1975–1976
	W. J. Usery	1976–1977
Secretary of Defense	James R. Schlesinger	1974–1975
	Donald Rumsfeld	1975–1977
Secretary of Health, Education, and Welfare	Casper Weinberger	1974–1975
	Forrest D. Mathews	1975–1977
Secretary of Housing and Urban Development	James T. Lynn	1974–1975
	Carla A. Hills	1975–1977
Secretary of Transportation	Claude Brinegar	1974–1975
	William T. Coleman	1975–1977

The Carter Administration

Title	Office Holder	Dates
President	Jimmy Carter	1977–1981
Vice President	Walter F. Mondale	1977–1981
Secretary of State	Cyrus R. Vance	1977–1980
	Edmund Muskie	1980–1981
Secretary of Treasury	W. Michael Blumenthal	1977–1979
	G. William Miller	1979–1981
Attorney General	Griffin Bell	1977–1979
	Benjamin R. Civiletti	1979–1981
Secretary of Interior	Cecil D. Andrus	1977–1981
Secretary of Agriculture	Robert Bergland	1977–1981
Secretary of Commerce	Juanita M. Kreps	1977–1979
	Philip M. Klutznick	1979–1981
Secretary of Labor	F. Ray Marshall	1977–1981
Secretary of Defense	Harold Brown	1977–1981
Secretary of Health, Education, and Welfare	Joseph A. Califano	1977–1979
	Patricia R. Harris	1979
Secretary of Health and Human Services	Patricia R. Harris	1979–1981
Secretary of Education	Shirley M. Hufstedler	1979–1981
Secretary of Housing and Urban Development	Patricia R. Harris	1977–1979
	Moon Landrieu	1979–1981
Secretary of Transportation	Brock Adams	1977–1979
	Neil E. Goldschmidt	1979–1981

| Secretary of Energy | James R. Schlesinger | 1977–1979 |
| | Charles W. Duncan | 1979–1981 |

The Reagan Administration

Title	Office Holder	Dates
President	Ronald Reagan	1981–1989
Vice President	George Bush	1981–1989
Secretary of State	Alexander M. Haig	1981–1982
	George P. Shultz	1982–1989
Secretary of Treasury	Donald Regan	1981–1985
	James A. Baker III	1985–1988
	Nicholas F. Brady	1988–1989
Attorney General	William F. Smith	1981–1985
	Edwin A. Meese III	1985–1988
	Richard L. Thornburgh	1988–1989
Secretary of Interior	James G. Watt	1981–1983
	William P. Clark, Jr.	1983–1985
	Donald P. Hodel	1985–1989
Secretary of Agriculture	John Block	1981–1986
	Richard E. Lyng	1986–1989
Secretary of Commerce	Malcolm Baldrige	1981–1987
	C. William Verity, Jr.	1987–1989
Secretary of Labor	Raymond J. Donovan	1981–1985
	William E. Brock	1985–1987
	Ann Dore McLaughlin	1987–1989
Secretary of Defense	Casper Weinberger	1981–1987
	Frank C. Carlucci	1987–1989
Secretary of Health and Human Services	Richard S. Schweiker	1981–1983
	Margaret Heckler	1983–1985
	Otis R. Bowen	1985–1989
Secretary of Education	Terrel H. Bell	1981–1984
	William J. Bennett	1985–1988
	Lauro F. Cavazos	1988–1989
Secretary of Housing and Urban Development	Samuel R. Pierce, Jr.	1981–1989
Secretary of Transportation	Drew Lewis	1981–1982
	Elizabeth Hanford Dole	1983–1987
	James H. Burnley IV	1987–1989
Secretary of Energy	James B. Edwards	1981–1982
	Donald P. Hodel	1982–1985
	John S. Herrington	1985–1989

The (George H. W.) Bush Administration

Title	Office Holder	Dates
President	George Bush	1989–1993
Vice President	Dan Quayle	1989–1993
Secretary of State	James A. Baker III	1989–1992
Secretary of Treasury	Nicholas F. Brady	1989–1993
Attorney General	Richard L. Thornburgh	1989–1991
Secretary of Interior	Manuel Lujan, Jr.	1989–1993
Secretary of Agriculture	Clayton K. Yeutter	1989–1991
Secretary of Commerce	Robert A. Mosbacher	1989–1992
Secretary of Labor	Elizabeth Hanford Dole	1989–1991
Secretary of Defense	Richard B. Cheney	1989–1993
Secretary of Health and Human Services	Louis W. Sullivan	1989–1993
Secretary of Education	Lauro F. Cavazos	1989–1991
Secretary of Housing and Urban Development	Jack F. Kemp	1989–1993
Secretary of Transportation	Samuel K. Skinner	1989–1991
Secretary of Energy	James D. Watkins	1989–1993
Secretary of Veterans Affairs	Edward J. Derwinski	1989–1992

Source: Congressional Quarterly, *The Presidency A to Z*, 528–32.

Vietnam, Watergate, and the Crisis of the Modern Presidency

The American presidency underwent a crisis in the 1970s and it remained a weakened and distrusted institution for at least the decade that followed. This weakening and loss of trust began with the Vietnam War because Vietnam had been a presidential war and it had gone so badly. Many observers by 1968 had concluded that the United States had been led into a conflict it could not win and perhaps should not win and that the war had left the country weakened, embarrassed, and sharply divided. While every president dating back to Harry Truman bore some responsibility for the entanglement in Indochina, the bulk of the blame came to rest with Lyndon Johnson, who had Americanized the war and misled the people as to the expected outcome and the principles for which it was fought. Johnson left office in 1969 discredited, if not humiliated, and the major reason was the effects of the Vietnam War.

In running for the presidency in 1968, Richard Nixon had promised to end the war, and soon after taking office he began a withdrawal of forces, but he took other steps—the bombing of North Vietnam and Cambodia, the invasion of Cambodia—that left his intentions and his honesty in question. The first and most substantial efforts to limit the presidency, such measures as the War Powers Act of 1973 and a tightening congressional control of the military budget, came because of Vietnam, and the armistice signed in January 1973 did not slow down the movement.

It so happened that the issue of Vietnam overlapped and became entangled with the domestic political scandal known as Watergate that emerged in the early 1970s. The issues that had surfaced during the war: excessive presidential power, lack of honesty, and presidential misuse of power, grew to heroic proportion as the sordid story of the Watergate episode unfolded between 1972 and 1974. The downfall of Richard Nixon came not because he ordered a break-in of the Democrat headquarters in Washington (he did not) and not officially because he lied to the people (which he did repeatedly) but because he misused the huge powers at his disposal. Needless to say, the fact that he lied and evidence of devious behind-the-scenes dealings, laid open by the Watergate tapes, cast an even darker shadow on an institution already under fire. The presidency had gotten out of hand, had become pampered, privilege laden, grandiose, and very powerful—if only because of technology. In the estimate of Arthur Schlesinger, Jr., the office of the American chief executive had evolved into the imperial presidency.

What followed in the post-Watergate period affirmed or reaffirmed that the Americans react sharply to immediate circumstances but that the collective memory often does not last. Simplicity, openness, and honesty became prized characteristics for leadership. Nixon already had acknowledged the theme in his choice of Gerald Ford, a dependable but unexceptional congressman from Michigan, to replace discredited vice president Spiro Agnew in 1973; although Agnew's ouster had no direct connection to Watergate, it did stand as another example of untrustworthy leadership. On August 9, 1974, clean Jerry Ford of Grand Rapids was on hand to take over when the secretive Nixon resigned. During the 1970s the reputation of previously much-maligned president Harry Truman underwent a revival. Truman's shortcomings in retrospect seemed minor and at least "give 'em hell Harry" had been open and brutally honest. The clearest and most obvious expression of a new-found presidential prerequisite appeared in the election in 1976 of Jimmy Carter. A little-known former governor of Georgia, Carter managed to identify himself as a small-town southern boy who had worked hard, remained a man of the people, and always told the truth. Another hint as to the mood of the time came in the fact that only 53.5 percent of the electorate voted in 1976, lowest for a presidential race since 1948.

The Carter administration had its ups and downs, successes and failures, but the new president's preoccupation with democratic simplicity soon began to wear thin. As problems surfaced in the economy and world affairs, the people again seemed to reorder priorities. Perhaps a little more power and a little less democracy were not so bad after all. In truth, much of what took place in world affairs during the late 1970s probably would have happened under any president, but the fact that major problems developed under Carter left the impression that they developed because of Carter. The crowing event was the absolute humiliation and appearance of impotence of the United States during the Iranian hostage crisis of 1979–81. For all his high ideals and good intentions, Carter did not strengthen the office of the presidency or enhance its popularity.

It is fairly commonly agreed that a period of national self-doubt, self-guilt, and reluctance to act in world affairs came to an end in the 1980s during the administration of Ronald Reagan. After a slow start, Reagan presided over a period of heightened, if poorly distributed, economic growth and reassertion of American power in world affairs. Otherwise his was a presidency marked with paradoxes. Running as an enemy of big government, he headed an administration larger than what preceded him. A foe of government spending and an unbalanced budget, he presided over a government marked with massive increases in spending and budget deficits. Reagan was essentially honest, a likeable individual, and a liked president, but his presidency was almost detached, guarded, and separated from public contact. A masterful communicator, Reagan rarely had press conferences. The supreme paradox is that while he recaptured some of the popularity and prestige the presidency had lost in the previous decade, Reagan at the same time diminished the office by in effect turning it over for others to run. Poorly informed on the issues and on the operations of government, he seemed little anxious to learn. The presidency gained popularity with Reagan in office, but it lost some of its substance.

Chronology of the Watergate Scandal

February 15, 1972   Attorney General John Mitchell resigns to become head of a Committee to Reelect the President, known as CRP or CREEP.

June 17, 1972   Police arrest five men who have broken into the headquarters of the Democratic Party in the Watergate Hotel Complex in Washington. It will develop that the men were commissioned by CRP.

August 29, 1972   President Nixon announces that his counsel, John Dean, had investigated the "bizarre" Watergate break-in and that no White House people had been involved.

October 10, 1972   The Washington *Post* reports existence of a Republican espionage organization headed by John Mitchell. *Post* reporters Bob Woodward and Carl Bernstein are able to trace break-in at the Watergate to the White House.

February 7, 1973   The Senate establishes a select committee, chaired by Democrat senator Sam Ervin of North Carolina, to investigate the Watergate episode.

March 23, 1973   Having been tried and convicted, six of seven Watergate conspirators (involved in the break-in) are sentenced to jail by Judge John Sirica.

April 20, 1973   L. Patrick Gray, acting director of the FBI, who admitted giving files on Watergate to John Dean, now admits that he had destroyed FBI Watergate documents and that Nixon's advisers had told him to do so.

April 30, 1973   Nixon announces the resignation of his highest aides, H. R. Haldeman and John Erlichman, as well as Attorney General Richard Kleindienst and that counsel John Dean had

The common touch. Jimmy and Rosalynn Carter walk to the White House after inauguration, January 20, 1977. (Courtesy: Jimmy Carter Library)

been fired. He denies advance knowledge of the break-in or that there was underway an effort to conceal the truth—a so-called cover-up.

May 25, 1973 Attorney General Elliot Richardson appoints Archibald Cox as special prosecutor in the Watergate affair.

June 25–29, 1973 Appearing before Ervin's Watergate Committee, Dean implicates Haldeman, Erlichman, Mitchell, and Nixon, as well as himself in an attempt to hide the truth about the growing scandal.

July 16, 1973 Before the Ervin committee, Alexander Butterfield, a White House aide, revealed almost in passing that conversations in the oval office were routinely recorded.

October 10, 1973 Under fire for financial corruption unrelated to Watergate, Spiro Agnew resigns the vice presidency; two days later Nixon will appoint Congressman Gerald R. Ford of Michigan to replace him; as stipulated in the Twenty-fifth Amendment, Congress gives approval.

October 14, 1973 Nixon continues to refuse to turn taped messages over to investigators, but he offers written (and as it turned out, sanitized) summaries.

October 20, 1973 "The Saturday Night Massacre." Attorney General Elliot Richardson and the Assistant Attorney General William Ruckelshaus refuse Nixon's order to dismiss special prosecutor Cox; both resign. Solicitor General Robert Bork then fires Cox who had persisted in efforts to get hold of the White House tapes.

November 5, 1973 Leon Jaworski is appointed new special prosecutor for the Watergate affair.

November 26, 1973 Nixon surrenders seven tapes to Judge Sirica, but he will continue to reject subpoenas for materials from both House and Senate committees. He continues to insist that he was guilty of no wrongdoing.

February 6, 1974 The House of Representatives authorizes its Judiciary Committee to conduct an inquiry into impeachment.

March 1, 1974   Seven former presidential aides, including Haldeman, Erlichman, and Mitchell, are indicated for conspiracy (the cover-up).

May 24, 1974   Faced with repeated rejection of appeals for the tapes from the Judiciary Committee and from the special prosecutor, Jaworski appeals to the Supreme Court.

July 24, 1974   In a unanimous vote the Supreme Court orders Nixon to turn over the tapes that had been requested.

July 27–30, 1974   The House Judiciary Committee passes three articles of impeachment of the president; the issue next is to go to the full House.

August 5, 1974   The White House releases transcripts of three taped conversations, the most critical of which was the tape of June 23, 1972, the "smoking pistol." The tapes revealed that Nixon knew about the break-in shortly after it happened, that he had been involved in a cover-up of more than two years, and had misused government agencies, such as the FBI and CIA to that end.

August 8, 1974   Faced with almost certain impeachment and probable removal from office, Nixon announced resignation to take effect the next day. He became the first U.S. president to take that step.

August 9, 1974   Gerald R. Ford becomes president.

September 8, 1974   President Ford pardons Nixon for any crimes he might have committed while in office.

Source: Kane, *Facts About the Presidents*, 249–50; Andre Kaspi, *Great Dates in United States History* (New York, 1994), 197–99.

Government Officials and Other Individuals Convicted As a Result of the Watergate Affair

Charles Colson, special counsel to the president
John Dean, counsel to the president
John Erlichman, chief presidential adviser on domestic policy
H. R. Haldeman, presidential Chief of Staff
Fred LaRue, member of CREEP
Robert C. Mardian, assistant attorney general and counsel for CREEP
John Mitchell, attorney general and head of CREEP
Dwight Chapin, Nixon's appointments secretary
Herbert Kalmbach, Nixon's personal attorney
Richard Kleindienst, attorney general
Egil Krough, assistant to Erlichman
Jeb Stuart Magruder, aide to Haldeman
Donald Segretti, head of "dirty tricks" division of the campaign
Maurice Stans, Secretary of Commerce, chief fund raiser
E. Howard Hunt, helped plan burglary
G. Gordon Liddy, coleader (with Hunt) of burglary team

Source: *Time*, June 14, 1982, 30, 32.

President Richard Nixon in the Oval Office with advisers: H. R. Haldeman (left), Dwight Chapin (center), and John Erlichman (right) (National Archives)

TABLE 9.3   PARTY STRENGTH IN CONGRESS, 1946–1990

Period	Congress	House Majority Party		House Minority Party		House Others	Senate Majority Party		Senate Minority Party		Senate Others	Party of President	
1945–47	79th	D	242	R	190	2	D	56	R	38	1	D	Truman
1947–49	80th	R	245	D	188	1	R	51	D	45	. . .	D	Truman
1949–51	81st	D	263	R	171	1	D	54	R	42	. . .	D	Truman
1951–53	82nd	D	234	R	199	1	D	49	R	47	. . .	D	Truman
1953–55	83rd	R	221	D	211	1	R	48	D	47	1	R	Eisenhower
1955–57	84th	D	232	R	203	. . .	D	48	R	47	1	R	Eisenhower
1957–59	85th	D	233	R	200	. . .	D	49	R	47	. . .	R	Eisenhower
1959–61	86th	D	284	R	153	. . .	D	65	R	35	. . .	R	Eisenhower
1961–63	87th	D	263	R	174	. . .	D	65	R	35	. . .	D	Kennedy
1963–65	88th	D	258	R	117	. . .	D	67	R	33	. . .	D	Kennedy
. . .	. . .	. . .	. . .	. . .	. . .	. . .	. . .	. . .	. . .	. . .	. . .	D	Johnson
1965–67	89th	D	295	R	140	. . .	D	68	R	32	. . .	D	Johnson
1967–69	90th	D	246	R	187	. . .	D	64	R	36	. . .	D	Johnson
1969–71	91st	D	245	R	189	. . .	D	57	R	43	. . .	R	Nixon
1971–73	92nd	D	254	R	180	. . .	D	54	R	44	2	R	Nixon
1973–75	93rd	D	239	R	192	1	D	56	R	42	2	R	Nixon
1975–77	94th	D	291	R	144	. . .	D	60	R	37	3	R	Ford
1977–79	95th	D	292	R	143	. . .	D	61	R	38	1	D	Carter
1979–81	96th	D	276	R	157	. . .	D	58	R	41	1	D	Carter
1981–83	97th	D	243	R	192	. . .	R	53	D	46	1	R	Reagan
1983–85	98th	D	267	R	168	. . .	R	55	D	45	. . .	R	Reagan
1985–87	99th	D	253	R	182	. . .	R	53	D	47	. . .	R	Reagan
1987–89	100th	D	258	R	177	. . .	D	55	R	45	. . .	R	Reagan
1989–91	101st	D	259	R	174	. . .	D	54	R	46	. . .	R	Bush

Source: Congressional Quarterly, *American Leaders 1789–1991*, 506.

TABLE 9.4   SPEAKER OF THE HOUSE, 1945–1991

Congress	Speaker
79th (1945–1947)	Sam Rayburn, Dem-Tex.
80th (1947–1949)	Joseph W. Martin, Jr., Rep-Mass.
81st (1949–1951)	Rayburn
82nd (1951–1953)	Rayburn
83rd (1953–1955)	Martin
84th (1955–1957)	Rayburn
85th (1957–1959)	Rayburn
86th (1959–1961)	Rayburn
87th (1961)	Rayburn
(1962–1963)	John W. McCormack, Dem-Mass.
88th (1963–1965)	McCormack
89th (1965–1967)	McCormack
90th (1967–1969)	McCormack
91st (1969–1971)	McCormack
92nd (1971–1973)	Carl Albert, Dem-Okla.
93rd (1973–1975)	Albert
94th (1975–1977)	Albert
95th (1977–1979)	Thomas P. O'Neill Jr., Dem-Mass.
96th (1979–1981)	O'Neill
97th (1981–1983)	O'Neill
98th (1983–1985)	O'Neill
99th (1985–1987)	O'Neill
100th (1987–1989)	Jim Wright, Dem-Tex.
101st (1989)	Wright
(1989–1991)	Thomas S. Foley, Dem-Wash.

Source: Stephen G. Christianson, *Facts About the Congress* (New York, 1996), 576.

TABLE 9.5 LEADERS OF THE HOUSE, 1946–1990

Congress	House Floor Leaders		House Whips	
	Majority	Minority	Majority	Minority
79th (1945–47)	John W. McCormack (D Mass.)	Joseph W. Martin Jr. (R Mass.)	John J. Sparkman (D Ala.)	Leslie C. Arends (R Ill.)
80th (1947–49)	Charles A. Halleck (R Ind.)	Sam Rayburn (D Texas)	Leslie C. Arends (R Ill.)	John W. McCormack (D Mass.)
81st (1949–51)	McCormack	Martin	J. Percy Priest (D Tenn.)	Arends
82d (1951–53)	McCormack	Martin	Priest	Arends
83d (1953–55)	Halleck	Rayburn	Arends	McCormack
84th (1955–57)	McCormack	Martin	Carl Albert (D Okla.)	Arends
85th (1957–59)	McCormack	Martin	Albert	Arends
86th (1959–61)	McCormack	Charles A. Halleck (R Ind.)	Albert	Arends
87th (1961–63)	McCormack/Carl Albert (D Okla.)	Halleck	Albert/Hale Boggs (D La.)	Arends
88th (1963–65)	Albert	Halleck	Boggs	Arends
89th (1965–67)	Albert	Gerald R. Ford (R Mich.)	Boggs	Arends
90th (1967–69)	Albert	Ford	Boggs	Arends
91st (1969–71)	Albert	Ford	Boggs	Arends
92d (1971–73)	Hale Boggs (D La.)	Ford	Thomas P. O'Neill Jr. (D Mass.)	Arends
93d (1973–75)	Thomas P. O'Neill Jr. (D Mass.)	Ford/John J. Rhodes (R Ariz.)	John J. McFall (D Calif.)	Arends
94th (1975–77)	O'Neill	Rhodes	McFall	Robert H. Michel (R Ill.)
95th (1977–79)	Jim Wright (D Texas)	Rhodes	John Brademas (D Ind.)	Michel
96th (1979–81)	Wright	Rhodes	Brademas	Michel
97th (1981–83)	Wright	Robert H. Michel (R Ill.)	Thomas S. Foley (D Wash.)	Trent Lott (R Miss.)
98th (1983–85)	Wright	Michel	Foley	Lott
99th (1985–87)	Wright	Michel	Foley	Lott
100th (1987–89)	Thomas S. Foley (D Wash.)	Michel	Tony Coelho (D Calif.)	Lott
101st (1989–91)	Foley/Richard A. Gephardt (D Mo.)	Michel	Coelho/William H. Gray III (D Pa.)	Dick Cheney (R Wyo.)/Newt Gingrich (R Ga.)

Source: Congressional Quarterly, *American Leaders 1789–1991*, 524–25.

TABLE 9.6 LEADERS OF THE SENATE, 1946–1990

Congress	Senate Floor Leaders		Senate Whips	
	Majority	Minority	Majority	Minority
79th (1945–47)	Alben W. Barkley (D Ky.)	Wallace H. White Jr. (R Maine)	Lister Hill (D Ala.)	Kenneth Wherry (R Neb.)
80th (1947–49)	Wallace H. White Jr. (R Maine)	Alben W. Barkley (D Ky.)	Kenneth Wherry (R Neb.)	Scott Lucas (D Ill.)
81st (1949–51)	Scott W. Lucas (D Ill.)	Kenneth S. Wherry (R Neb.)	Francis Myers (D Pa.)	Leverett Saltonstall (R Mass.)
82d (1951–53)	Ernest W. McFarland (D Ariz.)	Wherry/Styles Bridges (R N.H.)	Lyndon B. Johnson (D Texas)	Saltonstall
83d (1953–55)	Robert A. Taft (R Ohio)/ William F. Knowland (R Calif.)	Lyndon B. Johnson (D Texas)	Leverett Saltonstall (R Mass.)	Earle Clements (D Ky.)
84th (1955–57)	Lyndon B. Johnson (D Texas)	William F. Knowland (R Calif.)	Earle Clements (D Ky.)	Saltonstall
85th (1957–59)	Johnson	Knowland	Mike Mansfield (D Mont.)	Everett McKinley Dirksen (R Ill.)
86th (1959–61)	Johnson	Everett McKinley Dirksen (R Ill.)	Mansfield	Thomas H. Kuchel (R Calif.)
87th (1961–63)	Mike Mansfield (D Mont.)	Dirksen	Hubert H. Humphrey (D Minn.)	Kuchel
88th (1963–65)	Mansfield	Dirksen	Humphrey	Kuchel
89th (1965–67)	Mansfield	Dirksen	Russell Long (D La.)	Kuchel
90th (1967–69)	Mansfield	Dirksen	Long	Kuchel
91st (1969–71)	Mansfield	Dirksen/Hugh Scott (R Pa.)	Edward M. Kennedy (D Mass.)	Hugh Scott (R Pa.)/Robert P. Griffin (R Mich.)
92d (1971–73)	Mansfield	Scott	Robert C. Byrd (D W.Va.)	Griffin
93d (1973–75)	Mansfield	Scott	Byrd	Griffin
94th (1975–77)	Mansfield	Scott	Byrd	Griffin
95th (1977–79)	Robert C. Byrd (D W.Va.)	Howard H. Baker Jr. (R Tenn.)	Alan Cranston (D Calif.)	Ted Stevens (R Alaska)
96th (1979–81)	Byrd	Baker	Cranston	Stevens
97th (1981–83)	Howard H. Baker Jr. (R Tenn.)	Robert C. Byrd (D W.Va.)	Ted Stevens (R Alaska)	Alan Cranston (D Calif.)
98th (1983–85)	Baker	Byrd	Stevens	Cranston
99th (1985–87)	Robert J. Dole (R Kan.)	Byrd	Alan K. Simpson (R Wyo.)	Cranston
100th (1987–89)	Byrd	Robert J. Dole (R Kan.)	Alan Cranston (D Calif.)	Alan K. Simpson (R Wyo.)
101st (1989–91)	George J. Mitchell (D Maine)	Dole	Cranston	Simpson

Source: Congressional Quarterly, *American Leaders 1789–1991*, 526–27.

TABLE 9.7 INCUMBENTS TO THE U.S. HOUSE OR SENATE—HOW THEY FARED, 1946–1990

Years	Retired[a]	Number Seeking Reelection	Defeated Primaries	Defeated General Election	Reelected Total	Reelected Percentage of Those Seeking Reelection
House						
1946	32	398	18	52	328	82.4
1948	29	400	15	68	317	79.3
1950	29	400	6	32	362	90.5
1952	42	389	9	26	354	91.0
1954	24	407	6	22	379	93.1
1956	21	411	6	16	389	94.6
1958	33	396	3	37	356	89.9
1960	26	405	5	25	375	92.6
1962	24	402	12	22	368	91.5
1964	33	397	8	45	344	86.6
1966	22	411	8	41	362	88.1
1968	23	409	4	9	396	96.8
1970	29	401	10	12	379	94.5
1972	40	390	12	13	365	93.6
1974	43	391	8	40	343	87.7
1976	47	384	3	13	368	95.8
1978	49	382	5	19	358	93.7
1980	34	398	6	31	361	90.7
1982	40	393	10	29	354	90.1
1984	22	409	3	16	390	95.4
1986	38	393	2	6	385	98.0
1988	23	409	1	6	402	98.5
1990	27	407	1	15	391	96.1
Senate						
1946	9	30	6	7	17	56.7
1948	8	25	2	8	15	60.0
1950	4	32	5	5	22	68.8
1952	4	31	2	9	20	64.5
1954	6	32	2	6	24	75.0
1956	6	29	0	4	25	86.2
1958	6	28	0	10	18	64.3
1960	5	29	0	1	28	96.6
1962	4	35	1	5	29	82.9
1964	2	33	1	4	28	84.8
1966	3	32	3	1	28	87.5
1968	6	28	4	4	20	71.4
1970	4	31	1	6	24	77.4
1972	6	27	2	5	20	74.1
1974	7	27	2	2	23	85.2
1976	8	25	0	9	16	64.0
1978	10	25	3	7	15	60.0
1980	5	29	4	9	16	55.2
1982	3	30	0	2	28	93.3
1984	4	29	0	3	26	89.6
1986	6	28	0	7	21	75.0
1988	6	27	0	4	23	85.2
1990	3	32	0	1	31	96.9

[a] Does not include persons who died or resigned from office before the election.
Source: Harold W. Stanley and Richard G. Niemi, *Vital Statistics on American Politics,* (Washington, D.C., 1992), 204–05.

Money in Politics and Growth of the PAC

Money has always been a factor in politics on all levels, and as a rule the higher the level of office being contested the higher the price of winning the post. The most expensive campaign was for the U.S. presidency. Private contributions to campaigns were logical, inevitable, and seemingly the most democratic method of campaign finance, but they also carried an inherent contradiction. Simply put, the more money a person could contribute, the more influence that person would seem to have on the officeholder once she or he attained the post. The Political Action Committee (PAC), which emerged in the 1940s as an expression of the collective will, contained some of the same problems. Starting with labor unions as a device to promote the interests of a group, these organizations soon spread to other areas. After 1971 corporations, which often had huge sums at their disposal, joined the process. Legislation in the mid-1970s legitimized the PAC and set limits on contributions—$1,000 per person, $5,000 per committee—to individual candidates. The PACs circumvented the legislation by their distribution of "soft money" not to candidates but to state or national parties, for which no limits had been established. The parties then used the money to assist the individual candidates. Thus the PACs first raised the price of running for office and then placed themselves in a position to help pay the cost. It was the same old problem but on a higher scale. The people with the most money to offer had the best chance of having their message heard. Both parties complained about the PACs and about "soft money," but both took the funds.

TABLE 9.8 LOSSES BY PRESIDENT'S PARTY IN MIDTERM ELECTIONS, 1946–1990

Year	Party Holding Presidency	President's Party: Gain/Loss of Seats in House	President's Party: Gain/Loss of Seats in Senate
1946	D	−55	−12
1950	D	−29	−6
1954	R	−18	−1
1958	R	−48	−13
1962	D	−4	3
1966	D	−47	−4
1970	R	−12	2
1974	R	−48	−5
1978	D	−15	−3
1982	R	−26	1
1986	R	−5	−8
1990	R	−8	1

Source: Stanley and Niemi, *Statistics on Politics*, 203.

TABLE 9.9 CAMPAIGN SPENDING FOR WINNING CONGRESSIONAL CANDIDATES, 1975–1990

Years	Receipts[a]	Expenditures[a]	Political Action Committee Contributions Total[a]	Percentage of Receipts
House				
1975–1976	$42.5	$38.0	$10.9	25.6
1977–1978	60.0	55.6	17.0	28.3
1979–1980	86.0	78.0	27.0	31.4
1981–1982	123.1	114.7	42.7	34.7
1983–1984	144.8	127.0	59.5	41.1
1985–1986	172.7	154.9	72.8	42.2
1987–1988	191.0	171.0	86.4	45.2
1989–1990	197.6	178.4	91.6	46.4
Senate				
1975–1976	21.0	20.1	3.1	14.8
1977–1978	43.0	42.3	6.0	14.0
1979–1980	41.7	40.0	10.2	24.5
1981–1982	70.7	68.2	15.6	22.1
1983–1984	100.9	97.5	20.0	19.8
1985–1986	106.8	104.3	28.4	26.6
1987–1988	121.7	123.6	31.8	26.1
1989–1990	121.5	115.4	31.1	25.6

[a] In millions of current dollars.
Source: Stanley and Niemi, *Statistics on Politics*, 210.

TABLE 9.10 NUMBER OF WOMEN MEMBERS IN CONGRESS, 1947–1991

Listed below by Congress is the number of women members of the Senate and House of Representatives from the 80th Congress through the beginning of the 102nd Congress. The figures include women appointed to office, those chosen in general elections and special elections, and nonvoting delegates.

Congress	Years	Senate	House
80th	(1947–49)	1	7
81st	(1949–51)	1	9
82d	(1951–53)	1	10
83d	(1953–55)	3	12
84th	(1955–57)	1	16
85th	(1957–59)	1	15
86th	(1959–61)	1	16
87th	(1961–63)	2	17
88th	(1963–65)	2	11
89th	(1965–67)	2	10
90th	(1967–69)	1	11
91st	(1969–71)	1	10
92nd	(1971–73)	2	13
93d	(1973–75)	0	16
94th	(1975–77)	0	19
95th	(1977–79)	2	18
96th	(1979–81)	1	16
97th	(1981–83)	2	21
98th	(1983–85)	2	22
99th	(1985–87)	2	23
100th	(1987–89)	2	24
101st	(1989–91)	2	29

Source: Congressional Quarterly, *American Leaders 1789–1991*, 80.

TABLE 9.11 WOMEN IN CONGRESS, A ROSTER, 1946–1990

Senate	
Representative	Year
Vera C. Bushfield (R S.Dak.)	1948
Margaret Chase Smith (R Maine)	1949–73
Hazel H. Abel (R Neb.)	1954
Eva K. Bowring (R Neb.)	1954
Maurine B. Neuberger (D Ore.)	1960–67
Elaine S. Edwards (D La.)	1972
Maryon Pittman Allen (D Ala.)	1978
Muriel Buck Humphrey (D Minn.)	1978
Nancy Landon Kassebaum (R Kan.)	1978–97
Paula Hawkins (R Fla.)	1981–87
Barbara Mikulski (D Md.)	1987–
House	
Representative	Year
Mary T. Norton (D N.J.)	1925–51
Edith N. Rogers (R Mass.)	1925–60
Jessie Sumner (R Ill.)	1939–47
Frances P. Bolton (R Ohio)	1940–69
Florence R. Gibbs (D Ga.)	1940–41
Margaret Chase Smith (R Maine)	1940–49
Clare Boothe Luce (R Conn.)	1943–47
Winifred C. Stanley (R N.Y.)	1943–45
Willa L. Fulmer (D S.C.)	1944–45
Emily T. Douglas (D Ill.)	1945–47

Representative	Year
Helen G. Douglas (D Calif.)	1945–51
Chase G. Woodhouse (D Conn.)	1945–47
	1949–51
Helen D. Mankin (D Ga.)	1946–47
Eliza J. Pratt (D N.C.)	1946–47
Georgia L. Lusk (D N.M.)	1947–49
Katherine P. C. St. George (R N.Y.)	1947–65
Reva Z. B. Bosone (D Utah)	1949–53
Cecil M. Harden (R Ind.)	1949–59
Edna F. Kelly (D N.Y.)	1949–69
Vera D. Buchanan (D Pa.)	1951–55
Marguerite S. Church (R Ill.)	1951–63
Maude E. Kee (D W. Va.)	1951–65
Ruth Thompson (R Mich.)	1951–57
Gracie B. Pfost (D Idaho)	1953–63
Leonor K. Sullivan (D Mo.)	1953–77
Iris F. Blitch (D Ga.)	1955–63
Edith Green (D Ore.)	1955–75
Martha W. Griffiths (D Mich.)	1955–74
Coya G. Knutson (DFL Minn.)	1955–59
Kathryn E. Granahan (D Pa.)	1956–63
Florence P. Dwyer (R N.J.)	1957–73
Catherine D. May (R Wash.)	1959–71
Edna O. Simpson (R Ill.)	1959–61
Jessica McC. Weis (R N.Y.)	1959–63
Julia B. Hansen (D Wash.)	1960–74
Catherine D. Norrell (D Ark.)	1961–63
Louise G. Reece (R Tenn.)	1961–63
Corinne B. Riley (D S.C.)	1962–63
Charlotte T. Reid (R Ill.)	1963–71
Irene B. Baker (R Tenn.)	1964–65
Patsy T. Mink (D Hawaii)	1965–77
	1990–2002
Lera M. Thomas (D Texas)	1966–67
Margaret M. Heckler (R Mass.)	1967–83
Shirley Chisholm (D N.Y.)	1969–83
Bella S. Abzug (D N.Y.)	1971–77
Ella T. Grasso (D Conn.)	1971–75
Louise Day Hicks (D Mass.)	1971–73
Elizabeth B. Andrews (D Ala.)	1972–73
Yvonne B. Burke (D Calif.)	1973–79
Marjorie S. Holt (R Md.)	1973–87
Elizabeth Holtzman (D N.Y.)	1973–81
Barbara C. Jordan (D Texas)	1973–79
Patricia Schroeder (D Colo.)	1973–97
Corinne C. Boggs (D La.)	1973–91
Cardiss R. Collins (D Ill.)	1973–97
Marilyn Lloyd (D Tenn.)	1975–95
Millicent Fenwick (R N.J.)	1975–83
Martha E. Keys (D Kan.)	1975–79
Helen S. Meyner (D N.J.)	1975–79
Virginia Smith (R Neb.)	1975–91

Representative	Year
Gladys Noon Spellman (D Md.)	1975–81
Shirley N. Pettis (R Calif.)	1975–79
Barbara A. Mikulski (D Md.)	1977–87
Mary Rose Oakar (D Ohio)	1977–93
Beverly Byron (D Md.)	1979–93
Geraldine Ferraro (D N.Y.)	1979–85
Olympia Snowe (R Maine)	1979–95
Bobbi Fiedler (R Calif.)	1981–87
Lynn M. Martin (R Ill.)	1981–91
Marge Roukema (R N.J.)	1981–
Claudine Schneider (R R.I.)	1981–91
Jean Ashbrook (R Ohio.)	1982–83
Barbara B. Kennelly (D Conn.)	1982–99
Sala Burton (D Calif.)	1983–87
Barbara Boxer (D Calif.)	1983–93
Katie Hall (D Ind.)	1982–85
Nancy L. Johnson (R Conn.)	1983–
Marcy Kaptur (D Ohio)	1983–
Barbara Vucanovich (R Nev.)	1983–97
Helen Delich Bentley (R Md.)	1985–95
Jan Meyers (R Kan.)	1985–97
Cathy Long (D La.)	1985–87
Constance A. Morella (R Md.)	1987–
Elizabeth J. Patterson (D S.C.)	1987–93
Patricia Saiki (R Hawaii)	1987–91
Louise M. Slaughter (D N.Y.)	1987–
Nancy Pelosi (D Calif.)	1989–
Nita M. Lowey (D N.Y.)	1989–
Jolene Unsoeld (D Wash.)	1989–95
Ileana Ros-Lehtinen (R Fla.)	1989–97
Jill Long (D Ind.)	1989–95
Susan Molinari (R N.Y.)	1990–97

Source: Congressional Quarterly, *American Leaders 1789–2000* (Washington, D.C, 2000), 455–56.

TABLE 9.12 WOMEN IN ELECTIVE OFFICES, 1975–1989

Level of Office	1975	1977	1979	1981	1983	1985	1987	1989
U.S. Congress	4%	4%	3%	4%	4%	5%	5%	5%
Statewide Elective	10%	10%	11%	11%	11%	14%	14%	14%
State Legislatures	8%	9%	10%	12%	13%	15%	16%	17%
County Governing Boards	3%	4%	5%	6%	8%	8% (1984)	9%	9% (1988)
Mayors and Municipal Councils	4%	8%	10%	10%	NA	14%	NA	NA

Source: Linda Schmittroth, ed., *Statistical Record of Women Worldwide* (Detroit, 1995), 894.

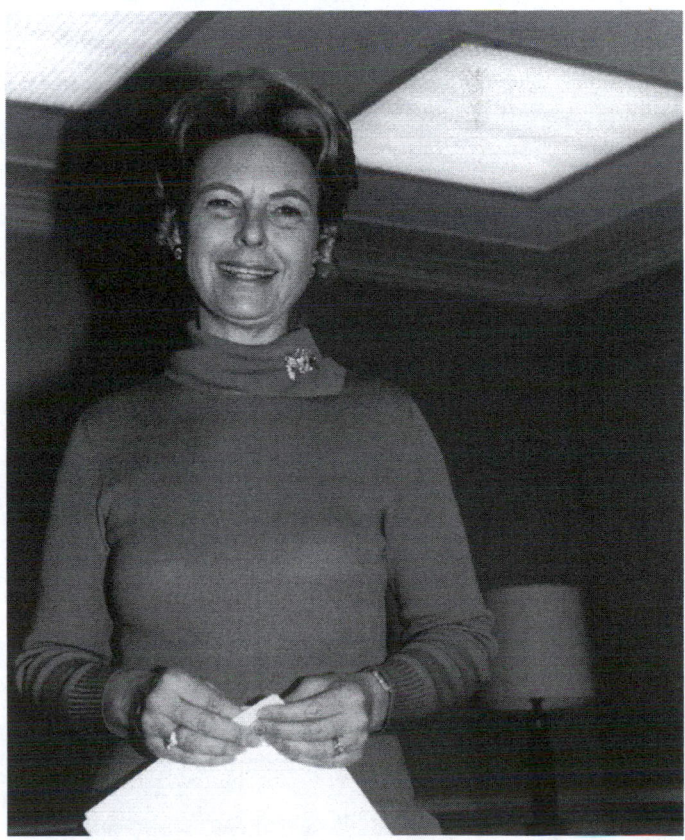

Author and conservative spokesperson, Phyllis Schlafly was a leader of opposition to the ERA. (Courtesy: Jimmy Carter Library)

TABLE 9.13   NUMBER OF BLACK MEMBERS IN CONGRESS, 1947–1990

Listed below by Congress is the number of black members of the Senate and House of Representatives from the 80th Congress through the beginning of the 102nd Congress. The figures do not include the nonvoting delegate from the District of Columbia.

Congress	Years	Senate	House
80th	1947–49	0	2
81st	1949–51	0	2
82d	1951–53	0	2
83d	1953–55	0	2
84th	1955–57	0	3
85th	1957–59	0	4
86th	1959–61	0	4
87th	1961–63	0	4
88th	1963–65	0	5
89th	1965–67	0	6
90th	1967–69	1	5
91st	1969–71	1	9
92d	1971–73	1	12
93d	1973–75	1	15
94th	1975–77	1	16
95th	1977–79	1	16
96th	1979–81	0	16
97th	1981–83	0	17
98th	1983–85	0	20
99th	1985–87	0	20
100th	1987–89	0	22
101st	1989–91	0	24

Source: Congressional Quarterly, *American Leaders 1789–1991*, 81.

TABLE 9.14   BLACK MEMBERS OF CONGRESS, A ROSTER, 1946–1990

Senate	
Edward W. Brooke (R Mass.)	1967–79

House	
William L. Dawson (D Ill.)	1943–70
Adam C. Powell Jr. (D N.Y.)	1945–67
	1969–71
Charles C. Diggs Jr. (D Mich.)	1955–80
Robert N. C. Nix (D Pa.)	1958–79
Augustus F. Hawkins (D Calif.)	1963–91
John Conyers Jr. (D Mich.)	1965–
Louis Stokes (D Ohio)	1969–99
William L. Clay (D Mo.)	1969–2000
Shirley Chisholm (D N.Y.)	1969–83
George W. Collins (D Ill.)	1970–72
Ronald V. Dellums (D Calif.)	1971–98
Ralph H. Metcalfe (D Ill.)	1971–78
Parren J. Mitchell (D Md.)	1971–87
Charles B. Rangel (D N.Y.)	1971–
Yvonne B. Burke (D Calif.)	1973–79
Cardiss Collins (D Ill.)	1973–97
Barbara C. Jordan (D Texas)	1973–79
Andrew Young (D Ga.)	1973–77
Harold E. Ford (D Tenn.)	1975–97
Julian C. Dixon (D Calif.)	1979–2000
William H. Gray (D Pa.)	1979–91
George T. Leland (D Texas)	1979–89
Bennett McVey Stewart (D Ill.)	1979–81
George W. Crockett Jr. (D Mich.)	1981–91
Mervin M. Dymally (D Calif.)	1981–93
Gus Savage (D Ill.)	1981–93
Harold Washington (D Ill.)	1981–83
Katie Hall (D Ind.)	1983–85
Charles A. Hayes (D Ill.)	1983–93
Major R. Owens (D N.Y.)	1983–

House	
Edolphus Towns (D N.Y.)	1983–
Alan Wheat (D Mo.)	1983–95
Alton R. Waldon Jr. (D N.Y.)	1986–87
Mike Espy (D Miss.)	1987–93
Floyd H. Flake (D N.Y.)	1987–97
John Lewis (D Ga.)	1987–
Kweisi Mfume (D Md.)	1987–96
Donald M. Payne (D N.J.)	1989–
Craig Washington (D Texas)	1990–95

Source: Congressional Quarterly, *American Leaders 1789–2000*, 458.

TABLE 9.15   HISPANICS IN CONGRESS, 1946–1990

Senate	
Dennis Chavez, D-N.M.	1935–1962
Joseph M. Monotoya, D-N.M.	1964–1977

House	
Antonio Manuel Fernandez, D-N.M.	1943–1956
Joseph Manuel Montoya, D-N.M.	1957–1964
Henry B. Gonzalez, D-Texas	1961–1999
Edward R. Roybal, D-Calif.	1963–1993
E. "Kika" de la Garza II, D-Texas	1965–1997
Manuel Lujan, Jr., R-N.M.	1969–1989
Herman Badillo, D-N.Y.	1971–1977
Robert Garcia, D-N.Y.	1978–1990
Anthony Lee Coelho, D-Calif.	1979–1989
Matthew G. Martinez, D-Calif.	1982– 1994
Solomon P. Ortiz, D-Texas	1983–
William B. Richardson, D-N.M.	1983–1997
Esteban E. Torres, D-Calif.	1983–1999
Albert G. Bustamante, D-Texas	1985–1993
Ileana Ros-Lehtinen, R-Fla.	1989–
José E. Serrano, D-N.Y.	1990–

Source: Congressional Quarterly, *American Leaders 1789–2000*, 460.

Expansion of the Electorate, 1946–1990

The first reason for growth of the number of people eligible to vote, of course, was expansion of the population. The number of people of voting age doubled between 1946 and 1990, and the people who voted in 1990 roughly equalled the number who had been eligible in 1946. Other factors included black people in the southern states at last being able to vote, largely because of the Civil Rights Acts of 1964 and 1965 and general intervention of national officials on their behalf, and a growing political awareness of women, beginning in the 1960s. Other than population growth, the most important single reason for increase in the franchise was reduction of the voting age from 21 to 18. One of the many reform movements of the 1960s, the 18-year-old vote might have been anticipated, if only because many of the reformers were under age 21. The issue also became bound up in the great emotion surrounding the war in Vietnam. "If you are old enough to fight," as the saying went, "you are old enough to vote—and drink." Reduction of age limits for both activities came to pass, but automobile accident statistics caused the states to restore the minimum drinking age to 21 in short order. The 18-year-old vote, a case for which could be made irrespective of the war, remained and was locked in as national policy through a constitutional amendment that took effect in 1971. Subsequent statistics indicated, however, that once they had the vote, young people were not anxious to use it. The lowest voting percentage consistently came from people age 18–24, and one suspects that the bulk of the nonvoters were 21 and lower.

TABLE 9.16 GROWING FRANCHISE IN THE UNITED STATES, 1946–1990

Year	Estimated Population of Voting Age	Vote Cast for Presidential Electors		Vote Cast for U.S. Representatives	
		Number	Percent	Number	Percent
1946	92,659,000	. . .	. . .	34,398,000	37.1
1948	95,573,000	48,793,826	51.1	45,933,000	48.1
1950	98,134,000	. . .	. . .	40,342,000	41.1
1952	99,929,000	61,550,918	61.6	57,571,000	57.6
1954	102,075,000	. . .	. . .	42,580,000	41.7
1956	104,515,000	62,026,908	59.3	58,426,000	55.9
1958	106,447,000	. . .	. . .	45,818,000	43.0
1960	109,672,000	68,838,219	62.8	64,133,000	58.5
1962	112,952,000	. . .	. . .	51,267,000	45.4
1964	114,090,000	70,644,592	61.9	65,895,000	57.8
1966	116,638,000	. . .	. . .	52,908,000	45.4
1968	120,285,000	73,211,875	60.9	66,288,000	55.1
1970	124,498,000	. . .	. . .	54,173,000	43.5
1972	140,777,000	77,718,554	55.2	71,430,000	50.7
1974	146,338,000	. . .	. . .	52,495,000	35.9
1976	152,308,000	81,555,889	53.5	74,422,000	48.9
1978	158,369,000	. . .	. . .	55,332,000	34.9
1980	164,595,000	86,515,221	52.6	77,995,000	47.4
1982	169,936,000	. . .	. . .	64,514,000	38.0
1984	174,468,000	92,652,842	53.1	83,231,000	47.7
1986	178,566,000	. . .	. . .	56,619,000	33.4
1988	182,779,000	91,594,809	50.1	81,786,000	44.7
1990	185,812,000	. . .	. . .	61,513,000	33.1

Source: Congressional Quarterly, *Presidential Elections, 1789–1992* (Washington, D.C., 1995), 80.

TABLE 9.17 VOTER REGISTRATION IN 11 SOUTHERN STATES, 1960–1971

In thousands, except percent. For 1960 to 1970, covers population 18 years old and older in Georgia, and 21 and older elsewhere; for 1971, covers population 18 years old and older for all the southern states.

Item	Total	Ala.	Ark.	Fla.	Ga.	La.	Miss.	N.C.	S.C.	Tenn.	Tex.	Va.
1960												
White	12,276	860	518	1,819	1,020	993	478	1,861	481	1,300	2,079	867
Black	1,463	66	73	183	180	159	22	210	58	185	227	100
Percent white	61.1	63.6	60.9	69.3	56.8	76.9	63.9	92.1	57.1	73.0	42.5	46.1
Percent Black	29.1	13.7	38.0	39.4	29.3	31.1	5.2	39.1	13.7	59.1	35.5	23.1
1964												
White	14,264	946	621	2,200	1,340	1,037	525	1,942	703	1,297	2,602	1,050
Black	2,164	111	95	300	270	165	29	258	144	218	375	200
1966												
White	14,310	1,192	598	2,093	1,378	1,072	471	1,654	718	1,375	2,600	1,159
Black	2,689	250	115	303	300	243	175	282	191	225	400	205
1968												
White	15,702	1,117	640	2,195	1,524	1,133	691	1,579	587	1,448	3,532	1,256
Black	3,112	273	130	292	344	350	251	305	189	228	540	255

(continued)

TABLE 9.17 (continued)

Item	Total	Ala.	Ark.	Fla.	Ga.	La.	Miss.	N.C.	S.C.	Tenn.	Tex.	Va.
1970												
White	16,985	1,311	728	2,495	1,615	1,143	690	1,640	668	1,600	3,599	1,496
Black	3,357	315	153	302	395	319	286	305	221	242	550	269
1971												
White	17,378	1,370	674	3,065[a]	1,598	1,330[a]	671	1,911[a]	681[a]	1,542	3,700	1,550
Black	3,449	290	165	349[a]	450	388[a]	268	35.1[a]	233[a]	245	575	275
Percent white	65.0	78.5	61.4	69.9[a]	68.8	74.0[a]	69.7	65.2[a]	50.2[a]	67.3	56.8	59.6
Percent Black	58.6	54.7	80.9	53.2[a]	64.2	58.9[a]	59.4	49.8[a]	49.2[a]	565.6	68.2	52.0

[a] Data for 1974.
Source: Jessie C. Smith and Carrell P. Horton, eds., *Historical Statistics of Black America* (Detroit, 1995), 1312–13.

TABLE 9.18 PERCENTAGE OF PERSONS WHO REPORTED VOTING, BY AGE, 1964–1990

Year	Age			
	18–24	25–44	45–64	65 and Older
1964	50.9	69.0	75.9	66.3
1966	31.2	53.1	64.5	56.1
1968	50.4	66.6	74.9	65.8
1970	40.9	65.0	77.5	73.7
1972	49.6	62.7	70.8	63.5
1974	23.8	42.2	56.9	51.4
1976	42.2	58.7	68.7	62.2
1978	23.5	43.1	58.5	55.9
1980	39.9	69.3	65.1	58.5
1982	24.8	45.4	62.2	59.9
1984	40.8	58.4	69.8	67.7
1986	21.9	41.4	58.7	60.9
1988	36.2	54.0	67.9	68.8
1990	20.4	40.7	55.8	60.3

Note: Data is for persons of voting age, which in most states prior to 1972 was 21 and older.
Source: Mark S. Littman, *A Statistical Portrait of the U.S., Social Conditions and Trends* (Lanham, Md., 1998), 366.

TABLE 9.19 PERCENTAGE OF PERSONS WHO REPORTED VOTING, BY AGE, RACE, AND HISPANIC ORIGIN, 1964–1990

Year	Age 18–24			Age 65 and Older		
	White	Black	Hispanic	White	Black	Hispanic
1964	52.1	44.2	. . .	68.1	45.3	. . .
1966	32.6	21.9	. . .	57.9	35.3	. . .
1968	52.8	38.9	. . .	67.4	49.9	. . .
1970	31.5	22.4	. . .	58.6	39.3	. . .
1972	51.9	34.7	30.9	64.8	50.6	26.7
1974	25.2	16.1	13.3	52.8	38.5	28.1
1976	44.7	27.9	21.8	63.2	54.3	29.9
1978	24.2	20.1	11.5	57.2	45.6	24.9
1980	41.8	30.1	15.9	66.0	59.4	36.8
1982	25.0	25.5	14.2	61.1	50.8	29.5
1984	41.6	40.6	21.9	68.7	61.5	40.5
1986	21.6	25.1	11.6	61.9	53.3	36.5
1988	37.0	35.0	16.8	69.8	63.5	45.6
1990	20.8	20.2	8.7	61.7	51.3	40.5

Note: Data is for persons of voting age, which in most states prior to 1972 was 21 and older.
Source: Littman, *Statistical Portrait of the U.S.*, 367–68.

TABLE 9.20 NUMBER OF CIVILIAN FEDERAL GOVERNMENT EMPLOYEES AND PERCENT UNDER MERIT CIVIL SERVICE, 1946–1990

Year	Total Number of Employees	Percentage Under Merit
1946	2,696,529	. . .
1947	2,111,001	80.2
1948	2,071,009	82.4
1949	2,102,109	84.3
1950	1,960,708	84.5
1951	2,482,666	86.4
1952	2,600,612	86.4
1953	2,558,416	83.6
1954	2,407,676	82.7
1955	2,397,309	83.6
1956	2,398,736	85.1
1957	2,417,565	85.5
1958	2,382,491	85.3
1959	2,382,807	85.7
1960	2,398,704	85.5
1961	2,435,804	86.1
1962	2,514,197	85.9
1963	2,527,960	85.6
1964	2,500,503	86.1
1965	2,527,915	85.2

Year	Total Number of Employees	Percentage Under Merit
1966	2,759,019	85.8
1967	3,002,461	82.8
1968	3,055,212	84.1
1969	3,076,414	82.9
1970	2,981,574	82.3
1971	2,862,894	84.1
1972	2,779,261	61.6
1973	2,732,377	62.0
1974	2,893,118	57.0
1975	2,896,944	57.4
1976	2,883,134	57.6
1977	2,893,334	57.1
1978	2,929,100	57.3
1979	2,949,630	56.6
1980	3,121,769	56.1
1981	2,947,428	58.7
1982	2,917,095	59.2
1983	2,920,514	59.2
1984	2,959,317	58.7
1985	3,059,987	57.2
1986	3,061,210	56.6
1987	3,125,635	56.2
1988	3,126,171	56.0
1989	3,151,334	56.2
1990	3,503,550	50.5

Source: Stanley and Niemi, *Statistics on Politics*, 268.

TABLE 9.21 BILLS, ACTS, AND RESOLUTIONS, 1947–1990

Congress	Measures Introduced			Measures Enacted		
	Bills	Joint Resolutions	Total	Public	Private	Total
80th (1947–1948)	10,108	689	10,797	906	457	1,363
81st (1949–1950)	14,219	769	14,988	921	1,103	2,024
82d (1951–1952)	12,062	668	12,730	594	1,023	1,617
83d (1953–1954)	14,181	771	14,952	781	1,002	1,783
84th (1955–1956)	16,782	905	17,687	1,028	893	1,921
85th (1957–1958)	18,205	907	19,112	936	784	1,720
86th (1959–1960)	17,230	1,031	18,261	800	492	1,292
87th (1961–1962)	17,230	1,146	18,376	885	684	1,569
88th (1963–1964)	16,079	1,401	17,480	666	360	1,026
89th (1965–1966)	22,483	1,520	24,003	810	473	1,283
90th (1967–1968)	24,786	1,674	26,460	640	362	1,002
91st (1969–1970)	24,631	1,672	26,303	695	246	941
92d (1971–1972)	21,363	1,606	22,969	607	161	768
93d (1973–1974)	21,950	1,446	23,396	651	123	774
94th (1975–1976)	19,762	1,334	21,096	588	141	729
95th (1977–1978)	18,045	1,342	19,387	633	170	803
96th (1979–1980)	11,722	861	12,583	613	123	736
97th (1981–1982)	10,582	908	11,490	473	56	529
98th (1983–1984)	10,134	1,022	11,156	623	54	677
99th (1985–1986)	8,697	1,188	9,885	664	24	688
100th (1987–1988)	8,515	1,073	9,588	713	48	761
101st (1989–1990)	9,257	1,095	10,352	404	7	411

Source: Stanley and Niemi, *Statistics on Politics*, 216.

TABLE 9.22 PRESIDENTIAL VETOES, 1945–1990

Years	President	Regular Vetoes	Vetoes Overridden	Pocket Vetoes	Total Vetoes
1945–1953	Truman	180	12	70	250
1953–1961	Eisenhower	73	2	108	181
1961–1963	Kennedy	12	0	9	21
1963–1969	L. Johnson	16	0	14	30
1969–1974	Nixon	26[a]	7	17	43
1974–1977	Ford	48	12	18	66
1977–1981	Carter	13	2	18	31
1981–1989	Reagan	39	9	39	78
1989–1990	Bush	12	0	4	16

[a] Two pocket vetoes, overruled in the courts, are counted here as regular vetoes.
Source: Stanley and Niemi, *Statistics on Politics,* 276.

Civil Rights

One of the great social and political undertakings of the 20th century, the Civil Rights Movement was designed to resolve what a scholar in the 1940s identified as an American dilemma: the contradiction between American ideals and constitutional principles and the reality of the status of black people. In its origins and most compelling stage, it involved mass action efforts to change the political, social, and economic structure of the southern states, where the color line remained, if not exactly rigid, at least the dominant fact of life. The Supreme Court's desegregation decision in the *Brown v. Board of Education of Topeka, Kansas* case of 1954 supplied the immediate encouragement and incentive for the movement to start. During the period from 1954 to approximately 1965, black and white demonstrators sought to dramatize and publicize the evils of segregation and denial of black peoples' right to vote in hope that public pressure would induce southern state governments to change. In the event that the southern power structure would not yield, the activists sought to induce the national government to superimpose its will over the states.

Battlegrounds were southern cities, small towns, and highways as the activists marched, rode, or sat in defiance of state laws and local ordinances, and southern whites, acting either through public institutions, such as the police, or as private individuals or organizations, resisted demands for change. Out of the movement came heroes and martyrs: Medgar Evers; James Meredith; Fred Schuttleworth; John Lewis; Martin Luther King, Jr. (both a hero and a martyr); and the resistors: J. Ross Barnet, "Bull" Connor, George Wallace, and others—these became not heroes, except in special circles, but at least national figures. In spite of murders, beatings, assaults from police dogs and firehoses, arrests, and humiliation, the reformers persisted until indeed the national government did step in. The most important measures were the Civil Rights Acts of 1964 and 1965, which were designed to strike not only at traditional forms of oppression and discrimination as manifested through organs of the state (laws that imposed segregation and prevented blacks from voting) but also at institutionalized racism as practiced by private individuals and organizations. The law of 1964, for example, forbade discrimination in hiring by private companies and discrimination in providing service by private restaurants and hotels.

At the point when it appeared that the Civil Rights Movement had achieved its immediate objectives, the focus shifted. That the activity that took place in the last half of the 1960s involved race, there could be no question; that it continued to be a matter of "civil rights" was at least subject to debate. Attention moved from South to North and West, objectives changed, slogans changed, leadership changed. Stokeley Carmichael seemed to eclipse King; the charismatic black nationalist Malcolm X attracted national attention in the early 1960s;

separatism superseded integration; passive resistance was replaced, at least temporarily, by confrontation. The Black Power movement of the late 1960s produced numerous consequences, of course, many of them difficult to measure. The most conspicuous reaction at the time was the creation of a white backlash, and a lessening of sympathy for the continuing plight of much of black America.

Part of what went on in race relations after 1970 involved implementation of laws and principles that the movement had produced. Black people did vote in the South, and black youth went to school with whites. The University of Alabama began to use black football players, and the University of Kentucky recruited blacks for the basketball team. It soon developed that the teams could not do without them. Passage of time allowed meaning and shortcomings of the various changes to become clear. The slowest gains came in economics—in some measure because of prejudice but also because of qualification (which also could have stemmed from prejudice). A renewed emphasis after 1970 on economics caused some terms to take on new meaning. the Civil Rights Act of 1964 had endorsed "affirmative action" to assure that there had been no form of discrimination; a law of 1972. the Equal Employment Opportunity Act, however, suggested that properly used, discrimination could be helpful: The measure endorsed employment practices preferential to racial and ethnic minority groups and women.

Integration probably remained the most commonly accepted objective, and a "color-blind" society the most noble objective of race relations, but it was doubtful that many people of any color were entirely oblivious to race, and some people had come to have doubts about aspects of integration. Associations based on race often seemed to be the normal and chosen order of events in settings that officially were biracial or multiracial. In some cases, segregation became a stated objective, as in requests for separate black dormitories in universities. The movement for racial and ethnic diversity that gathered such momentum in the 1980s was in no small measure a campaign to foster racial distinction. It might seem that the United States had moved from the doctrine of separate but equal—still, for nearly 20 years after 1946, the policy of the southern states—toward a policy of equal but separate. After nearly 40 years of close attention to race relations, marked with numerous laws, court rulings, expensive programs, noble and selfless acts by people of all races, the United States in 1990 still stood a great distance from effectively dealing with the issue of race. Americans did not agree on what effective dealing would be.

Development of the Civil Rights Movement and the Issue of Race Relations, 1954–1990

1954 The Supreme Court issues its epochal desegregation decision in the case of *Brown v. Board of Education of Topeka, Kansas.*

1955 A refusal by seamstress Rosa Parks to give up her bus seat to a white man, for which she will be arrested, touches off a bus boycott in Montgomery, Alabama—the first expression of mass action by blacks, an event that will produce the first appearance of Martin Luther King, Jr., as a leader.

1957 When the governor of Arkansas, Orval Faubus, blocked racial integration of Central High School in Little Rock, President Dwight Eisenhower nationalizes the national guard to keep order and protect the nine black students wishing to attend Central High.

1960 Four black college freshmen who, denied service at the segregated lunch counter of a Woolworth store in Greensboro, North Carolina, refuse to depart the structure—thus initiating the "sit-in" as a tactic of passive resistance to segregation in the South.

1960 Black and white activists form the Student Nonviolent Coordinating Committee (SNCC) to challenge segregation and denial of voting rights for blacks.

Civil rights advocates "sit-in" at a Woolworth lunch counter in Jackson, Mississippi, and are harassed by local whites, May 28, 1963. (State Historical Society of Wisconsin)

1961 The Congress of Racial Equality (CORE) begins "freedom rides" from one southern locality to another to dramatize segregation in the South.

1962 James Meredith, a black veteran, enrolls at the University of Mississippi, but not until after resistance by state officials and a riot in Oxford that caused two deaths, several injuries, numerous arrests, and intervention by the army.

1963 The governor of Alabama, George Wallace, is forced by national officials to cease resistance to token integration of the state university.

1963 Medgar Evers, a leader of the NAACP, is murdered in his home in Jackson, Mississippi.

1963 Some 200,000 demonstrators march to the Lincoln Memorial in Washington, D.C., and hear Martin Luther King, Jr.'s, "I Have a Dream" speech.

1964 The year of Mississippi Freedom Summer, which emphasizes voter registration of black people. The movement culminates in the murder of three civil rights workers near Philadelphia, Mississippi. National attention to the event will help promote passage of the sweeping Civil Rights Act of 1964, which had been stalled in Congress.

1964 A riot breaks out in Harlem.

1965 Aided by demonstrations in Selma, Alabama, another civil rights bill, the voting rights measure, passes Congress. The law is designed to foster registration of black people in the South.

1965 Black nationalist leader Malcolm X is assassinated in New York City, presumably by a faction of the Nation of Islam.

1965 A race riot in the Watts section of Los Angeles kills 35.

1966 Huey Newton and Bobby Seale found a social and political organization called the Black Panthers in Oakland, California.

1966 Stokeley Carmichael, an advocate of an aggressive Black Power replaces the more conciliatory John Lewis as head of SNCC.

1966 Appointed by President Johnson as head of the Department of Housing and Urban Development (HUD), Robert Weaver becomes the first black member of the Cabinet.

1967 Appointed by President Johnson, Thurgood Marshall becomes the first black justice of the Supreme Court.

1967 A race riot in Newark, New Jersey, leaves 26 dead and 1,400 injured.

1967 A race riot in Detroit kills 43, injures 2,000, and leaves many city blocks gutted.

1968 Martin Luther King, Jr., is shot and killed by a sniper as he stands outside a motel in Memphis.

1968 Congress passes a civil rights act designed to prevent discrimination in the transfer of residential property—the Equal Housing Law.

1968 An investigative body appointed by the president, the Kerner Commission, reports the existence of two nations, black and white, separate and unequal.

1973 Barbara Jordan of Texas becomes the first black woman, and the first southern African American in the 20th century, to be elected to Congress.

1980 Acquittal of white police officers accused of killing a black man causes rioting in Miami that leaves 18 dead.

1983 Harold Washington is elected first black mayor of Chicago.

1990 Continuing a long series of black "firsts" in politics on the state and national level, L. Douglas Wilder becomes first black governor of Virginia and David Dinkins becomes the first black mayor of New York City.

Source: Information compiled by the author from numerous materials.

The Supreme Court

Although the president and Congress received more attention, it could be argued that in the end the judiciary was the most powerful branch of government. Armed with the power of judicial review, the Supreme Court could not only establish boundaries of policy but also steer policy in a distinct direction. Many of the major issues and controversies developed as a consequence of a court ruling; an answer to large questions of national policy—to the extent that any such questions were fully answered—often took the form of a decision by the highest court in the land.

The court of the immediate postwar period, called the Vinson Court, after its chief justice, Fred Vinson, continued in an approach of judicial restraint, a philosophy coming out of the years of depression that allowed the government a great deal of latitude of action, especially in dealing with economic concerns. The court restrained itself from striking down actions of the other branches. Impressed by threats and dangers implicit in an emerging cold war, the court of the early 1950s tilted in the direction of security—permitting the government more power—at some cost in the area of free speech.

From the middle part of the 1950s through virtually the end of the 1960s a different Supreme Court, following a different judicial philosophy, supplied a new thrust to judicial decisions. Named the Warren Court after Chief Justice Earl Warren (appointed by Dwight Eisenhower in 1953), the court practiced a form of judicial activism that was designed to promote egalitarianism and realization of the civil liberties of all Americans. Criticized in some quarters for exercising powers it did not have (the power to make policy), the Warren Court did not hesitate to invalidate acts of a legislature that in its judgment encroached on the rights of its citizens. The bulk of such measures were acts of state legislatures, as opposed to action taken by Congress. The most striking examples included the *Brown* decision and other cases involving race relations; a series of decisions such as in the *Miranda* case, involving legal proceedings within state jurisdiction; and reapportionment decisions having to do with representation within state legislatures. The Warren Court fit the activist and reformist mood of the 1960s and even helped to make it.

Following the retirement of Warren in 1969, the Supreme Court came under the leadership of Warren Burger (appointed by Richard Nixon) until 1986 and afterward by William Rehnquist (appointed originally by Nixon; elevated to the chief justiceship by Ronald

TABLE 9.23   JUSTICES OF THE SUPREME COURT, 1946–1990

Justice	Term of Service	Years of Service	Life Span	Appointed By
Hugo L. Black	1937–71	34	1886–1971	F. Roosevelt
Stanley F. Reed	1938–57	19	1884–1980	F. Roosevelt
Felix Frankfurter	1939–62	23	1882–1965	F. Roosevelt
William O. Douglas	1939–75	36	1898–1980	F. Roosevelt
Frank Murphy	1940–49	9	1890–1949	F. Roosevelt
Harlan F. Stone[a]	1941–46	5	1872–1946	F. Roosevelt
Robert H. Jackson	1941–54	13	1892–1954	F. Roosevelt
Wiley B. Rutledge	1943–49	6	1894–1949	F. Roosevelt
Harold H. Burton	1945–58	13	1888–1964	Truman
Fred M. Vinson[a]	1946–53	7	1890–1953	Truman
Tom C. Clark	1949–67	18	1899–1977	Truman
Sherman Minton	1949–56	7	1890–1965	Truman
Earl Warren[a]	1953–69	16	1891–1974	Eisenhower
John M. Harlan	1955–71	16	1899–1971	Eisenhower
William J. Brennan	1956–90	33	1906–1997	Eisenhower
Charles E. Whittaker	1957–62	5	1901–1973	Eisenhower
Potter Stewart	1958–81	23	1915–1985	Eisenhower
Byron R. White	1962–93	31	1917–	Kennedy
Arthur J. Goldberg	1962–65	3	1908–1990	Kennedy
Abe Fortas	1965–69	4	1910–1982	Johnson
Thurgood Marshall	1967–91	24	1908–1993	Johnson
Warren C. Burger[a]	1969–86	17	1907–1995	Nixon
Harry A. Blackmun	1970–94	24	1908–1999	Nixon
Lewis F. Powell	1972–87	15	1907–1998	Nixon
William H. Rehnquist[a]	1971–	. . .	1924–	Nixon
John P. Stevens	1975–	. . .	1920–	Ford
Sandra Day O'Connor	1981–	. . .	1930–	Reagan
Antonin Scalia	1986–	. . .	1936–	Reagan
Anthony M. Kennedy	1988–	. . .	1936–	Reagan
David M. Souter	1990–	. . .	1939–	Bush

[a] Denotes Chief Justice.
Source: Commission on the Bicentennial of the United States Constitution, *The Supreme Court of the United States* (Washington, D.C., 1992), 273–276.

Reagan). There was, of course, overlapping of personnel in the various courts, but in the broad view, the significant factor was that all justices appointed between 1969 and 1990 (there were nine) and both chief justices were appointed by Republican presidents. Court watchers had reason to expect that liberal activism of the 1960s would give way to conservative jurisprudence.

In some measure a conservative reaction did set in beginning in the 1970s, but it never reached the expected proportion. The Court did loosen the fairly rigid guidelines of the *Miranda* decision and did allow local officials grounds for acting against obscenity, but most observers gave mixed reviews to both the Burger and Rehnquist courts. Both courts continued to supply striking expressions of activism, as in the abortion case of *Roe v. Wade* in 1973 and decisions in 1989 and 1990 declaring that burning the American flag was a right of free speech that had to be protected. The Burger Court more or less struck down capital punishment in 1972 and then brought it back in 1976. In judicial issues, as with society in general, the great battleground of the era came to be abortion and affirmative action. The Rehnquist Court gave no indication of moving sharply in any direction on either issue. The postwar court mirrored the flow of society in another way. Long considered the final citadel of old white men, the Supreme Court received its first black justice in the 1960s and its first female member in the 1980s.

President John F. Kennedy and Jackie Kennedy receive members of the Supreme Court and spouses on November 20, 1963, two days before Kennedy's assassination. (John Fitzgerald Kennedy Library)

Landmark Decisions of the Supreme Court

Dennis v. United States (1951) Heard in the early years of the cold war, during the "Red Scare" of the 1950s, this case tested the boundaries of First Amendment freedoms (the freedom of speech) in a time of great national and international insecurity. In upholding the conviction of 11 high-ranking American communists for advocating overthrow of the government by force (thus violating the Smith Act of 1940), the Vinson Court placed emphasis on security rather than freedom and barely stopped short of ruling that being a communist could be made illegal.

Brown v. Board of Education of Topeka, Kansas (1954) In perhaps its most famous decision, the Warren Court ruled that segregation on a basis of race in the public schools violated the equal protection clause of the Fourteenth Amendment. The decision overturned the principle of "separate but equal" set down in 1896 in *Plessy v. Ferguson,* ordered that segregation of southern schools (and by implication other public facilities) must stop, and touched off a civil rights revolution and a period of some 15 years of social and political unrest.

Baker v. Carr (1962) Here the Warren Court ruled that legislative apportionment within the states based on some geographic district (such as a county) violated the Fourteenth Amendment and that such issues came under the jurisdiction of the national courts. The decision laid the groundwork for the principle of "one man, one vote," applied in *Reynolds v. Sims,* the effect of which was to shift power within the states from rural areas to the populous cities.

Engel v. Vitale (1962) The Warren Court ruled that public school officials could not require students to recite even a nondenominational prayer, as it would constitute an effort to establish a religion. The ruling was one of several sensitive decisions designed to keep virtually all religious observances out of public schools.

Gideon v. Wainwright (1963) This case was one of several in which the Warren Court continued a practice of applying the protections of the Bill of Rights through the Fourteenth Amendment to the states. The Gideon decision established the principle that in state and local criminal proceedings, all accused persons must be supplied with an attorney, if they wished one.

New York Times v. Sullivan (1964) The Supreme Court gave broad meaning to the principle of freedom of the press. A public official, victim of a harsh or even incorrect statement in the media, could not sue for libel unless it could be demonstrated that the party (in this case a newspaper) knowingly and with malice had published false information.

Heart of Atlanta Motel v. United States (1964) In this decision the Warren Court upheld the sweeping Civil Rights Act of 1964, which prominent politicians had challenged on constitutional grounds. The essential point was the court's ruling that the commerce clause gave the national government jurisdiction in an area that critics claimed belonged to the states or to private individuals. The part of the law under review (Title II) involved regulation of privately owned facilities, such as restaurants, that served the public.

Miranda v. Arizona (1966) This case represented an extension of principles established in the *Gideon* case (1963) and *Escobido* case (1964). Not only did defendants in state courts have the right of silence and the right to have an attorney, but they must be advised of these rights before questioning could start. A failure to do so negated the criminal proceeding that followed. Even though Miranda had confessed to murder and rape, he was freed because he had not been so advised.

Roe v. Wade (1973) In the Burger Court's most important decision and one of the most controversial ever rendered, the Supreme Court ruled that because of an individual's right to privacy, state governments could not prevent a woman from having an abortion. Measures in several states that had made abortion illegal were from this point on inoperable. Only in the last three months of pregnancy could the state establish any guidelines, and even then it could not forbid abortion altogether.

United States v. Nixon (1974) In politics this decision sealed the fate of President Richard Nixon. The constitutional issue involved the meaning and extent of executive privilege of the president. The court (Burger Court) ruled that prevailing circumstances—such as national security—in this case did not justify the president's withholding evidence needed in a criminal trial. Thus Nixon was ordered to surrender the "Watergate" tapes—the messages secretly recorded in the Oval Office—that contained evidence of his guilt.

Gregg v. Georgia and other cases (1976) The Burger Court held that for a person convicted of first-degree murder, execution did not constitute cruel and unusual punishment, as stipulated in the Eighth Amendment. Judges and juries should weigh all circumstances carefully, but the death penalty hereafter was reinstated, if indeed it ever had been forbidden.

United States v. Weber and other cases (1979) The Burger Court decided that although the Civil Rights Act of 1964 forbade racial discrimination in employment, employers could utilize certain preferential practices in hiring members of minority groups. In other words, they could discriminate. The decision provided a legal rationale for affirmative action programs—one of the heated political issues in the years to come.

Bowers v. Hardwick (1986) In a narrow 5 to 4 decision, the Court ruled that an ill-defined right to privacy did not extent to homosexual relations. The Court upheld a law passed in Georgia in 1916 that made anal and oral sex a crime; to that point enforcement, to the extent it existed, had been restricted to homosexual behavior.

Source: Bernard Schwartz, *A History of the Supreme Court* (New York, 1993), many pages, especially 263–361.

TABLE 9.24   MEASURES HELD UNCONSTITUTIONAL BY THE SUPREME COURT, 1940–1989

Period	Federal Statutes	State Laws and Local Ordinances
1940–49	2	57
1950–59	5	61
1960–69	16	149
1970–79	20	193
1980–89	16	162
Totals	59	622

Source: Lawrence Baum, *The Supreme Court* (Washington, D.C., 1995), 201, 205.

Trends and Themes of Government Finance

The first trend that attracts attention was the enormous increase in the costs and expenditures of government in the United States. Spending of the national government grew from $55 billion in 1946 to $1 trillion, $250 billion in 1990. Combined expenses of the states went from $7 billion in 1946 to $570 billion in 1990. Frequently, and with increasing regularity, the government spent more money than it earned. Although deficit spending would become a familiar economic and political phenomenon, the condition took a while to develop. Budgets occasionally were balanced in the postwar years; the last surplus came in 1969. During the 1970s deficit spending became persistent but seemingly manageable. It was during the 1980s—the Ronald Reagan years—that the roof fell in. A sharp reduction in taxes accompanied by an increase in expenditures (mostly for military purposes) created annual budget deficits measured in the hundreds of billions. How many hundreds depended on the set of numbers one chose to use.

The government in effect kept two sets of books. One set applied to the expenditures and income for standard operations of government. There also was a separate category for a number of trust funds in the hands of the national government—of which Social Security was the most prominent—that had in some measure separate taxes

TABLE 9.25   NATIONAL GOVERNMENT RECEIPTS, OUTLAYS, AND SURPLUSES OR DEFICITS (–) BY FUND GROUP, 1945–1990

(in millions of dollars)

Fiscal Year	Receipts				Outlays				Surplus or Deficit (–)		
	Total	Federal Funds	Trust Funds	Interfund Transactions	Total	Federal Funds	Trust Funds	Interfund Transactions	Total	Federal Funds	Trust Funds
1945	45,159	41,875	5,045	−1,760	92,712	94,846	−374	−1,760	−47,553	−52,972	5,419
1946	39,296	36,357	5,144	−2,205	55,232	56,204	1,234	−2,205	−15,936	−19,847	3,910
1947	38,514	35,380	4,885	−1,751	34,496	34,803	1,444	−1,751	4,018	577	3,441
1948	41,560	37,822	4,894	−1,156	29,764	28,988	1,932	−1,156	11,796	8,834	2,962
1949	39,415	35,849	4,750	−1,184	38,835	37,686	2,333	−1,184	580	−1,838	2,417
1950	39,443	35,334	5,823	−1,715	42,562	38,389	5,888	−1,715	−3,119	−3,055	−65
1951	51,616	46,183	6,729	−1,296	45,514	43,732	3,078	−1,296	6,102	2,451	3,651
1952	66,167	59,989	7,744	−1,566	67,686	64,994	4,257	−1,566	−1,519	−5,005	3,486
1953	69,608	63,085	8,080	−1,557	76,101	73,006	4,652	−1,557	−6,493	−9,921	3,427
1954	69,701	62,774	8,297	−1,370	70,855	65,924	6,301	−1,370	−1,154	−3,151	1,997
1955	65,451	58,168	8,627	−1,344	68,444	62,341	7,447	−1,344	−2,993	−4,173	1,180
1956	74,587	65,594	10,745	−1,753	70,640	64,281	8,111	−1,753	3,947	1,313	2,634
1957	79,990	68,847	13,210	−2,067	76,578	67,189	11,456	−2,067	3,412	1,657	1,755
1958	79,636	66,720	15,082	−2,166	82,405	69,737	14,834	−2,166	−2,769	−3,017	248
1959	79,249	65,800	15,770	−2,321	92,098	77,071	17,348	−2,321	−12,849	−11,271	−1,578
1960	92,492	75,647	19,232	−2,387	92,191	74,856	19,722	−2,387	301	791	−490
1961	94,388	75,175	22,320	−3,107	97,723	79,368	21,462	−3,107	−3,335	−4,193	858
1962	99,676	79,700	22,981	−3,005	106,821	86,546	23,281	−3,005	−7,146	−6,847	−299
1963	106,560	84,013	25,792	−3,245	111,316	90,643	23,918	−3,245	−4,756	−6,630	1,874
1964	112,613	87,511	28,461	−3,358	118,528	96,098	25,788	−3,358	−5,915	−8,588	2,673
1965	116,817	90,943	29,202	−3,328	118,228	94,853	26,703	−3,328	−1,411	−3,910	2,499
1966	130,835	101,428	32,959	−3,552	134,532	106,590	31,495	−3,552	−3,698	−5,162	1,464
1967	148,822	111,835	42,213	−5,227	157,464	127,544	35,147	−5,227	−8,643	−15,709	7,066
1968	152,973	114,726	44,011	−5,764	178,134	143,100	40,799	−5,764	−25,161	−28,373	3,212
1969	186,882	143,322	51,108	−7,549	183,640	148,192	42,996	−7,549	3,242	−4,871	8,112
1970	192,807	143,159	58,425	−8,777	195,649	156,327	48,099	−8,777	−2,842	−13,168	10,326
1971	187,139	133,785	64,937	−11,583	210,172	163,681	58,074	−11,583	−23,033	−29,896	6,863
1972	207,309	148,846	71,619	−13,156	230,681	178,144	65,693	−13,156	−23,373	−29,299	5,926
1973	230,799	161,357	90,767	−21,325	245,707	187,044	79,988	−21,325	−14,908	−25,687	10,779
1974	263,224	181,228	103,789	−21,793	269,359	201,376	89,776	−21,793	−6,135	−20,148	14,013
1975	279,090	187,505	117,647	−26,061	332,332	248,174	110,220	−26,061	−53,242	−60,669	7,427
1976	298,060	201,099	132,509	−35,548	371,792	277,242	130,099	−35,548	−73,732	−76,143	2,410
TQ[a]	81,232	54,085	31,625	−4,478	95,975	66,878	33,575	−4,478	−14,744	−12,794	−1,950
1977	355,559	241,312	151,503	−37,256	409,218	304,474	142,000	−37,256	−53,659	−63,162	9,502
1978	399,561	270,490	166,468	−37,397	458,746	342,372	153,771	−37,397	−59,186	−71,882	12,697
1979	463,302	316,366	188,072	−41,136	504,032	375,435	169,733	−41,136	−40,729	−59,069	18,339
1980	517,112	350,856	212,106	−45,850	590,947	433,494	203,302	−45,850	−73,835	−82,639	8,804
1981	599,272	410,422	240,601	−51,751	678,249	496,222	233,778	−51,751	−78,976	−85,799	6,823
1982	617,766	409,253	270,138	−61,625	745,755	543,486	263,894	−61,625	−127,989	−134,233	6,244
1983	600,562	382,432	319,363	−101,233	808,380	613,331	296,282	−101,233	−207,818	−230,899	23,081
1984	666,457	420,370	338,661	−92,574	851,846	638,664	305,756	−92,574	−185,388	−218,293	32,905
1985	734,057	460,280	397,500	−123,723	946,391	726,763	343,351	−123,723	−212,334	−266,483	54,149
1986	769,091	474,001	423,377	−128,287	990,336	757,138	361,485	−128,287	−221,245	−283,138	61,892
1987	854,143	538,499	444,203	−128,559	1,003,911	760,885	371,585	−128,559	−149,769	−222,386	72,618
1988	908,954	561,098	491,202	−143,346	1,064,140	814,008	393,479	−143,346	−155,187	−252,909	97,723
1989	990,691	614,823	535,941	−160,073	1,143,172	890,787	412,458	−160,073	−152,481	−275,964	123,483
1990	1,031,321	635,190	566,931	−170,799	1,252,515	976,564	446,750	−170,799	−221,194	−341,374	120,180

[a] In the calender year 1976 the July–September period was a separate accounting period, known as the transition quarter or TQ.
Source: Office of Management and Budget, *The Budget for Fiscal Year 1997, Historical Tables* (Washington, D.C., 1996), 25.

TABLE 9.26 FEDERAL EXPENDITURES BY FUNCTION—SELECTED FISCAL YEARS, 1946–1990

(millions $)

Year	Total	National Defense	Postal Service	Public Education	High-ways	Public Welfare	Health & Hospitals	Police Protection	Natural Resource	Housing	Veterans Service	Admnis-tration	Interest on Debt	Insurance Trust	Payments to Other Gov'ts	Other
1946	66,534	50,461	1,381	355	8	26	324	70	2,809	107	2,534	460	3,865	1,086	894	2,154
1948	35,592	16,075	1,715	2,342	35	45	705	80	1,727	69	3,293	445	4,323	1,417	1,771	1,550
1950	44,800	18,355	2,270	2,470	69	24	963	88	4,335	121	2,796	514	4,404	4,515	2,371	1,505
1951	48,935	25,953	2,403	1,885	56	25	967	104	3,027	124	2,601	547	4,221	2,801	2,383	1,838
1952	71,568	48,187	2,612	1,280	64	42	1,014	141	2,476	106	2,428	608	4,262	3,790	2,585	1,973
1953	79,990	53,583	2,686	727	66	42	956	122	4,111	138	2,710	602	4,863	4,294	2,873	2,217
1954	77,692	49,265	2,669	639	60	43	959	124	5,615	131	2,811	622	4,796	5,061	2,967	1,930
1955	73,441	43,472	2,726	802	68	42	905	129	5,545	112	2,997	607	4,845	6,238	3,099	1,853
1956	75,991	43,388	2,899	940	82	45	967	156	5,724	125	3,097	675	5,311	7,200	3,347	2,036
1957	81,783	47,500	3,034	964	115	49	1,032	155	5,205	119	3,186	680	5,497	8,520	3,873	1,854
1958	86,054	47,626	3,327	917	135	48	1,104	159	5,161	200	3,455	693	6,116	10,356	4,835	1,922
1959	93,531	49,688	3,499	836	134	57	1,343	170	6,890	223	3,645	747	5,543	11,847	6,355	2,556
1960	97,284	48,922	3,730	685	137	58	1,450	173	5,898	284	3,689	746	7,662	13,565	6,994	3,290
1961	104,863	51,210	4,025	640	151	59	1,595	193	8,429	377	3,965	788	7,485	14,892	7,011	4,043
1962	113,428	55,172	4,101	598	151	63	1,793	196	9,097	548	4,129	850	7,162	16,740	7,735	5,093
1963	118,805	56,386	4,402	751	165	118	2,008	209	8,014	509	3,941	923	7,682	18,273	8,507	6,915
1964	125,949	57,326	4,775	1,056	164	114	2,169	220	8,207	895	4,189	1,016	8,293	19,067	10,097	8,360
1965	130,059	55,810	5,261	1,050	127	105	2,309	243	9,260	948	4,190	1,069	8,940	19,930	11,062	9,752
1966	143,022	60,832	5,706	1,550	125	208	2,452	257	8,262	1,009	4,510	1,131	9,589	23,342	13,115	10,933
1967	166,849	74,638	6,227	2,295	100	1,374	2,817	282	7,801	944	4,425	1,224	10,373	28,283	15,027	11,038
1968	184,464	83,874	6,485	2,456	173	1,388	3,033	290	6,729	1,209	4,740	1,319	11,607	32,474	18,053	10,634
1969	196,165	84,496	6,993	3,139	321	2,620	3,410	341	7,472	603	5,046	1,458	13,260	37,547	19,421	10,038
1970	208,190	84,253	7,722	3,053	319	2,837	3,919	409	8,737	1,051	5,388	1,688	14,037	41,248	23,257	10,272
1971	226,157	80,910	8,683	4,629	301	2,220	3,630	478	10,658	1,913	6,411	1,881	16,599	48,235	27,500	12,109
1972	242,186	79,258	9,366	5,104	432	2,488	4,166	554	11,105	2,630	6,882	2,245	17,114	54,086	33,584	13,172
1973	272,709	83,004	9,572	5,176	271	3,385	4,824	1,023	13,432	3,765	7,353	2,544	18,332	64,252	41,268	14,508
1974	295,488	85,444	11,235	5,820	243	6,286	5,723	988	13,697	2,416	7,523	2,448	22,450	74,075	42,854	14,286
1975	341,517	93,877	12,678	7,153	312	12,212	5,996	1,095	13,844	2,392	8,598	3,280	25,005	88,025	49,628	17,422
1976	391,085	98,000	13,748	9,039	294	13,694	6,884	1,204	14,710	2,284	9,289	3,680	29,306	101,433	69,057	18,463
1977	433,340	105,596	14,641	7,835	265	14,904	7,508	1,343	18,335	2,212	10,165	4,038	33,276	117,936	74,016	21,270
1978	479,297	114,811	15,271	7,992	277	16,540	8,135	1,571	22,073	2,345	10,776	4,365	39,330	131,297	79,172	25,342
1979	537,338	128,529	16,581	9,979	418	18,722	8,933	1,724	25,632	3,308	11,553	4,808	48,768	147,352	85,327	25,704
1980	617,166	149,459	18,177	10,619	434	19,212	11,136	1,739	29,734	6,080	12,443	5,330	61,286	170,576	90,836	30,105
1981	719,249	174,564	20,466	12,228	306	22,395	11,277	1,904	38,896	6,808	13,776	5,687	80,510	202,339	94,609	33,484
1982	796,483	204,275	21,761	11,484	576	22,564	12,507	2,000	40,349	4,585	14,959	6,040	101,816	228,110	89,339	36,118
1983	874,264	228,763	23,561	12,773	560	24,749	12,377	2,322	49,105	5,870	15,817	7,062	108,735	250,094	92,686	39,790
1984	928,188	248,040	26,619	12,496	792	23,715	12,966	2,092	59,415	8,325	16,020	7,556	109,209	264,142	99,015	37,786
1985	1,032,131	288,736	28,898	13,208	834	25,234	14,020	3,430	53,635	8,214	16,876	7,427	140,281	284,633	107,424	39,281
1986	1,096,401	312,183	30,985	13,581	568	25,790	14,552	3,543	60,075	7,925	17,139	8,619	144,167	300,192	115,632	41,450
1987	1,148,654	319,084	32,243	14,393	623	26,187	15,351	4,036	84,566	9,538	17,088	9,230	146,155	316,454	111,511	42,029
1988	1,214,812	329,993	33,892	14,552	377	28,656	16,849	4,657	81,481	11,969	18,340	10,691	158,119	336,289	118,906	50,041
1989	1,270,068	346,338	36,472	17,282	776	31,170	17,334	4,952	54,975	13,492	18,669	11,290	174,288	359,630	127,247	56,153
1990	1,393,121	344,069	39,065	17,830	856	33,447	17,852	5,344	70,266	16,951	17,353	12,710	187,952	390,897	146,990	91,539

Source: Scott Moody, Facts and Figures on Government Finance (Washington, D.C., 1999), 69–70. (A publication of the Tax Foundation)

and a separate accounting system. Although standard government operations during 1946–90 ran ever-increasing deficits every year but six, the trust fund ran a surplus every year but four. In 1990 the surplus was $120 billion. By placing Social Security and other trusts into the general accounting hopper, using the trust-fund surplus to reduce the budget deficit (if only as an accounting device), it was possible to make a terrible situation seem only reprehensible. In 1990 it was the difference between a budget unbalanced by $341 billion and one of $221 billion.

The same basic principle applied to the issue of the national debt, which was, of course, nothing more than accumulated deficit spending. Long considered a consequence of extraordinary times, such as war, the debt became a standard and regularly growing part of economic life. As with deficit spending, the debt increased steadily but

gradually until the 1980s when it soared—to nearly $3.3 trillion in 1990. By bringing in the trust-fund surplus, however, the debt became a mere $2.4 trillion.

With respect to expenditures, defense and military costs became a large obligation of the national government, and in the early years of the cold war, the military took more than half of the government's funds. Even though defense spending went up steadily in the years that followed, it did not keep pace with the increase in general spending. The final year that the military took half the budget was 1960; by 1990 its share of the budget had dropped beneath 25 percent. By that time social and welfare spending absorbed at least 50 percent of spending by the government in Washington. The states of course had special responsibilities for education and transportation, but their budgets also were

TABLE 9.27   FEDERAL RECEIPTS BY SOURCE, BY FISCAL YEAR, 1945–1990
(millions $)

Year	Total Receipts	Individual Income Taxes	Corporate Income Taxes	Social Insurance Taxes	Excise Taxes	Other
1945	45,159	18,372	15,988	3,451	6,265	1,083
1946	39,296	16,098	11,883	3,115	6,998	1,202
1947	38,514	17,935	8,615	3,422	7,211	1,331
1948	41,560	19,315	9,678	3,751	7,356	1,461
1949	39,415	15,552	11,192	3,781	7,502	1,388
1950	39,443	15,755	10,449	4,338	7,550	1,351
1951	51,616	21,616	14,101	5,674	8,648	1,578
1952	66,167	27,934	21,226	6,445	8,852	1,710
1953	69,608	29,816	21,238	6,820	9,877	1,857
1954	69,701	29,542	21,101	7,208	9,945	1,905
1955	65,451	28,747	17,861	7,862	9,131	1,850
1956	74,587	32,188	20,880	9,320	9,929	2,270
1957	79,990	35,620	21,167	9,997	10,534	2,672
1958	79,636	34,724	20,074	11,239	10,638	2,961
1959	79,249	36,719	17,309	11,722	10,578	2,921
1960	92,492	40,715	21,494	14,683	11,676	3,923
1961	94,388	41,338	20,954	16,439	11,860	3,796
1962	99,676	45,571	20,523	17,046	12,534	4,001
1963	106,560	47,588	21,579	19,804	13,194	4,395
1964	112,613	48,697	23,493	21,963	13,731	4,731
1965	116,817	48,792	25,461	22,242	14,570	5,753
1966	130,835	55,446	30,073	25,546	13,062	6,708
1967	148,822	61,526	33,971	32,619	13,719	6,987
1968	152,973	68,726	28,665	33,923	14,079	7,580
1969	186,882	87,249	36,678	39,015	15,222	8,718
1970	192,807	90,412	32,829	44,362	15,705	9,499
1971	187,139	86,230	26,785	47,325	16,614	10,185
1972	207,309	94,737	32,166	52,574	15,477	12,355
1973	230,799	103,246	36,153	63,115	16,260	12,026
1974	263,224	118,952	38,620	75,071	16,844	13,737
1975	279,090	122,386	40,621	84,534	16,551	14,998
1976	298,060	131,603	41,409	90,769	16,963	17,317
1977	355,559	157,626	54,892	106,485	17,548	19,008
1978	399,561	180,988	59,952	120,967	18,376	19,278
1979	463,302	217,841	65,677	138,939	18,745	22,101
1980	517,112	244,069	64,600	157,803	24,329	26,311
1981	599,272	285,917	61,137	182,720	40,839	28,659
1982	617,766	297,744	49,207	201,498	36,311	33,006
1983	600,562	288,938	37,022	208,994	35,300	30,309
1984	666,486	298,415	56,893	239,376	37,361	34,440
1985	734,088	334,531	61,331	265,163	35,992	37,072
1986	769,215	348,959	63,143	283,901	32,919	40,292
1987	854,353	392,557	83,926	303,318	32,457	42,095
1988	909,303	401,181	94,508	334,335	35,227	44,051
1989	991,190	445,690	103,291	359,416	34,386	48,407
1990	1,031,969	466,884	93,507	380,047	35,345	56,186

Source: Office of Management and Budget, *Historical Tables*, 27–28.

TABLE 9.28 **FEDERAL RECEIPTS BY SOURCE— PERCENTAGES, 1945–1990**

Year	Individual Income Taxes	Corporate Income Taxes	Social Insurance	Excise Taxes	Other
1945	40.7	35.4	7.6	13.9	2.4
1950	39.9	26.5	11.0	19.1	3.4
1955	43.9	27.3	12.0	14.0	2.8
1960	44.0	23.2	15.9	12.6	4.2
1965	41.8	21.8	19.0	12.5	4.9
1970	46.9	17.0	23.0	8.1	4.9
1975	43.9	14.6	30.3	5.9	5.4
1980	47.2	12.5	30.5	4.7	5.1
1985	45.6	8.4	36.1	4.9	5.1
1990	45.2	9.1	36.8	3.4	5.4

Source: Office of Management and Budget, *Historical Tables*, 29–30.

given over heavily to welfare spending. By 1990 such social programs took up more than 60 percent of state spending.

When it came to raising the money, simply put: The national government relied heavily on income taxes, the states on the sales tax, and local government on property taxes. With the passage of years, however, most states felt compelled to add some measure of income tax to the base for funding. Increasingly, the national tax policy stressed obligations of the individual. Corporation income taxes dropped sharply, although the firms did have to contribute to separate taxes for social insurance programs.

In general, spending on all levels of government continued to grow, and all levels constantly sought ways to find more money. More taxes always remained an alternative, of course, but taxation remained a delicate issue. For the Republican Party it often seemed to be the only issue. In 1990 the concept of a national balanced budget seemed a world away.

TABLE 9.29   FEDERAL DEBT AT THE END OF YEAR, 1945–1990

End of Fiscal Year	In Millions of Dollars			As Percentages of GDP		
	Gross Federal Debt	Less: Held by Federal Government Accounts	Equals Debt Held by Public	Gross Federal Debt	Less: Held by Federal Government Accounts	Equals Debt Held by Public
1945	260,123	24,941	235,182	122.7	11.8	110.9
1946	270,991	29,130	241,861	127.5	13.7	113.8
1947	257,149	32,810	224,339	115.4	14.7	100.6
1948	252,031	35,761	216,270	101.9	14.5	87.5
1949	252,610	38,288	214,322	96.2	14.6	81.6
1950	256,853	37,830	219,023	96.6	14.2	82.4
1951	255,288	40,962	214,326	81.4	13.1	68.4
1952	259,097	44,339	214,758	76.1	13.0	63.1
1953	265,963	47,580	218,383	73.1	13.1	60.0
1954	270,812	46,313	224,499	73.6	12.6	61.0
1955	274,366	47,751	226,616	71.3	12.4	58.9
1956	272,693	50,537	222,156	65.5	12.1	53.4
1957	272,252	52,931	219,320	62.1	12.1	50.0
1958	279,666	53,329	226,336	62.4	11.9	50.5
1959	287,465	52,764	234,701	59.9	11.0	48.9
1960	290,525	53,686	236,840	57.6	10.6	46.9
1961	292,648	54,291	238,357	56.6	10.5	46.1
1962	302,928	54,918	248,010	54.6	9.9	44.7
1963	310,324	56,345	253,978	53.1	9.6	43.5
1964	316,059	59,210	256,849	50.5	9.5	41.1
1965	322,318	61,540	260,778	48.0	9.2	38.9
1966	328,498	64,784	263,714	44.7	8.8	35.9
1967	340,445	73,819	266,626	42.9	9.3	33.6
1968	368,685	79,140	289,545	43.5	9.3	34.2
1969	365,769	87,661	278,108	39.5	9.5	30.0
1970	380,921	97,723	283,198	38.7	9.9	28.7
1971	408,176	105,140	303,037	38.8	10.0	28.8
1972	435,936	113,559	322,377	38.0	9.9	28.1
1973	466,291	125,381	340,910	36.6	9.8	26.8
1974	483,893	140,194	343,699	34.5	10.0	24.5
1975	541,925	147,225	394,700	35.9	9.8	26.1
1976	628,970	151,566	477,404	37.3	9.0	28.3
TQ	643,561	148,052	495,509	36.2	8.3	27.8
1977	706,398	157,295	549,103	36.8	8.2	28.6
1978	776,602	169,477	607,125	36.0	7.9	28.2
1979	829,470	189,162	640,308	34.1	7.8	26.4
1980	909,050	199,212	709,838	34.4	7.5	26.8
1981	994,845	209,507	785,338	33.6	7.1	26.5
1982	1,137,345	217,560	919,785	36.4	7.0	29.5
1983	1,371,710	240,114	1,131,596	41.4	7.2	34.1
1984	1,564,657	264,159	1,300,498	42.3	7.1	35.2
1985	1,817,521	317,612	1,499,908	45.8	8.0	37.8
1986	2,120,629	383,919	1,736,709	50.3	9.1	41.2
1987	2,346,125	457,444	1,888,680	52.7	10.3	42.4
1988	2,601,307	550,507	2,050,799	54.1	11.4	42.7
1989	2,868,039	678,157	2,189,882	55.4	13.1	42.3
1990	3,206,564	795,841	2,410,722	58.5	14.5	44.0

Source: Office of Management and Budget, *Historical Tables*, 102.

TABLE 9.30 FEDERAL, STATE, AND LOCAL TAX REVENUE BY SOURCE—A SUMMARY AND COMPARISON, 1957–1988

(in percent)

Jurisdiction/Year	Property Taxes	Sales, Gross Receipts, and Customs	Individual and Corporate Income Taxes	All Other Taxes
Federal				
1957	. . .	15.9	81.3	2.7
1967	. . .	13.7	83.0	3.3
1972	. . .	13.1	82.5	4.4
1977	. . .	9.5	86.8	3.7
1979	. . .	8.4	88.9	2.7
1981	. . .	12.0	85.5	2.5
1982	. . .	11.3	85.7	3.0
1983	. . .	11.7	85.5	2.8
1984	. . .	11.9	85.1	3.0
1985	. . .	10.8	86.4	2.8
1986	. . .	10.0	87.3	2.7
1987	. . .	9.0	88.3	2.7
1988	. . .	9.4	88.1	2.6
State				
1957	3.3	58.1	17.5	21.1
1967	2.7	58.2	22.4	16.8
1972	2.1	55.5	29.1	13.3
1977	2.2	51.8	34.3	11.7
1979	2.0	51.0	35.8	11.2
1981	2.0	48.6	36.8	12.6
1982	1.9	48.4	36.7	12.9
1983	1.9	48.9	36.7	12.4
1984	2.0	48.7	37.8	11.5
1985	1.9	48.9	37.7	11.5
1986	1.9	49.3	37.6	11.2
1987	1.9	48.5	39.2	10.4
1988	1.9	49.3	38.6	10.3
Local				
1957	86.7	7.2	1.3	4.8
1967	86.6	6.7	3.2	3.5
1972	83.7	8.6	4.5	3.3
1977	80.5	11.1	5.0	3.4
1979	77.5	13.1	5.3	4.0
1981	76.0	13.9	5.8	4.3
1982	76.0	14.3	5.9	3.9
1983	76.0	14.5	5.7	3.9
1984	75.0	14.8	5.8	4.3
1985	74.2	15.6	5.9	4.3
1986	74.0	15.6	5.9	4.5
1987	73.7	15.5	6.1	4.7
1988	74.1	15.2	6.0	4.7

Source: Stanley and Niemi, *Statistics on Politics,* 318.

(millions $)

Year	Total	Public Education	Highways	Public Welfare	Health & Hospitals	Police Protection	Adminis- tration	Insurance Trust	Payments to Other Governments	Other
1946	7,066	518	613	680	424	45	192	1,158	2,092	1,344
1948	11,181	1,081	1,510	962	663	65	266	1,020	3,283	2,331
1950	15,082	1,358	2,058	1,566	947	85	317	2,177	4,217	2,357
1952	15,834	1,494	2,556	1,410	1,132	106	361	1,413	5,044	2,318
1953	16,850	1,634	2,781	1,534	1,184	119	399	1,416	5,384	2,399
1954	18,686	1,715	3,254	1,548	1,276	130	419	2,096	5,679	2,569
1955	20,357	1,905	3,899	1,600	1,338	139	447	2,411	5,986	2,632
1956	21,686	2,138	4,367	1,603	1,470	159	477	1,984	6,538	2,950
1957	24,235	2,342	4,875	1,826	1,571	179	531	2,313	7,440	3,158
1958	28,080	2,728	5,507	1,944	1,760	214	569	3,675	8,089	3,594
1959	31,125	3,093	6,414	2,124	1,850	228	619	4,259	8,689	3,849
1960	31,596	3,396	6,070	2,221	1,896	245	654	3,461	9,443	4,210
1961	34,693	3,792	6,230	2,311	2,059	261	726	4,701	10,114	4,499
1962	36,402	4,270	6,635	2,509	2,161	276	763	4,238	10,906	4,644
1963	39,583	4,718	7,425	2,712	2,330	297	830	4,306	11,885	5,080
1964	42,583	5,465	7,850	2,796	2,464	315	871	4,364	12,968	5,490
1965	45,639	6,181	8,214	2,998	2,701	348	948	4,170	14,174	5,905
1966	51,123	7,572	8,624	3,138	2,966	385	1,024	3,952	16,928	6,534
1967	58,760	9,384	9,423	4,291	3,358	441	1,175	4,268	19,056	7,364
1968	66,254	10,957	9,819	5,122	3,832	516	1,310	4,626	21,950	8,122
1969	74,227	12,304	10,414	6,464	4,258	585	1,496	4,911	24,779	9,016
1970	85,055	13,780	11,044	8,203	4,788	688	1,720	6,010	28,892	9,930
1971	98,840	15,800	12,304	10,518	5,400	797	1,950	8,327	32,640	11,104
1972	109,255	17,153	12,747	12,247	6,008	900	2,134	8,950	36,759	12,357
1973	118,836	18,283	12,072	14,147	6,506	1,017	2,451	9,167	40,822	14,371
1974	132,134	19,753	12,636	15,169	7,494	1,145	2,799	10,590	45,941	16,607
1975	158,882	22,902	14,258	17,457	8,968	1,314	3,205	18,860	51,978	19,940
1976	180,926	25,546	14,860	20,157	9,851	1,412	3,539	25,455	57,858	22,248
1977	191,225	27,073	13,853	22,646	11,209	1,569	3,983	23,426	62,460	25,006
1978	203,832	29,577	14,658	25,729	12,319	1,683	5,288	20,495	67,287	26,796
1979	224,653	31,517	17,079	28,742	13,786	1,825	5,953	20,111	75,963	29,677
1980	257,812	35,251	20,661	33,242	15,666	2,060	6,840	24,981	84,504	34,607
1981	291,527	39,664	20,688	38,580	18,028	2,270	7,366	32,221	93,180	39,530
1982	310,358	42,301	20,103	41,513	19,398	2,396	8,308	34,730	98,743	42,866
1983	334,019	44,584	21,153	44,454	20,834	2,622	9,198	42,180	101,309	47,684
1984	351,446	48,573	23,250	49,122	21,567	2,793	9,837	34,632	108,373	53,299
1985	390,828	53,667	27,167	52,688	23,211	3,114	10,897	37,940	121,571	60,573
1986	424,216	58,260	30,191	56,256	25,471	3,328	12,221	39,749	131,966	66,774
1987	455,696	61,647	31,488	61,123	27,202	3,636	13,339	43,316	141,425	72,520
1988	485,005	64,110	33,732	66,570	29,381	3,914	14,569	44,217	151,662	76,850
1989	525,077	68,583	35,318	73,138	32,360	4,138	16,038	46,995	165,415	83,094
1990	572,318	75,497	36,464	83,336	35,543	4,487	17,707	54,452	175,028	89,806

Source: Moody, Facts and Figures, 164–65.

Social Insurance Programs

Programs of public assistance and social insurance did not emerge from a single grand scheme about needs of the people and responsibilities of government. Instead, they represented an accumulation of measures adopted piecemeal over the years in response to changing philosophy of government and pressure from various interest groups at various times. The basic starting point in several respects had been the Social Security Act of 1935, a part of Franklin D. Roosevelt's New Deal during the crisis of the Great Depression. Its original purpose had been twofold: to provide old-age benefits for retired workers and unemployment compensation for people out of work. Over coming years the program expanded, not only through adding new categories of workers but also by adding new grounds on which participants could claim support. Disability insurance was added in 1956, Medicare in 1965, a black-lung program (for coal miners) in 1970, a cost-of-living provision in 1972. Other programs continued to be introduced, either through the existing system or through new programs, such as food stamps in 1964 in the Department of Agriculture, or through grants of federal funds to the states. Aid to the nation's military veterans, one of the few concepts to precede the Social Security Act, continued to expand as a result of the permanence of a large standing military force, consequences of the nation's frequent military engagements, pressure from ever-powerful veterans groups, and inducements designed (after 1973) to keep an all-volunteer force up to strength.

The social and welfare responsibilities of the government grew so large and complex that hardly anyone understood its workings. The few individuals who might have mastered the system probably were in the best position to understand its weaknesses—the overlapping, the waste, and the opportunity for abuse, if not fraud. Much easier to grasp was the huge cost. By 1976, shortly after the end of the Vietnam

TABLE 9.32 SOCIAL WELFARE EXPENDITURES, BY CATEGORY, 1950–1988

Year	Social Insurance	Public Aid	Health and Medical Programs	Veterans Programs	Education	Housing	Other Social Welfare	All Health and Medical Care	Total Social Welfare Outlays
Federal (millions $)									
1950	2,103	1,103	604	6,386	157	15	174	1,362	10,541
1955	6,385	1,504	1,150	4,772	485	75	252	1,948	14,623
1960	14,307	2,117	1,737	5,367	868	144	417	2,918	24,957
1965	21,807	3,594	2,660	6,011	2,470	238	812	4,482	37,591
1970	45,246	9,649	4,568	8,952	5,876	582	2,259	16,363	77,130
1975	99,715	27,186	7,890	16,570	8,629	2,541	4,264	33,469	166,795
1980	191,162	48,666	12,840	21,254	13,452	6,278	8,786	68,939	302,438
1985	310,175	61,985	18,029	26,704	13,796	11,059	7,548	122,950	449,296
1986	326,016	65,722	19,433	27,072	15,022	10,090	7,822	130,664	471,177
1987	342,920	69,233	20,806	27,641	16,062	11,044	8,504	141,220	496,211
1988	358,412	74,137	22,681	28,845	16,952	14,006	8,112	149,102	523,145
State and Local (millions $)									
1950	2,844	1,393	1,460	480	6,517	. . .	274	1,704	12,967
1955	3,450	1,499	1,953	62	10,672	15	367	2,473	18,017
1960	4,999	1,984	2,727	112	16,758	33	723	3,478	27,337
1965	6,316	2,670	3,495	20	25,638	80	1,254	4,942	39,493
1970	9,446	6,839	5,038	126	44,970	120	1,886	8,698	68,425
1975	23,298	14,171	8,852	449	72,205	631	2,683	17,932	122,289
1980	38,592	23,309	14,423	212	107,597	601	4,813	31,320	189,548
1985	59,420	36,169	21,024	338	158,251	1,540	6,004	50,382	282,746
1986	64,754	39,026	24,512	373	174,253	1,872	6,338	57,220	311,128
1987	69,941	41,748	27,565	410	188,487	2,129	6,773	62,977	337,054
1988	73,783	46,237	29,859	409	202,416	2,550	7,368	70,511	362,622
Total (millions $)									
1950	4,947	2,496	2,064	6,866	6,674	15	448	3,065	23,508
1955	9,835	3,003	3,103	4,834	11,157	89	619	4,421	32,640
1960	19,307	4,101	4,464	5,479	17,626	177	1,139	6,395	52,293
1965	28,123	6,283	6,155	6,031	28,108	318	2,066	9,424	77,084
1970	54,691	16,488	9,606	9,078	50,846	701	4,145	25,061	145,555
1975	123,013	41,357	16,742	17,019	80,834	3,172	6,946	51,401	289,084
1980	229,754	71,975	27,263	21,466	121,050	6,879	13,599	100,259	491,986
1985	369,595	981,154	39,053	27,042	172,048	12,598	13,552	173,332	732,042
1986	390,770	104,747	43,495	27,445	189,276	11,962	14,161	187,884	782,305
1987	412,862	110,981	48,371	28,051	204,549	13,174	15,278	204,197	833,265
1988	432,195	120,375	52,540	29,254	219,368	16,556	15,480	219,613	885,767
Percentage of Total Expenditures									
1950	21.0	10.6	8.8	29.2	28.4	0.1	1.9	13.0	100.0
1955	30.1	9.2	9.5	14.8	34.2	0.3	1.9	13.5	100.0
1960	36.9	7.8	8.5	10.5	33.7	0.3	2.2	12.2	100.0
1965	36.4	8.2	8.0	7.8	36.5	0.4	2.7	12.2	100.1
1970	37.6	11.3	6.6	6.2	34.9	0.5	2.8	17.2	99.9
1975	42.6	14.3	5.8	5.9	28.0	1.1	2.4	17.8	100.1
1980	46.7	14.6	5.5	4.4	24.6	1.4	2.8	20.4	100.0
1985	50.5	13.4	5.3	3.7	23.5	1.6	1.9	23.7	99.9
1986	50.0	13.4	5.6	3.5	24.2	1.5	1.8	24.0	100.0
1987	49.5	13.3	5.8	3.4	24.5	1.6	1.8	24.5	99.9
1988	48.8	13.6	5.9	3.3	24.8	1.9	1.7	24.8	100.0
Percentage Federal of Total									
1950	42.5	44.2	29.2	93.0	2.3	100.0	38.9	44.4	44.8
1955	64.9	50.1	37.1	98.7	4.3	84.3	40.7	44.1	44.8
1960	74.1	51.6	38.9	98.0	4.9	81.4	36.6	45.6	47.7
1965	77.5	57.2	43.2	99.7	8.8	74.9	39.3	47.6	48.8
1970	82.7	58.5	47.6	98.6	11.6	82.9	54.5	65.3	53.0
1975	81.1	65.7	47.1	97.4	10.7	80.1	61.4	65.1	57.7
1980	83.2	67.6	47.1	99.0	11.1	91.3	64.6	68.8	61.5
1985	83.9	63.2	46.2	98.8	8.0	87.8	55.7	70.9	61.4
1986	83.4	62.7	44.7	98.6	7.9	84.4	55.2	69.5	60.2
1987	83.1	62.4	43.0	98.5	7.9	83.8	55.7	69.2	59.6
1988	82.9	61.6	43.2	98.6	7.7	84.6	52.4	67.9	59.1

Source: Stanley and Niemi, *Statistics on Politics*, 378–80.

War, payments reached nearly 57 percent of all federal expenditures. The proportion declined in the 1980s, but at the end of the decade social expenditures still absorbed approximately half of the money spent by the national government and 60 percent of what was spent by the states. An issue of growing concern was future solvency of the Social Security program, brought on by the massive baby-boom generation approaching retirement age and the much-smaller successive generations being left to pay for it.

TABLE 9.33 SOCIAL WELFARE EXPENDITURES, 1950–1988

Year	Federal		State and Local		Total Expenditures	
	Total (billions $)	Percentage of Total Federal Outlays	Total (billions $)	Percentage of Total State and Local Outlays	Total (billions $)	Percentage of Total GNP
1950	10.5	26.2	13.0	59.2	23.5	8.2
1955	14.6	22.3	18.0	55.3	32.6	8.2
1960	25.0	28.1	27.3	60.1	52.3	10.3
1965	37.6	32.6	39.5	61.7	77.1	11.5
1966	45.2	34.9	42.6	60.0	87.8	11.9
1967	51.2	35.0	46.3	57.8	99.5	12.5
1968	60.2	35.1	53.4	60.0	113.6	13.4
1969	68.1	37.5	58.8	58.8	127.0	13.7
1970	77.1	40.0	68.4	57.9	145.6	14.7
1971	92.3	44.8	78.9	59.3	171.3	16.2
1972	105.9	47.2	84.4	60.4	190.3	16.5
1973	122.2	50.3	91.1	59.3	213.3	16.7
1974	136.7	52.1	101.9	58.1	238.6	16.9
1975	166.8	53.6	122.3	61.6	289.1	19.0
1976	196.5	56.8	134.8	63.2	331.4	19.5
1977	217.6	56.1	142.4	63.2	360.1	18.6
1978	239.0	55.1	154.4	63.2	393.4	18.1
1979	262.9	54.7	166.6	62.1	429.5	17.6
1980	302.4	54.2	189.5	62.9	492.0	18.4
1981	345.6	54.2	207.4	62.3	553.0	18.5
1982	369.2	52.8	230.9	61.1	600.2	19.1
1983	401.1	52.9	247.1	61.0	648.2	19.5
1984	419.8	50.6	256.9	59.9	676.8	18.4
1985	449.3	48.6	282.7	60.2	732.0	18.5
1986	471.2	48.4	311.1	60.7	782.3	18.7
1987	496.2	50.0	337.1	60.0	833.3	18.8
1988	523.1	49.1	362.6	60.1	885.8	18.5

Source: Stanley and Niemi, *Statistics on Politics*, 377.

TABLE 9.34 SOCIAL SECURITY TAXES AND BENEFITS, 1945–1990
(millions $)

Year	Old-Age and Survivors Insurance Trust Fund									
	Total Receipts	Net Contributions (Taxes)	Income from Taxation of Benefits	Payments from the General Fund of the Treasury	Net Interest	Total Expenditures	Benefit Payments	Administrative Expenses	Transfer to Railroad Retirement Account	Balance in Fund at End of Year
1945	1,420	1,285	. . .	. . .	134	304	274	30	. . .	7,121
1946	1,447	1,295	. . .	. . .	152	418	378	40	. . .	8,150
1947	1,722	1,557	. . .	1	164	512	466	46	. . .	9,360
1948	1,969	1,685	. . .	3	281	607	556	51	. . .	10,722
1949	1,816	1,666	. . .	4	146	721	667	54	. . .	11,816
1950	2,928	2,667	. . .	4	257	1,022	961	61	. . .	13,721
1951	3,784	3,363	. . .	4	417	1,966	1,885	81	. . .	15,540
1952	4,184	3,819	. . .	. . .	365	2,282	2,194	88	. . .	17,442
1953	4,359	3,945	. . .	. . .	414	3,094	3,006	88	. . .	18,707
1954	5,610	5,163	. . .	. . .	447	3,741	3,670	92	(21)	20,576
1955	6,167	5,713	. . .	. . .	454	5,079	4,968	119	(7)	21,663
1956	6,697	5,172	. . .	. . .	526	5,841	5,715	132	(5)	22,519
1957	7,381	6,825	. . .	. . .	556	7,507	7,347	162	(2)	22,393
1958	8,117	7,566	. . .	. . .	552	8,646	8,327	194	124	21,864
1959	8,584	8,052	. . .	. . .	532	10,308	9,842	184	282	20,141

Old-Age and Survivors Insurance Trust Fund

Year	Total Receipts	Net Contributions (Taxes)	Income from Taxation of Benefits	Payments from the General Fund of the Treasury	Net Interest	Total Expenditures	Benefit Payments	Administrative Expenses	Transfer to Railroad Retirement Account	Balance in Fund at End of Year
1960	11,382	10,866	. . .	. . .	516	11,198	10,677	203	318	20,324
1961	11,833	11,285	. . .	. . .	548	12,432	11,862	239	332	19,725
1962	12,585	12,059	. . .	. . .	526	13,973	13,356	256	361	18,337
1963	15,063	14,541	. . .	. . .	521	14,920	14,217	281	423	18,480
1964	16,258	15,689	. . .	. . .	569	15,613	14,914	296	403	19,125
1965	16,610	16,017	. . .	. . .	593	17,501	16,737	328	436	18,235
1966	21,302	20,580	. . .	78	644	18,967	18,267	256	444	20,570
1967	24,034	23,138	. . .	78	818	20,382	19,468	406	508	24,222
1968	25,040	23,719	. . .	382	939	23,557	22,643	476	438	25,704
1969	29,554	27,947	. . .	442	1,165	25,176	24,210	474	491	30,082
1970	32,220	30,256	. . .	449	1,515	29,848	28,798	471	579	32,454
1971	35,877	33,723	. . .	488	1,667	34,542	33,414	514	613	33,789
1972	40,050	37,781	. . .	475	1,794	38,522	37,124	674	724	35,318
1973	48,344	45,975	. . .	442	1,928	47,175	45,745	647	783	36,487
1974	54,688	52,081	. . .	447	2,159	53,397	51,623	865	909	37,777
1975	59,605	56,816	. . .	425	2,364	60,395	58,517	896	982	36,987
1976	66,276	63,362	. . .	614	2,301	67,876	65,705	959	1,212	35,388
1977	72,412	69,572	. . .	613	2,227	75,309	73,121	981	1,208	32,491
1978	78,094	75,471	. . .	615	2,008	83,064	80,361	1,115	1,589	27,520
1979	90,274	87,919	. . .	557	1,797	93,133	90,573	1,113	1,448	24,660
1980	105,841	103,456	. . .	540	1,845	107,678	105,083	1,154	1,442	22,823
1981	125,361	122,627	. . .	675	2,060	126,695	123,803	1,307	1,585	21,490
1982	125,198	123,673	. . .	680	845	142,119	138,806	1,519	1,793	22,088
1983	150,584	138,337	. . .	5,541	6,706	152,999	149,221	1,528	2,251	19,672
1984	169,328	164,122	2,835	105	2,266	161,883	157,841	1,638	2,404	27,117
1985	184,239	176,958	3,208	2,203	1,871	171,150	167,248	1,592	2,310	35,842
1986	197,393	190,741	3,424	160	3,069	181,000	176,813	1,601	2,585	39,081
1987	210,736	202,735	3,257	55	4,690	187,668	183,587	1,524	2,557	62,149
1988	240,770	229,775	3,384	43	7,568	200,020	195,454	1,776	2,790	102,899
1989	264,653	250,195	2,439	34	11,985	212,489	207,971	1,673	2,845	155,063
1990	286,653	267,530	4,848	(2,089)	16,363	227,519	222,987	1,563	2,969	214,197

Disability Insurance Trust Fund

Year	Total Receipts	Net Contributions (Taxes)	Income from Taxation of Benefits	Payments from the General Fund of the Treasury	Net Interest	Total Expenditures	Benefit Payments	Administrative Expenses	Transfer to Railroad Retirement Account	Balance in Fund at End of Year
1957	709	702	. . .	. . .	7	59	57	3	. . .	649
1958	991	966	. . .	. . .	25	261	249	12	. . .	1,379
1959	931	891	. . .	. . .	40	485	457	50	(22)	1,825
1960	1,063	1,010	. . .	. . .	53	600	568	36	(5)	2,289
1961	1,104	1,038	. . .	. . .	66	956	887	64	5	2,437
1962	1,114	1,046	. . .	. . .	68	1,183	1,105	66	11	2,368
1963	1,165	1,099	. . .	. . .	66	1,297	1,210	68	20	2,235
1964	1,218	1,154	. . .	. . .	64	1,407	1,309	79	19	2,047
1965	1,247	1,188	. . .	. . .	59	1,687	1,573	90	24	1,606
1966	2,079	2,006	. . .	16	58	1,947	1,784	137	25	1,739
1967	2,379	2,286	. . .	16	78	2,089	1,950	109	31	2,029
1968	3,454	3,316	. . .	32	106	2,458	2,311	127	20	3,025
1969	3,792	3,599	. . .	16	177	2,716	2,557	138	21	4,100
1970	4,774	4,481	. . .	16	277	3,259	3,085	164	10	5,614
1971	5,031	4,620	. . .	50	361	4,000	3,783	205	13	6,645
1972	5,572	5,107	. . .	51	414	4,759	4,502	233	24	7,457
1973	6,443	5,932	. . .	52	458	5,973	5,764	190	20	7,927
1974	7,378	6,826	. . .	52	500	7,196	6,957	217	22	8,109
1975	8,035	7,444	. . .	90	502	8,790	8,505	256	29	7,354
1976	8,757	8,233	. . .	103	422	10,366	10,055	285	26	5,745
1977	9,570	9,138	. . .	128	304	11,945	11,547	399	(1)	3,370
1978	13,810	13,413	. . .	142	256	12,954	12,599	325	30	4,226
1979	15,520	15,114	. . .	118	358	14,186	13,786	371	30	5,630
1980	13,871	13,255	. . .	130	485	15,872	15,515	368	(12)	3,629
1981	17,078	16,738	. . .	168	172	17,658	17,192	436	29	3,049
1982	22,71	21,995	. . .	174	546	17,992	17,376	590	26	2,691
1983	20,680	17,991	. . .	1,121	1,569	18,177	17,524	625	28	5,195
1984	17,304	15,945	190	. . .	1,174	18,546	17,898	626	22	3,959

(continued)

TABLE 9.34 (continued)

Year	Total Receipts	Net Contributions (Taxes)	Income from Taxation of Benefits	Payments from the General Fund of the Treasury	Net Interest	Total Expenditures	Benefit Payments	Administrative Expenses	Transfer to Railroad Retirement Account	Balance in Fund at End of Year
				Disability Insurance Trust Fund						
1985	19,301	17,191	222	1,017	870	19,478	18,827	608	43	6,321
1986	19,439	18,399	238	. . .	803	20,522	19,853	600	68	7,780
1987	20,303	19,691	(36)	. . .	648	21,425	20,519	849	57	6,658
1988	22,699	22,039	61	. . .	600	22,494	21,695	737	61	6,864
1989	24,795	23,993	95	. . .	707	23,753	22,911	754	88	7,905
1990	28,791	28,539	144	(775)	883	25,616	24,829	707	80	11.079

Source: Moody, *Facts and Figures*, 119–20.

TABLE 9.35   SOCIAL SECURITY–COVERED WORKERS AND BENEFICIARIES, 1945–1990, WITH PROJECTIONS TO 2050

Year	Covered Workers[a] (thousands)	Beneficiaries[b]			Covered Workers per OASDI Beneficiary	Beneficiaries per 100 Covered Workers
		OASI	DI	Total		
1945	46,930	1,106	. . .	1,106	41.9	2
1950	48,280	2,930	. . .	2,930	16.5	6
1955	65,200	7,563	. . .	7,563	8.6	12
1960	72,530	13,740	522	14,262	5.1	20
1965	80,680	18,509	1,648	20,157	4.0	25
1970	93,090	22,618	2,568	25,186	3.7	27
1975	100,200	26,998	4,125	31,123	3.2	31
1980	112,212	30,385	4,734	35,119	3.2	31
1985	120,098	32,776	3,874	36,650	3.3	31
1986	122,960	33,349	3,972	37,321	3.3	30
1987	125,548	33,917	4,034	37,952	3.3	30
1988	129,564	34,343	4,077	38,421	3.4	30
1989	131,934	34,754	4,105	38,859	3.4	29
1990	132,824	35,377	4,174	39,551	3.4	30
1995	138,180	37,425	4,515	41,490	3.3	30
2000	143,357	38,962	5,308	44,270	3.2	31
2005	147,487	40,458	6,235	46,693	3.2	32
2010	150,903	43,599	7,143	50,742	3.0	34
2015	151,914	49,248	7,641	56,890	2.7	37
2020	151,456	56,367	7,888	64,254	2.4	42
2025	150,597	63,007	8,269	71,276	2.1	47
2030	150,310	68,126	8,208	76,334	2.0	51
2035	150,766	70,915	8,096	79,011	1.9	52
2040	151,143	71,475	8,141	79,617	1.9	53
2045	151,124	71,700	8,423	80,123	1.9	53
2050	150,729	72,499	8,584	81,083	1.9	54

Note: ". . ." indicates not available; "OASI" indicates Old-Age and Survivors' Insurance; "DI" indicates Disability Insurance.
[a] Workers who pay OASDI taxes at some time during the year.
[b] Beneficiaries with monthly benefits in current-payment status as of June 30.
Source: Stanley and Niemi, *Statistics on Politics*, 384.

CHAPTER 10　Military Forces and Wars: Hot and Cold

The United States and Origins of the Cold War

When the Second World War ended, the United States was astride the world. Alone among all major belligerents, it emerged from the war strengthened both absolutely and proportionately as an economic and military power. Its prewar rivals had either been destroyed (as in the case of Germany and Japan) or substantially weakened—despite being on the winning side—as in the case of Britain and France. One nation, to be sure, presented a paradox, at least at the start of the postwar era. In the process of defending the homeland and carrying the brunt of the war against Nazi Germany, the Soviet Union had constructed the largest army in the world. Because of the massive increase in its military strength and because its European and Asian rivals had experienced such enormous losses, the Soviet Union had undergone a proportionate gain in power during the course of the war. Political maneuvering in the immediate postwar period—in the new United Nations and outside it—left no doubt that if the United States stood supreme in power and influence, the Soviet Union was second and from all indications seemed determined to crawl, claw, or by any means necessary move itself to the top.

Even so, the Soviets ranked second in the postwar period and it was a distant second, save perhaps in the strength of their conventional military forces. If the Soviet Union had gained in some areas during the war, it had lost in others: in sheer loss of people, for example, and in the thousands of villages, towns, and cities destroyed in the gigantic struggle that had taken place on the eastern front. The nation faced a major task of reconstruction. There also was a need for the Soviet government to establish its legitimacy in the conduct of diplomacy, to show that after many years as an outcast it belonged in the family of nations, that the regime of Joseph Stalin and whomever should follow him could be effective in areas other than exercise of military force. Political philosophy—communist ideology—stood as both a useful instrument or a potential detriment in the Soviet quest for power, influence, and allies. In its anti-exploitation, egalitarian emphasis, the communist message in the early postwar years had great appeal worldwide—in impoverished and colonialized areas, of course, but also to intellectuals in the United States and to Americans who were not getting their share.

But the proof, as they say, would be in the pudding: How would Marxism-Leninism, or any version of communism, function beyond its philosophical foundations? How well would communism live up to its rhetorical promises? How well would the philosophy, which focused on distribution, serve the interests of production? Could it be possible that communism, as with any political system, would be utilized to promote the interests of the people who controlled it or the state that served as its sponsor? Answers to these questions, although not necessarily the final answers, would come in the half-century following the Second World War, and they would have great effect on American life and the position of the United States in world affairs.

The United States began the postwar period as the world's richest, most productive, and most powerful nation; 50 years later it was still foremost in each of these categories. By 1990, to be sure, American supremacy was under challenge, subject to qualification in several categories. Military supremacy had to be defined in broad, general terms, taking into account quality, diversity, and technology. Other nations had larger armies, more tanks, and more airplanes. The United States still had the most productive economy, but in several areas the nation did not produce the best goods or the most goods; in some traditional categories it did not produce any goods at all. Absolute power of the United States was at its peak, but its power relative to other nations

had declined. If other nations were gaining fast, the United States still was on top. In the year 1941 publishing magnate Henry Luce had proclaimed that the 20th century was and would be the "American Century." Looking back from near century's end in the 1990s, it was possible to say that Luce was right.

To protect that supremacy and to resist what was deemed serious, even deadly, threats to the nation and the world, the United States engaged in what came to be labeled as the cold war. People who spent much or all of their lives in that period came to think of the cold war as an ongoing phase of world history, something that seemingly would go on forever. By the 1990s it was possible to identify more specific boundaries for the phenomenon. The cold war lasted roughly 45 years—from 1945 to 1990, although it was possible to quibble about a year or so on either side of the equation. The cold war—the term originated in a speech of financier Bernard Baruch in 1947—could be defined as a long period of intense rivalry and hostility originally between the United States and the Soviet Union that constituted conflict in all respects but combat. The magnitude, intensity, and danger in the conflict qualified it to be called a war, but because for a war to be hot—by this definition—it had to involve military engagement, this one was cold. Starting in Europe, it moved to Asia, the Middle East, and over all the globe, affecting nearly everything the United States did in foreign policy. It produced two power blocs in Europe and a complex network of bilateral or multilateral agreements between a bloc leader and many of the world's nations. The cold war led the United States into regional hot engagements in Korea and Vietnam and various other ventures. Although the United States and the Soviet Union never came to blows, the threat of a nuclear holocaust maintained at least a nominal presence throughout the period. The threat intensified on a few occasions, most prominently the Cuban missile crisis of October 1962.

The origins of the cold war would become a subject of intense debate in academic circles in the United States. The late 1960s produced a school of young, leftist-oriented scholars who challenged a prevailing practice of blaming the cold war on the Soviet Union and communism. These individuals, who became known as revisionists, sought to at least distribute blame between the two adversaries, if not place the bulk of responsibility on an aggressive, expansive American capitalist system. The revisionist, or New Left, point of view maintained a substantial presence in American universities through the rest of the cold war. It might have become the dominant point of view in these circles. There is little indication, however, that this perspective had much impact on general American opinion.

American opinion might come to question later aspects of policy, notably in the Vietnam War, but it generally accepted the government's explanation of how the cold war started. Almost immediately after end of the Second World War, the United States and Soviet Union set to quarreling over several issues: control of nuclear energy, procedure within the United Nations, and the status of Germany among them. In the American perspective the events that established the basis for a breach with its wartime ally were developments that took place in eastern Europe. The Soviets had overrun the area during the war with Germany, and after the end of the conflict, the Red army remained. One by one the nations that bordered on the Soviet Union took on communist regimes and accepted—had to accept—a subservient relationship with the Soviet Union that the western world identified as satellites. A process that began with Poland in 1945 extended to a communist coup in Czechoslovakia in 1948; it also included the Soviet zone of occupation in Germany: territory—including the city of Berlin—that later became the state of East Germany.

The United States, then under the administration of President Harry S. Truman (Franklin D. Roosevelt had died in April 1945, at the start of his 13th year in office), responded with profound disapproval of developments in eastern Europe and with a policy designed to protect European nations not under communist domination. Named *containment* by George F. Kennan, a state department official who gave the policy much of its rationale, the approach steered a middle course between doing nothing and confronting the Soviet Union with military force. The objective, as Kennan put it, was to contain "Russian expansive tendencies" wherever they developed in Europe. Containment began with efforts to promote economic health and well-being of western and central European nations not already subject to Soviet influence and a communist regime; perhaps inevitably, the response took military form, with the creation of an alliance system designed to confront a possible threat from the East.

If the Americans considered their action in Europe to be a reaction to Soviet policy, the USSR produced countermeasures to whatever the United States or west Europeans did. And so it continued. By 1949 at the latest, the lines were drawn in Europe; the continent was divided East and West, into a Soviet and American sphere, by a long irregular line stretching from the Balkan countries to the Baltic Sea that Winston Churchill in 1946 had labeled an "iron curtain."

The existence of two power blocs, each with a clearly established leader, on the surface suggested symmetry and perhaps equal measures of virtue (or absence of virtue) on the part of the chief adversaries, both of whom were outsiders. In truth there were vast differences. The Americans were encouraged (by the Europeans) to maintain military presence in Europe after the occupation of Germany ended; the Europeans, at least at the start, were more interested in an alliance than the United States was. Nations in the western sphere maintained their independence, chose their governments, and could leave the alliance at will. The Soviets ruled the eastern sphere that they had created. All regimes had to be communist and to be acceptable to the USSR. No nation could withdraw from the eastern alliance, the Warsaw Pact—a principle that would be confirmed in Hungary in 1956, Czechoslovakia in 1968, and perhaps Poland in the 1980s. Although lines and some policies would soften with the passage of years, the division of Europe continued. For nearly a half-century the status of the continent rested upon two themes that signaled the continued duration of a cold war: (1) the division of Germany into two, seemingly permanent independent states—East and West Germany (and the continued partition of Berlin); (2) continued hypersensitivity of the Soviet Union about the governments of and attitudes within the eastern European states on its periphery. When attitudes on these issues changed, the cold war ended—in Europe and over the world.

Monster of the era: An atomic bomb explodes at Bikini Atoll, July 25, 1946. (National Archives)

Major Aspects of a Containment Policy for Europe

Truman Doctrine, 1947 Economic and military aid for Greeks who were fighting communist forces with aid from the outside and for Turks who faced threats from the Soviet Union, and a sweeping statement of the United States willingness to aid "free peoples."

Marshall Plan, 1948 Massive American economic support for war-ravaged European nations. Presented as a humanitarian program—as in fact it was—but it also had clear political overtones, designed to keep communism out of Western and Central Europe.

Berlin Airlift, 1948 Prompted by Soviet blockade of Berlin, 1948. The United States and allies supplied Berlin by air more than a year, 1948–49. Lines were being drawn in Europe, pressure-points identified.

NATO, 1949 North Atlantic Treaty Organization, an entangling military alliance that committed the United States to the defense of Western Europe and the Europeans to the defense of each other. Although unstated, the structure clearly was directed at the USSR. Twelve original members.

TABLE 10.1 MARSHALL PLAN AID ALLOTMENTS BY COUNTRY, APRIL 3, 1948–DECEMBER 31, 1951

(in millions of dollars)

Recipient Country	Total
Austria	634.8
Belgium-Luxembourg	546.6
Denmark	266.4
France	2,576.8
Germany (Federal Republic)	1,317.3
Greece	614.1
Iceland	26.8
Ireland	146.2
Italy	1,315.4
Netherlands	1,000.7
Norway	241.9
Portugal	50.5
Sweden	118.5
Trieste	33.0
Turkey	176.5
United Kingdom	2,865.8
Yugoslavia	61.5[a]
Prepaid freight account	42.5
European Payments Union—capital fund	350.0
Total	12,385.2

[a] Although Yugoslavia received aid, it was not a member of the Organization for European Economic Cooperation and Development.
Source: Bruce W. Jentleson and Thomas G. Paterson, *Encyclopedia of American Foreign Relations, Vol. III* (New York, 1997), 115.

TABLE 10.2 NATO

Supreme Allied Commanders, NATO	
Dates	Commander
Dec. 1950–Apr. 1952	Dwight D. Eisenhower (U.S.)
Apr. 1952–Jul. 1953	Matthew Ridgway (U.S.)
Jul. 1953–Nov. 1956	Alfred M. Gruenther (U.S.)
Nov. 1956–Jan. 1963	Lauris Norstad (U.S.)
Jan. 1963–Jul. 1969	Lyman L. Lemnitzer (U.S.)
Jul. 1969–Dec. 1974	Andrew J. Goodpaster (U.S.)
Dec. 1974–Jun. 1979	Alexander Haig (U.S.)
Jun. 1979–1987	Benard Rogers (U.S.)
Jun. 1987–	John R. Galvin (U.S.)

Members of NATO
Belgium
Canada
Denmark
France (withdrew from military committee in 1966 while remaining member of council)
W. Germany (1955)
Greece (joined 1952, withdrew from military structure after Turkish invasion of Cyprus in 1974, rejoined 1980)
Iceland
Italy
Luxembourg
Netherlands
Norway
Portugal
Spain (joined 1982)
Turkey (joined 195
United Kingdom
United States

Source: Chris Cook, *The Facts on File World Political Almanac* (New York, 1992), 20.

TABLE 10.3 NATO ARMED FORCES, TOTAL MILITARY PERSONNEL, 1981–1990

(figures are in thousands)

	1981	1982	1983	1984	1985	1986	1987	1988	1989	1990
North America										
Canada	81	82	81	82	83	85	86	88	88	87
U.S.A.	2,168	2,201	2,222	2,222	2,244	2,269	2,279	2,246	2,241	2,189
Europe										
Belgium	109	110	109	107	107	107	109	110	110	108
Denmark	33	30	30	31	29	28	28	30	31	30
France	575	577	578	571	563	558	559	558	554	550
FR Germany	493	490	496	487	493	495	495	495	503	503
Greece	187	188	177	197	201	202	199	199	201	203
Italy	505	517	498	508	531	529	531	533	533	520
Luxembourg	1	1	1	1	1	1	1	1	1	1
Netherlands	108	106	104	103	103	106	106	107	106	104
Norway	39	41	41	39	36	38	38	40	43	51
Portugal	88	89	93	100	102	101	105	104	104	95
Spain	366	372	355	342	314	314	314	304	277	295
Turkey	741	769	824	815	814	860	879	847	780	827
U.K.	341	334	333	336	334	331	328	324	318	313
European NATO total	**3,586**	**3,624**	**3,639**	**3,638**	**3,630**	**3,669**	**3,693**	**3,651**	**3,560**	**3,603**
NATO total	**5,835**	**5,607**	**5,942**	**5,942**	**5,957**	**6,023**	**6,058**	**5,985**	**5,888**	**5,876**

Source: Stockholm International Peace Research Institute, *SIPRI Yearbook, 1991: World Armaments and Disarmament* (New York, 1991), 134.

TABLE 10.4   MAKERS OF AMERICAN FOREIGN RELATIONS, 1945–1990

Presidents	Secretaries of State	Chairs of the Senate Foreign Relations Committee	Secretaries of Defense	Assistants to the President for National Security Affairs
Harry S. Truman (1945–1953)	Edward R. Stettinius, Jr. (1945) James F. Byrnes (1945–1947) George C. Marshall (1947–1949) Dean G. Acheson (1949–1953)	Tom Connally (1945–1947) Arthur H. Vandenberg (1947–1949) Tom Connally (1949–1953)	James V. Forrestal (1947–1949) Louis A. Johnson (1949–1950) George C. Marshall (1950–1951) Robert A. Lovett (1951–1953)	
Dwight D. Eisenhower (1953–1961)	John F. Dulles (1953–1959) Christian A. Herter (1959–1961)	Alexander Wiley (1953–1955) Walter F. George (1955–1957) Theodore F. Green (1957–1959) J. William Fulbright (1959–1963)	Charles E. Wilson (1953–1957) Neil H. McElroy (1957–1959) Thomas S. Gates, Jr. (1959–1961)	Robert Cutler (1953–1955 & 1957–1958) Dillon Anderson (1955–1956) William H. Jackson (1956) Gordon Gray (1958–1961)
John F. Kennedy (1961–1963)	Dean Rusk (1961–1963)	J. William Fulbright (1961–1963)	Robert S. McNamara (1961–1963)	McGeorge Bundy (1961–1963)
Lyndon B. Johnson (1963–1969)	Dean Rusk (1963–1969)	J. William Fulbright (1963–1969)	Robert S. McNamara (1963–1968) Clark M. Clifford (1968–1969)	McGeorge Bundy (1963–1966) Walt W. Rostow (1966–1969)
Richard M. Nixon (1969–1974)	William P. Rogers (1969–1973) Henry A. Kissinger (1973–1974)	J. William Fulbright (1969–1974)	Melvin R. Laird (1969–1973) Elliot L. Richardson (1973) James R. Schlesinger (1973–1974)	Henry A. Kissinger (1969–1974)
Gerald R. Ford (1974–1977)	Henry A. Kissinger (1974–1977)	J. William Fulbright (1974–1975) John Sparkman (1975–1977)	James R. Schlesinger (1974–1976) Donald Rumsfeld (1976–1977)	Henry A. Kissinger (1974–1975) Brent Scowcroft (1975–1977)
James E. Carter (1977–1981)	Cyrus R. Vance (1977–1980) Edmund Muskie (1980–1981)	John Sparkman (1977–1979) Frank Church (1979–1981)	Harold Brown (1977–1981)	Zbigniew Brzezinski (1977–1981)
Ronald W. Reagan (1981–1989)	Alexander M. Haig, Jr. (1981–1982) George P. Shultz (1982–1989)	Charles Percy (1981–1985) Richard G. Lugar (1985–1987) Claiborne Pell (1987–1989)	Casper Weinberger (1981–1987) Frank C. Carlucci (1987–1989)	Richard Allen (1981) William P. Clark, Jr. (1981–1983) Robert C. McFarlane (1983–1985) John M. Poindexter (1985–1986) Frank C. Carlucci (1986–1987) Colin L. Powell (1987–1989)
George H. W. Bush (1989–1993)	James A. Baker III (1989–1992)	Claiborne Pell (1989–1995)	Richard B. Cheney (1989–1993)	Brent Scowcroft (1989–1993)

Source: Thomas G. Paterson, J. Garry Clifford, Kenneth J. Hagan, *American Foreign Relations, A History, Since 1985* (Boston, 2000), 515–16.

TABLE 10.5   AMBASSADORS TO UN, DATES, AND ADMINISTRATION, 1945–1990

Ambassador to UN	Dates	Administration
Edward R. Stettinius, Jr.	1945–1946	Truman
Warren R. Austin	1947–1953	Truman
Henry Cabot Lodge, Jr.	1953–1960	Eisenhower
James J. Wadsworth	1960–1961	Eisenhower
Adlai E. Stevenson	1961–1965	Kennedy L. B. Johnson
Arthur J. Goldberg	1965–1968	L. B. Johnson
George W. Ball	1968	L. B. Johnson
James Russell Wiggins	1968–1969	L. B. Johnson
Charles W. Yost	1969–1971	Nixon
George Bush	1971–1973	Nixon
John A. Scali	1973–1975	Nixon Ford

Ambassador to UN	Dates	Administration
Daniel P. Moynihan	1975–1976	Ford
William W. Scranton	1976–1977	Ford
Andrew J. Young	1977–1979	Carter
Donald F. McHenry	1979–1981	Carter
Jeane J. Kirkpatrick	1981–1985	Reagan
Vernon A. Walters	1985–1989	Reagan Bush
Thomas R. Pickering	1989–1992	Bush

Source: Stephen A. Flanders and Carl N. Flanders, *Dictionary of American Foreign Affairs* (New York, 1993), 782.

TABLE 10.6 DIRECTOR OF CENTRAL INTELLIGENCE, 1946–1990

Director of Central Intelligence	Dates	Administration
Sidney W. Souers	1946	Truman
Hoyt S. Vandenberg	1946–1947	Truman
Roscoe H. Hillenkoetter	1947–1950	Truman
Walter Bedell Smith	1950–1953	Truman
		Eisenhower
Allen W. Dulles	1953–1961	Eisenhower
		Kennedy
John A. McCone	1961–1965	Kennedy
		L. B. Johnson
William F. Raborn, Jr.	1965–1966	L. B. Johnson
Richard M. Helms	1966–1973	L.B. Johnson
		Nixon
James R. Schlesinger	1973	Nixon
William E. Colby	1973–1976	Nixon
George H. W. Bush	1976–1977	Ford
Stansfield Turner	1977–1981	Carter
William J. Casey	1981–1987	Reagan
William H. Webster	1987–1991	Reagan
		Bush

Source: Flanders & Flanders, *Dictionary of Foreign Affairs*, 733.

TABLE 10.7 CHAIRMAN OF THE JOINT CHIEFS OF STAFF, 1946–1990

Date	Chairman	Administration
Jul. 1942–Mar. 1949	Fleet Adm. William D. Leahy, USN	Truman
Aug. 1949–Aug. 1953	Gen. of the Army Omar N. Bradley, USA	
		Truman/Eisenhower
Aug. 1953–Aug. 1957	Adm. Arthur W. Radford, USN	Eisenhower
Aug. 1957–Sep. 1960	Gen. Nathan F. Twining, USAF	Eisenhower
Oct. 1960–Sep. 1962	Gen. Lyman L. Lemnitzer, USA	Eisenhower/Kennedy
Oct. 1962–Jul. 1964	Gen. Maxwell D. Taylor, USA	Kennedy/Johnson
Jul. 1964–Jul. 1970	Gen. Earle G. Wheeler, USA	Johnson/Nixon
Jul. 1970–Jun. 1974	Adm. Thomas H. Moorer, USN	Nixon
Jul. 1974–Jun. 1978	Gen. George S. Brown, USAF	Ford/Carter
Jun. 1978–Jun. 1982	Gen. David C. Jones, USAF	Carter/Reagan
Jun. 1982–Sep. 1985	Gen. John W. Vessey, Jr., USA	Reagan
Oct. 1985–Sep. 1989	Adm. William J. Crowe, Jr., USN	Reagan/Bush
Oct. 1989–Oct. 1993	Gen. Colin L. Powell, USA	Bush/Clinton

Source: Polmar, *Cold War at Sea*, xvi.

The Cold War Moves East: China and Korea

The Chinese Civil War of 1946–49 was an extension of a conflict that went back to the 1920s. It had appeared that the Nationalists, the Guomindang (Kuomintang) under Jiang Jieshi (Chiang Kai-shek), had defeated the enemy, the Communists, eventually led by Mao Zedong, when the Second World War—the eight-year conflict between China and Japan—had interceded. A fraternal wartime truce, the "United Front," between the two Chinese adversaries was a patriotic pretense that fooled no one, but the war did relieve Nationalist pressure against the Communists and gave Mao's forces time to organize and recruit new followers. Equipped with a remarkably appealing program of agricultural reform, they made the most of it. By 1945 the Communists had raised a peasant army of considerable size and outstanding dedication. Not surprisingly, and despite American efforts to prevent it from happening, the end to the war against Japan led to the last phase of the Civil War between Nationalists and Communists.

Outward appearances at the start of the Chinese Civil War would seem to support two propositions: (1) Based on the size of its army, superiority of its weapons and its international connections, the Nationalist side—then the recognized government of China—should have won and perhaps with some dispatch; (2) based on ideological trappings of the adversaries, the United States should experience neither hesitation nor timidity in its support of the forces of Jiang. In this early stage of the cold war, Mao's forces after all were communists; the Nationalists were intensely anticommunist and pro-Western, with close American connections and at least claims to strong Christian influence in the highest rungs of leadership.

Appearances, as it turned out, were only appearances and a good distance from truth. Rarely paid, with corrupt and incompetent leadership, low morale, and nothing to fight for, the Nationalist army was largely a shell; the soldiers often surrendered in large bodies, taking their weapons with them. Marked with hope and other characteristics

TABLE 10.8 PUBLIC OPINION ON U.S. INVOLVEMENT IN WORLD AFFAIRS, 1945–1990

(percent)

Date	Active Part	Stay Out	No Opinion
Oct. 1945	70	19	11
Sep. 1947	65	26	9
Sep. 1949	67	25	8
Nov. 1950	64	25	11
Dec. 1950	66	25	9
Oct. 1952	68	23	9
Feb. 1953	73	22	5
Sep. 1953	71	21	8
Apr. 1954	69	25	6
Mar. 1955	72	21	7
Nov. 1956	71	25	4
Jun. 1965	79	16	5
Mar. 1973	66	31	3
Mar. 1975	61	36	4
Mar. 1976	63	32	5
Mar. 1978	64	32	4
Dec. 1978	59	29	12
Mar. 1982	61	34	5
Nov. 1982	53	35	12
Mar. 1983	65	31	4
Mar. 1984	65	29	6
Mar. 1985	70	27	2
Mar. 1986	65	32	4
Mar. 1988	65	32	4
Mar. 1989	68	28	4
Mar. 1990	69	27	4

Note: Question: "Do you think it would be best for the future of this country if we take an active part in world affairs or if we stay out of world affairs?"
Source: From various surveys, reported in Stanley and Niemi, *Statistics on Politics*, 342.

that often seemed to be the reverse of the Nationalists, the Communists started to win the war almost from the beginning. The truth about proposition one opened up an explanation about fallacies of proposition two. The United States had had trouble with Jiang for some time, especially during the Second World War. Constantly demanding money and equipment, he had exhibited little inclination to fight the Japanese. He was waiting for the next war, the real war, with the Communists. Corruption was rampant. It was said that Jiang loved power, not money, but plenty of people in his family and the Kuomindang regime used their position for personal enrichment. Although Mao held no illusions about what the future would bring, his forces at times had given the Japanese a great deal of difficulty. The Communists approached a new conflict with the Nationalists with confidence and momentum.

Even so, all American aid to China during 1942–45 had gone to Jiang and when the Civil War started, American assistance for the regime—formally called the Republic of China—was resumed, albeit with steadily diminishing enthusiasm. Although President Truman at one point remarked that sending money to China was like pouring it "down a rat hole," support for the Nationalists continued until the war came to a halt. The end came in 1949 when Communist forces overran the bulk of the provinces, occupied Beijing, and made it possible for Mao to proclaim on October 1, 1949, existence of the People's

Republic of China (PRC). The remainder of Nationalist forces and of the Nationalist cause fled the mainland some 100 miles across the strait to Taiwan, an island that the West then called Formosa. There the Kuomindang installed itself as the Republic of China.

It would appear that Truman and his secretary of state, Dean Acheson, were fed up with Chiang. In a report, really a large book called the China "White paper," Acheson blamed the outcome of the civil war on the Nationalists. Truman reported that his administration might supply some economic assistance for Taiwan, but there would be no military support, even if the Communists invaded. There were hints that the United States might consider granting diplomatic recognition of the PRC. Acheson recommended waiting "until the dust has settled."

As it developed, other events would intervene to make recognition out of the question and to harden substantially the U.S. position on Asia. Americans learned that in February 1950 Mao Zedong had been to Moscow, and after extensive discussion with Joseph Stalin had signed several treaties, one of which was a military alliance that came to be known as the Sino-Soviet pact. In popular American perception, Mao—in making a pact with the "devil"—had delivered himself into the hands of the world communist leader. Carried one step further, it was possible to argue that the arrangement probably had existed for some time and that the Chinese civil war had not been a social revolution after all, but an expression of Soviet imperialism.

F-80 "Shooting Star," one of the United States's first jet fighter planes, on a mission in the Korean War (National Archives)

TABLE 10.9 MILITARY CONTRIBUTIONS TO THE UNITED NATIONS COMMAND IN THE KOREAN WAR

Country	Ground Forces (Personnel)		
	Jun. 30, 1951	Jun. 30, 1952	Jul. 31, 1953
United States	253,250	265,864	302,483
Republic of Korea	273,266	376,418	590,911
Australia	912	1,844	2,282
Belgium	602	623	944
Canada	5,403	5,155	6,146
Colombia	1,050	1,007	1,068
Ethiopia	1,153	1,094	1,271
France	738	1,185	1,119
Greece	1,027	899	1,263
India[a]	333	276	70
Italy[a]	0	64	72
Netherlands	725	565	819
New Zealand	797	1,111	1,389
Norway[a]	79	109	105
Philippines	1,143	1,494	1,496
Sweden[a]	162	148	154
Thailand	1,057	2,274	1,294
Turkey	4,602	4,878	5,455
United Kingdom	8,278	13,043	14,198
Total	554,577	678,051	932,539

Country	Air Forces (Squadrons)		
	Jun. 30, 1951	Jun. 30, 1952	Jul. 31, 1953
United States	58	67	66
Australia	1	1	1
Canada	1	1	1
South Africa	1	1	1
Total	61	70	69

	Naval Forces (Ships)		
	Jun. 30, 1951	Jun. 30, 1952	Jul. 31, 1953
United States	186	195	261
Republic of Korea	34	67	76
		Jan. 15, 1952	Oct. 15, 1952
Australia		4	4
Canada		3	3
Colombia		1	1
Denmark		1	1
Netherlands		1	1
New Zealand		2	2
Thailand		2	2
United Kingdom		22	22

[a] Contributed noncombat medical units only.
Source: James I. Matray, *Historical Dictionary of the Korean War* (Westport, Conn., 1991), 552.

President-elect Eisenhower confers with commanders in the Korean War: (left to right) British Gen. Alston-Roberts West, Gen. James Van Fleet, and commanding Gen. Mark W. Clark. (Courtesy Dwight D. Eisenhower Library)

TABLE 10.10   BATTLE CASUALTIES OF KOREAN WAR

Korean and Chinese				
	Killed	Wounded	Missing/POW	Total
South Korea[a]	47,000	183,000	8,656	238,656
North Korea[b]	. . .	. . .	110,723	630,723
China[c]	. . .	. . .	21,374	381,374

United States					
	Total	Army	Navy	USMC	Air Force
Total Casualties	142,091	109,958	2,087	28,205	1,841
Deaths	33,629	27,704	458	4,267	1,200
Killed in Action	23,300	19,334	279	3,308	379
Wounded in Action	105,785	79,526	1,599	24,281	379
Died	2,501	1,930	23	537	11
Other	103,284	77,596	1,576	23,744	368
Missing in Action	5,866	4,442	174	391	859
Died	5,127	3,778	152	391	806
Returned	715	664	13	0	38
Captured or interned	7,140	6,656	35	225	224
Died	2,701	2,662	4	31	4
Returned	4,418	3,973	31	194	220
Refused repatriation	21	21	0	0	0

United Nations (other than United States)				
	Killed	Wounded	Missing/POW	Total
Australia	261	1,034	37	1,332
Britain	686	2,498	1,102	4,286
Canada	294	1,202	47	1,543
New Zealand	22	79	1	102
Others	1,931	6,484	1,582	9,997
Total	3,194	11,297	2,769	17,260

[a] There were approximately 1 million South Korean civilian casualties.
[b] The figure for total casualties includes estimates of dead and wounded. There also were approximately 1 million North Korean civilian casualties.
[c] Chinese casualties remain something of a mystery. Other sources estimate casualties at 900,000 or more.
Source: Matray, *Dictionary of the Korean War*, 553.

Then, in June 1950, came the Korean War. The conflict in Korea had grown out of a seemingly innocent Soviet-American agreement in 1945 to accept jointly surrender of Japanese forces in Korea in two areas divided north and south by the 38th parallel. Internal Korean divisions and emergence of Soviet-American hostility caused the two units to evolve into separate political entities: to the North a communist area, led by Kim Il-Sung, under Soviet influence; to the South a noncommunist regime, led by President Syngman Rhee, influenced by the Americans. All Koreans wanted unification, each Korean regime insisted it must lead the entire state. The better-armed and more aggressive of the two forced the issue. With the approval but no guarantee of protection from Stalin, North Korean units crossed the 38th parallel on June 25 and within a few days appeared to be in the process of overrunning the entire Korean Peninsula.

To the surprise of many people, probably including Kim and Stalin, Truman decided the time to act had come. Although he offered several reasons for intervention in the Korean War—the need to nip aggression in the bud, for example, and to enable an infant UN to survive a first major test (one should remember that the Korean War began only five years after the Second World War)—Truman clearly placed the issue of Korea in the broader context of Asian and international events. Influenced by conditions in Eastern Europe no less than what had happened in China, concerned that a communist onslaught would envelope all Asia, he committed U.S. forces—first in the form of air support and then ground troops hastily assembled in Japan. Officially the Korean War was a project of the United Nations, and 18 nations provided some form of support for South Korea, but the ground forces were mostly American or South Korean, nearly all the equipment came from the United States, and the Americans made all the decisions.

A conventional war, with forces facing each other in the field, the Korean conflict became a seesaw affair. The threat of North Korean conquest of the South brought in the Americans (and officially the UN); the threat of American and South Korean conquest of the North (which brought them to the border of Manchuria), brought in the Chinese. By the end of the first year, the war had become a stalemate,

with one side—China and North Korea—unable to win and the other—the Americans—unwilling to make a total commitment to an area that was important but not absolutely vital to national interest and security. The war was bloody and after the first year settled into a depressing slugging match, with little gain for what was being expended, somewhat on the order of the First World War. Americans became anxious to see it over, and the war probably represented the most important reason Dwight Eisenhower was elected president in 1952, while the war was still going on. Eisenhower had promised to end the war.

Armistice negotiations began in 1951, a year after the war started; they would last, with frequent interruptions, for two years. The primary issue was prisoner repatriation: Should all prisoners be forced to return to their original side, even if they did not want to? The issue bore most heavily on several thousand North Korean and Chinese captives, many of whom did not wish to return. Dumbfounded that 21 Americans also refused repatriation, Americans found an explanation in relentless efforts at mind control—brainwashing, as they called it—a fitting expression of the communist system. The armistice of July 1953 acknowledged that the conflict had been a draw. The Korean War would be defended in years to come as a successful application of containment, but many Americans would have trouble understanding what they had gained for the effort.

Consequences of Korea

The concept of monolithic communism in Asia rested on a premise that all communist movements were allied and all were traceable to a central headquarters in the Soviet Union. It followed that every communist movement, whatever the location, existed to serve the interests of the USSR. This attitude in considerable measure grew out of experiences gathered from events in Eastern Europe, where communism was monolithic and the will of the Soviet Union prevailed, and applying them to East Asia where conditions differed. The situation varied from place to place, but a major force in Asia was not the power of the Soviet army but of nationalist, anticolonial movements, some of which had connections to the Soviet Union, the Chinese Communists, or both.

None, however, were under control of the Russian bear. In its determination to resist communism in certain situations, the United States found itself opposing legitimate aspirations of various indigenous peoples. Curiously, the country that fit this model least effectively was Korea, where Soviet influence, if poorly defined in 1950, was unmistakable and had been since the end of the Second World War. The start of the Korean War was a major force behind large steps the United States would take in Asian policy.

Aspects of Asian Policy in 1950 and After

Korea   The United States fights a costly three-year war to preserve the independence of South Korea, after which it signs a security pact that commits the United States to defense of South Korea indefinitely. Some 35,000–40,000 American troops remain in the country to at least the end of the century.

China   Americans fight Chinese troops in Korea, and a long period of hostility follows that conflict. The United States keeps the People's Republic of China out of the UN for two decades and refuses recognition for three decades. Policy did not start to change until the 1970s.

Taiwan   On outbreak of the Korean War, Truman reverses an earlier position that the United States will not protect Taiwan. In 1950 the U.S. 7th fleet moves into the Straits of Taiwan to prevent a Chinese invasion. The United States signs a security pact in 1954 that will be in force until 1979.

Japan   The Chinese revolution and the Korean War speeds up an American decision to end the occupation of this conquered enemy and to begin to treat Japan as an ally. A formal peace treaty (ending the occupation) is signed in 1951, a security pact in 1952. The United States protects Japan; Japan permits U.S. bases on its soil. The two remain close allies throughout the century.

Indochina   The Korean War helps to induce the United States in 1950 to supply money and equipment to France, which also was fighting Asian Communists—in its colony of French Indochina. On defeat of the French in 1954, the United States moves in, en route to its fateful Vietnam War.

Southeastern Asia   In step with a broad policy of containing China in Asia, the United States signs in 1954 a multilateral security pact called SEATO—the Southeast Asia Treaty Organization.

A turning point: President Richard Nixon meets leader of the People's Republic of China, Mao Zedong, in February 1972. (National Archives)

Presidential Doctrines and American Foreign Policy

A curious feature of American foreign policy during the cold war was the propensity of presidents to proclaim policies that by one means or another became known as presidential doctrines. The practice of course had its origin in 1823 with James Monroe. Americans would come to think of the Monroe Doctrine as virtually holy writ, but between the years 1823 and 1946 no other president had introduced a doctrine that bore his name, or perhaps better put, no one—such as a news reporter—had seen fit to attach the president's name to a significant statement of policy. There had been, for example, no Wilson Doctrine about submarine warfare or the First World War in general, although Wilson certainly made important statements. During the cold war it was different. Between 1947 and the late 1980s, only John F. Kennedy and Gerald Ford—both of whom had very brief presidencies—failed to issue a major principle of foreign policy that bore their name. Although there appears to have been no plan of continuity, of linking the statements together, the presidential doctrines—with possible exception of the one associated with Richard Nixon—carried much sameness in description of problem and of the proposed response.

Presidential Doctrines

The Truman Doctrine (1947) In the early stages of the cold war, President Harry S. Truman announces his intention to assist "free peoples" threatened by armed minorities on the inside or by outside forces—in either case probably communist. One of the first steps in an emerging policy of containment, the statement prefaced economic and military aid to Greece and Turkey in March 1947.

The Eisenhower Doctrine (1957) Having proclaimed communism to be the primary threat to the Middle East in the wake of the Suez Crisis of 1956, President Dwight Eisenhower announces American intent to assist any Middle Eastern nation threatened by "international communism" to the point of using military force. The nation so threatened will have to request assistance.

The Johnson Doctrine (1965) Faced with a civil war in the Dominican Republic that President Lyndon Johnson claimed is being driven by communists, Johnson dispatches 20,000 troops to the island and proclaims that American nations "cannot, must not, and will not" permit another communist regime in the Western Hemisphere.

The Nixon Doctrine (1969) Responding to growing U.S. disenchantment with globalism and especially with the devastating entanglement in Vietnam, Richard Nixon in effect promises retrenchment. Henceforth the United States will support threatened nations with money and equipment, but troops will have to come from somewhere else.

The Carter Doctrine (1980) Inspired by the Soviet invasion of Afghanistan, the hostage crisis with Iran, and a need to toughen his image as an international leader, Jimmy Carter states that the area of the Persian Gulf (which contained huge oil reserves) is vital to American interests and that the United States will respond to any "outside force" that seek to control the region.

The Reagan Doctrine (1985) Influenced by local resistance to Soviet action in Afghanistan and internal conflict in several other places, Ronald Reagan proclaims that the United States had a right and a duty to support "freedom fighters" against Soviet or Soviet-assisted regimes wherever they exist.

Instruments of American Policy: The Armed Forces

The primary factor affecting U.S. armed forces after 1945 was the state of world affairs. Because the world remained unsettled, marked with change, revolution, nearly 50 years of rivalry with the Soviet Union, periods of armed conflict, and a standing threat of a major war, the United States committed itself to a large military force, equipped with the most modern weaponry and prepared to deal with a wide range of possible situations. The military establishment did not make a smooth transition from the Second World War to the challenges of the postwar era. Yielding to pressure to "bring the boys home," and apparently anticipating that an end to the war would bring a long period of peace, the government released 9 million service personnel in one year. By the time the Korean War started in 1950, military forces had dropped below 1.5 million, with an army of scarcely a half-million. The Korean War provoked a rapid increase in numbers, and for the rest of the cold war, military forces stood at between approximately 3.5 million and 2 million, with largest numbers coming, of course, during the wars in Korea and Vietnam. If these numbers suggest a careful and continuous concern about the security of the United States and a determination to meet any military challenge that might appear, they stand in striking contrast to the 12 million men in arms in the final years of the Second World War. While the government prosecuted a long and potentially deadly cold war with the Soviet Union and responded to numerous pressure points that emerged in world affairs, the nation and the people went about their business.

A second factor affecting U.S. military forces during the cold war was technology. Technology would do much to determine the number of troops (as a rule, the better the technology, the fewer the forces needed), the type of troops, and the distribution of personnel between the military branches. In the American Civil War nearly all the forces had been in the army; in the First World War approximately 80 percent of personnel served in ground forces; in the Second World War the army made up two-thirds of all personnel, although it must be added that a rapidly growing air force was classified as a part of the army. Even though the army remained "labor intensive" and many situations developed that called for traditional ground action, the demand for other forms of military readiness grew more rapidly. The army's share of military personnel hovered around 40 percent during much of the cold war, and in the 1980s the percentage dropped into the 30s. The proportionate increase in the size of the navy and the air force (which became a separate department in 1947) was to considerable extent an expression of increased reliance on technology.

The armed forces was a product of (and a part of) the national government, and it experienced most of the pressures that came to bear on the government. Such issues as size of the military, its personnel, its use, and especially its cost all had to be resolved in a political setting. The rationale behind raising troops through a draft was that it tapped into a huge reservoir of human resources and represented an extension of a tested system that supplied a measure of fairness and impartiality to a service that most people regarded as unpleasant and undesirable. Nonetheless, politics, influence, and power inevitably entered the conscription process and the pressures increased in proportion to the increase in danger in military service. Deferments, exceptions, other pressures and manipulations produced military forces with markings of race and class. President Truman had ordered an end to segregation in the armed forces in 1948, and the pace of desegregation accelerated during the Korean War. Nonetheless, charges of racial discrimination did not vanish and became more pronounced in the area of casualties during the Vietnam War. Lower-class men and lower-income men were more likely to serve than people in higher economic echelons. Young men from well-placed families seemed to find a way to avoid going to Vietnam. Distinction based on gender was widespread, taken for granted, and broadly accepted. Beginning in the late 1960s, however, the issue began to receive increased attention.

The final two decades of the cold war—1970–90—brought several changes to constituency of the armed forces. Public pressure and politics brought the draft to an end. Thereafter the branches, especially the army, at times would have trouble keeping its ranks filled. Most of the

TABLE 10.11 MILITARY FORCES OF THE UNITED STATES, 1945–1990

(In thousands, as of end of fiscal year. Includes National Guard, Reserve, and retired regular personnel on extended or continuous active duty; excludes Coast Guard)

Year	Total	Army Total	Army Officers	Army Enlisted	Navy Total	Navy Officers	Navy Enlisted	Marine Corps Total	Marine Corps Officers	Marine Corps Enlisted	Air Force Total	Air Force Officers	Air Force Enlisted
1945	12,123	8,267	891	7,376	3,380	331	3,049	475	37	437	a	a	a
1946	3,030	1,891	267	1,623	983	141	842	155	14	142	a	a	a
1948	1,445	554	68	485	419	45	373	84	6	78	387	49	338
1950	1,459	593	73	519	381	45	333	74	7	67	411	57	354
1952	3,635	1,596	148	1,447	824	82	742	231	16	215	983	128	854
1955	2,935	1,109	122	986	661	75	583	205	18	187	960	137	823
1960	2,475	873	101	770	617	70	545	171	16	154	815	130	683
1961	2,483	859	100	757	626	70	552	177	16	161	821	129	690
1962	2,806	1,066	116	949	664	75	585	191	17	174	884	135	746
1963	2,699	976	108	866	664	76	584	190	17	173	869	134	733
1964	2,686	973	111	861	666	76	585	190	17	173	857	133	721
1965	2,654	969	112	855	670	78	588	190	17	173	825	132	690
1966	3,092	1,200	118	1,080	743	80	659	262	21	241	887	131	753
1967	3,375	1,442	144	1,297	750	82	664	285	24	262	897	135	759
1968	3,546	1,570	166	1,402	764	85	674	307	25	283	905	140	762
1969	3,458	1,512	173	1,337	774	85	684	310	26	284	862	135	723
1970	3,065	1,323	167	1,153	691	81	606	260	25	235	791	130	657
1971	2,713	1,124	149	972	622	75	542	212	22	191	755	126	625
1972	2,322	811	121	687	587	73	511	198	20	178	726	122	600
1973	2,252	801	116	682	564	71	490	196	19	177	691	115	572
1974	2,162	783	106	674	546	67	475	189	19	170	644	110	529
1975	2,128	784	103	678	535	66	466	196	19	177	613	105	503
1976	2,082	779	99	678	525	64	458	192	19	174	585	100	481
1977	2,075	782	98	680	530	63	462	192	19	173	571	96	470
1978	2,062	772	98	670	530	63	463	191	18	172	570	95	470
1979	2,027	759	97	657	523	62	457	185	18	167	559	96	459
1980	2,051	777	99	674	527	63	460	188	18	170	558	98	456
1981	2,083	781	102	675	540	65	470	191	18	172	570	99	467
1982	2,109	780	103	673	553	67	481	192	19	173	583	102	476
1983	2,123	780	106	669	558	68	485	194	20	174	592	105	483
1984	2,138	780	108	668	565	69	491	196	20	176	597	106	486
1985	2,151	781	110	667	571	71	495	198	20	178	602	108	489
1986	2,169	781	110	667	581	72	504	199	20	179	608	109	495
1987	2,174	781	108	668	587	72	510	200	20	179	607	107	495
1988	2,138	772	107	660	593	72	516	197	20	177	576	105	467
1989	2,130	770	107	658	593	72	516	197	20	177	571	104	463
1990	2,044	732	104	624	579	72	503	197	20	177	535	100	431

a Included with army until 1948.

Source: Ben J. Wattenberg, *The Statistical History of the United States: From Colonial Times to the Present* (New York, 1976), 1141; Bureau of Census, *Statistical Abstract, 1992*, 343.

TABLE 10.12 MILITARY PERSONNEL ON ACTIVE DUTY, BY LOCATION, 1970–1990

(in thousands, 1970 and 1975, as of Dec. 31; thereafter, as of end of fiscal year)

Item	1970	1975	1980	1984	1985	1986	1987	1988	1989	1990
Total	3,066	2,128	2,051	2,138	2,151	2,169	2,174	2,138	2,130	2,044
Shore-based a	2,798	1,912	1,840	1,908	1,920	1,929	1,928	1,891	1,884	1,794
Afloat b	268	216	211	230	231	240	246	248	246	252
United States c	2,033	1,643	1,562	1,628	1,636	1,644	1,650	1,598	1,620	1,437
Foreign countries	1,033	485	488	510	516	526	524	541	510	609

a Includes navy personnel temporarily on shore.
b Includes marine corps.
c Includes outlying areas.

Source: Bureau of Census, *Statistical Abstract, 1992*, 343.

TABLE 10.13 NATIONAL DEFENSE OUTLAYS AND VETERANS BENEFITS, 1945–1990

(for fiscal year ending in year shown; includes outlays of Department of Defense, Department of Veterans Affairs, and other agencies for activities primarily related to national defense and veterans programs; minus sign (−) indicates decline.)

| Year | National Defense and Veterans Outlays | | | | Annual Percent Change | | | | Defense Outlays Percent of — | |
| | Total Outlays (billions $) | Defense Outlays | | Veterans Outlays (billions $) | Total Outlays | Defense Outlays | | Veterans Outlays | Federal Outlays | Gross National Product |
		Current Dollars (billions $)	Constant (1982) Dollars (billions $)			Current Dollars	Constant (1982) Dollars			
1945	82.7	81.6	. . .	.55	. . .	. . .	. . .	. . .	89.5	39.1
1950	21.2	12.2	. . .	8.8	. . .	. . .	. . .	. . .	32.2	5.1
1955	44.5	39.8	. . .	4.7	. . .	. . .	. . .	. . .	62.4	11.1
1960	53.5	48.1	192.1	5.4	2.5	2.4	−1.9	3.1	52.2	9.5
1962	58.0	52.3	202.2	5.6	4.0	4.3	2.6	1.7	49.0	9.4
1963	58.9	53.4	197.1	5.5	1.6	2.0	−2.5	−1.9	48.0	9.1
1964	60.4	54.8	198.8	5.7	2.6	2.5	0.9	2.9	46.2	8.7
1965	56.3	50.6	181.4	5.7	−6.8	−7.6	−8.8	0.7	42.8	7.5
1966	64.0	58.1	197.9	5.9	13.7	14.8	9.1	3.5	43.2	7.9
1967	78.2	71.4	235.1	6.7	22.1	22.9	18.8	13.8	45.4	9.0
1968	89.0	81.9	254.8	7.0	13.8	14.7	8.4	4.4	46.0	9.6
1969	90.1	82.5	243.4	7.6	1.3	0.7	−4.5	8.5	44.9	8.9
1970	90.4	81.7	225.6	8.7	0.3	−1.0	−7.3	13.6	41.8	8.3
1971	88.7	78.9	202.7	9.8	−1.9	−3.5	−10.2	12.7	37.5	7.5
1972	89.9	79.2	190.9	10.7	1.4	0.4	−5.8	9.8	34.3	6.9
1973	88.7	76.7	175.1	12.0	1.3	−3.1	−8.3	12.0	31.2	6.0
1974	92.7	79.3	163.3	13.4	4.6	3.5	−6.7	11.4	29.5	5.6
1975	103.1	86.5	159.8	16.6	11.2	9.0	−2.1	24.0	26.0	5.7
1976	108.1	89.6	153.6	18.4	4.8	3.6	−3.9	11.0	24.1	5.3
1976 TO[a]	26.2	22.3	37.1	4.0	. . .	. . .	. . .	. . .	23.2	5.0
1977	115.3	97.2	154.3	18.0	6.1	8.5	0.5	−2.1	23.8	5.0
1978	123.5	104.5	155.0	19.0	7.1	7.5	0.5	5.2	22.8	4.8
1979	136.3	116.3	159.1	19.9	10.4	11.3	2.6	5.0	23.1	4.8
1980	155.2	134.0	164.0	21.2	13.9	15.2	3.1	6.3	22.7	5.0
1981	180.5	157.5	171.4	23.0	16.3	17.6	4.5	8.5	23.2	5.3
1982	209.3	185.3	185.3	24.0	15.9	17.6	8.1	4.2	24.9	5.9
1983	234.7	209.9	201.3	24.8	12.1	13.3	8.6	3.3	26.0	6.3
1984	253.0	227.4	211.3	25.6	7.8	8.3	5.0	3.2	26.7	6.2
1985	279.0	252.7	230.0	26.3	10.3	11.1	8.8	2.7	26.7	6.4
1986	299.7	273.4	244.0	26.4	7.4	8.2	6.1	0.4	27.6	6.5
1987	308.8	282.0	251.0	26.8	3.0	3.1	2.9	1.5	28.1	6.4
1988	319.8	290.4	252.8	29.4	3.6	3.0	0.7	9.7	27.3	6.1
1989	333.7	303.6	256.6	30.1	4.3	4.5	1.5	2.4	26.2	5.9
1990	328.4	299.3	271.1	29.1	−1.6	−1.4	5.7	−3.3	23.9	5.5

[a] Transition quarter, Jul.–Sep.
Source: Bureau of the Census, *Statistical Abstract of the United States, 1992* (Washington, D. C., 1992), 336.

TABLE 10.14 FEDERAL BUDGET OUTLAYS FOR NATIONAL DEFENSE FUNCTIONS, 1970–1990

(in billions of dollars, except percent; for fiscal year ending in year shown)

Defense Function	1970	1980	1983	1984	1985	1986	1987	1988	1989	1990
Total	81.7	134.0	209.9	227.4	252.7	273.4	282.0	290.4	303.6	299.3
Percent change[a]	10.1	15.2	13.3	8.3	11.1	8.2	3.1	3.0	4.5	−1.4
Defense Dept., military	80.1	130.9	204.4	220.9	245.2	265.5	274.0	281.9	294.9	289.8
Military personnel	29.0	40.9	60.9	64.2	67.8	71.5	72.0	76.3	80.7	75.6
Percent of military	36.2	31.2	29.8	29.0	27.7	26.9	26.3	27.1	27.0	−1.7
Operation, maintenance	21.6	44.8	64.9	67.4	72.4	75.3	76.2	84.5	87.0	88.3
Procurement	21.6	29.0	53.6	61.9	70.4	76.5	80.7	77.2	81.6	81.0
Research and development	7.2	13.1	20.6	23.1	27.1	32.3	33.6	34.8	37.0	37.5
Military construction	1.2	2.5	3.5	3.7	4.3	5.1	5.9	5.9	5.3	5.1
Family housing	0.6	1.7	2.1	2.4	2.6	2.8	2.9	3.1	3.3	3.5
Other	−1.1	−1.1	−1.2	−1.7	0.6	2.0	2.6	0.2	0.1	−1.2
Atomic energy activities	1.4	2.9	5.2	6.1	7.1	7.4	7.5	7.9	8.1	9.0
Defense-related activities	0.2	0.2	0.3	0.4	0.5	0.5	0.6	0.5	0.6	0.6

[a] Change from immediate prior year; for 1970, change from 1965.
Source: Bureau of Census, *Statistical Abstract, 1992*, 336.

barriers to female service (with respect to numbers and type of duty) came down and the number of women increased in all branches. A disproportionately high number of black and Hispanic people in service suggested either that the armed forces had made considerable progress in a quest for equality or that society as a whole continued to be discriminatory. It was altogether likely that both answers applied. An end to the war in Vietnam and easing of cold-war tensions produced a slow reduction in the number of regular military personnel, and the government seemed willing to rely more on inactive forces, such as the reserves or National Guard. The costs, however, did not show corresponding shrinkage. To attract new recruits, it was necessary to offer higher wages. The technology race and modernization of weapons continued. A single top-of-the-line fighter plane in the 1980s cost $30 million. Only in the final year, 1990, did the Pentagon report a slight reduction in its budget.

Raising the Troops: Volunteers and Conscripts

The Second World War had been fought largely with conscripted forces. After the attack on Pearl Harbor, the term of duty had been defined as the "duration" of the war plus six months, and at war's end, as the government yielded to pressure to release its conquering warriors as quickly as possible, the draft continued to bring other young men into military service. The enabling legislation was extended piece-by-piece until March 31, 1947, when the draft was allowed to die. It did not stay dead long. Faced with rapidly developing difficulty with the Soviet Union, the Berlin blockade of January 1948, and a stunning communist coup in Czechoslovakia the following month, Congress enacted a new conscription measure that President Harry S. Truman signed into law on June 19, 1948. Under direction of Lewis B. Hershey, the Selective Service System resumed drafting qualified male citizens and residents aged 18 to 26. The draft thereupon became essentially a mechanism for keeping the army supplied with its rank-and-file soldiers, the "enlisted men;" the other military services normally could fill their quotas through volunteers, and the army's officers were either career soldiers or men whose service included some measure of volunteerism, as in the case of the ROTC program in force on many college campuses. Young men of that era came to regard a two-year hitch in military service as a routine part of reaching adulthood, not sought-after—even dreaded by some—but probably inevitable. The existence of deferments and exemptions, however, and sheer numbers alone indicated that not every one would have to go.

The Korean War started suddenly in 1950, and the first American troops in battle were men already in service or veterans in the reserve who could be recalled to duty. After the first year the bulk of combat troops were draftees. In 1951 nearly 600,000 came into the army through conscription. The draft also proved to be an inducement for volunteers. In an effort to avoid the bloody battlefields of Korea, young men offered themselves for service in the navy, the air force, or occasionally even the army if doing so would increase the opportunity for duty other than in combat arms. The Korean War ended in 1953, but the cold war did not, and conscription seemed to have become a permanent part of American life. The concept of universal military service, requiring every able young man to spend time in the armed forces, had much support.

Then in the 1960s came Vietnam and coming of age of the first layers of the baby-boom, or Vietnam, generation. Although the number of men inducted yearly never reached the level of the Korean War, the draft calls did increase after 1965, by which time the Vietnam conflict had become an American war. In short order the Vietnam War became unpopular, and one of the principal targets of a growing antiwar movement was compulsory military service. Many of the protestors were young men of draftable age. In popular perception, conscription placed the individual at the mercy of the army's command, which produced a real prospect of combat duty and the risk of injury or death.

Avoidance of the draft took many forms, starting with petitions for deferment, exemption, and finding some grounds for disqualification. Such ventures could include a claim of conscientious objector status, stressing—even creating—a medical problem, juggling of Selective Service classification, and exploiting to the fullest possible political influence. Attachment to complementary military units such as the National Guard or the reserves made much fewer demands on the participant and carried virtually no danger of combat. Rarely were these units called to active service. Persons who had access to or were willing to utilize none of these tactics or who genuinely wished to make a political statement simply resisted the draft. Perhaps encouraged by such slogans as "Hell no, we won't go" or by the poster urging that "Girls say yes to boys who say no," some burned draft cards in public; others less ostentatiously refused to participate in the induction process. Defenders of the movement would have every draft resister acting out of conscience and moral courage; critics, at least the harshest ones, saw them as spoiled-brat baby boomers who refused to accept anything not to their immediate liking. The truth surely included representatives from all the extremes and many others who acted out of different and more complex motivation.

The upshot was that although more than 2 million young men of the Vietnam era subjected themselves to compulsory induction, a much larger number found legal or illegal ways to avoid it, and the Selective Service System came close to breaking down. Of some 26.8 million men of the Vietnam generation, 2.2 million were drafted; 8.7 million (some of whom surely came from an earlier generation) enlisted; 16 million, about 60 percent, avoided induction by deferment, exemption, disqualification, or other means. Of some 570,000 apparent draft offenders (including people who never registered) and 209,517 accused draft offenders, 8,750 would be convicted and 3,250 imprisoned.

Under constant assault as being prejudicial, class-driven, racist (but, curiously, rarely sexist even though it took only males), and of course the sustaining force of an immoral war, the draft underwent change while the conflict was going on. In 1969 Curtis Tarr, who had replaced Hershey as director, reduced deferments and instituted a random lottery system. President Nixon ended the controversial student deferments in 1971; by that time the number of men in Vietnam was small, and draft calls shrank markedly. On January 27, 1973, the day of the armistice in Vietnam that officially ended U.S. participation, Nixon formally ended the draft.

Since that date the United States has relied on an all-volunteer military force: the AVF. Poor enlistment rates and the increased portion of minority groups in the armed forces led President Jimmy Carter in 1980 to reinstitute the registration requirement for 18-year-old males. The move did not constitute a first step toward resumption of conscription. In 1981 the Supreme Court ruled that registration (and presumably conscription) of males only was constitutional because women could not serve in combat duty. The AVF did undergo a substantial increase in the number of women and a disproportionately high representation of black Americans, but otherwise recruitment lagged at times. During the 1980s the Ronald Reagan administration relied on advertising, higher pay, and education benefits to attract volunteers. In 1990 the AVF seemed to be responding with enthusiasm to a developing operation in the Persian Gulf, but the experience did not suggest that the United States had found a way to staff its military forces once and for all. In the possibility of a future prolonged major military engagement, resumption of a draft remained a realistic option.

TABLE 10.15 TOTAL CALLS, DELIVERIES, AND INDUCTIONS OF SELECTIVE SERVICE REGISTRANTS BY FISCAL YEAR, 1949–1974

Fiscal Year	Calls for Inductions	Deliveries for Induction	Inductions
Total	4,750,873	5,635,878	4,894,462
1949	35,000	31,800	30,129
1950	0	0	0[a]
1951	550,397	608,246	587,444
1952	367,288	408,781	381,006
1953	523,000	589,308	560,798
1954	251,000	289,096	268,018
1955	211,000	232,407	213,716
1956	136,000	149,474	136,580
1957	175,000	196,875	179,321
1958	124,958	144,026	126,369
1959	109,000	137,745	111,889
1960	89,500	130,119	90,549
1961	58,000	85,274	61,070
1962	147,500	194,937	157,465
1963	70,000	98,971	71,744
1964	145,000	190,495	150,808
1965	101,300	137,588	103,328
1966	336,530	399,419	343,481
1967	288,900	345,622	298,559
1968	343,300	401,017	341,404
1969	266,900	329,272	262,646
1970	209,300	248,862	203,707
1971	152,000	204,446	153,631
1972	25,000	39,669	25,273
1973	35,000	51,429	35,527
1974 (first half)	0	0	0

[a] There were 219,765 inductions in calendar year 1950.
Source: Director of Selective Service, *Semiannual Report of the Director of Selective Service, Jul–Dec 1973* (Washington, D.C., 1974), 32.

TABLE 10.16 NUMBER OF REGISTRANTS CLASSIFIED AS CONSCIENTIOUS OBJECTORS, 1952–1973

Total as of Dec. 31	Total Classes 1–O, 1–W, and 4–W
1952	6,233
1953	7,196
1954	9,740
1955	11,282
1956	12,551
1957	14,011
1958	15,097
1959	16,060
1960	16,512
1961	17,253
1962	17,574
1963	15,712
1964	18,802
1965	19,397
1966	20,963
1967	24,238
1968	29,005
1969	35,326
1970	52,050
1971	65,478
1972	33,041
1973	26,043

Source: Director of Selective Service, *Report, Jul–Dec 1973*, 32.

TABLE 10.17 LEGAL CONSCIENTIOUS-OBJECTOR EXEMPTIONS IN THE VIETNAM PERIOD IN COMPARISON TO WORLD WAR I AND WORLD WAR II RATES

War/Year	Ratio of Objector Exemptions to Actual Inductions (per 100 inductions)
World War I	0.14
World War II	0.15
1966	6.10
1967	8.11
1968	8.50
1969	13.45
1970	25.55
1971	42.62
1972	130.72
1973	73.30

Source: Stephen M. Kohn, *Jailed for Peace: The History of American Draft Law Violations, 1658–1985* (Westport, Conn., 1986), 93.

TABLE 10.18 DISPOSITION OF DEFENDANTS CHARGED WITH VIOLATION OF SELECTIVE SERVICE ACTS, SHOWING TYPE OF SENTENCE, 1945–1971

Fiscal Year	Total Defendants	Not Convicted Total	Convicted and Sentenced Total	Imprisonment Total	1 Year and 1 Day and Under	Over 1 Year 1 Day to 3 Years	3–5 Years	5 Years and Over	Average Sentence of Imprisonment (months)	Probation	Fine and Other
1945	4,287	1,449	2,838	2,368	438	775	744	411	31.9	453	17
1946	2,651	999	1,652	1,339	547	501	244	47	20.6	301	12
1947	2,074	937	1,137	775	394	317	61	3	14.3	245	117
1948	833	529	304	212	133	69	9	1	14.1	84	8
1949	506	214	292	213	134	62	17	. . .	14.6	73	6
1950	449	274	175	109	78	24	6	1	13.4	65	1
1951	368	212	159	123	35	37	29	22	29.6	32	1

Fiscal Year	Total Defendants	Not Convicted Total	Convicted and Sentenced Total	Type of Sentence						Probation	Fine and Other
				Imprisonment							
				Total	1 Year and 1 Day and Under	Over 1 Year 1 Day to 3 Years	3–5 Years	5 Years and Over	Average Sentence of Imprisonment (months)		
1952	561	248	313	272	58	77	97	40	30.5	39	2
1953	630	285	345	280	61	101	84	34	29.3	64	1
1954	822	398	424	356	78	137	126	15	26.4	64	4
1955	719	430	289	217	54	105	47	11	24.8	70	2
1956	371	185	186	123	35	50	35	3	24.0	31	2
1957	357	95	262	194	60	85	41	8	23.7	68	...
1958	325	96	229	190	66	81	42	1	21.6	36	3
1959	258	56	202	152	46	63	39	4	23.2	49	1
1960	239	73	166	126	47	48	28	3	21.5	37	3
1961	244	45	199	141	45	59	35	2	22.6	57	1
1962	274	49	225	164	58	75	28	3	21.6	60	1
1963	339	73	265	189	79	65	36	9	21.5	74	2
1964	276	70	206	146	46	77	22	1	20.8	59	1
1965	341	99	212	189	64	90	30	5	21.0	52	1
1966	516	145	371	301	61	128	95	17	26.4	64	6
1967	996	248	748	666	47	270	291	58	32.1	78	4
1968	1,192	408	784	580	44	131	301	104	37.3	202	2
1969	1,744	844	900	544	40	155	261	88	36.3	350	6
1970	2,833	1,803	1,027	450	53	144	208	45	33.5	572	5
1971	2,973	1,937	1,036	377	79	140	129	29	29.1	650	9
1972	4,906	3,264	1,642	1,642	53	120	123	16	22.0	1,178	6

Source: Director of Selective Service, *Semiannual Report of the Director of Selective Service, Jul–Dec 1972* (Washington, D.C., 1973), 46.

Women and the Military

The status of women in postwar military forces was defined by the Woman's Armed Forces Integration Act of 1948, which gave permanent status to women in the armed forces, authorized service in the army, the navy, and the air force, imposed a 2 percent ceiling on women on active duty, prohibited women from combat duty and service on all naval vessels except hospital and transport ships. Military women in the 1950s and early 1960s served as part of a permanent and professional army and navy corps of nurses, or in duties, mostly clerical, as WACS, WAVES, or Lady Marines—elements of the army and the navy. Women who served in the Korean War were almost entirely nurses, as television viewers later would learn from the long-running popular series about a field medical unit, M*A*S*H.

Of the several thousand—estimates put it at between 6,000 and 12,000—women who served in the long Vietnam War, the vast majority were nurses. Eight servicewomen died in Vietnam, all of them nurses. Seven were killed in airplane accidents; one died of wounds from an enemy artillery attack. The era of Vietnam corresponded with a growing woman's movement that had as its most persistent objective gender equality in as many areas of society as possible. It was nearly inevitable that a linkage would be drawn to military operations, and so changes began to take place while the war was going on. In 1967 Congress lifted limitations on rank for servicewomen and abolished the 2 percent limit on the number of women who could serve. The air force opened its ROTC program to women in 1969; the army and the navy did so in 1972.

Institution of the All-Volunteer Force opened the door for more women to serve and in an ever-broadening range of activity. The army and navy produced their first female pilots in 1974, and the air force began pilot training for females two years later. In 1975 Congress admitted women into the service academies of the army, the navy, and the air force, and in that same year the practice of discharging pregnant females came to an end. In 1978 the separate Woman's Army Corps was abol-

TABLE 10.19 FEMALE ACTIVE-DUTY MILITARY PERSONNEL, 1965–1990

Year	Total	Army	Navy	Marine Corps	Air Force
1965	30,610	12,326	7,862	1,581	8,841
1970	41,479	16,724	8,683	2,418	13,654
1975	96,868	42,295	21,174	3,186	30,213
1980	171,418	69,338	34,980	6,706	60,394
1985	211,606	79,247	52,603	9,695	70,061
1990	227,018	83,621	59,907	9,356	74,134

Source: Ronald J. Alsop, *The Wall Street Journal Almanac, 1998* (New York, 1997), 126.

TABLE 10.20 WOMEN IN UNIFORM, 1988

Service	Officers		Enlisted	
	Number	Percent	Number	Percent
Army	11,436	10.4	71,343	10.6
Navy	7,210	10.1	46,195	9.1
Marine Corps	659	3.3	9,172	5.1
Air Force	12,595	11.5	61,640	12.4
Total	30,476	10.3	188,350	10.2

Source: Wright, *Universal Almanac, 1991*, 113.

ished, and women were integrated into the regular army. Most restrictions on service on navy ships ended. By the end of the 1980s virtually the only restriction on female activity in the armed forces involved active participation in combat arms. There did not appear to be a ground-swell movement for changing this rule, but women were getting close to combat anyway, if only in incidental circumstances. Women participated in the incursion into Grenada in 1983; nearly 800 went into Panama with the military operation of 1989; and among the large military force gathering for likely hostilities in the Persian Gulf in the winter of 1990, one could find several thousand female soldiers.

TABLE 10.21   U.S. ACTIVE-DUTY FORCES, BY SEX, RACE, AND HISPANIC ORIGIN, 1965–1990

(in percent)

Year	Female Officers	Female Enlisted	Female Total	Black Officers	Black Enlisted	Black Total	Hispanic Officers	Hispanic Enlisted	Hispanic Total	Total Officers (thousands)	Total Enlisted (thousands)
1965	3.1%	0.9%	1.2%	1.9%	10.5%	9.5%	...	...	...	339	2,317
1966	3.2	0.8	1.1	...	...	...	...	...	...	349	2,745
1967	3.3	0.8	1.0	2.1	9.9	8.9	...	...	...	385	2,992
1968	3.2	0.8	1.1	2.1	10.2	9.2	...	...	...	416	2,132
1969	3.1	0.9	1.1	2.1	9.6	8.7	...	...	...	419	3,041
1970	3.3	1.1	1.4	2.2	11.0	9.8	...	...	...	402	2,664
1971	3.5	1.3	1.6	2.3	12.1	10.7	1.3%	3.4%	3.1%	371	2,329
1972	3.8	1.6	1.9	2.4	13.5	11.9	1.2	4.0	3.6	336	1,987
1973	4.0	2.2	2.5	2.7	14.9	13.2	1.2	4.5	4.0	321	1,932
1974	4.3	3.3	3.5	3.0	16.2	14.4	1.3	4.5	3.9	303	1,860
1975	4.6	4.5	4.6	3.2	16.2	14.4	1.4	4.6	4.2	292	1,836
1976	5.0	5.3	5.2	3.6	17.1	15.2	1.3	4.6	4.2	281	1,801
1977	5.4	5.8	5.7	3.9	17.4	15.6	1.5	4.5	4.1	276	1,798
1978	6.2	6.5	6.5	4.3	19.3	17.3	1.6	4.5	4.1	274	1,788
1979	6.9	7.5	7.4	4.7	21.2	19.0	1.6	4.4	3.8	274	1,753
1980	7.7	8.5	8.4	5.0	21.9	19.6	1.2	4.0	3.6	278	1,759
1981	8.1	9.0	8.9	5.3	22.1	19.8	1.2	4.1	3.7	285	1,783
1982	8.6	9.0	9.0	5.3	22.0	19.7	1.2	4.1	3.7	292	1,804
1983	9.0	9.3	9.3	5.8	21.6	19.4	1.4	4.1	3.7	301	1,811
1984	9.4	9.5	9.5	6.2	21.1	19.0	1.4	3.9	3.6	304	1,820
1985	9.8	9.8	9.8	6.4	21.1	18.9	1.5	3.9	3.6	309	1,828
1986	10.1	10.0	10.1	6.5	21.2	19.1	1.7	4.1	3.7	311	1,845
1987	10.4	10.2	10.2	6.5	21.5	19.4	1.7	4.3	3.9	308	1,856
1988	10.7	10.4	10.4	6.7	22.0	19.8	1.8	4.5	4.1	305	1,819
1989	11.1	11.0	11.0	6.9	22.8	20.3	2.0	4.8	4.4	303	1,814
1990	11.4	10.9	10.9	6.9	22.9	20.5	2.1	5.0	4.6	304	1,762

Source: Stanley and Niemi, *Statistics on Politics*, 354–55.

TABLE 10.22   MINORITIES IN UNIFORM, 1988

Service	Black Americans Number	Black Americans Percent	Hispanic Americans Number	Hispanic Americans Percent	Other Number	Other Percent	Total Number	Total Percent
Officers								
Army	11,192	10.5%	1,687	1.6%	3,140	2.9%	16,019	15.0%
Navy	2,576	3.6	1,443	2.0	1,969	2.7	5,988	8.3
Marine Corps	983	4.9	416	2.1	363	1.8	1,762	8.7
Air Force	5,670	5.4	2,129	2.0	2,721	2.6	10,520	10.1
Total	20,421	6.7	5,675	1.9	8,193	2.7	34,289	11.3
Enlisted								
Army	200,912	30.7%	27,324	4.2%	28,692	4.4%	256,928	39.3%
Navy	80,984	16.0	25,871	5.1	28,532	5.6	135,387	26.8
Marine Corps	36,565	20.9	11,026	6.3	5,543	3.2	53,134	30.4
Air Force	81,633	17.4	17,607	3.7	15,753	3.4	114,993	24.5
Total	400,094	22.2	81,828	4.5	78,520	4.4	560,442	31.1

Source: John Wright, *The Universal Almanac, 1991* (New York, 1990), 113.

TABLE 10.23   U.S. ARMED FORCES WORLDWIDE, 1989

Location	Army	Navy	Marine Corps	Air Force	Total DOD
United States					
Continental U.S.	452,468	268,080	144,027	418,008	1,282,583
Hawaii	18,416	12,604	8,565	5,763	45,348
Alaska	9,373	2,315	173	10,928	22,789
Guam	35	4,405	360	3,424	8,224
Puerto Rico	379	3,511	154	45	4,089
Johnston Atoll	130	2	0	10	142
Transients	15,374	14,572	5,440	10,071	45,457
Afloat	0	187,708	1,038	0	188,746
Total	496,253	493,236	159,757	448,270	1,597,517
Europe					
Belgium	1,504	133	32	699	2,368
West Germany	214,087	339	106	40,170	254,702
Greece	406	550	16	2,283	3,255
Greenland	0	0	0	196	196
Iceland	2	1,823	101	1,382	3,308
Italy	3,860	5,596	305	6,052	15,813
Netherlands	794	17	10	2,028	2,849
Norway	36	36	17	119	208
Portugal	57	385	11	1,205	1,658
Spain	18	3,676	180	4,407	8,281
Turkey	1,169	109	19	3,580	4,877
United Kingdom	259	2,417	377	24,541	27,594
Afloat	0	16,657	2,049	0	18,706
Total	222,243	31,777	3,336	86,722	344,078
Eastern Europe	65	5	110	16	196

Location	Army	Navy	Marine Corps	Air Force	Total DOD
East Asia and Pacific					
Australia	20	429	10	274	733
Japan	2,176	7,196	24,288	15,931	49,591
Philippines	173	5,037	978	9,207	15,395
South Korea	32,052	391	2,233	11,495	46,171
Thailand	67	10	13	34	124
Afloat	0	31,595	2,193	0	33,788
Total	34,530	44,744	29,773	36,979	146,026
Africa, Near East, and South Asia					
Bahrain	7	124	9	10	150
British Indian Ocean Territory	3	933	82	24	1,042
Egypt	1,036	32	36	41	1,145
Saudi Arabia	150	47	23	213	433
Afloat	0	2,872	48	0	2,920
Total	1,413	4,047	603	394	6,457
Other Western Hemisphere					
Bermuda	0	1,787	74	0	1,861
Canada	12	388	8	127	535
Cuba (Guantanamo)	10	1,906	466	2	2,384
Honduras	2,628	5	13	161	2,807
Panama	6,953	517	484	2,854	10,808
Afloat	0	2,306	0	0	2,306
Total	9,749	7,058	1,281	3,223	21,311
Worldwide					
Ashore	764,259	339,912	189,532	575,604	1,869,307
Afloat	0	241,138	5,328	0	246,466
Total	764,259	581,050	194,860	575,604	2,115,773

Source: Wright, *Universal Almanac, 1991,* 111.

TABLE 10.24   MILITARY FORCES, RANKED BY COUNTRY, 1989

Armed Forces (thousands)			Military Expenditures (millions of dollars)		
Rank	Country	Number	Rank	Country	Dollars
1.	China — Mainland	3,903	1.	Soviet Union	311,000
2.	Soviet Union	3,700	2.	United States	304,100
3.	United States	2,241	3.	France	35,260
4.	India	1,257	4.	United Kingdom	34,630
5.	Korea, North	1,040	5.	Germany West	33,600
6.	Iraq	1,000	6.	Japan	28,410
7.	Vietnam	1,000	7.	China — Mainland	22,330
8.	Turkey	780	8.	Italy	20,720
9.	Korea, South	647	9.	Iraq	
10.	Iran	604	10.	Poland	15,480
11.	France	554	11.	Saudi Arabia	14,690
12.	Italy	533	12.	Germany, East	13,970
13.	Pakistan	520	13.	Canada	10,840
14.	Germany, West	503	14.	Korea, South	9,100
15.	Egypt	450	15.	Czechoslovakia	8,361
16.	Syria	400	16.	India	8,174
17.	China — Taiwan	379	17.	China — Taiwan	8,060
18.	Poland	350	18.	Spain	7,775
19.	Brazil	319	19.	Romania	6,916
20.	United Kingdom	318	20.	Netherlands	6,399
21.	Cuba	297	21.	Brazil	
22.	Indonesia	285	22.	Australia	6,153
23.	Spain	277	23.	Korea, North	6,000
24.	Thailand	273	24.	Bulgaria	5,885
25.	Germany, East	262	25.	Israel	5,745

Source: U.S. Arms Control and Disarmament Agency, *World Military Expenditures and Arms Transfers 1990* (Washington, D.C., 1991), 36.

Weapons and Equipment of the Armed Forces

The half-century after 1945 was not only the age of the cold war; it also became an era of revolution in world affairs. If the first objective of American military forces was to protect the nation in case of conflict with its perceived enemy, the Soviet Union, a second purpose was to prepare the nation to respond to diverse situations—related to American interests and security—that emerged throughout the world. The primary focus of the military establishment remained on the rapidly expanding world of nuclear technology, but it also had to pay attention to less dramatic and more familiar military equipment.

Weaponry of the United States came to be divided into two categories: conventional and nuclear, or weapons that could be and were used and weapons so destructive that they were held as a threat and deterrent to prevent the Soviet Union from using similarly destructive weapons on the United States. Thus, if the revolution in nuclear weapons brought terror and threat of massive, if not global, destruction, it also emerged as and remained a deterrent to war between the two principal adversaries.

Traditional weapons of course involved arms, albeit in improved varieties, that had been used in the past: rifles, artillery, tanks, airplanes, and warships designed to fight other warships. Nuclear weapons for the most part were classified as strategic—powerful, long-range explosive devices capable of inflicting large damage on an enemy country. The atomic bombing of Hiroshima and Nagasaki in 1945 in retrospect would be classified as strategic warfare, although small examples by standards of the cold war. Those two bombings contained the only documented evidence of the effect of strategic warfare

on populated areas. Knowledge of the destructive power of cold war weaponry remained the domain of speculation and calculation, but no one could doubt that the impact would be mind-boggling, going far beyond damage from the immediate explosion. A second, lesser, category of nuclear weapons was termed tactical—small, low-yield devices, probably a type of artillery—designed for close-combat battlefield use. Impact and complications of such weaponry could not be established because they never were used.

Perhaps the most utilitarian new weapon in the cold war era was the missile, or guided missile, as it was called in the early years. The self-propelled missile—the missile in fact was the vehicle—could transport nuclear or conventional explosive devices. Adaptable to various forms, sizes, and purposes, the missile became important to all military branches. There were air-to-air missiles: air-to-ground, or air-to-ship missiles; ground-to-air, ground-to-ground, ship-to-ship, ship-to-air, ship-to-ground missiles. They could travel several yards, intercontinental distances, or various ranges in between. Because they carried their own propulsion equipment and often guidance devices and were, of course, nonreusable, missiles were so expensive that armed services members trained in their use rarely, if ever, fired a live round, even in the small, hand-held versions. A fully equipped missile for a Trident submarine cost more than $35 million.

Of all the military forces, the army changed the least in character and mission during the years of the cold war. To settle a conflict truly and to win a military engagement, the ground forces had to go in and defeat the enemy, one-by-one if necessary, and take control of territory. The Korean War was largely a conventional war fought with equipment left over from the Second World War: the M-1 semiautomatic rifle, the jeep, and the medium tank. With passage of years, the army's technology changed more than its mission. The M-16 rifle that became standard in the early 1960s was not as accurate as the M-1 it replaced, but, fully automatic, it spewed out so many bullets that one of them was bound to hit. The tank of the Second World War gave way to the larger M-60 and then to the much larger, redesigned, and technologically advanced M-1 Abrams tank that would serve the army into the next century. Even the durable jeep had been replaced by a much larger, ugly beast called a HumVee that cost $28,000 apiece, about the same as a Cadillac. In terms of technology and change in tactics, probably the most important development had been improvement of the helicopter, which had performed mostly transportation service in Korea and came into widespread combat usage during the war in Vietnam. Clumsy looking for a flying machine, the "chopper" performed many services for the army. As an instrument of combat arms, it was most effective as a mobile platform for firing missiles. The army thus had changed, probably lost its position as the preeminent element of the armed forces, but in some ways it remained the same. There were hundreds of airplanes gathering to engage Iraq in the winter of 1990; the navy's carriers and even a couple of battleships stood off in waters nearby. But the people in charge suspected (and they were right) that it all would not be over until the foot soldiers went in and did their stuff.

The air force came of age as an independent entity in the years of the cold war. Separated from the army in the National Defense Act of 1947, it received its own department, secretary, and service academy (in Colorado Springs) and despite its youth zealously protected its position as partner equal to the army and the navy. Entrusted with operating land-based units of the strategic arsenal—the intercontinental missiles and long-range B-52 bombers of the Strategic Air Command (SAC)—it also adjusted itself to perform varied nonnuclear, limited conflict duties mandated by the cold war and other regional issues. These duties took air personnel—the pilots and support personnel—to bases around the globe that were made possible by the numerous treaties and security pacts accepted by the government.

The most important change in equipment of the air force was the development and continued improvement of jet propulsion. American forces had not used jet aircraft in the Second World War, but defense technology had been moving in that direction, and at war's end it could benefit from advanced German development and a prod from knowledge that the Soviets were hard at work in the same area. By the time the Korean War started in 1950, the United States had several jet fighters in production, notably the F-80 Shooting Star and F-86 Sabrejet, both of which participated in numerous engagements in Korean skies with the Soviet-built MIG 15. The air force in Korea also used many propeller-driven aircraft such as the P-51 Mustang, and propeller planes would not disappear from the air armada. Many propeller-type planes, such as the Dragonfly, flew throughout the Vietnam War, especially in the hands of South Vietnamese pilots. Jet power in the early 1950s could increase the speed of a fighter plane by 30 to 40 percent. By the 1960s a top-of-the-line jet fighter could double, even triple the speed of a P-51. Small wonder that starting in the late 1940s the air force moved to build progressively faster, more powerful, and technologically advanced jet aircraft. The airplane of the 1960s—the Vietnam War—was the noisy, dirty but powerful Phantom, the F-4. Beginning in the mid-1970s two aircraft, the twin-engine F-15 Eagle and the single-engine F-16 Falcon entered service on a regular basis.

Borrowing from experience in the Second World War, the air force had sought to build a separate fleet of heavy bombers. After experiment with several models—the speedy B-58 looked promising for a while—the Department of Defense settled on the massive, lumbering (for a jet plane) B-52. Introduced in 1952, this huge jet bomber provided the striking force for SAC: the airplanes that could bomb Moscow and return to their bases. A third leg (along with land- and submarine-based missiles) in the American TRIAD strategic defense system, counted in the SALT II treaty of 1979, the bombers officially

maintained their role into the 1990s. In truth a few B-52 bombers were kept in reserve for special missions; a nuclear war surely would have been fought with missiles.

The genuine workhorses of the air force were continuously updated F-15 and F-16 fighter-bombers. In conjunction with carrier-based naval aircraft—the F-14 Tomcat, F-18 Hornet, and other attack craft—the fighter-bombers were being summoned to take on an expanded field of operations. The Vietnam War had left American administrations acutely sensitive to the casualties that could come from ground operations. A small but bitter experience in Lebanon in 1983 had confirmed the apprehension. If the United States truly had to act in a military situation, it was better and far less costly in terms of casualties to act with airpower. There even emerged a growing hope (but not a conviction) that in many situations, air power alone would be enough.

Although the navy maintained elements of traditional ways of doing its job—the aircraft carrier *Midway*, for example, commissioned in 1945, was still at sea in 1990—it probably was the branch most changed by technology and demands of the era of the cold war. The navy shared in major developments in weaponry and added a wrinkle or two of its own. A deemphasis on large, heavily armored surface vessels continued. The battleships were retired as museums or cut up for scrap. The navy did place the four newest ones in protective coating called mothballs, making it possible for the government to return one or more to active service. Reagan pulled all four out for a while in the 1980s, and in fact two battleships were on hand for the Gulf Crisis of 1990. They ended up being expensive platforms for launching cruise missiles.

Alone among powers of the world, the United States continued to emphasize large aircraft carriers. The carriers performed important functions, although probably in ways that had been unanticipated. They did not engage enemy warships; there were no naval battles after 1945. The Soviet Union did not present a naval threat, other than with submarines, in which case the threat was considerable, if hardly the responsibility of large carriers. Aircraft carriers did not help much in the direct struggle with the Soviet Union, but they did provide exceptional service in the numerous global responsibilities the United States chose to undertake during this period. Carriers allowed the United States to transport its air bases to the scene of action—to wars in Korea or Vietnam or almost any area that gave cause for concern. The primary function of naval aircraft, and thus the carriers, was to strike land targets.

For several years the navy utilized warships constructed for the Second World War. It soon became apparent that many of the navy's war machines and certainly aircraft carriers were large enough to lend themselves to nuclear energy as a power source. The first nuclear-powered aircraft carrier, the *Enterprise*, was commissioned in 1961; it could sail for years without refueling. By the start of the 1970s all new carriers and cruisers were nuclear powered, and all new warships, except for carriers, came equipped with missile-firing capability.

The most striking development of naval technology took place in the area of submarines. Cold war submarines came in two varieties: First was the attack submarine that performed the traditional task of seeking out enemy ships. The most likely potential target would be enemy U-boats, for only in submarines did the Soviet Union seek to keep pace with the United States Navy; the Soviets in fact had more subs than the Americans. The first atomic-powered warship was the *Nautilus*, an attack submarine commissioned in 1954. After 1960 all submarines of any variety came equipped with nuclear power plants and were capable of staying submerged for months. Thereafter the navy employed a continuous program of upgrading the attack submarine fleet—modernizing vessels, retiring old models, building new ones.

Jewel of the fleet, if not of the American strategic arsenal, was a vessel that blended together all the major developments in naval technology. Designated SSBN, this nuclear-powered submarine fired ballistic missiles from tubes protruding downward from the deck, not at other ships but at land-based targets perhaps 3,000 miles away. The

B-58 "Hustler" supersonic bomber of the early cold war: It was as fast as the Concorde but not a cost-effective weapon. (author's photo)

first SSBN was identified by the class of its missile, Polaris. The Polaris submarine *George Washington,* armed with 16 nuclear-tipped missiles, set sail on November 1960. The final patrol of a Polaris submarine took place in 1981. By that time the second generation of SSBN, called the Poseidon (first tested in 1970), had taken over. Originally armed with Polaris missiles, 31 of the new submarines would be refitted to carry the newer Poseidon missile, which was equipped for multiple warheads (MIRV); each missile carried 10 warheads. In the late 1970s and 1980s, 12 of the newer Poseidon submarines were rearmed with the latest Trident C4 missile.

The start of the 1980s brought the appearance of the third and latest family of ballistic submarines: the "Ohio" class (all, save one, would be named after states), better known as Trident submarines. Improved in every way, almost twice the size of the Poseidon vessel, the Trident submarine carried 24 missiles, each equipped with eight warheads. The Poseidon submarines were scheduled to be decommissioned or assigned a new function by the start of the 1990s; those equipped with the latest missiles would sail until the end of the 1990s. What would be left for future maritime strategic defense was the new fleet of 18 Trident submarines that could carry an astonishing amount of destructive power and were capable—it was said—of surviving almost any humanmade or natural disaster, even a nuclear war.

The Nuclear Arms Race:
A Glossary

antiballistic missile (ABM)   A defensive missile designed to destroy an incoming enemy ballistic missile before its warhead reaches its target.

ballistic missile   A rocket-propelled missile that leaves the atmosphere and returns to Earth in a free fall.

cruise missile   A guided missile that flies to its target within the earth's atmosphere, close to the surface. The cruise missile can carry a nuclear warhead and can be launched from air, land, or sea.

delivery vehicle   A missile or strategic bomber that delivers a warhead to its target.

deployment   Installing weapons, making them ready for action.

first strike   An initial nuclear attack by one country intended to destroy an adversary's strategic nuclear forces.

intercontinental ballistic missile (ICBM)   A land-based missile capable of traveling more than 3,000 nautical miles to deliver one or more warheads.

intermediate-range nuclear forces (INF)   Sometimes called theater nuclear forces, these weapons have a range of about 3,000 miles.

missile experimental (MX)   An American ICBM capable of carrying as many as 10 MIRVs.

multiple independently targetable reentry vehicle (MIRV)   A vehicle loaded with a warhead and mounted, along with similar vehicles, on one ballistic missile. Once separated from the missile, each MIRV can be directed against a different target.

mutual assured destruction (MAD)   The ability of both the United States and the Soviet Union to inflict damage so severe that neither is willing to initiate a nuclear attack.

neutron bomb   An "enhanced radiation weapon," this nuclear bomb is designed primarily to kill people and to inflict less damage on buildings than other bombs.

nuclear freeze   The immediate halt to the development, production, transfer, and deployment of nuclear weapons.

second strike   A retaliatory nuclear attack launched after being hit by an opponent's first strike.

strategic defense initiative (SDI)   Popularly known as "Star Wars," SDI was President Ronald Reagan's 1983 proposal to build a space-based, defensive system that could establish a protective shield over the United States and its allies with the capability to shoot down incoming ballistic missiles.

strategic weapons or arms   Long-range weapons capable of hitting an adversary's territory. ICBMs, SLBMs, and strategic bombers are so classified.

submarine-launched ballistic missile (SLBM)   A ballistic missile carried in and launched from a submarine.

surface-to-air missile (SAM)   A missile launched from Earth's surface for the purpose of knocking down an adversary's airplanes.

tactical nuclear weapons   Low-yield nuclear weapons for battlefield use.

triad   The three-part structure of American strategic forces (ICBMs, SLBMs, and strategic bombers).

warhead   The part of a missile that contains the nuclear explosive intended to inflict damage.

Source: Paterson, Clifford, and Hagan, *American Foreign Relations, Vol. II*, 373.

TABLE 10.25   SELECT U.S., SOVIET, AND FRENCH BALLISTIC MISSILES TESTED AND DEPLOYED

Country	Type	First Flight	Maximum Range (km)	No. Tested Before Deployment	Highest No. Deployed	Total No. Built
U.S.A	Redstone	1953	500	37	. . .	. . .
	Atlas	1957	8 000	45	132	(300)[a]
	Titan-1	1960	11 000	47	54	163
	Pershing-1	1960	740	69	216	827
	Titan-2	1962	11 000	33	54	. . .
	Lance	1965	125	156	. . .	2 391
	Pershing-2	1982	1 800	26	108	336
	MX	1983	10 000	20	50	117
USSR	SS-13	1965	. . .	44	60	. . .
	SS-17	1972	. . .	30	150	. . .
	SS-18	1972	. . .	35	308	. . .
	SS-19	1973	. . .	27	360	. . .
	SS-20	1974	. . .	(40)[a]	405	(740)[a]
	SS-23	1976	. . .	(40)[a]	310	(420)[a]
France	S-2	1965	2 700	27	18	55
	S-3	1977	3 000	21	18	52
	Pluton	1968	120	36	44	106

[a] Data in parentheses are estimates.

Source: Aaron Karp, *Ballistic Missile Proliferation* (New York, 1996), 139.

TABLE 10.26   NUCLEAR ARSENALS—STRATEGIC DELIVERY SYSTEMS OF THE SUPERPOWERS, 1960–1990

United States

	1960	1961	1962	1963	1964	1965	1966	1967	1968	1969	1970	1971	1972	1973
ICBM	18	63	294	424	834	854	904	1054	1054	1054	1054	1054	1054	1054
SLBM	32	96	144	224	416	496	592	656	656	656	656	656	656	656
LRB	450	600	630	630	630	630	600	540	480	450	405	360	390	397

	1974	1975	1976	1977	1978	1979	1980	1981	1982	1983	1984	1985	1988	1990
ICBM	1054	1054	1054	1054	1054	1054	1054	1052	1052	1045	1037	1030	1000	1000
SLBM	656	656	656	656	656	656	656	576	520	568	592	616	640	592
LRB	397	397	387	373	366	365	338	316	316	272	241	324	396	311

Soviet Union

	1960	1961	1962	1963	1964	1965	1966	1967	1968	1969	1970	1971	1972	1973
ICBM	35	50	75	100	200	270	300	460	800	1050	1300	1510	1530	1575
SLBM	na	na	na	100	120	120	125	130	130	130	160	280	560	628
LRB	na	na	na	na	na	na	na	155	155	150	140	140	140	140

	1974	1975	1976	1977	1978	1979	1980	1981	1982	1983	1984	1985	1988	1990
ICBM	1618	1527	1477	1350	1400	1398	1398	1398	1398	1398	1398	1398	1382	1356
SLBM	720	784	845	909	1028	1028	1028	989	989	980	981	966	922	930
LRB	140	135	135	135	135	156	156	150	150	143	143	165	155	162

na   no statistics available
ICBM   Intercontinental ballistic missiles
SLBM   Submarine-launched ballistic missiles
LRB   Long-range bombers
Source: Cook, *Facts On File World Almanac*, 337.

TABLE 10.27 COMMISSIONED SHIPS OF THE U.S. NAVY, 1945–1990

Ship Type	1945	1950	1953	1955	1960	1965	1970	1975	1980	1985	1990
Submarines—conventional											
SS-SSK-SSR	237	73	122	121	113	83	59	11	6	4	—
SSG	...	...	1	2	4	...	...	...	...	...	...
auxiliary	...	...	7	18	20	15	26	2	1	1	1
Submarines–nuclear											
SSN-SSRN	...	...	...	1	7	22	48	64	73	94	87
SSGN	...	...	...	...	1	...	...	...	...	...	...
SSBN	...	...	...	...	2	29	41	41	40	37	34
auxiliary	...	...	...	...	...	...	...	...	...	2	2
(total submarines)	(237)	(73)	(130)	(142)	(147)	(149)	(174)	(118)	(120)	(138)	(124)
Aircraft carriers											
CVB-CVA-CVAN-CV-CVN	20	7	17	16	14	16	15	15	13	13	12
CVS	...	...	...	5	9	9	4	...	...	...	...
CVL	8	4	5	1	...	...	...	...	...	...	...
CVE	70	4	17	3	...	...	...	...	...	...	...
Battleships											
BB	25	1	4	3	...	...	...	...	...	2	3
Cruisers											
CAG-CG-CLG-CGN	...	...	...	...	6	12	10	27	27	30	43
CA (8-inch guns)	24	9	15	10	6	2	2	...	...	...	...
CL (6-inch guns)	42	3	3	3	...	...	...	...	...	...	...
CLAA (5-inch guns)	6	1	1	...	...	...	...	...	...	...	...
Frigates											
DL	...	...	...	5	5	5	...	...	...	...	...
DLG-DLGN	...	...	...	...	4	20	20	...	...	...	...
Destroyers											
DD-DDE-DDK-DDR	372	142	246	244	211	189+17	122	32	43	31+1	31
DDG	...	...	...	...		33	37	38	37	37	22
Escort Ships/Frigates											
DE-DER/FF-FFR	365	11	89	64	41	39+21	41	58	59	53+6	36+12
DEG/FFG	...	...	...	...	...	...	6	6	13	47+4	35+16
Flagships/Command Ships											
AGC-CC-CLC-LCC-AGF	18	6				7	3	3	3	4	4
AMPHIBIOUS SHIPS	~3,300	83	226	175	113	132	95	62	58+5	58+2	59+3

Note: Frigates (DL–DIG–DLGN) were classified as CG–CGN–DDG in 1975. The various designations within ship categories represent differences, sometimes small, in usage or construction of the vessel. Perhaps the most meaningful observation is that up to the 1960s ships largely were of Second World War vintage, armed with guns, powered with diesel engines. Beginning in and after the 1960s, they were likely to be larger, nuclear powered, armed with missiles (and fewer guns). Appearance of an "N" in ship classification mean that the vessel was nuclear powered; appearance of a "G" indicated it fired missiles. There also was a new kind of submarine, the SSBN, the nuclear, ballistic missile-firing submarine—a naval weapon with a nonnaval function.
Source: Norman Polmar, *The Naval Institute Guide to the Ships and Aircraft of the U.S. Fleet* (Annapolis, 1993), 611.

TABLE 10.28   AIRCRAFT CARRIERS—EARLY YEARS

Number	Name	Commissioned	Stricken
CV 9	*Essex*	1942	Jun. 1, 1973
CV 10	*Yorktown*	1943	Jun. 1, 1973
CV 11	*Intrepid*	1943	Sep. 30, 1980
CV 12	*Hornet*	1943	Jul. 25, 1989
CV 13	*Franklin*[a]	1944	Oct. 1, 1964
CV 14	*Ticonderoga*	1944	Nov. 16, 1973
CV 15	*Randolph*	1944	Jun. 1, 1973
CV 16	*Lexington*[b]	1943	
CV 17	*Bunker Hill*[a]	1943	Nov. 1, 1966
CV 18	*Wasp*	1943	Jul. 1, 1972
CV 19	*Hancock*	1944	Dec. 31, 1975
CV 20	*Bennington*	1944	Sep. 20, 1989
CV 21	*Boxer*	1945	Dec. 1, 1969
CVL 22–30	*Independence*-class light carriers		
CV 31	*Bon Homme Richard*	1944	Sep. 20, 1989
CV 32	*Leyte*[a]	1946	Jun. 1, 1969
CV 33	*Kearsarge*	1946	May 1, 1973
CV 34	*Oriskany*	1950	Jul. 25, 1989
CV 35	*Reprisal*	cancelled 1945	
CV 36	*Antietam*	1945	May 1, 1973
CV 37	*Princeton*	1945	Jan. 30, 1970
CV 38	*Shangri-La*	1944	Jul. 15, 1982
CV 39	*Lake Champlain*	1945	Dec. 1, 1969
CV 40	*Tarawa*[a]	1945	Jun. 1, 1967
CVB 41	*Midway* (large)	1945	...

[a] Aviation transports
[b] Training carrier
Source: Polmar, *Guide to Ships and Aircraft*, 96.

USS *Enterprise*, the first nuclear-powered aircraft carrier. Here in the Gulf of Tonkin, *Enterprise* prepares to recover Skyhawk aircraft from attack in Vietnam. (National Archives)

TABLE 10.29 AIRCRAFT CARRIERS—THE MODERN ERA

Ship Name	Type	Hull Builder	Laid Down			Launched			Completed		
			D	M	Y	D	M	Y	D	M	Y
Forrestal	CV	59 Newport News	14	07	52	11	12	54	01	10	55
Forrestal—Slep[a]	CV	59 Phila. N.Y.	21	01	83				19	05	85
Saratoga	CV	60 Brooklyn N.Y.	16	12	52	08	10	55	14	04	56
Saratoga—Slep[a]	CV	60 Phila. N.Y.	01	10	80				01	02	83
Ranger	CV	61 Newport News	02	07	54	29	09	56	10	08	57
Independence	CV	62 Brooklyn N.Y.	01	07	55	06	06	58	10	01	59
Independence—Slep[a]	CV	62 Phila. N.Y.	18	04	85				16	05	88
Kitty Hawk	CV	63 NYSB, Camden	27	12	56	21	05	60	29	04	61
Kitty Hawk—Slep[a]	CV	63 Phila. N.Y.	28	01	88						1991
Constellation	CV	64 Brooklyn N.Y.	14	09	57	08	10	60	27	10	61
Constellation—Slep[a]	CV	64 Phila. N.Y.	02	07	90						1993
Enterprise	CVN[b]	65 Newport News	04	02	58	24	09	60	25	11	61
Enterprise—Rcoh[c]	CVN[b]	65 Newport News			1991						1994
America	CV	66 Newport News	09	01	61	01	02	64	23	01	65
John F. Kennedy	CV	67 Newport News	22	11	64	27	05	67	07	09	68
Nimitz	CVN[b]	68 Newport News	22	06	68	13	05	72	03	05	75
Dwight D. Eisenhower	CVN[b]	69 Newport News	14	08	70	11	10	75	18	10	77
Carl Vinson	CVN[b]	70 Newport News	11	10	75	15	03	80	13	03	82
Theodore Roosevelt	CVN[b]	71 Newport News	31	10	81	27	10	84	25	10	86
Abraham Lincoln	CVN[b]	72 Newport News	03	11	84	13	02	88	11	11	89
George Washington	CVN[b]	73 Newport News	25	08	86	21	07	90			1991
John C. Stennis	CVN[b]	74 Newport News	in planning			in planning			in planning		
Harry S. Truman	CVN[b]	75 Newport News	in planning			in planning			in planning		
Ronald Reagan	CVN[b]	76 Newport News	in planning			in planning			in planning		

[a] Slep: Service Life-Extension Project.
[b] CVN: Nuclear-Powered Aircraft Carrier.
[c] Rcoh: Refueling and Complex Overhaul.
Source: Timothy M. Laur and Steven L. Llanso, *Encyclopedia of Modern U.S. Military Weapons* (New York, 1995), 469.

TABLE 10.30 STRATEGIC-MISSILE SUBMARINES—"LAFAYETTE" CLASS (POSEIDON)

Number	Name	FY	Builder	Laid down	Launched	Commis-sioned	Status
SSBN 616	*Lafayette*	61	General Dynamics/Electric Boat	Jan. 17, 1961	May 8, 1962	Apr. 23, 1963	decomm. (1990s)
SSBN 617	*Alexander Hamilton*	61	General Dynamics/Electric Boat	Jun. 26, 1961	Aug. 18, 1962	Jun. 27, 1963	decomm. (1990s)
SSBN 619	*Andrew Jackson*	61	Mare Island Naval Shipyard	Apr. 26, 1961	Sep. 15, 1962	Jul. 3, 1963	decomm./str. Sep. 6, 1989
SSBN 620	*John Adams*	61	Portsmouth Naval Shipyard	May 19, 1961	Jan. 12, 1963	May 12, 1964	decomm./str. Sep. 30, 1989
SSBN 622	*James Monroe*	S61	Newport News Shipbuilding	Jul. 31, 1961	Aug. 4, 1962	Dec. 7, 1963	decomm./str. Sep. 25, 1990
SSBN 623	*Nathan Hale*	S61	General Dynamics/Electric Boat	Oct. 2, 1961	Jan. 12, 1963	Nov. 23, 1963	decomm./str. Nov 3, 1986
SSBN 624	*Woodrow Wilson*	S61	Mare Island Naval Shipyard	Sep. 13, 1961	Feb. 22, 1963	Dec. 27, 1963	decomm. (1990s)
SSBN 625	*Henry Clay*	S61	Newport News Shipbuilding	Oct. 22, 1961	Nov 30, 1962	Feb. 20, 1964	decomm./str. Nov 6, 1990
SSBN 626	*Daniel Webster*	S61	General Dynamics/Electric Boat	Dec. 28, 1961	Apr. 27, 1963	Apr. 9, 1964	decomm.; to MTS 626[a]
SSBN 627	*James Madison*	62	Newport News Shipbuilding	Mar. 5, 1962	Mar. 15, 1963	Jul. 28, 1964	decomm. (1990s)
SSBN 628	*Tecumseh*	62	General Dynamics/Electric Boat	Jun. 1, 1962	Jun. 22, 1963	May 29, 1964	decomm. (1990s)
SSBN 629	*Daniel Boone*	62	Mare Island Naval Shipyard	Feb. 6, 1962	Jun. 22, 1963	Apr. 23, 1964	[b]
SSBN 630	*John C. Calhoun*	62	Newport News Shipbuilding	Jun. 4, 1962	Jun. 22, 1963	Sep. 15, 1964	[b]
SSBN 631	*Ulysses S. Grant*	62	General Dynamics/Electric Boat	Aug. 18, 1962	Nov 2, 1963	Jul. 17, 1964	decomm. (1990s)
SSBN 632	*Von Steuben*	62	Newport News Shipbuilding	Sep. 4, 1962	Oct. 18, 1963	Sep. 30, 1964	[b] decomm. (1990s)
SSBN 633	*Casimir Pulaski*	62	General Dynamics/Electric Boat	Jan. 12, 1963	Feb. 1, 1964	Aug. 14, 1964	[b]
SSBN 634	*Stonewall Jackson*	62	Mare Island Naval Shipyard	Jul. 4, 1962	Nov 30, 1963	Aug. 26, 1964	[b]
SSBN 635	*Sam Rayburn*	62	Newport News Shipbuilding	Dec. 3, 1962	Dec. 20, 1963	Dec. 2, 1964	decomm./str. Jul. 31, 1989; to MTS 635[a]
SSBN 636	*Nathanael Greene*	62	Portsmouth Naval Shipyard	May 21, 1962	May 12, 1964	Dec. 19, 1964	decomm. Dec. 12, 1986; str. Jan. 31, 1987
SSBN 640	*Benjamin Franklin*	63	General Dynamics/Electric Boat	May 25, 1963	Dec. 5, 1964	Oct. 22, 1965	[b]
SSBN 641	*Simon Bolivar*	63	Newport News Shipbuilding	Apr. 17, 1963	Aug. 22, 1964	Oct. 29, 1965	[b]
SSBN 642	*Kamehameha*	63	Mare Island Naval Shipyard	May 2, 1963	Jan. 16, 1965	Dec. 10, 1965	to transport submarine
SSBN 643	*George Bancroft*	63	General Dynamics/Electric Boat	Aug. 24, 1963	Mar. 20, 1965	Jan. 22, 1966	[b]
SSBN 644	*Lewis and Clark*	63	Newport News Shipbuilding	Jul. 29, 1963	Nov 21, 1964	Dec. 22, 1965	decomm. (1990s)
SSBN 645	*James K. Polk*	63	General Dynamics/Electric Boat	Nov 23, 1963	May 22, 1965	Apr. 16, 1966	to transport submarine
SSBN 654	*George C. Marshall*	64	Newport News Shipbuilding	Mar. 2, 1964	May 21, 1965	Apr. 29, 1966	decomm. (1990s)
SSBN 655	*Henry L. Stimson*	64	General Dynamics/Electric Boat	Apr. 4, 1964	Nov 13, 1965	Aug. 20, 1966	[b] decomm. (1990s)
SSBN 656	*George Washington Carver*	64	Newport News Shipbuilding	Aug. 24, 1964	Aug. 14, 1965	Jun. 15, 1966	decomm. (1990s)
SSBN 657	*Francis Scott Key*	64	General Dynamics/Electric Boat	Dec. 5, 1964	Apr. 23, 1966	Dec. 3, 1966	[b]
SSBN 658	*Mariano G. Vallejo*	64	Mare Island Naval Shipyard	Jul. 7, 1964	Oct. 23, 1965	Dec. 16, 1966	[b]
SSBN 659	*Will Rogers*	64	General Dynamics/Electric Boat	Mar. 20, 1965	Jul. 21, 1966	Apr. 1, 1967	decomm. (1990s)

Specifications

Displacement: 6,650 tons light
              7,250 tons standard
              8,250 tons submerged
Length: 425 feet (129.6 m) overall
Beam: 33 feet (10.06 m)
Draft: $31^{1}/_{2}$ feet (9.6 m)
Propulsion: 2 steam turbines; 15,000 shp; 1 shaft
Reactors: 1 pressurized-water S5W (Westinghouse)
Speed: *approx. 20 knots surface*
              approx. 25 knots submerged
Manning: approx. 150(15 officers + 135 enlisted)
Missiles: 16 tubes for Poseidon C-3 SLBM, each with 10 warheads. (Original equipment was the Polaris SLBM, each with a single warhead.)

[a] MTS means Moored Training Ships.
[b] Eventually rearmed with upgraded Trident C-4 missiles.
Source: Polmar, *Guide to Ships and Aircraft*, 59.

TABLE 10.31 NUCLEAR-PROPELLED STRATEGIC-MISSILE SUBMARINES—"OHIO" CLASS (TRIDENT)

Number	Name	FY	Builder	Laid Down	Launched	Commissioned
SSBN 726	Ohio	74	General Dynamics/Electric Boat	Apr. 10, 1976	Apr. 7, 1979	Nov. 11, 1981
SSBN 727	Michigan	75	General Dynamics/Electric Boat	Apr. 4, 1977	Apr. 26, 1980	Sep. 11, 1982
SSBN 728	Florida	75	General Dynamics/Electric Boat	Jun. 9, 1977	Nov. 14, 1981	Jun. 18, 1983
SSBN 729	Georgia	76	General Dynamics/Electric Boat	Apr. 7, 1979	Nov. 6, 1982	Feb. 11, 1984
SSBN 730	Henry M. Jackson	77	General Dynamics/Electric Boat	Jan. 19, 1981	Oct. 15, 1983	Oct. 6, 1984
SSBN 731	Alabama	78	General Dynamics/Electric Boat	Aug. 27, 1981	May 19, 1984	May 25, 1985
SSBN 732	Alaska	78	General Dynamics/Electric Boat	Mar. 9, 1983	Jan. 12, 1985	Jan. 25, 1986
SSBN 733	Nevada	80	General Dynamics/Electric Boat	Aug. 8, 1983	Sep. 14, 1985	Aug. 16, 1986
SSBN 734	Tennessee	81	General Dynamics/Electric Boat	Jun. 9, 1986	Dec. 13, 1986	Dec. 17, 1988
SSBN 735	Pennsylvania	83	General Dynamics/Electric Boat	Mar. 2, 1987	Apr. 23, 1988	Sep. 9, 1989
SSBN 736	West Virginia	84	General Dynamics/Electric Boat	Dec. 18, 1987	Oct. 14, 1989	Oct. 20, 1990
SSBN 737	Kentucky	85	General Dynamics/Electric Boat	Dec. 18, 1987	Aug. 11, 1990	. . .
SSBN 738	Maryland	86	General Dynamics/Electric Boat	Dec. 18, 1987	. . .	. . .
SSBN 739	Nebraska	87	General Dynamics/Electric Boat	Dec. 18, 1987	. . .	. . .
SSBN 740	Rhode Island	88	General Dynamics/Electric Boat	Apr. 23, 1988	. . .	. . .
SSBN 741	Maine	89	General Dynamics/Electric Boat	Apr. 4, 1989	. . .	. . .
SSBN 742	Wyoming	90	General Dynamics/Electric Boat	Jan. 27, 1990	. . .	. . .
SSBN 743	Louisiana	91	General Dynamics/Electric Boat	. . .	. . .	. . .

Specifications

Displacement:	16,764 tons standard
	18,750 tons submerged
Length:	560 feet (170.7 m) overall
Beam:	42 feet (12.8 m)
Draft:	36 1/4 feet (11.05 m)
Propulsion:	2 steam turbines (General Electric); 1 shaft
Reactors:	1 pressurized-reactor S8G (General Electric)
Speed:	28 knots surface
	approx. 30 knots submerged
Manning:	approx. 172 (16 officers + 156 enlisted)
Missiles:	24 tubes for Trident C-4 SLBM in SSBN 726–733; 24 Tubes Trident D-5 in 734–743
	Each missile carried 8 warheads.

Source: Polmar, *Guide to Ships and Aircraft*, 56.

Submarine *Ohio* with missile tubes open: It was the first of newest and largest class of Trident ballistic missile submarines. (Defense Visual Information Center)

TABLE 10.32   U.S./SOVIET MILITARY COMPARISON, 1960

Statistical Summary (January 1960)			
Manpower	U.S.	USSR	U.S. Standing
	2,476,000	3,623,000	−1,147,000
Strategic Nuclear			
Offense			
Bombers			
Long-range	540	160–190	+350–380
Medium-range	1,775	1,000	+775
Cruise missiles	30	A few	About +30
Ballistic missiles			
ICBMs	12	Under 50	About −38
SLBMs	48	48	Par
Warheads	60	Under 100	About −40
Defense			
ABM	0	0	Par
Interceptor aircraft	2,700	5,000	−2,300
Surface-to-air missiles	4,400	4,800	−400
Theater Nuclear	U.S.	USSR	U.S. Standing
MRBM/IRBM	51	200	−149
Other	Many	A few	+Many

Statistical Summary (January 1960)			
Land Power	U.S.	USSR	U.S. Standing
Manpower			
Army/Ground Forces	873,000	2,250,000	−1,377,000
Marines/Naval Infantry	170,600	A few	+170,600
Divisions			
Army/Ground Forces	14	136	−122
Marines/Naval Infantry	3	0	+3
Tanks	12,975	35,000	−22,025
Tactical Air Forces	U.S.	USSR	U.S. Standing
Fighter/attack			
Land-based	1,805	4,000	−2,195
Carrier-based	1,300	0	+1,300
Medium-range bombers	0	1,000	−1,000
Naval Forces	U.S.	USSR	U.S. Standing
Aircraft carriers	23	0	+23
Cruisers	13	23	−10
Destroyers	226	124	+102
Frigates/other escorts	41	13	+28
Attack submarines	111	404	−293
Amphibious ships	113	0	+113
Land-based bombers	0	500	−500
Mobility Forces	U.S.	USSR	U.S. Standing
Airlift	1,725	1,065	+660
Sealift	954	873	+81

Source: Ray Bonds, *The U.S. War Machine* (New York, 1983), 266.

TABLE 10.33   STRATEGIC OFFENSIVE FORCES OF THE SUPERPOWERS, 1990

Delivery Vehicle Type	United States				Soviet Union		
	Weapon	Launchers Deployed	Warheads/ Launchers	Total Warheads	Weapon	Launchers Deployed	Warheads/ Launcher
Ballistic missiles							
Intercontinental ballistic missiles (ICBM)	Minuteman II	450	1	450	SS-18	308	10
	Minuteman III	500	3	1,500	SS-24	60	10
	MX	50	10	500	SS-25	225	1
					SS-11	350	1
					SS-13	60	1
					SS-17	75	4
					SS-19	320	6
Submarine-launched ballistic missiles (SLBM)	Poseidon C-3	192	10	1,920	SS-N-6	192	1
	Trident C-4	384	8	3,072	SS-N-8	280	1
	Trident D-5	48	8	384	SS-N-17	12	1
					SS-N-18	224	7
					SS-N-20	120	10
					SS-N-23	96	4
Total ballistic missiles		1,624	. . .	7,826		2,322	. . .
START limit				(4,900)			
Bombers							
With air-launched cruise missiles	B-52G	77	10	770	Bear	75	8
	B-52H	95	10	950	Blackjack	15	8
Without air-launched cruise missiles	B-1B	95	1	95	Bear	95	1
	B-52G/H	39	1	39			
Total bombers		306	. . .	1,854		185	. . .
Grand total		1,930	. . .	9,680		2,497	. . .
START limit		(1,600)	. . .	(6,000)		(1,660)	. . .

Note: ". . ." indicates not applicable. Data as of June 1, 1990. "START" refers to the Strategic Arms Reduction Talks between the United States and Union. Shown are strategic forces under START counting rules.
Source: Stanley and Niemi, *Statistics on Politics,* 348.

F-117 Nighthawk Stealth fighter plane—modern technology that evaded detection by radar (Defense Visual Information Center)

TABLE 10.34   EXAMPLES OF U.S. WEAPON SYSTEM COSTS

(millions of 1988 U.S. dollars)

Weapon System	Unit Cost	Number	Program Cost
Nuclear aircraft carrier	3,046	2	6,092
Trident II submarine	1,486	11	16,350
Aegis cruiser	987	27	26,658
B-1B bomber	261	100	26,142
C-17A cargo aircraft	126	211	26,607
Trident II missile	36	845	30,451
F-15 fighter aircraft	33	1,286	41,904
F-16 fighter aircraft	16	2,737	43,147
UH-60 helicopter	6.5	1,121	7,233
M-1 tank	2.5	7,857	19,947
Harpoon antiship missile	1.2	4,023	4,996
Sparrow antiaircraft missile	0.19	14,309	2,724

Source: Trevor N. Dupuy, *International Military and Defense Encyclopedia, Vol. 6* (New York, 1993), 2687.

Instruments of American Policy: Alliances

The first military alliance of the United States had been a treaty signed with France in 1778, during the American Revolution. While the alliance had been helpful, possibly indispensable, in winning independence, it did become troublesome in its later stages, threatening to entangle the new nation in seemingly interminable quarrels of Europe. It was said that this unpleasant experience—fostered, one might add, by American isolation and a popular perception of the nation's uniqueness—caused the United States to avoid "foreign" alliances for more than 150 years.

The two world wars had produced temporary working arrangements with "allied" nations, but the government had assumed no commitment to guarantee any nation support for the future. The cold war and the pre-eminent postwar position of the United States changed that situation, abruptly and in a major way. America's second military alliance, the NATO Pact of 1949, committed the United States to defend much of a continent: 10 European nations (and Canada) at first and eventually there would be 15. The alliance remained in operation, if with modified objectives, as the century drew to a close. After the first step, other alliances came quickly, although—one would hope—not easily. Some were bilateral, with a single country; others involved regional groups of nations. The Rio Pact with Latin America in fact had preceded NATO, but while it carried a potential for military application, it did not constitute a hard and fast military agreement on the order of the Atlantic Alliance.

The upshot was that the United States found itself committed to the defense of many of the world's nations, the chief exceptions being the Soviet bloc, of course, and the nations of Africa. The arrangement produced a possible scenario of two nations contemplating war, as in the case of Greece and Turkey in the 1960s, and the United States would be committed to defend both. And there was more: The United States did not need a treaty to come to the protection of a country. It intervened on behalf of South Korea without a promise to do so; the treaty came later. The United States had no alliance with South Vietnam, but it fought an eight-year war on its behalf. No treaty with Israel existed, but virtually no one doubted that if Israel was about to go down, the Americans would step in. The government's duty to protect the nation, it would appear, had taken on peculiar meaning.

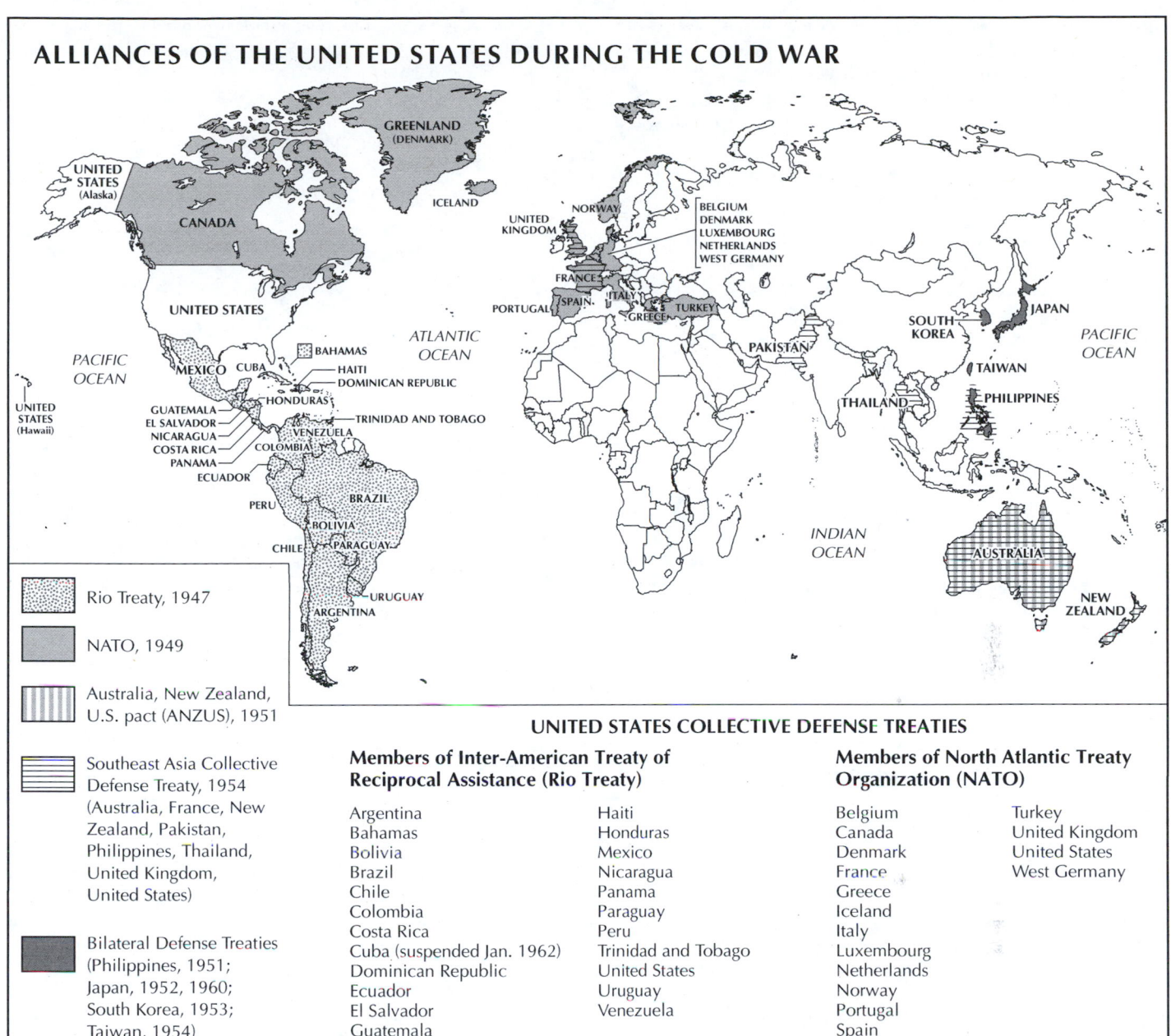

ALLIANCES OF THE UNITED STATES DURING THE COLD WAR

Rio Treaty, 1947

NATO, 1949

Australia, New Zealand, U.S. pact (ANZUS), 1951

Southeast Asia Collective Defense Treaty, 1954 (Australia, France, New Zealand, Pakistan, Philippines, Thailand, United Kingdom, United States)

Bilateral Defense Treaties (Philippines, 1951; Japan, 1952, 1960; South Korea, 1953; Taiwan, 1954)

UNITED STATES COLLECTIVE DEFENSE TREATIES

Members of Inter-American Treaty of Reciprocal Assistance (Rio Treaty)

Argentina	Haiti
Bahamas	Honduras
Bolivia	Mexico
Brazil	Nicaragua
Chile	Panama
Colombia	Paraguay
Costa Rica	Peru
Cuba (suspended Jan. 1962)	Trinidad and Tobago
Dominican Republic	United States
Ecuador	Uruguay
El Salvador	Venezuela
Guatemala	

Members of North Atlantic Treaty Organization (NATO)

Belgium	Turkey
Canada	United Kingdom
Denmark	United States
France	West Germany
Greece	
Iceland	
Italy	
Luxembourg	
Netherlands	
Norway	
Portugal	
Spain	

The Secret Cold War: World of the CIA

Among the many fronts of the cold war was the shadowy, secret domain of intelligence, a realm that the American government largely assigned to the Central Intelligence Agency (CIA). The long duration, global dimension, and multiple contested points of the cold war perhaps made it inevitable that the CIA would move beyond gathering information. Secrecy of operations left the agency in a position to execute policy, even initiate it by spreading propaganda in a foreign land, influencing elections, organizing coups—even the assassination of a leader. The most aggressive covert activities of the 1950s and 1960s produced both successes and failures. The post-Vietnam syndrome of the 1970s inspired investigations of the CIA and congressional efforts to halt most clandestine operations. The Reagan administration attempted to reinvigorate "the Company" under an aggressive director, William Casey, and the examples of not-so-secret activity in Afghanistan and Nicaragua suggested that the results, again, were mixed. The cold war's end seemed certain to change the role of the CIA, but in 1990 one could not tell how much or in what ways.

Instruments of American Policy: Covert Activity[a]

Iran (1953)   *President:* Eisenhower. CIA efforts to encourage opposition to leftist, nationalist prime minister, Mohammad Mossadegh.
Result: success—Mossadegh is deposed; the king (shah) returns to power, grateful to the Americans.

Guatemala (1954)   *President:* Eisenhower. CIA helps undermine leftist, reformist president, Jacobo Arbenz Guzmán, who had seized American property.
Result: Arbenz is deposed in favor of conservative military leader, Col. C. Castillo Armas, but troubles in Guatemala continue.

Cuba (1961)   *President:* Eisenhower/Kennedy. The Bay of Pigs Project. Poorly kept CIA effort to overthrow Castro regime in Cuba, using counterrevolutionary Cuban forces.
Result: failure—plot is foiled; rebels captured; United States is embarrassed.

Cuba (1961–63)   *President:* Kennedy. Various, often bizarre, CIA plots to assassinate Castro.

Result: failure—all plots fail; Castro lives on.

Chile (1973)   *President:* Nixon. CIA organizes opposition to Salvador Allende, popularly elected Marxist president who seized American copper assets.

Result: success—Allende is deposed (and assassinated), to be replaced by ultraconservative military leader.

Nicaragua (1980s)   *President:* Reagan. Not-so-secret American effort to organize a counterforce, called the Contras, to leftist Sandinista government.

Result: Controversial project fails, but it does weaken the Nicaraguan regime.

Afghanistan (1980s)   *President:* Reagan. CIA-managed program to funnel military aid, notably the Stinger ground-to-air missile, to Afghans who are resisting Soviet intervention.

Result: general success as Soviets become bogged down and then pull out; the Afghan victors, however, were neither saints nor democrats.

Iran-Contra episode (1985–86)   *President:* Reagan. A conspiracy within a conspiracy. When Congress refused aid for Contras in Nicaragua, people in the National Security Council, that is, Lt. Col. Oliver North, secretly sold arms to Iran, presumably the U.S.'s bitterest foe, and used the money to aid the Contras.

Result: Plot was exposed; Reagan presidency threatened; a $40 million investigation followed, but no one was punished.

ª Secret or not-so-secret activity, usually by the Central Intelligence Agency, to influence events in a foreign country. Projects extended to support for, weakening, even assassinating, a country's leader or deposing its government.

Instruments of American Foreign Policy: Armed Intervention

Korea (1950–1953)   *President:* Truman/Eisenhower. The United States fought a three-year war against communist forces of North Korea and China.

Result: a draw, no victor, but independence of South Korea was preserved; government claimed that containment succeeded.

Lebanon (1958)   *President:* Eisenhower. Some 14,000 marines sent ostensibly to keep communism out, in truth to prevent victory of anti-Western regime.

Result: status quo preserved, but Arab nationalists were furious.

Dominican Republic (1965)   *President:* Johnson. Some 20,000 soldiers sent to prevent a leftist regime coming to power.

Result: conservatives will achieve power, but Latin Americans saw more Yankee imperialism.

Vietnam (1965–73)   *President:* Johnson/Nixon. More than 500,000 troops engaged in long war to keep communism from Southern Vietnam and Southeast Asia.

Result: failure in all respects—casualties high; United States is divided; communists win.

Grenada (1983)   *President:* Reagan. Perhaps partly a move to recapture American military morale. Forces sent to rescue American students caught in a civil conflict and to keep out a leftist, Pro-Cuban regime.

Result: success but at huge cost in money and casualties.

Lebanon (1983)   *President:* Reagan. Some 1,200 marines sent as peace keepers in Syrian-Palestinian-Israeli-internal Lebanese conflict in Lebanon—a real mess. Objective is honorable but unobtainable.

Result: failure—some 250 marines killed; Americans are driven out. Not directly part of cold war.

Panama (1989)   *President:* Bush: 23,000 troops sent to depose and capture Manuel Noriega, corrupt, defiant dictator engaged in drug traffic.

Result: Noriega is captured and imprisoned in the United States, but costs are very high for United States and Panamanians. Not directly part of the cold war.

Persian Gulf (1990)   *President:* Bush. Half-million Americans lead a multinational force to protect Saudi Arabia and liberate Kuwait from conquest by Iraq. Oil has much to do with it.

Result: Outcome not determined, but allied force should win. Not directly part of cold war; venture perhaps made possible by its ending.

The Vietnam War

The Vietnam War grew out of the paranoia and perceptions of the early years of the cold war when conclusions that years later would be proven false seemed altogether valid. At the time the United States first established a policy toward French Indochina—of which Vietnam was a major part—communism was indeed a powerful world force; the Soviet Union was the acknowledged leader (even Mao Zedong in China had recognized that point), and in Eastern Europe the USSR was the dominant fact of political life. Its will prevailed. Specialists in the history and culture of East Asia could explain that that continent was different, that postwar revolutions in Asia were independent, largely anticolonial movements, and to the extent that communism became a force (as it frequently did), it was nationalistic and pluralistic, as opposed to being part of the large monolithic undertaking that the government of the United States claimed to have detected. Such observations at the time could only be offered as interpretation, even speculation; communism was a new force, untested in many ways, but showing a great deal of momentum in the years following the Second World War. So it was that the United States came to oppose communist-led revolutions in Asia, finding them at least oppressive, ineffective in the long run, and contrary to the general interests of the United States. The worst-case scenario identified them as agents—consciously or not—of Soviet imperialism.

The American war in Vietnam developed in increments, with the failure of one step providing a basis for another, larger move. Jargon of the Vietnam era termed the process "escalation." Every president from Harry Truman to Richard Nixon had a hand in building the war into the nightmare that it would become in the late 1960s. Probably the most important moves were the commitments to a separate South Vietnamese state assumed by the Dwight Eisenhower administration at the time of the ouster of the French in 1954–55 and the massive increase in military forces sent to Vietnam (more than 500,000)—in effect making the conflict an American war—undertaken by Lyndon Johnson during the years 1965–68. If Richard Nixon received credit for ending the American part in the war, the process took four years, entailed massive bombing campaigns, and came at large loss of life by Americans and people in both Vietnams.

By 1967 at latest, the war had become the largest issue in national American life and politics, and matters would continue to worsen. American deaths and injuries multiplied in proportion to the increase in soldiers committed and their engagement in combat. Casual-ties, homelessness, and general suffering of the Vietnamese people increased as the war expanded. Evidence mounted to challenge presumptions and perceptions of the early years of the cold war: about the fraternal unity of all communists, for example. (The Chinese and Russians at that time were almost at one another's throats.) The case seemed increasingly clear that the conflict in Vietnam was, and always had been, a nationalist, anticolonial revolution. To be sure, the situation was complicated by considerable brutality on the enemy's side (really on both sides) and by the fact that the Vietnamese differed among themselves on how their land should be run. Many Vietnamese did object to a communist regime imposed by people from the north. But, as one frequently heard it put at the time, "their Vietnamese" seemed substantially more determined and effective than "our Vietnamese." The nationalist inspiration seemed to be all on the other side.

The F-4 "Phantom" fighter-bomber, top-of-the line of the U.S. Air Force in the 1960s, was the main plane of the Vietnam War. (author's photo)

Finally, if the war devastated Vietnam, it also appeared to carry a danger of destroying the United States. Between 1967 and 1973 the nation experienced a division sharper than at any time since the American Civil War, and the most obvious reason was the war. At first glance it would appear that the division existed along generational lines—the newly emerging baby boomers who provided the troops, but not necessarily the leadership, of the antiwar movement—against the previous generation, or generations, who had grown up in circumstances different from their offspring. It would be interesting to know what direction the 1960s (really the late 1960s and early 1970s) would have taken had there been no war. The Civil Rights Movement earlier had sent out signals of a broadening revolution, and the new generation was giving notice that it wished to make its own rules of social behavior. As it was, the Vietnam War served to broaden, intensify, and validate a revolution in social activity that already had been building. The war was deemed so reprehensible that it explained and legitimized any activity undertaken in the name of opposition—ranging from hair styles and wearing apparel, sexual laxity, and illegal drug use to defying draft laws and the bombing of military recruitment offices, centers for weapons research, and corporation headquarters, places marked out by self-appointed radical leaders as agents of the "establishment." Many Americans came to fear that the country was coming apart and to conclude that people associated with the revolution did not bother to notice or did not seem

to care if it happened. The few genuine, dedicated revolutionaries took satisfaction in the prospect of national rebirth.

Whatever the antiwar movement did or did not do, it left a clear message that the United States had to get out of Vietnam. Negotiations to that end had been going on, intermittently, for nearly four years. The armistice agreement finalized in January 1973 by Henry Kissinger for the United States and Le Duc Tho for North Vietnam (for which both would receive the Nobel Peace Prize) would be merciful only for the United States. The final American troops came home; released prisoners-of-war followed shortly. The draft ended on January 27, the day the armistice took effect. The antiwar movement vanished almost overnight and the spirit of revolution died in the land. In Vietnam, however, the killing continued; 1974 produced more deaths than any other year. Nixon's policy of Vietnamization had been designed to allow South Vietnam to stand indefinitely, but in fact it lasted only some two years. Once the enemy began a major offensive in January 1975, the regime in the south collapsed with remarkable speed. After fighting a substantial battle in early April, South Vietnamese forces either fled or fell back to the capital. The surrender of Saigon on April 30, 1975, brought the war to an end. Combined with victory of leftist revolutionaries (the Khmer Rouge) in Cambodia two weeks earlier and of leftists in Laos (the Pathet Lao) the following year, the defeat sealed not merely a failure of American policy in South Vietnam but in all former French Indochina.

TABLE 10.35 U.S. MILITARY PERSONNEL IN SOUTH VIETNAM, 1960–1973

Date	Number
Dec. 31, 1960	900
Dec. 31, 1961	3,205
Dec. 31, 1962	9,000
Dec. 31, 1963	16,500
Dec. 31, 1964	23,300
Dec. 31, 1965	184,300
Jun. 30, 1966	267,500
Dec. 31, 1966	385,300
Jun. 30, 1967	448,800
Dec. 31, 1967	485,600
Jun. 30, 1968	534,700
Dec. 31, 1968	536,100
Apr. 30, 1969	543,400
Jun. 30, 1969	538,700
Dec. 31, 1969	475,200
Jun. 30, 1970	414,900
Dec. 31, 1970	334,600
Jun. 30, 1971	239,200
Dec. 31, 1971	156,800
Jun. 30, 1972	47,000
Dec. 31, 1972	24,200
Mar. 30, 1973	240

Source: Defense Department statistics, reported in George Donelson Moss, *Vietnam: An American Ordeal* (Englewood Cliffs, N.J., 1994), 415.

TABLE 10.36 REPUBLIC OF VIETNAM MILITARY STRENGTH, 1955–1972

Year	Army	Air Force	Navy	Regional Forces	Marine Corps	Popular Forces
1955	170,000	3,500	2,200	1,500	54,000	48,000
1960	136,000	4,600	4,300	2,000	49,000	48,000
1964	220,000	11,000	12,000	7,000	96,000	168,000
1967	303,000	16,000	16,000	8,000	151,000	149,000
1968	380,000	19,000	19,000	9,000	220,000	173,000
1969	416,000	36,000	30,000	11,000	190,000	214,000
1970	416,000	46,000	40,000	13,000	207,000	246,000
1972	410,000	50,000	42,000	14,000	284,000	248,000

Source: Spence C. Tucker, *Encyclopedia of the Vietnam War* (3 Vols., Santa Barbara, 1998), 526.

Flame-throwing tank of the American First Battalion burns an unidentified village in South Vietnam. (National Archives)

An American soldier is lowered into an enemy tunnel by comrades of the First Cavalry Division. Near Duc Pho, Vietnam. (National Archives)

TABLE 10.37 COMPARATIVE MILITARY CASUALTY FIGURES, 1960–1974

Year	Killed in Action		Wounded in Action	
	U.S.	RVNAF	U.S.	RVNAF
1960	0	2,223	0	2,788
1961	11	4,004	2	5,449
1962	31	4,457	41	7,195
1963	78	5,665	218	11,488
1964	147	7,457	522	17,017
1965	1,369	11,242	3,308	23,118
1966	5,008	11,953	16,526	20,975
1967	9,377	12,716	32,370	29,448
1968	14,589	27,915	46,797	70,696
1969	9,414	21,833	32,940	65,276
1970	4,221	23,346	15,211	71,582
1971	1,381	22,738	4,767	60,939
1972	300	39,587	587	109,960
1973	237	27,901	24	131,936
1974	207	31,219	0	155,735
Totals	46,370	254,256	153,313[a]	783,602

[a] Pertains only to persons who required hospital care. Another 150,000 did not.
Source: Moss, Vietnam, 416.

TABLE 10.38 CASUALTIES, JANUARY 1, 1961– JANUARY 28, 1973

Country	Number
United States	
Killed in action	45,941
Wounded	300,635
Missing	2,330
Killed or died, noncombat-related	10,420
South Vietnam	
Military: Killed in action	220,357
Military: Wounded	499,026
Civilian: Killed	415,000
Civilian: Wounded	935,000
Vietcong/North Vietnam	
Military: Killed	851,000
Civilian: North Vietnam	65,000
Third-Country Forces	
Military: Killed in action	
Korea	4,407
Australia/New Zealand	469
Thailand	351

Source: Moss, Vietnam, 416.

TABLE 10.39 STATISTICAL PORTRAIT OF U.S. CASUALTIES IN INDOCHINA

Type	Number
Killed in combat	45,941
Wounded in combat	300,635
Died in noncombat situations	10,420
90% of combat deaths were enlisted men	41,003
10% of combat deaths were officers	4,938
60% of combat deaths were age 19–21	26,931
22% of combat deaths were age 22–25	10,421
18% of combat deaths were age 26+	8,589
33% of the dead had served less than 1 year	14,995
33% of the dead had served between 1 and 2 years	14,853
Blacks accounted for 12% of the combat deaths	5,662
Other nonwhites accounted for 1% of the combat deaths	469
Whites accounted for 87% of the combat deaths	39,827
Draftees accounted for 33% of the combat deaths	15,404

Source: Moss, Vietnam, 417.

TABLE 10.40 U.S. CASUALTIES BY MILITARY SERVICE

Service	Battle Deaths	Nonbattle Deaths	WIA*	Total
Army	30,905	7,275	96,802	134,974
Navy	1,626	923	4,178	6,697
Marine Corps	13,082	1,754	51,392	66,213
Air Force	1,739	842	931	3,435
Coast Guard	5	2	n.a.	7
Total	47,357	10,796	153,303	211,326

* Wounded in action
Source: Michael Clodfelter, Vietnam in Military Statistics, 1772–1991 (Jefferson, N.C., 1995), 255.

TABLE 10.41 CASUALTIES BY AGE

Age	Number KIA
17	11
18	2,602
19	7,015
20	11,989
21	7,953
22	3,872
23	2,841
24	2,161
25	1,602
26	1,116

Source: Clodfelter, Vietnam Statistics, 255.

TABLE 10.42 CAUSES OF COMBAT AND NON-COMBAT DEATHS

Deaths	Number
Combat Deaths	45,941
Aircraft loss	4,178
Gunshot or small arms fire	18,385
Artillery/rocket/other explosion	12,350
Multiple fragmentation wounds	8,465
Other causes/unknown	2,563
Noncombat Deaths	10,420
Accidents	8,483
Illness	929
Murder	190
Suicide	379
Other	439

Source: Moss, Vietnam, 417.

TABLE 10.43 U.S. AIR SORTIES IN SOUTH VIETNAM, 1966–1973[a]

Year	Fixed-Wing Aircraft	Helicopters
1966	170,044	2,989,546
1967	222,276	5,479,518
1968	281,730	7,415,452
1969	254,841	8,208,099
1970	129,855	7,564,064
1971	40,616	4,212,251
1972	118,575	1,061,842
1973	10,977	67,383

[a] A sortie is a single plane flying a single mission.
Source: Clodfelter, Vietnam Statistics, 227, 229.

TABLE 10.44 TOTAL AIRCRAFT LOSSES, 1962–1973

Type	Number
Fixed-wing Aircraft	3,719
Helicopters	4,869
Total Aircraft	8,588

Source: Clodfelter, Vietnam Statistics, 228.

Miscellaneous Information about the Vietnam Military Experience

Desertion

Number of men who fled (to another country, or in hiding) to escape the draft: 30,000
Number of men who deserted their military unit: 20,000
Number of men who deserted in, or in route to, Vietnam: 12,000

Desertion rate per 1,000 men:	Army	Marines
In 1966:	14.7	16.1
In 1971:	73.5	56.1
Desertion rate in Korean War (1953):	22.3	29.6
Desertion at highest point in WW II (1944):	63.0	6.9

Number of deserters from Vietnamese army: 1968–71: 491,000

Venereal Disease

Estimated number of prostitutes in South Vietnam (1969): 600,000
Venereal disease rate per 1,000 servicemen in Vietnam (1969) 200
Venereal disease rate per 1,000 servicemen in Vietnam (1972) 700
Venereal disease rate per 1,000 adults in the U.S. (1969): 32

Selected Drug Use

Estimated percent of servicemen in Vietnam who smoked marijuana:	
In 1967:	29%
In 1969:	50.1
In 1971:	58.5

Number of Vietnam veterans addicted to heroin in 1970: 70,000

Fragging[a]

	1969	1970	1971	Total
Number of documented incidents:	126	271	333	1,017[b]
Number of documented deaths:	37	34	12	. . .

[a] An attack by a serviceman on a person in command: an officer or noncommissioned officer—named after a fragmentation grenade, a favorite weapon of assault.
[b] Estimates put the number (many were unreported) much higher.

Less than Honorable Discharges, 1965–73

General discharge:	300,000
Bad conduct discharges:	31,800
Dishonorable discharges:	2,200
Undesirable discharges:	215,000
Total:	563,000

Source: Clodfelter, Vietnam Statistics, 242, 246–48.

TABLE 10.45   U.S. AIRCRAFT LOSSES IN VIETNAM, 1966–1973

Losses	1966	1967	1968	1969	1970	1971	1972	1973
Fixed-Wing Aircraft								
Lost in North Vietnam	284	333	143	2	4	6	149	4
Lost in South Vietnam	118	141	239	156	59	29	63	3
Total lost in combat	402	474	382	158	63	35	212	7
Operational losses	232	254	275	308	199	110	88	24
Total combat and operational	634	728	657	466	262	145	300	31
Helicopters								
Lost in North Vietnam	1	4	2				1	
Lost in South Vietnam	127	276	558	521	431	224	128	4
Total lost in combat	128	280	560	521	431	224	129	4
Operational losses	193	383	452	527	422	278	50	5
Total combat and operational	321	663	1,012	1,048	853	502	179	9

Source: Clodfelter, *Vietnam Statistics,* 229.

"Home is where you dig it" says the sign over a bunker of soldiers of the Seventh Infantry Regiment, Vietnam. (National Archives)

Aftermath of Vietnam: The Syndrome

The Vietnam War had been a terrible experience for the people of the United States. The war had occupied some eight years of national life, caused the death of more than 58,000 service members and the expenditure of many billions of dollars; it had fractured the body politic in ways that previously had been unthinkable; and all these great costs had produced worse than nothing. Although it would be an error to classify the Vietnam War as a defeat for American military forces, it was an unqualified defeat for the policy of the United States. The reaction was immediate. The people had had enough of noble adventurism in world affairs, or whatever it was, and they were not going to do it again. The mood in the United States after 1973 resembled the attitude after the Great War in 1919, although the anger probably was greater. The United States, after all, had been on the winning side in the First World War.

What was deemed the post-Vietnam syndrome manifested itself in several ways. The government was hesitant to become deeply involved in episodes abroad, and if it found reason for activity, it likely would face opposition from Congress, the people, or both. The people distrusted its government, and especially the presidency, in issues pertaining to world affairs, if not generally. The tragedy of Vietnam did correspond with the Watergate scandal, which also reflected upon the integrity of the executive branch. In general the nation seemed to experience a lack of confidence in world affairs, a fear of being burned again, making a mistake similar to the catastrophe of Vietnam. Henry Kissinger, who would be an observer, and as secretary of state under presidents Nixon and Ford, in some measure a victim of this attitude, remarked in his memoirs that Americans wanted to withdraw from world politics in the 1920s because of a belief that the world was not good enough for the United States, but in the post-Vietnam years the Americans pulled back out of a feeling that they were not good enough for the world.

Examples of, or What Could Be Interpreted as, Expressions of the Post Vietnam Mentality

1973 War Powers Act. Passed over President Nixon's veto, designed to restrict sharply presidential war-making power.

1973 Gulf of Tonkin Resolution (of 1964—in support of policy in Vietnam) is repealed. Congress, it appears, is trying to take back the war.

1975 President Ford asks for 100 million to assist anticommunist forces in Cambodia. Congress refuses; Cambodia falls to the radical Khmer Rouge.

1975 President Ford asks for nearly $1 billion to assist the regime in South Vietnam. Congress refuses; South Vietnam falls to the enemy in April.

1975 President Ford and Secretary Kissinger seek congressional support for influencing a civil war in Angola; Congress refuses.

1975 Senate Intelligence Committee (Frank Church Committee) investigates activities of intelligence agencies, FBI and CIA, especially in foreign policy. Revelations about brazen behavior (attempts to assassinate Fidel Castro, for example) leads to restraints placed on CIA.

1977 President Carter completes negotiation of a treaty that will relinquish control of the canal to Panama; doubtless a proper policy, but critics see it (probably correctly) as another surrender of American world power.

1979 President Carter recognizes the People's Republic of China, completing a policy started by Nixon; the agreement requires that the United States abrogate a security pact—and break relations—with Taiwan.

1979 SALT II arms limitation agreement with the USSR. Critics charge that Carter surrendered to the Russians; treaty never will be ratified.

1979 Iranian Revolution ousts the shah, paving the way for a radical, Islamic theocracy. Probably inevitable, but the United States nonetheless loses a loyal and powerful ally in the Persian Gulf. Carter administration barely lifts a finger.

1979 Nicaraguan revolution. Ousts Anastasio Somoza, a brutal, oppressive, but pro-American dictator. Carter's acquiescence is honorable, but even so, the United States will face a leftist, anti-American regime of the Sandinistas.

1979 Beginning of the Iranian hostage crisis. The ultimate humiliation, compounded by Iranian celebration and defiance on television and by a bungled rescue effort in 1980. Carter is held responsible for impotence of the United States in world affairs. The people have had enough of self-condemnation, and the pendulum of attitude starts to swing back, even before Reagan administration arrives.

1980s Ronald Reagan comes to the presidency pledged to sweep away guilt and self-doubt in favor of a restoration of American power, prestige, and confidence. His rhetoric and gestures in world politics are mostly cosmetic but nonetheless impressive and very popular. Even so, the memory of the past war lingers. For all his preoccupation with influencing events in El Salvador and Nicaragua, Reagan refrains from commiting American military forces; the people still do not want "another Vietnam."

1990 Popular support for a substantial military undertaking in the Persian Gulf is solid; international support is widespread.

Instruments of American Policy: Foreign Aid and Sale of Military Goods

The United States was rich at the start of the postwar period, and much of the world was not only poor but—partly because of its poverty—vulnerable to movements that in the American assessment would be hazardous to its welfare and to the interests and well-being of the United States. The primary cause of poverty, at least at the start, was the destruction resulting from the Second World War; the primary threat came from communism, either through deceptive enticements in its literature and rhetoric or from its serving as a front for Soviet imperialism. So the Americans, or many of them, saw it. The United States responded with foreign aid—economic, military, or both. Some of it was humanitarian; much of it was political. Usually the United States did not see a conflict or even a distinction between the two. Humanitarian aid could serve another worthy end—keeping the communists or Russians out of a place.

Foreign economic and military aid and its cousin, sale of military goods, became familiar parts of cold-war policies of the United States and, of course, of the Soviet Union. Critics looked at some of it as bribery, as indeed it was. Which country received what kind of aid depended on circumstances. Many nations needed both economic and military help. The program probably started in Greece and Turkey and the Truman Doctrine of 1947. With passage of time and economic recovery, more countries could pay for goods received, and military aid became sale of arms. In many cases aid represented an implementation of the global alliance system. In other cases the nation was friendly but not formally an ally of the United States. Saudi Arabia, which fell into such a category, did not need aid, but it wanted arms and was prepared to pay. The nation that received the largest amount of military aid was South Vietnam. South Korea was second. Selling arms, of course, constituted a business transaction, and there persisted a possibility for business considerations to prevail. But arms sales also had become part of the foreign policy of the United States, and the government would not authorize sales to nations it did not wish to have the goods. As a rule, (there were a few exceptions) the major determinant of a nation's status with respect to economic or military aid or purchase of American arms was its position in the alignments of the cold war.

Summit Conferences, 1955–1990

For all the tension and competition in Soviet-American relations during the cold war, the two sides never stopped talking with each other. The words, to be sure, were harsh at times, especially during the contentious first 10 years: One side assailed the other for an aspect of the relationship or for some activity in world affairs; almost invariably, the other side replied in kind. Threats were implied, calmly stated, or blurted out, as in Nikita Khrushchev's often-quoted and probably misunderstood assertion: "We shall bury you." In 1962 President John F. Kennedy calmly threatened to begin a nuclear war against the USSR. But communication never ceased; neither side threatened to break relations—not in the Hungarian rebellion of 1956 or the Cuban missile crisis of October 1962.

The most dramatic discourse took place at the highest level: direct, personal discussion between the recognized leaders of the two states. Doubtless built on conferences during the Second World War between Franklin D. Roosevelt, Winston Churchill, and Joseph Stalin (Harry Truman and Clement Atlee each attended one), the meetings during the cold war, which did not begin until 1955, came to be heralded as *summit conferences*. Closely followed in the national and international press, the effect was more symbolic than substantive. The first summit in Geneva in 1955, after 10 years of troubled dealings, with new leaders on both sides, gave off special meaning. The four leaders (France and Britain also participated) considered major issues, notably arms control, but they reached agreement on nothing. Even so, the mere fact that the adversaries could meet and talk was enormously encouraging. The "spirit of Geneva" had been born. Thereafter, every American president met with a Soviet leader at intervals ranging from several months to six or seven years. Curiously, of 17 summits between 1955 and 1990, Republican presidents represented the United States in 14, Democrats in only 3. Topics varied, of course, depending on circumstance, but two issues—the arms race and status of Europe, especially Germany and Berlin—always were on the agenda, if they did not dominate discussion altogether.

TABLE 10.46 U.S. FOREIGN ECONOMIC AND MILITARY AID PROGRAMS, 1946–1990

(in millions of dollars)

Period or Year and Region	Total Economic and Military Aid	Economic Aid			Military Aid		
		Total	Loans	Grants	Total	Loans	Grants
1946–1990, total	374,046	232,971	56,364	176,607	141,075	40,983	100,092
1946–1952	41,661	31,116	8,518	22,598	10,545	b	10,545
1953–1961	43,358	24,053	5,850	18,203	19,305	161	19,144
1962–1969	50,254	33,392	15,421	17,972	16,862	1,620	15,242
1970–1979	65,714	26,902	9,995	16,907	38,812	14,179	24,633
1980–1986	96,368	63,081	10,941	52,140	33,287	19,758	13,529
1980–1987	111,650	73,261	12,194	61,067	38,389	20,711	17,678
1980–1988	125,442	82,222	13,046	69,176	43,220	21,474	21,746
1980–1989	140,130	92,082	13,740	78,342	48,048	21,884	26,164
1980–1990	155,857	102,916	14,496	88,420	52,941	22,288	30,653
1970	6,568	3,676	1,389	2,288	2,892	70	2,822
1975	6,916	4,908	1,679	3,229	2,009	750	1,259
1976	6,412	3,878	1,759	2,119	2,535	1,442	1,093
1976, TQ[a]	2,603	1,931	840	1,091	672	494	178
1977	7,784	5,594	2,083	3,511	2,190	1,411	779
1978	9,014	6,661	2,530	4,131	2,353	1,601	752
1979	13,845	7,120	1,900	5,220	6,725	5,173	1,552
1980	9,695	7,573	1,993	5,580	2,122	1,450	672
1981	10,550	7,305	1,460	5,845	3,245	2,546	699
1982	12,324	8,129	1,454	6,675	4,195	3,084	1,111
1983	14,202	8,603	1,619	6,984	5,599	3,932	1,667
1984	15,524	9,038	1,621	7,417	6,486	4,401	2,085
1985	18,128	12,327	1,579	10,748	5,801	2,365	3,436
1986	16,739	10,900	1,330	9,570	5,839	1,980	3,859
1987	14,488	9,386	1,138	8,248	5,102	953	4,149
1988	13,792	8,961	852	8,109	4,831	763	4,068
1989	14,688	9,860	694	9,166	4,828	410	4,418
1990	15,727	10,834	756	10,078	4,893	404	4,489
Near East and South Asia	7,377	3,136	373	2,763	4,241	404	3,837
East Asia	687	535	21	514	152	b	152
Europe	373	284	64	220	89	b	89
Latin-America	2,144	1,910	184	1,726	234	b	234
Africa	1,176	1,062	111	951	114	b	114
Oceania and other	25	25	b	25	. . .	b	. . .
Non-regional	3,945	3,883	3	3,880	63	b	63

[a] Transition quarter, July–September
[b] Represents zero.
Source: Bureau of Census, *Statistical Abstract, 1992,* 794.

TABLE 10.47 PRINCIPAL RECIPIENTS OF U.S. FOREIGN AID, 1962–1989

(millions of dollars)

Region/Country	1962–1985	1986	1987	1988	1989
Near East and South Asia[a]	31,976	3,728	2,763	2,523	2,562
Egypt	8,573	1,069	820	718	817
India	3,713	94	64	26	46
Israel	9,721	1,898	1,200	1,200	1,200
Jordan	1,150	95	111	24	16
Pakistan	2,816	263	276	384	265
Turkey	2,458	120	102	32	60
East Asia[a]	10,203	518	440	225	541
Indonesia	1,405	66	88	42	50
Korea	1,080	0	0	0	0
Philippines	1,046	351	253	78	347
Vietnam	4,490	0	0	0	0
Europe	1,026	142	106	77	54
Latin America[a]	11,774	1,126	1,310	967	937
Brazil	1,480	0	0	0	0
Costa Rica	718	139	161	101	115
Dominican Republic	739	67	20	33	20
El Salvador	1,135	268	415	266	253
Honduras	690	112	175	130	53
Jamaica	554	85	44	40	65
ROCAP[b]	448	63	58	59	48
Africa[a]	7,594	766	620	644	748
Cameroon	143	25	31	19	33
Chad	65	16	11	17	16
Kenya	404	43	37	43	56
Morocco	302	37	28	31	32
Niger	159	24	27	35	24
Senegal	189	50	35	24	49
Somalia	285	45	36	10	13
Sudan	766	71	21	17	5
Zaire	399	48	33	31	36
Zambia	225	20	17	13	7
Zimbabwe	266	13	6	13	29
Oceania and other	17	8	9	20	18
Total	77,699	7,446	6,355	5,705	6,136

Note: Amounts in current dollars. Shown are loans and grants made by the U.S. Agency for International Development and its predecessor agencies. Excluded are Food for Peace and "other" economic assistance.
[a] Includes countries not shown separately.
[b] Regional programs covering Costa Rica, El Salvador, Guatemala, Honduras, Nicaragua, and Panama.
Source: Stanley and Niemi, *Statistics on Politics*, 363.

TABLE 10.48 U.S. MILITARY SALES AND ASSISTANCE TO FOREIGN GOVERNMENTS, 1950–1990

(in millions of dollars; for end of fiscal year)

Item	1950–81	1982	1983	1984	1985	1986	1987	1988	1989	1990
Military sales agreements	91,066	16,558	14,444	12,872	10,559	6,540	6,449	11,739	10,747	13,948
Weapons and ammunition	38,699	6,651	7,697	5,936	3,433	2,208	1,838	5,058	4,386	5,341
Support equipment	11,513	3,631	1,048	1,847	1,720	664	783	997	997	1,843
Spare parts and mods	20,066	3,263	3,036	2,544	2,371	1,544	1,626	3,125	2,534	2,806
Support services	20,788	3,013	2,663	2,545	3,035	2,124	2,202	2,559	2,830	3,958
Military construction sales agreements	14,569	86	22	404	958	69	133	208	74	234
Military sales deliveries	64,761	10,547	12,948	9,659	8,473	7,882	11,399	9,212	7,313	7,533
Military sales financing	24,849	3,884	5,107	5,716	4,940	4,947	4,053	4,049	4,273	4,813
Military assistance programs	54,178	395	413	700	812	841	976	702	542	137
Military assist. program deliveries	53,804	416	173	129	76	76	84	56	53	29
IMET program/deliveries	1,999	44	47	52	54	51	54	46	46	47
Students trained (1,000)	506	6	7	6	7	6	6	6	5	5

Source: Bureau of Census, *Statistical Abstract, 1992*, 341.

TABLE 10.49   PRINCIPAL RECIPIENTS OF U.S. MILITARY SALES AND MILITARY ASSISTANCE TO FOREIGN GOVERNMENTS, 1950–1989

(millions of dollars)

Country	Military Sales						Military Assistance, 1950–1989
	1950–1984	1985	1986	1987	1988	1989	
Australia	2,825.8	522.0	409.0	608.5	862.4	400.8	0.0
Belgium	1,657.2	119.3	27.8	27.0	222.5	153.4	1,203.8
Canada	1,838.1	73.1	113.7	126.8	213.7	161.2	0.0
China (Taiwan)	2,629.0	339.4	247.3	375.7	494.3	352.1	2,554.6
France	463.4	45.1	142.7	99.4	37.2	36.8	4,045.1
Germany, Federal Republic	7,794.9	222.2	206.0	324.5	323.6	571.8	884.8
Greece	1,826.2	115.0	73.4	79.1	129.0	138.7	1,673.5
Indochina	8.5	0.0	0.0	0.0	0.0	0.0	709.0
Iran	10,653.9	0.0	0.0	0.0	0.0	0.0	766.7
Israel	8,486.2	479.2	192.3	1,295.0	753.3	233.1	0.0
Italy	882.3	54.9	65.7	75.2	62.0	65.4	2,243.7
Korea	2,588.5	258.1	353.8	353.2	335.4	330.6	5,471.7
The Netherlands	2,386.2	339.3	284.0	424.7	299.3	440.7	1,178.1
Saudi Arabia	14,991.2	1,369.1	2,240.6	3,232.8	1,004.4	760.6	23.9
Thailand	1,183.3	118.0	116.6	95.4	313.7	214.0	1,169.0
Turkey	1,433.6	389.5	280.0	279.0	734.6	697.0	3,138.7
United Kingdom	4,034.3	386.4	361.1	199.0	180.8	132.8	1,012.9
Vietnam	1.2	0.0	0.0	0.0	0.0	0.0	14,773.9
Total	85,278.9	7,570.6	7,341.0	11,240.4	8,896.4	7,321.4	54,950.7

Source: Stanley and Niemi, *Statistics on Politics,* 361–62.

TABLE 10.50   LEADING EXPORTERS OF CONVENTIONAL WEAPONS, 1986–1990

(millions of dollars; 1985 prices)

Exporters	1986	1987	1988	1989	1990	1986–90
	To all countries					
USSR	14,731	14,916	12,559	12,220	6,373	60,799
U.S.A.	10,304	12,596	10,503	11,669	8,738	53,811
France	4,096	3,011	2,300	2,577	1,799	13,783
UK	1,500	1,817	1,401	1,816	1,220	7,752
China	1,463	2,553	1,868	874	926	7,684
Germany, FR	1,120	676	1,270	716	963	4,745
Czechoslovakia	497	570	548	437	355	2,408
Netherlands	240	265	532	725	152	1,915
Sweden	324	489	575	311	115	1,813
Italy	457	389	471	169	96	1,582
Brazil	150	507	356	152	24	1,189
Israel	269	340	127	318	39	1,094
Spain	172	139	199	506	74	1,090
Canada	317	265	106	54	60	802
Egypt	159	194	216	65	33	668
Others	656	1,047	735	900	760	4,097
Total	36,453	39,777	33,767	33,509	21,726.	165,232

Source: Stockholm Peace Institute, *SIPRI Yearbook, 1991,* 198.

These were, of course, difficult and complicated matters, the business of diplomats and specialists. Not qualified to handle such detail, the leaders spoke in generality and broad principle. The first 17 years of summit meeting produced no agreements. The first arms agreement, SALT I, (Strategic Arms Limitation Treaty I) was capped by a ceremonious signing by President Nixon and Leonid Brezhnev in a meeting in Moscow in summer 1972. Thereafter the leaders preferred to have something to sign when they met, and indeed subsequent presidents were able to produce meaningful agreement, usually in the area of arms control. Staged signings, smiling handshakes, even embraces, however, represented only the culmination of long, arduous work behind the scene by lower-level diplomats. The summits thus remained important symbols of the status of Soviet-American relations. If the absence of a conference between 1945 and 1955 suggested a time of much trouble, the frequency of top-level meetings in the late 1980s (between 1985 and 1990 there were six summit conferences) indicated that something remarkable was taking place in Soviet-American relations and in the affairs of the world.

Strategic Arms Agreements

Nuclear arms had no more than been introduced than the parties involved questioned what to do with them, pondering the possibility of regulation or even their destruction. The United States and the Soviet Union began to talk about control of nuclear energy in 1945. They reached no agreement for 18 years. The United States had a monopoly of nuclear weapons and on knowledge of how to build them. The Soviet Union would accept no agreement that left this monopoly in place, and after 1949, when the Soviet exploded their first bomb, they would entertain no restrictions that left their nuclear weaponry inferior—in numbers and in technology—to the Americans. There probably could be no limits on an arms race until the two sides had reasonable parity.

The definition of parity, as it developed, kept changing. Both sides set to building newer, larger, more sophisticated weapons. The hydrogen bomb, the Super, eclipsed the atomic bomb. Missiles made their appearance in the 1950s as vehicles for delivering the explosives, and they soon spread to submarines. Negotiators came to be as concerned about the missiles as with the explosive—the "payload," in terminology of the day. At some early point both sides had acquired enough weapons to destroy their enemy, if not the world, but the race continued nonetheless out of fear that one side would fall behind technologically, leaving the adversary capable of neutralizing its threat. There were

countless other hypothetical scenarios. The decade of the 1960s did produce agreement, not in reducing weapons but on peripheral issues. In 1963 the Kennedy administration agreed to a test-ban treaty that forbade testing nuclear weapons under water, in outer space, or the atmosphere; tests thereafter would be underground. China and France refused to sign, but eventually 128 nations did. In 1968 the Johnson administration obtained agreement on a nonproliferation treaty that forbade the spread of nuclear weapons to states that did not have them.

By the 1970s the superpowers had achieved basic parity in their strategic arsenals. Both were massive, if formulated differently, and both countries were prepared to impose some restraint on growth with an assurance that the adversary would respond in like manner. Nuclear technology, after all, had become exceptionally expensive. The 1970s thus became the era of SALT: Strategic Arms Limitation Talks, that would lead to a treaty with the same acronym. The difficulty in reaching agreement stemmed partly from methods of verification, partly in the difficulty of measuring technology, and in the fact that the two sides had different strategic arsenals: The Soviets relied on land-based missiles, the Americans on a TRIAD system of ICBMs, submarine missiles, and bombers. SALT I in 1972 under the Nixon

TABLE 10.51   U.S.–SOVIET SUMMITS

Summit	Date	Nations	Participants	Significance
Geneva Summit	1955	United States Great Britain France Soviet Union	President Dwight D. Eisenhower Prime Minister Anthony Eden Premier Edgar Faure Premier Nikolai A. Bulganin	Discussion German reunification, European security, disarmament, U.S. Open Skies proposal
Camp David Summit	1959	United States Soviet Union	President Eisenhower Premier Nikita S. Khrushchev	Moderation Berlin Crisis
Paris Summit	1960	United States Great Britain France Soviet Union	President Eisenhower Prime Minister Harold MacMillan President Charles de Gaulle Premier Khrushchev	Terminated over U-2 Incident
Vienna Summit	1961	United States Soviet Union	President John F. Kennedy Premier Khrushchev	Discussion Berlin Crisis
Glassboro Summit	1967	United States Soviet Union	President Lyndon B. Johnson Premier Aleksei N. Kosygin	Discussion Middle East, Vietnam War, East-West relations
Moscow Summit	1972	United States Soviet Union	President Richard M. Nixon General Secretary Leonid I. Brezhnev	Detente, Salt I arms control agreement, U.S.-Soviet trade pact.
Washington Summit	1973	United States Soviet Union	President Nixon General Secretary Brezhnev	Prevention of Nuclear War Agreement
Moscow Summit	1974	United States Soviet Union	President Nixon General Secretary Brezhnev	Threshold Test Ban Treaty
Vladivostok Summit	1974	United States Soviet Union	President Gerald R. Ford General Secretary Brezhnev	Vladivostok Accord
Vienna Summit	1979	United States Soviet Union	President Jimmy Carter General Secretary Brezhnev	Salt II arms control agreement
Geneva Summit	1985	United States Soviet Union	President Ronald W. Reagan General Secretary Mikhail S. Gorbachev	Resumption top-level U.S.–Soviet contracts
Reykjavik Summit	1986	United States Soviet Union	President Reagan General Secretary Gorbachev	Discussion arms control
Washington Summit	1987	United States Soviet Union	President Reagan General Secretary Gorbachev	INF Treaty
Moscow Summit	1988	United States Soviet Union	President Reagan General Secretary Gorbachev	Discussion arms control, human rights, regional issues
Malta Summit	1989	United States Soviet Union	President George Bush President Gorbachev	Discussion collapse of communism in Eastern Europe, ending cold war
Washington Summit	1990	United States Soviet Union	President Bush President Gorbachev	Post–cold war East–west relations, U.S.–Soviet trade pact
Helsinki Summit	1990	United States Soviet Union	President Bush President Gorbachev	Coordinated response to Iraqi invasion of Kuwait

Source: Flanders & Flanders, *Dictionary of Foreign Affairs*, 805–06.

administration called for no more than two defensive missile (ABM) sites and froze offensive missile deployment for five years. Thus, there was to be equivalency in striking power and in vulnerability. A nation that went further in protecting its people from attack would be breaking the rules. SALT II in 1979 by the Jimmy Carter administration allowed each side 2,400 delivery systems and produced a complicated system of counting missiles, warheads, and bombers. Denounced in the United States and affected by other aspects of the relationship, SALT II never received ratification in the Senate.

Sharply critical of the SALT approach, Ronald Reagan favored a new strategy he called Strategic Arms Reduction Talks, which carried the catchy acronym of START (another official wittily suggested they be called Faster Arms Reduction Talks). Reagan also came to propose a complicated, questionable, and very costly defensive missile system called Strategic Defense Initiative (SDI) or "Star Wars." On the surface START seemed more aggressive than its predecessor, but Reagan had been so distrustful of the Soviets and so determined to promote American military supremacy that had other conditions remained equal, there would have been little chance of progress in arms control. The second Reagan administration, however, happened to correspond with the start of a new era in the Soviet Union and with a new leader who meant business about changing policy on, among other issues, strategic arms. Mikhail Gorbachev strongly opposed SDI, but he favored substantive arms reduction. Thus in 1987 the United States and the Soviet Union agreed to the INF (intermediate force) treaty, which eliminated all missiles with a range of 300 to 3,400 miles. The treaty left most of both nations' arsenals (the long-range and short-range missiles) in place, but it represented a breakthrough in its destruction of a weapons system and in its provision for on-site verification. And at the start of the 1990s, the prospect for further serious arms reduction seemed more promising than in any decade since the cold war began.

Strategic Arms Agreements, 1946–1990

Limited Test Ban Treaty (1963)   First treaty affecting nuclear weapons, in which the United States, Great Britain, and the Soviet Union agreed to forgo testing in the atmosphere, outer space, and underwater; Senate debate also reflected presidential need to pledge continued strong defense programs to ensure passage.

Nuclear Nonproliferation Treaty (1968)   Banned the spread of nuclear weapons, provided for safeguard arrangements, and ensured nondiscriminatory access to peaceful uses of nuclear energy. Signators included the United States, the Soviet Union, and 60 other nations.

Antiballistic Missile Systems (ABM) Treaty; Strategic Arms Limitation Talks (SALT I, Interim Agreement on Strategic Offensive Arms) (1972)   First U.S.–USSR arms control agreements under détente, serving to "cap" nuclear arms race quantitatively by limiting deployments of ABM systems, initially to two sites, and setting upper limits on the number of strategic nuclear missile launchers; also led to Jackson amendment, requiring equal levels in future agreements. ABM treaty was also the subject of a constitutional debate between the Reagan administration and the Senate over treaty interpretation as it related to Strategic Defense Initiative (SDI; Star Wars) testing.

SALT II Treaty (1979)   Follow-up to SALT I, extending limits to include bombers, and beginning qualitative limits as well; never brought to vote in Senate because of Soviet invasion of Afghanistan, signaling the end of détente.

Intermediate Nuclear Forces (INF) Treaty (Treaty on the Elimination of Intermediate-Range and Shorter-Range Missiles) (1987)   First U.S.–USSR arms control agreement to eliminate (rather than cap or reduce) an entire class of nuclear weapons systems.

Source: Stanley I. Kutler, et al., *Encyclopedia of the United States in the Twentieth Century, Vol. II* (New York, 1966), 566.

TABLE 10.52   NUCLEAR EXPLOSIONS SINCE 1945

Year	U.S. a	U.S. u	USSR a	USSR u	UK a	UK u	France a	France u	China a	China u	India a	India u	Total
1945	3	0											3
1946	1	1											2
1947	0	0											0
1948	3	0											3
1949	0	0	1	0									1
1950	0	0	0	0									0
1951	15	1	2	0									18
1952	10	0	0	0	1	0							11
1953	11	0	2	0	2	0							15
1954	6	0	2	0	0	0							8
1955	16	2	4	0	0	0							22
1956	18	0	7	0	6	0							31
1957	27	5	13	0	7	0							52
1958	61	16	26	0	5	0							108
1959	0	0	0	0	0	0							0
1960	0	0	0	0	0	0	3	0					3
1961	0	10	30	2	0	0	1	1					44
1962	37	59	41	1	0	2	0	1					141
1963	4	43	0	0	0	0	0	3					50
1964	0	29	0	6	0	1	0	3	1	0			40
1965	0	29	0	9	0	1	0	4	1	0			44
1966	0	40	0	15	0	0	5	1	3	0			64
1967	0	29	0	15	0	0	3	0	2	0			49
1968	0	39	0	13	0	0	5	0	1	0			58
1969	0	29	0	15	0	0	0	0	1	1			46
1970	0	33	0	12	0	0	8	0	1	0			54
1971	0	15	0	19	0	0	5	0	1	0			40
1972	0	15	0	22	0	0	3	0	2	0			42
1973	0	14	0	14	0	0	5	0	1	0			34
1974	0	12	0	19	0	1	7	0	1	0	0	1	41
1975	0	17	0	15	0	0	0	2	0	1	0	0	35
1976	0	15	0	17	0	1	0	3	3	1	0	0	40
1977	0	12	0	18	0	0	0	6	1	0	0	0	37
1978	0	16	0	27	0	2	0	7	2	1	0	0	55
1979	0	15	0	29	0	1	0	9	0	0	0	0	54
1980	0	14	0	21	0	3	0	11	1	0	0	0	50
1981	0	16	0	21	0	1	0	11	0	0	0	0	49
1982	0	18	0	31	0	1	0	5	0	0	0	0	55
1983	0	17	0	27	0	1	0	7	1	0	0	0	53
1984	0	17	0	27	0	2	0	7	0	2	0	0	55
1985	0	15	0	7	0	1	0	8	0	0	0	0	31
1986	0	14	0	0	0	1	0	8	0	0	0	0	23
1987	0	14	0	23	0	1	0	8	0	1	0	0	47
1988	0	14	0	17	0	0	0	8	0	1	0	0	40
1989	0	11	0	7	0	1	0	8	0	0	0	0	27
1990	0	8	0	7	0	1	0	8	0	0	0	0	18

Note: The Soviet Union conducted 33 other tests in the atmosphere during 1949–58, for which dates were unavailable.
a: atmosphere
u: underground
Source: Cook, *World Political Almanac*, 352. Updated by author.

TABLE 10.53   ESTIMATED NUMBER OF NUCLEAR EXPLOSIONS, JULY 16, 1945–DECEMBER 31, 1990

USA	USSR	UK	France	China	India	Total
929	715	43	183	36	1	1,907

Source: Stockholm Peace Institute, *SIPRI Yearbook of 1991*, 47.

The End to the Cold War

All signals at the start of the 1980s suggested that the cold war would continue indefinitely and probably would intensify in the immediate future. The United States had at its helm a doctrinaire right-winger, a strong anticommunist and anti-Russian who saw it as his mission to rescue the United States from self-doubt of the immediate past and reestablish American supremacy in world affairs. Calling the Soviet Union an "evil empire" that was prepared to "commit any crime, to lie, to cheat" to achieve its ends, Ronald Reagan sponsored a massive increase in the military budget, ordered formation of a force to challenge, or at least pester, the Soviet-supported Sandinista regime in Nicaragua, deployed new Pershing II missiles in Europe, and looked to El Salvador, Afghanistan, or any place where he might make matters difficult for the communists and the Soviets. Headed by a quick succession of old-line, cold war-hardened bureaucrats (three leaders died in office between 1982 and 1985), the Soviet Union did its best to keep up with the Americans. Even though the effort was taking the country into bankruptcy, the Soviets probably would have continued on the course for a while longer had not new leadership taken control in the Kremlin.

The immediate events that brought the cold war to an end with remarkable speed started with the assumption of power by Mikhail Gorbachev on the death of his aged predecessor, Konstantin Chernenko, in 1985. Virtually every step between 1985 and 1990 that produced a new era in Soviet-American (or Russian-American) relations constituted either a move of the Soviet leader or came as the fruit of a decision Gorbachev had made. Willing to face the facts about the state of his country, Gorbachev insisted that the Soviet Union had to change its political and economic system if it was to survive. In the area of world affairs and relations with the United States, Gorbachev reached a few critical decisions that emerged piece-by-piece in the diplomacy between 1985 and 1990: (1) The Soviet Union would relinquish its satellite empire in Eastern Europe in place, in one form or another, since the Second World War; (2) the USSR would tolerate the reunification of Germany and the end of controls in Berlin; (3) the Soviet Union would relinquish its far-flung client states, such as Cuba or Syria or Nicaragua; they were not productive anyway; (4) the Soviet government would take a hard look at basic requirements for national security and defense.

All these issues were of major interest to the United States. As the Americans saw it, they had been basic reasons for start of the trouble in the first place and for keeping it going. Satisfaction—mixed, no doubt, with a measure of skepticism—the United States experienced in watching these positions develop was surpassed only by surprise. The Americans liked the first three changes; they were willing to explore the fourth. The primary contribution of the United States and of the Reagan and Bush administrations to these immediate developments was more flexibility and willingness to deal than Reagan had intended or expected to need. The primary negotiation had been in arms control, but the flurry of summit meetings contributed to the changes underway. Most observers agreed that the cold war had ended by 1990. Gorbachev had given up his empire and abandoned traditional cornerstones of Soviet security; he had not anticipated that he also would lose his country and his job.

For all the emphasis on armies, bombs, and missiles, on alliances and intervention, the cold war had not been settled on a military basis after all. The Soviet Union had not been defeated; its military forces remained powerful, even ominous. It was the economy and social structure that was falling apart. Gorbachev merely admitted and moved to change weaknesses in a system that had been building for a long time. In doing so he set in motion events that went beyond his control. George F. Kennan had prophesied in his famous essay of 1947 that, effectively contained by the United States, the Soviet system would collapse under its own weight. Kennan in the end had been right, but the process took

Cold war thaws: President Reagan chats with President Mikhail Gorbachev in Red Square, Moscow, 1988. (Courtesy Ronald Reagan Library)

a great deal longer than he had imagined. If the Soviet Union lost the cold war, it was not clear that there had been a winner. When one considered the huge American budget and trade deficits at the end of the 1980s, the loss of jobs to other nations, and the unrest with segments of the population, one at least could say that an American gain at the end was in no way proportionate to the Soviet loss.

Selected Chronological Developments in the End of the Cold War

March 1985 Mikhail Gorbachev becomes first secretary of Soviet Communist Party. Conceding almost immediately that the Soviet system had failed, he announces major programs of *glasnost* (political liberalization) and *perestroika* (economic restructuring).

November 1985 Reagan and Gorbachev meet in Geneva. No agreements emerge, but the leaders establish good communication.

1986 Gorbachev continues replacing old-line bureaucrats with new people. Eduard Shevardnadze replaces Andrei Gromyko as foreign minister.

1987 Demands for change in the Baltic states, the Crimea, and Poland are allowed to take place.

December 1987 In their third meeting, Reagan and Gorbachev sign a significant INF arms reduction treaty.

May 1988   Gorbachev orders Soviet troops from Afghanistan—ending the Soviets' "Vietnam."

December 1988   Liberal, anticommunist "Solidarity" movement gains strength in Poland; Soviets do not resist.

December 1988   Gorbachev orders unilateral reduction of 500,000 troops and 10,000 tanks.

January 1989   The year of miracles in eastern Europe. Hungary adopts new anticommunist constitution.

July 1989   Having been legalized, Solidarity forms the first noncommunist government in Poland.

1989   Gorbachev denounces Brezhnev Doctrine of 1968, which had legitimized Soviet intervention in the east European states. A Soviet official explained that new Soviet policy could be called the Frank Sinatra Doctrine, a reference to Sinatra's signature song. East European states thereafter could do things "their way." No Soviet position was more important in ending the cold war.

September 1989   Hungary opens its border to Austria, allowing flight of East Germans, via Hungary and Austria, into West Germany.

October 1989   Gorbachev advises East Germans to open the Berlin Wall.

November 1989   The wall comes down (Nov 9); government of East Germany resigns; change also comes in governments of Bulgaria and Czechoslovakia. Uprising in Bucharest leads to fighting, arrest and execution of communist leader Nicolae Ceausescu and his wife. Free to act for the first time since the 1940s, East Europe, it is clear, is dumping communism and all Soviet connections.

December 1989   Gorbachev and President George H. W. Bush meet in Malta summit to declare an end to the cold war.

October 1990   Germany is reunified with Soviet acceptance: a logical extension of destruction of the Berlin Wall—a move as significant as it was stunning, a final validation that the cold war had ended.

1990   Signals do not bode well for the man who set these events in motion. Gorbachev was, after all, leader of the Soviet Union. Lithuania, Estonia, and Latvia proclaim their independence from the USSR; there are rumblings in the Ukraine and other Soviet Republics, even in Russia. Gorbachev was becoming a leader without a country.

Source: Information gathered by author.

One big happy family: President George H. W. Bush (third from left) and President Mikhail Gorbachev (fifth from left), wives, and advisers smile as the cold war ends, at Camp David, Maryland, June 2, 1990. (George Bush Presidential Library)

CHAPTER 11 States

This chapter supplies selected basic information about the fifty states of America. Except for a brief discussion of the early background of each state, the emphasis of the information is on each state during the post–Second World War era, 1946–1990. The data is both absolute and comparative. Except in a few circumstances, identification of "famous natives" pertains to individuals born in the state under question, whose noteworthy activity came largely, if not entirely, in the 45 years after 1945. Sources are: Bureau of the Census, *Statistical Abstract of the United States, 1953* (Washington, D.C., 1953); Bureau of the Census, *Statistical Abstract of the United States, 1993* (Washington, D.C., 1993); Council of State Governments, *The Book of the States, 1946–1990* (Chicago, 1946–1990); Robert H. Ferrell and Joan Hoff, eds., *Dictionary of American History: Supplement, Parts I and II* (New York, 1996); Timothy L. Gall, ed., *Worldmark Encyclopedia of the States* (Detroit, 1995); Mark S. Hoffman, *The World Almanac and Book of Facts, 1992* (New York, 1991); Edith R. Hornor, ed., *Almanac of the 50 States: Basic Data Profiles with Comparative Tables* (Palo Alto, Calif., 1993); Kathleen O'Leary Morgan, Scott Morgan, and Neil Quitno, eds., *State Rankings 1992* (Lawrence, Kansas, 1992); John W. Wright, ed., *The Universal Almanac 1995* (New York, 1994).

Alabama

Native American groups, especially the Creek, had a large presence in the Alabama area. The Spanish arrived around 1519 and Hernando DeSoto came later. The area was ceded to Britain in 1763, and the United States gained control in 1783. White control led to suppression and removal of the Indians. Alabama entered the union on December 22, 1819, the 22nd state, and became fully a part of the culture of the Deep South, with cotton farming and a slave-driven society. The capital is Montgomery. The origin of the name was a Choctaw term meaning "vegetable gatherers" or "thicket cleaners." Nickname is The Heart of Dixie. Motto: "We defend our rights." Flower: goldenrod. Tree: southern pine. Bird: yellowhammer. Song: "Alabama."

Land

Area: 51,705 sq. mi. (29th). Rivers: Alabama, Chattahoochee, Mobile, Tennessee, Tensaw, Tombigbee. Mountains: Cumberland, Lookout, Raccoon, Sand. Cities (With 1990 pop.): Birmingham (265,968), Mobile (196,278), Montgomery (187,106), Huntsville (159,789), Tuscaloosa (77,759.

People

Population, 1945: 2,812,301 (17th); 1990: 4,040,587 (22nd). Breakdown, 1990: 73.6% white, 25.3% black, 0.6% Hispanic, 0.4% American Indian, 43.8% urban, 56.2% rural (1950); 60.4% urban, 39.6% rural, (1990). Famous natives: Hank Aaron (baseball player), Tallulah Bankhead (actress), Nat "King" Cole (singer), Coretta Scott King (civil rights worker), George Wallace (politician), Hank Williams (singer and songwriter).

Economics

Gross state product, 1990: $70.4 billion (24); per capita income: $14,826. Leading agricultural products: cattle, eggs, chickens, greenhouse products. Industry: iron and steel, retail industries, manufacturing. Minerals: aluminium, coal, iron ore, fertilizer, limestone.

Major Developments, 1946–1990

After the Second World War Alabama gradually shifted away from an agriculture-oriented, cotton economy to more reliance on industry, especially in Birmingham. The state became more urbanized. Alabama was at the center of the Civil Rights Movement in the 1950s and 1960s as Governor George Wallace sought to preserve a segregated society. Such special economic projects as the power facilities at Muscle Shoals and the space center at Huntsville did not remove Alabama from the ranks of one of the poorest states.

Alaska

Alaska was originally inhabited by Inuit and Aleut in the north and other Indian groups to the south. European interests stemmed from the efforts of Vitus Bering, a Dane working for Russia in 1741. Russian fur traders also helped establish claim to this frigid land. Strapped for cash, the Russian government sold Alaska to the United States for $7.2 million in 1867, the deal negotiated by Secretary of State William F. Seward. Discovery of gold in 1896 brought a brief rush of people to the area, but Alaska remained a sparsely populated, remote area until the 1940s. Alaska became a state, the 49th, on January 3, 1959. Its capital is Juneau. The name originated in an Aleut word meaning "great land." Nickname: The Last Frontier. Motto: "North to the Future." State flower: forget-me-not. Tree: sitka spruce. Bird: yellow ptarmigan. State song: "Alaska's Flag."

Land

Area: 591,000 sq. mi. (1). Rivers: Colville, Porcupine, Noatak, Yukon, Susitna, Kobuk, Koyukuk, Kuskokwim, Tanana. Mountains: Alaska Range (Mt. McKinley, highest in North America), Aleutian Range, Brooks Range, Kuskokwim, St. Elias. Cities (with 1990 pop.): Anchorage (226,338), Fairbanks (30,843), Juneau (26,751), Ketchikan (8,263), Sitka (8,588).

People

Population, 1950: 126,643 (no rank); 1990: 550,043 (49th). Breakdown, 1990: 75.5% white, 3.2% black, 15.6% Indian, 3.2% Hispanic, 32.5% urban, 67.5% rural, (1990). Famous natives: Ernest Gruening (politician), Walter Hickel (politician), Carl Ben Eielson (pilot).

Economics

Gross state product, 1990: $26.4 billion (40th); per capita income: $21,761. Leading agricultural products: barley, hay, potatoes, lettuce, cattle, sheep, reindeer. Industry: fish products, lumber, pulp, furs. Minerals: gold, oil, sand and gravel.

Major Developments, 1946–1990

The Second World War, which had brought people north, helped facilitate a statehood movement that succeeded on January 3, 1959. It was the discovery of oil on the North Slope in 1968 and completion of the 800-mile Alaska pipeline in 1977 that boosted the economy and allowed for more population growth. Environmentalists' worries about effects on the natural habitat materialized in March 1989 when the tanker *Exxon Valdez* struck a reef and spilled 10 million gallons of oil into Prince William Sound. For the first year since the oil boom, production at Prudhoe Bay declined in 1989. State leaders were looking for new ways to carry on when income for oil ceased.

Arizona

Arizona was home to Hopi, Apache, Navajo (Dineh), Tohono O'odham (then known as Papago) and other Indian tribes. Francisco

Vásquez de Coronado and other searchers for gold came to the area in the mid-16th century and helped establish Spanish claim. The area became a part of Mexico and later part of the Mexican cession to the United States in 1848. The area became the organized Arizona Territory and part of the legendary old West, but heat and absence of rainfall did not attract a large population. Many of the people living there were Indians, and Arizona did not become a state—last of the original 48—until February 14, 1912. The state capital is Phoenix. The name originated with the Akimel O'odham (Pima) or Tohono O'odham term for "place of small springs." Nickname: Grand Canyon State. Motto: *Ditat Deus* (God Enriches). State flower: saguaro cactus blossom. Tree: paloverde. Bird: cactus wren. Song: "Arizona."

Land

Area: 114,000 sq. mi. (6th). Rivers: Colorado, Gila, Little Colorado, Salt, Zuni. Mountains: Black, Gila, Hualapai, Mohawk, San Francisco Peaks. Cities (with 1990 pop.): Phoenix (983,403), Tucson (405,390), Mesa (288,091), Glendale (148,134), Tempe (141,865), Scottsdale (130,069).

People

Population 1945: 630,298 (37th); 1990: 3,665,228 (24th). Breakdown, 1990: 80.8% white, 3.0% black, 5.6% American Indian, 18.8% Hispanic, 55.5% urban, 44.5% rural (1950); 87.5% urban, 12.5% rural (1990). Famous natives: Bruce Babbitt (politician), Cesar Chavez (labor leader), Barry Goldwater (politician), Sandra Day O'Connor (jurist), Linda Ronstadt (singer).

Economics

Gross state product, 1990: $67.3 billion (26th); per capita income: $16,297. Leading agricultural products: cotton, wheat, corn, citrus fruits, livestock. Industry: aircraft and missiles, electronics, publishing, metals. Minerals: copper, gold, silver.

Major Developments, 1946–1990

Post-Second World War Arizona owed its prosperity to modern technology, notably methods of irrigation, that made the desert bloom and air conditioning that could make a searing heat almost irrelevant. Now it was the warm winters, not the hot summers, that established the state's identity. Such natural features as the Grand Canyon, the Painted Desert, and the Petrified Forest attracted visitors, and the new cities attracted new residents, especially retired people. Arizona experienced a rate of growth larger than any state in the first half of the 1980s.

Arkansas

Numerous Indian tribes—Choctaw, Chickasaw, Caddo, Quapaw, and others—inhabited the Arkansas area before the Europeans came. Spanish and French explorers crossed the area, and the French claimed it as part of Louisiana. Arkansas was part of the United States's purchase of Louisiana in 1803 and later was incorporated into the Missouri and Arkansas territories. Admitted as 25th state in the union (and a slave state) on June 15, 1836, Arkansas seceded 25 years later, fought for the Confederacy, and had to be reaccepted in 1868. Thereafter Arkansas experienced a fate similar to other southern states: a long period of agriculture-oriented economic stagnation. The state capital is Little Rock. The origin of the name is a French word for the Quapaw tribe. Nickname is Land of Opportunity. Motto: *Regnat Populus* (The People Rule). Flower: apple blossom. Tree: pine. Bird: mockingbird. Song: "Arkansas."

Land

Area: 53,187 sq. mi. (27th). Rivers: Arkansas, Mississippi, Ouachita, Red, St. Francis, White. Mountains: Ozark, Ouachita. Cities (with 1990 population): Little Rock (175,795), Ft. Smith (72,798), Pine Bluff (57,140), Fayetteville (42,099).

People

Population, 1945: 1,779,817 (29th); 1990: 2,350,725 (33rd). Breakdown, 1990: 82.7% white, 15.9% black, 0.8% Hispanic, 33% urban, 67% rural (1950); 53.5% urban, 46.5% rural (1990). Famous natives: Glen Campbell (singer), Dizzy Dean (baseball player), Johnny Cash (singer), William Fulbright (statesman), Douglas MacArthur (general), Alan Ladd (actor).

Economics

Gross state product, 1990: $38.7 billion (33rd); per capita income: $14,218. Leading agricultural products: soybeans, rice, cotton, fruit, watermelons, wheat. Industry: food products, chemicals, furniture, automobile and airplane parts. Minerals: bauxite, bromine, bauxite.

Major Developments, 1946–1990

With limited natural resources, Arkansas continued to develop slowly. A less-than-Deep-South southern state with no striking identity of any sort, Arkansas received national publicity in an unexpected way during the 1950s. When Governor Orval Faubus refused to permit black students to enroll in Central High School in Little Rock in 1957, the state became known as a leader of forces against racial integration. In later years Arkansas attracted some industry; the retail giant Walmart retained its base there, but the state still possessed low marks in most economic and educational categories.

California

Before the arrival of Europeans, many Indian tribes inhabited this Pacific coastal area. The Spanish arrived in 1542 and began to establish Catholic missions and institutions for control. Spanish place names still predominate. California was part of an independent Mexico after 1821, and it became U.S. property after the United States war with Mexico in 1846–48. Discovery of gold and the rush in by the "forty-niners" helped prepare the area for statehood. California became the 31st state on September 9, 1850, the move a part of the pre–Civil War Compromise of 1850. The state capital is Sacramento. The name probably originated from a volume of the 16th century by Garci Rodrìguez de Montalvo. State nickname: Golden State. Motto: *Eureka* (I have found it). Flower: golden poppy. Tree: California redwood. Bird: California valley quail. Song: "I Love You, California."

Land

Area: 158,706 sq. mi. (3rd). Rivers: American, Colorado, Colorado River Aqueduct, Eel, Klamath, Russian, Sacramento, Salinas, San Joaquin. Mountains: Coast Ranges, Klamath, Lassen Peak, Sierra Nevada. Cities (with 1990 pop.): Los Angeles (3,485,398), San Diego (1,110,549), San Jose (782,248), San Francisco (723,959), Long Beach (429,433).

People

Population, 1945: 8,822,688 (3rd); 1990: 26,760,021 (1st). Breakdown, 1990: 69% white, 7.4% black, 25.8% Hispanic, 9.6% Asian, 80.7% urban, 19.7% rural (1950), 92.6% urban, 7.4% rural (1990). Famous natives: John Steinbeck (writer), Earl Warren (jurist), Shirley Temple (actress), Mark McGuire (baseball player), Richard Nixon (politician), George Patton, Jr. (general), Joe DiMaggio (baseball player).

Economics

Gross state product, 1990: $744 billion (1st); per capita income: $20,795. Leading agricultural products: specialized fruit and

Besides other attributes, California was a major agricultural state. This 600-acre ranch in the San Joaquin Valley raised 100,000 cattle in 400 feeding pens. (U.S. Department of Agriculture)

vegetable farming supplies much of winter produce, grapes, nuts. Industry: manufacturing of many kinds: aircraft and automobiles, machinery, high technology and electronic equipment. Minerals: petroleum, natural gas, gold, silver, cement.

Major Developments, 1946–1990

Blessed with pleasant climate, attractive geographic features, and the glamorous film industry, California grew in leaps and bounds, became the most populous state in 1964, and left competitors far behind. Even the Brooklyn Dodgers and New York Giants went West in the 1950s. Silicon Valley became synonymous with high technology. Growing pains do develop from crowding caused by internal emigration and external immigration, mostly from Asia and Latin America. The state led a growing rebellion against taxes with Proposition 13 in 1978. The Loma Prieta earthquake of 1989 killed 67 and caused much damage, leaving people still to wait for the "big one." The most pressing problem for agriculture and perhaps for the state was the shortage of water. The same water needed for popular consumption was needed to irrigate farmlands and of course there was too little of it.

Colorado

Indian groups that inhabited this land included Cheyenne, Arapaho, Pueblo, and others. France, having claimed the area, turned it over to Spain in 1763, took it back in 1801, and then sold the huge territorial domain to the United States in what the Americans called the Louisiana Purchase of 1803. Part of Colorado made up the western reaches of this land; the other part of Colorado came to the United States in the Mexican cession of 1848. Americans who explored the area included Zebulon Pike, Kit Carson, John C. Fremont, and later, John Wesley Powell. Discovery of gold and silver, the Homestead Act of 1862, and expansion west of the railroad all facilitated in the peopling of Colorado. War with the Indians continued through the 1870s. Colorado became a state on August 1, 1876, the 38th state. The capital is Denver. The state name originated in the Spanish word for red. Nickname: Centennial State. Motto: *Nil sine numine* (Nothing without providence). Flower: Rocky Mountain columbine. Tree: Colorado blue spruce. Bird: lark bunting. Song: "Where the Columbines grow."

Land

Area: 104,091 sq. mi. (8th). Rivers: Arkansas, Colorado, Green, Platte, Rio Grande. Mountains: Front Range, Laramie, Sangre de Cristo, San Juan, Sawatch Range. Cities (with 1990 pop.): Denver (467,610), Colorado Springs (281,140), Aurora (222,103), Lakewood (126,481), Pueblo (98,640).

People

Population, 1945: 1,120,595 (34th); 1990: 3,294,394 (26th). Breakdown, 1990: 88.2% white, 4.0% black, 12.9% Hispanic, 62.7% urban, 37.3% rural (1950); 82.4% urban, 17.6% rural (1990). Famous natives: Jack Dempsey (boxer), Douglas Fairbanks (actor), Scott Carpenter (astronaut), Lon Chaney (actor), Lowell Thomas (broadcaster), Byron White (jurist).

Economics

Gross state product, 1990: $71.4 billion (23rd); per capita income: $18,794. Agricultural products: corn, wheat, hay, vegetables, fruits. Industry: aerospace items, computer and electronics equipment, food products, machinery. Minerals: gold, silver, gravel, sand, stone.

Major Developments, 1946–1990

Growth of Colorado corresponded with the general movement west. Discovery of uranium in 1946, establishment of the Air Force Academy (at Colorado Springs, 1958), interest in shale oil development in the 1970s, all provided economic benefits. Perhaps most striking was the majestic scenery provided in large measure by the Rocky Mountains. Such locations as Aspen and Vail became among the most prestigious U.S. locations for winter sports. In the 1980s Colorado was one of the most attractive states for people either to visit or to make a new place of residence.

Connecticut

Home to various Indian tribes, such as Pequot and Mohegan, the Connecticut territory was a site of Dutch exploration, but it was mostly the English who settled the area. Thomas Hooker and other dissenters to the rigid Massachusetts Bay Colony defected and eventually formed a separate Connecticut Colony in 1736. Many men from Connecticut fought in the American Revolution, and representatives of the state were active in debates over the federal constitution, usually assuming a "small state" point of view. Thereupon, Connecticut became the fifth state to enter the union, on January 9, 1788. The capital is Hartford. The name originated with a Mohegan word meaning "beside the long tidal river." Nickname: Constitution State. Motto: *Qui Translulit Sustinet* (He Who Transplanted Still Sustains). Flower: mountain laurel. Tree: white oak. Bird: robin. Song: "Yankee Doodle Dandy."

Land

Area: 5,018 sq. mi. (48th). Rivers: Connecticut, Hoasatonic, Mianus, Naugatuck, Thames. Cities (with 1990 pop.): Bridgeport (141,686), Hartford (139,739), New Haven (130,474), Waterbury (108,961), Stamford (108,056).

People

Population, 1945: 1,786,300 (28th); 1990: 3,287,116 (27th). Breakdown, 1990: 87% white, 8.3% black, 6.5% Hispanic, 77.6% urban, 23.4% rural (1950); 79.1% urban, 20.9% rural (1990). Famous natives: Robert Mitchum (actor), J. P. Morgan (financier), Katharine Hepburn (actress), Samuel Colt (gun manufacturer), Mark Twain (writer).

Economics

Gross state product, 1990: $93.9 billion (28th); per capita income: $25,358. Agricultural products: vegetables, tobacco, apples and other fruits. Industry: computers and electronics, helicopters, submarines, aircraft engines, machinery. Minerals: stone, sand and gravel.

Major Developments, 1946–1990

During the long period of development, Connecticut acquired several marks of distinction. Samuel Colt produced the revolver in 1835, and the state had a long association with firearms. Hartford established a long-running domination of the insurance industry. Groton built atomic submarines during the cold-war era. Proximity to New York City allowed economic activity to spill over and help give the state the highest per capita income. Many people from Connecticut work in, or have economic connections to, New York City.

Delaware

The first Europeans to arrive, the Dutch in 1631, were expelled by local Indians. Swedes came to the area next, and the Dutch returned in 1651. The British seized the Delaware area and the entire Dutch holdings in 1664. The territory was part of the land granted to William Penn before it broke off from Pennsylvania. Delaware had the distinction of being the first state to ratify the new Constitution on December 7, 1787. The capital is Dover. The name comes from a governor of Virginia, Sir Thomas West—Lord De La Warr. Nickname: First State. Motto: Liberty and Independence. Flower: peach blossom. Tree: American holly. Bird: blue hen chicken. Song: "Our Delaware."

Land

Area: 2,396 sq. mi. (49th). Rivers: Chesapeake and Delaware Canal, Delaware, Nantacoke. Cities (with 1990 pop.): Wilmington (71,529), Dover (27,630), Newark (25,098), Milford (6,040).

People

Population, 1945: 286,832 (46th); 1990: 666,168 (46th). Breakdown, 1990: 80.3% white, 16.9% black, 2.4% Hispanic, 62.6% urban, 37.4% rural (1950); 73% urban, 27% rural (1990). Famous natives: E. I. DuPont (manufacturer), Pete DuPont (politician), Edward Squibb (doctor), Howard Pyle (Illustrator).

Economics

Gross state product, 1990: $19.6 billion (44th); per capita income: $20,039. Agricultural products: soybeans, potatoes, corn, vegetables, livestock. Industry: fishing, automobiles, railroad and aircraft equipment, nylon, wearing apparel. Minerals: magnesium, sand, and gravel.

Major Developments, 1946–1990

A tiny state, smaller than many counties, Delaware in its early years acquired a most prominent family in the DuPonts. Beginning as a producer of gunpowder and then other munitions, the DuPonts later expanded into other manufactures, property, finance, even politics. Liberal corporation laws induced numerous large firms to incorporate in the state—a set of circumstances that attracted criticism from reformers but promoted the economic well-being of the state. The per capita income was high.

Florida

Several Native American tribes, the Calusa, Apalachee, Timucua, and especially the more numerous Seminole inhabited the Florida area before the Spanish arrived, claimed the area and gave it its current name. Having found little gold, the Spanish did little to develop the swampy land within an empire that in the early 19th century was rapidly disintegrating. The Spanish were induced to cede the land to an expanding United States in 1819. The Seminole were mostly pushed out. Florida entered the union on March 3, 1845, the 27th state, and seceded some 16 years later in support of the losing cause of the Confederacy. The state capital is Tallahassee. The name originated in the Spanish word meaning "feast of flowers." Nickname: Sunshine State. Motto: In God We Trust. Flower: orange blossom. Tree: sabal palmetto palm. Bird: mockingbird. Song: "Swanee River" (Old Folks at Home).

Land

Area: 58,644 sq. mi. (22nd). Rivers: Apalachicola, Caloosahatchee, Indian, Kissimmee, Perdido, St. Johns, St. Marys, Swanee, Withlacoochee. Cities (with 1990 pop.): Jacksonville (672,971), Miami (358,548), Tampa (280,015), St. Petersburg (238,629), Hialeah (188,004).

People

Population, 1945: 2,385,917 (21st); 1990: 12,937,926 (4th). Breakdown, 1990: 83.1% white, 13.6% black, 12.2% Hispanic, 65.5% urban, 34.5% rural (1950), 84.8% urban, 15.2% rural (1990). Famous natives: Joseph Stilwell (general), Sidney Poitier (actor), Ben Vereen (dancer), James Weldon Johnson (author), A. Philip Randolph (labor leader), Faye Dunaway (actress).

Economics

Gross state product, 1990: $244.6 billion (6th); per capita income: $18,586. Agricultural products: citrus fruits, vegetables, melons, potatoes, sugarcane. Industry: tourism, electronic equipment, lumber, chemicals, publishing, industrial machinery. Minerals: phosphate, rock, crushed stone, sand and gravel, titanium.

Major Developments, 1946–1990

In geography and in its Confederate background, Florida was a southern state; in other respects it projected a different image. An enormous oceanfront and year-round warm weather were feature enticements to people from the North. Thus it attracted "snow birds" and other visitors in winter months and retirees year-round. The number grew as the expanding economy made it possible. Disney World moved in as did Cyprus Gardens; the Daytona 500 race, a growing national event, came early each year. Cubans fled the Castro revolution in several waves after 1959; most came to Florida. Floridians multiplied and the state prospered. But all was not paradise. The land was being trampled; animal habitat and the animals faced destruction. Both of Florida's peninsulas were targets for hurricanes in the autumn; drug sellers from the South found Florida a logical staging ground for markets up north.

Georgia

Hernando de Soto explored this area, populated by Cherokee and other Indian tribes, in the mid-16th century. The English began to colonize the land under the leadership of James Oglethorpe in 1733; Georgia was to be a home and new starting place for debtors and poor English. Oglethorpe extinguished Spanish claims in 1742. Many Georgians supported the cause of the American Revolution, and afterward the state became the fourth to join the union, on January 2, 1788. The Cherokee Indians were pushed out on the Trail of Tears in the 1830s. Georgia seceded in 1860 and suffered mightily from the Civil War. The capital is Atlanta. The name originated with George II, the king who granted the colonial charter. Nickname: Peach State. Motto: Wisdom, Justice, and Moderation. Flower: Cherokee rose. Tree: live oak. Bird: brown thrasher. Song: "Georgia on my Mind."

Land

Area: 58,910 sq. mi. (21st). Rivers: Altamaha, Apalachicola, Chattahoochee, Flint, Ocmulgee, Oconee, Savannah, Suwanee. Mountains: Blue Ridge. Cities (with 1990 pop.): Atlanta (394,017), Columbus (179,278), Savannah (137,560), Macon (106,612), Albany (78,122).

People

Population, 1945: 3,191,766 (13th); 1990: 6,478,216 (11th). Breakdown, 1990: 71% white, 27% black, 1.7% Hispanic, 45.3% urban, 54.7% rural (1950); 63.2% urban, 36.8% rural (1990). Famous natives: Erskine Caldwell (writer), Jimmy Carter (president), Ray Charles (singer), Jackie Robinson (baseball player), Joanne Woodward (actress), Margaret Mitchell (writer).

Economics

Gross state product, 1990: $135.9 billion (13th); per capita income: $16,944. Agricultural products: peanuts, cotton, corn, tobacco,

peaches. Industry: lumber, paper products, textiles, food products. Minerals: limestone, sand and gravel, clay, cement.

Major Developments, 1946–1990

In the postwar period Georgia carried many of the burdens of poor economic development and racial division that marked most southern states. The state did provide leadership in many agricultural areas, such as poultry, peanuts, and pecans. Rural areas were slow to change, but Atlanta was different. In the 1970s it elected Andrew Young, first black member of Congress, and Maynard Jackson, first black mayor since Reconstruction. Atlanta also had the booming Coca-cola headquarters; it obtained professional athletic teams of the first order and housed the sprawling communications empire of Ted Turner.

Hawaii

Polynesians arrived in the sixth and 10th centuries and established a basic population of these five main islands in the Central Pacific. Europeans landed in 1778 with the arrival of James Cook (a Briton). Large numbers of Japanese came in the late 19th and early 20th centuries. Whites, mostly from the United States, operated the major financial enterprises, and many of the same people supported a revolution in 1893 that ended the reign of a local monarchy. The United States annexed the islands in 1898. Governed as a territory after 1900, Hawaii became the major United States military base in the Pacific area. The Japanese attack in 1941 created a strong American sentimental attachment and boosted the statehood movement after the war. Hawaii became the 50th state on August 21, 1950. The capital is Honolulu. Origin of the name is unclear; perhaps it stemmed from the discoverer of the islands, Hawaii Loa. Nickname: The Aloha State. Motto: The life of the land is perpetuated in righteousness. Flower: yellow hibiscus. Tree: candlenut. Bird: Hawaiian goose. Song: "Hawaii Ponoi."

Land

Area: 6,471 sq. mi. (47th). Rivers: Kaukonahua stream, Wailuku stream. Mountains: Hualalai, Kilauea, Mauna Kea and Mauna Loa volcanoes. Cities (with 1990 population): Honolulu (365,272), Hilo (37,808), Kailua (36,818), Kaneohe (35,448), Waipahu (31,435).

People

Population, 1945: 502,122 (unranked); 1990: 1,108,229 (41st). Breakdown, 1990: 33.4% white, 2.5% black, 7.3% Hispanic, 61.8% Asian, 89% urban, 11% rural (1990). Famous natives: Daniel J. Inouye (politician), Don Ho (singer), Bette Midler (singer), Bernice Bishop (philanthropist), Victoria Kaiulani (claimed heiress to Hawaiian throne).

Economics

Gross state product, 1990: $28.6 billion (37th); per capita income: $20,254. Agricultural products: sugar, pineapples, melons, fruits, nuts. Industry: tourism, military bases, sugar refining, printing, food products. Minerals: crushed stone, cement.

Major Developments, 1946–1990

If Americans did not know much about Hawaii before 1941, they did so afterward, with the Japanese attack on December 7 and with many thousands of military personnel passing through to the Pacific war. It was an enchanting place but a long way off. Development of jet passenger travel supplied the last link in the chain. The islands continued to supply sugar, tropical fruits, and vegetables. The pentagon poured in large sums to maintain the military bases there. The government established a nostalgic *Arizona* (a sunken battleship in Pearl Harbor near Honolulu) war memorial. But it was as a Pacific paradise that most Americans perceived Hawaii, and with jet aircraft and growing income for millions of mainlanderers, many could make the trip, and they did.

Idaho

Indian tribes that had lived in the area that became Idaho included the Bannock, Coeur d'Alene, and Nez Perce. Lewis and Clark moved through the territory and helped assert U.S. claim to what would be called the Oregon Territory. Rival British and American claims would be resolved in a treaty of 1846 that legitimized U.S. possession of land up to the 49th parallel. Conflicts between whites and Indians, mostly the Nez Perce, would continue through the 1860s and 1870s. Idaho entered the union on July 3, 1890, in conjunction with five other silver-producing states. It was the 43rd member of the union. The capital is Boise. The name means "gem of the mountains." Nickname: Gem State. Motto: *Esta Perpetua* (It Is Perpetual). Flower: syringa. Tree: white pine. Bird: mountain bluebird. Song: "Here We Have Idaho."

Land

Area: 83,564 sq. mi. (13th). Rivers: Bear, Clearwater, Payette, Salmon, Snake. Mountains: Bitterroot Range, Centennial, Clearwater, Salmon River, Sawtooth Range, Wasatch Range. Cities (with 1990 pop.): Boise (125,738), Pocatello (46,080), Idaho Falls (42,929), Nampa (28,365), Lewiston (28,082).

People

Population, 1945: 500,109 (42nd); 1990: 1,006,749 (42nd). Breakdown, 1990: 94.4% white, 0.3% black, 5.3% Hispanic, 42.9% urban, 57.1% rural (1950); 57.4% urban, 42.6% rural (1990). Famous natives: Frank Church (politician), Lana Turner (actress), Ezra Pound (poet), Harmon Killebrew (baseball player), Jerry Kramer (football player).

Economics

Gross state product, 1990: $18.6 billion (45th); per capita income: $15,160. Agricultural products: potatoes, hay, wheat, sugar beets, fruits. Industry: lumber and wood products, chemicals, machinery, metal products. Minerals: phosphates, silver, gold, sand, coal.

Major Developments, 1946–1990

Idaho had very rugged terrain, including Hell's Canyon on the Snake River, the deepest canyon in North America, at which place a huge dam was built in the 1950s. Areas of attraction included Sun Valley, a favorite resort of novelist Ernest Hemingway; Shoshone Falls; Lava Hot Springs; and River of No Return. The state subsisted on agriculture, mining of precious metals, and development in the 1970s and the 1980s of high-technology industries.

Illinois

Numerous Indian tribes, such as the Illinois, Kaskaskia, Peoria, and others lived in this Great Lakes territory. The first Europeans were French trappers. Louis Jolliet and Jacques Marquette explored the area, and the French were the first to claim it. The British seized control in 1763, and the area of Illinois was a sort of backwater of the American Revolution. The area was part of the Northwest Territory after independence. Illinois then followed an orderly path to statehood, the journey completed on December 3, 1819, when Illinois became the 21st state. The capital is Springfield. The name came from the Indian term *iliniwek,* tribe of the superior men. Nickname: Prairie State. Motto: State sovereignty—national unity. Flower: native violet. Tree: white oak. Bird: cardinal. Song: "Illinois."

Land

Area: 56,345 sq. mi. (24th). Rivers: Fox, Illinois, Illinois Waterway, Kankakee, Kaskaskia, Mississippi, Ohio, Rock, Vermillion, Wabash. Cities (with 1990 pop.): Chicago (2,783,726), Rockford (139,426), Peoria (113,504), Springfield (105,227), Aurora (99,581).

People

Population, 1945: 7,721,099 (4th); 1990: 11,430,602 (6th). Breakdown, 1990: 78.3% white, 14.8% black, 7.9% Hispanic, 77.6% urban, 22.4% rural (1950); 84.6% urban, 15.4% rural (1990). Famous natives: Ray Bradbury (author), Saul Bellow (author), Enrico Fermi (scientist), Carl Sandburg (poet), Ernest Hemingway (novelist), Gloria Swanson (actress), Miles Davis (musician).

Economics

Gross state product, 1990: $272.2 billion (4th); per capita income: $20,303. Agricultural products: corn, wheat, soybeans, hay, vegetables and fruit. Industry: machinery, electronics, metals, chemicals, automobiles. Minerals: stone, sand and gravel, coal, oil.

Major Developments, 1946–1990

Illinois continued to possess many diverse features that would make it prosperous and strong: Rich prairie soil remained productive. In the south one found coal and gas fields. Rivers were plentiful, the climate moderate. Railroads, interstate highways, and aircraft lines crisscrossed the state. Lake Michigan graced the state's northern tip. Illinois had

Illinois had Chicago, and Chicago had Lake Michigan and skyscrapers. Here is the beautifully proportioned Hancock Building. (National Archives)

only one large city, but it was a whopper. Chicago experienced a relative decline from its once proud position of second city, but it remained large, bustling, and attractive. Chicago frequently hosted national political conventions, and the Democrat gathering in 1968 was memorable. The city insisted on having the tallest skyscraper—Sears Tower, finished in 1973, and the busiest airport: first Midway and then O'Hare. If the population had shrunk, it had not gone far away; Chicago was parent to a metropolitan area that stretched for miles and miles.

Indiana

Some of the earliest Indian artifacts were of the mound builders near Evansville that dated to the year 1,000. Afterward, the Kickapoo, Miami, and other tribes settled in the area. The French explored the territory and established a settlement at Vincennes, in the southwest part of the state. The area passed to Britain in the settlement of 1763. George Rogers Clark's conquest of Vincennes in 1779 was one of the few revolutionary engagements in the West. The postrevolutionary period was marked with numerous battles between whites and Indians, notably the Miami. The defeat of Tecumseh's Confederacy in 1811 in the north-central area helps pave the way for statehood. Indiana became the 19th state on December 11, 1816. The state capital is Indianapolis. The origin of the name is "land of Indians," as observed by early settlers. Nickname: Hoosier State. Motto: The Crossroads of America. Flower: peony. Tree: tulip poplar. Bird: cardinal. Song: "On the Banks of the Wabash."

Land

Area: 36,185 sq. mi. (38th). Rivers: Kankakee, Ohio, Tippecanoe, Wabash, White, Whitewater. Cities (with 1990 pop.): Indianapolis (741,952), Ft. Wayne (173,072), Evansville (126,272), Gary (116,646), South Bend (105,511).

People

Population, 1945: 3,437,745 (12th); 1990: 5,544,159 (14th). Breakdown, 1990: 90.6% white, 7.8% black, 1.8% Hispanic, 59.9% urban, 40.1% rural (1950); 64.9% urban, 35.9% rural (1990). Famous natives: Larry Bird (basketball player), Hoagy Carmichael (composer), Michael Jackson (singer), David Letterman (comedian), Kurt Vonnegut (author), Carole Lombard (actress), James Dean (actor), Cole Porter (composer), Jane Pauley (television host).

Economics

Gross state product, 1990: $111.9 billion (14th); per capita income: $16,866. Agricultural products: corn, wheat, soybeans, hay, hogs and cattle. Industry: machinery, electronics, steel, chemicals, automobile parts. Minerals: coal, limestone, sand and gravel.

Major Developments, 1946–1990

Long known as an agricultural state, Indiana continued to diversify, combining good prairie farmland in the north with growing industrialization, especially in such cities as Gary, East Chicago, Indianapolis, and Evansville. Southern Indiana produced increasing amounts of coal, although, sadly, much of it came from strip mines. Southern Indiana also produced much of the nation's limestone. Once home for several automobile manufacturers, the state had to accept their departure. The last Indiana-based company, Studebaker, closed in 1963, but several Hoosier cities attracted factories from companies headquartered in Detroit. Hoosiers continued to like their basketball. High school competition was unlike any in the nation, and now the girls joined in the action. Indiana University's men's team won four national championships between 1946 and 1990.

Iowa

The early Indian groups in the area that became Iowa included the mound builders. Marquette and Jolliet claimed the land for France. Iowa was within the territory the United States acquired in the Louisiana Purchase (from France) in 1803. Later it was a part of the Missouri Compromise of 1820 that scarcely concealed a festering problem of slavery. Settlers to this rich land had to contend with Indians during the Black Hawk Wars in the 1830s. Iowa entered the union as a free state on December 28, 1846, (the 29th state) as the United States entered its pre–Civil War period. The capital is Des Moines. The name originated with the Iowa tribe of Indians. Nickname: Hawkeye State. Motto: Our liberties we prize, and our rights we will maintain. Flower: wild rose. Tree: oak. Bird: eastern goldfinch. Song: "The Song of Iowa."

Land

Area: 52,275 sq. mi. (25th). Rivers: Big Sioux, Des Moines, Mississippi, Missouri. Cities (with 1990 pop.): Des Moines (193,187), Cedar Rapids (108,751), Davenport (95,333), Sioux City (80,505), Waterloo (66,467).

People

Population, 1945: 2,259,526 (22nd); 1990: 2,776,755 (30th). Breakdown, 1990: 96.6% white, 1.7% black, 1.2% Hispanic, 47.7% urban, 52.3% rural (1950): 60.6% urban, 39.4% rural (1990). Famous natives: George Gallup (pollster), Herbert Hoover (president), John L. Lewis (labor leader), Grant Wood (artist), John Wayne (actor).

Economics

Gross state product, 1990: $56.0 billion (29th); per capita income: $17,249. Agricultural products: corn, soybeans, wheat, hay, canola. Industry: farm machinery, electronics, chemicals, fertilizer. Minerals: sand and gravel, stone, cement.

Major Developments, 1946–1990

Iowa long has been synonymous with agriculture and for good reason. The state was blessed with exceptionally rich, deep, and productive topsoil. Several of the industries in the state were related to aspects of farming. Mechanization of farming was a reason why the population grew slowly in some years and between 1980 and 1986 Iowa lost more than 2 percent of its people. Farming has booms and busts, of course, and is vulnerable to drought (as in 1988) and the danger of floods from the great Missouri and Mississippi Rivers, both of which border the state.

Kansas

The Spanish explorer Coronado had passed through the territory that contained the future state of Kansas, as had the French, who claimed the land. Native Americans already in residence included some of the more familiar tribes of the Great Plains: the Pawnee, Kiowa, Osage, Cheyenne, Comanche, Apache. The Kansas area came to the United States through the Louisiana Purchase of 1803. The territory and later the state became a part of the Old West, with cattle drives and Indian wars. In the pre–Civil War era Kansas became a battleground of sorts before there was a battle. The antislavery people won this contest, and Kansas entered the union on January 29, 1861, as the great American conflict was getting underway. The 34th state, Kansas also was a free state, although many proslavery people inhabited the area. The capital is Topeka. The name came from Kansa, people of the south wind. Nickname: Sunflower State. Motto: *Ad astra per aspera* (To the stars through adversity). Flower: sunflower. Tree: cottonwood. Bird: western meadowlark. Song: "Home on the Range."

Land

Area: 82,277 sq. mi. (14th). Rivers: Arkansas, Kansas, Missouri, Republican, Saline, Smoky Hill, Solomon. Cities (with 1990 pop.): Wichita (304,011), Kansas City (149,767), Topeka (119,883), Overland Park (111,790), Lawrence (65,608).

People

Population, 1945: 1,740,379 (30th); 1990: 2,477,574 (32nd). Breakdown, 1990: 90.1% white, 5.8% black, 3.8% Hispanic, 52.1% urban, 47.9% rural (1950); 69.1% urban, 30.9% rural (1990). Famous natives: Bob Dole (politician), Dwight Eisenhower (general and president), Nancy Landon Kassebaum (politician), Charlie Parker (musician), Gale Sayers (football player), Dennis Hopper (actor).

Economics

Gross state product, 1990: $51.1 billion (31st); per capita income: $17,986. Agricultural products: wheat, corn, hay, soybeans, livestock. Industry: machinery, food products, publishing, airplanes. Minerals: sand and gravel, cement, petroleum, zinc, lead, coal.

Major Developments, 1946–1990

Wheat fields, spacious prairie lands, and herds of cattle continued to mark the landscape of Kansas. Oil derricks in specified places suggested economic activity of a different sort. Industrialization in many cases was related to agriculture. Kansas City was involved in milling, meat-packing, and other such enterprises. A lively aircraft industry that had grown up in Wichita during the Second World War continued to operate, placing an emphasis on private aircraft. Places of historic interest were largely connected to Kansas's position in development of the West: Dodge City, Ft. Riley, and John Brown's cabin at Osawatomie. The construction of the Dwight Eisenhower Museum and Library at Abilene attracted much interest.

Kentucky

The area of Kentucky was a part of Virginia Colony and an early target for colonists moving west beyond the Appalachian Mountains. Daniel Boone led an expedition in 1769, and the first settlement was established in 1774. The area also had been claimed by the French until 1763, and Native Americans were numerous. The British and Indians collaborated until the victory of George Rogers Clark in 1779. After the American Revolution, Virginia was persuaded to cede its western lands to the central government, opening the door for the Kentucky area to petition for statehood. Kentucky became the 15th state in the union on June 1, 1792. The state capital was Frankfort. The name Kentucky was a corruption of Indian words meaning "meadowland" or "land of tomorrow." Nickname: Bluegrass State. Motto: United we stand, divided we fall. Flower: goldenrod. Tree: Kentucky coffee tree. Bird: cardinal. Song: "My Old Kentucky Home."

Land

Area: 40,409 sq. mi. (37th). Rivers: Cumberland, Ohio, Kentucky, Licking, Tennessee. Mountains: Appalachian, Cumberland. Cities (with 1990 pop.): Louisville (269,063), Lexington-Fayette (225,366), Owensboro (53,549), Covington (43,264), Bowling Green (40,641).

People

Population, 1945: 2,578,179 (18th); 1990: 3,685,296 (23rd). Breakdown, 1990: 92% white, 7.1% black, 0.6% Hispanic, 36.8% urban, 63.2% rural (1950); 51.8% urban, 48.2% rural (1990). Famous natives: Muhammad Ali (boxer), Louis D. Brandeis (jurist), Robert Penn Warren (author), Colonel Harlan Sanders (restaurant-chain owner), Fred Vinson (jurist), Diane Sawyer (television reporter).

Economics

Gross state product, 1990: $67.5 billion (25th); per capita income: $14,929. Agricultural products: tobacco, corn, soybeans, livestock. Industry: lumber, food products, automobiles, electronics. Minerals: coal, sand and gravel.

Major Developments, 1946–1990

Throughout the period Kentucky retained a distinction in several areas. It remained a center of breeding and raising horses and a home to the Kentucky Derby, America's most famous horse race. It continued, if at a different pace and using different methods, to mine coal in the mountains; to produce bourbon whiskey; and to produce tobacco in spite of growing hostility to smoking. Diminished activity in all these areas and a growing shortage of good farmland added to economic woes for which new industry, such as Japanese automobile factories, did not entirely compensate. Kentucky was a part of the economic ramifications inherent in the term *Appalachia*.

Louisiana

The Spanish were the first Europeans to travel this southern coastal area, but LaSalle claimed the area for France in 1682. By 1731 it had become a French crown colony. Some 4,000 Acadians, French living in Nova Scotia, were transported by the British to Louisiana and settled in the bayou country in 1755. The land west of the Mississippi River was ceded to Spain in 1763, retroceded in 1800, and then sold to the United States in 1803. The southernmost portion of this territory contained the future state of Louisiana. The land east of the river was ceded to Britain in 1763, and it became American as a result of the revolution. Louisiana became a state, the 18th, on April 8, 1812—during the postrevolutionary years. At the end of the War of 1812 the Americans defeated the British in the celebrated battle of New Orleans—an event that perhaps reconfirmed United States possession of the territory. The capital of Louisiana is Baton Rouge. The name originated with King Louis XIV of France. Nickname: Pelican State. Motto: Union, justice, confidence. Flower: magnolia. Tree: cyprus. Bird: eastern brown pelican. Song: "Give Me Louisiana."

Land

Area: 47,751 sq. mi. (31st). Rivers: Atchafalaya, Mississippi, Ouachita, Pearl, Red, Sabine. Cities (with 1990 pop.): New Orleans (496,938), Baton Rouge (219,531), Shreveport (198,525), Lafayette (94,440), Kenner (72,033).

People

Population, 1945: 2,456,057 (20th); 1990: 4,219,973 (21st). Breakdown, 1990: 67.3% white, 30.8% black, 2.2% Hispanic, 54.8% urban, 45.2% rural (1950); 68.1% urban, 31.9% rural (1990). Famous natives: Louis Armstrong (singer and musician), Truman Capote (author), Mahalia Jackson (singer), Jerry Lee Lewis (singer), Michael De Bakey (surgeon), Fats Domino (entertainer).

Economics

Gross state product, 1990: $90.9 billion (22nd); per capita income: $14,391. Agricultural products: sugar, soybeans, pecans, corn, sweet potatoes, cotton. Industry: chemical goods, lumber, electronics, petroleum products. Minerals: salt, sulphur, gravel, oil, natural gas.

Major Developments, 1946–1990

Louisiana continued to have a diverse population of whites, Cajuns (originally the Acadians), Creoles, Indians, and blacks. The petrochemical industry situated along the Mississippi River between Baton Rouge and New Orleans remained critical, if controversial, and it shifted with the industry's ups and downs after the 1970s. A downturn in 1987 was devastating. Low taxes meant less money for schools and state services. New Orleans guarded the Mississippi River, and it was an important port for seagoing ships. In the 1970s and 1980s the state made a major pitch to attract foreign and domestic tourists to the unique culture of the southern part of the state and to "the sportsman's paradise."

Maine

The Penobscot, Passamaquoddy, and Abenaki Indians, among others, lived in this northeasternmost portion of the future United States. The Vikings explored the area, and in the 17th century some 1,000 French settlers arrived. The land nonetheless became part of a grant made by the English king to the Plymouth Colony; it later would be attached to the larger Massachusetts Bay Colony. The area was on the frontier of repeated quarrels between the British and French, a conflict resolved, of course, in favor of the British. Massachusetts relinquished its claim to the land after the American Revolution, thus opening a door for separate statehood. Maine became the 23rd state on March 15, 1820. Capital: Augusta. Origin of the name: the French province of Mayne. Nickname: Pine Tree State. Motto: *Dirigo* (I Direct). Tree: eastern white pine. Bird: chickadee. Song: "State of Maine Song."

Land

Area: 33,265 sq. mi. (39th). Rivers: Alagash, Androscoggin, Aroostook, Kennebec, Machias, Penobscot, Piscatqua, Salmon Falls, St. John. Mountains: Longfellow, Appalachian. Cities (with 1990 pop.): Portland (64,358), Lewiston (39,757), Bangor (33,181), Auburn (24,309), South Portland (23,163).

People

Population, 1945: 785,913 (35th); 1990: 1,227,928 (38th). Breakdown, 1990: 98.4% white, 0.4% black, 0.6% Hispanic, 51.7% urban, 48.3% rural (1950); 44.6% urban, 55.4% rural (1990). Famous natives: Edmund Muskie (politician), Kenneth Roberts (novelist), Nelson Rockefeller (politician), Henry Wadsworth Longfellow (poet).

Economics

Gross state product, 1990: $23.3 billion (42nd); per capita income: $17,200. Agricultural products: potatoes, blueberries, hay, fruit. Industry: wood products, leather goods, paper, fishing, iron and steel, ships. Minerals: sand and gravel, cement, limestone.

Major Developments, 1946–1990

Maine stretches far to the north, the coast is craggy, the soil often infertile, and for many inhabitants life was a struggle. Lumber, fishing, farming—especially hay and potatoes—continued to be major means of subsistence. Lumber companies owned huge portions of land. Reduction in defense spending caused layoffs at Bath Iron Works and the Portsmouth Naval Yard, but light industry multiplied in the 1970s and 1980s. Politics became more evenly divided between Democrats and Republicans (as opposed to being staunchly Republican). Democrat Edmund Muskie (vice presidential candidate in 1968) brought recognition to the state, as did George Mitchell, another Democrat, who became Senate majority leader in 1988.

Maryland

Home of coastal Indian tribes, the Maryland area had been explored by English settlers from Jamestown; later (in 1632) it was given to Cecilius Calvert, Lord Baltimore, to be a haven in the colonies for Roman Catholics. One of the original colonies, it also became one of the first round of states in the union. Ratifying the Constitution on April 28, 1788, Maryland became the seventh state. Lodged between North and South and classified as a border state in the Civil War, Maryland nonetheless was held in the Union camp. It also was the site of the battle of Antietam in 1862, one of the two major battles fought outside the South. The state capital is Annapolis. The name came from Henrietta Maria, queen consort of King Charles I. Nickname: Old Line State. Motto: *Fatti Maschii, Parole Femine* (Manly Deeds, Womanly Words). Flower: black-eyed Susan. Tree: white oak. Bird: Baltimore oriole. Song: "Maryland, My Maryland."

Land

Area: 10,460 sq. mi. (42nd). Rivers: Chester, Choptank, Nanticoke, Patapsco, Patuxent, Pocomoke, Potomac, Susquehanna. Mountains: Allegheny, Blue Ridge. Cities (with 1990 pop.): Baltimore (736,014), Rockville (44,835), Frederick (40,148), Gaithersburg (39,542), Bowie (37,589).

People

Population, 1945: 2,1235,419 (23rd); 1990: 4,781,468 (19th). Breakdown, 1990: 71% white, 24.9% black, 2.9% Asian, 2.6% Hispanic, 69% urban, 31% rural (1950); 81.3% urban, 18.7% rural (1990). Famous natives: Russell Baker (journalist), Eubie Blake (musician), Billie Holiday (singer), Babe Ruth (baseball player), Thurgood Marshall (jurist).

Economics

Gross state product, 1990: $108.6 billion (16th); per capita income: $21,864. Agricultural products: tobacco, corn, soybeans, livestock. Industry: metals, electronics, machinery, ships, aircraft, food products, fishing. Minerals: coal, sand and gravel.

Major Developments, 1946–1990

Maryland continued to be affected by two major geographic features: the Chesapeake Bay, which brought fishing, boating, and other water enterprises, and proximity to the national capital. Maryland nearly surrounded Washington, D.C. A native son, Spiro Agnew, served as vice president starting in 1969, although he would be forced out of office in 1973. George Wallace was shot in Maryland while running for the presidency in 1972. The naval academy remained at Annapolis and despite losses in population, Baltimore remained one of the major cities of the United States. By 1990 two-thirds of the people lived in six counties adjacent to Washington and Baltimore.

Massachusetts

The Pequot, Massachuset, and Nipmuc Indians lived in this northeastern coastal area. Some of the first English settlers coming to the New World came to Massachusetts: to Plymouth in 1620 (the Pilgrims) and to Massachusetts Bay Colony after 1628 (the Puritans). A large colony with a tightly structured, church-dominated government, Massachusetts Bay was a major player in the affairs of the colonies and in the revolutionary period—providing leadership in politics, education, and other areas. It was fitting that several revolutionary leaders and two early presidents came from this area. Ratifying the Constitution of February 6, 1788, Massachusetts became the sixth state and one of the first large states to enter the union. The capital is Boston. The name originated with Algonquian words meaning "great mountain place." Nickname: Bay State. Motto: *Ense Petit Placidani Sub Libertate Ouietem* (By the Sword We Seek Peace, But Peace Only under Liberty). Flower: mayflower. Tree: American elm. Bird: chickadee. Song: "All Hail to Massachusetts."

Land

Area: 8,284 sq. mi. (45th). Rivers: Cape Cod Canal, Connecticut, Merrimack, Taunton. Cities (with 1990 pop.): Boston (574,283),

Worchester (169,759), Springfield (156,983), Lowell (103,439), New Bedford (99,932).

People

Population, 1945: 4,493,281 (9th); 1990: 6,016,425 (13th). Breakdown, 1990: 89.8% white, 5% black, 4.8% Hispanic, 84.4% urban, 15.6% rural (1950); 84.3% urban, 15.7% rural (1990). Famous natives: Leonard Bernstein (conductor, composer), Richard Cardinal Cushing (religious leader), John F. Kennedy (president), Bette Davis (actress), Jack Kerouac (author), Samuel E. Morrison (historian), Ted Kennedy (politician), Thomas O'Neill (politician).

Economics

Gross state product, 1990: $153.9 billion (9th); per capita income: $22,642. Agricultural products: cranberries, potatoes, dairy products, nursery plants. Industry: cutlery, leather goods, electronics, machinery, ships, shoes, publishing. Minerals: babingtonite, limestone, coke, sand and gravel.

Major Developments, 1946–1990

Massachusetts continued to be a national leader in business, education, arts and sciences, and politics. Many of the traditional industries, such as textiles, shoes, and machinery declined or left the state altogether. But the state rebounded with growth of high technology, electronics, and military research. Some called it the Massachusetts Miracle, as unemployment dropped from 11 percent in 1975 to 3.2 percent in 1987. The state added many new structures devoted to education and the arts, of which the John F. Kennedy Library was a part. Massachusetts could claim numerous powerful politicians throughout this period. Several came from the Kennedy family, but another Democrat, John McCormack was Speaker of the House, and still another Irish Democrat, Thomas P. "Tip" O'Neill, held that post from 1977 to 1987.

Michigan

French fur traders who traversed this area in between the Great Lakes encountered numerous Indian tribes, among them the Potawatomi, Menominee, Huron, and Chippewa. The French left such place names as Detroit and Marquette, but they lost the area to the British in 1763. After the Revolutionary War, the area became part of the Northwest Territory and followed the orderly process toward statehood laid down in the Northwest Ordinance. Michigan thereupon became the 26th state on January 26, 1837. The capital is Lansing. The name originated in the Fox Indian word *meskiani,* meaning "large lake." Nickname: Wolverine State. Motto: *Si Quaeris Peninsulam Amoenam Circumspice* (If You Seek a Pleasant Peninsula, Look about You). Flower: apple blossom. Tree: white pine. Bird: robin. Song: "Michigan, My Michigan."

Land

Area: 58,527 sq. mi. (23rd). Rivers: Brule, Detroit, Kalamazoo, Menominee, Montreal, Muskegon, St. Joseph, St. Mary's. Cities (with 1990 pop.): Detroit (1,027,974), Grand Rapids (189,126), Warren (144,864), Flint (140,761), Lansing (127,321).

People

Population, 1945: 5,471,744 (7th); 1990: 9,295,297 (8th). Breakdown, 1990: 83.4% white, 13.9% black, 2.2% Hispanic, 70.7% urban, 29.3% rural (1950); 70.5% urban, 29.5% rural (1990). Famous natives: Henry Ford (manufacturer), Charles Lindbergh (aviator), William Upjohn (scientist), Ralph Bunche (diplomat), Joe Louis (boxer), Gerald Ford, (president), Madonna (singer), Diana Ross (singer), Tom Selleck (actor), Aretha Franklin (singer).

Economics

Gross state product, 1990: $188 billion (9th); per capita income: $18,346. Agricultural products: corn, potatoes, dairy goods, soybeans, fruit, blueberries, grapes. Industry: automobiles, metals, machinery, chemicals, plastics. Minerals: iron ore, copper, sand and gravel.

Major Developments, 1946–1990

Long associated with the automobile industry, Michigan experienced booms and busts tracable in many ways to production and sale of motor vehicles. Many plants remained in the state, but some relocated to other states or foreign countries. Another jolt came in the oil embargo of 1973 and the sharp rise in competition from Japanese auto firms. The old industrial cities such as Detroit and Flint became centers of unemployment, crime, and racial unrest. Michigan began to bounce back in the late 1970s as car sales returned and the tourist industry boomed. Politics was evenly split between the two parties, but the Republicans seemed to have the most prominent leaders, including Governor George Romney, William Millikan (governor 14 years), and Congressman and President Gerald Ford. Farming continued to decline, but Michigan remained a leader in public education.

Minnesota

The area of Minnesota had been home of northern Plains Indians, notably the Ojibway and Santee Dakota (Sioux). Britain controlled part of this area between 1763 and 1783; the western part was acquired from France in the Louisiana Purchase. Settlement and development came slowly and often involved conflict with Indians of the area, usually the Dakota Sioux. Minnesota entered the union as the 32nd state on May 1, 1858, on the eve of the Civil War. Later development, especially in farming, came at the hands of people descended from Scandanavian countries: Swedes and Norwegians. The capital is St. Paul. The name originated in the Sioux word *minisota,* "sky-tinted waters." Nickname: North Star State. Motto: *L. Étoile du Nord* (The Star of the North). Flower: pink and white lady slipper. Tree: red pine. Bird: common loon. Song: "Hail! Minnesota."

Land

Area: 84,402 sq. mi. (12th). Rivers: Minnesota, Mississippi, Red River of the North, St. Croix. Cities (with 1990 pop.): Minneapolis (368,383), St. Paul (272,285), Bloomington (86,335), Duluth (85,493), Rochester (70,745).

People

Population, 1945: 2,497,485 (19th); 1990: 4,375,099 (20th). Breakdown, 1990: 94.4% white, 2.2% black, 1.2% Hispanic, 1.8% Asian, 54.9% urban, 45.1% rural (1950); 69.9% urban, 31.1% rural (1990). Famous natives: Bob Dylan (singer), Warren Burger (jurist), Judy Garland (actress and singer), Garrison Keillor (humorist), Hubert Humphrey (politician), Charles Schulz (cartoonist), Walter Mondale (politician).

Economics

Gross state product, 1990: $100 billion (19th); per capita income: $18,731. Agricultural products: corn, wheat, hay, grain, livestock. Industry: food processing, wood products, metals, printing, machinery. Minerals: iron ore, granite, limestone, taconite.

Major Developments, 1946–1990

Minnesota depended on economic activity in foodstuffs, wood products, and iron ore. The Mesabi range still produced 60 percent of the nation's iron ore, but in the postwar period the state branched out into numerous high technology areas. As with nearly all states, the small towns declined and the cities became larger. Minnesota had the first indoor shopping mall in Edina in 1956 and later it acquired the largest mall: Mall of the Americas. Minnesota established a tradition of liberal politics, with such leaders as Hubert Humphrey, Walter Mondale, Eugene McCarthy, Orville Freeman. The situation became somewhat muddled beginning in the mid-1970s when such issues as abortion and homosexuality drove some conservatives out of the Democrat-Farmer-Labor Party. The state remained predominantly white, but nonwhite groups grew. Minneapolis had the largest urban population of Native Americans in the country. The largest growth in the 1970s and 1980s was in Asians, especially from Indochina.

Mississippi

DeSoto explored this area in 1540, discovered the Mississippi River, and traced it upstream. LaSalle later claimed the entire general area for France. The territory was ceded to Britain in 1763. American settlers gradually moved in and displaced the Indians living there. Mississippi was part of original United States territory, but the Spanish claimed part of the land for several years after the American Revolution. They did not depart until 1798. Mississippi entered the union as the 20th state on December 10, 1817. In years to come it developed a Deep South economy and culture in all respects. The state seceded in 1861, and the northern part of the state was a battleground. The capital is Jackson. The name stemmed from the Ojibway term: *misi sipi*—"great river." Nickname: Magnolia State. Motto: *Virtute et armis* (By Valor and arms). Flower: Southern magnolia. Tree: Southern magnolia. Bird: Northern mockingbird. Song: "Go Mississippi."

Land

Area: 47,689 sq. mi. (32nd). Rivers: Big Black, Mississippi, Pearl, Tennessee, Yazoo. Cities (with 1990 pop.): Jackson (196,637), Biloxi (46,319), Greenville (45,226), Hattiesburg (41,882), Meridian (41,036).

People

Population 1945; 2,080,377 (25th); 1990: 2,573,216 (31st). Breakdown, 1990: 63.5% white, 35.6% black, 0.6% Hispanic, 27.9% urban, 72.1% rural (1950); 47.1% urban, 52.9% rural (1990). Famous natives: William Faulkner (author), James Earl Jones (actor), Elvis Presley (singer), Charlie Pride (singer), Tennessee Williams (writer), Oprah Winfrey (television host).

Economics

Gross state product, 1990: $39.8 billion (32nd); per capita income: $12,735. Agricultural products: cotton, corn, soybeans, wheat, rice, livestock. Industry: wood products, food products, textiles, metals. Minerals: bauxite, iron ore, oil, natural gas.

Major Developments, 1946–1990

Mississippi in many ways mirrored the Deep South in the postwar period. A poor state, rural, agricultural, segregated at the start of the 1950s, Mississippi hosted some of the most intense civil rights battles of the era: James Meredith's efforts to desegregate "Ol' Miss," the murder of Medgar Evers, violent resistance to voter registration of blacks, Mississippi Freedom Summer of 1964. Victorious politicians in those days all were Democrats. Mississippi did change. The economy became more diverse, with growth of manufacturing and trade. Few people still farmed in 1990. Segregation ended—in schools, politics, and to lesser extent, in general social relations. Blacks ran for office; many of the whites shifted to the Republicans. But Mississippi still was a poor state in 1990, with low population and economic growth. Schools were improved and integrated but still rated among the weakest in the land.

Missouri

Home originally to the Missouri Indians and other tribes, Missouri was much affected by its rivers: the large Missouri that ran east and west and the Mississippi that formed its eastern border. Explored by the French and for many years a part of New France, the area became American in the Louisiana Purchase of 1803. Missouri became a state (the 24th) on August 21, 1821, as part of a major compromise over slavery. Missouri was a border state, but it was held in line by Union forces during the Civil War. The capital is Jefferson City. Origin of the name: from Iliniwek term *missouri*—"owner of big canoes." Nickname: Show Me State. Motto: *Salus populi Suprema lex esto* (Let the good of the people be the supreme law). Flower: blossom of the hawthorne. Tree: dogwood. Bird: bluebird. Song: "Missouri Waltz."

Land

Area: 69,697 sq. mi. (21st). Rivers: Des Moines, Mississippi, Missouri, Osage, St. Francis. Mountains: Ozark. Cities (with 1990 pop.): Kansas City (435,146), St. Louis (396,685), Springfield (140,494), Independence (112,301), St. Joseph (71,852).

People

Population, 1945: 3,556,693 (10th); 1990: 5,117,073 (15th). Breakdown, 1990: 87.7% white, 10.7% black, 1.2% Hispanic, 61.5% urban, 38.5% rural (1950); 68.7% urban, 31.3% rural (1990). Famous natives: Omar Bradley (general), Walter Cronkite (news reporter), Walt Disney (film producer), Langston Hughes (poet), Ginger Rogers (actress), Casey Stengel (baseball manager), Yogi Berra (baseball player), Harry S. Truman (president).

Economics

Gross state product, 1990: $103.7 billion (17th); per capita income: $17,497. Agricultural products: corn, wheat, livestock, soybeans. Industry: chemicals, automobiles, airplanes and airplane parts. Minerals: limestone, iron ore, lead.

Major Developments, 1946–1990

Missouri presented a familiar division between rural and urban areas. The St. Louis and Kansas City metropolitan areas had much of the people, but many still farmed, especially in the northern part of the state. The most famous city, St. Louis, best known for its breweries and the St. Louis Cardinals baseball team, suffered a sharp loss in population in the 1960s and 1970s. Winston Churchill made his "iron curtain" speech at Fulton in 1946. The Gateway Arch at St. Louis, a nationally known landmark, opened in 1964. The state's many signs that native son Harry S. Truman had been president from 1945 to 1953 included the Truman Library and Museum at Independence.

Montana

The area that included Montana was the northern portion of the Great Plains, a territory inhabited by the Crow and Flathead Indians. The United States acquired the territory in the Purchase of Louisiana in 1803. The course of development was part of the long story of exploration, westward expansion of the American population, and the discovery of precious metals that sparked more expansion and the inevitable conflict with Indians in the area. The storied Battle of Little Bighorn of 1876 was in Montana. Montana became a state on November 8, 1889, the 41st state and one of six so-called silver states (all contained silver deposits) brought into the union at approximately the same time. The capital is Helena. The name originated in the Spanish word *montana,* meaning "mountainous." Nickname: Treasure State or Big Sky Country. Motto: *Oro y Plata* (Gold and Silver). Tree: ponderosa pine. Bird: western meadowlark. Song: "Montana."

Land

Area: 147,046 sq. mi. (4th). Rivers: Kootenai, Milk, Missouri, Musselshell, Powder, Yellowstone. Mountains: Absaroka Range, Beartooth Range, Big Belt, Bitteroot Range, Centennial, Crazy, Lewis Range, Little Belt. Cities (with 1990 pop.): Billings (81,151), Great Falls (55,097), Missoula (42,918), Butte-Silver Bow (33,941), Helena (24,569).

People

Population, 1945: 457,624 (43rd); 1990: 799,065 (44th). Breakdown, 1990: 92.7% white, 0.3% black, 1.5% Hispanic, 6% American Indian, 43.7% urban, 56.3% rural (1950); 52.5% urban, 47.5% rural (1990). Famous natives: Gary Cooper (actor), Chet Huntley (newsman), Myrna Loy (actress), Mike Mansfield (politician), Charles Russell (artist).

Economics

Gross state product, 1990: $13.3 billion (46th); per capita income: $15,110. Agricultural products: livestock, wheat, corn, barley, oats, sugar beets. Industry: wood products, paper, oil, foodstuffs. Minerals: coal, oil, gas, copper, gravel, gypsum, phosphates.

Major Developments, 1946–1990

Montana underwent major changes between 1946 and 1990. Tourism expanded as visitors came to the state's many lakes and streams and to Yellowstone and Glacier National Parks. A boom in coal mining in the 1950s and 1960s produced a backlash in the 1970s when the state passed several measures designed to protect the land. A traditional economic giant, Anaconda Copper, sold out in the 1970s; Atlantic Richfield, which took over, stopped copper operation in 1983—a devastating event. Some promise appeared in the discovery of petroleum reserves in the 1970s and 1980s, but the basic enterprise remained agriculture, and it remained accountable to the large market forces.

Nebraska

Home of the Pawnee and other Indian tribes, Nebraska was part of the territory purchased from France in 1803. It was set aside as an Indian domain in 1834, but whites continued to cross the territory on the way west and enough of them stayed for Nebraska to become a territory in 1854 in the political struggles of the pre–Civil War era. The land was opened to settlement, and the railroad came in, making it possible for Nebraska to become the 37th state on March 1, 1867. The capital is Lincoln. The name's origin is a Siouan term meaning "flat water." Nickname: Cornhusker State. Motto: Equality Before the Law. Flower: goldenrod. Tree: cottonwood. Bird: western Meadowlark. Song: "Beautiful Nebraska."

Land

Area: 77,355 sq. mi. (15th). Rivers: Missouri, North Platte, Republican, South Platte. Cities (with 1990 pop.): Omaha (335,795), Lincoln (191,972), Grand Island (39,386), Bellvue (30,982), Kearney (24,396).

People

Population, 1945: 1,984,920 (33rd); 1990: 1,578,385 (36th). Breakdown, 1990: 93.8% white, 3.6% black, 2.3% Hispanic, 0.8% American Indian, 46.9% urban, 53.1% rural (1950); 66.1% urban, 33.9% rural (1990). Famous natives: Fred Astaire (dancer), Marlon Brando (actor), Henry Fonda (actor), Johnny Carson (comedian), Rollin Kirby (cartoonist).

Economics

Gross state product, 1990: $33.4 billion (34th); per capita income: $17,221. Agricultural products: sugar beets, corn, wheat, hay, soybeans, cattle. Industry: chemicals, food products, metals, machinery, electronics. Minerals: petroleum, coal.

Major Developments, 1946–1990

Nebraska is a Great Plains state that experiences great extremes of weather: cold winters and hot summers. Its chief enterprise continued to be agriculture; 95 percent of the land is used for agricultural purposes. Farming came to be so dominated by large operations that the legislature passed a law in 1982 restricting expansion of agricultural corporations. Industry often was related to food processing, although Omaha by 1990 had become a center for producing communications equipment. A growing problem was contamination of the environment, especially the water. The University of Nebraska was making a name for itself as a powerhouse of college football.

Nevada

Set in a desert, Nevada was barren, with less rainfall than any other American state. The Spanish explored the area but did not stay, although the territory did become a part of New Spain. The territory passed to the United States in 1848, a consequence of the Mexican cession after the war with Mexico. It was discovery of the Comstock Lode in 1859 that brought in people by the thousands, all of them seeking either to find the precious metal or to profit from its availability. Nevada came into the union on October 31, 1864, the 36th state. Further discoveries of gold, silver, and copper helped keep the economy going until gambling came in. The state capital is Carson City. The name originated from a Spanish word meaning "snow-covered sierra." Nickname: Silver State, Sagebrush State. Motto: All For Our Country. Flower: sagebrush. Tree: pinon pine and bristlecone pine. Bird: mountain bluebird. Song: "Home Means Nevada."

Land

Area: 110,561 sq. mi. (7th). Rivers: Colorado, Humboldt. Cities (with 1990 pop.): Las Vegas (258,295), Reno (133,850), Henderson (64,942), Sparks (53,367), North Las Vegas (64,942).

People

Population, 1945: 159,804 (48th); 1990: 1,201,833 (39th). Breakdown, 1990: 84.3% white, 6.6% black, 10.4% Hispanic, 3.2% Asian, 57.2% urban, 42.8% rural (1950); 88.3% urban, 11.7% rural (1990). Famous natives: Paul Laxalt (politician), Pat McCarran (politican), Key Pittman (politician), Andre Agassi (tennis player).

Economics

Gross state product, 1990: $30.8 billion (35th); per capita income: $19,416. Agricultural products: cattle, hay, potatoes, dairy products, onions. Industry: gambling, publishing and printing, tourism. Minerals: gold, silver, mercury, copper, barite.

Major Developments, 1946–1990

Surely the driest of the states, Nevada did very well with what it had. The area continued to produce precious metals. The national government, which owned a large portion of the land, found the climate and terrain suitable for testing weapons and training pilots. Growth in the population was astounding: nearly 600 percent between 1950 and 1990. The bulk of the growth came in the population centers of Las Vegas and Reno, the culture of which came to resemble urban California. Nevada subsisted largely on income from gambling and tourism. One of the most remarkable transformations in the nation since the Second World War has been in the creation of Las Vegas as a gambling, entertainment, and tourist center.

New Hampshire

Home of the Pennacook Indians, the area of New Hampshire was explored by Champlain for France, but the first settlers in 1623 near Portsmouth were English. The area remained part of Massachusetts Bay Colony until 1679, and the Massachusetts governor had authority until 1744. The Patriots drove the royal governor out in 1775. New Hampshire was the ninth state to join the union, on June 21, 1788. The state capital is Concord. Origin of the name is a county in England (Hampshire). Nickname: Granite State. Motto: Live Free or Die. Flower: purple lilac. Tree: white birch. Bird: purple finch. Song: "Old New Hampshire."

Land

Area: 9,279 sq. mi. (44th). Rivers: Connecticut, Merrimack, Piscataqua, Saco, Salmon Falls. Mountains: White. Cities (with 1990 pop.): Manchester (99,567), Nashua (79,662), Concord (36,006), Rochester (26,630), Dover (25,042).

People

Population, 1945: 452,174 (44th); 1990: 1,109,252 (40th). Breakdown, 1990: 98% white, 0.6% black, 1% Hispanic, 57.5% urban, 42.5% rural (1950); 51% urban, 49% rural (1990). Famous natives: Robert Frost (poet), Alan Shepard (astronaut), Sarah Buell Hale (author), Franklin Pierce (president), David Souter (jurist).

Economics

Gross state product, 1990: $23.9 billion (41st); per capita income: $20,789. Agricultural products: maple syrup, fruits and vegetables, dairy products. Industry: wood products, electronics, paper, maple syrup. Minerals: granite, limestone, sand, gravel.

Major Developments, 1946–1990

New Hampshire underwent striking changes in the postwar era. The population grew markedly, especially in the 1970s and 1980s, and reached 1 million for the first time in 1990. Some of the growth came in Hispanic Americans, Asian Americans and African Americans. Some of it was attracted by the increase in high-technology firms in the south-central part of the state; some of it was a product of people working in Boston and living in New Hampshire. Not that all change was acceptable to everyone. Local opposition in 1974 stopped construction of a massive oil refinery at Durham. Opposition did not halt construction of a nuclear power plant at Seabrook, which went on line in 1990. John Sununu, who served three terms as governor, was probably the most prominent politician of the later period.

New Jersey

Giovanni da Verrazano and Henry Hudson explored the eastern coastal area of North America that would include the future New Jersey. Dutch settlers established Ft. Nassau in 1623, and it became a Dutch colony. The English seized the area and established New Jersey colony in 1665. New Jersey played an important part in the American Revolution, with some 100 battles within the state/colony, including important engagements at Princeton, Trenton, and Monmouth. An area with a "small-state" point of view, New Jersey was the third state to ratify the Constitution, on December 18, 1787. In years to come, Jersey will develop as an overflow from New York City. The capital is Trenton. The name originated in an English Channel island of the same name. Nickname: Garden State. Motto: Liberty and Prosperity. Flower: purple violet. Tree: red oak. Bird: eastern goldfinch. Song: "New Jersey Loyalty" (unofficial).

Land

Area: 7,787 sq. mi. (46th). Rivers: Delaware, Hackensack, Hudson, Passaic. Mountains: Kittatinny, Ramapo. Cities (with 1990 pop.): Newark (275,221), Jersey City (228,537), Paterson (140,591), Elizabeth (110,002), Edison CDP (Census Designated Place) (88,630).

People

Population, 1945: 4,200,941 (8th); 1990: 7,730,188 (9th). Breakdown, 1990: 79.3% white, 13.4% black, 9.6% Hispanic, 3.5% Asian, 86.6% urban, 13.4% rural (1950); 89.4% urban, 10.6% rural (1990). Famous natives: Count Basie (orchestra leader), Paul Robeson (singer), Albert Einstein (scientist), Jack Nicholson (actor), Walter Schirra (astronaut), Meryl Streep (actress), Frank Sinatra (singer).

Economics

Gross state product, 1990: $208.4 billion (8th); per capita income: $24,968. Agricultural products: nursery and greenhouse plants, fruits and vegetables. Industry: chemicals, electronic equipment, sporting goods, glasswares, textiles. Minerals: glass, stone, gravel.

Major Developments, 1946–1990

New Jersey was surprisingly important as a producer of garden products, for its identity was closely associated with New York City. The state emerged as a center for chemical and pharmaceutical companies as well as petroleum and textile firms. The New Jersey Turnpike connecting Philadelphia and New York opened in 1952. Newark had a major race riot in 1967. Besides hosting the Miss America Pageant, Atlantic City and its landmark Boardwalk moved into legalized gambling in 1978. Senator Bill Bradley, basketball player at Princeton University and the professional New York Knicks, was probably the most prominent state politician.

New Mexico

Southwestern Indians were numerous, especially the Apache, Comanche, Navajo (Dineh), in the New Mexico area. The Spanish first established settlements at Santa Fe and San Juan Pueblo. Trade with non-Spanish America grew, and Americans trickled into the area from the East. The United States acquired possession of the land in the war with Mexico. Thereafter, the territory stood as a dry, sparsely populated part of 19th-century western culture. Billy the Kid was born there. Mexican revolutionary Pancho Villa raided into the territory in 1916. New Mexico became a state on January 6, 1912, the 47th and next-to-last of the original 48. The capital is Santa Fe. The name, attached by the Spanish, came from the larger Mexican area. Nickname: Land of Enchantment. Motto: *Crecit Eundo* (It Grows As It Goes.) Flower: yucca. Tree: pine. Bird: roadrunner. Song: "O, Fair New Mexico."

Land

Area: 121,593 sq. mi. (5th). Rivers: Gila, Pecos, Rio Grande, Zuni. Mountains: Chuska, Guadalupe, Sacramento, San Andres, Sangre de Cristo. Cities (with 1990 pop.): Albuquerque (384,736), Las Cruces (62,126), Santa Fe (55,859), Roswell (44,654), Farmington (33,997).

People

Population, 1945: 535,220 (40th); 1990: 1,515,069 (37th). Breakdown, 1990: 75.6% white, 2% black, 38.2% Hispanic, 8.9% American Indian, 50% urban, 49.8% rural (1950); 73% urban, 27% rural (1990). Famous natives: Nancy Lopez (golfer), Bill Mauldin (cartoonist), Georgia O'Keeffe (artist), Al Unser (race-car driver), Bob Unser (race-car driver).

Economics

Gross state product, 1990: $26.7 billion (39th); per capita income: $14,228. Agricultural products: cattle, hay, dairy products. Industry: oil refining, food products, electronics, machinery. Metals: petroleum, natural gas, uranium, potash, coal.

Major Developments, 1946–1990

Los Alamos became a research center for nuclear weapons, and the first nuclear bomb had been tested at Alamogordo. New Mexico benefited from a brief oil boom in the 1970s, by expansion of military bases and nuclear research, and by the manufacture of computers, appliances and communication equipment in the Albuquerque–Santa Fe area. The tourist industry also expanded. New Mexico brought together three cultures: Indian, Mexican, and Anglo.

New York

The area that became New York was home for the powerful Iroquois and other Indian tribes. Giovanni da Verrazano explored the area, and under the leadership of an Englishman, Henry Hudson, the Dutch founded New Amsterdam for which land Peter Minuit paid the Indians in trinkets. Britain seized the area in 1664 and renamed it New York. Aided by its fine port, New York grew in colonial affairs and became a major force in the Revolution and in the new nation. Among the original founders of the United States, New York entered the union on July 26, 1788, the 11th state. The capital is Albany. The state was named for the Duke of York, future King James II. Nickname: Empire State. Motto: *Excelsior* (Ever Upward). Flower: rose. Tree: sugar maple. Bird: red-breasted bluebird. Song: "I Love New York."

Land

Area: 49,108 sq. mi. (30th). Rivers: Allegheny, Delaware, Genesee, Hudson, Mohawk, New York State Barge Canal, Niagara, St. Lawrence, Susquehanna. Mountains: Adirondack, Allegheny, Berkshire Hills, Catskill, Kittatinny, Ramapo. Cities (with 1990 pop.): New York (7,322,564), Buffalo (328,123), Rochester (231,636), Yonkers (188,082), Syracuse (163,860).

People

Population, 1945: 12,584,913 (1st); 1990: 17,990,455 (2nd). Breakdown, 1990: 74.4% white, 15.9% black, 12.3% Hispanic, 3.9% Asian, 85.5% urban, 14.5% rural (1945); 84.3% urban, 15.7% rural (1990). Famous natives: Humphrey Bogart (actor), George Gershwin (composer), Vince Lombardi (football coach), Nelson A. Rockefeller (politician), Richard Rodgers (song writer), Jonas Salk (scientist), Eleanor Roosevelt (stateswoman), Franklin D. Roosevelt (president).

Economics

Gross state product, 1990: $466.8 billion (2nd); per capita income: $21,975. Agricultural products: apples and fruits, hay, corn, potatoes, dairy products. Industry: machinery, paper products, metals, optical goods, electronics, computers. Minerals: zinc, salt, sand and gravel.

Major Developments, 1946–1990

Traditionally the most vigorous and powerful of the states, national leader in numerous categories, New York had to surrender some of its power after 1946. California crept up and then zoomed past in population and by 1990 Texas was catching up fast. Several cities lost population; many industries moved out. New York City had major problems with crime and other social issues. But New York remained a very important state. It moved into service industries and was still vital in trade and as a producer of farm goods. The St. Lawrence Seaway opened in 1959. Per capita income still was among the highest.

New York City remained the nation's largest and most vibrant city and leader in world affairs. The United Nations kept its home there. New York's highest ranking politicians—Thomas E. Dewey, Jacob Javits, Robert Kennedy (elected to the Senate in 1964), Daniel P. Moynihan, Andrew Cuomo, and others—were national political figures.

North Carolina

The colony of North Carolina, which was home to the Cherokee and other Indian tribes, grew out of a land grant to eight English noblemen by King Charles II in 1663. The territory became a royal colony in 1729 when the proprietors sold their rights to the Crown. North Carolina was the first colony to declare independence explicitly and several battles were fought in the state during the American Revolution. After the war, North Carolina became the 12th state to ratify the Constitution, on November 21, 1789. The state thereupon gave up claim to its western lands, much of which would become Tennessee. The state capital is Raleigh. The name originated with King Charles I (*Carolus* is Latin for "Charles"). Nickname: Tarheel State. Motto: *Esse Quam Videri* (To Be Rather Than To Seem.) Flower: dogwood. Tree: pine. Bird: cardinal. Song: "The Old North State."

Land

Area: 52,669 sq. mi. (11th). Rivers: Albemarle, Pee Dee, Roanoke, Yadkin. Mountains: Black, Blue Ridge, Great Smoky, Unaka. Cities (with 1990 pop.): Charlotte (395,934), Raleigh (207,951), Greensboro (183,521), Winston Salem (143,485), Durham (136,611).

People

Population, 1945: 3,504,626 (11th); 1990: 6,628,637 (10th). Breakdown, 1990: 75.6% white, 22% black, 1.2% American Indian, 1.2% Hispanic, 33.7% urban, 66.3% rural (1950); 50.4% urban, 49.6% rural (1990). Famous natives: Billy Graham (evangelist), Edward R. Murrow (newsman), Jesse Jackson (civil rights leader), Ava Gardner (actress), Michael Jordan (basketball player), Richard Petty (race-car driver).

Economics

Gross state product, 1990: $141.2 billion (12th); per capita income: $16,207. Agricultural products: tobacco, peanuts, corn, soybeans, sweet potatoes. Industry: textiles, wood products, furniture, chemicals. Minerals: limestone, copper, phosphate, granite, kaolin, feldspar.

Major Developments, 1946–1990

North Carolina followed the path of other southern states, although it did so with much more speed and success. It confronted the civil rights revolution (the sit-ins started in Greensboro in 1960) but seemed to yield more gracefully. The state continued to grow tobacco and to face the great upheaval over smoking. The state moved to manufacturing and service industries. North Carolina shifted from a solid-South Democrat state to a two-party state, with the prominent Republican Senator Jesse Helms, first elected in 1972, still going strong in 1990. The state stood out in two other areas: in its fine university system that focused on the University of North Carolina, Duke, and North Carolina State, and as a growing sports mecca in college basketball and capital of a stock-car racing enterprise that reached full bloom.

North Dakota

Dakota was Sioux (Dakota, Lakota, Nakota) territory; even the name was of Sioux origin. But of course the whites kept coming. The United States acquired claim to the eastern half of the land in the

Louisiana Purchase. The western part came in agreement with Britain in 1818. Arrival of the railroad enhanced movement of people into the area, many of them immigrants from such countries as Norway and Germany. Defeat of the Sioux in the 1870s and 1880s and the politics of silver in Washington, D.C., paved the way for statehood, which came on November 2, 1889. North Dakota was the 39th state. Its capital is Bismarck. The name originated in the Sioux word for "allies." Nickname: Sioux State, Peace Garden State. Motto: Liberty and Union, now and forever, one and inseparable. Flower: wild prairie rose. Tree: American elm. Bird: western meadowlark. Song: "North Dakota Hymn."

Land

Area: 70,703 sq. mi. (17th). Rivers: Missouri, Red River of the North. Cities (with 1990 pop.): Fargo (74,111), Grand Forks (49,425), Bismarck (49,256), Minot (35,544), Dickinson (16,097).

People

Population, 1945: 520,935 (41st); 1990: 638,800 (47th). Breakdown, 1990: 94.6% white, 0.6% black, 0.7% Hispanic, 4.1% American Indian, 26.6% urban, 73.4% rural (1950); 53.3% urban, 46.7% rural (1990). Famous natives: Angie Dickinson (actress), Peggy Lee (singer), Eric Sevareid (newsman), Lawrence Welk (orchestra leader), Louis L'Amour (novelist).

Economics

Gross state product, 1990: $12.1 billion (49th); per capita income: $15,255. Agricultural products: wheat, corn, potatoes, livestock, sunflowers. Industry: food products, farm machinery. Minerals: lignite coal, oil, natural gas.

Major Developments, 1946–1990

In some measure the well-being of North Dakota depended on the weather and the price of wheat. Production of wheat ranged from 156 million bushels in 1970 to 328 million in 1981. Otherwise, the state relied heavily on the national government through price subsidies and funding of military facilities. Cold war North Dakota was sprinkled with air bases and Minuteman silos. Strip-mined coal also brought employment and generation of electric power that could be sold to other states. The population did not change much, and when it did, it often meant a reduction. There were fewer people in 1990 than there had been in 1970. Nearly 95 percent were white, and most of the rest were American Indians.

Ohio

The Miami, Lenni Lenape (Delaware), and Wyandot Indians had resided in the general domain that would become Ohio, and the power of the Iroquois reached into the area as well. Both British and French explorers had moved through the territory, and rival colonial claims were not resolved until 1763 after the British had defeated the French. The Ohio territory was part of the West in the new United States, and new settlers steadily moved in along the excellent Ohio River waterway. A river town, Cincinnati, was one of the first settlements. Ohio became a state on February 19, 1803, the 17th state. In the immediate years to come, Ohio would continue to benefit from the rivers, canals, and good farmland. The capital is Columbus. The name originated in the Iroquois word *oheo,* which meant "beautiful." Nickname: Buckeye State. Motto: With God, all things are possible. Flower: scarlet carnation. Tree: buckeye. Bird: cardinal. Song: "Beautiful Ohio."

Land

41,330 sq. mi. (35th). Rivers: Cuyahoga, Maumee, Miami, Muskingum, Ohio, Sandusky, Scioto. Mountains: Allegheny. Cities (with

1990 pop.): Columbus (632,910), Cleveland (515,616), Cincinnati (364,040), Toledo (332,943), Akron (223,019).

People

Population, 1945: 6,873,448 (5th); 1990: 10,847,115 (7th). Breakdown, 1990: 87.8% white, 10.6% black, 1.3% Hispanic, 0.8% Asian, 70.2% urban, 29.8% rural (1950); 74.1% urban, 25.9% rural (1990). Famous natives: John Glenn (astronaut and politician), Neil Armstrong (astronaut), Bob Hope (comedian), Dean Martin (singer), Roy Rogers (actor), Clark Gable (actor), Steven Spielberg (director), Robert A. Taft (politician).

Economics

Gross state product, 1990: $222.1 billion (7th); per capita income: $17,473. Agricultural products: corn, soybeans, wheat, poultry, livestock, fruit. Industry: rubber goods, electrical equipment, automobiles, plumbing equipment. Minerals: coal, oil, gas, limestone, shale, gypsum, salt.

Major Developments, 1946–1990

Ohio continued to prosper in the postwar period with its coal in the south, farms in the center, and industry in such cities as Cleveland, Akron, and Youngstown. Efforts to retain these traditional industries were only modestly successful, but Ohio scored victories in acquiring a Volkswagen plant in the 1970s and a factory to build Honda automobiles in the early 1980s. In the 1970s the state set forth on major programs to clean up the water and air, which included reclaiming Lake Erie, the Ohio River, and bespoiled strip-mined land in the south. Ohio received its mark of the Vietnam era when national-guard soldiers fired on demonstrators at Kent State University in 1970. Ohioans divided politics between the parties: Republican Senator Robert A. Taft was most prominent at the start of the period as was probably Democrat Senator John Glenn at the end.

Oklahoma

Oklahoma had been Indian land. The Kiowa, Apache, and other tribes had lived in the area for many years. A part of New France in the colonial era, the territory followed the changes in ownership that had characterized all the land that would be involved in the Louisiana Purchase of 1803. Under control of the United States, the area was set aside for the "Five Civilized Indian Tribes": Creek, Cherokee, Chickasaw, Choctaw, and Seminole. In 1889 the Oklahoma Territory was opened to non-Indian settlers—a blow, needless to say, to Native American interests; many thousands of "boomers" rushed in. The discovery of oil in the 1890s established an economic focus for years to come. The state entered the union on November 16, 1907, the 46th state, although large portions of land remained in Indian hands. The capital is Oklahoma City. The name originated with the Choctaw term: *okla humma*— "land of the red people." Nickname: Sooner State. Motto: *Labor omnia vinat* (Work overcomes all obstacles.). Flower: mistletoe. Tree: redbud. Bird: scissor-tailed flycatcher. Song: "Oklahoma!"

Land

Area: 69,956 sq. mi. (18th). Rivers: Arkansas, Canadian, Cimarron, Red. Mountains: Ouachita, Ozark Plateau, Staked Plain, Wichita. Cities (with 1990 pop.): Oklahoma City (444,719), Tulsa (367,302), Lawton (80,5651), Norman (80,071), Broken Arrow (58,043).

People

Population, 1945: 2,034,460 (26th); 1990: 3,145,585 (28th). Breakdown, 1990: 82.1% white, 7.4% black, 2.7% Hispanic, 8% American

Indian, 51% urban, 49% rural (1950); 67.7% urban, 32.3% rural (1990). Famous natives: Tony Randall (actor), Mickey Mantle (baseball player), Oral Roberts (evangelist), Ralph Ellison (author), Johnny Bench (baseball player), Gene Autry (actor), Walter Cronkite (newsman), Reba McIntire (singer).

Economics

Gross state product, 1990: $56 billion (28th); per capita income: $15,444. Agricultural products: wheat, corn, oats, hay, peanuts, cattle. Industry: plastic goods, machinery, metal products, rubber goods. Minerals: petroleum, natural gas, coal, stone, gravel.

Major Developments, 1946–1990

Oklahoma received a boost at the start of the period with appearance of *Oklahoma!* as a popular Broadway show in the early 1940s and a popular movie in the 1950s. If nothing else, the show provided a rousing new tune that quickly was adopted as the state song. The state's economy was based on oil production, farming, especially cattle ranches to the west, and growth of industry in the two major cities, Oklahoma City and Tulsa. A booming economy in the late 1970s, produced by high oil and grain prices, was followed by a devastating crash in the mid-1980s when these same forces reversed themselves. Many jobs vanished, and many farms were lost. In the 1970s and 1980s the state was struck with a remarkable display of political corruption, at the end of which, nearly 250 officials were convicted of national crimes, and others, including two governors and several state legislators, were convicted of various state offenses.

Oregon

Sir Francis Drake touched this area of northwest North America in the 16th century, and James Cook visited there in the 18th century. Meriwether Lewis and James Clark reached the Oregon territory in 1805, and they encountered various Indian tribes. A long-standing dispute between the United States and Great Britain was settled by a treaty in 1846 that awarded what now is Oregon to the United States. Oregon fever, as it was called, produced a migration of settlers to the area. Territorial status came in 1848, statehood on February 14, 1859 (the 33rd state), and the railroad in 1883. The capital is Salem. Origin of name: unknown. Nickname: Beaver State. Motto: The Union. Flower: Oregon grape. Tree: Douglas fir. Bird: western meadowlark. Song: "Oregon, My Oregon."

Land

Area: 97,073 sq. mi. (10th). Rivers: Columbia, Snake, Willamette. Mountains: Cascade Range, Coast Range, Klamath. Cities (with 1990 pop.): Portland (437,319), Eugene (112,669), Salem (107,786), Gresham (68,235), Beaverton (53,310).

People

Population, 1945: 1,206,322 (32nd); 1990: 2,842,321 (29th). Breakdown, 1990: 92.8% white, 1.6% black, 4% Hispanic, 1.4% American Indian, 2.4% Asian, 53.9% urban, 46.1% rural (1950); 70.5% urban, 29.5% rural (1990). Famous natives: Linus Pauling (chemist), Edwin Markham (poet), John Reed (author), Bob Packwood (politician), Mary Decker Slaney (runner).

Economics

Gross state product, 1990: $55.4 billion (30th); per capita income: $17,156. Agricultural products: fruit, vegetables, wheat, livestock, potatoes. Industry: wood and paper products, aluminium, metal goods, fish processing, electronic equipment. Minerals: sand gravel, cement, nickel.

Major Developments, 1946–1990

Oregon's economy rested on agriculture, tourism, and, above all, wood products, in this area that received much rainfall. As happened in several states, manufacturing jobs departed after 1970, and many people had to take lower-paying service work. The state became known in the 1960s and 1970s for its efforts to protect the environment and clean up its rivers. In 1972 Oregon was the first state to enact a "bottle act," which encouraged recycling of certain types of containers. In the 1980s the state became an outlet for dissatisfied Californians and for high-technology computer companies. In 1990 the state adopted and added to its constitution a sharp restriction on taxation. Prominent politicians were moderate Republican Senators Mark Hatfield and Robert Packwood. A well-known political maverick of the 1960s and 1970s was Senator Wayne Morse, who at various times had been Republican, Democrat, and somewhere in between.

Pennsylvania

Various European explorers visited this eastern coastal territory before it was awarded by England's King Charles II to William Penn in 1681. Penn, a Quaker, wished to make his colony a haven for religious toleration. The colony benefited from its port facilities and varied natural resources. The centrally placed and largest city, Philadelphia, became a major force in colonial affairs and in the new government of the United States. The Declaration of Independence (1776) and the Constitution (1789) were signed there. Pennsylvania became the second state to ratify the Constitution, on December 12, 1789, and the first state (1780) to abolish slavery. The capital is Harrisburg. Origin of the name: Admiral William Penn, father of William and founder of the colony. Nickname: Keystone State. Motto: Virtue, Liberty, and Independence. Flower: mountain laurel. Tree: hemlock. Bird: ruffled grouse. Song: "Hail Pennsylvania."

Land

Area: 45,308 sq. mi. (33rd). Rivers: Allegheny, Delaware, Juniata, Monongahela, Ohio, Schuylkill, Susquehanna. Mountains: Allegheny, Kittatinny, Laurel Hills, Pocono. Cities (with 1990 pop.): Philadelphia (1,585,718), Pittsburgh (369,879), Erie (108,718), Allentown (105,090), Scranton (78,380).

People

Population, 1945: 9,193,957 (2nd); 1990: 11,881,643 (5th). Breakdown, 1990: 88.5% white, 9.2% black, 2% Hispanic, 1.2% Asian, 70.5% urban, 29.5% rural (1950); 68.9% urban, 31.1% rural (1990). Famous natives: Bill Cosby (actor), George C. Marshall (general and statesman), Andy Warhol (artist), Alexander Calder (sculptor), Wilt Chamberlain (basketball player), Marian Anderson (singer).

Economics

Gross state product, 1990: $244.6 billion (3rd); per capita income: $18,672. Agricultural products: corn, hay, fruits, livestock, poultry, mushrooms. Industry: steel, chemicals, machinery, electronic equipment, food products. Minerals: coal, petroleum, natural gas, limestone, iron ore, cobalt, copper, zinc.

Major Developments, 1946–1990

In the early part of the postwar period, Pennsylvania exploited its traditional resources of agriculture, coal in the south, and manufacturing and the steel industry in large cities. Beginning in approximately 1970, the state had to shift to service industries and tourism (especially Philadelphia, Gettysburg, and the Pocono Mountains) as mining and steel making suffered devastating losses. Agriculture remained very important. Politics stood generally in the center, with tilting to moderate left or moderate right at various times. In the 1970s the state adopted major legislation to deal with the aged and women's rights and also passed a rigorous antiabortion measure. The state reestablished capital punishment in the 1970s but did not execute anyone. In the 1970s and 1980s several high officials engaged in corruption, including Senator Hugh Scott. Convicted of accepting a bribe, State Treasurer R. Budd Dwyer shot himself before a televised press conference in 1987. His death before being sentenced left his family entitled to pension benefits of $1 million.

Rhode Island

Most of the Indians that had inhabited the Rhode Island area were of the Narragannsett tribe. The colony grew out of defection from the restrictive religious atmosphere of Massachusetts Bay Colony. Roger Williams left and went to Providence in 1636. Other dissenters joined Williams in founding Rhode Island as a separate colony in 1647. Smallest of the colonies, it would be one of the first to declare independence in 1776 and the last of the original 13 colonies to ratify the Constitution—on May 29, 1790. The capital is Providence. The name originated with Rhode Island in Narragannsett Bay, itself named after the island of Rhodes in the Mediterranean Sea. Nickname: Ocean State or Little Rhody. Motto: Hope. Flower: violet. Tree: red maple. Bird: Rhode Island Red (a chicken). Song: "Rhode Island."

Land

Area: 1,212 sq. mi. (50th). Rivers: Blackstone, Pawcatuck, Providence, Sakonnet. Cities (with 1990 pop.): Providence (160,728), Warwick (85,427), Cranston (76,060), Pawtucket (72,644), East Providence (50,380).

People

Population, 1945: 758,222 (36th); 1990: 1,003,464 (43rd). Breakdown, 1990: 91.4% white, 3.9% black, 4.6% Hispanic, 1.8% Asian, 84.3% urban, 15.7% rural (1950); 86% urban, 14% rural (1990). Famous natives: Nelson Eddy (singer), George M. Cohan (song writer), Matthew Perry (admiral).

Economics

Gross state product, 1990: $21 billion (43rd); per capita income: $18,841. Agricultural products: potatoes, poultry, dairy products, greenhouse plants. Industry: textiles, clothing, jewelry, electronics, fish processing. Minerals: granite, limestone, gravel, bowemite cumberlandite.

Major Developments, 1946–1990

Tiny Rhode Island long had subsisted on manufacturing, but beginning in the 1960s the economic base began to leave. By 1990 only about one-fifth of the workforce was so employed. Half were in the jewelry business, and only two firms employed more than 1,000 people. More people worked in the lower-paying service area, which included tourism, health services, and education. A long-time Democrat stranglehold on politics was broken in the 1970s with election of a Republican mayor of Providence and a Republican U.S. senator and congressman (in 1980). Several officeholders were found guilty of corruption in the 1980s.

South Carolina

French and Spanish explorers had visited this southern coastal area in the 16th century, but it was part of the territory King Charles II of England granted to eight proprietors in 1663. South Carolina became a royal colony in 1729. Carolina had many of the markings of the southern colonies, especially slavery. It became the eighth state to enter the union, on May 23, 1788, and would be the first to try to leave it in 1860. Perhaps the most rabid of the secessionist states in the Civil War era, South Carolina would pay the price. The capital is Columbia. The name originated with King Charles (Carolus) II. Nickname: Palmetto State. Motto: *Amis opibusque parati* (Prepared in mind and deed). Flower: yellow jessamine. Tree: palmetto. Bird: Carolina wren. Song: "Carolina."

Land

Area: 31,113 sq. mi. (40th). Rivers: Congaree, Edisto, Pee Dee, Savannah, Tugalos, Wateree. Mountains: Blue Ridge. Cities (with 1990 pop.): Columbia (98,052), Charleston (80,414), North Charleston (70,218), Greenville (58,282), Spartanburg (43,467).

People

Population, 1945: 1,905,597 (27th); 1990: 3,486,703 (25th). Breakdown, 1990: 69% white, 29.8% black, 0.9% Hispanic, 0.6% Asian, 36.7% urban, 63.3% rural (1950); 54.6% urban, 45.4% rural (1990). Famous natives: Dizzy Gillespie (musician), Althea Gibson (athlete), Eartha Kitt (singer), James Byrnes (politician), Strom Thurmond (politician), Ernest Hollings (politician).

Economics

Gross state product, 1990: $63.8 billion (27th); per capita income: $15,099. Agricultural products: tobacco, peanuts, watermelons, peaches, wheat, cattle, poultry. Industry: textiles, chemicals, clothing, tourism. Minerals: cement, sand, gravel, stone, clay.

Major Developments, 1946–1990

South Carolina changed as much as any southern state between 1946 and 1990. It began as an agricultural, segregated state where whites and Democrats reigned. Mechanization, starting in the 1960s, destroyed thousands of jobs. By 1990 only 2 percent of the population lived on farms. Reapportionment in the 1970s took away rural domination of state government. The Voting Rights Act of 1965 gave black people substantial political power. Blacks were elected to office, but so was seemingly perpetual old-line Senator J. Strom Thurmond, who switched in 1964 to the Republicans. Decline of agriculture has more than been replaced by a booming tourist industry along the coastal areas and by the state's ability after 1975 to attract foreign companies, such as Michelin Rubber, to take up roots in the state. In September 1989 Hurricane Hugo took 26 lives and destroyed billions of dollars worth of property.

South Dakota

The French had claimed this northern Plains territory, which was home to the Sioux (Dakota, Lakota, Nakota) Indians. The United States acquired technical ownership in the Louisiana Purchase, but control of the land would take time. Whites were slow to move in until gold was discovered in the Black Hills in the 1870s. The scramble of settlers to get to the area provoked some of the last rounds in the conflict with the Sioux and other tribes. What was regarded as the last engagement—in truth, it was a massacre—came at Wounded Knee in 1890. By that time South Dakota had become the 40th state—on November 2, 1889. The capital is Pierre. The name came from the Sioux word for "allies." Nickname: Coyote State or Sunshine State. Motto: Under God, the people rule. Flower: pasque flower. Tree: Blue Hills spruce. Bird: ringnecked pheasant. Song: "Hail, South Dakota."

Land

Area: 77,116 sq. mi. (16th). Rivers: Cheyenne, James, Missouri, Moreau, White. Mountains: Black Hills. Cities (with 1990 pop.): Sioux

Falls (100,814), Rapid City (54,523), Aberdeen 24,927), Watertown 17,592), Brookings (16,270).

People

Population, 1945: 589,702 (39th); 1990: 696,004 (45th). Breakdown, 1990: 91.6% white, 0.5% black, 0.8% Hispanic, 7.3% American Indian, 33.2% urban, 66.8% rural (1950); 50% urban, 50% rural (1990). Famous natives: Tom Brokaw (newsman), Alvin Hansen (economist), George McGovern (politician), Cheryl Ladd (actress), Sparky Anderson (baseball manager).

Economics

Gross state product, 1990: $13.1 billion (47th); per capita income: $15,872. Agricultural products: sunflowers, wheat, oats, corn, livestock. Industry: machinery, food products, meatpacking, tourism. Minerals: gold, rose quartz, coal.

Major Developments, 1946–1990

South Dakota grew slowly in population, but the state changed after 1946. Agriculture remained important, but tourism (the Badlands and Mount Rushmore, for example, were attractions), mining, lumber, and assistance from the national government—agricultural subsidies, air-force bases, and work of the army corps of engineers—aided the economy. South Dakota has used tax policy (there was no income tax) and other incentives to attract outside business, but environmental concerns took high priority. There was an extended standoff at Wounded Knee between federal officials and the American Indian Movement (AIM) in 1973, but generally the plight of some 75,500 Indians, mostly Sioux, improved during this period. The state contained nine reservations.

Tennessee

French claim to the area of Tennessee was based on the travels of DeSoto; the British claimed the same territory. The dispute was not resolved until the end of the French and Indian War in 1763 when French claims were extinguished. The territory then passed to the United States as a result of the peace treaty of 1783 that ended the Revolutionary War. Enough settlers moved into the area as a part of the general westward expansion to raise the prospect of a new state. The final ingredient was willingness of the coastal states, in this case, North Carolina, to give up claim to their western lands. Tennessee then became a state on June 1, 1796, the 16th member of the new union. Soon thereafter the native Cherokee Indians were pushed out. A southern state and a slave state, Tennessee seceded in 1861. Several important battles of the Civil War took place in Tennessee, and afterward the state had to go through the painful process of reconstruction. The capital is Nashville. The origin of the name was in the term *tesase*: the principal village of the Cherokee. Nickname: Volunteer State. Motto: agriculture and commerce. Flower: iris. Tree: tulip poplar. Bird: mockingbird. Song: "The Tennessee Waltz."

Land

Area: 42,144 sq. mi. (34th). Rivers: Clinch, Cumberland, Mississippi, Tennessee. Mountains: Cumberland, Great Smoky, Unaka Mountains. Cities (with 1990 pop.): Memphis (610,337), Nashville–Davidson CC (510,784), Knoxville (165,121), Chattanooga (152,466), Clarksville (75,494).

People

Population, 1945: 2,878,777 (16th); 1990: 4,877,185 (17th). Breakdown, 1990: 83% white, 16% black, 0.7% Hispanic, 0.7% Asian, 44.1% urban, 55.9% rural (1950); 60.9% urban, 39.1% rural (1990). Famous natives: Aretha Franklin (singer), Cordell Hull (politician), Dolly Parton (singer), James Agee (author), Dinah Shore (singer), Roy Acuff (singer), Ernie Ford (singer).

Economics

Gross state product, 1990: $95.5 billion (20th); per capita income: $15,789. Agricultural products: cotton, tobacco, corn, soybeans, fruits, livestock. Industry: food processing, chemicals, automobiles, wood products, mining. Minerals: coal, zinc, lead.

Major Developments, 1946–1990

Tennessee benefited from the power facilities (and other functions) of the Tennessee Valley Authority, constructed in the 1930s. Farming of traditional crops continued to be important, but Tennessee also moved into industrialization. Its success in attracting foreign—mostly Japanese—firms was exemplified by the Nissan automobile factory near Murfreesboro, built in the 1980s. Starting as a segregated state and a Democrat state, Tennessee underwent changes that became familiar throughout the former Confederacy. Black people voted in large numbers, especially after 1965. Segregation for the most part ended. Republicans competed with Democrats on an essentially even basis. Evidence that old feelings died slowly was revealed in the assassination of Martin Luther King, Jr., at Memphis in 1968.

Texas

The Spanish, who had explored the area earlier, established a settlement in the area of Texas in the 17th century. The United States in 1819 renounced a shadowy claim inherited from France, but Americans moving west came into the area of Texas nonetheless; at one point the Spanish welcomed them with open arms. Mexican independence in 1821 left Texas as its northernmost province; quarrels with the Mexican government led Americans in the province to proclaim and then claim independence in 1936. Acceptance into the American union on December 29, 1845, the 28th state, helped provoke a war between the United States and Mexico, the outcome of which reconfirmed Texas as a state and added more territory as well. Curiously, only 16 years later, the Texans would seek to leave the union they had gone to so much trouble to enter. The state capital is Austin. The name came from an Indian word meaning "friends." Nickname: Lone-Star State. Motto: friendship. Flower: bluebonnet. Tree: pecan. Bird: mockingbird. Song: "Texas, Our Texas."

Land

Area: 266,807 sq. mi. (2nd). Rivers: Brazos, Colorado, Natchez, Nueces, Red, Rio Grande, Sabine, Trinity. Mountains: Guadalupe. Cities (with 1990 pop.): Houston (1,630,510), Dallas (1,006,877), San Antonio (935,933), El Paso (515,342), Austin (465,622).

People

Population, 1945: 6,786,740 (6th); 1990: 16,986,510 (3rd). Breakdown, 1990: 75.2% white, 11.9% black, 25.5% Hispanic, 1.9% Asian, 62.7% urban, 37.3% rural (1950); 80.3% urban, 19.7% rural (1990). Famous natives: Carol Burnette (comedian), Lyndon B. Johnson (politician), Barbara Jordan (politician), Chester Nimitz (admiral), Katherine Anne Porter (author), Audie Murphy (soldier, actor), Janis Joplin (singer), Dan Rather (newsman).

Economics

Gross state product, 1990: $372 billion (3rd); per capita income: $16,759. Agricultural products: cotton, grains, cattle, sheep, sorghum. Industry: petrochemicals, petroleum, electronic goods and equipment, airplanes. Minerals: petroleum, natural gas, sulphur.

Major Developments, 1946–1990

Boosted by the Second World War and defense spending in the cold war, Texas grew rapidly. The population doubled between 1950 and 1980 and still was going strong. The oil industry had ups and downs, but much of the time it boomed, and other technical and industrial development helped the economy to grow. The Manned Space Center opened in Houston in 1963, the same year that President John Kennedy was assassinated in Dallas. A large portion of the population growth was Hispanics, who by 1990 made up a quarter of the state's population. Texas gave up segregation and one-party rule by the Democrats. Sam Rayburn, Lyndon Johnson, and other Texan Democrats were national leaders, but so were such Republicans as George Bush. Texas received professional teams in all major sports, even hockey. The Dallas Cowboys of the National Football League proclaimed themselves "America's Team."

Utah

Utah's earliest residents were the Shoshone, the Paiute, and the Ute who gave the land its name. The area had been a part of New Spain and later of the state of Mexico. Morman leader Brigham Young brought his followers to the Salt Lake area in 1847 and created a state Young called Deseret. The territory came under jurisdiction of the United States the following year, at the end of the war with Mexico. The Mormon practice of polygamy stalled the movement to statehood, which finally came on January 4, 1896. Utah was the 45th state. Mormons continued to dominate for years to come, but a good portion of the land belonged to the national government. The capital is Salt Lake City. The name orginated with a Ute term meaning "people of the mountains." Nickname: Beehive State or Mormon State. Motto: Industry. Flower: sego lily. Tree: blue spruce. Bird: seagull. Song: "Utah, We Love Thee."

Land

Area: 84,899 sq. mi. (11th). Rivers: Bear, Colorado, Green, Sevier. Cities (with 1990 pop.): Salt Lake City (159,936), West Valley City (86,976), Provo (86,835), Sandy (75,058), Orem (67,561).

People

Population, 1945: 616,989 (38th); 1990: 1,722,850 (35th). Breakdown, 1990: 93.8% white, 0.7% black, 4.9% Hispanic, 65.3% urban, 34.7% rural (1950); 87% urban, 13% rural (1990). Famous natives: Maude Adams (actress), Philo Farnsworth (engineer), Merlin Olsen (football player and actor), Loretta Young (actress), Ivy Baker Priest (U.S. Treasurer), Donny Osmond (singer), Marie Osmond (singer).

Economics

Gross state product, 1990: $30.6 billion (37th); per capita income: $14,083. Agricultural products: hay, wheat, corn, livestock. Industry: food processing, metals, refining, computer equipment. Minerals: copper, gold, silver, lead, uranium, coal, oil, beryllium.

Major Developments, 1946–1990

As with many states, Utah had to undergo an economic transition in the cold war era. In the last part of the period, the state acquired some new industry in computers, electronics, and aircraft, but a large portion of the workforce had to shift over to service industries. The state's ski areas, national parks, and monuments made tourism a major enterprise. Utah's hospitals pioneered in medical technology, including the first renal transplant in 1965 and the first artificial heart implant in 1982. The Mormon Church claimed some 70 percent of the population and was in itself a sizeable industry. In 1978 the church opened itself to leadership from nonwhites—but not from females.

Starting in 1979 the Utah Jazz basketball team gave the state national publicity, as did the Mormon Tabernacle Choir.

Vermont

Home of the Mahican and other tribes, settled by the English from Massachusetts Bay Colony, claimed by New Hampshire and New York, the area of Vermont was moved by leadership of Ethan Allen to become a separate entity. Allen's Green Mountain Boys fought the British in the Revolution and proclaimed an independent Republic of New Connecticut. After the ouster of Allen, the territory entered the union on March 4, 1791, as the 14th state, thus the first new entity beyond the original 13. Even before statehood, the area had provided leadership in abolishing slavery and in proclaiming full manhood suffrage. The capital is Montpelier. The name came from the French words *vert mont,* meaning "green mountain." Nickname: Green Mountain State. Motto: Freedom and Unity. Flower: red clover. Tree: sugar maple. Bird: hermit thrush. Song: "Hail, Vermont."

Land

Area: 9,614 sq. mi. (43rd). Rivers: Connecticut, Lamoille, Otter Creek, Poultney, White, Winooski. Mountains: Green, Taconic. Cities (with 1990 pop.): Burlington (37,712), Rutland (18,436), South Burlington (10,679), Barre (9,824), Montpelier (8,241).

People

Population, 1945: 310,352 (45th); 1990: 562,758 (48th). Breakdown, 1990: 98.6% white, 0.2% black, 0.5% Hispanic, 36.4% urban, 63.6% rural (1950); 67.8% urban, 32.2% rural (1990). Famous natives: Calvin Coolidge (president), John Deere (manufacturer), George Dewey (naval officer), John Dewey (philosopher), Rudy Vallee (singer).

Economics

Gross state product, 1990: $11.2 billion (50th); per capita income: $17,436. Agricultural produce: dairy goods, corn, soybeans, maple syrup, fruits, livestock. Industry: wood and paper products, printing, tourism, machine tools. Minerals: granite, marble, slate.

Major Developments, 1946–1990

Although Vermont's rank in population dropped three places, to 48, in the postwar era, the state in fact underwent a sizeable growth after 1946. The state changed in other ways. An emphasis on such minerals as marble gave way to high technology manufacturing. Farming receded but did not vanish; tourism, especially in the ski areas, boomed. Normally a solid Republican state, Vermont began to elect some Democrats, such as Senator Patrick Leahy. There even was a woman governor, Madeleine Kunin, elected in 1984. Bernie Sanders, Socialist mayor of Burlington from 1981 to 1989, was elected to Congress in 1990. An interstate highway system truly brought the state into the nation and population centers nearby. Beginning in 1982, the stores opened on Sundays.

Virginia

Virginia, of course, built a rich legacy as a colony and leader within the budding new nation. Jamestown was the first successful colony, started in 1607, and Virginia was the most prominent of the southern colonies, with such remarkable leaders as Patrick Henry, who fired up the Patriots. Thomas Jefferson in his writings justified the Revolution, and George Washington led the army. Virginia's ratification of the Constitution on June 25, 1788, the 10th state, added mightily to the status of the new nation. Four of the first five presidents came from Virginia.

Unfortunately, Virginia also was a slave state and in 1861 it seceded to preserve the institution. The state capital, Richmond, now became the capital of another purported new nation. The origin of the name was Elizabeth I, the "Virgin Queen" of England. Nickname: Old Dominion. Motto: *Sic semper tyrannis* (Thus always to tyrants.) Flower: dogwood. Tree: dogwood. Bird: cardinal. Song: "Carry Me Back to Old Virginia."

Land

Area: 40,767 sq. mi. (36th). Rivers: James, Potomac, Rappahannock, Roanoke, Shenandoah, York. Mountains: Allegheny, Blue Ridge, Cumberland, Unaka. Cities (with 1990 pop.): Virginia Beach (393,069), Norfolk (261,229), Richmond (203,056), Newport News (170,045), Chesapeake (151,976).

People

Population, 1945: 3,079,706 (14th); 1990: 6,187,358 (12th). Breakdown, 1990: 77.4% white, 18.8% black, 2.6% Hispanic, 2.6% Asian, 47% urban, 53% rural (1950); 69.4% urban, 30.6% rural (1990). Famous natives: George C. Scott (actor), Bill Robinson (dancer), Jerry Falwell (minister), George Washington (president), Thomas Jefferson (president), James Madison (president), James Monroe (president).

Economics

Gross state product, 1990: $141.7 billion (11th); per capita income: $19,746. Agricultural products: tobacco, cotton, dairy products, fruits, vegetables, corn, soybeans. Industry: tobacco products, food products, textiles, chemicals, furniture and wood products. Minerals: coal, clay, stone, gravel and sand.

Major Developments, 1946–1990

Virginia underwent changes familiar to nearly all southern states. It yielded reluctantly but more gracefully than other states to an end to segregation. Blacks voted in larger numbers; many whites fled to the Republicans, leaving a fairly balanced two-party system. Blacks held several offices including, starting in 1989, the governorship. Status of the coastal area varied. Virginia Beach grew rapidly; Norfolk and Newport News lost some of their power as ports and ship-building centers, but they continued to be important to the economy. Tobacco remained important despite growing assaults on smoking. Tourism was big and growing bigger.

Washington

Sir Francis Drake came by the area in his travels for Britain; another Briton, James Cook, arrived in 1778. Robert Gray sailed up the Columbia River and claimed the territory for the United States. The area soon came to be known for its furs, timber, and fishing. Long-standing rival claims of Britain and the United States over what was called the Oregon Territory were resolved by treaty in 1846. Many of the settlers who followed the Oregon Trail to the area would have Washington (the northern portion of the territory) as a destination. Territorial status began in 1853. The Northern Pacific Railway arrived at Puget Sound in 1883, and the stage was set for full statehood. It came to Washington (the 42nd state) on November 11, 1889. The capital is Olympia. The name came as an honor to George Washington. Nickname: Evergreen State. Motto: *Alki* (By and By). Flower: western rhododendron. Tree: western hemlock. Bird: willow goldfinch. Song: "Washington, My Home."

Washington State featured the volcanic peaks of the Cascades, largest of which was Rainier, here standing as a backdrop for the waterfront of Tacoma. (National Archives)

Land

Area: 68,138 sq. mi. (20th). Rivers: Chehalis, Columbia, Pend Oreille, Snake, Yakima. Mountains: Cascade Range, Coast Range, Kettle River Range, Olympic. Cities (with 1990 pop.): Seattle (516,259), Spokane (177,196), Tacoma (176,664), Bellevue (86,874), Everett (69,961).

People

Population, 1945: 2,088,574 (24th); 1990: 4,866,692 (18th). Breakdown, 1990: 88.5% white, 3.1% black, 4.4% Hispanic, 4.3% Asian, 63.2% urban, 36.8% rural (1950); 76.4% urban, 26.4% rural (1990). Famous natives: Bing Crosby (singer), Jimi Hendrix (singer), Henry Jackson (politician), William O. Douglas (jurist), Edward R. Murrow (media pioneer).

Economics

Gross state product, 1990: $109.4 billion (15th); per capita income: $18,858. Agricultural products: wheat, apples, potatoes, lumber, vegetables. Industry: airplanes and parts, wood products, food products. Minerals: lead, zinc, gold, coal, magnesium.

Major Developments, 1946–1990

The center of population of the state was the Puget Sound where shipbuilding and industry had collected. The dominant firm was Boeing Aircraft, builder of such warplanes as the B-17 and the B-29. In the 1950s, Boeing built the long-range monsters, B-52 jet bombers, and thereafter it constructed mostly civilian jet liners, starting with the 707 in 1957. A court decision in 1974 awarded half of the salmon and steelhead catch to Native Americans of the area. Mount St. Helens underwent a spectacular, deadly, and destructive eruption in 1980. The Washington Public Power Supply Company defaulted on an $8 billion bond issue in 1983. Washington suffered its blows, but it still produced apples and lumber. Naval and other military facilities remained. Boeing fluctuated but generally remained strong; a computer company named Microsoft was starting to make a mark.

West Virginia

The West Virginia area (really western Virginia) had been a hunting ground for Shawnee, Lenni Lenape (Delaware), and Cherokee Indians. Virtually everything that related to colonial Virginia applied to the rugged western part of the state—except, perhaps, for slavery and secession. The mountainous west resisted attachment to the Confederacy in 1861 and insisted on detaching itself from a land that had gone to war with the United States. The Congress of that era agreed, and so on June 20, 1863, during the Civil War, West Virginia became the 35th state. The capital is Charleston. The name came from the western part of Virginia. Nickname: Mountain State. Motto: *Montani semper liberi* (Mountaineers are always free.) Flower: big rhododendron. Tree: sugar maple. Bird: cardinal. Song: "The West Virginia Hills."

Land

Area: 24,231 sq. mi. (41st). Rivers: Big Sandy, Guayandotte, Kanahwa, Little Kanahwa, Ohio, Potomac, Monogahela. Mountains: Allegheny, Blue Ridge, Cumberland. Cities (with 1990 pop.): Charleston (57,287), Huntington (54,844), Wheeling (34,882), Parkersburg (33,862), Morgantown (25,879).

People

Population, 1945: 1,724,677 (31st); 1990: 1,793,477 (34th). Breakdown, 1990: 96.2% white, 3.1% black, 0.5% Hispanic, 34.6% urban, 65.4% rural (1950); 36.1% urban, 63.9% rural (1990). Famous natives: Cyrus Vance (diplomat), Pearl Buck (author), Walter Reuther (labor leader), Chuck Yeager (pilot), Jerry West (basketball player), Don Knotts (actor).

Economics

Gross state product, 1990: $28.3 billion (38th); per capita income: $13,747. Agricultural products: cattle, poultry, greenhouse plants, corn, soybeans. Minerals: coal, natural gas, limestone, oil, rock-salt.

Major Developments, 1946–1990

West Virginia was the only state to experience an absolute loss of population between 1946 and 1990. The loss to considerable extent resulted from changes in economics. Underground mining, long the staple of the state's economy, continued to produce large amounts of coal, but nearly everything became mechanized, requiring fewer people. Even between the years 1980 and 1990, the number was virtually cut in half. Several chemical companies left the state. In 1985 West Virginia experienced devastating flooding from a tropical storm that reached far into the interior. Even so, not all information was dismal. West Virginia had help from powerful politicians, beginning with Robert Byrd, who went to Congress in 1953 and still was going strong (as a senator) in 1990. Byrd was joined in 1984 by John D. Rockefeller IV. The state received many miles of interstate highway that threaded through the mountains, even though the cost of construction was staggering.

Wisconsin

The area west of Lake Michigan had been home to numerous Indian tribes: the Winnebago, Fox, Sauk and others. The Ojibway gave the state its name. The French explored and claimed the territory and then lost it to Britain in 1763. Although Wisconsin had been a part of original United States territory, the British controlled part of it until 1812, and afterward the Black Hawk Wars lasted until the 1830s. Many of the settlers came from northern Europe; the German and Scandinavian influence lasted until the present time. On May 29, 1848, Wisconsin became the 30th state. The capital is Madison. The name came from the Ojibway word *wishkonsing*—"place of the bearer." Nickname: Badger State. Motto: Forward. Flower: wood violet. Tree: sugar maple. Bird: robin. Song: "On Wisconsin!"

Land

Area: 56,153 sq. mi. (26th). Rivers: Black, Chippewa, Menominee, Mississippi, St. Croix, Wisconsin. Cities (with 1990 pop.): Milwaukee (628,088), Madison (191,262), Green Bay (96,466), Racine (84,298), Kenosha (80,352).

People

Population, 1945: 3,137,587 (15th); 1990: 4,891,769 (16th). Breakdown, 1990: 92.2% white, 5% black, 1.9% Hispanic, 1.1 Asian, 0.8% American Indian, 57.9% urban, 42.1% rural (1950); 65.7% urban, 34.3% rural (1990). Famous natives: Liberace (musician), Alfred Lunt (actor), Joseph McCarthy (politician), Spencer Tracy (actor), Orson Welles (actor), Frank Lloyd Wright (architect).

Economics

Gross state product: 1990: $100.6 billion (18th); per capita income: $17,503. Agricultural products: dairy products, hay, wheat, corn, soybeans, cattle. Industry: industrial machinery, food products, printing and publishing. Minerals: stone, gravel, lime.

Major Developments, 1946–1990

Wisconsin remained the nation's chief producer of dairy products, despite a decline in the industry after 1970. As with many states with a traditional manufacturing base, Wisconsin had to watch as firms moved out, cut back, or, as in the case of Allis Chalmers (a producer of farm machinery), simply quit. To hold on, the state used tax and other incentives to attract new industry; it maintained shipping facilities at Superior, Green Bay, and Milwaukee. It broadcast tourist attractions, such as the Dells, the Milwaukee Brewers in baseball, the Bucks in basketball, and, of course, the Green Bay Packers. Wisconsin had a reputation for progressive politics, and leadership in the postwar period was perhaps not quite up to par. Senator William Proxmire was effective and respected in the 1960s and 1970s; his immediate predecessor, Senator Joseph McCarthy, had been highly dubious during the years 1947–59.

Wyoming

Wyoming had been the domain of northern Plains Indians. The Sioux (Dakota, Lakota, Nakota), Arapaho, Crow, and other tribes had lived or hunted there for hundreds of years. Originally in the colonial era a part of New France, the United States established claim in the Louisiana Purchase. Many people had come through on the way to the Oregon territory, but not many stopped. Wyoming's story thereafter was part of the story of the trans-Mississippi west—struggles with Native Americans who lived there and the struggle to establish a political identity and an economic foundation. The 44th state, Wyoming came into the union on July 10, 1890, a part of a group of six new states. The capital is Cheyenne. The name came from the Delaware Indian term *maugh-wau-wa-ma*—"large plains or mountains and valleys alternating." Nickname: Equality State. Motto: Equal Rights. Flower: Indian paintbrush. Tree: cottonwood. Bird: meadowlark. Song: "Wyoming."

Land

Area: 97,809 sq. mi. (9th). Rivers: Bighorn, Green, North Platte, Powder, Snake, Yellowstone. Mountains: Absaroka, Bighorn, Black Hills, Laramie, Owl Creek, Teton Range, Wind River Range, Wyoming Range. Cities (with 1990 pop.): Cheyenne (50,008), Casper (46,742), Laramie (26,687), Rock Springs (19,050), Gillette (17,635).

People

Population, 1945: 246,766 (47th); 1990: 453,588 (50th). Breakdown, 1990: 94.2% white, 0.8% black, 5.7% Hispanic, 2.1% American Indian, 49.8% urban, 50.2% rural (1950); 65% urban, 35% rural (1990). Famous natives: Jackson Pollock (artist), Nellie Tayloe Ross (politician), Alan Simpson (politician), Dick Cheney (politician).

Economics

Gross state product, 1990: $13 billion (48th); per capita income: $16,398. Agricultural products: hay, all grains, sugar beets, potatoes, beans. Industry: refining, chemicals, wool, fertilizer, glass, electrical equipment. Minerals: coal, petroleum, gas, uranium, iron ore, bentomite.

Major Developments, 1946–1990

Wyoming is a large state with few people. Oil, uranium, and especially coal had aided the economy until the 1950s when the demand for coal slowed. Then, after 1973, a new boom occurred as many industries shifted back to coal. Low energy prices in the 1980s turned the boom into a depression, and the state's population dropped to 50th in the land. Wyoming received the first ICBM base in 1951. Tourism was aided by Grand Teton National Park, Devil's Tower Monument, and especially Yellowstone National Park, the nation's first, which had suffered from devastating forest fires in the late 1880s. Prominent political leaders were Senator Gale McGee, Senator Alan Simpson, and Congressman (Wyoming had only one) Dick Cheney, who in 1989 became President George H. W. Bush's secretary of defense.

CHAPTER 12 Cities of the United States

The purpose of this chapter is to provide basic information about major urban areas of the United States and to emphasize change that took place in America's cities between 1946 and 1990. A continuing objective, needless to say, is to detect what urban change revealed about the broader national history during approximately the last half of the 20th century. The emphasis is on size and change of size, as opposed to detailed sociological and economic data, some of which appears in other chapters. The history of urbanization after 1945 affirmed the scenario of a nation moving south and southwest to the so-called sunbelt. It was an ever-recurring account of a city rising or declining, growing or shrinking, based on location. Southern and southwestern cities grew; eastern and midwestern cities shrank in population, often markedly so. Location, it must be said, suggested supplementary information. Eastern cities were not only colder; they also were older and worn down if not worn out. Western cities were still being built, in the case of a city such as Phoenix, almost from the ground up. To the extent that a major city bucked, at least modified the trend, it would have to be New York, which continued to be a city in a class to itself.

A powerful secondary theme, identified in the largest cities but not explored in detail in this chapter, was growth in the numbers and power of racial and ethnic minority groups. Much of the growth took place with blacks and Hispanics, although Asians became conspicuous in some western cities. Of the five older cities that remained in the top 10 (Los Angeles counted as one), four had a black mayor in 1990, and the fifth, Chicago, had recently had one. The growth frequently was more proportionate than absolute, a state of affairs produced when white people fled the inner city and left the others behind. The metropolitan populations produced ethnic and racial proportions much different from the inner city. Within the territorial limits of many cities, a condition rapidly approached in which everyone would be a person of color. When one considers that the Census Bureau's classification of "white" included many individuals also identified as Hispanics, it was evident that several places by 1990 already had reached that point.

Sources for the cities include: Bureau of the Census, appropriate volumes in the 17th through 21st *Census of the United States* (1950–1990); Bureau of the Census, *Statistical Abstracts*, especially for 1955 (Washington, D.C., 1955) and 1993 (Washington, D.C., 1993); Harry Hansen, ed., *World Almanac and Book of Facts for 1950* (New York, 1950); Mark Hoffman, ed., *World Almanac and Book of Facts 1992* (New York, 1991); Otto Johnson, ed., *The 1992 Information Please Almanac, Atlas and Yearbook* (Boston, 1991); Robert H. Ferrell and Joan Hoff, eds., *Dictionary of American History, Supplement, Parts I and II* (New York, 1996); and *The World Book Encyclopedia*, 1997 edition (Chicago, 1997).

TABLE 12.1   POPULATION OF 100 LARGEST U.S. CITIES, 1950–1990
(ranked in April 1990 census)

Rank	City	1990	1980	1970	1960	1950
1.	New York, N.Y.	7,322,564	7,071,639	7,895,563	7,781,984	7,891,957
2.	Los Angeles, Calif.	3,485,398	2,966,850	2,811,801	2,479,015	1,970,358
3.	Chicago, Ill.	2,783,726	3,005,072	3,369,357	3,550,404	3,620,962
4.	Houston, Tex.	1,630,553	1,595,138	1,233,535	938,219	596,163
5.	Philadelphia, Pa.	1,585,577	1,688,210	1,949,996	2,002,512	2,071,605
6.	San Diego, Calif.	1,110,549	875,538	697,471	573,224	334,387
7.	Detroit, Mich.	1,027,974	1,203,339	1,514,063	1,670,144	1,849,568
8.	Dallas, Tex.	1,006,877	904,078	844,401	679,684	434,462
9.	Phoenix, Ariz.	983,403	789,704	584,303	439,170	106,818
10.	San Antonio, Tex.	935,933	785,880	654,153	587,718	408,442
11.	San Jose, Calif.	782,248	629,442	459,913	204,196	95,280
12.	Indianapolls, Ind.	741,952	700,807	736,856	476,258	427,173
13.	Baltimore, Md.	736,014	786,775	905,787	939,024	949,708
14.	San Francisco, Calif.	723,959	678,974	715,674	740,316	775,357
15.	Jacksonville, Fla.	672,971	540,920	504,265	201,030	204,517
16.	Columbus, Ohio	632,910	564,871	540,025	471,316	375,901
17.	Milwaukee, Wis.	628,088	636,212	717,372	741,324	637,392
18.	Memphis, Tenn.	610,337	646,356	623,988	497,524	396,000
19.	Washington, D.C.	606,900	638,333	756,668	763,956	802,178
20.	Boston, Mass.	574,283	562,994	641,071	697,197	801,444
21.	Seattle, Wash.·	516,259	493,846	530,831	557,087	467,591
22.	El Paso, Tex.	515,342	425,259	322,261	276,687	130,485
23.	Nashville-Davidson, Tenn.	510,784	455,651	426,029	170,874	174,307
24.	Cleveland, Ohio	505,616	573,822	750,879	876,050	914,808
25.	New Orleans, La.	496,938	557,515	593,471	627,525	570,445
26.	Denver, Colo.	467,610	492,365	514,678	493,887	415,786
27.	Austin, Tex.	465,622	345,496	253,539	186,545	132,459
28.	Fort Worth, Tex.	447,619	385,164	393,455	356,268	278,778
29.	Oklahoma City, Okla.	444,719	403,213	368,164	324,253	243,504
30.	Portland, Oreg.	437,319	366,383	379,967	372,676	373,628
31.	Kansas City, Mo.	435,146	448,159	507,330	475,539	456,622
32.	Long Beach, Calif.	429,433	361,334	358,879	344,168	250,767
33.	Tucson, Ariz.	405,390	330,537	262,933	212,892	45,454
34.	St. Louis, Mo.	396,685	453,085	622,236	750,026	856,796
35.	Charlotte, N.C.	395,934	314,447	241,420	201,564	134,042

Rank	City	1990	1980	1970	1960	1950
36.	Atlanta, Ga.	394,017	425,022	495,039	487,455	331,314
37.	Virginia Beach, Va.	393,069	262,199	172,106	8,091	5,390
38.	Albuquerque, N.Mex.	384,736	331,767	244,501	201,189	96,815
39.	Oakland, Calif.	372,242	339,337	361,561	367,548	384,575
40.	Pittsburgh, Pa.	369,879	423,938	520,089	604,332	676,806
41.	Sacramento, Calif.	369,365	275,741	257,105	191,667	137,572
42.	Minneapolis, Minn.	368,383	370,951	434,400	482,872	521,718
43.	Tulsa, Okla.	367,302	360,919	330,350	261,685	182,740
44.	Honolulu, CDP, Hawaii	365,272	762,874	630,528	294,194	248,034
45.	Cincinnati, Ohio	364,040	385,457	453,514	502,550	503,998
46.	Miami, Fla.	358,548	346,865	334,859	291,688	249,276
47.	Fresno, Calif.	354,202	218,202	165,655	133,929	91,669
48.	Omaha, Nebr.	335,795	314,255	346,929	301,598	251,117
49.	Toledo, Ohio	332,943	354,635	383,062	318,003	303,616
50.	Buffalo, N.Y.	328,123	357,670	462,768	532,759	580,132
51.	Wichita, Kans.	304,011	279,272	276,554	254,698	168,279
52.	Santa Ana, Calif.	293,742	203,713	155,710	100,350	45,533
53.	Mesa, Ariz.	288,091	152,453	63,049	33,772	16,790
54.	Colorado Springs, Colo.	281,140	215,150	135,517	70,194	45,472
55.	Tampa, Fla.	280,015	271,523	277,714	274,970	124,681
56.	Newark, N.J.	275,221	329,248	381,930	405,220	438,776
57.	St. Paul, Minn.	272,235	270,230	309,866	313,411	311,349
58.	Louisville, Ky.	269,063	298,451	361,706	390,639	369,129
59.	Anaheim, Calif.	266,406	219,311	166,408	104,184	14,556
60.	Birmingham, Ala.	265,968	284,413	300,910	340,887	326,037
61.	Arlington, Tex.	261,721	160,113	90,229	44,775	7,692
62.	Norfolk, Va.	261,229	266,979	307,951	304,869	213,513
63.	Las Vegas, Nev.	258,295	164,674	125,787	64,405	24,624
64.	Corpus Christi, Tex.	257,453	231,999	204,525	167,690	108,287
65.	St. Petersburg, Fla.	238,629	238,647	216,159	181,298	96,738
66.	Rochester, N.Y.	231,636	241,741	295,011	318,611	332,488
67.	Jersey City, N.J.	228,537	223,532	260,350	276,101	299,017
68.	Riverside, Calif.	226,505	170,876	140,089	84,332	46,764
69.	Anchorage, Alaska	226,338	174,431	48,081	44,237	11,254
70.	Lexington-Fayette, Ky.	225,366	204,165	108,137	62,810	55,534
71.	Akron, Ohio	223,019	237,177	275,425	290,351	274,605
72.	Aurora, Colo.	222,103	158,588	74,974	48,548	11,421
73.	Baton Rouge, La.	219,531	346,029	165,921	152,419	125,629
74.	Stockton, Calif.	210,943	149,779	109,963	86,321	70,853
75.	Raleigh, N.C.	207,951	150,255	122,830	93,931	65,679
76.	Richmond, Va.	203,056	219,214	249,332	219,958	230,310
77.	Shreveport, La.	198,525	205,820	182,064	164,372	127,206
78.	Jackson, Miss.	196,637	202,895	153,968	144,422	98,271
79.	Mobile, Ala.	196,278	200,452	190,026	194,856	129,009
80.	Des Moines, Ia.	193,187	191,003	201,404	208,982	177,965
81.	Lincoln, Neb.	191,972	171,932	149,518	128,521	98,884
82.	Madison, Wis.	191,262	170,616	171,809	126,706	96,056
83.	Grand Rapids, Mich.	189,126	181,843	197,649	177,313	176,515
84.	Yonkers, N.Y.	188,082	195,351	204,297	190,634	152,798
85.	Hialeah, Fla.	188,004	145,254	102,452	66,972	19,676
86.	Montgomery, Ala.	187,106	177,857	133,386	134,393	106,525
87.	Lubbock, Tex.	186,206	173,979	149,101	126,691	71,747
88.	Greensboro, N.C.	183,521	170,279	144,076	119,574	74,389
89.	Dayton, Ohio	182,044	203,371	243,023	262,332	243,872
90.	Huntington Beach, Calif.	181,519	170,505	115,960	11,492	5,237
91.	Garland, Tex.	180,650	138,857	81,437	38,501	10,571
92.	Glendale, Calif.	180,038	139,060	133,000	119,000	96,000
93.	Columbus, Ga.	179,278	169,441	155,028	116,779	79,611
94.	Spokane, Wash.	177,196	171,300	170,516	181,608	161,721
95.	Tacoma, Wash.	176,664	158,501	154,407	147,979	143,673
96.	Little Rock, Ark.	175,795	158,461	132,483	107,813	102,213
97.	Bakersfield, Calif.	174,820	105,611	. . .	56,848	. . .
98.	Fremont, Calif.	173,339	131,945	100,869	43,790	. . .
99.	Fort Wayne, Ind.	173,072	172,196	178,269	161,776	133,607
100.	Newport News, Va.	170,045	144,903	138,000	114,000	42,000

Source: Mark Hoffman, ed., *The World Almanac and Book of Facts 1992* (New York, 1991), 132–33.

Beach crowds seen from the parachute jump at Steeplechase Park, Coney Island, New York, 1950 (National Archives)

TABLE 12.2   FORMER TOP 10 CITIES, 1950

City	Population 1950	Rank 1950	Population 1990	Change	Rank 1990
Baltimore	949,708	6.	736,014	−213,694	12.
Cleveland	914,808	7.	505,014	−409,192	23.
St. Louis	856,796	8.	396,685	−460,111	34.
Washington, D.C.	802,178	9.	606,900	−195,278	19.
Boston	801,444	10.	574,283	−227,161	20.

Source: World Almanac, 1992, 132.

TABLE 12.3   CITIES, BY POPULATION SIZE, 1960–1990

Population Size	Number of Cities				Population (mil.)				Percent of Total			
	1960	1970	1980	1990	1960	1970	1980	1990	1960	1970	1980	1990
Total	18,088	18,666	19,097	19,289	115.9	131.9	140.3	152.9	100.0	100.0	100.0	100.0
1,000,000 or more	5	6	6	8	17.5	18.8	17.5	20.0	15.1	14.2	12.5	13.0
500,000 to 999,999	16	20	16	15	11.1	13.0	10.9	10.1	9.6	9.8	7.8	6.6
250,000 to 499,999	30	30	33	40	10.8	10.5	11.8	14.2	9.3	7.9	8.4	9.3
100,000 to 249,999	79	97	114	131	11.4	13.9	16.6	19.1	9.8	10.5	11.8	12.5
50,000 to 99,999	180	232	250	309	12.5	16.2	17.6	21.2	10.8	12.2	12.3	13.9
25,000 to 49,999	366	455	526	567	12.7	15.7	18.4	20.0	11.0	11.9	13.1	13.0
10,000 to 24,999	978	1,127	1,260	1,290	15.1	17.6	19.8	20.3	13.1	13.3	14.1	13.3
Under 10,000	16,434	16,699	16,892	16,929	24.9	26.4	28.0	28.2	21.5	20.0	20.0	18.4

Source: Bureau of the Census, *Statistical Abstract of the United States 1992* (Lanham, Md., 1993), 35.

TABLE 12.4 FASTEST-GROWING CITIES, 1980–1990

(cities of more than 100,000 in 1990 that had the largest percentage increases in population from 1980)

Rank	City	Suburb of . . .	1990	1980	Change (percent)
1.	Moreno Valley, Calif.	Riverside	118.779	28,309	319.6
2.	Mesa, Ariz.	Phoenix	288,091	152,404	89.0
3.	Rancho Cucamonga, Calif.	Los Angeles	101,409	55,250	83.5
4.	Plano, Tex.	Dallas	128,713	72,331	77.9
5.	Irvine, Calif.	Los Angeles	110,330	62,134	77.6
6.	Escondido, Calif.	San Diego	108,635	64,355	68.8
7.	Oceanside, Calif.	Los Angeles	128,398	76,698	67.4
8.	Santa Clarita, Calif.	Los Angeles	110,642	66,730	65.8
9.	Bakersfield, Calif.	. . .	174,820	105,611	65.5
10.	Arlington, Tex.	Dallas	261,721	160,113	63.5
11.	Fresno, Calif	. . .	354,202	217,491	62.9
12.	Chula Vista, Calif.	San Diego	135,163	83,927	61.0
13.	Las Vegas, Nev.	. . .	258,295	164,674	56.9
14.	Modesto, Calif.	. . .	164,730	106,963	54.0
15.	Tallahassee, Fla.	. . .	124,773	81,548	53.0
16.	Glendale, Ariz.	Phoenix	148,134	97,172	52.4
17.	Mesquite, Tex.	Dallas	101,484	67,053	51.3
18.	Ontario, Calif.	Los Angeles	133,179	88,820	49.9
19.	Virginia Beach, Va.	Norfolk	393,069	262,199	49.9
20.	Scottsdale, Ariz.	Phoenix	130,069	88,622	46.5
21.	Santa Ana, Calif.	Los Angeles	293,742	204,023	44.0
22.	Stockton, Calif.	. . .	210,943	148,283	42.3
23.	Pomona, Calif.	Los Angeles	131,723	92,742	42.0
24.	Irving, Tex.	Dallas	155,037	109,943	41.0
25.	Aurora, Colo.	Denver	222,103	158,588	40.1
26.	Raleigh, N.C.	. . .	207,951	150,255	38.4
27.	San Bermardino, Calif.	. . .	164,164	118,794	38.2
28.	Santa Rosa, Calif.	San Francisco	113,313	82,658	37.1
29.	Overland Park, Kan.	Kansas City	111,790	81,784	36.7
30.	Vallejo, Calif	San Francisco	109,199	80,303	36.0
31.	Thousand Oaks, Calif.	Los Angeles	104,352	77,072	35.4
32.	Salinas, Calif.	. . .	108,777	80,479	35.2
33.	Durham, N.C.	. . .	136,611	101,149	35.1
34.	Austin, Tex.	. . .	465,622	345,890	34.6
35.	Laredo, Tex.	. . .	122,899	91,449	34.4
36.	Sacramento, Calif.	. . .	369,365	275,741	34.0
37.	El Monte, Calif.	Los Angeles	106,209	79,494	33.6
38.	Reno, Nev.	. . .	133,850	100,756	32.8
39.	Riverside, Calif.	. . .	226,505	170,591	32.8
40.	Chesapeake, Va.	Norfolk	151,967	114,486	32.7
41.	Tempe, Artz.	Phoenix	141,865	106,919	32.7
42.	Oxnard, Calif.	Los Angeles	142,216	108,195	31.4
43.	Fremont, Calif.	San Jose/Oakland	173,339	131,945	31.4
44.	Colorado Springs, Colo.	. . .	281,140	215,105	30.7
45.	Garland, Tex.	Dallas	180,650	138,857	30.1

Source: Hoffman, *World Almanac, 1992,* 131.

TABLE 12.5 CITIES WITH LARGEST PERCENTAGE LOSS IN POPULATION, 1980–1990

Rank	City	1990	1980	Change (percent)
1.	Gary, Ind.	116,646	151,968	−23.2
2.	Newark	275,221	329,248	−16.4
3.	Detroit	1,027,974	1,203,369	−14.6
4.	Pittsburgh	369,879	423,960	−12.8
5.	St. Louis	396,685	452,804	−12.4
6.	Cleveland	505,616	573,822	−11.9
7.	Flint, Mich.	140,761	159,611	−11.8
8.	New Orleans	496,938	557,927	−10.9
9.	Warren, Mich.	144,864	161,134	−10.1
10.	Chattanooga, Tenn.	152,466	169,514	−10.1
11.	Louisville, Ky.	269,063	298,694	−9.9
12.	Peoria, Ill.	113,504	124,813	−9.1
13.	Macon, Ga.	106,612	116,896	−8.8
14.	Erie, Pa.	108,718	119,123	−8.7
15.	Buffalo	328,123	357,870	−8.3
16.	Birmingham, Ala.	265,968	288,297	−7.7
17.	Richmond	203,056	219,214	−7.4
18.	Chicago	2,783,726	3,005,072	−7.4
19.	Atlanta	394,017	425,022	−7.3
20.	Kansas City, Kan.	149,767	161,148	−7.1
21.	Baltimore	736,014	786,741	−6.4
22.	Akron, Ohio	223,019	237,590	−6.1
23.	Toledo, Ohio	332,943	354,635	−6.1
24.	Philadelphia	1,585,577	1,688,210	−6.1
25.	Dayton, Ohio	182,044	193,549	−5.9
26.	Knoxville, Tenn.	165,121	175,045	−5.7
27.	Memphis	610,337	646,170	−5.5
28.	Cincinnati	364,040	385,410	−5.5
29.	Denver	467,610	492,694	−5.1
30.	District of Columbia	606,900	638,432	−4.9

Source: Hoffman, *World Almanac, 1992,* 133.

The cities keep moving out. This farm outside Richmond, Virginia, has its days numbered. (U.S. Department of Agriculture)

TABLE 12.6 75 LARGEST METROPOLITAN AREAS—RACIAL AND HISPANIC ORIGIN POPULATIONS, 1990

Metropolitan Area[a]	Total Population (1,000)	Percent of Total Metropolitan Population			
		Black	American Indian, Eskimo, Aleut	Asian and Pacific Islander	Hispanic Origin[b]
New York–Northern New Jersey–Long Island, N.Y.-N.J.-CT CMSA	18,087	18.2	0.3	4.8	15.4
Los Angeles–Anaheim–Riverside, Calif. CMSA	14,532	8.5	0.6	9.2	32.9
Chicago–Gary–Lake County, Ill.-Ind.-Wis. CMSA	8,066	19.2	0.2	3.2	11.1
San Francisco–Oakland–San Jose, Calif. CMSA	6,253	8.6	0.7	14.8	15.5
Philadelphia-Wilmington-Trenton, Pa.-N.J.-Del.-Md. CMSA	5,899	18.7	0.2	2.1	3.8
Detroit–Ann Arbor, Mich. CMSA	4,665	20.9	0.4	1.5	1.9
Boston-Lawrence-Salem, Mass.-N.H. CMSA	4,172	5.7	0.2	2.9	4.6
Washington D.C.–Md.–Va. MSA	3,924	26.6	0.3	5.2	5.7
Dallas–Fort Worth, Tex. CMSA	3,885	14.3	0.5	2.5	13.4
Houston-Galveston-Brazoria, Tex. CMSA	3,711	17.9	0.3	3.6	20.8
Miami–Fort Lauderdale, Fla. CMSA	3,193	18.5	0.2	1.4	33.3
Atlanta, Ga. MSA	2,834	26.0	0.2	1.8	2.0
Cleveland-Akron-Lorain, Ohio. CMSA	2,760	16.0	0.2	1.0	1.9
Seattle-Tacoma, Wash. CMSA	2,559	4.8	1.3	6.4	3.0
San Diego, Calif. MSA	2,498	6.4	0.8	7.9	20.4
Minneapolis–St. Paul, Minn. Wis. MSA	2,464	3.6	1.0	2.6	1.5
St. Louis, Mo.–Ill. MSA	2,444	17.3	0.2	1.0	1.1
Baltimore, Md. MSA	2,382	25.9	0.3	1.8	1.3
Pittsburgh–Beaver Valley, Pa. CMSA	2,243	8.0	0.1	0.7	0.6
Phoenix, Ariz. MSA	2,122	3.5	1.8	1.7	16.3

Metropolitan Area[a]	Total Population (1,000)	Percent of Total Metropolitan Population			
		Black	American Indian, Eskimo, Aleut	Asian and Pacific Islander	Hispanic Origin[b]
Tampa–St. Petersburg–Clearwater, Fla. MSA	2,068	9.0	0.3	1.1	6.7
Denver-Boulder, Colo. CMSA	1,848	5.3	0.8	2.3	12.2
Cincinnati-Hamilton, Ohio.-Ky.-Ind. CMSA	1,744	11.7	0.1	0.8	0.5
Milwaukee-Racine, Wis. CMSA	1,607	13.3	0.5	1.2	3.8
Kansas City, Mo.-Kans. MSA	1,566	12.8	0.5	1.1	2.9
Sacramento, Calif. MSA	1,481	6.9	1.1	7.7	11.6
Portland-Vancouver, Oreg.-Wash. CMSA	1,478	2.8	0.9	3.5	3.4
Norfolk–Virginia Beach–Newport News, Va. MSA	1,396	28.5	0.3	2.5	2.3
Columbus, Ohio. MSA	1,377	12.0	0.2	1.5	0.8
San Antonio, Tex. MSA	1,302	6.8	0.4	1.2	47.6
Indianapolis, Ind. MSA	1,250	13.8	0.2	0.8	0.9
New Orleans, La. MSA	1,239	34.7	0.3	1.7	4.3
Buffalo-Niagara Falls, N.Y. CMSA	1,189	10.3	0.6	0.9	2.0
Charlotte–Gastonia–Rock Hill, N.C.-S.C. MSA	1,162	19.9	0.4	1.0	0.9
Providence–Pawtucket–Fall River, R.I.-Maine CMSA	1,142	3.3	0.3	1.8	4.2
Hartford–New Britain–Middletown, CT CMSA	1,086	8.7	0.2	1.5	7.0
Orlando, Fla. MSA	1,073	12.4	0.3	1.9	9.0
Salt Lake City–Ogden, Utah MSA	1,072	1.0	0.8	2.4	5.8
Rochester, N.Y. MSA	1,002	9.4	0.3	1.4	3.1
Nashville Tenn. MSA	985	15.5	0.2	1.0	0.8
Memphis, Tenn.-Ark.-Mass. MSA	982	40.6	0.2	0.8	0.8
Oklahoma City, Okla. MSA	959	10.5	4.8	1.9	3.6
Louisville, Ky.-Ind. MSA	953	13.1	0.2	0.6	0.6
Dayton-Springfield, Ohio MSA	951	13.3	0.2	1.0	0.8
Greensboro–Winston-Salem–High Point, N.C. MSA	942	19.3	0.3	0.7	0.8
Birmingham, Ala. MSA	908	27.1	0.2	0.4	0.4
Jacksonville, Fla. MSA	907	20.0	0.3	1.7	2.5
Albany-Schenectady-Troy, N.Y. MSA	874	4.7	0.2	1.2	1.8
Richmond-Petersburg, Va. MSA	866	29.2	0.3	1.4	1.1
West Palm Beach–Boca Raton–Delray Beach, Fla. MSA	864	12.5	0.1	1.0	7.7
Honolulu, Hawaii MSA	836	3.1	0.4	63.0	6.8
Austin, Tex. MSA	782	9.2	0.4	2.4	20.5
Las Vegas, Nev. MSA	741	9.5	0.9	3.5	11.2
Raleigh-Durham, N.C. MSA	735	24.9	0.3	1.9	1.2
Scranton–Wilkes-Barre, Pa. MSA	734	1.0	0.1	0.5	0.8
Tulsa, Okla. MSA	709	8.2	6.8	0.9	2.1
Grand Rapids, Mich. MSA	688	6.0	0.5	1.1	3.3
Allentown-Bethlehem, Pa.-N.J. MSA	687	2.0	0.1	1.1	4.2
Fresno, Calif. MSA	667	5.0	1.1	8.6	35.5
Tucson, Ariz. MSA	667	3.1	3.0	1.8	24.5
Syracuse, N.Y. MSA	660	5.9	0.6	1.2	1.4
Greenville-Spartanburg, S.C. MSA	641	17.4	0.1	0.7	0.8
Omaha, Neb.–Iowa MSA	618	8.3	0.5	1.0	2.6
Toledo, Ohio MSA	614	11.4	0.2	1.0	3.3
Knoxville, Tenn. MSA	605	6.0	0.2	0.8	0.5
El Paso, Tex. MSA	592	3.7	0.4	1.1	69.6
Harrisburg-Lebanon-Carlisle, Pa. MSA	588	6.7	0.1	1.1	1.7
Bakersfield, Calif. MSA	543	5.5	1.3	3.0	28.0
New Haven–Meriden, CT MSA	530	12.1	0.2	1.6	6.2
Springfield, Mass. MSA	530	6.6	0.2	1.0	9.0
Baton Rouge, La. MSA	528	29.6	0.2	1.1	1.4
Little Rock–North Little Rock, Ark. MSA	513	19.9	0.4	0.7	0.8
Charleston, S.C. MSA	507	30.2	0.3	1.2	1.5
Youngstown-Warren, Ohio MSA	493	11.1	0.2	0.4	1.5
Wichita, Kans. MSA	485	7.6	1.1	1.9	4.1

[a] Metropolitan areas are shown in rank order of total population of consolidated metropolitan statistical areas (CMSA) and metropolitan statistical areas (MSA).
[b] Persons of Hispanic origin may be of any race.
Source: *Statistical Abstract 1992, 34.*

The Most, and Least, Promising Metropolitan Counties, 1990

The following tables, produced by *American Demographics* magazine, measured the business potential of counties and their independent cities with a formula that included population change between 1970 and 1990, percent change in per capita money income between 1979 and 1987, and each area's deviation from the median density for all metropolitan counties in 1990. The 411 counties and independent cities from metros and consolidated metros of 500,000 or more population were ranked on each viable. Scores were assigned based on rank. The maximum score for population change was 480 points, for income growth 320 points, and for density deviation 200 points. The final ranking was determined by summing each area's scores for each variable.

TABLE 12.7   THE MOST PROMISING 50 COUNTIES

Rank	County (metropolitan area)	Population Change, 1970–90 (percent)	Per Capita Income Change, 1979–87 (percent)	Persons per Square Mile, 1990
1.	Fayette, Ga. [Atlanta]	449.2	79.2	316
2.	Collin, Tex. [Dallas–Fort Worth]	294.6	76.8	311
3.	Gwinnett, Ga. [Atlanta]	387.8	76.0	815
4.	Hernando, Fla. [Tampa–St. Petersburg–Clearwater]	494.7	66.3	211
5.	Denton, Tex. [Dallas–Fort Worth]	261.6	59.9	308
6.	Cherokee, Ga. [Atlanta]	190.4	86.3	213
7.	James City, Va. [Norfolk–Virginia Beach–Newport News]	95.3	94.0	244
8.	Osceola, Fla. [Orlando]	326.4	77.9	81
9.	Howard, Md. [Baltimore]	202.6	81.6	743
10.	Loudoun, Va. [Washington]	131.8	94.6	166
11.	Stafford, Va. [Washington]	149.1	85.7	227
12.	Pasco, Fla. [Tampa–St. Petersburg–Clearwater]	270.1	78.1	377
13.	Forsyth, Ga. [Atlanta]	160.4	90.0	195
14.	Paulding, Ga. [Atlanta]	137.5	82.4	133
15.	Douglas, Colo. [Denver-Boulder]	618.3	56.2	72
16.	Henry, Ga. [Atlanta]	147.6	77.0	182
17.	Seminole, Fla. [Orlando]	243.6	77.2	933
18.	Chesterfield, Va. [Richmond-Petersburg]	172.3	75.5	492
19.	Prince William, Va. [Washington]	94.1	82.1	637
20.	Palm Beach, Fla. [W. Palm Beach–Boca Raton–Delray Beach]	147.6	79.4	424
21.	Calvert, Md. [Washington]	148.4	84.4	239
22.	Rockdale, Ga. [Atlanta]	198.0	75.9	414
23.	St. Johns, Fla. [Jacksonville]	172.8	84.8	138
24.	Clay, Fla. [Jacksonville]	230.6	71.4	176
25.	St. Charles, Md. [St. Louis]	129.0	69.7	379
26.	Wake, N.C. [Raleigh-Durham]	85.3	85.4	508
27.	Riverside, Calif. [Los Angeles–Anaheim–Riverside]	155.0	53.8	162
28.	Williamson, Tex. [Austin]	274.1	56.0	124
29.	Orange, Fla. [Orlando]	96.8	79.0	746
30.	Dakota, Minn. [Minneapolis–St. Paul]	96.9	68.0	483
31.	Hunterdon, N.J. [New York–Northern New Jersey–Long Island]	54.6	101.6	251
32.	Shelby, Ala. [Birmingham]	161.2	70.8	125
33.	Manassas, Va. [Washington]	205.1	87.5	2,793
34.	Cobb, Ga. [Atlanta]	127.5	83.0	1,316
35.	Chesapeake Va. [Norfolk–Virginia Beach–Newport News]	69.7	77.0	446
36.	Clark, Nev. [Las Vegas]	171.3	51.8	94
37.	Fort Bend, Tex. [Houston-Galveston-Brazoria]	330.9	37.4	258
38.	Solano, Calif. [San Francisco–Oakland–San Jose]	100.3	57.6	411
39.	Charles, Md. [Washington]	112.2	76.8	219
40.	Williamson, Tenn. [Nashville]	136.0	81.9	139
41.	Harford, Md. [Baltimore]	57.9	77.6	414
42.	Rutherford, Tenn. [Nashville]	99.5	74.8	192
43.	Hamilton, Ind. [Indianapolis]	99.8	73.6	274
44.	Ocean, N.J. [New York–Northern New Jersey–Long Island]	107.8	86.1	681
45.	Douglas, Ga. [Atlanta]	148.2	73.1	357
46.	Washington, Minn. [Minneapolis–St. Paul]	75.9	73.0	372
47.	Frederick, Md. [Washington]	76.9	76.1	227
48.	Carroll, Md. [Baltimore]	78.8	76.3	275
49.	Queen Anne's, Md. [Baltimore]	84.3	88.7	91
50.	Somerset, N.J. [New York–Northern New Jersey–Long Island]	21.1	99.3	789

Source: American Demographics, September, 1991, 36.

TABLE 12.8   THE LEAST PROMISING 20 COUNTIES

(The least promising metropolitan counties are mostly central cities that are losing people and have below-average purchasing power; bottom-ranked counties, population growth 1970–1990, per capita income growth 1979–1987, and density in 1990, within metropolitan areas including consolidated metros of 500,000 or more.)

Rank	County (metropolitan area)	Population Change, 1970–90 (percent)	Per Capita Income Change, 1979–87 (percent)	Persons per Square Mile, 1990
411.	Orleans, La. [New Orleans]	−16.3	44.5	2,751
410.	Denver, Colo. [Denver-Boulder]	−9.1	51.8	3,051
409.	Cuyahoga, Ohio [Cleveland-Akron-Lorain]	−18.0	54.7	3,081
408.	Cook, Ill. [Chicago–Gary–Lake County]	−7.1	55.7	5,398
407.	Wayne, Mich. [Detroit–Ann Arbor]	−20.8	54.7	3,438
406.	Milwaukee, Wis. [Milwaukee-Racine]	−9.0	54.4	3,971
405.	Hopewell, Va. [Richmond-Petersburg]	−1.6	58.8	2,254
404.	St. Louis, Mo. [St. Louis]	−36.2	65.4	6,406
403.	Washington, D.C. [Washington]	−19.8	65.0	9,883
402.	Philadelphia, Pa. [Philadelphia-Wilmington-Trenton]	−18.6	65.2	11,734
401.	Portsmouth, Va. [Norfolk–Virginia Beach–Newport News]	−6.4	60.7	3,135
400.	Norfolk, Va. [Norfolk–Virginia Beach–Newport News]	−15.2	64.7	4,859
399.	Osage, Okla. [Tulsa]	40.0	37.2	19
398.	Baltimore, Md. [Baltimore]	−18.7	70.0	9,108
397.	Hamilton, Ohio [Cincinnati-Hamilton]	−6.3	62.2	2,126
396.	Richmond, Va. [Richmond-Petersburg]	−18.7	72.6	3,377
395.	Allegheny, Pa. [Pittsburgh–Beaver Valley]	−16.7	58.5	1,830
394.	Queens, N.Y. [New York–Northern New Jersey–Long Island]	−1.8	67.9	17,839
393.	Kings, N.Y. [New York–Northern New Jersey–Long Island]	−11.6	70.4	32,619
392.	San Francisco, Calif. [San Francisco–Oakland–San Jose]	1.2	63.4	15,502

Source: *American Demographics*, September, 1991, 37.

Ten Largest Cities of the United States
New York City

Profile

Founded: 1613, incorporated 1653

Population: 1990, 7,322,564, rank: 1; 1950, 7,891,957, rank: 1

Population change, 1950–1990: −569,393

Racial/ethnic mix, 1990: white, 3,827,088; black, 2,102,512 (28.7%); American Indian, Eskimo, or Aleut, 27,531 (0.4%); Asian or Pacific Islander, 512,719 (7%); Hispanic origin, 1,783,511 (24.4%)

Per capita income (1989) by race: all races, $16,281; white, $21,972; black, $10,505; American Indian, Eskimo, or Aleut, $10,861; Asian or Pacific Islander, 12,851; Hispanic, $8,430

Land area: 309 sq. mi.; Elevation: 87 ft. above sea level

Counties: Bronx, Kings, New York, Queens, Richmond

Average temperature*: January, 31.5°F; July, 76.8°F; annual average, 54.7°F

Annual precipitation*: 47.25 inches (snowfall: 28.2 inches)

Clear days*: 107; precipitation days: 121

Type of government: mayor-council; mayor in 1990: David N. Dinkins

History and Develoment

The area of New York was explored in 1524 by Giovanni da Verrazano, an Italian sailing for France. Henry Hudson, an Englishman sailing for the Dutch, sailed into the area and claimed it as New Netherlands. The Indians living there, as the story goes, sold Manhattan Island for $24 worth of trinkets. The English seized the Dutch colony in 1664, and renamed it New York after the duke of York, the

future King James II. New York colony and later New York State stood out because they contained New York City. The factor that did most to promote New York as a major colonial city and soon thereafter as the dominant city in the nation was its harbor. Virtually everyone going to or coming from Europe went through New York. There is where the immigrants landed; many of them stayed.

In the 19th and early 20th centuries, New York maintained its status of being not only the most populous city but center of much of what went on in American culture and economics. As the United States grew in power and wealth and its culture reached into other continents, New York probably deserved a title of first city of the world. When the United Nations was established in 1945, it was fitting that the headquarters would be in New York.

The story of New York in the postwar period was a tale of contrasts. The city gave off signals similar to developments in other older urban areas. It lost some 100,000 residents in the 1950s, many of them going to bedroom communities nearby. Some businesses moved or closed, especially in the garment industries. The city appeared to be unwieldy, impossible to govern. Transit workers struck for 12 days in 1966, stopping public transportation. Sanitation workers would not work in 1968, letting garbage pile up for a week and a half. The police struck in 1971, and the city approached bankruptcy in 1975. By 1990 five major racial and ethnic groups—blacks, Irish, Italians, Jewish and Puerto Ricans—seemed to constitute five separate cities.

But the city held on. It reversed a population loss in the 1960s and again in the 1980s. The Port of New York (and New Jersey) lost traffic to the St. Lawrence Seaway system, but it remained a major port. Many companies did not leave. New York dominated publishing in all respects. It was the nation's broadcasting center. Broadway stage productions, especially the musicals, buckled somewhat in the 1960s, but survived. New York's Stock Exchange and the Financial District gave national economics much of its thrust. Despite racial divisions the city managed to elect mayors and they came in all stripes—Jews (Abe Beame and Ed Koch); in 1988 an African American, David Dinkins, defeated an Italian, Rudolph Giuliani, and became the first person of his

* *Note:* Climatological data for the most populous 10 cities has been based on a standard 30-year average. For the largest nine cities the period used was 1961–1990. For the 16th city, San Antonio, the period was 1951–1980.

Iron workers raise steel at the 32nd floor of the Esso Building, New York City, 1954. (National Archives)

race to hold the office. There even had been an Anglo, John Lindsay, in the 1960s. New York remained in 1990 a place of large forces and momentous developments, still first city of the nation, if not the world.

Los Angeles

Profile

Founded: 1781, incorporated 1850

Population: 1990, 3,485,557, rank: 2; 1950, 1,970,358, rank 4

Population change, 1950–1990: +1,515,199

Racial/ethnic mix, 1990: white, 1,841,182; black, 487,674 (14%); American Indian, Eskimo, or Aleut, 16,379 (0.5%), Asian or Pacific Islander, 341,807 (7.8%); Hispanic origin, 1,391,411 (39.9%)

Per capita income (1989) by race: all races, $16,188; white, $22,191; black, $11,257; American Indian, Eskimo, or Aleut, $12,901; Asian or Pacific Islander, $13,875; Hispanic, $7,111

Land area: 469.3 sq. mi.; Elevation: 104 ft

County: Los Angeles

Average temperature: January, 56.8°F; July, 69.1°F; annual average, 63°F

Annual precipitation: 12.01 inches (snowfall: trace)

Clear days: 143; precipitation days: 35

Type of government: mayor-council; mayor in 1990: Tom Bradley

History and Development

Several Native American groups lived in what is Los Angeles many years before arrival of the Europeans. A Spanish explorer passed through in 1542, and then the area was ignored for more than 200 years until 1769 when other Spaniards appeared, and a Franciscan priest gave what he called a "delightful place" its name. In 1781 a party of 44 people from Spanish Mexico arrived and established the pueblo of Los Angeles. Spanish rule transferred to Mexico in 1821, the year of Mexican independence, and the general area of California fell into the United States's hands in the treaty of 1848 that ended the U.S.-Mexican War. Growth of Los Angeles paralleled growth of the new state of California. Farming and ranching expanded. Arrival of the transcontinental railroads in the 1870s facilitated commerce and brought in people from the East. Completion of an artificial harbor in 1914 made Los Angeles a major Pacific port. There followed the development of an oil industry, the opening of new factories, and the establishment in the 1920s of Los Angeles as base for the glamorous new film industry. The Depression of the 1930s and world war of the 1940s provided major new economic incentive for people to move west.

The population boom continued into the postwar period. Los Angeles grew by approximately 1 million people between 1945 and 1960. Beginning in the 1970s, if not earlier, the city became destination for many immigrants from Asia and Latin America. What had stood as a mark of appeal and success also became the measure of growing problems. More people meant need for more water—for irrigation or simply for living. Completion of the California Aqueduct in 1973 helped, but water shortages continued to appear. The city's freeways were jammed and downright dangerous; in 1987 the city began long-term work on a mass-transit rail system. Air pollution, serious since the 1950s, induced expensive corrective measures. By the end of the 1980s Los Angeles was home to four major racial/ethnic groups—Asians, blacks, Hispanics, non-Hispanic whites—and many other subgroupings. The racial mix provided diversity to be sure, but it also produced gang competition, drive-by shootings, and racial unrest in general. It seemed that every major issue had its racial aspect. In 1973 Los Angelans elected Tom Bradley as its first African-American mayor. He still was in office in 1990.

Chicago

Profile

Founded: 1803, incorporated 1837
Population: 1990, 2,783,726, rank 3; 1950, 3,620,902, rank 2
Population change, 1950–1990: −837,236
Racial/ethnic mix, 1990: white 1,263,524; black, 1,087,711 (39.1%); American Indian, Eskimo, or Aleut, 7,064 (0.3%); Asian or Pacific Islander, 104,118 (3.7%); Hispanic origin, 545,852 (19.6%)
Per capita income (1989) by race: all races, $12,899; white, $18,258; black, $8,596; Indian, Eskimo, or Aleut, $11,251; Asian or Pacific Islander, $11,581; Hispanic, $7,438
Land area: 227 sq. mi.; Elevation: 623 ft
County: Cook
Average temperature: January, 21°F; July, 73.2°F; annual average, 49°F
Annual precipitation: 35.82 inches (snowfall: 38.5 inches)
Clear days: 94; precipitation days: 123
Type of government: mayor-council; mayor in 1990: Richard M. Daley

History and Development

The area that became Chicago was a crossroads for American Indians moving from one waterway to another. The Wyandot had been there, and the Potawatomi. Later a trading post, the area on the south shore of Lake Michigan was ceded by the Indians to the United States, where soldiers proceeded to build Fort Dearborn, a place that also would be known as Chicago, a derivative from a Potawatomi name. Aided by its excellent location, the Chicago settlement grew and prospered as the nation moved west. Establishment of a railroad network enabled Chicago to build further on its identity as a crossroads. One of the first major industries was meatpacking.

In the period between the two world wars, Chicago established a reputation for racial tension, based on the Red Summer of 1919, and especially as a hotbed of political corruption and brutal gang violence, brought on in many respects by the national experiment in prohibition. Chicago meanwhile had become a major manufacturing center, a city that boasted of tall buildings and, far-and-away the second-largest city of the United States.

In the postwar period Chicago moved to continue in the tradition of building and growth. When Midway Airport on the southside, the nation's busiest, was deemed too small to handle large jet aircraft, the city build O'Hare on the northwest side, which then became the busiest. There was also a network of expressways—the Dan Ryan and Kennedy, Eisenhower, Eden's Expressway, and the Stevenson. Seeking to stay ahead of New York in the height of structures, Chicago built the Hancock Building in 1969, the Standard Oil Building in 1973, and—taking care to assure that it would be the tallest—the Sears Tower in 1974.

Chicago unfortunately revealed that it would not be spared the problems facing the so-called rustbelt urban areas. Faced with foreign competition, inefficient equipment or high labor costs, several traditional manufacturers closed shop or moved out. Faced with congestion, racial tension, simply wanting more space and a new start, Chicagoans left the city limits, probably going to suburban areas that pushed farther and farther from the central city. Chicago still might be the "second city" in people's minds and hearts, but it no longer ranked number two in population. The people left behind were increasingly nonwhite, unskilled, with limited education. Chicago's politics also changed. The mayor during the building boom, in office some 20 years, was Richard J. Daley. A political boss of the old style, Daley ran things as head of the Democrat Committee in Cook County. Clear evidence of his authority came in the tumultous events during the Democrat National Convention of 1968. Daley's death in 1976 destroyed a political coalition and personal control of city politics. There followed the brief tenure of Daley's protege, Michael Bilandic; a single term by "Calamity Jane" Byrne, the first female mayor; and in 1983 the victory of Congressman Harold Washington, the first black mayor. Reelected in 1987, Washington was preparing to start a second term when he died of a heart attack. Politics then seemed to return to "normalcy." Elected in a special election in 1989 was Richard M. Daley, son of "the boss."

Houston

Profile

Founded: 1836, incorporated 1837
Population: 1990, 1,630,553, rank 4; 1950, 596,163, rank 14
Population change, 1950–1990: +1,034,701
Racial/ethnic mix, 1990: white, 859,069; black, 457,990 (28.1%); American Indian, Eskimo, or Aleut, 4,126 (0.3%); Asian or Pacific Islander, 67,113 (4.1%); Hispanic origin, 450,483 (27.6%)
Per capita income (1989) by race: all races, $14,261; white, $19,817; black, $8,366; Indian, Eskimo, or Aleut, $12,239; Asian or Pacific Islander, $12,250; Hispanic, $7,021
Land area: 539.9 sq. mi.; Elevation, 49 ft
Counties: Fort Bend, Harris, Montgomery
Average temperature: January, 50.4°F; July, 82.6°F; annual average, 67.9°F
Annual precipitation: 46.07 inches (snowfall: 0.4 inches)
Clear days: 94; precipitation days: 107
Type of government: mayor-council; mayor in 1990: Katherine J. Whitmire

History and Development

Before arrival of the whites, the Karankawa Indians lived near what became Houston. The area became part of New Spain and after 1821 was in the province of Texas within the new state of Mexico. Two brothers, August C. and John K. Allen, founded Houston in 1836 and named it after Sam Houston, who led the army in the Texan war for independence and who was president of the Republic of Texas. Houston was capital of the new nation until 1840. As part of a state of the United States, Houston depended on agriculture, notably cotton, and a growing commerce—the railroad arrived in the 1850s and work was to begin on constructing a pathway by water to the sea. The Houston ship canal, finished in 1914, made the city a port even though it was 50 miles inland. Discovery of oil in the early 20th century did much to determine Houston's economy for many years to come.

The population soared between 1950 and 1980 when nearly everything seemed to go right. Factories expanded; a large petrochemical industry grew up. NASA established its center for the space program in Houston in 1964, and the following year, the pioneering Astrodome—pioneering because it is an indoor baseball and football stadium—opened. The economy boomed when oil prices soared after the first energy crisis of 1973. Thirty-two buildings of 500 or more feet high went up downtown, all but one of them built in the 1970s and 1980s. A glut in petroleum supplies and sharp drop in energy prices was devastating in the early 1980s, and it took the city several years to recover. Houston remained dependent on oil and oil-related industries, but there had been some effort to diversify the economy. The Manned Space Center—after 1973 the Lyndon B. Johnson Center—helped a great deal, as did expansion of industry and activities related to health and medical care.

Philadelphia

Profile

Founded: 1682, chartered 1701
Population: 1990, 1,585,577, rank 5; 1950, 2,071,605, rank 3
Population change, 1950–1990: −486,028
Racial/ethnic mix, 1990: white, 848,586; black, 631,936 (39.9%); American Indian, Eskimo, or Aleut, 3,434 (0.2%); Asian or Pacific Islander, 43,522 (2.7%); Hispanic origin, 89,193 (5.6%)
Per capita income (1989) by race: all races, $12,091; white, $15.027; black, $9,061; Indian, Eskimo, or Aleut, $10,146; Asian or Pacific Islander, $8,285; Hispanic, $6,053
Land area: 135.1 sq. mi.; Elevation: 28 ft
County: Philadelphia
Average temperature: January, 30.4°F; July, 76.7°F; annual average, 54.3°F
Annual precipitation: 41.4 inches (snowfall: 21.1 inches)
Clear days: 92; precipitation days: 116
Type of government: mayor-council; mayor in 1990: W. Wilson Goode

History and Development

The location of Philadelphia had much to do with its emergence as a leader in colonial America and in the life of the new nation. Located near the Atlantic coast, less than 100 miles from New York and slightly more than 100 from Washington, D.C., with two rivers to aid transportation, Philadelphia was in the midst of things. William Penn had founded the city; a pacifist and Quaker, he called it the city of brotherly love. With Benjamin Franklin as its most famous resident, Philadelphia was deeply enmeshed in the revolution and events that followed. Home of the Continental Congress, capital of the new nation, Philadelphia produced the Declaration of Independence and the Constitution. The Liberty Bell is still there.

Philadelphia grew into a large—second in population for many years—and influential city partly, again, because of location and because it could have access to a good mix of economic and social resources. Within its state one could find good farmland, coal and oil fields, and good transportation and manufacturing plants. The city probably reached its peak at approximately the time of the Second World War.

The decline that developed in the postwar period was slow and remarkably consistent with what went on in the nation as a whole. It came in spite of efforts in the 1950s and 1960s to clean up and restore what clearly had become an aged and worn-down inner city. But the better-educated and better-employed Philadelphians—most of them white—were going to the suburbs as they had been doing in many places. Factories moved to another state or another country. The city lost some of its tax base, and remaining residents found a city beset by racial tension. The power struggles played out in the contests for the highest local office. The mayor of the 1970s was Frank Rizzo, a white, aggressive, former police commissioner, and in the 1980s it was W. Wilson Goode, an African American who had good scores in race relations but left doubt about administrative competence.

In spite of its divisions and a major loss of population between 1970 and 1990, Philadelphia still had the markings of a first-class city, with museums and remarkable historic districts, competitive professional teams in all major sports, a new convention center, a marina, a trade center, and ongoing efforts to improve the center city.

San Diego

Profile

Founded: 1769, incorporated 1850
Population: 1990, 1,110,549, rank 6; 1950, 334,387, rank 31
Population change, 1950–1990: +726,236
Racial/ethnic mix, 1990: white, 745,406; black, 104,261 (9.4%); American Indian, Eskimo, or Aleut, 6,800 (0.6%); Asian or Pacific Islander, 130,945 (11.8%); Hispanic origin, 229,519 (20.7%)
Per capita income (1989) by race: all races, $16,401; white, $19,807; black, $10,375; Indian, Eskimo, or Aleut, $11,893; Asian or Pacific Islander, $10,628; Hispanic, $8,242
Land area: 324 sq. mi.; Elevation: 13 ft
County: San Diego
Average temperature: January, 57.4°F; July, 71°F; annual average, 64.2°F
Annual precipitation: 9.9 inches (snowfall: 0)
Clear days: 150; precipitation days: 41
Type of government: council-manager; mayor in 1990: Maureen O'Connor

History and Development

The Pacific coastal area that became San Diego was home to Native Americans known as Kumeyaay. Spaniards entered the harbor in 1542, and 60 years later the site was named in honor of San Diego de Alcalá, a Franciscan brother. In 1769 a Spanish official placed a military outpost and a mission in the bay area. The territory became part of Mexico in 1821 and in 1848 was part of the land lost to the United States in the U.S.-Mexican War. This area near the Mexican border developed slowly until the railroad, the Santa Fe, arrived in 1884. San Diego grew more rapidly in the early 20th century as a center for processing tuna and because its excellent deep-water harbor served as a major Pacific base for the U.S. Navy. During the Second World War, which included a Pacific war, the naval base expanded and numerous war-related industries, such as Consolidated Aircraft (later called General Dynamics), set up shop in the area.

Growth of the city after the Second World War stemmed from three major factors and several smaller ones. First was expansion of the industrial base, in which shipbuilding, production of electronic and oceanographic equipment joined with airplane factories. Military establishments continued to be a major force, as manifested in the huge San Diego Naval Base and the Marine station nearby. The third factor was a remarkable tourist industry that offered the ocean, the prestigious San Diego Zoo, a wild animal park in Escondido, the nationally famous Sea World, and professional sports teams. An end to the cold war left apprehension about how long southern California could count on continued presence of so many service personnel and the factories that produced goods for a war machine that was likely to shrink.

Detroit

Profile

Founded: 1701, incorporated 1806
Population: 1990, 1,017,974, rank 7; 1950, 1,849,568, rank 5
Population change, 1950–1990: −821,594
Racial/ethnic mix, 1990: white, 222,316; black, 777,916 (75.7%); American Indian, Eskimo, or Aleut, 3,655 (0.4%); Asian or Pacific Islander, 8,461 (0.8%); Hispanic origin, 28,473 (2.8%)
Per capita income (1989) by race: all races, $9,443; white, $11,947; black, $8,809; Indian, Eskimo, or Aleut, $8,241; Hispanic, $7,518
Land area: 138.7 sq. mi.; Elevation: 581 ft
County: Wayne
Average temperature: January, 22.4°F; July, 72.3°F; annual average, 48.6°F
Annual precipitation: 32.62 inches (snowfall: 41.1 inches)

Clear days: 75; precipitation days: 133
Type of government: mayor-council; mayor in 1990: Coleman A. Young

History and Development

When French explorers and fur traders reached the area that they would name Detroit, they met Wyandot, Ottawa, and other Indian tribes. Situated on Lake Saint Claire, close to Lakes Huron and Erie, Detroit was well located for commerce and other economic enterprise. The French explorer, Sieur de Cadillac, founded the area as a fur-trading post and eventually a fort. The British took control in 1760, and although the territory legally became American in 1783, the British did not depart until 1796. Friction with Indian tribes, and with the British, continued until at least the end of the War of 1812. Presence of the lakes, opening of the Erie Canal in 1925, and westward expansion of the railroad all helped Detroit move into manufacturing at an early stage.

It was of course development of the automobile that gave the city its identity, much of its livelihood, and many of its people in the 20th century. The automobile factories allowed Detroit to became the nation's third-largest city in the 1920s, and the automobile industry or its shrinkage would guide fortunes of the city for the rest of the century. The dismal times of the 1930s when people could not buy cars ended with return of prosperity during the Second World War. The people still could not buy cars, but the factories operated at full steam, producing war materials.

The postwar period produced an immediate burst of activity as factories strained to keep pace with pent-up demand. By 1950 Detroit's population approached the 2 million mark. Troubles soon began to surface. Schools were crowded, crime increased, and racial tension mounted. As had begun to happen to in other eastern and midwestern cities, people who could afford to do so, mostly whites, began to flee to the suburbs. The large and destructive race riot of 1967 gutted a portion of the city and drove more people away. The 1970s produced more bad news. Two energy crises (1973–74 and 1978–1980) depressed the demand for cars and introduced American car producers on a major scale to competition from factories abroad, notably Japan. Between 1972 and 1987 the city lost half of its stores and manufacturing plants. The population shrank to scarcely 1 million in 1990, three-fourths of whom were black people. There was a concerted effort to begin a recovery, largely under leadership of Coleman Young, the first black mayor, during the years 1973–90. From this effort came an impressive high-rise inner-city complex called Renaissance Center and such other structures as the Joe Louis arena, where the Red Wings played hockey. The "big three" American automobile companies reaffirmed an intent to maintain their headquarters inthe area. Detroit's bleeding seemed to have stopped, or slowed, and the city probably would end the century ranked in the top 10—but not for much longer.

Dallas

Profile

Founded: 1841, chartered 1871
Population: 1990, 1,006,877, rank 8; 1950, 296,994, rank 22
Population change, 1950–1990: +573,156
Racial/ethnic mix, 1990: white, 556,760; black, 296,994 (29.5%); American Indian, Eskimo, or Aleut, 4,792 (0.5%); Asian or Pacific Islander, 21,952 (2.2%); Hispanic origin, 210,240 (20.9%)
Per capita income (1989) by race: all races, $16,300; white, $22,898; black, $8,444; Indian, Eskimo, or Aleut, $10,048; Asian or Pacific Islander, $12,628; Hispanic, $7,093
Land area: 342.4 sq. mi.; Elevation: 596 ft
Counties: Collin, Dallas, Denton, Kaufman, Rockwell
Average temperature: January, 43.4°F; July, 85.3°F; annual average, 65.4°F

Annual precipitation: 33.7 inches (snowfall: 2.9 inches) Clear days: 138; precipitation days: 79
Type of government: council-manager; mayor in 1990: Annette Strauss

History and Development

This portion of Texas was still part of Mexico in 1841 when John Neely Bryan, a lawyer from Tennessee, built a log cabin alongside the Trinity River. The town that grew up Bryan named Dallas, probably in honor of George M. Dallas, vice president of the United States, 1845–49. By the time the village began to grow, Dallas was part of the state of Texas in the American union. The town's future was made promising in the 1870s when two railroads formed a union at Dallas. Cotton production and manufacture of farm tools aided the economy, and the discovery in 1930 of the huge East Texas oil field some 100 miles away provided a major boost.

The Second World War brought defense manufacturing and an aircraft industry, some of which remained after 1945. Vought Aircraft moved to Dallas; such companies as Texas Instruments expanded their operations. Dallas also became home to Southern Methodist University, a branch of the University of Texas, and other educational facilities. A "Goals for Dallas" campaign that in 1967 entailed a $175 million bond issue helped build Dallas–Ft. Worth International Airport (opened in 1974), a new city hall, and the Martin Luther King, Jr., Community Center. As with any area that depended heavily on the production and sale of oil, the city's fortunes fluctuated. Boom times in the 1970s gave way to a considerable economic downturn in the next decade. For many people Dallas remained memorable for a football organization that claimed to be "America's team," a long-running television series of the 1980s, and an exceptionally sorrowful afternoon in November 1963 when President John F. Kennedy was gunned down.

Phoenix

Profile

Founded: 1867, incorporated 1881
Population: 1990, 983,403, rank 9; 1950, 106,818, rank 98
Population change, 1950–1990: +876,585
Racial/ethnic mix, 1990: white, 803,332; black, 51,053 (5.2%); American Indian, Eskimo, or Aleut, 18,225 (1.9%); Asian or Pacific Islander, 16,303 (1.7%); Hispanic origin, 197,103 (20%)
Per capita income (1989) by race; all races, $14,096; white, $15,497; black, $8,734; Indian, Eskimo, or Aleut, $7,076; Asian or Pacific Islander, $12,643; Hispanic, $7,213
Land area: 419 sq. mi.; Elevation: 1,117 ft
County: Maricopa
Average temperature: January, 53.5°F; July, 93.5°F; annual average, 72.6°F
Annual precipitation: 7.66 inches (snowfall: trace)
Clear days: 214; precipitation days: 34
Type of government: mayor-council; mayor in 1990: Paul Johnson

History and Development

Jack Swilling and Darrel Dupa, two settlers who in 1860 had happened onto the valley now known as Phoenix, noted that many years earlier, the grand civilization of the Hohokam Indians had thrived in this parched land. Convinced that another great civilization would grow in this area, Dupa named the settlement after that bird of mythology that rose from the ashes every 500 years. Explored by the Spanish, claimed by Spain from 1539 to 1821, the area became part of Mexico and was part of that land awarded to the United States in the Mexican cession of 1848. Part of the New Mexico Territory until 1863 and afterward within the Territory of Arizona, the Phoenix settlement developed slowly. The weather was too hot, water too scarce; making a living left much to the imagination. Small wonder that Arizona was last of the original 48 states to join the union, and that in 1920, the largest city in the state, Phoenix, had fewer than 30,000 people.

Several forces combined to change the status of the city. One was the Second World War, which brought people to the area for military purposes. Second and probably most important was postwar development and mass production of air conditioning. The winters were pleasant enough to attract a growing tourist traffic, and with air conditioning the summers also became enjoyable. The third factor was establishment of an adequate supply of water—a process that began with completion of the Roosevelt Dam, 53 miles away, in 1911 and finished with a national project in 1986 to bring water in from the Colorado River. The foundation was laid for multifaceted industrial growth and for a city that could welcome droves of visitors or retirees flocking to the sunbelt where the living was easy and no one had to shovel snow. The population of Phoenix quadrupled between 1950 and 1960, and satellite suburbs such as Mesa, Tempe, and Sun City sprang up; by 1980 the population had doubled again, and Phoenix became the nation's ninth-largest city.

San Antonio

Profile

Founded: 1718, incorporated 1837

Population: 1990, 935,933, rank 10; 1950, 408,442, rank 25

Population change, 1950–1990: +590,463

Racial/ethnic mix, 1990: white, 676,082; black, 65,884 (7%); American Indian, Eskimo, or Aleut, 3,303 (0.4%); Asian or Pacific Islander, 10,703 (1.1%); Hispanic origin, 520,282 (55.6%)

Per capita income (1989) by race: all races, $10,884; white, $12,322; black, $8,730; Indian, Eskimo, or Aleut, $9,561; Asian or Pacific Islander, $11,075; Hispanic, $7,032

Land area: 333 sq. mi.; Elevation: 701 ft

County: Bexar

Average temperature: January, 50.4°F; July, 84.6°F; annual average, 68.7°F

Annual precipitation: 29.2 inches (snowfall: 0.5 inches)

Clear days: 110; precipitation days: 81

Type of government: council-mayor; mayor in 1990: Nelson Wolff

History and Development

The Coahuiltec Indians lived in the area of San Antonio for hundreds of years. Spaniard explorers traveled through the area in the 16th century and returned near the end of the 17th century to establish a village at a bend in the river. They named the village and the river San Antonio, and a nearby mission and military outpost was called the Alamo. Spanish rule ended in 1821 on establishment of Mexican independence. Settlers from the United States, some of whom had been invited in—first by the Spanish and later by Mexico—joined more recent American immigrants in protesting what they deemed unjust treatment by the Mexican government. In the Texan war of independence that followed in 1835–36 the most famous battle was the 13-day seige of the Alamo, which ended on March 6, 1836, with death of all Texan defenders. After Texas became a state, San Antonio grew as a stopping place for cattle drives and later, after 1877, as a railroad town. Discovery of oil in the 1890s aided growth, as did two world wars, during both of which the city served as a military center.

Development of San Antonio after 1945 continued to be connected to the national government. The area contained the headquarters of the Fifth Army at Ft. Sam Houston and no fewer than four air force bases, including Lackland. The military presence helped the area become a center for medical research. The city also benefited from tourism, the oil industry, good transportation facilities, and numerous manufacturing firms. The residents, more than half of whom were of Hispanic origin, elected in 1981 its first Mexican-American mayor. Henry G. Cisneros would serve four terms, reaching to 1989. San Antonio exploited to the fullest the river that meandered through and around the inner city. The river banks were lined with shops and restaurants, and the riverfront downtown featured the *Villita,* a square block of quaint houses and shops preserved in the Spanish tradition.

CHAPTER 13 Prominent and Representative Americans

Rachel Carson

Born in Springdale, Pennsylvania, on May 27, 1907, Rachel Louise Carson received a bachelor's degree from Pennsylvania College for Women in 1929 and a master's in biology from Johns Hopkins University in 1932. After college she taught at the University of Maryland and in the summer studied at Marine Biological Laboratory at Woods Hole, Massachusetts. In 1936 she began a long period of service as aquatic biologist with the U.S. Bureau of Fisheries.

From this post Carson developed an impressive reputation as editor of the agency's publications and as a writer about sea life. *Under the Sea* (1941) was followed by *The Sea Around Us,* which won the National Book Award for nonfiction in 1951, and *The Edge of the Sea* in 1955. Carson then shifted course. Four years of study into the use of pesticides led her to conclude that human efforts to conquer nature, to make life more comfortable and convenient had had a devastating effect on the earth and the living beings that shared the planet with people. To cite a single example, the use of chemical sprays, especially DDT, to destroy bugs and other pests had rendered birds who ate the bugs incapable of reproducing. If the process continued, the United States and the world would face a time when birds would fail to exist. Publication of this message, in the volume *Silent Spring,* which appeared in 1962, had an immediate profound effect. The government began an investigation into use of pesticides. The general public began to notice habits previously taken for granted. New organizations, public and private—notably the national Environmental Protection Agency (EPA)—sprang up. The movement probably culminated in (but did not end with) the year 1970, when Congress passed the Clean Air Act and National Environment Act, the EPA banned use of DDT, and the first celebration of Earth Day took place. The person who started these developments, by most accounts the founder of the modern environmentalist movement, was not on hand to to see what she had done. Rachel Carson died in April 1964.

Cesar Chavez

Cesar Estrada Chavez was born on March 31, 1927, on a small farm near Yuma, Arizona. Losing the land in the Great Depression of

Cesar Chavez, Hispanic leader and founder of the United Farm Workers Union (National Archives)

the 1930s, the Chavez family set out for California, becoming in effect, migrant workers. Cesar left school in seventh grade and worked in the fields until he joined the navy in 1944. Returning home at war's end, Chavez seemed destined for a life of following the cycles of the crops.

Chavez gradually came to the conclusion that farm workers' conditions could be improved through organization. Affiliated between 1952 and 1962 with the Community Service Organization, he became acquainted with methods of recruitment and organization that he would utilize in starting his own farm workers union in 1962—the United Farm Workers (UFW). The zenith of his campaign came between 1965 and 1970 when he won major contracts with grape companies and led a five-year national boycott of table grapes that ended in success. He had become nationally known and had acquired support and friendship of Senator Robert Kennedy of New York, who ran for the presidency in 1968.

Then Chavez' star began to fall. Kennedy was assassinated in June 1968. When contracts with the grape growers expired, many of them chose to affiliate with the Teamsters Union that had emerged as a rival to the UFW. Chavez's union became torn with factionalism, and new recruitment campaigns and another grape boycott failed to recapture the previous strength. Even so, he kept trying. Chavez was busy at work when he died suddenly in 1993. Still recognized nationally as a humanitarian and spokesman for the downtrodden, he was awarded posthumously the nation's highest civilian award, the Presidential Medal of Freedom in 1995.

Vine Deloria, Jr.

One of the most prolific Native American scholars and writers about Native Americans, Vine Deloria, Jr., was born on March 26, 1933, in Martin, South Dakota. A member of the Yankton Nakota (Sioux) tribe, he came from a distinguished family. His great grandfather had been a medicine man, his aunt Ella Deloria, a prominent ethnologist, his grandfather an Episcopal missionary, and his father a high official in the Episcopal Church. Vine, Jr., graduated from high school in Kent, Connecticut, spent two years (1954–56) in the U.S. Marine Corps, and received a B.A. (1958) from Iowa State University, a B.D. in theology from Augustana Lutheran Seminary in Rock Island, Illinois (1963), and a law degree from the University of Colorado (1970).

In his work and in his writing, Deloria became a spokesman for the rights, interests, welfare, and culture of Native Americans. His most famous publication, *Custer Died for Your Sins: An Indian Manifesto* (1969), was followed by *We Talk, You Listen* (1970), *God Is Red: A Native View of Religion* (1973), *Behind the Trail of Broken Treaties* (1974), and several others. His works constituted an attack on the injustice and treachery of the white man, but they also represented an appeal for Indian nationalism, against Indian assimilation into decadent American culture and in favor of Indian ethnicity and self-government.

Deloria was significant in the attention he drew to the status of Native Americans in the United States. His life also stands as an example of the supreme dilemma faced in seeking to remain Indian when the path to fortune, even a decent standard of living, ran down the white man's road. A vigorous defender of Indian culture, Deloria's education came from the public schools; he made his living selling books on the market and teaching in state universities.

Clint Eastwood

Tall, with rugged good looks, with a seemingly passive but in the end decisive demeanor, Clint Eastwood became one of the most popular movie actors in the United States by the the 1980s. Born on May 31, 1930, in San Francisco, he endured high school, worked vari-

ous menial jobs, spent four years in the army, and briefly attended Los Angeles City College before, in the mid-1950s, beginning to inquire into the possibility of a career as an actor. Success came slowly, and work at first involved bit parts based entirely on his physical appearance.

Eastwood's break came in 1959 with his being signed to a television series, a "new" western, *Rawhide*, which had a large cast of continuing characters of fairly equal rank. He was to be Rowdy Yates, the "ramrod," second in command to the "trail boss," played by Eric Fleming. *Rawhide* ran eight years, to 1966, and made Eastwood a familiar face to television audiences. The series also attracted the attention of Sergio Leone, an Italian director who enticed Eastwood to star in a series of openly violent and brutal Italian films about the old West that came to be known as spaghetti westerns. After three such movies between 1964 and 1967, Eastwood returned to the United States, started his own company, Malpaso, and began to produce an American version of the spaghetti western. Starting with *Hang 'em High,* he continued the image of the strong, silent loner, probably with a score to settle. One might not like the methods, but he got the job done. In 1971 Eastwood moved his character to the city, dressed him in a suit, gave him a badge, and named him Harry Callahan. The "Dirty Harry" series—there would be five films in all—helped project him to the top of the charts. Even President Reagan, never hesitant to steal someone else's lines, quoted Harry Callahan. Eastwood starred in and produced other types of films as well. There was a war movie, *Where Eagles Dare;* a musical, *Paint Your Wagon;* a drama, *Play Misty for Me;* and a film with an orangutan as a companion, *Any Which Way But Loose.* A tumultuous private life slowed him not at all. A long-running open affair with actress Sandra Locke led to a divorce from his wife and a split with, and later a suit by, Locke; an illegitimate child with another woman was followed by marriage to still another woman and another child. Clint simply squinted and went about his business.

Chris Evert

Chris Evert was one of the best American tennis players and one of the most popular female athletes in the second half of the 20th century. Born Christine Marie Evert on December 21, 1954, in Ft. Lauderdale, Florida, she began to play tennis at age six, with her father, a teaching professional, as coach. By age 15 she was the top amateur player in the country; at age 18, in December 1972, after defeating some of the best professional players and winning two major tournaments, she turned professional.

In the course of a professional career of 17 years, Chris, or Chrissy, put up superlative numbers in many categories. She did not have superior athletic talent, but she made the most of what she had. A dedicated baseline player, preferring hard courts, especially clay, she won the French Open, played on clay, seven times and in one stretch won 125 straight matches on clay courts. Even though her worst surface probably was grass, she won three singles titles on Wimbledon's prestigious grass courts. There also would be six U.S. Open titles and two Australian, a total of 157 singles titles and, starting in 1975, a period of 133 consecutive weeks ranked number one in the world. Some of her most monumental battles were with Martina Navratilova; there would be 80 such matches, at the conclusion of which Navratilova had a small edge of 43 wins to 37.

Evert's popularity began with competence on the court, but she also scored with demeanor and charm. Always poised and self-composed, she took wins and losses, good calls and bad, with grace. She was pretty and photogenic, and the press followed all aspects of her private life that it was able to see. Her engagement at age 19 to dashing tennis firebrand Jimmy Connor, age 21, seemed a match made in heaven, but the wedding never came off. Marriage to British tennis player John Lloyd in 1979 lasted eight years.

Evert retired in 1989, still ranked fourth in the world. She had remarried—to skier Andy Mill—in 1988, and the couple would produce three children. The popularity of women's tennis continued to grow and became perhaps more interesting than the men's game, which often was dominated by an overpowering serve. Knowledgeable observers knew that Chris Evert, ever the steady ground stroker, had much to do with it.

Ella Fitzgerald

She became known as "The First Lady of Song," and during the period from the 1940s through the 1960s, she probably was the foremost female musical technician and jazz vocalist in the country. Born in Newport News, Virginia, in 1918, growing up in Yonkers, New York, in the era of segregation, Ella Fitzgerald began her career in what would be deemed "black" circumstances: singing at the Apollo Theater and Savoy Ballroom in Harlem, as a vocalist for Chick Webb's band.

Blessed with perfect pitch and clear, masterfully controlled voice, Ella went on to establish a national and international reputation as a genuine musical artist. Commonly identified as a jazz singer, adept at improvisation and extemporaneous "scat" vocalizing, she seemed to prefer what she called the Great American Songbook—the music of Cole Porter, George Gershwin, Irving Berlin, and other composers of the midtwentieth century. Although she often appeared with such black big band leaders as Duke Ellington, Count Basie, and Louis Armstrong, she went far beyond the color line in her recordings, concerts, and guest appearances on radio and television with Bing Crosby, Dinah Shore, Ed Sullivan, and popular variety shows of the 1940s, 1950s, and 1960s. Her music, in fact, was mostly white people's music.

Starting in 1938 with a playful tune, "A-Tisket, A-Tasket," she recorded countless singles and more than 250 albums. Winner of 13 Grammy Awards, Ella was a singer's singer, a musical artist, as opposed to someone who simply was pleasant to listen to. Her highest praise came from such musical technicians as Frank Sinatra and Mel Tormé. Her concerts at home and abroad were peopled with not merely jazz enthusiasts but students of the artform. While at the peak of her career in the 1950s, she continued to perform into the 1990s. She died in 1995 at age 78 from complications emerging from diabetes.

Betty Friedan

Although Betty Friedan would accumulate a long list of publications, titles, awards, and honors, she is and will be known for a single piece of work, her book, The Feminine Mystique, published in 1963. Born Betty Goldstein on February 4, 1921, in Peoria, Illinois, she grew up in a family of comfort and means. After graduating from prestigious Smith College in 1942 and graduate work at Berkeley, she—in the fashion of most young women in the budding world of postwar America—married (in 1947, to Carl Friedan), had three children, and settled into life as the middle-class mother and housewife.

On the whole, Betty found that lifestyle disappointing. Marriage and motherhood created a place and offered its rewards, but it did not leave her fulfilled, challenged, able to use her considerable education and talents. A survey she sent in 1957 by chance to 200 graduates of Smith College revealed remarkably similar feelings in former academic sisters. Now Friedan had validation of her feelings and a thesis for what would become a seminal book: the difference between appearance and reality in postwar suburban America, the loss of identity, the anxiety and hopelessness of the modern female. The home had become, she wrote, a "comfortable concentration camp."

Critics made their points about The Feminine Mystique. The survey was notoriously narrow and surely elitist. The alternative for many women in that day was not being a brain surgeon, fashion designer, or—as in the case of Friedan—a successful writer and public speaker but long hours in one spot on an assembly line, beside which "staying at home," as they put it, was not so bad. But Friedan had clearly put her finger on something, and her points took on greater meaning as the economy expanded, more women went to work, society opened up, and work became more automated, technical, and less physically demanding.

Remarkable success of The Feminine Mystique led to countless speaking engagements, more publications on feminism, equality, aging. She helped found National Organization for Women (NOW) in 1966, Woman's Strike for Equality (1970), and National Woman's Political Caucus (1971). Betty Friedan's name always appears in the highest ranking of founders of the modern feminist movement. Many people date its origin to 1963.

Billy Graham

The evangelism of Billy Graham extended through the entire second half of the 20th century. Except possibly for the pope, he became the religious leader best-known to Americans. During the 1970s and 1980s he faced competition from a group of more dynamic and colorful televangelists. He survived that challenge, if with a somewhat diminished following, partly because of the shortcomings of his competitors, partly because of the steadiness of his program and his reputation.

William Franklin Graham was born in Charlotte, North Carolina, on November 7, 1918. He attended Bob Jones University and Florida Bible Institute and in 1943 graduated from Wheaton (Illinois) College. An ordained Baptist minister, he pastored a Baptist Church in Western Springs, a suburb of Chicago, in 1943, and in 1944 he began to hold open-air preachings in Chicago to returning armed-service members. He joined the national Crusade for Youth for Christ, also based in Chicago, and led his first bonafide crusade, a two-month series of rallies designed to recharge the faithful and convert the uncommitted, in Los Angeles in 1949.

In 1950 he formed the Billy Graham Evangelistic Association and began to speak on Hour of Decision on ABC radio. During the next half-century, he traveled to virtually every continent and in many countries held rallies during which he urged people to make a "decision for Christ." Audiences at these gatherings were huge, almost without exception, and although it was impossible to measure the level of influence or of personal commitment, the number who responded at the end to an invitation to come forward—taken as an interest in conversion—also was impressive.

Graham's evangelism stood out because it was long lasting and far reaching, consistent, appealing but not grandiose, and free of personal or financial scandal. He was an adviser to every president beginning with Eisenhower, up to the 1990s, and although he considered himself a Democrat, he seemed to do better with the Republicans. Visibly aging and suffering from Parkinson's disease as the century ended, unsteady afoot but still mentally sharp, he denied any intent to retire. Even so, he turned more routine duties over to subordinates and to his son, Franklin, the heir apparent. Billy Graham was as close as one could come to being America's preacher.

Bob Hope

Bob Hope came to symbolize several themes: the golden age of radio in the 1930s and 1940s, triviality of the comedy films of the 1940s and 1950s, patriotism and service to country in his many trips to entertain servicemen abroad, and longevity in the American entertainment business.

Born Leslie Townes Hope in Eltham, England, on May 29, 1903, son of an English stonemason and Welsh concert singer, he came with his family to the United States, settling in Cleveland. Bob, who became a citizen in 1920, had his mind set on show business from the beginning. For a period of 15 years he traveled the vaudeville circuit, trying almost anything that would bring a laugh—dancing (he had taken lessons), blackface routines—but what seemed to work best was his stand-up, rapid-fire jokes. His big break came in 1934 when, after appearance at the Capitol Theater in New York and on radio, NBC signed him to a weekly radio show with Pepsodent toothpaste as sponsor. Appearing on Tuesday nights for 15 years, he became one of the giants of radio and of the American entertainment business. A film career of some 70 movies extended from the 1930s to the end of the 1960s. Except for a brief experiment with drama in the 1950s, Hope's films entailed light-hearted comedy. Although he received several special Academy Awards, he won no Oscar for acting—never even had a nomination, but his films remained a big screen fixture for a quarter-century.

Hope's celebrated trips to entertain troops abroad began with the Second World War and were in tune with the philosophy that everyone should do something to assist in the war effort. After the war they continued and became annual events at Christmas, extending through the Gulf War of 1990–91. In time they became the subject of television specials. His style was to appear on stage in loose-fitting shirt, carrying a golf club, telling jokes about the military, his colleagues, and conditions in the United States, many of the jokes carrying sexual innuendoes. The appeal of Hope's humor surely diminished with passage of years, but he tried to keep his troupe staffed with contemporary performers, particularly sexy women.

A very wealthy man, recipient of virtually every civilian award, friend and golfing partner of presidents, especially the Republicans, Hope saw the end of the century and people hoped that he would make it to 100. They knew that he represented the last of the lot.

Hubert H. Humphrey

Born in Wallace, South Dakota, on May 27, 1911, Hubert Horatio Humphrey would establish an identity as a socially active, liberal Democrat from Minnesota. Son of a small-town pharmacist, he took a crash course in pharmacy in Denver, studied political science at the University of Minnesota (B.A., 1939) and Louisiana State University (M.A., 1940), and did work on the Ph.D. at Minnesota. Rejected by the armed forces, he worked for state government and taught college during the war. After promoting a merger of the Democrat and Farmer-Labor Parties in Minnesota, he was elected mayor of Minneapolis in 1945 and began his political career.

Cofounder of the liberal Americans for Democratic Action (ADA), sponsor of a strong civil-rights position in the contentious Democrat Convention of 1948, and elected to the Senate in that year, Humphrey would become the most persistent and conspicuous spokesman for liberal social and economic causes in the quarter-century that would follow. He was always at the forefront of the struggle for civil-rights legislation. Essentially a New Deal activist, an advocate of reforming (not destroying) capitalism, and a strong anticommunist, Humphrey nonetheless became a target for conservative politicians and private citizens looking for someone to brand as pink if not red.

Selected by Lyndon Johnson as his running mate in 1964, Humphrey spent an uneasy four years as vice president—delighted, no doubt, with social legislation of the Great Society in 1964–65, but deeply troubled with the deepening crevasse of the Vietnam War. Johnson's decision to not seek reelection in 1968 largely left the Democrat candidacy for Humphrey, but this prize that he long had sought now became a mixed blessing at best. The irony of the election of 1968 came in the intensity with which the activist left attacked this man who—before they were old enough to know—had been their

spokesman, their labeling of this individual who usually had been a step ahead of the political crowd as agent of the establishment. Humphrey could not escape the Vietnam War; his party and the country were so divided that it was remarkable that the election of 1968 was so close. After defeat Humphrey came back to the senate (in 1970) and served for the rest of his life. His death from cancer in January 1978 was prolonged enough for him to receive the acolades he deserved. Some believed that in the two decades following the Second World War no one in government had been better.

Daniel K. Inouye

Daniel K. Inouye was as legitimate a war hero as one could imagine; he has been since 1959 the most prominent Japanese American in the politics and government of the United States. Born on September 7, 1924, in Honolulu, Hawaii, of Japanese immigrant parents, he grew up on the island of Oahu and graduated from high school in 1942, shortly after the Second World War began. At a time when his ethnic brothers and sisters in the United States were interned in camps, Inouye enlisted in the army in 1943 and became a member of an all-volunteer, all-Japanese 442nd Regimental Combat Team. Assigned to the war in Europe, he spent many months in combat. The courage he displayed and the wounds he received left him with many medals and without a right arm. Arguably, he deserved a Medal of Honor.

After the war, he graduated from the University of Hawaii and George Washington law school, entered politics in Hawaii, became the new state's first congressman in 1959, and has been a U.S. senator since 1962. A Democrat, he consistently supported liberal social and economic programs in Washington. Highlights of his career included being keynote speaker at the Democrat Convention of 1968, member of the Watergate Committee, and chair of the Intelligence Committee

Danny Inouye, before he became a badly wounded war hero, a U.S. senator from Hawaii, and a Medal of Honor recipient (Courtesy Senator Daniel K. Inouye)

in 1976 and of the Senate Iran-Contra Committee in 1987. Inouye has been an illustrious defender of his nation and a worthy and effective representative of his state and ethnic grouping. In the year 2000 a special government organization reviewed the military record of the Japanese Americans during the Second World War. Taking into account prejudice and other wartime circumstances, the government concluded that several Japanese who had received the second-highest military award, the Distinguished Service Cross, in fact deserved the nation's highest medal. By these means Danny Inouye finally received the Congressional Medal of Honor.

Lyndon B. Johnson

Lyndon Baines Johnson was born on a ranch near Stonewall, Texas, on August 27, 1908. He studied at Southwest State Teachers College, taught school briefly, married heiress Claudia "Lady Bird" Taylor, entered Texan politics, and was elected as a Democrat, New Deal congressman in 1936. He spent eight years in the House, had very brief military service during the Second World War. In the House and as United States senator 1949–61, he developed considerable political skills; becoming Senate majority leader in 1955 made him, still in his 40s, the second most powerful man in government. Placed on the victorious national ticket in 1960, he became on John F. Kennedy's assassination in November 1963 the 36th president of the United States.

During a presidency that lasted five years Johnson established a mixed legacy. Building on his contacts and knowledge of Congress and

The "Johnson Treatment." President Johnson "confers" with Abe Fortas, friend, adviser, short-time justice of the Supreme Court. (LBJ Library Photo by Yoichi Okamoto)

his reputation as a Democrat centrist, and strengthened by bountiful victories—for the presidency and in Congress—in the election of 1964, Johnson compiled a list of legislative victories second in the 20th century only to the first two terms of the presidency of Franklin D. Roosevelt. Two civil-rights laws, Medicare, and an Equal Opportunity Act were major ingredients in the program of the Great Society of 1964–65. The undoing of Johnson's presidency came largely but not entirely from the course of the Vietnam War. Having inherited from Kennedy a losing situation in South Vietnam, he chose to try to win the war by vastly increasing American participation. Commitment of a force of 500,000 probably staved off a South Vietnamese defeat, but it caused mounting American casualties and produced—and gave no prospect of producing—neither a victory nor a foreseeable end. Escalation of the war corresponded with growing social and political tension that took two forms: racial tension in the cities and antiwar demonstrations and a general unruliness by college-based activists and their fellow travelers. However one defined and explained this multisided restiveness, under the presidency of Lyndon Johnson the country seemed to be coming apart. Johnson's decision to not seek reelection in 1968 (announced in March) was stunning but not unwise. He left office in January 1969 a discredited president and a troubled man. Speculation that passage of time—with better understanding of his legislative record, a broader distribution of blame for Vietnam—would cause Johnson's reputation to improve. No such transformation had taken place, or even started, at the time of his death on January 22, 1973.

Barbara Jordan

Barbara Charline Jordan was born on February 21, 1936, the third and youngest daughter of Benjamin Jordan, a black Baptist minister in Houston. An honors student in high school, she graduated magna cum laude from Texas Southern University in 1956. Her major was political science, and her speciality, in high school as in college, was debating. After earning a law degree from Boston University in 1959, she returned to Houston to practice law.

Elected as a Democrat in 1966, she became the first black person in the state senate of Texas since 1883 in the immediate aftermath of the period of Reconstruction. After six years in the state senate, near the end of which she was chosen president pro tem, she ran for Congress in 1972. Her election from the 18th district in Houston made her the first southern black elected to Congress in the 20th century and the first black and the first woman ever elected from Texas. During three terms in Congress, she focused on social legislation, workman's compensation, voting rights, and the interests of poor people and minority groups. She participated in the preimpeachment hearings for Richard Nixon. The highlight of her political career came when she gave a riveting keynote address at the Democrat National Convention of 1976. Rhetoric was her forte.

She retired from politics in 1979 to return to Texas where she added to her considerable collection of awards and distinctions, and taught political ethics at the Lyndon B. Johnson School of Public Affairs at the University of Texas. Eventually confined to a wheelchair by multiple sclerosis, she died from pneumonia in January 1996.

A pathfinder for her race and gender, Jordan was a spokesperson for disadvantaged people of all kinds. She made her case vigorously, with decorum and absence of rancor, and always with eloquence.

George F. Kennan

George Frost Kennan had two overlapping careers. He served 26 years as a professional foreign service officer, much of the time at very high level; he was a scholar and author of many publications about diplomacy and especially American relations with the Soviet Union.

Born in Milwaukee on February 16, 1904, he graduated from Princeton University in 1925 and joined the foreign service in 1926. His assignments took him to Geneva, Hamburg, the three Baltic States, and Berlin and, after two years' (1929–31) study of Russian language, culture, and history, to the Soviet Union in 1933 and again at the end of the Second World War in 1944–46.

Kennan attracted attention in Washington in 1946 when he sent to the state department a "long telegram" explaining the sources of emerging trouble with the Soviet Union and recommending a response. Called to the United States, he became head of the Policy Planning Staff in the Department of State, in which capacity he began implementation of the policy he had recommended. In 1947 he anonymously explained the policy to the public in an article in the periodical *Foreign Affairs*. In this essay, signed only by "X," (he did not want the piece to appear as a statement of the government) he revealed dislike and distrust of the Soviet government but not of the Russian people, and he recommended the application of counterpressure to Soviet expansionism. Kennan thus unofficially became, and to the end of the cold war remained, identified as author of a policy that would last, in one form or another, as long as the cold war lasted. The policy was called containment.

Thereafter Kennan's career fluctuated for a few years. He was appointed ambassador to the Soviet Union, but when the Soviets refused to accept him, Kennan, becoming displeased with the increasing military tone of American policy, retired and went to Princeton to study. Appointed by President Kennedy, he would be ambassador to Yugoslavia during the years 1961–63, after which he returned to Princeton and remained as a teacher and scholar until he retired at the end of the 1980s.

There he produced several volumes and other pieces about diplomacy and the Soviet Union. *Russia Leaves the War* (1956), about the First World War, and *Memoirs* (1967) won Pulitzer Prizes. His *Sketches from a Life* (1989) was a best-seller. Considered one of the wisest and most experienced individuals about Eastern European affairs, his opinion often was sought out. The collapse of communism and the Soviet Union—which, in a fashion he had predicted in 1947—seemed to reaffirm, however belatedly, the depth of his wisdom.

John F. Kennedy

John Fitzgerald Kennedy had the distinction of being the youngest man elected to the presidency (but not the youngest to serve), the first president born in the 20th century, and to the end of the 20th century the first and only Catholic to be president. He was born on May 29, 1917, into what would be a large Irish-American family headed by Joseph P. Kennedy, a wealthy businessman, financier, and operator in local and national Democrat politics. After attending several prestigious private schools, Kennedy graduated from Harvard in 1940 and saw significant combat duty as a PT boat commander in the Second World War, which left him with a back injury and several decorations.

With much help from his father and the Kennedy clan, he was elected to the House of Representatives in 1946, serving three terms in the House and then as a U.S. senator between 1953 and 1961. Effective campaigning, organization, and generous financing made it possible for him to narrowly defeat Vice President Richard Nixon in the presidential election of 1960. As a legislator, Kennedy had been anticommunist,

Kennedy at the wall. In the aftermath of a third Berlin crisis, President Kennedy visits the recently constructed Berlin Wall, June 26, 1963. (John Fitzgerald Kennedy Library)

centrist, practical, and not particularly outstanding; as president he exuded a refreshing and inspiring youthfulness, confidence, and vigor. He approached pressing issues of the time with caution but usually ended up on the side of the reformers. His New Frontier legislative program, which included such measures as Medicare and a major civil rights act, did not pass, but most of it became part of Lyndon Johnson's program of the Great Society. In foreign affairs he confronted a succession of challenges and tensions that included such crises as the Bay of Pigs episode of 1961, the third confrontation over Berlin in 1961, and the harrowing crisis over Soviet missiles in Cuba in October 1962. Kennedy began his presidency a cold warrior and ended it a cold warrior, albeit a more sober and cautious one. His assassination on November 22, 1963, ended a presidency of approximately 1,000 days and provoked enormous national mourning for a charismatic young leader who seemed to be reaching his stride. Later revelations about Kennedy's sexual escapades and other aspects of scandal in the family raised serious questions about character, but they did not appear to destroy the mystique and appeal of this knight of Camelot.

Martin Luther King, Jr.

Martin Luther King, Jr., was born in the Deep South, in Atlanta, Georgia, in 1929, at a time of segregation of the races. A stable and loving family life (his father was a Baptist minister) helped spare him from from the hopelessness that afflicted many young black men of that era. He graduated from Morehouse College in 1948, from Grozer Theological Seminary (with a divinity degree) in Chester, Pennsylvania, in 1951, and from Boston University with a Ph.D. in theology in 1955. His selection as new pastor of the Dexter Avenue Baptist Church in Montgomery, Alabama, by chance placed him "at the creation" of the Civil Rights Movement. The year he arrived, 1955, was the year of the boycott of the segregated Montgomery bus system, perhaps the earliest expression of black activism against the racial system of the South. The young minister was asked to lead the movement. From this point until his death in 1968, King would stand at the forefront of the movement against racial discrimination in the United States (chiefly the South) as its eloquent spokesman. Seeking to combine Christian love with an aggressive but peaceful activism, he moved to achieve clearly stated objectives of his Civil Rights movement: integration and equal treatment of his people. In a later stage he attacked the American war in Vietnam and injustice on all fronts.

King's principal attributes were eloquence, persistence, and raw courage. Combining the style and spirit of the African-American preacher with the content of a social reformer, he gave numerous quotable speeches, the most moving of which was the "I Have a Dream" address during the march on Washington in 1963. Assailed by segments of the white population and by a new chorus of separatist, militant blacks, faced with constant danger—his house was bombed in

Martin Luther King, Jr., answers questions in Kalamazoo, Michigan, October 18, 1963. (Western Michigan University Archives and Regional Collections)

1956, he was stabbed (by a black woman) in 1958 and was repeatedly jailed and threatened—he stuck to his message and to the strategy of nonviolent passive resistance. He was on a segment of his mission when he was assassinated by a white man in Memphis on March 10, 1968.

In the aftermath of his death, King's reputation—somewhat on the order of Abraham Lincoln and John F. Kennedy—would soar. He had been experiencing a mixed public reception and serious internal challenges to his leadership, but a brutal and tragic ending essentially put these assaults to rest. Surely the most celebrated African American in U.S. history, King—living or dead—would accumulate honors ranking from a Nobel Peace Prize (in 1964) to an astonishing number of streets, schools, and buildings bearing his name and the designation of his birthday as a national holiday, with public ceremonies and commemorations that went beyond even the greatest of America's great: Abraham Lincoln and George Washington.

Henry Kissinger

Henry Alfred Kissinger was born in Färth, Germany, on May 23, 1923. Of German-Jewish parentage, he fled with his family in 1938 to the United States to escape the regime of Adolf Hitler. He studied at City College of New York, served in the army between 1942 and 1947, and studied at Harvard, where in 1954 he received the Ph.D. in political science. Remaining at Harvard, he held several posts and eventually became professor of government in the Center for International Affairs in 1962. A for-

eign-policy specialist and an author (*Nuclear Weapons and Foreign Policy, 1957*), he frequently advised politicians, both Republican and Democrat.

Appointed by Richard Nixon as assistant to the president for National Security in 1969, he immediately eclipsed secretary of state William Rogers in running foreign policy of the Nixon administration. In 1973, at the start of his second term, Nixon made him secretary of state. He stayed on to the end of the administration of Gerald Ford, who had replaced Nixon in 1974. Thus Kissinger had eight years at the helm of American foreign policy.

In his studies, experience, and preference, Kissinger placed emphasis on traditional European-style diplomacy, called *Realpolitik,* or realism. The objectives were pursuit of national interest and international stability and order. The tools were unemotional diplomacy, the search for a convergence of interests, and the use, or willingness to use, simple power. Stability was expected to come through a balance of power. In the 1970s Kissinger received the bulk of credit for a series of moves in foreign policy: opening dialogue with China (1972), détente with the USSR (1972), withdrawal from Vietnam and an armistice (1973) for which he received a Nobel Peace Prize, armistice between Israel and Egypt (1973) and between Israel and Syria (1974), and disengagement in Sinai (1975). President Ford was in awe of these maneuvers, and so were many people abroad and in the United States. There even emerged a Kissinger for president movement—which, of course, would have entailed changing the Constitution, which forbade a foreign-born person from holding the office.

Ray Kroc's first McDonald's franchise, Des Plaines, Illinois, 1955 (Used with permission from McDonald's Corporation)

Kissinger left office in 1977 after Ford had been defeated, and there was little interest later in bringing him back. His style was criticized for being secretive, too personal, and indifferent to human rights and human suffering. He wrote penetrating books on diplomacy (*Memoirs*, 1979 and 1982, and *Diplomacy*, 1994), headed a consulting firm, and advised Republican leaders. Whenever a major issue of world affairs came up, the press sought him out, and—Kissinger always had something perceptive to say.

Ray Kroc

Raymond Albert Kroc spent much of his life seemingly in a hurry to make it big—or at least to make it. Born on October 5, 1902, in Oak Park, Illinois, he spent many childhood days watching the Chicago Cubs play baseball and learning to play the piano. He lied himself into the army at age 15 as the First World War was coming to an end. Kroc spent the long interwar years in enterprises that included playing the piano in clubs and on radio, but mostly as a traveling salesman. He believed that he had found his niche in the late 1930s when he helped found and then became sole owner of Prince Castle, a company that produced a multi-spindled milk-shake mixer called a multimixer.

Anxious to get his share of a booming post–Second World War economy by selling multimixers, Kroc in April 1954 investigated a small drive-in restaurant in San Bernardino, California, that used no fewer than eight of his mixers. The owners, the McDonald brothers, had made the place a model of simplicity, efficiency, and spotless cleanliness. It served only hamburgers, french fries, and drinks; all business was carry-out, service time was approximately a minute, and the line reached outside the door. Kroc quickly surmised that if this idea could be expanded, he would be able to sell many multimixers. Having persuaded the McDonald brothers to make him exclusive agent of franchising, he opened his own store at Des Plains, near his home in Chicago, and continued selling franchises. In 1960 there were 238 units, and a year later Kroc bought the McDonald brothers out. By the end of the sixties 1,500 McDonald hamburger stores operated worldwide, and by the mid-1980s a new store was literally opening somewhere every day. In a quest to sell mixers, he had become a master at marketing franchises; to sell franchises, of course, it was necessary to sell hamburgers. Shifting his attention, Kroc established a reputation for truly notable charitable work and as a colorful businessman and owner of a baseball team. The Cubs were not for sale so he bought the San Diego Padres. But when he died in January 1984, he still was known as the hamburger man, the individual who had made McDonald's and in some considerable measure the mushrooming American fast-food industry.

Nancy Lopez

Nancy Marie Lopez was born to Mexican-American parents on January 6, 1957, in Torrence, California. She grew up in lower-middle class surroundings in Roswell, New Mexico. As a little girl she began to play golf, a game she learned from her parents, who went to the links as often as they found the time. Her father, detecting that she had talent and temperament for the game, became her coach. She won her first tournament at age 9; by the time she was 11, she could beat her father. Nancy was the only female and the best player on the state championship golf team at Godland High School in Roswell. She accepted a golf scholarship at the University of Tulsa, and after winning amateur and intercollegiate titles as well as athletic awards, she left school after two years in 1977 to become, at age 19, a professional golfer.

From the beginning she was the dominant player and feature attraction on a fledgling LPGA tour. By 1987 she had won 35 titles and numerous awards and was inducted into the LPGA Hall of Fame. Mar-

rying major league baseball player Ray Knight in 1982, Nancy tried to balance a professional and family life, but bearing three children between 1983 and 1988 was demanding and surely reduced her time on the course. No longer dominant, she remained a competitive player through the 1990s. Nancy Lopez probably contributed more than anyone to make professional woman's golf popular; she was for the woman's game what Arnold Palmer was for the men's. Some people stressed her contribution to gender, others to ethnicity; to many observers she simply was a skilled athlete and an admirable individual who carried herself with modesty and grace.

Malcolm X

He was born Malcolm Little in Omaha, Nebraska, on May 19, 1925. He grew up in Lansing, Michigan, until age 16 when he went to live with a half-sister in Roxbury, Massachusetts, a black district of Boston. Between 1941 and 1946 he held various "negro" jobs and soon became involved in the rackets—drugs, prostitution, robbery—of Boston and Harlem. Convicted in 1946 of larceny and burglary, he was sentenced to prison in Charlestown, Massachusetts, where he became acquainted with the Black Muslim faith as manifested in the Nation of Islam. Released in 1952, he went to Detroit, abandoned his "slave name," became Malcolm X, and went to work for the Muslims.

In the process of recruiting for his organization, Malcolm set a tone vastly different from Martin Luther King, Jr., and other accommodationist leaders who were active at that time. The white man was the devil, he said, and must pay for his sins. Blacks should win their freedom "by any means necessary," which included armed confrontation if it came to that point. An articulate and compelling speaker, he favored separation from whites, even moving to Africa, but he also was a vigorous spokesman for black pride, self-help, and freedom from drugs and other vices that once had been a part of his life.

Malcolm's confrontational style and expression of delight at any misfortune that befell the whites produced uneasiness in the Nation of Islam, as well as jealousy with his growing popularity. His open satisfaction with the assassination of President Kennedy in 1963—"chickens coming home to roost," he said—led to his suspension from the group. The year 1964 produced Malcolm's formation of a new organization called "Muslim Mosque, Inc.," two trips to Africa and the Middle East, his conversion to orthodox Islam, a softening of his racial line, and intensification of the split with the parent Muslim sect. His home in New York was firebombed in February 1965, and on February 21, while addressing followers at the Audubon Ballroom in Harlem, he was cut down by assassins. In 1966 three Black Muslims were convicted of the murder.

Malcolm became markedly more popular in death than in life. With passage of time and opening up of the dialogue about race, he was honored as a black man willing to speak the truth without equivocation. Publication in 1965, after his death, of his autobiography did wonders for his reputation, as did appearance in 1992 of a movie about Malcolm, directed by Spike Lee. No one could rival King as leader of the struggle for black equality, but Malcolm, who offered an alternative course, by the 1990s surely ranked second.

Thurgood Marshall

The Civil Rights movement in the postwar period was in its immediate objectives an effort to change the law. No black person—probably no person—had more to do with law as pertaining to African Americans than Thurgood Marshall. Born in Baltimore on July 3, 1908, he graduated from Lincoln University, a black school, in 1930; received a law degree from Howard University, also a school for blacks, in 1933; and joined the NAACP in 1936; and became the organization's legal counsel in 1938. From the start of the 1940s to the early

1960s, Marshall carried the load in the effort to overturn the system of segregation in the southern states. Point-by-point and step-by-step, Marshall won his case. In 1944 (Smith v. Allwright) black people gained the right to vote in primaries in Texas; in 1950 (Sweatt v. Painter) segregation—in truth, exclusion—of black people ended in the law school of the University of Texas. The crowning achievement for Marshall and the movement was the Brown decision of 1954 that overturned segregation in the public school system. The Supreme Court's unanimous decision borrowed generously from the sociological and psychological argument Marshall had made before the court.

In the 1960s Marshall moved into the second phase of his career: as a public servant of the government of the United States. Between 1961 and 1967 he was judge of the United States Court of Appeals and solicitor general of the United States. In 1967 President Johnson afforded him the high honor of becoming the first African American on the Supreme Court of the United States. Interpretations differed, of course, about Marshall's 25 years on the bench, but there has been little effort to define him as a penetrating and perceptive legal scholar. Some critics were downright brutal, calling him incompetent, a justice who found in law and the Constitution what he thought should be there. He joined the liberal activist majority in the last phase of the Warren Court and generally stuck to his guns. Placing the rights of individuals in a privileged position, he wished to see the Civil Rights movement continue. He dissented in the Bakke decision of 1978 that opposed racial quotas in college admission, strongly supported affirmative action, and adamantly opposed the death penalty. He retired at age 82 in 1991 and died two years later, no doubt proud to be labeled the black people's lawyer.

Joe McCarthy

Joseph Raymond McCarthy is noted for the period from 1947 to 1957 that he spent as a U.S. senator. In the middle of that tenure, during the years 1950–1954, he began a major movement, became one of the most prominent people in the country, and added at least one new word to the English language. Born on November 14, 1908, in Grand Chute, Wisconsin, he graduated from Marquette University in 1935, served as a circuit court judge before the Second World War, served as a marine in the South Pacific, returned to the judiciary after the war, and was elected as a Republican to the U.S. Senate in the election of 1946.

Undistinguished in his first term in office, McCarthy searched for a theme that would attract attention and secure reelection in 1952. Settling on the issue of the internal threat of communism, he began in 1950 to charge that the national government had several disloyal communist employees that the Harry Truman administration allowed to remain in office. Already a sensitive topic in this time of spy trials and an emerging cold war, communism in government became a major battle cry in the period preceeding and immediately following the election of 1952. McCarthy's role was as chief and most reckless accusor, making charges he could not prove and citing numbers he could not support. Oblivious to injury that might result for person or group, he used the tactic of guilt by association and the power of the big bluff. As long as he functioned as a member of Congress, he was immune from personal lawsuits. It worked for a while. McCarthy became a popular man, a powerful and feared senator, credited with influencing the outcome of several elections. He was reelected in 1952.

His downfall came in 1954 when he began to attack elements of his own Republican administration. A conflict with army officials led to a series of public, televised hearings in 1954 that exposed his brutality and evasiveness to a national audience. At the end of the proceedings, President Eisenhower issued a statement of criticism and the Senate officially censured McCarthy for his behavior. Although he stayed on in the Senate until his death (at age 49) in 1957, his power had vanished. McCarthy exemplifies the paranoia and all-encompassing demand for

conformity that pervaded the early years of the the cold war. He had given his name to a process that most people associated with character assassination, reckless, and irresponsible use of political power. From that point on, to be accused of McCarthyism was a serious charge indeed.

James Michener

James Albert Michener was one of the most popular and prolific novelists of the last half of the 20th century. Once he had hit his stride in the years following the Second World War, most of his books became best-sellers; many of them provided a basis for theater productions, movies, or television shows. Born an orphan on February 3, 1907, in New York City, he was adopted by a Quaker family in Doylestown, Pennsylvania, who gave him a home and a last name. A graduate of Swarthmore College in Philadelphia in 1929, he taught English in high school, got a master's degree, and became a professor at Colorado State College of Education.

Spending the Second World War with the navy in the Pacific Theater of Operations provided a foundation for his first and most memorable book, Tales of the South Pacific, published in 1947. Winner of a Pulitzer Prize, basis for a long-running Broadway play and movie (South Pacific), the volume made his reputation. There followed nearly a half-century of works about widely varied places, cultures and social and political issues: The Bridges at Toko-Ri (1953) and Sayonara (1954), both of which became movies, were set in Asia. The Bridge at Andau (1957) was about the Hungarian Rebellion, and Iberia (1967) was set in Spain. That he did not neglect his homeland could be seen in the autobiographical The Fires of Spring (1949); Kent State: What Happened and Why (1971): the epic Centennial (1976) about Colorado that became a television miniseries with 26 episodes: and Texas (1985), another epic and television hit.

A major philanthropist, Michener had donated some $25 million by the time of his death in 1997 to charities, schools, and institutes, including $5 million each to museums in Texas and Doylestown, Pennsylvania. An outspoken liberal and political activist, he ran unsuccessfully as a Democrat candidate for Congress in 1962; yet he accompanied Richard Nixon to historic visits to China and the Soviet Union in 1972, and Republican president Gerald Ford awarded him the Presidential Medal of Freedom in 1977. One could tell that James Michener was going to be a forerunner for civil rights and racial tolerance by listening in 1949 to the song from South Pacific, "You've Got to Be Taught."

Marilyn Monroe

Born Norma Jean Mortensen (her father's surname), out of wedlock, she would change her name to Norma Jean Baker, her mother's surname. Her mother's mental illness consigned her to years of foster parentage, which ended in 1942, when at age 16 she married James Dougherty, a factory worker. The marriage lasted four years. Possessing a pretty face and striking sex appeal, she began to model and posed for photographers while working at an aircraft factory. Appearance on the cover of national magazines led to a movie contract and between 1946 and 1950 several bit parts. Now cast as Marilyn Monroe, her acting left something to be desired, but the innocent good looks, blonde hair, and well-sculptured body caused the audience to take notice, especially of her brief appearance in 1950 in a movie named The Asphalt Jungle.

Her studio, 20th Century-Fox, which also took notice, began to cast her in larger but artistically undemanding roles and embarked on a publicity campaign to produce Hollywood's new sex goddess. It worked. Her appearance in 1952 as the first centerfold for a new men's magazine called *Playboy* did her image no harm. (The nude photo had been taken as a calendar shot in 1949.) Between 1953 and 1961 Marilyn starred in several films such as *Niagara, Gentlemen Prefer Blondes, The Seven Year Itch,* and the meatier *Bus Stop,* and *The Misfits.* She had become a national phenomenon.

Despite all Monroe had, she could not get her life straightened out. Storybook marriages to baseball icon Joe DiMaggio and playwright Arthur Miller failed (DiMaggio after nine months; Miller after five years). She could not advance beyond being defined as a sex object and beyond a film identity as the pretty, sexy blonde without talent and without brains. One of her last, and most memorable performances was singing happy birthday to President John F. Kennedy on May 19, 1963, and it perpetuated the image. Frustrated with the outcome of her film career, depressed with the state of her personal life, the object of rumors of many kinds, including affairs with two (John and Robert) Kennedys, she died from an overdose of sleeping pills in August 1962 at age 36, evidently a suicide. Thereupon the legend, the tragedy of Marilyn Monroe—of Norma Jean—began, in film, book, and song.

Richard M. Nixon

Richard Milhous Nixon had a long and contentious political career that came to an end in a controversial presidency. Born on January 9, 1913, in Yorba Linda, California, he graduated from Whittier College and Duke University law school, saw military service in the Second World War, and came to Congress in the Republican landslide of 1946. Between 1946 and 1968 he served as congressman, U.S. senator, and vice-president for eight years. He was defeated for the presidency in 1960 and for governorship of California in 1962. In the course of this career he acquired a reputation as intelligent and opportunist, a red-baiting, modestly conservative, but skillful politician who had a mean streak that he tried to keep hidden.

Aided by unusual circumstances in both the political parties, Nixon scored a remarkable political comeback in being elected president in a close race in 1968 and was reelected in a landslide in 1972. His presidency of five and one-half years was marked with high points, mostly in foreign policy: an overdue reversal of a long-standing hostility with China, an end—albeit belatedly—to the Vietnam War, and effective dealings with the USSR and the Middle East. His low point largely had to do with the Watergate episode, and it was devastating. This political scandal occupied nearly all of Nixon's second administration, and it exposed the deceit, mean-spirited, illegal, and dangerous behavior of the man and his regime. Facing impeachment and removal from office, Nixon resigned on August 8, 1974. In the years that followed resignation and disgrace, he was remarkably active: traveling, writing, observing and advising on politics. When he died in 1994 at age 81 he had gone some distance in rebuilding a reputation. But he could not remove the signal distinction of his career—being the only president forced to resign from the office.

Sandra Day O'Connor

Sandra Day O'Connor was the first female appointed to the Supreme Court of the United States. Contrary to expectation, the breaking of this final gender barrier in the judiciary and the closure to the final one in the government, came in the act of a conservative Republican president. Born on March 30, 1930, in El Paso, Texas, O'Connor grew up in Arizona and went to college in California. She

Sandra Day O'Connor, first woman justice of the Supreme Court, sits with the president who appointed her, Ronald Reagan. (Courtesy Ronald Reagan Library)

graduated from Stanford University in 1950 and from Stanford Law School in 1952, ranking third in her class. One law school classmate was her future husband; another was her future boss on the high court, William Rhenquist.

Finding a less-than-friendly welcome from private law firms, O'Connor found work with the state of California and, as a civilian attorney with the army, with the U.S. government. After spending some eight years as a full-time wife and mother, she turned to politics, becoming a Republican state senator and majority leader in Arizona; between 1975 and 1981 she held various judicial posts in the state. Ronald Reagan came to office in 1981, and pledged to appoint a woman to the Supreme Court. From a Republican perspective, Sandra O'Connor had a less than unblemished record on the issues (she had equivocated on abortion, for example), but she was an able Republican lawyer with judicial experience, and Reagan did not find an abundance of qualified females who were Republican, so in 1981 she got the call.

As a justice of the high court, O'Connor fit no single ideological philosophy. She generally supported aggressive change in cases involving gender, was less of a reformer in cases involving race. She favored protecting, if not extending, power of the states, straddled the ever-explosive abortion issue, but opposed overturning the decision in the case of *Roe v. Wade*. Identified by the time of the 1990s as a centrist, a swing judge, she probably disappointed the conservatives who put her in power. Although liberals found her to be much less than what they wanted, she was more than they had expected from an appointee of Ronald Reagan.

I. M. Pei

Son of a banker, Ieoh Ming Pei (Pei Ieoh-ming) was born on April 26, 1917, in Canton (Guangzhou) in southwestern China. He grew up in Hong Kong and Shanghai, where he attended Saint John's Middle School, operated by Protestant missionaries. Interested in architecture and fascinated by watching movies about American life, he came to the United States in 1935 and graduated with a degree in architectural engineering from Massachusetts Institute of Technology in 1939. Unable, because of the war with Japan, to return to China, Pei taught and studied at the Harvard Graduate School of Design, under, among other teachers, German architect Walter Gropius.

After the Second World War, with China still in turmoil, he became head of the architecture division of the real estate firm of Webb and Knapp. For seven years he designed large housing complexes, shopping centers, and such urban projects as Mile High Center in Denver. In 1955 he started Pei and Associates, which in 1989 was changed to the firm of Pei, Cobb, and Freed. Over the years Pei designed or had a hand in design of such prominent structures as Society Hill apartment towers in Philadelphia, the National Airlines Termi-

East wing of the National Gallery of Art in Washington, D.C., is one of the more familiar projects of architect I. M. Pei. (Courtesy Linda Gregory)

nal at Kennedy Airport, New York; the National Center for Atmospheric Research in Boulder, Colorado; the East Wing of the National Gallery of Art in Washington; the Kennedy Library at Harvard; an addition to the Louvre in Paris, and the skyscraper Bank of China in Hong Kong.

Although Pei had been influenced by the formalism of Gropius, the key to his formula was that he had no formula. The structures varied widely in shape and use of materials. The Dallas City Hall was a seven-story inverted pyramid; the Javits Conventation Center in New York had an all-glass facade. Pei wanted his buildings to be useful and joyful to see.

By the start of the 1990s Pei, in his 70s, was ready to turn major jobs over to his associates. Interested in doing work in his native land, he was distressed with events in Tiananmen Square in 1989 and their aftermath. By this time he had received almost every architectural award available. A citizen of the United States since 1954, he received the Medal of Liberty from President Reagan in 1986 and the Medal of Freedom from President Bush in 1990.

Jackson Pollock

Born on a sheep ranch near Cody, Wyoming, on January 28, 1912, Jackson Pollock grew up on farms in Arizona and California. He moved to New York City in 1929 to study at the Art Students League under the regionalist painter Thomas Hart Benton. After roaming the West for several years he returned to New York and worked between 1935 and 1942 for the Federal Art Project, a depression-era, work-relief project of Franklin Roosevelt's New Deal. Influenced by Benton's realist work, he also began to develop a different style of abstract painting. His first showing, at the Art of this Century Gallery in New York in 1943, revealed a stage in evolution as an artist. By 1947 he had gone all the way to a new type of painting. Shunning brush and easel, he spread the canvas on the floor, walked around and proceeded to pour, drip, or splatter paint right out of a can, allowing the colors to go where they would. To create direction, he used a stick, a trowel, or a knife, sometimes throwing in sand, broken glass, or other objects. Pollock's work had, if nothing else, spontaneity and originality. He often did not know where he was going until he arrived, and once there he was not sure from where he had come.

Pollock's first "drip" or "action" painting appeared at Betty Parson's Gallery in 1948. Most viewers were stunned; to some it represented the absurdity to which modern art had come. Other people found no message or pattern in the work; critics would call Pollock "Jack, the Dripper." Many artists saw dynamism and originality—the work of a genius. The drip paintings became the centerpiece of an emerging school called abstract expressionism, and Jackson Pollock became its messiah. During the 1950s Pollock was the best-known contemporary artist in the United States, if not the world, and the representative of a school of work.

Action painting did not last long, and Pollock himself had moved away from it; his work, after all, had reconfirmed the idea that art had virtually no bounds. An unstable man, he was given to drinking bouts, sexual escapades, and unpredictable behavior. At the end of one such binge in August 1956, Pollock, age 44, and a female companion died when his Oldsmobile convertible crashed. As frequently happened in the world of art, death enhanced the artist's reputation and the value of the work. In 1973 Pollock's *Blue Poles* sold for $2 million, the highest price ever paid for an American painting to that date.

Colin Powell

Colin Luther Powell was born in Harlem, New York, on April 5, 1937, the son of Jamaican immigrants who worked in the garment dis-

trict. Colin graduated from high school in 1954 and City College of New York in 1958, where he majored in geology but his best area of study was ROTC, the military officer's training familiar to nearly all campuses in that era. He attained the highest rank offered in the program, cadet colonel. Powell later would receive an MBA (masters degree in business) from George Washington University.

Entering the army as a second lieutenant in 1958, Powell moved through the ranks as he held a series of posts remarkably balanced between combat arms and as military attaché to civilian officials. He served two tours of duty in Vietnam (1962–63 and 1968–69), from which he received two Purple Hearts and other medals, spent a tour in Korea, and served as a corps commander stationed in Germany. Service with civilian agencies included assistant to the deputy secretary of defense and to the secretary of defense, deputy assistant to the president for national security, and assistant to the president for national security during 1987–89—a post Henry Kissinger once had—which placed him in the inner workings of the White House of Ronald Reagan. In 1989 he became the first black man to be chairman of the Joint Chiefs of Staff, the highest ranking military official in the land.

The timing could not have been better. Powell's ascendency corresponded with an emerging crisis in the Persian Gulf, an episode that evoked large pent-up American patriotism and placed the military forces and its leading general at the center of things. Powell was so handsome, poised, articulate, patriotic, and qualified that he could have been a star in any color, but to be a black man in this age of diversity made his appeal nearly boundless. Although most of his dealings had been with Republican administrations, both political parties probably would have offered him anything he wanted. In 1990, Colin Powell's future seemed to be limited only by his ambition.

General Colin Powell, shown here as U.S. Army, National Security Advisor, Chairman of Joint Chiefs of Staff (National Defense Information Center)

Elvis Presley

Elvis Aron Presley was one of the most remarkable forces in popular culture in the last half of the 20th century. Born in virtual poverty on January 8, 1935, in Tupelo, Mississippi—a twin, his brother was stillborn—he grew up singing at the local Assembly of God Church. The family moved to Memphis in 1948, and in Elvis's effort to get through Humes High School (graduation, 1953), the most memorable moment was a stage appearance in his senior year singing "Old Shep," a familiar country song about a dog.

In the year of his graduation Presley recorded two songs as a gift for his mother. Sam Phillips, head of the local Sun Record Company, hear the recording, signed Elvis to a contract and in 1954 released the label with "I'm All Right, Mama" on one side and "Blue Moon of Kentucky" on the other. Presley's career had been set in motion, and in the two years that followed, one plateau came after another with dazzling speed. Tom Parker took charge of promotions; RCA Victor bought his contract. Jackie Gleason introduced him to national television in 1955 and his appearance on the Ed Sullivan Sunday night variety show in 1956 became a national event. Behind it all, of course, were the hit single records: "Don't be Cruel," "Heartbreak Hotel," "Hound Dog," "Love Me Tender," "Blue Suede Shoes," and others.

Presley clearly had become a cultural phenomenon that defied a simple explanation. His music was fast paced, was emotional, and had a heavy beat. In musical parlance of "crossover," blending, or switching from one genre to another, he was all over the place: country to rock, rock to rhythm and blues, country to pop, white music to black. At the start he was described as a white boy who sounded like a black. With bountiful combed-back hair, a curl, almost a snarl to his lips, and sexual gyrations released while singing, he appeared more of a rebel than he was.

Through a career of some 20 years that included movies, personal appearances, television specials, and of course record sales (some 500 million and counting), he retained remarkable popularity. Appealing at the start to adolescents, especially females, his fans grew older, but they remained loyal, even in the final years when Elvis became bloated and somewhat withdrawn. He died suddenly in August 1972, apparently of a drug overdose; his estate, "Graceland," in Memphis then became and remains a shrine to the king of rock and roll. A performer so familiar that he needed only one name, Elvis did more than anyone to change popular music in the United States.

Ronald Reagan

Born on February 6, 1911 in Tampico, Illinois, Ronald Wilson Reagan graduated from Eureka (Illinois) College in 1932, and went to work as a sports announcer on radio in Des Moines, Iowa; among other assignments, his duties included broadcasting baseball games of the Chicago Cubs by teletype or, as they called it, ticker. A screen test in 1937 led to a film career that was prolific—more than 50 movies—if unspectacular. Reagan often played "second banana" to the leading man. President of the Screen Actors Guild in the 1940s and 1950s, he also was involved in national politics. For many years a New Deal Democrat, he came under the influence of his corporation contacts (he was pitchman for General Electric in the 1950s) and such people as actor-turned-U.S.-Senator George Murphy. In 1960 he made the shift to the Republican Party and he went all the way over. A powerful speech made on behalf of Barry Goldwater in the presidential election of 1964 gave him recognition and momentum to seek office on his own. He served two terms as governor of California, 1966–74. His impressive victory over a weakened President Jimmy Carter in 1980 seemed to place American leadership in the hands of a superpatriot and genuine doctrinaire economic conservative.

Reagan's formula was simple: Reduce taxes sharply, eliminate many government controls, and give military leaders whatever they wanted. Assisted by simplistic but nonetheless impressive rhetoric on his part, by "Boll-weevil" southern Democrats who shifted over and, curiously, by public sympathy from an assassin's attempt on his life in 1981, Reagan received largely what he wanted. Taxes went down, military spending went up, inflation and interest rates declined. The economy began a period of sustained growth. Side effects of these policies—massive budget and trade deficits, a shift of income from the poor to the rich—were indeed serious, but they did not produce an end to "Reaganomics."

Reagan also set out to restore American power and influence in world affairs, and he did so by rhetoric, huge defense expenditures, and such military gestures as feuding with Libya and invading Grenada in 1982. But his foreign policy experienced as many defeats as victories; the centerpiece—efforts to oust the Sandinistas in Nicaragua—failed, and the Iran-Contra scandal that surfaced in 1987 threatened the entire presidency. Fortunately Mikhail Gorbachev arrived on the scene, almost unilaterally ended the cold war and essentially on America's terms. By being a coparticipant in arms negotiation, Reagan appeared to be a coinstigator in everything that took place. Being in office when the cold war ended made him appear to have won it. Reagan did make the presidency a more popular office, but he also turned it over for others to run.

Jackie Robinson

Jackie Robinson's national reputation came from being the most important pioneer for African Americans in professional sports. Born Jack Roosevelt Robinson in Cairo, Georgia, on January 31, 1919, he starred in high school athletics in a time when it was unusual for a black man from the segregated South to attend any high school at all. His skill in sports brought him to U.C.L.A. between 1939 and 1941. Drafted into the army in 1942, he left military service near the end of the war in 1944, as a first lieutenant. He was playing baseball for the Kansas City Monarchs of the Negro American Baseball League when President Branch Rickey of the Brooklyn Dodgers signed him to a professional contract in 1945.

After a year in the minor leagues in 1946—in Montreal, where he batted .349—Robinson joined the Dodgers in 1947, the first black player in the modern era in the major leagues of America's premier professional sport. His appearance opened the door and the effect was immediate. Two other black players, Larry Doby of the Cleveland Indians and Hank Thompson of the St. Louis Browns, came into the majors before the year was out. Robinson batted .297 in 1947 and was National League Rookie of the Year. Playing either second or first base, he was a fine fielder, a daring base runner, and of course an excellent batter. He won the batting title at .342 in 1949 and was the league's Most Valuable Player. During Robinson's years with the Dodgers between 1947 and 1956, the team won six pennants and the World Series in 1955. Through it all he carried himself with dignity, courage, and pride and was aggressive without being deliberately provocative. He retired in 1957 with a lifetime battling average of .311.

Life after retirement was spent in New York as corporation executive, banker, civil rights activist, and political operative on the Republican side. His many honors included election to the Baseball Hall of Fame in 1962. His death in October 1972 at only 53 did not halt the awards. Surely the most unique distinction came in the 50th anniversary of his joining the Dodgers, in 1997, when all the major league teams permanently retired his number: 42.

Jonas Salk

Jonas Salk was born in the Bronx, New York, on October 28, 1914, son of a garment worker. An intellectually gifted young man, he attended an advanced high school (Townsend Harris), City College of New York (bachelor's degree, 1934), and New York University Medical School, where he became deeply interested in viral research. After graduation in 1939 he spent three years researching influenza at the University of Michigan. In 1947 he moved to the University of Pittsburgh Medical School, where he shifted focus from the flu to polio, one of the most dreaded diseases of the time.

Poliomeylitis, polio, was also called infantile paralysis because it often struck children. Highly contagious, it killed (3,300 in 1952), crippled, or left victims disabled for life, in some cases confined to an ugly machine called an iron lung that covered the body except for the head sticking out. The most illustrious victim had been Franklin D. Roosevelt, who contacted the disease in his late 30s and was crippled for the rest of his life. The Health Service reported nearly 58,000 cases of polio in 1952. Supported by funds from the Polio Foundation and the March of Dimes Campaign, Salk avoided the dangerous, sometimes deadly live virus, and searched for a vaccine using the killed virus. His work was ready for testing in 1952. Thousands of people, including Salk and his family, volunteered. The vaccine was ready for popular use in 1955. Distribution was slower than it needed to be, but nonetheless the results were remarkable. In 1962 only 910 cases of polio were reported and eradication in the United States was not far away.

Salk became an immediate national hero. He received the highest medals, new awards were created on his behalf; numerous scholarships received the name Jonas Salk. He had to reject a ticker tape parade in New York City.

Salk considered such commotion distasteful, a huge distraction, and other problems would follow. The Salk vaccine, administered by injection, necessitated periodic booster shots. Albert Sabin produced a slightly more risky live virus vaccine to be taken orally and it lasted for life. Salk and Sabin then engaged in a bitter intellectual and personal dispute that never was resolved. Ever the medical scientist, Salk went back to the laboratory, eventually developing a widely used flu vaccine, and when he died in June 1995 at age 80, he was hard at work on a cure for AIDS. Jonas Salk's name lived on as the man who conquered polio.

Charles M. Schulz

Charles M. Schulz became the most durable, the most persistent, and in the end the most popular and admired practitioner of comic-strip art in the last half of the 20th century. His characters were a band of small children, a dog, and a bird, but his readers mostly were adults. The strips offered humor, but they also carried philosophy and sociology and exposure into human nature. Schulz was born on November 26, 1922, in Minneapolis; a poor student, he never went to college but did take art instruction through correspondence courses. After service with the infantry in the Second World War, he tried his hand at what he wanted to do: produce a continuing comic strip. He called it *Li'l Folks,* and it appeared in 1948. In 1950 he renamed the strip Peanuts—in those days a child was often called Peanut—and it came out in seven newspapers. A half-century later, Schulz still was drawing *Peanuts,* and the coverage had expanded to more than 2,500 papers in 75 countries and 21 languages.

Schulz's cartoon did not succeed because of exquisite artwork. Crudely drawn, the characters hardly constituted art at all, if one used likeness as a measurement. Contrary to the trend of "comics" of the 1950s, the strip had no sexual references and virtually no violence, unless one counted Snoopy's ongoing imaginary air battles with the Red Baron. Peanuts was about people Schulz had known as a child and knew as an adult and about Schulz himself. "All my fears, my anxieties, my joys and almost even all my experience go into that strip," he said. In sum, readers could see themselves and people they knew in Charlie Brown, Linus, the Little Red-Haired Girl, even in Snoopy.

Peanuts went from being a comic strip, which of course it remained, seven days a week, to the end, to an industry with stationery, T-shirts, books, ashtrays, a Broadway play, and movies. A television special, *A Charlie Brown Christmas,* first appeared in 1965, and a Thanksgiving special started in 1973. Others followed. Schulz became a very rich man. Suffering from cancer, Schulz had to announce with some suddenness at the start of 2000 that he intended to retire and that *Peanuts* was not to be continued by someone else. With his death in February 2000 readers knew they had lost not a single friend but four little girls, three little boys, a bird named Woodstock, and a dog named Snoopy.

William B. Shockley

William Bradford Shockley was born in London, England, on February 13, 1910. His higher education and his lifework all came in the United States. After graduating from Caltech—California Institute of Technology—in 1932, he became a teacher and advanced graduate student at Massachusetts Institute of Technology (MIT). He received the Ph.D. in physics from MIT in 1936. Joining the well-funded Bell Telephone Laboratory as a research scientist, he became a member of a group working on electrical conduction in solids and semiconductors. After wartime work for the navy and the Department of War, he resumed his research at Bell Lab. In 1947 the Bell team under his leadership announced development of a solid-state amplifier known as the transistor, a tiny but highly efficient replacement for the bulky and expendable vacuum tube. Suitable for use in hearing aid, radio, television, computers—indeed, in almost any form of communication—the invention set the stage for the computer age and for the revolution in global, even celestial, communication that followed.

Shockley, who would share the Nobel Prize for Physics with two colleagues in 1956, left Bell to teach at Stanford. In forming his own laboratory and transistor company near Palo Alto, California, he unknowingly planted the seed of a technological and cultural phenomenon known as Silicon Valley. A member of the president's Scientific Advisory Board beginning in 1962, he stayed at Stanford until 1975.

By that time Shockley had left a mark of a different sort. Shifting his studies to genetics, Shockley concluded that intelligence was passed on genetically, that blacks were less capable than whites of transmitting intelligence, and because he believed that blacks reproduced more rapidly than whites, evolution was in a state of retrogression. Needless to say, such an idea did not set well with America in the late 20th century. Shockley was harshly denounced by many people, not necessarily because they had superior scientific knowledge but because they did not want the information to be true. On a more impressive level, the theory of "retrogressive evolution" found few, if any, takers in the community of science. By a strange twist of fate this brilliant scientist who had done so much to start the electronics revolution was at the time of his death in August 1989 angrily denounced in certain circles as a racist and crackpot.

Frank Sinatra

Francis Albert Sinatra was born of Italian-American parentage of modest means in Hoboken, New Jersey, on December 12, 1915. He came of age in the Great Depression when times were hard but one still could dream of making it big. Sinatra's agent for success was to be singing popular music, and he put all his efforts in adolescence and early adult years toward finding the path. It probably started with winning the Major Bowes Amateur Hour Competition on radio in 1937, which led to three months of touring, more radio, and a job with Harry James's big band in 1939. Between 1939 and 1942 Sinatra had an engagement as a regular singer with the orchestra of Tommy Dorsey, one of the most popular on the circuit. Setting out on his own in 1942, he made records, did personal appearances, and performed on such radio shows as the popular weekly program, *Your Hit Parade*. His youthful appearance, sexy and flirtatious style, and high-pitched voice made him an idol of adolescent females—the bobbysoxers. The movies in which he had begun to appear were mostly frivolous musicals.

A brief lull in his career ended in the mid-1950s with his first film appearance in a nonsinging role, as Maggio in *From Here to Eternity*, which won him an Oscar. Many other films—in all he would appear in 58—followed over the course of many years, many of them dramas. The more mature Sinatra as a vocalist probably began with "Young at Heart" in 1954 and, except for a brief retirement in 1971, continued for the rest of his life. Approaching 80 in the year 1995, he still could pack them in.

In personal life there was much to admire, much to dislike. He could be warm, charming, supportive, and generous. He lived life as he wished, with no apologies. A heavy smoker and drinker, something of a brawler and womanizer, he could be mean, dirty, and brutal. He liked power and people with power. A friend and supporter of President John Kennedy until the Kennedys, because of Sinatra's alleged connections with organized crime, cut ties. Sinatra then moved over to the Republicans, and in the 1980s he was a welcome guest in the White House of Ronald Reagan.

As a musical performer, however, covering almost the entire last half of the 20th century, Sinatra had no peer. Whether it was "Love and Marriage," "Chicago," "Come Fly with Me," "Strangers in the Night," "New York, New York," the signature "My Way," or one of dozens of other hits, his singing could evoke a mood, his phrasing was exquisite, and one could understand every word of the song. He died at 82 in May 1998 not far removed from his last performance.

Harry S. Truman

Harry S. Truman came from modest circumstances. Born on May 8, 1884, into a farming family near Independence, Missouri, he graduated from high school, farmed, tried various business activities, went to France as an artillery officer in the National Guard during the First World War, and courted his beloved Bess Wallace, who for several years refused his offers of marriage. Truman entered local politics courtesy of the Pendergast Machine of Kansas City and, with the help of Pendergast, was elected to the United States Senate in 1934 and reelected in 1940. He was a respectable, honest, but not outstanding Democrat senator. His placement on the national ticket with Franklin D. Roosevelt in 1944 was another of those accidents that happen in politics, especially when the vice presidency was involved. The Democrats wanted to dump incumbent Henry A. Wallace, and Truman's name came up.

Truman barely had settled into the vice presidency when Roosevelt died suddenly on April 12, 1945, at the start of his fourth term. To say that Truman was shocked and unprepared would be a considerable understatement. After a rocky start as president, Truman gained confidence and displayed a propensity for making large, far-reaching decisions. He ordered dropping of the atomic bomb in 1945, instituted the

President Harry S. Truman returns from a conference with Gen. Douglas MacArthur during the Korea War in 1950. Pictured from the left: Averell Harriman, Gen. George Marshall, Truman, Dean Acheson, John Snyder, Frank Pace, Gen. Omar Bradley. (National Park Service photograph by Abbie Rowe, Courtesy Harry S. Truman Library)

cold-war policy of containment and in 1949 committed the United States to the NATO alliance. He sent troops to Korea in 1950 and during that war fired the majestic general Douglas MacArthur, for insubordination assailed the "do-nothing" Republicans in Congress, and survived the assaults of Senator Joseph McCarthy. His election to a second term in 1948 was perhaps the largest upset in presidential politics. Although considered probably outside his element at the start, and criticized throughout his time in office, his reputation and his policies generally have stood the test of time. His basic honesty, frank and open manner have made the Truman presidency in retrospect even more appealing. Truman died in December 1972 in the house that Bess had inherited.

Wernher von Braun

To Americans during much of the cold war, Wernher Magnus Maximilian von Braun (Werner von Braun) was the rocket man, our rocket man, and his name and German heritage made his mystique and the perception of his brilliance all the greater. Born in Wirsitz, Germany, on March 23, 1912, this Prussian nobleman became fascinated in youth with space flight. Eventually earning a Ph.D. in physics at University of Berlin in 1934, he was a rocket scientist before there was a Nazi Germany, and because Hitler's regime eagerly sought his services, he joined the party (1937) and even the SS (1940). His work found fullest expression in the V-2 rocket that produced horror in London in the final months of the war with Germany.

Even before Germany's official surrender, von Braun delivered himself to the American army, came to Ft. Bliss, Texas, bringing several dozen members of his rocket team in Germany. Later moving to the Redstone Arsenal at Huntsville, Alabama, von Braun and his men led the way in developing propulsion devices for the military (the missiles) and for space travel (the rockets). His rocket put the first American satellite in orbit in 1958, and sent Alan Shephard into space in 1960; his *Saturn V* rocket sent Neil Armstrong on the way to the Moon in 1969. Von Braun also became a spokesman for missile weapons and the space program, if not for study of science in general. He liked appearing on television, and Americans liked having him on their side in the cold war. Inevitably, later—after the space race and missile program were well in hand— more shadowy aspects of his early career would receive attention: the ease with which he became a Nazi and the use of slave labor in making the V-2. Von Braun's example reemphasized the need for pursuers of pure science to explore deeply into consequences of their efforts. He died in Alexandria, Virginia, on June 16, 1977, not long after receiving the National Medal of Science from President Gerald Ford.

George C. Wallace

Born on August 25, 1919 in Clio, Alabama, George Corley Wallace was an Alabaman and a southerner to the core. He graduated from the University of Alabama law school in 1942 and almost immediately went into the army, serving on a B-29 bomber in the Pacific war. To be successful in Alabama politics in those days, one needed to be a Democrat and a segregationist. Wallace easily met these terms as, in the postwar period, he began to move up the steps of the state political ladder—from assistant attorney general to state legislator, circuit court judge, unsuccessful candidate for governor (in Alabama the primary was the election) in 1958, and the governorship in 1962.

Wallace thus came on the scene in the immediate aftermath of the *Brown* desegregation decision, when civil-rights crusaders had placed the southern Jim Crow system under full assault. In this compelling and (outside the South) nationally popular movement, George Wallace not only appeared as a member of the decadent and bigoted opposition, he came to be its symbol: the most defiant, determined, outspo-

ken, and shrewdest leader of the forces seeking to keep black people "in their place." The immediate objective was to prevent desegregation of the public schools. One might forget such compatriot southern governors as Ross Barnet (Mississippi) and even the colorful Lester Maddox (Georgia), but one did not forget the feisty, "banty" rooster Wallace, and he wished it so. Leader of the segregationists, although he had to yield to national power, he also was leader of Alabama politics—was governor most of the time—between 1962 and 1987.

This long period in politics did produce some changes. In running for the presidency in 1968 (as an independent) and 1972 (as a regular Democrat), he sought to broaden his appeal by defining himself as a populist—a man of the common people, unlike the other agents of the elite—and a patriot and nationalist determined to win the war in Vietnam. That this pitch had appeal can be seen in the fact that he received 13 percent of the popular vote (electoral vote of five states) in 1968, and before being shot in Maryland in the primary campaign of 1972, he had scored several victories, including in the primary in Michigan.

The assassination effort placed him in a wheelchair in much pain the rest of his life. He nonetheless served three more terms as governor of Alabama, in the latter stages of which he projected a new demeanor. He apologized for segregation, said it was wrong, appointed black people to office, and courted their friendship. Before his death on September 13, 1998, some people offered forgiveness and support; some did not. For people familiar with the era, the most memorable image of George Wallace still was the angry little man standing in the doorway, keeping the "Nigras" out of his schools.

Ryan White

The short life of Ryan White was a tale of inner strength, courage, and a primer in the effects and consequences of AIDS. A native of Kokomo, Indiana, he had been born (on December 6, 1971) with hemophilia, a serious disease that restricted capacity of the blood to clot. To control that condition and provide some semblance of a normal life, Ryan for years had received blood transfusions. At age 13, he was diagnosed at Riley Hospital in Indianapolis with having AIDS; the agent of transmission was contaminated blood. Determined to make the most of the life he had, Ryan also was prepared to offer himself as an expression of what the disease was and what it was not.

The young man unfortunately had to deal with a society ill-prepared to face this mysterious and deadly new disease. It was not commonly understood, for example, that AIDS was not spread by casual contact or that it could be transferred through blood products. Popular perception confined the disease to homosexual activity or intravenous drug use, in either case a product of "degenerate" lifestyle. Once the news was out, Ryan White in effect was driven out of Kokomo. The school board would not allow him back in school. A court ruling later reversed that decision, but at school Ryan was ostracised and insulted, his family so harassed and threatened that the Whites decided to leave the area.

Moving some 25 miles to Cicero, Indiana, Ryan and his family received a warm and sympathetic reception. In the following two or so years, Ryan became an agent for understanding AIDS. He appeared with officials of the AIDS Foundation and with numerous celebrities in the entertainment business. Often interviewed on television, he was modest, articulate, and photogenic as he sought to debunk myths about the disease and to instruct young people about how to prevent it. A television movie of his life appeared in 1988. A too-brief life came to an end in April 1990 when he died of a respiratory infection. Present at the funeral were Barbara Bush, wife of the president; singer Michael Jackson; TV personality Phil Donahue; and other celebrities. Singer Elton John, a good friend, sang a special song. Governor Evan Bayh ordered Indiana's flags flown at half-mast. Ryan White gave AIDS a human face, and he demonstrated that the afflicted deserved not derision but understanding and compassion.

CHAPTER 14 Education

The Course of American Education

Education in the United States was in a constant state of flux during the half-century following the Second World War. If the task of providing schooling for a large and growing population was not enough, it seemed that all the nation's social and political problems, the differing philosophies and objectives, found their way into—indeed, often had first airing in—the public schools. Education on all levels remained largely the responsibility of the states, and while the states differed significantly in their ability and willingness to support education, the tendency with the passage of years was for states to imitate one another. Pressures and demands and financial shortages of the era provided a rationale and probably a need for the national government to become involved in education in ever-increasing ways. The Supreme Court made a continuing series of decisions having to do with the rights of students and the responsibilities of government that applied to all the states. If by the end of the period there still existed no national education policy for the United States, the nation, at least in some areas, had come closer to identification of national goals. There existed, needless to say, considerable differences on how to achieve them.

Much of what went on in education aroused controversy, but some manifestations of change stood virtually, if not entirely, beyond dispute. The United States entered the period with a population that was not well educated. Only one-third of the people older than 25 (and only 14 percent of black people) had graduated from high school in 1947; the number did not reach 50 percent until 1967; by 1990 it was approximately 75 percent. The percentage of people who received a high school diploma increased steadily (but not year-after-year)—from approximately 50 percent of people of graduation age at the start of the period to 75 percent at the end. Following a long tradition, more females graduated than males, even though there probably were more males of high school age. The males gradually did catch up, and by 1990 the sexes were nearly equal in numbers graduated. In terms of the percent of people older than 25 with diplomas, the males reached parity in 1972 and occasionally did surpass females afterward. The explanation probably has to do with the propensity of older, less-educated men to die off faster than females, thus increasing the percentage of males.

Race and ethnicity did affect education, especially at the start of the period. The dropout rates for blacks, and more strikingly for Hispanics, was higher than for whites throughout the era. In median years of education, blacks stood approximately three years below whites though the 1960s (Hispanics were not counted separately), but they narrowed the gap, and by 1990 African Americans had nearly pulled even with whites.

Other changes of the postwar period included the following:

1. The cost of everything from teacher's salaries to chalk and textbooks increased manifold.
2. The demands and requirements in special-education programs grew sharply in terms of numbers of programs, numbers within the program, and amount spent.
3. Long an issue within the education community, the ratio between number of students per teacher did gradually decline. Student-teacher ratios were highest in the 1950s (approximately 30 students per teacher in elementary schools) and by the end of the 1980s had dropped to fewer than 20.
4. The states still differed sharply in their support of elementary and secondary education: from a low of $2,700 per student per year in Utah in 1990 to a high of nearly $9,000 in Washington, D.C.
5. Although clearly below earnings of college graduates in other fields, teachers' salaries on the surface increased significantly, some

16-fold between 1946 and 1990. In terms of current dollars (the sum actually paid in a given year), salaries nearly doubled in the 1980s. Using constant dollars—which took inflation into account—as a measurement, the increase was much less dramatic, barely more than a twofold gain, with a more modest increase of 20 percent in the final decade.

The end of the Second World War produced the baby boom, and the babies, of course, grew into children—a lot of them—who needed education. It is possible to trace the course of that demographic phenomenon in enrollment statistics. The surge began in the early 1950s when the first "boomer" children started to go to school. The increase was steady until the early 1970s when the last crop came of school age. The record in elementary and secondary enrollment came in 1970 and 1971. Then the slide began, and it was steady until 1985 when enrollment leveled off, albeit at numbers considerably below the peak years of the early 1970s.

The first postwar "crisis" in education stemmed from a surplus of students and shortages of almost everything else—classrooms, teachers (because college graduates opted for better-paying careers), and ultimately money in the hands of the states. The problem created a new political issue, a debate over larger involvement of the national government, "federal aid to education" as it was called in those days. As logical and sensible as the case for national participation in education seemed to be, the issue inspired multifaceted opposition, based partly on constititional grounds, partly religious and racial grounds. The Soviet Union's launching of *Sputnik* in 1957, which suggested that the United States had fallen behind in scientific education, prompted passage of a National Defense Education Act, the only measure that got through Congress in the 1950s, which appropriated national money to support education, mostly in study of the sciences. The issue probably reached a peak in the presidential election of 1960. Lyndon Johnson's program of the Great Society in the mid-1960s, which contained several measures directed at schools and students, seemingly affirmed the legitimacy of the national government's role in education. In fact, much of the national activity would come in the area of college education, and the bulk of funding for the public schools continued to come from within the individual states.

The era of the 1960s and early 1970s brought new moods and challenges. The corporation became the enemy, the establishment, in that time of student-based rebellion and high idealism in many of the nation's colleges. A new priority given to study of the humanities, and a new respect for the honorable profession of teaching caused the shortage of teachers to end, to be replaced, except in unusual circumstances, by a surplus. An era of living life by one's feelings, of few rules, or no rules—and in a classroom setting, perhaps of no grades—inspired a revival of "progressive" or "needs-based" education that emphasized self-development and adjustment as opposed to learning substantive information. Placing childrens' chairs (or desks) in rows, requiring permission before one could speak, even compulsory reading assignments or homework, came to be perceived as regimentation; discipline was the way the Nazis had done it. The new system continued to have its defenders, and the students seemed to have a good time, but parents began to complain that their children were not learning anything.

The late 1970s and 1980s produced growing concerns about weaknesses and failures of the system. The general dropout rate remained fairly steady, but with African Americans and especially Hispanics, it either increased or remained at a high rate. Although some statistics suggested that illiteracy virtually had vanished, other studies indicated that perhaps 20 percent of the population was functionally

The U.S. government made efforts to improve students' scientific skills. Although still lagging, scientific knowledge grew rapidly after 1945, as exemplified by photographs of Earth from space and from the Moon. This one was taken by the crew of *Apollo 17* in December 1972. (National Archives)

illiterate, unable to read beyond fifth-grade level, if that high. Student scores on the Scholastic Aptitude Test (SAT) used by nearly all colleges in admissions policy, which never had been high in the first place, decreased with almost every year. American students continued to perform poorly, embarrassingly so, in standardized international examinations, especially in science and mathematics. Various blue-ribbon panels studied the system in the 1980s, most of them recommending better training for teachers, especially in subject matter, a longer school year, and an emphasis on basic subjects. Many school systems sought to move in these directions, but they continued to have to deal with socially and politically based aspects of the education process and such newer concerns as drugs and even violence within the schoolyard.

Some parents who blamed a purportedly uncontrollable public-school system opted for a new experimental structure, said to be more creative and designed to meet students' needs, called an alternative school. Some school systems established "magnet" schools that specialized in one area of study. A few hearty and ambitious parents, probably grounded in religious concerns, undertook the task of "home-schooling" their children. Most parents in search of a different educational experience turned to the private school, which could entail traditional church-based institutions, many of them Roman Catholic, or the newer idea of a private, for profit, establishment sanctioned by the state, called a charter school.

A problem with private schools, of course, always had been money; they were expensive, with no public support, and the funds often came out of the pocket of the parents. It was inevitable that advocates of private schools—not to mention the schools or the churches themselves—would seek ways to use public money to fund private institutions. A tax deducation for education expenses represented a conservative approach, but something was better than nothing. The idea with greatest appeal within private-school circles was the voucher, a system through which the state would allow parents of every child a sum that could be spent at any school they chose. Private schools loved the voucher and saw it as their salvation, as did the parents who wished to make use of the system. The idea fed the suspicions of political conservatives who were skeptical about anything run by the state. Of questionable constitutionality, the voucher threatened the public-school system. Presumably, any public money committed to a private school would be subtracted from the sum previously allotted to public schools. Devotees of the public school gave notice that they were not going to submit gracefully to this challenge, and they had in their corner millions of dedicated supporters, the powerful National Education Association (the teachers' union) and, in some assessments, virtually the entire United States Department of Education. The future of American education remained murky at the start of the 1990s, but no one could doubt that it would be a large national issue for as far as one could see.

TABLE 14.1 ENROLLMENT IN REGULAR PUBLIC AND PRIVATE ELEMENTARY AND SECONDARY SCHOOLS, BY GRADE LEVEL, 1946–1947 TO FALL 1990

(enrollment in thousands)

Year	All Schools			Public Schools			Private Schools[a]			All Public and Private Schools		
	Total	Kinder-garten to Grade 8	Grades 9 to 12	Total	Kinder-garten to Grade 8	Grades 9 to 12	Total	Kinder-garten to Grade 8	Grades 9 to 12	Ratio of Kinder-garten to Grade 12 Enrollment to 5- to 17-Year-Olds	Ratio of Kinder-garten to Grade 8 Enrollment to 5- to 13-Year-Olds	Ratio of Grade 9 to 12 Enrollment to 14- to 17-Year-Olds
1946–47	26,598	20,177	6,421	23,659	17,821	5,838	2,939	2,355	584	93.1	102.6	72.0
1947–48	26,998	20,743	6,256	23,945	18,291	5,653	3,054	2,451	602	93.2	103.2	70.5
1948–49	27,694	21,398	6,296	24,477	18,818	5,658	3,217	2,580	637	93.4	102.1	72.3
1949–50	28,492	22,095	6,397	25,111	19,387	5,725	3,380	2,708	672	94.3	102.1	74.5
1950–51	29,301	22,831	6,470	25,706	19,900	5,806	3,595	2,931	664	95.4	102.5	76.6
1951–52	30,372	23,834	6,538	26,563	20,681	5,882	3,809	3,154	656	97.0	104.6	76.7
1952–53	31,581	24,997	6,584	27,507	21,625	5,882	4,074	3,373	702	95.7	103.0	75.5
1953–54	33,175	26,138	7,038	28,836	22,546	6,290	4,339	3,592	747	96.7	102.7	79.4
1954–55	34,569	27,210	7,359	30,045	23,471	6,574	4,524	3,739	785	97.0	102.1	81.8
1955–56	35,872	28,177	7,696	31,163	24,290	6,873	4,709	3,886	823	97.1	101.7	83.5
1956–57	37,303	29,107	8,195	32,334	25,016	7,318	4,968	4,092	877	97.4	101.2	86.0
1957–58	38,756	29,966	8,790	33,529	25,669	7,860	5,227	4,297	931	97.7	101.4	86.6
1958–59	40,290	31,040	9,250	34,839	26,581	8,258	5,451	4,459	993	97.9	101.6	87.2
1959–60	41,762	32,242	9,520	36,087	27,602	8,485	5,675	4,640	1,035	98.0	101.8	86.9
1960–61	43,070	33,191	9,879	37,260	28,439	8,821	5,810	4,752	1,058	97.5	100.4	89.0
1961–62	44,146	33,451	10,694	38,253	28,686	9,566	5,893	4,765	1,128	97.5	100.7	88.8
1962–63	45,798	34,224	11,574	39,746	29,374	10,372	6,052	4,850	1,202	98.2	101.0	90.8
1963–64	47,199	34,825	12,375	41,025	29,915	11,110	6,174	4,910	1,265	98.2	100.7	91.7
1964–65	48,580	35,652	12,928	42,280	30,652	11,628	6,300	5,000	1,300	98.1	101.2	90.6
Fall 1965	48,368	35,366	13,002	42,068	30,466	11,602	6,300	4,900	1,400	96.9	98.9	91.9
Fall 1966	49,242	35,962	13,280	43,042	31,162	11,880	6,200	4,800	1,400	97.2	99.1	92.2
Fall 1967	49,890	36,243	13,647	43,890	31,643	12,247	6,000	4,600	1,400	97.1	98.9	92.7
Fall 1968	50,703	36,581	14,123	44,903	32,181	12,723	5,800	4,400	1,400	97.6	99.4	93.1
Fall 1969	51,050	36,713	14,337	45,550	32,513	13,037	5,500	4,200	1,300	97.5	99.7	92.2
Fall 1970	51,257	36,610	14,647	45,894	32,558	13,336	5,363	4,052	1,311	97.5	99.8	92.0
Fall 1971	51,271	36,218	15,053	46,071	32,318	13,753	5,200	3,900	1,300	97.5	100.0	92.2
Fall 1972	50,726	35,579	15,148	45,726	31,879	13,848	5,000	3,700	1,300	97.0	99.7	91.0
Fall 1973	50,445	35,101	15,344	45,445	31,401	14,044	5,000	3,700	1,300	97.2	100.2	91.0
Fall 1974	50,073	34,671	15,403	45,073	30,971	14,103	5,000	3,700	1,300	97.2	100.6	90.4
Fall 1975	49,819	34,215	15,604	44,819	30,515	14,304	5,000	3,700	1,300	97.6	100.9	91.1
Fall 1976	49,478	33,822	15,656	44,311	29,997	14,314	5,167	3,825	1,342	97.7	100.9	91.5
Fall 1977	48,717	33,172	15,546	43,577	29,375	14,203	5,140	3,797	1,343	97.6	101.0	91.2
Fall 1978	47,637	32,195	15,441	42,551	28,463	14,088	5,086	3,732	1,353	97.1	100.3	91.1
Fall 1979	46,651	31,734	14,916	41,651	28,034	13,616	5,000	3,700	1,300	97.1	101.0	89.8
Fall 1980	46,208	31,639	14,570	40,877	27,647	13,231	5,331	3,992	1,339	97.8	101.7	90.3
Fall 1981	45,544	31,380	14,164	40,044	27,280	12,764	5,500	4,100	1,400	98.3	102.0	90.8
Fall 1982	45,166	31,361	13,805	39,566	27,161	12,405	5,600	4,200	1,400	98.9	102.4	91.8
Fall 1983	44,967	31,296	13,671	39,252	26,981	12,271	5,715	4,315	1,400	99.6	102.9	92.9
Fall 1984	44,908	31,205	13,704	39,208	26,905	12,304	5,700	4,300	1,400	99.9	103.2	93.2
Fall 1985	44,979	31,229	13,750	39,422	27,034	12,388	5,557	4,195	1,362	100.0	103.7	92.5
Fall 1986	45,205	31,536	13,669	39,753	27,420	12,333	5,452	4,116	1,336	100.1	103.9	92.4
Fall 1987	45,486	32,162	13,324	40,007	27,930	12,077	5,479	4,232	1,247	100.4	104.3	92.1
Fall 1988	45,430	32,535	12,896	40,189	28,499	11,690	5,241	4,036	1,206	100.1	103.6	92.2
Fall 1989	45,898	33,314	12,583	40,543	29,152	11,390	5,355	4,162	1,193	101.3	104.6	93.2
Fall 1990	46,450	33,978	12,472	41,224	29,888	11,336	5,226	4,090	1,136	102.5	106.2	93.7

[a] Data for most years was at least partially estimated.
Source: Center for Education Statistics, *120 Years of American Education: A Statistical Portrait* (Washington, D.C., 1993), 37.

TABLE 14.2 HIGH SCHOOL GRADUATES, BY SEX AND CONTROL OF INSTITUTION, 1946–1990

(numbers in thousands)

School Year	Population 17 Years Old	High School Graduates					Graduates per 100 17-Year-Olds[a]
		Sex			Control		
		Total	Male	Female	Public	Private[a]	
1945–46	2,278	1,080	467	613	. . .	. . .	47.4
1947–48	2,261	1,190	563	627	1,073	117	52.6
1949–50	2,034	1,200	571	629	1,063	136	59.0
1951–52	2,086	1,197	569	627	1,056	141	57.4
1953–54	2,135	1,276	613	664	1,129	147	59.8
1955–56	2,242	1,415	680	735	1,252	163	63.1
1956–57	2,272	1,434	690	744	1,270	164	63.1
1957–58	2,325	1,506	725	781	1,332	174	64.8
1958–59	2,458	1,627	784	843	1,435	192	66.2
1959–60	2,672	1,858	895	963	1,627	231	69.5
1960–61	2,892	1,964	955	1,009	1,725	239	67.9
1961–62	2,768	1,918	938	980	1,678	240	69.3
1962–63	2,740	1,943	956	987	1,710	233	70.9
1963–64	2,978	2,283	1,120	1,163	2,008	275	76.7
1964–65	2,684	2,658	1,311	1,347	2,360	298	72.1
1965–66	3,489	2,665	1,323	1,342	2,367	298	76.4
1966–67	3,500	2,672	1,328	1,344	2,374	298	76.3
1967–68	3,532	2,695	1,338	1,357	2,395	300	76.3
1968–69	3,659	2,822	1,399	1,423	2,522	300	77.1
1969–70	3,757	2,889	1,430	1,459	2,589	300	76.9
1970–71	3,872	2,937	1,454	1,483	2,637	300	75.9
1971–72	3,973	3,001	1,487	1,514	2,699	302	75.5
1972–73	4,049	3,036	1,500	1,536	2,730	306	75.0
1973–74	4,132	3,073	1,512	1,561	2,763	310	74.4
1974–75	4,256	3,133	1,542	1,591	2,823	310	73.6
1975–76	4,272	3,148	1,552	1,596	2,837	311	73.7
1976–77	4,272	3,155	1,548	1,607	2,840	315	73.9
1977–78	4,286	3,127	1,531	1,596	2,825	302	73.0
1978–79	4,327	3,117	1,523	1,594	2,817	300	72.0
1979–80	4,262	3,043	1,491	1,552	2,748	295	71.4
1980–81	4,207	3,020	1,483	1,537	2,725	295	71.8
1981–82	4,121	2,995	1,471	1,524	2,705	290	72.7
1982–83	3,939	2,888	1,437	1,451	2,598	290	73.3
1983–84	3,753	2,767	[b]1,313	[b]1,454	2,495	272	73.7
1984–85	3,658	2,677	[b]1,291	[a]1,386	2,414	263	73.2
1985–86	3,621	2,643	[b]1,263	[b]1,380	2,383	260	73.0
1986–87	3,697	2,694	[b]1,301	[b]1,393	2,429	265	72.9
1987–88	3,781	2,773	[b]1,384	[b]1,389	2,500	273	73.4
1988–89	3,761	2,727	[b]1,343	[b]1,384	2,459	268	72.5
1989–90	3,485	2,587	[b]1,285	[b]1,302	2,320	268	74.2

[a] For most years, private school data has been estimated based on surveys.
[b] Estimates based on data from the Bureau of Labor Statistics.
Source: Center for Education Statistics, *120 Years of Education*, 55.

TABLE 14.3 PERCENT OF POPULATION WITH LESS THAN 12 YEARS OF SCHOOL AND WITH FOUR YEARS OF COLLEGE OR MORE, BY RACE AND HISPANIC ORIGIN, 1970–1990

(persons 25 years old and over; as of April 1970 and 1980, and March beginning 1985)

Race and Hispanic Origin	Less Than 12 Years of School					4 Years of College or More				
	1970	1980	1985	1989	1990	1970	1980	1985	1989	1990
All races	**47.7**	**33.5**	**26.1**	**23.1**	**22.4**	**10.7**	**16.2**	**19.4**	**21.1**	**21.3**
White	45.5	31.2	24.5	21.6	20.9	11.3	17.1	20.0	21.8	22.0
Black	68.6	48.8	40.2	35.4	33.8	4.4	8.4	11.1	11.8	11.3
Hispanic origin	67.9	56.0	52.1	49.1	49.2	4.5	7.6	8.5	9.9	9.2
Mexican	75.8	62.4	58.7	57.3	55.9	2.5	4.9	5.5	6.1	5.5
Puerto Rican	76.6	59.9	53.7	46.0	44.5	2.2	5.6	7.0	9.8	9.6
Cuban	56.1	44.7	48.9	37.0	36.5	11.1	16.2	16.7	19.8	20.2
Other	55.1	42.6	35.8	34.9	37.9	7.0	12.4	16.4	15.7	15.5

Source: Bureau of Census, *Statistical Abstract of the United States, 1992* (Lanham, Md., 1992), 145.

TABLE 14.4   PERSONS 25 AND OLDER WHO HAVE COMPLETED HIGH SCHOOL, 1947–1990
(in percent)

Year	All Races			White			Black			Hispanic		
	Both Sexes	Male	Female	Both Sexes	Male	Female	Both Sexes	Male	Female	Both Sexes	Male	Female
1947	33.1	31.4	34.7	35.0	33.2	36.7	13.6	12.7	14.5	...	...	...
1950	34.3	32.6	36.0	...	...	...	13.7	12.5	14.7	...	...	...
1952	38.8	36.9	40.5	...	...	...	15.0	14.0	15.7	...	...	...
1957	41.6	39.7	43.3	43.2	41.1	45.1	18.4	16.9	21.6	...	...	...
1959	43.7	42.2	45.2	46.1	44.5	47.7	20.7	19.6	19.7	...	...	...
1962	46.3	45.0	47.5	48.7	47.4	49.9	24.8	23.2	26.2	...	...	...
1964	48.0	47.0	48.9	50.3	49.3	51.2	25.7	23.7	27.4	...	...	...
1966	49.9	49.0	50.8	52.2	51.3	53.0	27.8	25.8	29.5	...	...	...
1968	52.6	52.0	53.2	54.9	54.3	55.5	30.1	28.9	31.0	...	...	...
1970	55.2	55.0	55.4	57.4	57.2	57.6	33.7	32.4	34.8	...	...	...
1972	58.2	58.2	58.2	60.4	60.3	60.5	36.6	35.7	37.2	...	...	...
1974	61.2	61.6	60.9	63.3	63.6	63.0	40.8	39.9	41.5	36.5	38.3	34.9
1976	64.1	64.7	63.5	66.1	66.7	65.5	43.8	42.3	45.0	39.3	41.4	37.3
1978	65.9	66.8	65.2	67.9	68.6	67.2	47.6	47.9	47.3	40.8	42.2	39.6
1980	68.6	69.2	68.1	70.5	71.0	70.1	51.2	51.1	51.3	45.3	46.4	44.1
1982	71.0	71.7	70.3	72.8	73.4	72.3	54.9	55.7	54.3	45.9	48.1	44.1
1984	73.3	73.7	73.0	75.0	75.4	74.6	58.5	57.1	59.7	47.1	48.6	45.7
1986	74.7	75.1	74.4	76.2	76.5	75.9	62.3	61.5	63.0	48.5	49.2	47.8
1988	76.2	76.4	76.0	77.7	77.7	77.6	63.5	63.7	63.4	51.0	52.0	50.0
1990	77.6	77.7	77.5	79.1	79.1	79.0	66.2	65.8	66.5	50.8	50.3	51.3

Source: Mark S. Littman. *A Statistical Portrait of the U.S., Social Conditions and Trends* (Lanham, Md., 1998), 233.

TABLE 14.5   AGES FOR COMPULSORY SCHOOL ATTENDANCE AND COMPULSORY PROVISION OF SERVICES FOR SPECIAL EDUCATION STUDENTS, BY STATE, 1989–1990

State	Compulsory Attendance (November 1989)	Compulsory Provision of Service for Special Education (1989–90)
Ala.	7 to 16	5 to 20
Alaska	7 to 16	3 to 21
Ariz.	8 to 16	5 to 21
Ark.	5 to 17	5 to 20
Calif.	6 to 16	5 to 21
Colo.	7 to 16	5 to 20
Conn.	7 to 16	3 to 21
Del.	5 to 16	3 to 20
D.C.	7 to 17	3 to 21
Fla.	6 to 16	5 to 18
Ga.	7 to 16	5 to 21
Hawaii	6 to 18	3 to 20
Idaho	7 to 16	3 to 20
Ill.	7 to 16	3 to 21
Ind.	7 to 16	5 to 17
Iowa	7 to 16	Birth to 20
Kans.	7 to 16	5 to 21
Ky.	[b]6 to 16	5 to 20
La.	7 to 17	3 to 21
Maine	7 to 17	5 to 19
Md.	6 to 16	Birth to 20
Mass.	6 to 16	3 to 21
Mich.	6 to 16	Birth to 25
Minn.	[a]7 to 18	Birth to 20
Miss.	6 to 14	5 to 20

State	Compulsory Attendance (November 1989)	Compulsory Provision of Service for Special Education (1989–90)
Mo.	7 to 16	5 to 20
Mont.	[c]7 to 16	6 to 18
Nebr.	7 to 16	Birth to 20
Nev.	7 to 17	5 to 21
N.H.	6 to 16	3 to 20
N.J.	6 to 16	3 to 21
N.Mex.	6 to 18	3 to 21
N.Y.	[d]6 to 16	3 to 21
N.C.	7 to 16	5 to 20
N.Dak.	7 to 16	3 to 20
Ohio	6 to 18	5 to 21
Okla.	7 to 16	4 to 21
Oreg.	7 to 18	5 to 20
Pa.	8 to 17	5 to 21
R.I.	6 to 16	3 to 20
S.C.	5 to 17	5 to 20
S.Dak.	[c]7 to 16	3 to 20
Tenn.	7 to 17	4 to 21
Tex.	[e]7 to 17	3 to 21
Utah	6 to 18	3 to 21
Vt.	7 to 16	5 to 21
Va.	5 to 17	2 to 21
Wash.	8 to 18	3 to 21
W.Va.	6 to 16	5 to 22
Wis.	6 to 18	3 to 20
Wyo.	7 to 16	3 to 20

[a] Must have parental signature to leave school between 16 and 18.
[b] Takes effect in 2000; currently, 7–16.
[c] May leave after finishing eighth grade.
[d] Ages 6–17 for New York City and Buffalo.
[e] Must complete academic year in which 16th birthday occurs.
Source: National Center for Education Statistics, *Digest of Education Statistics. 1991*, (Washington, D.C., 1991), 137.

TABLE 14.6 **PERCENTAGE OF HIGH SCHOOL DROPOUTS AMONG PERSONS 16 TO 24 YEARS OLD, BY SEX AND RACE/ETHNICITY, OCTOBER 1967–OCTOBER 1990[a]**

	Total				Men				Women			
Year	All Races	White, Non-Hispanic	Black Non-Hispanic	Hispanic origin	All Races	White, Non-Hispanic	Black, Non-Hispanic	Hispanic Origin	All Races	White, Non-Hispanic	Black Non-Hispanic	Hispanic Origin
1967	17.0	15.4	28.6	. . .	16.5	14.7	30.6	. . .	17.3	16.1	26.9	. . .
1968	16.2	14.7	27.4	. . .	15.8	14.4	27.1	. . .	16.5	15.0	27.6	. . .
1969	15.2	13.6	26.7	. . .	14.3	12.6	26.9	. . .	16.0	14.6	26.7	. . .
1970	15.0	13.2	27.9	. . .	14.2	12.2	29.4	. . .	15.7	14.1	26.6	. . .
1971	14.7	13.4	23.7	. . .	14.2	12.6	25.5	. . .	15.2	14.2	22.1	. . .
1972	14.6	12.3	21.3	34.3	14.1	11.7	22.3	33.7	15.1	12.8	20.5	34.9
1973	14.1	11.6	22.2	33.5	13.7	11.5	21.5	30.4	14.5	11.8	22.8	36.4
1974	14.3	11.9	21.2	33.0	14.2	12.0	20.1	33.8	14.4	11.8	22.1	32.2
1975	13.9	11.4	22.9	29.2	13.3	11.0	23.0	26.7	14.5	11.8	22.9	31.6
1976	14.1	12.0	20.5	31.4	14.1	12.1	21.2	30.3	14.2	11.8	19.9	32.3
1977	14.1	11.9	19.8	33.0	14.5	12.6	19.5	31.6	13.8	11.2	20.0	34.3
1978	14.2	11.9	20.2	33.3	14.6	12.2	22.5	33.6	13.9	11.6	18.3	33.1
1979	14.6	12.0	21.1	33.8	15.0	12.6	22.4	33.0	14.2	11.5	20.0	34.5
1980	14.1	11.4	19.1	35.2	15.1	12.3	20.8	37.2	13.1	10.5	17.7	33.2
1981	13.9	11.4	18.4	33.2	15.1	12.5	19.9	36.0	12.8	10.2	17.1	30.4
1982	13.9	11.4	18.4	31.7	14.5	12.1	21.2	30.5	13.3	10.9	15.9	32.8
1983	13.7	11.2	18.0	31.6	14.9	12.2	19.9	34.3	12.5	10.1	16.2	29.1
1984	13.1	11.0	15.5	29.8	14.0	12.0	16.8	30.6	12.3	10.1	14.3	29.0
1985	12.6	10.4	15.2	27.6	13.4	11.1	16.1	29.9	11.8	9.8	14.3	25.2
1986	12.2	9.7	14.2	30.1	13.1	10.3	15.0	32.8	11.4	9.1	13.5	27.2
1987	12.7	10.4	14.4	28.6	13.3	10.8	15.5	29.1	12.2	10.0	13.4	28.1
1988	12.9	9.6	14.5	35.8	13.5	10.3	15.0	36.0	12.2	8.9	14.0	35.4
1989	12.6	9.4	13.9	33.0	13.6	10.3	14.9	34.4	11.7	8.5	13.0	31.6
1990	12.1	9.0	13.2	32.4	12.3	9.3	11.9	34.3	11.8	8.7	14.4	30.3

[a] "Status" dropouts—persons not enrolled in school and not high school graduates.
Source: Center for Education Statistics, *Digest of Education, 1992,* 109.

TABLE 14.7 **CHILDREN SERVED IN SPECIAL EDUCATION PROGRAMS, BY TYPE OF DISABILITY, 1947–1948 TO 1989–1990**

(in thousands)

Year	Total	Percent of Public School Enroll-ment	Learning Disabled	Speech Impaired	Mentally Retarded	Seriously Emoti-onally Disturbed	Hard-of Hearing and Deaf	Ortho-pedically Handi-capped	Other Health Impaired	Visually Handi-capped	Multi-Handi-capped	Deaf—Blind	Pre-school Handi-capped	Other Handi-capped
1947–48	356	1.5	. . .	182	87	15	14	50	. . .	8	. . .	. . .	. . .	. . .
1952–53	475	1.7	. . .	307	114	. . .	16	29	. . .	9	. . .	. . .	. . .	. . .
1957–58	838	2.5	. . .	490	223	29	20	52	. . .	12	. . .	. . .	. . .	12
1962–63	1,469	3.7	. . .	802	432	80	46	65	. . .	22	. . .	. . .	. . .	22
1965–66	1,794	4.3	. . .	990	540	88	51	69	. . .	23	. . .	. . .	. . .	33
1969–70	2,677	5.9	. . .	1,237	830	113	78	269	. . .	24	. . .	. . .	. . .	126
1976–77	3,692	8.3	796	1,302	959	283	87	87	141	38	. . .	. . .	. . .	. . .
1977–78	3,751	8.6	964	1,223	933	288	85	87	135	35	. . .	. . .	. . .	. . .
1978–79	3,889	9.1	1,130	1,214	901	300	85	70	105	32	50	2	. . .	. . .
1979–80	4,005	9.6	1,276	1,186	869	329	80	66	106	31	60	2	. . .	. . .
1980–81	4,142	10.1	1,462	1,168	829	346	79	58	98	31	68	3	. . .	. . .
1981–82	4,198	10.5	1,622	1,135	786	339	75	58	79	29	71	2	. . .	. . .
1982–83	4,255	10.8	1,741	1,131	757	352	73	57	50	28	63	2	. . .	. . .
1983–84	4,298	10.9	1,806	1,128	727	361	72	56	53	29	65	2	. . .	. . .
1984–85	4,315	11.0	1,832	1,126	694	372	69	56	68	28	69	2	. . .	. . .
1985–86	4,317	11.0	1,862	1,125	660	375	66	57	57	27	86	2	. . .	. . .
1986–87	4,374	11.0	1,914	1,136	643	383	65	57	52	26	97	2	. . .	. . .
1987–88	4,447	11.1	1,928	953	582	373	56	47	45	22	77	1	363	. . .
1988–89	4,544	11.3	1,987	967	564	376	56	47	43	23	85	2	394	. . .
1989–90	4,641	11.4	2,050	973	548	381	57	48	52	22	86	2	422	. . .

Source: Center for Education Statistics, *120 Years of Education,* 44.

School Year	Total Expenditures, in Millions	Current Expenditures, Day Schools (in millions)					Capital Outlay, in Millions	Interest on School Debt, in Millions	Other Expenditures in Millions	Expenditures in Current Dollars				Expenditures in Constant 1989–90 Dollars			
		Total	Administration	Instruction	Plant Operation and Maintenance	Other				Total: Per Capita	Total: Per Pupil Enrolled	Total: Per Pupil in ADA	Current Per Pupil in ADA	Total: Per Capita	Total: Per Pupil Enrolled	Total: Per Pupil in ADA	Current Per Pupil in ADA
1945–46	2,907	2,707	133	1,854	372	349	111	77	11	21	125	145	136	145	870	1,007	949
1947–48	4,311	3,795	170	2,572	526	527	412	76	28	30	180	203	179	163	981	1,105	978
1949–50	5,838	4,687	220	3,112	642	713	1,014	101	36	39	232	259	209	210	1,244	1,388	1,120
1951–52	7,344	5,722	266	3,782	757	917	1,477	114	30	48	276	313	244	230	1,333	1,511	1,180
1953–54	9,092	6,791	311	4,552	908	1,020	2,055	154	92	57	315	351	265	269	1,487	1,657	1,250
1955–56	10,955	8,251	373	5,502	1,072	1,304	2,387	216	101	66	352	388	294	313	1,663	1,833	1,390
1957–58	13,569	10,252	443	6,901	1,302	1,605	2,853	342	123	79	405	449	341	352	1,801	1,995	1,517
1959–60	15,613	12,329	528	8,351	1,508	1,943	2,662	490	133	88	433	472	375	381	1,871	2,040	1,621
1961–62	18,373	14,729	648	10,016	1,760	2,304	2,862	588	194	100	480	530	419	424	2,028	2,238	1,770
1963–64	21,325	17,218	745	11,750	1,985	2,738	2,978	701	428	113	519	559	460	466	2,137	2,300	1,895
1965–66	26,248	21,053	938	14,445	2,386	3,284	3,755	792	648	136	613	654	537	540	2,439	2,602	2,138
1967–68	32,977	26,877	1,249	18,376	2,864	4,388	4,256	978	866	167	737	786	658	624	2,752	2,936	2,458
1969–70	40,683	34,218	1,607	23,270	3,512	5,829	4,659	1,171	636	202	877	955	816	679	2,948	3,210	2,743
1970–71	45,500	39,630	1,789	26,224	3,960	7,657	4,552	1,318	973	223	970	1,049	911	713	3,100	3,353	2,912
1971–72	48,050	41,818	1,876	28,148	4,325	7,469	4,459	1,378	396	232	1,034	1,128	990	717	3,191	3,481	3,055
1972–73	51,852	46,213	2,018	30,119	4,677	9,399	4,091	1,547	1,698	248	1,116	1,211	1,077	735	3,310	3,592	3,195
1973–74	56,970	50,025	2,276	32,609	5,291	9,849	4,978	1,514	453	270	1,244	1,364	1,207	734	3,388	3,715	3,287
1974–75	64,846	57,363	2,670	36,482	6,136	12,075	5,746	1,737	702	304	1,424	1,545	1,365	745	3,491	3,788	3,346
1975–76	70,601	62,054	2,808	39,687	6,675	12,884	6,146	1,846	553	328	1,564	1,697	1,504	750	3,581	3,885	3,444
1976–77	74,194	66,864	3,273	41,869	7,331	14,391	5,344	1,953	853	341	1,673	1,816	1,638	738	3,619	3,929	3,544
1977–78	80,844	73,058	3,867	45,024	8,096	16,071	5,245	1,952	589	368	1,842	2,002	1,823	746	3,734	4,059	3,696
1978–79	86,712	78,951	3,896	48,403	8,565	18,087	5,448	1,955	357	390	2,029	2,210	2,020	724	3,761	4,097	3,744
1979–80	95,962	86,984	4,264	53,258	9,745	a	6,506	1,874	598	427	2,290	2,491	2,272	699	3,745	4,074	3,716
1980–81	104,125	94,321	a	a	a	a	a	a	a	b458	b2,529	b2,742	2,502	b672	b3,707	b4,019	3,667
1981–82	111,186	101,109	a	a	a	a	a	a	a	b484	b2,754	b2,973	2,726	b653	b3,716	b4,011	3,678
1982–83	118,425	108,268	a	a	a	a	a	a	a	b510	b2,966	b3,203	2,955	b660	b3,837	b4,144	3,823
1983–84	127,500	115,392	a	a	a	a	a	a	a	b544	b3,216	b3,471	3,173	b679	b4,012	b4,330	3,958
1984–85	137,000	126,337	a	a	a	a	a	a	a	b579	b3,456	b3,722	3,470	b696	b4,149	b4,468	4,166
1985–86	148,600	137,165	a	83,463	a	a	a	a	a	b622	b3,724	b4,020	3,756	b726	b4,345	b4,691	4,383
1986–87	160,900	146,365	a	89,559	a	a	a	a	a	b667	b3,995	b4,308	3,970	b762	b4,560	b4,918	4,532
1987–88	172,400	157,098	a	96,967	a	a	a	a	a	b708	b4,310	b4,654	4,240	b776	b4,724	b5,101	4,647
1988–89	192,977	173,099	a	101,016	a	a	14,101	3,213	2,564	785	4,738	5,109	4,645	823	4,964	5,353	4,866
1989–90	211,731	187,384	a	108,964	a	a	17,685	3,693	2,969	853	5,149	5,526	4,960	853	5,149	5,526	4,960

a Not available.
b Estimated.
Source: Center for Education Statistics, *120 Years of Education,* 60–61.

TABLE 14.9 CURRENT EXPENDITURE PER PUPIL IN AVERAGE DAILY ATTENDANCE IN PUBLIC ELEMENTARY AND SECONDARY SCHOOLS, BY STATE, 1959–1960 TO 1989–1990

State or Other Area	Unadjusted Dollars											
	1959–60	1969–70	1979–80	1980–81	1981–82	1983–84	1984–85	1985–86	1986–87	1987–88	1988–89	1989–90
United States	$375	$816	$2,272	$2,502	$2,726	$3,173	$3,470	$3,756	$3,970	$4,240	$4,645	$4,960
Ala.	241	544	1,612	1,985	2,063	2,055	2,325	2,565	2,573	2,718	3,197	3,327
Alaska	546	1,123	4,728	5,688	6,312	8,627	7,843	8,304	8,010	7,971	7,716	8,374
Ariz.	404	720	1,971	2,258	2,462	2,751	3,009	3,336	3,544	3,744	3,902	4,057
Ark.	225	568	1,574	1,701	1,841	2,235	2,482	2,658	2,733	2,989	3,273	3,485
Calif.	³424	867	2,268	2,475	2,671	2,963	3,256	3,543	3,728	3,840	4,135	4,391
Colo.	396	738	2,421	2,693	2,914	3,373	3,697	3,975	4,147	4,220	4,521	4,720
Conn.	436	951	2,420	2,876	3,188	4,023	4,738	4,743	5,435	6,230	6,857	7,604
Del.	456	900	2,861	3,018	3,198	3,849	4,184	4,610	4,825	5,017	5,422	5,696
D.C.	431	1,018	3,259	3,441	3,792	4,766	5,103	5,337	5,742	6,132	7,850	8,904
Fla.	318	732	1,889	2,401	2,443	2,932	3,241	3,529	3,794	4,092	4,563	4,997
Ga.	253	588	1,625	1,708	2,019	2,352	2,657	2,966	3,181	3,434	3,852	4,187
Hawaii	325	841	2,322	2,604	2,862	3,334	3,465	3,807	3,787	3,919	4,121	4,448
Idaho	290	603	1,659	1,856	1,945	2,146	2,362	2,484	2,585	2,667	2,833	3,078
Ill.	438	909	2,587	2,704	2,936	3,298	3,538	3,781	4,106	4,369	4,906	5,118
Ind.	369	728	1,882	2,010	2,306	2,725	3,051	3,275	3,556	3,794	4,284	4,549
Iowa	368	844	2,326	2,668	2,874	3,274	3,467	3,619	3,770	4,124	4,285	4,453
Kans.	348	771	2,173	2,559	2,815	3,284	3,560	3,829	3,933	4,076	4,443	4,752
Ky.	233	545	1,701	1,784	1,906	2,311	2,390	2,486	2,733	3,011	3,347	3,675
La.	372	648	1,792	2,469	2,590	2,694	2,990	3,187	3,069	3,138	3,317	3,855
Maine	283	692	1,824	1,934	2,221	2,700	3,024	3,472	3,850	4,258	4,744	5,373
Md.	393	918	2,598	2,914	3,234	3,858	4,102	4,447	4,777	5,201	5,758	6,196
Mass.	409	859	2,819	2,940	3,137	3,595	4,026	4,562	5,145	5,471	5,972	6,237
Mich.	415	904	2,640	3,037	3,140	3,556	3,848	4,176	4,353	4,692	5,150	5,546
Minn.	425	904	2,387	2,673	2,905	3,395	3,674	3,941	4,180	4,386	4,755	4,971
Miss.	206	501	1,664	1,605	1,706	2,244	2,350	2,362	2,350	2,548	2,861	3,096
Mo.	344	709	1,936	2,172	2,342	2,748	2,958	3,189	3,472	3,786	4,263	4,507
Mont.	411	782	2,476	2,683	2,998	3,604	3,847	4,091	4,194	4,246	4,293	4,736
Nebr.	337	736	2,150	2,384	2,704	3,221	3,471	3,634	3,756	3,943	4,360	4,842
Nev.	430	769	2,088	2,078	2,424	2,690	2,829	3,440	3,440	3,623	3,871	4,117
N.H.	347	723	1,916	2,265	2,509	2,980	3,271	3,542	3,933	4,457	4,807	5,304
N.J.	388	1,016	3,191	3,254	3,674	4,496	4,504	5,570	5,953	6,564	7,549	7,991
N.Mex.	363	707	2,034	2,329	2,703	2,928	3,153	3,195	3,558	3,691	3,473	3,518
N.Y.	562	1,327	3,462	3,741	4,280	5,117	5,492	6,011	6,497	7,151	7,663	8,062
N.C.	237	612	1,754	2,001	2,107	2,303	2,625	2,948	3,129	3,368	3,874	4,268
N.Dak.	367	690	1,920	2,275	2,727	3,028	3,339	3,483	3,437	3,519	3,952	4,189
Ohio	365	730	2,075	2,303	2,492	2,982	3,285	3,527	3,673	3,998	4,686	5,136
Okla.	311	604	1,926	2,199	2,673	2,859	2,850	3,146	3,099	3,093	3,379	3,512
Oreg.	448	925	2,692	3,100	3,299	3,677	3,889	4,141	4,337	4,789	5,182	5,521
Pa.	409	882	2,535	2,824	3,050	3,648	4,237	4,325	4,616	4,989	5,597	6,061
R.I.	413	891	2,601	2,927	3,040	3,938	4,287	4,667	4,985	5,329	6,064	6,249
S.C.	220	613	1,752	1,734	1,907	2,183	2,783	3,058	3,214	3,408	3,736	4,088
S.Dak.	347	690	1,908	1,991	2,300	2,685	2,892	3,051	3,097	3,249	3,585	3,732
Tenn.	238	566	1,635	1,794	1,895	2,101	2,385	2,612	2,827	3,068	3,491	3,664
Tex.	332	624	1,916	2,006	2,229	2,784	3,124	3,298	3,409	3,608	3,877	4,150
Utah	322	626	1,657	1,819	1,872	2,053	2,220	2,390	2,415	2,454	2,588	2,730
Vt.	344	807	1,997	2,475	2,793	3,359	3,651	4,031	4,399	5,207	5,481	6,227
Va.	274	708	1,970	2,179	2,384	2,870	3,155	3,520	3,780	4,149	4,539	4,612
Wash.	420	915	2,568	2,542	2,650	3,465	3,725	3,881	3,964	4,164	4,359	4,681
W.Va.	258	670	1,920	2,146	2,593	2,879	3,244	3,528	3,784	3,858	3,883	4,359
Wis.	413	883	2,477	2,738	2,935	3,513	3,815	4,168	4,523	4,747	5,266	5,524
Wyo.	450	856	2,527	2,967	3,417	4,523	4,799	5,114	5,201	5,051	5,375	5,577
Outlying areas												
A.S.	. . .	. . .	. . .	. . .	. . .	. . .	1,262	1,387	1,846	1,908	1,988	2,570
Guam	236	820	. . .	. . .	2,133	2,301	2,489	3,383	3,344	3,295	4,067	. . .
Northern Marianas	. . .	. . .	. . .	. . .	. . .	1,142	1,693	2,552	3,099	3,366	2,414	3,646
P.R.	106	. . .	. . .	. . .	961	1,247	1,319	1,325	1,384	1,504	1,692	1,825
V.I.	271	. . .	. . .	. . .	2,646	2,710	. . .	3,223	4,277	4,036	5,281	6,767

Source: Center for Education Statistics, *Digest of Education, 1992,* 160.

TABLE 14.10 REVENUES FOR PUBLIC ELEMENTARY AND SECONDARY SCHOOLS, BY SOURCE OF FUNDS, 1945–1946 TO 1989–1990

School Year	In Thousands				Percentage Distribution			
	Total	Federal	State	Local (including intermediate)	Total	Federal	State	Local (including intermediate)
1945–46	3,059,845	41,378	1,062,057	1,956,409	100.0	1.4	34.7	63.9
1947–48	4,311,534	120,270	1,676,362	2,514,902	100.0	2.8	38.9	58.3
1949–50	5,437,044	155,848	2,165,689	3,115,507	100.0	2.9	39.8	57.3
1951–52	6,423,816	227,711	2,478,596	3,717,507	100.0	3.5	38.6	57.9
1953–54	7,866,852	355,237	2,944,103	4,567,512	100.0	4.5	37.4	58.1
1955–56	9,686,677	441,442	3,828,886	5,416,350	100.0	4.6	39.5	55.9
1957–58	12,181,513	486,484	4,800,368	6,894,661	100.0	4.0	39.4	56.6
1959–60	14,746,618	651,639	5,768,047	8,326,932	100.0	4.4	39.1	56.5
1961–62	17,527,707	760,975	6,789,190	9,977,542	100.0	4.3	38.7	56.9
1963–64	20,544,182	896,956	8,078,014	11,569,213	100.0	4.4	39.3	56.3
1965–66	25,356,858	1,996,954	9,920,219	13,439,686	100.0	7.9	39.1	53.0
1967–68	31,903,064	2,806,469	12,275,536	16,821,063	100.0	8.8	38.5	52.7
1969–70	40,266,923	3,219,557	16,062,776	20,984,589	100.0	8.0	39.9	52.1
1970–71	44,511,292	3,753,461	17,409,086	23,348,745	100.0	8.4	39.1	52.5
1971–72	50,003,645	4,467,969	19,133,256	26,402,420	100.0	8.9	38.3	52.8
1972–73	52,117,930	4,525,000	20,843,520	26,749,412	100.0	8.7	40.0	51.3
1973–74	58,230,892	4,930,351	24,113,409	29,187,132	100.0	8.5	41.4	50.1
1974–75	64,445,239	5,811,595	27,211,116	31,422,528	100.0	9.0	42.2	48.8
1975–76	71,206,073	6,318,345	31,776,101	33,111,627	100.0	8.9	44.6	46.5
1976–77	75,322,532	6,629,498	32,688,903	36,004,134	100.0	8.8	43.4	47.8
1977–78	81,443,160	7,694,194	35,013,266	38,735,700	100.0	9.4	43.0	47.6
1978–79	87,994,143	8,600,116	40,132,136	39,261,891	100.0	9.8	45.6	44.6
1979–80	96,881,165	9,503,537	45,348,814	42,028,813	100.0	9.8	46.8	43.4
1980–81	105,949,087	9,768,262	50,182,659	45,998,166	100.0	9.2	47.4	43.4
1981–82	110,191,257	8,186,466	52,436,435	49,568,356	100.0	7.4	47.6	45.0
1982–83	117,497,502	8,339,990	56,282,157	52,875,354	100.0	7.1	47.9	45.0
1983–84	126,055,419	8,576,547	60,232,981	57,245,892	100.0	6.8	47.8	45.4
1984–85	137,294,678	9,105,569	67,168,684	61,020,425	100.0	6.6	48.9	44.4
1985–86	149,127,779	9,975,622	73,619,575	65,532,582	100.0	6.7	49.4	43.9
1986–87	158,523,693	10,146,013	78,830,437	69,547,243	100.0	6.4	49.7	43.9
1987–88	169,561,974	10,716,687	84,004,415	74,840,873	100.0	6.3	49.5	44.1
1988–89	192,016,374	11,902,001	91,768,911	88,345,462	100.0	6.2	47.8	46.0
1989–90	207,583,910	12,750,530	98,059,659	96,773,720	100.0	6.1	47.2	46.6

Source: Center for Education Statistics, Digest of Education, 1992, 150.

TABLE 14.11 MEDIAN ANNUAL INCOME OF YEAR-ROUND FULL-TIME WORKERS 25 YEARS OLD AND OLDER, BY YEARS OF SCHOOL COMPLETED AND SEX, 1970–1990

Year	Total	Elementary School			High School		College		
		Less Than 8 Years	8 Years	8 Years or Less	1 to 3 Years	4 Years	1 to 3 Years	4 Years	5 Years or More
Men									
1970	$9,521	$6,043	$7,535	. . .	$8,514	$9,567	$11,183	$13,264	$14,747
1971	10,038	6,310	7,838	. . .	8,945	9,996	11,701	13,730	15,300
1972	11,148	7,042	8,636	. . .	9,462	11,073	12,428	14,879	16,877
1973	12,088	7,521	9,406	. . .	10,401	12,017	13,090	15,503	17,726
1974	12,786	7,912	9,891	. . .	11,225	12,642	13,718	16,240	18,214
1975	13,821	8,647	10,600	. . .	11,511	13,542	14,989	17,477	19,658
1976	14,732	8,991	11,312	. . .	12,301	14,295	15,514	18,236	20,597
1977	15,726	9,419	12,083	. . .	13,120	15,434	16,235	19,603	21,941
1978	16,882	10,474	12,965	. . .	14,199	16,396	17,411	20,941	23,578
1979	18,711	10,993	14,454	. . .	15,198	18,100	19,367	22,406	25,860
1980	20,297	11,753	14,674	. . .	16,101	19,469	20,909	24,311	27,690
1981	21,689	12,866	16,084	. . .	16,938	20,598	22,565	26,394	30,434
1982	22,857	12,386	16,376	. . .	17,496	21,344	23,633	28,030	32,325
1983	23,891	14,093	16,438	. . .	17,685	21,823	24,613	29,892	34,643
1984	25,497	14,624	16,812	. . .	19,120	23,269	25,831	31,487	36,836
1985	26,365	14,766	18,645	. . .	18,881	23,853	26,960	32,822	39,335
1986	27,337	14,485	18,541	. . .	20,003	24,701	28,025	34,391	39,592
1987	28,232	. . .	. . .	$16,691	20,863	25,490	29,820	35,527	41,973
1988	29,331	. . .	. . .	17,190	20,777	26,045	30,129	36,434	43,938
1989	30,465	. . .	. . .	17,555	21,065	26,609	31,308	38,565	46,842
1990	30,733	. . .	. . .	17,394	20,902	26,653	31,734	39,238	49,304

Year	Total	Elementary School			High School		College		
		Less Than 8 Years	8 Years	8 Years or Less	1 to 3 Years	4 Years	1 to 3 Years	4 Years	5 Years or More
Women									
1970	5,616	3,798	4,181	. . .	4,655	5,580	6,604	8,156	9,581
1971	5,872	3,946	4,400	. . .	4,889	5,808	6,815	8,451	10,581
1972	6,331	4,221	4,784	. . .	5,253	6,166	7,020	8,736	11,036
1973	6,791	4,369	5,135	. . .	5,513	6,623	7,593	9,057	11,340
1974	7,370	5,022	5,606	. . .	5,919	7,150	8,072	9,523	11,790
1975	8,117	5,109	5,691	. . .	6,355	7,777	9,126	10,349	13,138
1976	8,728	5,644	6,433	. . .	6,800	8,377	9,475	11,010	13,569
1977	9,257	6,074	6,564	. . .	7,387	8,894	10,157	11,605	14,338
1978	10,121	6,648	7,489	. . .	7,996	9,769	10,634	12,347	15,310
1979	11,071	7,414	7,788	. . .	8,555	10,513	11,854	13,441	16,693
1980	12,156	7,742	8,857	. . .	9,676	11,537	12,954	15,143	18,100
1981	13,259	8,419	9,723	. . .	10,043	12,332	14,343	16,322	20,148
1982	14,477	8,424	10,112	. . .	10,661	13,240	15,594	17,405	21,449
1983	15,292	9,385	10,337	. . .	11,131	13,787	16,536	18,452	22,877
1984	16,169	9,828	10,848	. . .	11,843	14,569	17,007	20,257	25,076
1985	17,124	9,736	11,377	. . .	11,836	15,481	17,989	21,389	25,928
1986	17,675	10,153	11,183	. . .	12,267	15,947	18,516	22,412	27,279
1987	18,608	. . .	. . .	11,018	12,939	16,549	19,946	23,399	30,060
1988	19,497	. . .	. . .	11,358	13,104	16,810	20,845	25,187	30,136
1989	20,570	. . .	. . .	12,188	13,923	17,528	21,631	26,709	32,050
1990	21,372	. . .	. . .	12,251	14,429	18,319	22,227	28,017	33,750

Source: Center for Education Statistics, *Digest of Education, 1992,* 391.

TABLE 14.12   SELECTED CHARACTERISTICS OF PUBLIC SCHOOL TEACHERS, SPRING 1961–SPRING 1986

Item	1961	1966	1971	1976	1981	1986
Number of teachers, in thousands	**1,408**	**1,710**	**2,055**	**2,196**	**2,184**	**2,207**
Sex (percent)						
Men	31.3	31.1	34.3	32.9	33.1	31.2
Women	68.7	69.0	65.7	67.0	66.9	68.8
Median age (years)						
All teachers	41	36	35	33	37	41
Men	34	33	33	33	38	42
Women	46	40	37	33	36	41
Race (percent)						
White	. . .	. . .	88.3	90.8	91.6	89.6
Black	. . .	. . .	8.1	8.0	7.8	6.9
Other	. . .	. . .	3.6	1.2	0.7	3.4
Marital status (percent)						
Single	22.3	22.0	19.5	20.1	18.5	12.9
Married	68.0	69.1	71.9	71.3	73.0	75.7
Widowed, divorced, or separated	9.7	9.0	8.6	8.6	8.5	11.4
Highest degree held (percent)						
Less than bachelor's	14.6	7.0	2.9	0.9	0.4	0.3
Bachelor's	61.9	69.6	69.6	61.6	50.1	48.3
Master's or specialist degree	23.1	23.2	27.1	37.1	49.3	50.7
Doctor's	0.4	0.1	0.4	0.4	0.3	0.7
College credits earned in last 3 years						
Percent who earned credits	. . .	. . .	60.7	63.2	56.1	53.1
Mean number of credits earned	. . .	. . .	14	. . .	9	4
Median years of teaching experience	11	8	8	8	12	15
Teaching for first year (percent)	8.0	9.1	9.1	5.5	2.4	3.1
Average number of pupils per class						
Elementary teachers, not departmentalized	29	28	27	25	25	24
Elementary teachers, departmentalized	. . .	. . .	25	23	22	. . .
Secondary teachers	28	26	27	25	23	25
Mean number of students taught per day by secondary teachers	138	132	134	126	118	94

(continued)

TABLE 14.12 (continued)

Item	1961	1966	1971	1976	1981	1986
Average number of hours in required school day	7.4	7.3	7.3	7.3	7.3	7.3
Average number of hours per week spent on all teaching duties.						
All teachers	47	47	47	46	46	49
Elementary teachers	49	47	46	44	44	47
Secondary teachers	46	48	48	48	48	51
Average number of days of classroom teaching in school year	. . .	181	181	180	180	180
Average number of nonteaching days in school year	. . .	5	4	5	6	5
Average annual salary as classroom teacher	$5,264	$6,253	$9,261	$12,005	$17,209	$24,504
Total income, including spouse's (if married)	. . .	. . .	$15,021	$19,957	$29,831	$43,413
Willingness to teach again (percent)						
Certainly would	49.9	52.6	44.9	37.5	21.8	22.7
Probably would	26.9	25.4	29.5	26.1	24.6	26.3
Chances about even	12.5	12.9	13.0	17.5	17.6	19.8
Probably would not	7.9	7.1	8.9	13.4	24.0	22.0
Certainly would not	2.8	2.0	3.7	5.6	12.0	9.3

Source: Center for Education Statistics, *Digest of Education*, 1991, 75.

TABLE 14.13   AVERAGE STARTING SALARIES OF PUBLIC SCHOOLTEACHERS COMPARED WITH SALARIES IN PRIVATE INDUSTRY, BY SELECTED POSITION, 1975–1990

(Except as noted, salaries represent what corporations plan to offer graduates graduating in the year shown with bachelors' degrees. Based on a survey of approximately 200 companies.)

Item and Position	1975	1980	1983	1984	1985	1986	1987	1988	1989	1990
Salaries (dollars)										
Teachers[a]	8,233	10,764	13,366	14,500	15,460	16,500	17,500	19,400	. . .	20,985
College graduates:										
Engineering	12,744	20,136	25,800	26,844	26,880	28,512	28,932	29,856	30,852	32,304
Accounting	11,880	15,720	19,476	20,172	20,628	21,216	22,512	25,140	25,908	27,408
Sales—marketing	10,344	15,936	18,648	19,620	20,616	20,688	20,232	23,484	27,768	27,828
Business administration	9,768	14,100	18,564	19,416	19,896	21,324	21,972	23,880	25,344	26,496
Liberal arts	9,312	13,296	18,264	19,344	18,828	21,060	20,508	25,608	26,364	. . .
Chemistry	11,904	17,124	22,344	24,192	24,216	24,264	27,048	27,108	27,552	29,088
Mathematics—statistics	10,980	17,604	21,696	22,416	22,704	23,976	25,548	28,416	28,944	. . .
Economics—finance	10,212	14,472	19,740	20,484	20,964	22,284	21,984	23,928	25,812	26,712
Computer science	. . .	17,712	23,208	24,864	24,156	26,172	26,280	26,904	28,608	29,100

[a] Estimate. Minimum mean salary.
Source: Bureau of Census, *Statistical Abstract*, 1991, 146.

TABLE 14.14   AVERAGE ANNUAL SALARY OF INSTRUCTIONAL STAFF IN PUBLIC ELEMENTARY AND SECONDARY SCHOOLS, BY STATE, 1939–1940 TO 1988–1989[a]

State or Other Area	Current Dollars								Constant 1989–90 Dollars						
	1939–40	1949–50	1959–60	1969–70	1979–80	1987–88	1988–89	1989–90	1939–40	1949–50	1959–60	1969–70	1979–80	1987–88	1988–89
United States	**1,441**	**3,010**	**5,174**	**8,840**	**16,715**	**29,231**	**31,003**	**32,574**	**13,093**	**16,138**	**22,359**	**29,714**	**27,339**	**32,040**	**32,482**
Ala.	744	2,111	4,002	6,954	13,338	24,210	26,150	26,700	6,760	11,318	17,294	23,375	21,815	26,537	27,398
Alaska	...	...	6,859	10,993	27,697	41,531	42,818	43,500	...	...	29,640	36,951	45,301	45,522	44,861
Ariz.	1,544	3,556	5,590	8,975	16,180	30,550	31,985	33,592	14,029	19,065	24,156	30,168	26,464	33,486	33,511
Ark.	584	1,801	3,295	6,445	12,704	21,097	22,193	22,693	5,306	9,656	14,239	21,664	20,778	23,125	23,252
Calif.	2,351	...	6,600	9,980	18,626	34,304	35,882	37,640	21,361	...	28,521	33,546	30,464	37,601	37,594
Colo.	1,393	2,821	4,997	7,900	16,840	29,626	34,918	35,586	12,657	15,125	21,594	26,555	27,543	32,473	36,584
Conn.	1,861	3,558	6,008	9,400	16,989	34,802	38,708	41,909	16,909	19,076	25,963	31,597	27,787	38,147	46,555
Del.	1,684	3,273	5,800	9,300	16,845	30,614	32,736	34,700	15,301	17,548	25,064	31,261	27,551	33,556	34,298
D.C.	2,350	3,920	6,280	11,075	23,027	39,616	42,310		21,352	21,017	27,138	37,237	37,663	43,423	44,329
Fla.	1,012	2,958	5,080	8,600	14,875	27,052	28,697	30,197	9,195	15,859	21,953	28,908	24,329	29,652	30,066
Ga.	770	1,963	3,904	7,372	14,547	27,606	29,752	31,685	6,996	10,525	16,871	24,780	23,793	30,259	31,172
Hawaii	...	...	5,390	9,829	20,436	29,510	31,945	32,956	...	...	23,292	33,039	33,425	33,346	33,469
Idaho	1,057	2,481	4,216	7,257	14,110	23,105	23,640	24,444	9,604	13,302	18,219	24,393	23,078	25,326	24,768
Ill.	1,700	3,458	5,814	9,950	18,271	30,673	32,207	34,139	15,446	18,540	25,124	33,445	29,884	33,621	33,744
Ind.	1,433	3,401	5,542	9,574	16,256	27,188	30,357	30,472	13,020	18,234	23,949	32,182	26,588	29,801	31,806
Iowa	1,017	2,420	4,030	8,200	15,776	25,592	26,590	27,619	9,240	12,975	17,415	27,563	25,803	28,052	27,859
Kans.	1,014	2,628	4,450	7,811	14,513	26,309	29,248	30,154	9,213	14,090	19,230	26,256	23,737	28,837	30,644
Ky.	826	1,936	3,327	7,624	15,350	25,327	26,026	27,431	7,505	10,380	14,377	25,627	25,106	27,761	27,268
La.	1,006	2,983	4,978	7,220	14,020	21,802	23,150	23,754	9,100	15,993	21,512	24,269	22,931	23,897	24,255
Maine	894	2,115	3,694	8,059	13,743	24,161	25,779	27,829	8,123	11,339	15,963	27,089	22,478	26,483	27,009
Md.	1,642	3,594	5,557	9,885	18,308	31,932	35,072	37,515	14,919	19,269	24,014	33,227	29,944	35,001	36,746
Mass.	2,037	3,338	5,545	9,175	18,900	35,327	37,898	40,377	18,508	17,896	23,962	30,840	30,912	38,722	39,706
Mich.	1,576	3,420	5,654	10,125	20,682	33,151	35,741	37,286	14,319	18,336	24,433	34,034	33,827	36,337	37,446
Minn.	1,276	3,013	5,275	9,957	16,654	30,960	31,750	33,340	11,594	16,154	22,795	33,469	27,239	33,935	33,265
Miss.	559	1,416	3,314	6,012	12,274	21,175	23,297	25,156	5,079	7,592	14,321	20,208	20,208	23,210	24,409
Mo.	1,159	2,581	4,536	8,091	14,543	25,666	27,020	28,381	10,531	13,838	19,602	27,197	23,786	28,133	28,309
Mont.	1,184	2,962	4,425	8,100	15,080	28,042	28,415	29,526	10,758	15,881	19,122	27,227	24,665	30,737	29,771
Nebr.	829	2,292	3,876	7,855	14,236	24,100	25,335	26,198	7,532	12,288	16,750	26,403	23,284	26,416	26,544
Nev.	1,557	3,209	5,693	9,689	17,290	28,860	30,150	31,810	14,147	17,205	24,602	32,568	28,279	31,634	31,589
N.H.	1,258	2,712	4,455	8,018	13,508	24,690	27,448	28,958	11,430	14,540	19,252	22,093	26,951	27,063	28,758
N.J.	2,093	3,511	5,871	9,500	18,851	32,101	34,627	37,777	19,017	18,824	25,371	31,933	30,832	35,196	36,279
N.Mex.	1,144	3,215	5,382	8,125	15,406	24,797	25,003	25,988	10,394	17,237	23,258	27,311	25,198	27,180	26,196
N.Y.	2,604	3,706	6,537	10,200	20,400	35,400	38,100	40,300	23,660	19,869	28,249	34,286	33,366	38,802	39,918
N.C.	946	2,688	4,178	7,744	14,445	25,900	26,833	28,947	8,595	14,412	18,055	26,030	23,626	28,389	28,113
N.Dak.	745	2,324	3,695	6,900	13,684	22,370	22,994	23,788	6,769	12,460	15,967	23,193	22,381	24,520	24,091
Ohio	1,587	3,088	5,124	8,594	16,100	29,322	30,934	32,380	14,419	16,556	22,143	28,887	26,333	32,140	32,410
Okla.	1,014	2,736	4,659	7,139	13,500	22,400	23,200	23,944	9,213	14,669	20,133	23,997	22,080	24,553	24,307
Oreg.	1,333	3,323	5,535	9,200	16,996	29,300	30,680	31,887	12,111	17,816	23,919	30,924	27,798	32,116	32,144
Pa.	1,640	3,006	5,308	9,000	17,060	29,881	31,555	33,219	14,901	16,116	22,938	30,252	27,903	32,753	33,061
R.I.	1,809	3,294	5,499	8,900	18,425	33,326	35,564	36,704	16,436	17,661	23,763	29,916	30,136	36,529	37,261
S.C.	743	1,891	3,450	7,000	13,670	25,608	26,762	28,266	6,751	10,138	14,909	23,529	22,358	28,069	28,039
S.Dak.	807	2,064	3,725	6,700	13,010	21,420	21,250	22,120	7,332	11,066	16,097	22,521	21,279	23,479	22,264
Tenn.	862	2,302	3,929	7,290	14,193	24,536	26,512	27,949	7,832	12,342	16,979	24,504	23,214	26,894	27,777
Tex.	1,079	3,122	4,708	7,503	14,729	26,572	27,565	28,558	9,804	16,738	20,345	25,220	24,090	29,126	28,880
Utah	1,394	3,103	5,096	8,049	17,403	23,655	23,955	24,793	12,666	16,637	22,022	27,056	28,464	25,928	25,098
Vt.	981	2,348	4,466	8,225	13,300	25,525	27,265	29,159	8,913	12,589	19,299	27,647	21,753	27,978	28,566
Va.	899	2,328	4,312	8,200	14,655	27,833	27,667	31,862	8,168	12,481	18,634	27,563	23,969	30,508	31,083
Wash.	1,706	3,487	5,643	9,500	19,735	29,468	30,527	31,825	15,500	18,695	24,386	31,933	32,278	32,300	31,984
W.Va.	1,170	2,425	3,952	7,850	14,395	22,711	22,897	23,842	10,630	13,001	17,078	26,387	23,544	24,894	23,990
Wis.	1,379	3,007	4,870	9,150	16,335	30,958	32,500	33,788	12,529	16,122	21,045	30,756	26,717	33,933	34,051
Wyo.	1,169	2,798	4,937	8,532	16,830	28,327	28,844	29,304	10,621	15,001	21,335	28,679	27,527	31,049	30,220

[a]Includes supervisors, principals, classroom teachers, and other instructional staff.
Source: Center for Education Statistics. Digest of Education, 1990, 86–87.

TABLE 14.15 **PUBLIC AND PRIVATE ELEMENTARY AND SECONDARY TEACHERS AND PUPIL-TEACHER RATIOS, BY LEVEL, FALL 1955–FALL 1990**

Year	Public and Private Elementary and Secondary Schools			Public Elementary and Secondary Schools			Private Elementary and Secondary Schools		
	Kindergarten to Grade 12	Elementary	Secondary	Kindergarten to Grade 12	Elementary	Secondary	Kindergarten to Grade 12	Elementary	Secondary
Number of Teachers, in Thousands									
1955	1,286	827	459	1,141	733	408	145	94	51
1956	1,354	854	499	1,199	751	447	155	103	52
1957	1,424	898	526	1,259	786	473	165	112	53
1958	1,475	931	544	1,306	815	491	169	116	53
1959	1,531	952	580	1,355	832	524	176	120	56
1960	1,600	991	609	1,408	858	550	192	133	59
1961	1,643	992	651	1,461	869	592	182	123	59
1962	1,708	1,021	686	1,508	886	621	200	135	65
1963	1,790	1,050	739	1,578	908	669	212	142	70
1964	1,865	1,086	779	1,648	940	708	217	146	71
1965	1,933	1,112	822	1,710	965	746	223	147	76
1966	2,012	1,153	859	1,789	1,006	783	223	147	76
1967	2,079	1,188	891	1,855	1,040	815	224	148	76
1968	2,161	1,223	938	1,936	1,076	860	225	147	78
1969	2,245	1,260	986	2,016	1,109	908	229	151	78
1970	2,292	1,283	1,009	2,059	1,130	929	233	153	80
1971	2,293	1,263	1,030	2,063	1,111	952	230	152	78
1972	2,337	1,296	1,041	2,106	1,142	964	231	154	77
1973	2,372	1,308	1,064	2,136	1,151	985	236	157	79
1974	2,410	1,330	1,079	2,165	1,166	998	245	164	81
1975	2,453	1,353	1,100	2,198	1,181	1,017	255	172	83
1976	2,457	1,351	1,106	2,189	1,168	1,021	268	183	85
1977	2,488	1,375	1,113	2,209	1,185	1,024	279	190	89
1978	2,479	1,376	1,103	2,207	1,191	1,016	272	185	87
1979	2,461	1,379	1,082	2,185	1,191	994	276	188	88
1980	2,486	1,402	1,084	2,185	1,190	995	301	212	89
1981	2,440	1,404	1,037	2,127	1,183	945	313	221	92
1982	2,458	1,413	1,045	2,133	1,182	951	325	231	94
1983	2,476	1,426	1,050	2,139	1,186	953	337	240	97
1984	2,508	1,451	1,057	2,168	1,208	960	340	243	97
1985	2,549	1,483	1,066	2,206	1,237	969	343	246	97
1986	2,592	1,521	1,071	2,244	1,271	973	348	250	98
1987	2,632	1,564	1,068	2,279	1,307	973	353	257	95
1988	2,668	1,604	1,064	2,323	1,353	970	345	251	94
1989	2,734	1,662	1,072	2,357	1,387	970	377	275	102
1990	2,751	1,680	1,072	2,397	1,426	972	354	254	100
Pupil-Teacher Ratios									
1955	27.4	31.4	20.3	26.9	30.2	20.9	31.7	40.4	15.7
1956	27.0	30.7	20.8	26.5	29.6	21.2	31.6	38.8	17.3
1957	26.8	30.3	20.9	26.2	29.1	21.3	31.5	38.4	17.0
1958	26.8	30.0	21.4	26.1	28.7	21.7	32.5	38.8	18.9
1959	26.7	30.0	21.2	26.0	28.7	21.5	32.2	38.7	18.5
1960	26.4	29.4	21.4	25.8	28.4	21.7	30.7	36.1	18.6
1961	26.4	29.6	21.5	25.6	28.3	21.7	32.5	39.0	19.0
1962	26.3	29.5	21.4	25.7	28.5	21.7	30.5	36.3	18.5
1963	26.0	29.3	21.2	25.5	28.4	21.5	29.7	35.2	18.6
1964	25.6	28.7	21.2	25.1	27.9	21.5	29.0	34.2	18.3
1965	25.1	28.4	20.6	24.7	27.6	20.8	28.3	33.3	18.4
1966	24.5	27.7	20.2	24.1	26.9	20.3	27.8	32.7	18.4
1967	24.0	26.9	20.1	23.7	26.3	20.3	26.8	31.1	18.4
1968	23.5	26.0	20.2	23.2	25.4	20.4	25.8	29.9	17.9
1969	22.7	25.1	19.7	22.6	24.7	20.0	24.0	27.8	16.7
1970	22.4	24.6	19.5	22.3	24.3	19.8	23.0	26.5	16.4
1971	22.4	25.0	19.1	22.3	24.9	19.3	22.6	25.7	16.7
1972	21.7	23.9	18.9	21.7	23.9	19.1	21.6	24.0	16.9
1973	21.3	23.0	19.1	21.3	23.0	19.3	21.2	23.6	16.5
1974	20.8	22.6	18.5	20.8	22.6	18.7	20.4	22.6	16.0

Year	Public and Private Elementary and Secondary Schools			Public Elementary and Secondary Schools			Private Elementary and Secondary Schools		
	Kindergarten to Grade 12	Elementary	Secondary	Kindergarten to Grade 12	Elementary	Secondary	Kindergarten to Grade 12	Elementary	Secondary
1975	20.3	21.7	18.6	20.4	21.7	18.8	19.6	21.5	15.7
1976	20.1	21.7	18.3	20.2	21.8	18.5	19.3	20.9	15.8
1977	19.6	20.9	17.9	19.7	21.1	18.2	18.4	20.0	15.1
1978	19.2	20.9	17.1	19.3	21.0	17.3	18.7	20.2	15.6
1979	19.0	20.5	17.0	19.1	20.6	17.2	18.1	19.7	14.8
1980	18.6	20.1	16.6	18.7	20.3	16.8	17.7	18.8	15.0
1981	18.7	20.0	16.8	18.8	20.3	16.9	17.6	18.6	15.2
1982	18.4	19.8	16.4	18.6	20.2	16.6	17.2	18.2	14.9
1983	18.2	19.6	16.2	18.4	19.9	16.4	17.0	18.0	14.4
1984	17.9	19.3	16.0	18.1	19.7	16.1	16.8	17.7	14.4
1985	17.6	19.1	15.6	17.9	19.5	15.8	16.2	17.1	14.0
1986	17.4	18.8	15.5	17.7	19.3	15.7	15.7	16.5	13.6
1987	17.3	18.8	15.0	17.6	19.3	15.2	15.5	16.4	13.1
1988	17.0	18.6	14.7	17.3	19.0	14.9	15.2	16.1	12.8
1989	16.8	18.4	14.3	17.2	19.0	14.6	14.2	15.1	11.7
1990	16.9	18.5	14.3	17.2	19.0	14.6	14.7	16.0	11.3

Source: Center for Education Statistics, *Digest of Education, 1992*, 73.

TABLE 14.16 MICROCOMPUTERS FOR STUDENT INSTRUCTION IN ELEMENTARY AND SECONDARY SCHOOLS, 1981–1990

	Public Schools										Private Schools			
	Number of Schools (1,000)				Percent with Micros				Number of Micros (1,000)	Students per Micro	Number of Schools (1,000)	Percent with Micros	Number of Micros (1,000)	Students per Micro
Year	Total	Elementary	Junior	Senior	Total	Elementary	Junior	Senior						
1981	84.2	53.3	10.1	15.6	18.2	11.1	25.6	42.7	. . .	. . .	. . .	. . .	. . .	. . .
1982	82.4	51.9	9.9	15.3	30.0	20.2	39.8	57.8	. . .	. . .	. . .	. . .	. . .	. . .
1983	81.5	51.3	9.8	15.2	68.4	62.4	80.5	86.1	324.4	92.3	22.8	23.8	. . .	. . .
1984	81.1	51.0	9.8	15.2	85.1	82.2	93.1	94.6	569.8	63.5	24.4	53.0	62.2	56.2
1985	80.8	50.8	9.7	15.1	92.2	91.0	97.3	97.4	842.6	45.5	23.4	70.3	101.2	41.6
1986	80.5	50.7	9.7	15.1	95.6	94.9	98.5	98.7	1,081.9	36.5	22.7	77.1	129.2	33.7
1987	80.6	50.9	9.7	15.0	96.4	96.0	98.6	99.0	1,354.0	30.8	22.7	78.7	151.1	28.8
1988	80.8	51.0	9.8	15.0	97.1	96.8	98.8	99.1	1,522.9	26.9	22.3	82.8	185.5	23.5
1989	81.7	49.5	11.5	13.7	97.0	96.8	98.5	99.1	1,706.4	24.1	23.4	81.8	222.8	20.1
1990, total	82.0	49.7	11.7	13.8	97.2	97.3	98.4	98.8	2,028.7	20.9	22.3	88.2	241.8	19.5
Number of micros	2,028.7	863.0	369.8	646.5	. . .	. . .	. . .	. . .	. . .	. . .	241.8	. . .	. . .	. . .
Students per micro	20.9	25.6	19.2	16.4	. . .	. . .	. . .	. . .	. . .	. . .	19.5	. . .	. . .	. . .

Source: Bureau of Census, *Statistical Abstract, 1992*, 155.

TABLE 14.17 PRIVATE ELEMENTARY AND SECONDARY ENROLLMENT AND SCHOOLS, BY AMOUNT OF TUITION, LEVEL, AND ORIENTATION OF SCHOOL, 1987–1988

Orientation and Tuition	Kindergarten Through 12th Grade Enrollment				Schools				Average Tuition Paid by Students (dollars)			
	Total	Elementary	Secondary	Combined	Total	Elementary	Secondary	Combined	Total	Elementary	Secondary	Combined
Total	**5,479,368**	**3,174,760**	**896,478**	**1,408,132**	**26,807**	**17,087**	**2,425**	**7,296**	**1,915**	**1,357**	**2,552**	**2,767**
Catholic	2,901,809	2,096,779	731,922	73,107	9,527	7,760	1,420	348	1,327	1,005	2,045	3,382
Less than $1,000	1,230,392	1,186,981	. . .	. . .	4,860	4,619	. . .	. . .	. . .	. . .	. . .	. . .
$1,000 to $2,499	1,456,418	881,701	556,150	. . .	4,113	3,017	1,037	. . .	. . .	. . .	. . .	. . .
$2,500 or more	214,998	. . .	. . .	. . .	554	. . .	. . .	. . .	. . .	. . .	. . .	. . .
Other religious	1,714,852	768,372	93,058	853,424	12,132	6,859	501	4,771	1,941	1,619	3,592	2,052
Less than $1,000	283,399	169,765	. . .	110,996	4,407	2,794	. . .	1,601	. . .	. . .	. . .	. . .
$1,000 to $2,499	1,034,471	480,903	. . .	537,175	6,377	3,497	. . .	2,751	. . .	. . .	. . .	. . .
$2,500 or more	396,984	117,704	74,027	205,253	1,347	568	360	419	. . .	. . .	. . .	. . .
Non-sectarian	862,707	309,609	71,498	481,601	5,148	2,468	504	2,177	3,839	3,091	6,391	3,941
Less than $1,000	96,326	. . .	. . .	74,401	805	. . .	. . .	619	. . .	. . .	. . .	. . .
$1,000 to $2,499	214,168	73,424	. . .	140,434	1,388	836	. . .	520	. . .	. . .	. . .	. . .
$2,500 or more	552,214	219,304	66,144	266,766	2,984	1,518	428	1,038	. . .	. . .	. . .	. . .

Source: Center for Education Statistics, *Digest of Education, 1992*, 71.

TABLE 14.18 **SUMMARY STATISTICS ON CATHOLIC ELEMENTARY AND SECONDARY SCHOOLS, BY LEVEL, 1949–1950 TO 1989–1990**

School Year	Number of Schools			Enrollment			Instructional Staff		
	Total	Elementary	Secondary	Total	Elementary	Secondary	Total	Elementary	Secondary
1949–50	10,778	8,589	2,189	3,066,387	2,560,815	505,572	94,295	66,525	27,770
Fall 1960	12,893	10,501	2,392	5,253,791	4,373,422	880,369	151,902	108,169	43,733
1969–70	11,771	9,695	2,076	4,658,098	3,607,168	1,050,930	195,400	133,200	62,200
1970–71	11,350	9,370	1,980	4,363,566	3,355,478	1,008,088	166,208	112,750	53,458
1974–75	10,127	8,437	1,690	3,504,000	2,602,000	902,000	150,179	100,011	50,168
1975–76	9,993	8,340	1,653	3,415,000	2,525,000	890,000	149,276	99,319	49,957
1979–80	9,640	8,100	1,540	3,139,000	2,293,000	846,000	147,294	97,724	49,570
1980–81	9,559	8,043	1,516	3,106,000	2,269,000	837,000	145,777	96,739	49,038
1981–82	9,494	7,996	1,498	3,094,000	2,266,000	828,000	146,172	96,847	49,325
1982–83	9,432	7,950	1,482	3,026,000	2,225,000	801,000	146,460	97,337	49,123
1983–84	9,380	7,917	1,463	2,969,000	2,179,000	790,000	146,913	98,591	48,322
1984–85	9,325	7,876	1,449	2,903,000	2,119,000	784,000	149,888	99,820	50,068
1985–86	9,220	7,790	1,430	2,821,000	2,061,000	760,000	146,594	96,741	49,853
1986–87	9,102	7,693	1,409	2,726,000	1,998,000	728,000	141,930	93,554	48,376
1987–88	8,992	7,601	1,391	2,623,000	1,942,000	681,000	139,887	93,199	46,688
1988–89	8,867	7,505	1,362	2,551,000	1,912,000	639,000	137,700	93,154	44,546
1989–90	8,719	7,395	1,324	2,499,000	1,894,000	606,000	136,900	94,197	42,703

Source: Center for Education Statistics, *Digest of Education, 1992*, 71.

TABLE 14.19 **SCHOLASTIC APTITUDE TEST SCORE AVERAGES, BY RACE/ETHNICITY, 1975–1976 TO 1989–1990**

Racial/Ethnic Background	1975–76	1976–77	1977–78	1978–79	1979–80	1980–81	1981–82	1982–83	1983–84	1984–85	1986–87	1987–88	1988–89	1989–90
SAT—Verbal[a]														
All students	431	429	429	427	424	424	426	425	426	431	430	428	427	424
White	451	448	446	444	442	442	444	443	445	449	447	445	446	442
Black	332	330	332	330	330	332	341	339	342	346	351	353	351	352
Mexican-American	371	370	370	370	372	373	377	375	376	382	379	382	381	380
Puerto Rican	364	355	349	345	350	353	360	358	358	368	360	355	360	359
Asian-American	414	405	401	396	396	397	398	395	398	404	405	408	409	410
American Indian	388	390	387	386	390	391	388	388	390	392	393	393	384	388
Other	410	402	399	393	394	388	392	386	388	391	405	410	414	410
SAT—Mathematical[a]														
All students	472	470	468	467	466	466	467	468	471	475	476	476	476	476
White	493	489	485	483	482	483	483	484	487	490	489	490	491	491
Black	354	357	354	358	360	362	366	369	373	376	377	384	386	385
Mexican-American	410	408	402	410	413	415	416	417	420	426	424	428	430	429
Puerto Rican	401	397	388	388	394	398	403	403	405	409	400	402	406	405
Asian-American	518	514	510	511	509	513	513	514	519	518	521	522	525	528
American Indian	420	421	419	421	426	425	424	425	427	428	432	435	428	437
Other	458	457	450	447	449	447	449	446	450	448	455	460	467	467

[a] Minimum score 200; maximum score 800.
Source: Center for Education Statistics, *Digest of Education, 1992*, 125.

Aspects of Education: An International Comparison

Comparative international statistics, of course, depend upon many variables, one of which involved the countries with which the United States compared itself. Nations in the tables listed below varied, but as a rule they included countries with which the United States has had the most in common: Western European nations mostly, along with Canada and Japan. Although the tables stand in isolation, their results were generally consistent with competitive measurements taken in other years.

The United States by far had the largest number of students among the nations listed (China, India, and the Soviet Union did not appear) and had by far the largest expenditure. In expenditure per pupil the United States ranked high: near the top—fourth out of 21—in 1980; second in 1989. In expenditure as a percent of government spending, the nation stood in the upper-middle rank in most years between 1960 and 1980 and near the top during the 1980s. In expenditure as a percent of Gross National Product, the United States ranked in the upper-middle class of nations. In number of students per teacher the nation also stood in the upper-middle ranks—the fewer the students per teacher, the higher the rank. The United States spent huge sums of money for education, but in terms of its wealth and extent of government expenditure, the nation stood higher than average, but not the highest.

In selected international testing, American 12th grade students ranked low, near the bottom, in all aspects of mathematics: average score, algebra, geometry, and calculus. In fifth grade science and ninth grade science, American students also were near the bottom. In a test of geographic knowledge Americans age 18–24 ranked rock-bottom in a group that included Japan, Canada, Mexico, and five western European countries. Older age groups performed slightly better. American geographic knowledge, never good at any time, seemingly with each succeeding generation became progressively worse. It would appear, in sum, that results of education in the United States were not commensurate with its expenditure of funds.

TABLE 14.20   PUPILS PER TEACHER IN PUBLIC AND PRIVATE ELEMENTARY AND SECONDARY SCHOOLS— SELECTED COUNTRIES, 1970–1989

Country	All Schools				Elementary Schools				Secondary Schools			
	1970	1980	1985	1989	1970	1980	1985	1989	1970	1980	1985	1989
Australia	. . .	16.0	13.9	14.6	28.0	18.8	15.9	16.8	. . .	12.9	12.1	12.6
Brazil	. . .	23.5	22.3	21.6	23.6	25.6	23.8	23.0	13.2	14.2	14.6	14.4
Canada	20.9	. . .	. . .	14.9	23.4	. . .	37.5	15.7	16.9	. . .	. . .	14.2
China	30.1	23.4	22.1	19.4	33.3	26.6	24.9	22.3	21.8	17.9	17.2	14.8
Egypt	33.2	. . .	26.2	24.0	38.0	. . .	31.9	29.9	25.0	24.0	20.4	18.0
France	20.0	21.4	. . .	13.7	26.0	24.0	20.3	15.7	15.8	19.6	. . .	12.4
Germany, (former) West	19.4	. . .	. . .	14.8	25.5	. . .	17.0	17.5	12.3	. . .	. . .	14.0
Indonesia	30.1	26.7	21.8	20.2	28.9	32.4	25.3	23.6	13.1	14.9	15.3	14.8
Iran, Islamic Republic of	32.8	. . .	. . .	21.6	32.4	. . .	21.9	24.4	34.2	. . .	. . .	17.7
Italy	15.6	12.3	10.8	10.1	21.6	16.2	13.5	12.2	11.5	10.2	9.5	9.2
Japan	21.8	20.9	20.5	18.8	26.2	25.1	23.9	21.2	18.4	17.2	17.9	17.1
Korea	49.9	43.5	36.2	29.7	56.9	47.5	38.3	35.6	36.5	39.1	34.3	25.2
Mexico	34.8	30.2	26.1	24.5	45.9	39.1	33.6	31.1	14.5	17.7	17.2	16.9
Nigeria	32.3	35.7	. . .	32.1	34.1	37.2	44.1	36.9	21.2	28.8	. . .	19.9
Pakistan	32.1	27.9	. . .	30.8	41.5	36.5	38.7	41.1	19.8	17.5	. . .	19.3
Philippines	29.4	. . .	31.2	33.1	28.6	. . .	30.9	33.0	33.1	34.1	32.3	33.4
Poland	17.5	16.6	14.0	14.0	23.0	19.7	15.6	15.6	10.2	12.0	10.6	10.8
Spain	28.5	23.9	22.6	22.3	34.0	28.3	25.3	24.7	21.5	20.9	21.0	20.9
Sweden	13.6	. . .	. . .	. . .	20.0	. . .	. . .	6.2	10.1	. . .	. . .	. . .
Thailand	30.5	. . .	. . .	18.2	34.7	24.7	19.3	18.7	15.5	. . .	. . .	16.8
United Kingdom	19.6	. . .	. . .	. . .	23.3	18.9	17.6	20.5	15.9	. . .	. . .	. . .
United States	22.4	18.9	17.8	17.0	24.6	20.7	19.5	18.0	19.6	17.3	16.3	15.7
USSR	. . .	. . .	. . .	. . .	10.9	9.4	9.4	8.3	19.6	. . .	. . .	. . .
Yugoslavia	24.3	20.2	19.6	18.7	27.1	24.1	23.6	22.6	22.4	18.5	17.7	16.9

Source: Center for Education Statistics, *Digest of Education, 1992*, 408.

TABLE 14.21   ELEMENTARY AND SECONDARY ENROLLMENT AND CURRENT EXPENDITURES—SELECTED COUNTRIES, 1980 AND 1989

Country	1980			1989		
	Pre- elementary, Elementary and Secondary Enrollment	Pre-elementary, Elementary and Secondary Expenditures in Millions of U.S. Dollars	Expenditure per Student	Pre-elementary Elementary and Secondary Enrollment	Pre-elementary Elementary and Secondary Expenditures in Millions of U.S. Dollars	Expenditure per Student
United States	46,208,481	94,321	2,041	45,897,707	187,384	4,083
Australia	2,984,562	4,749	1,591	2,982,727	6,552	2,197
Austria	1,305,710	2,498	1,913	1,161,092	4,195	3,613
Belgium	2,061,596	3,877	1,881	1,905,874	4,804	2,521
Canada	4,814,413	10,973	2,279	5,074,654	18,929	3,730
Denmark	996,515	1,993	2,000	898,347	3,598	4,005
Finland	848,794	1,436	1,692	849,421	2,868	3,377
France	12,007,492	17,367	1,446	12,071,005	29,971	2,483
Germany, (former West)	10,881,123	18,750	1,723	10,253,112	25,497	2,487
Ireland	858,132	719	838	908,211	1,276	1,405
Italy	11,601,354	11,287	973	10,512,792	20,634	1,963
Japan	23,791,229	27,911	1,173	23,224,369	52,090	2,243
Netherlands	3,134,403	5,239	1,671	2,717,945	6,558	2,413
New Zealand	790,547	837	1,058	717,994	1,202	1,675
Norway	829,151	1,468	1,770	797,174	2,659	3,336
Portugal	1,738,805	1,183	680	1,677,389	2,580	1,538
Spain	8,768,795	3,594	410	9,099,233	8,531	938
Sweden	1,500,083	3,624	2,416	1,484,327	5,997	4,040
Switzerland	1,030,847	2,751	2,669	894,854	4,336	4,845
Turkey	7,879,094	1,136	144	10,581,118	20,672	1,954
United Kingdom	10,578,973	16,231	1,534	9,496,878	27,517	2,897

Source: Center for Education Statistics, *Digest of Education, 1992*, 419.

TABLE 14.22 PUBLIC EXPENDITURES FOR EDUCATION AS A PERCENTAGE OF GOVERNMENT EXPENDITURES FOR ALL PURPOSES—SELECTED COUNTRIES, 1960–1989

Country	1960	1970	1975	1980	1981	1982	1983	1984	1985	1986	1987	1988	1989
Australia	...	13.3	14.8	14.8	14.5	14.0	13.6	13.2	12.8	12.6	12.5	...	...
Canada	14.3	24.1	17.8	17.3	17.0	...	...	15.2	12.7	15.5	15.4	15.9	15.3
Chile	12.6	22.0	12.0	11.9	...	...	...	...	15.3	...	...	...	...
France	...	...	...	...	...	...	18.0	...	...	...	...	...	...
Germany, (former) Federal Republic of	...	9.2	10.7	10.1	...	...	9.5	9.2	9.2	9.2	9.0	8.8	...
Hungary	8.4	6.9	4.2	5.2	5.5	5.8	6.6	6.4	6.4	6.4	6.3	6.4	7.1
Italy	...	11.9	9.4	...	...	...	9.6	8.5	8.3	8.3	...	...	...
Japan	...	20.4	22.4	19.6	19.4	19.1	18.7	18.1	17.9	17.7	16.8	16.2	...
Mexico	...	8.5	11.9	16.7	17.2	14.6	6.4	...	13.2	...	8.0	7.6	...
Netherlands	...	...	23.7	23.1	19.6	18.8	18.1	16.8	16.4	...	...	...	...
Nigeria	...	...	...	...	...	9.6	9.3	11.6	8.7	12.0	...	...	...
Norway	...	15.5	14.7	13.8	13.5	13.5	12.9	12.8	13.6	13.6	13.8	13.5	13.4
Sweden	...	...	13.4	14.1	13.9	13.0	12.5	12.2	12.6	12.6	12.8	12.3	13.1
Thailand	...	17.3	21.0	20.6	20.0	20.1	21.1	...	18.5	19.4	17.9	16.6	...
United Kingdom	...	14.1	14.3	13.9	12.2	11.9	11.5	11.3	...	...	...	...	...
United States	15.1	20.3	18.1	19.9	19.1	18.1	17.7	17.7	17.3	17.5	17.5	17.6	18.2
USSR (former)	11.7	12.8	12.9	11.2	10.9	10.3	10.2	10.2	...	...	...	...	...
Yugoslavia	...	23.3	24.4	32.5	...	...	...	...	...	...	...	...	...

Source: Center for Education Statistics, *Digest of Education, 1992*, 419.

TABLE 14.23 PUBLIC EXPENDITURES FOR EDUCATION AS A PERCENT OF GROSS NATIONAL PRODUCT—SELECTED COUNTRIES, 1960–1989

Country	1960	1970	1975	1980	1981	1982	1983	1984	1985	1986	1987	1988	1989
Australia	2.9	4.2	6.5	5.9	5.9	5.9	6.3	6.0	5.9	5.7	5.5	...	...
Canada	4.6	8.9	7.6	7.3	7.8	8.3	7.7	7.2	7.0	7.5	7.3	7.2	7.0
Chile	2.7	5.1	4.1	4.6	5.4	5.7	4.9	4.8	4.4	...	3.6	3.6	...
France	2.4	4.9	5.2	5.0	5.6	5.8	5.8	5.8	5.8	5.6	5.5	5.3	...
Germany, (former) Federal Republic of	...	3.5	5.1	4.7	4.7	4.6	4.8	4.6	4.5	4.4	4.4	4.2	...
Hungary	4.4	4.4	4.1	4.7	5.1	5.0	5.8	5.4	5.4	5.7	5.5	5.4	6.0
Italy	3.6	4.0	4.1	...	...	...	4.8	5.1	5.0	5.0	...	...	...
Japan	4.1	3.9	5.5	5.8	5.9	5.6	5.6	5.2	5.1	5.0	4.9	4.8	...
Mexico	1.3	2.4	3.6	3.0	4.2	5.2	2.8	2.5	3.8	3.8	3.4	3.3	3.8
Netherlands	4.9	7.3	8.2	7.9	7.8	7.6	7.4	6.8	6.8	6.9	7.3	6.8	...
Nigeria	2.2	...	4.3	...	5.5	2.1	1.6	1.2	1.0	1.5	...	...	...
Norway	4.2	6.0	7.1	7.2	6.9	7.0	7.0	6.7	6.5	6.8	7.1	7.4	7.5
Sweden	4.6	7.7	7.3	9.0	9.2	9.0	8.4	8.0	7.7	7.5	7.3	6.7	7.3
Thailand	2.5	3.5	3.5	3.4	3.7	3.9	3.9	...	3.9	3.8	3.6	3.2	...
United Kingdom	4.3	5.3	6.6	5.6	5.5	5.4	5.2	5.1	4.9	5.0	4.9	4.7	...
United States	4.0	5.9	6.6	5.8	5.4	5.6	5.6	5.5	5.5	5.6	5.7	5.7	5.8
USSR	5.9	6.8	7.6	7.3	6.9	6.7	6.8	6.8	7.0	7.2	7.5	7.8	7.9
Yugoslavia	2.5	4.9	5.4	4.7	4.5	4.4	3.7	3.5	3.4	3.8	4.2	3.6	4.4

Source: Center for Education Statistics, *Digest of Education, 1992*, 420.

TABLE 14.24 SCIENCE TEST SCORES FOR 10- AND 14-YEAR-OLDS, PERCENTAGE OF AGE GROUPS IN SCHOOL, AND MEAN AGES OF STUDENTS TESTED IN SELECTED COUNTRIES, 1983–1986

Country	10-Year-Olds					14-Year-Olds				
	Grade Tested	Average Test Scores	Percent of Age Group in school	Mean Age in Years and Months	Standard Deviation of age in Months	Grade Tested	Average Test Scores	Percent of Age Group in School	Mean Age in Years and Months	Standard Deviation of Age in Months
Australia	4,5,6	12.9	99	10:6	3.3	8,9,10	17.8	98	14:5	3.3
Canada (English)	5	13.7	99	11:1	7.1	9	18.6	99	15:0	6.1
England	5	11.7	99	10:3	3.6	9	16.7	98	14:2	3.6
Finland	4	15.3	99	10:1	4.1	8	18.5	99	14:1	4.1
Hong Kong	4	11.2	99	10:5	9.8	8	16.4	99	14:7	10.9
Hungary	4	14.4	99	10:3	5.2	8	21.7	98	14:3	4.7
Italy	5	13.4	99	10:9	5.2	8,9	16.7	99	14:7	5.4
Japan	5	15.4	99	10:7	3.5	9	20.2	99	14:7	3.5
Korea (South)	5	15.4	99	11:2	7.4	9	18.1	99	15:0	7.2
Netherlands	...	...	...	...	...	9	19.8	99	15:6	12.5
Norway	4	12.7	99	10:1	4.0	9	17.9	99	15:1	4.0
Philippines	5	9.5	97	11:1	11.3	9	11.5	60	16:1	18.9
Poland	4	11.9	99	10:1	5.4	8	18.1	91	15:0	5.8
Singapore	5	11.2	99	10:1	5.7	9	16.5	91	15:3	9.0
Sweden	4	14.7	99	10:1	4.1	8	18.4	99	14:9	3.8
Thailand	...	...	...	...	...	9	16.5	32	15:4	8.9
United States	5	13.2	99	11:3	6.9	9	16.5	99	15:4	9.1

Source: Center for Education Statistics, *Digest of Education, 1991*, 399.

TABLE 14.25 INTERNATIONAL MATHEMATICS TEST SCORES AND PERCENTAGE OF AGE GROUP TAKING TESTS IN THE 12TH GRADE—SELECTED COUNTRIES, 1981–1982

Country or Province	Average Age of Students	Percent of Age Group Taking Test	Percent of Analysis items Students had Been Taught	Achievement Scores for Top 5 Percent of Age Group			
				Average Score	Algebra	Geometry	Analysis (calculus)
Average	**17**	**16**	**76**	**57.1**	**57.6**	**57.2**	**56.4**
Belgium							
Flemish	17	10	88	56.3	57.5	55.9	55.5
French	17	10	. . .	54.2	55.3	53.6	53.7
Canada							
British Columbia	17	30	32	57.3	60.9	59.2	51.8
Ontario	18	19	83	59.4	59.6	59.3	59.4
England and Wales	17	6	85	55.5	54.9	55.5	56.1
Finland	18	15	87	60.5	60.7	59.8	61.0
Hungary	17	50	67	59.9	60.9	61.1	57.7
Israel	17	6	78	50.0	51.5	47.7	50.9
Japan	17	12	92	65.0	63.7	64.9	66.5
New Zealand	17	11	93	57.2	56.8	57.0	57.7
Scotland	16	18	. . .	55.7	56.2	58.0	52.9
Sweden	18	12	86	58.9	58.5	59.0	59.2
Thailand	. . .	. . .	63	. . .	. . .	. . .	. . .
United States	17	13	54	52.2	52.8	53.0	50.9

Source: Center for Education Statistics, *Digest of Education, 1991*, 398.

TABLE 14.26 MEAN NUMBER OF AREAS CORRECTLY IDENTIFIED IN A TEST OF GEOGRAPHY KNOWLEDGE, BY COUNTRY AND AGE, 1988

Country	Age				
	18–24	25–34	35–44	45–54	55 and Over
Canada	9.3	9.2	10.5	8.3	8.7
France	9.2	9.6	10.1	9.0	8.8
Germany, West	11.2	11.2	11.0	11.8	10.9
Italy	9.3	9.3	8.4	7.8	5.5
Japan	9.5	10.8	10.5	9.7	7.9
Mexico	8.2	6.9	7.6	6.4	5.7
Sweden	11.9	12.3	12.5	11.5	10.3
United Kingdom	9.0	8.4	9.2	8.9	7.8
United States	6.9	8.8	9.6	8.8	8.4

Source: Center for Education Statistics, *Digest of Education, 1991*, 400.

TABLE 14.27 AVERAGE GRADE THAT THE PUBLIC WOULD GIVE THE SCHOOLS IN THEIR COMMUNITY AND IN THE NATION AT LARGE, 1974–1990[a]

Year	All Adults		No Children in School		Public School Parents		Private School Parents	
	Nation	Local Community	Nation	Local Community	Nation	Local Community	Nation	Local Community
1974	. . .	2.63	. . .	2.57	. . .	2.80	. . .	2.15
1975	. . .	2.38	. . .	2.31	. . .	2.49	. . .	1.81
1976	. . .	2.38	. . .	2.34	. . .	2.48	. . .	2.22
1977	. . .	2.33	. . .	2.25	. . .	2.59	. . .	2.05
1978	. . .	2.21	. . .	2.11	. . .	2.47	. . .	1.69
1979	. . .	2.21	. . .	2.15	. . .	2.38	. . .	1.88
1980	. . .	2.26	. . .	. . .	. . .	. . .	. . .	. . .
1981	1.94	2.20	. . .	2.12	. . .	2.36	. . .	1.88
1982	2.01	2.24	2.04	2.18	2.01	2.35	2.02	2.20
1983	1.91	2.12	1.92	2.10	1.92	2.31	1.82	1.89
1984	2.09	2.36	2.11	2.30	2.11	2.49	2.04	2.17
1985	2.14	2.39	2.16	2.36	2.20	2.44	1.93	2.00
1986	2.13	2.36	. . .	2.29	. . .	2.55	. . .	2.14
1987	2.18	2.44	2.20	2.38	2.22	2.61	2.03	2.01
1988	2.08	2.35	2.02	2.32	2.13	2.48	2.00	2.13
1989	2.01	2.35	1.99	2.27	2.06	2.56	1.93	2.12
1990	1.99	2.29	1.98	2.27	2.03	2.44	1.85	2.09

[a] Average based on scale of: A = 4, B = 3, C = 2, D = 1, F = 0.
Source: National Center for Education Statistics, *Digest of Education Statistics, 1992* (Washington, D.C., 1992), 28.

TABLE 14.28   ITEMS MOST FREQUENTLY CITED BY THE GENERAL PUBLIC AS A MAJOR PROBLEM FACING THE LOCAL PUBLIC SCHOOLS, 1970–1990

Problems	Percent												
	1970	1975	1980	1981	1982	1983	1984	1985	1986	1987	1988	1989	1990
Use of drugs	11	9	14	15	20	18	18	18	28	30	32	34	38
Lack of discipline	18	23	26	23	27	25	27	25	24	22	19	19	19
Lack of financial support	17	14	10	12	22	13	14	9	11	14	12	13	13
Getting good teachers	12	11	6	11	10	8	14	10	6	9	11	7	7
Poor curriculum/standards	6	5	11	14	11	14	15	11	8	8	11	8	8
Large schools/overcrowding	. . .	10	7	5	4	3	4	5	5	8	6	8	7
Moral standards	. . .	. . .	. . .	1	2	4	1	2	5	7	6	3	3
Parents' lack of interest	3	2	6	5	5	6	5	3	4	6	7	6	4
Pupils' lack of interest/truancy	. . .	3	5	4	5	5	4	5	3	6	5	3	6
Drinking/alcoholism	. . .	. . .	2	2	3	3	4	3	5	6	5	4	4
Low teacher pay	. . .	. . .	. . .	. . .	. . .	. . .	4	2	3	5	4	4	6
Integration/busing	17	15	10	11	6	5	6	4	3	4	4	4	5
Teachers' lack of interest	. . .	. . .	6	4	7	8	5	4	4	5	3	4	4
Lack of proper facilities	11	3	2	2	2	1	2	1	1	2	1	1	2

Source: Center for Education Statistics, *Digest of Education, 1992,* 128.

Education and Racial Segregation

Between 1946 and 1954 the prevailing concept in the school systems of the southern and border states was the principle, modified in a few specific circumstances, of separate but equal. The purpose and the effect was to impose a separation of the races, an arrangement that facilitated keeping blacks subordinate to whites. Southern schools were separate for blacks and whites, but contrary to a Supreme Court ruling of some 60 years earlier, they were scarcely equal. As a whole the poorest in the land, southern schools for African Americans easily constituted the poorest of the poor.

In the *Brown* decision of May 1954 the high court abolished separate but equal, and in a complementary ruling it decreed that desegregation should begin quickly but could proceed "with all deliberate speed," which in fact meant gradually. Many southerners took gradually to mean never. The border states began movement, however slow and grudging, toward mixing the races, but states of the Deep South proclaimed resistance and looked for means to circumvent the court's decision. The years 1954 to 1965 marked high tide of the Civil Rights movement, and it also produced the most determined southern resistance to desegregation of the public schools. In 1957 the governor of Arkansas openly prevented integration of Central High School in Little Rock, and when President Dwight Eisenhower sent military forces to enforce the court's order, the governor, Orvil Faubus, closed the schools. Several counties in Virginia pursued the same course in 1958 and 1959. Resistance to token desegregation on the university level by the state governors and resident whites provoked major incidents in Louisiana in 1960, Mississippi in 1962, and Alabama in 1963.

Justified as an expression of states' rights, action of state officials had the effect of interposing the will of the national government upon the states. Tardy but persistent intervention of national officials in specific situations, passage of the Civil Rights Act of 1964 (which contained special provisions for school desegregation), and continuing decisions by the Supreme Court gradually broke the wall of southern resistance and induced local officials and much of the populace to yield to the inevitable outcome. The portion of southern black students attending totally or almost totally black schools nosedived to 25 percent by 1972. Very few blacks went to schools that did not also have white classmates.

Desegregation efforts in the 1970s centered on public schools of the North and Midwest, where racial separation had not been rooted in law (de jure), but was de facto, a product of residential patterns and neighborhood schools that had grown from them. Court-ordered busing to achieve racial balance in the 1970s produced angry white protest in Cleveland, Detroit, Denver, Kansas City, and especially in Boston. A growing "white flight" to school districts in the suburbs in several cases produced more segregation than there had been in the first place. Some 10,000 students fled the Boston school district in the late 1970s. An often-mentioned antidote, cross-district busing, from suburbs to inner city and vice versa, carried such prospect for violence that it never was extensively tried. The courts began to relax rulings on busing and desegregation.

By the end of the 1980s the status of desegregation lended itself to no simple generalization. Officially, segregation was illegal in all publicly supported institutions, and few students attended school with only people of their race. Opinion polls suggested that nearly everyone accepted the principle of integration. The most racially mixed schools were in the South, the least in the North and Midwest. Schools of the inner city had mostly black or Hispanic students; even at a time of a teacher surplus, it was difficult to get teachers to go there. Suburban schools contained mostly white students and were safer and better funded; in several states, school finance came partly from locally driven funding: millage—a public referendum on the rate of taxation for schools. Traditional civil-rights reformers and white liberals still formally endorsed integration, but the reformers were not as adamant as they once had been, and many of the whites in Congress probably sent their children to private schools. The most radical activists favored, even demanded, black schools for black students with black teachers and black programs. On many college campuses black students wanted racially exclusive dormitories, fraternities and sororities, and officially recognized social organizations. Multiculturalism had clear separatist overtones. To blacks and whites the answers in 1990 were not as simple as they had appeared in 1959.

SEGREGATION IN THE SOUTH: PERCENT OF BLACK STUDENTS ATTENDING SCHOOL WITH WHITE STUDENTS

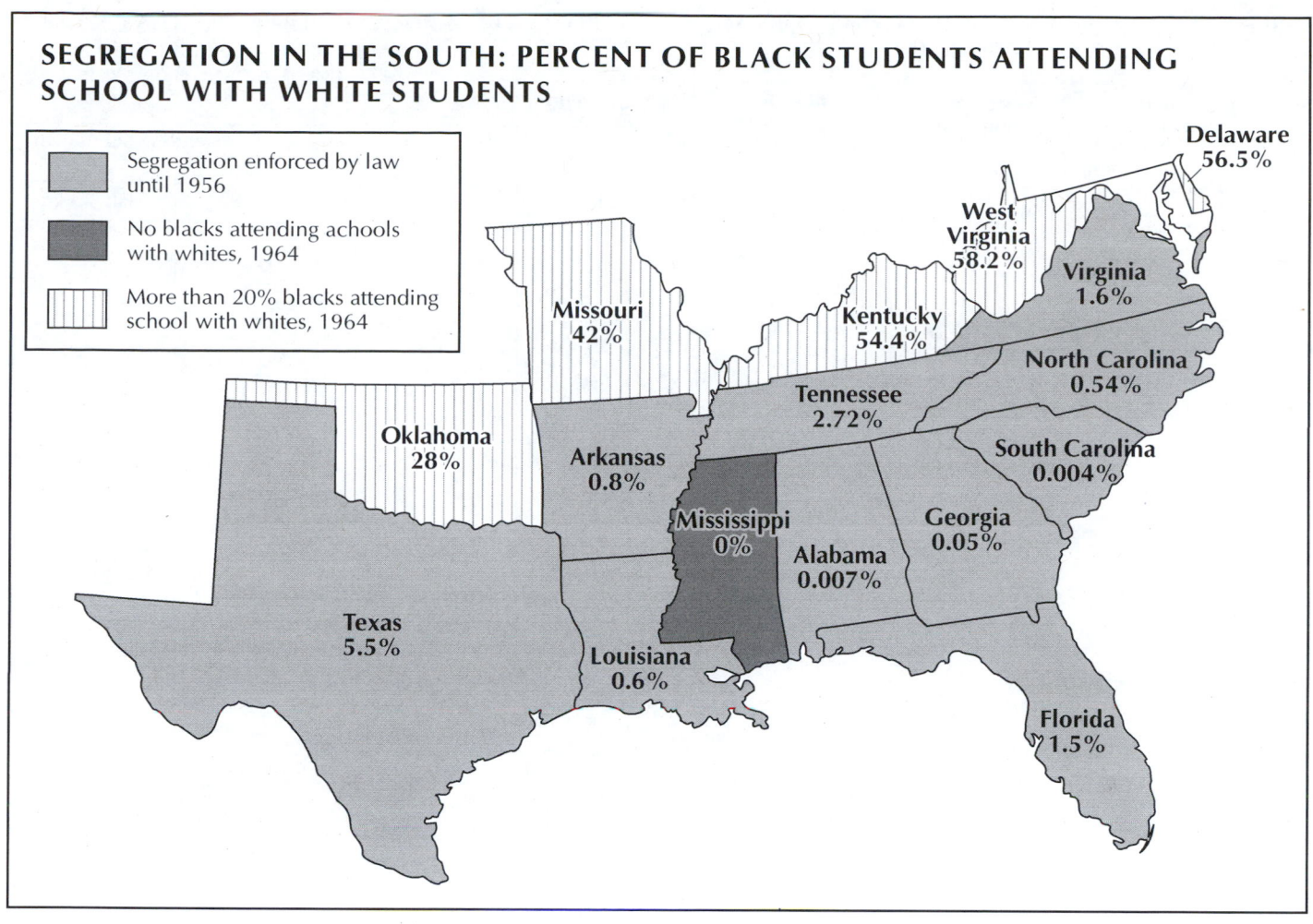

Legend:
- Segregation enforced by law until 1956
- No blacks attending schools with whites, 1964
- More than 20% blacks attending school with whites, 1964

Delaware 56.5%
West Virginia 58.2%
Virginia 1.6%
Kentucky 54.4%
North Carolina 0.54%
Missouri 42%
Tennessee 2.72%
South Carolina 0.004%
Oklahoma 28%
Arkansas 0.8%
Mississippi 0%
Georgia 0.05%
Alabama 0.007%
Texas 5.5%
Louisiana 0.6%
Florida 1.5%

TABLE 14.29   GALLUP POLL ON SCHOOL INTEGRATION, SEPTEMBER 19–24, 1957

Question: *The United States Supreme Court has ruled that racial segregation in the public schools is illegal. This means that all children, no matter what their race, must be allowed to go to the same schools. Do you approve or disapprove of this decision?*

Answer	Percent
Approve	59
Disapprove	35
No opinion	6
South Only	
Approve	23
Disapprove	72
No opinion	5
Southern Blacks	
Approve	69
Disapprove	13
No opinion	18

Source: George H. Gallup, *The Gallup Poll, Public Opinion 1935–1971, Volume Two, 1949–1958* (New York, 1972), 1518, 1527.

TABLE 14.30   PERCENTAGES OF BLACK ELEMENTARY AND SECONDARY STUDENTS GOING TO SCHOOL WITH ANY WHITES, IN 11 SOUTHERN STATES, 1954–1973

School Year	Percentage
1954–1955	0.001
1956–1957	0.14
1958–1959	0.13
1960–1961	0.16
1962–1963	0.45
1964–1965	2.25
1966–1967	15.9
1968–1969	32.0
1970–1971	85.6
1972–1973	91.3

Note: The states are Alabama, Arkansas, Florida, Georgia, Louisiana, Mississippi, North Carolina, South Carolina, Tennessee, Texas, and Virginia.
Source: Laurence Baum, *The Supreme Court* (Washington, D.C., 1995), 233.

TABLE 14.31 YEARS OF SCHOOL COMPLETED, BY AGE, RACE, AND ETHNIC ORIGIN, 1940–1989

Age/ Year	Median School Years Completed by All Persons	Median School Years Completed by Black Persons	Median School Years Completed by Hispanic Persons
25 years and Older			
1940	8.6	5.7	. . .
1950	9.3	6.8	. . .
1960	10.6	8.0	. . .
1970	12.1	9.8	9.1
1980	12.5	12.0	10.8
1989	12.7	12.4	12.0
25–29 Years			
1940	10.3	7.0	. . .
1950	12.0	8.6	. . .
1960	12.3	9.9	. . .
1970	12.6	12.1	. . .
1980	12.9	12.6	. . .
1989	12.9	12.7	12.3

Source: Harold W. Stanley and Richard G. Niemi, *Vital Statistics on American Politics* (Washington, D.C., 1992), 388.

TABLE 14.32 PUBLIC OPINION OF WHITES ON SCHOOL INTEGRATION, BY RACIAL COMPOSITION OF SCHOOL, 1958–1990

(percent)

Date	Objection to Own Children Attending School with		
	A Few Blacks	Half Blacks	More Than Half Blacks
Sep. 1958	25	53	70
Feb. 1959	20	47	71
May 1963	25	52	75
Apr. 1965	16	42	67
Jun. 1965	20	44	68
May 1966	11	41	67
Jul. 1969	11	38	66
Mar. 1970	8	32	66
Apr. 1970	10	34	63
Mar. 1972	6	25	55
Aug. 1973	9	36	67
Mar. 1974	4	33	67
Mar. 1975	6	38	66
Sep. 1975	7	35	62
Mar. 1977	7	26	64
Mar. 1978	4	24	61
Jul. 1978	7	36	67
Dec. 1980	6	28	62
Mar. 1982	4	21	54
Mar. 1983	3	25	65
Mar. 1985	4	22	60
Mar. 1986	4	24	64
Mar. 1988	3	21	52
Mar. 1989	4	23	59
Mar. 1990	2	20	59

Note: Question: "Would you, yourself, have any objection to sending your children to a school where a few of the children are (Negroes/blacks)?" If no: "Where half of the children are (Negroes/blacks)?" If no: "Where more than half of the children are (Negroes/blacks)?" Those saying "don't know" were assumed to have expressed some objection. Question asked of whites with school-age children only.
Source: Various surveys compiled in Stanley and Niemi, *Statistics on Politics*, 392.

TABLE 14.33 PUBLIC OPINION OF WHITES ON SCHOOL AND NEIGHBORHOOD INTEGRATION, 1942–1990

(percent)

Date	Blacks and Whites Should Attend		
	Same Schools	Separate Schools	Don't Know
Jun. 1942	30	66	4
Apr. 1956	49	47	4
Jun. 1956	49	49	2
Sep. 1956	48	49	3
May 1963	63	32	5
Dec. 1963	65	29	6
Jun. 1964	62	32	5
Oct. 1964	64	34	2
Jun. 1965	67	30	3
Oct. 1965	68	28	4
Apr. 1970	74	24	3
Mar. 1972	85	14	2
Nov. 1972	80	15	5
Mar. 1976	83	15	3
Mar. 1977	85	14	2
Mar. 1980	86	12	2
Mar. 1982	88	9	2
Mar. 1984	90	8	2
Mar. 1985	92	7	1

Date	If Blacks Lived Next Door			
	Would Definitely Move	Might Move	Would Not Move	Don't Know
1963	20	25	55	. . .
1965	13	22	65	. . .
1966	13	21	66	. . .
1967	12	23	65	. . .
1978	4	9	84	3
1990	1	4	93	2

Date	If Many Blacks Lived in Neighborhood			
	Would Definitely Move	Might Move	Would Not Move	Don't Know
1963	49	29	22	. . .
1965	40	29	31	. . .
1966	39	31	30	. . .
1967	40	31	29	. . .
1978	20	31	45	4
1990	8	18	68	6

Note: ". . ." indicates not available. Neighborhood questions: "If (colored/black) people came to live next door, would you move?" "Would you move if (colored/black) people came to live in great numbers in your neighborhood?" Asked of non-blacks only.
Source: Various surveys compiled in Stanley and Niemi, *Statistics on Politics*, 391.

TABLE 14.34 **SCHOOL DESEGREGATION, BY REGION, 1968–1988**

Region/Year	Percentage of Black Students in Schools with More Than Half Minority Students	Percentage of Hispanic Students in Schools with More Than Half Minority Students	Percentage of Black Students in Schools 90–100 Percent Minority	Percentage of Hispanic Students in Schools 90–100 Percent Minority
South 1968	80.9	69.6	77.8	33.7
1972	55.3	69.9	24.7	31.4
1976	54.9	70.9	22.4	32.2
1980	57.1	76.0	23.0	37.3
1984	56.9	75.4	24.2	37.3
1986	58.0	75.2	25.1	38.6
1988	56.5	80.2	24.0	37.9
Change 1968 to 1988	−24.4	+10.6	−53.8	+4.2
Border 1968	71.6	. . .	60.2	. . .
1972	67.2	. . .	54.7	. . .
1976	60.1	. . .	42.5	. . .
1980	59.2	. . .	37.0	. . .
1984	62.5	. . .	37.4	. . .
1986	59.3	29.9	35.6	. . .
1988	59.6	. . .	34.5	. . .
Change 1968 to 1988	−12.0	. . .	−25.7	. . .
Northeast 1968	66.8	74.8	42.7	44.0
1972	69.9	74.4	46.9	44.1
1976	72.5	74.9	51.4	45.8
1980	79.9	76.3	48.7	45.8
1984	73.1	77.5	47.4	47.1
1986	72.8	78.2	49.8	46.4
1988	77.3	79.7	48.0	44.2
Change 1968 to 1988	+10.5	+4.9	+5.3	+0.2
Midwest 1968	77.3	31.8	58.0	6.8
1972	75.3	34.4	57.4	9.5
1976	70.3	39.3	51.1	14.1
1980	69.5	46.6	43.6	19.6
1984	70.7	53.9	43.6	24.2
1986	69.8	54.3	38.5	23.5
1988	70.1	52.3	41.8	24.9
Change 1968 to 1988	−7.2	+20.5	−16.2	+18.1
West 1968	72.2	42.4	50.8	11.7
1972	68.1	44.7	42.7	11.5
1976	67.4	52.7	36.3	13.3
1980	66.8	63.5	33.7	18.5
1984	66.9	68.4	29.4	22.9
1986	68.2	69.9	28.3	24.7
1988	67.1	71.3	28.6	27.5
Change 1968 to 1988	−5.1	+28.9	−22.2	+15.8
Total 1968	76.6	54.8	64.3	23.1
1972	63.6	56.6	38.7	23.3
1976	62.4	60.8	35.9	24.8
1980	62.9	68.1	33.2	28.8
1984	63.5	70.6	33.2	31.0
1986	63.3	71.5	32.5	32.2
1988	63.2	. . .	32.1	. . .
Change 1968 to 1988	−13.4	+16.7	−32.2	+9.1

Source: Harold W. Stanley and Richard G. Niemi, *Vital Statistics on American Politics* (Washington, D.C., 1994), 395–96.

The School and Greater American Society

American society in the last half of the 20th century was in an almost constant state of change. The most concrete statement of change often took the form of an act of Congress or a state legislature or a decision by the national or a state Supreme Court. Decreeing change was one step; carrying it out was another matter. Often the forum of debate or the battleground was the schoolyard, the portal to the building, or what went on inside. Although the stated objectives usually were worthwhile and meritorious, at least in theory, putting them into force placed a heavy burden on the public school system, turning them into proving grounds and social laboratories for addressing the problems of American society. The following represent a few examples.

1. The long overdue civil-rights revolution began with a Supreme Court decision about schools, and it often was played out in an educational setting in such places as Little Rock, Arkansas; Oxford, Mississippi; Tuscaloosa, Alabama; New York City; or Boston.
2. In 1975 Congress ordered the states to provide free education for all disabled children. If they could not be "mainstreamed" (taught in regular classes), they would have to receive special treatment, whatever it cost in terms of money and personnel.
3. Congress in 1968 passed a law to help low-income, non-English-speaking children learn English, and in 1974 the Supreme Court sustained that principle. A form of bilingual education, the concept gradually turned into a program of separate instruction in a student's native tongue. By 1990 the number of language groups that received special bilingual instruction had grown to 145.

4. Title IX of the Education Amendments Act of 1972 forbade sexual discrimination in schools, and ensuing regulations bordered on a decree that the sexes were in all respects the same. Boys took home economics; girls took shop. Girls could compete for boys athletic teams or form their own teams (rarely, if ever, were boys allowed to try out for girls basketball or volleyball squads). Valid in its most basic principle, philosophically appealing, and politically correct, the policy created situations that were awkward, unsettling, and often expensive.

5. Preoccupation with multiculturalism starting in the 1970s introduced a maze of philsophical, substantive, and political issues with respect to hiring, selection of courses, how and what the students were taught—a system that in its most stringent application could come close to thought and speech control.

Although it would seem unjust and inappropriate to expect the school system, the teachers, and even the students to resolve these complex issues, it often appeared that conditions evolved in that fashion. With so many distractions, with continuing disintegration of the family and increasing extracurricular social enticements, one perhaps should not be surprised that test scores were low.

Colleges and Universities

The postwar era began on college campus with a bang. In one of the most enlightened moves of the century, a wartime Congress in 1944 passed the Serviceman's Readjustment Act. Intended as payment from a grateful nation and designed to promote an orderly passage into peacetime, the measure offered veterans of the Second World War a package of benefits that became known as the G.I. Bill of Rights. Surely the most important provision offered financial support for veterans wishing to expand their education, including—if armed service members were so inclined—four full years of college. More than 1 million showed up on campus in 1946, roughly doubling the student clientele, and producing a crisis in teachers, classrooms, and places to live. Many of the veterans were married and already had

begun work on a baby boom. By the time benefits ended on July 25, 1956 (an extension would be added for veterans of the Korean War), some 7.8 million had received education and training assistance; 2.2 million attended two- or four-year colleges. In addition to training national leadership for decades to come, the G.I. Bill gave an egalitarian mark to the idea of a college education, and it got the schools off and running.

One of the most striking features of higher education between 1946 and 1990 was the sheer increase in numbers—of institutions, of students, and in the percentage of the commonly accepted college-age population that went to college. The number of schools approximately doubled during the period, and the largest increase came in two-year colleges, which nearly trebled. The student body underwent an expansion of nearly sevenfold, which meant, among other themes, that the change was more in size of institutions than in numbers. Some campuses became virtual cities in themselves, larger in population than the towns that housed them.

A majority of female students that had marked the schools during the years of war abruptly gave way to the wave of former soldiers that flooded the campus in 1946. A continuation of the male majority was consistent with social and cultural priorities of the 1950s, and the trend continued through the 1960s as well. The largest difference between male and female students, more than 1.5 million, came in the year 1970. Thereafter the male lead begins to erode, and the most rapid change would come in the late 1970s. A male majority of 1 million in 1974 dropped to 600,000 in 1976. By 1979 the women had passed the men; the lead expanded through the rest of the period. By 1990 females on campus outnumbered males by more than 1.2 million.

Complete numbers did not exist for the racial and ethnic mix of students in the early part of the period. Hispanics had no numbers at all until the 1970s. The start of the Civil Rights movement produced much opposition to identification by race or ethnicity on grounds that it could invite discrimination. No one could doubt, however, that except for clearly marked African-American institutions, most of which were in the South, the college population was overwhelmingly white. With

Colleges scrambled for married veterans' housing during the rush to campus after 1945. These facilities were at Western Michigan College, where enrollment grew from 1,839 to 4,034 in one year. (Western Michigan University Archives and Regional History Collections)

growing emphasis on race and ethnicity, with development of numerous state and national funding programs that targeted minority groups, and with the impact of affirmative-action preferences in enrollment practices, conditions begin to change in the 1970s. Statistics varied fairly sharply from year-to-year, but after 1975 the proportion of black and Hispanic high school graduates who enrolled in college frequently approximated the percentage of whites. Perhaps the most compelling numbers had to do with the fact that the portion of college-age people (18–24) who enrolled in college went from 12.5 percent in 1946 to 51.1 percent in 1990. Attending college had gone from being an elitist enterprise to a common part of the American experience.

The college experience changed with passage of time, emergence of new issues, and appearance on campus of new generations of students. Military veterans probably had different treatment, but postwar colleges often served as surrogate parents for young people away from home, perhaps for the first extended period in their lives. Campus living arrangements remained strictly segregated. Younger students—at least the young women—had to live in campus facilities. Rules were elaborate and usually enforced. Many schools had dress codes. Uniforms remained a conspicuous part of the campus landscape, a continuing reminder of the cold war and that young men had certain (ROTC) obligations.

As the baby boomers came of college age in the mid-to-late 1960s, and as pressing national problems took center stage, the universities became settings for intellectual discourse and social and political upheaval. Starting with the free speech (and filthy speech) movement at Berkeley in 1964, few major schools did not experience some form of turmoil in the late 1960s and early 1970s. Extreme examples were the seizure of Columbia University in 1968, which closed the school for the

semester, and conditions at Kent State University in 1970 that led to the killing of four people and wounding of 11 by the Ohio National Guard.

Sanctity of the movements for civil rights and against the war in Vietnam seemed to legitimize anything student protestors wished to do or not do, and as the closest and most continuing object of authority—the "establishment"—the university itself became a target. Unaccustomed to such pressure, the schools quickly abandoned the social restrictions and many canceled the ROTC programs. Demands for curricular change ranged from new, more "relevant" courses and instructors—especially having to do with gender, race, and ethnicity—to an end to required courses—compulsory reading assignments, examinations and even grades, which in that heady atmosphere were charged with being class-ridden and elitist. Timid adminstrators and individual instructors often yielded rather than face having their place torn up.

Some of the changes of the 1960s and 1970 were long overdue, and they became lasting parts of university operations. Many schools had become impersonal diploma mills, many professors concerned largely, if not entirely, with individual projects. Courses, if not departments, in such areas as gender, ethnicity, and especially African-American studies—now part of permanent offerings—date their origins to that era. Other measures that seemed to represent student efforts to make their life easier and more fun were soon abandoned.

With the Vietnam War, and the draft, ending in 1973, with the Civil Rights movement in a state of limbo, with students now into their 20s and facing a need to make a living, conditions changed on campus. The spirit of revolution died, to be replaced with more practical concerns about preparing for a good job. As with society itself, however, the universities did not go back to what they had

Closeup of a veteran's residential "trailer," Western Michigan College, 1946 (Western Michigan Archives and Regional History Collections)

been. In the 1980s the colleges seek to adapt to a new technology, the ramifications of which scarcely could be imagined. Computer usage expanded rapidly, but the reaches of an Internet had yet to be established. The schools continue to grow, and the students come from more varied backgrounds. With a growing emphasis on multiculturalism, with the concept of affirmative action taking on a substantive meaning, diversity will be a major driving force in university activity through the 1980s.

TABLE 14.35 INSTITUTIONS OF HIGHER EDUCATION, BY CONTROL AND TYPE OF INSTITUTION, 1949–1950 TO 1989–1990

Year	All Institutions			Public			Private		
	Total	4-Year	2-Year	Total	4-Year	2-Year	Total	4-Year	2-Year
Excluding Branch Campuses									
1949–50	1,851	1,327	524	641	344	297	1,210	983	227
1950–51	1,852	1,312	540	636	341	295	1,216	971	245
1951–52	1,832	1,326	506	641	350	291	1,191	976	215
1952–53	1,882	1,355	527	639	349	290	1,243	1,006	237
1953–54	1,863	1,345	518	662	369	293	1,201	976	225
1954–55	1,849	1,333	516	648	353	295	1,201	980	221
1955–56	1,850	1,347	503	650	360	290	1,200	987	213
1956–57	1,878	1,355	523	656	359	297	1,222	996	226
1957–58	1,930	1,390	540	666	366	300	1,264	1,024	240
1958–59	1,947	1,394	553	673	366	307	1,274	1,028	246
1959–60	2,004	1,422	582	695	367	328	1,309	1,055	254
1960–61	2,021	1,431	590	700	368	332	1,321	1,063	258
1961–62	2,033	1,443	590	718	374	344	1,315	1,069	246
1962–63	2,093	1,468	625	740	376	364	1,353	1,092	261
1963–64	2,132	1,499	633	760	386	374	1,372	1,113	259
1964–65	2,175	1,521	654	799	393	406	1,376	1,128	248
1965–66	2,230	1,551	679	821	401	420	1,409	1,150	259
1966–67	2,329	1,577	752	880	403	477	1,449	1,174	275
1967–68	2,374	1,588	786	934	414	520	1,440	1,174	266
1968–69	2,483	1,619	864	1,011	417	594	1,472	1,202	270
1969–70	2,525	1,639	886	1,060	426	634	1,465	1,213	252
1970–71	2,556	1,665	891	1,089	435	654	1,467	1,230	237
1971–72	2,606	1,675	931	1,137	440	697	1,469	1,235	234
1972–73	2,665	1,701	964	1,182	449	733	1,483	1,252	231
1973–74	2,720	1,717	1,003	1,200	440	760	1,520	1,277	243
1974–75	2,747	1,744	1,003	1,214	447	767	1,533	1,297	236
1975–76	2,765	1,767	998	1,219	447	772	1,546	1,320	226
1976–77	2,785	1,783	1,002	1,231	452	779	1,554	1,331	223
1977–78	2,826	1,808	1,018	1,241	454	787	1,585	1,354	231
1978–79	2,954	1,843	1,111	1,308	463	845	1,646	1,380	266
1979–80	2,975	1,863	1,112	1,310	464	846	1,665	1,399	266
1980–81	3,056	1,861	1,195	1,334	465	869	1,722	1,396	326
1981–82	3,083	1,883	1,200	1,340	471	869	1,743	1,412	331
1982–83	3,111	1,887	1,224	1,336	472	864	1,775	1,415	360
1983–84	3,117	1,914	1,203	1,325	474	851	1,792	1,440	352
1984–85	3,146	1,911	1,235	1,329	461	868	1,817	1,450	367
1985–86	3,155	1,915	1,240	1,326	461	865	1,829	1,454	375
Including Branch Campuses									
1974–75	3,004	1,866	1,138	1,433	537	896	1,571	1,329	242
1975–76	3,026	1,898	1,128	1,442	545	897	1,584	1,353	231
1976–77	3,046	1,913	1,133	1,455	550	905	1,591	1,363	228
1977–78	3,095	1,938	1,157	1,473	552	921	1,622	1,386	236
1978–79	3,134	1,941	1,193	1,474	550	924	1,660	1,391	269
1979–80	3,152	1,957	1,195	1,475	549	926	1,677	1,408	269
1980–81	3,231	1,957	1,274	1,497	552	945	1,734	1,405	329
1981–82	3,253	1,979	1,274	1,498	558	940	1,755	1,421	334
1982–83	3,280	1,984	1,296	1,493	560	933	1,787	1,424	363
1983–84	3,284	2,013	1,271	1,481	565	916	1,803	1,448	355
1984–85	3,331	2,025	1,306	1,501	566	935	1,830	1,459	371
1985–86	3,340	2,029	1,311	1,498	566	932	1,842	1,463	379
1986–87	3,406	2,070	1,336	1,533	573	960	1,873	1,497	376
1987–88	3,587	2,135	1,452	1,591	599	992	1,996	1,536	460
1988–89	3,565	2,129	1,436	1,582	598	984	1,983	1,531	452
1989–90	3,535	2,127	1,408	1,563	595	968	1,972	1,532	440

Source: Center for Education Statistics, *Digest of Education, 1991,* 230.

TABLE 14.36 ENROLLMENT IN INSTITUTIONS OF HIGHER EDUCATION, BY SEX, ATTENDANCE STATUS, AND TYPE AND CONTROL OF INSTITUTION, FALL 1946–FALL 1990

(in thousands)

Year	Total Enrollment	Enrollment as a Percent of 18- to 24-Year-Old Population	Male	Female	Full-Time	Part-Time	4-Year	2-Year	Public Institutions Total	Public 4-Year	Public 2-Year	Private Institutions Total	Private 4-Year	Private 2-Year
Fall 1946	2,078	12.5	1,418	661	...	...	...	...	...	...	...	...	...	...
Fall 1947	2,338	14.2	1,659	679	...	...	2,116	222	1,152	989	163	1,186	1,127	59
Fall 1948	2,403	14.7	1,709	694	...	...	2,192	211	1,186	1,032	154	1,218	1,161	57
Fall 1949	2,445	15.2	1,722	723	...	...	2,216	229	1,207	1,036	171	1,238	1,179	58
Fall 1950	2,281	14.3	1,560	721	...	...	2,064	217	1,140	972	168	1,142	1,092	50
Fall 1951	2,102	13.4	1,391	711	...	...	1,902	200	1,038	882	156	1,064	1,020	44
Fall 1952	2,134	13.8	1,380	754	...	...	1,896	238	1,101	910	192	1,033	986	47
Fall 1953	2,231	14.7	1,423	808	...	...	1,973	258	1,186	976	210	1,045	997	48
Fall 1954	2,447	16.2	1,563	883	...	...	2,164	282	1,354	1112	241	1,093	1,052	41
Fall 1955	2,653	17.7	1,733	920	...	...	2,345	308	1,476	1211	265	1,177	1,134	43
Fall 1956	2,918	19.5	1,911	1,007	...	...	2,571	347	1,656	1359	298	1,262	1,212	50
Fall 1957	3,324	22.0	2,171	1,153	...	...	...	...	1,973	...	...	1,351	...	...
Fall 1959	3,640	23.8	2,333	1,307	...	...	...	...	2,181	...	...	1,459	...	...
Fall 1961	4,415	23.6	2,586	1,559	...	...	...	...	2,561	...	...	1,584	...	...
Fall 1963	4,780	27.7	2,962	1,818	3,184	1,596	3,929	850	3,081	2341	740	1,698	1,588	111
Fall 1964	5,280	28.7	3,249	2,031	3,573	1,707	4,291	989	3,468	2593	875	1,812	1,698	114
Fall 1965	5,921	29.8	3,630	2,291	4,096	1,825	4,748	1,173	3,970	2928	1,041	1,951	1,820	132
Fall 1966	6,390	30.7	3,856	2,534	4,439	1,951	5,064	1,326	4,349	3160	1,189	2,041	1,904	137
Fall 1967	6,912	32.2	4,133	2,779	4,793	2,119	5,399	1,513	4,816	3444	1,372	2,096	1,955	141
Fall 1968	7,513	34.1	4,478	3,035	5,210	2,303	5,721	1,792	5,431	3784	1,646	2,082	1,937	146
Fall 1969	8,005	35.0	4,746	3,258	5,499	2,506	5,937	2,068	5,897	3963	1,934	2,108	1,975	133
Fall 1970	8,581	35.8	5,044	3,537	5,816	2,765	6,262	2,319	6,428	4,233	2,195	2,153	2,029	124
Fall 1971	8,949	35.3	5,207	3,742	6,077	2,871	6,369	2,579	6,804	4,347	2,457	2,144	2,022	122
Fall 1972	9,215	35.8	5,239	3,976	6,072	3,142	6,459	2,756	7,071	4,430	2,641	2,144	2,029	115
Fall 1973	9,602	36.5	5,371	4,231	6,189	3,413	6,590	3,012	7,420	4,530	2,890	2,183	2,060	122
Fall 1974	10,224	37.9	5,622	4,601	6,370	3,853	6,820	3,404	7,989	4,703	3,285	2,235	2,117	119
Fall 1975	11,185	40.3	6,149	5,036	6,841	4,344	7,215	3,970	8,835	4,998	3,836	2,350	2,217	134
Fall 1976	11,012	38.8	5,811	5,201	6,717	4,295	7,129	3,883	8,653	4,902	3,752	2,359	2,227	132
Fall 1977	11,286	39.0	5,789	5,497	6,793	4,493	7,243	4,043	8,847	4945	3,902	2,439	2,298	141
Fall 1978	11,260	38.3	5,641	5,619	6,668	4,592	7,232	4,028	8,786	4,912	3,874	2,474	2,319	155
Fall 1979	11,570	38.8	5,683	5,887	6,794	4,776	7,353	4,217	9,037	4,980	4,057	2,533	2,373	160
Fall 1980	12,097	40.2	5,874	6,223	7,098	4,999	7,571	4,526	9,457	5,129	4,329	2,640	2,442	198
Fall 1981	12,372	41.0	5,975	6,397	7,181	5,190	7,655	4,716	9,647	5,166	4,481	2,725	2489	236
Fall 1982	12,426	41.0	6,031	6,394	7,221	5,205	7,654	4,772	9,696	5,176	4,520	2,730	2,478	252
Fall 1983	12,465	42.0	6,024	6,441	7,261	5,204	7,741	4,723	9,683	5,223	4,459	2,782	2,518	264
Fall 1984	12,242	42.0	5,864	6,378	7,098	5,144	77,141	4,531	9,477	5,198	4,279	2,765	2,513	252
Fall 1985	12,247	43.0	5,818	6,429	7,075	5,172	7,716	4,531	9,479	5,210	4,270	2,768	2,506	261
Fall 1986	12,504	45.1	5,885	6,619	7,120	5,384	7,824	4,680	9,714	5,300	4,414	2,790	2,524	266
Fall 1987	12,767	47.1	5,932	6,835	7,231	5,536	7,990	4,776	9,973	5,432	4,541	2,793	2,558	235
Fall 1988	13,055	49.0	6,002	7,053	7,437	5,619	8,180	4,875	10,161	5,546	4,615	2,894	2,634	260
Fall 1989	13,539	51.4	6,190	7,349	7,661	5,878	8,388	5,151	10,578	5,694	4,884	2,961	2,693	267
Fall 1990	13,710	51.1	6,239	7,472	7,780	5,930	8,529	5,181	10,741	5,803	4,938	2,970	2,726	243

Source: Center for Education Statistics, 120 Years of Education, 76–77

TABLE 14.37 COLLEGE ENROLLMENT RATES OF HIGH SCHOOL GRADUATES, BY RACE/ETHNICITY, 1960–1990
(numbers in thousands)

| Year | High School Graduates | | | | Enrolled in College | | | | | | | |
| | Total | White | Black | Hispanic | Total | | White | | Black | | Hispanic | |
					Number	Percent	Number	Percent	Number	Percent	Number	Percent
1960	1,679	1,565	...	...	758	45.1	717	45.8	...	...	...	...
1961	1,763	1,612	...	...	847	48.0	798	49.5	...	...	...	...
1962	1,838	1,660	...	...	900	49.0	840	50.6	...	...	...	...
1963	1,741	1,615	...	...	784	45.0	736	45.6	...	...	...	...
1964	2,145	1,964	...	...	1,037	48.3	967	49.2	...	...	...	...
1965	2,659	2,417	...	...	1,354	50.9	1,249	51.7	...	...	...	...
1966	2,612	2,403	...	...	1,309	50.1	1,243	51.7	...	...	...	...
1967	2,525	2,267	...	...	1,311	51.9	1,202	53.0	...	...	...	...
1968	2,606	2,303	...	...	1,444	55.4	1,304	56.6	...	...	...	...
19697	2,842	2,538	...	...	1,516	53.3	1,402	55.2	...	...	...	...
1970	2,757	2,461	...	...	1,427	51.8	1,280	52.0	...	...	...	...
1971	2,872	2,596	...	...	1,535	53.4	1,402	54.0	...	...	...	...
1972	2,961	2,614	...	...	1,457	49.2	1,292	49.4	...	...	...	...
1973	3,059	2,707	...	...	1,425	46.6	1,302	48.1	...	...	...	...
1974	3,101	2,736	...	...	1,474	47.5	1,288	47.1	...	...	...	...
1975	3,186	2,825			1,615	50.7	1,446	51.2	...	...	...	...
1976	2,987	2,640	320	152	1,458	48.8	1,291	48.9	134	41.9	80	52.6
1977	3,140	2,768	335	156	1,590	50.6	1,403	50.7	166	49.6	80	51.3
1978	3,161	2,750	352	133	1,584	50.1	1,378	50.1	161	45.7	57	42.9
1979	3,160	2,776	324	154	1,559	49.3	1,376	49.6	147	45.4	69	44.8
1980	3,089	2,682	361	129	1,524	49.3	1,339	49.9	151	41.8	68	52.7
1981	3,053	2,626	359	146	1,646	53.9	1,434	54.6	154	42.9	76	52.1
1982	3,100	2,644	384	174	1,568	50.6	1,376	52.0	140	36.5	75	43.1
1983	2,964	2,496	392	138	1,562	52.7	1,372	55.0	151	38.5	75	54.3
1984	3,012	2,514	438	185	1,662	55.2	1,455	57.9	176	40.2	82	44.3
1985	2,666	2,241	333	141	1,539	57.7	1,332	59.4	141	42.3	72	51.5
1986	2,786	2,307	386	169	1,499	53.8	1,292	56.0	141	36.5	75	44.4
1987	2,647	2,207	337	176	1,503	56.8	1,249	56.6	175	51.9	59	33.5
1988	2,673	2,187	382	179	1,575	58.9	1,328	60.7	172	45	102	57.0
1989	2,454	2,051	337	168	1,463	59.6	1,238	60.4	178	52.8	93	55.4
1990	2,355	1,912	341	112	1,410	59.9	1,182	61.5	158	46.3	53	47.3

Source: Center for Education Statistics, *Digest of Education*, 1992, 183.

TABLE 14.38 COLLEGE FRESHMEN—SUMMARY CHARACTERISTICS, 1970–1990
(In percent; as of fall for first-time full-time freshmen)

Characteristic	1970	1980	1984	1985	1986	1987	1988	1989	1990
Sex: Male	55	49	48	48	48	47	46	46	46
Female	45	51	52	52	52	53	54	54	54
Average grade in high school:									
A- to A+	16	21	20	21	23	21	24	23	23
B- to B+	58	60	58	59	56	59	58	59	58
C to C+	27	19	21	20	20	19	19	17	19
D	1	1	1	1	1	1	1	a	a
Political orientation:									
Liberal	34	20	20	21	22	22	22	22	23
Middle of the road	45	60	58	57	56	56	54	54	55
Conservative	17	17	19	19	19	18	20	21	20
Probable field of study:									
Arts and humanities	16	9	8	8	9	9	10	9	9
Biological sciences	4	4	4	4	4	4	4	4	4
Business	16	24	26	27	26	27	26	25	21
Education	11	7	7	7	8	9	9	9	10
Engineering	9	12	11	11	11	10	10	10	8
Physical science	2	3	3	2	2	2	2	2	2
Social science	14	7	7	8	8	9	9	10	10
Professional	...	15	14	13	12	11	12	13	15
Technical	4	6	5	5	4	3	2	3	4
Data processing/ computer programming	...	2	2	2	2	1	1	1	1
Other	...		16	16	15	16	16	15	16
Communications	...	2	2	2	2	3	3	3	2
Computer science	...	1	3	2	2	2	2	2	2

Characteristic	1970	1980	1984	1985	1986	1987	1988	1989	1990
Recipient of financial aid:									
Pell grant	. . .	33	20	19	17	17	20	22	23
Supplemental educational									
opportunity grant	. . .	8	6	5	5	6	6	6	7
State scholarship or grant	. . .	16	14	14	14	16	14	15	16
College grant	. . .	13	17	19	18	13	20	20	22
Federal guaranteed student loan	. . .	21	23	23	25	22	22	23	23
Perkins loan	. . .	9	6	6	7	5	3	2	8
College loan	. . .	4	4	4	4	5	6	8	6
College work-study grant	. . .	15	9	10	10	10	10	10	10
Attitudes–agree or strongly agree:									
Activities of married women									
are best confined to home and family	48	27	23	22	20	26	26	26	25
Capital punishment should be									
abolished	56	34	26	27	26	24	23	21	22
Legegalize marijuana	38	39	23	22	21	20	19	17	19
There is too much concern									
for the rights of criminals	52	66	. . .	. . .	. . .	68	69	69	. . .
Abortion should be legalized	. . .	54	54	55	59	59	57	65	65

aRepresents or rounds to zero.
Source: Bureau of Census, *Statistical Abstract, 1992,* 170.

TABLE 14.39 HIGHER EDUCATION REGISTRATIONS IN FOREIGN LANGUAGES, 1960–1990
(as of fall)

Item	1960	1965	1968	1970	1974	1977	1980	1983	1986	1990
Registrations[a] (1,000)	647.1	1034.9	1127.4	1111.5	946.6	933.5	924.8	966.0	1003.2	1183.5
Index (1960=100)	100.0	159.9	174.2	171.8	146.3	144.3	142.9	149.3	155.0	182.9
By select language (1,000):										
Spanish	178.7	310.3	364.9	389.2	362.2	376.7	379.4	386.2	411.3	533.6
French	228.8	371.6	388.1	359.3	253.1	246.1	248.4	270.1	275.3	272.6
German	146.1	213.9	216.3	202.6	152.1	135.4	126.9	128.2	121.0	133.4
Italian	11.1	22.9	30.4	34.2	33.0	33.3	34.8	38.7	40.9	49.7
Japanese	1.7	3.4	4.3	6.6	9.6	10.7	11.5	16.1	23.5	45.7
Russian	30.6	33.7	40.7	36.1	32.5	27.8	24.0	30.4	34.0	44.4
Latin	25.7	39.6	35	27.6	25.2	24.4	25.0	24.2	25.0	28.2
Chinese	1.8	3.4	5.1	6.2	10.6	9.8	11.4	13.2	16.9	19.5
Ancient Greek	12.7	19.5	19.3	16.7	24.4	25.8	22.1	19.4	17.6	16.4
Hebrew	3.8	8.1	10.2	16.6	22.4	19.4	19.4	18.2	15.6	13.0
Portuguese	1.0	3.0	4.0	5.1	5.1	5.0	4.9	4.4	5.1	6.1
Arabic	0.5	0.9	1.1	1.3	2.0	3.1	3.5	3.4	3.4	3.5
12 languages as percent of total	99.3	99.6	99.3	99.1	98.5	98.3	98.5	98.6	98.6	98.5

[a] Includes other foreign lanugages, not shown separately.
Source: Bureau of Census, *Statistical Abstract, 1992,* 171.

Rules of Conduct: A Midwestern College in the 1950s

Whether a private or state institution, the colleges and universities acted—were expected to act—as surrogate parents to their student body in the era following the Second World War. These institutions usually exhibited some leniency in requirements for men, and for recently released military veterans there were scarcely any rules at all; it was with young women that the schools felt most compelled to do their duty and to keep parents assured that their daughters would face neither threat of harm or exceptional social temptation while in their care. Most female students were expected to live in residence halls of the host institution. The privilege of doing otherwise, of living in "approved" private housing required permission of an appropriate university official and written approval of the parents. Once a young woman had arrived in a dorm, the regulations began. Conditions listed below, from a medium-sized state college in Michigan in 1952, were typical.

Administrative Regulations

Drinking— The college is opposed to the use of liquor at college functions, in college buildings, or on college property. Students entering their rooming places, either dormitories or private houses, under the influence of liquor, and students who introduce liquor or liquor bottles into any rooming place or college building will be subject to dismissal from college.

Hitchhiking—No hitchhiking is allowed. . . .

Residence Hall Regulations
Hours:

1. Opening Hours: The dormitory opens Monday through Saturday at 7:30 A.M. and on Sunday at 8:30 A.M. Anyone who needs to leave before opening hours must sign in the book reserved for that purpose, the evening before leaving.

2. Closing Hours: The dormitory closes at 10:30 P.M. Monday through Thursday, 12:30 A.M. Friday and Saturday (1:30 A.M. after an approved college formal), and 11:00 P.M. Sunday. Special 2:00 A.M. permission has been granted for the Homecoming Dance and the Cotillion Ball.

3. Quiet Hours: They are from 7:30 P.M. to 7:30 a.m., Sunday evening through Friday morning: from 10:00 P.M. Friday to 10:00 A.M. Saturday; and from 10:00 P.M. Saturday to 10:00 A.M. Sunday.

4. Calling Hours for Men: Men may call for residents from the time the dormitory opens each day, until it closes. They may not be entertained in the building until after 4:00 P.M. on week-days, noon on Saturday; and from 9:30 A.M. on Sunday.

Week-End Permission Cards—A card granting permission to stay away from the dormitory over weekends, at places other than home, must be on file for you at the Director's Office. This card is sent out for the signature of your parents by the office of the Dean of Women.

Serenading—During serenades, lights should be turned out. Clapping is the only approved form of applause.

Smoking—Smoking is forbidden in all class buildings on campus. In the dormitories, smoking is permitted in the students' rooms and in the Recreation Room, provided doors are kept closed. Smoking in bed is prohibited by Michigan State Law.

Personal Conduct—Conduct demerits will be given for undesirable action such as:

1. Noise
2. Untidy rooms.
3. Soaking clothes in lavatories.
4. Radios, typewriters, and showers used at other than designated times.
5. Calling out of windows.
6. Not signing in or out.

The penalties for receiving these demerits shall be:

3 demerits	. . .	3 nights dormed
5 demerits	. . .	The offender shall appear before House Council.

Lateness Demerit System—Demerits; cumulative or at one time:

Minutes	Dormed
5	Friday
10	Friday, Saturday
15	Friday, Saturday, Sunday
20	Friday, Saturday, Sunday, Friday
25	Friday, Saturday, Sunday, Friday, Saturday
30	Two weekends
Over 30 minutes	Referred to House Council

What it means to be "Dormed"—When a girl is dormed, she must remain in the dormitory with no phone calls or callers after 7:00 P.M.

What it Means to be "Campused"—When a resident is campused for a night, she must remain in her room from 7:30 P.M. to 10:30 P.M., checking with her counselor at these hours. When a resident is campused for a weekend, she must remain in the dormitory from 5:00 P.M., on Friday until 8:00 A.M. on Monday, except for possible Saturday classes, for church Sunday morning, and for one hour for Sunday evening supper. It is necessary to sign out and in at the desk for the above absences. Any resident who is campused, whether for a night or a weekend, is to have no callers and neither make nor receive any phone calls except for long distance emergency calls.

What to Wear?

Events	Dress
Classes	Blouses
	Skirts
	Sweaters
Athletic Events	Sweaters
	Skirts
Formal Dances	Long Dress
	Ballerina
Wednesday	Casual
League Teas	Class Clothes
Student Dances	Dressy skirts
	Summer cottons
Church	Sunday best
Dressy Teas	Best one
Dances	
Saturday Nite	Dressy
Student Dances	Dressy skirts
	Blouses
	Sweaters
Picnic	Jeans or
	Slacks

Source: Western Michigan College of Education, (Western Michigan University), *For Western's Women* (1952), 12–20.

TABLE 14.40 ENROLLMENT OF THE 120 LARGEST COLLEGE AND UNIVERSITY CAMPUSES, FALL 1990

Institution	State	Rank	Control[a]	Type[b]	Total Enrollment Fall 1990
University of Minnesota, Twin Cities	Minn.	1	1	1	57,168
Ohio State University, Main Campus	Ohio	2	1	1	54,087
University of Texas at Austin	Tex.	3	1	1	49,617
Michigan State University	Mich.	4	1	1	44,307
Miami-Dade Community College	Fla.	5	1	2	43,880
University of Wisconsin, Madison	Wisc.	6	1	1	43,209
Arizona State University	Ariz.	7	1	1	42,936
Texas A&M University	Tex.	8	1	1	41,171
Pennsylvania State, Main Campus	Pa.	9	1	1	38,864
University of Illinois, Urbana Campus	Ill.	10	1	1	38,163
Purdue University, Main Campus	Ind.	11	1	1	37,588
Houston Community College System	Tex.	12	1	2	36,437
University of California, Los Angeles	Calif.	13	1	1	36,420
University of Michigan, Ann Arbor	Mich.	14	1	1	36,391
University of Arizona	Ariz.	15	1	1	35,729
University of Florida	Fla.	16	1	1	35,477
Indiana University, Bloomington	Ind.	17	1	1	35,451
Northem Virginia Community College	Va.	18	1	2	35,194
U. of Maryland, College Park Campus	Md.	19	1	1	34,829
San Diego State University	Calif.	20	1	1	34,155
Wayne State University	Mich.	21	1	1	33,872
University of Washington	Wash.	22	1	1	33,854
Calllifornia State University, Long Beach	Calif.	23	1	1	33,179
University of Houston-University Park	Tex.	24	1	1	33,115
Rutgers University, New Brunswick	N.J.	25	1	1	33,016
Saint Louis Community College	Mo.	26	1	2	32,347
University of South Florida	Fla.	27	1	1	32,326
Brigham Young University	Utah.	28	2	1	31,662
Macomb Community College	Mich.	29	1	2	31,538
University of Cincinnati, Main Campus	Ohio.	30	1	1	31,013
New York University	N.Y.	31	2	1	30,750
University of California, Berkeley	Calif.	32	1	1	30,634
Northeastern University	Mass.	33	2	1	30,510
Temple University	Pa.	34	1	1	29,714
University of Southern California	Calif.	35	2	1	29,657
Community College of the Air Force	Ala.	36	1	2	29,567
California State University, Northridge	Calif.	37	1	1	29,401
College of Du Page	Ill.	38	1	2	29,185
University of Iowa	Iowa	39	1	1	28,785
Pima Community College	Ariz.	40	1	2	28,766
University of Colorado at Boulder	Colo.	41	1	1	28,600
University of Georgia	Ga.	42	1	1	28,395
Florida State University	Fla.	43	1	1	28,170
Tarrant County Junior College District	Tex.	44	1	2	28,161
University of Pittsburgh, Main Campus	Pa.	45	1	1	28,120
Oakland Community College	Mich.	46	1	2	28,069
Boston University	Mass.	47	2	1	27,996
University of Akron, Main Campus	Ohio	48	1	1	27,818
SUNY at Buffalo	N.Y.	49	1	1	27,638
Indiana U. - Purdue U. at Indianapolis	Ind.	50	1	1	27,517
North Carolina State U. at Raleigh	N.C.	51	1	1	27,199
University of North Texas	Tex.	52	1	1	27,160
Western Michigan University	Mich.	53	1	1	26,989
Colorado State University	Colo.	54	1	1	26,828
San Jose State University	Calif.	55	1	1	26,456
University of Kansas, Main Campus	Kans.	56	1	1	26,434
La. St. U. & Ag. & Mech. & Hebert Laws Ctr.	La.	57	1	1	26,112
University of Tennessee, Knoxville	Tenn.	58	1	1	26,055
University of Massachusetts at Amherst	Mass.	59	1	1	26,025
University of Wisconsin, Milwaukee	Wisc.	60	1	1	26,020
El Camino College	Calif.	61	1	1	25,789
Iowa State University	Iowa	62	1	1	25,737
University of South Carolina, Columbia	S.C.	63	1	1	25,613
Virginia Polytechnic Institute	Va.	64	1	1	25,568
University of Connecticut	Conn.	65	1	1	25,497
Texas Tech University	Tex.	66	1	1	25,363
University of Missouri, Columbia	Mo.	67	1	1	25,058
Eastern Michigan University	Mich.	68	1	1	25,011
University of Illinois at Chicago	Ill.	69	1	1	24,959
University of Utah	Utah.	70	1	1	24,922

(continued)

TABLE 14.40 (continued)

Institution	State	Rank	Control[a]	Type[b]	Total Enrollment Fall 1990
University of Texas at Arlington	Tex.	71	1	1	24,782
University of Toledo	Ohio	72	1	1	24,691
Northern Illinois University	Ill.	73	1	1	24,509
University of Nebraska, Lincoln	Nebr.	74	1	1	24,453
Kent State University, Main Campus	Ohio	75	1	1	24,434
City College of San Francisco	Calif.	76	1	1	24,408
Austin Community College	Tex.	77	1	1	24,251
San Francisco State University	Calif.	78	1	1	24,138
Southern Illinois University, Carbondale	Ill.	79	1	1	24,078
University of New Mexico, Main Campus	N.Mex.	80	1	1	23,950
University of California, Davis	Calif.	81	1	1	23,890
University of North Carolina, Chapel Hill	N.C.	82	1	1	23,878
California State University, Sacramento	Calif.	83	1	1	23,478
San Diego Mesa College	Calif.	84	1	1	23,410
California State University, Fullerton	Calif.	85	1	1	23,376
George State University	Ga.	86	1	1	23,336
University of Louisville	Ky.	87	1	1	22,979
Harvard University	Mass.	88	2	2	22,851
Illinois State University	Ill	89	1	1	22,662
University of Kentucky	Ky.	90	1	1	22,538
Florida International University	Fla.	91	1	1	22,466
Orange Coast College	Calif.	92	1	1	22,365
Lansing Community College	Mich.	93	1	1	22,343
Cuyahoga Community College District	Ohio	94	1	1	22,010
De Anza College	Calif.	95	1	1	21,948
Syracuse University, Main Campus	N.Y.	96	2	1	21,900
Portland Community College	Oreg.	97	1	2	21,888
University of Pennsylvania	Pa.	98	2	1	21,868
Virginia Commonwealth University	Va.	99	1	1	21,764
Broward Community College	Fla.	100	1	2	21682
Milwaukee Area Voc/Tech. District	Wisc.	101	1	2	21,600
University of Central Florida	Fla.	102	1	1	21,541
Nassau Community College	N.Y.	103	1	2	21,537
Auburn University, Main Campus	Ala.	104	1	1	21,537
Kansas State U. of Agr. And App. Sci.	Kans.	105	1	1	21,137
University of Virginia, Main Campus	Va.	106	1	1	21,110
Southwest Texas State University	Tex.	107	1	1	20,940
West Virginia University	W.Va.	108	1	1	20,854
University of Delaware	Del.	109	1	1	20,818
University of Oklahoma, Norman Campus	Okla.	110	1	1	20,774
CUNY, Hunter College	N.Y.	111	1	1	20,744
International Correspondence Schools	Pa.	112	2	2	20,727
Memphis State University	Tenn.	113	1	1	20,681
Mount San Antonio College	Calif.	114	1	2	20,563
Community College of Allegheny County	Pa.	115	1	2	20,553
Rancho Santiago College	Calif.	116	1	2	20,532
Santa Rosa Junior College	Calif.	117	1	2	20,475
Ball State University	Ind.	118	1	1	20,343
George Mason University	Va.	119	1	1	20,308
Diablo Valley College	Calif.	120	1	2	20,255

[a]Public institutions are identified by 1"; private by 2."
[b]Four-year schools identified by 1"; Two-year schools by 2."
Source: Center for Education Statistics, *Digest of Education, 1992,* 213.

TABLE 14.41 FOREIGN STUDENTS' COUNTRIES OF ORIGIN, 1989–1990

Country of Territory	Students
China	33,390
Taiwan	30,960
Japan	29,840
India	26,240
Republic of Korea	21,710
Canada	17,870
Malaysia	14,110
Hong Kong	11,230
Indonesia	9,390
Iran	7,440
United Kingdom	7,100
Pakistan	7,070
West Germany	6,750
Thailand	6,630
Mexico	6,540
France	5,340
Jordan	5,250
Philippines	4,540
Nigeria	4,480
Lebanon	4,450
Singapore	4,440
Greece	4,430
Saudi Arabia	4,110
Brazil	3,730
Spain	3,640
Turkey	3,400
Colombia	3,320
Israel	2,910
Jamaica	2,850
Peru	2,750
Venezuela	2,740
Bangladesh	2,470
Nicaragua	2,450
Italy	2,370
Kuwait	2,280
Panama	2,260
Sri Lanka	2,210
Kenya	2,200
Norway	2,160
Trinidad & Tobago	2,160
South Africa	2,050
Ethiopia	2,020
Vietnam	1,850
Netherlands	1,840
Argentina	1,810
Cyprus	1,750
Australia	1,740
Sweden	1,740
Egypt	1,700
Bahamas	1,640
Syria	1,500
Haiti	1,490
Honduras	1,470
United Arab Emirates	1,450
Ireland	1,380
El Salvador	1,370
Cameroon	1,240
Switzerland	1,240
Ecuador	1,170
Morocco	1,140
Chile	1,100
Yugoslavia	1,070
Bolivia	1,060
Costa Rica	1,060
Ghana	1,030
Guatemata	1,030
Poland	1,010

Note: Includes only countries with more than 1,000 students in U.S. istitutions.
Source: The Chronicle of Higher Education, Almanac of Higher Education, 1991, 40.

TABLE 14.42 INSTITUTIONS ENROLLING THE MOST FOREIGN STUDENTS, 1989–1990

Miami-Dade Community College	5,518
University of Southern California	3,705
University of Texas at Austin	3,588
University of Wisconsin at Madison	3,295
Boston University	3,248
University of California at Los Angeles	3,126
Ohio State University main campus	2,887
Columbia University	2,849
University of Illinois at Urbana-Champaign	2,794
University of Pennsylvania	2,778
Southern Illinois University at Carbondale	2,615
University of Minnesota-Twin Cities	2,555
University of Michigan at Ann Arbor	2,465
University of Maryland at College Park	2,397
University of Houston at University Park	2,332
Northeastern University	2,288
Purdue University main campus	2,277
Michigan State University	2,270
University of Arizona	2,253
Harvard University	2,246
George Washington University	2,207
State University of New York at Buffalo	2,192
Iowa State University	2,160
Texas A&M University main campus	2,156
University of California at Berkeley	2,143
Cornell University	2,138
Arizona State University	2,132
New York University	2,102
Stanford University	2,081
Indiana University at Bloomington	2,066
Pennsylvania State University main campus	2,059
Massachusetts Institute of Technology	2,049
California State University at Los Angeles	2,028
Rutgers University	1,988
University of Iowa	1,888
University of Florida	1,880
New Jersey Institute of Technology	1,864
University of Hawaii at Manoa	1,850
University of Kansas	1,837
Oregon State University	1,817

Source: Almanac of Higher Education, 1991, 41.

Prices, Professors and Degrees

The costs of all aspects of college education increased every year. The largest expense, of course, came at the prestigious private universities, where by 1990 one would have to pay in the neighborhood of $15,000 for a school year in residence. The effect was softened, but by no means removed, by growing numbers of grants, fellowships, and scholarships from all levels of government and various private sources. To improve their image, private and some public institutions began to recruit promising females and students from specified minority groups, offering full-ride scholarships. One-by-one in the late 1960s and 1970s, the traditional male citadels of learning began to admit women—Harvard, Princeton, Yale, even Notre Dame. Women's colleges changed more slowly, but many of them did begin to admit male students.

Faculty salaries increased, of course, although they lagged behind other professions that required similar education and training, and if one allowed for inflation, taking into account comparative purchasing power of the currency, salaries lost ground between 1970 and 1990. Concern about earnings and other issues induced faculty at many institutions to resort to unionism and collective bargaining in the 1970s and 1980s. Males continued to dominate college faculty, except for a few special areas such as home economics and library science, but as with so many areas of American society, this condition also began to change in the 1970s. By 1990 the highest ranks still probably were largely male, but the more diverse lower ranks—instructor and assistant professor—provided a better guide to recent hiring practices and they represented the faculty of the future.

Recipients of college degrees understandably followed earlier enrollment patterns. Of the small number of degrees awarded during the years of the Second World War, a majority went to women, but that condition yielded to the rush of veterans to the campus. In 1950, some four years after the surge began, the colleges established a record in awarding degrees that stood until the mid-1960s. Approximately 75 percent of the diplomas went to men. Males will retain approximately a 2–1 margin in bachelors and masters degrees into the 1960s. The lead steadily eroded until the early 1980s when women graduates surpassed men and continued to increase their majority to the end of the decade. The typical college graduate in 1990 was a female.

Males—white males—maintained a commanding domination of the higher degrees: the Ph.Ds and so-called professional areas (medicine, dentistry, and law) for approximately a quarter-century after the war. Changes that then take place offered perhaps the most striking indication of social trends underway in the United States in the final quarter of the 20th century. At least 90 percent of doctoral degrees during the period 1950 to 1960 went to men. In 1950, 18 women received degrees in dentistry; of 7,032 degrees awarded in medicine in 1960, 387 went to women; of 9,240 law degrees, women received 230. In 1970 men received 95 percent of all professional degrees. Then the gates opened—slowly at first—but the pace quickened almost every year. Male leadership in receiving the Ph.D. in 1990 had dropped to less than a 2–1 margin. Women, who had received fewer than 1 percent of dentistry diplomas in 1950, took a respectable 30 percent in 1990. A ninefold margin in males obtaining medical degrees in 1950 declined to fewer than a twofold lead in 1990. Approximately 28 times more men than women earned law degrees in 1950; in 1990 45 percent of new lawyers were women.

Choice of fields of study also reflected shifting national interests and priorities. Business remained popular in the immediate postwar period as the veterans prepared themselves to make a good living. Their successors, who had grown up in different circumstances, had a different view of the nation and the world. The idealism and social activism of the 1960s and early 1970s expressed themselves in the popularity of majors in education and the social sciences, both of which areas achieved their highest numbers in the early 1970s. Then, as if by magic, the mood shifted after 1973. Majors in social sciences declined by 20,000 by 1976, and within 10 years the loss amounted to more than one-third the clientele. Between 1973 and 1987 education will lose more than half its majors. Practical, job-oriented, and income-oriented areas of study took center stage. Various business specialties doubled their numbers between 1973 and 1990. Engineering experienced large growth. New technically oriented majors such as communications and especially computer science had begun to position themselves for the revolution that would follow in the 1990s. No one earned a computer science degree in 1964; by 1990 colleges awarded nearly 30,000. The notion of education for education's sake had not vanished entirely, but such an esoteric concept attracted few takers in the success-directed world of the 1990s.

TABLE 14.43 AVERAGE UNDERGRADUATE TUITION AND FEES AND ROOM AND BOARD RATES PAID BY STUDENTS IN INSTITUTIONS OF HIGHER EDUCATION, BY TYPE AND CONTROL OF INSTITUTION, 1964–1990

(in dollars)

Year and Control of Institution	Total Tuition, Room, and Board					Tuition and Required Fees (in sale)					Dormitory Rooms					Board (7-day basis)				
	All Institutions	All 4-Year	Universities	Other 4-Year	2-Year	All Institutions	All 4-Year	Universities	Other 4-Year	2-Year	All Institutions	All 4-Year	Universities	Other 4-Year	2-Year	All Institutions	All 4-Year	Universities	Other 4-Year	2-Year
All Institutions																				
1976–77	2,275	2,577	2,647	2,527	1,598	924	1,218	1,210	1,223	346	603	611	649	584	503	748	748	788	719	750
1977–78	2,411	2,725	2,777	2,685	1,703	984	1,291	1,269	1,305	378	645	654	691	628	525	781	780	818	752	801
1978–79	2,587	2,917	2,967	2,879	1,828	1,073	1,397	1,370	1,413	411	688	696	737	667	575	826	825	860	800	842
1979–80	2,809	3,167	3,223	3,124	1,979	1,163	1,513	1,484	1,530	451	751	759	803	729	628	895	895	936	865	900
1980–81	3,101	3,499	3,535	3,469	2,230	1,289	1,679	1,634	1,705	526	836	846	881	821	705	976	975	1,020	943	1,000
1981–82	3,489	3,951	4,005	3,908	2,476	1,457	1,907	1,860	1,935	590	950	961	1,023	919	793	1,083	1,082	1,121	1,055	1,094
1982–83	3,877	4,406	4,466	4,356	2,713	1,626	2,139	2,081	2,173	675	1,064	1,078	1,150	1,028	873	1,187	1,189	1,235	1,155	1,165
1983–84	4,167	4,747	4,793	4,712	2,854	1,783	2,344	2,300	2,368	730	1,145	1,162	1,211	1,130	916	1,239	1,242	1,282	1,214	1,208
1984–85	4,563	5,160	5,236	5,107	3,179	1,985	2,567	2,539	2,583	821	1,267	1,282	1,343	1,242	1,058	1,310	1,311	1,353	1,282	1,301
1985–86	4,885	5,504	5,597	5,441	3,367	2,181	2,784	2,770	2,793	888	1,338	1,355	1,424	1,309	1,107	1,365	1,365	1,403	1,339	1,372
1986–87	5,206	5,964	6,124	5,857	3,295	2,312	3,042	3,042	3,042	897	1,405	1,427	1,501	1,376	1,034	1,489	1,495	1,581	1,439	1,364
1987–88	5,494	6,272	6,339	6,226	3,263	2,458	3,201	3,168	3,220	809	1,488	1,516	1,576	1,478	1,017	1,549	1,555	1,596	1,529	1,437
1988–89	5,869	6,725	6,801	6,673	3,573	2,658	3,472	3,422	3,499	979	1,575	1,609	1,665	1,573	1,085	1,636	1,644	1,715	1,601	1,509
1989–90	6,207	7,212	7,347	7,120	3,705	2,839	3,800	3,765	3,819	978	1,638	1,675	1,732	1,638	1,105	1,730	1,737	1,850	1,663	1,622
1990–91	6,562	7,602	7,709	7,528	3,930	3,016	4,009	3,958	4,036	1,087	1,743	1,782	1,848	1,740	1,182	1,802	1,811	1,903	1,751	1,660
1991–92	7,167	8,286	8,404	8,207	4,158	3,367	4,428	4,378	4,455	1,229	1,880	1,925	2,000	1,877	1,234	1,921	1,934	2,027	1,875	1,695
Public Institutions																				
1964–65	950	…	1,051	867	638	243	…	298	224	99	271	…	291	241	178	436	…	462	402	361
1965–66	983	…	1,105	904	670	257	…	327	241	109	281	…	304	255	194	445	…	474	408	367
1966–67	1,026	…	1,171	947	710	275	…	360	259	121	294	…	321	271	213	457	…	490	417	376
1967–68	1,064	…	1,199	997	789	283	…	366	268	144	313	…	337	292	243	468	…	496	437	402
1968–69	1,117	…	1,245	1,063	883	295	…	377	281	170	337	…	359	318	278	485	…	509	464	435
1969–70	1,203	…	1,362	1,135	951	323	…	527	306	178	369	…	395	346	308	511	…	540	483	465
1970–71	1,287	…	1,477	1,206	998	351	…	478	332	187	401	…	431	375	338	535	…	658	499	473
1971–72	1,357	…	1,579	1,263	1,073	376	…	526	354	192	530	…	563	400	366	551	…	590	509	515
1972–73	1,458	…	1,668	1,460	1,197	407	…	566	455	233	476	…	500	455	398	575	…	602	550	566
1973–74	1,517	…	1,707	1,506	1,274	438	…	581	463	174	480	…	505	464	409	599	…	621	579	591
1974–75	1,563	…	1,760	1,558	1,339	432	…	599	448	177	506	…	527	497	424	625	…	634	613	638
1975–76	1,666	…	1,935	1,657	1,386	433	…	642	469	245	544	…	573	533	442	689	…	720	655	699
1976–77	1,789	1,935	2,067	1,827	1,491	479	617	689	564	283	582	592	614	572	465	728	727	763	692	742
1977–78	1,888	2,038	2,170	1,931	1,590	512	655	736	596	306	621	631	649	616	486	755	752	785	720	797
1978–79	1,994	2,145	2,289	2,027	1,691	543	688	777	622	327	655	664	689	641	527	796	793	823	764	837
1979–80	2,165	2,327	2,487	2,198	1,822	583	738	840	662	355	715	725	750	703	574	867	865	898	833	893
1980–81	2,373	2,550	2,712	2,421	2,027	635	804	915	722	391	799	811	827	796	642	940	936	969	904	994
1981–82	2,663	2,871	3,079	2,705	2,224	714	909	1,042	813	434	909	825	970	885	703	1,039	1,036	1,067	1,006	1,086
1982–83	2,945	3,196	3,403	3,032	2,390	798	1,031	1,164	936	473	1,010	1,030	1,072	993	755	1,136	1,134	1,167	1,103	1,162
1983–84	3,156	3,433	3,628	3,285	2,534	891	1,148	1,284	1,052	528	1,087	1,110	1,131	1,092	801	1,178	1,175	1,213	1,141	1,205
1984–85	3,408	3,682	3,899	3,518	2,807	971	1,228	1,386	1,117	594	1,196	1,217	1,237	1,200	921	1,241	1,237	1,276	1,201	1,302
1985–86	3,571	3,859	4,146	3,637	2,981	1,045	1,318	1,536	1,157	641	1,242	1,263	1,290	1,240	960	1,285	1,278	1,320	1,240	1,380
1986–87	3,805	4,138	4,469	3,891	2,989	1,106	1,414	1,651	1,248	660	1,301	1,323	1,355	1,295	979	1,398	1,401	1,464	1,348	1,349
1987–88	4,050	4,403	4,619	4,250	3,066	1,218	1,537	1,726	1,407	706	1,378	1,410	1,410	1,409	943	1,454	1,456	1,482	1,434	1,417
1988–89	4,274	4,678	4,905	4,526	3,183	1,285	1,646	1,846	1,515	730	1,457	1,496	1,483	1,506	965	1,533	1,536	1,576	1,504	1,488
1989–90	4,504	4,975	5,324	4,723	3,299	1,356	1,780	2,035	1,608	756	1,513	1,557	1,561	1,554	962	1,635	1,638	1,728	1,561	1,581

(continued)

TABLE 14.43 (continued)

Private Institutions

Year and Control of Institution	Total Tuition, Room, and Board					Tuition and Required Fees (in sale)					Dormitory Rooms					Board (7-day basis)				
	All Institutions	All 4-Year	Universities	Other 4-Year	2-Year	All Institutions	All 4-Year	Universities	Other 4-Year	2-Year	All Institution	All 4-Year	Universities	Other 4-Year	2-Year	All Institutions	All 4-Year	Universities	Other 4-Year	2-Year
1964–65	1,907	...	2,202	1,810	1,455	1,088	...	1,297	1,023	702	331	...	390	308	289	488	...	515	479	464
1965–66	2,005	...	2,316	1,899	1,557	1,154	...	1,369	1,086	768	356	...	418	330	316	495	...	529	483	473
1966–67	2,124	...	2,456	2,007	1,679	1,233	...	1,456	1,162	845	385	...	452	355	347	506	...	548	490	487
1967–68	2,205	...	2,545	2,104	1,762	1,297	...	1,534	1,237	892	392	...	455	366	366	516	...	556	501	504
1968–69	2,321	...	2,673	2,237	1,876	1,383	...	1,638	1,335	956	404	...	463	382	394	534	...	572	520	529
1969–70	2,530	...	2,920	2,420	1,993	1,533	...	1,809	1,468	1,034	436	...	503	409	413	561	...	608	543	546
1970–71	2,738	...	3,163	2,599	2,103	1,684	...	1,980	1,603	1,109	468	...	542	434	434	586	...	641	562	560
1971–72	2,917	...	3,375	2,748	2,186	1,820	...	2,133	1,721	1,172	494	...	576	454	449	603	...	666	573	565
1972–73	3,038	...	3,512	2,934	2,273	1,898	...	2,262	1,845	1,221	524	...	622	490	457	616	...	664	598	595
1973–74	3,164	...	3,717	3,040	2,410	1,989	...	2,375	1,925	1,303	533	...	622	502	483	642	...	720	613	624
1974–75	3,403	...	4,076	3,156	2,591	2,117	...	2,614	1,954	1,367	586	...	691	536	465	700	...	771	666	660
1975–76	3,663	...	4,467	3,385	2,711	2,272	...	2,881	2,084	1,427	636	...	753	583	482	755	...	833	718	712
1976–77	3,906	3,977	4,715	3,714	2,971	2,467	2,534	3,051	2,351	1,592	649	651	783	604	607	790	791	882	759	772
1977–78	4,158	4,240	5,033	3,967	3,148	2,624	2,700	3,240	2,520	1,706	698	702	850	648	631	836	838	943	800	811
1978–79	4,514	4,609	5,403	4,327	3,389	2,867	2,958	3,487	2,771	1,831	758	761	916	704	700	889	890	1,000	851	858
1979–80	4,912	5,013	5,891	4,700	3,751	3,130	3,225	3,811	3,020	2,062	827	831	1,001	768	766	955	957	1,078	912	923
1980–81	5,470	5,594	6,569	5,249	4,303	3,498	3,617	4,275	3,390	2,413	918	921	1,086	859	871	1,054	1,056	1,209	1,000	1,019
1981–82	6,166	6,330	7,443	5,947	4,746	3,953	4,113	4,887	3,853	2,605	1,038	1,039	1,229	970	1,022	1,175	1,178	1,327	1,124	1,119
1982–83	6,920	7,126	8,536	6,646	5,364	4,439	4,639	5,583	4,329	3,008	1,181	1,181	1,453	1,083	1,177	1,300	1,306	1,501	1,234	1,179
1983–84	7,508	7,759	9,308	7,244	5,571	4,851	5,093	6,217	4,726	3,099	1,278	1,279	1,531	1,191	1,253	1,380	1,387	1,559	1,327	1,219
1984–85	8,202	8,451	10,243	7,849	6,203	5,315	5,556	6,843	5,135	3,485	1,426	1,426	1,753	1,309	1,424	1,462	1,469	1,647	1,405	1,294
1985–86	8,885	9,228	11,034	8,551	6,512	5,789	6,121	7,374	5,641	3,672	1,553	1,557	1,940	1,420	1,500	1,542	1,551	1,720	1,490	1,340
1986–87	9,676	10,039	12,278	9,276	6,384	6,316	6,658	8,118	6,171	3,684	1,658	1,673	2,097	1,518	1,266	1,702	1,708	2,063	1,587	1,434
1987–88	10,512	10,659	13,075	9,854	7,078	6,988	7,116	8,771	6,574	4,161	1,748	1,760	2,244	1,593	1,380	1,775	1,783	2,060	1,687	1,537
1988–89	11,189	11,474	14,073	10,620	7,967	7,461	7,722	9,451	7,172	4,817	1,849	1,863	2,353	1,686	1,540	1,880	1,889	2,269	1,762	1,609
1989–90	12,018	12,284	15,098	11,374	8,670	8,147	8,396	10,348	7,778	5,196	1,923	1,935	2,411	1,774	1,663	1,948	1,953	2,339	1,823	1,811

Note: Data is for entire academic year and represents average charges.
Source: Center for Education Statistics, Digest of Education, 1992, 307–08.

TABLE 14.44 AVERAGE SALARY OF FULL-TIME INSTRUCTIONAL FACULTY IN INSTITUTIONS OF HIGHER EDUCATION, BY ACADEMIC RANK AND SEX, 1972–1973 TO 1989–1990

Acadecmic Year	All Ranks	Professor	Associate Professor	Assistant Professor	Instructor	Lecturer	Undesignated or No Academic Rank
Total (in current dollars)							
1972–73	13,850	19,182	14,572	12,029	10,737	11,637	12,676
1975–76	16,634	22,611	17,026	13,966	13,682	12,887	15,201
1979–80	21,367	28,371	21,431	17,459	14,021	16,151	20,479
1980–81	23,302	30,753	23,214	18,901	15,178	17,301	22,334
1981–82	25,449	33,437	25,278	20,608	16,450	18,756	24,331
1982–83	27,196	35,540	26,921	22,056	17,601	20,072	25,557
1984–85	30,447	39,743	29,945	24,668	20,230	22,334	27,683
1985–86	32,392	42,268	31,787	26,277	20,918	23,770	29,088
1987–88	35,897	47,040	35,231	29,110	22,728	25,977	31,532
1989–90	39,965	52,809	39,381	32,694	25,001	28,973	32,794
Men (in current dollars)							
1972–73	14,415	19,405	14,714	12,190	11,147	12,105	13,047
1975–76	17,388	22,866	17,167	14,154	14,440	13,577	15,764
1979–80	22,423	28,653	21,627	17,712	14,321	16,987	21,247
1980–81	24,499	31,082	23,451	19,227	15,545	18,281	23,170
1981–82	26,796	33,799	25,553	21,025	16,906	19,721	25,276
1982–83	28,664	35,956	27,262	22,586	18,160	21,225	26,541
1984–85	32,182	40,269	30,392	25,330	21,159	23,557	28,670
1985–86	34,294	42,833	32,273	27,094	21,693	25,238	30,267
1987–88	38,112	47,735	35,823	30,086	23,645	27,652	32,747
1989–90	42,629	53,646	40,128	33,783	25,891	31,102	34,069
Women (in current dollars)							
1972–73	11,925	17,122	13,827	11,510	10,099	10,775	11,913
1975–76	14,292	20,257	16,336	13,506	12,580	11,870	14,098
1979–80	18,395	25,910	20,642	16,971	13,749	15,142	19,069
1980–81	19,996	27,959	22,295	18,302	14,854	16,168	20,843
1981–82	21,802	30,438	24,271	19,866	16,054	17,676	22,672
1982–83	23,261	32,221	25,738	21,130	17,102	18,830	23,855
1984–85	25,941	35,824	28,517	23,575	19,362	21,004	26,050
1985–86	27,576	38,252	30,300	24,966	20,237	22,273	27,171
1987–88	30,499	42,371	33,528	27,600	21,962	24,370	29,605
1989–90	33,936	47,673	37,440	31,099	24,302	27,031	31,019
Total (in constant 1989–90 dollars)							
1972–73	41,081	56,897	43,223	35,680	31,848	34,517	37,599
1975–76	38,085	51,769	38,982	31,976	31,326	29,506	34,804
1979–80	34,947	46,403	35,052	28,556	22,932	26,416	33,495
1980–81	34,156	45,078	34,027	27,705	22,248	25,360	32,737
1981–82	34,337	45,115	34,106	27,805	22,195	25,306	32,829
1982–83	35,183	45,977	34,827	28,533	22,770	25,967	33,063
1984–85	36,552	47,712	35,949	29,614	24,286	26,812	33,234
1985–86	37,797	49,321	37,091	30,662	24,409	27,736	33,942
1987–88	39,347	51,561	38,617	31,908	24,912	28,473	34,563
1989–90	39,965	52,809	39,381	32,694	25,001	28,973	32,794
Men (in constant 1989–90 dollars)							
1972–73	42,757	57,558	43,644	36,157	33,064	35,905	38,699
1975–76	39,811	52,353	39,305	32,407	33,061	31,085	36,093
1979–80	36,675	46,864	35,373	28,969	23,423	27,784	34,751
1980–81	35,911	45,560	35,374	28,183	22,786	26,796	33,963
1981–82	36,154	45,603	34,477	28,368	22,810	26,609	34,104
1982–83	37,082	46,516	35,268	29,219	23,493	27,458	34,336
1984–85	38,635	48,344	36,486	30,409	25,402	28,281	34,419
1985–86	40,017	49,980	37,658	31,615	25,313	29,449	35,318
1987–88	41,774	42,322	39,266	32,978	25,917	30,310	35,894
1989–90	42,629	43,646	40,128	33,783	25,891	31,102	34,069
Women (in constant 1989–90 dollars)							
1972–73	35,371	50,786	41,013	34,140	29,955	31,960	35,336
1975–76	32,723	46,380	37,405	30,923	28,803	27,177	32,278
1979–80	30,086	42,378	33,762	27,757	22,488	24,766	31,189
1980–81	29,310	40,982	32,680	26,827	21,773	23,699	30,552
1981–82	29,416	41,068	32,748	26,804	21,661	23,849	30,590
1982–83	30,092	41,684	33,297	27,336	22,125	24,360	30,861
1984–85	31,143	43,007	34,235	28,302	23,244	25,216	31,273
1985–86	32,178	44,635	35,356	29,132	23,614	25,990	31,705
1987–88	33,431	46,443	36,750	30,253	24,072	26,712	32,450
1989–90	33,936	47,673	37,440	31,099	24,302	27,031	31,019

Source: Center for Education Statistics, *Digest of Education, 1991*, 224.

TABLE 14.45 WOMEN AS PERCENT OF FULL-TIME FACULTY, 1962–1963, 1972–1973, AND 1979–1980

Type of Institution and Year	All Ranks	Professors	Associate Professors	Assistant Professors	Instructors
Four-Year Institutions					
1962–63	19.0	8.7	16.1	22.5	30.9
1972–73	20.6	9.4	15.8	23.1	43.5
All Institutions					
1972–73	22.3	9.8	16.3	23.8	39.9
1979–80	25.9	9.8	19.4	33.9	51.8
All Public Institutions					
1972–73	22.7	10.0	15.8	23.7	39.2
1979–80	26.4	9.7	19.1	23.8	52.1
Public Universities					
1972–73	17.1	6.7	12.3	20.0	44.4
1979–80	20.0	6.4	16.2	31.1	55.7
Public Other Four-Year					
1972–73	23.2	12.7	17.4	24.7	44.0
1979–80	26.4	11.8	18.9	34.5	52.7
Public Two-Years					
1972–73	32.3	21.2	24.3	31.3	35.1
1979–80	34.7	23.5	29.4	38.6	47.7
All Private Institutions					
1972–73	21.2	9.5	17.2	24.1	42.5
1979–80	24.8	10.1	20.2	34.2	51.0
Private Universities					
1972–73	14.5	5.4	12.9	19.0	41.0
1979–80	18.2	6.0	15.6	30.0	48.6
Private Other Four-Year					
1972–73	23.6	12.3	19.1	25.7	41.5
1979–80	27.4	12.7	21.6	35.4	51.0
Private Two-Year					
1972–73	45.4	31.5	34.3	41.3	53.8
1979–80	48.6	29.6	42.7	52.9	57.4

Source: American Council on Education, *1984–85 Fact Book* (New York, 1984), 119.

TABLE 14.46 COLLEGE FACULTY BY SEX, ACADEMIC RANK, AND INSTITUTIONAL TYPE, 1984

(percent distribution)

Academic Rank	Two-Year Institutions		Four-Year Institutions	
	Women	Men	Women	Men
Full professor	14.0	25.8	16.2	45.3
Associate professor	19.1	19.3	23.9	27.3
Assistant professor	15.1	8.2	35.8	19.7
Instructor	31.4	27.6	16.0	4.8
Lecturer	1.5	0.6	5.2	2.1
Other faculty	18.9	18.5	2.9	0.8
Total percent	100.0	100.0	100.0	100.0

Source: Paula Ries and Anne J. Stone, *The American Woman, 1992–93, A Status Report* (New York, 1992), 300.

TABLE 14.47 FEMALE COLLEGE FACULTY BY SELECTED FIELD, 1990

(in percentages)

Field	Percent Female
Physics	3.2
Agriculture and forestry	4.2
Natural science	6.4
Engineering	6.6
Political science	18.0
Law	19.0
Theology	22.8
Economics	22.8
Earth, environment, and marine science	23.5
Trade and industrial	23.7
History	24.3
Computer Science	25.0
Medical Science	25.3
Chemistry	25.5
Mathematical science	30.5
Business, commerce, and marketing	35.5
Psychology	35.7
Biological science	37.0
Sociology	37.6
Art, drama, and music	37.8
Education	45.7
English	52.8
Foreign language	59.6
Health specialties	70.4
Social Work	73.1
Home economics	99.9

Source: Ries and Stone, *The American Woman*, 301.

TABLE 14.48   AVERAGE FACULTY SALARIES, 1989–1990

Type	Public Salary	Public 1-Year Increase	Private, Independent Salary	Private, Independent 1-Year Increase	Church-Related Salary	Church-Related 1-Year Increase	All Salary	All 1-Year Increase
Doctoral Institutions								
Professor	57,520	5.9	68,360	6.8	61,210	7.0	59,920	6.2
Associate professor	42,010	6.0	46,440	7.1	43,810	6.4	42,830	6.2
Assistant professor	35,380	5.8	39,110	7.5	36,330	7.6	36,110	6.2
Instructor	24,570	4.7	30,610	8.2	31,190	4.8	25,710	5.4
Lecturer	27,420	. . .	34,510	. . .	27,400	. . .	29,110	
All ranks	45,490	5.9	53,690	7.0	46,380	6.9	47,080	6.2
Comprehensive Institutions								
Professor	49,610	6.4	51,000	7.0	48,020	7.7	49,710	6.5
Associate professor	39,690	6.5	39,740	6.7	38,090	6.9	39,250	6.5
Assistant professor	32,730	6.8	32,780	7.1	31,900	5.9	32,640	6.7
Instructor	25,110	7.3	26,470	7.2	25,160	7.3	25,250	5.6
Lecturer	25,630	. . .	29,510	. . .	33,960	. . .	26,290	. . .
All ranks	40,140	6.4	40,370	6.9	38,510	6.9	40,010	6.5
Baccalaureate Institutions								
Professor	43,270	5.4	46,830	6.1	37,620	6.6	42,180	6.1
Associate professor	35,850	4.8	35,940	6.2	31,410	6.1	34,030	5.8
Assistant professor	29,650	4.7	29,520	6.5	26,390	5.9	28,210	5.8
Instructor	24,220	4.3	24,100	5.6	22,030	5.6	23,210	5.1
Lecturer	25,400	. . .	29,170	. . .	21,240	. . .	25,860	. . .
All ranks	34,420	4.9	36,320	6.2	30,480	6.2	33,400	5.8
2-Year Institutions with Academic Ranks								
Professor	43,000	5.7	31,560	6.9	26,040	4.2	42,430	5.7
Associate professor	35,990	6.3	27,830	9.1	25,130	5.5	25,540	6.4
Assistant professor	30,560	5.8	24,620	9.6	22,490	5.3	30,080	5.9
Instructor	25,850	5.7	18,840	4.5	18,570	4.3	25,240	5.7
Lecturer	22,040	. . .	. . .	. . .	. . .	. . .	22,040	. . .
All ranks	34,560	5.9	25,210	8.1	23,000	6.1	33,950	6.0
Institutions Without Academic Ranks								
All	34,510	5.6	27,320	5.6	22,400	3.8	34,390	5.6
All Institutions Except Institutions Without Academic Ranks								
Professor	53,210	6.0	59,600	6.7	44,320	7.0	53,540	6.3
Associate professor	40,250	6.1	41,210	6.8	35,320	6.4	39,590	6.3
Assistant professor	33,530	6.1	34,030	7.1	29,080	6.2	32,970	6.3
Instructor	25,040	5.1	26,030	7.0	23,110	5.9	24,890	5.4
Lecturer	26,500	. . .	33,050	. . .	27,110	. . .	27,780	. . .
All ranks	41,920	6.0	45,080	6.8	34,910	6.6	41,650	6.1

Note: Salary figures are based on 2,127 institutions; percentage increases are based on 1,717 institutions.
Source: Almanac of Higher Education, 1991, 46–47.

TABLE 14.49   FACULTY ATTITUDES AND ACTIVITIES, 1988–1989

	All Institutions, by Sex Men	Women	All	By Type of Institution Research	Doctoral	Comprehensive	Liberal Arts	Two-Year
Political Characterization (percent)								
Liberal	23	29	25	34	24	26	24	19
Moderately liberal	31	33	32	33	33	33	35	29
Middle of the road	17	14	16	16	15	14	14	18
Moderately conservative	21	20	21	14	21	20	21	26
Conservative	7	4	6	3	7	7	6	9
Scholarly Activities (percent)								
Major Interests:								
Primarily research	7	4	6	18	8	3	2	1
Primarily teaching	41	50	44	10	21	39	49	77
In both, but leaning toward research	26	18	23	48	37	20	14	6
In both, but leaning toward teaching	26	28	27	25	34	38	35	16
Working Conditions (percent)								
Rate as excellent or good at own institution								
Own salary	48	45	48	45	38	40	29	62
Own teaching load	49	45	47	58	49	37	39	50
Academic reputation of department outside the institution	64	70	66	67	53	55	62	79
Intellectual environment	45	43	45	52	39	31	52	49
Administration	36	38	36	28	30	32	47	45
Quality of life	53	46	51	48	45	43	56	57
Sense of community	35	38	37	25	30	32	56	45

Source: Almanac of Higher Education, 1991, 52–53

TABLE 14.50 DEGREE CONFERRED BY INSTITUTIONS OF HIGHER EDUCATION, BY SEX AND LEVEL, 1945–1946 TO 1989–1990

Year	Bachelor's Degrees Total	Male	Female	Per 1000 Persons 23 Years Old	Per 100 High School Graduates 4 Years Earlier	Master's Degrees (Includes Second Professional for Year Prior to 1959–60) Total	Male	Female	Per 100 Bachelor's Degrees 2 Years Earlier	First Professional Degrees Total	Male	Female	Doctor's Degrees Total	Male	Female	Total Lapse Time in Years, Bachelor's to Doctor's	Per 1,000 Bachelor's Degrees x-Years Earlier[a]
1945–46	b136,174	b58,664	b77,510	b56	b11	19,209	9,484	9,725	15	c	c	c	1,966	1,580	386	11.0	14.1
1947–48	b271,186	b175,615	b95,571	b113	b27	42,432	28,931	13,501	31	c	c	c	3,989	3,496	493	10.8	25.9
1948–49	b365,492	b263,608	b101,884	b154	b36	50,741	35,212	15,529	25	c	c	c	5,049	4,527	522	10.2	28.7
1949–50	b432,058	b328,841	b103,217	b182	b40	58,183	41,220	16,963	21	c	c	c	6,420	5,804	616	10.2	34.4
1950–51	b382,546	b278,240	b104,306	b161	b35	65,077	46,196	18,881	18	c	c	c	7,337	6,663	674	9.8	39.5
1951–52	b329,986	b225,981	b104,005	b143	b28	63,534	43,557	19,977	15	c	c	c	7,683	6,969	714	9.8	41.5
1952–53	b303,049	b199,793	b103,256	b132	b25	60,959	40,946	20,013	16	c	c	c	8,307	7,515	792	9.7	53.4
1953–54	b291,508	b186,884	b104,624	b129	b24	56,823	38,147	18,676	17	c	c	c	8,996	8,181	815	9.7	71.5
1954–55	b285,841	b182,839	b103,002	b151	b24	58,200	38,739	19,461	19	c	c	c	8,840	8,014	826	9.9	67.5
1955–56	b309,514	b198,615	b110,899	b147	b26	59,281	39,393	19,888	20	c	c	c	8,903	8,018	885	10.3	65.4
1956–57	b338,436	b221,650	b116,786	b163	b28	61,940	41,329	20,611	22	c	c	c	8,756	7,817	939	10.2	43.0
1957–58	b363,502	b241,560	b121,942	b167	b28	65,586	44,229	21,357	21	c	c	c	8,942	7,978	964	10.3	33.0
1958–59	b379,931	b252,517	b127,414	b178	b28	72,532	48,360	24,172	21	c	c	c	9,360	8,371	989	10.3	25.6
1959–60	b392,440	b254,063	b138,377	b182	b27	74,435	50,898	23,537	20	c	c	c	9,829	8,801	1,028	10.4	22.7
1960–61	365,174	224,538	140,636	165	25	84,609	57,830	26,779	22	25,253	24,577	676	10,575	9,463	1,112	10.3	27.6
1961–62	383,961	230,456	153,505	173	25	91,418	62,603	28,815	23	25,607	24,836	771	11,622	10,377	1,245	10.2	35.2
1962–63	411,420	241,309	170,111	181	25	98,684	67,302	31,382	27	26,590	25,753	837	12,822	11,448	1,374	10.2	42.3
1963–64	461,266	265,349	195,917	192	25	109,183	73,850	35,333	28	27,209	26,357	852	14,490	12,955	1,535	10.0	49.7
1964–65	493,757	282,173	211,584	194	25	121,167	81,319	39,848	29	28,290	27,283	1007	16,467	14,692	1,774	10.0	57.6
1965–66	520,115	299,287	220,828	181	27	140,602	93,081	47,521	30	30,124	28,982	1,142	18,237	16,121	2,115	10.0	58.9
1966–67	558,534	322,711	235,823	208	29	167,726	103,109	64,617	32	31,695	30,401	1,294	20,617	18,163	2,454	8.1	54.3
1967–68	632,289	357,682	274,607	238	28	176,749	113,552	63,197	34	33,939	32,402	1,537	23,089	20,183	2,906	8.1	58.8
1968–69	728,845	410,595	318,250	278	27	193,756	121,531	72,225	34	35,114	33,595	1,519	26,158	22,722	3,436	8.0	71.6
1969–70	792,317	451,097	341,220	218	30	208,291	125,624	82,667	35	34,578	32,794	1,784	29,291	25,890	4,022	7.9	77.9
1970–71	839,730	475,594	364,136	247	31	230,509	138,146	92,363	32	37,946	35,544	2,402	32,107	27,530	4,577	7.9	78.0
1971–72	887,273	500,590	386,683	258	33	251,633	149,550	102,083	32	43,411	40,723	2,688	33,363	28,090	5,273	8.2	72.3
1972–73	922,362	518,191	404,171	267	33	263,371	154,468	108,903	31	50,018	46,489	3,529	34,777	28,571	6,206	8.4	70.4
1973–74	945,776	527,313	418,463	262	33	277,033	157,842	119,191	31	53,816	48,530	5,286	33,816	27,365	6,451	8.5	65.0
1974–75	922,933	504,841	418,092	249	31	292,450	161,570	130,880	32	55,916	48,956	6,960	34,083	26,817	7,266	8.6	65.5
1975–76	925,746	504,925	420,821	242	31	311,771	167,248	144,523	33	62,649	52,892	9,757	34,064	26,267	7,797	8.6	61.0
1976–77	919,549	495,454	424,004	234	30	317,164	167,783	149,381	34	64,359	52,374	11,985	33,232	25,142	8,090	8.7	52.6
1977–78	921,204	487,347	433,857	229	30	311,620	161,212	150,408	34	66,581	52,270	14,311	32,131	23,658	8,473	8.9	44.1
1978–79	921,390	477,344	444,046	225	29	301,079	153,370	147,709	33	68,848	52,652	16,196	32,730	23,541	9,189	9.0	41.3
1979–80	929,417	473,611	455,806	218	30	298,081	150,749	147,332	32	70,131	52,716	17,415	32,615	22,943	9,672	9.3	38.8
1980–81	935,140	469,883	465,257	218	30	295,739	147,043	148,696	32	71,956	52,792	19,164	32,958	22,711	10,247	9.4	37.1
1981–82	952,998	473,364	479,634	222	30	295,546	145,532	150,014	32	72,032	42,223	19,809	32,707	22,224	10,483	9.6	36.9
1982–83	969,510	479,140	490,370	227	31	289,921	144,697	145,224	31	73,136	51,310	21,826	32,775	21,902	10,873	9.8	35.5
1983–84	974,309	482,319	491,990	225	32	284,263	143,595	140,668	30	74,407	51,334	23,073	33,209	22,064	11,145	10.0	35.1
1984–85	979,477	482,528	496,949	230	32	286,251	143,390	142,861	30	75,063	50,455	24,608	32,943	21,700	11,243	10.2	35.7
1985–86	987,823	485,923	501,900	236	33	288,567	143,508	145,059	30	73,910	49,261	24,649	33,653	21,819	11,834	10.4	36.4
1986–87	991,339	480,854	510,485	241	34	289,557	141,363	148,194	30	72,750	47,460	25,290	34,120	22,099	12,021	10.4	37.1
1987–88	994,829	477,203	517,626	252	36	299,317	145,163	154,154	30	70,735	45,484	25,251	34,870	22,615	12,255	10.5	37.9
1988–89	1,018,755	483,346	535,409	272	38	310,621	149,354	161,267	31	70,853	45,046	25,810	35,720	22,648	13,022	10.5	38.8
1989–90	1,049,657	491,488	558,169	282	40	323,844	153,643	170,201	33	70,980	44,002	26,978	38,238	24,371	13,867	10.5	41.1

[a]Represents the number of years from the receipt of the bachelor's degree to the receipt of the doctorate degree. See column 17.
[b]Includes first-professional degrees.
[c]First professional degrees included with bachelor's degrees.
Source: Center for Education Statistics, *120 Years of Education,* 83–84.

TABLE 14.51 **PERCENTAGE DISTRIBUTION OF BACHELOR AND HIGHER DEGREES, BY GENDER, 1948–1990**

Year	Percentage of Degrees							
	Bachelor's		1st-Professional		Master's		Doctorate	
	Men	Women	Men	Women	Men	Women	Men	Women
1947–48	65	35	na	na	68	32	88	13
1949–50	76	24	na	na	71	29	91	9
1954–55	65	36	na	na	66	34	91	9
1959–60	65	35	na	na	68	32	90	10
1964–65	57	43	96	4	68	32	89	11
1969–70	57	43	95	5	60	40	87	13
1974–75	55	45	88	13	55	45	79	21
1979–80	51	49	75	25	51	49	70	30
1981–82	50	50	73	28	49	51	68	32
1983–84	50	50	69	31	51	49	67	33
1984–85	49	51	67	33	50	50	66	34
1985–86	49	51	67	33	50	50	65	35
1987–88	48	52	64	36	49	52	65	35
1989–90	47	53	62	38	47	53	64	36

Source: American Council on Education, *The Fact Book on Higher Education,* 1997 Edition (Phoenix, 1998), 185.

TABLE 14.52 **PERSONS 25 OR OLDER WHO HAVE COMPLETED FOUR OR MORE YEARS OF COLLEGE, 1947–1990**
(in percent)

Year	All Races			White			Black			Hispanic		
	Both Sexes	Male	Female	Both Sexes	Male	Female	Both Sexes	Male	Female	Both Sexes	Male	Female
1947	5.4	6.2	4.7	5.7	6.6	4.9	2.5	2.4	2.6	. . .	. . .	. . .
1950	6.2	7.3	5.2	. . .	. . .	. . .	2.3	2.1	2.4	. . .	. . .	. . .
1952	7.0	8.3	5.8	. . .	. . .	. . .	2.4	2.0	2.7	. . .	. . .	. . .
1957	7.6	9.6	5.8	8.0	10.1	6.0	2.9	2.7	3.0	. . .	. . .	. . .
1959	8.1	10.3	6.0	8.6	11.0	6.2	3.3	3.8	2.9	. . .	. . .	. . .
1962	8.9	11.4	6.7	9.5	12.2	7.0	4.0	3.9	4.0	. . .	. . .	. . .
1964	9.1	11.7	6.8	9.6	12.3	7.1	3.9	4.5	3.4	. . .	. . .	. . .
1966	9.8	12.5	7.4	10.4	13.3	7.7	3.8	3.9	3.7	. . .	. . .	. . .
1968	10.5	13.3	8.0	11.0	14.1	8.3	4.3	3.7	4.8	. . .	. . .	. . .
1970	11.0	14.1	8.2	11.6	15.0	8.6	4.5	4.6	4.4	. . .	. . .	. . .
1972	12.0	15.4	9.0	12.6	16.2	9.4	5.1	5.5	4.8	. . .	. . .	. . .
1974	13.3	16.9	10.1	14.0	17.7	10.6	5.5	5.7	5.3	5.5	7.1	4.0
1976	14.7	18.6	11.3	15.4	19.6	11.6	6.6	6.3	6.8	6.1	8.6	4.0
1978	15.7	19.7	12.2	16.4	20.7	12.6	7.2	7.3	7.1	7.0	8.6	5.7
1980	17.0	20.9	13.6	17.8	22.1	14.0	7.9	7.7	8.1	7.9	9.7	6.2
1982	17.7	21.9	14.0	18.5	23.0	14.4	8.8	9.1	8.5	7.8	9.6	6.2
1984	19.1	22.9	15.7	19.8	23.9	16.0	10.4	10.4	10.4	8.3	9.5	7.0
1986	19.4	23.2	16.1	20.1	23.1	16.4	10.9	11.2	10.7	8.4	9.5	7.4
1988	20.3	24.0	17.0	20.9	25.0	17.3	11.2	11.1	11.4	10.1	12.3	8.1
1990	21.3	24.4	18.4	22.0	25.3	19.0	11.3	11.9	10.8	9.2	9.8	8.7

Source: Littman, *Statistical Portrait of the U.S.,* 233–345

TABLE 14.53   BACHELOR'S DEGREES CONFERRED BY INSTITUTIONS OF HIGHER EDUCATION, BY FIELD OF STUDY, 1959–1960 TO 1989–1990

Year	Total	Agricultural and Natural Resources	Architecture and Environmental Design	Business and Management	Communications	Computer and Information Sciences	Education	Engineering	Foreign Languages	Health Science	Letters	Library Science	Life Sciences	Mathematics	Physical Sciences	Psychology	Public Affairs	Social Science	Visual and Performing Arts	Others[a]
1959–60	392,440	6,241	1,801	51,076	1,548	0	89,002	37,679	5,405	24,455	22,457	1,938	15,576	11,399	16,007	8061	3,714	48,002	13,163	34,916
1960–61	365,174	5,649	1,674	48,074	1,830	0	91,028	35,698	6,364	11,314	24,003	439	16,060	13,097	15,452	8460	1,688	50,221	12,942	21,181
1961–62	383,961	5,841	1,774	49,017	1,519	0	96,280	34,735	7,906	11,366	26,609	423	16,915	14,570	15,851	9578	1,560	55,296	13,609	21,112
1962–63	422,420	6,013	2,028	50,639	1,687	0	101,338	33,458	9,707	11,854	30,225	462	19,114	16,078	16,215	10,993	1,957	63,104	14,518	22,030
1963–64	461,266	6,169	2,059	55,474	2,001	0	111,215	35,226	12,160	11,527	35,146	510	22,723	18,624	17,456	13,258	2,032	74,729	16,459	24,798
1964–65	493,757	6,734	2,333	59,288	1,928	87	117,137	36,795	13,859	11,611	38,836	623	25,166	19,460	17,861	14,626	2,320	81,919	17,391	25,783
1965–66	520,115	7,178	2,663	62,721	2,357	89	116,448	35,615	15,186	14,965	42,262	619	26,916	19,977	17,129	16,897	2,960	90,632	18,679	26,822
1966–67	558,534	7,866	2,937	69,032	2,741	222	118,955	35,954	16,706	15,908	45,900	701	28,849	21,207	17,739	19,364	3,242	101,550	21,548	28,113
1967–68	632,289	8,308	3,057	79,074	3,173	459	133,965	37,368	19,128	17,429	52,467	814	31,826	23,513	19,380	23,819	4,912	117,093	25,521	30,983
1968–69	728,845	9,965	3,477	93,094	4,269	933	150,985	41,248	21,493	19,825	59,674	1,000	35,308	27,209	21,480	29,332	5,282	137,517	31,588	35,166
1969–70	792,317	11,321	4,105	104,706	5,199	1,544	164,080	44,479	20,895	21,674	62,583	1,054	37,389	27,442	21,439	33,606	5,762	150,331	35,901	38,807
1970–71	839,730	12,682	5,570	114,865	10,802	2,388	176,614	50,046	19,945	25,190	64,933	1,013	35,743	24,801	21,412	37,880	6,252	155,236	30,394	43,974
1971–72	887,273	13,516	6,440	121,360	12,340	3,402	191,220	51,164	18,849	28,570	64,670	989	37,293	23,713	20,745	43,093	8,221	158,037	33,831	49,820
1972–73	922,362	14,856	6,962	126,263	14,317	4,304	194,229	51,265	18,964	33,523	61,799	1,159	42,233	23,067	20,696	47,695	11,346	155,922	36,017	57,845
1973–74	945,776	16,253	7,822	13,166	17,096	4,756	185,225	50,286	18,840	41,394	55,469	1,164	48,340	21,635	21,178	51,821	12,671	150,298	39,730	70,032
1974–75	922,933	17,528	8,226	133,010	19,248	5,033	167,015	46,852	17,606	48,858	48,534	1,069	51,741	18,181	20,778	50,988	14,730	135,165	40,782	77,589
1975–76	925,746	19,402	9,146	142,379	21,282	5,652	154,807	46,331	15,471	53,813	43,019	843	54,275	15,984	21,465	49,908	16,751	126,287	42,138	86,793
1976–77	919,549	21,467	9,222	150,964	23,214	6,407	143,722	49,283	13,944	57,122	38,849	781	53,605	14,196	22,497	47,373	17,627	116,879	41,793	90,604
1977–78	921,204	22,650	9,250	160,187	25,400	7,201	136,141	55,654	12,730	59,168	36,365	693	51,502	12,569	22,986	44,559	18,078	112,827	40,951	72,293
1978–79	921,390	23,134	9,273	171,764	26,457	8,719	126,109	62,375	11,825	61,819	34,557	558	48,846	11,806	23,207	42,461	18,882	107,922	40,969	90,707
1979–80	929,417	22,802	9,132	185,361	28,616	11,154	118,169	68,893	11,133	63,607	33,497	398	46,370	11,378	23,410	41,962	18,422	106,519	40,892	90,702
1980–81	935,140	21,886	9,455	199,338	31,282	15,121	108,309	75,000	10,319	63,348	33,208	375	43,216	11,078	23,952	40,833	18,714	100,345	40,479	88,882
1981–82	852,998	21,029	9,728	214,001	34,222	20,267	101,113	80,005	9,851	63,385	34,334	307	41,639	11,599	24,052	41,031	18,739	99,545	40,422	87,739
1982–83	969,510	20,909	9,823	226,893	38,602	24,510	97,991	89,270	9,685	64,614	32,743	258	39,982	12,453	23,405	40,364	16,290	95,088	39,469	87,161
1983–84	974,309	19,317	9,186	230,031	40,165	32,172	92,382	94,444	9,479	64,338	33,739	255	38,640	13,211	23,671	39,872	14,396	93,121	39,833	85,966
1984–85	979,477	18,107	9,325	233,351	42,083	38,878	88,161	96,105	9,954	64,513	34,091	202	38,445	15,146	23,732	39,811	13,838	91,461	37,936	84,338
1985–86	987,823	16,823	9,119	238,160	43,091	41,889	87,221	95,953	10,102	64,535	35,434	157	38,524	16,306	21,731	40,521	13,878	93,703	36,949	83,727
1986–87	991,339	14,991	8,922	241,156	45,408	39,664	87,115	93,074	10,184	63,206	37,133	139	38,114	16,489	19,974	42,868	14,161	96,185	36,223	86,333
1987–88	994,829	14,222	8,603	243,725	46,726	34,523	91,287	88,706	10,045	60,754	39,551	123	36,755	15,904	17,806	45,003	14,294	100,288	36,638	89,876
1988–89	1,018,755	13,492	9,150	247,175	48,645	30,454	97,082	85,225	10,780	59,138	43,387	122	36,059	15,218	17,186	48,737	15,270	107,914	37,925	95,796
1989–90	1,049,657	13,070	9,261	249,081	51,434	27,434	104,715	82,110	11,326	58,816	48,075	84	37,170	14,597	16,131	53,586	16,241	116,925	39,695	100,057

[a]Other includes degrees in area and ethnic studies, home economics, law, liberal/general studies, military sciences, multi/interdisciplinary studies, parks and recreation, philosophy and religion, protective services, theology, and degrees not classified by field of study.

Source: Center for Education Statistics, 120 Years of Education, 85.

TABLE 14.54   MASTER'S DEGREES CONFERRED BY INSTITUTIONS OF HIGHER EDUCATION, BY FIELD OF STUDY, 1959–1960 TO 1989–1990

Year	Total	Agricultural and Natural Resources	Architecture and Environmental Design	Business and Management	Communications	Computer and Information Sciences	Education	Engineering	Foreign Languages	Health Science	Letters	Library Science	Life Sciences	Mathematics	Physical Sciences	Psychology	Public Affairs	Social Science	Visual and Performing Arts	Others[a]
1959–60	74,435	1,203	319	4643	0	0	33,433	7,159	1,055	1,838	3,262	305	2,154	1,757	3,376	1,406	568	5,448	2,892	3,617
1960–61	84,609	1,241	378	6723	37	0	34,368	8,178	1,274	1,632	3,556	1,931	2,358	2,231	3,790	1,719	2,706	5,825	2,910	3,752
1961–62	91420	1,357	311	7691	44	0	36,182	8,909	1,480	1,632	3,947	2,140	2,642	2,680	3,925	1,832	2,841	6,678	3,151	3,978
1962–63	98684	1,261	356	8334	32	0	37,878	9,635	1,849	2,011	4,490	2,363	2,921	3,313	4,123	1,918	3,180	7,637	3,363	4,020
1963–64	109,183	1,344	383	9251	32	0	41,091	10,827	2,196	2,279	5,006	2,717	3,296	3,597	4,561	2,059	3,651	8,493	3,673	4,727
1964–65	121,167	1,366	373	10,602	38	146	44,314	12,055	2,690	2,493	5,745	3,211	3,598	4,141	4,914	2,241	4,085	9,565	4,244	5,346
1965–66	140,602	1,661	702	12,959	44	238	50,397	13,675	3,393	2,833	7,033	3,939	4,232	4,769	4,987	2,530	4,769	11,477	5,019	5,945
1966–67	157,726	1,750	812	14,892	107	449	55,760	13,880	4,017	3,398	8,231	4,489	4,996	5,278	5,405	3,138	5,087	13,460	5,812	6,765
1967–68	176,749	1,797	1,021	17,795	65	548	63,399	15,182	4,511	3,677	9,021	5,165	5,506	5,527	5,499	3,479	5,858	14,539	6,563	7,597
1968–69	193,756	2,070	1,143	19,281	129	1,012	70,967	15,240	4,691	4,067	9,684	5,932	5,743	5,713	5,895	4,011	6,318	16,068	7,413	8,379
1969–70	208,291	1,793	1,427	21,287	130	1,459	79,293	15,593	4,803	4,488	9,713	6,511	5,800	5,636	5,935	4,111	7,067	16,281	7,849	9,115
1970–71	230,509	2,457	1,705	26,481	1,856	1,588	88,952	16,443	4,755	5,445	11,148	7,001	5,728	5,191	6,367	4,431	8,215	16,476	6,675	9,595
1971–72	251,633	2,680	1,899	30,367	2,200	1,977	98,143	16,960	4,616	6,875	11,074	7,383	6,101	5,198	6,287	5,289	9,183	17,416	7,537	10,448
1972–73	263,371	2,807	2,307	31,007	2,406	2,113	105,565	16,619	4,289	7,879	10,808	7,696	6,263	5,028	6,257	5,831	10,899	17,288	7,254	11,055
1973–74	277,033	2,928	2,702	32,644	2,640	2,276	112,610	15,379	3,964	9,090	10,384	8,134	6,552	4,834	6,062	6,588	12,077	17,249	8,001	12,919
1974–75	292,450	3,067	2,938	36,247	2,794	2,299	120,169	15,348	3,807	9,901	10,068	8,091	6,550	4,327	5,807	7,066	14,610	16,892	8,362	14,107
1975–76	311,771	3,340	3,215	42,512	3,126	2,603	128,417	16,342	3,531	11,885	9,468	8,037	6,582	3,857	5,466	7,811	16,117	15,824	8,817	14,812
1976–77	317,164	3,724	3,213	46,420	3,091	2,798	126,825	16,245	3,147	12,323	8,701	7,572	7,114	3,695	5,331	8,301	17,917	15,395	8,636	16,716
1977–78	311,620	4,023	3,115	48,326	3,296	3,038	119,038	16,398	2,726	13,619	8,306	6,914	6,806	3,373	5,561	8,160	18,341	14,578	9,036	16,966
1978–79	301,079	3,994	3,113	50,372	2,882	3,055	111,995	15,495	2,426	14,781	7,289	5,906	6,831	3,036	5,451	8,003	18,300	12,807	8,524	16,819
1979–80	298,081	3,976	3,139	55,006	3,082	3,647	103,951	16,243	2,236	15,068	6,807	5,374	6,510	2,860	5,219	7,806	18,413	12,101	8,708	17,935
1980–81	295,739	4,003	3,153	57,898	3,105	4,218	98,938	16,709	2,104	16,004	6,515	4,859	5,978	2,567	5,284	7,998	18,524	11,855	8,629	17,398
1981–82	295,546	4,163	3,327	61,299	3,327	4,935	93,757	17,939	2,008	15,942	6,421	4,506	5,874	2,727	5,514	7,791	18,216	11,892	8,746	17,162
1982–83	289,921	4,254	3,357	65,319	3,604	5,321	84,853	19,350	1,759	17,068	5,767	3,979	5,696	2,837	5,290	8,378	18,245	11,112	8,742	16,990
1983–84	284,263	4,178	3,223	66,653	3,656	6,190	77,187	20,661	1,773	17,443	5,818	3,805	5,406	2,741	5,576	8,002	15,373	10,465	8,520	17,593
1984–85	286,251	3,928	3,275	67,527	3,669	7,101	76,137	21,557	1,724	17,383	5,934	3,893	5,059	2,882	5,796	8,408	16,045	10,380	8,714	16,839
1985–86	288,567	3,801	3,260	67,137	3,823	8,070	76,353	21,661	1,721	18,624	6,291	3,626	5,013	3,159	5,902	8,293	16,300	10,428	8,416	16,689
1986–87	289,557	3,523	3,142	67,496	3,937	8,491	75,501	22,693	1,746	18,426	6,123	3,815	4,954	3,221	5,652	8,204	17,032	10,397	8,506	16,598
1987–88	299,317	3,479	3,159	69,655	3,925	9,197	77,867	23,388	1,844	18,665	6,194	3,713	4,784	3,442	5,733	7,872	17,290	10,294	7,937	20,879
1988–89	310,621	3,245	3,383	73,521	4,257	9,414	82,533	24,572	1,898	19,293	6,676	3,953	4,961	3,447	5,723	8,552	17,918	10,867	8,265	18,143
1989–90	323,844	3,373	3,492	77,203	4,369	9,643	86,057	24,848	1,995	20,354	7,223	4,349	4,861	3,677	5,447	9,231	17,993	11,419	8,546	19,764

a"Other" includes degrees in area and ethnic studies, home economics, law, liberal/general studies, military sciences, multi/interdisciplinary studies, parks and recreation, philosophy and religion, protective services, theology, and degrees not classified by field of study.

Source: Center for Education Statistics, *120 Years of Education,* 85.

TABLE 14.55   DOCTOR'S DEGREES CONFERRED BY INSTITUTIONS OF HIGHER EDUCATION, BY FIELD OF STUDY, 1959–1960 TO 1989–1990

Year	Total	Agricultural and Natural Resources	Architecture and Environmental Design	Business and Management	Communications	Computer and Information Sciences	Education	Engineering	Foreign Languages	Health Science	Letters	Library Science	Life Sciences	Mathematics	Physical Sciences	Psychology	Public Affairs	Social Science	Visual and Performing Arts	Others[a]
1959–60	9,829	440	17	135	0	0	1,591	786	203	107	431	19	1,205	303	1,838	641	43	1,211	292	567
1960–61	10,575	450	3	172	16	0	1,742	943	232	133	439	14	1,193	344	1,991	703	66	1,302	303	529
1961–62	11,622	465	1	226	9	0	1,898	1,207	228	148	526	10	1,338	396	2,122	781	67	1,309	311	580
1962–63	12,822	449	3	250	7	0	2,075	1,378	237	157	565	17	1,455	490	2,380	844	77	1,461	379	598
1963–64	14,490	555	3	275	12	0	2,348	1,693	326	192	618	13	1,625	596	2,455	939	72	1,719	422	627
1964–65	16,467	529	10	321	9	6	2,705	2,124	376	173	766	12	1,928	682	2,829	847	87	1,913	428	722
1965–66	18,237	588	12	387	11	19	3,065	2,304	426	251	801	19	2,097	782	3,045	1,046	108	2,033	476	767
1966–67	20,617	637	18	437	5	38	3,529	2,614	478	250	972	16	2,255	832	3,462	1,231	123	2,388	504	828
1967–68	23,089	648	15	441	1	36	4,078	2,932	610	243	1,116	22	2,784	947	3,593	1,268	129	2,684	528	1,014
1968–69	26,158	699	32	530	14	64	4,830	3,377	659	283	1,275	17	3,051	1,097	3,859	1,551	137	3,016	684	983
1969–70	29,866	823	35	601	10	107	5,895	3,681	760	357	1,339	40	3,289	1,236	4,312	1,668	152	3,638	734	1,189
1970–71	32,107	1,086	36	807	145	128	6,403	3,638	781	459	1,857	39	3,645	1,199	4,390	1,782	185	3,659	621	1,247
1971–72	33,363	971	50	896	111	167	7,044	3,671	841	425	2,023	64	3,653	1,128	4,103	1,881	219	4,078	572	1,466
1972–73	34,777	1,059	58	923	139	196	7,318	3,492	991	643	2,170	102	3,636	1,068	4,006	2,089	214	4,230	616	1,827
1973–74	33,816	930	69	981	175	198	7,293	3,312	923	568	2,076	60	3,439	1,031	3,626	2,336	214	4,123	585	1,877
1974–75	34,083	991	69	1009	165	213	7,446	3,108	857	609	1,951	56	3,384	975	3,626	2,442	271	4,209	649	2,053
1975–76	34,064	928	82	953	204	244	7,778	2,821	864	577	1,884	71	3,392	856	3,431	2,581	298	4,154	620	2,326
1976–77	33,232	893	73	863	171	216	7,963	2,586	752	538	1,723	75	3,397	823	3,341	2,761	316	3,784	662	2,295
1977–78	32,131	971	73	866	191	196	7,595	2,440	649	638	1,616	67	3,309	805	3,133	2,587	385	3,583	708	2,319
1978–79	32,730	950	96	860	192	236	7,736	2,506	641	705	1,504	70	3,542	730	3,102	2,662	344	3,358	700	2,796
1979–80	32,615	991	79	792	193	240	7,941	2,507	549	771	1,500	73	3,636	724	3,089	2,768	372	3,219	655	2,516
1980–81	32,958	1,067	93	842	182	252	7,900	2,561	588	827	1,380	71	3,718	728	3,141	2,955	388	3,114	654	2,497
1981–82	32,707	1,079	80	855	200	251	7,680	2,636	536	910	1,313	84	3,743	681	3,286	2,780	389	3,061	670	2,473
1982–83	32,775	1,149	97	809	214	262	7,551	2,831	488	1,155	1,176	52	3,341	698	3,269	3,108	347	2,931	692	2,605
1983–84	33,209	1,172	84	977	219	251	7,473	2,981	462	1,163	1,215	74	3,437	695	3,306	2,973	421	2,911	728	2,667
1984–85	32,943	1,213	89	866	234	248	7,151	3,230	437	1,199	1,239	87	3,432	699	3,403	2,908	431	2,851	693	2,533
1985–86	33,653	1,158	73	969	223	344	7,110	3,410	448	1,241	1,215	62	3,358	742	3,551	3,088	385	2,955	722	2,599
1986–87	34,120	1,049	92	1,098	275	374	6,909	3,820	441	1,213	1,181	57	3,423	725	3,672	3,123	398	2,916	792	2,562
1987–88	34,870	1,142	98	1,109	234	428	6,553	4,191	411	1,261	1,172	46	3,629	750	3,809	2,987	470	2,781	725	3,074
1988–89	35,720	1,183	86	1,149	253	551	6,800	4,523	420	1,436	1,234	61	3,520	866	3,858	3,222	429	2,885	752	2,492
1989–90	38,238	1,272	97	1,142	269	623	6,922	4,965	512	1,543	1,266	41	3,844	915	4,168	3,353	495	3,023	842	2,946

[a]"Other" includes degrees in area and ethnic studies, home economics, law, liberal/general studies, military sciences, multi/interdisciplinary studies, parks and recreation, philosophy and religion, protective services, theology, and degrees not classified by field of study.
Source: Center for Education Statistics, *120 Years of Education,* 87.

TABLE 14.56 FIRST-PROFESSIONAL DEGREES IN DENTISTRY, MEDICINE, AND LAW, BY SEX, 1949–1950 TO 1989–1990

Year	Dentistry (D.D.S. or D.M.D.) Number of Institutions Conferring Degrees	Degrees Conferred Total	Men	Women	Medicine (M.D.) Number of Institutions Conferring Degrees	Degrees Conferred Total	Men	Women	Law (LL.B. or J.D.) Number of Institutions Conferring Degrees	Degrees Conferred Total	Men	Women
1949–50	40	2,579	2,561	18	72	5,612	5,028	584	. . .	. . .	. . .	. . .
1951–52	41	2,918	2,895	23	72	6,201	5,871	330	. . .	. . .	. . .	. . .
1953–54	42	3,102	3,063	39	73	6,712	6,377	335	. . .	. . .	. . .	. . .
1955–56	42	3,009	2,975	34	73	6,810	6,464	346	131	8,262	7,974	288
1957–58	43	3,065	3,031	34	75	6,816	6,469	347	131	9,394	9,122	272
1959–60	45	3,247	3,221	26	79	7,032	6,645	387	134	9,240	9,010	230
1961–62	46	3,183	3,166	17	81	7,138	6,749	389	134	9,364	9,091	273
1963–64	46	3,180	3,168	12	82	7,303	6,878	425	133	10,679	10,372	307
1965–66	47	3,178	3,146	32	84	7,673	7,170	503	136	13,246	12,776	470
1967–68	48	3,422	3,375	47	85	7,944	7,318	626	138	16,454	15,805	649
1969–70	48	3,718	3,684	34	86	8,314	7,615	699	145	14,916	14,115	801
1970–71	48	3,745	3,703	42	89	8,919	8,110	809	147	17,421	16,181	1,240
1971–72	48	3,862	3,819	43	92	9,253	8,423	830	147	21,764	20,266	1,498
1972–73	51	4,047	3,992	55	97	10,307	9,388	919	152	27,205	25,037	2,168
1973–74	52	4,440	4,355	85	99	11,356	10,093	1,263	151	29,326	25,986	3,340
1974–75	52	4,773	4,627	146	104	12,447	10,818	1,629	154	29,296	24,881	4,415
1975–76	56	5,425	5,187	238	107	13,426	11,252	2,174	166	32,293	26,085	6,208
1976–77	57	5,138	4,764	374	109	13,461	10,891	2,570	169	34,104	26,447	7,657
1977–78	57	5,189	4,623	566	109	14,279	11,210	3,069	169	34,402	25,457	8,945
1978–79	58	5,434	4,794	640	109	14,786	11,381	3,405	175	35,206	25,180	10,026
1979–80	58	5,258	4,558	700	112	14,902	11,416	3,486	179	35,647	24,893	10,754
1980–81	58	5,460	4,672	788	116	15,505	11,672	3,833	176	36,331	24,563	11,768
1981–82	59	5,282	4,467	815	119	15,814	11,867	3,947	180	35,991	23,965	12,026
1982–83	59	5,585	4,631	954	118	15,484	11,350	4,134	177	36,853	23,550	13,303
1983–84	60	5,353	4,302	1,051	119	15,813	11,359	4,454	179	37,012	23,382	13,630
1984–85	59	5,339	4,233	1,106	120	16,041	11,167	4,874	181	37,491	23,070	14,421
1985–86	59	5,046	3,907	1,139	120	15,938	11,022	4,916	181	35,844	21,874	13,970
1986–87	58	4,741	3,603	1,138	121	15,428	10,431	4,997	179	36,056	21,561	14,495
1987–88	57	4,477	3,300	1,177	122	15,358	10,278	5,080	180	35,397	21,067	14,330
1988–89	58	4,265	3,124	1,141	124	15,460	10,310	5,150	182	35,634	21,069	14,565
1989–90	57	4,100	2,834	1,266	124	15,075	9,923	5,152	182	36,485	21,079	15,406

Source: Cynthia M. Taeuber, *Statistical Handbook on Women, 1996* (Phoenix, 1996), 312.

TABLE 14.57 BARRON'S TOP 50 AMERICAN COLLEGES, 1990[a]

School	Reputation
Amherst College	First-rate Liberal Arts School
Boston College	Jesuit Ivy
Bowdoin College	Innovative/Well-regarded Liberal Arts
Brown University	Top-notch Liberal Arts
Bryn Mawr College	Best Women's College
California Institute of Technology	Leading Edge Science Tech
Carleton College	A Renaissance School
Carnegie Mellon University	The Professional Choice
Claremont McKenna College	On the Verge of Greatness
College of William and Mary	Strong Liberal Arts—Well Balanced
Columbia University	Top-notch Liberal Arts
Cornell University	Diversified Academic Excellence
Dartmouth College	Top Rate Liberal Arts
Davidson College	Demanding Liberal Arts Curriculum
Duke University	Thorough Coursework/Versatility of Graduates
Georgetown University	Traditional/Value Oriented
Georgia Institute of Technology	Hell of an Engineer
Harvard University	Internationally Premier College
Harvey Mudd College	Best Specialty Engineering College
Haverford College	Liberal Arts Center
Johns Hopkins University	Academic Think Tank
Massachusetts Institute of Technology	Premier Science and Engineering Institution
Middlebury College	Liberal Arts Personified
Northwestern University	Midwest Ivy
Pomona College	Best Liberal Arts West of Mississippi
Princeton University	Quintessential Ivy League
Reed College	Best Liberal Arts School
Rice University	Top-notch Science and Engineering

School	Reputation
Stanford University	Ivy League/Best
Swarthmore College	Best Liberal College
Tufts University	Strong All Around
University of California/Berkeley	International Intellectual Center
University of California/Irvine	Up and Coming
University of California/Los Angeles	World-class University
University of Chicago	High-powered Academics
University of Illinois/Urbana-Champaign	MIT of the Midwest
University of Michigan/Ann Arbor	Best All Around
University of North Carolina/Chapel Hill	Public Ivy
University of Notre Dame	Top-notch Undergraduate Program
University of Pennsylvania	Strong Multifaceted University
University of Texas/Austin	University of the First Class
University of Virginia	Great Academics
Vanderbilt University	Liberal Arts Stronghold
Vassar College	Innovative and Independent
Wake Forest University	Liberal Arts Bastion
Washington and Lee University	Best Kept Secret in the South
Wellesley College	Intellectual Haven
Wesleyan University	Top-notch Liberal Arts
Williams College	Top-notch Liberal Arts
Yale University	Finest Liberal Arts—creative

[a]The highest-ranked undergraduate colleges and universities, based on three measures: percent accepted (number of applicants accepted vs. number who applied); percent enrolled (number who enrolled vs. number accepted); SAT scores (combined verbal and quantitative). Listing is alphabetically, not by rank.
Source: Tom Fischgrund, ed., *Barron's Top 50: An Inside Look at America's Best Colleges* (Hauppauge, N.Y., 1991), xv, 666–67.

It would be an act of folly to attempt in a single chapter to explore the dimensions of science and technology in the United States during the 45 years following the Second World War. Much of what went on in the country involved science and technology in one fashion or another, albeit in degrees that varied from area to area. Much of the information in this volume represents a manifestation in some form of science or technology. Obvious examples include measurement and understanding of weather; all aspects of transportation and communication; many aspects of economics and of birth, death, and health care; politics; and education. The state of military forces at any time was directly related to the level of military technology. This unit thus does not purport to address all sciences and technology, aspects of which are explored in other parts of the volume. It focuses on selected themes, chosen for their significance, their propensity to stretch the bounds of knowledge and imagination, their importance to the functioning and future of the basic culture, and their relationship to the way Americans lived daily lives.

The United States possessed several advantages in the pursuit of scientific inquiry and technological change. It had an expanding system of colleges and universities, in which the value of professional inquiry had become a staple. Intellectual curiosity aside, producing new information allowed one to advance within the system. The nation had extensive research facilities and an intellectual and political climate that as a rule fostered free inquiry. The government wanted certain subjects pursued, as did private industry, but much of what went on in research was voluntary. The competitive American economic and business system fostered continuous development and improvement of goods and services. Failure to do so usually meant, well, failure. Whether it came from government or private organizations the United States had money, and financial support was the parent of research. Such an atmosphere attracted some of the world's best minds to the United States.

Statistics on research and development reveal a few themes. The amount of money spent increased each year, but its percentage of the Gross National Product remained steady. A large portion of funds went to defense-related purposes at the start of the period, but the percentage decreased markedly though the passage of years. The largest contributor of funds for research and development each year after 1970 was private industry. The number of patents issued in the United States increased nearly every year between 1946 and 1990, but the rate of growth usually was small. The largest recipients of patents

TABLE 15.1 RESEARCH AND DEVELOPMENT (R&D)—EXPENDITURES, 1960–1990

| Year or Period | Current Dollars (billions) | | | Constant (1982) Dollars | | Annual Percent Change | | Percent of Total R&D Outlays | | | | | |
| | Total | Defense Space Related | Other | Total (billions) | Percent of GNP | Current Dollars | Constant Dollars | Federally Funded Defense/Space-Related | | | Other Outlays | | |
								Total	Defense	Space	Total	Non-federal	Federal
1960	13.5	7.4	6.1	43.6	2.6	9.4	7.5	55	52	3	45	35	10
1961	14.3	'8.0	6.3	45.8	2.7	5.9	4.9	56	50	6	44	35	9
1962	15.4	8.6	6.8	48.2	2.7	7.5	5.2	56	49	7	44	36	8
1963	17.1	9.2	7.8	52.6	2.8	10.8	9.2	54	41	13	46	34	12
1964	18.9	10.6	8.3	57.2	2.9	10.5	8.8	56	37	19	44	34	10
1965	20.0	10.8	9.2	59.4	2.8	6.3	3.8	54	33	21	46	35	11
1966	21.8	11.1	10.7	62.6	2.8	9.0	5.5	51	32	19	49	36	13
1967	23.1	11.3	11.8	64.4	2.8	6.0	2.9	49	35	14	51	38	13
1968	24.6	12.1	12.5	65.5	2.8	6.3	1.6	49	35	14	51	39	12
1969	25.6	11.5	14.1	64.7	2.7	4.2	−1.2	45	34	11	55	42	13
1970	26.1	11.2	14.9	62.4	2.6	2.0	−3.5	43	33	10	57	43	14
1971	26.7	11.5	15.2	60.4	2.4	2.1	−3.2	43	33	10	57	44	13
1972	28.5	11.7	16.8	61.4	2.4	6.7	1.7	41	33	8	59	44	15
1973	30.7	12.0	18.7	62.4	2.3	7.9	1.7	39	32	7	61	47	14
1974	32.9	11.8	'21.0	61.5	2.2	7.0	−1.5	36	29	7	64	49	15
1975	35.2	12.0	23.2	59.9	2.2	7.2	−2.6	34	27	7	66	49	17
1976	39.0	13.7	25.4	62.1	2.2	10.8	3.8	35	27	8	65	49	16
1977	42.8	14.5	28.2	63.7	2.2	9.6	2.4	34	27	7	66	50	16
1978	48.1	15.4	32.7	66.8	2.1	12.5	4.9	32	26	6	68	50	18
1979	55.0	17.0	37.9	70.1	2.2	14.2	5.0	31	25	6	69	51	18
1980	62.6	18.2	44.5	73.3	2.3	13.9	4.5	29	24	5	71	53	18
1981	71.9	20.8	51.0	76.6	2.4	14.8	4.6	29	24	5	71	54	17
1982	80.0	24.0	56.0	80.0	2.5	11.3	4.4	30	26	4	70	54	16
1983	89.1	26.7	62.4	85.8	2.6	11.4	7.2	30	27	3	70	54	16
1984	101.1	31.4	69.8	93.8	2.7	13.5	9.4	31	28	3	69	55	14
1985	113.8	37.6	76.3	102.5	2.8	12.5	9.2	33	30	3	67	54	13
1986	119.5	40.6	78.9	104.9	2.8	5.0	2.3	34	31	3	66	55	11
1987	125.4	43.9	81.5	106.6	2.8	4.9	1.7	35	32	3	65	54	11
1988	133.7	45.5	88.3	110.2	2.7	6.7	3.3	34	31	3	66	54	12
1989	140.5	46.4	94.1	111.1	2.7	5.0	0.9	33	29	4	67	55	12
1990	145.5	46.5	98.9	110.5	2.7	3.5	−0.6	32	28	4	68	56	12

Note: Includes basic research, applied research, and development. Defense-related outlays comprise all research and development spending by Department of Defense, including space activities, and a portion of Department of Energy funds. Space-related outlays are those of the National Aeronautics and Space Administration; they exclude space activities of other federal agencies, estimated at less shan 5 percent of all space research tech development spending. Minus sign (−) indicates decrease.
Source: Bureau of the Census, *Statistical Abstract of the United States, 1992* (Washington, D.C., 1993), 585.

year-after-year was American corporations, but foreign companies pick up the pace after 1970 and by 1990 foreign firms virtually had drawn even with the Americans. Japanese firms dominated foreign recipients of patents. There probably existed no equivalent of Thomas Edison in the last half of the 20th century, and if by chance one could be found, he or she likely worked for a corporation.

TABLE 15.2   RESEARCH AND DEVELOPMENT (R&D)—SOURCE OF FUNDS AND PERFORMANCE SECTOR, 1970–1990

(millions of dollars)

Year	Total	Source of Funds				Performance Sector				
		Federal Govt.	Industry	Univ., Colleges	Other[a]	Federal Govt.	Industry	Univ., Colleges	Associated FFRDC's[b]	Other[a]
Current Dollars										
1970	26,134	14,891	10,444	462	337	4,079	18,067	2,335	737	916
1975	35,213	18,109	15,820	749	535	5,354	24,187	3,409	987	1,276
1980	62,610	29,461	30,912	1,334	903	7,632	44,505	6,077	2,246	2,150
1982	80,018	36,578	40,692	1,731	1,017	9,141	58,650	7,323	2,479	2,425
1983	89,139	40,832	45,251	1,929	1,127	10,582	65,268	7,877	2,737	2,675
1984	101,139	45,641	52,204	2,104	1,190	11,572	74,800	8,617	3,150	3,000
1985	113,818	52,120	57,977	2,376	1,345	12,945	84,239	9,686	3,523	3,425
1986	119,529	54,273	61,056	2,790	1,410	13,535	87,823	10,926	3,895	3,350
1987	125,352	57,904	62,642	3,200	1,606	13,413	92,155	12,153	4,206	3,425
1988	133,741	61,499	66,953	3,473	1,816	14,281	97,889	13,465	4,531	3,575
1989	140,486	62,688	71,767	3,948	2,083	15,121	101,599	14,987	4,729	4,050
1990	145,450	64,000	74,700	4,450	2,300	16,100	104,200	16,000	4,800	4,350
Constant (1982) Dollars										
1970	62,403	35,632	24,851	1,114	807	9,833	42,986	5,629	1,777	2,179
1975	59,882	30,985	26,679	1,302	916	9,308	40,781	5,926	1,716	2,151
1980	73,255	34,557	36,065	1,574	1,059	9,006	51,919	7,171	2,650	2,508
1981	76,641	35,690	38,257	1,667	1,027	9,040	55,140	7,345	2,667	2,448
1982	80,018	36,578	40,692	1,731	1,017	9,141	58,650	7,323	2,479	2,425
1983	85,753	39,251	43,568	1,851	1,083	10,152	62,842	7,557	2,626	2,576
1984	93,790	42,286	48,456	1,945	1,102	10,696	69,433	7,965	2,912	2,785
1985	102,462	46,870	52,252	2,130	1,209	11,606	75,925	8,684	3,159	3,087
1986	104,866	47,555	53,639	2,436	1,235	11,820	77,160	9,542	3,401	2,943
1987	106,616	49,201	53,341	2,711	1,364	11,364	78,477	10,296	3,563	2,917
1988	110,166	50,635	55,181	2,856	1,495	11,742	80,680	11,072	3,726	2,947
1989	111,129	49,553	56,815	3,115	1,646	11,931	80,436	11,825	3,731	3,206
1990	110,470	48,591	56,757	3,376	1,746	12,213	79,173	12,137	3,641	3,305

[a] Nonprofit institutions.
[b] University-associated federally funded R&D centers.
Source: Bureau of Census, *Statistical Abstract, 1992,* 585.

TABLE 15.3   PATENTS AND TRADEMARKS, 1946–1990

(in thousands)

Item	1946–50	1951–1955	1960	1965	1970	1980	1985	1990
Patent Applications	400.3	379.1	64.4	100.4	109.4	113.0	127.1	176.7
Inventions	360.1	351.6	79.6	94.6	102.9	104.3	117.0	164.6
Designs	39.1	26.0	4.5	5.4	6.0	7.8	9.6	11.3
Botanical plants	.4	.5	.1	.1	.2	.2	.2	.4
Reissues	.7	1.0	.2	.3	.3	.6	.3	.5
Patents Issued	163.0	209.0	50.0	66.6	68.0	66.2	77.3	99.2
Inventions	144.1	192.7	47.2	62.9	64.4	61.8	71.7	90.4
Individuals	59.0	78.5	13.1	16.1	13.5	13.8	12.9	17.3
Corporations								
U.S.	78.4	100.3	28.2	37.2	36.9	27.7	31.2	36.1
Foreign	4.7	10.5	4.7	8.1	12.3	19.1	26.4	36.0
U.S. Government	1.8	3.4	1.2	1.5	1.7	1.2	1.1	1.0
Designs	18.0	15.1	2.5	3.4	3.2	3.9	5.1	8.0
Botanical plants	.3	.4	.1	.1	.1	.1	.2	.3
Reissues	.6	.8	.2	.2	.3	.3	.3	.4
Trademarks issued	85.6	100.9	22.4	21.7	27.8	24.7	71.5	60.8
Trademarks	61.3	83.3	18.4	18.5	21.7	18.9	65.8	53.6
Renewals	24.3	17.6	3.9	3.2	6.1	5.9	5.9	7.2

Source: Bureau of the Census, *Statistical Abstract of the United States, 1971* (Washington, D.C., 1971), 518; Bureau of Census, *Statistical Abstract of the United States, 1993* (Washington, D.C., 1993), 544.

TABLE 15.4 FOREIGN RECIPIENTS OF UNITED STATES PATENTS, 1990

(includes only U.S. patents granted to residents of areas outside of the United States and its territories)

Top Countries	Total	Inventions	Designs
Total, foreign country residents	46,223	42,973	2,956
Japan	20,726	19,524	1,137
Germany	7,858	7,610	182
France	3,093	2,866	184
United Kingdom	3,015	2,790	202
Canada	2,089	1,861	213
Italy	1,499	1,260	227
Switzerland	1,347	1,284	57
Netherlands	1,044	958	46
Sweden	885	768	114
China: Taiwan	861	732	129
Australia	517	432	81
Austria	423	393	29
Belgium	352	313	37
Israel	311	299	7
Denmark	204	158	43
Finland	315	304	10
South Korea	289	224	65
Other countries	1,395	1,197	193

Source: Bureau of Census, *Statistical Abstract, 1992*, 840.

TABLE 15.5 TOP 74 CORPORATIONS RECEIVING U.S. PATENTS IN 1990

Rank	Company	Number
1.	Hitachi	908
2.	Toshiba Corp.	891
3.	Canon K.K.	868
4.	Mitsubishi Denki K.K.	862
5.	General Electric Co.	785
6.	Fuji Photo Film Co., Ltd.	767
7.	Eastman Kodak Co.	720
8.	U.S. Philips Corp.	637
9.	IBM Corp.	608
10.	Siemens A.G.	506
11.	Bayer A.G.	499
12.	E.I. du Pont de Nemours & Co.	481
13.	NEC Corp.	436
14.	Westinghouse Electric Co.	435
15.	AT&T Co.	429
16.	Ciba—Geigy Corp.	409
17.	Dow Chemical Co.	400
18.	BASF A.G.	394
19.	Motorola Inc.	394
20.	General Motors Corp.	379
21.	Minolta Camera Co., Ltd.	376
22.	Nissan Motor Co., Ltd.	372
23.	Honda Motor Co., Ltd.	363
24.	Mobil Oil Corp.	353
25.	Sharp Corp.	349
26.	Matsushita Electric Industrial Co.	340
27.	3M Corp.	323
28.	Ricoh Co., Ltd.	292
29.	Texas Instruments, Inc.	284
30.	Hoechst A.G.	278
31.	Shell Oil Co.	263
32.	Fujitsu Ltd.	260
33.	Xerox Corp.	252
34.	Hughes Aircraft Co.	248
35.	Allied Signal Inc.	243
36.	Sony Corp.	238
37.	AMP Inc.	223
38.	Hewlett–Packard Co.	218
39.	Robert Bosch GmbH	204
40.	Boeing Co.	192
41.	Amoco Corp.	187
42.	Hoechst Celanese Corp.	182
43.	Olympus Optical Co., Ltd.	179
44.	Brother Kogyo K.K.	178
45.	Imperial Chemical Industries PLC	176
46.	Honeywell Inc.	167
47.	Sunstrand	155
48.	Ford Motor Co.	154
49.	Pioneer Electronic Corp.	154
50.	United Technologies Corp.	151
51.	Toyota Jidosha K.K.	149
52.	Konica Corp.	147
53.	Eaton Corp.	143
54.	American Cyanamid Co.	136
55.	Merck & Co., Inc.	134
56.	Mazda Motor Corp.	132
57.	Aisin Seiki K.K.	131
58.	Phillips Petroleum Co.	131
59.	Procter & Gamble Co.	127
60.	Exxon Research & Engineering Co.	126
61.	Digital Equipment Corp.	124
62.	Fancu Ltd.	123
63.	Sumitomo Electric Industries	123
64.	Dow Corning Corp.	122
65.	GTE Products Corp.	122
66.	Henkel KGAA	117
67.	Fuji Jukogyo K.K.	116
68.	Rockwell International Corp.	115
69.	Sumitomo Chemical Co., Ltd.	114
70.	Texaco Inc.	114
71.	Thomson–CSF	114
72.	Chrysler Motors Corp.	112
73.	Sanyo Electric Co., Ltd.	111
74.	Massachusetts Inst. of Tech.	110

Source: Richard C. Levy, *Inventing & Patenting Sourcebook* (Detroit, 1992), 977.

U.S. Winners of Nobel Prizes in the Sciences

The Nobel Prizes grew out of the will of Alfred B. Nobel, a Swedish scientist (the inventor of dynamite) and philanthropist who, on his death in 1896, left the sum of $9.2 million, the interest from which was to be distributed yearly to the individuals who had contributed the most to chemistry, physics, medicine/physiology, as well as to the individual who had produced the most distinguished literary work and the person who had contributed most to world peace. An award in economics was added in 1969. Worth $38,000 in 1945, each award by 1990 brought its recipient $710,000. In the first 45 years of the 20th century, Americans won 20 of the awards in the sciences; in the second 45 years Americans received 142. Assisted by generous funding for research from government, private industry, and the universities and able to attract some of the sharpest minds from other nations, the United States had established absolute domination of Nobel Prizes in the sciences.

TABLE 15.6 NOBEL PRIZE LAUREATES IN CHEMISTRY, PHYSICS, AND PHYSIOLOGY/MEDICINE—SELECTED COUNTRIES, 1901–1990

(presented by location of award-winning research and by date of award)

| Country | 1901–90 | | | | 1901–15 | 1916–30 | 1931–45 | 1946–60 | 1961–75 | 1976–90 |
	Total	Physics	Chemistry	Physiology/ Medicine						
Total	406	140	115	151	52	41	49	74	92	98
United States	162	57	36	69	3	3	14	38	41	63
United Kingdom	69	21	24	24	7	8	11	14	20	9
West Germany[a]	57	17	28	12	15	12	11	4	8	7
France	22	8	7	7	10	3	. . .	0	5	2
Soviet Union	10	7	1	2	2	0	0	4	3	1
Japan	4	3	1	0	0	0	0	1	2	1
Other countries	82	27	18	37	15	15	11	13	13	15

[a] Includes East Germany before 1946.
Source: Bureau of Census, *Statistical Abstract, 1992,* 594.

The Space Program

But for the cold war the U.S. space program might never have left the ground. This undertaking that called for efforts both sublime and delicate and produced the most spectacular results in science and technology at least would have proceeded at a more deliberate pace, starved as inevitably it would have been, for funding either from government or private enterprise. A propulsion team headed by Werner von Braun had been working on a missile program for the army, but the Department of Defense in the early 1950s had rejected the idea of placing a satellite in space. The Soviet Union's launching of *Sputnik I* in October 1957 and *Sputnik II* (or *Muttnik*—a dog was aboard) a month later jolted the United States into the space race. There followed a crash program of spending for space activity, creation of the National Aeronautics and Space Administration (NASA) in 1958, the initial Mercury program (1960–63) to place an American in Earth orbit, and the two-man Gemini program of 1965–66 that made great strides in orbital docking.

The three-man Apollo program that followed constituted implementation of President John Kennedy's pledge in 1961 to place an American on the Moon before the end of the decade. Despite a tragic fire aboard the grounded spacecraft in 1967 that took the lives of astronauts Virgil Grissom, Edward White, and Roger Chaffee, the Apollo program progressed step-by-step toward its objective. The voyage of *Apollo 8* that orbited the Moon with its three-man crew and sent back a Christmas message in December 1968 helped prepare the populace for the ultradramatic voyage of *Apollo 11* in July 1969, at the end of which Neil Armstrong and Edwin "Buzz" Aldrin set foot on the Moon—and all this for people on Earth to see on live television. One of the great scientific and technological feats of humankind, the Moon landing manifested, among other miracles, a revolution in the technology of communication.

Six other Moon missions would follow *Apollo 11;* five of them would achieve lunar landing—*Apollo 13,* having experienced a near-tragic malfunction, had to abort its journey to the surface. Each landing sent back marvelous pictures; each expanded the scope of investigation of the Moon and of space, but none—*Apollo 13* the closest to an exception—approached the drama and excitement of the first landing on the Moon. After *Apollo 11,* the moon landings were anticlimactic. Now anything was believable.

By the time the Apollo program ended in December 1972, NASA was at work on its next project, a huge delta-winged spacecraft, able to accommodate a crew of several persons, go into space, and return to be used again, called the space shuttle or orbiter. Having received approval of President Richard Nixon, NASA constructed an experimental vessel it called *Enterprise.* Named after a starship in the venerable television series *Star Trek* (which was itself named after a U.S. aircraft carrier), *Enterprise* never went into space. The first fully functional orbiter, *Columbia,* took off April 12, 1981, and returned as planned two days later. Plagued with problems of many sorts, delays, and cost-overruns, the shuttle program completed only 24 missions between 1981 and 1986, far fewer than had been anticipated. Then a condition that had been disappointing became a disaster. Failure of an O-ring seal of a booster rocket on January 28, 1986, caused destruction in flight of shuttle *Challenger* and death of its crew of seven. There followed a two-year period of recrimination, investigation, reshuffling leadership in NASA, and redesign of the vehicle. With launch of *Discovery* in September 1988, the shuttle program seemed back on track as the focus of space travel in the 1990s, albeit with more modest and realistic expectations. An immediate benefit of the program was launching into orbit (from a shuttle) of the revolutionary 94-inch Hubble telescope in April 1990. Early reports of a defect in the telescope, which had cost $2 billion, set off a new round of cynicism and pessimism about the space program generally, but in time the malfunction proved to be correctable.

The "right stuff"—original seven astronauts stand in front of the Mercury capsule, June 1963. *Left-to-right:* L. Gordon Cooper, Walter Schirra, Alan Shepard, Virgil Grissom, John Glenn, Donald Slayton, and Scott Carpenter (NASA)

TABLE 15.7 FEDERAL SPACE ACTIVITIES BUDGET AUTHORITY, BY FISCAL YEAR, 1955–1990

(millions of current dollars)

Year	Total	NASA	DOD[a]	Energy	Commerce	Other[b]
1955	75	74	1	. . .	. . .	. . .
1956	100	71	17	. . .	. . .	12
1957	150	76	48	. . .	. . .	26
1958	249	89	136	. . .	. . .	24
1959	521	146	341	. . .	. . .	34
1960	960	401	518	. . .	. . .	41
1961	1,518	744	710	68	. . .	64
1962	3,295	1,797	1,298	148	51	1
1963	5,435	3,626	1,550	214	43	2
1964	6,831	5,016	1,599	210	3	3
1965	6,956	5,138	1,574	229	12	3
1966	6,970	5,065	1,689	187	27	3
1967	6,710	4,830	1,664	184	29	3
1968	6,529	4,430	1,922	145	28	4
1969	5,976	3,822	2,013	118	20	3
1970	5,341	3,547	1,678	103	8	4
1971	4,741	3,101	1,512	95	27	5
1972	4,575	3,071	1,407	55	31	10
1973	4,825	3,093	1,623	54	40	15
1974	4,640	2,759	1,766	42	60	14
1975	4,914	2,915	1,892	30	64	13

Year	Total	NASA	DOD[a]	Energy	Commerce	Other[b]
1976	5,320	3,225	1,983	23	72	16
Tr. Qtr.[c]	1,341	849	460	5	22	4
1977	5,983	3,440	2,412	22	91	18
1978	6,518	3,623	2,738	34	103	20
1979	7,244	4,030	3,036	59	98	21
1980	8,689	4,680	3,848	40	93	28
1981	9,978	4,992	4,828	41	87	30
1982	12,441	5,528	6,679	61	145	29
1983	15,589	6,328	9,019	39	178	25
1984	17,136	6,648	10,195	34	236	22
1985	20,167	6,925	12,768	34	423	17
1986	21,659	7,165	14,126	35	309	25
1987	26,448	9,809	16,287	48	278	27
1988	26,607	8,302	17,679	241	352	33
1989	28,443	10,098	17,906	97	301	42
1990	31,854	12,142	19,382	79	202	50

[a] DOD: Department of Defense.
[b] Departments of Interior and Agriculture and National Science Foundation. NSF transferred to NASA after 1982. Commerce was included until 1962.
[c] Transition Quarter: July 1–September 30, 1976.
Source: Aerospace Industries of America, *Aerospace Facts & Figures 1973–74* (Washington, D.C., 1973), 61; Aerospace Industries of America, *Aerospace Facts & Figures 91–92* (Washington, D.C., 1991), 66.

TABLE 15.8 NATIONAL AERONAUTICS AND SPACE ADMINISTRATION BUDGET AUTHORITY IN CONSTANT DOLLARS,[a] BY FISCAL YEAR, 1963–1990

(millions of constant dollars, 1982 = 100)

Year	Total	Research and Development	Space Flight Control and Data Communications[b]	Construction of Facilities	Research Program Management
1963	11,274	8,990	. . .	2,284	[c]
1964	15,428	11,770	. . .	2,157	1,501
1965	15,556	12,919	. . .	791	1,846
1966	14,896	12,959	. . .	176	1,733
1967	13,827	11,787	. . .	237	1,804
1968	12,339	10,519	. . .	102	1,718
1969	10,191	8,454	. . .	84	1,653
1970	9,038	7,216	. . .	128	1,695
1971	7,586	5,854	. . .	60	1,672
1972	7,182	5,478	. . .	115	1,589
1973	7,049	5,375	. . .	163	1,510
1974	5,828	4,206	. . .	194	1,428
1975	5,617	4,039	. . .	249	1,330
1976	5,722	4,314	. . .	132	1,276
Tr. Qtr.[d]	1,444	1,084	. . .	17	342
1977	5,697	4,261	. . .	176	1,261
1978	5,666	4,200	. . .	226	1,241
1979	5,852	4,463	. . .	190	1,199
1980	6,187	4,824	. . .	188	1,175
1981	5,924	4,650	. . .	126	1,149
1982	6,020	4,772	. . .	114	1,134
1983	6,596	5,314	. . .	133	1,148
1984	6,762	1,908[b]	3,486	206	1,161
1985	6,790	2,213	3,222	160	1,194
1986	6,818	2,287	3,205	154	1,172
1987	9,254	2,672	5,168	184	1,231
1988	7,450	2,697	3,129	175	1,449
1989	8,655	3,324	3,594	217	1,520
1990	9,349	3,963	3,523	165	1,535

[a] Constant dollars measured, not dollars spent in a given year, but purchasing power of money relative to other years.
[b] Separate budget category beginning in FY 84; funds formerly included under Research and Development.
[c] Included in Research and Development for one year.
[d] Transition quarter: July 1–September 30, 1976.
Source: Aerospace Industries, Aerospace Facts & Figures 91–92, 69.

TABLE 15.9 U.S. SPACECRAFT RECORD[a]

(calendar years 1957–1990)

Year	Earth Orbit[b] Success	Earth Orbit[b] Failure	Earth Escape[b] Success	Earth Escape[b] Failure
1957	. . .	1	. . .	. . .
1958	5	8	. . .	4
1959	9	9	1	2
1960	16	12	1	2
1961	35	12	. . .	2
1962	55	12	4	1
1963	62	11	. . .	. . .
1964	69	8	4	. . .
1965	93	7	4	1
1966	94	12	7	1[c]
1967	78	4	10	. . .
1968	61	15	3	. . .
1969	58	1	8	1
1970	36	1	3	. . .
1971	45	2	8	1
1972	33	2	8	. . .
1973	23	2	3	. . .
1974	27	2	1	. . .
1975	30	4	4	. . .
1976	33	. . .	1	. . .
1977	27	2	2	. . .
1978	34	2	7	. . .
1979	18	. . .	. . .	. . .
1980	16	4	. . .	. . .
1981	20	1	. . .	. . .
1982	21	. . .	. . .	. . .
1983	31	. . .	. . .	. . .
1984	35	3	. . .	. . .
1985	37	1	. . .	. . .
1986	11	4	. . .	. . .
1987	9	1	. . .	. . .
1988	16	1	. . .	. . .
1989	24	. . .	2	. . .
1990	36	. . .	1	. . .
Total	1,187	144	82	15

[a] Payloads, rather than launchings; some launches account for multiple spacecraft. Includes spacecraft from cooperating countries launched on U.S. launch vehicles.
[b] The criterion of success is attainment of Earth orbit or Earth escape rather than judgment of mission success. "Escape" flights include all that were intended to go at least an altitude equal to the lunar distance from the Earth.
[c] This Earth-escape failure did attain Earth orbit and therefore is included in the Earth-orbit success totals.
Source: Aerospace Industries, Aerospace Facts & Figures 91–92, 60.

TABLE 15.10 WORLDWIDE SPACE LAUNCHINGS[a] THAT ATTAINED EARTH ORBIT OR BEYOND

(calendar years 1957–1990)

Country	Total 1957–90	1986	1987	1988	1989	1990
Total	3,308	103	110	116	100	116
USSR	2,256	91	95	90	74	75
United States	923	6	8	12	17	27
Japan	41	2	3	2	2	3
People's Republic of China	28	2	2	4	. . .	5
European Space Agency	35	2	2	7	7	5
Israel	2	. . .	. . .	1	. . .	1
Other[b]	23	. . .	. . .	. . .	. . .	. . .

[a] Number of launchings rather than spacecraft; some launches orbited multiple spacecraft.
[b] Includes 10 by France, 8 by Italy (6 were U.S. spacecraft), 3 by India, 1 by Australia, and 1 by the United Kingdom.
Source: Aerospace Industries, Aerospace Facts & Figures 91–92, 60.

Harrison Schmitt and the lunar rover on the Moon, December 1972: *Apollo 17,* the last mission (NASA)

TABLE 15.11 NOTABLE U.S. PLANETARY SCIENCE MISSIONS

Spacecraft	Launch Date (Coordinated Universal Time)	Mission	Remarks
Mariner 2	Aug. 27,1962	Venus	Passed within 22,000 mi of Venus 12/14/62: contact lost 1/3/63 at 54 million mi
Ranger 7	Jul. 28, 1964	Moon	Yielded more than 4,000 photos of lunar surface
Mariner 4	Nov. 28, 1964	Mars	Passed behind Mars 7/14/65; took 22 photos from 6,000 mi
Ranger 8	Feb. 17, 1965	Moon	Yielded more than 7,000 photos of lunar surface
Surveyor 3	Apr. 17, 1967	Moon	Scooped and tested lunar soil
Mariner 5	Jun. 14, 1967	Venus	In solar orbit; closest Venus flyby 10/19/67
Mariner 6	Feb. 24, 1969	Mars	Came within 2,000 mi of Mars 7/31/69; collected data, photos
Mariner 7	Mar. 27, 1969	Mars	Came within 2,000 mi of Mars 8/5/69
Mariner 9	May 30, 1971	Mars	First craft to orbit Mars 11/13/71; sent back more than 7,000 photos
Pioneer 10	Mar. 2, 1972	Jupiter	Passed Jupiter 12/14/73; exited the planetary system 6/13/83; transmission ended 3/31/97 at 6.39 billion mi
Pioneer 11	Apr. 5, 1973	Jupiter, Saturn	Passed Jupiter 12/3/74; Saturn 9/1/79; discovered an additional ring and two moons around Saturn; operating in outer solar system: transmission ended 9/95
Mariner 10	Nov. 3 1973	Venus, Mercury	Passed Venus 2/5/74; arrived Mercury 3/29/74. First time gravity of one planet (Venus) used to whip spacecraft towad another (Mercury)
Viking 1	Aug. 20, 1975	Mars	Landed on Mars 7/20/76: did scientific research, sent photos; functioned 6$\frac{1}{2}$ years
Viking 2	Sep. 9, 1975	Mars	Landed on Mars 9/3/76: functioned 3$\frac{1}{2}$ years
Voyager 1	Sep. 5, 1977	Jupiter, Saturn	Encountered Jupiter 3/5/79, provided evidence of Jupiter ring: passed near Saturn 11/12/80
Voyager 2	Aug. 20, 1977	Jupiter, Saturn Uranus, Neptune	Encountered Jupiter 7/9/79; Saturn 8/25/81; Uranus 1/24/86; Neptune 8/25/89
Pioneer Venus 1	May 20, 1978	Venus	Entered Venus orbit 12/4/78; spent 14 years strudying planet; ceased operating 10/19/92
Pioneer Venus 2	Aug. 8, 1978	Venus	Encountered Venus 12/9/78; probes impacted on surface
Magellan	May 4, 1989	Venus	Landed on Venus 8/10/90; orbited and mapped Venus: monitored geological activity on surface: ceased operating 10/11/94
Galileo	Oct. 18, 1989	Jupiter	Used Earth's gravity to propel it toward Jupiter; encountered Venus Feb. 1990; scheduled to reach Jupiter in 1995.

Source: Robert Famighetti, ed., *The World Almanac and Book of Facts, 1999* (Mahwah, N. J., 1998), 215.

The first space shuttle, *Enterprise,* atop its 747 carrier, en route to its first "free-flight" test, October 12, 1977 (NASA)

TABLE 15.12 MANNED SOVIET AND U.S. SPACEFLIGHTS, 1961–1990

Dates	Mission	Crew (no. of flights)	Duration (hr:min)	Features
4/12/61	*Vostok 1*	Yuri A. Gagarin	1:48	1st human orbital flight
5/5/61	*Mercury-Redstone 3*[a]	Alan B. Shepard, Jr.	0:15	1st American in space
7/21/61	*Mercury-Redstone 4*	Virgil I. Grissom	0:15	Spacecraft sank, Grissom rescued
8/6/1961–8/7/61	*Vostok 2*	Gherman S. Titov	25:18	1st spaceflight of more than 24 hrs
2/20/62	*Mercury-Atlas 6*[a]	John H. Glenn, Jr.	4:55	1st American in orbit; 3 orblts
5/24/62	*Mercury-Atlas 7*	M. Scott Carpenter	4:56	Manual retrofire error caused 250-mi landing overshoot
8/11/62–8/15/62	*Vostok 3*	Andrian G. Nikolayev	94:22	*Vostok 3* and *4* made 1st group flight
8/12/62–8/15/62	*Vostok 4*	Pavel R. Popovich	70:57	On 1st orbit it came within 3 mi of *Vostok 3*
10/3/62	*Mercury-Atlas 8*	Walter M. Schirra, Jr.	9:13	Landed 5 mi from target
5/15/63–5/16/63	*Mercury-Atlas 9*	L. Gordon Cooper	34:19	1st U.S. evaluation of effects of one day in space on a person; 22 orbits
6/14/63–6/19/63	*Vostok 5*	Valery F. Bykovsky	119:06	Vostok 5 and 6 made 2d group flight
6/16/63–6/19/63	*Vostok 6*	Valentina V. Tereshkova	70:50	1st woman in space: passes within 3 mi of Vostok 5
10/12/64–10/13/64	*Voskhod 1*	Vladimir M. Komarov, Konstantin P. Feoktistov, Boris B. Yegorov	24:17	1st 3-person orbital flight; 1st without space suits
3/18/65–3/19/65	*Voskhod 2*	Pavel I. Belyayev, Aleksei A. Leonov	26:02	Leonov made 1st "space walk" (10 min)
3/23/65	*Gemini-Titan 3*[a]	Grissom (2), John W. Young	4:53	1st piloted spacecraft to change its orbital path
6/3/65–6/7/65	*Gemini-Titan 4*	James A. McDivitt, Edward H. White 2d	97:56	White was 1st American to "walk in space" (36 min)
8/21/65–8/29/65	*Gemini-Titan 5*	Cooper (2), Charles Conrad, Jr.	190:55	Longest-duration human flight to date
12/15/65–12/16/65	*Gemini-Titan 6A*	Schirra (2), Thomas P. Stafford	25:51	Completed 1st U.S. space rendezvous, with *Gemini 7*
12/4/65–12/18/65	*Gemini-Titan 7*	Frank Borman, James A. Lovell	330:35	Longest-duration Gemini flight
3/16/66	*Gemini-Titan 8*	Neil A. Armstrong, David R. Scott	10:41	1st docking of one space vehicle with another; mission aborted, control malfunction; 1st Pacific landing
6/3/66–6/6/66	*Gemini-Titan 9A*	Stafford (2), Eugene A. Cernan	72:21	Performed rendezvous maneuvers, including simulation of lunar module randezvous
7/18/66–7/21/66	*Gemini-Titan 10*	Young (2), Michael Collins	70:47	1st use of Agena target vehicle's propulsion systems; 1st orbital docking
9/12/66–9/15/66	*Gemini-Titan 11*	Conrad (2), Richard F. Gordon, Jr.	71:17	1st tethered flight; highest Earth-orbit altitude (850 mi)
11/11/66–11/15/66	*Gemini-Titan 12*	Lovell (2), Edwin W. "Buzz" Aldrin, Jr.	94:34	Final Gemini mission; 5½ hr EVA[b]
4/23/67–4/24/67	*Soyuz 1*	Komarov (2)	26:40	Crashed on reentry, killing Komarov
10/11/68–10/22/68	*Apollo-Saturn 7*[a]	Schirra (3), Donn F. Eisele, R. Walter Cunningham	260:09	1st piloted flight of Apollo spacecraft command-service module only; live TV footage of crew
12/21/68–12/27/68	*Apollo-Saturn 8*	Borman (2), Lovell (3), William A. Anders	147:00	1st lunar orbit and piloted lunar return reentry (command-service module only); views of lunar surface televised to Earth
1/14/69–1/17/69	*Soyuz 4*	Vladimir A. Shatalov	71:21	Docked with *Soyuz 5*
1/15/69–1/18/69	*Soyuz 5*	Boris V. Volyanov, Aleksei S. Yeliseyev, Yevgeny V. Khrunov	72:54	Docked with 4; Yeliseyev and Khrunov transferred to Soyuz 4 via a spacewalk
3/3/69–3/13/69	*Apollo-Saturn 9*	McDivitt (2), D. Scott (2), Russell L. Schweickart	241:00	1st piloted flight of lunar module
5/18/69–5/26/69	*Apollo-Saturn 10*	Stafford (3), Young (3), Cernan (2)	192:03	1st lunar module orbit of Moon, 50,000 ft from Moon surface
7/16/69–7/24/69	*Apollo-Saturn 11*	Armstrong (2), Collins (2), Aldrin (2)	195:18	1st lunar landing made by Armstrong and Aldrin (7/20); collected 48.5 lb of soil, rock samples; lunar stay time 21:36:21
10/11/69–10/16/69	*Soyuz 6*	Georgi S. Shonin, Valery N. Kubasov	118:43	1st welding of metals in space
10/12/69–10/17/69	*Soyuz 7*	Anatoly V. Flipchenko, Vladislav N. Volkov, Viktor V. Gorbatko	118:40	Space lab construction test made; *Soyuz 6, 7,* and *8*: 1st time 3 spacecraft, 7 crew members orbited the Earth at once
10/13/69	*Soyuz 8*	Shatalov (2), Yeliseyev (2)	118:51	Part of space lab construction team
11/14/69–11/24/69	*Apollo-Saturn 12*	Conrad (3), Richard F. Gordon, Jr. (2), Alan L. Bean	244:36	Conrad and Bean made 2d Moon landing (11/18); collected 74.7 lb of samples, lunar stay time 31:31
4/11/70–4/17/70	*Apollo-Saturn 13*	Lovell (4), Fred W. Hase, Jr., John L. Swigart, Jr.	142:54	Aborted after service module oxygen tank ruptured; crew returned safely using lunar module
6/1/70–6/19/70	*Soyuz 9*	Nikolayev (2), Vitaliy I. Sevastyanov	424:59	Longest human spaceflight to date
1/31/71–2/9/71	*Apollo-Saturn 14*	A. Shepard (2), Stuart A. Roosa, Edgar D. Mitchell	216:01	Shepard and Mitchell made 3d Moon landing (2/3); collected 96 lb of lunar samples; lunar stay 33:31
4/19/71–4/22/71	*Salyut 1*	(Occupied by Soyuz 11 crew)		1st space station
	Soyuz 10	Shatalov (3), Yeliseyev (3), Nikolay N. Rukavishnikov	47:46	1st successful docking with a space station; failed to enter space station
6/6/71–6/30/71	*Soyuz 11*	Georgi T. Dobrovolskiy, V. Volkov (2), Viktor I. Patsayev	570:22	Docked and entered *Salyut 1* space station; orbited in *Salyut 1* for 23 days, crew died during reentry from loss of pressurization

Dates	Mission	Crew (no. of flights)	Duration (hr:min)	Features
7/26/71–8/7/71	Apollo-Saturn 15	D. Scott (3), James B. Irwin, Alfred M. Worden	295:12	Scott and Irwin made 4th Moon landing (7/30); 1st lunar rover use; 1st deep space walk; 170 lb of samples; 66:55 stay
4/16/72–4/27/72	Apollo-Saturn 16	Young (4), Charles M. Duke, Jr., Thomas K. Mattingly 2d	265:51	Young and Duke made 5th Moon landing (4/20); collected 213 lb of lunar samples; lunar stay 71:2
12/7/72–12/19/72	Apollo-Saturn 17	Cernan (3), Ronald E. Evans, Harrison H. Schmitt	301:51	Cernan and Schmitt made 6th lunar landing (12/11); collected 243 lb of samples; record lunar stay of more than 75 hr
5/14/73	Skylab 1	(Occupied by Skylab 2, 3, and 4 crews)		1st U.S. space station
5/25/73–6/22/73	Skylab 2	Conrad (4), Joseph P. Kerwin, Paul J. Weitz	672:49	1st Amer. piloted orbiting space station; crew repaired damage caused during boost
7/28/73–9/25/73	Skylab 3	Bean (2), Owen K. Garriott, Jack R. Lousma	1,427:09	Crew systems and operational tests; exceeded pre-mission plans for scientific activities; 13 hrs EVA 13:44[b]
11/16/73–2/8/74	Skylab 4	Gerald P. Carr, Edward G. Gibson, William Pogue	2,017:15	Final Skylab mission
7/15/75–7/21/75	Soyuz 19 (ASTP)	Leonov (2), Kubasov (2)	143:31	U.S.-USSR joint flight; crews linked up in space (7/17), conducted experiments, shared meals, and held a joint news conference
7/15/75–7/24/75	Apollo (ASTP)	Vance Brand, Stafford (4), Donald K. Slayton	217:28	Joint flight with Soyuz 19
12/10/77	Soyuz 26	Yuri V. Romanenko, Georgiy M. Grechko (2)	2,314:00	1st multiple docking to a space station (Soyuz 26 and 27 docked at Salyut 6)
1/10/78	Soyuz 27	Vladimir A. Dzhanibekov	142:59	See Soyuz 26
3/2/78	Soyuz 28	Aleksei A. Gubarev (2), Vladimir Remek	190:16	1st international crew launch; Remek was 1st Czech in space
4/12/81–4/14/81	Columbia [c] (STS-1)	Young (5), Robert L. Crippen	54:21	1st space shuttle to fly into Earth orbit
11/12/81–11/14/81	Columbia (STS-2)	Joe H. Engle, Richard H. Truly	54:13	1st scientific payload; 1st reuse of space shuttle
11/11/82–11/16/82	Columbia (STS-5)	Brand (2), Robert Overmyer, William Lenoir, Joseph Allen	122:14	1st 4-person crew
6/18/83–6/24/83	Challenger (STS-7)	Crippen (2), Frederick Hauck, Sally K. Ride, John M. Fabian, Norman Thagard	146:24	Ride was 1st U.S. woman in space; 1st 5-person crew
6/27/83	Soyuz T-9	Vladimir A. Lyakhov (2), Aleksandr Pavlovich Aleksandrov	3,585:46	Docked at Salyut 7; 1st construction in space
8/30/83–9/5/83	Challenger (STS-8)	Truly (2), Daniel Brandenstein, William Thornton, Guion Bluford, Dale Gardner	145:09	Bluford was 1st U.S. black in space
11/28/83–12/8/83	Columbia (STS-9)	Young (6), Brewster Shaw, Jr., Robert Parker, Garriott (2), Byron Lichtenberg, Ulf Merbold	247:47	1st 6-person crew; 1st Spacelab mission
2/3/84–2/11/84	Challenger (41-B)	Brand (3), Robert Gibson, Ronald McNair, Bruce McCandless, Robert Stewart	191:16	1st untethered EVA[b]
2/8/84–4/11/84	Soyuz T-10B	Leonid Kizim, Vladimir Solovyov, Oleg Atkov	1,510:43	Docked with Salyut 7; crew set space duration record of 237 days
4/3/84–10/2/84	Soyuz T-11	Yury Malyshev (2), Gennady Strekalov (3), Rakesh Sharma	4,365:48	Docked with Salyut 7; Sharma 1st Indian in space
4/6/84–4/13/84	Challenger (41-C)	Crippen (3), Francie R. Scobee, George D. Nelson, Terry J. Hart, James D. van Hoften	167:40	1st in-orbit satellite repair
7/17/84	Soyuz T-12	Dzhanibekov (4), Svetlana Y. Savitskaya (2), Igor P. Volk	283:14	Docked at Salyut 7; Savitskaya was 1st woman to perform EVA
8/30/84–9/5/84	Discovery (41-D)	Henry W. Hartsfield (2), Michael L. Coats, Richard M. Mullane, Steven A. Hawley, Judith A. Resnik, Charles D. Walker	144:56	1st flight of U.S. nonastronaut (Walker)
10/5/84–10/13/84	Challenger (41-G)	Crippen (4), Jon A. McBride, Kathryn D. Sullivan, Ride (2), Marc Garneau, David C. Leestma, Paul D. Scully-Power	197:24	1st 7-person crew
11/8/84–11/16/84	Discovery (51-A)	Hauck (2); David M. Walker, Dr. Anna L. Fisher, J. Allen (2), D. Gardner (2)	191:45	1st satellite retrieval/repair
4/12/85–4/19/85	Discovery (51-D)	Karol J. Bobko, Donald E. Williams, Jake Garn, Walker (2), Jeffrey A. Hoffman, S. David Griggs, M. Rhea Seddon	167:55	Garn was 1st senator in space
6/17/85–6/24/85	Discovery (51-G)	Brandenstein (2), John O. Creighton, Shannon W. Lucid, Steven R. Nagel, Fabian (2), Prince Sultan Salman al-Saud, Patrick Baudry	169:39	Launched 3 satellites; Salman al-Saud was 1st Arab in space; Baudry was 1st French person on U.S. mission
10/3/85–10/7/85	Atlantis (51-J)	Bobko (3), Ronald J. Grabe, David C. Hilmers, Stewart (2), William A. Pailes	97:47	1st Atlantis flight

(continued)

TABLE 15.12 (continued)

Dates	Mission	Crew (no. of flights)	Duration (hr:min)	Features
10/30/85–11/6/85	*Challenger (61-A)*	Hartsfield (3), Nagel (2), Buchli (2), Bluford (2), Bonnie J. Dunbar, Wubbo J. Ockels, Richard Furrer, Ernst Messerschmid	168:45	1st 8-person crew; 1st German Spacelab mission
11/26/85–12/3/85	*Atlantis (61-B)*	Shaw (2), Bryan D. O'Connor, Sherwood C. Spring, Mary L. Cleave, Jerry L. Ross, C. Walker (3), Rodolfo Neri	165:05	Space structure assembly test; Neri was 1st Mexican in space
1/12/86–1/18/86	*Columbia (61-C)*	R. Gibson (2), Charles F. Bolden, Jr., Hawley (2), G. Nelson (2), Franklin R. Chang-Diaz, Robert J. Cenker, Bill Nelson	146:04	B. Nelson was 1st U.S. representative in space; material and astronomy experiments conducted
1/28/86	*Challenger (51-L)*	Scobee (2), Michael J. Smith, Resnik (2), Ellison S. Onizuka (2), Ronald E. McNair, Gregory B. Jarvis, Christa McAuliffe	–	Exploded 73 sec after liftoff; all were killed
2/20/86	*Mir*	–	–	Space station with 6 docking ports launched
3/13/86	*Soyuz T-15*	Kizim (3), Solovyov (2)	3,000:01	Ferry between stations; docked at *Mir*
2/5/87–12/29/87	*Soyuz TM-2*	Romanenko (3), Aleksandr I. Laveikin	7,835:38	Romanenko set endurance record, since broken
7/22/87–12/29/87	*Soyuz TM-3*	Aleksandr Vildorenko, Aleksandr Pavlovich Aleksandrov (2), Mohammed Faris	3,847:16	Docked with *Mir*, Faris 1st Syrian in space
12/21/87–12/21/88	*Soyuz TM-4*	V. Titov (2), Muso Manarov, Anatoly Levchenko	8,782:39	Docked with *Mir*
6/7/88–6/17/88	*Soyuz TM-5*	Viktor Savinykh (3), Anatoly Solovyev, Aleksandr Panayotov Aleksandrov	236:13	Docked with *Mir*, Aleksandrov 1st Bulgarian in space
9/29/88–10/3/88	*Discovery (STS-26)*	Hauck (3), Richard O. Covey (2), Hilmers (2), G. Nelson (2), John M. Lounge (2)	97:00	Redesigned shuttle makes 1st flight
5/4/89–5/8/89	*Atlantis (STS-30)*	D. Walker (2), Grabe (2), Thagard (2), Cleave (2), Mark C. Lee	96:56	Launched Venus orbiter *Magellan*
10/18/89–10/23/89	*Atlantis (STS-34)*	Williams (2), Michael J. McCulley, Lucid (2), Chang-Diaz (2), Ellen S. Baker	119:39	Launched Jupiter probe and orbiter *Galileo*
4/24/90–4/29/90	*Discovery (STS-31)*	McCandless (2), Sullivan (2), Loren J. Shriver (2), Bolden (2), Hawley (3)	121:16	Launched Hubble Space Telescope
10/6/90–10/10/90	*Discovery (STS-41)*	Richard N. Richards (2), Robert D. Cabana, Bruce E. Melnick, William M. Shepherd (2), Thomas D. Akers	98:10	Launched *Ulysses* spacecraft to investigate interstellar space and the Sun

[a] In American missions, the first name designated the spacecraft, the second the rocket: i.e., Mercury spacecraft, Redstone rocket; Gemini spacecraft, Titan rocket; Apollo spacecraft, Saturn rocket.

[b] EVA: extravehicular activity

[c] Beginning in 1981, all U.S. missions were in returnable space shuttles.

Source: Bureau of the Census, *Statistical Abstract of the United States, 1971* (Washington, D.C., 1971), 521; Famighetti, *World Almanac, 1999,* 210–212.

Crew of *Challenger* that perished when the space shuttle blew up on January 28, 1986. *Front row, left-to-right:* Michael J. Smith, Dick Scobie, and Ronald McNair; *back row, left-to-right:* Ellison Onizuka, Christa McAuliffe (a teacher), Gregory Jarvis (of Hughes Corporation), and Judith Resnik (NASA)

An Undelivered Speech

Of the many milestones and accomplishments in America's first age of space travel, nothing rivaled the landing on the Moon on July 20, 1969, for significance, impact, and popular appeal. This scientific and technological marvel seemingly went off without a hitch. Neil Armstrong and Buzz Aldrin exited the lunar lander, tramped around the Moon's surface, returned to the command module and—with Pete Conrad, who stayed with the mother vessel—flew off to virtually universal and everlasting adulation of Earth. The mission might have developed differently. Each phase of the adventure into space carried risks, of course, if only because each step carried problems that could not always be anticipated. The most harrowing task of *Apollo 11,* evidently, was getting the lunar vehicle back to the command module. A failure of that procedure and absence of a plan of rescue would have condemned Armstrong and Aldrin to remain forever on the Moon.

People in and connected to the White House of Richard Nixon agreed that however unthinkable it might seem, preparation should be made for the possibility of such a disaster. Frank Borman, one of the first astronauts to reach, but not land on, the Moon, broached the idea

to William Safire, a columnist who doubled as Nixon's speech writer. Nixon's aide, Peter Flanigan, and his chief of staff, H. R. Haldeman, told Safire to get something ready. Safire proposed the president's telephoning spouses of the condemned men, a religious service sort of like burial at sea, that commended the men's souls "to the deepest of the deep," and a brief message from the president. "These brave men, Neil Armstrong and Buzz Aldrin, know there is no hope for their recovery," Nixon was to say, "but they also know that there is hope for mankind in their sacrifice." "Man's search will not be denied," the president would promise, later in the speech. "But these were the first and will remain foremost in our hearts." And there would be a poetic ending: "Every human being who looks up at the Moon in the nights to come will know that there is some corner of another world that is forever mankind." Nixon, of course, never had to give that speech. Armstrong and Aldrin were blessed with long, fruitful lives, doubtless content in the knowledge that if their mission had ended in a different way, they at least would have gone out in style.

Source: William Safire, *"The Speech That Never Was Given," Kalamazoo Gazette,* July 13, 1999, A-10.

Computers

Scientists and technicians for many years had been in quest of a mechanical or automatic calculator—an electronic brain, as it sometimes had been called. An army team at the University of Pennsylvania that included John Mauchly and J. Presper Eckert in 1945 made a major if somewhat cumbersome step when it produced the first functioning electronic digital computer. Named ENIAC (Electronic Numerical Integrator and Computer), it weighed 60,000 pounds, occupied an entire large room and, equipped with vacuum tubes, drained enough electricity to dim the lights in the surrounding territory. Although ENIAC and subsequent calculating machines were imposing in size, expensive to construct and operate, and limited in memory and scope of activity, they became progressively important in large business and industrial operations. One such device, in the employ of CBS News, made a speedy and remarkably accurate determination of the outcome of the presidential election of 1952. Advances in solid-state technology, especially with development of the transistor and integrated circuits, reduced the size and cost and vastly increased speed and capacity of operations. Transistors began to replace vacuum tubes in the late 1950s, and technology continued to improve to the point in the 1980s when the size of electronic devices had been reduced by a factor of 100,000.

Miniaturization of components enabled a new direction in the world of electronic business devices that in short order exploded into a genuine revolution. A new company, Apple Computer, organized by Stephen Wozniak and Steven P. Jobs, set the stage in 1977 when it introduced a fully equipped unit that weighed 12 pounds and was small enough to sit on an individual desk. Apple II, as it was called, produced a realization that a computer could be a personal tool, a household device. There followed an astonishing proliferation of new "high tech" companies—Microsoft, Intel, Tandy, D.E.C., and many others—each pursuing a niche in the expanding world of electronics, each seeking to gain a step on competitors. Even the electronic giant and master of the mainframe, IBM, moved into the personal computer (PC) market. Within less than 15 years the number of computers in service grew from fewer than a half-million to well beyond 100 million, and the pace of technological advance—or the reverse, the speed of obsolescence—moved accordingly. By the start of the 1990s a single quarter-inch silicon chip could outperform ENIAC by a factor of approximately 1 million. One computer expert determined that equivalent improvements in automobile manufacturing would have enabled production of a Rolls Royce car that cost $1.00 and would deliver a million miles per gallon of gasoline. A separate information revolution associated with the Internet in 1990 had little more than begun.

The personal computers and mainframes were only the start of it. Traffic signals in any city, the lighting system of New York, the space shuttle *Discovery* and the Hubble telescope, the Trident submarine *Ohio,* the ignition system of nearly all cars, and the hand-held calculator, everything, it seemed, that made American society func-

ENIAC, in 1946. The first large-scale, general-purpose electronic computer filled a large room at the University of Pennsylvania. (John W. Mauchly Papers, Rare Book and Manuscript Library, University of Pennsylvania)

tion, operated because of—and was at the mercy of—the transistor and the computer.

As with any technological change, there would be problems, hazards, and casualties. With machines doing everything, critics wondered about the fate of the human mind. Would children learn multiplication tables anymore? Television commercials began to speak a different language, incomprehensible to many of the viewers; indeed the whole business of computer jargon would be provocative, as anything that left one feeling ignorant would be. Familial relationships shifted and perhaps suffered when children of eight knew more about something than their parents or grandparents. The self-educated mechanic discovered that he could not fix his car anymore. Older folks, regular visitors to the library, found themselves unable to find the books. Embarrassed to ask for instructions about the new machines or perhaps having failed to fully grasp the speedy lesson offered, they simply stopped coming. Large computer systems retained at least a measure of questionable security; the word *hacker* took on new meaning. A power outage could shut everything down. To people who had jumped aboard the computer special these problems were, if not irrelevant, at least unlikely to ever develop. It was a marvelous ride, and the object was not to look back but to position oneself for the next technological miracle.

Computerese: A Primer

bit   means binary digit, smallest unit of information in a computer.

bug   an error that exists in a computer's program or in an electrical unit.

byte   group of eight bits that represent one character—a letter, number, etc.; smallest unit for measuring computer storage capacity.

CD-ROM   means compact disk, read only memory; a spinning disk with permanent information that can be read by a laser inside a computer.

central processing unit (CPU)   mechanism inside the unit that responds to instructions and makes the computer perform.

cursor   blinking marker on computer screen that shows where operator is working.

database   organized information stored in computer by a certain type of software that is subject to recall and use by operator.

download   process of transferring information from central computer or file server to a personal computer.

floppy disk   a small magnetic plate that can record and store information and from which data can be recalled.

gigabyte   data storage capacity of one billion bytes.

hacker   an individual skilled in computer operations who can gain unlawful or unauthorized access into data banks and computer systems.

hard drive   the main drive of a computer, built in, as opposed to the floppy drive, which uses disks, or the CD drive.

hardware   equipment and devices that make up the computer: monitor, keyboard, CPI—as opposed to the programs and procedures.

language   sets of commands and instructions compatible with a computer.

laptop   a small self-sustaining microcomputer that can be carried around and can operate on a person's lap.

mainframe computer   largest, most sophisticated and expensive units that can accommodate hundreds of users at the same time; mostly owned by large companies.

megabyte   storage capacity of 1 million bytes.

memory   capacity of a computer to store information, rendering it available for retrieval.

menu   list of possible actions that computer can perform, subject to operator's command; possible programs that can be run; possible files that can be accessed.

microcomputer   small and least costly units, can operate on a table—the standard personal computer (PC).

microprocessor   a complete processing unit on a single silicon chip.

minicomputer   medium-size computer system, used by small companies.

monitor   the screen that displays what one is working on with the computer.

mouse   a small device that the operator manipulates by hand to direct commands to the computer.

password   a word or code, preferably kept secret, that identifies an authorized user of computer information.

PC   the standard personal computer, a microcomputer used on a desk or person's lap.

semiconductor   solid-state substance that can be electrically altered, as with a transistor.

silicon chip   tiny wafers of silicon covered with layers of chemicals, each of which serves as an electrical component.

software   the programs and procedures that tell the computer (which is the hardware) what to do, usually bought on disks or CDs and then installed onto a computer hard drive.

spreadsheet   a type of software that arranges numbers or text in lines and columns.

superconductor   the most exquisite of the mainframe computers, the fastest and best designed for complex calculations.

transistor   a tiny piece of semiconducting material that acts as a switching device for electrons, vastly superior to previously used vacuum tubes.

user friendly   perhaps the first, and worst, cliche of the industry—simply means a computer, software, or anything that is easy to use.

virus   a foreign program, introduced from the outside to a computer system; it can produce major damage.

word processor   probably the first marvel produced by computers: a text-producing and editing system that allows immediate rewriting and correction of errors.

Source: Famighetti, *World Almanac, 1999*, 621–23; Wright, *Universal Almanac, 1995*, 598–600.

A Selected Short List of Milestones in Computer Technology

1946   John Mauchly and J. Presper Eckert develop ENIAC (Electronic Numerical Integrator and Computer) at the University of Pennsylvania. With 18,000 vacuum tubes, it weighs 80 tons and fills a large room.

1948   IBM builds the Selective Sequence Electronic Calculator.

1948   William Shockley, John Bareen, and Walter Brattain invent the transistor.

1951   UNIVAC, an 18-ft-long computer using magnetic tape, is installed at the Bureau of Census.

1952   Employed by CBS News, UNIVAC predicts a large victory for Eisenhower, one hour after polls close, using only 7% of the votes.

1953   IBM produces its first stored-program computer, the 701.

1957   Ken Olsen founds Digital Equipment Corporation (DEC).

1958   Jack Kirby of Texas Instruments makes the first integrated circuit.

1959   IBM sells the 1620 and 1790, its first computers using transistors, not tubes.

1964   The number of computers in the United States increases to 18,000, up from 2,500 in 1958.

1965   DEC ships the PDP-8, the first truly successful minicomputer.

1965   Richard L. Wexelblat at the University of Pennsylvania receives the first Ph.D. degree in computer science.

1965   IBM produces System 360, a third-generation, integrated circuit-based computer.

1968   Gordon Moore and Robert Noyce found Integrated Electronics Corp., to be known as Intel, which in 1969 produces Intel 4004, the first microprocessor—miniature circuits on one chip.

1971   Floppy disks, a mobile system for storing information, are developed to load IBM's 370, a fourth-generation computer.

1972	At Texas Instruments, Jack Kirby, Jerry Merryman, and Tim Van Tassel develop the electronic pocket calculator.
1975	The first computer store opens in Santa Monica, California.
1976	Stephen Wozniak and Steven Jobs found Apple Computer in a family garage; Apple II is marketed the following year and becomes the first widely accepted personal computer.
1977	Bill Gates and Paul Allen form Microsoft, to produce microcomputer operating systems.
1978	Computers in use in the United States pass the half-million mark.
1980	Computers in use in the United States pass the 1 million mark.
1981	IBM introduces a first personal computer, the IBM PC. Using Microsoft's operating system called PC-DOS (personal computer disk operating system), it becomes standard of the industry.
1981	Osborne Computer produces a first portable machine, a forerunner of the laptop.
1982	In adopting Microsoft's MS-DOS operating system, many manufacturers are able to produce clones of the successful IBM machine.
1982	*Time* magazine names the computer its Man of the Year.
1983	Computers in use in the United States surpass 10 million.
1983	Apple introduces the mouse, a hand-maneuvered device that gives commands to the computer.
1984	Apple introduces the Macintosh personal computer that includes Apple's first software systems. A portable version will appear in 1989.
1985	Toshiba produces the first widely used laptop computer.
1985	Apple and Aldus Corporation introduce printers that begin an era of electronic desktop publishing.
1986	Computers in use in the United States pass 30 million.
1987	IBM offers Personal System/2 (PS 2) that provides high resolution VGA display; it soon will be cloned by competitors.
1989	Intel introduces the 80486 microprocessor and 1860 RISC/coprocessor chip, each of which has 1 million transistors. Microcomputers now have the speed of supercomputers.
1989	Computers in the United States pass 50 million; in the world there are more than 100 million.
1990	Microsoft introduces a software program called Windows 3.0. Microsoft's revenue for the fiscal year ending in June topped $1 billion.

Source: Karen P. Juliussen and Egil Juliussen, *The Computer Industry 1993 Almanac* (Austin, Texas, 1993), 375–79; John Wright, *The Universal Almanac, 1995* (New York, 1994), 596–98.

TABLE 15.13   DOMESTIC SHIPMENTS OF MICRO-, MINI-, AND MAINFRAME COMPUTERS

Year	Micros Units	Micros $ (in millions)	Minis Units	Minis $ (in millions)	Mainframe Units	Mainframe $ (in millions)	Total Units	Total $ (in millions)
1960	. . .	. . .	. . .	. . .	1,790	590	1,790	590
1965	. . .	. . .	600	66.0	5,350	1,770	5,950	1,836
1970	. . .	. . .	6,060	485.0	5,700	3,600	11,760	4,085
1975	10,500	19.0	26,990	1,484.0	6,700	4,960	44,190	6,463
1976	53,100	97.0	39,320	1,887.0	6,750	5,060	99,170	7,044
1977	120,400	223.0	56,780	2,780.0	8,900	6,940	186,080	9,943
1978	237,900	440.0	68,340	3,690.0	7,500	6,230	313,740	10,360
1979	329,400	630.0	81,250	4,712.0	7,200	6,340	417,850	11,682
1980	796,000	1,550.0	105,870	6,238.0	9,900	8,840	911,770	16,628
1981	1,157,000	2,550.0	121,990	7,290.0	10,700	9,640	1,289,690	19,480
1982	1,950,000	4,390.0	128,000	7,770.0	10,600	9,860	2,088,600	22,020
1983	3,249,000	7,470.0	146,800	8,979.0	9,980	9,780	3,405,780	26,229
1984	5,190,000	11,940.0	205,400	12,817.0	11,330	11,900	5,406,730	36,657
1985	4,750,000	11,260.0	190,800	11,696.0	10,910	11,890	4,951,710	34,846
1986	5,060,000	12,060.0	198,200	11,872.0	10,990	12,200	5,269,190	36,132
1987	5,460,000	12,890.0	205,800	12,000.0	11,200	12,660	5,677,000	37,630
1988	5,990,000	14,050.0	218,100	12,656.0	11,540	13,270	6,219,640	39,976
1989	6,530,000	15,963.0	227,700	13,093.0	11,890	13,790	6,769,590	42,846
1990	7,050,000	17,980.0	232,000	12,650.0	12,130	14,190	7,294,130	44,820

Source: Juliussen and Juliussen, *1993 Computer Almanac*, 323.

TABLE 15.14   NATIONS WITH MOST COMPUTING POWER, 1988

Rank	Country	Estimated MIPS[a] (millions)	Share of Total MIPS[a] (%)
1.	U.S.A	22.81	55.2
2.	Japan	4.09	9.9
3.	United Kingdom	2.59	6.3
4.	West Germany	1.57	3.8
5.	France	1.33	3.2
6.	Canada	1.01	2.4
7.	Italy	0.89	2.2
8.	Australia	0.36	0.86
9.	Netherlands	0.35	0.84
10.	Brazil	0.25	0.61

[a] Calculations are based on estimated numbers of all kinds of computers in each country and the average processing power per computer in MIPS (million instructions per second).
Source: Egil Juliussen and Karen Juliussen, *The Computer Industry Almanac, 1989*, (New York, 1988) 17.10.

TABLE 15.15   NATIONS WITH MOST COMPUTING POWER PER CAPITA, 1988

Rank	Country	Computers in Use per 1,000 People[a,b]	Computing Power MIPS/1000 People[a]
1.	U.S.A.	167	93.5
2.	United Kingdom	95	45.5
3.	Canada	82	38.9
4.	Norway	73	35.1
5.	Japan	71	33.5
6.	Ireland	66	32.0
7.	Singapore	65	24.8
8.	Switzerland	61	29.7
9.	Denmark	61	29.3
10.	Sweden	60	29.1

[a] Calculations based on estimated number of computers in use per person and computing power in MIPS (million instructions per second) per person.
[b] World average of computers per 1,000 people was 16. Western Europe had 51; the USSR had 0.1.
Source: Juliussen & Juliussen, *Computer Industry Almanac, 1989*, 17.10–17.11

Weapons Technology: An Example

Weapons activity dominated the government's research and development expenditures for many years, and it was at any time an expensive undertaking. The process had no end. At an early date the arms race ceased to be a mere matter of destructive capacity (why make provision to blow up Earth several times over?), and it became a contest for maintaining a competitive edge, for assuring that one's weapons could not be neutralized by an enemy, and for equipping forces for multiple circumstances they might have to face. The research and development program involved all branches of military forces, although new equipment for the navy and air force seemed to be the most spectacular.

Technological development best could be exemplified in the area of missiles, for it was the most complex, was probably most sophisticated and effective, and was exceptionally expensive. The missile brought together three aspects of technological development. It began with propulsion, the driving force that carried the missile a range that differed from a few yards to 7,000 miles. The guidance system pointed the instrument in the right direction and steered it to a specific target: a city, a tank, a ship, a plane, a detachment of soldiers, or another missile. At the end there was the explosive device or warhead—nuclear

TABLE 15.16   MAJOR U.S. MISSILES

Missile	Type	Guidance	Length (feet)	Diameter (feet)	Weight (pounds)	Stage	Propellant	Speed	Range (miles)
Asroc	Surface-to-underwater	None	15	1	1,000	1	Solid	. . .	5+
Bullpup A	Air-to-surface	Command	10.5	1.0	570	1	Liquid	Mach 2	6
Bullpup B	Air-to-surface	Command	13.6	1.5	1,785	1	Liquid	. . .	9
Chaparral	Surface-to-air	Infrared	9.5	0.42	185	1	Solid	. . .	. . .
Condor	Air-to-surface	TV command	. . .	. . .	. . .	1	Solid	. . .	40+
Dragon	Antitank	Command	2.5	1	13.5	1	Solid	. . .	. . .
Entac	Antitank	Wire-guided	2.6	0.5	27	2	Solid	180 mph	1+
Falcon	Air-to-air	Radar or infrared	6.5	0.5	134	1	Solid	Supersonic	5
Genie	Air-to-air	None	9	1.5	835	1	Solid	Mach 3	6
Hawk	Surface-to-air	Rader homing	17	1.2	1,275	1	Solid	Mach 2	22
Honest John	Surface-to-surface	None	24.8	2.5	4,500	1	Solid	1,200 mph	20
Hound Dog	Air-to-surface	Inertial	42.5	2.25	9,600	1	Turbojet	Mach 1 +	600
Lance	Surface-to-surface	Inertial	20	1.8	3,200	2	Liquid	. . .	30
Little John	Surface-to-surface	None	14.5	1	780	1	Solid	Mach 1 +	10
Maverick	Air-to-surface	TV homing	8.1	1	500	1	Solid	. . .	. . .
Minuteman 1	Surface-to-surface	Inertial	59.8	6.2	69,000	3	Solid	. . .	6,300
Minuteman 2	Surface-to-surface	Inertial	59.8	6.2	70,000	3	Solid	15,000 mph	7,000+
Minuteman 3	Surface-to-surface	Inertial	. . .	6.2	. . .	3	Solid	Mach 2 +	7,000+
Nike-Hercules	Surface-to-air	Command	41	2.6	10,000	2	Solid	Mach 3+	75+
Pershing 1	Surface-to-surface	Inertial	34	3.25	10,000	2	Solid	Mach 1+	400
Pershing 2	Surface-to-surface	Inertial and radar terminal	35.3	3.3	16,820	2	Solid	Mach 1+	1,120
Phoenix	Air-to-air	Command	13	1.3	838	1	Solid	Supersonic	. . .
Polaris A1	Underwater-to-surface	Inertial	28	4.5	28,000	1	Solid	. . .	1,200
Polaris A2	Underwater-to-surface	Inertial	31	4.5	30,000	2	Solid	. . .	1,500
Polaris A3	Underwater-to-surface	Inertial	31	4.5	35,000	2	Solid	8,000 mph	2,500
Poseidon	Underwater-to-surface	Inertial	34	6	. . .	2	Solid	. . .	2,500
Quail	Air-to-surface	Autopilot	12.9	2.5	1,100	1	Turbojet	600 mph	230
Redeye	Surface-to-air	Infrared	4	0.25	20	1	Solid	. . .	. . .
SCAD	Armed decoy	Inertial	. . .	. . .	. . .	1	Turbojet	subsonic	1,000
Sergeant	Surface-to-surface	Inertial	34.5	2.6	10,000	1	Solid	Mach 1+	75
Shillelagh	Surface-to-surface	Command	—	0.5	40	1	Solid	. . .	10
Shrike	Air-to-surface	Infrared	10	0.75	390	1	Solid	. . .	. . .
Sidewinder 1C	Air-to-air	Infrared	9.5	0.42	185	1	Solid	Mach 2 +	10
Sparrow 3	Air-to-air	Radar homing	12	0.67	450	1	Solid	Mach 2+	12
Spartan	Surface-to-air	Command	54	9.9	28,600	3	Solid	Supersonic	400
Sprint	Surface-to-air	Command	27	4.6	7,500	2	Solid	Hypersonic	30+
SRAM	Air-to-surface	Autopilot	14	1.5	. . .	1	Solid	Supersonic	100
SS-11B1	Antitank	Wire-guided	3.8	0.5	63	1	Solid	400+ mph	1.6
Standard ARM	Air-to-surface	Radar homing	26	. . .	3,000	2	Solid	. . .	35
Subroc	Underwater-to-underwater	Inertial	22	1.75	4,000	1	Solid	. . .	5+
Super Falcon	Air-to-air	Radar	7.2	0.55	150	1	Solid	Mach 3	5
Talos	Surface-to-air	Beam-rider	33	2.5	7,000	1	Ramjet	Mach 2.5	65+
Tartar	Surface-to-air	Semiactive homing	15	1.1	1,500	1	Solid	Mach 2+	10+
Terrier	Surface-to-air	Beam-rider	26.5	1.1	3,000	1	Solid	Mach 2.5	20+
Titan 2	Surface-to-surface	Inertial	102	10	330,000	2	Liquid	. . .	6,300
TOW	Antitank	Wire-guided	. . .	. . .	48	1	Solid	. . .	. . .
Trident 1	Underwater-to-surface	Stellar-inertial	. . .	. . .	. . .	. . .	Solid	. . .	4,000
Trident 2	Underwater-to-surface	Stellar-inertial	. . .	. . .	. . .	. . .	Solid	. . .	6,000+
Walleye	Air-to-surface	Television	11.3	1.25	1,100	1	[Glider]	. . .	. . .

Note: This list does not include some of the most modern missiles, such as the *Stinger*, a shoulder–fired antiaircraft weapon, first supplied to the army in 1981, or the MX or Peacekeeper, an ICBM, the first 50 of which were deployed in 1986, or the Patriot, a surface-to-air weapon.
Source: Bernard Johnston, *Colliers Encyclopedia* (New York, 1995), 508.

or conventional, multiple or singular, small or large—appropriate to the target. Built in many shapes and sizes for army, navy, and air force, missiles remained in a state of continuous development. In all their applications, missiles surely represented the largest change in military technology since the Second World War.

Environmentalism

An environmental movement did not emerge suddenly in the United States in the last half of the 20th century. For many years there had been at least passing concern with consequences of the way Americans were using the land and with byproducts of a modern industrial nation. Regret over rapid destruction of forests had led presidents to exclude tracts of national forests from exploitation by private economic interests. Farmers who noticed that soil unprotected by vegetation washed away in heavy rains or blew away in windstorms of the Great Plains began to seek ways to halt these forms of erosion.

During the administration of Franklin D. Roosevelt, the national government became directly involved in these efforts. In those days they called it conservation. An agency of the era of Roosevelt bore the title, Civilian Conservation Corps. Industrial pollution was as old as industry itself, and while factory operations contaminated water and soil, urban residents first saw, smelled, and breathed pollution of the air. They even devised a word for it, *smog*, technically a combination of fog and smoke, although fog often had little to do with it; the air was filled with smoke, soot, and tiny particles of varying compounds. Attempts to regulate factory emissions dated to the 1880s, and in 1952 Oregon acted on a statewide basis.

Environmental concerns—in some instances they would constitute alarms—of the last half of the 20th century developed from these original problems being multiplied and compounded by the growth of the population, national economic expansion, and changes in lifestyle and in the production processes, which meant that the social system found more things to do with machines and more machines to do what previously had been done without them. The machines that built the machines polluted

Three Mile Island nuclear plant near Middletown, Pennsylvania, site in March 1979 of a partial meltdown and near radioactive disaster (National Archives)

some aspect of the environment and then the machines themselves became new agents of contamination. The postwar era did introduce one new force and it was a whopper: nuclear power and consequences of its use as an instrument of peacetime society. Any suggestion of nuclear accident set off alarms that would be heard worldwide. Scientists warned of long-range catastrophic effects of global warming, a condition that developed from sunlight being trapped in Earth's atmosphere. This "greenhouse effect" was largely the product of four gases: carbon dioxide, chlorofluorocarbons, methane, and nitrous oxide being released into the atmosphere. Attending to the problem depended on a reduction of these gases, but all were byproducts of modern, industrial society.

Many people dated the modern environmental movement to the first celebration of Earth Day in 1970. Others credited the origins to Rachel Carson, whose highly influential scientific study *Silent Spring* warned in 1962 that in the effort to conquer and utilize nature's offerings, humankind was destroying its habitat. The movement would be fed by the energy crises of the 1970s; nuclear accidents at the Three Mile Island plant in Pennsylvania in 1979 and at Chernobyl in the Soviet Union in 1986; by oil spills on the international waterways; and by

mounting evidence of health hazards in contaminants of many kinds. Public awareness and concern inspired books and articles, movies and film documentaries, rallies, submovements and campaigns—such as recycling. It produced new organizations, such as Greenpeace, and energized older ones, such as the Sierra Club. It prompted new lesson plans for elementary and high schools, new courses for colleges and universities. Environmentalism produced many state and national laws and at least one major new institution in the government of the United States, the Environmental Protection Agency (EPA). It stopped certain practices in their tracks—the use of leaded gasoline, for example, and the construction of nuclear power plants—and it produced marked improvement in some categories of health hazards. In many areas the efforts merely illuminated the magnitude and complexities of the problems. A contaminated environment came from people living their lives. Environment efforts often collided with economic interests that went beyond a fat corporation that wished to feed at the public trough. It also revealed that if science and technology had produced many problems in the living space, it would take a great deal more work in science and technology to bring them under control.

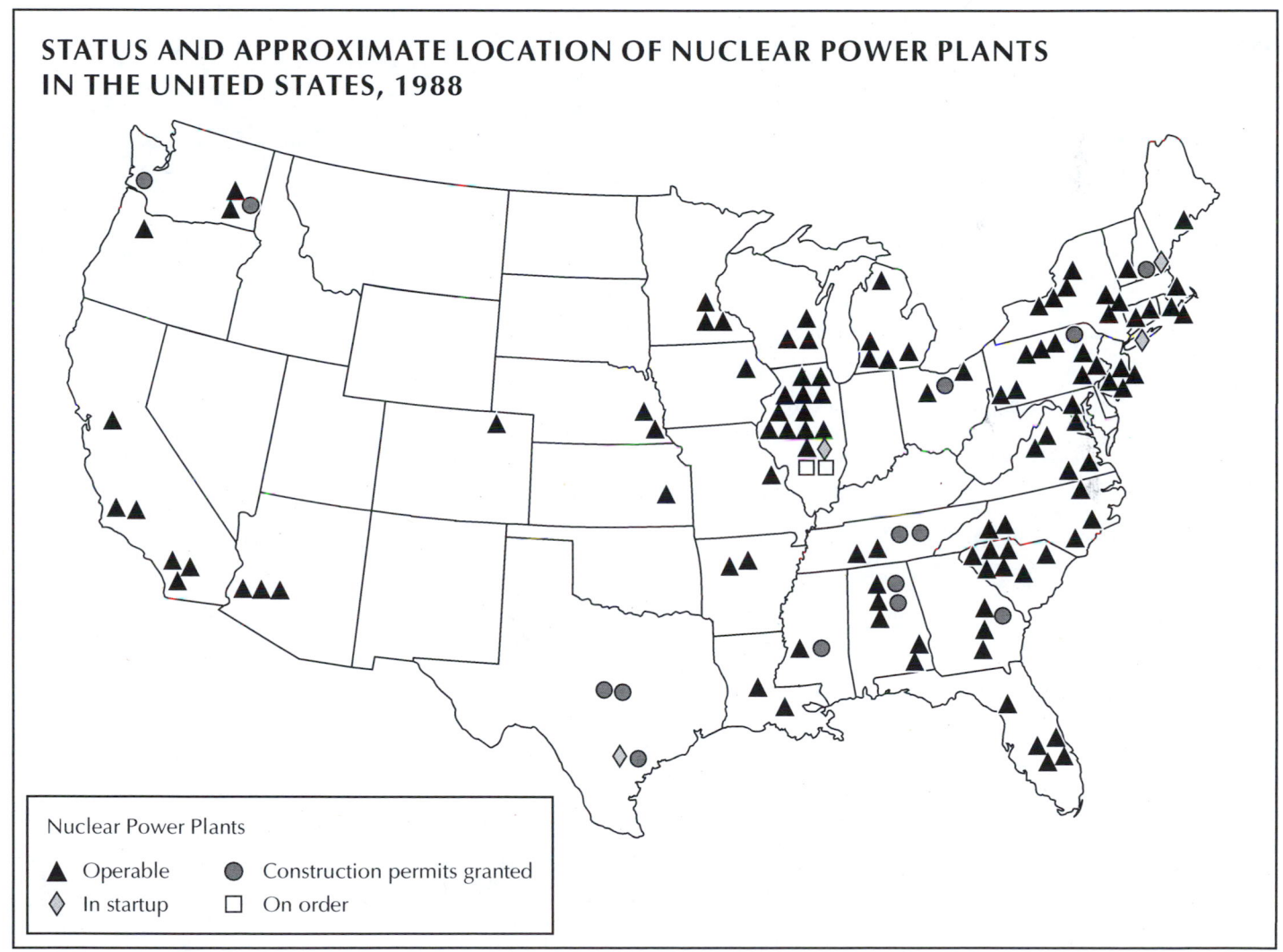

STATUS AND APPROXIMATE LOCATION OF NUCLEAR POWER PLANTS IN THE UNITED STATES, 1988

Nuclear Power Plants

▲ Operable   ● Construction permits granted
◇ In startup   ☐ On order

Some Developments in Environmental History in the United States, 1948 to 1985

1948 Several days of air pollution kill 20 people in Donora, Pennsylvania.

1952 Americans learn that smog was blamed for 4,000 deaths in London.

1953 Officials blame 200 deaths in New York on smog.

1962 Rachel Carson publishes exceptionally influential book, *Silent Spring,* about environmental damage by pesticides.

1963 Congress passes original Clean Air Act; federal funds are to be used on air pollution.

Concern about nuclear fallout leads to Test-Ban Treaty, signed by the United States and the Soviet Union. Testing is banned in atmosphere, under water, or in outer space.

1964 Congress passes Wilderness Act, designed to preserve specified wilderness areas.

1965 Congress passes Highway Beautification Law, a favorite of President Johnson's wife Lady Bird, which bans many billboards that contaminate highway landscape settings.

1966 Congress passes Rare and Endangered Species Act.

1970 First Earth Day is celebrated on April 22.

The Environmental Protection Agency (EPA) is established in national government to establish and oversee antipollution efforts.

Congress passes Water Quality Act, to clean up waterways.

1972 Congress extends and expands upon the Clean Air Act. Virtually all use of pesticide DDT is banned.

1974 Construction begins on Trans Alaska Pipeline, extensive measures having been taken to protect local environment and wildlife.

Scientists warn that the protective ozone layer is being destroyed by chlorofluorocarbons.

Energy crisis caused by Middle East war prompts movement toward smaller automobile engines and shift from petroleum products to coal for generating energy.

1976 Toxic Substances Act is designed to control hazardous chemicals.

1978 Buried hazardous waste forces residents to evacuate homes and move permanently from Love Canal area of New York State.

1979 Accident at nuclear reactor at Three Mile Island plant in Pennsylvania produces partial meltdown and a severe national reaction against additional nuclear power plants.

1980 Congress passes law creating the Superfund, and a program for cleaning up the most hazardous toxic-waste sites.

1983 Community of Times Beach, Missouri, has to evacuate upon learning that oil to control road dust has contaminated soil.

1985 Canada and the United States sign agreement to investigate causes of acid rain.

Scientists warn that a hole has appeared in the ozone layer over Antarctica.

1986 News of explosion of nuclear reactor at Chernobyl in the Ukraine (USSR) that killed 31, contaminated thousands, and made hundreds of square miles uninhabitable is stunning and is a reconfirmation of the hostility toward nuclear plants.

1987 Congress passes Clean Water Act to combat pollution of rainwater and estuaries in the United States.

Officials trap and confine the last-known California condor in the wild to prevent assumed extinction of species.

1989 American-owned tanker, *Exxon Valdez*, runs aground in Alaska, spilling its oil and despoiling pristine Prince William Sound. Worst oil spill in the United States.

Source: Bruce Wetterau, *The New York Public Library Book of Chronologies* (New York, 1990), 422–24; Wright, *Universal Almanac, 1991*, 531.

Air Pollution

Contamination of the air attracted some of the first efforts in a fledgling movement to promote healthy living conditions in the United States. The reasons were obvious: One could see, smell, even feel the pollution in and around many of the major cities. In some cases it left a coating of soot on cars and anything out of doors. Some people found it difficult to breathe in such conditions, and in the worst cases—as in Donora, Pennsylvania, in 1952—it could be deadly. The principal causes of urban pollution were motor vehicles, industrial factories, and power plants. A more broadly based atmospheric problem that gradually entered public consciousness between 1960 and 1980 became known as acid rain. Consisting mostly of the sulfur dioxide produced by the burning of coal and oil, the particles came to the ground attached to rainfall or any form of precipitation, in effect, making sulfuric acid. Acid rain could travel great distances with the wind and weather systems—from state to state or across national boundaries, as in the case of Canada and the United States. The effects included excessive, unwanted algae growth. Acid rain tarnished and discolored bronze, marble, and limestone. The military park at Gettysburg, Pennsylvania, marked with hundreds of stone monuments, showed signs of premature weathering. In extreme cases, acid rain could contaminate lakes and streams, rendering them incapable of sustaining fish or other natural life. One of its worst effects was killing trees.

The solution, needless to say, involved ridding the air of the pollutants. Natural gas burned cleaner than coal or oil. Filtering devices on smokestacks called scrubbers removed sulfur dioxide. Catalytic converters and other emission devices softened the environmental impact of vehicular exhaust. All these changes cost a great deal of money. They were not necessarily consistent with energy options that were most appealing during the crises of the 1970s. Nuclear power, a clean energy alternative, encountered public disfavor from different points of view. Congress passed a Clean Air Act as early as 1963, a measure that charged the Public Health Service with investigating the issue and organizing elementary efforts to control it. A stronger law in 1970 handed authority over to the newly created Environmental Protection Agency, which was to act in concert with the states in approaching the pollution problem on several fronts. The EPA set quality standards for pollutants that posed the largest threat to air quality. The most dangerous offenders were deemed "criteria pollutants"—the EPA named six—and standards were set consistent with acceptable living conditions. The EPA also produced a second list of "hazardous pollutants"—asbestos was an example—that could be harmful, even deadly, and it established guidelines for their use. Utilizing a variety of restraints and changes that affected industry, public and private power plants, and the general public, the EPA could claim uneven but nonetheless marked progress by the start of the 1990s.

TABLE 15.17   MAJOR INDOOR AIR POLLUTANTS

Pollutant	Sources
Asbestos	Old, damaged insulation, acoustical tiles.
Biological pollutants	Bacteria, mold, animal residue, mites, pollen.
Carbon monoxide	Kerosene, gas stoves, fireplaces, auto exhaust, tobacco smoke.
Formaldehyde	Textiles, glue, paneling, foam insulation.
Lead	Automobile exhaust, soldering, burning lead paint.
Mercury	Latex paint.
Nitrogen dioxide	Tobacco smoke, kerosene and gas heaters.
Organic gases	Paint, solvents, aerosol spray, cleaners, air fresheners, stored fuel.
Particles (soot)	Tobacco smoke, wood, kerosene heaters, stoves, fireplaces.
Pesticides	Bug and insect killers for indoors and lawns.
Radon	Well water, building material, soil and rocks under house.
Tobacco smoke	Cigarettes, cigars, pipes.

Source: Wright, *Universal Almanac, 1991*, 536–37.

The primary cause of air pollution was emissions from motor vehicles, as one would discover in any city. (U.S. Department of Agriculture)

TABLE 15.18   HEALTH EFFECTS OF THE REGULATED AIR POLLUTANTS

Criteria Pollutants	Health Concerns
Ozone	Respiratory-tract problems such as difficult breathing and reduced lung function. Asthma, eye irritation, nasal congestion, reduced resistance to infection and possibly premature aging of lung tissue.
Particulate Matter	Eye and throat irritation, bronchitis, lung damage, and impaired visibility
Carbon Monoxide	Ability of blood to carry oxygen impaired. Cardiovascular, nervous, and pulmonary systems affected.
Sulfur Dioxide	Respiratory tract problems; permanent harm to lung tissue.
Lead	Retardation and brain damage, especially in children.
Nitrogen Dioxide	Respiratory illness and lung damage.
Hazardous Air Pollutants	
Asbestos	A variety of lung diseases, particularly lung cancer.
Beryllium	Primary lung disease although also affects liver, spleen, kidneys, and lymph glands.
Mercury	Several areas of the brain as well as the kidneys and bowels affected.
Vinyl chloride	Lung and liver cancer
Aresenic	Causes cancer
Radionuclides	Cause cancer
Benzene	Leukemia
Coke Oven Emissions	Respiratory cancer

Source: Environmental Protection Agency, *Environmental Progress and Challenge: EPA's Update* (Washington, D.C., 1988), 13.

TABLE 15.19   NATIONAL AIR POLLUTANT EMISSIONS, 1940–1990

(In millions of metric tons, except lead in thousands of metric tons. Metric ton = 1.1023 short tons, PM = Particulate matter, SO_x = Sulfur oxides, NO_x = Nitrogen oxides, VOC = volatile organic compound, CO = Carbon monoxide, Pb = Lead. NA not available)

Year	Emissions						Percent Change from Prior Year					
	PM	SO_x	NO_x	VOC	CO	Pb	PM	SO_x	NO_x	VOC	CO	Pb
1940	23.1	17.6	6.9	15.2	82.6	(NA)	(NA)	(NA)	(NA)	(NA)	(NA)	(NA)
1950	24.9	19.8	9.4	18.1	87.6	(NA)	7.8	12.5	36.2	19.1	6.1	(NA)
1960	21.6	19.7	13.0	21.0	89.7	(NA)	−13.3	−0.5	38.3	16.0	2.4	(NA)
1970	18.5	28.3	18.5	25.0	101.4	203.8	−14.4	43.7	42.3	19.0	13.0	(NA)
1980	8.5	23.4	20.9	21.1	79.6	70.6	−54.1	−17.3	13.0	−15.6	−21.5	−65.4
1981	8.0	22.6	20.9	19.8	77.4	56.4	−5.9	−3.4	0.0	−6.2	−2.8	−20.1
1982	7.1	21.4	20.0	18.4	72.4	54.4	−11.3	−5.3	−4.3	−7.1	−6.5	−3.5
1983	7.1	20.7	19.3	19.3	74.5	46.4	1.0	−3.3	−3.5	4.9	2.9	−14.7
1984	7.4	21.5	19.8	20.3	71.8	40.1	4.2	3.9	2.6	5.2	−3.6	−13.6
1985	7.2	21.1	19.9	20.1	68.7	20.1	−2.7	−1.9	0.5	−1.0	−4.3	−49.9
1986	6.7	20.9	19.1	19.0	63.2	8.4	−6.9	−0.9	−4.0	−5.5	−8.0	−58.2
1987	6.9	20.5	19.4	19.3	63.4	8.0	3.0	−1.9	1.6	1.6	0.3	−4.8
1988	7.5	20.6	20.0	19.4	64.7	7.6	8.7	0.5	3.1	0.5	−2.1	−5.0
1989	7.2	20.8	19.8	18.5	60.4	7.2	−4.0	1.0	−1.0	−4.6	−6.6	−5.3
1990	7.5	21.2	19.6	18.7	60.1	7.1	4.2	1.9	−1.0	1.1	−0.5	−1.4

Source: Bureau of Census, *Statistical Abstract, 1992*, 213.

TABLE 15.20   AIR POLLUTANT EMISSIONS, BY POLLUTANT AND SOURCE, 1970–1990

(in millions of metric tons, except lead in thousands of metric tons, metric ton = 1.1023 short tons)

Pollutant	Total Emissions	Controllable Emissions								Percent of Total		
		Transportation		Fuel Combustion								
		Total	Road Vehicles	Total	Electric Utilities	Industrial Processes	Solid Waste Disposal	Misc. Uncontrollable		Transportation	Fuel Combustion	Industrial
1970												
Carbon monoxide	101.4	74.4	65.3	4.5	0.2	8.9	6.4	7.2		73.4	4.4	8.8
Sulfur oxides	28.4	0.6	0.3	21.3	15.8	6.4	. . .	0.1		2.1	75.0	22.5
Volatile organic compounds	25.0	10.3	9.1	0.6	. . .	8.9	1.8	3.3		41.2	2.4	35.6
Particulates	18.5	1.2	0.9	4.6	2.3	10.5	1.1	1.1		6.5	24.9	56.8
Nitrogen oxides	18.5	8.0	6.3	9.1	4.4	0.7	0.4	0.3		43.2	49.2	3.8
Lead	203.8	163.6	156.0	9.6	0.3	23.9	6.7	. . .		80.3	4.7	11.7
1980												
Carbon monoxide	79.6	56.1	48.7	7.4	0.3	6.3	2.2	7.6		70.5	9.3	7.9
Sulfur oxides	23.4	0.9	0.4	18.7	15.5	3.8	. . .	0.0		3.8	79.9	16.2
Volatile organic compounds	21.1	7.5	6.2	0.9	. . .	9.2	0.6	2.9		35.5	4.3	43.6
Particulates	8.5	1.3	1.1	2.4	0.8	3.3	0.4	1.1		15.3	28.2	38.8
Nitrogen oxides	20.9	9.8	7.9	10.1	6.4	0.7	0.1	0.2		46.9	48.3	3.3
Lead	70.6	59.4	56.4	3.9	0.1	3.6	3.7	. . .		84.1	5.5	5.1
1990												
Carbon monoxide	60.1	37.6	30.3	7.5	0.3	4.7	1.7	8.6		62.6	12.5	7.8
Sulfur oxides	21.2	0.9	0.6	17.1	14.2	3.1	. . .	. . .		4.2	80.7	14.6
Volatile organic compounds	18.7	6.4	5.1	0.9	. . .	8.1	0.6	2.7		34.2	4.8	43.3
Particulates	7.5	1.5	1.3	1.7	0.4	2.8	0.3	1.2		20.0	22.7	37.3
Nitrogen oxides	19.6	7.5	5.6	11.2	7.3	0.6	0.1	0.3		38.3	57.1	3.1
Lead	7.1	2.2	2.0	0.5	0.1	2.2	2.2	. . .		31.0	7.0	31.0

Note: ". . ." represents zero.
Source: Bureau of Census, *Statistical Abstract, 1992*, 213.

TABLE 15.21 **POLLUTION ABATEMENT AND CONTROL EXPENDITURES, IN CURRENT AND CONSTANT (1987) DOLLARS, 1972–1990, AND BY MEDIA, 1990**

(in millions of dollars)

| Year | Total Expenditures | Pollution Abatement | | | | | | | Regulation and Monitoring | Research and Development |
| | | Total | Personal Consumption | Business | Government | | | | | |
					Total	Federal	State and Local	Govt Enterprise		
Current Dollars										
1972	17,037	15,848	1,349	11,090	3,409	139	1,311	1,959	367	823
1975	28,424	26,668	3,231	16,531	6,906	432	1,752	4,722	653	1,104
1977	35,123	32,812	4,286	21,101	7,426	490	1,965	4,971	833	1,478
1978	39,457	36,860	4,772	23,266	8,822	472	2,212	6,139	949	1,647
1979	45,593	42,750	5,423	27,285	10,042	548	2,461	7,033	1,067	1,777
1980	51,478	48,432	6,568	30,618	11,246	494	2,778	7,973	1,296	1,751
1981	56,472	53,346	8,140	34,453	10,752	506	3,053	7,194	1,378	1,749
1982	56,576	53,395	8,309	34,151	10,935	550	3,274	7,111	1,397	1,783
1983	60,002	56,283	9,758	35,357	11,167	795	3,547	6,825	1,385	2,335
1984	66,445	62,746	10,771	39,467	12,508	944	3,886	7,679	1,362	2,337
1985	70,941	67,250	11,839	41,559	13,852	1,225	4,324	8,304	1,279	2,412
1986	74,178	70,074	12,244	42,636	15,195	1,346	4,793	9,056	1,532	2,573
1987	76,672	72,506	10,875	44,501	17,130	1,237	5,356	10,538	1,519	2,648
1988	81,081	76,605	12,044	46,928	17,633	1,402	6,149	10,082	1,695	2,781
1989	85,407	80,630	10,636	50,817	19,177	1,381	7,076	10,720	1,803	2,974
1990, prel.	89,967	85,087	9,247	54,674	21,166	1,394	8,015	11,757	1,784	3,097
Air	29,499	26,969	9,247	17,369	352	71	13	268	476	2,053
Water	37,260	36,202	. . .	23,473	12,729	737	503	11,489	649	409
Solid Waste	24,110	23,504	. . .	15,770	7,735	304	7,431	. . .	408	197
Constant (1987) Dollars										
1972	46,298	43,080	3,449	30,553	9,098	402	3,669	5,028	959	2,259
1975	57,333	53,673	6,165	33,113	14,395	937	3,737	9,720	1,346	2,313
1977	62,011	57,792	7,147	37,101	13,545	917	3,726	8,902	1,514	2,705
1978	64,863	60,296	7,412	38,151	14,734	809	3,892	10,032	1,788	2,779
1979	66,796	62,424	7,156	40,224	15,044	840	3,931	10,273	1,624	2,747
1980	67,291	63,005	7,311	40,148	15,546	679	4,051	10,816	1,873	2,414
1981	66,536	62,556	8,494	40,470	13,592	627	3,984	8,981	1,810	2,170
1982	63,219	59,457	8,518	37,790	13,150	649	4,068	8,434	1,709	2,053
1983	65,052	60,870	10,016	38,042	12,813	911	4,203	7,698	1,608	2,574
1984	69,981	65,996	10,967	41,178	13,851	1,048	4,381	8,422	1,507	2,478
1985	72,656	68,802	11,780	42,408	14,615	1,300	4,646	8,668	1,361	2,493
1986	76,384	72,163	12,685	43,797	15,681	1,402	4,990	9,289	1,589	2,633
1987	76,672	72,506	10,875	44,501	17,130	1,237	5,356	10,538	1,519	2,648
1988	79,086	74,785	11,831	45,963	16,991	1,340	5,875	9,777	1,643	2,658
1989	80,106	75,720	10,147	47,755	17,818	1,273	6,502	10,043	1,657	2,730
1990, prel.	81,838	77,472	8,665	49,688	19,118	1,232	6,994	10,893	1,636	2,370
Air	27,313	25,053	8,665	16,077	310	62	11	237	446	1,814
Water	34,391	33,435	. . .	21,621	11,814	660	498	10,656	597	359
Solid Waste	20,938	20,393	. . .	13,699	6,695	269	6,425	. . .	372	173

Note: ". . ." represents or rounds to zero.
Source: Bureau of Census, *Statistical Abstract, 1993,* 229.

TABLE 15.22 AIR AND WATER POLLUTION ABATEMENT EXPENDITURES IN CONSTANT (1987) DOLLARS, 1980–1990

(in millions of dollars, excludes agricultural production of crops and livestock except feedlots)

Year	Air Total	Mobile Sources[a] Total	Cars[b]	Trucks[b]	Stationary Sources Total	Industrial Facilities	Operations	Water Total	Industrial Facilities	Operations	Public Sewer Systems Facilities	Operations
1980	25,661	12,367	9,103	2,840	13,294	6,011	6,443	26,482	3,696	3,988	10,148	5,148
1981	27,012	13,932	11,092	2,700	13,080	5,951	6,295	24,251	3,405	4,025	8,270	5,297
1982	25,719	13,754	10,914	2,777	11,965	5,501	5,601	23,337	3,284	3,844	7,679	5,616
1983	26,085	15,456	12,756	3,177	10,629	3,893	5,911	23,751	2,666	4,264	7,063	5,959
1984	27,659	16,896	14,119	4,090	10,763	3,820	6,151	25,382	2,865	4,482	7,791	6,149
1985	29,041	18,073	14,896	4,463	10,968	3,539	6,320	26,542	2,879	4,658	8,124	6,550
1986	30,270	19,513	15,424	4,670	10,757	3,573	6,732	27,765	2,392	4,866	8,807	7,285
1987	28,548	17,629	13,166	4,433	10,919	3,728	6,575	29,695	2,354	5,383	10,053	7,792
1988	29,531	19,190	14,727	4,607	10,341	3,342	6,436	29,107	2,381	5,310	9,376	8,269
1989	27,742	17,181	12,511	3,910	10,561	3,463	6,553	30,618	2,923	5,777	9,661	8,554
1990, prel.	26,104	15,201	10,768	3,362	10,903	3,900	6,546	33,435	3,799	5,988	10,566	9,534

[a] Excludes expenditures from sources other than cars and trucks.
[b] Includes expenditures for devices such as catalytic converters.
Source: Bureau of Census, *Statistical Abstract, 1993,* 229.

TABLE 15.23 AIR QUALITY TRENDS IN SELECTED U.S. URBAN AREAS, 1985–1990

(number of PSI Days Greater than 100)

PMSA	Trend Sites Number	1985	1986	1987	1988	1989	1990
Atlanta	7	9	18	27	21	3	17
Baltimore	15	25	23	28	43	9	12
Boston	24	3	2	5	15	4	1
Chicago	40	9	9	17	22	4	3
Cleveland	25	1	2	7	21	6	2
Dallas	9	27	9	13	14	7	8
Denver	20	38	49	37	19	11	9
Detroit	25	2	5	9	17	10	3
El Paso	16	32	43	32	16	33	27
Houston	28	64	55	67	61	42	61
Kansas City	19	3	4	6	4	2	2
Los Angeles	37	208	226	201	239	226	178
Miami	7	5	4	4	5	4	1
Minn./ St. Paul	22	14	13	7	1	5	1
New York	24	65	58	44	46	18	18
Philadelphia	36	31	23	36	35	20	14
Phoenix	22	88	88	42	26	30	9
Pittsburgh	31	9	8	13	25	9	11
San Diego	21	88	70	61	84	90	60
San Francisco	11	5	4	1	2	1	1
Seattle	13	25	13	14	20	8	5
St Louis	46	10	13	17	18	13	8
Washington, D.C.	32	17	12	26	37	8	5
Subtotal	522	778	751	714	791	563	456
Other Sites	682	878	816	824	1,163	687	552
All Sites	1,204	1,656	1,567	1,538	1,954	1,250	1,008

Notes: PMSA=Primary Metropolitan Statistical Area. PSI=Pollutant Standards Index. Minn=Minneapolis. The PSI index integrates information from many pollutants across an entire monitoring network into a single number which represents the worst daily air quailty experienced in an urban area. Only carbon monoxide and ozone monitoring sites with adequate historical data are included in the PSI trend analysis above, except for Pittsburgh, where sulfur dioxide contributes a significant number of days in the PSI high range. PSI index ranges and health effect descriptor words are as follows: 0–50 (good): 51–100 (moderate); 101–199 (unhealthful); 202–299 (very unhealthful); and 300 and above (hazardous). The table above shows the number of days when the PSI was greater than 100 (=unhealthy or worse days).
Source: Littman, *Statistical Portrait of U.S.,* 381.

TABLE 15.24 METROPOLITAN AREAS FAILING TO MEET NATIONAL AMBIENT AIR-QUALITY STANDARDS FOR CARBON MONOX-IDE—NUMBER OF DAYS EXCEEDING STANDARDS, 1989 AND 1990

(areas generally represent the officially defined metropolitan area, but may, in some cases, not have all the counties indentified as part of the area)

Metropolitan Areas	1989	1990
Albuquerque, N.Mex.	6	3
Anchorage, Alaska	3	12
Baltimore, Md.	. . .	1
Boston, Mass.–N.H. CMSA	. . .	. . .
Chico, Calif.	1	1
Cleveland, Ohio CMSA	1	. . .
Colorado Springs, Colo.	1	. . .
Denver-Boulder, Colo. CMSA	6	3
Duluth, Minn.	2	. . .
El Paso, Tex.	5	4
Fairbanks, Alaska	3	2
Fort Collins, Colo.	1	. . .
Fresno, Calif.	13	1
Grant Pass, Oreg.	. . .	1
Greensboro–Winston-Salem, N.C.	. . .	. . .
Hartford, Conn. CMSA	1	. . .
Klamath County, Oreg.	2	. . .
Lake Tahoe S. Shore, Calif.	. . .	5
Las Vegas, Nev.	26	17
Longmont, Colo.	. . .	. . .
Los Angeles, Calif. CMSA	72	47
Medford, Oreg.	15	. . .
Memphis, Tenn.–Ark.–Miss.	2	1
Minneapolis–St. Paul, Minn.–Wis.	2	1
Missoula County, Mont.	2	1
Modesto, Calif.	8	2
New York, N.Y.–N.J.–Conn. CMSA	16	4
Ogden, Utah	. . .	3
Philadelphia, Pa.–N.J.–Del.–Md. CMSA	2	. . .
Phoenix, Ariz.	9	4
Portland, Oreg.–Wash. CMSA	2	2
Provo-Orem, Utah	12	11
Raleigh-Durham, N.C.	2	2
Reno, Nev.	2	7
Sacramento, Calif.	18	11
San Diego, Calif.	4	. . .
San Francisco, Calif. CMSA	6	2
Seattle-Tacoma, Wash. CMSA	2	2
Spokane, Wash.	11	6
Stockton, Calif.	4	2
Syracuse, N.Y.	2	1
Washington, D.C.–Md.–Va.	1	. . .

Note: ". . ." Represents zero. CMSA = Consolidated Metropolitan Statistical Area
Source: Bureau of Census, Statistical Abstract, 1992, 214.

Chemical Contaminants

The postwar cultural and economic revolution in the United States probably would have been impossible without chemicals. Chemicals had much to do with many aspects of manufacture and product production and innovation, with green lawns and pretty flowers and with remarkable growth in the productivity of American farms. With progress, however, often come problems, and it often appeared that chemical usage constituted the most obvious example of contradictions in modern society. Chemicals generally were considered hazardous if they caught fire quickly, reacted to other chemicals, were corrosive or toxic, or were proven to produce health problems, including cancer. Some chemicals produced such danger that they had to be banned. In the case of many others the government and society tried to strike a balance, permitting continued usage of a substance but placing it subject to careful regulation. Chemicals listed below were legal but closely regulated by the EPA, which might require regular reports from owners in possession of large amounts of a substance.

TABLE 15.25 ACID-RAIN TROUBLE AREAS, 1990

Area	No. of Lakes over 10 Acres	No Acidified	Percent
Adirondacks			
Southwest Lakes	450	171	38
New England			
Seaboard Lowlands Lakes	848	68	8
Highland Lakes	3,574	71	2
Appalachia			
Forested Lakes	433	43	10
Forested Streams	11,631	1,396	12
Atlantic Coastal Plain			
Northeast Lakes	187	21	11
Pine Barrens Streams	675	378	56
Other streams	7,452	745	10
Florida			
Nothern Highland Lakes	522	329	63
Northern Highland Streams	669	187	28
Eastern Upper Midwest			
Low Silica Lakes	1,254	201	16
High Silica Lakes	1,673	50	3

Source: Mark Hoffman, ed., The World Almanac and Book of Facts, 1991 (New York, 1990), 250.

TABLE 15.26 SOME COMMON HAZARDOUS CHEMICALS

Substance	Use
Acetic acid	Vinegar and manufacturing processes
Acetone	Solvent for resins and fats
Aluminum sulfate	Fire extinguishers, dyes
Ammonia	Fertilizer, cleaning and disinfectant agents
Benzene	Detergents, dyes, plastics, paint remover, explosives
Chlorine	Water disinfectant (gas is very toxic)
Cumene	High octane fuel
Ethylene dichloride	Plastics, "ethyl" gasoline
Ethylene oxide	Plastics
Formaldehyde	Plastics, wood substitutes
Hydrodrochloric acid	Metals, petroleum, manufacturing processes
Methanol	Anti-freeze, solvent, many compounds
Nitric acid	Fertilizers, explosives
Phenol	Plastics
Phosphoric acid	Fertilizers, flavoring substances
Sodium hydroxide	Lye, caustic soda
Styrene	Plastics, rubber substitutes
Sulfuric acid	Many products and processes
Toluene	Drugs, dyes, explosives
Vinyl chloride	Aerosols, plastics

Source: Wright, Universal Almanac, 1991, 541.

TABLE 15.27 MAJOR TOXIC CHEMICAL LAWS ADMINISTERED BY EPA, 1988

Statute	Provisions
Toxic Substances Control Act	Requires that EPA be notified of any new chemical prior to its manufacture and authorizes EPA to regulate production, use, or disposal of a chemical.
Federal Insecticide, Fungicide, and Rodenticide Act	Authorizes EPA to register all pesticides and specify the terms and conditions of their use and to remove unreasonably hazardous pesticides from the marketplace.
Federal Food, Drug, and Cosmetic Act	Authorizes EPA in cooperation with FDA to establish tolerance levels for pesticide residues on food and food products.
Resource Conservation and Recovery Act	Authorizes EPA to identify hazardous wastes and to regulate their generation, transportation, treatment, storage, and disposal.
Comprehensive Environmental Response, Compensation, and Liability Act	Requires EPA to designate hazardous substances that can present substantial danger and authorizes the cleanup of sites contaminated with such substances.
Clean Air Act	Authorizes EPA to set emission standards to limit the release of hazardous air pollutants.
Clean Water Act	Requires EPA to establish a list of toxic water pollutants and to set standards.
Safe Drinking Water Act	Requires EPA to set drinking water standards to protect public health from hazardous substances.
Marine Protection Research and Sanctuaries Act	Regulates ocean dumping of toxic contaminants.
Asbestos School Hazard Act	Authorizes EPA to provide loans and grants to schools with financial need for abatement of severe asbestos hazards.
Asbestos Hazard Emergency Response Act	Requires EPA to establish a comprehensive regulatory framework for controlling asbestos hazards in schools.
Emergency Planning and Community Right-to-Know Act	Requires states to develop programs for responding to hazardous chemical releases and requires industries to report on the presence and release of certain hazardous substances.

Source: Environmental Protection Agency, *EPA Update* (1988), 113.

TABLE 15.28 U.S. COMMERCIAL PESTICIDE USE, BY SECTOR AND TYPE, 1979–1990

(million pounds of active ingredients)

Year	Agriculture				Industry, Commercial, and Government				Home and Garden				Total			
	Herbi-cides	Insect-icides	Fung-icides	Total	Herbi-cides	Insect-icides	Fungi-cides	Total	Herbi-cides	Insect-icides	Fungi-cides	Total	Herbi-cides	Insecti-cides	Fungi-cides	Total
1979	488	302	90	840	84	38	18	140	28	38	12	77	560	378	120	1,058
1980	445	306	95	846	82	47	18	147	28	42	12	82	555	395	125	1,075
1981	456	309	95	860	86	48	19	153	28	48	12	85	570	405	126	1,101
1982	430	295	90	815	86	48	19	153	28	48	12	88	544	391	121	1,056
1983	445	185	103	733	105	40	20	165	25	30	10	65	575	255	133	963
1984	545	200	105	850	105	40	20	165	25	30	10	65	675	270	135	1,080
1985	525	225	111	861	115	40	21	176	30	35	10	75	670	300	142	1,112
1986	500	210	110	820	125	45	25	195	30	40	11	81	655	395	146	1,096
1887	505	179	130	814	115	45	40	200	25	36	12	73	645	260	182	1,087
1988	510	185	150	845	120	45	40	205	30	38	12	80	660	268	202	1,130
1989	520	151	135	806	110	45	40	195	25	30	14	78	655	226	189	1,070
1990	516	173	145	834	103	42	38	183	25	30	14	69	644	245	197	1,086

Note: Estimates for total fungicide use also include other pesticides. Totals may not agree with sum of components due to independent rounding.
Source: Littman, *Statistical Portrait of U.S.*, 387.

TABLE 15.29   PESTICIDE RESIDUES IN DOMESTIC SURVEILLANCE FOOD SAMPLES, 1978–1990

(percent of samples with residues found)

Year	Grains and Grain Products	Eggs, Milk, Dairy Products	Fish, Shell-fish, and Meats	Fruits	Vegetables	Other	Total
1978	54	43	80	48	34	42	47
1979	54	47	81	58	35	47	49
1980	52	36	71	53	40	36	46
1981	43	32	77	56	37	34	44
1982	42	34	72	49	36	32	41
1983	42	32	61	52	41	31	43
1984	54	31	75	38	33	31	37
1985	52	22	65	36	34	22	35
1986	60	21	68	57	39	48	44
1987	57	24	73	50	37	37	42
1988	49	19	72	51	35	28	40
1989	44	13	65	44	32	20	35
1990	46	9	68	49	38	21	40

Note: Food samples are collected as close as possible to production point. Fresh produce is whole, raw, unwashed. Although a percent of samples have pesticide residue, the percent with overtolerance amounts (as set by EPA) is low. Between 1973 and 1986, 0.3 percent of samples were classified as violative; since 1987, less than 0.1 percent were violative.
Source: Littman, *Statistical Portrait of U.S.*, 390.

TABLE 15.30   PESTICIDES TAKEN OFF THE MARKET BY 1988

Pesticides	Use	Concerns
Aldrin	Insecticide	Oncogenicity[a]
Chlordane (Agricultural uses; termiticide uses suspended or canceled)	Insecticide/Termites, Ants	Oncogenicity; reduction in[a] nontarget and endangered species
Compound 1080 (Livestock collar retained; rodenticide use under review)	Coyote control; Rodenticide	Reductions in nontarget and endangered species; no known antidote
Dibromochloropropane (DBCP)	Soil Fumigant—Fruits and vegetables	Oncogenicity; mutagenicity[a,b]; reproductive effects
DDT and Related Compounds	Insecticide	Ecological (eggshell thinning); carcinogenicity[c]
Dieldrin	Insecticide	Oncogenicity[a]
Dinoseb (in hearings)	Herbicide/Crop dessicant	Fetotoxicity; reproductive effects[d]; acute toxicity
Endrin (Avicide use retained)	Insecticide/Avicide	Oncogenicity; teratogenicity;[a,e] reductions in nontarget and endangered species
Ethylene Dibromide (EDB) (Very minor uses and use on citrus for export retained)	Insecticide/Fumigant	Oncogenicity; mutagenicity;[a,b] reproductive effects
Heptachlor (Agricultural uses; termiticide uses suspended or canceled)	Insecticide	Oncogenicity; reductions in[a] nontarget and endangered species
Kepone	Insecticide	Oncogenicity[a]
Lindane (Indoor smoke bomb canceled; some uses restricted)	Insecticide/Vaporizer	Oncogenicity; teratogenicity;[a,e] reproductive effects; acute toxicity; other chronic effects
Mercury	Microbial Uses	Cumulative toxicant causing brain damage
Mirex	Insecticide/Fire Ant Control	Nontarget species; potential oncogenicity
Silvex	Herbicide/Forestry, rights-of-way, weed control	Oncogenicity; teratogenicity;[a,e] fetotoxicity[d]
Strychnine (Rodenticide use and livestock collar retained)	Mammalian predator control; rodenticide	Reductions in nontarget and endangered species
2,4,5,-T	Herbicide/Forestry, rights-of-way, weed control	Oncogenicity; teratogenicity;[a,e] fetotoxicity[d]
Toxaphene (Livestock dip retained)	Insecticide – Cotton	Oncogenicity; reductions in[a] nontarget species; acute toxicity to aquatic organisms; chronic effects on wildlife

[a] Oncogenicity: causes tumors.
[b] Mutagenicity: causes mutation.
[c] Carinogenicity: causes cancer.
[d] Fetotoxicity: causes toxicity to unborn fetus.
[e] Teratogenicity: causes major birth defects.
Source: Environmental Protection Agency, *EPA Update* (1988), 118.

Solid Municipal Waste

Some called it junk; everyone called it garbage, and the problem of what to do with the standard byproducts, the leftovers from normal living continued to grow with the passage of time. The issue became compounded and complicated with the increase in population, a growing scarcity of places suitable for waste disposal, changing features of the waste itself, and the uncomfortable realization that there was no entirely satisfactory way of getting rid of the garbage.

All standard practices of waste disposal carried objectionable features. Traditionally, the trash collectors simply had hauled the stuff away to what might be called the city dump or to a junkyard. In the

Looked on as an environmental disaster, a strip-mine coal pit in Pennsylvania (Special Collections, Indiana University of Pennsylvania)

modern era the site became a landfill, and city planners had taken means to remove the smell, unsightly appearance, and presumably any threat to health. Landfills often took the form of craters with earth-moving equipment constantly at work, keeping the garbage covered up. Unfortunately the waste simply laid there, did not decay and degrade itself, as it long had been assumed. The propensity to use more plastic containers and more paper and paperboard and to dispose of smaller amounts of food waste and metal containers made the problem larger. Of course when one landfill reached capacity, another had to open up somewhere; the cities and states were running out of usable space. Given the fact that the amount of land was fixed and that the number of people and amount of garbage not only continued to grow but also were being added to what already existed, one was left with the proposition, projected far enough into the future, that a time would come when all America would be a landfill.

Burning trash, another long-used practice, also carried its burdens. Simply setting garbage afire replaced one kind of pollution with another, and many—if not most—municipal administrations found the practice unthinkable. Most municipalities and towns by the start of the 1990s had banned burning refuse and fallen leaves in the autumn. More sophisticated incineration equipment did a better job of it; they separated materials, burned waste at very high temperatures, and some even produced a form of usable energy. But this technology was expensive; it produced its own—albeit smaller amounts of—waste in the form of ash, and it was impossible to filter all toxic gases from the exhaust.

Recycling as a means of reducing disposable waste had stood as at least a theoretical alternative for several years, and the more seriously people and city officials began to take the condition of their homes and territory, the more appealing the possibility of reusing materials became. Many local communities established programs for regular collection of specified items and for yard waste that then could be composted. A few states, by requiring a deposit, established a financial incentive for return and reuse of plastic, glass, and aluminum beverage containers. An increase in recycling from less than 7 percent of all waste generated in 1960 to more than 17 percent in 1990 suggested that collecting and reworking certain materials had its place in future environmental practices. As with all aspects of waste disposal, recycling was in need of more and newer technology.

Hazardous Waste

While environmentalists focused much of their attention on halting objectionable practices, they also had to contend with damage already done. Sobered and stunned by news in 1978 that houses along the Love Canal area near Buffalo, New York, had been built on top of contaminated soil, by the close call at the Three Mile Island nuclear plant in 1979, and by report of the EPA about thousands of dangerously contaminated sites in the United States, Congress in 1980 passed a measure with the cumbersome title: the Comprehensive Environmen-

TABLE 15.31   GENERATION AND RECOVERY OF SELECTED MATERIALS IN MUNICIPAL SOLID WASTE, 1960–1990

(in millions of tons, except as indicated)

Item and Material	1960	1970	1980	1985	1986	1987	1988	1989	1990
Waste generated, total	**87.8**	**121.9**	**151.5**	**164.4**	**170.7**	**178.1**	**184.2**	**191.4**	**195.7**
Paper and paperboard	29.9	44.2	54.7	61.5	65.6	69.6	71.7	71.9	73.3
Ferrous metals	9.9	12.6	11.6	10.9	11.1	11.3	11.6	12.0	12.3
Aluminum	0.4	0.8	1.8	2.3	2.4	2.4	2.5	2.5	2.7
Other nonferrous metals	0.2	0.7	1.1	1.0	1.0	1.1	1.1	1.2	1.2
Glass	6.7	12.7	45.0	13.2	13.0	12.3	12.5	12.9	13.2
Plastics	0.4	3.1	7.9	11.6	12.2	13.4	14.4	15.4	16.2
Yard waste	20.0	23.2	27.5	30.0	30.2	31.0	31.6	34.7	35.0
Other wastes	20.3	24.6	31.9	33.9	35.2	37.0	38.8	40.8	41.8
Materials recovered, total	**5.9**	**8.6**	**14.5**	**16.4**	**18.3**	**20.1**	**23.5**	**29.9**	**33.4**
Paper and paperboard	5.4	7.4	11.9	13.1	14.8	16.3	18.4	19.1	20.9
Ferrous metals	0.1	0.1	0.4	0.4	0.4	0.4	0.7	1.5	1.9
Aluminum	. . .	. . .	0.3	0.6	0.6	0.7	0.8	0.9	1.0
Other nonferrous metals	0	0.3	0.5	0.5	0.6	0.6	0.7	0.8	0.8
Glass	0.1	0.2	0.8	1.0	1.1	1.3	1.5	2.5	2.6
Plastics	. . .	. . .	. . .	0.1	0.1	0.1	0.2	0.3	0.4
Yard waste	. . .	. . .	. . .	. . .	. . .	. . .	0.5	3.5	4.2
Other wastes	0.3	0.6	0.6	0.7	0.7	0.7	0.7	1.3	1.6
Percent of generation recovered, total	**6.7**	**7.1**	**9.6**	**10.0**	**10.7**	**11.2**	**12.8**	**15.6**	**17.1**
Paper and paperboard	18.1	16.7	21.8	21.3	22.6	23.4	25.6	26.6	28.6
Ferrous metals	1.0	0.8	3.4	3.7	3.6	3.5	5.8	12.6	15.4
Aluminum	. . .	. . .	16.7	26.1	25.0	29.2	31.7	35.5	38.1
Other nonferrous metals	. . .	42.9	45.5	50.0	60.0	54.5	65.1	68.3	67.7
Glass	1.5	1.6	5.3	7.6	8.5	10.6	12.0	19.5	19.9
Plastics	. . .	. . .	. . .	0.9	0.8	0.7	1.1	1.7	2.2
Yard waste	. . .	. . .	. . .	. . .	. . .	. . .	1.6	10.0	12.0
Other wastes	1.5	2.4	1.9	2.1	2.0	1.9	1.8	3.2	3.8

Note: Covers postconsumer residential and commercial solid wastes, which comprise the major portion of typical municipal collections. Excludes mining, agricultural and industrial processing, demolition and construction wastes, sewage sludge, and junked autos and obsolete equipment wastes. Based on material-flows estimating procedure and wet weight as generated. ". . ." represents zero.
Source: Bureau of Census, *Statistical Abstract, 1993*, 227.

TABLE 15.32   SUPERFUND HAZARDOUS SITES, 1981–1990

Date	Number of Sites
October 23, 1981	115
December 30, 1982	418
September 8, 1983	406
October 15, 1984	538
June 10, 1986	703
July 22, 1987	802
October 4, 1989	981
February 21, 1990	1,081

Source: John Wright, *NY Times Almanac, 1998* (New York, 1997), 803.

TABLE 15.33   ACTIVITY AT TOXIC-WASTE SITES, 1990

Activity	Number of Sites
Surface impoundments	453
Landfills, commercial/industrial	423
Containers/drums	305
Other manufacturing/industrial	241
Landfills, municipal	233
Spills	200
Chemical processing/manufacturing	173
Waste piles	124
Leaking containers	117
Tanks, above ground	113
Tanks, below ground	83
Groundwater plumes	77
Electroplating	72
Military testing and maintenance	62
Wood-preserving	57

Note: The Environmental Protection Agency published its first "Interim Priorities List" of hazardous waste sites in 1981, and in 1983 it instituted the National Priorities List, which included 406 sites. As of February 1990, there were 1,218 places that the EPA deemed must be cleaned up immediately. These are the most common activities—several of which can occur at one site.
Source: Wright, *Universal Almanac, 1991*, 540.

tal Response, Compensation, and Liability Act. Mercifully shortened to the Superfund, the measure was designed to begin immediate efforts to clean up the most hazardous waste sites in the country. The EPA assumed responsibility for compiling a priority list of dan-gerous places, for establishing responsibility, whenever possible, for the damage, and for getting the cleanup underway, if necessary doing the work itself. Initially a five-year program, the Superfund was extended five more years in 1986 with other renewals likely to follow.

TABLE 15.34   THE WORST TOXIC-WASTE SITES, 1990

State	Site	City/County	Rank	When Listed
Ala.	Triana/Tennessee River	Limestone/Morgan	31	Oct. 1981
Ark.	Vertac, Inc.	Jacksonville	18	Oct. 1981
Calif.	Riverbank Army Ammunition Plant	Riverbank	Fed.	Jun. 1988
Calif.	Stringfellow	Glen Avon Heights	32	Oct. 1981
Colo.	Rocky Flats Plant (USDOE)	Golden	Fed.	Oct. 1984
Colo.	Sand Creek Industrial	Commerce City	36	Dec. 1982
Del.	Army Creek Landfill	New Castle County	9	Oct. 1981
Del.	Tybouts Corner Landfill	Mantua Township	2	Oct. 1981
Fla.	Reeves Southeast Galvanizing Corp.	Tampa	47	Oct. 1981
Fla.	Schuylkill Metals Corp.	Plant City	41	Dec. 1982
Iowa	LaBounty Site	Charles City	8	Dec. 1982
Maine	McKin Co.	Gray	33	Dec. 1982
Mass.	Baird & McGuire	Holbrook	14	Dec. 1982
Mass.	Industri-Plex	Woburn	5	Oct. 1981
Mass.	Nyanza Chemical Waste Dump	Ashland	11	Oct. 1981
Mass.	W.R. Grace & Co. Inc. (Acton Plant)	Acton	38	Dec. 1982
Mich.	Berlin & Farro	Swartz Creek	13	Jul. 1982
Mich.	Liquid Disposal, Inc.	Utica	23	Jul. 1982
Minn.	FMC Corp. (Fridley Plant)	Fridley	17	Jul. 1982
Minn.	New Brighton/Arden Hills	New Brighton	40	Jul. 1982
Minn.	Reilly Tar (St. Louis Park Plant)	St. Louis Park	39	Oct. 1981
Mo.	Weldon Spring (USDOE/Army)	St. Charles County	Fed.	Oct. 1984
Mont.	Anaconda Co. Smelter	Anaconda	48	Dec. 1982
Mont.	East Helena Site	East Helena	29	Sep. 1983
Mont.	Silver Bow Creek/Butte Area	Deer Lodge	20	Dec. 1982
N.H.	Keefe Environmental Services	Epping	19	Oct. 1981
N.H.	Somersworth Sanitary Landfill	Somersworth	16	Dec. 1982
N.H.	Sylvester	Nashua	24	Oct. 1981
N.J.	Bridgeport Rental & Oil Services	Bridgeport	35	Sep. 1983
N.J.	Burnt Fly Bog	Marlboro Township	43	Oct. 1981
N.J.	CPS/Madison Industries	Old Bridge Township	10	Dec. 1982
N.J.	GEMS Landfill	Gloucester Township	12	Jul. 1982
N.J.	Helen Kramer Landfill	Mantua Township	4	Jul. 1982
N.J.	Lipari Landfill	Pitman	1	Oct. 1981
N.J.	Lone Pine Landfill	Freehold Township	15	Sep. 1983
N.J.	Price Landfill	Pleasantville	6	Sep. 1983
N.J.	Shieldalloy Corp.	Newfield Borough	46	Sep. 1983
N.J.	Vineland Chemical Co., Inc.	Vineland	42	Sep. 1983
N.Mex.	Cal West Metals (USSBA)	Lemitar	Fed.	Jun. 1988
N.Y.	Old Bethpage Landfill	Oyster Bay	45	Oct. 1981
N.Y.	Pollution Abatement Services	Oswego	7	Oct. 1981
Ohio	Arcanum Iron & Metal	Darke County	28	Dec. 1982
Pa.	Bruin Lagoon	Bruin Borough	3	Oct. 1981
Pa.	McAdoo Associates	McAdoo Borough	26	Oct. 1981
Pa.	Publicker Industries, Inc	Philadelphia	44	May 1989
Pa.	Tysons Dump	Upper Merion Twp.	25	Sep. 1983
S.Dak.	Whitewood Creek	Whitewood	21	Oct. 1981
Tex.	Crystal Chemical Co.	Houston	34	Jul. 1982
Tex.	French, Ltd.	Crosby	22	Oct. 1981
Tex.	Geneva Industries/Furtherman Energy	Houston	37	Sep. 1983
Tex.	Motco, Inc.	La Marque	27	Oct. 1981
Tex.	Sikes Disposal Pits	Crosby	30	Oct. 1981
Wash.	Hanford 200-Area (USDOE)	Benton County	Fed.	Jun. 1988
Wash.	Hanford 300-Area (USDOE)	Benton County	Fed.	Jun. 1988
Wash.	Western Processing Co., Inc.	Kent	49	Jul. 1982
Wis.	Omega Hills North Landfill	Germantown	50	Sep. 1983

Source: EPA *Priorities List*, produced in Wright, *Universal Almanac, 1991*, 540.

TABLE 15.35   HAZARDOUS WASTE SITES ON THE NATIONAL PRIORITY LIST, BY STATE, 1990

State	Total Sites	Rank	Percent Distribution
Total	1,207	N/A	N/A
United States	**1,197**	**N/A**	**100.0**
Ala.	12	27	1.0
Alaska	6	43	0.5
Ariz.	11	29	0.9
Ark.	10	34	0.8
Calif.	88	3	7.4
Colo.	16	22	1.3
Conn.	15	24	1.3
Del.	20	19	1.7
D.C.	0	N/A	0
Fla.	51	6	4.3
Ga.	13	26	1.1
Hawaii	7	42	0.6
Idaho	9	38	0.8
Ill.	37	10	3.1
Ind.	35	11	2.9
Iowa	21	18	1.8
Kans.	11	29	0.9
Ky.	17	21	1.4
La.	11	29	0.9
Maine	9	38	0.8
Md.	10	34	0.8
Mass.	25	14	2.1
Mich.	78	5	6.5
Minn.	42	8	3.5
Miss.	2	48	0.2
Mo.	24	15	2.0
Mont.	10	34	0.8
Nebr.	6	43	0.5
Nev.	1	50	0.1
N.H.	16	22	1.3
N.J.	109	1	9.1
N.Mex.	10	34	0.8
N.Y.	83	4	6.9
N.C.	22	17	1.8
N.Dak.	2	48	0.2
Ohio	33	12	2.8
Okla.	11	29	0.9
Oreg.	8	40	0.7
Pa.	95	2	7.9
R.I.	11	29	0.9
S.C.	23	16	1.9
S.Dak.	3	46	0.3
Tenn.	14	25	1.2
Tex.	28	13	2.3
Utah	12	27	1.0
Vt.	8	40	0.7
Va.	20	19	1.7
Wash.	45	7	3.8
W.Va.	5	45	0.4
Wis.	39	9	3.3
Wyo.	3	46	0.3
Guam	1	N/A	N/A
P.R.	9	N/A	N/A

Note: Includes both proposed and final sites listed on the National Priorities List for the Superfund program as authorized by the Comprehensive Environmental Response, Compensation, and Liability Act of 1980 and the Superfund Amendments and Reauthorization Act of 1986.
Source: Bureau of Census, *Statistical Abstract, 1991,* 211.

TABLE 15.36   MAJOR SOURCES OF GROUNDWATER CONTAMINATION REPORTED BY STATES, 1986

Source	No. of States Reporting Source	No. of States Reporting as Primary Source
Septic Tanks	46	9
Underground Storage Tanks	43	13
Agricultural Activities	41	6
On-site Landfills	34	5
Surface Impoundments	33	2
Municipal Landfills	32	1
Abandoned Waste Sites	29	3
Oil and Gas Brine Pits	22	2
Saltwater Intrusion	19	4
Other Landfills	18	0
Road Salting	16	1
Land Application of Sludge	12	0
Regulated Waste Sites	12	1
Mining Activities	11	1
Underground Injection Wells	9	0
Construction Activities	2	0

Source: Environmental Protection Agency, *EPA Update* (1988), 48.

Endangered Species

The environmental movement concerned itself with more than the status of human beings. Birds, animals, fish, and plants not only affected the environment; they also made up the environment, and conditions harmful to their existence probably foretold danger for the livelihood of humans. Doubtless influenced by Rachel Carson's ground-breaking volume *Silent Spring,* Congress in the 1960s began to legislate about environmental conditions generally and about the status of identified species specifically. First passed in 1966, amended in 1973 and several other times, the Endangered Species Act authorized the Fish and Wildlife Service to compile two lists: First was of endangered species, at risk of becoming extinct, and the other was a list of threatened species, deemed likely soon to become at risk. The law forebade action harmful to the species—killing an animal, fowl, or fish—or, more far-reaching, damage to its habitat. Implementation of the Endangered Species Act often produced battles that pitted forces favoring or depending upon some form of economic development against those determined to protect the living space for a bird, fish, or animal. Two publicized examples involved a tiny fish called the snail darter, which stalled construction of the Tellico Dam in the Tennessee Valley, and the spotted owl, efforts to protect the habitat of which threatened lumbering operations in the Northwest. Placed on the threatened list in 1990, the spotted owl produced a controversy yet to be resolved.

TABLE 15.37   ENDANGERED AND THREATENED SPECIES AND RECOVERY PLANS

Group	Endangered U.S. Only	Endangered U.S. & Foreign	Endangered Foreign Only	Threatened U.S. Only	Threatened U.S. & Foreign	Threatened Foreign Only	Listed Species Total	Species with Plans
Mammals	32	19	241	6	2	23	323	24
Birds	61	15	145	7	3	0	231	57
Reptiles	8	7	59	14	4	14	106	22
Amphibians	5	0	8	3	1	0	17	5
Fishes	45	2	11	24	6	0	88	47
Snails	3	0	1	6	0	0	10	7
Clams	32	0	2	0	0	0	34	22
Crustaceans	8	0	0	1	0	0	9	4
Insects	10	0	0	7	0	0	17	12
Arachnids	3	0	0	0	0	0	3	0
Plants	153	6	1	40	6	2	208	85
Total	360	49	468	108	22	39	1,046	285

Total U.S. Endangered	409	Approved recovery plans	245
Total U.S. Threatened	130	Species/populations in above plans	301
Total U.S. Listed	539	Percentage of listed species covered by 1 or more plans.	52.9

Source: Hoffman, World Almanac, 1991, 251.

TABLE 15.38   SOME ENDANGERED SPECIES IN NORTH AMERICA
(U.S. Fish and Wildlife Service, U.S. Interior Department: as of April 15, 1990)

Common Name	Scientific Name	Range
Mammals		
Ozark big-eared bat	*Plecotus townsendii ingens*	U.S. (Mo., Okla., Ariz.)
Brown or grizzly bear	*Ursus arctos horribilis*	U.S. (48 conterminous states)
Eastern cougar	*Felis concolor cougar*	Eastern N.A.
Columbian white-tailed deer	*Odocoileus virginianus leucurus*	U.S. (Wash., Ore.)
San Joaquin kit fox	*Vulpes macrotis mutica*	U.S. (Calif.)
Southeastern beach mouse	*Peromyscus polionotus phasma*	U.S. (Fla.)
Ocelot	*Felis paradalis*	U.S. (Tex., Ariz.)
Southern sea otter	*Enhydra lutris hereis*	U.S. (Wash., Ore., Calif.)
Florida panther	*Felis concolor coryi*	U.S. (La., Ark. east to S.C., Fla.)
Utah prairie dog	*Cynomys parvidens*	U.S. (Utah)
Morro Bay kangaroo rat	*Dipodomys heermanni morroensis*	U.S. (Calif.)
Carolina northern flying squirrel	*Glaucomys sabrinus coloratus*	U.S. (N.C., Tenn.)
Hualapai Mexican vole	*Microtus mexicanus hualapaiensis*	U.S. (Ariz.)
Red wolf	*Canis rufus*	U.S. (Southeast to central Tex.)
Birds		
Masked bobwhite (quail)	*Colinus virginianus ridgwayi*	U.S. (Ariz.)
California condor	*Gymnogyps californianus*	U.S. (Ore., Calif.)
Whooping crane	*Grus americana*	U.S. (Rky. Mtns. east to Carolinas), Canada
Eskimo curlew	*Numenius borealis*	Alaska and N. Canada
Bald eagle	*Haliaeetus leucocephalus*	U.S. (most states). Canada
American peregrine falcon	*Falco peregrinus anatum*	Canada to Mexico
Hawaiian hawk	*Buteo solitartius*	U.S. (Hawaii)
Attwater's greater prairie-chicken	*Tympanuchus cupido attwateri*	U.S. (Tex.)
Bachman's warbler (wood)	*Vermivora bachmanii*	U.S. (Southeast), Cuba
Kirtland's warbler (wood)	*Dendroica kirtlandii*	U.S., Canada, Bahama Is.
Ivory-billed woodpecker	*Campephilus principalis*	U.S. (Southcentral and Southeast), Cuba
Reptiles		
American alligator	*Alligator mississippiensis*	U.S. (Southeast)
American crocodile	*Crocodylus acutus*	U.S. (Fla.)
Atlantic salt marsh snake	*Nerodia fasciatia taeniata*	U.S. (Fla.)
Plymouth red-bellied turtle	*Pseudemys rubiventris bangsi*	U.S. (Mass.)
Fishes		
Yaqui catfish	*Ictalupus pricei*	U.S. (Ariz.)
Bonytail chub	*Gila elegans*	U.S. (Ariz., Calif., Col., Nev., Utah, Wyo.)
Gila trout	*Salmo gilae*	U.S. (Ariz., N.Mex.)

Source: Hoffman, World Almanac, 1991, 251.

Domestic Technology

Domestic technology in the postwar years focused mostly on making life easier, safer, more comfortable, and convenient. The basic processes began with continued application of electric power to virtually all aspects of living; it culminated at the end of the period with expansion of computerization into many agents of lifestyle. Whether one was cooling a room, turning a wrench, or opening a garage door, the new devices almost always began with electricity. Several of the innovations had their foundation in wartime, when shortages of basic materials inspired development of substitutes that often proved superior to the product they replaced. Chemical compounds that replaced scarce metal goods established a basis for a postwar revolution in plastics. Wartime efforts to find substitutes for silk, then vital to female stockings and undergarments, gave birth to an ever-growing family of synthetic fabrics that at one point threatened to replace conventional cotton or wool clothing and then ended up in a blend between the old fabrics and the new. Researchers discovered that such commodities as nylon and polyester had many uses. After the mid-1940s rubber tires were not rubber any more, and wool carpets, or at least carpets, probably were not wool.

Among major household items the refrigerator always came first because it was the most utilitarian. Adoption of television, another of the truly remarkable developments of the era, was stalled somewhat by cost, but more likely by availability of a clear, reliable signal. Once a nationwide network of sending stations had emerged, nearly everyone would get a TV, although color units had to wait until the 1960s. Utilization of other appliances depended on cost, adaptability to existing facilities, and perception of their importance. Bulky and noisy, automatic washers and dryers often did not fit the space within an existing residence. There needed to be modification for drainage, venting, and possibly electric power. The washer and dryer worked best in new housing construction, although some of the postwar housing projects did not include them. As late as 1990 only 35 percent of households had a separate freezer—partly because of space, buying habits, and the fact that newer refrigerators came equipped with a sizable freezing compartment. Residential air conditioning, virtually unheard of before 1946 and long perceived as an ultimate household luxury, took hold in steps that depended on product technology, status of the economy, and changing expectations in life. The most desirable method, central air conditioning, evoked some of the same complications as automatic laundering. Installation in existing facilities was expensive, always requiring a substantial new unit of some sort and in some cases a new routing system. Most residences began with window units, which were noisy, overcooled some rooms and undercooled others. Fewer than 40 percent of homes had central air conditioning in 1990, and many people continued to view the service as uneconomical if not unnecessary. Nonetheless, with passage of each year fewer and fewer new houses were built, even in the northern states, without "central air" facilities.

Some of the most significant products of domestic technology involved small items that passed almost without notice into the mainstream of American living. Thomas Jefferson did not use a ballpoint pen and neither did Franklin D. Roosevelt. Writing instruments that had been used throughout the ages carried a measure of artistry, as with a Japanese calligraphic painting, but they had to be filled regularly: from an inkwell, bottle, or cartridge, and they could be messy and inconvenient. The ballpoint pen might have been regarded as crass at the time of its introduction, but it was effective, durable, handy, and, once its novelty had passed, very inexpensive.

People old enough to recall, associated Gillette razor blades with the World Series of professional baseball. Gillette sponsored radio and television broadcasts for many years. Gillette's promotional jingles were catchy and effective, but the products—even state of the art "blue" blades—would rarely provide the user more than a single shave. Messiness from used, sometimes rusting, razor blades was the order of the day

in many a bathroom cabinet. Stainless steel blades, introduced by Wilkinson in the 1950s and adopted by such major competitors as Gillette and Schick, came into common usage by the 1960s. Capable of lasting weeks if not months, stainless steel blades produced a silent, minor revolution in grooming of men's faces and women's legs.

The standard lawnmower before the 1950s was a simple machine with revolving scissor blades activated by the wheels that made it move. Manual power thus provided both the movement and the cutting action. Operating a lawnmower in good cutting condition took a measure of effort; pushing a machine with dull blades took considerable exertion and perhaps left grass only partly severed. The new technology emerged from rearrangement of equipment already available. By attaching a flat piece of steel, sharpened at both ends, directly to a small Briggs and Stratton gasoline engine, covering the blade for safety, and putting the unit on wheels, one had the lawnmower of the future. The blade whirled so fast that it could cut even when dull; with no linkage to the cutting action the wheels ran so freely that male, female, or child of 10 or so could move the machine along. The simple technology was so effective that it remained basically unchanged decades after introduction. For all its noise, pollutant exhaust, risk of injury from incautious exposure to the whirling blade, the rotary lawnmower occupied a conspicuous place in the landscape of cold war America.

Selected Examples of Domestic Technology, 1946–1990

1946 Bikini, a name associated with atomic testing, now is applied to a skimpy female swimsuit, introduced by a French designer.

Procter and Gamble introduces Tide, first "built" detergent.

Timex corporation introduces a wristwatch.

1947 Raytheon manufactures a microwave oven.

"New Look" long skirts become fashionable.

Reynolds Metal begins production of aluminum foil.

1948 DuPont begins production of a nonstick coating called Teflon.

Instant tea reaches the American market.

DuPont introduces Orlon, a polyester fiber.

Dishpans and utility containers made of polyethylene appear, part of an emerging revolution in plastics.

Burton Baskins and Irving Robbins agree to combine their ice cream businesses.

The MacDonald brothers develop a self-service restaurant in California.

Vinyl floor tiles, another form of plastic, become available.

1949 General Mills and Pillsbury introduce premixed cake preparations.

Tufted carpet reaches the market.

Sara Lee baked products are introduced by Charles Lubin.

1950 A zigzag sewing machine (the Necchi) reaches the market. Portable typewriters become available.

The principle of the Bikini swimsuit now expands to standard female undergarments.

1951 DuPont produces Orlon polyester, and dacron polyester comes out in men's suits.

White fluorescent lighting tubes become available.

1952 Chemistrand introduces acrilan, acrylic fiber.

A nylon stretch fiber is now used in men's socks.

Kirsch Beverages introduces a sugar-free soft drink called NoCal.

1953 Sunbeam markets an automatic electric frying pan.

A felt-tipped pen called Magic Marker is patented.

A tiny hearing aid with a transistor becomes available.

An inexpensive plastic valve enhances appeal of the aerosol spray can.

1954 M&M candy with peanuts hits the market.

The first frozen "TV" dinners are marketed.

A petroleum-based synthetic fabric called polypropylene becomes an effective component of carpeting.

<table>
<thead>
<tr><td>1955</td><td></td></tr>
</thead>
</table>

1955   A freezer ("deep freeze," in popular terminology) capable of freezing fresh food from scratch becomes marketable.

     Franchiser Ray Kroc opens his first McDonald's "hamburger joint" in Des Plaines, Illinois.

     A buttonless and zipperless fastener called velcro is patented. Wilkinson Sword introduces a remarkably effective stainless steel blade for safety razors.

     The McNeil company begins to sell Tylenol pain medicine.

1956   After years of testing at Indiana University, Procter and Gamble introduces a toothpaste with a decay resistant component called stannous fluoride; it is named Crest.

     Smith-Corona produces an electric portable typewriter.

     Southdale Center, first enclosed shopping mall, opens near Minneapolis.

1957   Steam/spray iron is produced by General Electric.

     StaPuf and NuSoft, both fabric softeners in the laundering process, are introduced.

     A plastic saucer suitable for tossing from person to person makes an appearance in California. Called a Frisbee, its use becomes a fad and then a sport.

     Hamilton introduces the electric watch.

1958   DuPont markets a tough, durable synthetic elastic called lycra.

     Hush Puppies reach the American market, as does panty hose.

     Wolf Company introduces an electric lawnmower with rotating blade. The first Pizza Hut restaurant opens in Wichita.

     A simple plastic hoop, called a hula hoop, becomes a marketing bonanza. Twenty million sell in a year.

1959   Tomato-harvesting machines are marketed.

     Kleenex introduces a container that easily dispenses tissues.

     Johnson and Johnson buys the rights to Tylenol.

1960   Cooking pans coated with Teflon reach the market.

     Soft drinks are now sold in aluminum cans.

     IBM introduces the Selectric typewriter.

     Tylenol goes on sale "over the counter."

     The first oral contraceptive pill, Enovid, is marketed.

     L'Oreal develops hair spray called Elnett.

     Seamfree women's stockings are for sale.

1961   Pampers becomes the first successful disposable diapers on the market.

     Coca-Cola introduces lemon-lime soft drink: Sprite.

     Squibb produces first electric toothbrush.

     Liquid fabric softener called Downy comes on sale.

1962   Plastic bags for various uses appear; Baggies are first.

     Silicone rubber gel sacs are utilized as breast implants.

     DEC produces first desktop computer.

     The standard two-pronged electric plug-in now is replaced by a three-pronged receptacle; third prong is for grounding.

1963   Valium appears on the market, courtesy of Roche Laboratories.

     Diet soft drinks appear from Coca-Cola (Tab) and Pepsi Cola (Diet Pepsi).

1964   Irradiation approved for preservation of certain foodstuffs.

     Permanent-press fabrics reach the market; parents will be pleased; producers of irons will not.

     Rudi Gernreich designs a topless swimsuit—for women!

     Corning's photochronomatic glass darkens with exposure to light.

1965   Microwave ovens for domestic consumption reach the market.

     The daring miniskirt makes an appearance, an import from England.

     The water bed makes an appearance in San Francisco.

     Cranapple juice is introduced, as is Gatorade, a rehydrant.

1966   Gerald Moyer introduces Water-Pik.

     Nestle produces freeze-dried Taster's Choice coffee.

1970   Self-cleaning ovens reach the market.

     Corning introduces soon-to-be-popular Corelle dinnerware.

1971   Rival company markets the Crock Pot slow-cooker.

1973   McDonald's restaurant chain turns to breakfast, introduces the Egg McMuffin.

     A new form of cosmetic surgery, of face-lifting, is introduced by a French surgeon.

1974   Computerized product scanners, to replace slower, mistake-prone key-punching by cashiers, appear at Marsh Supermarkets in Troy, Ohio.

TABLE 15.39   NUMBER AND PERCENT OF WIRED HOMES WITH MAJOR ELECTRICAL APPLIANCES, SELECTED YEARS, 1960–1979[a]

Year	Room Air Conditioners	Dishwashers	Clothes Dryers (Electric & Gas)	Electric Ranges	Home Freezers	Refrigerators	Color Televisions	Washers	Total Wired Homes
				Number (million)					
1960	7.8	3.7	10.1	18.4	12.1	50.7	N.A.	28.6	51.7
1965	13.9	7.8	15.2	24.2	13.9	57.3	5.5	33.1	57.6
1970	26.0	17.0	28.6	35.5	20.0	63.9	27.2	39.8	64.0
1975	38.4	27.9	42.0	49.8	31.6	72.6	54.1	50.8	72.7
1976	40.3	29.4	43.4	52.0	32.9	73.9	57.5	53.7	74.1
1977	42.0	31.1	45.0	54.5	34.0	75.8	61.7	55.6	75.9
1978	43.1	32.6	46.9	54.9	34.9	77.6	66.3	58.5	77.8
1979	44.1	34.2	48.8	55.2	35.5	79.2	71.3	61.4	79.4
				Percent					
1960	15.1	7.1	19.6	35.6	23.4	98.0	NA	55.4	. . .
1965	24.2	13.5	26.4	42.0	24.2	99.5	9.5	57.4	. . .
1970	40.6	26.5	44.6	55.5	31.2	99.8	42.5	62.1	. . .
1975	52.8	38.3	57.7	68.5	43.5	99.9	74.4	69.9	. . .
1976	54.4	39.6	58.6	70.1	44.4	99.8	77.7	72.5	. . .
1977	55.3	40.9	59.3	71.9	44.8	99.9	81.3	73.3	. . .
1978	55.4	41.9	60.3	70.6	44.9	99.7	85.2	75.2	. . .
1979	55.5	43.0	61.5	69.5	44.7	99.8	89.8	77.3	. . .

[a] For houses to have electric appliances, it was necessary, of course, to have power brought into the house. Although most houses were wired for electricity in 1960, there were many thousands, especially in the rural south, that were not, although the number diminished every year. In 1978, nearly 55% of wired houses had an electric range, but only 53% of all homes did. Virtually all wired homes had a refrigerator, the first acquired and most important appliance, but when all homes were counted, the number dropped to 84%.

Source: U.S. Department of Energy, *1980 Annual Report to Congress*, Vol. 2 (Washington, D.C., 1981), 199.

1976   Bic and Gillette companies begin to sell disposable razors in the United States.

     The Apple corporation introduces Apple I, a personal micro computer.

1977   The convection oven becomes available.

     Warner-Lambert produces a home pregnancy test.

1979   Halogen lamps are introduced in the United States.

1981   Searle produces a new artificial sweetener with brand name, Equal, that utilized an aspartame substance named Nutrasweet. Many products labeled as "diet," "lo-cal," "no-cal," or "fat-free" will turn to Nutrasweet as a sweetening agent.

     A new modestly alcoholic beverage, the wine cooler, comes on the market.

1982   Alarm caused by poisoning from Tylenol products produces speedy efforts at product security and tamper-proof packaging of nonprescription drugs.

     A disposable watch, Swatch, appears on the market.

1983   Maytag manufactures its last wringer-type washer; the automatic machines, of course, have captured the industry.

     Introduction of French-style yogurt by Dannon signals growing interest in low-fat, "health" foods.

1984   Major producers of no-calorie soft drinks—Diet Pepsi and Diet Coke are the best examples—have adopted nutrasweet.

Many companies now produce personal computers, and more and more computer-related businesses appear on the scene.

CompuServe experiments with Electronic Mall, an early form of shopping by computer.

1985   Burger King, MacDonald's competitor, moves into breakfast business.

     Gillette produces a twin-blade razor cartridge.

     With much fanfare, Coca-Cola changes its Coke formula; popular outcry causes the company then to reintroduce the original beverage as Classic Coke; it also added Cherry Coke to the product line.

     Scientists report on plants, yeasts, and bacteria that are capable of combating air pollutants.

     Research in various quarters produces advanced individual devices for determing pregnancy and female peak fertility.

1986   Warner-Lambert reintroduced some classic, but suspended, chewing gum brands: Black Jack, Beemans, Clove.

     Soft bifocal contact lens are developed separately by two companies.

     Separate companies develop the Container-Mate closure and MicroMatch system for use in packaging.

     French scientists attract attention with a "morning after" contraceptive pill, not yet approved in the United States.

TABLE 15.40   HOUSEHOLDS WITH SELECTED APPLIANCES, SELECTED YEARS, 1978–1990

Appliance	Percent of Households								Percent Change
	1978	1979	1980	1981	1982	1984	1987	1990	1980 to 1990
Total Households	100	100	100	100	100	100	100	100	
Type of Appliances									
Electric Appliances									
Television Set (Color)	. . .	. . .	82	82	85	88	93	96	14
Television Set (B/W)	. . .	. . .	51	48	47	43	36	31	−20
Clothes Washer	75	. . .	75	74	72	74	76	76	1
Range (Stove-Top Burner)	53	. . .	54	54	53	54	57	58	4
Oven, Regular or Microwave	54	. . .	59	58	59	63	79	88	29
Oven, Microwave	8	. . .	14	17	21	34	61	79	65
Clothes Dryer	45	. . .	47	45	45	46	51	53	6
Separate Freezer	35	. . .	38	38	37	37	34	35	−3
Dishwasher	35	. . .	37	37	36	38	43	45	8
Dehumidifier	. . .	. . .	9	9	9	9	10	12	3
Waterbed Heaters	. . .	. . .	. . .	. . .	. . .	10	14	15	. . .
Window or Ceiling Fan	. . .	. . .	. . .	. . .	28	35	46	51	. . .
Whole House Fan	. . .	. . .	. . .	. . .	8	8	9	10	. . .
Evaporative Cooler	. . .	. . .	.4	4	4	4	3	4	a
Personal Computer	. . .	. . .	. . .	. . .	. . .	. . .	. . .	16	. . .
Pump for Well Water	. . .	. . .	. . .	. . .	. . .	. . .	. . .	15	. . .
Swimming-Pool Pump	. . .	. . .	4	4	3	. . .	. . .	5	1
Gas Appliances									
Range (Stove-Top or Burners)	48	. . .	46	46	47	45	43	42	−4
Oven	47	. . .	42	40	42	42	41	41	−1
Clothes Dryer	14	. . .	14	16	15	16	15	16	2
Outdoor Gas Grill	. . .	. . .	9	9	11	13	20	26	17
Outdoor Gas Light	2	. . .	2	2	2	1	1	1	−1
Swimming Pool Heater	. . .	. . .	. . .	. . .	. . .	1	1	2	. . .
Refrigerators									
One	86	. . .	86	87	86	88	86	84	−2
Two or More	14	. . .	14	13	13	12	14	15	1
Air Conditioning (A/C)									
Central	23	24	27	27	28	30	36	39	12
Individual Room Units	33	31	30	31	30	30	30	29	−1
None	44	45	43	42	42	40	36	32	−11
Portable Kerosene Heaters	a	. . .	a	1	3	6	6	5	5

a Less than 1 percent.

Source: Department of Energy, *Annual Energy Review, 1991*, 47.

Procter & Gamble introduces a disposable bib for infants, deftly named "Dribbles."

1987 Richard Davis of Kansas City begins to market a condiment, K.C. Masterpiece Barbeque Sauce, on a national basis.

The Kroger grocery chain uses a customer-operated scanner as a check-out instrument.

A new cholesterol-lowering drug appears on the market.

1988 Prozac, a promising new antidepressant medication, makes an appearance.

The Chicago Cubs baseball team plays its first home night game at Wrigley Field, heretofore a storied ballpark alone in the Major Leagues in the absence of nighttime illumination.

Egg-Watchers, a liquid low-cholesterol substitute for eggs, made from soybeans, reaches the market.

Source: Nell DuVall, *Domestic Technology: A Chronology of Development* (Boston, 1988), 445–465; Bruce Wetterau, *The New York Public Library Book of Chronologies* (New York, 1990), 436.

Science, Technology, and Change in the American Diet

Throughout the 20th century government agencies and private groups had been active in study and policing of popular dietary habits. The activity accelerated in the postwar era with emergence of new agencies and private interest groups and the availability of growing quantities of scientific information. The Food and Drug Administration in 1973 required nutrient labeling on all foods that carry nutrient claims. The Department of Agriculture for years had recommended balance between the five food groups and a diet low in fats, sugar, and sodium. Studies of the 1980s produced a better, albeit still incomplete understanding of blood cholesterol and its connection to heart disease. They also confirmed that cholesterol had its origin in animal fats and dairy products. Food consumptive practices remained mixed, although they contained some evidence of popular attention to new available information. Americans consumed declining amounts of beef, pork, milk, and all dairy products except cheese, of which consumption increased markedly. They ate higher amounts of fish—a highly recommended meat substitute—and such safer meats as chicken and turkey, but the taste for healthy fresh fruits and vegetables improved not at all.

American dietary practices, in fact, were moving in opposite directions. At the same time that some people became involved in—even obsessed with—scientific nutrition, health food, and low cholesterol campaigns, others (or perhaps even the same people) succumbed to the wares of a booming fast-food industry seemingly interested only in taste, speed, and convenience in dining and, of course, profit. Starting with White Castle hamburger stands in the 1920s, the fast-food chains that followed operated in a familiar fashion: standardized operations, scientifically planned goods—each McDonald's hamburger weighed 1.6 ounces—that would produce tasty food speedily, preferably carried out, at low cost. A fast-moving, machine-driven culture of the postwar decades, with tight schedules, mothers and fathers both with jobs, was ideally suited to dine in, delivery, or carry-out foods that left nothing to cook and virtually nothing to clean up. Hamburger places led the way at the start and after 1955 McDonald's led the hamburgers. Competition followed, especially in burgers and then chicken—starting with Col. Harlan Sanders's "finger lickin' good" Kentucky Fried Chicken; by the 1970s it was possible to buy almost every American food and nearly any ethnic specialty—Italian, Chinese, and Mexican were most popular—on the run.

Then there was pizza. This simple, inexpensive dish had been available in Italian districts of large cities for many years, but most Americans probably had their first taste in the 1950s. More likely than not, they liked what they ate. Pizzarias (or pizzerias) began to move into college towns where one found a large number of people on limited budget (the students) eating out on a regular basis in the postwar period. Starting perhaps as a fad, on the order of the espresso-coffee movement, pizza caught on quickly as tasty food on which one could make a meal at a cost not substantially greater than hamburgers. In the same fashion as hamburgers and other fast-food specialties, the pizza business lended itself to national franchise operations. Shakey's started the practice, followed by Pizza Hut (both founded in the 1950s), Domino's (exclusively for delivery), Little Caesar's, and others. A successful pizza chain or other fast-food chain likely then would sell out to a larger, broadly based restaurant enterprise. Pizza franchises substantially outnumbered hamburger stands by the 1980s, and their numbers did not include the frozen pizza business, such as Totino's, operating through grocery stores. Many a youngster proudly proclaimed pizza as the favorite meal, and rarely could one find an adult who did not enjoy some variety of this new "American" food. In the half-century following the Second World War, no other food product changed eating habits as much as pizza.

TABLE 15.41 APPARENT CIVILIAN PER CAPITA CONSUMPTION OF MEAT, FAT, AND FRUIT, 1946–1990
(in pounds, except eggs; calendar years, except as noted)

Year	Meats (carcass weight)			Edible Fats and Oils				Fresh Fruits (farm weight)		
	Total	Beef and Veal	Pork, Excluding Lard	Fish (edible weight)	Total (fat content)	Margarine (actual weight)	Butter, Farm and Factory (actual weight)	Total	Citrus	Apples
1946	154.1	71.6	75.8	12.8	40.0	3.9	10.5	133.9	59.1	23.0
1950	144.6	71.4	69.2	13.8	45.9	6.1	10.7	108.8	41.7	22.7
1955	162.8	91.4	66.8	12.9	45.9	8.2	9.0	99.4	41.8	19.6
1960	160.9	91.2	64.9	13.2	45.3	9.4	7.5	93.4	33.7	18.3
1965	167.1	104.7	58.7	13.9	47.8	9.9	6.4	81.1	29.1	16.3
1970	186.3	116.6	66.4	14.8	53.2	11.0	5.3	81.0	28.6	18.3
1975	180.5	123.7	54.8	12.2	52.6	11.0	4.7	85.0	29.4	19.5
1980	126.4	73.4	52.1	12.5	57.2	11.3	4.5	90.0	28.9	19.2
1985	124.9	76.1	47.7	15.1	64.3	10.8	4.9	89.3	22.6	17.5
1990	112.3	64.9	46.3	15.5	62.7	10.9	4.4	92.3	22.6	19.8

Source: George T. Kurian, *Datapedia of the United States 1790–2000: America Year by Year* (Lanham, Md., 1994), 113.

TABLE 15.42   APPARENT CIVILIAN PER CAPITA CONSUMPTION OF VEGETABLES, DAIRY, POULTRY, AND OTHER, 1946–1990

(in pounds, except eggs; calendar years, except as noted)

Year	Potatoes (farm weight)	Fresh Vegetables (farm weight)	Dairy Products Fluid Milk and Cream	Dairy Products Cheese	Dairy Products Ice Cream (product weight)	Eggs (number)	Chicken and Turkey (ready to-cook)	Wheat Flour	Peanuts (shelled)	Coffee (green-bean basis)
1946	123.0	129.9	389.0	6.7	23.1	379	23.1	156.0	5.3	20.1
1950	106.0	115.2	348.0	7.7	18.0	389	24.7	135.0	4.5	16.1
1955	106.0	105.2	348.0	7.9	18.0	371	26.3	123.0	4.1	15.3
1960	101.0	105.9	322.0	8.3	18.3	335	34.2	118.0	4.9	15.8
1965	93.0	98.6	302.0	9.6	18.5	314	40.9	113.0	5.6	14.8
1970	91.0	98.9	264.0	11.5	17.7	319	49.5	110.0	5.9	13.8
1975	122.2	89.9	261.4	14.3	18.6	276	48.9	114.5	6.0	12.2
1980	114.2	92.7	245.6	17.5	17.5	271	42.6	116.9	4.8	10.3
1985	122.4	100.2	241.0	22.5	18.1	255	49.4	124.7	6.3	10.5
1990	127.2	111.0	233.2	24.7	15.7	233	63.6	137.8	6.0	10.2

Source: Kurian, *Datapedia*, 115.

TABLE 15.43   NUTRITION—NUTRIENTS IN FOODS AVAILABLE FOR CIVILIAN CONSUMPTION PER CAPITA PER DAY AND PERCENT CHANGE, 1955–1988

Nutrient	Unit	1955–59	1965–69	1975–79	1985–88	Percent Change, 1985–88 1955–59	Percent Change, 1985–88 1965–69	Percent Change, 1985–88 1975–79
Food energy	Calories	3,100	3,200	3,300	3,600	13.9	11.1	8.3
Protein	Grams	94	97	99	104	9.6	6.7	4.8
Total fat	Grams	142	154	157	169	16.0	8.9	7.1
Saturated	Grams	60	62	58	61	1.6	−1.6	4.9
Monounsaturated	Grams	56	62	63	67	16.4	7.5	6.0
Polyunsaturated	Grams	19	23	29	34	44.1	32.4	14.7
Cholesterol	Milligrams	510	490	450	440	−15.9	−11.4	−2.3
Carbohydrate	Grams	380	380	390	420	9.5	9.5	7.1
Vitamin A	Retinol equivalents	1,320	1,350	1,540	1,630	19.0	17.2	5.5
Carotenes	Retinol equivalents	430	430	600	750	42.7	42.7	20.0
Vitamin E	Milligram α-TE	11.3	12.7	14.5	16.3	30.7	22.1	11.0
Ascorbic acid	Milligrams	100	96	111	116	13.8	17.2	4.3
Thiamin	Milligrams	1.9	1.9	2.1	2.2	13.6	13.6	4.5
Riboflavin	Milligrams	2.3	2.2	2.4	2.4	4.2	8.3	0.0
Niacin	Milligrams	20	22	24	26	23.1	15.4	7.7
Vitamin B_6	Milligrams	1.9	2.0	2.1	2.1	9.5	4.8	0.0
Folacin	Micrograms	282	267	277	283	0.4	5.7	2.1
Vitamin B_{12}	Micrograms	9.4	10.0	10.0	9.2	−2.2	−8.7	−8.7
Calcium	Milligrams	920	850	850	900	−2.2	5.6	5.6
Phosphorus	Milligrams	1,470	1,460	1,470	1,530	3.9	4.6	3.9
Magnesium	Milligrams	320	310	310	330	3.0	6.1	6.1
Iron	Milligrams	13.8	14.3	15.1	17.0	18.8	15.9	11.2
Zinc	Milligrams	11.8	12.3	12.5	12.6	6.3	2.4	0.8
Copper	Milligrams	1.6	1.5	1.6	1.6	0.0	6.3	0.0
Potassium	Milligrams	3,530	3,380	3,370	3,460	−2.0	2.3	2.6

Note: Based on estimates of per capita food consumption at the retail level, on imputed consumption data for foods no longer reported, and on estimates of quantities of home grown produce. Food supply estimates do not reflect loss of food or nutrients from further marketing or home processing. Enrichment and fortification levels of iron, thiamin, riboflavin, niacin, vitamin A, vitamin B_6 vitamin B_{12}, and ascorbic acid are included. Minus sign (−) indicates decrease.
Source: Bureau of Census, *Statistical Abstract, 1992*, 134.

TABLE 15.44   EATING OUT, 1950–1990

Type	1950	1960	1970	1980	1990
Percent of all food expenditures away from home	24.2	26.6	33.7	39.4	45.7
Percent of food expenditures away from home that was fast food	6.2	7.1	18.4	27.9	34.4

Source: *Restaurant Business*, November 20, 1991, 2.

TABLE 15.45 TAKE-OUT FOOD BUSINESS, BY SPECIALTY, 1987 AND 1990

Concept	1987 Units	1990 Units	% Change
Pizza	41,270	49,526	20
Hamburger	31,920	34,269	7
Oriental	17,859	23,221	30
Mexican	14,646	17,238	18
Chicken	12,161	12,047	−1
Fish/Seafood	9,970	10,870	9
Sub Sandwiches	6,153	9,836	60
Italian	5,142	8,735	70
Yogurt	1,341	3,310	147
Biscuit/Buns	306	908	196

Source: *Restaurant Business,* November 1, 1990, 2.

TABLE 15.46 TOP 25 RESTAURANT COMPANIES, 1990

Rank	Company	1990 U.S. Sales Dollars ('000s)	1990 U.S. Sales % Change	U.S. Units Number	U.S. Units % Change	Unit Rank
1.	**McDonald's Corp.**	12,251,600	2.0	8,576	3.7	2
	McDonald's	12,251,600	2.0	8,576	3.7	...
2.	**PepsiCo Food Service**	9,434,300	13.7	14,997	5.0	1
	Pizza Hut	3,800,000	15.2	6,688	7.1	...
	Kentucky Fried Chicken	3,200,000	6.7	5,006	0.9	...
	Taco Bell	2,400,000	20.0	3,227	4.7	...
	Hot 'N Now Hamburgers	34,300	50.8	76	68.9	...
3.	**Grand Metropolitan, PCL**	5,329,000	3.4	5,764	1.6	3
	Burger King	5,250,000	3.4	5,469	1.7	...
	Häagen-Dazs	79,000	2.6	295	0.0	...
4.	**Imasco, Ltd.**	3,360,000	15.9	4,022	22.2	8
	Hardee's/Roy Rogers	3,360,000	15.9	4,022	22.2	...
5.	**Wendy's International Inc.**	2,835,000	0.3	3,436	−1.5	9
	Wendy's	2,835,000	0.3	3,436	−1.5	...
6.	**TW Services, Inc.**	2,670,757	9.6	2,221	3.6	12
	Denny's Restaurants	1,686,720	10.2	1,294	1.6	...
	Hardee's	510,457	9.3	483	3.9	...
	Quincy's Family Steakhouse	281,510	6.9	212	−0.5	...
	El Pollo Loco	192,070	9.8	232	20.8	...
7.	**Domino's Pizza, Inc.**	2,500,000	12.7	5,003	3.6	5
	Domino's Pizza	2,500,000	12.7	5,003	3.6	...
8.	**International Dairy Queen, Inc.**	2,142,600	2.6	5,277	−1.4	4
	Dairy Queen	2,025,000	3.1	4,622	−0.1	...
	Orange Julius of America	85,000	−3.4	466	−7.9	...
	Karmel Korn	17,600	12.0	138	−15.9	...
	Golden Skillet	15,000	0.0	51	−5.6	...
9.	**General Mills Restaurant Group**	1,913,985	14.8	703	13.9	24
	Red Lobster	1,362,000	6.4	475	6.3	...
	Olive Garden	551,985	42.6	228	34.1	...
10.	**Shoney's, Inc.**	1,584,695	10.3	1,658	4.6	15
	Shoney's	991,279	14.9	734	7.9	...
	Captain D's	413,537	5.4	633	4.3	...
	Lee's Famous Recipe	140,754	−3.1	274	−2.8	...
	Specialty Dinnerhouses	39,125	8.5	17	6.3	...
11.	**Allied-Lyons, PLC**	1,438,336	18.3	4,433	13.6	7
	Dunkin' Donuts	790,722	10.6	1,680	7.3	...
	Baskin-Robbins	490,000	2.7	2,278	−2.0	...
	Mister Donut	127,648	−17.6	460	−8.7	...
	Chili's	29,966	27.7	15	25.0	...
12.	**Little Caesar Enterprises, Inc.**	1,400,000	23.9	3,173	17.5	10
	Little Caesars	1,400,000	23.9	3,173	17.5	...

Rank	Company	1990 U.S. Sales		U.S. Units		Unit Rank
		Dollars ('000s)	% Change	Number	% Change	
13.	**Foodmaker, Inc.**	1,372,272	12.1	1,241	7.3	17
	Jack in the Box	944,000	13.2	1,040	5.5	...
	Chi-Chi's	428,272	9.8	201	17.5	...
14.	**DWG**	1,366,500	9.3	2,314	8.6	11
	Arby's Restaurants	1,363,000	9.0	2,309	8.4	...
	Daddy-O's Express	3,500	45.8	5	66.7	...
15.	**Doctor's Associates, Inc.**	1,123,000	39.9	4,866	23.1	6
	Subway Sandwiches	1,100,000	37.5	4,777	21.3	...
	Cajun Joe's	23,000	666.7	89	456.3	...
16.	**Metromedia**	1,097,000	−6.0	1,147	−5.5	19
	Ponderosa	651,000	0.2	727	3.3	...
	Bonanza	446,000	−13.8	420	−17.6	...
17.	**Elias Brothers Restaurants, Int.**	1,046,700	0.0	923	−0.1	21
	Big Boy	1,040,000	0.0	915	0.0	...
	Top Hat	6,700	−6.9	8	−11.1	...
18.	**Collins Foods Intl., Inc.**	1,041,584	6.7	849	2.3	22
	Sizzler	903,100	6.2	640	2.7	...
	Kentucky Fried Chicken	138,484	9.7	209	1.0	...
19.	**Copeland, A., Enterprises**	1,032,500	−1.0	1,845	−0.7	13
	Popeye's Fried Chicken	541,000	3.8	778	5.3	...
	Church's Fried Chicken	468,000	−6.2	1,059	−4.7	...
	Copeland's	23,500	4.4	8	0.0	...
20.	**Tennessee Restaurant Co.**	992,000	1.2	1,198	0.4	18
	Friendly	520,000	−6.6	799	−3.0	...
	Perkins Family Restaurants	472,000	11.5	399	8.1	...
21.	**Restaurant Enterprises Group**	907,600	3.7	521	−1.9	32
	El Torito	393,500	2.4	180	−0.6	...
	R.E.G. Coffee Shops	319,800	9.0	252	−1.6	...
	Far West Dinnerhouses	194,300	−1.5	89	−5.3	...
22.	**Long John Silver's Holdings, Inc.**	777,336	−0.3	1,434	−2.1	16
	Long John Silver's	777,336	−0.3	1,434	−2.1	...
23.	**Benale Holding Corp.**	735,000	5.0	380	0.3	48
	Bennigan's	535,000	5.9	225*	2.3	...
	Steak N Ale	200,000	2.6	155*	−2.5	...
24.	**Carlson Companies, Inc.**	672,167	8.7	410	1.7	43
	TGI Friday's	470,950	12.3	159	7.4	...
	Country Kitchen	173,467	1.3	240	−0.8	...
	Dalts	27,750	0.9	11	−15.4	...
25.	**Morrison, Inc.**	668,900	12.0	349	14.4	51
	Morrison's Cafeterias	365,000	−0.8	171	−2.3	...
	Ruby Tuesday	226,100	36.2	133	35.7	...
	L & N Seafood	63,800	20.8	34	41.7	...
	Silver Spoon	14,000	37.3	11	37.5	...

Source: *Restaurant Business,* November 20, 1991, 116–120.

CHAPTER 16 Art and Architecture

Art in the United States: Who Pays for It

Historically, art in the United States had largely been an extension of the capitalist system. Art institutions, organizations, and the artists themselves had the responsibility of finding their own funding. They had relied on ticket sales: to museums, for example, or special exhibitions; artist sold, or tried to sell, their works. Private patronage provided a sometimes lucrative but always unreliable source of income. If the national or a state government occasionally agreed to support a project it usually was to decorate a building or other public property or to celebrate a person or a cause. The Civil War had inspired a virtually countless number of monuments, scattered mostly about the eastern half of the nation. During the depression era of the 1930s, an agency of Franklin D. Roosevelt's New Deal, the Works Progress Administration (WPA) had sponsored several art-related programs in the form of work relief for artists in need of subsistence.

In the period following the Second World War, funding for the arts expanded in several areas. Private patronage grew with growth of surplus wealth and with changes in tax policy that placed gifts to artistic functions within the category of tax-deductible charitable donations. Since the 1960s major support came from philanthropic foundations and from corporations. Private companies created the Business Committee for the Arts in 1967 and contributions from this source increased markedly nearly every year. Many business people regarded assistance to the arts as a tasteful and, because of tax policy, an inexpensive way of promoting public relations.

The national government had long had a hand in the world of art, if only to act as a collector and depository of national and historic works. The Smithsonian Institution, the National Gallery of Art, and the Institute of Museum Services, all in Washington, D.C., represented the most obvious examples. In the 1960s the national government became involved in the arts in a different fashion. Inspired by a favorable reaction to the WPA in the 1930s, influenced by President John F. Kennedy and especially his wife, Jacqueline, Congress set to work on creating a different sort of art agency. As frequently happened in the 1960s, what had been proposed during the shortened presidency of Kennedy came to fruition in the administration of Lyndon B. Johnson. Congress in 1965 created the National Endowment on the Arts and Humanities, which had two branches—the Humanities and the National Endowment for the Arts (NEA). Subject of course to appropriation from the legislature—at the start it was only $8 million a year—the N.E.A. began to make grants to organizations, to state agencies, and to individual artists for specific artistic projects. During the remarkably sympathetic administration of Richard Nixon, funding increased sharply—to $65 million in the mid-1970s, more than $150 million by the end of the decade.

In the 1980s the N.E.A. had to contend with several serious challenges. First came an effort by the administration of Ronald Reagan to reduce, or at least reallocate, government expenditures by making sharp cuts in specific programs. The first proposal had called for a 50 percent reduction in funding for the N.E.A., and it took vigorous efforts to trim the cut to 10 percent. Near the end of the 1980s the government's arts program provoked strong opposition to some of the projects that it chose to support. First came the photography of Andrés Serrano, who had received a grant and whose exhibit included pictures of a crucifix submerged in urine. A second furor then erupted over a N.E.A.–sponsored exhibition of photographs of Robert Mapplethorpe, which included pictures of men engaged in homosexual behavior and of naked children. Charged with supporting sacrilegious and obscene activity, the N.E.A. faced legislators who threatened tight controls on what constituted art, a reduction in funding, if not—as some senators demanded—outright abolition of the agency. The N.E.A. weathered the storm but only barely. The agency had to impose restrictions on use of its funds; it faced a threat to reclaim any money improperly spent, and legislation passed in 1990 reauthorized the N.E.A. for three years instead of the customary five.

TABLE 16.1 GIVING TO THE ARTS, 1965–1990
(in billions of current dollars)

Year	Total	Percent Change
1965	0.44	
1966	0.54	22.94
1967	0.56	4.29
1968	0.60	8.05
1969	0.72	18.87
1970	0.66	−7.66
1971	1.01	52.34
1972	1.10	8.91
1973	1.26	14.55
1974	1.20	−4.76
1975	1.56	30.00
1976	2.27	45.51
1977	2.32	2.20
1978	2.40	3.45
1979	2.73	13.75
1980	3.15	15.38
1981	3.66	16.19
1982	4.96	35.52
1983	4.21	−15.12
1984	4.50	6.89
1985	5.08	12.89
1986	5.83	14.76
1987	6.31	8.23
1988	6.79	7.61
1989	7.50	10.46
1990	7.89	5.20

Source: American Association of Fund-Raising Counsel, *Giving USA* (New York, 1996), 23.

TABLE 16.2 TOTAL CORPORATE CONTRIBUTIONS TO THE ARTS, 1975–1985

Year	Estimated Amount Given to the Arts ($millions)	Percentage of Total Contributions Given to Arts
1975	90	7.5
1976	122	8.2
1977	161	9.0
1978	211	10.1
1979	227	9.9
1980	257	10.9
1981	299	11.9
1982	331	11.4
1983	413	11.4
1984	428	10.7
1985	488	11.1

Source: Robert A. Porter, ed., *Corporate Giving to the Arts 4* (New York, 1987), x.

TABLE 16.3 PERCENTAGE DOLLAR ALLOCATION AMONG BENEFICIARIES OF CORPORATE SUPPORT FOR THE ARTS, 1984

Beneficiaries	Percentage
Museums	19.6
Music	12.7
Public TV and radio	12.1
Cultural centers	9.5
Theaters	6.0
Employee matching gifts	5.8
Arts funds and councils	5.4
Dance	2.3
Libraries	1.6
Other	25.0
(Number of companies)	(415)

Source: Porter, Corporate Giving 4, xiii.

TABLE 16.4 FINANCIAL SUPPORT OF THE ARTS BY PRIVATE CORPORATE BUSINESS— SUMMARY, 1984–1988

(in millions of dollars)

Type of Art Category	1984	1985	1988
Direct cash support	**482.4**	**559.0**	**634.0**
Museums	104.5	133.2	101.4
Symphony orchestras	66.8	79.8	101.4
Performing arts and cultural facilities	52.0	59.4	31.7
Theaters	67.2	49.5	76.1
Art funds—general support	28.5	37.9	. . .
Other music	25.3	30.2	44.4
Dance	20.7	25.4	50.7
Public TV and radio, program underwriting	17.9	23.6	25.4
Opera	24.8	22.7	50.7
Films (noncommercial)	15.7	13.2	. . .
Arts-in-education programs	3.8	11.8	19.0
Historic and cultural preservation projects	9.7	11.3	. . .
Libraries	4.8	8.8	44.4
Commercial TV and radio, cultural programming	6.5	5.6	. . .
Public TV and radio, general support	16.5	4.5	25.4
Crafts	2.3	1.8	. . .
Artist-in-residence programs	1.1	1.0	. . .
Poetry and writing	1.4	1.0	. . .
Video projects (noncommercial)	0.2	0.2	. . .
Folk art	. . .	. . .	. . .
Other (excluding commercial activities)	12.7	38.0	63.4

Source: Bureau of the Census, Statistical Abstract of the United States, 1992 (Washington, D.C., 1992), 243.

TABLE 16.5 SELECTED MAJOR PRIVATE GIFTS TO THE ARTS

Amount	Year	Donor	Recipient
$40 million[a]	1974	John Paul Getty	Getty Museum
$1.2 billion	1976	Getty Estate	Getty Museum
$5 million	1983	Mr. & Mrs. Joe Price	Los Angeles County Museum of Art
$3 million	1983	Philip Morris Co.	Metropolitan Museum of Art (N.Y.)
$1 million	1983	Vincent Astor Foundation	Brooklyn Museum of Art
93 works of art	1983	Paul Mellon	National Gallery of Art
$15 million	1989	Walter Annenberg	Metropolitan Museum of Art
$5 million	1989	Walter Annenberg	National Gallery of Art
$5 million	1989	Walter Annenberg	Philadelphia Museum of Art

[a] Donation also included $2 million annual operating fund.

Source: American Association of Fund-Raising Counsel, Inc., Giving USA, 1983 (New York, 1984), 87, 94; Richard B. Morris and Jeffrey B. Morris, Encyclopedia of American History (New York, 1996), 912.

TABLE 16.6 FEDERAL AID—NATIONAL ENDOWMENT FOR THE ARTS, 1970–1990

(in millions of dollars)

Type of Fund and Program	1970	1975	1980	1984	1985	1986	1987	1988	1989	1990
Funds available	15.7	86.9	188.1	169.9	171.7	167.1	170.9	171.1	166.7	170.8
Program appropriation	6.3	67.3	97.0	119.0	118.7	115.7	120.8	122.2	123.5	124.3
Matching funds	2.0	7.5	42.9	27.4	29.5	30.0	29.3	32.9	23.6	32.4
Grants awarded (number)	556	3,071	5,505	5,056	4,801	4,484	4,542	4,628	4,604	4,475
Funds obligated	12.9	81.7	166.4	147.4	149.4	146.6	151.4	156.3	148.3	157.6
Music	2.5	14.9	13.6	15.2	15.3	14.6	15.1	15.3	15.3	16.5
State programs	1.9	14.7	22.1	24.6	24.4	23.8	24.6	24.9	25.5	26.1
Museums	. . .	10.8	11.2	12.5	11.9	11.5	11.5	12.6	12.7	12.1
Theater	2.8	6.4	8.4	10.7	10.6	10.2	10.8	10.7	10.7	10.6
Dance	1.7	6.1	8.0	9.1	9.0	9.0	9.1	9.2	9.5	9.6
Media arts	0.2	5.4	8.4	9.5	9.9	12.3	12.9	12.4	12.7	13.9
Challenge	. . .	. . .	50.8	18.8	20.7	20.7	20.8	24.8	15.4	19.7
Visual arts	1.0	3.2	7.3	6.6	6.2	5.7	6.2	6.0	6.1	5.9
Other	2.8	20.1	36.6	40.6	41.3	38.8	40.4	40.4	40.2	43.1

Source: Bureau of Census, Statistical Abstract, 1992, 244.

TABLE 16.7 BUDGET—NATIONAL ENDOWMENT FOR THE ARTS, 1983 AND 1984

(in dollars)

Programs	1983	1984
Artists-in-Education	4,800,000	5,200,000
Dance	9,039,000	9,000,000
Design Arts	4,200,000	4,500,000
Expansion Arts	7,500,000	7,000,000
Folk Arts	2,800,000	3,000,000
Inter-Arts	3,300,000	4,200,000
Literature	4,300,000	4,500,000
Media Arts	9,100,000	9,500,000
Museum	10,139,000	12,200,000
Music	13,039,000	15,300,000
Opera—Musical Theater	5,040,000	6,100,000
State Program	21,039,000	24,300,000
Locals Test	. . .	2,000,000
Theater	9,439,000	10,600,000
Visual Arts	6,000,000	6,400,000
Policy, Planning, and Research	940,000	1,000,000
Regional Representatives	600,000	700,000
Advancement	1,600,000	2,400,000
Subtotal (Program and Treasury Funds)	112,875,000	127,900,000
Administration	10,910,000	13,100,000
Challenge	18,400,000	21,000,000

Source: AAFRC, Giving USA, 1983, 91.

TABLE 16.8 STATE ARTS AGENCIES LEGISLATIVE APPROPRIATIONS, FISCAL YEARS 1983 AND 1984

State	Per Capita (¢)			Appropriations ($)		
	Rank	1984	1983	1984	1983	% Change
Ala.	46.	19.0	14.6	750,000	570,000	31.6
Alaska	1.	1025.0	1207.7	4,489,500	4,975,800	−9.8
Amer. Samoa	10.	111.4	147.1	36,750	47,500	−22.6
Ariz.	52.	14.9	15.0	426,000	419,100	1.6
Ark.	34.	31.9	32.4	730,904	742,946	−1.6
Calif.	33.	34.0	44.0	8,401,000	10,649,000	−21.1
Colo.	40.	27.7	28.5	843,242	844,027	−.1
Conn.	35.	31.0	28.1	978,000	881,663	10.9
Del.	14.	69.2	71.6	416,300	428,140	−2.8
D.C.	9.	145.2	139.8	916,400	882,400	3.9
Fla.	18.	50.5	39.3	5,264,106	3,997,724	31.7
Ga.	39.	28.5	29.5	1,605,796	1,641,521	−2.2
Guam	4.	175.5	108.9	192,924	115,445	67.1
Hawaii	7.	147.8	161.6	1,468,779	1,585,509	−7.4
Idaho	56.	10.6	10.8	102,000	103,300	−1.3
Ill.	21.	48.0	24.0	5,492,440	2,751,900	99.6
Ind.	42.	26.5	25.7	1,450,128	1,403,286	3.3
Iowa	51.	16.5	12.9	479,706	372,776	28.7
Kans.	48.	17.6	17.2	422,978	410,660	3.0
Ky.	26.	40.6	35.4	1,489,000	1,295,564	14.9
La.	29.	38.0	45.9	1,658,892	1,978,007	−16.1
Maine	45.	21.9	19.2	248,529	217,039	14.5
Md.	24.	42.4	42.5	1,807,983	1,810,603	−.1
Mass.	8.	147.4	95.3	8,523,671	5,500,000	55.0
Mich.	13.	78.2	56.7	7,126,200	5,217,200	36.6
Minn.	19.	48.9	37.7	2,020,600	1,542,472	31.0
Miss.	47.	18.0	17.2	459,408	435,324	5.5
Mo.	20.	48.5	50.5	2,401,307	2,494,442	−3.7
Mont.	15.	67.6	17.6	541,662	139,456	288.4
Nebr.	36.	31.0	29.5	491,857	465,994	5.6
Nev.	54.	13.1	11.2	115,647	94,282	22.7
N.H.	53.	13.3	10.3	126,424	96,347	31.2
N.J.	22.	47.7	48.5	3,546,322	3,589,842	−1.2
N.Mex.	30.	37.6	39.2	510,700	521,100	−2.0
N.Y.	2.	198.8	200.8	35,100,000	35,340,000	−.7
N.C.	28.	39.4	35.5	2,370,611	2,113,672	12.2
N.Dak.	43.	26.1	20.7	174.972	136,466	28.2
N.M.	5.	173.4	59.6	30,000	10,000	200.0
Ohio	17.	51.8	46.6	5,594,547	5,024,452	11.3
Okla.	16.	55.1	57.2	1,751,226	1,773,517	−1.3

State	Per Capita (¢)			Appropriations ($)		
	Rank	1984	1983	1984	1983	% Change
Oreg.	50.	16.6	12.9	440,787	342,460	28.7
Pa.	27.	40.1	40.1	4,759,000	4,758,000	0
P.R.	3.	180.2	162.2	5,859,200	5,186,240	13.0
R.I.	31.	35.5	41.5	339,616	395,262	−14.1
S.C.	23.	47.4	42.2	1,516,644	1,337,610	13.4
S.Dak.	37.	30.8	29.0	212,779	199,271	6.8
Tenn.	55.	11.3	10.4	527,700	481,600	9.6
Tex.	44.	25.9	12.2	3,951,718	1,803,313	119.1
Utah	12.	79.3	84.2	1,233,043	1,277,853	−3.5
Vt.	25.	42.1	35.8	217,028	184,500	17.6
V.I.	6.	157.7	156.2	156,761	150,856	3.9
Va.	41.	27.2	25.8	1,495,215	1,400,710	6.7
Wash.	32.	35.1	17.5	1,488,742	738,752	101.5
W.Va.	11.	87.8	92.6	1,709,792	1,807,690	−5.4
Wis.	49.	17.0	17.1	808,300	809,000	−.1
Wy.	38.	30.1	29.0	151,064	142,902	5.7
Total				135,423,900	123,634,495	9.5

Source: AAFRC, *Giving USA, 1983*, 93.

Directions of American Art

Art underwent multiple major changes in the United States in the period following the Second World War. The emergence of fascism and the war had induced many European artists to find refuge in the United States. American form and style began to take on unprecedented international significance, as did artists born and trained in the United States or others who had adopted the country as their own. Older patterns of social realism and regionalism ran their course as style in painting, and other art forms, became increasingly abstract. The movement culminated during the immediate postwar era in the emergence in grandiose fashion of a new, distinctly American form called abstract expressionism, an approach that was most distinct in what was absent: There were seemingly no rules as to style, subject, message, or even tools of the trade. The abstract expressionist painter did not have to use a brush. The most prominent such artist, Jackson Pollock, spread his canvas on the floor and walked about pouring paint from the bucket or applying it any way he felt like doing. The rage of the art-world in the 1950s, Pollock's "action" or "drip" painting (colleagues called him Jack the Dripper) did not remain long in vogue, but he had at least made a point of total abstraction. Painting, or art in general, was what the artist said it was.

Art thus could carry barely recognizable form, as in the works of Willem de Kooning, no form at all, or it could be precise representations of mundane aspects of life, as in a theme called pop art that caught on in the 1960s. Andy Warhol did a series of Campbell soup cans, Roy Lichtenstein painted comic-strip characters, Claes Oldenburg did hamburgers (of fabric and stuffing), and sculptor Jasper Johns worked with beer cans. Driven apparently by the dictum "anything goes," art forms proliferated during the rest of the 20th century. Conventional patterns had periodic revivals, and there also was op art (optical art) that combined colors in geometric shapes, minimal art that might feature geometric shapes or flat areas of color, color field paintings, or the fluorescent-light works by Dan Flavin or neon lights by Chryssa. Earth art, or earthworks, appreciated best when viewed from the air, was exemplified by Robert Smithson's "Spiral Jetty," a jetty that spiraled 1,500 feet, ending in the Great Salt Lake.

As the population and national wealth expanded, so also did the world of art. Major art exhibitions attracted audiences numbering in hundreds of thousands, if not millions; with internationalization of the

Woman and Bicycle (1952–53), by Willem de Kooning, one of the most prominent abstract expressionist painters (Whitney Museum of American Art and Willem de Kooning Revocable Trust/Artists Rights Society, New York)

Alexander Calder's sculpture in Grand Rapids, Michigan, completed in 1969—the first work of public art supported by the NEA (author's photo)

art market—Japanese buyers, if inconspicuous, were exceptionally active—famous paintings brought mammoth prices at auction, the highest amounts going for traditional European masters. Wealthy contributors provided large donations, either in cash or artworks, to art institutions. New museums opened, such as the Getty Museum in California in the 1970s; older ones were renovated, rebuilt, or underwent expansion. The Guggenheim in New York moved into new quarters that were designed by Frank Lloyd Wright, in 1959; the National Gallery in Washington, D.C., received an East Annex in 1978; the Metropolitan Museum of Art in New York expanded in 1987. Developments in art made national news. More than 200 unknown works of Andrew Wyeth—the Helga paintings—were discovered in 1987. Skillful thieves robbed the Gardner Museum in Boston of $200 million worth of uninsured paintings in 1990. It was likely that a large portion of the American population remained either ignorant of, amused by, or disinterested in purported new directions in art, but it appeared that the world center of art—as with so many other centers in previous years—had moved west from Europe and that an artistic revolution had taken place in the United States since the Second World War.

One did not need to visit a museum to be exposed to art in the United States. It became nearly impossible to avoid. The period since the Second World War has been marked with growth in what became known as public art: conspicuously placed pieces of art, usually

sculpture, although wall paintings called murals, earthworks, and other forms also qualified. Public art, of course, was not new. The Statue of Liberty represented such a structure, as did the faces carved at Mount Rushmore in South Dakota. The most common examples probably had been statues of American heroes in public places. Beginning especially in the 1960s, public art expanded rapidly in numbers, sources of funding, and form. One found art pieces everywhere—in front of or near public buildings and at corporation headquarters, college campuses, city parks, or almost any conspicuous place in urban areas. The National Endowment for the Arts made its first grant in public art in 1969—for Alexander Calder's sculpture *La Grande Vitesse* in Grand Rapids, Michigan. After that time the N.E.A. made at least 20 public art awards each year. Beginning in 1963 the national government customarily has reserved 1 percent of the cost of construction of virtually all public buildings for artwork.

A part of the local environment in nearly every city, the public artworks doubtless received a mixed reception. Much of the native populace probably became accustomed to their presence, treating them as they would a building or a tree. Art lovers approved of the idea, if not the piece itself. Other people might consider the structure a waste of money but not necessarily offensive. The rub came when the wish for sophistication and environment enrichment came together with the free-wheeling spirit in the world of art in the last half of the 20th century. What moved and inspired the artist was not necessarily in step with the mood and taste of the people who had to pass by the structure every day. Two examples stood out. The Vietnam War Memorial, the work of Maya Ying Lin, was unveiled in Washington in 1982. A stark, black granite wall 500 feet long, inscribed with names of the war's dead, the memorial at first was criticized as shameful and no fitting expression of the dedication and sacrifice of the people whose names appeared on the structure. Only after construction of a more traditional sculpture of three soldiers in 1984 and another bearing a female army nurse in 1988 did the memorial come to be treated as hallowed ground. The second case emerged from the national government's wish to decorate the Javits Center, a federal building in New York City. The General Services Administration approved an ambitious project proposed by sculptor Richard Serra, a slight curving wall 120 feet long, 12 feet high called *Tilted Arc*. Erected in 1982, the wall represented to Serra and apparently to the G.S.A. a piece of art. What much of the public saw was an enormous piece of metal that rusted with age, a hulking eyesore that cut off vision and destroyed normal operations of the plaza in which it stood. Serra defended his artwork, claimed that he was exercising the artist's right to free expression, and took his case to court, but it was to no avail. Criticized and ridiculed from the time of its appearance, *Tilted Arc* was dismantled in 1989.

TABLE 16.9   MAJOR AMERICAN PAINTERS, ACTIVE DURING 1946–1990

Artist	Example of Work
Josef Albers	Homage to the Square (series)
Stuart Davis	Colonial Cubism
Willem de Kooning	Woman (series)
Helen Frankenthaler	Mountains and Sea
Hans Hofmann	The gate
Edward Hopper	Nighthawks
Robert Indiana	Love (series)
Jasper Johns	Three Flags
Franz Kline	Mahoning
Roy Lichtenstein	Masterpiece
Morris Louis	Unfurled (series)
Grandma Moses	Sugaring-Off
Robert Motherwell	Elegy for the Spanish Republic (series)
Barnett Newman	Concord
Georgia O'Keeffe	Cow's Skull
Jackson Pollock	Lavender Mist
Robert Rauschenberg	Gloria
Adolph (Ad) Reinhardt	Black Paintings
Larry Rivers	Dutch Masters (series)
Norman Rockwell	*Saturday Evening Post* Covers
Mark Rothko	No. 10
Ben Shahn	Sacco-Vanzetti Trial (series)
Charles Sheeler	Steel-Croton
Theodore Stamos	High Snow, Low Sun II
Frank Stella	Jill
Andy Warhol	Campbell Soup Cans (series)
Andrew Wyeth	Helga (series)

Source: The New York Public Library Desk Reference (New York, 1993), 165–68; Les Krantz, *American Artists: An Illustrated Survey of Contemporary Americans* (New York, 1985), many pages.

TABLE 16.10   MAJOR ART MUSEUMS IN THE UNITED STATES

Museum	Location	Year of Foundation
Art Institute of Chicago	Chicago, Ill.	1879
Brooklyn Museum of Art	Brooklyn, N.Y.	1889
Busch-Reisinger Museum	Cambridge, Mass.	1901
Carnegie Institute	Pittsburgh, Pa.	1896
Cincinnati Art Museum	Cincinnati, Ohio	1880
City Art Museum	St. Louis, Mo.	1912
Cleveland Museum of Art	Cleveland, Ohio	1913
Corcoran Gallery of Art	Washington, D.C.	1869
Currier Gallery of Art	Manchester, N.H.	1915
Dallas Museum of Art	Dallas, Tex.	1903
Denver Art Museum	Denver, Colo.	1917
Detroit Institute of Arts	Detroit, Mich.	1884
Fine Arts Museum of San Fran.	San Francisco, Calif.	1924
Freer Gallery of Art	Washington, D.C.	1923
Frick Collection	New York, N.Y.	1935
High Museum of Art	Atlanta, Ga.	1926
Huntington Library and Gallery	San Marino, Calif.	1919
John Herron Art Museum	Indianapolis, Ind.	1883
Los Angeles County Mus. of Art	Los Angeles, Calif.	1910
Metropolitan Museum of Art	New York, N.Y.	1870
Milwaukee Art Center	Milwaukee, Wis.	1888
Minneapolis Institute of Art	Minneapolis, Minn.	1915
Museum of Contemporary Art	Los Angeles, Calif.	1979
Museum of Fine Arts	Boston, Mass.	1870
Museum of Modern Art	New York, N.Y.	1929
Museum of the City of New York	New York, N.Y.	1923
National Collection, Fine Arts	Washington, D.C.	1906
National Gallery of Art	Washington, D.C.	1937
Nelson-Atkins Museum of Art	Kansas City, Mo.	1933
New-York Historical Society	New York, N.Y.	1804
Pennsylvania Academy Fine Arts	Philadelphia, Pa.	1805
Philadelphia Museum of Art	Philadelphia, Pa.	1975
Public Museum of Grand Rapids	Grand Rapids, Mich.	1854
San Diego Museum of Art	San Diego, Calif.	1925
San Fran. Museum of Modern Art	San Francisco, Calif.	1921
Scottsdale Center for Arts	Scottsdale, Ariz.	1975
Toledo Museum of Art	Toledo, Ohio	1901
Virginia Museum of Fine Arts	Richmond, Va.	1910
Walker Art Center	Minneapolis, Minn.	1879
Whitney Museum American Art	New York, N.Y.	1930
William H. Fogg Art Museum	Cambridge, Mass.	1895
Worcester Art Museum	Worcester, Mass.	1896

Source: The American Association of Museums, The Official Museum Directory, 1990 (Wilmette, Ill., 1989), numerous pages.

TABLE 16.11 TOP WORKS OF ART AT AUCTION, TO 1990

(paintings that sold for the highest prices)

Artist	Title/Date	Sale Date	Hammer Price	With[a] Premium
Vincent van Gogh	*Portrait du Dr. Gachet* (1890)	05/15/90	$75,000,000	$82,500,000
Pierre-Auguste Renoir	*Le Moulin de la Galette* (1876)	05/17/90	71,000,000	78,100,000
Pablo Picasso	*Les Noces de Pierrette* (1905)	11/30/89	49,200,000	49,200,000
Vincent van Gogh	*Irises* (1889)	11/11/87	49,000,000	53,900,000
Pablo Picasso	*Yo Picasso* (c. 1901)	05/09/89	43,500,000	47,850,000
Pablo Picasso	*Au Lapin Agile* (1905)	11/15/89	37,000,000	40,700,000
Vincent van Gogh	*Sunflowers* (1889)	03/30/87	36,292,500	39,921,750
Pablo Picasso	*Acrobate et Jeune Arlequin* (1905)	11/28/88	34,960,000	38,456,000
Pontormo	*Portrait of Duke Cosimo I de Medici*	05/31/89	32,000,000	35,200,000
Vincent van Gogh	*Autoportrait* (1888)	05/15/90	24,000,000	26,400,000
Edouard Manet	*La Rue Mosnier aux Drapeaux* (1878)	11/14/89	24,000,000	26,400,000
Pablo Picasso	*Le Miroir* (1932)	11/15/89	24,000,000	26,400,000
Pablo Picasso	*Maternité* (1901)	11/14/88	22,500,000	24,750,000
Claude Monet	*Dans la Prairie* (1876)	06/28/88	22,230,000	24,453,000
Paul Gauguin	*Mata Mua* (1892)	05/09/89	22,000,000	24,200,000
Pablo Picasso	*Les Tuileries* (1901)	06/25/90	21,612,500	23,773,750
John Constable	*The Lock*	11/14/90	19,230,540	21,153,594
Wassili Kandinsky	*Fugue* (1914)	05/17/90	19,000,000	20,900,000
Willem de Kooning	*Interchange* (1955)	11/08/89	18,800,000	20,680,000
Vincent van Gogh	*Le Pont de Trinquetaille* (1888)	06/29/87	18,515,000	20,366,500
Vincent van Gogh	*Le Vieil If* (1888)	11/14/89	18,500,000	20,350,000

[a] A premium is the 10% added to hammer price by auctioneer at most auctions.
Source: Ronald Alsop, ed., *The Wall Street Journal Almanac, 1998* (New York, 1997), 405.

TABLE 16.12 PERFORMING ARTS—SELECTED DATA, 1955–1969

(for season ending in year shown, except as indicated)

Item	1955	1960	1964	1965	1966	1967	1968	1969
Theater, legitimate, New York City								
Broadway shows	72	76	82	77	87	82	87	80
New productions, including revivals	58	58	63	67	68	69	73	67
Performances	8,917	9,214	7,975	10,000	10,360	10,152	10,056	9,672
Off Broadway productions	41	114	131	86	82	91	79	99
New	41	100	107	75	75	80	77	118
Performances	1,883	6,803	9,296	6,637	4,865	6,326	5,140	5,828
Dance groups								
Professional	. . .	139	196	. . .	. . .	. . .	. . .	. . .
Tours, October (towns and cities visited)	106	142	117	229	176	136	. . .	. . .
Performances	115	192	191	265	230	199	. . .	. . .
Performances, New York City Oct.–Feb.	197	191	222	340	. . .	. . .	. . .	. . .
Opera companies	543	754	754	732	752	918	. . .	. . .
Performances	3,217	4,232	3,877	4,176	4,777	5,487	. . .	. . .
Orchestras								
Symphony	1,029	1,226	1,363	1,385	. . .	. . .	1,441	1,441
College	240	250	284	290	. . .	. . .	298	298
Community	761	933	1,025	1,032	. . .	. . .	1,020	1,021
Urban	. . .	. . .	. . .	. . .	. . .	31	36	81
Metropolitan	. . .	18	29	38	48	48	59	63
Major	28	25	25	25	26	28	28	28
Musicians	2,079	. . .	2,207	2,216	2,343	[a]2,465	[b]2,396	[a]2,512
Concerts played	2,257	. . .	2,877	2,987	3,488	[a]3,658	[b]3,984	[a]3,976
Attendance 1,000	4,900	. . .	6,400	6,750	7,747	[c]8,393	[b]8,229	[a]8,176
Gross expenditures $1,000	13,838	. . .	24,100	27,700	38,384	41,245	[a]46,123	[a]51,746

[a] 27 orchestras reporting
[b] 26 orchestras reporting
[c] 25 orchestras reporting
Source: Bureau of Census, *Statistical Abstract of the United States, 1970* (Washington, D.C., 1970), 204.

TABLE 16.13 PERFORMING ARTS—SELECTED DATA, 1970–1990

(receipts and expenditures in millions of dollars; for season ending in year shown, except as indicated)

Item	1970	1975	1980	1984	1985	1986	1887	1988	1989	1990
Legitimate theater:										
Broadway shows:										
New productions	62	59	67	36	31	33	40	31	29	35
Playing weeks	1,047	1,101	1,541	1,119	1,062	1,049	1,031	1,114	1,097	1,062
Number of tickets sold (1,000)	. . .	. . .	9,380	7,898	7,156	6,527	6,968	8,142	7,968	8,039
Gross box office receipts	53.3	57.4	143.4	226.5	208.0	190.6	207.2	253.4	262.0	283.3
Road shows										
Playing weeks	1,024	799	1,351	1,057	993	983	901	893	869	944
Gross box office receipts	48.0	50.9	181.2	206.2	225.9	235.6	224.2	222.9	255.5	367.1
Nonprofit professional theatres:										
Companies reporting	. . .	39	147	230	217	201	188	189	192	185
Gross income	. . .	34.5	113.6	226.6	234.7	263.8	271.2	276.4	349.0	307.6
Earned income	. . .	21.8	67.3	145.7	146.1	160.8	165.2	167.0	224.6	188.4
Contributed income	. . .	12.7	46.3	80.9	88.6	103.0	106.0	109.4	124.4	119.2
Gross expenses	. . .	34.3	113.6	230.3	239.3	263.3	272.8	277.9	349.2	306.3
Productions	. . .	398	1,852	3,434	2,710	2,944	2,427	2,369	2,469	2,265
Performances	. . .	11,952	42,109	56,735	52,341	57,727	46,768	46,149	53,263	46,131
Total attendance (mil.)	. . .	5.4	14.2	15.5	14.2	14.8	14.6	13.9	18.7	15.2
Opera companies	648	807	986	1,051	1,123	1,176	1,224	1,250	1,285	. . .
Major	35	54	109	154	168	170	174	187	209	. . .
Expenditures	36.5	. . .	133.6	236.7	256.5	270.3	321.1	352.3	403.8	. . .
Other companies	266	335	458	491	576	602	658	654	658	. . .
Workshops	347	418	419	406	379	404	392	409	418	. . .
Opera performances	4,779	6,428	9,391	10,421	10,642	11,080	11,794	12,361	15,098	. . .
Operas performed	341	387	497	576	578	660	622	658	731	. . .
Musical performances	. . .	. . .	1,397	2,787	4,983	6,993	7,759	8.,836	9,825	1
Musicals performed	. . .	. . .	104	129	242	301	278	296	279	. . .
World premieres	17	16	79	101	121	116	129	141	165	. . .
Attendance (mil.)	4.6	8.0	10.7	13.0	14.1	14.4	16.4	17.7	21.4	. . .
Symphony orchestras	1,441	1,463	1,572	1,572	1,572	1,572	1,572	1,572	1,666	1,666
College	298	300	385	380	371	371	365	350	422	. . .
Community	1,019	1,003	926	937	946	927	936	903	924	. . .
Urban	24	41	85	89	89	93	92	103	103	. . .
Metropolitan	72	90	115	96	96	107	102	123	121	. . .
Regional	. . .	. . .	29	40	40	43	45	57	59	. . .
Major	28	29	32	30	30	31	32	36	37	. . .
Concerts	6,599	14,171	22,229	19,086	19,969	20,272	20,059	17,774	17,361	16,725
Attendance (mil.)	12.7	18.3	22.6	23.2	23.7	25.4	25.1	23.6	22.4	22.2
Gross income	73.3	124.5	246.3	379.0	435.4	480.5	523.6	561.8	619.5	679.9
Earned income	43.1	70.9	141.2	220.2	250.7	282.4	305.9	332.9	363.3	405.4
Contributed income	30.2	53.6	105.1	158.8	184.7	198.1	217.7	228.9	256.2	274.5
Gross expenses	76.4	129.5	252.1	389.8	441.8	491.2	525.4	571.3	600.0	665.4

Source: Bureau of the Census, *Statistical Abstract of the United States, 1993* (Washington, D.C., 1993), 256.

TABLE 16.14   ATTENDANCE AT ARTS ACTIVITIES, 1987
(percentage of people who attended specified arts activities in previous 12 months)

	Jazz	Classical Music	Opera	Musicals	Plays	Ballet	Museums
Total	10	13	3	18	12	4	22
Age							
18–24	16	12	2	16	12	4	22
25–34	15	12	2	18	12	5	26
35–44	9	16	4	22	15	6	27
45–54	8	15	4	20	13	4	22
55–64	5	2	3	18	11	4	19
65–74	3	13	3	14	10	3	15
75 & Older	1	8	2	9	. . .	2	9
Sex							
Male	10	11	3	16	11	3	21
Female	9	14	3	20	13	6	23
Education							
Grade School	1	2	1	4	2	1	3
Some H.S.	4	3	1	6	4	1	7
H.S. Grad.	7	7	2	13	7	2	15
Some College	14	17	3	23	16	6	31
Coll. Grad.	19	29	7	36	26	10	45
Grad. School	22	40	10	42	36	14	56
Income							
Under $5,000	9	9	2	10	8	3	14
$5,000–9,999	7	7	2	8	5	2	13
$10,000–14,999	7	9	2	12	6	3	16
$15,000–24,999	9	11	2	15	10	4	20
$25,000–49,999	11	17	3	25	16	5	29
$50,000 & Over	18	30	9	39	30	11	46
Unknown	9	13	4	18	11	4	21
Region							
Northeast	8	13	4	20	14	5	21
Midwest	10	15	1	17	11	4	21
South	9	10	2	13	10	4	19
West	12	15	4	19	13	5	30

Source: Dow Jones Inc., *American Demographics*, September 1987, 45.

Architecture

Architecture had some similarity with art. Both were creative activities that represented an expression of individualism. As with artists, architects were identified with their work. The two differed in several ways, not the least of which was the element of utilitarianism. The architect had to be concerned with function as well as form. The painter or sculptor of the post-1950 era largely did what he or she wanted. Architecture was a profession; part of the world of competitive business and industry, it could count on a steady clientele but was also accountable to the same crowd. Of the many people who considered themselves artists, few would call art their profession; an even smaller number made their living in the production of creative art.

In perhaps the most mundane level of architecture, residential housing, designs remained basically conservative and traditional throughout the period. The Levittowns of the immediate postwar era offered only two styles, ranch and Cape Cod. The late 1950s and 1960s produced a split-level design that featured living space at the expense of storage (closets, cupboards, and the like). Once that fad had passed, most housing returned to variations of the one-story ranch, Cape Cod, or two-story colonial structures. Rental apartment complexes followed similarly conventional styles and newer condominiums—sort of enlarged privately owned apartments—showed little more creativity. The size of houses increased with passage of years and expansion of the economy. By the 1990s builders were erecting entire subdivisions of privately owned single-family homes, each of which resembled what once had been a multifamily complex or office building.

An architect rarely left a mark in residential buildings, unless it was his or her own house. Reputations and careers came from public structures. In this area the artistic aspect of architecture suggested a continuing measure of diversity and individuality. The practical and commercial aspect imposed restraints and lended the profession to trends and at least loosely defined schools of style. The dominant architectural theme in the years following the Second World War consisted largely of extending and building upon what had been identified as the International Style. Stressing clean, reasonably simple, functional designs, the style originated in the fact that its principles had received widespread approval in several areas, notably in North America and Europe. In the United States it also meant that the profession contained a generous sprinkling of architects from abroad. Ludwig Mies van der Rohe, from Germany, and Eliel Saarinen and his son, Eero, from Finland, were examples. Most architects heavily utilized steel and glass in their structures. The United Nations buildings in New York, the product of a committee of international architects, stood as an example.

U.S. architects, or perhaps it was their customers, continued a fascination with tall buildings, and the prewar competition in height—mostly between New York and Chicago—continued through much of the century. For all its attributes, the Empire State Building in New York, completed in 1931, was best known for many years as the nation's, indeed the world's, tallest building. Construction of the twin World Trade Centers in 1973 shifted the crown, but it also seemed to solidify New York's leadership. In short order, however, Chicago, evidently not content with being the "second city" in everything, could boast of its Sears Tower, 101 feet taller than any building in New York. Architects showed an inclination toward diversity in the construction of skyscrapers. The Transamerica building in San Francisco, completed in 1973, was a pyramid; the Pennzoil Place in Houston (1976) had twin trapezoidal towers. Many people considered the tapered John Hancock Building in Chicago, constructed in the late 1960s, to be the most impressive of the postwar skyscrapers.

As a new generation of architects began to come on line in the 1960s, the influence of the International Style waned somewhat. Movement away from the rectangular building opened the door for freedom of choice in building shape. An emphasis on steel-supported concrete beginning in the 1960s produced new "brutalist" forms and finishes. The arrival in the 1970s and 1980s of a postmodernist element to architecture stimulated much disagreement as to merit. Although the theme by definition suggested variation of style, the postmodernist thrust generally was away from the sleek, simple style of the Hancock building and in the direction of more ornamentation and greater recognition of the contributions of history. The historic preservation movement that began in the 1970s called for restructuring and rebuilding dilapidated waterfront areas in such cities as St. Louis and Baltimore, in the preservation of old buildings and restoration of whole areas of inner cities. Although diversity and freedom did mark the contruction of buildings and cities at the start of the 1990s, architecture remained a part of the world of business, commerce, and living space of middle-class America. One thus would not find the extent of individuality and creativity present in such categories of art as painting and sculpture.

I. M. Pei's design: the John F. Kennedy Library in Boston, Massachusetts, 1965–79 (Courtesy April Summitt)

TABLE 16.15 MAJOR AMERICAN ARCHITECTS, ACTIVE DURING 1946–1990

Architect	Example of Project	Location
Max Abramovitz	Corning Glass Building	N.Y.C.
Pietro Belluschi	Juilliard School of Music	N.Y.C.
Marcel Breuer	Whitney Museum of Art	N.Y.C.
Gordon Bunshaft	Lever House	N.Y.C.
Joseph Esherick	U.S. Embassy	Bolivia
James Freed	Holocaust Museum	Washington, D.C.
R. Buckminster Fuller	Expo 67	Montreal
Bruce Graham	Sears Tower	Chicago
Walter Gropius	Pan Am Building	N.Y.C.
Wallace K. Harrison	Metropolitan Opera House	N.Y.C.
Philip K. Johnson	A.T. & T. Sony Bldg.	N.Y.C.
Fay E. Jones	Pinecote Pavilion	Picayune, Miss.
Louis Kahn	Yale Art Gallery	New Haven
William Lescaze	Borg-Warner Building	Chicago
Charles M. McKim	Lutheran Church of Redeemer	Houston
Ludwig Mies van der Rohe	Buildings 845–860	Chicago
Richard J. Neutra	Orange Co. Courthouse	Santa Ana, Calif.
Gyo Obata	Air & Space Museum	Washington, D.C.
William Pedersen	333 Wacker Drive	Chicago
I. M. Pei	Addition to the Louvre	Paris
William Pereira	TransAmerica Building	San Francisco
John C. Portman	Renaissance Center	Detroit
Kevin Roche	Air Force Museum	near Dayton, Ohio
John W. Root	Palmolive Building	Chicago)
Paul Rudolph	Art & Architecture Bldg.	Yale U.
Eero Saarinen	Gateway Arch	St. Louis
Der Scutt	Trump Tower	N.Y.C.
Josep Sert	Holyoke Center	Harvard U.
Louis Skidmore	Terrace Plaza Hotel	Cincinnati
Clarence S. Stein	Temple Emanu-el	N.Y.C.
Adrian Smith	A.T.&T. Center	Chicago
Ralph T. Walker	IBM Research Lab.	Poughkeepsie, N.Y.
Roland A. Wank	Union Terminal	Cincinnati
Frank Lloyd Wright	Guggenheim Museum	N.Y.C.
William Wurster	Bank of America Hq.	San Francisco
Minoru Yamasaki	World Trade Center	N.Y.C.

Source: Les Krantz, *American Architects* (New York, 1989), many pages; Mark Hoffman, *The World Almanac and Book of Facts, 1992* (New York, 1991), 340–41.

TABLE 16.16 AMERICAN INSTITUTE OF ARCHITECTS GOLD MEDALISTS, 1947–1990

(First awarded in 1907, the American Institute of Architects Gold Medal recognizes outstanding lifetime achievement.)

Year	Medalists
1947	Eliel Saarinen, Bloomfield Hills, Mich.
1948	Charles Donagh Maginnis, Boston
1949	Frank Lloyd Wright, Spring Green, Wis.
1950	Sir Patrick Abercrombie, London
1951	Bernard Ralph Maybeck, San Francisco
1952	Auguste Perret, Paris
1953	Williams Adams Delano, New York
1955	Willem Marinus Dudok, Hilversum, Holland
1956	Clarence S. Stein, New York
1957	Ralph Walker, New York
1957	Louis Skidmore, New York
1958	John Wellborn Root, Chicago
1959	Walter Gropius, Cambridge, Mass.
1960	Ludwig Mies van der Rohe, Chicago
1961	Le Corbusier (Charles Edouard Jeanneret-Gris), Paris
1962[a]	Eero Saarinen, Bloomfield Hills, Mich.
1963	Alvar Aalto, Helsinki
1964	Pier Luigi Nervi, Rome
1966	Kenzo Tange, Tokyo
1967	Wallace K. Harrison, New York
1968	Marcel Breuer, New York
1969	William Wilson Wurster, San Francisco
1970	Richard Buckminster Fuller, Carbondale, Ill.
1971	Louis I. Kahn, Phildadelphia
1972	Pietro Belluschi, Boston
1977[a]	Richard Joseph Neutra, Los Angeles
1978	Philip Johnson, New York
1979	Ieoh Ming Pei, New York
1981	Josep Lluis Sert, Cambridge, Mass.
1982	Romaldo Giurgola, New York
1983	Nathaniel A. Owings, San Francisco
1985[a]	William Caudill, Houston
1986	Arthur Erickson, Canada
1989	Joseph Esherick, San Francisco
1990	Fay Jones, Fayetteville, Ark.

[a] Awarded posthumously.

Source: John Wright, *The Universal Almanac, 1995* (New York, 1994), 643.

TABLE 16.17 TALLEST BUILDINGS IN THE UNITED STATES, 1990

Rank	Building	City	Year Built	Stories	Height (in feet)
1.	Sears Tower	Chicago	1974	110	1,454
2.	World Trade Center, North	New York	1972	110	1,368
3.	World Trade Center, South	New York	1973	110	1,362
4.	Empire State Building	New York	1931	102	1,250
5.	Amoco	Chicago	1973	80	1,136
6.	John Hancock Building	Chicago	1968	100	1,127
7.	Chrysler Building	New York	1930	77	1,046
8.	First Interstate Center	Los Angeles	1989	75	1,018
9.	Texas Commerce Tower	Houston	1982	79	1,000
10.	Two Prudential Plaza	Chicago	1990	64	995
11.	Allied Bank Plaza	Houston	1983	71	972
12.	333 S. Wacker Drive	Chicago	1990	65	970
13.	Columbia Center	Seattle	1984	76	954
14.	American International	New York	1932	67	950
15.	One Liberty Place	Philadelphia	1987	60	945
16.	40 Wall Tower	New York	1966	71	927
17.	Interfirst Plaza Tower	Dallas	1985	71	921
18.	Citicorp Center	New York	1977	55	915
19.	Transco Tower	Houston	1983	64	901
20.	AT&T Corporate Center	Chicago	1988	60	875
21.	900 N. Michigan Avenue	Chicago	1989	66	875
22.	Water Tower Place	Chicago	1976	74	859
23.	First Interstate Bank	Los Angeles	1974	62	858
24.	Transamerica Pyramid	San Francisco	1972	48	853
25.	First National Bank	Chicago	1969	60	850
26.	GE Rockefeller Center	New York	1933	70	850
27.	Two Liberty Place	Philadelphia	1990	58	848
28.	USX Tower	Pittsburgh	1970	64	841
29.	Atlantic Center (IBM)	Atlanta	1988	50	820
30.	City Spire	New York	1987	72	814

Note: Antennas and flagpoles not included.
Source: Wright, *Universal Almanac, 1995,* 347.

TABLE 16.18 LONGEST AMERICAN BRIDGES, 1969

Name	Location	Type	Length (ft) Main Span	Year Completed
Verrazano-Narrows	Lower N.Y. Bay	S	4,260	1964
Golden Gate	San Francisco Bay	S	4,200	1937
Mackinac	Northern Michigan	S	3,800	1957
George Washington	Hudson River, N.Y.C.	S	3,500	1931
Tacoma Narrows	Puget Sound, Wash.	S	2,800	1950
Transbay (2 spans)	San Francisco Bay	S	2,310	1936
Bronx Whitestone	East River, N.Y.C.	S	2,300	1939
Delaware Memorial (2 spans)	Wilmington	S	2,150	1951–68
Seaway Skyway	Ogdensburg, N.Y.	S	2,150	1960
Gas Pipe Line	Atchafalaya River, La.	S	2,000	1951
Walt Whitman	Delaware River, Philadelphia	S	2,000	1957
Ambassador	Detroit River, Detroit	S	1,850	1929
Throgs Neck	East River, N.Y.C.	S	1,800	1961
Benjamin Franklin	Delaware River, Philadelphia	S	1,750	1926
New River Gorge	Fayetteville, W.Va.	SA	1,700	1977
Bayonne	Bayonne, N.J.	SA	1,675	1931
Commodore J. Barry	Chester, Pa.	C	1,644	1974
Bear Mountain	Peekskill, N.Y.	S	1,632	1924
Wm. Preston Lane Jr. (2 spans)[a]	Annapolis, Md.	S	1,600	1952–73
Williamsburg	East River, N.Y.C.	S	1,600	1903
Newport	Newport, R.I.	S	1,600	1969
Brooklyn	East River, N.Y.C.	S	1,595	1883
Greater N. Orleans	Miss. River, La.	C	1,576	1958
Jesse Jones Mem.	Houston Ship Canal	CA	1,500	1982

Note: S=Suspension; SA=Steel Arch; C=Cantilever; CA=Concrete Arch.
[a] The second span of these structures completed in 1973, is called the Chesapeake Bay Bridge.
Source: Otto Johnson, *The 1988 Information Please Almanac* (Boston, 1987), 587–88.

Bridges

Bridge building represented a different sort of architecture that demanded no less skill in arts and science than the construction of buildings. The postwar era was a time of bridge building, and while size of bridges depended upon need and surroundings, there existed a form of competition for the longest span. To an extent greater than in prewar years, the suspension bridge, with its massive moorings and undulating steel cables, remained the favorite for long stretches. Bridge building otherwise produced several highlights between 1950 and 1980. The Verrazano-Narrows bridge in New York, completed in 1964, nudged out the Golden Gate bridge for longest span. The most striking "new" bridge, where none previously had existed, was over Mackinac Straits in northern Michigan. "Big Mac," a compelling structure in its own right, linked Michigan's two peninsulas together in 1957. A new bridge over Tacoma Narrows in Washington, finished in 1950, proved to be more stable than its predecessor, "Galloping Gertie," which twisted in a storm and fell into Puget Sound in 1940, the year it had opened. One of the most scenic, and despite a somewhat remote location, most popular structures was the bridge over the New River Gorge in West Virginia, completed in 1977. One day each year, the state opened the bridge to regulated "recreational" jumping (bungee jumping and mini-parachute jumping). None of the new structures, however, could dethrone the monarch, and it grew grander with age. The president and the nation paused in 1983 to celebrate the 100th birthday of the Brooklyn Bridge.

"Big Mac," over the Straits of Mackinac in northern Michigan. Completed in 1957, it was the second longest bridge in the United States. (Linda Norris, Michigan Department of Transportation)

Bridge over scenic New River Gorge, Fayetteville, West Virginia. Completed in 1977, it was, at 1,700 feet, the longest steel arch bridge in the United States. (David Bowen)

CHAPTER 17 Entertainment

Entertainment, the occupying of time not devoted to obligatory or needed duties, depended in the first instance upon preference, of course, and in the flourishing, ever-changing American culture it also depended on money. One did in spare time what one preferred to do, what was accessible and affordable; in a competitive society, what other people were doing also had an influence. Driven by businesspeople ever watchful for new products to sell, American society passed through a neverending series of fads and preoccupations in recreational activity. Purchase of a new house or a first house after World War II led to backyard cooking as a form of recreation. Families with a comfortable income or who were willing to stretch the budget might have a swimming pool installed in the back. Homeowners whose parents, or at least grandparents, never had taken a vacation, began to set aside money and a week or two for a family trip; with each year the trip took longer, and it carried the family farther. Some individuals or families took to boating and spent much of summer weekends on the lake; others took to camping. By the 1980s the popularity of camping was such that for one to be assured of a campsite on a summertime holiday weekend, it was necessary to make a reservation months in advance. Capitalism kept turning out the machines and devices: The boats and camping equipment were followed, starting in the 1960s, by snowmobiles; by 1990 one could acquire a Jet Ski, what amounted to a snowmobile that traveled on water. Each of these instruments of culture commanded a following in the American populace, each created its own industry and each cost quite a bit of money. In the broadest sense, entertainment encompassed an exceptionally broad range of personal choices in how to spend leisure time. In a more narrow and probably more familiar sense, it pertained to a special entertainment industry.

Superimposed over the various individualized entertainment activities spread a vast, ever-expanding commercialized establishment designed to attract a mass audience. If one excluded professional and some aspects of nonprofessional sports—which will be addressed in a separate unit—this empire was composed largely of five units: movies, radio, television, popular music, and live theater as exemplified by the Broadway stage. Four of the five were a part of the revolution in electronics that took place after 1950. Broadway, the weakest sibling in terms of audience, did not rely on new technology, but because of links to the other four elements, it claimed a spot in the empire.

Up-and-coming young actress Lauren Bacall chats with her accompanist, Vice President Harry S. Truman, in 1945. (Harry S. Truman Library, courtesy Stock Montage)

All the forces that had driven a commercial entertainment industry in previous decades remained in place and were vastly enlarged in the postwar era. The entertainment industry thus benefited from a large increase in population, an enormous increase in disposable wealth, and an increase in the population financially able to partake of commercial entertainment. Technological change transformed the industry in several categories. Performers in entertainment continued to be viewed as larger than life, the object of popular adulation, and the recipients of great sums of money. More than ever before, the entertainment industry took on international dimension. Although the United States remained the world leader in professional entertainment and it continued to have access to foreign markets, the Americans drew heavily upon foreign—mostly European—talent, especially in the segments that featured acting and popular music. Perhaps to a greater degree than at any time, the United States—and Americans—continued to be defined in the world by what its entertainment industry produced.

Original Names of Selected People in the Entertainment Business

Many people in entertainment found it wise to select a name to substitute for what they had been given at the start of life. The purpose in most cases was to promote simplicity, a name that was easier to pronounce and to remember, or simply something that sounded better. There is as well some indication that name change could represent an act of anglicization of an "ethnic sounding" name, for the purpose of facilitating acceptance in mainstream American culture. Whatever the reason for change, the substitute name usually became the only one that the public remembered or even knew about. The list below contains a few examples.

Alan Alda: Alphonso D'Abruzzo
Woody Allen: Allen Konigsberg
Fred Astaire: Frederick Austerlitz
Lauren Bacall: Betty Joan Perske
Anne Bancroft: Anna Maria Italiano
Tony Bennett: Anthony Benedetto
Irving Berlin: Israel Baline
Jack Benny: Benjamin Kubelsky
Boy George: George Alan O'Dowd
Albert Brooks: Albert Einstein
Ellen Burstyn: Edna Gilhooley
Nicolas Cage: Nicholas Coppola
Maria Callas: Maria Kalogeropoulos
Chubby Checker: Ernest Evans
Cher: Cherilyn Sarkisian
Michael Connors: Kreker Ohanian
Alice Cooper: Vincent Furnier
Joan Crawford: Lucille Le Sueur
Tom Cruise: Thomas Mapother IV
Bobby Darin: Walden Robert Cassotto
Doris Day: Doris von Kappelhoff
John Denver: Henry John Deutschendorf, Jr.
Kirk Douglas: Issur Danielovitch
Dale Evans: Francis Smith
Jamie Farr: Jameel Farah
Arlene Francis: Arlene Kazanjian
Connie Francis: Concetta Franconero
Judy Garland: Frances Gumm
Kathie Lee Gifford: Kathie Epstein
Cary Grant: Archibald Leach
Lee Grant: Lyova Rosenthal
Rex Harrison: Reginald Carey
Barbara Hershey: Barbara Herzstein
William Holden: William Beedle
Elton John: Reginald Dwight

Larry King: Larry Zeigler
Ted Knight: Tadeus Wladyslaw Konopka
Michael Landon: Eugene Horowitz
Queen Latifah: Dana Owens
Bruce Lee: Lee Yuen Kam
Peggy Lee: Norma Egstrom
Jerry Lewis: Joseph Levitch
Hal Linden: Harold Lipshitz
Sophia Loren: Sophia Scicolone
Madonna: Madonna Louise Ciccone
Lee Majors: Harvey Lee Yeary II
Walter Matthau: Walter Matuschanskayasky
Dean Martin: Dino Crocetti
Ray Milland: Reginald Truscott-Jones
Marilyn Monroe: Norma Jean Mortenson (later Baker)
Demi Moore: Demetria Guynes
Minnie Pearl: Sarah Ophelia Cannon
Stefanie Powers: Stefania Federkiewicz
Tony Randall: Leonard Rosenberg
Edward G. Robinson: Emmanuel Goldenberg
Martin Sheen: Ramon Estevez
Ringo Starr: Richard Starkey
Sting: Gordon Sumner
Robert Taylor: Spangler Brugh
Danny Thomas: Muzyad Yakhoob
Sid Vicious: John Simon Ritchie
John Wayne: Marion Morrison
Natalie Wood: Natasha Gurdin

Source: Robert Famighetti, *The World Almanac and Book of Facts, 1999* (Mahwah, N.J., 1998), 371–72.

The Broadway Stage

Live American theatre had its most illustrious expression on the stages of Broadway in New York City, and the Broadway stage began the postwar era with a bang. In both drama and in musical production Broadway reached a golden age that ran from the 1940s into the 1960s. Led by the work of such playwrights as Arthur Miller (*Death of a Salesman, The Crucible*) and Tennessee Williams (*A Streetcar Named Desire, Cat on a Hot Tin Roof*), Broadway drama gave professional birth to individuals who would become stalwarts of entertainment for years to come: Marlon Brando, Montgomery Clift, Paul Newman, Joanne Woodward. The string of successes in musical theatre was even more striking. There were the composers: Rodgers and Hammerstein, Lerner and Loewe, Frank Loesser, Cole Porter, Jule Styne, Bernstein and Sondheim, and the shows: *South Pacific, Carousel, My Fair Lady, Guys and Dolls, Camelot, West Side Story,* and many others. The Broadway setting probably constituted elitist entertainment, but its effect went beyond elitism. Broadway musicals supplied some of the nation's most popular music, and the Broadway stage served as training ground for what the general public would see in movies, and in time on television.

The golden age did not last long. Having lost some of its premier agents—to death or through defection to Hollywood—Broadway experienced, although not as profoundly as movies, competition from television. The popularity of live theatre declined sharply in the 1970s, and after a brief recovery in the early 1980s, attendance leveled off at approximately what it had been at the end of the 1950s—a disappointing level, perhaps, in view of the growth in population but still enough to leave the institution with a great deal of life, creativity, and excitement.

During those years Broadway set off into several new avenues. Rock music arrived, as inevitably it would, in *Godspell* and *Jesus Christ*

Superstar; profanity on stage became commonplace; nudity made an appearance in *Hair* and *Oh! Calcutta*. Homosexuality became a common theme in the 1980s, if only because of empathy produced by the spread of AIDS, which had a profound effect on the Broadway community. The void left by Rodgers and Hammerstein and Lerner and Loewe was at least partly filled by Stephen Sondheim (*Company, Follies, A Little Night Music*) and British composer Andrew Lloyd Webber (*Cats, Evita, Phantom of the Opera*). In something of a reversal of practices of the 1950s, Broadway began to attract some of the best of filmdom to the live stage (although most had begun on the stage). Proliferation of revivals in the late 1980s perhaps suggested a shortage of original material, but even so, a new edition of *Guys and Dolls* still was delightful. Good new music continued to originate from the stage, if at a pace slower than in the 1940s and 1950s. Broadway held on and maintained

a special niche in American entertainment. There was a semipermanent clientele, of course, and the most prestigious American stage stood as a continuing tourist attraction. After all, one had not truly visited New York until one had been to a Broadway musical.

TABLE 17.1 BROADWAY OVER THE YEARS, 1945–1991

Theatre Season	Number of Productions	Ticket Prices
1945–46	98	$6.60
1950–51	88	$7.20
1955–56	73	$7.50
1960–61	63	$8.60
1965–66	76	$11.90
1970–71	56	$15.00
1975–76	65	$17.50
1980–81	63	$32.00
1985–86	42	$43.00
1990–91	27	$55.00

Source: Thomas S. Hischak, *The Theatregoers Almanac* (Westport, Conn., 1997), 3–4.

TABLE 17.2 BROADWAY SEASON STATISTICS, 1959–1990

Season	Gross (mil $)	Attendance (mil)	Playing Weeks	New Productions
1959–1960	46	7.9	1,156	58
1960–1961	44	7.7	1,210	48
1961–1962	44	6.8	1,168	53
1962–1963	44	7.4	1,134	54
1963–1964	40	6.8	1,107	63
1964–1965	50	8.2	1,250	67
1965–1966	54	9.6	1,295	68
1966–1967	55	9.3	1,269	69
1967–1968	59	9.5	1,259	74
1968–1969	58	8.6	1,209	67
1969–1970	53	7.1	1,047	62
1970–1971	55	7.4	1,107	49
1971–1972	52	6.5	1,157	55
1972–1973	45	5.4	889	55
1973–1974	46	5.7	907	43
1974–1975	57	6.6	1,101	54
1975–1976	71	7.3	1,136	55
1976–1977	93	8.8	1,349	54
1977–1978	114	9.6	1,433	42
1978–1979	134	9.6	1,542	50
1979–1980	146	9.6	1,540	61
1980–1981	197	11.0	1,544	60
1981–1982	223	10.1	1,455	48
1982–1983	209	8.4	1,258	50
1983–1984	227	7.9	1,097	36
1984–1985	208	7.3	1,075	33
1985–1986	190	6.5	1,045	33
1986–1987	206	7.0	1,038	41
1987–1988	252	8.1	1,116	32
1988–1989	265	8.0	1,097	30
1989–1990	282	8.0	1,061	35

Source: Famighetti, *The World Almanac, 1999,* 179.

TABLE 17.3 RECORD LONG-RUN BROADWAY PLAYS[a], AS OF 1990

Play	Performances
Chorus Line	6,137
Oh, Calcutta (revival)	5,959
42nd Street	3,486
Grease	3,388
Fiddler on the Roof	3,242
Cats	3,237
Life With Father	3,224[b]
Tobacco Road	3,182
Hello, Dolly!	2,844
My Fair Lady	2,717
Annie	2,377
Man of La Mancha	2,328
Abie's Irish Rose	2,327
Oklahoma!	2,212
Pippin	1,944
South Pacific	1,925
Magic Show	1,920
Deathtrap	1,792
Gemini	1,788
Harvey	1,775
Dancin'	1,774
La Cage aux Folles	1,761
Hair	1,750
The Wiz	1,672
Born Yesterday	1,642
Ain't Misbehavin'	1,604
Best Little Whorehouse in Texas	1,584
Mary, Mary	1,572
Evita	1,567
Voice of the Turtle	1,557
Barefoot in the Park	1,530
Dreamgirls	1,521
Mame	1,508
Same Time, Next Year	1,453
Arsenic and Old Lace	1,444
The Sound of Music	1,443
How To Succeed in Business Without Really Trying	1,417
Me and My Girl	1,412
Hellzapoppin	1,404
The Music Man	1,375
Funny Girl	1,348
Mumenschanz	1,326
Les Miserables	1,319[b]
Oh! Calcutta! (Original)	1,314
Brighton Beach Memoirs	1,299
Angel Street	1,295
Lightnin'	1,291
Promises, Promises	1,281
The King and I	1,246
Cactus Flower	1,234
Sleuth	1,222
Torch Song Trilogy	1,222
"1776"	1,217
Equus	1,209
Sugar Babies	1,208
Guys and Dolls	1,200
Amadeus	1,181
Cabaret	1,165
Mister Roberts	1,157
Annie Get Your Gun	1,147
Seven Year Itch	1,141
Butterflies Are Free	1,128
Pins and Needles	1,108

[a] Performances through July 2, 1990.
[b] Still running July 2, 1990.
Source: Mark S. Hoffman, *The World Almanac and Book of Facts, 1992* (New York, 1991), 309.

The Tony Awards

The Tony Awards began modestly in 1947 as an opportunity for the family of Broadway performers to recognize excellence in the art. Named after Antoinette Perry, former chair of the American Theater Wing, sponsor of the program, the Tony Awards at first discouraged a spirit of competition. Nominations were not announced; persons honored (no mention of a winner) received a scroll and either a compact or a cigarette lighter. The selection committee recognized not only an actress and actor but also "best featured" performers of either gender, which generally referred to a supporting role. In 1956 Tony nominations were made public, and the contest was on. With television coverage beginning in 1967, the awards ceremony became a show, and the Tony emerged as a sibling—albeit a younger and smaller one—to the Oscar.

TABLE 17.4 TONY AWARDS—BEST PLAYS AND MUSICALS, 1947–1990

Year	Play	Musical
1947	No award	No award
1948	Mister Roberts	No award
1949	Death of a Salesman	Kiss Me, Kate
1950	The Cocktail Party	South Pacific
1951	The Rose Tattoo	Guys and Dolls
1952	The Fourposter	The King and I
1953	The Crucible	Wonderful Town
1954	The Teahouse of the August Moon	Kismet
1955	The Desperate Hours	The Pajama Game
1956	The Diary of Anne Frank	Damn Yankees
1957	Long Day's Journey Into Night	My Fair Lady
1958	Sunrise at Campobello	The Music Man
1959	J.B.	Redhead
1960	The Miracle Worker	Tie: Fiorello! and The Sound of Music
1961	Becket	Bye Bye Birdie
1962	A Man for All Seasons	How to Succeed in Business Without Really Trying
1963	Who's Afraid of Virginia Woolf?	A Funny Thing Happened On the Way to the Forum
1964	Luther	Hello, Dolly!
1965	The Subject Was Roses	Fiddler on the Roof
1966	Marat/Sade	Man of La Mancha
1967	The Homecoming	Cabaret
1968	Rosencrantz and Guildenstern Are Dead	Hallelujah, Baby!
1969	The Great White Hope	1776
1970	Borstal Boy	Applause
1971	Sleuth	Company
1972	Sticks and Bones	Two Gentlemen of Verona
1973	That Championship Season	A Little Night Music
1974	The River Niger	Raisin
1975	Equus	The Wiz
1976	Travesties	A Chorus Line
1977	The Shadow Box	Annie
1978	Da	Ain't Misbehavin'
1979	The Elephant Man	Sweeney Todd
1980	Children of a Lesser God	Evita
1981	Amadeus	42nd Street
1982	Nicholas Nickleby	Nine
1983	Torch Song Trilogy	Cats
1984	The Real Thing	La Cage Aux Folles
1985	Biloxi Blues	Big River
1986	I'm Not Rappaport	The Mystery of Edwin Drood
1987	Fences	Les Misérables
1988	M. Butterfly	Phantom of the Opera
1989	The Heidi Chronicles	Jerome Robbins' Broadway
1990	The Grapes of Wrath	City of Angels

Source: Hischak, Theatregoers Almanac, 167–68.

TABLE 17.5 BEST ACTRESS—PLAYS, 1947–1990

Year	Actress	Play
1947	Tie: Ingrid Bergman / Helen Hayes	Joan of Lorraine; / Happy Birthday
1948	Tie: Judith Anderson / Katharine Cornell / Jessica Tandy	Medea; / Antony and Cleopatra; / A Streetcar Named Desire
1949	Martita Hunt	The Madwoman of Chaillot
1950	Shirley Booth	Come Back, Little Sheba
1951	Uta Hagen	The Country Girl
1952	Julie Harris	I Am a Camera
1953	Shirley Booth	Time of the Cuckoo
1954	Audrey Hepburn	Ondine
1955	Nancy Kelly	The Bad Seed
1956	Julie Harris	The Lark
1957	Margaret Leighton	Separate Tables
1958	Helen Hayes	Time Remembered
1959	Gertrude Berg	A Majority of One
1960	Anne Bancroft	The Miracle Worker
1961	Joan Plowright	A Taste of Honey
1962	Margaret Leighton	The Night of the Iguana
1963	Uta Hagen	Who's Afraid of Virginia Woolf?
1964	Sandy Dennis	Any Wednesday
1965	Irene Worth	Tiny Alice
1966	Rosemary Harris	The Lion in Winter
1967	Beryl Reid	The Killing of Sister George
1968	Zoe Caldwell	The Prime of Miss Jean Brodie
1969	Julie Harris	Forty Carats
1970	Tammy Grimes	Private Lives
1971	Maureen Stapleton	The Gingerbread Lady
1972	Sada Thompson	Twigs
1973	Julie Harris	The Last of Mrs. Lincoln
1974	Colleen Dewhurst	A Moon for the Misbegotten
1975	Ellen Burstyn	Same Time, Next Year
1976	Irene Worth	Sweet Bird of Youth
1977	Julie Harris	The Belle of Amherst
1978	Jessica Tandy	The Gin Game
1979	Tie: Constance Cummings / Carole Shelley	Wings / The Elephant Man
1980	Phyllis Frehlich	Children of a Lesser God
1981	Jane Lapotaire	Piaf
1982	Zoe Caldwell	Medea
1983	Jessica Tandy	Foxfire
1984	Glenn Close	The Real Thing
1985	Stockard Channing	Joe Egg
1986	Lily Tomlin	The Search for Signs of Intelligent Life in the Universe
1987	Linda Lavin	Broadway Bound
1988	Joan Allen	Burn This
1989	Pauline Collins	Shirley Valentine
1990	Maggie Smith	Lettice & Lovage

Source: Hischak, Theatregoers Almanac, 171–73.

TABLE 17.6 BEST ACTOR—PLAYS, 1947–1990

Year	Actor	Play
1947	Tie: José Ferrer / Fredric March	Cyrano de Bergerac / Years Ago
1948	Tie: Henry Fonda / Paul Kelly / Basil Rathbone	Mister Roberts / Command Decision / The Heiress
1949	Rex Harrison	Anne of the Thousand Days
1950	Sidney Blackmer	Come Back, Little Sheba
1951	Claude Rains	Darkness at Noon
1952	José Ferrer	The Shrike
1953	Tom Ewell	The Seven Year Itch
1954	David Wayne	The Teahouse of the August Moon
1955	Alfred Lunt	Quadrille
1956	Paul Muni	Inherit the Wind
1957	Fredric March	Long Day's Journey Into Night
1958	Ralph Bellamy	Sunrise at Campobello
1959	Jason Robards, Jr.	The Disenchanted

Year	Actor	Play
1960	Melvyn Douglas	The Best Man
1961	Zero Mostel	Rhinoceros
1962	Paul Scofield	A Man for All Seasons
1963	Arthur Hill	Who's Afraid of Virginia Woolf?
1964	Alec Guinness	Dylan
1965	Walter Matthau	The Odd Couple
1966	Hal Holbrook	Mark Twain Tonight!
1967	Paul Rogers	The Homecoming
1968	Martin Balsam	You Know I Can't Hear You When the Water's Running
1969	James Earl Jones	The Great White Hope
1970	Fritz Weaver	Child's Play
1971	Brian Bedford	The School for Wives
1972	Cliff Gorman	Lenny
1973	Alan Bates	Butley
1974	Michael Moriarty	Find Your Way Home
1975	John Kani and Winston Ntshona	Sizwe Banzi Is Dead and The Island
1976	John Wood	Travesties
1977	Al Pacino	The Basic Training of Pavlo Hummel
1978	Bernard Hughes	Da
1979	Tom Conti	Whose Life Is It Anyway?
1980	John Rubenstein	Children of a Lesser God
1981	Ian McKellen	Amadeus
1982	Roger Rees	Nicholas Nickleby
1983	Harvey Fierstein	Torch Song Trilogy
1984	Jeremy Irons	The Real Thing
1985	Derek Jacobi	Much Ado About Nothing
1986	Judd Hirsch	I'm Not Rappaport
1987	James Earl Jones	Fences
1988	Ron Silver	Speed-the-Plow
1989	Philip Bosco	Lend Me a Tenor
1990	Robert Morse	Tru

Source: Hischak, Theatregoers Almanac, 173–75.

TABLE 17.7 BEST ACTRESS—MUSICALS, 1947–1990

Year	Actress	Musical
1947	No award	
1948	Grace Hartman	Angel in the Wings
1949	Nanette Fabray	Love Life
1950	Mary Martin	South Pacific
1951	Ethel Merman	Call Me Madam
1952	Gertrude Lawrence	The King and I
1953	Rosalind Russell	Wonderful Town
1954	Dolores Gray	Carnival in Flanders
1955	Mary Martin	Peter Pan
1956	Gwen Verdon	Damn Yankees
1957	Judy Holliday	Bells Are Ringing
1958	Tie: Thelma Ritter / Gwen Verdon	New Girl in Town
1959	Gwen Verdon	Redhead
1960	Mary Martin	The Sound of Music
1961	Elizabeth Seal	Irma La Douce
1962	Tie: Anna Maria Alberghetti / Diahann Carroll	Carnival / No Strings
1963	Vivien Leigh	Tovarich
1964	Carol Channing	Hello, Dolly!
1965	Liza Minnelli	Flora, the Red Menace
1966	Angela Lansbury	Mame
1967	Barbara Harris	The Apple Tree
1968	Tie: Patricia Routledge / Leslie Uggams	Darling of the Day; Hallelujah, Baby!
1969	Angela Lansbury	Dear World
1970	Lauren Bacall	Applause
1971	Helen Gallagher	No, No, Nanette
1972	Alexis Smith	Follies
1973	Glynis Johns	A Little Night Music
1974	Virginia Capers	Raisin
1975	Angela Lansbury	Gypsy
1976	Donna McKechnie	A Chorus Line
1977	Dorothy Loudon	Annie
1978	Liza Minnelli	The Act
1979	Angela Lansbury	Sweeney Todd, the Demon Barber of Fleet Street

Year	Actress	Musical
1980	Patti LuPone	Evita
1981	Lauren Bacall	Woman of the Year
1982	Jennifer Holliday	Dreamgirls
1983	Natalia Makarova	On Your Toes
1984	Chita Rivera	The Rink
1985	No award	
1986	Bernadette Peters	Song and Dance
1987	Maryann Plunkett	Me and My Girl
1988	Joanna Gleason	Into the Woods
1989	Ruth Brown	Black and Blue
1990	Tyne Daly	Gypsy

Source: Hischak, Theatregoers Almanac, 175–76.

TABLE 17.8 BEST ACTOR—MUSICALS, 1947–1990

Year	Actor	Musical
1947	No award	
1948	Paul Hartman	Angel in the Wings
1949	Ray Bolger	Where's Charley?
1950	Ezio Pinza	South Pacific
1951	Robert Alda	Guys and Dolls
1952	Phil Silvers	Top Banana
1953	Thomas Mitchell	Hazel Flagg
1954	Alfred Drake	Kismet
1955	Walter Slezak	Fanny
1956	Ray Walston	Damn Yankees
1957	Rex Harrison	My Fair Lady
1958	Robert Preston	The Music Man
1959	Richard Kiley	Redhead
1960	Jackie Gleason	Take Me Along
1961	Richard Burton	Camelot
1962	Robert Morse	How to Succeed in Business Without Really Trying
1963	Zero Mostel	A Funny Thing Happened on the Way to The Forum
1964	Bert Lahr	Foxy
1965	Zero Mostel	Fiddler on the Roof
1966	Richard Kiley	Man of La Mancha
1967	Robert Preston	I Do! I Do!
1968	Robert Goulet	The Happy Time
1969	Jerry Orbach	Promises, Promises
1970	Cleavon Little	Purlie
1971	Hal Linden	The Rothschilds
1972	Phil Silvers	A Funny Thing Happened on the Way to the Forum
1973	Ben Vereen	Pippin
1974	Christopher Plummer	Cyrano
1975	John Cullum	Shenandoah
1976	George Rose	My Fair Lady
1977	Barry Bostwick	The Robber Bridegroom
1978	John Cullum	On the Twentieth Century
1979	Len Cariou	Sweeney Todd, the Demon Barber of Fleet Street
1980	Jim Dale	Barnum
1981	Kevin Kline	The Pirates of Penzance
1982	Ben Harney	Dreamgirls
1983	Tommy Tune	My One and Only
1984	George Hearn	La Cage aux Folles
1985	No award	
1986	George Rose	The Mystery of Edwin Drood
1987	Robert Lindsay	Me and My Girl
1988	Michael Crawford	Phantom of the Opera
1989	Jason Alexander	Jerome Robbins' Broadway
1990	James Naughton	City of Angels

Source: Hischak, Theatregoers Almanac, 177–78.

Memorable Losers

Prominent performances that did not win a Tony:

Actor	Play
Julie Andrews	My Fair Lady
Barbara Bel Geddes	Cat on a Hot Tin Roof
Vivian Blaine and Sam Levene	Guys and Dolls

(continued)

Actor	Play
Marlon Brando	*A Streetcar Named Desire*
Georgia Brown	*Oliver!*
Carol Burnett	*Once Upon a Mattress*
Richard Burton	*Hamlet*
Sid Caesar	*Little Me*
Carol Channing	*Gentlemen Prefer Blondes*
Lee J. Cobb	*Death of a Salesman*
Alfred Drake	*Kiss Me, Kate*
Frances Eldridge	*Long Day's Journey Into Night*
Henry Fonda	*Clarence Darrow*
Joel Grey	*George M!*
Julie Harris	*A Member of the Wedding*
Lena Horne	*Jamaica*
Josephine Hull	*The Solid Gold Cadillac*
Burl Ives	*Cat on a Hot Tin Roof*
Deborah Kerr	*Tea and Sympathy*
Alfred Lunt and Lynn Fontanne	*The Visit*
Claudia McNeil and Sidney Poitier	*A Raisin in the Sun*
Laurence Olivier	*The Entertainer*
Jason Robards	*A Moon for the Misbegotten*
Rosalind Russell	*Auntie Mame*
Barbra Streisand	*Funny Girl*
Elaine Stritch	*Company*
Gwen Verdon	*Sweet Charity*

Source: Hischak, *Theatregoers Almanac,* 179–80.

Motion Pictures

Motion pictures underwent many changes in the period following the Second World War. Emergence of television as mass media in the 1950s produced a sharp decline in theater attendance. Moviemakers tried to compensate with film extravaganzas, such costly movies as *Cleopatra* and *Mutiny on the Bounty,* that all lost money. Neither did the movement into new technology, with various widescreen innovations such as Cinerama and CinemaScope and the experiment with three-dimensional projection (3-D), which necessitated wearing funny-looking little glasses, produce the desired turnaround. Film studios lost control of their actors, but the star system continued. In time the high cost of large-name performers induced producers to make movies with lesser-known or unknown entities. Standardized heroes and standardized endings yielded somewhat to the more naturalized "method" actors, as exemplified by Marlon Brando, Montgomery Clift, and Rod Steiger. National cynicism in the 1960s and early 1970s enhanced the popularity of antihero films, such as *Catch 22* and *M*A*S*H,* but the strong, silent man never went away, as could be seen in the continuing popularity of John Wayne and Clint Eastwood's westerns or Eastwood's bluntly, even brutally stated series of Dirty Harry movies. Lifting of restrictive production codes in the 1960s produced two immediate reactions: efforts to address sensitive issues and older themes in a realistic way, and attempts to attract audiences through "shock" effect—nudity, explicit sex, and gratuitous scenes of blood, violence, and horror.

Moviemakers were not far behind social themes that surfaced throughout the period. Black people appeared more frequently, starting in the 1970s and in more positive roles. There were black heroes and even a few movies about black people. After the 1950s women appeared less frequently solely as sex objects (although they continued to be used to dress up the scenery) or as a supporter of the male hero—someone to be protected and rescued. More and more women appeared in strong roles and increasingly they engaged in the same activity as men. In a film environment given over to hypersensitivity it was becoming difficult to find someone to villainize without offending some group. The safest course, it often appeared, was to "nail the white male."

Movies moved a great distance after the Second World War, and for many people aboard it had been a bumpy ride. Statistics on attendance at

TABLE 17.9   MOTION PICTURE STATISTICS— ADMISSIONS, 1946–1990

Year	Gross ($ millions)	Admissions (millions)	Per Week (millions)
1946	1,692.0	4,067.3	78.2
1947	1,594.0	3,664.4	70.5
1948	1,506.0	3,422.7	65.8
1949	1,448.0	3,168.5	60.9
1950	1,379.0	3,017.5	58.0
1951	1,332.0	2,840.1	54.6
1952	1,325.0	2,777.7	53.4
1953	1,339.0	2,630.6	50.6
1954	1,251.0	2,270.4	43.7
1955	1,204.0	2,072.3	39.9
1956	1,125.0	1,893.9	36.4
1957	1,078.0	1,727.6	33.2
1958	1,010.0	1,553.8	29.9
1959	1,006.0	1,488.2	28.6
1960	984.4	1,304.5	25.1
1961	945.5	1,224.7	23.6
1962	874.9	1,080.1	20.8
1963	925.0	1,093.4	21.0
1964	947.6	1,024.4	19.7
1965	1,041.8	1,031.5	19.8
1966	1,067.1	975.4	18.8
1967	1,110.0	926.5	17.8
1968	1,282.0	978.6	18.8
1969	1,294.0	911.9	17.5
1970	1,429.2	920.6	17.7
1971	1,349.5	820.3	15.8
1972	1,583.1	934.1	18.0
1973	1,523.5	864.6	16.6
1974	1,908.5	1,010.7	19.4
1975	2,114.8	1,032.8	19.9
1976	2,036.4	957.1	18.4
1977	2,372.3	1,063.2	20.4
1978	2,643.4	1,128.2	21.7
1979	2,821.3	1,120.9	21.6
1980	2,748.5	1,021.5	19.6
1981	2,965.6	1,067.0	20.5
1982	3,452.7	1,175.4	22.6
1983	3,766.0	1,196.9	23.0
1984	4,030.6	1,199.1	23.1
1985	3,749.4	1,056.1	20.3
1986	3,778.0	1,017.2	19.6
1987	4,252.9	1,088.5	20.9
1988	4,458.4	1,084.8	20.9
1989	5,033.4	1,262.8	24.3
1990	5,021.8	1,188.6	22.9

Source: James D. Moser, ed., *1997 International Motion Picture Almanac* (New York, 1997), 15A.

TABLE 17.10   NUMBER OF THEATERS AND AVERAGE ADMISSION PRICE, 1945–1990

Year	Theaters		Admission Price ($)
	Indoor	Drive In	
1945	20,355	102	0.35
1950	16,904	2,202	0.53
1955	19,106[a]	. . .	0.50
1960	16,999[a]	. . .	0.69
1965	10,150	4,150	1.01
1970	10,335	3,720	1.55
1975	12,168[b]	3,801[b]	2.05
1980	14,029[b]	3,561[b]	2.69
1985	18,327[b]	2,820[b]	3.55
1990	22,774[b]	915[b]	4.23

[a] Includes theaters of all kinds, including drive-ins.
[b] Numbers after 1975 pertain to screens, not theaters. Most new theaters had multiple screens.
Source: John Wright, *Universal Almanac, 1995* (New York, 1994), 235; Thomas Schatz, *Boom and Bust: The American Cinema in the 1940s* (New York, 1997), 461; David Oak, *Lost Illusions: American Cinema in the Shadow of Watergate and Vietnam, 1970–1979* (New York, 2000), 491.

theaters suggested a virtual disaster. While the numbers increased slightly at the end of the 1980s, they still stood a great distance from the glory days of the 1940s. Theater statistics, however, represented only part of the story. As with nearly everything in the last part of the 20th century, the condition of the film industry had become remarkably complex. Film companies made their peace with television by becoming part of it. They sold their movies to television networks and began to make movies and other shows specially for the small screen. Popularity after the 1970s of the videocassette recorder (VCR) made it possible for anyone to pick out a movie, rent it at the store, and watch it at home. One did not need to go to a theater to see the work of Hollywood and most people did not do so.

What Can Be Seen on Screen: Changes in Production Rules

Since 1934 Hollywood had policed its operations in a production code administered by a special branch of the Motion Picture Producers and Distributors of America (MPPDA) headed by Will Hays. The Hays Office had established elaborate rules that forbade treatment of sensitive topics, banned virtually all profanity—Clark Gable's saying "I don't give a damn" in *Gone With the Wind* in 1939 had been a rare expression of leniency—and above all there was to be no showing of uncovered intimate parts of the body, a proviso most commonly applied to women's breasts. The code was revised in 1956, but the ban on nudity, profanity, and obscenity remained. With emergence of *Playboy* magazine in the 1950s, Supreme Court rulings that subjected censorship to a narrow definition (if it allowed it at all), and gradual loosening of social taboos, producers stretched the bounds of the code in such films as *Baby Doll*, *Peyton Place*, and *Lolita*. Appearance of the contraceptive pill and the dash into liberalized social standards in the 1960s seemingly gave movie producers license to make the sort of films that previously had been forbidden. In showing nudity, explicit sex, and violence, filmmakers doubtless hoped to recoup at least some of the huge losses in recent years to television. In 1966 Jack Valenti, a former member of the Lyndon Johnson administration, became head of what was now called the Motion Picture Association of America (MPAA), and he encouraged efforts to produce a new production code, not so much to forbid certain forms of behavior but to classify films as to their suitability for various segments of the population. In November 1968 the MPA introduced a new voluntary system that carried four rating symbols.

MPAA Film Rating System and Symbols

1. 1968—G: for General Audiences; M: for Mature Audiences, parental guidance advised; R: Restricted, admission limited to persons older than 16, unless accompanied by parent or adult guardian; X: no one younger than 16 admitted.
2. 1970—M changed to GP (later PG), parental guidance advised.
3. 1984—new rating, PG-13, special guidance advised for children younger than 13.
4. 1990—X rating changed to NC-17; no persons younger than 17 admitted.

Summary of ratings procedure (number of films in each category) for the year 1990: G: 8; PG: 74; PG-13: 103; R: 365; NC-17 or X: 20. Ratings totals for the years 1968–1990: G: 952; PG: 2,996; PG-13: 508; R: 4,862; X or NC-17: 381.

Source: Barry Monush, ed., *1992 International Motion Picture Almanac* (New York, 1992), 25A.

TABLE 17.11   TOP FIVE MOST POPULAR MOTION PICTURE STARS, BY YEAR AND RANK, 1946–1990

1946	1947	1948	1949	1950
Bing Crosby Ingrid Bergman Van Johnson Gary Cooper Bob Hope	Bing Crosby Betty Grable Ingrid Bergman Gary Cooper Humphrey Bogart	Bing Crosby Betty Grable Abbott & Costello Gary Cooper Bob Hope	Bob Hope Bing Crosby Abbott & Costello John Wayne Gary Cooper	John Wayne Bob Hope Bing Crosby Betty Grable James Stewart
1951	**1952**	**1953**	**1954**	**1955**
John Wayne Martin & Lewis Betty Grable Abbott & Costello Bing Crosby	Martin & Lewis Gary Cooper John Wayne Bing Crosby Bob Hope	Gary Cooper Martin & Lewis John Wayne Alan Ladd Bing Crosby	John Wayne Martin & Lewis Gary Cooper James Stewart Marilyn Monroe	James Stewart Grace Kelly John Wayne William Holden Gary Cooper
1956	**1957**	**1958**	**1959**	**1960**
William Holden John Wayne James Stewart Burt Lancaster Glenn Ford	Rock Hudson John Wayne Pat Boone Elvis Presley Frank Sinatra	Glenn Ford Elizabeth Taylor Jerry Lewis Marlon Brando Rock Hudson	Rock Hudson Cary Grant James Stewart Doris Day Debbie Reynolds	Doris Day Rock Hudson Cary Grant Elizabeth Taylor Debbie Reynolds
1961	**1962**	**1963**	**1964**	**1965**
Elizabeth Taylor Rock Hudson Doris Day John Wayne Cary Grant	Doris Day Rock Hudson Cary Grant John Wayne Elvis Presley	Doris Day John Wayne Rock Hudson Jack Lemmon Cary Grant	Doris Day Jack Lemmon Rock Hudson John Wayne Cary Grant	Sean Connery John Wayne Doris Day Julie Andrews Jack Lemmon
1966	**1967**	**1968**	**1969**	**1970**
Julie Andrews Sean Connery Elizabeth Taylor Jack Lemmon Richard Burton	Julie Andrews Lee Marvin Paul Newman Dean Martin Sean Connery	Sidney Poitier Paul Newman Julie Andrews John Wayne Clint Eastwood	Paul Newman John Wayne Steve McQueen Dustin Hoffman Clint Eastwood	Paul Newman Clint Eastwood Steve McQueen John Wayne Elliott Gould

(continued)

TABLE 17.11   (continued)

1971	1972	1973	1974	1975
John Wayne Clint Eastwood Paul Newman Steve McQueen George C. Scott	Clint Eastwood George C. Scott Gene Hackman John Wayne Barbra Streisand	Clint Eastwood Ryan O'Neal Steve McQueen Burt Reynolds Robert Redford	Robert Redford Clint Eastwood Paul Newman Barbra Streisand Steve McQueen	Robert Redford Barbra Streisand Al Pacino Charles Bronson Paul Newman

1976	1977	1978	1979	1980
Robert Redford Jack Nicholson Dustin Hoffman Clint Eastwood Mel Brooks	Sylvester Stallone Barbra Streisand Clint Eastwood Burt Reynolds Robert Redford	Burt Reynolds John Travolta Richard Dreyfuss Warren Beatty Clint Eastwood	Burt Reynolds Clint Eastwood Jane Fonda Woody Allen Barbra Streisand	Burt Reynolds Robert Redford Clint Eastwood Jane Fonda Dustin Hoffman

1981	1982	1983	1984	1985
Burt Reynolds Clint Eastwood Dudley Moore Dolly Parton Jane Fonda	Burt Reynolds Clint Eastwood Sylvester Stallone Dudley Moore Richard Pryor	Clint Eastwood Eddie Murphy Sylvester Stallone Burt Reynolds John Travolta	Clint Eastwood Bill Murray Harrison Ford Eddie Murphy Sally Field	Sylvester Stallone Eddie Murphy Clint Eastwood Michael J. Fox Chevy Chase

1986	1987	1988	1989	1990
Tom Cruise Eddie Murphy Paul Hogan Rodney Dangerfield Bette Midler	Eddie Murphy Michael Douglas Michael J. Fox A. Schwarzenegger Paul Hogan	Tom Cruise Eddie Murphy Tom Hanks A. Schwarzenegger Paul Hogan	Jack Nicholson Tom Cruise Robin Williams Michael Douglas Tom Hanks	A. Schwarzenegger Julia Roberts Bruce Willis Tom Cruise Mel Gibson

Note: Rankings compiled annually by Quigley Publishing Company.
Source: Monush, *1993 Motion Picture Almanac,* 44A.

Symbolically in the spotlight and still alone, film sensation Marilyn Monroe sings "Happy Birthday" to President John Kennedy in 1962—the final year of her life. (John Fitzgerald Kennedy Library)

Sons of the Golden West

The postwar era seemed poised to carry on an honored tradition in the world of American films. The B-grade western, standard fare since the 1920s, had followed an unchanging pattern: cheap, short, black-and-white movies, many of them made by Republic Studios, that featured a vigorous, well-tailored, unflinchingly moral male hero accompanied by a scruffy and erratic sidekick to provide humor and occasionally help the lead actor out of a tight spot. Such loyal companions as Gabby Hayes, Smiley Burnette, and Andy Devine became nearly as popular as the star. Usually part of a package offering for Saturday afternoons, the B-grade western had attracted a steady audience, mostly of young boys, and early signs suggested that the pace would continue after the Second World War. Gene Autry returned from a stint in the army, but he had to yield top ranking to Roy Rogers, who had stayed home and made movies.

It was not to be. After a good start in the postwar era, the Saturday westerns passed into obsolescence much quicker than had been expected. It was partly a matter of attrition. Several cowboy heroes reached back well into the 1930s, if not earlier, and they simply were becoming too old and too fat. Some moved on. John Wayne—at one time a member of the "Three Mesquiteers" hero gang—graduated to become a grade-A player of the first order. As happened in many areas of entertainment, the coup de grace came from television, although in rare cases the cowboy stars, such as Rogers and William Boyd, were able to ride that new territory for a while.

TABLE 17.12 COWBOY STARS—MOST POPULAR PERFORMERS IN GRADE B WESTERN MOVIES, BY YEAR AND RANK, 1946–1954

1946	1947	1948
Roy Rogers	Roy Rogers	Roy Rogers
William Elliott	Gene Autry	Gene Autry
Gene Autry	William Boyd[a]	William Elliott
"Gabby" Hayes	William Elliott	"Gabby" Hayes
Smiley Burnette	"Gabby" Hayes	William Boyd[a]
Charles Starrett	Charles Starrett	Charles Starrett
Johnny Mack Brown	Smiley Burnette	Tim Holt
Sunset Carson	Johnny Mack Brown	Johnny Mack Brown
Fuzzy Knight	Dale Evans[b]	Smiley Burnette
Eddie Dean	Eddie Dean	Andy Devine
1949	**1950**	**1951**
Roy Rogers	Roy Rogers	Roy Rogerss
Gene Autry	Gene Autry	Gene Autry
"Gabby" Hayes	"Gabby" Hayes	Tim Holt
Tim Holt	Bill Elliott	Charles Starrett
William Elliott	William Boyd[a]	Rex Allen
Charles Starrett	Tim Holt	Bill Elliott
William Boyd[a]	Charles Starrett	Smiley Burnette
Johnny Mack Brown	Johnny Mack Brown	Allan Lane
Smiley Burnette	Smiley Burnette	Dale Evans[b]
Andy Devine	Dale Evans[b]	"Gabby" Hayes
1952	**1953**	**1954**
Roy Rogers	Roy Roger	Roy Rogers
Gene Autry	Gene Autry	Gene Autry
Rex Allen	Rex Allen	Rex Allen
Bill Elliott	Bill Elliott	Bill Elliott
Tim Holt	Allan "Rocky" Lane	"Gabby" Hayes
"Gabby" Hayes		
Smiley Burnette		
Dale Evans[b]		
Charles Starrett		
William Boyd[a]		

Note: Rankings based on poll of movie exhibitors by *Motion Picture Herald.*
[a] Better known by his stage or movie name: Hopalong Cassidy.
[b] The only female in the listing, Dale Evans was not, of course, a gunslinger but a proper friend and companion of Roy Rogers in the movies. Later in "real" life, after Rogers' first wife died, Dale and Roy married.
Source: Richard Gertner, ed., *1975 International Motion Picture Almanac* (New York, 1975), 44A.

TABLE 17.13   TOP EARNING FILMS BY YEAR, 1947–1990
(in millions of dollars)

1947[a]	1948	1949	1950
Best Years of Our Lives (11.5)	*Road to Rio* (4.5)	*Jolson Sings Again* (5.5)	*Samson and Delilah* (11)
Duel in the Sun (10.7)	*Easter Parade* (4.2)	*Pinky* (4.2)	*Battleground* (4.55)
The Jolson Story (8)	*Red River* (4.15)	*I Was a Male War Bride* (4.1)	*King Solomon's Mines* (4.4)
Forever Amber (8)	*The Three Musketeers* (4.1)	*The Snake Pit* (4.1)	*Cheaper by the Dozen* (4.3)
Unconquered (7.5)	*Johnny Belinda* (4.1)	*Joan of Arc* (4.1)	*Annie Get Your Gun* (4.2)
Life with Father (6.3)	*Cass Timberlane* (4.05)	*The Stratton Story* (3.7)	*Cinderella* (4.15)
Welcome Stranger (6.1)	*The Emperor Waltz* (4)	*Mr. Belvedere Goes to College* (3.65)	*Father of the Bride* (4.15)
The Egg and I (5.8)	*Gentleman's Agreement* (3.9)	*Little Women* (3.6)	*Sands of Iwo Jima* (3.9)
The Yearling (5.3)	*Date with Judy* (3.7)	*Words and Music* (3.5)	*Broken Arrow* (3.55)
Green Dolphin Street (5)	*Captain from Castile* (3.65)	*Neptune's Daughter* (3.45)	*Twelve O'Clock High* (3.225)

1951	1952	1953	1954
David and Bathsheba (7)	*Greatest Show on Earth* (12)	*The Robe* (20–30)	*White Christmas* (12)
Showboat (5.2)	*Quo Vadis* (10.5)	*From Here to Eternity* (12.5)	*The Caine Mutiny* (8.7)
An American in Paris (4.5)	*Ivanhoe* (7)	*Shane* (8)	*The Glenn Miller Story* (7)
The Great Caruso (4.5)	*Snows of Kilimanjaro* (6.5)	*How to Marry a Millionaire* (7.5)	*The Egyptian* (6)
A Streetcar Named Desire (4.15)	*Sailor Beware* (4.3)	*Peter Pan* (7)	*Rear Window* (5.3)
Born Yesterday (4.25)	*The African Queen* (4)	*Hans Christian Andersen* (6)	*The High and the Mighty* (5.2)
That's My Boy (3.8)	*Jumping Jacks* (4)	*House of Wax* (5.5)	*Magnificent Obsession* (5)
A Place in the Sun (3.5)	*High Noon* (3.4)	*Mogambo* (5.2)	*Three Coins in the Fountain* (5)
At War with the Army (3.35)	*Son of Paleface* (3.4)	*Gentlemen Prefer Blondes* (5.1)	*Seven Brides for Seven Brothers* (4.8)
Father's Little Dividend (3.1)	*With a Song in My Heart* (2.85)	*Moulin Rouge* (5)	*Desiree* (4.5)

1955	1956	1957	1958
Cinerama Holiday (10)	*Guys and Dolls* (9)	*The Ten Commandments* (18.5)	*Bridge on the River Kwai* (18)
Mister Roberts (8.5)	*The King and I* (8.5)	*Around the World in 80 Days* (16.2)	*Peyton Place* (12)
Battle Cry (8)	*Trapeze* (7.5)	*Giant* (12)	*Sayonara* (10.5)
20,000 Leagues Under the Sea (8)	*High Society* (6.5)	*Pal Joey* (6.7)	*No Time for Sergeants* (7.2)
Not as a Stranger (7.1)	*I'll Cry Tomorrow* (6.5)	*Seven Wonders of the World* (6.5)	*The Vikings* (7)
The Country Girl (6.9)	*Picnic* (6.3)	*Teahouse of the August Moon* (5.6).	*Search for Paradise* (6.5)
The Lady and the Tramp (6.5)	*War and Peace* (6.25)	*The Pride and the Passion* (5.5)	*South Pacific* (6)
Strategic Air Command (6.5)	*The Eddy Duchin Story* (5.3)	*Anastasia* (5)	*Cat on a Hot Tin Roof* (6.1)
To Hell and Back (6)	*Moby Dick* (5.2)	*Island in the Sun* (5)	*Raintree County* (6)
Sea Chase (6)	*The Searchers* (4.8)	*Love Me Tender* (4.5)	*Old Yeller* (5.9)
A Star is Born (6)			

1959	1960	1961	1962
Auntie Mame (8.8)	*Ben-Hur* (17.3)	*The Guns of Navarone* (8.6)	*Spartacus* (13.5)
Shaggy Dog (7.8)	*Psycho* (8.5)	*The Absent-Minded Professor* (8.2)	*West Side Story* (11)
Some Like It Hot (7)	*Operation Petticoat* (6.8)	*The Parent Trap* (8)	*Lover Come Back* (8.5)
Imitation of Life (6.2)	*Suddenly, Last Summer* (5.5)	*Swiss Family Robinson* (7.5)	*That Touch of Mink* (8.5)
The Nun's Story (6)	*On the Beach* (5.3)	*Exodus* (7.35)	*El Cid* (8)
Anatomy of a Murder (5.25)	*Solomon and Sheba* (5.25)	*The World of Suzie Wong* (7.3)	*The Music Man* (8)
North by Northwest (5.25)	*The Apartment* (5.1)	*Alamo* (7.25)	*King of Kings* (7.5)
Rio Bravo (5.2)	*From the Terrace* (5)	*Gone With the Wind* (reissue, 6)	*Hatari* (6)
Sleeping Beauty (4.3)	*Please Don't Eat the Daisies* (5)	*101 Dalmatians* (5.8)	*The Flower Drum Song* (5)
Some Came Running (4.2)	*Ocean's 11* (4.9)	*Splendor in the Grass* (5.1)	*The Interns* (5)

1963	1964	1965	1966
Cleopatra (15.7)	*The Carpetbaggers* (13)	*Mary Poppins* (28.6)	*Thunderball* (26)
The Longest Day (12.75)	*It's a Mad, Mad, Mad, Mad World* (10)	*The Sound of Music* (20)	*Doctor Zhivago* (15)
Irma La Douce (9.25)	*Unsinkable Molly Brown* (7.5)	*Goldfinger* (19.7)	*Who's Afraid of Virginia Woolf?* (10.3)
Lawrence of Arabia (9)	*Charade* (6.15)	*My Fair Lady* (19)	*That Darned Cat* (9.2)
How the West Was Won (8)	*The Cardinal* (5.3)	*What's New Pussycat?* (7.15)	*The Russians Are Coming . . .* (7.75)
Mutiny on the Bounty (7.7)	*Move Over, Darling* (5.1)	*Shenandoah* (6.4)	*Lt. Robin Crusoe, USN* (7.5)
Son of Flubber (6.9)	*My Fair Lady* (5)	*The Sandpiper* (6.4)	*The Silencers* (7)
To Kill a Mockingbird (6.7)	*What a Way to Go* (5)	*Father Goose* (6)	*Torn Curtain* (7)
Bye Bye Birdie (5.6)	*Good Neighbor Sam* (4.95)	*Von Ryan's Express* (5.6)	*Our Man Flint* (6.5)
Come Blow Your Horn (5.45)	*The Pink Panther* (4.85)	*The Yellow Rolls-Royce* (5.4)	*A Patch of Blue* (6.3)

1967	1968	1969	1970
The Dirty Dozen (18.2)	*The Graduate* (39)	*The Love Bug* (17)	*Airport* (37.6)
You Only Live Twice (16.3)	*Guess Who's Coming to Dinner* (25)	*Funny Girl* (16.5)	*M*A*S*H* (22)
Casino Royale (10.2)	*Gone With the Wind* (reissue, 23)	*Bullitt* (16.4)	*Patton* (21)
A Man for All Seasons (9.25)	*The Valley of the Dolls* (20)	*Butch Cassidy and Sundance Kid* (15)	*Bob & Carol & Ted & Alice* (14)
Thoroughly-Modern Millie (8.5)	*The Odd Couple* (18.5)	*Romeo and Juliet* (14.5)	*Woodstock* (13.5)
Barefoot in the Park (8.25)	*Planet of the Apes* (15)	*True Grit* (11.5)	*Hello, Dolly!* (13)
Georgy Girl (7.3)	*Rosemary's Baby* (12.3)	*Midnight Cowboy* (11)	*Cactus Flower* (11.3)
To Sir With Love (7.2)	*The Jungle Book* (11.5)	*Oliver!* (10.5)	*Catch 22* (9.25)
Grand Prix (7)	*Yours, Mine, and Ours* (11)	*Goodbye Columbus* (10.5)	*On Her Majesty's Secret Service* (9)
Hombre (6.5)	*The Green Berets* (8.7)	*Chitty Chitty Bang Bang* (7.5)	*The Reivers* (8)

1971	1972	1973	1974
Love Story (50)	The Godfather (81.5)	The Poseidon Adventure (40)	The Sting (68.5)
Little Big Man (15)	Fiddler on the Roof (25.1)	Deliverance (18)	The Exorcist (66.3)
Summer of '42 (14)	Diamonds Are Forever (21)	The Getaway (17.5)	Papillon (19.75)
Ryan's Daughter (13.4)	What's Up, Doc? (17)	Live and Let Die (15.5)	Magnum Force (18.3)
The Owl and the Pussycat (11.5)	Dirty Harry (16)	Paper Moon (13)	Herbie Rides Again (17.5)
The Aristocats (10.1)	The Last Picture Show (12.75)	Last Tango in Paris (12.6)	Blazing Saddles (16.5)
Carnal Knowledge (9.35)	A Clockwork Orange (12)	The Sound of Music (reissue, 11)	Trial of Billy Jack (15)
Willard (8.2)	Cabaret (10.89)	Jesus Christ Superstar (10.8)	The Great Gatsby (14.2)
The Andromeda Strain (7.5)	The Hospital (9)	The World's Greatest Athlete (10.6)	Serpico (14.1)
Big Jake (7.5)	Everything You Always Wanted to Know About Sex (8.5)	American Graffiti (10.3)	Butch Cassidy and the Sundance Kid (reissue, 13.8)

1975	1976	1977	1978
Jaws (102.65)	One Flew Over Cuckoo's Nest (56.5)	Star Wars (127)	Grease (83.1)
The Towering Inferno (55)	All the President's Men (29)	Rocky (54)	Close Encounters of the Third Kind (54)
Benji (30.8)	The Omen (27.85)	Smokey and the Bandit (39.7)	National Lampoon's Animal House (52.4)
Young Frankenstein (30)	The Bad News Bears (22.3)	A Star Is Born (37.1)	Jaws 2 (49.3)
The Godfather Part II (28.9)	Silent Movie (20.3)	King Kong (35.9)	Heaven Can Wait (42.6)
Shampoo (22)	Midway (20.3)	The Deep (31)	The Goodbye Girl (41)
Funny Lady (19)	Dog Day Afternoon (19.8)	Silver Streak (27.1)	Star Wars (reissue, 38.4)
Murder on Orient Express (17.8)	Murder by Death (18.8)	The Enforcer (24)	Hooper (31.5)
Return of the Pink Panther (17)	Jaws (reissue, 16.1)	Close Encounters of the Third Kind (23)	Foul Play (25.1)
Tommy (16)	Blazing Saddles (reissue, 13.8)	In Search of Noah's Ark (23)	Revenge of Pink Panther (25)

1979	1980	1981	1982
Superman (81)	The Empire Strikes Back (120)	Raiders of the Lost Ark (90.4)	E.T.: The Extra-Terrestrial (187)
Every Which Way But Loose (48)	Kramer vs. Kramer (60.5)[c]	Superman II (64)	Rocky III (63.4)
Rocky II (43)	The Jerk (43)[c]	Stir Crazy (58.4)[c]	On Golden Pond (63)[c]
Alien (40.1)	Airplane (38)	9 To 5 (57.8)[c]	Porky's (53.5)
The Amityville Horror (35)	Smokey and the Bandit (37.5)	Stripes (39.5)	An Officer and a Gentleman (52)
Star Trek (35)	Coal Miner's Daughter (35)	Any Which Way You Can (39.5)	The Best Little Whorehouse in Texas (48)
Moonraker (33.9)	Private Benjamin (33.5)	Arthur (37)	Star Trek II: The Wrath of Khan (40)
The Muppet Movie (32)	The Blues Brothers (31)	The Cannonball Run (35.4)	Poltergeist (36)
California Suite (29.2)	The Electric Horseman (30.9)	Four Seasons (26.8)	Annie (35)
The Deer Hunter (26.9)	The Shining (30.2)	For Your Eyes Only (25.4)	Chariots of Fire (27.6)

1983	1984	1985	1986
Return of the Jedi (165.5)	Ghostbusters (127)	Back to the Future (94)	Top Gun (82)
Tootsie (94.6)	Indiana Jones and the Temple of Doom (109)	Rambo: First Blood, Part II (80)	The Karate Kid. Part II (56.9)
Trading Places (40.6)	Gremlins (78.5)	Rocky IV (65)	"Crocodile" Dundee (51)
War Games (36.6)	Beverly Hills Cop (58)	Beverly Hills Cop (50)[d]	Star Trek IV: The Voyage Home (45)
Superman III (36.4)	Terms of Endearment (50.3)[c]	Cocoon (40)	Aliens (42.5)
Flashdance (36.2)	The Karate Kid (41.7)	The Goonies (29.9)	The Color Purple[b] (41.9)
Staying Alive (33.6)	Star Trek III: The Search for Spock (39)	Witness (28)	Back to School (41.7)
Octopussy (33.2)	Police Academy (38.5)	Police Academy 2 (27.2)	The Golden Child (33)
Mr. Mom (31.5)	Romancing the Stone (36)	National Lampoon's European Vacation (25.6)	Ruthless People (31)
48 Hours (30.3)	Sudden Impact (34.6)	A View to a Kill (25.2)	Out of Africa[d] (30)

1987	1988	1989	1990
Beverly Hills Cop II (80.8)	Who Framed Roger Rabbit (78)	Batman (150.5)	Ghost (94)
Platoon (66.7)[d]	Coming to America (65)	Indiana Jones and the Last Crusade (115.5)	Pretty Woman (81.9)
Fatal Attraction (60)	Good Morning, Vietnam (58.1)	Lethal Weapon 2 (79.5)	Home Alone (81.9)
Three Men and a Baby (45)	"Crocodile" Dundee II (57.3)	Honey, I Shrunk the Kids (71)	Die Hard 2 (66.5)
The Untouchables (36.8)	Big (50.8)	Rain Man (65)	Total Recall (65)
The Witches of Eastwick (31.8)	Three Men and a Baby[b] (36.3)	Back to the Future, Part II (63)	Teenage Mutant Ninja Turtles (62)
Predator (31)	Die Hard (35)	Ghostbusters II (61.6)	Dick Tracy (59.5)
Dragnet (30.1)	Cocktail (35)	Look Who's Talking (55)	The Hunt for Red October (58.5)
The Secret of My Success (29.5)	Moonstruck (34.4)	Parenthood (48.6)	Driving Miss Daisy (49.5)
Lethal Weapon (29.5)	Beetlejuice (33.3)	Dead Poets Society (47.6)	Back to the Future, Part III (49)

[a] All statistics are based on revenues, "rentals," returned to the distributors and reported in *Variety Magazine*. From 1947 to 1958 numbers represent total anticipated domestic earnings.

[b] After 1959 the numbers represent only rental fees to the end of the calendar year, which of course placed films released late (Oct.–Dec.) at a disadvantage.

[c] Represents films released late in the previous year.

[d] Represents films released late in previous year, but rentals for only the current year are reported.

Source: Cobbett Steinberg, *Film Facts* (New York, 1980), 20–28; Oak, *Lost Illusions*, 447–48.

TABLE 17.14 TOP FIVE MONEYMAKING FILMS BY DECADE, 1940s–1980s

Top Five Moneymaking Films from the Forties

Rank	Title	Amount
1.	Bambi (1942)	$18,735,000
2.	Fantasia (1940)	15,500,000
3.	Pinocchio (1940)	13,000,000
4.	Song of the South (1946)	12,800,000
5.	Cinderella (1949)	12,450,000

Top Five Moneymaking Films from the Fifties

Rank	Title	Amount
1.	The Ten Commandments (1956)	$43,000,000
2.	Ben-Hur (1959)	36,650,000
3.	Around the World in 80 Days (1956)	23,120,000
4.	The Robe (1953)	17,500,000
5.	South Pacific (1958)	17,500,000

Top Five Moneymaking Films from the Sixties

Rank	Title	Amount
1.	The Sound of Music (1965)	$79,000,000
2.	The Graduate (1968)	49,078,000
3.	Doctor Zhivago (1965)	46,550,000
4.	Butch Cassidy (1969)	46,039,000
5.	Mary Poppins (1964)	41,000,000

Top Five Moneymaking Films from the Seventies

Rank	Title	Amount
1.	Star Wars (1977)	$175,849,013
2.	Jaws (1975)	133,429,000
3.	Grease (1978)	93,292,000
4.	The Exorcist (1973)	88,100,000
5.	The Godfather (1972)	86,275,000

Top Five Moneymaking Films from the Eighties

Rank	Title	Amount
1.	E.T.–The Extra-Terrestrial (1982)	$228,170,000
2.	Return of the Jedi (1983)	168,190,000
3.	Batman (1989)	150,500,000
4.	The Empire Strikes Back (1980)	141,670,000
5.	Ghostbusters (1984)	132,720,000

Note: Films of the 1940s through 1970s reflect earnings through the year 1979 and thus are little affected by the video rentals that would blossom near the end of the 20th century. Films of the 1980s reflect earnings to February 1994.
Source: Steinberg, *Film Facts,* 13–15; Wright, *Universal Almanac,* 1995, 235.

TABLE 17.15 BEST-SELLING PRERECORDED VIDEOS, 1989

Rank	Title	Distributor	Unit sold ('000s)
1.	Batman	Warner	11,500
2.	Bambi	Disney	10,500
3.	Who Framed Roger Rabbit	Touchstone	8,500
4.	The Land Before Time	MCA	5,000
5.	The Wizard of Oz: The 50th Anniversary Edition	MGM/UA	3,600
6.	Michael Jackson's Moonwalker	CBS	800
7.	Sports Illustrated's 25th Anniversary Swimsuit Video	HBO	600
8.	Jane Fonda's Complete Workout	Warner	500
9.	Rain Man	MGM/UA	490
10.	Lawrence of Arabia	RCA/Columbia	450

Source: Wright, *Universal Almanac,* 1991, 242.

TABLE 17.16 TOP-RENTING PRERECORDED VIDEOS, 1989

Rank	Title	Distributor
1.	Big	CBS-Fox
2.	Die Hard	CBS-Fox
3.	A Fish Called Wanda	CBS-Fox
4.	Three Men and a Baby	Touchstone
5.	Beetlejuice	Warner
6.	Coming to America	Paramount
7.	Cocktail	Touchstone
8.	Twins	MCA
9.	Bull Durham	Orion
10.	Crocodile Dundee II	Paramount

Source: Wright, *Universal Almanac,* 1991, 242.

TABLE 17.17 BEST-SELLING PRERECORDED VIDEOS OF ALL TIME

Rank	Title	Distributor	Units sold (millions)
1.	E.T.–The Extra-Terrestrial	MCA	15.1
2.	Batman	Warner	11.5
3.	Bambi	Disney	10.5
4.	Who Framed Roger Rabbit	Touchstone	8.5
5.	Cinderella	Disney	7.5
6.	Honey, I Shrunk the Kids	Disney	5.7
7.	Indiana Jones and the Last Crusade	Paramount	5.5
8.	The Land Before Time	MCA	5.0
9.	The Wizard of Oz	MGM/UA	3.6
10.	Top Gun	Paramount	3.5

Note: As of Apr. 1990.
Source: Wright, *Universal Almanac,* 1991, 242.

The Academy Awards

The Academy of Motion Picture Arts and Sciences, founded in 1927, set out immediately to promote its popularity and image by honoring the most distinguished work in aspects of the field. Starting with only four awards in 1928, the categories in 1934 began to increase until they reached the point in 1990 when Academy Awards—also known as Oscars—were given to winners in 19 areas. The academy divided itself into 13 branches and entrusted each branch with making up to five nominations in its given area of specialization. The entire membership made nominations in the best film category and the entire membership voted on all categories. The large decline in made-for-theater movies as a means of entertainment seemingly had little effect on the appeal of the Academy Awards. Enhanced substantially by the emergence of television coverage, "Oscar Night" maintained continuing national appeal, marked with lavish and daring costumes by female attendees, acceptance speeches that competed in measure of predictability, creativity, and outright effrontery, and a rare snub by such rebels as Marlon Brando or George C. Scott. The table below lists winners of awards by year in each of arguably the seven most popular categories.

TABLE 17.18 THE ACADEMY AWARDS, 1946–1990

Year	Best Picture	Best Director	Best Actor	Best Actress	Best Supporting Actor	Best Supporting Actress	Best Song (from film)
1946	*The Best Years of Our Lives*	William Wyler *The Best Years of Our Lives*	Fredric March *The Best Years of Our Lives*	Olivia de Havilland *To Each His Own*	Harold Russell *The Best Years of Our Lives*	Anne Baxter *The Razor's Edge*	"On the Atchison, Topeka and Santa Fe" *The Harvey Girls*
1947	*Gentleman's Agreement*	Elia Kazan *Gentleman's Agreement*	Ronald Colman *A Double Life*	Loretta Young *The Farmer's Daughter*	Edmund Gwenn *Miracle on 34th Street*	Celeste Holm *Gentleman's Agreement*	"Zip-A-Dee-Doo-Dah" *Song of the South*
1948	*Hamlet*	John Huston *Treasure of the Sierra Madre*	Laurence Olivier *Hamlet*	Jane Wyman *Johnny Belinda*	Walter Huston *Treasure of the Sierra Madre*	Claire Trevor *Key Largo*	"Buttons and Bows" *The Paleface*
1949	*All the King's Men*	Joseph L. Mankiewicz *A Letter to Three Wives*	Broderick Crawford *All the King's Men*	Olivia de Havilland *The Heiress*	Dean Jagger *Twelve O'Clock High*	Mercedes McCambridge *All the King's Men*	"Baby, It's Cold Outside" *Neptune's Daughter*
1950	*All About Eve*	Joseph L. Mankiewicz *All About Eve*	Jose Ferrer *Cyrano de Bergerac*	Judy Holliday *Born Yesterday*	George Sanders *All About Eve*	Josephine Hull *Harvey*	"Mona Lisa" *Captain Carey, USA*
1951	*An American in Paris*	George Stevens *A Place in the Sun*	Humphrey Bogart *The African Queen*	Vivien Leigh *A Streetcar Named Desire*	Karl Malden *A Streetcar Named Desire*	Kim Hunter *A Streetcar Named Desire*	"In the Cool, Cool, Cool of the Evening" *Here Comes the Groom*
1952	*The Greatest Show on Earth*	John Ford *The Quiet Man*	Gary Cooper *High Noon*	Shirley Booth *Come Back, Little Sheba*	Anthony Quinn *Viva Zapata!*	Gloria Grahame *The Bad and the Beautiful*	"High Noon (Do not Forsake Me, Oh My Darlin')" *High Noon*
1953	*From Here to Eternity*	Fred Zinnemann *From Here to Eternity*	William Holden *Stalag 17*	Audrey Hepburn *Roman Holiday*	Frank Sinatra *From Here to Eternity*	Donna Reed *From Here to Eternity*	"Secret Love" *Calamity Jane*
1954	*On the Waterfront*	Elia Kazan *On the Waterfront*	Marion Brando *On the Waterfront*	Grace Kelly *The Country Girl*	Edmond O'Brien *The Barefoot Contessa*	Eva Marie Saint *On the Waterfront*	"Three Coins in the Fountain" *Three Coins in the Fountain*
1955	*Marty*	Delbert Mann *Marty*	Ernest Borgnine *Marty*	Anna Magnani *The Rose Tattoo*	Jack Lemmon *Mister Roberts*	Jo Van Fleet *East of Eden*	"Love Is a Many-Splendored Thing" *Love Is a Many-Splendored Thing*
1956	*Around the World in 80 Days*	George Stevens *Giant*	Yul Brynner *The King and I*	Ingrid Bergman *Anastasia*	Anthony Quinn *Lust for Life*	Dorothy Malone *Written on the Wind*	"Whatever Will Be, Will Be (Que Sera, Sera)" *The Man Who Knew Too Much*
1957	*The Bridge on the River Kwai*	David Lean *The Bridge on the River Kwai*	Alec Guinness *The Bridge on the River Kwai*	Joanne Woodward *The Three Faces of Eve*	Red Buttons *Sayonara*	Miyoshi Umeki *Sayonara*	"All the Way" *The Joker Is Wild*
1958	*Gigi*	Vincente Minnelli *Gigi*	David Niven *Separate Tables*	Susan Hayward *I Want to Live!*	Burl Ives *The Big Country*	Wendy Hiller *Separate Tables*	"Gigi" *Gigi*
1959	*Ben-Hur*	William Wyler *Ben-Hur*	Charlton Heston *Ben-Hur*	Simone Signoret *Room at the Top*	Hugh Griffith *Ben-Hur*	Shelley Winters *The Diary of Anne Frank*	"High Hopes" *A Hole in the Head*
1960	*The Apartment*	Billy Wilder *The Apartment*	Burt Lancaster *Elmer Gantry*	Elizabeth Taylor *Butterfield 8*	Peter Ustinov *Spartacus*	Shirley Jones *Elmer Gantry*	"Never on Sunday" *Never on Sunday*
1961	*West Side Story*	Jerome Robbins, Robert Wise *West Side Story*	Maximilian Schell *Judgment at Nuremberg*	Sophia Loren *Two Women*	George Chakiris *West Side Story*	Rita Moreno *West Side Story*	"Moon River" *Breakfast at Tiffany's*
1962	*Lawrence of Arabia*	David Lean *Lawrence of Arabia*	Gregory Peck *To Kill a Mockingbird*	Anne Bancroft *The Miracle Worker*	Ed Begley *Sweet Bird of Youth*	Patty Duke *The Miracle Worker*	"Days of Wine and Roses" *Days of Wine and Roses*
1963	*Tom Jones*	Tony Richardson *Tom Jones*	Sidney Poitier *Lilies of the Field*	Patricia Neal *Hud*	Melvyn Douglas *Hud*	Margaret Rutherford *The V.I.P.s*	"Call Me Irresponsible" *Papa's Delicate Condition*
1964	*My Fair Lady*	George Cukor *My Fair Lady*	Rex Harrison *My Fair Lady*	Julie Andrews *Mary Poppins*	Peter Ustinov *Topkapi*	Lila Kedrova *Zorba the Greek*	"Chim Chim Cher-ee" *Mary Poppins*
1965	*The Sound of Music*	Robert Wise *The Sound of Music*	Lee Marvin *Cat Ballou*	Julie Christie *Darling*	Martin Balsam *A Thousand Clowns*	Shelley Winters *A Patch of Blue*	"The Shadow of Your Smile" *The Sandpiper*
1966	*A Man for All Seasons*	Fred Zinnemann *A Man for All Seasons*	Paul Scofield *A Man for All Seasons*	Elizabeth Taylor *Who's Afraid of Virginia Woolf?*	Walter Matthau *The Fortune Cookie*	Sandy Dennis *Who's Afraid of Virginia Woolf?*	"Born Free" *Born Free*
1967	*In the Heat of the Night*	Mike Nichols *The Graduate*	Rod Steiger *In the Heat of the Night*	Katharine Hepburn *Guess Who's Coming to Dinner*	George Kennedy *Cool Hand Luke*	Estelle Parsons *Bonnie and Clyde*	"Talk to the Animals" *Doctor Dolittle*
1968	*Oliver!*	Carol Reed *Oliver!*	Cliff Robertson *Charly*	Katharine Hepburn *The Lion in Winter*, Barbra Streisand *Funny Girl*	Jack Albertson *The Subject Was Roses*	Ruth Gordon *Rosemary's Baby*	"The Windmills of Your Mind" *The Thomas Crown Affair*
1969	*Midnight Cowboy*	John Schlesinger *Midnight Cowboy*	John Wayne *True Grit*	Maggie Smith *The Prime of Miss Jean Brodie*	Gig Young *They Shoot Horses, Don't They?*	Goldie Hawn *Cactus Flower*	"Raindrops Keep Fallin' on My Head" *Butch Cassidy and the Sundance Kid*

(continued)

TABLE 17.18 (continued)

Year	Best Picture	Best Director	Best Actor	Best Actress	Best Supporting Actor	Best Supporting Actress	Best Song (from film)
1970	Patton	Franklin Schaffner *Patton*	George C. Scott *Patton*	Glenda Jackson *Women in Love*	John Mills *Ryan's Daughter*	Helen Hayes *Airport*	"For All We Know" *Lovers and Other Strangers*
1971	The French Connection	William Friedkin *The French Connection*	Gene Hackman *The French Connection*	Jane Fonda *Klute*	Ben Johnson *The Last Picture Show*	Cloris Leachman *The Last Picture Show*	"Theme from Shaft" *Shaft*
1972	The Godfather	Bob Fosse *Cabaret*	Marlon Brando *The Godfather*	Liza Minnelli *Cabaret*	Joel Grey *Cabaret*	Eileen Heckart *Butterflies Are Free*	"The Morning After" *The Poseidon Adventure*
1973	The Sting	George Roy Hill *The Sting*	Jack Lemmon *Save the Tiger*	Glenda Jackson *A Touch of Class*	John Houseman *The Paper Chase*	Tatum O'Neal *Paper Moon*	"The Way We Were" *The Way We Were*
1974	The Godfather, Part II	Francis Ford Coppola *The Godfather, Part II*	Art Carney *Harry and Tonto*	Ellen Burstyn *Alice Doesn't Live Here Anymore*	Robert DeNiro *The Godfather, Part II*	Ingrid Bergman *Murder on the Orient Express*	"We May Never Love Like This Again" *The Towering Inferno*
1975	One Flew over the Cuckoo's Nest	Milos Forman *One Flew Over the Cuckoo's Nest*	Jack Nicholson *One Flew over the Cuckoo's Nest*	Louise Fletcher *One Flew over the Cuckoo's Nest*	George Burns *The Sunshine Boys*	Lee Grant *Shampoo*	"I'm Easy" *Nashville*
1976	Rocky	John G. Avildsen *Rocky*	Peter Finch *Network*	Faye Dunaway *Network*	Jason Robards *All the President's Men*	Beatrice Straight *Network*	"Evergreen" (love theme) *A Star Is Born*
1977	Annie Hall	Woody Allen *Annie Hall*	Richard Dreyfuss *The Goodbye Girl*	Diane Keaton *Annie Hall*	Jason Robards *Julia*	Vanessa Redgrave *Julia*	"You Light Up My Life" *You Light Up My Life*
1978	The Deer Hunter	Michael Cimino *The Deer Hunter*	Jon Voight *Coming Home*	Jane Fonda *Coming Home*	Christopher Walken *The Deer Hunter*	Maggie Smith *California Suite*	"Last Dance" *Thank God It's Friday*
1979	Kramer vs. Kramer	Robert Benton *Kramer vs. Kramer*	Dustin Hoffman *Kramer vs. Kramer*	Sally Field *Norma Rae*	Melvyn Douglas *Being There*	Meryl Streep *Kramer vs. Kramer*	"It Goes Like It Goes" *Norma Rae*
1980	Ordinary People	Robert Redford *Ordinary People*	Robert DeNiro *Raging Bull*	Sissy Spacek *Coal Miner's Daughter*	Timothy Hutton *Ordinary People*	Mary Steenburgen *Melvin and Howard*	"Fame" *Fame*
1981	Chariots of Fire	Warren Beatty *Reds*	Henry Fonda *On Golden Pond*	Katharine Hepburn *On Golden Pond*	John Gielgud *Arthur*	Maureen Stapleton *Reds*	"Arthur's Theme" (Best That You Can Do) *Arthur*
1982	Gandhi	Richard Attenborough *Gandhi*	Ben Kingsley *Gandhi*	Meryl Streep *Sophie's Choice*	Lou Gossett, Jr. *An Officer and a Gentleman*	Jessica Lange *Tootsie*	"Up Where We Belong" *An Officer and a Gentleman*
1983	Terms of Endearment	James L. Brooks *Terms of Endearment*	Robert Duvall *Tender Mercies*	Shirley MacLaine *Terms of Endearment*	Jack Nicholson *Terms of Endearment*	Linda Hunt *The Year of Living Dangerously*	"Flashdance . . . What a Feeling" *Flashdance*
1984	Amadeus	Milos Forman *Amadeus*	F. Murray Abraham *Amadeus*	Sally Field *Places in the Heart*	Haing S. Ngor *The Killing Fields*	Peggy Ashcroft *A Passage to India*	"I Just Called to Say I Love You" *The Woman in Red*
1985	Out of Africa	Sydney Pollack *Out of Africa*	William Hurt *Kiss of the Spider Woman*	Geraldine Page *The Trip to Bountiful*	Don Ameche *Cocoon*	Anjelica Huston *Prizzi's Honor*	"Say You, Say Me" *White Nights*
1986	Platoon	Oliver Stone *Platoon*	Paul Newman *The Color of Money*	Marlee Matlin *Children of a Lesser God*	Michael Caine *Hannah and Her Sisters*	Dianne Wiest *Hannah and Her Sisters*	"Take My Breath Away" *Top Gun*
1987	The Last Emperor	Bernardo Bertolucci *The Last Emperor*	Michael Douglas *Wall Street*	Cher *Moonstruck*	Sean Connery *The Untouchables*	Olympia Dukakis *Moonstruck*	"(I've Had) the Time of My Life" *Dirty Dancing*
1988	Rain Man	Barry Levinson *Rain Man*	Dustin Hoffman *Rain Man*	Jodie Foster *The Accused*	Kevin Kline *A Fish Called Wanda*	Geena Davis *The Accidental Tourist*	"Let the River Run" *Working Girl*
1989	Driving Miss Daisy	Oliver Stone *Born on the Fourth of July*	Daniel Day-Lewis *My Left Foot*	Jessica Tandy *Driving Miss Daisy*	Denzel Washington *Glory*	Brenda Fricker *My Left Foot*	"Under the Sea" *The Little Mermaid*
1990	Dances With Wolves	Kevin Costner *Dances With Wolves*	Jeremy Irons *Reversal of Fortune*	Kathy Bates *Misery*	Joe Pesci *GoodFellas*	Whoopi Goldberg *Ghost*	"Sooner or Later (I Always Get My Man)" *Dick Tracy*

Other categories for which Oscars were awarded in 1990

Foreign Film	Cinematography
Costume Design	Feature Documentary
Make Up	Original Score
Original Screenplay	Adapted Screenplay
Editing	Short Subject Live Action
Art Direction	Short Subject Documentary

Source: For detailed information on yearly awards see Robert Osborne, *65 Years of the Oscar: The Official History of the Academy Awards* (New York, 1994), 90–307.

Giants of postwar movies, Gary Cooper (right) and Ingrid Bergman appear with director Sam Wood while filming *For Whom the Bell Tolls*. (National Archives)

TABLE 17.19   FILMS NOMINATED FOR THE MOST OSCARS, TO 1990

Film	Year	Awards	Nominations
All About Eve	1950	6	14
Gone With the Wind	1939	8	13
From Here to Eternity	1953	8	13
Mary Poppins	1964	5	13
Who's Afraid of Virginia Woolf	1966	5	13
Mrs Miniver	1942	6	12
The Song of Bernadette	1943	4	12
Johnny Belinda	1948	1	12
A Streetcar Named Desire	1951	4	12
On the Waterfront	1954	8	12
Ben-Hur	1959	11	12
Becket	1964	1	12
My Fair Lady	1964	8	12
Reds	1981	3	12
Dances With Wolves	1990	7	12

Source: Russell Ash, *The Top Ten of Everything* (New York, 1994), 176.

TABLE 17.20   FILMS THAT WON THE MOST OSCARS, TO 1990

Film	Year	Awards
Ben-Hur	1959	11
West Side Story	1961	10
Gigi	1958	9
The Last Emperor	1987	9
Gone With the Wind	1939	8
From Here to Eternity	1953	8
On the Waterfront	1954	8
My Fair Lady	1964	8
Cabaret	1972	8
Gandhi	1982	8
Amadeus	1984	8

Source: Ash, *Top Ten,* 176.

Radio

Radio's position at the start of the postwar period was at the same time commanding and precarious. For more than two decades the universal form of entertainment for the American populace, radio approached the late 1940s as an extension of earlier years: the same basic schedule of diverse offerings, often the same shows and performers. For a short time, radio received the same results in audience approval: The comedy-variety programs, featuring large-name performers, such as Jack Benny or Bob Hope, remained the most popular. The end came with remarkable speed, and some people could see it coming. Freed of wartime shortages and government-imposed priorities, the television industry developed rapidly once it got started, with expansion of stations, improvement of quality, and affordability of receiving sets. Television pioneers became national figures, and then one-by-one or group-by-group, the top people of radio, and many of the most popular shows shifted over to television. The golden age of radio had largely ended by the mid-1950s or at latest the end of the decade, and the future of the medium seemed much in doubt.

It developed in short order that there was still fire in the ashes, as radio set to reestablishing itself as a meaningful part of the American system of communication, information, and entertainment. In large measure it meant that radio would have to shift into different forms of programming. Having yielded virtually the entire realm of prime-time network shows to television, radio emphasized programs that one could enjoy while performing some other function. Music, after all, is

music, an audio expression that one did not need to see to appreciate. Almost immediately recorded music and disc-jockey shows became a staple of the new radio, and offerings varied as tastes and times changed. Fortunately, rock music arrived at about the same time that radio was searching for new territory, in the mid-1950s. Rock and roll music and its later variations doubtless helped radio survive, but in time one could find on the dial something for every musical taste. "Talk" radio, which came somewhat later, took on new life in the 1980s when such personalities as Larry King, Rush Limbaugh, and Howard Stern came on the air. Even in areas where radio duplicated television, as in coverage of sporting events, it became evident that there was an audience for both forms of broadcast.

Well positioned to benefit from many of the technological advances in electronics, radio advanced its range, clarity, and quality of sound through such developments as the transistor, expansion of frequency modulation (FM) broadcasting, which lent itself to stereophonic sound (stereo), and the transmission miracles associated with space satellites. Every automobile had a radio, and one could find scarcely a household that did not have at least one portable unit. The Walkman (early versions of which had a radio) and the "boom box" were familiar parts of popular culture and excellent gifts for almost any occasion. Radio networks remained, but they stopped controlling programs, often confining their attention to brief hourly news summaries, special developments, and national sporting events, such as the World Series of baseball. Whether it offered music, sports, talk shows, or some combination of varied programs, radio in the last half of the 20th century became regionalized and localized, geared to ethnic, geographic, political, or cultural interests. As a consequence it became nearly impossible to identify, as once had been the practice, the most popular national radio programs, although some talk-show hosts did develop a national following. One could identify only popular formats.

TABLE 17.21 MOST POPULAR NETWORK RADIO PROGRAMS, SEASON OF 1946–1947

Program	Format	Hooper Rating[a]
Bob Hope	Comedy–Variety	30.2
Fibber McGee & Molly	Comedy–Drama	30.2
Charlie McCarthy	Comedy–Variety	27.4
Jack Benny	Comedy–Variety	27.0
Red Skelton	Comedy–Variety	25.4
Fred Allen	Comedy–Variety	24.9
Lux Radio Theater	Drama	23.8
Screen Actors Guild	Drama	23.8
Amos 'n Andy	Comedy–Drama	22.5
Phil Harris / Alice Faye	Comedy–Variety	21.0
Duffy's Tavern	Comedy–Drama	19.6
George Burns / Gracie Allen	Comedy–Drama	17.9
Judy Canova	Comedy–Variety	17.8
Bob Hawk	Quiz Show	17.6
Blondie	Comedy–Drama	17.3
Take It or Leave It	Quiz Show	17.2
Eddie Cantor	Comedy–Drama	17.1
Great Gildersleeve	Comedy–Drama	16.9
Henry Aldrich	Comedy–Drama	16.8
Truth or Consequences	Audience Part.	16.5
Bing Crosby	Comedy–Variety	16.1
Date with Judy	Comedy–Drama	16.0
Fannie Brice	Comedy–Drama	15.9
Abbott & Costello	Comedy–Variety	15.7
Big Town	Thriller-Drama	15.4
Life of Riley	Comedy–Drama	15.3
Joan Davis Show	Comedy–Drama	14.9
Your Hit Parade	Music–Variety	14.6
Jimmy Durante	Comedy–Variety	14.6
Eddie Foy	Comedy–Variety	14.5
Jack Haley	Comedy–Variety	14.4
Manhattan Merry Go Round	Comedy–Variety	14.0

[a] The Hooper Ratings, used during 1934–49, were based on telephone calls in major cities to learn the programs to which people were listening.
Source: Harry B. Summers, ed., *A Thirty-year History of Programs Carried on National Networks in the United States 1926–1956* (New York, 1971), 141–43.

TABLE 17.22 MOST POPULAR NETWORK RADIO PROGRAMS, SEASON OF 1955–1956

Program	Format	Nielsen Rating[a]
Guiding Light	Daytime Drama[b]	4.7
Helen Trent	Daytime Drama[b]	4.7
Young Dr. Malone	Daytime Drama[b]	4.7
Ma Perkins	Daytime Drama[b]	4.5
Arthur Godfrey	Daytime Variety	4.4
Our Miss Brooks	Comedy Drama	4.3
Nora Drake	Daytime Drama[b]	4.2
Road of Life	Daytime Drama[b]	4.1
Charlie McCarthy	Comedy–Drama	3.9
Two for the Money	Quiz	3.9
Brighter Day	Daytime Drama[b]	3.9
Wendy Warren	Daytime Drama[b]	3.9
Aunt Jenny's Stories	Daytime Drama[b]	3.7
Dragnet	Thriller Drama	3.6
People Are Funny	Audience Part.	3.5
Art Linkletter	Human Interest	3.4
Lowell Thomas	News	3.4
Second Mrs. Burton	Daytime Drama[b]	3.3
Gunsmoke	Thriller Drama	3.3
Morgan Beatty	News	3.3
Robert Q. Lewis	Daytime Variety	3.2
Great Gildersleeve	Comedy Drama	3.2
One Man's Family	Homey Drama	3.2
When a Girl Marries	Daytime Drama[b]	3.2
Gunsmoke	Daytime Thriller	3.2

Program	Format	Nielsen Rating[a]
Gene Autry	Semi-Variety	3.2
Groucho Marx	Quiz	3.2
Pepper Young's Family	Daytime Drama[b]	3.1
My True Story	Daytime Drama[b]	3.0
Woman in My House	Daytime Drama[b]	2.9
Lone Ranger	Daytime Thriller	2.7
Young Widder Brown	Daytime Drama[b]	2.6
Don McNeill, Breakfast Club	Daytime Variety	2.6
Fibber McGee & Molly	Comedy–Drama	2.5

[a] The Nielsen ratings that began in 1949–50 used new technology—a device attached to radios—to answer the same question as the Hooper survey: How many radios were tuned to specific programs? The much lower numbers in these Nielsen ratings reflected not a difference in systems but that conventional radio entertainment had collapsed.
[b] So-called soap operas, the last shows to defect to television.
Source: Summers, History of Programs, 221–27.

TABLE 17.23   RECORD OF RADIO-STATION GROWTH SINCE TELEVISION BEGAN, 1946–1990

Date	AM Authorized	On Air	FM Authorized	On Air
Jan. 1, 1949[a]	1,004		456	55
Jun. 30, 1946[a]	. . .	. . .	. . .	. . .
Jan. 1, 1947[a]	1,517	. . .	. . .	. . .
Jun. 30, 1947	. . .	. . .	918	238
Jan. 1, 1948[a]	1,962	1,621	926	458
Jan. 1, 1949	2,127	1,912	966	700
Jan. 1, 1950	2,234	2,086	788	733
Jan. 1, 1951	2,351	2,232	703	676
Jan. 1, 1952	2,408	2,331	650	637
Jan. 1, 1953[a]	2,524	2,391	. . .	. . .
Jun. 30, 1953[a]	. . .	. . .	601	580
Jan. 1, 1954	2,636	2,521	580	560
Jan. 1, 1955	2,774	2,669	559	552
Jan. 1, 1956	2,935	2,824	557	540
Jan. 1, 1957	3,125	3,008	554	530
Jan. 1, 1958	3,295	3,196	590	537
Jan. 1, 1959	3,440	3,326	695	578
Jan. 1, 1960	3,527	3,398	838	688
Jan. 1, 1961	3,667	3,539	1,018	815
Jan. 1, 1962	3,911	3,693	1,128	960
Jan. 1, 1963	3,924	3,810	1,128	1,081
Jan. 1, 1964	4,039	3,937	1,249	1,146
Jan. 1, 1965	4,077	4,009	1,468	1,270
Jan. 1, 1966	4,129	4,049	1,657	1,446
Jan. 1, 1967	4,190	4,121	1,865	1,643
Jan. 1, 1968	4,249	4,156	3,005	1,753
Jan. 1, 1969	4,300	4,237	2,114	1,938
Jan. 1, 1970	4,344	4,269	2,651	2,476
Jan. 1, 1971	4,383	4,323	2,795	2,636
Jan. 1, 1972	4,411	4,355	2,971	2,783
Jan. 1, 1973	4,431	4,382	3,162	2,965
Jan. 1, 1974	4,448	4,395	3,360	3,151
Jan. 1, 1975	4,477	4,432	3,617	3,353
Jan. 1, 1976	4,513	4,463	3,752	3,571
Jan. 1, 1977	4,536	4,497	3,969	3,743
Jan. 1, 1978	4,569	4,513	4,130	3,972
Jan. 1, 1979	4,599	4,549	4,310	4,089
Jan. 1, 1980	4,651	4,558	4,463	4,190
Jan. 1, 1981	4,700	4,589	4,588	4,374
Jan. 1, 1982	4,763	4,634	4,736	4,467
Jan. 1, 1983	4,828	4,685	4,970	4,505
Jan. 1, 1984	4,897	4,733	5,240	4,649
Jan. 1, 1985	4,924	4,754	5,479	4,888
Oct. 30, 1985	4,975	4,805	5,657	5,066
Oct. 31, 1986	5,026	4,856	5,781	5,190
Jan. 1, 1988	5,072	4,902	5,933	5,342
Jan. 1, 1989	5,199	4,932	6,434	5,529
Jan. 1, 1990	5,223	4,966	6,705	5,665

[a] Comparable figures for all services not available this date.
Source: R. R. Bowker Co., Broadcasting and Cable Market Place, 1992 (New Providence, N.J., 1992), E–15.

TABLE 17.24   RADIO AND TELEVISION OWNERSHIP—A COMPARISON, 1949–1990

Year	Radio Homes (millions)	TV Homes (millions)
1949	40.8	1.6
1950	42.1	5.9
1951	43.6	17.3
1952	44.8	17.3
1953	45.0	23.4
1954	45.4	28.2
1955	46.2	32.3
1956	47.2	36.7
1957	48.2	40.3
1958	48.9	43.0
1959	49.5	46.9
1960	49.5	45.2
1961	49.5	46.9
1962	51.1	49.0
1963	52.3	51.3
1964	54.9	52.6
1965	55.2	53.8
1966	57.0	54.9
1967	57.5	56.0
1968	58.5	57.0
1969	60.6	58.5
1970	62.0	60.1
1971	62.6	62.1
1972	64.1	64.8
1973	67.4	66.2
1974	68.9	68.5
1975	70.4	69.6
1976	71.4	71.2
1977	72.9	72.9
1978	74.6	74.5
1979	76.5	76.3
1980	78.6	77.3
1981	80.5	81.5
1982	84.3	83.3
1983	84.6	83.8
1984	84.6	84.9
1985	86.7	85.9
1986	87.1	87.4
1987	88.1	88.6
1988	89.9	90.4
1989	91.1	92.1
1990	92.8	93.1

Source: The Broadcasting Yearbook, 1991, G–16.

TABLE 17.25   RADIO FACTS, 1989

Radios in Use
533.2 million (up 17% since 1980)
343.0 million in homes
131.4 million in cars
37.8 million in trucks and vans
20.8 million at work
Households with Radios
99% of U.S. Total
Who Listens and How Long
95.3% of Americans older then 12 listen an average of 3 hours and 21 minutes each weekday.

Source: Wright, Universal Almanac, 1991, 242.

TABLE 17.26 RADIO STATIONS IN THE UNITED STATES, BY FORMAT, 1990

Type	Number
AM Stations	4,941
FM Stations	5,995
Commercial Stations	9,447
Noncommercial Stations	1,489
Country	2,577
Adult Contemporary	2,359
Religious	1,070
Oldies	934
Contemporary Hit/Top-40	905
Middle-of-the-Road (MOR)	555
Variety/Diverse	542
Rock/AOR	502
News	449
Classical	413
News/Talk	386
Jazz	342
Talk	326
Beautiful Music	311
Spanish	300
Gospel	266
Educational	241
Classic Rock	240
Urban Contemporary	235
Progressive	213
Big Band	181
Black	173
Other	157
Agriculture & Farm	105
Nostalgia	98
Public Affairs	53
Foreign Language/Ethnic	46
New Age	45
Blues	30
Bluegrass	18
Portuguese	8
Polka	7
Folk	6
Greek	3
Children	3
American Indian	3
Drama/Literature	2
Polish	2
Comedy	2
Filipino	1
Reggae	1
French	1

Source: *Broadcasting Yearbook, 1991*, F–103.

Television

The development of television was the most important new factor in American entertainment in the last half of the 20th century. It was one of the most important forces affecting the culture of the United States in the entire century. Television came to dominate the way people spent their leisure time; it affected all other means of entertainment in various ways—in some cases enhancing growth and expansion, as with several professional sports, in other cases producing decline of near catastrophic proportion, as in the case of theater-based motion pictures. Because of television, every competing agent of entertainment in some fashion had to change its format.

The evolution, or was it revolution, of television conformed almost perfectly with the classic tale of rags to riches—an industry that began the postwar era with virtually nothing and exploded to a state in 1990 where it was on top of everything in entertainment. Developed in the 1920s, television for many years stood as an unproven technological novelty left behind by another, simpler marvel of communication, radio. In the mid-1940s there were only six television stations and barely 30,000 receiving sets in the country, most of them in the New York City area. The first full year of the postwar period, 1946, brought sales of only 7,000 units. Then everything seemed to fall into place in terms of technological improvement, increase in family income, public policy, and a culture given over to anything new that made life easier and fun. By 1950 television sales zoomed to 5 million. Within 10 years 90 percent of the people had television, and by 1990 the number without a set was negligible—probably a consequence of accessibility or of intellectual or idiosyncratic choice. Even more fully than radio a few decades earlier, television became universal American entertainment.

Quality of the medium, and the cost, improved with competition and advances in technology. The transistor, so critical to the computer, also affected the quality, durability, and price of television sets. The industry began to broadcast in color in the mid-1950s, and in a relatively short time color was all it did. In the 1970s production of units began to shift abroad, starting with Japan, which first mastered the business of low-cost, precision manufacture, especially of electronics, and then it spread to other Asian states. In time nearly all television sets, or at least most of their components, came from abroad.

It soon became evident that television, as with radio earlier, would focus its attention on entertainment as opposed to information and that economics would guide the selection of shows. The system remained overwhelmingly private, although in time a limited public television would appear. Sponsors, companies that paid for programs to have them interspersed with commercial messages, and advertisers wanted shows that would cause the least offense and produce the largest audience. Radio had faced this issue earlier, and at first television programming was composed of shifting radio's lineup of shows—and often the people—over to TV. Aspects of this arrangement became almost permanent in the schedule. The basic philosophy of scheduling for parts of the day did not change much. Soap operas, for example, appeared on weekday afternoons on television as they had done on radio. But listener taste did change, with shifting emphases, the rise and fall of cultural attitudes. The westerns and variety shows that had been popular in the 1950s and 1960s at last ran their course. The appeal of certain forms remained fairly constant, even if the content within them changed: situation comedies; drama series that more often than not featured activities of police or doctors; movies, either made for television or adapted from films originally designed for theaters. Professional or intercollegiate sports maintained continuing and expanding appeal, although except for championship engagements, television sports coverage remained local or regional.

In its first quarter-century of operation, television broadcasting was in the hands of three companies that started in radio, reincarnated as America's established television networks: ABC, NBC, and CBS. Confinement of broadcasting largely to 12 Very High Frequency (VHF) channels and government concern about multiple stations interfering with one another discouraged expansion, making it possible for the Big Three to control 90 percent of prime-time broadcasting by the early 1970s.

What technology gives, however, more technology perhaps can take away. Domination by ABC, NBC, and CBS began to loosen with improvement in the UHF (Ultra High Frequency) bands—channels that numbered 14 and above. Then came video cable and satellite technology that enhanced the distance of signals and created a foundation for a virtual explosion of stations and networks.

In 1975 Home Box Office (HBO) began to use satellites to feed cable systems, thus becoming in effect a fourth national network, albeit committed to a limited form of programming and available only to those who paid for cable. In 1980 Ted Turner started CNN, Cable

News Network, a channel that truly came of age in the Gulf crisis that began in 1990. In 1981 MTV, an around-the-clock music channel targeted at the rock generation and its successors was made available for cable systems.

Originally designed for rural and suburban customers, cable moved into the cities in the 1980s. At that time the typical household without cable had seven channels; equipped with cable the average was 33, and the process of proliferation had only started. In the late 1980s a new regular broadcast network, Fox, entered the picture and began to gear up for full-scale competition with the traditional giants. The share of prime-time broadcasting held by CBS, NBC, and ABC had slipped to 60 percent and only a fool would argue that it would not go lower, probably much lower. By 1990 television continued to command a lion's share of the time Americans allotted to entertainment, and yet because of changes in television coverage, entertainment had taken on meaning vastly broader than in the 1950s and 1960s when the prime-time viewer as a rule had three choices.

TABLE 17.27 TELEVISION HOUSEHOLDS IN THE UNITED STATES, 1949–1990

Year	Total Households (1,000)	Total TV Households (1,000)	Percent with TV
1949–1950	43,000	3,880	9.0
1950–1951	43,890	10,320	23.5
1951–1952	44,760	15,300	34.2
1952–1953	45,640	20,400	44.7
1953–1954	46,660	26,000	55.7
1954–1955	47,620	30,700	64.5
1955–1956	48,600	34,900	71.8
1956–1957	49,500	38,900	78.6
1957–1958	50,370	41,920	83.2
1958–1959	51,150	43,950	85.9
1959–1960	52,500	45,750	87.1
1960–1961	53,170	47,200	88.8
1961–1962	54,300	48,855	90.0
1962–1963	55,100	50,300	91.3
1963–1964	55,900	51,600	92.3
1964–1965	56,900	52,700	92.6
1965–1966	57,900	53,850	93.0
1966–1967	58,900	55,130	93.6
1967–1968	59,900	56,670	94.6
1968–1969	61,300	58,250	95.0
1969–1970	61,410	58,500	95.3
1970–1971	62,910	60,100	95.5
1971–1972	64,850	62,100	95.8
1972–1973	67,210	64,800	96.4
1973–1974	68,310	66,200	96.9
1974–1975	70,520	68,500	97.1
1975–1976	71,460	69,600	97.4
1976–1977	73,100	71,200	97.4
1977–1978	74,700	72,900	97.6
1978–1979	76,240	74,500	97.7
1979–1980	77,900	76,300	97.9
1980–1981	81,480	79,900	98.1
1981–1982	83,120	81,500	98.1
1982–1983	84,940	83,300	98.1
1983–1984	85,430	83,800	98.1
1984–1985	86,530	84,900	98.1
1985–1986	87,590	85,900	98.1
1986–1987	89,125	87,400	98.1
1987–1988	90,270	88,600	98.1
1988–1989	92,030	90,400	98.1
1989–1990	93,760	92,100	98.1

Source: Les Brown, *Les Brown's Encyclopedia of Television* (Detroit, 1992), 652–53.

TABLE 17.28 TV VIEWING PER HOUSEHOLD, 1949–1990

Year	Hours per Day
1949–1950	4:35
1950–1951	4:43
1951–1952	4:49
1952–1953	4:40
1953–1954	4:46
1954–1955	4:51
1955–1956	5:01
1956–1957	5:09
1957–1958	5:05
1958–1959	5:02
1959–1960	5:06
1960–1961	5:07
1961–1962	5:06
1962–1963	5:11
1963–1964	5:25
1964–1965	5:29
1965–1966	5:32
1966–1967	5:42
1967–1968	5:46
1968–1969	5:50
1969–1970	5:56
1970–1971	6:02
1971–1972	6:12
1972–1973	6:15
1973–1974	6:14
1974–1975	6:07
1975–1976	6:18
1976–1977	6:10
1977–1978	6:17
1978–1979	6:28
1979–1980	6:36
1980–1981	6:45
1981–1982	6:48
1982–1983	6:55
1983–1984	7:08
1984–1985	7:07
1985–1986	7:10
1986–1987	7:05
1987–1988	6:59
1988–1989	7:02
1989–1990	6:55

Source: *Les Brown's Encyclopedia*, 668–69.

TABLE 17.29 U.S. CABLE SYSTEMS, BY SUBSCRIBER SIZE, AS OF APRIL 1, 1988

Size by Subscribers	Systems	Percent of Total	Subscribers	Percent of Total
50,000 & Over	149	1.77	13,387,749	32.27
20,000–49,999	358	4.26	10,938,683	26.37
10,000–19,999	486	5.78	6,630,808	15.99
5,000–9,999	610	7.25	4,250,525	10.24
3,500–4,999	400	4.75	1,669,758	4.02
1,000–3,499	1,617	19.22	3,108,321	7.50
500–999	1,169	13.90	831,619	2.00
250–499	1,183	14.06	425,944	1.02
249 & under	1,759	20.91	247,813	0.59
Not available	682	8.10	-	-
Total	8,413	100%	41,491,270	100%

Source: Warren Publishing Co., *Television & Cable Factbook: Cable and Services 1988* (New York, 1988), C-539.

TABLE 17.30 TOP-RANKED TELEVISION PROGRAMS— SELECTED SEASONS, 1950–1990

The following table contains the highest-ranked continuing evening television programs, based on the size of the audience. The rankings came from the A.C. Nielsen Company and measure the percent of homes with television that watched a show on a given night. A rating of 50, for example, meant that half the homes with televison watched this program. A modification of the system in 1960 made it difficult to compare popularity of shows before that time with shows afterward, but relative standing of a program within a given season remained the same. The television season lasted from October of one year through April of the following year.

Top 10, October 1950–April 1951

Rank	Program	Network	Rating
1.	Texaco Star Theater	NBC	61.6
2.	Fireside Theatre	NBC	52.6
3.	Philco TV Playhouse	NBC	45.3
4.	Your Show of Shows	NBC	42.6
5.	The Colgate Comedy Hour	NBC	42.0
6.	Gillette Cavalcade of Sports	NBC	41.3
7.	The Lone Ranger	ABC	41.2
8.	Arthur Godfrey's Talent Scouts	CBS	40.6
9.	Hopalong Cassidy	NBC	39.9
10.	Mama	CBS	39.7

Top 10, 1952–1953

Rank	Program	Network	Rating
1.	I Love Lucy	CBS	67.3
2.	Arthur Godfrey's Talent Scouts	CBS	54.7
3.	Arthur Godfrey and His Friends	CBS	47.1
4.	Dragnet	NBC	46.8
5.	Texaco Star Theater	NBC	46.7
6.	The Buick Circus Hour	NBC	46.0
7.	The Colgate Comedy Hour	NBC	44.3
8.	Gangbusters	NBC	42.4
9.	You Bet Your Life	NBC	41.6
10.	Fireside Theatre	NBC	40.6

Top 10, 1955–1956

Rank	Program	Network	Rating
1.	The $64,000 Question	CBS	47.5
2.	I Love Lucy	CBS	46.1
3.	The Ed Sullivan Show	CBS	39.5
4.	Disneyland	ABC	37.4
5.	The Jack Benny Show	CBS	37.2
6.	December Bride	CBS	37.0
7.	You Bet Your Life	NBC	35.4
8.	Dragnet	NBC	35.0
9.	The Millionaire	CBS	33.8
10.	I've Got a Secret	CBS	33.5

Top 10, 1957–1958

Rank	Program	Network	Rating
1.	Gunsmoke	CBS	43.1
2.	The Danny Thomas Show	CBS	35.3
3.	Tales of Wells Fargo	NBC	35.2
4.	Have Gun Will Travel	CBS	33.7
5.	I've Got a Secret	CBS	33.4
6.	The Life and Legend of Wyatt Earp	ABC	32.6
7.	General Electric Theater	CBS	31.5
8.	The Restless Gun	NBC	31.4
9.	December Bride	CBS	30.7
10.	You Bet Your Life	NBC	30.6

Top 10, October 1959-April 1960

Rank	Program	Network	Rating
1.	Gunsmoke	CBS	40.3
2.	Wagon Train	NBC	38.4
3.	Have Gun Will Travel	CBS	34.7
4.	The Danny Thomas Show	CBS	31.1
5.	The Red Skelton Show	CBS	30.8
6.	Father Knows Best	CBS	29.7
7.	77 Sunset Strip	ABC	29.7
8.	The Price Is Right	NBC	29.2
9.	Wanted: Dead or Alive	CBS	28.7
10.	Perry Mason	CBS	28.3

Top 10, 1962–1963

Rank	Program	Network	Rating
1.	The Beverly Hillbillies	CBS	36.0
2.	Candid Camera	CBS	31.1
3.	The Red Skelton Show	CBS	31.1
4.	Bonanza	NBC	29.8
5.	The Lucy Show	CBS	29.8
6.	The Andy Griffith Show	CBS	29.7
7.	Ben Casey	ABC	28.7
8.	The Danny Thomas Show	CBS	28.7
9.	The Dick Van Dyke Show	CBS	27.1
10.	Gunsmoke	CBS	27.0

Top 10, 1965–1966

Rank	Program	Network	Rating
1.	Bonanza	NBC	31.8
2.	Gomer Pyle, U.S.M.C.	CBS	27.8
3.	The Lucy Show	CBS	27.7
4.	The Red Skelton Hour	CBS	27.6
5.	Batman (Thurs.)	ABC	27.0
6.	The Andy Griffith Show	CBS	26.9
7.	Bewitched	ABC	25.9
8.	The Beverly Hillbillies	CBS	25.9
9.	Hogan's Heroes	CBS	24.9
10.	Batman (Wed.)	ABC	24.7

Top 10, 1967–1968

Rank	Program	Network	Rating
1.	The Andy Griffith Show	CBS	27.6
2.	The Lucy Show	CBS	27.0
3.	Gomer Pyle, U.S.M.C.	CBS	25.6
4.	Gunsmoke	CBS	25.5
5.	Family Affair	CBS	25.5
6.	Bonanza	NBC	25.5
7.	The Red Skelton Show	CBS	25.3
8.	The Dean Martin Show	NBC	24.8
9.	The Jackie Gleason Show	CBS	23.9
10.	Saturday Night at the Movies	NBC	23.6

Top 10, October 1969–April 1970

Rank	Program	Network	Rating
1.	Rowan & Martin's Laugh-In	NBC	26.3
2.	Gunsmoke	CBS	25.9
3.	Bonanza	NBC	24.8
4.	Mayberry R.F.D.	CBS	24.4
5.	Family Affair	CBS	24.2
6.	Here's Lucy	CBS	23.9
7.	The Red Skelton Hour	CBS	23.8
8.	Marcus Welby, M.D.	ABC	23.7
9.	Walt Disney's Wonderful World of Color	NBC	23.6
10.	The Doris Day Show	CBS	22.8

Top 10, 1972–1973

Rank	Program	Network	Rating
1.	All in the Family	CBS	33.3
2.	Sanford and Son	NBC	27.6
3.	Hawaii Five-O	CBS	25.2
4.	Maude	CBS	24.7
5.	Bridget Loves Bernie	CBS	24.2
6.	The NBC Sunday Mystery Movie	NBC	24.2
7.	The Mary Tyler Moore Show	CBS	23.6
8.	Gunsmoke	CBS	23.6
9.	The Wonderful World of Disney	NBC	23.5
10.	Ironside	NBC	23.4

Top 10, 1975–1976

Rank	Program	Network	Rating
1.	All in the Family	CBS	30.1
2.	Rich Man, Poor Man	ABC	28.0
3.	Laverne & Shirley	ABC	27.5
4.	Maude	CBS	25.0
5.	The Bionic Woman	ABC	24.9
6.	Phyllis	CBS	24.5
7.	Sanford and Son	NBC	24.4
8.	Rhoda	CBS	24.4
9.	The Six Million Dollar Man	ABC	24.3
10.	ABC Monday Night Movie	ABC	24.2

Top 10, 1977–1978			
Rank	Program	Network	Rating
1.	Laverne & Shirley	ABC	31.6
2.	Happy Days	ABC	31.4
3.	Three's Company	ABC	28.3
4.	60 Minutes	CBS	24.4
5.	Charlie's Angels	ABC	24.4
6.	All in the Family	CBS	24.4
7.	Little House on the Prairie	NBC	24.1
8.	Alice	CBS	23.2
9.	M*A*S*H	CBS	23.2
10.	One Day at a Time	CBS	23.0

Top 10, September 1979–April 1980			
Rank	Program	Network	Rating
1.	60 Minutes	CBS	28.4
2.	Three's Company	ABC	26.3
3.	That's Incredible	ABC	25.8
4.	Alice	CBS	25.3
5.	M*A*S*H	CBS	25.3
6.	Dallas	CBS	25.0
7.	Flo	CBS	24.4
8.	The Jeffersons	CBS	24.3
9.	The Dukes of Hazzard	CBS	24.1
10.	One Day at a Time	CBS	23.0

Top 10, 1982–1983			
Rank	Program	Network	Rating
1.	60 Mintues	CBS	25.5
2.	Dallas	CBS	24.6
3.	M*A*S*H	CBS	22.6
4.	Magnum, P.I.	CBS	22.6
5.	Dynasty	ABC	22.4
6.	Three's Company	ABC	21.2
7.	Simon & Simon	CBS	21.0
8.	Falcon Crest	CBS	20.7
9.	The Love Boat	ABC	20.3
10.	The A–Team	NBC	20.1

Top 10, 1985–1986			
Rank	Program	Network	Rating
1.	The Cosby Show	NBC	33.7
2.	Family Ties	NBC	30.0
3.	Murder, She Wrote	CBS	25.3
4.	60 Minutes	CBS	23.9
5.	Cheers	NBC	23.7
6.	Dallas	CBS	21.9
7.	Dynasty	ABC	21.8
8.	The Golden Girls	NBC	21.8
9.	Miami Vice	NBC	21.3
10.	Who's the Boss	ABC	21.1

Top 10, 1987–1988			
Rank	Program	Network	Rating
1.	The Cosby Show	NBC	27.8
2.	A Different World	NBC	25.0
3.	Cheers	NBC	23.4
4.	The Golden Girls	NBC	21.8
5.	Growing Pains	ABC	21.3
6.	Who's the Boss?	ABC	21.2
7.	Night Court	NBC	20.8
8.	60 Minutes	CBS	20.6
9.	Murder, She Wrote	CBS	20.2
10.	Alf	NBC	18.8

Top 10, September 1989–April 1990			
Rank	Program	Network	Rating
1.	The Cosby Show	NBC	23.1
2.	Roseanne	ABC	23.1
3.	Cheers	NBC	22.7
4.	A Different World	NBC	21.1
5.	America's Funniest Home Videos	ABC	20.9
6.	The Golden Girls	NBC	20.1
7.	60 Minutes	CBS	19.7
8.	The Wonder Years	ABC	19.2
9.	Empty Nest	NBC	18.9
10.	Monday Night Football	ABC	18.1

Source: Tim Brooks and Earle Marsh, *The Complete Directory to Prime Time Network and TV Shows, 1995* (New York, 1995), 1258–71

Bill Cosby, comedian, singer, actor, costar of NBC television series, *I Spy*, on tour in 1969 (Western Michigan University Archives and Regional History Collections)

TABLE 17.31   HIGHEST RANKING NETWORK SERIES, BY YEAR, 1950–1990

Season	Program	Network	Rating
1950–51	Texaco Star Theatre	NBC	61.6
1951–52	Godfrey's Talent Scouts	CBS	53.8
1952–53	I Love Lucy	CBS	67.3
1953–54	I Love Lucy	CBS	58.8
1954–55	I Love Lucy	CBS	49.3
1955–56	$64,000 Question	CBS	47.5
1956–57	I Love Lucy	CBS	43.7
1957–58	Gunsmoke	CBS	43.1
1958–59	Gunsmoke	CBS	39.6
1959–60	Gunsmoke	CBS	40.3
1960–61	Gunsmoke	CBS	37.3
1961–62	Wagon Train	NBC	32.1
1962–63	Beverly Hillbillies	CBS	36.0
1963–64	Beverly Hillbillies	CBS	39.1
1964–65	Bonanza	NBC	36.3
1965–66	Bonanza	NBC	31.8
1966–67	Bonanza	NBC	29.1
1967–68	Andy Griffith	CBS	27.6
1968–69	Rowan & Martin Laugh-in	NBC	31.8
1969–70	Rowan & Martin Laugh-in	NBC	26.3
1970–71	Marcus Welby, MD	ABC	29.6
1971–72	All In The Family	CBS	34.0
1972–73	All In The Family	CBS	33.3
1973–74	All In The Family	CBS	31.2
1974–75	All In The Family	CBS	30.2
1975–76	All In The Family	CBS	30.1
1976–77	Happy Days	ABC	31.5
1977–78	Laverne & Shirley	ABC	31.6
1978–79	Laverne & Shirley	ABC	30.5
1979–80	60 Minutes	CBS	28.2
1980–81	Dallas	CBS	31.2
1981–82	Dallas	CBS	28.4
1982–83	60 Minutes	CBS	25.5
1983–84	Dallas	CBS	25.7
1984–85	Dynasty	ABC	25.0
1985–86	Bill Cosby Show	NBC	33.8
1986–87	Bill Cosby Show	NBC	34.9
1987–88	Bill Cosby Show	NBC	27.8
1988–89	Roseanne	ABC	25.5
1989–90	Roseanne	ABC	23.4

Source: Ronald Alsop, ed., *The Wall Street Journal Almanac, 1998* (New York, 1997), 907.

TABLE 17.32   TOP 50 TV SERIES OF ALL TIME, THROUGH THE SEASON OF 1987–1988

Rank	Program	Network(s)	From	To
1.	*Gunsmoke*	CBS	1955	1975
2.	*The Red Skelton Show*	CBS, NBC	1951	1971
3.	*60 Minutes*	CBS	1968	. . .
4.	*Bonanza*	NBC	1959	1973
5.	*All in the Family / Archie Bunker's Place*	CBS	1971	1983
6.	*The Ed Sullivan Show / Toast of the Town*	CBS	1948	1971
7.	*Walt Disney*	ABC, NBC, CBS	1954	. . .
8.	*The Lucy Show / Here's Lucy*	CBS	1962	1974
9.	*M*A*S*H*	CBS	1972	1983
10.	*Dallas*	CBS	1978	. . .
11.	*The Andy Griffith Show*	CBS	1960	1968
12.	*The Jack Benny Show*	CBS, NBC	1950	1965
13.	*Three's Company / Three's a Crowd*	ABC	1977	1985
14.	*I Love Lucy*	CBS	1951	1961
15.	*The Danny Thomas Show*	ABC, CBS	1953	1971
16.	*The Beverly Hillbillies*	CBS	1962	1971
17.	*You Bet Your Life*	NBC	1950	1961
18.	*Happy Days*	ABC	1974	1984
19.	*I've Got a Secret*	CBS	1952	1967
20.	*Dragnet / Dragnet '67*	NBC	1952	1970
21.	*Arthur Godfrey's Talent Scouts*	CBS	1948	1958
22.	*The Jeffersons*	CBS	1975	1985
23.	*Hawaii Five-O*	CBS	1968	1980
24.	*The Jackie Gleason Show*	CBS	1952	1970
25.	*One Day at a Time*	CBS	1975	1984
26.	*Laverne & Shirley*	ABC	1976	1983
27.	*The Milton Berle Show*	NBC, ABC	1948	1967
28.	*Sandford and Son*	NBC	1972	1977
29.	*Gomer Pyle, U.S.M.C.*	CBS	1964	1970
30.	*Alice*	CBS	1976	1985
31.	*Dynasty*	ABC	1981	. . .
32.	*Wagon Train*	NBC, ABC	1957	1965
33.	*My Three Sons*	ABC, CBS	1960	1972
34.	*Bewitched*	ABC	1964	1972
35.	*The Love Boat*	ABC	1977	1986
36.	*Fireside Theatre*	NBC, ABC	1949	1963
37.	*Little House on the Prairie*	NBC	1974	1983
38.	*The Cosby Show*	NBC	1984	. . .
39.	*The Waltons*	CBS	1972	1981
40.	*Have Gun, Will Travel*	CBS	1957	1963
41.	*Candid Camera*	CBS, NBC, ABC	1948	1967
42.	*General Electric Theater*	CBS	1953	1962
43.	*Arthur Godfrey and His Friends*	CBS	1949	1959
44.	*The Mary Tyler Moore Show*	CBS	1970	1977
45.	*Falcon Crest*	CBS	1981	. . .
46.	*Maude*	CBS	1972	1978
47.	*Marcus Welby, M.D.*	ABC	1969	1976
48.	*Magnum, P.I.*	CBS	1980	1988
49.	*Cheers*	NBC	1982	. . .
50.	*Family Ties*	NBC	1982	. . .

Note: The list was compiled by authors of *The Complete Directory to . . . TV Shows* who developed a point system based on duration and popularity of each television series. Shows still running in 1988 of course could improve their ranking. The most significant change involved *60 Minutes,* which ran strong through the rest of the century and replaced *Gunsmoke* in the early 1990s as the most popular series.
Source: Tim Brooks and Earle Marsh, *The Complete Directory to Prime Time Network and Cable TV Shows, 1995* (New York, 1995), 979–80.

TABLE 17.33   TOP-RATED INDIVIDUAL NETWORK PROGRAMS

Rank	Program	Telecast Date	Network	Duration (minutes)	Average Audience[a] %	Share[b]	Average Audience (1,000)
1.	M*A*S*H Special	Feb 28, 1983	CBS	150	60.2	77	50,150
2.	Dallas	Nov 21, 1980	CBS	60	53.3	76	41.470
3.	Roots Pt. VIII	Jan 30, 1977	ABC	115	51.1	71	36,380
4.	Super Bowl XVI Game	Jan 24, 1982	CBS	213	49.1	73	40,020
5.	Super Bowl XVII Game	Jan 30, 1983	NBC	204	48.6	69	40.480
6.	Super Bowl XX Game	Jan 26, 1986	NBC	231	48.3	70	41,490
7.	Gone With the Wind Pt. 1	Nov 7, 1976	NBC	179	47.7	65	33,960
8.	Gone With the Wind Pt. 2	Nov 8, 1976	NBC	119	47.4	64	33,750
9.	Super Bowl XII Game	Jan 15, 1978	CBS	218	47.2	67	34,410
10.	Super Bowl XIII Game	Jan 21, 1979	NBC	230	47.1	74	35,090
11.	Bob Hope Christmas Show	Jan 15, 1970	NBC	90	46.6	64	27,260
12.	Super Bowl XVIII Game	Jan 22, 1984	CBS	218	46.4	71	38,800
13.	Super Bowl XIX Game	Jan 20, 1985	ABC	218	46.4	63	39,390
14.	Super Bowl XIV Game	Jan 20, 1980	CBS	178	46.3	67	35,330
15.	ABC Theater (The Day After)	Nov 20, 1983	ABC	144	46.0	62	38,550
16.	Roots Pt. VI	Jan 28, 1977	ABC	120	45.9	66	32,680
17.	The Fugitive	Aug 29, 1967	ABC	60	45.9	72	25,700
18.	Super Bowl XXI Game	Jan 25, 1987	CBS	206	45.8	66	40,030
19.	Roots Pt. V	Jan 27, 1977	ABC	60	45.7	71	32,540
20.	Ed Sullivan	Feb 9, 1964	CBS	60	45.3	60	23,240
21.	Bob Hope Christmas Show	Jan 14, 1971	NBC	90	45.0	61	27,050
22.	Roots Pt. III	Jan 25, 1977	ABC	60	44.8	68	31,900
23.	Super Bowl XI Game	Jan 9, 1977	NBC	204	44.4	73	31,610
24.	Super Bowl XV Game	Jan 25, 1981	NBC	220	44.4	63	34,540
25.	Super Bowl VI Game	Jan 16, 1972	CBS	170	44.2	74	27,450
26.	Roots Pt. II	Jan 24, 1977	ABC	120	44.1	62	31,400
27.	Beverly Hillbillies	Jan 8, 1964	CBS	30	44.0	65	22,570
28.	Roots Pt. IV	Jan 26, 1977	ABC	60	43.8	66	31,190
29.	Ed Sullivan	Feb 16, 1964	CBS	60	43.8	60	22,445
30.	Super Bowl XXIII Game	Jan 22, 1989	NBC	213	43.5	68	39,320
31.	Academy Awards	Apr 7, 1970	ABC	145	43.4	78	25,390
32.	Thorn Birds Pt. III	Mar 29, 1983	ABC	120	43.2	62	35,990
33.	Thron Birds Pt. IV	Mar 30, 1983	ABC	180	43.1	62	35,900
34.	CBS NFC Champ. Game	Jan 10, 1982	CBS	195	42.9	62	34,960
35.	Beverly Hillbillies	Jan 15, 1964	CBS	30	42.8	62	21,960
36.	Super Bowl VII Game	Jan 14, 1973	NBC	185	42.7	72	27,670
37.	Thorn Birds Pt. II	Mar 28, 1983	ABC	120	42.5	59	35,400
38.	Super Bowl IX Game	Jan 12, 1975	NBC	190	42.4	72	29,040
39.	Beverly Hillbillies	Feb 26, 1964	CBS	30	42.4	60	21,750
40.	Super Bowl X Game	Jan 18, 1976	CBS	200	42.3	78	29,440
41.	Airport (Movie Specials)	Nov 11, 1973	ABC	170	42.3	63	28,000
42.	Love Story (Sun. Night Mov.)	Oct 1, 1972	ABC	120	42.3	62	27,410
43.	Cinderella	Feb 22, 1965	CBS	90	42.3	59	22,250
44.	Roots Pt. VII	Jan 29, 1977	ABC	60	42.3	65	30,120
45.	Beverly Hillbillies	Mar 25, 1964	CBS	30	42.2	59	21,650
46.	Beverly Hillbillies	Feb 6, 1964	CBS	30	42.0	61	21,550
47.	Beverly Hillbillies	Jan 29, 1964	CBS	30	41.9	62	21,490
48.	Super Bowl XXII Game	Jan 31, 1988	ABC	229	41.9	62	37,120
49.	Miss America Pageant	Sep 9, 1961	CBS	150	41.8	75	19,600
50.	Beverly Hillbillies	Jan 1, 1964	CBS	30	41.8	59	21,440

Note: Rankings based on reports made from July 1960 through December 1990. List includes neither shows lasting fewer than 30 minutes nor programs, such as political conventions, covered by more than one network.
[a] Average audience, or ratings, pertains to the percent of all households with TV that are tuned to a program.
[b] Share pertains to portion of the audience received from all households that are watching TV in a given time slot.
Source: Les Brown's Encyclopedia, 650–51.

TABLE 17.34 TOP-RATED NETWORK SPORTS EVENTS, THROUGH THE YEAR 1990

Rank	Program	Date	Net.	Household Rating	Share
1.	Super Bowl XVI (San Francisco vs. Cincinnati)	1/24/82	CBS	49.1	73
2.	Super Bowl XVII (Washington vs. Miami)	1/30/83	NBC	48.6	69
3.	Super Bowl XX (Chicago vs. New England)	1/26/86	NBC	48.3	70
4.	Super Bowl XII (Dallas vs. Denver)	1/15/78	CBS	47.2	67
5.	Super Bowl XXIII (Dallas vs. Pittsburgh)	1/21/79	NBC	47.1	74
6.	Super Bowl XVIII (L.A. Raiders vs. Washington)	1/22/84	CBS	46.4	71
7.	Super Bowl XIX (San Francisco vs. Miami)	1/20/85	ABC	46.4	63
8.	Super Bowl XIV (L.A. Rams vs. Pittsburgh)	1/20/80	CBS	46.3	67
9.	Super Bowl XXI (N.Y. Giants vs. Denver)	1/25/87	CBS	45.8	66
10.	Super Bowl XI (Minnesota vs. Oakland Raiders)	1/9/77	NBC	44.4	73
11.	Super Bowl XV (Philadelphia vs. Oakland Raiders)	1/25/81	NBC	44.4	63
12.	Super Bowl VI (Dallas vs. Miami)	1/16/72	CBS	44.2	74
13.	Super Bowl XXIII (Cincinnati vs. San Francisco)	1/22/89	NBC	43.5	68
14.	NFC Championship Game (Dallas vs. San Francisco)	1/10/82	CBS	42.9	62
15.	Super Bowl VII (Washington vs. Miami)	1/14/73	NBC	42.7	72
16.	Super Bowl IX (Minnesota vs. Pittsburgh)	1/12/75	NBC	42.4	72
17.	Super Bowl X (Dallas vs. Pittsburgh)	1/8/76	CBS	42.3	78
18.	Super Bowl XXII (Washington vs. Denver)	1/31/88	ABC	41.9	62
19.	Super Bowl VIII (Minnesota vs. Miami)	1/13/74	CBS	41.6	73
20.	World Series Game #6 (Kansas City vs. Philadelphia)	10/21/80	NBC	40.0	60
21.	Super Bowl V (Dallas vs. Baltimore)	1/17/71	NBC	39.9	75
22.	World Series Game #7 (Boston vs. Cincinnati)	10/22/75	NBC	39.6	60
23.	World Series Game #4 (Yankees vs. Dodgers)	10/6/63	NBC	39.5	87
24.	Super Bowl IV (Minnesota vs. Kansas City)	1/11/70	CBS	39.4	69

Source: Les Brown's Encyclopedia, 648.

TABLE 17.35 SUPER BOWL RATING HISTORY, 1967–1990

Year	Game	Network	Total Rating	Audience Share
1967	Green Bay–Kansas City	CBS	33.1	43
1968	Green Bay–Oakland	CBS	48.3	68
1969	N.Y. Jets–Baltimore	NBC	47.1	71
1970	Kansas City–Minnesota	CBS	52.7	69
1971	Baltimore–Dallas	NBC	50.7	75
1972	Dallas–Miami	CBS	55.0	74
1973	Miami–Washington	NBC	54.1	72
1974	Miami–Minnesota	CBS	51.9	73
1975	Minnesota–Pittsburgh	NBC	53.9	72
1976	Dallas–Pittsburgh	CBS	53.7	78
1977	Oakland–Minnesota	NBC	44.4	73
1978	Dallas–Denver	CBS	47.2	67
1979	Dallas–Pittsburgh	NBC	47.1	74
1980	Los Angeles–Pittsburgh	CBS	46.3	67
1981	Oakland–Philadelphia	NBC	44.4	63
1982	Cincinnati–San Francisco	CBS	49.1	73
1983	Washington–Miami	NBC	48.6	69
1984	Washington–L.A. Raiders	CBS	46.4	71
1985	San Francisco–Miami	ABC	46.4	63
1986	Chicago–New England	NBC	48.3	70
1987	Denver–N.Y. Giants	CBS	45.8	66
1988	Washington–Denver	ABC	41.9	62
1989	San Francisco–Cincinnati	NBC	43.5	68
1990	San Francisco–Denver	CBS	39.0	63

Source: Les Brown's Encyclopedia, 649.

TABLE 17.36 LONGEST-RUNNING TELEVISION GAME SHOWS, THROUGH THE YEAR 1990

Show	Showing	Length	Debut
The Price Is Right[a]	daytime	18 years	Sep. 1972
What's My Line	prime time	17+ years	Feb. 1950
Wheel of Fortune (syndication began 1983)[a]	daytime	15 years	Jan. 1975
I've Got a Secret	prime time	15 years	Jun. 1952
Concentration	daytime	14+ years	Aug. 1958
Hollywood Squares	daytime	13+ years	Oct. 1966
Let's Make a Deal	daytime	12+ years	Dec. 1963
G.E. College Bowl	weekend	11+ years	Jan. 1959
You Bet Your Life	prime time	11 years	Oct. 1950
Jeopardy (syndication began 1984)[a]	daytime	10+ years	Mar. 1964
To Tell the Truth (syndication began 1969)	prime time	10+ years	Dec. 1956
Pantomime Quiz	seasonal	9+ years	Jul. 1950
Truth or Consequences	syndicated	9 years	Sep. 1966
The Joker's Wild	syndicated	9 years	Sep. 1977
Family Feud (syndicated 1977)	day time	9 years	Jul. 1976
The Price Is Right	daytime	8+ years	Nov. 1956
Queen for a Day	daytime	8+ years	Jan. 1956
Truth or Consequences	daytime	8+ years	Dec. 1956
Newlywed Game	daytime	8+ years	Jul. 1966
Break the Bank	prime time	8+ years	Oct. 1948
Masquerade Party	prime time	8+ years	July 1952
Tic Tac Dough	syndicated	8 years	Sep. 1978
Beat the Clock	prime time	8 years	Mar. 1950
The Big Payoff	daytime	7+ years	Dec. 1951
The Dating Game	daytime	7+ years	Dec. 1965
$10,000/20,000 Pyramid	daytime	7+ years	Mar. 1973
Sports Challenge	syndicated	7 years	Jan. 1971
Name that Tune	syndicated	7 years	Sep. 1968
Celebrity Bowling	syndicated	7 years	Jan. 1971
The Match Game	daytime	6+ years	Dec. 1962

[a] Still running, 1990.

Source: Danny Schwartz, Steven Ryan and Fred Wostrock, *The Encyclopedia of TV Game Shows* (New York, 1995), 273–74.

TABLE 17.37   THE EMMY AWARDS, 1948–1990

Intended as TV's equivalent of the Oscars, the Emmy Awards were presented first in 1949. The number has grown over the years. Listed below are some of the most popular awards.

1948	1949	1950
Outstanding TV Personality: Shirley Dinsdale (and her puppet Judy Splinters) (KTLA) Most Popular TV Program: *Pantomime Quiz Time* (KTLA) Best Film Made for Television: "The Necklace,' *Your Show Time* (NBC) Special Award: Louis McManus, original designer of the Emmy.	Best Live Show: *The Ed Wynn Show* (CBS) Best Kinescope Show: *Texaco Star Theater* (NBC) Outstanding Live Personality: Ed Wynn (CBS) Outstanding Kinescope Personality: Milton Berle (NBC) Best Film Made for TV: *The Life of Riley* (NBC)	Best Actor: Alan Young (CBS) Best Actress: Gertrude Berg (CBS) Outstanding Personality: Groucho Marx (NBC) Best Variety Show: *The Alan Young Show* (CBS) Best Dramatic Show: *Pulitzer Prize Playhouse* (ABC) Best Game Show: *Truth or Consequences* (CBS)

1951	1952	1953
Best Dramatic Show: *Studio One* (CBS) Best Comedy Show: *The Red Skelton Show* (CBS) Best Variety Show: *Your Show of Shows* (NBC) Best Actor: Sid Caesar (NBC) Best Actress: Imogene Coca (NBC) Best Comedian or Comedienne: Red Skelton (NBC)	Best Dramatic Program: *Robert Montgomery Presents* (NBC) Best Variety Program: *Your Show of Shows* (NBC) Best Mystery, Action, or Adventure Program: *Dragnet* (NBC) Best Situation Comedy: *I Love Lucy* (CBS) Best Actor: Thomas Mitchell Best Actress: Helen Hayes	Best Dramatic Program: *The U.S. Steel Hour* (ABC) Best Situation Comedy: *I Love Lucy* (CBS) Best Variety Program: *Omnibus* (CBS) Best Male Star of Regular Series: Donald O'Connor, *Colgate Comedy Hour* (NBC) Best Female Star of Regular Series: Eve Arden, *Our Miss Brooks* (CBS) Best Mystery, Action, or Adventure Program: *Dragnet* (NBC)

1954	1955	1956
Best Actor Starring in a Regular Series: Danny Thomas, *Make Room for Daddy* (ABC) Best Actress Starring in a Regular Series: Loretta Young, *The Loretta Young Show* (NBC) Best Mystery or Intrigue Series: *Dragnet* (NBC) Best Variety Series including Musical Varieties: *Disneyland* (ABC) Best Situation Comedy Series: *Make Room for Daddy* (ABC) Best Dramatic Series: *The U.S. Steel Hour* (ABC)	Best Action or Adventure Series: *Disneyland* (ABC) Best Comedy Series: *The Phil Silvers Show* (CBS) Best Variety Series: *The Ed Sullivan Show* (CBS) Best Dramatic Series: *Producers' Showcase* (NBC) Best Actor (Continuing Performance): Phil Silvers, *The Phil Silvers Show* (CBS) Best Actress (Continuing Performance): Lucille Ball, *I Love Lucy* (CBS)	Best Single Program of the Year: "Requiem for a Heavy-weight," *Playhouse 90* (CBS) Best Series (Half Hour or Less): *The Phil Silvers Show* (CBS) Best Series (One Hour or More): *Caesar's Hour* (NBC) Best Continuing Performance by an Actor in a Dramatic Series: Robert Young, *Father Knows Best* (NBC) Best Continuing Performance by an Actress in a Dramatic Series: Loretta Young, *The Loretta Young Show* (NBC)

1957	1958–59	1959–60
Program of the Year: "The Comedian," *Playhouse 90* (CBS) Best Dramatic Series with Continuing Characters: *Gunsmoke* (CBS) Best Comedy Series: *The Phil Silvers Show* (CBS) Best Musical, Variety, Audience Participation, or Quiz Series: *The Dinah Shore Chevy Show* (NBC) Best Continuing Performance by an Actor in a Leading Role in a Dramatic or Comedy Series: Robert Young, *Father Knows Best* (NBC) Best Continuing Performance by an Actress in a Leading Role in a Dramatic or Comedy Series: Jane Wyatt, *Father Knows Best* (NBC)	Program of the Year: "An Evening with Fred Astaire" (NBC) Best Dramatic Series (One Hour or Longer): *Playhouse 90* (CBS) Best Dramatic Series (Less Than One Hour): *Alcoa-Goodyear Theatre* (NBC) Best Comedy Series: *The Jack Benny Show* (CBS) Best Musical or Variety Series: *The Dinah Shore Chevy Show* (NBC) Best Western Series: *Maverick* (ABC) Best Actor in a Leading Role (Continuing Character) in a Dramatic Series: Raymond Burr, *Perry Mason* (CBS) Best Actress in a Leading Role (Continuing Character) in Dramatic Series: Loretta Young, *The Loretta Young Show* (NBC) Best Actor in a Leading Role (Continuing Character) in a Comedy Series: Jack Benny, *The Jack Benny Show* (CBS) Best Actress in a Leading Role (Continuing Character) in a Comedy Series: Jane Wyatt, *Father Knows Best* (CBS and NBC)	Outstanding Program Achievement in the Field of Humor: "The Art Carney Special" (NBC) Outstanding Program Achievement in the Field of Drama: *Playhouse 90* (CBS) Outstanding Program Achievement in the Field of Variety: "The Fabulous Fifties" (CBS) Outstanding Performance by an Actor in a Series (Lead or Support): Robert Stack, *The Untouchables* (ABC) Outstanding Performance by an Actress in a Series (Lead or Support): Jane Wyatt, *Father Knows Best* (CBS) Oustanding Performance in a Variety or Musical Program or Series: Harry Belafonte, "Tonight with Belafonte," *The Revlon Revue* (CBS)

1960–61	1961–62	1962–63
Program of the Year: "Macbeth," *Hallmark Hall of Fame* (NBC) Outstanding Program Achievement in the Field of Humor: *The Jack Benny Show* (CBS) Outstanding Program Achievement in the Field of Drama: "Macbeth," *Hallmark Hall of Frame* (NBC) Outstanding Program Achievement in the Field of Variety: "Astaire Time" (NBC) Outstanding Performance by an Actor in a Series (Lead): Raymond Burr, Perry Mason (CBS) Outstanding Performance by an Actress in a Series (Lead): Barbara Stanwyck, *The Barbara Stanwyck Show* (NBC) Outstanding Performance in a Variety or Musical Program or Series: Fred Astaire, "Astaire Time" (NBC)	Program of the Year: "Victoria Regina," *Hallmark Hall of Fame* (NBC) Outstanding Program Achievement in the Field of Humor: *The Bob Newhart Show* (NBC) Outstanding Program Achievement in the Field of Drama: *The Defenders* (CBS) Outstanding Program Achievement in the Field of Variety: *The Garry Moore Show* (CBS) Outstanding Performance by an Actor in a Series (Lead): E.G. Marshall, *The Defenders* (CBS) Outstanding Continued Performance by an Actress in a Series (Lead): Shirley Booth, *Hazel* (NBC) Outstanding Performance in a Variety or Musical Program or Series: Carol Burnett, *The Garry Moore Show* (CBS)	Program of the Year: "The Tunnel" (NBC) Outstanding Program Achievement in the Field of Humor: *The Dick Van Dyke Show* (CBS) Outstanding Program Achievement in the Field of Drama: *The Defenders* (CBS) Outstanding Program Achievement in the Field of Music: "Julie and Carol At Carnegie Hall" (CBS) Outstanding Program Achievement in the Field of Variety: *The Andy Williams Show* (NBC) Outstanding Continued performance by an Actor in a Series (Lead) E.G. Marshall, *The Defenders* (CBS) Outstanding Continued Performance by an Actress in a Series (Lead): Shirley Booth, *Hazel* (NBC) Outstanding Performance in a Variety or Musical Program or Series: Carol Burnett, "Julie and Carol at Carnegie Hall" (CBS) and "Carol and Company" (CBS)

1963–64	1964–65	1965–66
Program of the Year: "The Making of the President 1960" (ABC) Outstanding Program Achievement in the Field of Comedy: *The Dick Van Dyke Show* (CBS)	Outstanding Achievements in Entertainment: *The Dick Van Dyke Show* (CBS); "The Magnificent Yankee," *Hallmark Hall of Fame* (NBC); "My Name Is Barbra" (CBS) Outstanding Individual Achievements in Entertainment	Outstanding Comedy Series: *The Dick Van Dyke Show* (CBS Outstanding Variety Series: *The Andy Williams Show* (NBC) Outstanding Dramatic Series: *The Fugitive* (ABC) Outstanding Continued Performance by an Actor in a

(continued)

TABLE 17.37   (continued)

1963–64	1964–65	1965–66
Outstanding Program Achievement in the Field of Drama: *The Defenders* (CBS) Outstanding Program Achievement in the Field of Variety: *The Danny Kaye Show* (CBS) Outstanding Continued Performance by an Actor in a Series (lead): Dick Van Dyke, *The Dick Van Dyke Show* (CBS) Outstanding Continued Performance by an Actress in a Series (lead): Mary Tyler Moore, *The Dick Van Dyke Show* (CBS) Outstanding Performance in a Variety or Musical Program or Series: Danny Kaye, *The Danny Kaye Show* (CBS)	(Actors and Performers): Lynn Fontanne, "The Magnificent Yankee," *Hallmark Hall of Fame* (NBC); Barbra Streisand, "My Name Is Barbra" (CBS); Dick Van Dyke, *The Dick Van Dyke Show* (CBS)	Leading Role in a Dramatic Series: Bill Cosby, *I Spy* (NBC) Outstanding Continued Performance by an Actress in a Leading Role in a Dramatic Series: Barbara Stanwyck, *The Big Valley* (ABC) Outstanding Continued Performance by an Actor in a Leading Role in a Comedy Series: Dick Van Dyke, *The Dick Van Dyke Show* (CBS) Outstanding Continued Performance by an Actress in a Leading Role in a Comedy Series: Mary Tyler Moore, *The Dick Van Dyke Show* (CBS)

1966–67	1967–68	1968–69
Outstanding Comedy Series: *The Monkees* (NBC) Outstanding Variety Series: *The Andy Williams Show* (NBC) Outstanding Dramatic Series: *Mission: Impossible* (CBS) Outstanding Continued Performance by an Actor in a Leading Role in a Dramatic Series: Bill Cosby, *I Spy* (NBC) Outstanding Continued Performance by an Actress in a Leading Role in a Dramatic Series: Barbara Bain, *Mission: Impossible* (CBS) Outstanding Continued Performance by an Actor in a Leading Role in a Comedy Series: Don Adams, *Get Smart* (NBC) Outstanding Continued Performance by an Actress in a Leading Role in a Comedy Series: Lucille Ball, *The Lucy Show* (CBS)	Outstanding Comedy Series: *Get Smart* (NBC) Outstanding Dramatic Series: *Mission: Impossible* (CBS) Outstanding Continued Performance by an Actor in a Leading Role in a Dramatic Series: Bill Cosby, *I Spy* (NBC) Outstanding Continued Performance by an Actress in a Leading Role in a Dramatic Series: Barbara Bain, *Mission: Impossible* (CBS) Outstanding Continued Performance by an Actor in a Leading Role in a Comedy Series: Don Adams, *Get Smart* (NBC) Outstanding Continued Performance by an Actress in a Leading Role in a Comedy Series: Lucille Ball, *The Lucy Show* (CBS)	Outstanding Comedy Series: *Get Smart* (NBC) Outstanding Dramatic Series: *NET Playhouse* (NET) Outstanding Musical or Variety Series: *Rowan and Martin's Laugh-In* (NBC) Outstanding Continued Performance by an Actor in a Leading Role in a Dramatic Series: Carl Betz, *Judd, for the Defence* (ABC) Outstanding Continued Performance by an Actress in a Leading Role in a Dramatic Series: Barbara Bain, *Mission: Impossible* (CBS) Outstanding Continued Performance by an Actor in a Leading Role in a Comedy Series: Don Adams, *Get Smart* (NBC) Outstanding Continued Performance by an Actress in a Leading Role in a Comedy Series: Hope Lange, *The Ghost and Mrs. Muir* (NBC)

1969–70	1970–71	1971–72
Outstanding Comedy Series: *My World and Welcome to It* (NBC) Outstanding Dramatic Series: *Marcus Welby, M.D.* (ABC) Outstanding Variety or Musical Series: *The David Frost Show* (syndicated) Outstanding Continued Performance by an Actor in a Leading Role in a Dramatic Series: Robert Young, *Marcus Welby, M.D.* (ABC) Outstanding Continued Performance by an Actress in a Leading Role in a Dramatic Series: Susan Hampshire, *The Forsythe Saga* (NET) Outstanding Continued Performance by an Actor in a Leading Role in a Comedy Series: William Windom, *My World and Welcome to It* (NBC) Outstanding Continued Performance by an Actress in a Leading Role in a Comedy Series: Hope Lange, *The Ghost and Mrs. Muir* (ABC)	Outstanding Series—Comedy: *All in the Family* (CBS) Outstanding Series—Drama: *The Senator* (NBC) Outstanding Variety Series—Musical: *The Flip Wilson Show* (NBC) Outstanding Continued Performance by an Actor in a Leading Role in a Dramatic Series: Hal Holbrook, *The Senator* (NBC) Outstanding Continued Performance by an Actress in a Leading Role in a Dramatic Series: Susan Hampshire, *The First Churchills (Masterpiece Theatre)* (PBS) Outstanding Continued Performance by an Actor in a Leading Role in a Comedy Series: Jack Klugman, *The Odd Couple* (CBS) Outstanding Continued Performance by an Actress in a Leading Role in a Comedy Series: Jean Stapleton, *All in the Family* (CBS)	Outstanding Series—Comedy: *All in the Family* (CBS) Outstanding Series—Drama: *Elizabeth R (Masterpiece Theatre)* (PBS) Outstanding Variety Series—Musical: *The Carol Burnett Show* (CBS) Outstanding Variety Series—Talk: *The Dick Cavett Show* (ABC) Outstanding Continued Performance by an Actor in a Leading Role in a Dramatic Series: Peter Falk, *Columbo* (NBC) Outstanding Continued Performance by an Actor in a Leading Role in a Comedy Series: Carroll O'Connor, *All in the Family* (CBS) Outstanding Continued Performance by an Actress in a Leading Role in a Comedy Series: Jean Stapleton, *All in the Family* (CBS)

1972–73	1973–74	1974–75
Outstanding Comedy Series: *All in the Family* (CBS) Outstanding Drama Series: *The Waltons* (CBS) Outstanding Variety Musical Series: *The Julie Andrews Hour* (ABC) Outstanding Continued Performance by an Actor in a Leading Role (Drama Series—Continuing): Richard Thomas, *The Waltons* (CBS) Outstanding Continued Performance by an Actress in a Leading Role (Drama Series—Continuing): Michael Learned, *The Waltons* (CBS) Outstanding Continued Performance by an Actor in a Leading Role in a Comedy Series: Jack Klugman, *The Odd Couple* (ABC) Outstanding Continued Performance by an Actress in a Leading Role in a Comedy Series: Mary Tyler Moore, *The Mary Tyler Moore Show* (CBS)	Outstanding Comedy Series: *M*A*S*H* (CBS) Outstanding Drama Series: *Upstairs, Downstairs (Masterpiece Theatre)* (PBS) Outstanding Music Variety Series: *The Carol Burnett Show* (CBS) Best Lead Actor in a Comedy Series: Alan Alda, *M*A*S*H* (CBS) Best Lead Actor in a Drama Series: Telly Savalas, *Kojak* (CBS) Best Lead Actress in a Comedy Series: Mary Tyler Moore, *The Mary Tyler Moore Show* (CBS) Best Lead Actress in a Drama Series: Michael Learned, *The Waltons* (CBS)	Outstanding Comedy Series: *The Mary Tyler Moore Show* (CBS) Outstanding Drama Series: *Upstairs, Downstairs (Masterpiece Theatre)* (PBS) Outstanding Comedy-Variety or Music Series: *The Carol Burnett Show* (CBS) Outstanding Lead Actor in a Comedy Series: Tony Randall, *The Odd Couple* (ABC) Outstanding Lead Actor in a Drama Series: Robert Blake, *Baretta* (ABC) Outstanding Lead Actress in a Comedy Series: Valerie Harper, *Rhoda* (CBS) Outstanding Lead Actress in a Drama Series: Jean Marsh, *Upstairs, Downstairs (Masterpiece Theatre)* (PBS)

1975–76	1976–77	1977–78
Outstanding Comedy Series: *The Mary Tyler Moore Show* (CBS) Outstanding Drama Series: *Police Story* (NBC) Outstanding Comedy-Variety or Music Series: *NBC's Saturday Night Live* (NBC) Outstanding Lead Actor in a Comedy Series: Jack Albertson, *Chico and the Man* (NBC) Outstanding Lead Actor in a Drama Series: Peter Falk, *Columbo* (NBC) Outstanding Lead Actress in a Comedy Series: Mary Tyler Moore, *The Mary Tyler Moore Show* (CBS) Outstanding Lead Actress in a Drama Series: Michael Learned, *The Waltons* (CBS)	Outstanding Comedy Series: *The Mary Tyler Moore Show* (CBS) Outstanding Drama Series: *Upstairs, Downstairs (Masterpiece Theatre)* (PBS) Outstanding Comedy-Variety or Music Series: *Van Dyke and Company* (NBC) Outstanding Lead Actor in a Comedy Series: Carroll O'Connor, *All in the Family* (CBS) Outstanding Lead Actor in a Drama Series: James Garner, *The Rockford Files* (NBC) Outstanding Lead Actress in a Comedy Series: Beatrice Arthur, *Maude* (CBS) Outstanding Lead Actress in a Drama Series: Lindsay Wagner, *The Bionic Woman* (ABC)	Outstanding Comedy Series: *All in the Family* (CBS) Outstanding Drama Series: *The Rockford Files* (NBC) Outstanding Comedy-Variety or Music Series: *The Muppet Show* (syndicated) Outstanding Lead Actor in a Comedy Series: Carroll O'Connor, *All in the Family* (CBS) Outstanding Lead Actor in a Drama Series: Ed Asner, *Lou Grant* (CBS) Outstanding Lead Actress in a Comedy Series: Jean Stapleton, *All in the Family* (CBS) Outstanding Lead Actress in a Drama Series: Sada Thompson, *Family* (ABC)

1978–79	1979–80	1980–81
Outstanding Comedy Series: *Taxi* (ABC) Outstanding Drama Series: *Lou Grant* (CBS) Outstanding Comedy-Variety or Music Program (Special or Series): *Steve & Eydie Celebrate Irving Berlin* (NBC) Outstanding Lead Actor in a Comedy Series (Continuing or Single Performance): Carroll O'Connor, *All in the Family* (CBS) Outstanding Lead Actor in a Drama Series (Continuing or Single Performance): Ron Leibman, *Kaz* (CBS) Outstanding Lead Actress in a Comedy Series (Continuing or Single Performance): Ruth Gordon, *Taxi* ("Sugar Mama") (ABC) Outstanding Lead Actress in a Drama Series (Continuing or Single Performance): Mariette Hartley, *The Incredible Hulk* ("Married") (CBS)	Outstanding Comedy Series: *Taxi* (ABC) Outstanding Drama Series: *Lou Grant* (CBS) Outstanding Variety or Music Program (Special or Series): *IBM Presents Baryshnikov on Broadway* (ABC) Outstanding Lead Actor in a Comedy Series (Continuing or Single Performance): Richard Mulligan, *Soap* (ABC) Outstanding Lead Actor in a Drama Series (Continuing or Single Performance): Ed Asner, *Lou Grant* (CBS) Outstanding Lead Actress in a Comedy Series (Continuing or Single Performance): Cathryn Damon, *Soap* (ABC) Outstanding Lead Actress in a Drama Series (Continuing or Single Performance): Barbara Bel Geddes, *Dallas* (CBS)	Outstanding Comedy Series: *Taxi* (ABC) Outstanding Drama Series: *Hill Street Blues* (NBC) Outstanding Variety, Music, or Comedy Program: *Lily: Sold Out* (CBS) Outstanding Lead Actor in a Drama Series: Daniel J. Travanti, *Hill Street Blues* (NBC) Outstanding Lead Actor in a Comedy Series: Judd Hirsch, *Taxi* (ABC) Outstanding Lead Actress in a Drama Series: Barbara Babcock, *Hill Street Blues* (NBC) Outstanding Lead Actress in a Comedy Series: Isabel Sanford, *The Jeffersons* (CBS)
1981–82	**1982–83**	**1983–84**
Outstanding Comedy Series: *Barney Miller* (ABC) Outstanding Drama Series: *Hill Street Blues* (NBC) Outstanding Variety, Music, or Comedy Program: *Night of 100 Stars* (ABC) Outstanding Lead Actor in a Drama Series: Daniel J. Travanti, *Hill Street Blues* (NBC) Outstanding Lead Actor in a Comedy Series: Alan Alda *M*A*S*H* (CBS) Outstanding Lead Actress in a Drama Series: Michael Learned, *Nurse* (CBS) Outstanding Lead Actress in a Comedy Series: Carol Kane, *Taxi* ("Simka Returns") (ABC)	Outstanding Comedy Series: *Cheers* (NBC) Outstanding Drama Series: *Hill Street Blues* (NBC) Outstanding Variety, Music, or Comedy Program: *Motown 25: Yesterday, Today, Forever* (NBC) Outstanding Lead Actor in a Drama Series: Ed Flanders, *St. Elsewhere* (NBC) Outstanding Lead Actor in a Comedy Series: Judd Hirsch, *Taxi* (ABC) Outstanding Lead Actress in a Drama Series: Tyne Daly, *Cagney & Lacey* (CBS) Outstanding Lead Actress in a Comedy Series: Shelley Long, *Cheers* (NBC)	Outstanding Comedy Series: *Cheers* (NBC) Outstanding Drama Series: *Hill Street Blues* (NBC) Outstanding Variety, Music, or Comedy Program: "The 6th Annual Kennedy Center Honors: A Celebration of the Performing Arts" (CBS) Outstanding Lead Actor in a Drama Series: Tom Selleck, *Magnum, P.I.* (CBS) Outstanding Lead Actor in a Comedy Series: John Ritter *Three's Company* (ABC) Outstanding Lead Actress in a Drama Series: Tyne Daly, *Cagney & Lacey* (CBS) Outstanding Lead Actress in a Comedy Series: Jane Curtin, *Kate & Allie* (CBS)
1984–85	**1985–86**	**1986–87**
Outstanding Comedy Series: *The Cosby Show* (NBC) Outstanding Drama Series: *Cagney & Lacey* (CBS) Outstanding Variety, Music, or Comedy Program: "Motown Returns to the Apollo" (NBC) Outstanding Lead Actor in a Drama Series: William Daniels, *St. Elsewhere* (NBC) Outstanding Lead Actor in a Comedy Series: Robert Guillaume, *Benson* (ABC) Outstanding Lead Actress in a Drama Series: Tyne Daly, *Cagney & Lacey* (CBS) Outstanding Lead Actress in a Comedy Series: Jane Curtin, *Kate & Allie* (CBS)	Outstanding Comedy Series: *The Golden Girls* (NBC) Outstanding Drama Series: *Cagney & Lacey* (CBS) Outstanding Variety, Music, or Comedy Program: "The Kennedy Center Honors: A Celebration of the Performing Arts" (CBS) Outstanding Lead Actor in a Drama Series: William Daniels, *St. Elsewhere* (NBC) Outstanding Lead Actor in a Comedy Series: Michael J. Fox, *Family Ties* (NBC) Outstanding Lead Actress in a Drama Series: Sharon Gless, *Cagney & Lacey* (CBS) Outstanding Lead Actress in a Comedy Series: Betty White, *The Golden Girls* (NBC)	Outstanding Comedy Series: *The Golden Girls* (NBC) Outstanding Drama Series: *L.A. Law* (NBC) Outstanding Variety, Music, or Comedy Program: "The 1987 Tony Awards" (CBS) Outstanding Lead Actor in a Drama Series: Bruce Willis, *Moonlighting* (ABC) Outstanding Lead Actor in a Comedy Series: Michael J. Fox, *Family Ties* (NBC) Outstanding Lead Actress in a Drama Series: Sharon Gless, *Cagney & Lacey* (CBS) Outstanding Lead Actress in a Comedy Series: Rue McClanahan, *The Golden Girls* (NBC)
1987–88	**1988–89**	**1989–90**
Outstanding Comedy Series: *The Wonder Years* (ABC) Outstanding Drama Series: *thirtysomething* (ABC) Outstanding Variety, Music, or Comedy Program: "Irving Berlin's 100th Birthday Celebration" (CBS) Outstanding Lead Actor in a Comedy Series: Michael J. Fox, *Family Ties* (NBC) Outstanding Lead Actor in a Drama Series: Richard Kiley, *A Year in the Life* (NBC) Outstanding Lead Actress in a Comedy Series: Beatrice Arthur, *The Golden Girls* (NBC) Outstanding Lead Actress in a Drama Series: Tyne Daly, *Cagney & Lacey* (CBS)	Outstanding Comedy Series: *Cheers* (NBC) Outstanding Drama Series: *L.A. Law* (NBC) Outstanding Variety, Music, or Comedy Program: *The Tracey Ullman Show* (Fox) Outstanding Lead Actor in a Comedy Series: Richard Mulligan, *Empty Nest* (NBC) Outstanding Lead Actor in a Drama Series: Carroll O'Connor, *In the Heat of the Night* (NBC) Outstanding Lead Actress in a Comedy Series: Candice Bergen, *Murphy Brown* (CBS) Outstanding Lead Actress in a Drama Series: Dana Delany, *China Beach* (ABC)	Outstanding Comedy Series: *Murphy Brown* (CBS) Outstanding Drama Series: *L.A Law* (NBC) Outstanding Variety, Music, or Comedy Series: *In Living Color* (Fox) Outstanding Lead Actor in a Comedy Series: Ted Danson, *Cheers* (NBC) Outstanding Lead Actor in a Drama Series: Peter Falk, *Columbo* (ABC) Outstanding Lead Actress in a Comedy Series: Candice Bergen, *Murphy Brown* (CBS) Outstanding Lead Actress in a Drama Series: Patricia Wettig, *thirtysomething* (ABC)

Source: A detailed list of awards appears in Brooks and Marsh, *Directory to TV Shows, 1995,* 1216–52; this abridged version was published in Wright, *Universal Almanac, 1991,* 555–57.

Top Television Commercials, from 1960 to 1990

1. Wendy's: "Where's the Beef?"— competitors have little meat on their burgers. (1984)
2. California Raisin Board: "Lunch Box"—Raisins dancing to "I Heard It Through the Grapevine." (1986)
3. Alka Seltzer: "Spicy Meatball"—actor exclaims, "Mamma mia, that's a spicy meatball." (1969)
4. Hallmark: "100th Birthday"—100-year-old grandmother surprised with birthday card. (1990)
5. Life cereal: "Hey Mikey"—child likes cereal. (1971)
6. 7Up: "un-cola"—white-suited actor pitches "un-cola." (1969)
7. Coca-Cola: "Mean Joe Greene"—kid gives Coke to famous football player. (1979)
8. Coca-Cola: "Hilltop song"—group sings song of harmony, "I'd like to buy the world a Coke." (1971)
9. Federal Express: "Fast Talker"—rapid talker John Moschitta pitches the company. (1982)
10. Budweiser: "Christmas Commercial"—Clydesdales beer wagon rolls through snow-covered small town. (1986)
11. Nike: "Bo and Bo"—Bo Diddley says to Bo Jackson, "Bo, you don't know Diddley." (1990)
12. AT&T: "Joey calls Mom"—son called "just to say I love you, Mom." (1980)
13. Eastman Kodak: "Father and Daughter"—as daughter prepares to marry, father recalls her life through photographs." (1989)
14. Maxwell House: "Perking Coffee Pot"—Music replicates sound of perking coffee. (1960)
15. Bartles & Jaymes: "Bartles & Jaymes in New York"—fictional wine-cooler salesmen thank customers "for your support." (1986)

Note: Titles selected from a broad survey of advertising and trade specialists prepared by *USA TODAY.*
Source: USA TODAY, March 22, 1999, 3B.

Popular Music

The postwar era in popular music began as an extension of the period that came before it, but it would not take long for changes to surface. The swing era in the age of the big bands had nearly run its course when the Second World War started, and the war served to extend its life a few more years. As the swing era waned beginning in 1945, the vocalists, many of whom had been band singers, came to the forefront. Bing Crosby had been carrying his music for many years, and now such vocalists as Frank Sinatra, Doris Day, and several others began to establish identities apart from being—as they had begun their careers—part of the band. Much of the best popular music had its origin on stage, appearing as part of Broadway musicals.

The postwar period promoted the band singers, and it also produced a new crop of male and female vocalists as well as group singers: the trios, as with Nat "King" Cole, or the quartets—the Four Aces, Four Freshmen, Four Lads, and others. The singers, or the groups, could be black or white, although most were white. A part of the general popular music scene and yet existing on its fringes were various specialty groups, such as people involved in jazz, either Dixieland or Progressive. In 1949 *Billboard* magazine changed its category of "race records" to "rhythm and blues," a music that began in black quarters of the South, expanded to the urban North, and under leadership of such persons as Count Basie, B.B. King, the Ink Spots, Ray Charles, and many others moved closer to the mainstream and attracted a national multiracial audience. Somewhat further from the center stood a music that had originated largely in the South and uplands of the border area. Called country, country and western, or simply Hillbilly, this music was

still largely in its "she (or he) done me wrong" stage, but radio had done much to broaden its exposure, and its newer singers had impressed a varied audience.

By the 1950s, "crossing over" from one musical specialty to another was taking place with some regularity. Louis Armstrong, a jazz trumpeter who also played blues, established himself as a vocalist of mainstream popular music. Patti Page, a pop singer, had a hit with "Tennessee Waltz." Tony Bennett, an emerging pop vocalist, recorded "Cold, Cold Heart," written by Hank Williams, a genuine pioneer of country music. Both Eddie Fisher, a new popular artist, and Eddie Arnold, an established country singer, scored with recordings of "Any Time."

The most significant musical shift of the era—the development of rock and roll—had its origin in crossover, largely by whites to black rhythms, although the movement went several directions. Bill Haley, who helped establish the new music with his records "Rock Around the Clock" and "Shake, Rattle and Roll," had started with a country and western group called the Saddlemen. Elvis Presley, perhaps the single giant of the formative years of rock, impressed his backers as a white boy who sang like a black. Presley would rank high on the musical charts, whether it was popular music, rock and roll, rhythm and blues, or even country. What Elvis began, a quartet of young men from Liverpool, the Beatles, some 10 years later would expand considerably. Surely the dominant performers of the era of early rock and roll, the Beatles offered repeatable sounds to be sure, and they led the music into new social and political themes. The Beatles also established a practice of giving themselves a name that in no way attempted to describe the entertainers involved—a departure from earlier practices exemplified in the King Cole Trio or Four Lads or Four Aces. The Beatles inspired many imitators of their music, and names of many rock bands, which, while occasionally catchy, seemed to carry little meaning beyond attracting attention.

Rock music in time became the dominant popular music in the United States, but traditional musical patterns remained popular with people from pre-rock generations. Needless to say the size of that audience steadily shrank with passage of time, and the number of people to whom rock music was conventional music continued to increase. The mainstream disk jockey shows on radio gradually gave way to programs devoted to rock and roll in some form or to country music. By the start of the 1970s, rock music had begun to fragment. Folk-rock performers such as Bob Dylan, Simon and Garfunkel, and then Paul Simon alone combined message with melody. Disco seemed to attract more critics than followers, but it held on for a short while. Heavy metal bands, such as Led Zeppelin, stressed the "rock" in rock and roll; there also was punk rock and new-wave music. In the 1980s Madonna depended as much on sexual shock as talent, and it worked. African-American-inspired hip-hop and rap seemed to reintroduce a measure of racial segregation to music, and then some whites took up the nonmelodic, staccato, crudely poetic rhythms of rap, and some black artists came out against it. By the 1990s there seemed to be an audience for everything and toleration of almost anything in popular music but broad agreement on nothing.

As with so much of change in the last half of the 20th century, development in music depended on technology. It began with improvement in recording devices. The breakable and scratchable 78 rpm disk gave way in the 1940s and 1950s to the 45 rpm single and 33 rpm album-length vinyl records that were almost unbreakable. Then came the tape deck and cassette and finally the compact disk. The recording and playback equipment, virtually all musicians' instruments, the radio and television and public sound systems that carried the music all utilized highly technical electronic devices that produced clear, stereophonic sound and as much noise as the ear could take. Volume, it would appear, was vital to the age of rock.

TABLE 17.38   MOST POPULAR AMERICAN SINGERS, 1950

The following lists indicate the most popular American singers as measured in a Gallup Poll taken in November 1950. People surveyed simply were asked: Who is your favorite male (and female) singer? The results suggested continuity, not change, in popular music. Persons on the lists mostly had been active for several years in movies, record sales, radio, and—in smaller measure—television. There appeared to be little differentiation based on age. Seven of the women ranked highest by people in their 20s also appeared in the top 10 suggested by people older than 50.

Favorite Female Vocalists (listed by frequency of mention)	Favorite Male Vocalists (listed by frequency of mention)
Dinah Shore	Bing Crosby
Jeanette MacDonald	Perry Como
Kate Smith	Dennis Day
Jo Stafford	Nelson Eddy
Doris Day	Frank Sinatra
Lily Pons	Vaughn Monroe
Marian Anderson	Ezio Pinza
Judy Garland	Tony Martin
Margaret Whiting	Gene Autry
Rise Stevens	Billy Eckstine

Female Vocalists by Age of Respondents, 21–29 years	Female Vocalists by Age of Respondents, 50 Years and Older
Dinah Shore	Jeanette MacDonald
Jo Stafford	Dinah Shore
Doris Day	Kate Smith
Kay Starr	Lily Pons
Jeanette MacDonald	Judy Garland
Kate Smith	Marian Anderson
Margaret Whiting	Jo Stafford
Lily Pons	Doris Day
Marian Anderson	Kay Armen
Betty Hutton	Rise Stevens

Source: American Institute of Public Opinion, *The Gallup Poll: Public Opinion 1935–1971, Vol. 2, 1949–1958* (New York, 1972), 954, 957.

TABLE 17.39   SELECTED POPULAR SONGS FROM THE POSTWAR, PRE–ROCK AND ROLL ERA, 1946–1954

1946	1947	1948	1949
"Come Rain or Come Shine"	"But Beautiful"	"'A'—You're Adorable"	"Bali Ha'i"
"Do You Love Me?"	"Feudin' and Fightin'"	"Baby, It's Cold Outside"	"Cry of the Wild Goose"
"Doin' What Comes Natur'lly"	"Heartaches"	"Buttons and Bows"	"Dear Hearts, Gentle People"
"The Gypsy"	"Mam'selle"	"Candy Kisses"	"Daddy's Little Girl"
"Linda"	"Open the Door, Richard"	"I Love You So Much It Hurts"	"I Can Dream, Can't I?"

1950	1951	1952	1953	1954
"American Beauty Rose"	"Any Time"	"Auf Wiedersehen, Sweetheart"	"Baubles, Bangles & Beads"	"Hernando's Hideaway"
"Autumn Leaves"	"Beacause of You"	"Because You're Mine"	"Crying in the Chapel"	"Hey There"
"A Bushel and a Peck"	"Cold, Cold Heart"	"Blue Tango"	"Ebb Tide"	"The High and the Mighty"
"Chattanooga Shoe Shine Boy"	"Come on-a My House"	"Don't Let Stars Get in Your Eyes"	"I Believe"	"Let Me Go, Lover"
"Dearie"	"I Get Ideas"	"Gandy Dancers' Ball"	"I Love Paris"	"Little Things Mean a Lot"

Source: Julius Mattfeld, *Variety Music Cavalcade, 1620–1969* (Englewood Cliffs, N.J., 1971), 559–611.

TABLE 17.40 TOP FIVE SINGLE RECORDS, BY YEAR, 1955–1990

The *Billboard* ranking of singles combined performances on the charts of best-sellers, disc jockeys, juke boxes, and the Top 100. The date indicated when a record achieved #1 on any chart. The weeks category pertained to the weeks a record reached #1 on whichever chart its total was highest.

1955

Date	Weeks	Rank	Record Title	Artist
1/01	4	1.	Let Me Go Lover	Joan Weber
2/05	3	2.	Hearts of Stone	The Fontane Sisters
2/12	10	3.	Sincerely	The McGuire Sisters
3/26	5	4.	The Ballad Of Davy Crockett	Bill Hayes
4/30	10	5.	Cherry Pink And Apple Blossom White	Perez Prado

1956

Date	Weeks	Rank	Record Title	Artist
1/07	6	1.	Memories Are Made of This	Dean Martin
2/18	6	2.	Rock and Roll Waltz	Kay Starr
2/18	2	3.	The Great Pretender	The Platters
2/25	4	4.	Lisbon Antigua	Nelson Riddle
3/17	6	5.	The Poor People of Paris	Les Baxter

1957

Date	Weeks	Rank	Record Title	Artist
2/09	3	1.	Too Much	Elvis Presley
2/09	1	2.	Don't Forbid Me	Pat Boone
2/09	1	3.	Young Love	Sonny James
2/16	6	4.	Young Love	Tab Hunter
3/30	3	5.	Butterfly	Andy Williams

1958

Date	Weeks	Rank	Record Title	Artist
1/06	7	1.	At the Hop	Danny & the Juniors
2/10	5	2.	Don't	Elvis Presley
2/17	4	3.	Sugartime	The McGuire Sisters
2/24	2	4.	Get A Job	The Silhouettes
3/17	5	5.	Tequila	The Champs

1959

Date	Weeks	Rank	Record Title	Artist
1/19	3	1.	Smoke Gets in Your Eyes	The Platters
2/9	4	2.	Stagger Lee	Lloyd Price
3/9	5	3.	Venus	Frankie Avalon
4/13	4	4.	Come Softly to Me	Fleetwoods
5/11	1	5.	The Happy Organ	Dave 'Baby' Cortez

1960

Date	Weeks	Rank	Record Title	Artist
1/4	2	1.	El Paso	Marty Robbins
1/18	3	2.	Running Bear	Johnny Preston
2/8	2	3.	Teen Angel	Mark Dinning
2/22	9	4.	The Theme From "A Summer Place"	Percy Faith
4/25	4	5.	Stuck On You	Elvis Presley

1961

Date	Weeks	Rank	Record Title	Artist
1/9	3	1.	Wonderland by Night	Bert Kaempfert
1/30	2	2.	Will You Love Me Tomorrow	The Shirelles
2/13	2	3.	Calcutta	Lawrence Welk
2/27	3	4.	Pony Time	Chubby Checker
3/20	2	5.	Surrender	Elvis Presley

1962

Date	Weeks	Rank	Record Title	Artist
1/13	2	1.	The Twist	Chubby Checker first entered #1 position in 1960 for 1 week
1/27	3	2.	Peppermint Twist — Part I	Joey Dee & the Starliters
2/17	3	3.	Duke of Earl	Gene Chandler
3/10	3	4.	Hey! Baby	Bruce Channel
3/31	1	5.	Don't Break the Heart That Loves You	Connie Francis

1963

Date	Weeks	Rank	Record Title	Artist
1/12	2	1.	Go Away Little Girl	Steve Lawrence
1/26	2	2.	Walk Right In	The Rooftop Singers
2/9	3	3.	Hey Paula	Paul & Paula
3/2	3	4.	Walk Like a Man	The 4 Seasons
3/23	1	5.	Our Day Will Come	Ruby & The Romantics

1964

Date	Weeks	Rank	Record Title	Artist
1/4	4	1.	There! I've Said It Again	Bobby Vinton
2/1	7	2.	I Want to Hold Your Hand	The Beatles
3/21	2	3.	She Loves You	The Beatles
4/4	5	4.	Can't Buy Me Love	The Beatles
5/9	1	5.	Hello, Dolly!	Louis Armstrong

1965

Date	Weeks	Rank	Record Title	Artist
1/23	2	1.	Downtown	Petula Clark
2/6	2	2.	You've Lost That Lovin' Feelin'	The Righteous Brothers
2/20	2	3.	This Diamond Ring	Gary Lewis & The Playboys
3/6	1	4.	My Girl	The Temptations
3/13	2	5.	Eight Days a Week	The Beatles

1966

Date	Weeks	Rank	Record Title	Artist
1/1	2	1.	The Sounds of Silence	Simon & Garfunkel
1/8	3	2.	We Can Work It Out	The Beatles
2/5	2	3.	My Love	Petula Clark
2/19	1	4.	Lightnin' Strikes	Lou Christie
2/26	1	5.	These Boots Are Made for Walkin'	Nancy Sinatra

1967

Date	Weeks	Rank	Record Title	Artist
2/18	2	1.	Kind of a Drag	The Buckinghams
3/4	1	2.	Ruby Tuesday	The Rolling Stones
3/11	1	3.	Love Is Here and Now You're Gone	The Supremes
3/18	1	4.	Penny Lane	The Beatles
3/25	3	5.	Happy Together	The Turtles

1968

Date	Weeks	Rank	Record Title	Artist
1/20	2	1.	Judy in Disguise (With Glasses)	John Fred & His Playboy Band
2/3	1	2.	Green Tambourine	The Lemon Pipers
2/10	5	3.	Love is Blue	Paul Mauriat
3/16	4	4.	(Sittin' on) the Dock of the Bay	Otis Redding
4/13	5	5.	Honey	Bobby Goldsboro

1969

Date	Weeks	Rank	Record Title	Artist
2/1	2	1.	Crimson and Clover	Tommy James & The Shondells
2/15	4	2.	Everyday People	Sly & The Family Stone
3/15	4	3.	Dizzy	Tommy Roe
4/12	6	4.	Aquarius / Let the Sunshine In	The 5th Dimension
5/24	5	5.	Get Back	The Beatles with Billy Preston

1970

Date	Weeks	Rank	Record Title	Artist
1/3	4	1.	Raindrops Keep Fallin' On My Head	B. J. Thomas
1/31	1	2.	I Want You Back	The Jackson 5
2/7	1	3.	Venus	The Shocking Blue
2/14	2	4.	Thank You (Falettinme Be Mice Elf Agin)	Sly & the Family Stone
2/28	6	5.	Bridge Over Troubled Water	Simon & Garfunkel

1971

Date	Weeks	Rank	Record Title	Artist
1/23	3	1.	Knock Three Times	Dawn
2/13	5	2.	One Bad Apple	The Osmonds
3/20	2	3.	Me and Bobby McGee	Janis Joplin
4/3	2	4.	Just My Imagination (Running Away with Me)	The Temptations
4/17	6	5.	Joy to the World	Three Dog Night

1972

Date	Weeks	Rank	Record Title	Artist
1/15	4	1.	American Pie - Parts I & II	Don McLean
2/12	1	2.	Let's Stay Together	Al Green
2/19	4	3.	Without You	Nilsson
3/18	1	4.	Heart of Gold	Neil Young
3/25	3	5.	A Horse with No Name	America

1973

Date	Weeks	Rank	Record Title	Artist
1/6	3	1.	You're So Vain	Carly Simon
1/27	1	2.	Superstition	Stevie Wonder
2/3	3	3.	Crocodile Rock	Elton John
2/24	5	4.	Killing Me Softly with His Song	Roberta Flack
3/24	1	5.	Love Train	O'Jays

1974

Date	Weeks	Rank	Record Title	Artist
1/12	1	1.	The Joker	Steve Miller Band
1/19	1	2.	Show and Tell	Al Wilson
1/26	1	3.	You're Sixteen	Ringo Starr
2/2	3	4.	The Way We Were	Barbra Streisand
2/9	1	5.	Love's Theme	Love Unlimited Orchestra

1975

Date	Weeks	Rank	Record Title	Artist
1/4	2	1.	Lucy in the Sky With Diamonds	Elton John
1/18	1	2.	Mandy	Barry Manilow
1/25	1	3.	Please Mr. Postman	Carpenters
2/1	1	4.	Laughter in the Rain	Neil Sedaka
2/8	1	5.	Fire	Ohio Players

1976

Date	Weeks	Rank	Record Title	Artist
1/3	1	1.	Saturday Night	Bay City Rollers
1/10	1	2.	Convoy	C.W. McCall
1/17	1	3.	I Write the Songs	Barry Manilow
1/24	1	4.	Theme from Mahogany (Do You Know Where You're Going To)	Diana Ross
1/31	1	5.	Love Rollercoaster	Ohio Players

1977

Date	Weeks	Rank	Record Title	Artist
1/8	1	1.	You Don't Have to Be a Star (To Be in My Show)	Marilyn McCoo & Billy Davis. Jr
1/15	1	2.	You Make Me Feel Like Dancing	Leo Sayer
1/22	1	3.	I Wish	Stevie Wonder
1/29	1	4.	Car Wash	Rose Royce
2/5	2	5.	Torn Between Two Lovers	Mary MacGregor

1978

Date	Weeks	Rank	Record Title	Artist
1/14	3	1.	Baby Come Back	Player
2/4	4	2.	Stayin' Alive	Bee Gees
3/4	2	3.	(Love Is) Thicker Than Water	Andy Gibb
3/18	8	4.	Night Fever	Bee Gees
5/13	1	5.	If I Can't Have You	Yvonne Elliman

1979

Date	Weeks	Rank	Record Title	Artist
1/6	2	1.	Too Much Heaven	Bee Gees
2/10	4	2.	Da Ya Think I'm Sexy?	Rod Stewart
3/10	3	3.	I Will Survive	Gloria Gaynor
3/24	2	4.	Tragedy	Bee Gees
4/14	1	5.	What a Fool Believes	The Doobie Brothers

1980

Date	Weeks	Rank	Record Title	Artist
1/5	1	1.	Please Don't Go	K.C. & The Sunshine Band
1/19	4	2.	Rock with You	Michael Jackson
2/16	1	3.	Do That to Me One More Time	The Captain & Tennille
2/23	4	4.	Crazy Little Thing Called Love	Queen
3/22	4	5.	Another Brick in the Wall (Part II)	Pink Floyd

1981

Date	Weeks	Rank	Record Title	Artist
1/31	1	1.	The Tide Is High	Blondie
2/7	2	2.	Celebration	Kool & The Gang
2/21	2	3.	9 To 5	Dolly Parton
2/28	2	4.	I Love A Rainy Night	Eddie Rabbitt
3/21	1	5.	Keep On Loving You	REO Speedwagon

1982

Date	Weeks	Rank	Record Title	Artist
1/30	1	1.	I Can't Go for That (No Can Do)	Daryl Hall & John Oates
2/6	6	2.	Centerfold	The J. Geils Band
3/20	7	3.	I Love Rock 'N Roll	Joan Jett & the Blackhearts
5/8	1	4.	Chariots of Fire—Titles	Vangelis
5/15	7	5.	Ebony and Ivory	Paul McCartney with Stevie Wonder

(continued)

TABLE 17.40 (continued)

1983

Date	Weeks	Rank	Record Title	Artist
1/15	4	1.	Down Under	Men At Work
2/5	1	2.	Africa	Toto
2/19	2	3.	Baby, Come to Me	Patti Austin with James Ingram
3/5	7	4.	Billie Jean	Michael Jackson
4/23	1	5.	Come On Eileen	Dexys Midnight Runners

1984

Date	Weeks	Rank	Record Title	Artist
1/21	2	1.	Owner of a Lonely Heart	Yes
2/4	3	2.	Karma Chameleon	Culture Club
2/25	5	3.	Jump	Van Halen
3/31	3	4.	Footloose	Kenny Loggins
4/21	3	5.	Against All Odds (Take a Look at Me Now)	Phil Collins

1985

Date	Weeks	Rank	Record Title	Artist
2/2	2	1.	I Want to Know What Love Is	Foreigner
2/16	3	2.	Careless Whisper	Wham! Featuring George Michael
3/9	3	3.	Can't Fight This Feeling	REO Speedwagon
3/30	2	4.	One More Night	Phil Collins
4/13	4	5.	We Are the World	USA for Africa

1986

Date	Weeks	Rank	Record Title	Artist
1/18	4	1.	That's What Friends Are For	Dionne & Friends
2/15	2	2.	How Will I Know	Whitney Houston
3/1	2	3.	Kyrie	Mr. Mister
3/15	1	4.	Sara	Starship
3/22	1	5.	These Dreams	Heart

1987

Date	Weeks	Rank	Record Title	Artist
1/17	1	1.	Shake You Down	Gregory Abbott
1/24	2	2.	At This Moment	Billy Vera & the Beaters
2/7	1	3.	Open Your Heart	Madonna
2/14	4	4.	Livin' on a Prayer	Bon Jovi
3/14	1	5.	Jacob's Ladder	Huey Lewis & the News

1988

Date	Weeks	Rank	Record Title	Artist
1/9	1	1.	So Emotional	Whitney Houston
1/16	1	2.	Got My Mind Set on You	George Harrison
1/23	1	3.	The Way You Make Me Feel	Michael Jackson
1/30	1	4.	Need You Tonight	INXS
2/6	2	5.	Could've Been	Tiffany

1989

Date	Weeks	Rank	Record Title	Artist
1/14	1	1.	My Prerogative	Bobby Brown
1/21	2	2.	Two Hearts	Phil Collins
2/4	1	3.	When I'm With You	Sheriff
2/11	3	4.	Straight Up	Paula Abdul
3/4	3	5.	Lost in Your Eyes	Debbie Gibson

1990

Date	Weeks	Rank	Record Title	Artist
1/20	3	1.	How Am I Supposed to Live Without You	Michael Bolton
2/10	3	2.	Opposites Attract	Paula Abdul with the Wild Pair
3/3	3	3.	Escapade	Janet Jackson
3/24	2	4.	Black Velvet	Alannah Myles
4/7	1	5.	Love Will Lead You Back	Taylor Dayne

Source: Joel Whitburn, *The Billboard Book of Top 40 Hits* (New York, 1989), 602–03; Joel Whitburn, *Top Pop Singles* (Menomonee Falls, Wisc., 1991), 818–27.

TABLE 17.41 THE TOP 10 ARTISTS BY DECADE
(based on popularity of single records)

1950s ('55–'59)

Rank	Artist	Points
1.	Elvis Presley	3595
2.	Pat Boone	2836
3.	Perry Como	2022
4.	Fats Domino	1905
5.	Nat "King" Cole	1782
6.	The Platters	1662
7.	Frank Sinatra	1428
8.	Ricky Nelson	1427
9.	The McGuire Sisters	1358
10.	Bill Haley & His Comets	1209

1960s

Rank	Artist	Points
1.	The Beatles	4657
2.	Elvis Presley	4144
3.	Ray Charles	2679
4.	Brenda Lee	2575
5.	The Supremes	2465
6.	The 4 Seasons	2316
7.	Connie Francis	2253
8.	The Beach Boys	2230
9.	James Brown	2204
10.	Marvin Gaye	2069

1970s

Rank	Artist	Points
1.	Elton John	2164
2.	Paul McCartney / Wings	2148
3.	Bee Gees	2003
4.	Carpenters	1887
5.	Chicago	1777
6.	The Jackson 5	1727
7.	James Brown	1639
8.	Stevie Wonder	1614
9.	Neil Diamond	1574
10.	Elvis Presley	1562

1980s

Rank	Artist	Points
1.	Michael Jackson	2095
2.	Prince	2020
3.	Madonna	1970
4.	Daryl Hall & John Oates	1923
5.	George Michael / Wham!	1796
6.	Billy Joel	1634
7.	Elton John	1600
8.	Lionel Richie	1567
9.	Phil Collins	1492
10.	John Cougar Mellencamp	1461

Source: Whitburn, *Top Pop Singles*, 802.

TABLE 17.42 TOP ARTIST ACHIEVEMENTS—SINGLE RECORDS, 1955–1990

	Most Charted Singles			Most Top 40 Hits			Most Top 10 Hits	
Rank	Number	Artist	Rank	Number	Artist	Rank	Number	Artist
1.	149	Elvis Presley	1.	107	Elvis Presley	1.	38	Elvis Presley
2.	94	James Brown	2.	49	The Beatles	2.	33	The Beatles
3.	76	Ray Charles	3.	48	Elton John	3.	28	Stevie Wonder
4.	72	Aretha Franklin	4.	46	Stevie Wonder	4.	23	Elton John
5.	69	The Beatles	5.	44	James Brown	5.	23	The Rolling Stones
6.	67	Frank Sinatra	6.	41	The Rolling Stones	6.	22	Paul McCartney/Wings
7.	66	Fats Domino	7.	41	Aretha Franklin	7.	21	Michael Jackson
8.	61	Stevie Wonder	8.	40	Marvin Gaye	8.	20	The Supremes
9.	60	Pat Boone	9.	38	Pat Boone	9.	20	Chicago
10.	58	Nat "King" Cole	10.	37	Fats Domino	10.	20	Madonna
11.	56	Marvin Gaye	11.	37	Neil Diamond	11.	19	Ricky Nelson
12.	56	The Beach Boys	12.	37	The Temptations	12.	18	Pat Boone
13.	56	Neil Diamond	13.	35	Paul McCartney/Wings	13.	18	Marvin Gaye
14.	56	Connie Francis	14.	35	The Beach Boys	14.	17	Aretha Franklin
15.	55	Dionne Warwick	15.	35	Ricky Nelson	15.	17	George Michael/Wham!
16.	54	Ricky Nelson	16.	35	Connie Francis	16.	16	Connie Francis
17.	54	Jackie Wilson	17.	34	Chicago	17.	16	Daryl Hall & John Oates
18.	53	Paul Anka	18.	33	Ray Charles	18.	15	The Beach Boys
19.	52	The Rolling Stones	19.	33	The Supremes	19.	15	The Temptations
20.	52	The Temptations	20.	33	Paul Anka	20.	15	Bee Gees
21.	52	Brenda Lee	21.	31	Dionne Warwick	21.	15	The 4 Seasons
22.	51	Elton John	22.	31	Billy Joel	22.	15	Olivia Newton-John
23.	49	Brook Benton	23.	30	The 4 Seasons	23.	15	The Everly Brothers
24.	48	Chicago	24.	30	Bobby Vinton	24.	15	Prince
25.	48	Johnny Cash						

	Most #1 Hits			Most Weeks at #1 Position	
Rank	Number	Artist	Rank	Number	Artist
1.	20	The Beatles	1.	80	Elvis Presley
2.	18	Elvis Presley	2.	59	The Beatles
3.	12	The Supremes	3.	30	Paul McCartney/Wings
4.	11	Michael Jackson	4.	29	Michael Jackson
5.	10	Stevie Wonder	5.	27	Bee Gees
6.	9	Paul McCartney/Wings	6.	25	Stevie Wonder
7.	9	Bee Gees	7.	22	The Supremes
8.	9	George Michael/Wham!	8.	22	George Michael/Wham!
9.	8	The Rolling Stones	9.	21	Pat Boone
10.	8	Madonna	10.	21	Lionel Richie
11.	8	Whitney Houston	11.	20	Diana Ross
12.	7	Elton John	12.	19	Elton John
13.	7	Phil Collins	13.	18	The 4 Seasons
14.	6	Pat Boone	14.	18	Olivia Newton-John
15.	6	Diana Ross	15.	18	Madonna
16.	6	Daryl Hall & John Oates	16.	17	The Rolling Stones
17.	5	The 4 Seasons	17.	17	Rod Stewart
18.	5	Olivia Newton-John	18.	15	The Everly Brothers
19.	5	Barbra Streisand	19.	15	Phil Collins
20.	5	Lionel Richie	20.	14	Daryl Hall & John Oates
21.	5	Eagles	21.	14	The McGuire Sisters
22.	5	KC & the Sunshine Band	22.	14	Whitney Houston
23.	5	Bon Jovi	23.	13	Barbra Streisand
			24.	13	Donna Summer
			25.	13	Andy Gibb

	Most Consecutive #1 Hits			Most Consecutive Top 10 Hits	
Rank	Number	Artist	Rank	Number	Artist
1.	10	Elvis Presley	1.	30	Elvis Presley
2.	7	Whitney Houston	2.	24	The Beatles
3.	6	The Beatles	3.	17	Michael Jackson
4.	6	Bee Gees	4.	17	Madonna
5.	5	The Supremes	5.	14	Pat Boone
6.	5	Michael Jackson	6.	13	Phil Collins
7.	4	The Jackson 5	7.	13	Lionel Richie
8.	4	George Michael	8.	11	Whitney Houston
9.	4	Paula Abdul	9.	10	Brenda Lee
			10.	10	George Michael

Source: Whitburn, *Top Pop Singles*, 804.

TABLE 17.43 TOP ARTISTS OF THE ROCK ERA: ALBUM SALES DURING THE YEARS, 1955–1990

Ranking of performers in various kinds of popular music was based on a system devised by *Billboard Magazine* that measured success in terms of the standing of albums on the charts of the Top 40. Points were allocated for appearance in the No. 1 position, for each additional week at the top; points also were distributed on a descending scale for appearance on the charts in positions 2 through 40; points also were allocated for number of weeks in the list of Top 40 albums during this 35-year period. Names in the ranking clearly indicated that while *Billboard* termed the period the "Era of Rock," not all successful performers were active with rock and roll music.

Rank	Artists	Points
1.	The Beatles	3267
2.	Elvis Presley	2699
3.	Frank Sinatra	2383
4.	The Rolling Stones	2128
5.	Barbra Streisand	1836
6.	The Kingston Trio	1757
7.	Elton John	1516
8.	Johnny Mathis	1422
9.	Herb Alpert/The Tijuana Brass	1387
10.	Harry Belafonte	1320
11.	Mitch Miller	1316
12.	Chicago	1136
13.	Bob Dylan	1080
14.	Andy Williams	1063
15.	Paul McCartney/Wings	1051
16.	Mantovani	1022
17.	Henry Mancini	1021
18.	Michael Jackson	1009
19.	Bee Gees	1008
20.	Fleetwood Mac	1001
21.	Led Zeppelin	988
22.	Enoch Light	937
23.	The Monkees	926
24.	Prince	901
25.	Stevie Wonder	897
26.	Ray Conniff	891
27.	The Temptations	891
28.	Lawrence Welk	891
29.	Ray Charles	852
30.	The Beach Boys	832
31.	Simon and Garfunkel	825
32.	Billy Joel	824
33.	Eagles	805
34.	Peter, Paul and Mary	786
35.	The Supremes	774
36.	Rod Stewart	742
37.	Bruce Springsteen	716
38.	Jefferson Airplane/Starship	698
39.	Olivia Newton-John	680
40.	Neil Diamond	679
41.	Carole King	671
42.	Pink Floyd	661
43.	Billy Vaughn	660
44.	Aretha Franklin	651
45.	Linda Ronstadt	634
46.	Santana	632

Source: Joel Whitburn, *The Billboard Book of Top 40 Albums* (New York, 1991), 320–321.

TABLE 17.44 TOP ARTIST ACHIEVEMENTS—ALBUMS, 1955–1990

The Most No. 1 Albums			The Most Top 10 Albums		
Rank	Artist	Total	Rank	Artist	Total
1.	The Beatles	15	1.	Frank Sinatra	31
2.	Elvis Presley	9	2.	The Rolling Stones	31
3.	The Rolling Stones	9	3.	Elvis Presley	25
4.	Elton John	7	4.	The Beatles	23
5.	Paul McCartney/Wings	7	5.	Barbra Streisand	22
6.	Barbra Streisand	6	6.	Johnny Mathis	16
7.	Led Zeppelin	6	7.	The Kingston Trio	14
8.	The Kingston Trio	5	8.	Mitch Miller	14
9.	Herb Alpert/The Tijuana Brass	5	9.	Bob Dylan	14
10.	Chicago	5	10.	Elton John	13
11.	Frank Sinatra	4	11.	The Beach Boys	13
12.	The Monkees	4	12.	Chicago	12
13.	Eagles	4	13.	Andy Williams	12
14.	Bruce Springsteen	4	14.	Paul McCartney/Wings	12
15.	Mitch Miller	3	15.	Ray Conniff	12
16.	Bob Dylan	3	16.	Neil Diamond	12
17.	Bee Gees	3	17.	Mantovani	11
18.	Fleetwood Mac	3	18.	Led Zeppelin	10
19.	Prince	3	19.	Stevie Wonder	10
20.	Stevie Wonder	3	20.	The Temptations	10
21.	Simon and Garfunkel	3	21.	Lawrence Welk	10
22.	Billy Joel	3	22.	Linda Ronstadt	10
23.	The Supremes	3	23.	Herb Alpert/The Tijuana Brass	9
24.	Olivia Newton-John	3	24.	Harry Belafonte	9
25.	Carole King	3	25.	Henry Mancini	9
26.	Pink Floyd	3	26.	Billy Joel	9
27.	Linda Ronstadt	3	27.	The Who	9
28.	Madonna	3			
29.	John Denver	3			
30.	Donna Summer	3			
31.	John Lennon	3			
32.	Crosby, Stills, Nash & Young	3			
33.	Allan Sherman	3			

Source: Whitburn, *Top 40 Albums,* 324.

TABLE 17.45   TOP 50 ALBUMS OF THE ROCK ERA, 1955–1990

Rank	Weeks Ch	40	10	#1	Peak Year	Album Title	Artist
1.	198	144	106	54	62	*West Side Story*	Soundtrack
2.	122	91	78	37	83	*Thriller*	Michael Jackson
3.	262	161	90	31	58	*South Pacific*	Soundtrack
4.	99	72	58	31	56	*Calypso*	Harry Belafonte
5.	134	60	52	31	77	*Rumours*	Fleetwood Mac
6.	120	54	35	24	78	*Saturday Night Fever*	Bee Gees/Soundtrack
7.	72	42	32	24	84	*Purple Rain*	Prince & the Revolution/Soundtrack
8.	79	53	39	20	61	*Blue Hawaii*	Elvis Presley/Soundtrack
9.	33	32	28	19	90	*Please Hammer Don't Hurt 'Em*	M.C. Hammer
10.	96	68	48	18	87	*Dirty Dancing*	Soundtrack
11.	96	45	25	18	67	*More of the Monkees*	The Monkees
12.	75	50	40	17	83	*Synchronicity*	The Police
13.	28	28	25	17	55	*Love Me Or Leave Me*	Doris Day/Soundtrack
14.	276	168	105	16	60	*The Sound of Music*	Original Cast
15.	107	61	23	16	63	*Days of Wine and Roses*	Andy Williams
16.	480	292	173	15	56	*My Fair Lady*	Original Cast
17.	302	68	46	15	71	*Tapestry*	Carole King
18.	175	63	33	15	67	*Sgt. Pepper's Lonely Hearts Club Band*	The Beatles
19.	90	48	31	15	82	*Business As Usual*	Men at Work
20.	118	43	31	15	59	*The Kingston Trio at Large*	The Kingston Trio
21.	101	50	30	15	81	*Hi Infidelity*	REO Speedwagon
22.	123	35	27	15	80	*The Wall*	Pink Floyd
23.	114	78	48	14	65	*Mary Poppins*	Soundtrack
24.	162	78	46	14	86	*Whitney Houston*	Whitney Houston
25.	108	67	44	14	60	*The Button-Down Mind of Bob Newhart*	Bob Newhart
26.	89	55	38	14	61	*Exodus*	Soundtrack
27.	80	44	35	14	76	*Songs in the Key of Life*	Stevie Wonder
28.	101	59	33	14	62	*Modern Sounds in Country and Western Music*	Ray Charles
29.	51	40	28	14	64	*A Hard Day's Night*	The Beatles/Soundtrack
30.	124	105	43	13	60	*Persuasive Percussion*	Enoch Light/Terry Snyder and the All-Stars
31.	95	73	37	13	61	*Judy at Carnegie Hall*	Judy Garland
32.	102	49	32	13	66	*The Monkees*	The Monkees
33.	151	59	28	13	69	*Hair*	Original Cast
34.	245	123	63	12	58	*The Music Man*	Original Cast
35.	87	69	51	12	88	*Faith*	George Michael
36.	96	69	46	12	62	*Breakfast at Tiffany's*	Henry Mancini/Soundtrack
37.	73	42	29	12	60	*Sold Out*	The Kingston Trio
38.	77	39	29	12	78	*Grease*	Olivia Newton-John/Soundtrack
39.	49	26	17	12	62	*The First Family*	Vaughn Meader
40.	64	50	33	11	61	*Calcutta!*	Lawrence Welk
41.	85	51	31	11	87	*Whitney*	Whitney Houston
42.	129	32	27	11	69	*Abbey Road*	The Beatles
43.	71	27	21	11	64	*Meet the Beatles!*	The Beatles
44.	34	22	18	11	85	*Miami Vice*	TV Soundtrack
45.	118	78	64	10	89	*Forever Your Girl*	Paula Abdul
46.	88	88	54	10	57	*Around the World in 80 Days*	Soundtrack
47.	172	78	54	10	58	*Gigi*	Soundtrack
48.	97	55	52	10	76	*Frampton Comes Alive!*	Peter Frampton
49.	48	48	43	10	56	*Elvis Presley*	Elvis Presley
50.	119	47	43	10	59	*The Music From Peter Gunn*	Henry Mancini/TV Soundtrack

Note: Ranking based on *Billboard's* point system that counted weeks at No. 1, weeks in top 10, top 40 and total weeks on the charts.
Abbreviated headings have the following meanings:
   Peak Year: Year album reached peak position
   Weeks Ch: Total weeks charted
   Weeks 40: Total weeks in Top 40
   Weeks 10: Total weeks in Top 10
   Weeks #1: Total weeks in no. 1 position
Source: Whitburn, *Top 40 Albums*, 325–26.

TABLE 17.46   THE TOP 10 ARTISTS BY DECADE
(albums on the charts)

	The Fifties (1955–59)			The Seventies	
Rank	Artist	Points	Rank	Artist	Points
1.	Harry Belafonte	1,103	1.	Elton John	1,329
2.	Frank Sinatra	1,015	2.	Chicago	944
3.	Elvis Presley	927	3.	Paul McCartney/Wings	833
4.	Johnny Mathis	851	4.	Bee Gees	831
5.	The Kingston Trio	749	5.	The Rolling Stones	820
6.	Mitch Miller	747	6.	Eagles	769
7.	Mantovani	585	7.	Fleetwood Mac	732
8.	Roger Williams	418	8.	Led Zeppelin	720
9.	Tennessee Ernie Ford	384	9.	Carole King	671
10.	Doris Day	356	10.	Bob Dylan	642
	The Sixties			The Eighties	
1.	The Beatles	2,817	1.	Prince	881
2.	Elvis Presley	1,469	2.	Michael Jackson	860
3.	Frank Sinatra	1,309	3.	Bruce Springsteen	632
4.	Herb Alpert/The Tijuana Brass	1,302	4.	Whitney Houston	574
5.	The Kingston Trio	1,008	5.	Madonna	566
6.	Andy Williams	999	6.	The Rolling Stones	550
7.	Enoch Light	930	7.	Billy Joel	501
8.	The Monkees	904	8.	The Police	499
9.	Ray Charles	852	9.	U2	473
10.	Barbra Streisand	808	10.	John Cougar Mellencamp	455

Source: Whitburn, *Top 40 Albums,* 33.

Elvis Presley

Arguably the most popular and most significant single performer of popular music during the half-century following the Second World War, Elvis Presley set many ratings and sales records, especially in the category of single songs and records. While it appeared for the rest of the 20th century that Presley's impact was timeless, his most profound effect came shortly after he burst onto the scene in the mid-1950s. Of his 50 most popular songs, 39 were released during the 10-year period between 1956 and 1965. After that point, his popularity waned somewhat but by no means died as American pop/rock music proceeded on its never-ending process of evolution, and a new competitor, the Beatles, arrived to jolt the measurement charts in much the same fashion as "the King" had done nearly 10 years earlier.

Elvis Presley meets President Richard M. Nixon in the White House. (Richard M. Nixon Library)

TABLE 17.47 THE TOP 50 SONGS OF ELVIS PRESLEY

Rank	Song	Year Song Was Introduced
1.	"Don't Be Cruel/Hound Dog"	1956
2.	"Heartbreak Hotel"	1956
3.	"All Shook Up"	1957
4.	"Jailhouse Rock/Treat Me Nice"	1957
5.	"(Let Me Be Your) Teddy Bear"	1957
6.	"Love Me Tender"	1956
7.	"I Want You, I Need You, I Love You"	1956
8.	"It's Now or Never"	1960
9.	"Are You Lonesome Tonight?"	1960
10.	"Don't/I Beg of You"	1958
11.	"Stuck On You"	1960
12.	"Too Much"	1957
13.	"Return to Sender"	1962
14.	"Wear My Ring Around Your Neck"	1958
15.	"One Night"	1958
16.	"Love Me"	1957
17.	"Suspicious Minds"	1969
18.	"Good Luck Charm"	1962
19.	"Surrender"	1961
20.	"A Big Hunk O' Love"	1959
21.	"Hard Headed Woman"	1958
22.	"Can't Help Falling in Love"	1962
23.	"Burning Love"	1972
24.	"(Now and Then There's) a Fool Such As I"	1959
25.	"In the Ghetto"	1969
26.	"I Got Stung"	1958
27.	"Crying in the Chapel"	1965
28.	"Don't Cry Daddy"	1970
29.	"I Need Your Love Tonight"	1959
30.	"The Wonder of You"	1970
31.	"(You're the) Devil in Disguise"	1963
32.	"She's Not You"	1962
33.	"Little Sister"	1961
34.	"If I Can Dream"	1969
35.	"My Wish Came True"	1959
36.	"One Broken Heart for Sale"	1963
37.	"Ask Me"	1964
38.	"Fame and Fortune"	1960
39.	"Promised Land"	1974
40.	"Steamroller Blues/Fool"	1973
41.	"I Feel So Bad"	1961
42.	"Bossa Nova Baby"	1963
43.	"You Don't Have to Say You Love Me"	1970
44.	"I'm Yours"	1965
45.	"(Marie's the Name) His Latest Flame"	1961
46.	"Puppet on a String"	1965
47.	"Kentucky Rain"	1970
48.	"Ain't That Loving You Baby"	1964
49.	"Follow That Dream"	1962
50.	"Way Down"	1977

Source: Fred Bronson, *Billboard's Hottest 100 Hits* (New York, 1995), 5–6.

Rock Music: Booming Business, Vulnerable Lifestyle

The rock music business lended itself to overnight success, lavish wealth, and adulation, and also unhealthy living conditions, emotional stress, and sudden, untimely, frequently unnatural death of its participants. Many of the difficulties appeared to be either inherent in the entertainment business or a creation of the culture that rock music had done much to produce. Show business and especially popular music subjected performers to frequent travel and thus made them vulnerable to accident. Rock musicians faced erratic schedules and too little sleep that sometimes came, so it appeared, only with "a little help." Rock music was an emotional exercise, given to sharp and sudden highs and lows on the part of both performers and audience. Rock music showed remarkable toleration of—even preference for—performers who experienced success at very early age, partly because, it would appear, the listeners and admirers were themselves very young. The setting fostered a great deal of freedom, too much temptation, and too little maturity to handle new situations. Almost from the beginning, rock music intermingled closely with the culture of mind-altering drugs, and the entanglement intensified as the culture grew. All sudden deaths from that culture were tragic, but many came as a consequence of the victim's behavior, and those related to drugs seem to carry special meaning. The following list contains names of several musicians of the era who failed to survive the era, whose end came suddenly and in most cases at very young age.

TABLE 17.48 SOME CASUALTIES FROM THE AGE OF ROCK, IN ORDER OF THEIR DEATH

Artist	Age	Band/ Description	Cause of Death	Date of Death
Buddy Holly	22	The Crickets	plane crash	February 1959
Sam Cooke		singer	shot	December 1964
Bobby Fuller	23	singer	auto asphyxiation	July 1966
Otis Redding	26	blues singer	plane crash	December 1967
Frankie Lymon	25	singer	drug overdose	February 1968
Brian Jones	27	Rolling Stones	drowning in pool	July 1969
Jimi Hendrix	27	singer	drug-related choking	September 1970
Janis Joplin	27	singer	drug overdose	October 1970
Jim Morrison	27	Doors	alcohol-related heart attack	July 1971
Duane Allman	24	Allman Brothers	motorcycle crash	October 1971
Berry Oakley	24	Allman Brothers	motorcycle crash	November 1972
Jim Croce	30	singer	plane crash	September 1973
Bobby Darin	37	singer	heart attack	December 1973
Cass Elliot	30	Mamas and Papas	choking and heart attack	July 1974
Peter Ham	27	Badfinger	suicide	April 1975
Tim Buckley	28	singer	drug overdose	June 1975
Phil Ochs	35	singer	suicide	April 1976
Elvis Presley	42	singer	drug-related heart attack	August 1977
Marc Bolan	29	T. Rex	auto accident	September 1977
Ronnie Van Zant	28	Lynyrd Skynyrd	plane crash	October 1977
Keith Moon	31	The Who	drug overdose	September 1978
Sid Vicious	21	Sex Pistols	drug overdose	February 1979
Gram Parsons	26	Byrds	drug overdose	September 1979
Bon Scott		AC/DC	heavy drinking	February 1980
John Bonham		Led Zeppelin	inhale vomit	September 1980
John Lennon	40	Beatles	murdered	December 1980
Bob Marley	36	Reggae	cancer	May 1981
Harry Chapin	38	singer	auto accident	July 1981
Karen Carpenter	32	The Carpenters	heart attack from anorexia	February 1983
Tom Evans		Badfinger	suicide	November 1983
Marvin Gaye	45	soul singer	drugs, depression, murder	April 1984
Rick Nelson	45	singer	plane crash	December 1985
Richard Manuel	42	The Band	suicide	March 1986
Stevie Ray Vaughan	35	bluesman	plane crash	August 1990

Source: *USA Today*, April 17, 1998, 1E–2E; Michael Weatley, *The Ultimate Encyclopedia of Rock* (New York, 1993), 326–27.

Greatest Rock 'n' Roll Songs: An Opinion Poll

Unlike various charts that based popularity of music on raw statistics, the following table is based on a quest for the best 100 rock and roll songs that measured opinion. The survey, conducted by the television music channel VH1, polled some 700 people in the music business. As with any such survey, it was subjective, and results would bear markings of the people being polled: their age, race, ethnicity, gender, and the mere fact that they were in the music business. Several themes accompanied the outcome. The songs were rock and roll songs, as identified by beat and arrangement and also by the themes or message and not merely songs that appeared during the era. Frank Sinatra was not on the list; neither were the Everly Brothers nor surprisingly Fleetwood Mac, U2, or Madonna. The giant of the list was the Beatles, and that group probably would have received the No. 1 ranking but for the fact that respondents split their vote among nine Beatles selections. Another message that rang clear was that the years 1955–90 composed the era of rock and roll. No song came before that period and although the poll was taken at the end of the 1990s (and published in January 2000), only one song that appeared after 1990 made the list—and even then only barely; "Smells Like Teen Spirit," number 41 and by Nirvana, came out in 1991.

TABLE 17.49   100 GREATEST ROCK 'N' ROLL SONGS— AN OPINION POLL

The 100 greatest rock 'n' roll songs, as determined by a panel of 700 voters assembled by the music network VH1

Rank	Song	Artist
1.	"(I Can't Get No) Satisfaction"	The Rolling Stones
2.	"Respect"	Aretha Franklin
3.	"Stairway to Heaven"	Led Zeppelin
4.	"Like a Rolling Stone"	Bob Dylan
5.	"Born to Run"	Bruce Springsteen
6.	"Hotel California"	The Eagles
7.	"Light My Fire"	The Doors
8.	"Good Vibrations"	The Beach Boys
9.	"Hey Jude"	The Beatles
10.	"Imagine"	John Lennon
11.	"Louie Louie"	The Kingsmen
12.	"Yesterday"	The Beatles
13.	"My Generation"	The Who
14.	"What's Going On"	Marvin Gaye
15.	"Johnny B. Goode"	Chuck Berry
16.	"Layla"	Derek and the Dominos
17.	"Won't Get Fooled Again"	The Who
18.	"Jailhouse Rock"	Elvis Presley
19.	"American Pie"	Don McLean
20.	"A Day in the Life"	The Beatles
21.	"I Got You (I Feel Good)"	James Brown
22.	"Superstition"	Stevie Wonder
23.	"I Want to Hold Your Hand"	The Beatles
24.	"Brown Sugar"	The Rolling Stones
25.	"Purple Haze"	Jimi Hendrix
26.	"Sympathy for the Devil"	The Rolling Stones
27.	"Bohemian Rhapsody"	Queen
28.	"You Really Got Me"	The Kinks
29.	"Oh, Pretty Woman"	Roy Orbison
30.	"Bridge Over Troubled Water"	Simon & Garfunkel
31.	"Hound Dog"	Elvis Presley
32.	"Let It Be"	The Beatles
33.	"(Sittin' On) the Dock of the Bay"	Otis Redding
34.	"All Along the Watchtower"	The Jimi Hendrix Experience
35.	"Walk This Way"	Aerosmith
36.	"My Girl"	The Temptations
37.	"Rock Around the Clock"	Bill Haley & His Comets
38.	"I Heard It Through the Grapevine"	Marvin Gaye
39.	"Proud Mary"	Creedence Clearwater Revival
40.	"Born to Be Wild"	Steppenwolf
41.	"Smells Like Teen Spirit"	Nirvana[a]
42.	"Every Breath You Take"	The Police
43.	"What'd I Say"	Ray Charles
44.	"Free Bird"	Lynyrd Skynyrd
45.	"That'll Be the Day"	Buddy Holly and the Crickets
46.	"Whole Lotta Love"	Led Zeppelin
47.	"Dream On"	Aerosmith
48.	"California Dreamin'"	The Mamas and the Papas
49.	"Brown Eyed Girl"	Van Morrison
50.	"Wild Thing"	The Troggs

Rank	Song	Artist
51.	"Suite: Judy Blue Eyes"	Crosby, Stills and Nash
52.	"Beat It"	Michael Jackson
53.	"Great Balls of Fire"	Jerry Lee Lewis
54.	"Stayin' Alive"	The Bee Gees
55.	"For What It's Worth"	The Buffalo Springfield
56.	"Blowin' in the Wind"	Bob Dylan
57.	"Twist and Shout"	The Beatles
58.	"Piano Man"	Billy Joel
59.	"She Loves You"	The Beatles
60.	"Space Oddity"	David Bowie
61.	"Strawberry Fields Forever"	The Beatles
62.	"Kashmir"	Led Zeppelin
63.	"Crazy"	Patsy Cline
64.	"London Calling"	The Clash
65.	"Jumpin' Jack Flash"	The Rolling Stones
66.	"Rock & Roll"	Led Zeppelin
67.	"Let's Stay Together"	Al Green
68.	"All Shook Up"	Elvis Presley
69.	"Maggie May"	Rod Stewart
70.	"Your Song"	Elton John
71.	"Heartbreak Hotel"	Elvis Presley
72.	"God Only Knows"	The Beach Boys
73.	"The Twist"	Chubby Checker
74.	"Good Golly, Miss Molly"	Little Richard
75.	"Sunshine of Your Love"	Cream
76.	"California Girls"	The Beach Boys
77.	"Summertime Blues"	Eddie Cochran
78.	"Blue Suede Shoes"	Carl Perkins
79.	"A Hard Day's Night"	The Beatles
80.	"Fire and Rain"	James Taylor
81.	"Gloria"	Them
82.	"Sexual Healing"	Marvin Gaye
83.	"Start Me Up"	The Rolling Stones
84.	"More Than a Feeling"	Boston
85.	"Roxanne"	The Police
86.	"We Are the Champions"	Queen
87.	"Tangled Up in Blue"	Bob Dylan
88.	"Somebody to Love"	Jefferson Airplane
89.	"Stand By Me"	Ben E. King
90.	"Whole Lotta Shakin' Going On"	Jerry Lee Lewis
91.	"You Shook Me All Night Long"	AC/DC
92.	"When Doves Cry"	Prince & the Revolution
93.	"In the Midnight Hour"	Wilson Pickett
94.	"Gimme Some Lovin'"	Spencer Davis Group
95.	"Jump"	Van Halen
96.	"Thunder Road"	Bruce Springsteen
97.	"No Woman No Cry"	Bob Marley & the Wailers
98.	"La Bamba"	Ritchie Valens
99.	"We've Only Just Begun"	The Carpenters
100.	"Papa Was a Rolling Stone"	The Temptations

[a] Released in 1991 and thus not a part of the years 1955–1990.
Source: Published in Kalamazoo (Mich.) *Gazette*, January 7, 2000, D6.

TABLE 17.50 GRAMMY AWARDS, 1958–1990

Seeking to keep in step with other areas of comercial entertainment, a growing music recording industry formed its own organization, the National Academy of Recording Arts and Sciences, to publicize its wares by honoring its most effective and successful members. Beginning in the year 1958, members of the academy, in time some 6,000 strong, voted on recipients of "Grammy" awards in a few categories. The name stemming from the term *gramophone,* or phonograph—as record players originally were called—the Grammy at first was awarded in only a few areas of mainstream popular music. By 1990 honorees came from approximately 70 categories. The five areas listed below remained the persistent headliners of the occasion.

Year	Record of the Year	Album of the Year	Song of the Year	Best Male Vocal Performance	Best Female Vocal Performance
1958	Domenico Modugno, "Nel Blu Dipinto di Blu (*Volare*)"	Henry Mancini, *The Music from Peter Gunn*	Domenico Modugno, "Nel Blu Dipinto di Blu (*Volare*)"	Perry Como, "Catch a Falling Star"	Ella Fitzgerald, *Ella Fitzgerald Sings the Irving Berlin Songbook*
1959	Bobby Darin, "Mack the Knife"	Frank Sinatra, *Come Dance with Me*	Jimmy Driftwood, "The Battle of New Orleans"	Frank Sinatra, "Come Dance with Me"	Ella Fitzgerald, *But Not for Me*
1960	Percy Faith, "Theme from a Summer Place"	Bob Newhart, *Button-Down Mind*	Ernest Gold, "Theme from Exodus"	Ray Charles, "Georgia on My Mind"	Ella Fitzgerald, *Mack the Knife*
1961	Henry Mancini, "Moon River"	Judy Garland, *Judy at Carnegie Hall*	Henry Mancini, Johnny Mercer, "Moon River"	Jack Jones, "Lollipops and Roses"	Judy Garland, *Judy at Carnegie Hall*
1962	Tony Bennett, "I Left My Heart in San Francisco"	Vaughn Meader, *The First Family*	Leslie Bricusse, Anthony Newley, "What Kind of Fool Am I?"	Tony Bennett, *I Left My Heart in San Francisco*	Ella Fitzgerald, *Ella Swings Brightly with Nelson Riddle*
1963	Henry Mancini, "The Days of Wine and Roses"	Barbra Streisand, *The Barbra Streisand Album*	Henry Mancini, Johnny Mercer, "The Days of Wine and Roses"	Jack Jones, "Wives and Lovers"	Barbra Streisand, *The Barbra Streisand Album*
1964	Stan Getz, Astrud Gilberto, "The Girl from Ipanema"	Stan Getz, Astrud Gilberto, *Getz/Gilberto*	Jerry Herman, "Hello, Dolly!"	Louis Armstrong, "Hello, Dolly!"	Barbra Streisand, *People*
1965	Herb Alpert & the Tijuana Brass "A Taste of Honey"	Frank Sinatra, *September of My Years*	Paul Francis Webster, Johnny Mandel, "The Shadow of Your Smile"	Frank Sinatra, "It Was a Very Good Year"	Barbra Streisand, *My Name is Barbra*
1966	Frank Sinatra, "Strangers in the Night"	Frank Sinatra, *A Man and His Music*	John Lennon, Paul McCartney, "Michelle"	Frank Sinatra, "Strangers in the Night"	Eydie Gorme, *If He Walked into My Life*
1967	5th Dimension, "Up, Up and Away"	The Beatles, *Sgt. Pepper's Lonely Hearts Club Band*	Jim Webb, "Up, Up, and Away"	Glen Campbell, "By the Time I Get to Phoenix"	Bobbie Gentry, *Ode to Billie Joe*
1968	Simon & Garfunkel, "Mrs. Robinson"	Glen Campbell, *By the Time I Get to Phoenix*	Bobby Russell, "Little Green Apples"	Jose Feliciano, "Light My Fire"	Dionne Warwick, *Do You Know the Way to San Jose?*
1969	5th Dimension, "Aquarius/Let the Sunshine In"	Blood, Sweat & Tears, *Blood, Sweat & Tears*	Joe South, "Games People Play"	Harry Nilsson, "Everybody's Talkin'"	Peggy Lee, *Is That All There Is?*
1970	Simon & Garfunkel, "Bridge over Troubled Water"	Simon & Garfunkel, *Bridge over Troubled Water*	Paul Simon, "Bridge over Troubled Water"	Ray Stevens, "Everything Is Beautiful"	Dionne Warwick, *I'll Never Fall in Love Again*
1971	Carole King, "It's Too Late"	Carole King, *Tapestry*	Carole King, "You've Got a Friend"	James Taylor, "You've Got a Friend"	Carole King, *Tapestry*
1972	Roberta Flack, "The First Time Ever I Saw Your Face"	George Harrison, Ravi Shankar, Bob Dylan et al., *Concert for Bangladesh*	Ewan McColl, "The First Time Ever I Saw Your Face"	Harry Nilsson, "Without You"	Helen Reddy, *I Am Woman*
1973	Roberta Flack, "Killing Me Softly with His Song"	Stevie Wonder, *Innervisions*	Norman Gimbel, Charles Fox, "Killing Me Softly with His Song"	Stevie Wonder, "You Are the Sunshine of My Life"	Roberta Flack, *Killing Me Softly with His Song*
1974	Olivia Newton-John, "I Honestly Love You"	Stevie Wonder, *Fulfillingness' First Finale*	Marilyn & Alan Bergman, Marvin Hamlisch, "The Way We Were"	Stevie Wonder, *Fulfillingness' First Finale*	Olivia Newton-John, *I Honestly Love You*
1975	Captain & Tennille, "Love Will Keep Us Together"	Paul Simon, *Still Crazy After All These Years*	Stephen Sondheim, "Send in the Clowns"	Paul Simon, *Still Crazy after All These Years*	Janis Ian, *At Seventeen*
1976	George Benson, "This Masquerade"	Stevie Wonder, *Songs in the Key of life*	Bruce Johnston, "I Write the Songs"	Stevie Wonder, *Songs in the Key of Life*	Linda Ronstadt, *Hasten Down the Wind*
1977	The Eagles, "Hotel California"	Fleetwood Mac, *Rumours*	Barbra Streisand, Paul Williams, "Evergreen"	James Taylor, "Handy Man"	Barbra Streisand, *Evergreen*
1978	Billy Joel, "Just the Way You Are"	Various Artists, *Saturday Night Fever*	Billy Joel, "Just the Way You Are"	Barry Manilow, "Copacabana (At the Copa)"	Anne Murray, *You Needed Me*
1979	The Doobie Brothers, "What a Fool Believes"	Billy Joel, *52nd Street*	Kenny Loggins, Michael McDonald, "What a Fool Believes"	Billy Joel, *52nd Street*	Dionne Warwick, *I'll Never Love This Way Again*
1980	Christopher Cross, "Sailing"	Christopher Cross, *Christopher Cross*	Christopher Cross, "Sailing"	Kenny Loggins, "This Is It"	Bette Midler, *The Rose*
1981	Kim Carnes, "Bette Davis Eyes"	John Lennon/Yoko Ono, *Double Fantasy*	Donna Weiss, Jackie DeShannon, "Bette Davis Eyes"	Al Jarreau, *Breakin' Away*	Lena Horne, *The Lady and Her Music Live on Broadway*
1982	Toto, "Rosanna"	Toto, *Toto IV*	Johnny Christopher, Mark James, Wayne Carson, "Always on My Mind"	Lionel Richie, "Truly"	Melissa Manchester, *You Should Hear How She Talks About You*

(continued)

TABLE 17.50   (continued)

Year	Record of the Year	Album of the Year	Song of the Year	Best Male Vocal Performance	Best Female Vocal Performance
1983	Michael Jackson, "Beat It"	Michael Jackson, *Thriller*	Sting, "Every Breath You Take"	Michael Jackson, *Thriller*	Irene Cara, *Flashdance . . .What a Feeling*
1984	Tina Turner, "What's Love Got to Do with It?"	Lionel Richie, *Can't Slow Down*	Graham Lyle, Terry Britten, "What's Love Got to Do With It?"	Phil Collins, *Against All Odds (Take a Look at Me Now)*	Tina Turner, *What's Love Got to Do with It?*
1985	USA for Africa, "We Are the World"	Phil Collins, *No Jacket Required*	Michael Jackson, Lionel Richie, "We Are the World"	Phil Collins, *No Jacket Required*	Whitney Houston, *Saving All My Love for You*
1986	Steve Winwood, "Higher Love"	Paul Simon, *Graceland*	Various Artists, "That's What Friends Are For"	Steve Winwood, *Higher Love*	Barbra Streisand, *The Broadway Album*
1987	Paul Simon, "Graceland"	U2, *The Joshua Tree*	Linda Ronstadt, James Ingram, "Somewhere Out There"	Sting, *Bring on the Night*	Whitney Houston, *I Wanna Dance with Somebody (Who Loves Me)*
1988	Bobby McFerrin, "Don't Worry, Be Happy"	George Michael, *Faith*	Bobby McFerrin, "Don't Worry, Be Happy"	Bobby McFerrin, *Don't Worry, Be Happy*	Tracy Chapman, *Fast Car*
1989	Bette Midler, "Wind Beneath My Wings"	Bonnie Raitt, *Nick of Time*	Bette Midler, "Wind Beneath My Wings"	Michael Bolton, *How Am I Supposed to Live Without You*	Bonnie Raitt, *Nick of Time*
1990	Phil Collins, "Another Day in Paradise"	Quincy Jones, *Back on the Block*	Julie Gold, "From a Distance"	Roy Orbison, *Oh, Pretty Woman*	Mariah Carey, *Vision of Love*

Source: John Wright, *The New York Times Almanac, 2000* (New York, 1999), 837–38.

President Ronald Reagan, a former actor, cuts in on singer Frank Sinatra, dancing with his wife, Nancy, also a former actress, at the White House. (Courtesy Ronald Reagan Library)

Empty at the Grammys

The following artists had not won prior to 1990 or have never won a Grammy Award in a competitive category, although many have been nominated. Some have received special or honorary prizes.

Roy Acuff[a]
Beach Boys
Chuck Berry
Jackson Browne
Byrds
Benny Carter[a]
Pablo Casals[a]
Cher
Patsy Cline
Sam Cooke
Elvis Costello
Creedence Clearwater Revival
Cream
Jim Croce
Bing Crosby[a]
Fats Domino[a]
Doors
Drifters
Four Tops
Peter Frampton
Benny Goodman[a]
Grateful Dead
Lionel Hampton
Jimi Hendrix
Jackson 5
Jefferson Airplane/Starship
Janis Joplin
Led Zeppelin
"Little Richard" Penniman
Mitch Miller
Van Morrison
Buck Owens
Pretenders
Queen
Ramones
Santana
Cat Stevens
Rolling Stones[a]
Diana Ross
Sex Pistols
Rod Stewart
Supremes
Talking Heads
Three Dog Night
Lawrence Welk
Kitty Wells[a]
Who
Hank Williams, Sr.

[a] Lifetime Achievement Awards.
Source: O'Neil, *The Grammys,* 548.

Popular Country Songs

Measurement of the popularity of country records was based on statistics compiled by *Billboard* that began with juke-box records, until 1948, and between 1948 and 1958 they combined record sales, disk-jockey playings, and juke-box statistics. Between 1958 and 1990 the charts depended upon playlists supplied by radio stations. Beginning in 1990 *Billboard* utilized electronic monitors placed on radio stations.

TABLE 17.51 TOP 100 COUNTRY SINGLES, 1944–1990

Rank	Wks @#1	Pk Yr	Title	Artist
1.	21	50	"I'm Moving On"	Hank Snow
2.	21	47	"I'll Hold You in My Heart (Till I Can Hold You in My Arms)"	Eddy Arnold
3.	21	55	"In the Jailhouse Now"	Webb Pierce
4.	20	56	"Crazy Arms"	Ray Price
5.	20	54	"I Don't Hurt Anymore"	Hank Snow
6.	19	48	"Bouquet of Roses"	Eddy Arnold
7.	19	61	"Walk On By"	Leroy Van Dyke
8.	17	54	"Slowly"	Webb Pierce
9.	17	49	"Slipping Around"	Margaret Whiting & Jimmy Wakely
10.	17	56	"Heartbreak Hotel"	Elvis Presley
11.	16	49	"Lovesick Blues"	Hank Williams with His Drifting Cowboys
12.	16	46	"Guitar Polka"	Al Dexter and His Troopers
13.	16	63	"Love's Gonna Live Here"	Buck Owens
14.	16	46	"New Spanish Two Step"	Bob Wills & His Texas Playboys
15.	16	47	"Smoke! Smoke! Smoke! (That Cigarette)"	Tex Williams and His Western Caravan
16.	15	51	"Slow Poke"	Pee Wee King and his Golden West Cowboys
17.	15	52	"The Wild Side of Life"	Hank Thompson
18.	14	60	"Please Help Me, I'm Falling"	Hank Locklin
19.	14	60	"He'll Have to Go"	Jim Reeves
20.	14	52	"Jambalaya (On the Bayou)"	Hank Williams with his Drifting Cowboys
21.	14	51	"The Shot Gun Boogie"	Tennessee Ernie Ford
22.	14	46	"Divorce Me C.O.D."	Merle Travis
23.	14	47	"So Round, So Firm, So Fully Packed"	Merle Travis
24.	13	44	"So Long Pal"	Al Dexter and His Troopers
25.	13	55	"Love, Love, Love"	Webb Pierce
26.	13	56	"Singing the Blues"	Marty Robbins
27.	13	44	"Smoke on the Water"	Red Foley
28.	13	58	"City Lights"	Ray Price
29.	13	58	"Alone with You"	Faron Young
30.	13	50	"Chattanooga Shoe Shine Boy"	Red Foley
31.	13	53	"Kaw-Liga"	Hank Williams
32.	12	55	"I Don't Care"	Webb Pierce
33.	12	51	"Always Late (With Your Kisses)"	Lefty Frizzell
34.	12	53	"There Stands the Glass"	Webb Pierce
35.	12	60	"Alabam"	Cowboy Copas
36.	12	49	"Don't Rob Another Man's Castle"	Eddy Arnold
37.	11	48	"One Has My Name (The Other Has My Heart)"	Jimmy Wakely
38.	11	51	"I Want to Be with You Always"	Lefty Frizzell
39.	11	51	"I Wanna Play House with You"	Eddy Arnold
40.	11	51	"There's Been a Change in Me"	Eddy Arnold
41.	11	62	"Don't Let Me Cross Over"	Carl Butler and Pearl
42.	11	45	"You Two-Timed Me One Time Too Often"	Tex Ritter and His Texans
43.	10	60	"Wings of a Dove"	Ferlin Husky
44.	10	54	"More and More"	Webb Pierce
45.	10	56	"Don't Be Cruel/Hound Dog"	Elvis Presley
46.	10	50	"Why Don't You Love Me"	Hank Williams with His Drifting Cowboys
47.	10	57	"Gone"	Ferlin Husky
48.	10	58	"Ballad of a Teenage Queen"	Johnny Cash
49.	10	55	"Sixteen Tons"	Tennessee Ernie Ford
50.	10	59	"The Battle Of New Orleans"	Johnny Horton

(continued)

TABLE 17.51   (continued)

Rank	Wks @#1	Pk Yr	Title	Artist
51.	10	61	"Don't Worry"	Marty Robbins
52.	10	59	"The Three Bells"	The Browns
53.	9	48	"Anytime"	Eddy Arnold and His Tennessee Plowboys
54.	9	45	"Shame on You"	Spade Cooley
55.	9	53	"Mexican Joe"	Jim Reeves and the Circle O Ranch Boys
56.	9	62	"Wolverton Mountain"	Claude King
57.	9	57	"Young Love"	Sonny James
58.	9	61	"Hello Walls"	Faron Young
59.	9	66	"Almost Persuaded"	David Houston
60.	8	51	"Let Old Mother Nature Have Her Way"	Carl Smith
61.	8	48	"Just a Little Lovin' (Will Go a Long, Long Way)"	Eddy Arnold
62.	8	51	"The Rhumba Boogie"	Hank Snow
63.	8	58	"Oh Lonesome Me"	Don Gibson
64.	8	53	"Hey Joe!"	Carl Smith
65.	8	53	"I Forgot More Than You'll Ever Know"	The Davis Sisters
66.	8	57	"Four Walls"	Jim Reeves
67.	8	51	"Hey, Good Lookin'"	Hank Williams with His Drifting Cowboys
68.	8	52	"(When You Feel Like You're in Love) Don't Just Stand There"	Carl Smith
69.	8	45	"At Mail Call Today"	Gene Autry
70.	8	53	"It's Been So Long"	Webb Pierce
71.	8	50	"Long Gone Lonesome Blues"	Hank Williams with His Drifting Cowboys
72.	8	58	"Guess Things Happen That Way"	Johnny Cash
73.	8	57	"Wake Up Little Susie"	The Everly Brothers
74.	8	64	"Once a Day"	Connie Smith
75.	8	62	"Devil Woman"	Marty Robbins
76.	7	55	"Loose Talk"	Carl Smith
77.	7	61	"Tender Years"	George Jones
78.	7	64	"My Heart Skips a Beat"	Buck Owens
79.	7	59	"El Paso"	Marty Robbins
80.	7	62	"Mama Sang a Song"	Bill Anderson

Rank	Wks @#1	Pk Yr	Title	Artist
81.	7	57	"Bye Bye Love"	The Everly Brothers
82.	7	45	"I'm Losing My Mind Over You"	Al Dexter and His Troopers
83.	7	63	"Still"	Bill Anderson
84.	7	63	"Ring of Fire"	Johnny Cash
85.	7	64	"I Guess I'm Crazy"	Jim Reeves
86.	7	66	"There Goes My Everything"	Jack Greene
87.	7	66	"Waitin' in Your Welfare Line"	Buck Owens
88.	6	56	"I Walk the Line"	Johnny Cash
89.	6	53	"A Dear John Letter"	Jean Shepard & Ferlin Husky
90.	6	44	"Your Cheatin' Heart"	Hank William with His Drifting Cowboys
91.	6	44	"I'm Wastin' My Tears on You"	Tex Ritter and His Texans
92.	6	62	"She Thinks I Still Care"	George Jones
93.	6	45	"Oklahoma Hills"	Jack Guthrie
94.	6	64	"I Don't Care (Just as Long as You Love Me)"	Buck Owens
95.	6	52	"It Wasn't God Who Made Honky Tonk Angels"	Kitty Wells
96.	6	64	"Understand Your Man"	Johnny Cash
97.	6	64	"Dang Me"	Roger Miller
98.	6	59	"Don't Take Your Guns to Town"	Johnny Cash
99.	6	44	"Straighten Up and Fly Right"	The King Cole Trio
100.	6	66	"Giddyup Go"	Red Sovine

Note: Ranking is based on the number of weeks a record held the #1 position on the charts. Ties would be broken by number of weeks in Top 10, Top 40, and Top 100. Abbreviations have the following meanings:

Pk Yr: year record reached peak position.
Wks @ #1: total weeks in number 1 position.

Source: Joel Whitburn, *The Billboard Book of Top 40 Country Hits* (New York, 1996), 502–04.

TABLE 17.52   TOP COUNTRY ARTISTS BY DECADE, 1940s–1980s

Forties (1944–49)		Fifties		Sixties		Seventies		Eighties	
Artist	Points	Artist	Points	Artist	Points	Artist	Points	Artist	Points
Eddy Arnold	3,587	Webb Pierce	5,041	Buck Owens	4,729	Conway Twitty	4,082	Willie Nelson	3,219
Ernest Tubb	2,612	Eddy Arnold	4,422	George Jones	3,872	Merle Haggard	3,464	Conway Twitty	3,201
Bob Wills	2,143	Hank Snow	3,913	Jim Reeves	3,311	Charley Pride	3,245	Alabama	3,196
Al Dexter	1,986	Carl Smith	3,519	Johnny Cash	2,898	Loretta Lynn	3,145	Ronnie Milsap	3,105
Red Foley	1,746	Red Foley	3,424	Eddy Arnold	2,685	Dolly Parton	3,124	Kenny Rogers	2,916
Gene Autry	1,741	Hank Williams	3,203	Marty Robbins	2,525	Tammy Wynette	3,081	Merle Haggard	2,907
Jimmy Wakely	1,415	Johnny Cash	2,648	Bill Anderson	2,406	Mel Tillis	2,991	Oak Ridge Boys	2,835
Tex Ritter	1,344	Elvis Presley	2,624	Webb Pierce	2,362	Waylon Jennings	2,899	Hank Williams, Jr.	2,735
Tex Williams	1,203	Kitty Wells	2,528	Sonny James	2,320	George Jones	2,875	George Strait	2,674
Merle Travis	1,172	Ernest Tubb	2,503	Ray Price	2,312	Sonny James	2,573	Earl Thomas Conley	2,661

Source: Whitburn, *Top Country Hits*, 506.

TABLE 17.53 COUNTRY MUSIC ASSOCIATION AWARDS, 1967–1990

The Country Music Association to promote country music began in Nashville in 1958. The association founded the Country Music Hall of Fame and Museum in 1961, and in 1967, when the museum opened, the association began its program of annual awards.

Entertainer of the Year		Female Vocalist of the Year		Male Vocalist of the Year		Musician of the Year*		Single of the Year	
Year	Artist	Year	Artist	Year	Artist	Year	Artist	Year	Song/Artist
1967	Eddy Arnold	1967	Loretta Lynn	1967	Jack Greene	1967	Chet Atkins	1967	"There Goes My Everything," Jack Greene
1968	Glen Campbell	1968	Tammy Wynette	1968	Glen Campbell	1968	Chet Atkins	1968	"Harper Valley P.T.A.," Jeannie C. Riley
1969	Johnny Cash	1969	Tammy Wynette	1969	Johnny Cash	1969	Chet Atkins	1969	"A Boy Named Sue," Johnny Cash
1970	Merle Haggard	1970	Tammy Wynette	1970	Merle Haggard	1970	Jerry Reed	1970	"Okie from Muskogee," Merle Haggard
1971	Charley Pride	1971	Lynn Anderson	1971	Charley Pride	1971	Charley Pride	1971	"Help Me Make It Through the Night," Sammi Smith
1972	Loretta Lynn	1972	Loretta Lynn	1972	Charley Pride	1972	Charlie McCoy	1972	"The Happiest Girl in the Whole U.S.A.," Donna Fargo
1973	Roy Clark	1973	Loretta Lynn	1973	Charlie Rich	1973	Charlie Mccoy	1973	"Behind Closed Doors," Charlie Rich
1974	Charlie Rich	1974	Olivia Newton-John	1974	Ronnie Milsap	1974	Don Rich	1974	"Country Bumpkin," Cal Smith
1975	John Denver	1975	Dolly Parton	1975	Waylon Jennings	1975	Johnny Gimble	1975	"Before the Next Teardrop Falls," Freddy Fender
1976	Mel Tillis	1976	Dolly Parton	1976	Ronnie Milsap	1976	Hargus "Pig" Robbins	1976	"Good Hearted Woman," Waylon Jennings & Willie Nelson
1977	Ronnie Milsap	1977	Crystal Gayle	1977	Ronnie Milsap	1977	Roy Clark	1977	"Lucille," Kenny Rogers
1978	Dolly Parton	1978	Crystal Gayle	1978	Don Williams	1978	Roy Clark	1978	"Heaven's Just a Sin Away," The Kendalls
1979	Willie Nelson	1979	Barbara Mandrell	1979	Kenny Rogers	1979	Charlie Daniels	1979	"The Devil Went Down to Georgia," Charlie Daniels Band
1980	Barbara Mandrell	1980	Emmylou Harris	1980	George Jones	1980	Roy Clark	1980	"He Stopped Loving Her Today," George Jones
1981	Barbara Mandrell	1981	Barbara Mandrell	1981	George Jones	1981	Chet Atkins	1981	"Elvira," The Oak Ridge Boys
1982	Alabama	1982	Janie Frickie	1982	Ricky Skaggs	1982	Chet Atkins	1982	"Always on My Mind," Willie Nelson
1983	Alabama	1983	Janie Frickie	1983	Lee Greenwood	1983	Chet Atkins	1983	"Swingin'," John Anderson
1984	Alabama	1984	Reba McEntire	1984	Lee Greenwood	1984	Chet Atkins	1984	"A Little Good News," Anne Murray
1985	Ricky Skaggs	1985	Reba McEntire	1985	George Strait	1985	Chet Atkins	1985	"Why Not Me," The Judds
1986	Reba McEntire	1986	Reba McEntire	1986	George Strait	1986	Johnny Gimble	1986	"Bop," Dan Seals
1987	Hank Williams, Jr.	1987	Reba McEntire	1987	Randy Travis	1987	Johnny Gimble	1987	"Forever and Ever, Amen," Randy Travis
1988	Hank Williams, Jr.	1988	K.T. Oslin	1988	Randy Travis	1988	Chet Atkins	1988	"Eighteen Wheels and a Dozen Roses," Kathy Mattea
1989	George Strait	1989	Kathy Mattea	1989	Ricky Van Shelton	1989	Johnny Gimble	1989	"I'm No Stranger to the Rain," Keith Whitley
1990	George Strait	1990	Kathy Mattea	1990	Clint Black	1990	Johnny Gimble	1990	"When I Call Your Name," Vince Gill

* changed from instrumentalist of the year in 1988.
Source: Tom Biracree, *The Country Music Almanac* (New York, 1993), 267–71.

TABLE 17.54 COUNTRY MUSIC'S SHARE OF THE RECORDED MUSIC MARKET, 1973–1990

(dollars spent [in millions] and percent of total dollars spent)

Year	Gross Country Sales	Country Portion of Dollars Spent on Recorded Music
1973	$150.2	10.5%
1974	$255.2	11.6%
1975	$276.1	11.7%
1976	$331.2	12.1%
1977	$451.6	12.4%
1978	$426.5	10.2%
1979	$437.5	9.0%
1980	$526.5	12.0%
1981	$529.3	15.0%
1982	$538.8	15.0%
1983	$496.0	13.0%
1984	$393.3	10.0%
1985	$438.8	10.0%
1986	$415.6	10.0%
1987	$528.9	9.5%
1988	$425.3	6.8%
1989	$447.4	6.8%
1990	$663.6	8.8%

Source: Paul Kingsbury, *The Encyclopedia of Country Music* (New York, 1998), 615.

TABLE 17.55 FULL-TIME COUNTRY RADIO STATIONS IN THE UNITED STATES, 1961–1990

(number of country stations and their percentage of all United States stations)

Year	Full-time Country Stations	Percentage of All United States Stations
1961	81	1.7
1963	97	1.9
1965	208	3.8
1969	606	9.0
1971	525	7.8
1972	633	8.6
1973	764	10.2
1974	856	11.0
1975	1,116	13.9
1977	1,140	13.6
1978	1,150	13.4
1979	1,434	16.4
1980	1,534	17.2
1981	1,785	19.6
1982	2,114	23.1
1983	2,266	24.3
1984	2,265	23.5
1985	2,289	23.2
1986	2,275	22.6
1987	2,212	21.6
1988	2,169	20.7
1989	2,086	19.6
1990	2,108	19.5

Source: Kingsbury, *Encyclopedia of Country Music*, 615.

Reading

Modern audio and video technology and great popularity of the performing arts did not mean that the most traditional, and perhaps most honored, instrument of spending leisure time—the printed word—would pass into oblivion. Society in the last half of the 20th century made room for almost everything. The publishing industry utilized evolving printing and copying technology and anything related to modern business and office techniques. Electronic communication allowed the press to keep abreast of new stories. Use of satellites enabled publications, such as the newspaper *USA Today,* to print in several locations at the same time. By the 1980s the writers or other print operatives had access to new and improving computer-driven methods of communication, research, storage, and composition. The simple word processor was a marvel in itself.

In addition to these factors, the writing and publishing establishment drew on all the forces driving public entertainment in the United States: a large, rapidly growing population, national wealth, and income that provided funds for inessential activity; a culture in which censorship had become a dirty word—something to be suppressed, it would appear—especially in publication; and a society that by the 1970s and 1980s treated the word *diversity* as almost holy writ.

Major themes of publication entertainment thus would be size, volume, variety, and diversity, even though in aspects of diversity, it took a few years to get there. The United States produced winners of the Nobel Prize in literature—the supreme expression of literary accomplishment—and it produced authors of unexceptional, even trashy works in all sizes and shapes. One could succeed by applying skill, perception, and originality to the noble art of writing or by finding a

TABLE 17.56   BEST-SELLERS IN AMERICA, 1946–1990

Year	Fiction Title	Fiction Author	Nonfiction Title	Nonfiction Author
1946	The King's General	Daphne du Maurier	The Egg and I	Betty MacDonald
1947	The Miracle of the Bells	Russell Janney	Peace of Mind	Joshua L. Liebman
1948	The Big Fisherman	Lloyd C. Douglas	Crusade in Europe	Dwight D. Eisenhower
1949	The Egyptian	Mika Waltari	White Collar Zoo	Clare Barnes, Jr.
1950	The Cardinal	Henry Morton Robinson	Betty Crocker's Picture Cookbook	
1951	From Here to Eternity	James Jones	Look Younger, Live Longer	Gayelord Hauser
1952	The Silver Chalice	Thomas B. Costain	The Holy Bible: Revised Standard Version	
1953	The Robe	Lloyd C. Douglas	The Holy Bible: Revised Standard Version	
1954	Not As a Stranger	Morton Thompson	The Holy Bible: Revised Standard Version	
1955	Marjorie Morningstar	Herman Wouk	Gift from the Sea	Anne Morrow Lindbergh
1956	Don't Go Near the Water	William Brinkley	Arthritis and Common Sense	Dan Dale Alexander
1957	By Love Possessed	James Gould Cozzens	Kids Say the Darndest Things!	Art Linkletter
1958	Doctor Zhivago	Boris Pasternak	Kids Say the Darndest Things!	Art Linkletter
1959	Exodus	Leon Uris	'Twixt Twelve and Twenty	Pat Boone
1960	Advise and Consent	Allen Drury	Folk Medicine	D.C. Jarvis
1961	The Agony and the Ecstasy	Irving Stone	The New English Bible: The New Testament	
1962	Ship of Fools	Katherine Anne Porter	Calories Don't Count	Dr. Herman Taller
1963	The Shoes of the Fisherman	Morris L. West	Happiness Is a Warm Puppy	Charles M. Schulz
1964	The Spy Who Came in From the Cold	John le Carré	Four Days	American Heritage
1965	The Source	James A. Michener	How to Be a Jewish Mother	Dan Greenburg
1966	Valley of the Dolls	Jacqueline Susann	How to Avoid Probate	Norman F. Dacey
1967	The Arrangement	Elia Kazan	Death of a President	William Manchester
1968	Airport	Arthur Hailey	Better Homes & Gardens New Cook Book	
1969	Portnoy's Complaint	Philip Roth	American Heritage Dictionary of the English Language	ed. William Morris
1970	Love Story	Erich Segal	Everything You Wanted to Know About Sex but Were Afraid to Ask	David Reuben, M.D.
1971	Wheels	Arthur Hailey	The Sensuous Man	"M."
1972	Jonathan Livingston Seagull	Richard Bach	The Living Bible	Kenneth Taylor
1973	Jonathan Livingston Seagull	Richard Bach	The Living Bible	Kenneth Taylor
1974	Centennial	James A. Michener	The Total Woman	Marabel Morgan
1975	Ragtime	E.L. Doctorow	Angels: God's Secret Agents	Billy Graham
1976	Trinity	Leon Uris	The Final Days	Bob Woodward, Carl Bernstein
1977	The Silmarillion	J.R.R. Tolkien	Roots	Alex Haley
1978	Chesapeake	James A. Michener	If Life Is a Bowl of Cherries—What Am I Doing in the Pits?	Erma Bombeck
1979	The Matarese Circle	Robert Ludlum	Aunt Erma's Cope Book	Erma Bombeck
1980	The Covenant	James Michener	Crisis Investing	Douglas R. Casey
1981	Noble House	James Clavell	The Beverly Hills Diet	Judy Mazel
1982	E.T. The Extra-Terrestrial Storybook	Willam Kotzwinkle	Jane Fonda's Workout Book	Jane Fonda
1983	Return of the Jedi Storybook	Joan D. Vinge	In Search of Excellence	Thomas J. Peters, Robert H. Waterman, Jr.
1984	The Talisman	Stephen King, Peter Straub	Iacocca: An Autobiography	Lee Iacocca with William Novak
1985	The Mammoth Hunters	Jean M. Auel	Iacocca: An Autobiography	Lee Iacocca with William Novak
1986	It	Stephen King	Fatherhood	Bill Cosby
1987	The Tommyknockers	Stephen King	Time Flies	Bill Cosby
1988	The Cardinal of the Kremlin	Tom Clancy	The Eight-Week Cholesterol Diet	Robert Kowalski
1989	Clear and Present Danger	Tom Clancy	All I Really Need to Know I Learned in Kindergarten	Robert Fulghum
1990	The Plains of Passage	Jean Auel	A Life on the Road	Charles Kuralt

Source: Wright, *New York Times Almanac, 1998,* 404–05.

timely subject or pushing the boundaries of acceptability, given the nation's loosening moral standards. As with the nation itself, literature went through a process of transition from domination by white males to a state of affairs in the 1980s in which virtually every attitude and orientation had its agents of expression. The late 1960s and early 1970s produced works about change, rebellion, and fullest expression of freedom in all its forms, especially social and cultural. The later 1970s and early 1980s featured works on introspection, self-development, and how to do almost anything, in which category sexual behavior seemed to command major attention.

The most prominent new voices came from the largest and most powerful groups that had been underrepresented in the past: women and black people, many of whose works were understandably politicized and radical, although a few, such as Shelby Steele and Glenn Loury, were not. Hispanics, Native Americans, and other minority groups had their spokespeople; writers representing the homosexual community were among the last to put their view forward, but once the process started the easier it became.

Some groups had to rely on special publishers and sales outlets, especially at the start. As a rule the successful writers used major commercial publishing houses, mostly based in New York, and they marketed their books many ways, including through an expanding group of mass-market retail bookstore chains, such as B. Dalton, Crown, Borders, and Barnes and Noble. Virtually every press established provisions for paperback editions, and after hardback sales had run their course, a volume with prospect for more circulation would be released in the compact, less-costly paperback version.

Magazines followed a pattern present in other areas of publication. The postwar period started as an extension of the earlier 1940s and then began to fragment, and proliferation became a theme. Led by the Big Three of *Time, Newsweek* and *U.S. News & World Report,* the newsmagazines held on to their following by subscription and retail sales, but the popular, general interest weeklies, such as *The Saturday Evening Post, Collier's, Life, Look,* and others declined and eventually stopped publication. One or two of them later returned in modified format, but their role in shaping American culture largely had come to an end. What followed was a mighty multitude of titles, with many of them targeted at specific interest groups. The enormously popular comic books—little magazines that started with children's stories, moved to the superheroes, mostly in the 1940s, and in the 1950s shocked parents and members of Congress with their blatant exploitation of sex and violence—returned to popularity in the 1980s. *Sports Illustrated* was the most popular of several magazines devoted to sports generally and of course each sport had special publications. *Ebony* was designed for black people, *Essence* for black women and so on. There were women's magazines for every female interest or attitude. Mention of men's magazines invariably led one to Hugh Hefner's revolutionary *Playboy,* which started publication in 1953 and attracted many imitators or competitors, but men's interests and their publications were not confined to naked women.

Traditional newsstands shrank in number and all but disappeared (except in New York City perhaps), but they were replaced by more broadly based retail outlets, including grocery supermarkets that set aside broad aisles for periodical publications. An old standard, *Reader's Digest,* was the largest seller in open competition, but in the 1980s *Modern Maturity,* under the auspices of its parent, American Association of Retired People (AARP), circulated more copies. Also, there was one type of publication so popular that it had to be placed up front, near the checkout lane or cash register to be seen as people left the store. These shrunken tabloid newspapers, classified as magazines, were exemplified by the *National Enquirer.* Eager watchdogs for (or creators of?) scandal, perpetually on the edge of slander, the tabloids sold several million copies every week.

Newspapers remained much alive in the United States. They attracted a hefty portion of advertising patronage; many of them did well financially. But a huge increase in national population did not produce a corresponding increase in the newspaper business. Neither the number of newspapers nor the circulation changed much between the 1950s and 1990. Only the large cities had more than one newspaper. The trend toward consolidation, into large newspaper chains, continued into the 1990s. Newspapers and most aspects of the print media frequently crossed the boundary between entertainment, communication, and information. Indeed, those portions of printed material that constituted entertainment depended on the reader. (For fuller data about published materials, one should consult the tables under the subheading "Printed Media" in Chapter 6, "Communication.")

TABLE 17.57 THE NATIONAL BOOK AWARDS, 1950–1990

The National Book Awards are given annually or outstanding literary works by American citizens. In the past the number of prizes has varied and has included such categories as poetry, fiction, biography, science, philosophy, religion, and history. Currently only two awards are made each year, one for fiction and one for nonfiction.

National Book Awards for Fiction, 1950–1990

Year	Author	Title
1950	Nelson Algren	The Man with the Golden Arm
1951	William Faulkner	The Collected Stories
1952	James Jones	From Here to Eternity
1953	Ralph Ellison	Invisible Man
1954	Saul Bellow	The Adventures of Augie March
1955	William Faulkner	A Fable
1956	John O'Hara	Ten North Frederick
1957	Wright Morris	Field of Vision
1958	John Cheever	The Wapshot Chronicle
1959	Bernard Malamud	The Magic Barrel
1960	Philip Roth	Goodbye, Columbus
1961	Conrad Richter	The Waters of Kronos
1962	Walker Percy	The Moviegoer
1963	J.F. Powers	Morte d'Urban
1964	John Updike	The Centaur
1965	Saul Bellow	Herzog
1966	Katherine Anne Porter	The Collected Stories
1967	Bernard Malamud	The Fixer
1968	Thornton Wilder	The Eighth Day
1969	Jerzy Kosinski	Steps
1970	Joyce Carol Oates	Them
1971	Saul Bellow	Mr. Sammler's Planet
1972	Flannery O'Connor	The Complete Stories
1973	John Barth	Chimera
1974	Thomas Pynchon	Gravity's Rainbow
	Isaac Bashevis Singer	A Crown of Feathers & Other Stories
1975	Robert Stone	Dog Soldiers
	Thomas Williams	The Hair of Harold Roux
1976	William Gaddis	JR
1977	Wallace Stegner	The Spectator Bird
1978	Mary Lee Settle	Blood Ties
1979	Tim O'Brien	Going After Cacciato
1980	William Styron	Sophie's Choice
1981	Wright Morris	Plains Song
1982	John Updike	Rabbit Is Rich
1983	Alice Walker	The Color Purple
1984	Ellen Gilchrist	Victory Over Japan
1985	Don DeLillo	White Noise
1986	E.L. Doctorow	World's Fair
1987	Larry Heinemann	Paco's Story
1988	Pete Dexter	Paris Trout
1989	John Casey	Spartina
1990	Charles Johnson	The Middle Passage

National Book Awards for Nonfiction, 1950–1990

Year	Author	Title
1950	Ralph L. Rusk	Ralph Waldo Emerson
1951	Newton Arvin	Herman Melville
1952	Rachel Carson	The Sea Around Us
1953	Bernard De Voto	Course of Empire
1954	Bruce Catton	A Stillness at Appomattox
1955	Joseph Wood Krutch	The Measure of Man
1956	Herbert Kubly	An American in Italy
1957	George F. Kennan	Russia Leaves the War
1958	Catherine Drinker Bowen	The Lion and the Throne
1959	J. Christopher Herold	Mistress to an Age
1960	Richard Ellman	James Joyce
1961	William L. Shirer	The Rise and Fall of the Third Reich
1962	Lewis Mumford	The City in History
1963	Leon Edel	Henry James, vols. 2 and 3
1964	Aileen Ward	John Keats: The Making of a Poet
1965	Louis Fisher	The Life of Lenin
1966	Arthur M. Schlesinger, Jr.	A Thousand Days: JFK in the White House
1967	Justin Kaplan	Mr. Clemens and Mark Twain
1968	Jonathan Kozol	Death at an Early Age
1969	Norman Mailer	The Armies of the Night
1970	Lillian Hellman	An Unfinished Woman, a Memoir
1971	James MacGregor Burns	Roosevelt: The Soldier of Freedom
1972	Joseph P. Lash	Eleanor and Franklin
1973	Frances Fitzgerald	Fire in the Lake: The Vietnamese and the Americans in Vietnam
1974	Pauline Kael	Deeper into the Movies
1975	Richard B. Sewall	The Life of Emily Dickinson
	Lewis Thomas	The Lives of a Cell
1976	Paul Fussell	The Great War and Modern Memory
1977	Bruno Bettelheim	The Uses of Enchantment: The Meaning and Importance of Fairy Tales
1978	Walter Jackson Bate	Samuel Johnson
1979	Arthur M. Schlesinger, Jr.	Robert Kennedy and His Times
1980	Tom Wolfe	The Right Stuff
1981	Maxine Hong Kingston	China Men
1982	Tracy Kidder	The Soul of a New Machine
1983	Fox Butterfield	China: Alive in the Bitter Sea
1984	Robert V. Remini	Andrew Jackson and the Course of American Democracy, 1833–1845, vol. 5
1985	J. Anthony Lukas	Common Ground: A Turbulent Decade in the Lives of Three American Families
1986	Barry Lopez	Arctic Dreams
1987	Richard Rhodes	The Making of the Atom Bomb
1988	Neil Sheehan	A Bright and Shining Lie: John Paul Vann and America in Vietnam
1989	Thomas L. Friedman	From Beirut to Jerusalem
1990	Ron Chernow	The House of Morgan: An American Banking Dynasty and the Rise of Modern Finance

National Book Awards for Poetry, 1950–1984

Year	Author	Title
1950	William Carlos Williams	Paterson: Book III and Selected Poems
1951	Wallace Stevens	The Auroras of Autumn
1952	Marianne Moore	Collected Poems
1953	Archibald MacLeish	Collected Poems 1917–1952
1954	Conrad Aiken	Collected Poems
1955	Wallace Stevens	The Collected Poems
1956	W.H. Auden	The Shield of Achilles
1957	Richard Wilbur	Things of This World
1958	Robert Penn Warren	Promises: Poems, 1954–1956
1959	Theodore Roethke	Words for the Wind
1960	Robert Lowell	Life Studies
1961	Randall Jarrell	The Woman at the Washington Zoo
1962	Alan Dugan	Poems
1963	William Stafford	Traveling Through the Dark
1964	John Crowe Ransom	Selected Poems
1965	Theodore Roethke	The Far Field
1966	James Dickey	Buckdancer's Choice
1967	James Merrill	Nights and Days
1968	Robert Bly	The Light Around the Body
1969	John Berryman	His Toy, His Dream, His Rest
1970	Elizabeth Bishop	The Complete Poems
1971	Mona Van Duyn	To See, To Take
1972	Howard Moss	Selected Poems
1973	A.R. Ammons	Collected Poems: 1951-1971
1974	Allen Ginsberg	The Fall of America: Poems of These States, 1965–1971
	Adrienne Rich	Diving into the Wreck: Poems, 1971–72
1975	Marilyn Hacker	Presentation Piece
1976	John Ashbery	Self-Portrait in a Convex Mirror
1977	Richard Eberhart	Collected Poems, 1930–1976
1978	Howard Nemerov	The Collected Poems
1979	James Merrill	Mirabell: Books of Number
1980	Philip Levine	Ashes
1981	Liesl Mueller	The Need to Hold Still
1982	William Bronk	Life Supports
1983	Galway Kinnell	Selected Poems
1984	Charles Wright	Country Music

Note: No awards were given for poetry during 1985–1990.
Source: Wright, Universal Almanac, 1992, 562–63.

The Pulitzer Prizes

The Pulitzer Prizes had their origin in the will of Joseph Pulitzer, Hungarian immigrant who established a newspaper empire targeted at mass readership that included the New York World and St. Louis Post-Dispatch. Pulitzer bequeathed the sum of $2 million to found the Columbia University School of Journalism. The trustees in 1917 began to make annual awards in journalism. The categories would change and increase over the years, although virtually all of them fell within the classification of journalism or literature. In 1990 each award carried a stipend of $3,000, but the value in terms of prestige was much greater.

TABLE 17.58 PULITZER PRIZE FOR MERITORIOUS PUBLIC SERVICE, 1946–1990

Year	Publication
1946	*Scranton (Pa.) Times*
1947	*Baltimore Sun*
1948	*St. Louis Post-Dispatch*
1949	*Nebraska State Journal*
1950	*Chicago Daily News; St. Louis Post-Dispatch*
1951	*Miami (Fla.) Herald; Brooklyn Eagle*
1952	*St. Louis Post-Dispatch*
1953	*Whiteville (N.C.) News Reporter; Tabor City (N.C.) Tribune*
1954	*Newsday (Long Island, N.Y.)*
1955	*Columbus (Ga.) Ledger and Sunday Ledger-Enquirer*
1956	*Watsonvile (Calif.) Register-Pajaronian*
1957	*Chicago Daily News*
1958	*Arkansas Gazette (Little Rock)*
1959	*Utica (N.Y.) Observer-Dispatch and Utica Daily Press*
1960	*Los Angeles Times*
1961	*Amarillo (Tex.) Globe-Times*
1962	*Panama City (Fla.) News-Herald*
1963	*Chicago Daily News*
1964	*St. Petersburg (Fla.) Times*
1965	*Hutchinson (Kans.) News*
1966	*Boston Globe*
1967	*Louisville (Ky.) Courier-Journal; Milwaukee Journal*
1968	*Riverside (Calif.) Press-Enterprise*
1969	*Los Angeles Times*
1970	*Newsday (Long Island, N.Y.)*
1971	*Winston Salem (N.C.) Journal & Sentinel*
1972	*New York Times*
1973	*Washington Post*
1974	*Newsday (Long Island, N.Y.)*
1975	*Boston Globe*
1976	*Anchorage (Alaska) Daily News*
1977	*Lufkin (Tex.) News*
1978	*Philadelphia Inquirer*
1979	*Point Reyes (Calif.) Light*
1980	*Gannett News Service*
1981	*Charlotte (N.C.) Observer*
1982	*Detroit News*
1983	*Jackson (Miss.) Clarion-Ledger*
1984	*Los Angeles Times*
1985	*Ft. Worth (Tex.) Star-Telegram*
1986	*Denver Post*
1987	*Pittsburgh Press*
1988	*Charlotte (N.C.) Observer*
1989	*Anchorage (Alaska) Daily News*
1990	*Philadelphia Inquirer*, Gilbert M. Gaul; *Washington (N.C.)*

Source: Columbia University; tables essentially as arranged in *World Almanac, 1999,* 669–72.

TABLE 17.59 PULITZER PRIZE IN REPORTING, 1946–1990

Year	Publication
1946	William L. Laurence, *New York Times*
1947	Frederick Woltman, *New York World-Telegram*
1948	George E. Goodwin, *Atlanta Journal*
1949	Malcolm Johnson, *New York Sun*
1950	Meyer Berger, *New York Times*
1951	Edward S. Montogomery, *San Francisco Examiner*
1952	George de Carvalho, *San Francisco Chronicle* (1) General or Spot; (2) Special or Investigative;
1953	(1) *Providence (R.I.) Journal and Evening Bulletin;* (2) Edward J. Mowery, *New York World-Telegram & Sun*
1954	(1) *Vicksburg (Miss.) Sunday Post-Herald;* (2) Alvin Scott McCoy. *Kansas City Star*
1955	(1) Mrs. Caro Brown, *Alice (Tex.) Daily Echo;* (2) Roland K. Towery, *Cuero (Tex.) Record*
1956	(1) Lee Hills, *Detroit Free Press,* (2) Arthur Daley, *New York Times*
1957	(1) *Salt Lake Tribune;* (2) Wallace Turner and William Lambert, *Portland Oregonian*
1958	(1) *Fargo (N.Dak.) Forum;* (2) George Beveridge, *Washington (D.C.) Evening Star*
1959	(1) Mary Lou Werner, *Washington (D.C.) Evening Star;* (2) John Harold Brislin, *Scranton (Pa.) Tribune,* and *The Scrantonian*
1960	(1) Jack Nelson, *Atlanta Constitution;* (2) Miriam Ottenberg, *Washington (D.C.) Evening Star*
1961	(1) Science de Gramont, *New York Herald-Tribune;* (2) Edgar May, *Buffalo (N.Y.) Evening News*
1962	(1) Robert D. Mullins, *Deseret News,* Salt Lake City; (2) George Bliss, *Chicago Tribune*
1963	(1) Sylvan Fox, William Longgood, Anthony Shannon, *New York World-Telegram & Sun;* (2) Oscar Griffin, Jr., *Pecos (Tex.) Independent and Enterprise*
1964	(1) Norman C. Miller, *Wall Street Journal;* (2) James V. Magee, Albert V. Gaudiosi, Frederick A. Meyer, *Philadelphia Bulletin.*
1965	(1) Melvin H. Ruder, *Hungry Horse News,* Columbia Falls, Mont.; (2) Gene Goltz, *Houston Post*
1966	(1) *Los Angeles Times* staff; (2) John A. Frasca, *Tampa (Fla.) Tribune*
1967	(1) Robert V. Cox, *Chambersburg (Pa.) Public Opinion;* (2) Gene Miller, *Miami (Fla.) Herald*
1968	(1) *Detroit Free Press* staff; (2) J. Anthony Lukas, *New York Times*
1969	(1) John Fetterman, *Louisville Courier-Journal and Times;* (2) Albert L. Delugach, *St. Louis Globe Democrat,* and Denny Walsh, *Life*
1970	(1) Thomas Fitzpatrick, *Chicago Sun-Times;* (2) Harold Eugene Martin, *Montgomery Advertiser & Alabama Journal*
1971	(1) *Akron (Ohio) Beacon Journal* staff; (2) William Hugh Jones, *Chicago Tribune*
1972	(1) Richard Cooper, John Machacek, *Rochester (N.Y.) Times-Union;* (2) Timothy Leland, Gerard M. O'Neill, Stephen A. Kurkjian, Anne De Santis, *Boston Globe*
1973	(1) *Chicago Tribune;* (2) Sun Newspapers of Omaha
1974	(1) Hugh F. Hough, Arthur M. Petacque, *Chicago Sun-Times;* (2) William Sherman, *New York Daily News*
1975	(1) *Xenia (Ohio) Daily Gazette;* (2) Indianapolis Star
1976	(1) Gene Miller, *Miami (Fla.) Herald;* (2) Chicago Tribune
1977	(1) Margo Huston, *Milwaukee Journal;* (2) Acel Moore, Wendell Rawis, Jr., *Philadelphia Inquirer*
1978	(1) Richard Whitt, *Louisville (Ky.) Courier-Journal;* (2) Anthony R. Dolan, *Stamford (Conn.) Advocate*
1979	(1) *San Diego (Calif.) Evening Tribune;* (2) Gilbert M. Gaul, Elliot G. Jaspin, *Pottsville (Pa.) Republican*
1980	(1) *Philadelphia Inquirer;* (2) Stephen A. Kurkjian, Alexander B. Hawes, Jr., Nils Bruzelius, Joan Vennochi, Robert M. Porterfield, *Boston Globe*
1981	(1) *Longview (Wash.) Daily News* staff; (2) Clark Hallas, Robert B. Lowe, *Arizona Daily Star*
1982	(1) *Kansas City Star, Kansas City Times;* (2) Paul Henderson, *Seattle Times*
1983	(1) *Fort Wayne (Ind.) News-Sentinel;* (2) Loretta Tofani, *Washington Post*
1984	(1) *New York Newsday;* (2) Boston Globe
1985	(1) Thomas Turcol, *Virginian-Pilot and Ledger-Star,* Norfolk, Va.; (2) William K. Marimow, *Philadelphia Inquirer;* Lucy Morgan, Jack Reed, St. Petersburg (Fla.) *Times*
1986	(1) Edna Buchanan, *Miami (Fla.) Herald;* (2) Jeffrey A. Marx, Michael M. York, *Lexington (Ky.) Herald-Leader*
1987	(1) *Akron (Ohio) Beacon Journal;* (2) Daniel R. Biddle, H.G. Bissinger, Fredric N. Tulsky, *Philadelphia Inquirer,* John Woestendiek, *Philadelphia Inquirer*
1988	(1) *Alabama Journal;* Lawrence (Mass.) *Eagle-Tribune;* (2) Walt Bogdanich, *Wall Street Journal*
1989	(1) *Louisville (Ky.) Courier-Journal;* (2) Bill Dedman, *Atlanta Journal and Constitution*
1990	(1) *San Jose (Calif.) Mercury News;* (2) Lon Kilzer, Chris Ison, *Minneapolis-St. Paul Star Tribune*

* This category originally embraced all fields. Later, separate categories were made for national and international reporting.
Source: Columbia University; tables essentially as arranged in *World Almanac, 1999,* 669–72.

TABLE 17.60 PULITZER PRIZE IN NATIONAL REPORTING, 1946–1990

Year	Publication
1946	Edward A. Harris, *St. Louis Post-Dispatch*
1947	Edward T. Folliard, *Washington Post*
1948	Bert Andrews, *New York Herald-Tribune;* Nat S. Finney, *Minneapolis Tribune*
1949	Charles P. Trussell, *New York Times*
1950	Edwin O. Guthman, *Seattle Times*
1951	No award
1952	Anthony Leviero, *New York Times*
1953	Don Whitehead, AP
1954	Richard Wilson, *Des Moines Register*
1955	Anthony Lewis, *Washington Daily News*
1956	Charles L. Bartlett, *Chattanooga (Tenn.) Times*
1957	James Reston, *New York Times*
1958	Relman Morin, AP; Clark Mollenhoff, *Des Moines Register & Tribune*
1959	Howard Van Smith, *Miami (Fla.) News*
1960	Vance Trimble, Scripps-Howard, Washington D.C.
1961	Edward R. Cony, Wall Street Journal
1962	Nathan G. Caldwell, Gene S. Graham, *Nashville Tennessean*
1963	Anthony Lewis, *New York Times*
1964	Merriman Smith, *UPI*
1965	Louis M. Kohlmeier, *Wall Street Journal*
1966	Haynes Johnson, *Washington (D.C.) Evening Star*
1967	Monroe Karmin, Stanley Penn, *Wall Street Journal*
1968	Howard James, *Christian Science Monitor;* Nathan K. Kotz, *Des Moines Register*
1969	Robert Cahn, *Christian Science Monitor*
1970	William J. Eaton, *Chicago Daily News*
1971	Lucinda Franks, Thomas Powers, UPI
1972	Jack Anderson, United Features Syndicate
1973	Robert Boyd, Clark Hoyt, Knight Newspapers
1974	James R. Polik, *Washington (D.C.) Star-News;* Jack White, *Providence (R.I.) Journal-Bulletin*
1975	Donald L. Barlett, James B. Steele, *Philadelphia Inquirer*
1976	James Risser, *Des Moines Register*
1977	Walter Mears, AP
1978	Gaylord D. Shaw, *Los Angeles Times*
1979	James Risser, *Des Moines Register*
1980	Charles Stafford, Bette Swenson Orsini, *St. Petersburg (Fla.) Times*
1981	John M. Crewdson, *New York Times*
1982	Rick Atkinson, *Kansas City Times*
1983	*Boston Globe*
1984	John Noble Wilford, *New York Times*
1985	Thomas I. Knudson, *Des Moines Register*
1986	Craig Flournoy, George Rodrigue, *Dallas Morning News;* Arthur Howe, *Philadelphia Inquirer*
1987	*Miami (Fla.) Herald; New York Times*
1988	Tim Weiner, *Philadelphia Inquirer*
1989	Donald L. Barlett, James B. Steele, *Philadelphia Inquirer*
1990	Ross Anderson, Bill Dietrich, Mary Ann Gwinn, Eric Nalder, *Seattle Times*

Source: Columbia University; tables essentially as arranged in *World Almanac, 1999,* 669–72.

TABLE 17.61 PULITZER PRIZE IN INTERNATIONAL REPORTING, 1946–1990

Year	Publication
1946	Homer W. Bigart, *New York Herald-Tribune*
1947	Eddy Gilmore, AP
1948	Paul W. Ward, *Baltimore Sun*
1949	Price Day, *Baltimore Sun*
1950	Edmund Stevens, *Christian Science Monitor*
1951	Keyes Beech, Fred Sparks, *Chicago Daily News;* Homer Bigart, Marguerite Higgins, *New York Herald-Tribune;* Relman Morin, Don Whitehead, AP
1952	John M. Hightower, AP
1953	Austin C. Wehrwein, *Milwaukee Journal*
1954	Jim G. Lucas, Scripps-Howard Newspapers
1955	Harrison Salisbury, *New York Times*
1956	William Randolph Hearst Jr., Frank Conniff, Hearst Newspapers; Kingsbury Smith, INS
1957	Russell Jones, UPI
1958	*New York Times*
1959	Joseph Martin, Philip Santora, *New York Daily News*
1960	A.M. Rosenthal, *New York Times*
1961	Lynn Heinzerling, AP
1962	Walter Lippmann, New York Herald Tribune Syndicate
1963	Hal Hendrix, *Miami (Fla.) News*
1964	Malcolm W. Browne, AP, David Halberstam, *New York Times*
1965	L. A. Livingston, *Philadelphia Bulletin*
1966	Peter Arnett, AP
1967	R. John Hughes, *Christian Science Monitor*
1968	Alfred Friendly, *Washington Post*
1969	William Tuohy, *Los Angeles Times*
1970	Seymour M. Hersh. Dispatch News Service
1971	Jimmie Lee Hoagland, *Washington Post*
1972	Peter R. Kann, *Wall Street Journal*
1973	Max Frankel, *New York Times*
1974	Hedrick Smith, *New York Times*
1975	William Mullen and Oyle Carter, *Chicago Tribune*
1976	Sydney H. Schanberg, *New York Times*
1978	Henry Kamm, *New York Times*
1979	Richard Ben Cramer, *Philadelphia Inquirer*
1980	Joel Brinkley, Jay Mather, *Louisville (Ky.) Courier-Journal*
1981	Shirley Christian, *Miami (Fla.) Herald*
1982	John Darnton, *New York Times*
1983	Thomas L. Friedman, *New York Times;* Loren Jenkins, *Washington Post*
1984	Karen Elliot House, *Wall Street Journal*
1985	Josh Friedman, Dennis Bell, Ozier Muhammad, *New York Newsday*
1986	Lewis M. Simons, Pete Carey, Katherine Ellison, *San Jose (Calif.) Mercury News*
1987	Michael Parks, *Los Angeles Times*
1988	Thomas L. Friedman, *New York Times*
1989	Glenn Frankel, *Washington Post;* Bill Keller, *New York Times*
1990	Nicholas D. Kristof, Sheryl Wu Dunn, *New York Times*

Source: Columbia University; tables essentially as arranged in *World Almanac, 1999,* 669–72.

TABLE 17.62 PULITZER PRIZE FOR EDITORIAL WRITING, 1946–1990

Year	Publication
1946	Hodding Carter, Greenville (Miss.) *Delta Democrat-Times*
1947	William H. Grimes, *Wall Street Journal*
1948	Virginius Dabney, Richmond (Va.) *Times-Dispatch*
1949	John H. Crider, *Boston Herald;* Herbert Elliston, *Washington Post*
1950	Carl M. Saunders, *Jackson* (Miss.) *Citizen-Patriot*
1951	William H. Fitzpatrick, *New Orleans States*
1952	Louis LaCoss, *St. Louis Globe Democrat*
1953	Vermont C. Royster, *Wall Street Journal*
1954	Don Murray, *Boston Herald*
1955	Royce Howes, *Detroit Free Press*
1956	Lauren K. Soth, *Des Moines Register & Tribune*
1957	Buford Boone, *Tuscaloosa* (Ala.) *News*
1958	Harry S. Ashmore, *Arkansas Gazette*
1959	Ralph McGill, *Atlanta Constitution*
1960	Lenoir Chambers, *Norfolk Virginian-Pilot*
1961	William J. Dorvillier, *San Juan* (Puerto Rico) *Star*
1962	Thomas M. Storke, *Santa Barbara* (Calif.) *News-Press*
1963	Ira B. Harkey, Jr., *Pascagoula* (Miss.) *Chronicle*
1964	Harzel Brannon Smith, *Lexington* (Miss.) *Advertiser*
1965	John P. Harrison, *Gainesville* (Fla.) *Sun*
1966	Robert Lasch, *St. Louis Post-Dispatch*
1967	Eugene C. Patterson, *Atlanta Constitution*
1968	John S. Knight, *Knight Newspapers*
1969	Paul Greenberg, *Pine Bluff* (Ark.) *Commercial*
1970	Philip J. Geyelin, *Washington Post*
1971	Horance G. Davis, Jr., *Gainesville* (Fla.) *Sun*
1972	John Strohmeyer, *Bethlehem* (Pa.) *Globe-Times*
1973	Roger B. Linscott, *Berkshire Eagle,* Pittsfield, Mass.
1974	F. Gilman Spencer, *Trentonian,* Trenton, N.J.
1975	John D. Maurice, *Charleston* (W.Va.) *Daily Mail*
1976	Phillp Kerby, *Los Angeles Times*
1977	Warren L Lerude, Foster Church, Norman F. Cardoza. *Reno Evening Gazette* and *Nevada State Journal*
1978	Meg Greenfield, *Washington Post*
1979	Edwin M. Yoder, *Washington Star*
1980	Robert L. Bartley, *Wall Street Journal*
1982	Jack Rosenthal, *New York Times*
1983	Editorial board, *Miami Herald*
1984	Albert Scardino, *Georgia Gazette*
1985	Richard Aregood, *Philadelphia Daily News*
1986	Jack Fuller, *Chicago Tribune*
1987	Jonathan Freedman, *Tribune* (San Diego)
1988	Jane Healy, *Orlando* (Fla.) *Sentinel*
1989	Lois Wille, *Chicago Tribune*
1990	Thomas J. Hylton, *Pottstown* (Pa.) *Mercury*

Source: Columbia University; tables essentially as arranged in *World Almanac,* 1999, 669–72.

TABLE 17.63 PULITZER PRIZE FOR CRITICISM (1) OR COMMENTARY (2), 1970–1990

Year	Publication
1970	(1) Ada Louise Huxtable, *New York Times;* (2) Marquis W. Childs, *St. Louis Post-Dispatch*
1971	(1) Harold C. Schonberg, *New York Times;* (2) William A. Caldwell, *The Record,* Hackensack, N.J.
1972	(1) Frank Peters, Jr., *St. Louis Post-Dispatch;* (2) Mike Royko, *Chicago Daily News*
1973	(1) Ronald Powers, *Chicago Sun-Times;* (2) David S. Broder *Washington Post*
1974	(1) Emily Genauer, *New York Newsday;* (2) Edwin A. Roberts, Jr., *National Observer.*
1975	(1) Roger Ebert, *Chicago Sun-Times;* (2) Mary McGrory, *Washington Star*
1976	(1) Alan M. Kriegsman, *Washington Post;* (2) Walter W. (Red) Smith, *New York Times*
1977	(1) William McPherson, *Washington Post;* (2) George F. Will, *Washington Post* Writers Group
1978	(1) Walter Kerr, *New York Times;* (2) William Safire, *New York Times*
1979	(1) Paul Gapp, *Chicago Tribune;* (2) Russell Baker, *New York Times*

Year	Publication
1980	(1) William A. Henry III, *Boston Globe;* (2) Ellen Goodman, *Boston Globe*
1981	(1) Jonathan Yardley, *Washington Star;* (2) Dave Anderson, *New York Times*
1982	(1) Martin Bernheimer, *Los Angeles Times;* (2) Art Buchwald, Los Angeles Times Syndicate
1983	(1) Manuela Hoelterhoff, *Wall Street Journal;* (2) Claude Sitton, *Raleigh* (N.C.) *News and Observer*
1984	(1) Paul Goldberger, *New York Times;* (2) Vermont Royster, *Wall Street Journal*
1985	(1) Howard Rosenberg, *Los Angeles Times;* (2) Murray Kempton, *New York Newsday*
1986	(1) Donal J. Henthan, *New York Times;* (2) Jimmy Breslin, *New York Daily News*
1987	(1) Richard Eder, *Los Angeles Times;* (2) Charles Krauthammer, *Washington Post*
1988	(1) Tom Shales, *Washington Post;* (2) Dave Barry, *Miami* (Fla.) *Herald*
1989	(1) Michael Skube, *Raleigh, N.C. News and Observer;* (2) Clarence Page, *Chicago Tribune*
1990	(1) Allan Temko, *San Francisco Chronicle;* (2) Jim Murray, *Los Angeles Times*

Source: Columbia University; tables essentially as arranged in *World Almanac,* 1999, 669–72.

TABLE 17.64 PULITZER PRIZE IN EDITORIAL CARTOONING, 1946–1990

Year	Publication
1946	Bruce Alexander Russell, *Los Angeles Times*
1947	Vaughn Shoemaker, *Chicago Daily News*
1948	Reuben L. (Rube) Goldberg, *New York Sun*
1949	Lute Pease, *Newark* (N.J.) *Evening News*
1950	James T. Berryman, *Washington Star*
1951	Reginald W. Manning, *Arizona Republic*
1952	Fred L. Packer, *New York Mirror*
1953	Edward D. Kuekes, *Cleveland Plain Dealer*
1954	Herbert L. Block, *Washington Post & Times-Herald*
1955	Daniel B. Fitzpatrick, *St Louis Post-Dispatch*
1956	Robert York, *Louisville* (Ky.) *Times*
1957	Tom Little, *Nashville Tennessean*
1958	Bruce M. Shanks, *Buffalo Evening News*
1959	Bill Mauldin, *St. Louis Post-Dispatch*
1961	Carey Orr, *Chicage Tribune*
1962	Edmund S. Valtman, *Hartford Times*
1963	Frank Miller, *Des Monies Register*
1964	Paul Conrad, *Denver Post*
1966	Don Wright, *Miami* (Fla.) *News*
1967	Patrick B. Oliphant, *Denver Post*
1968	Eugene Gray Payne, *Charlotte* (N.C.) *Observer*
1969	John Fischetti, *Chicago Daily News*
1970	Thomas F. Darcy, *New York Newsday*
1971	Paul Conrad, *Los Angeles Times*
1972	Jeffrey K. MacNelly, *Richmond News-Leader*
1974	Paul Szep, *Boston Globe*
1975	Garry Trudeau, Universal Press Syndicate
1976	Tony Auth, *Philadelphia Inquirer*
1977	Paul Szep, *Boston Globe*
1978	Jeffrey K. MacNelly, *Richmond News-Leader*
1979	Herbert L. Block, *Washington Post*
1980	Don Wright, *Miami* (Fla.) *News*
1981	Mike Peters, *Dayton* (Ohio) *Daily News*
1982	Ben Sargent, *Austin American-Statesman*
1983	Richard Locher, *Chicago Tribune*
1984	Paul Conrad, *Los Angeles Times*
1985	Jeffrey K. MacNelly, *Chicago Tribune*
1986	Jules Feiffer, *Village Voice* (N.Y.)
1987	Berke Breathed, *Washington Post*
1988	Doug Marlette, *Atlanta Constitution, Charlotte* (N.C.) *Observer*
1989	Jack Higgins, *Chicago Sun-Times*
1990	Tom Toles, *Buffalo News*

TABLE 17.65 PULITZER PRIZE IN SPOT NEWS PHOTOGRAPHY, 1947–1990

Year	Publication
1947	Arnold Hardy, amateur, Atlanta, Ga.
1948	Frank Cushing, *Boston Traveler*
1949	Nathaniel Fein, *New York Herald-Tribune*
1950	Bill Crouch, *Oakland (Calif.) Tribune*
1951	Max Desfor, AP
1952	John Robinson, Don Ultang, *Des Moines Register & Tribune*
1953	William M. Gallagher, *Flint (Mich.) Journal*
1954	Mrs. Walter M. Schau, amateur
1955	John L. Gaunt Jr., *Los Angeles Times*
1956	*New York Daily News*
1957	Harry A. Trask, *Boston Traveler*
1958	William C. Beall, *Washington Daily News*
1959	William Seaman, *Minneapolis Star*
1960	Andrew Lopez, UPI
1961	Yasushi Nagao, *Mainichi Newspapers*, Tokyo
1962	Paul Vathis. AP
1963	Hector Rondon, *La Republica*, Caracas, Venezuela
1964	Robert H. Jackson, *Dallas Times-Herald*
1965	Horst Faas, AP
1966	Kyoichi Sawada, UPI
1967	Jack R. Thornell, AP
1968	Rocco Morabito, *Jacksonville (Fla.) Journal*
1969	Edward Adams, AP
1970	Steve Starr, AP
1971	John Paul Filo, *Valley Daily News & Daily Dispatch of Tarentum & New Kensington, Pa.*
1972	Horst Faas, Michel Laurent, AP
1973	Huynh Cong, Utah, AP
1974	Anthony K. Roberts, AP
1975	Gerald H. Gay, *Seattle Times*
1976	Stanley Forman, *Boston Herald American*
1977	Neal Ulevich, AP; Stanley Forman, *Boston Herald American*
1978	John H. Blair, UPI
1979	Thomas, J. Kelly III, *Pottstown (Pa.) Mercury*
1980	UPI
1981	Larry C. Price, *Ft. Worth (Tex.) Star-Telegram*
1982	Ron Edmonds, AP
1983	Bill Foley, AP
1984	Stan Grossfeld, *Boston Globe*
1985	*The Register*, Santa Ana, Calif.
1986	Carol Guzy, Michel duCille, *Miami (Fla.) Herald*
1987	Kim Komenich, *San Francisco Examiner*
1988	Scott Shaw, *Odessa (Tex.) American*
1989	Ron Olshwanger, *St. Louis Post-Dispatch*
1990	*Oakland (Calif.) Tribune* photo staff

Source: Columbia University; tables essentially as arranged in *World Almanac, 1999*, 669–72.

TABLE 17.66 PULITZER PRIZE SPECIAL CITATION, 1947–1987

Year	Publication
1947	(Pulitzer centennial year) Columbia Univ. and the Graduate School of Journalism; St. Louis Post-Dispatch
1948	Dr. Frank Diehl Fackenthal
1951	C(yrus) L. Sulzberger, *New York Times*
1952	Max Kase, *New York Journal-American; Kansas City Star*
1953	*New York Times*, Lester Markel
1958	Walter Lippmann, *New York Herald-Tribune*
1964	Gannett Newspapers, "The Road to Integration"
1976	Prof. John Hohenberg, Admin. of Pulitzer Prizes
1978	Richard Lee Strout, *Christian Science Monitor* and *New Republic*
1987	Joseph Pulitzer Jr.

TABLE 17.67 PULITZER PRIZE IN FEATURE PHOTOGRAPHY, 1968–1990

Year	Publication
1968	Toshio Sakai, UPI
1969	Moneta Sleet Jr., *Ebony*
1970	Dallas Kinney, *Palm Beach (Fla.) Post*
1971	Jack Dykinga, *Chicago Sun-Times*
1972	Dave Kennerly, UPI
1973	Brian Lanker, *Topeka (Kans.) Capitol-Journal*
1974	Slava Veder, AP
1975	Matthew Lewis, *Washington Post*
1976	*Louisville (Ky.) Courier-Journal* and *Louisville Times*
1977	Robin Hood, *Chattanooga (Tenn.) News-Free Press*
1978	J. Ross Baughman, AP
1979	Staff photographers, *Boston Herald American*
1980	Erwin H. Hagler, *Dallas Times-Herald*
1981	Taro M. Yamasaki, *Detroit Free Press*
1982	John H. White, *Chicago Sun-Times*
1983	James B. Dickman, *Dallas Times-Herald*
1984	Anthony Suad, *Denver Post*
1985	Stan Grossfeld, *Boston Globe*; Larry C. Price. *Phila. Inquirer*
1986	Tom Gralish, *Philadelphia Inquirer*
1987	David Peterson, *Des Moines Register*
1988	Michel duCille, *Miami (Fla.) Herald*
1989	Manny Crisostomo, *Detroit Free Press*
1990	David C. Turnley, *Detroit Free Press*

Source: Columbia University; tables essentially as arranged in *World Almanac, 1999*, 669–72.

TABLE 17.68 PULITZER PRIZE IN FEATURE WRITING, 1979–1990

Year	Publication
1979	Jon D. Franklin, *Baltimore Evening Sun*
1980	Madeleine Blais, *Miami (Fla.) Herald Tropic* Magazine
1981	Teresa Carpenter, *Village Voice*, New York City
1982	Saul Pett, AP
1984	Peter M. Rinearson, *Seattle Times*
1985	Alice Steinbach, *Baltimore Sun*
1986	John Camp, *St. Paul Pioneer Press & Dispatch*
1987	Steve Twomey, *Philadelphia Inquirer*
1988	Jacqui Banaszynski, *St. Paul Pioneer Press Dispatch*
1989	David Zucchino, *Philadelphia Inquirer*
1990	Dave Curtin, *Colorado Springs Gazette Telegraph*

Source: Columbia University; tables essentially as arranged in *World Almanac, 1999*, 669–72.

TABLE 17.69 PULITZER PRIZE IN EXPLANATORY REPORTING, 1985–1990

Year	Publication
1985	Jon Franklin, *Baltimore Evening Sun*
1986	*New York Times* staff
1987	Jeff Lyon, Peter Gorner, *Chicago Tribune*
1988	Daniel Hertzberg, James B. Stewart, *Wall Street Journal*
1989	David Hanners, William Snyder, Karen Blessen, *Dallas Morning News*
1990	David A. Vise, Steve Coll, *Washington Post*

Source: Columbia University; tables essentially as arranged in *World Almanac, 1999*, 669–72.

TABLE 17.70 PULITZER PRIZE IN SPECIALIZED REPORTING, 1985–1990

Year	Publication
1985	Randall Savage, Jackie Crosby, *Macon (Ga.) Tel. & News*
1986	Andrew Schneider & Mary Pat Flaherty, *Pittsburgh Press*
1987	Alex S. Jones, *New York Times*
1988	Dean Baquet, William Gaines, Ann Marie Lipinski, *Chicago Tribune*
1989	Edward Humes, *Orange County (Calif.) Register*
1990	Tamar Stieber, *Albuquerque Journal*

Source: Columbia University; tables essentially as arranged in *World Almanac, 1999*, 669–72.

TABLE 17.71 PULITZER PRIZE IN FICTION, 1947–1990

Year	Author	Work
1947	Robert Penn Warren	All the King's Men
1948	James A. Michener	Tales of the South Pacific
1949	James Gould Cozzens	Guard of Honor
1950	A.B. Guthrie Jr.	The Way West
1951	Conrad Richter	The Town
1952	Herman Wouk	The Caine Mutiny
1953	Ernest Hemingway	The Old Man and the Sea
1955	William Faulkner	A Fable
1956	MacKinlay Kantor	Andersonville
1958	James Agee	A Death in the Family
1959	Robert Lewis Taylor	The Travels of Jaimie McPheeters
1960	Allen Drury	Advise and Consent
1961	Harper Lee	To Kill a Mockingbird
1962	Edwin O'Connor	The Edge of Sadness
1963	William Faulkner	The Reivers
1965	Shirley Ann Grau	The Keeper of the House
1966	Katherine Anne Porter	Collected Stories
1967	Bernard Malamud	The Fixer
1968	William Styron	The Confessions of Nat Turner
1969	N. Scott Momaday	House Made of Dawn
1970	Jean Stafford	Collected Stories
1972	Wallace Stegner	Angle of Repose
1973	Eudora Welty	The Optimist's Daughter
1975	Michael Shaara	The Killer Angels
1976	Saul Bellow	Humboldt's Gift
1978	James Alan McPherson	Elbow Room
1979	John Cheever	The Stories of John Cheever
1980	Norman Mailer	The Executioner's Song
1981	John Kennedy Toole	A Confederacy of Dunces
1982	John Updike	Rabbit Is Rich
1983	Alice Walker	The Color Purple
1984	William Kennedy	Ironweed
1985	Alison Lurie	Foreign Affairs
1986	Larry McMurtry	Lonesome Dove
1987	Peter Taylor	A Summons to Memphis
1988	Toni Morrison	Beloved
1989	Anne Tyler	Breathing Lessons
1990	Oscar Hijuelos	The Mambo Kings Play Songs of Love

Source: World Almanac, 1999, 672–73.

TABLE 17.72 PULITZER PRIZE IN DRAMA, 1946–1990

Year	Author	Work
1946	Russel Crouse and Howard Lindsay	State of the Union
1948	Tennessee Williams	A Streetcar Named Desire
1949	Arthur Miller	Death of a Salesman
1950	Richard Rodgers, Oscar Hammerstein II and Joshua Logan	South Pacific
1952	Joseph Kramm	The Shrike
1953	William Inge	Picnic
1954	John Patrick	Teahouse of the August Moon
1955	Tennessee Williams	Cat on a Hot Tin Roof
1956	Frances Goodrich and Albert Hackett	The Diary of Anne Frank
1957	Eugene O'Neill	Long Day's Journey Into Night
1958	Ketti Frings	Look Homeward, Angel
1959	Archibald MacLeish	J. B.
1960	George Abbott, Jerome Weidman, Sheldon Harnick, and Jerry Bock	Fiorello!
1961	Tad Mosel	All the Way Home
1962	Frank Loesser and Abe Burrows	How to Succeed in Business Without Really Trying
1965	Frank D. Gilroy	The Subject Was Roses
1967	Edward Albee	A Delicate Balance
1969	Howard Sackler	The Great White Hope
1970	Charles Gordone	No Place to Be Somebody

Year	Author	Work
1971	Paul Zindel	The Effect of Gamma Rays on Man-in-the-Moon Marigolds
1973	Jason Miller	That Championship Season
1975	Edward Albee	Seascape
1976	Michael Bennett, James Kirkwood, Nicholas Dante, Marvin Hamlisch, and Edward Kleban	A Chorus Line
1977	Michael Cristofer	The Shadow Box
1978	Donald L. Coburn	The Gin Game
1979	Sam Shepard	Buried Child
1980	Lanford Wilson	Talley's Folly
1981	Beth Henley	Crimes of the Heart
1982	Charles Fuller	A Soldier's Play
1983	Marsha Norman	'night, Mother
1984	David Mamet	Glengarry Glen Ross
1985	Stephen Sondheim and James Lapine	Sunday in the Park With George
1987	August Wilson	Fences
1988	Alfred Uhry	Driving Miss Daisy
1989	Wendy Wasserstein	The Heidi Chronicles
1990	August Wilson	The Piano Lesson

Source: World Almanac, 1999, 673.

TABLE 17.73 PULITZER PRIZE IN GENERAL NONFICTION, 1962–1990

Year	Author	Work
1962	Theodore H. White	The Making of the President 1960
1963	Barbara W. Tuchman	The Guns of August
1964	Richard Hofstadter	Anti-Intellectualism in American Life
1965	Howard Mumford Jones	O Strange New World
1966	Edwin Way Teale	Wandering Through Winter
1967	David Brion Davis	The Problem of Slavery in Western Culture
1968	Will and Ariel Durant	Rousseau and Revolution
1969	Norman Mailer	The Armies of the Night
	Rene Jules Dubos,	So Human an Animal: How We Are Shaped by Surroundings and Events
1970	Eric H. Erikson	Gandhi's Truth
1971	John Toland	The Rising Sun
1972	Barbara W. Tuchman	Stilwell and the American Experience in China, 1911–1945
1973	Frances FitzGerald	Fire in the Lake: The Vietnamese and the Americans in Vietnam
	Robert Coles	Children of Crisis, Volumes II & III
1974	Ernest Becker	The Denial of Death
1975	Annie Dillard	Pilgrim at Tinker Creek
1976	Robert N. Butler	Why Survive? Being Old in America
1977	William W. Warner	Beautiful Swimmers
1978	Carl Sagan	The Dragons of Eden
1979	Edward O. Wilson	On Human Nature
1980	Douglas R. Hofstadter	Gödel, Escher, Bach: An Eternal Golden Braid
1981	Cart E. Schorske	Fin-de-Siecle Vienna: Politics and Culture
1982	Tracy Kidder	The Soul of a New Machine
1983	Susan Sheehan	Is There No Place on Earth for Me?
1984	Paul Starr	Social Transformation of American Medicine
1985	Studs Terkel	The Good War
1986	Joseph Lelyveld	Move Your Shadow
	J. Anthony Lukas	Common Ground
1987	David K. Shipler	Arab and Jew
1988	Richard Rhodes	The Making of the Atomic Bomb
1989	Neil Sheehan	A Bright Shining Lie: John Paul Vann and America in Vietnam
1990	Dale Maharidge and Michael Williamson	And Their Children After Them

Source: World Almanac, 1999, 675.

TABLE 17.74 PULITZER PRIZE IN (U.S.) HISTORY, 1946–1990

Year	Author	Work
1946	Arthur M. Schlesinger Jr.	*The Age of Jackson*
1947	James Phinney Baxter 3d	*Scientists Against Time*
1948	Bernard De Voto	*Across the Wide Missouri*
1949	Roy F. Nichols	*The Disruption of American Democracy*
1950	O. W. Larkin	*Art and Life in America*
1951	R. Carlyle Buley	*The Old Northwest: Pioneer Period 1815–1840*
1952	Oscar Handlin	*The Uprooted*
1953	George Dangerfield	*The Era of Good Feelings*
1954	Bruce Catton	*A Stillness at Appomattox*
1955	Paul Horgan	*Great River: The Rio Grande in North American History*
1956	Richard Hofstadter	*The Age of Reform*
1957	George F. Kennan	*Russia Leaves the War*
1958	Bray Hammond	*Banks and Politics in America—From the Revolution to the Civil War*
1959	Leonard D. White and Jean Schneider	*The Republican Era: 1869–1901*
1960	Margaret Leech	*In the Days of McKinley*
1961	Herbert Feis	*Between War and Peace: The Potsdam Conference*
1962	Lawrence H. Gibson	*The Triumphant Empire: Thunderclouds Gather in the West*
1963	Constance McLaughlin Green	*Washington: Village and Capital, 1800–1878*
1964	Sumner Chilton Powell	*Puritan Village: The Formation of a New England Town*
1965	Irwin Unger	*The Greenback Era*
1966	Perry Miller	*Life of the Mind in America*
1967	William H. Goetzmann	*Exploration and Empire: The Explorer and Scientist in the Winning of the American West*
1968	Bernard Bailyn	*The Ideological Origins of the American Revolution*
1969	Leonard W. Levy	*Origin of the Fifth Amendment*
1970	Dean Acheson	*Present at the Creation: My Years in the State Department*
1971	James McGregor Burns	*Roosevelt: The Soldier of Freedom*
1972	Carl N. Degler	*Neither Black nor White*
1973	Michael Kammen	*People of Paradox: An Inquiry Concerning the Origins of American Civilization*
1974	Daniel J. Boorstin	*The Americans: The Democratic Experience*
1975	Dumas Malone	*Jefferson and His Time*
1976	Paul Horgan	*Lamy of Santa Fe*
1977	David M. Potter	*The Impending Crisis*
1978	Alfred D. Chandler Jr.	*The Visible Hand: The Managerial Revolution in American Business*
1979	Don E. Fehrenbacher	*The Dred Scott Case: Its Significance in American Law and Politics*
1980	Leon F. Litwack	*Been in the Storm So Long*
1981	Lawrence A. Cremin	*American Education: The National Experience, 1783–1876*
1982	C. Vann Woodward, ed.	*Mary Chesnut's Civil War*
1983	Rhys L. Isaac	*The Transformation of Virginia, 1740–1790*
1985	Thomas K. McCraw	*Prophets of Regulation*
1986	Walter A. McDougall	*The Heavens and the Earth*
1987	Bernard Bailyn	*Voyagers to the West*
1988	Robert V. Bruce	*The Launching of Modern American Science, 1846–1876*
1989	Taylor Branch	*Parting the Waters: America in the King Years, 1954–63;*
1990	James M. McPherson Stanley Karnow	*Battle Cry of Freedom: The Civil War Era In Our Image: America's Empire in the Philippines*

Source: World Almanac, 1999, 673–74.

TABLE 17.75 PULITZER PRIZE IN BIOGRAPHY OR AUTOBIOGRAPHY, 1946–1990

Year	Author	Work
1946	Linny Marsh Wolfe	*Son of the Wilderness (John Muir)*
1947	William Allen White	*Autobiography of William Allen White*
1948	Margaret Clapp	*Forgotten First Citizen: John Bigelow*
1949	Robert E. Sherwood	*Roosevelt and Hopkins*
1950	Samuel Flag Bemis	*John Quincy Adams and the Foundations of American Foreign Policy*
1951	Margaret Louise Colt	*John C. Calhoun: American Portrait*
1952	Merlo J. Pusey	*Charles Evans Hughes*
1953	David J. Mays	*Edmund Pendleton; 1721–1803*
1954	Charles A. Lindbergh	*The Spirit of St. Louis*
1955	William S. White	*The Taft Story*
1956	Talbot F. Hamlin	*Benjamin Henry Latrobe*
1957	John F. Kennedy	*Profiles in Courage*
1958	Douglas Southall Freeman (Vols. I–VI) and John Alexander Carroll and Mary Wells Ashworth (Vol. VII)	*George Washington*
1959	Arthur Walworth	*Woodrow Wilson: American Prophet*
1960	Samuel Eliot Morison	*John Paul Jones*
1961	David Donald	*Charles Sumner and the Coming of the Civil War*
1963	Leon Edel	*Henry James: Vols. 2–3*
1964	Walter Jackson Bate	*John Keats*
1965	Ernest Samuels	*Henry Adams*
1966	Arthur M. Schlesinger Jr.	*A Thousand Days*
1967	Justin Kaplan	*Mr. Clemens and Mark Twain*
1968	George F. Kennan	*Memoirs (1925–1950)*
1969	B.L. Reid	*The Man From New York: John Quinn and His Friends*
1970	T. Harry Williams	*Huey Long*
1971	Lawrence Thompson	*Robert Frost: The Years of Triumph, 1915–1938*
1972	Joseph P. Lash	*Eleanor and Franklin*
1973	W.A. Swanberg	*Luce and His Empire*
1974	Louis Sheaffer	*O'Neill, Son and Artist*
1975	Robert A. Caro	*The Power Broker: Robert Moses and the Fall of New York*
1976	R.W.B. Lewis	*Edith Wharton: A Biography*
1977	John E. Mack	*A Prince of Our Disorder: The Life of T.E. Lawrence*
1978	Walter Jackson Bate	*Samuel Johnson*
1979	Leonard Baker	*Days of Sorrow and Pain: Leo Baeck and the Berlin Jews*
1980	Edmund Morris	*The Rise of Theodore Roosevelt*
1981	Robert K. Massie	*Peter the Great: His Life and World*
1982	William S. McFeely	*Grant: A Biography*
1983	Russel Baker	*Growing Up*
1984	Louis R. Harlan	*Booker T. Washington*
1985	Kenneth Silverman	*The Life and Times of Cotton Mather*
1986	Elizabeth Frank	*Louise Bogan: A Portrait*
1987	David J. Garrow	*Bearing the Cross: Martin Luther King Jr. and the Southern Christian Leadership Conference*
1988	David Herbert Donald	*Look Homeward: A Life of Thomas Wolfe*
1989	Richard Ellmann	*Oscar Wilde*
1990	Sebastian de Grazia	*Machiavelli in Hell*

Source: World Almanac, 1999, 674.

TABLE 17.76 PULITZER PRIZE IN AMERICAN POETRY, 1947–1990

Year	Author	Work
1947	Robert Lowell	Lord Weary's Castle
1948	W. H. Auden	The Age of Anxiety
1949	Peter Viereck	Terror and Decorum
1950	Gwendolyn Brooks	Annie Allen
1951	Carl Sandburg	Complete Poems
1952	Marianne Moore	Collected Poems
1953	Archibald MacLeish	Collected Poems
1954	Theodore Roethke	The Waking
1955	Wallace Stevens	Collected Poems
1956	Elzabeth Bishop	Poems, North and South
1957	Richard Wilbur	Things of This World
1958	Robert Penn Warren	Promises: Poems 1954–1956
1959	Stanley Kunitz	Selected Poems 1928–1958
1960	W. D. Snodgrass	Heart's Needle
1961	Phyllis McGinley	Times Three: Selected Verse From Three Decades
1962	Alan Dugan	Poems
1963	William Carlos Williams	Pictures From Breughel
1964	Louis Simpson	At the End of the Open Road
1965	John Berryman	77 Dream Songs
1966	Richard Eberhart	Selected Poems
1967	Anne Sexton	Live or Die
1968	Anthony Hecht	The Hard Hours
1969	George Oppen	Of Being Numerous
1970	Richard Howard	United Subjects
1971	William S. Merwin	The Carrier of Ladders
1972	James Wright	Collected Poems
1973	Maxine Winokur Kumin	Up Country
1974	Robert Lowell	The Dolphin
1975	Gary Snyder	Turtle Island
1976	John Ashbery	Self-Portrait in a Convex Mirror
1977	James Merrill	Divine Comedies
1978	Howard Nemerov	Collected Poems
1979	Robert Penn Warren	Now and Then: Poems 1976–1978
1980	Donald Justice	Selected Poems
1981	James Schuyler	The Morning of the Poem
1982	Sylvia Plath	The Collected Poems
1983	Galway Kinnell	Selected Poems
1984	Mary Oliver	American Primitive
1985	Carolyn Kizer	Yin
1986	Henry Taylor	The Flying Change
1987	Rita Dove	Thomas and Beulah
1988	William Meredith	Partial Accounts: New and Selected Poems
1989	Richard Wilbur	New and Collected Poems
1990	Charles Simic	The World Doesn't End

Source: World Almanac, 1999, 675.

TABLE 17.77 PULITZER PRIZE SPECIAL CITATIONS, 1957–1984

Year	Author	Work
1957	Kenneth Roberts	for his historical novels
1960	Garrett Mattingly	The Armada
1961		American Heritage Picture History of the Civil War
1973	James Thomas Flexner	George Washington, Vols. I–IV
1977	Alex Haley	Roots
1978	E. B. White	
1984	Theodore Seuss Geisel	Dr. Seuss books

Source: World Almanac, 1999, 675.

TABLE 17.78 AMERICAN WINNERS OF THE NOBEL PRIZE IN LITERATURE, 1949–1990

Year	Author	Reason for Award
1949	William Faulkner	For his "unique contribution to the modern American novel."
1954	Ernest M. Hemingway	For his "mastery of the art of narrative," as expressed in The Old Man and the Sea.
1962	John Steinbeck	For "his realistic and imaginative writings."
1976	Saul Bellow	For "human understanding," and "subtle analysis of contemporary culture."
1978	Isaac B. Singer	For "impassioned narrative art," which "brings universal human conditions to life."
1980	Czeslaw Milosz	(U.S. and Poland) For voicing "man's exposed condition in a world of severe conflicts."
1987	Joseph Brodsky	For "authorship inbued with clarity of thought and poetic intensity."

Source: Wright, Universal Almanac, 1995, 664–65.

TABLE 17.79 THE OLDEST AUTHORS TO REACH NO. 1 ON THE NEW YORK TIMES BEST-SELLERS LIST, TO 1990

Author	Age at #1	Book
George Burns	92.9	Gracie
Helen H. Santmeyer	88.7	'. . . and Ladies of the Club."
Bernard Baruch	87.2	Baruch: My Own Story
Agatha Christie	86.2	Sleeping Murder
Dr. Seuss	86.1	Oh, the Places You'll Go
J. R. R. Tolkien	85.8	The Silmarillion
Agatha Christie	85.3	Curtain
Douglas MacArthur	84.8	Reminiscences
Katharine Hepburn	83.9	Me
Rose Kennedy	83.9	Times to Remember
Dr. Seuss	82.1	You're Only Old Once!
Winston Churchill	81.5	The Birth of Britain
James Michener	81.5	Alaska
Louis L'Amour	79.2	The Haunted Mesa
James Michener	78.7	Texas
Louis L'Amour	78.3	Last of the Breed
James Michener	76.7	Poland
James Michener	75.7	Space
Harry Overstreet	74.4	The Mature Mind
James Michener	73.8	The Covenant
Winston Churchill	73.7	The Gathering Storm
Sidney Sheldon	73.6	Memories of Midnight
Hedda Hopper	73.0	The Whole Truth and Nothing But
Sidney Sheldon	71.8	The Sands of Time
Peter Wright	71.6	Spycatcher
James Michener	71.5	Chesapeake
Lloyd C. Douglas	71.4	The Big Fisherman
Somerset Maugham	70.5	Razor's Edge
Thornton Wilder	70.2	The Eighth Day
Sidney Sheldon	70.0	Windmills of the Gods

Source: John Bear, The #1 New York Times Best Sellers (New York, 1992), 50.

TABLE 17.80 AUTHORS WHO REACHED NO. 1 ON THE *NEW YORK TIMES* BEST-SELLERS LIST BEFORE THEY WERE 35, TO 1990

Author	Age	Title
Francoise Sagan	19.9	*Bonjour Tristesse*
Amy Wallace	22.0	*The Book of Lists*
Marion Hargrove	23.0	*See Here, Private Hargrove*
Bill Mauldin	23.8	*Up Front*
Norman Mailer	25.4	*The Naked and the Dead*
Richard Tregaskis	26.3	*Guadalcanal Diary*
Ralph Martin	26.4	*Jennie*
Joe McGinnis	27.0	*The Selling of the President 1968*
Kathleen Winsor	28.1	*Forever Amber*
James Jones	29.3	*From Here to Eternity*
David Wallechinsky	29.5	*The Book of Lists*
Michael Jackson	29.7	*Moonwalk*
Carl Bernstein	30.4	*All the President's Men*
Ken Follett	30.5	*Triple*
"J"	30.7	*The Sensuous Woman*
Ken Follett	31.4	*The Key to Rebecca*
Stephen King	32.1	*The Dead Zone*
Grace Metalious	32.2	*Peyton Place*
Gwethalyn Graham	32.3	*Earth and High Heaven*
John le Carré	32.4	*The Spy Who Came in from the Cold*
Germaine Greer	32.5	*The Female Eunuch*
Richard Simmons	32.7	*Never Say Diet*
Erich Segal	32.9	*Love Story*
Stephen King	33.0	*Firestarter*
Bob Woodward	33.1	*The Final Days*
Frederick Forsyth	33.2	*The Day of the Jackal*
André Schwarz-Bart	33.3	*The Last of the Just*
Stephen King	33.9	*Cujo*
Ross Lockridge	34.0	*Raintree County*
Maurice Herzog	34.1	*Annapurna*
Patrick Dennis	34.3	*Auntie Mame*
Douglas Casey	34.4	*Crisis Investing*
John Roy Carlson	34.4	*Under Cover*
Jean Kerr	34.6	*Please Don't Eat the Daisies*
Frederick Forsyth	34.6	*The Odessa File*
Leon Uris	34.8	*Exodus*
Stephen King	34.9	*Different Seasons*

Source: Bear, *#1 On Times List,* 8.

The Most Influential Books

The Library of Congress and Book-of-the-Month Club in 1991 conducted a survey that asked readers to name the book that had been most influential in their lives. The following 13 volumes were most frequently mentioned.

1. *The Bible* (No version or edition mentioned)
2. *Atlas Shrugged*, Ayn Rand
3. *The Road Less Traveled*, M. Scott Peck
4. *To Kill a Mockingbird*, Harper Lee
5. *The Lord of the Rings*, J.R.R. Tolkien
6. *Gone with the Wind*, Margaret Mitchell
7. *How to Win Friends and Influence People*, Dale Carnegie
8. *The Book of Mormon* (No author listed)
9. *The Feminine Mystique*, Betty Friedan
10. *A Gift from the Sea*, Anne Lindbergh (tie)
11. *Man's Search for Meaning*, Viktor Frankl (tie)
12. *Passages*, Gail Sheehy (tie)
13. *When Bad Things Happen to Good People*, Harold Kushner (tie)

Source: Bear, *#1 On Times List,* 44.

CHAPTER 18 Sports

In its broadest dimension, American competitive athletics occupied a vast domain of almost immeasurable size. In its most elementary expression, it sponsored participatory activity of many millions of people of all ages, but mostly young men and women, boys and girls, from college age down to four or five. Every state had well-established programs for sports competition between schools at every level—the most intense and best organized coming, of course, in high school. In the period after 1945 the number of sports expanded and the number of participants multiplied, most conspicuously in the 1970s to include female competitors.

What was exercise and competition for one was entertainment for another. The spectator aspect of sports reached much further than the participation. Behind nearly every youthful athlete stood a legion of excitable parents, other relatives, friends, and simply interested observers. The Friday game remained part of the routine of life, probably a highlight of the week, and it was not uncommon for the local gymnasium and certainly the football field to hold more people than the town's population. College athletics represented mass entertainment, and football and basketball competition in Division I schools carried many of the markings of big business, except that the players were not paid (but coaches and all phases of management were) and the system did not operate on the profit motive. Week-after-week and year-after-year, the University of Michigan drew more football fans than the Detroit Lions of the professional National Football League (NFL).

As a rule, however, commercial sports activity pertained to professional teams and professional competition. In these categories the half-century after 1945 produced growth and expansion entirely commensurate with the numerous social, cultural, and economic revolutions underway in the nation. Those professional sports with a well-established and respected structure underwent increase in number of participants and expansion to nationwide markets. Major league baseball, the best example, which in 1946 was confined to an area north of the Mason-Dixon Line and east of the Mississippi River (except for the St. Louis Cardinals and Browns, barely on the other side of the river), moved to the West Coast in the 1950s and then, by moving teams or adding new ones, began to fill the area in between. Professional football, starting several steps behind baseball, underwent a long national building program, as did professional basketball, which had to start from scratch.

Except possibly for boxing, which could not shed charges of being brutal and shadowy if not crooked, every organized professional sport underwent growth of national scope. The National Hockey League (NHL), normally associated with the frigid north and with Canada, placed teams in Dallas and Los Angeles. Other activities that were either sketchily structured or nonexistent in 1946 arose to claim a share of the growing business of spectator sports. Automobile racing, especially that form loosely defined as "stock" cars, represented the most striking example.

The explosion of professional sports drew on familiar forces. Air travel in general and jet aircraft travel in particular made national expansion possible. The Yankees could play in New York one day and California the next if need be. Invariably, success in any sport came down to a matter of money. In simplest terms the population increased rapidly in cold war America and, the economy being what it was, people had money to spend on entertainment. The world of sports moved either to meet or to create demand through new forms of activity. The development would be registered in larger numbers of people attending sporting events. As time went on more dramatic evidence came in revenue produced from media coverage of sporting events—radio and television, although, of course, television became the most important. Behind every case of spectacular growth in sporting enterprise—be it the big three of professional baseball, football, and basketball, or golf, tennis, or auto

racing—one would find a large television contract, if not more than one. The traditional commercial networks competed for rights to carry sporting events. In 1979 a new network, ESPN, devoted exclusively to sports, began to offer competition, and the end of the 1980s brought signs of other broadcast enterprises preparing to enter the race.

Postwar society brought prosperity to professional sports, and prosperity did not necessarily bring peace. Demanding a larger share of a team's revenues, and later, as it appeared, as much money as they could get, players in the major sports formed unions, hired professional negotiators, while at the same time reserving the right to negotiate individually with management—a process that also became the job of a professional agent. Club owners pleaded impending bankruptcy, screamed bloody murder, and then tried to outbid each other for the services of—in the lexicon of the age—a valued "free agent." The result, beginning largely in the 1970s, was a succession of deadlines and crises that occasionally produced strikes or lockouts, all these continuously interspersed with players leaving one team for another and teams trading prized players for a pittance, out of fear of losing them to free agency in the near future or to unload a burdensome contract. Perhaps the single constant theme was that salaries kept going up, the highest ones—even the players would admit—reaching far beyond any reasonable measure of fairness or worth.

In terms of the quality of personnel the most significant change to the world of sports was its opening on nearly all fronts to African-American athletes. The transformation differed with the sport. Boxing

Willie Mays, arguably the best baseball player of them all. He was centerfielder of the New York Giants and San Francisco Giants in 1950s and 1960s. (National Baseball Hall of Fame Library, Cooperstown, N.Y.)

had had black participants since the start of the century. African-American athletes had been visible but by no means fairly represented in college and high school teams in the northern states. In the three high-profile professional sports, the emergence of black players was a phenomenon of the postwar era. Although it began with football, the integration of major league baseball in 1947 received the most attention and probably was the most important step. Black players moved gradually but with some dispatch to dominate professional basketball and football rosters. The pool of baseball players did not contain as proportionately large a number of blacks, but lists of best players and recipients of postseason awards had heavy representation of African-American names. Arrival of black baseball players called to question presumptions about the grand standard bearers of the past. How good in contemporary terms was Babe Ruth? Was Ty Cobb as good a base runner as Ricky Henderson? In the case of football, where tradition was skimpy, and with basketball, where there was none at all, black players became part of the tradition from the start. In a few other sports, where it would appear that factors other than physical ability came more prominently to bear—hockey, golf, tennis, for example—the number of black participants remained small.

In all, sports competition faced large challenges and shocks in the postwar era, especially on the professional level. Fans became enraged at the strikes and work stoppages, bitter about players' salaries and correspondingly high ticket prices, cynical, if not rebellious, about the entire enterprise. However worthy and long overdue the racial integration of sports, the process required an adjustment in many white spectators, even in the North. It took an adjustment from blacks, too, albeit a happy one, as one could detect in the crowds as Jackie Robinson made the circuit of National League cities in 1947 and 1948. But the anger over disruption of the season would subside; however grudgingly, most—but not all—fans would return to the ballpark or watch the game on television. Everything considered, the process or racial integration went reasonably smooth. The fans in, of all places, Atlanta cheered mightily in 1975 when Henry Aaron hit his 715th home run, breaking perhaps the most hallowed tradition of all.

TABLE 18.1 MOST POPULAR SPORTS—A GALLUP POLL, 1948

(in percent)

Sport	National	Men	Women
Baseball	39	45	31
Football	17	20	15
Basketball	10	8	12
Horse racing	4	3	5
Boxing	3	4	2
Ice skating, hockey	2	2	4
Swimming, diving	2	1	3
Tennis	2	1	2
Bowling	1	1	1
Auto racing	1	1	. . .
Others	7	7	9
None	12	7	16

Note: Based on a Gallup Survey of April 1948 which asked the question: What sport do you, yourself, enjoy watching most?
Source: George E. Gallup, *The Gallup Poll, Public Opinion 1935–1971* (New York, 1972), 733.

TABLE 18.2 MOST POPULAR SPORTS, 1986

(in percent)

Sport	Americans Interested
Pro football	60
Baseball	59
Fishing	43
College football	42
Bowling	35
Pro basketball	32
Pro boxing	32
Auto racing	31
College basketball	30
Hunting	26
Pool/billiards	26
Ice skating	25
Tennis	22
Horse racing	20
Hockey	18

Note: Based on a survey conducted in 1986 for *Sports Illustrated* magazine which asked in which sports respondents were interested.
Source: Tom and Nancy Biracree, *Almanac of the American People* (New York, 1988), 292–93.

TABLE 18.3 RACIAL COMPOSITION OF MAJOR PROFESSIONAL SPORTS TEAMS, 1989 AND 1990

(in percent)

Sport	Year	
	1989	1990
National Basketball Association		
Black	75	72
White	25	28
Latino	0	0
Other	0	0
National Football League		
Black	60	61
White	40	39
Latino	0	0
Other	0	0
Major League Baseball		
Black	NA	17
White	NA	70
Latino	NA	13
Other	NA	0

Source: Jessie C. Smith and Robert L. Johns, *Statistical Record of Black America* (Detroit, 1995), 1085–86.

TABLE 18.4 MOST POPULAR SPORTS ON TELEVISION, 1985

Sport	Number of Viewers	% of Adult
Pro football	63,200,000	37
Baseball	62,700,000	37
College football	48,900,000	29
Boxing	32,200,000	22
College basketball	36,200,000	21
Pro basketball	34,700,000	21
Pro wrestling	28,800,000	17
Bowling	28,600,000	17
Tennis	26,300,000	16
Auto racing	25,800,000	15
Golf	25,800,000	15
Drag racing	18,400,000	11
Thoroughbred horse racing	18,100,000	11
Hockey	16,600,000	10
Track and field	16,100,000	10
Rodeo	13,200,000	8
Weight lifting	12,900,000	8
Harness horse racing	9,800,000	6
Pro soccer	8,100,000	5
Roller derby	6,600,000	4

Note: Based on a survey in August 1985 by Simmons Market Research Bureau, which asked which sports adult Americans "frequently" or "almost always" watched on television.
Source: Biracree, *Almanac of American People*, 293–94.

TABLE 18.5   RACIAL COMPOSITION OF MAJOR PROFESSIONAL COACHES AND MANAGERS, 1989 AND 1990

(in percent; numbers in parentheses)

Sports	Year	
	1989	1990
National Basketball Association		
Black	22 (6)	22 (6)
White	78 (21)	78 (21)
Latino	0 (0)	0 (0)
National Football League		
Black	4 (1)	4 (1)
White	96 (27)	86 (27)
Latino	0 (0)	0 (0)
Major League Baseball		
Black	4 (1)	4 (1)
White	96 (27)	96 (27)
Latino	0 (0)	0 (0)

Source: Smith and Johns, *Black America,* 1085.

Sports remained an important part of American entertainment, an entity in itself that had inseparable ties to such other entertainment as radio and television, with lesser ties to movies and Broadway. It was as well an integral part of American society and culture and of increasing importance to the economy. For better or worse, sports stood as an expression of the competitive spirit of American society and people. Competitive athletics provided a source of personal identity and a channel of linkage to other forms of identity. The association with a school or university, a town, city, or state, often—if not most commonly—found expression through athletic teams.

Baseball

Organized baseball began the postwar era as the best organized and most popular national sport, perhaps not the "national pastime," as advocates claimed, but as close to that status as one could find. The institution experienced challenges and pressures so formidable that at times it seemed possible that the professional game might not survive. The largest challenges came in two forms: competition from several fronts—most prominently television and such other organized sports as basketball and football—and, starting in the 1970s, internal divisions so intense that they seemed to place the major leagues on a course of self-destruction.

As for the game itself, the period produced minor tinkering, some of it cosmetic, with no fundamental change in the way baseball was played. In 1954 the major leagues recognized the sacrifice fly—a small scoring adjustment that affected batting statistics, but not the production of runs. In the 1960s fielders had to bring in their gloves at the end of a half-inning, rather than flinging them onto the outfield grass. In 1973 the commissioner's office offered leagues the option of using a substitute hitter continuously through the game in place of one batter in the lineup, almost invariably the pitcher. In response the American League in 1974 adopted the designated hitter, or D.H.; in the National League the pitcher still had to bat. Beginning in 1974 all batters had to don a protective helmet when at the plate, and in 1988 similar head-gear was required of the catcher. There continued to be a mysterious tampering with the territory encompassed in a called strike. Tradition-ally regarded as the area over the plate, between the letters and the knees, the strike zone steadily shrank, and by the 1980s umpires seemed hesitant to designate as a strike any pitch that passed above the batter's beltline.

Otherwise uniforms, previously loose and baggy, became form fit-ting, knees and leg stockings all but disappearing; the conventional white for home uniforms and gray for the road gave way to experi-ments with color and design. Fielder's gloves became almost as large as a bushel basket, batter's gloves became commonplace, even on a hot summer day. Relief pitchers developed into a new type of specialty—young power-pitchers, raised from the ground up, as opposed to being the wise and grizzled former starter with a used-up arm. Players pro-gressively appeared larger and stronger; the good ones could play—if they wished—to almost 40.

The most meaningful change in personnel, of course, stemmed from the belated, grudging, and gradual racial integration of the sport. Jackie Robinson broke the color line in April 1947 when he took the field for the Brooklyn Dodgers. Other African-American players fol-lowed almost immediately, but this black migration hardly developed into a gusher. It took 12 years to achieve even minimal integration of all 16 teams, and black players remained clearly in the minority. Those blacks who did make it represented some of the best players in the game. African Americans dominated nearly all statistics in the National League except pitching. In the American League, where integration proceeded slowly, African Americans were less prominent. Another form of integration had been underway in the major leagues for some time. At a time when blacks were banned, a few good Latin American players had found their way into the big leagues. Beginning in the 1960s they began to appear in larger numbers from several Hispanic nations, most commonly Mexico, Venezuela, the Dominican Republic, and other Caribbean Islands. To the familiar African-American names one also would add a growing list of Latinos: Rod Carew, Orlando Cepeda, Juan Marichal, David Concepcion, Tony Armas, Tony Perez, Fernando Valenzuela, Jose Canseco, and many others. Before it became a fashionable term, baseball was leading the way in promoting multiculturalism.

In time the major leagues showed some balance between the teams, but not at the start of the period. Continuing a dominance that went back some two decades, the New York Yankees after 1946 won 14 of the first 20 American League championships and then settled into a period of mediocrity for the next 20 or so years. There followed brief spurts by Baltimore, Oakland, and the Yankees again and then a period of nine years, each of which produced a different winner. To the extent that the National League had a most successful team, it would be the franchise of the Brooklyn Dodgers, transplanted to Los Angeles in 1958. Between 1946 and 1990 the Dodgers won 15 pen-nants. Otherwise, virtually every one of the traditional eight National League teams had at least a taste of glory, either in the original city or a new location. The only National League expansion teams to win were the New York Mets, twice, and the San Diego Padres. The longest-suffering major league franchise continued to be Chicago of the National League, which still played games in quaint and historic Wrigley Field on the city's north side. Only in 1988 did the club suc-cumb to the modern world by allowing installation of lights for night games. The Cubbies nonetheless remained suffering, claiming not a single National League pennant between 1946 and 1990.

Expansion of the two leagues and the city-hopping that some teams experienced represented a reasonable expression of the need to make major league baseball a truly national venture. But movement of teams also came to be a manifestation of the extent to which economics had come to dominate all aspects of this game originally intended as fun time for boys. Owners moved teams to cities that offered the most incentives or the largest market. Harsh reality could have been made no more clear than in the sudden departure in 1958 of the storied and generally successful Brooklyn Dodger ballclub to antiseptic, sunny Los Angeles, which to the baseball purist offered nothing but money. Team movement represented only a part of the perception of betrayal, broken loyalty, and greed that beset organized baseball in the postwar era.

The 1970s produced the start of a series of struggles between players and owners, the outcome of which was nowhere in sight at the end of the 1980s. The players revived their union, hired a hard-driving trade-union professional, Marvin Miller, and set out to make more money and maintain control over all their activities. What one might call D-day for baseball, and perhaps professional sports, came on December 23, 1975, when independent arbitrator Peter Seitz ruled that the so-called reserve clause, which had bound a player to a team that "owned" him, was no longer operable and that the players who brought the suit—Dave McNally and Andy Messersmith—were free to sign with any team. The Seitz decision had two immediate effects. It touched off a bidding war for prized, unsigned players, in which

owners became victims of their most aggressive competitors—owners anxious to buy a team quickly by offering high prices, in this instance Ted Turner of the Atlanta Braves and George Steinbrenner of the New York Yankees. The second consequence was the need for owners and the players' association to negotiate a contract, called the basic agreement, that identified new terms of employment. The owners wanted limits on salaries, probably through a team "salary cap"; the players wanted none. The owners wanted various restraints on free agency; the players opposed any provision that might limit their freedom to negotiate the best terms possible.

An immediate result was escalating salaries. The average pay, $45,000 in 1975, went to $371,000 in 1985, and to $600,000 in

TABLE 18.6   MAJOR LEAGUE TEAMS—1946, 1965, AND 1990

League Standings, 1946

National League					American League				
Team	Wins	Losses	Percent	Games Back	Team	Wins	Losses	Percent	Games Back
ªSt. Louis	98	58	.628		Boston	104	50	.675	
Brooklyn	96	60	.615	2	Detroit	92	62	.597	12
Chicago	82	71	.536	14.5	New York	87	67	.565	17
Boston	81	72	.529	15.5	Washington	76	78	.494	28
Philadelphia	69	85	.448	28	Chicago	74	80	.481	30
Cincinnati	67	87	.435	30	Cleveland	68	86	.442	36
Pittsburgh	63	91	.409	34	St. Louis	66	88	.429	38
New York	61	93	.396	36	Philadelphia	49	105	.318	55

ª Defeated Brooklyn in playoff 2 games to 0.

League Standings, 1965

National League					American League				
Team	Wins	Losses	Percent	Games Back	Team	Wins	Losses	Percent	Games Back
Los Angeles	97	65	.599		Minnesota	102	60	.630	
San Francisco	95	67	.586	2	Chicago	95	67	.586	7
Pittsburgh	90	72	.556	7	Baltimore	94	68	.580	8
Cincinnati	89	73	.549	8	Detroit	89	73	.549	13
Milwaukee	86	76	.531	11	Cleveland	87	75	.537	15
Philadelphia	85	76	.528	11.5	New York	77	85	.475	25
St. Louis	80	81	.497	16.5	California	75	87	.463	27
Chicago	72	90	.444	25	Washington	70	92	.432	32
Houston	65	97	.401	32	Boston	62	100	.383	40
New York	50	112	.309	47	Kanas City	59	103	.364	43

League Standings, 1990

National League					American League				
Team	Wins	Losses	Percent	Games Back	Team	Wins	Losses	Percent	Games Back
East					East				
Pittsburgh	95	67	.586		Boston	88	74	.543	
New York	91	71	.562	4	Toronto	86	76	.531	2
Montreal	85	77	.525	10	Detroit	79	83	.488	9
Chicago	77	85	.475	18	Cleveland	77	85	.475	11
Philadelphia	77	85	.475	18	Baltimore	76	85	.472	11.5
St. Louis	70	92	.432	25	Milwaukee	74	88	.457	14
					New York	67	95	.414	21
West					West				
Cincinnati	91	71	.562		Oakland	103	59	.636	
Los Angeles	86	76	.531	5	Chicago	94	68	.580	9
San Francisco	85	77	.525	6	Texas	83	79	.512	20
Houston	75	87	.463	16	California	80	82	.494	23
San Diego	75	87	.463	16	Seattle	77	85	.475	26
Atlanta	65	97	.401	26	Kansas City	75	86	.466	27.5
					Minnesota	74	88	.457	29

Source: Rick Wolff, The Baseball Encyclopedia (New York, 1993), 302, 304, 374, 376, 506, 509.

1990, with a million-dollar average only a step away. Loyalty to a team, or city—even a hometown—seemingly became an attitude of the past. Pete Rose, a native of Cincinnati whose lifelong ambition had been to be a "$100,000 singles hitter," left the Reds at age 37 for more money than he had dreamed of receiving. Difficulty in agreeing to a basic contract produced a strike in 1981 that canceled a third of the season, and another shorter work stoppage came in 1985.

While frustrated fans vented their feelings on both sides, it appeared that deepest anger increasingly was directed at the players who, at one time seemingly embarrassed with their soaring incomes, now defended them as an expression of right and justice. Baseball fans, as it developed, showed themselves to be remarkably forgiving, willing, once the trouble had passed, to return to their beloved game. Television contracts made it possible for most teams to absorb high salaries, but a breach continued to widen between the earnings, and thus the buying power, of teams from large market centers, such as New York and Los Angeles, and small market cities, such as Pittsburgh and St. Louis. The decision by the owners and the players' union in 1990 to extend the basic agreement for three years merely bought time. It solved none of baseball's problems.

Changes in Major League Baseball Teams, 1946–1990

1953   Boston Braves (N) move to Milwaukee.

1954   St. Louis Browns (A) move to Baltimore and become the Orioles; Cincinnati Reds (N) are renamed Redlegs.

1955   Philadelphia Athletics (A) move to Kansas City.

1958   Brooklyn Dodgers (N) move to Los Angeles: New York Giants (N) move to San Francisco.

1961   Washington Senators (A) move to Bloomington, Minnesota, and become the Minnesota Twins; a new Washington Senators joins the American League as an expansion team; the Los Angeles Angels join the American League; Cincinnati Redlegs (N) restore the name of Reds.

1962   Houston Colt 45s and New York Mets join the National League.

1965   Houston Colt 45s (N) are renamed Astros; Los Angeles Angels are renamed California Angels.

1966   California Angels (A) move to Anaheim; Milwaukee Braves move to Atlanta.

1968   Kansas City Athletics (A) move to Oakland and become A's.

1969   Kansas City Royals and Seattle Pilots join the American League; Montreal Expos and San Diego Padres join the National League.

1970   Seattle Pilots (A) move to Milwaukee and become the Brewers.

1972   Washington Senators (A) move to Arlington, Texas, and become the Rangers.

1977   Seattle Mariners and Toronto Blue Jays join the American League.

1982   Minnesota Twins (A) move to Minneapolis.

1987   Oakland A's (A) are renamed Athletics.

Sources: Mike Meserole, ed., *The 1993 Information Please Sports Almanac* (Boston, 1992), 97.

TABLE 18.7   MAJOR LEAGUE ATTENDANCE, 1950–1990
(in millions)

Year	Number of Clubs	Total Attendance	Attendance per Club
1950	16	17.5	1.09
1955	16	16.6	1.04
1960	16	19.9	1.24
1965	20	22.4	1.12
1970	24	28.8	1.20
1975	24	29.8	1.24
1976	24	31.3	1.31
1977	26	38.7	1.49
1978	26	40.6	1.56
1984	26	44.7	1.70
1985	26	46.8	1.80
1986	26	47.5	1.83
1987	26	52.0	2.00
1988	26	53.0	2.04
1989	26	55.2	2.12
1990	26	54.8	2.11

Source: Andrew Zimbalist, *Baseball and Billions* (New York, 1992), 52.

TABLE 18.8   AVERAGE BASEBALL TICKET PRICES, 1950–1990

Year	Box	General Admission	Overall	Overall (1990 prices)
1950	. . .	. . .	$1.60	$8.74
1960	. . .	. . .	$2.05	$9.11
1970	. . .	. . .	$3.18	$10.79
1980	. . .	. . .	$4.53	$7.23
1984	$7.71	$3.33	$5.93	$7.51
1985	$8.19	$3.48	$6.21	$7.60
1986	$8.57	$3.61	$6.70	$8.04
1987	$8.95	$3.96	$6.89	$7.98
1988	$9.60	$4.53	$7.17	$7.98
1989	$9.84	$4.59	$7.61	$8.07
1990	$10.26	$4.47	$7.95	$7.95

Source: Zimbalist, *Baseball and Billions*, 52.

TABLE 18.9 AMERICAN LEAGUE PENNANT WINNERS, 1946–1990

Year	Club	Manager	W.	L.	Pct.	G.A.
1946	Boston	Joe Cronin	104	50	.675	12
1947	New York	Bucky Harris	97	57	.630	12
1948	Cleveland[a]	Lou Boudreau	97	58	.626	1
1949	New York	Casey Stengel	97	57	.630	1
1950	New York	Casey Stengel	98	56	.636	3
1951	New York	Casey Stengel	98	56	.636	5
1952	New York	Casey Stengel	95	59	.617	2
1953	New York	Casey Stengel	99	52	.656	8½
1954	Cleveland	Al Lopez	111	43	.721	8
1955	New York	Casey Stengel	96	58	.623	3
1956	New York	Casey Stengel	97	57	.630	9
1957	New York	Casey Stengel	98	56	.636	8
1958	New York	Casey Stengel	92	62	.597	10
1959	Chicago	Al Lopez	94	60	.610	5
1960	New York	Casey Stengel	97	57	.630	8
1961	New York	Ralph Houk	109	53	.673	8
1962	New York	Ralph Houk	96	66	.593	5
1963	New York	Ralph Houk	104	57	.646	10½
1964	New York	Yogi Berra	99	63	611	1
1965	Minnesota	Sam Mele	102	60	.630	7
1966	Baltimore	Hank Bauer	97	63	.606	9
1967	Boston	Dick Williams	92	70	.568	1
1968	Detroit	Mayo Smith	103	59	.636	12
1969	Baltimore (E)	Earl Weaver	109	53	.673	19
1970	Baltimore (E)	Earl Weaver	108	54	.667	15
1971	Baltimore (E)	Earl Weaver	101	57	.639	12
1972	Oakland (W)	Dick Williams	93	62	.600	5½
1973	Oakland (W)	Dick Williams	94	68	.580	6
1974	Oakland (W)	Al Dark	90	72	.556	5
1975	Boston (E)	Darrell Johnson	95	65	.594	4½
1976	New York (E)	Billy Martin	97	62	.610	10½
1977	New York (E)	Billy Martin	100	62	.617	2½
1978	New York (E)	Billy Martin, Bob Lemon	100	63	.613	1
1979	Baltimore (E)	Earl Weaver	102	57	.642	8
1980	Kansas City (W)	Jim Frey	97	65	.599	14
1981	New York (E)	Gene Michael, Bob Lemon	59	48	.551	5
1982	Milwaukee (E)	Buck Rodgers, Harvey Kuenn	95	67	.586	1
1983	Baltimore (E)	Joe Altobelli	98	64	.605	6
1984	Detroit (E)	Sparky Anderson	104	58	.642	15
1985	Kansas City (W)	Dick Howser	91	71	.562	1
1986	Boston (E)	John McNamara	95	66	.590	5½
1987	Minnesota (W)	Tom Kelly	85	77	.525	2
1988	Oakland (W)	Tony La Russa	104	58	.642	13
1989	Oakland (W)	Tony La Russa	99	63	.611	7
1990	Oakland (W)	Tony La Russa	103	59	636	9

GA: Games ahead of second place team.
[a] Defeated Boston in one-game playoff.
Source: Craig Carter, *The Sporting News Complete Baseball Record Book, 1993 Edition* (St. Louis, 1992), 176–77.

TABLE 18.10 NATIONAL LEAGUE PENNANT WINNERS, 1946–1990

Year	Club	Manager	W.	L.	Pct.	G.A.
1946	St. Louis[a]	Eddie Dyer	98	58	.628	2
1947	Brooklyn	Burt Shotton	94	60	.610	5
1948	Boston	Billy Southworth	91	62	.595	6½
1949	Brooklyn	Burt Shotton	97	57	.630	1
1950	Philadelphia	Eddie Sawyer	91	63	.591	2
1951	New York[b]	Leo Durocher	98	59	.624	1
1952	Brooklyn	Charlie Dressen	96	57	.627	4½
1953	Brooklyn	Charlie Dressen	105	49	.682	13
1954	New York	Leo Durocher	97	57	.630	5
1955	Brooklyn	Walter Alston	98	55	.641	13½
1956	Brooklyn	Walter Alston	93	61	.604	1
1957	Milwaukee	Fred Haney	95	59	.617	8
1958	Milwaukee	Fred Haney	92	62	.597	8
1959	Los Angeles[c]	Walter Alston	88	68	.564	2
1960	Pittsburgh	Danny Murtaugh	95	59	.617	7
1961	Cincinnati	Fred Hutchinson	93	61	.604	4
1962	San Francisco[d]	Al Dark	103	62	.624	1
1963	Los Angeles	Walter Alston	99	63	.611	6
1964	St. Louis	Johnny Keane	93	69	.574	1
1965	Los Angeles	Walter Alston	97	65	.599	2
1966	Los Angeles	Walter Alston	95	67	.586	1½
1967	St. Louis	Red Schoendienst	101	60	.627	10½
1968	St. Louis	Red Schoendienst	97	65	.599	9
1969	New York (E)	Gil Hodges	100	62	.617	8
1970	Cincinnati (W)	Sparky Anderson	102	60	.630	14½
1971	Pittsburgh (E)	Danny Murtaugh	97	65	.599	7
1972	Cincinnati (W)	Sparky Anderson	95	59	.617	10½
1973	New York (E)	Yogi Berra	82	79	.509	1½
1974	Los Angeles (E)	Walter Alston	102	60	.630	4
1975	Cincinnati (W)	Sparky Anderson	108	54	.667	20
1976	Cincinnati (W)	Sparky Anderson	102	60	.630	10
1977	Los Angeles (W)	Tommy Lasorda	98	64	.605	10
1978	Los Angeles (W)	Tommy Lasorda	95	67	.586	2½
1979	Pittsburgh (E)	Chuck Tanner	98	64	.605	2
1980	Philadelphia (E)	Dallas Green	91	71	.562	1
1981	Los Angeles (W)	Tommy Lasorda	63	47	.573	[e]
1982	St. Louis (E)	Whitey Herzog	92	70	.568	3
1983	Philadelphia (E)	Pat Corrales, Paul Owens	90	72	.556	6
1984	San Diego (W)	Dick Williams	92	70	.568	12
1985	St. Louis (E)	Whitey Herzog	101	61	.623	3
1986	New York (E)	Dave Johnson	108	54	.667	21½
1987	St. Louis (E)	Whitey Herzog	95	67	.586	3
1988	Los Angeles (W)	Tommy Lasorda	94	67	.584	7
1989	San Francisco (W)	Roger Craig	92	70	.568	3
1990	Cincinnati (W)	Lou Piniella	91	71	.562	5

GA: Games ahead of second place team.
[a] Defeated Brooklyn two games to one in pennant playoff.
[b] Defeated Brooklyn two games to none in pennant playoff.
[c] Defeated Milwaukee two games to none in pennant playoff.
[d] Defeated Los Angeles two games to one, in pennant playoff.
Source: Carter, *Sporting News Record Book, 1993,* 178.

TABLE 18.11   LEAGUE CHAMPIONSHIP SERIES, 1969–1990

Division play came to the major leagues in 1969 when both the American and National Leagues expanded to 12 teams. With an East and West Division in each league, League Championship Series (LCS) became necessary to determine the NL and AL pennant winners. In the charts below, the East Division champions are noted by the letter E and the West Division champions by W. Also, each playoff winner's wins and losses are noted in parentheses after the series score. The LCS changed from best-of-5 to best-of-7 in 1985.

Year	Winner	Manager	Series	Loser	Manager
National League					
1969	E-New York	Gil Hodges	3–0	W-Atlanta	Lum Harris
1970	W-Cincinnati	Sparky Anderson	3–0	E-Pittsburgh	Danny Murtaugh
1971	E-Pittsburgh	Danny Murtaugh	3–1 (LWWW)	W-San Francisco	Charlie Fox
1972	W-Cincinnati	Sparky Aderson	3–2 (LWLWW)	E-Pittsburgh	Bill Virdon
1973	E-New York	Yogi Berra	3–2 (LWWLW)	W-Cincinnati	Sparky Anderson
1974	W-Los Angeles	Walter Alston	3–1 (WWLW)	E-Pittsburgh	Danny Murtaugh
1975	W-Cincinnati	Sparky Anderson	3–0	E-Pittsburgh	Danny Murtaugh
1976	W-Cincinnati	Sparky Anderson	3–0	E-Philadelphia	Danny Ozark
1977	W-Los Angeles	Tommy Lasorda	3–1 (LWWW)	E-Philadelphia	Danny Ozark
1978	W-Los Angeles	Tommy Lasorda	3–1 (WWLW)	E-Philadelphia	Danny Ozark
1979	E-Pittsburgh	Chuck Tanner	3–0	W-Cincinnati	John McNamara
1980	E-Philadelphia	Dallas Green	3–2 (WLLWW)	W-Houston	Bill Virdon
1981	W-Los Angeles	Tommy Lasorda	3–2 (WLLWW)	E-Montreal	Jim Fanning
1982	E-St. Louis	Whitey Herzog	3–0	W-Atlanta	Joe Torre
1983	E-Philadelphia	Paul Owens	3–1 (WLWW)	W-Los Angeles	Tommy Lasorda
1984	W-San Diego	Dick Williams	3–2 (LLWWW)	E-Chicago	Jim Frey
1985	E-St. Louis	Whitey Herzog	4–2 (LLWWWW)	W-Los Angeles	Tommy Lasorda
1986	E-New York	Davey Johnson	4–2 (LWWLWW)	W-Houston	Hal Lanier
1987	E-St. Louis	Whitey Herzog	4–3 (WLWLLWW)	W-San Francisco	Roger Craig
1988	W-Los Angeles	Tommy Lasorda	4–3 (LWLWWLW)	E-New York	Davey Johnson
1989	W-San Francisco	Roger Craig	4–1 (WLWWW)	E-Chicago	Don Zimmer
1990	W-Cincinnati	Lou Piniella	4–2 (LWWWLW)	E-Pittsburgh	Jim Leyland
American League					
1969	E-Baltimore	Earl Weaver	3–0	W-Minnesota	Billy Martin
1970	E-Baltimore	Earl Weaver	3–0	W-Minnesota	Bill Rigney
1971	E-Baltimore	Earl Weaver	3–0	W-Oakland	Dick Williams
1972	W-Oakland	Dick Williams	3–2 (WWLLW)	E-Detroit	Billy Martin
1973	W-Oakland	Dick Williams	3–2 (LWWLW)	E-Baltimore	Earl Weaver
1974	W-Oakland	Alvin Dark	3–1 (LWWW)	E-Baltimore	Earl Weaver
1975	E-Boston	Darrell Johnson	3–0	W-Oakland	Alvin Dark
1976	E-New York	Billy Martin	3–2 (WLWLW)	W-Kansas City	Whitey Herzog
1977	E-New York	Billy Martin	3–2 (LWLWW)	W-Kansas City	Whitey Herzog
1978	E-New York	Bob Lemon	3–1 (WLWW)	W-Kansas City	Whitey Herzog
1979	E-Baltimore	Earl Weaver	3–1 (WWLW)	W-California	Jim Fregosi
1980	W-Kansas City	Jim Frey	3–0	E-New York	Dick Howser
1981	E-New York	Bob Lemon	3–0	W-Oakland	Billy Martin
1982	E-Milwaukee	Harvey Kuenn	3–2 (LLWWW)	W-Calfornia	Gene Mauch
1983	E-Baltimore	Joe Altobelli	3–1 (LWWW)	W-Chicago	Tony La Russa
1984	E-Detroit	Sparky Anderson	3–0	W-Kansas City	Dick Howser
1985	W-Kansas City	Dick Howser	4–3 (LLWLWWW)	E-Toronto	Bobby Cox
1986	E-Boston	John McNamara	4–3 (LWLWWW)	W-California	Gene Mauch
1987	W-Minnesota	Tom Kelly	4–1 (WWLWW)	E-Detroit	Sparky Anderson
1988	W-Oakland	Tony La Russa	4–0	E-Boston	Joe Morgan
1989	W-Oakland	Tony La Russa	4–0 (WWLWW)	E-Toronto	Cito Gaston
1990	W-Oakland	Tony La Russa	4–0	E-Boston	Joe Morgan

Source: 1993 Information Please Sports Almanac, 95.

TABLE 18.12   THE WORLD SERIES, 1946–1990

Year	Winner	Manager	Series	Loser	Manager
1946	ST. LOUIS CARDINALS	Eddie Dyer	4–3 (LWLWLWW)	Boston Red Sox	Joe Cronin
1947	N.Y. Yankees	Bucky Harris	4–3 (WWLLWLW)	BROOKLYN DODGERS	Burt Shotton
1948	Cleveland	Lou Boudreau	4–2 (LWWWLW)	BOSTON BRAVES	Billy Southworth
1949	N.Y. Yankees	Casey Stengel	4–1 (WLWWW)	BROOKLYN DODGERS	Burt Shotton
1950	N.Y. Yankees	Casey Stengel	4–0	PHILADELPHIA PHILLIES	Eddie Sawyer
1951	N.Y. Yankees	Casey Stengel	4–2 (LWLWWW)	N.Y. GIANTS	Leo Durocher
1952	N.Y. Yankees	Casey Stengel	4–3 (LWLWLWW)	BROOKLYN DODGERS	Charlie Dressen
1953	N.Y. Yankees	Casey Stengel	4–2 (WWLLWW)	BROOKLYN DODGERS	Charlie Dressen
1954	N.Y. GIANTS	Leo Durocher	4–0	Cleveland	Al Lopez
1955	BROOKLYN DODGERS	Walter Alston	4–3 (LLWWWLW)	N.Y. Yankees	Casey Stengel
1956	N.Y. Yankees	Casey Stengel	4–3 (LLWWWLW)	BROOKLYN DODGERS	Walter Alston
1957	MILWAUKEE BRAVES	Fred Haney	4–3 (LWLWWLW)	N.Y. Yankees	Casey Stengel
1958	N.Y. Yankees	Casey Stengel	4–3 (LLWLWWW)	MILWAUKEE BRAVES	Fred Haney
1959	L.A. DODGERS	Walter Alston	4–2 (LWWWLW)	Chicago White Sox	Al Lopez
1960	PITTSBURGH	Danny Murtaugh	4–3 (WLLWWLW)	N.Y. Yankees	Casey Stengel
1961	N.Y. Yankees	Ralph Houk	4–1 (WLWWW)	CINCINNATI	Fred Hutchinson
1962	N.Y. Yankees	Ralph Houk	4–3 (WLWLWLW)	S.F. GIANTS	Alvin Dark
1963	L.A. DODGERS	Walter Alston	4–0	N.Y. Yankees	Ralph Houk
1964	ST. LOUIS CARDINALS	Johnny Keane	4–3 (WLLWWLW)	N.Y. Yankees	Yogi Berra
1965	L.A. DODGERS	Walter Alston	4–3 (LLWWWLW)	Minnesota	Sam Mele
1966	Baltimore	Hank Bauer	4–0	L.A. DODGERS	Walter Alston
1967	ST. LOUIS CARDINALS	Red Schoendienst	4–3 (WLWWLLW)	Boston Red Sox	Dick Williams
1968	Detroit	Mayo Smith	4–3 (LWLLWWW)	ST. LOUIS CARDINALS	Red Schoendienst
1969	N.Y. METS	Gil Hodges	4–1 (LWWWW)	Baltimore	Earl Weaver
1970	Baltimore	Earl Weaver	4–1 (WWWLW)	CINCINNATI	Sparky Anderson
1971	PITTSBURGH	Danny Murtaugh	4–3 (LLWWWLW)	Baltimore	Earl Weaver
1972	Oakland A's	Dick Williams	4–3 (WWLWLLW)	CINCINNATI	Sparky Anderson
1973	Oakland A's	Dick Williams	4–3 (WLWLLWW)	N.Y. METS	Yogi Berra
1974	Oakland A's	Alvin Dark	4–1 (LWWWW)	L.A. DODGERS	Walter Alston
1975	CINCINNATI	Sparky Anderson	4–3 (LWWLWLW)	Boston Red Sox	Darrell Johnson
1976	CINCINNATI	Sparky Anderson	4–0	N.Y. Yankees	Billy Martin
1977	N.Y. Yankees	Billy Martin	4–2 (WLWWLW)	L.A. DODGERS	Tommy Lasorda
1978	N.Y. Yankees	Bob Lemon	4–2 (LLWWWW)	L.A. DODGERS	Tommy Lasorda
1979	PITTSBURGH	Chuck Tanner	4–3 (LWLLWWW)	Baltimore	Earl Weaver
1980	PHILADELPHIA PHILLIES	Dallas Green	4–2 (WWLLWW)	Kansas City	Jim Frey
1981	L.A. DODGERS	Tommy Lasorda	4–2 (LLWWWW)	N.Y. Yankees	Bob Lemon
1982	ST. LOUIS CARDINALS	Whitey Herzog	4–3 (LWWLLWW)	Milwaukee Brewers	Harvey Kuenn
1983	Baltimore	Joe Altobelli	4–1 (LWWWW)	PHILADELPHIA PHILLIES	Paul Owens
1984	Detroit	Sparky Anderson	4–1 (WLWWW)	SAN DIEGO	Dick Williams
1985	Kansas City	Dick Howser	4–3 (LLWLWWW)	ST. LOUIS CARDINALS	Whitey Herzog
1986	N.Y. METS	Davey Johnson	4–3 (LLWWLWW)	Boston Red Sox	John McNamara
1987	Minnesota	Tom Kelly	4–3 (WWLLLWW)	ST. LOUIS CARDINALS	Whitey Herzog
1988	L.A. DODGERS	Tommy Lasorda	4–1 (WWLWW)	Oakland A's	Tony La Russa
1989	Oakland A's	Tony La Russa	4–0	S.F. GIANTS	Roger Craig
1990	CINCINNATI	Lou Piniella	4–0	Oakland A's	Tony La Russa

Note: National League teams are listed in CAPITAL letters. Series champion's wins and losses are noted in parentheses.
Source: 1993 Information Please Sports Almanac, 91–92.

TABLE 18.13 BATTING CHAMPIONS, 1946–1990

American League				National League			
Year	Player	Club	B.A.	Year	Player	Club	B.A.
1946	James (Mickey) Vernon	Washington	.353	1946	Stanley Musial	St. Louis	.365
1947	Theodore Williams	Boston	.343	1947	Harry Walker	St. Louis-Philadelphia	.363
1948	Theodore Williams	Boston	.369	1948	Stanley Musial	St. Louis	.376
1949	George Kell	Detroit	.343	1949	Jack Robinson	Brooklyn	.342
1950	William Goodman	Boston	.354	1950	Stanley Musial	St. Louis	.346
1951	Ferris Fain	Philadelphia	.344	1951	Stanley Musial	St. Louis	.355
1952	Ferris Fain	Philadelphia	.327	1952	Stanley Musial	St. Louis	.336
1953	James (Mickey) Vernon	Washington	.337	1953	Carl Furillo	Brooklyn	.344
1954	Roberto Avila	Cleveland	.341	1954	Willie Mays	New York	.345
1955	Albert Kaline	Detroit	.340	1955	Richie Ashburn	Philadelphia	.338
1956	Mickey Mantle	New York	.353	1956	Henry Aaron	Milwaukee	.328
1957	Theodore Williams	Boston	.388	1957	Stanley Musial	St. Louis	.351
1958	Theodore Williams	Boston	.328	1958	Richie Ashburn	Philadelphia	.350
1959	Harvey Kuenn	Detroit	.353	1959	Henry Aaron	Milwaukee	.355
1960	James (Pete) Runnels	Boston	.320	1960	Richard Groat	Pittsburgh	.325
1961	Norman Cash	Detroit	.361	1961	Roberto Clemente	Pittsburgh	.351
1962	James (Pete) Runnels	Boston	.326	1962	H. Thomas Davis	Los Angeles	.346
1963	Carl Yastrzemski	Boston	.321	1963	H. Thomas Davis	Los Angeles	.326
1964	Pedro (Tony) Oliva	Minnesota	.323	1964	Roberto Clemente	Pittsburgh	.339
1965	Pedro (Tony) Oliva	Minnesota	.321	1965	Roberto Clemente	Pittsburgh	.329
1966	Frank Robinson	Baltimore	.316	1966	Mateo Alou	Pittsburgh	.342
1967	Carl Yastrzemski	Boston	.326	1967	Roberto Clemente	Pittsburgh	.357
1968	Carl Yastrzemski	Boston	.301	1968	Peter Rose	Cincinnati	.335
1969	Rodney Carew	Minnesota	.332	1969	Peter Rose	Cincinnati	.348
1970	Alexander Johnson	California	.329	1970	Ricardo Carty	Atlanta	.366
1971	Pedro (Tony) Oliva	Minnesota	.337	1971	Joseph Torre	St. Louis	.363
1972	Rodney Carew	Minnesota	.318	1972	Billy Williams	Chicago	.333
1973	Rodney Carew	Minnesota	.350	1973	Peter Rose	Cincinnati	.338
1974	Rodney Carew	Minnesota	.364	1974	Ralph Garr	Atlanta	.353
1975	Rodney Carew	Minnesota	.359	1975	Bill Madlock	Chicago	.354
1976	George Brett	Kansas City	.333	1976	Bill Madlock	Chicago	.339
1977	Rodney Carew	Minnesota	.388	1977	David Parker	Pittsburgh	.338
1978	Rodney Carew	Minnesota	.333	1978	David Parker	Pittsburgh	.334
1979	Fredric Lynn	Boston	.333	1979	Keith Hernandez	St. Louis	.344
1980	George Brett	Kansas City	.390	1980	William Buckner	Chicago	.324
1981	Carney Lansford	Boston	.336	1981	Bill Madlock	Pittsburgh	.341
1982	Willie Wilson	Kansas City	.332	1982	Albert Oliver	Montreal	.331
1983	Wade Boggs	Boston	.361	1983	Bill Madlock	Pittsburgh	.323
1984	Donald Mattingly	New York	.343	1984	Anthony Gwynn	San Diego	.351
1985	Wade Boggs	Boston	.368	1985	Willie McGee	St. Louis	.353
1986	Wade Boggs	Boston	.357	1986	Timothy Raines	Montreal	.334
1987	Wade Boggs	Boston	.363	1987	Anthony Gwynn	San Diego	.370
1988	Wade Boggs	Boston	.366	1988	Anthony Gwynn	San Diego	.313
1989	Kirby Puckett	Minnesota	.339	1989	Anthony Gwynn	San Diego	.336
1990	George Brett	Kansas City	.329	1990	Willie McGee	St. Louis	.335

Source: Sporting News Record Book, 1993, 179–80.

TABLE 18.14   HOME-RUN LEADERS, 1946–1990

National League				American League			
Year	Player	Club	HR	Year	Player	Club	HR
1946	Ralph Kiner	Pittsburgh	23	1946	Hank Greenberg	Detroit	44
1947	Ralph Kiner	Pittsburgh	51	1947	Ted Williams	Boston	32
	John Mize	New York					
1948	Ralph Kiner	Pittsburgh	40	1948	Joe DiMaggio	New York	39
	John Mize	New York					
1949	Ralph Kiner	Pittsburgh	54	1949	Ted Williams	Boston	43
1950	Ralph Kiner	Pittsburgh	47	1950	Al Rosen	Cleveland	37
1951	Ralph Kiner	Pittsburgh	42	1951	Gus Zernial	Chicago-Philadelphia	33
1952	Ralph Kiner	Pittsburgh	37	1952	Larry Doby	Cleveland	32
	Hank Sauer	Chicago					
1953	Ed Mathews	Milwaukee	47	1953	Al Rosen	Cleveland	43
1954	Ted Kluszewski	Cincinnati	49	1954	Larry Doby	Cleveland	32
1955	Willie Mays	New York	51	1955	Mickey Mantle	New York	37
1956	Duke Snider	Brooklyn	43	1956	Mickey Mantle	New York	52
1957	Hank Aaron	Milwaukee	44	1957	Roy Sievers	Washington	42
1958	Ernie Banks	Chicago	47	1958	Mickey Mantle	New York	42
1959	Ed Mathews	Milwaukee	46	1959	Rocky Colavito	Cleveland	42
					Harmon Killebrew	Washington	
1960	Ernie Banks	Chicago	41	1960	Mickey Mantle	New York	40
1961	Orlando Cepeda	San Francisco	46	1961	Roger Maris	New York	61
1962	Willie Mays	San Francisco	49	1962	Harmon Killebrew	Minnesota	48
1963	Hank Aaron	Milwaukee	44	1963	Harmon Killebrew	Minnesota	45
	Willie McCovey	San Francisco					
1964	Willie Mays	San Francisco	47	1964	Harmon Killebrew	Minnesota	49
1965	Willie Mays	San Francisco	52	1965	Tony Conigliaro	Boston	32
1966	Hank Aaron	Atlanta	44	1966	Frank Robinson	Baltimore	49
1967	Hank Aaron	Atlanta	39	1967	Carl Yastrzemski	Boston	44
					Harmon Killebrew	Minnesota	
1968	Willie McCovey	San Francisco	36	1968	Frank Howard	Washington	44
1969	Willie McCovey	San Francisco	45	1969	Harmon Killebrew	Minnesota	49
1970	Johnny Bench	Cincinnati	45	1970	Frank Howard	Washington	44
1971	Willie Stargell	Pittsburgh	48	1971	Bill Melton	Chicago	33
1972	Johnny Bench	Cincinnati	40	1972	Dick Allen	Chicago	37
1973	Willie Stargell	Pittsburgh	44	1973	Reggie Jackson	Oakland	32
1974	Mike Schmidt	Philadelphia	36	1974	Dick Allen	Chicago	32
1975	Mike Schmidt	Philadelphia	38	1975	George Scott	Milwaukee	36
					Reggie Jackson	Oakland	
1976	Mike Schmidt	Philadelphia	38	1976	Graig Nettles	New York	32
1977	George Foster	Cincinnati	52	1977	Jim Rice	Boston	39
1978	George Foster	Cincinnati	40	1978	Jim Rice	Boston	46
1979	Dave Kingman	Chicago	48	1979	Gorman Thomas	Milwaukee	45
1980	Mike Schmidt	Philadelphia	46	1980	Reggie Jackson	New York	41
					Ben Oglivie	Milwaukee	
1981	Mike Schmidt	Philadelphia	31	1981	Bobby Grich,	California;	22
					Tony Armas	Oakland	
					Dwight Evans	Boston	
					Eddie Murray	Baltimore	
1982	Dave Kingman	New York	37	1982	Gorman Thomas,	Milwaukee	39
					Reggie Jackson	California	
1983	Mike Schmidt	Philadelphia	40	1983	Jim Rice	Boston	39
1984	Mike Schmidt	Philadelphia	36	1984	Tony Armas	Boston	43
	Dale Murphy	Atlanta					
1985	Dale Murphy	Atlanta	37	1985	Darrell Evans	Detroit	40
1986	Mike Schmidt	Philadelphia	37	1986	Jesse Barfield	Toronto	40
1987	Andre Dawson	Chicago	49	1987	Mark McGwire	Oakland	49
1988	Darryl Strawberry	New York	39	1988	Jose Canseco	Oakland	42
1989	Kevin Mitchell	San Francisco	47	1989	Fred McGriff	Toronto	36
1990	Ryne Sandberg	Chicago	40	1990	Cecil Fielder	Detroit	51

Source: Mark S. Hoffman, *The World Almanac and Book of Facts, 1992* (New York, 1991), 921–22.

TABLE 18.15   RUNS-BATTED-IN LEADERS, 1946–1990

American League				National League			
Year	Player	Club	RBI	Year	Player	Club	RBI
1946	Henry Greenberg	Detroit	127	1946	Enos Slaughter	St. Louis	130
1947	Theodore Williams	Boston	114	1947	John Mize	New York	138
1948	Joseph DiMaggio	New York	155	1948	Stanley Musial	St. Louis	131
1949	Theodore Williams	Boston	159	1949	Ralph Kiner	Pittsburgh	127
	Vernon Stephens	Boston	159				
1950	Walter Dropo	Boston	144	1950	Delmer Ennis	Philadelphia	126
	Vernon Stephens	Boston	144				
1951	Gus Zernial	Chicago-Philadelphia	129	1951	Monford Irvin	New York	121
1952	Albert Rosen	Cleveland	105	1952	Henry Sauer	Chicago	121
1953	Albert Rosen	Cleveland	145	1953	Roy Campanella	Brooklyn	142
1954	Lawrence Doby	Cleveland	126	1954	Theodore Kluszewski	Cincinnati	141
1955	Raymond Boone	Detroit	116	1955	Edwin (Duke) Snider	Brooklyn	136
	Jack Jensen	Boston	116				
1956	Mickey Mantle	New York	130	1956	Stanley Musial	St. Louis	109
1957	Roy Sievers	Washington	114	1957	Henry Aaron	Milwaukee	132
1958	Jack Jensen	Boston	122	1958	Ernest Banks	Chicago	129
1959	Jack Jensen	Boston	112	1959	Ernest Banks	Chicago	143
1960	Roger Maris	New York	112	1960	Henry Aaron	Milwaukee	126
1961	Roger Maris	New York	142	1961	Orlando Cepeda	San Francisco	142
1962	Harmon Killebrew	Minnesota	126	1962	H. Thomas Davis	Los Angeles	153
1963	Richard Stuart	Boston	118	1963	Henry Aaron	Milwaukee	130
1964	Brooks Robinson	Baltimore	118	1964	Kenton Boyer	St. Louis	119
1965	Rocco Colavito	Cleveland	108	1965	Deron Johnson	Cincinnati	130
1966	Frank Robinson	Baltimore	122	1966	Henry Aaron	Atlanta	127
1967	Carl Yastrzemski	Boston	121	1967	Orlando Cepeda	St. Louis	111
1968	Kenneth Harrelson	Boston	109	1968	Willie McCovey	San Francisco	105
1969	Harmon Killebrew	Minnesota	140	1969	Willie McCovey	San Francisco	126
1970	Frank Howard	Washington	126	1970	Johnny Bench	Cincinnati	148
1971	Harmon Killebrew	Minnesota	119	1971	Joseph Torre	St. Louis	137
1972	Richard Allen	Chicago	113	1972	Johnny Bench	Cincinnati	125
1973	Reginald Jackson	Oakland	117	1973	Wilver Stargell	Pittsburgh	119
1974	Jeffrey Burroughs	Texas	118	1974	Johnny Bench	Cincinnati	129
1975	George Scott	Milwaukee	109	1975	Gregory Luzinski	Philadelphia	120
1976	Lee May	Baltimore	109	1976	George Foster	Cincinnati	121
1977	Larry Hisle	Minnesota	119	1977	George Foster	Cincinnati	149
1978	James Rice	Boston	139	1978	George Foster	Cincinnati	120
1979	Donald Baylor	California	139	1979	David Winfield	San Diego	118
1980	Cecil Cooper	Milwaukee	122	1980	Michael Schmidt	Philadelphia	121
1981	Eddie Murray	Baltimore	78	1981	Michael Schmidt	Philadelphia	91
1982	Harold McRae	Kansas City	133	1982	Dale Murphy	Atlanta	109
					Albert Oliver	Montreal	109
1983	Cecil Cooper	Milwaukee	126	1983	Dale Murphy	Atlanta	121
	James Rice	Boston	126				
1984	Antonio Armas	Boston	123	1984	Gary Carter	Montreal	106
					Michael Schmidt	Philadelphia	106
1985	Donald Mattingly	New York	145	1985	David Parker	Cincinnati	125
1986	Joseph Carter	Cleveland	121	1986	Michael Schmidt	Philadelphia	119
1987	George Bell	Toronto	134	1987	Andre Dawson	Chicago	137
1988	Jose Canseco	Oakland	124	1988	William Clark	San Francisco	109
1989	Ruben Sierra	Texas	119	1989	Kevin Mitchell	San Francisco	125
1990	Cecil Fielder	Detroit	132	1990	Matthew Williams	San Francisco	122

Source: Sporting News Record Book, 1993, 191–92.

TABLE 18.16   CY YOUNG AWARD, 1956–1990

Year	Player	Club	Year	Player	Club	Year	Player	Club
1956	Don Newcombe	Dodgers	1971	(NL) Ferguson Jenkins	Cubs	1981	(NL) Fernando Valenzuela	Dodgers
1957	Warren Spahn	Braves		(AL) Vida Blue	A's		(AL) Rollie Fingers	Brewers
1958	Bob Turley	Yankees	1972	(NL Steve Carlton	Phillies	1982	(NL) Steve Carlton	Phillies
1959	Early Wynn	White Sox		(AL) Gaylord Perry	Indians		(AL) Pete Vuckovich	Brewers
1960	Vernon Law	Pirates	1973	(NL) Tom Seaver	Mets	1983	(NL) John Denny	Phillies
1961	Whitey Ford	Yankees		(AL) Jim Palmer	Orioles		(AL) LaMarr Hoyt	White Sox
1962	Don Drysdale	Dodgers	1974	(NL) Mike Marshall	Dodgers	1984	(NL) Rick Sutcliffe	Cubs
1963	Sandy Koufax	Dodgers		(AL) Jim (Catfish) Hunter	A's		(AL) Willie Hernandez	Tigers
1964	Dean Chance	Angels	1975	(NL) Tom Seaver	Mets	1985	(NL) Dwight Gooden	Mets
1965	Sandy Koufax	Dodgers		(AL) Jim Palmer	Orioles		(AL) Bret Saberhagen	Royals
1966	Sandy Koufax	Dodgers	1976	(NL) Randy Jones	Padres	1986	(NL) Mike Scott	Astros
1967	(NL) Mike McCormick	Giants		(AL) Jim Palmer	Orioles		(AL) Roger Clemens	Red Sox
	(AL) Jim Lonborg	Red Sox	1977	(NL) Steve Carlton	Phillies	1987	(NL) Steve Bedrosian	Phillies
1968	(NL) Bob Gibson	Cardinals		(AL) Sparky Lyle	Yankees		(AL) Roger Clemens	Red Sox
	(AL) Dennis McLain	Tigers	1978	(NL) Gaylord Perry	Padres	1988	(NL) Orel Hershiser	Dodgers
1969	(NL) Tom Seaver	Mets		(AL) Ron Guidry	Yankees		(AL) Frank Viola	Twins
	(AL) (tie) Dennis McLain	Tigers	1979	(NL) Bruce Sutter	Cubs	1989	(NL) Mark Davis	Padres
	Mike Cuellar	Orioles		(AL) Mike Flanagan	Orioles		(AL) Bret Saberhagan	Royals
1970	(NL) Bob Gibson	Cardinals	1980	(NL) Steve Carlton	Phillies	1990	(NL) Doug Drabek	Pirates
	(AL) Jim Perry	Twins		(AL) Steve Stone	Orioles		(AL) Bob Welch	A's

Note: This pitcher's award has been presented since 1956 by the Baseball Writers' Association of America. Between 1956 and 1966 one award was given. After 1967 an award was given to the best pitcher in each league.
Source: World Almanac, 1992, 924.

Sandy Koufax of the Brooklyn and Los Angeles Dodgers celebrates his fourth no-hit game. Unhittable when he was "right," Koufax's career (1955–66) was brief but sensational. (National Baseball Hall of Fame Library, Cooperstown, N.Y.)

TABLE 18.17   MOST VALUABLE PLAYER, 1946–1990
(voted by Baseball Writers' Association)

National League		
Year	Player	Team
1946	Stan Musial	St. Louis
1947	Bob Elliott	Boston
1948	Stan Musial	St. Louis
1949	Jackie Robinson	Brooklyn
1950	Jim Konstanty	Philadelphia
1951	Roy Campanella	Brooklyn
1952	Hank Sauer	Chicago
1953	Roy Campanella	Brooklyn
1954	Willie Mays	New York
1955	Roy Campanella	Brooklyn
1956	Don Newcombe	Brooklyn
1957	Henry Aaron	Milwaukee
1958	Ernie Banks	Chicago
1959	Ernie Banks	Chicago
1960	Dick Groat	Pittsburgh
1961	Frank Robinson	Cincinnati
1962	Maury Wills	Los Angeles
1963	Sandy Koufax	Los Angeles
1964	Ken Boyer	St. Louis
1965	Willie Mays	San Francisco
1966	Roberto Clemente	Pittsburgh
1967	Orlando Cepeda	St. Louis
1968	Bob Gibson	St. Louis
1969	Willie McCovey	San Francisco
1970	Johnny Bench	Cincinnati
1971	Joe Torre	St. Louis
1972	Johnny Bench	Cincinnati
1973	Pete Rose	Cincinnati
1974	Steve Garvey	Los Angeles
1975	Joe Morgan	Cincinnati
1976	Joe Morgan	Cincinnati
1977	George Foster	Cincinnati
1978	Dave Parker	Pittsburgh
1979	(tie) Willie Stargell	Pittsburgh
	Keith Hernandez	St. Louis
1980	Mike Schmidt	Philadelphia

Year	Player	Team
1981	Mike Schmidt	Philadelphia
1982	Dale Murphy	Atlanta
1983	Dale Murphy	Atlanta
1984	Ryne Sandberg	Chicago
1985	Willie McGee	St. Louis
1986	Mike Schmidt	Philadelphia
1987	Andre Dawson	Chicago
1988	Kirk Gibson	Los Angeles
1989	Kevin Mitchell	San Francisco
1990	Barry Bonds	Pittsburgh

American League

Year	Player	Team
1946	Ted Williams	Boston
1947	Joe DiMaggio	New York
1948	Lou Boudreau	Cleveland
1949	Ted Williams	Boston
1950	Phil Rizzuto	New York
1951	Yogi Berra	New York
1952	Bobby Shantz	Philadelphia
1953	Al Rosen	Cleveland
1954	Yogi Berra	New York
1955	Yogi Berra	New York
1956	Mickey Mantle	New York
1957	Mickey Mantle	New York
1958	Jackie Jensen	Boston
1959	Nellie Fox	Chicago
1960	Roger Maris	New York
1961	Roger Maris	New York
1962	Mickey Mantle	New York
1963	Elston Howard	New York
1964	Brooks Robinson	Baltimore
1965	Zollo Versalles	Minnesota
1966	Frank Robinson	Baltimore
1967	Carl Yastrzemski	Boston
1968	Denny McLain	Detroit
1969	Harmon Killebrew	Minnesota
1970	John (Boog) Powell	Baltimore
1971	Vida Blue	Oakland
1972	Dick Allen	Chicago
1973	Reggie Jackson	Oakland
1974	Jeff Burroughs	Texas
1975	Fred Lynn	Boston
1976	Thurman Munson	New York
1977	Rod Carew	Minnesota
1978	Jim Rice	Boston
1979	Don Baylor	California
1980	George Brett	Kansas City
1981	Rollie Fingers	Milwaukee
1982	Robin Yount	Milwaukee
1983	Cal Ripken Jr.	Baltimore
1984	Willie Hernandez	Detroit
1985	Don Mattingly	New York
1986	Roger Clemens	Boston
1987	George Bell	Toronto
1988	Jose Canseco	Oakland
1989	Robin Yount	Milwaukee
1990	Rickey Henderson	Oakland

Source: World Almanac, 1992, 925.

Johnny Bench, catcher of Cincinnati's "Big Red Machine," a giant of baseball in the 1970s (National Baseball Hall of Fame Library, Cooperstown, N.Y.)

TABLE 18.18 MAJOR LEAGUE PLAYERS' SALARIES— MINIMUM AND MEAN, 1950–1990

Year	Minimum Salary	Mean Salary
1950	$5,000	$14,000
1952	5,000	13,600
1953	5,000	14,580
1954	5,000	14,740
1955	5,000	14,870
1956	5,000	14,750
1967	6,000	19,000
1968	10,000	. . .
1969	10,000	24,909
1970	12,000	29,303
1971	12,750	31,543
1972	13,500	34,092
1973	15,000	36,566
1974	15,000	40,839
1975	16,000	44,676
1976	19,000	51,501
1977	19,000	76,066
1978	21,000	99,876
1979	21,000	113,558
1980	30,000	143,756
1981	32,500	185,651
1982	33,500	241,497
1983	35,000	289,194
1984	40,000	329,408
1985	60,000	371,157
1986	60,000	412,520
1987	62,500	412,454
1988	62,500	438,729
1989	68,000	497,254
1990	100,000	597,537

Source: Patrick J. Harrigan, The Detroit Tigers: Club and Community, 1945–1995 (Toronto, 1997), 301.

TABLE 18.19 HIGHEST-SALARY MILESTONES, 1947–1990

Year	Salary	Player
1947	$100,000	Hank Greenberg
1950	$125,000	Ted Williams
1972	$225,000	Dick Allen
1975	$250,000	Dick Allen
1975	$578,000	Catfish Hunter
1979	$1,000,000	Dave Winfield
1979	$1,300,000	Nolan Ryan
1981	$1,450,000	George Foster
1981	$2,200,000	Dave Winfield
1989	$3,000,000	Kirby Puckett
1990	$4,700,000	Jose Canseco

Source: Jonathan F. Light, *The Cultural Encyclopedia of Baseball* (Jefferson, N. C., 1997), 341–42.

TABLE 18.20 SALARY SHARE IN TEAM REVENUES, 1946–1989

Year	Salary Share[a] (%)
1946	24.8
1950	22.1
1974	17.6
1977	20.5
1978	25.1
1979	28.1
1980	31.3
1981	39.1
1982	41.1
1983	41.1
1984	40.3
1985	39.7
1986	40.0
1987	35.2
1988	34.2
1989	31.6

[a] Includes salaries of coaches and managers.
Source: Zimbalist, *Baseball and Billions*, 87.

TABLE 18.21 FIRST DATES ON WHICH A BLACK PLAYER PLAYED FOR EACH MAJOR LEAGUE BASEBALL TEAM

Team	Player	Date
Brooklyn Dodgers	Jackie Robinson	April 15, 1947
Cleveland Indians	Larry Doby	July 5, 1947
St. Louis Browns	Hank Thompson	July 17, 1947
New York Giants	Hank Thompson	July 8, 1949
Boston Braves	Sam Jethro	April 18, 1950
Chicago White Sox	Sam Hairston	July 21, 1951
Philadelphia Athletics	Bob Trice	September 13, 1953
Chicago Cubs	Ernie Banks	September 17, 1953
Pittsburgh Pirates	Curt Roberts	April 13, 1954
St. Louis Cardinals	Tom Alston	April 13, 1954
Cincinnati Reds	Nino Escalera	April 17, 1954
Washington Senators	Carlos Paula	September 6, 1954
New York Yankees	Elston Howard	April 14, 1955
Philadelphia Phillies	John Kennedy	April 22, 1957
Detroit Tigers	Ossie Virgil	June 6, 1958
Boston Red Sox	Pumpsie Green	July 21, 1959

Source: Harrigan, *Detroit Tigers*, 316.

TABLE 18.22 PERCENTAGE OF BLACK PLAYERS ON MAJOR LEAGUE TEAMS, 1960–1971

	National League												
	Average												
Team	1960–71	1971	1970	1969	1968	1967	1966	1965	1964	1963	1962	1961	1960
Atlanta	27	40	40	32	28	28	24	32	16	24	20	16	24
Chicago	19	12	20	20	24	24	28	16	20	16	20	16	16
Cincinnati	25	32	28	36	28	32	24	24	16	20	20	20	20
Houston	24	36	36	32	28	28	32	16	12	12	12	. . .	. . .
Los Angeles	22	24	24	16	20	12	32	24	20	24	20	24	20
New York	18	16	16	20	16	12	16	24	16	20	20	. . .	. . .
Philadelphia	26	20	24	28	24	28	20	32	20	20	24	32	28
Pittsburgh	35	48	44	36	44	56	44	32	28	32	28	16	16
San Francisco	28	24	20	28	32	32	32	32	32	28	28	20	28
St. Louis	28	32	44	36	36	40	24	24	16	24	20	16	24
Montreal	20	8	20	32	. . .	. . .	. . .	. . .	. . .	. . .	. . .	. . .	. . .
San Diego	24	16	24	32	. . .	. . .	. . .	. . .	. . .	. . .	. . .	. . .	. . .
Average	25	26	28	29	28	29	28	26	20	22	21	20	22

Team	American League Average												
	1960–71	1971	1970	1969	1968	1967	1966	1965	1964	1963	1962	1961	1960
Baltimore	17	36	36	36	24	12	12	8	12	8	8	4	12
Boston	14	12	12	12	24	24	24	12	12	12	8	8	4
California	17	24	20	20	16	16	20	24	16	16	8	8	...
Chicago	18	28	20	24	16	20	20	20	20	12	12	20	8
Cleveland	21	20	16	24	40	32	20	16	16	28	12	20	12
Detroit	18	16	20	28	16	20	24	20	20	16	20	16	4
Minnesota	22	24	32	24	24	32	24	24	20	16	16	12	16
New York	17	20	20	28	20	20	20	16	16	12	12	12	8
Oakland	21	24	28	24	12	24	24	16	24	24	20	8	...
Washington	17	28	24	16	24	16	16	12	16	16	8	16	...
Kansas City	24	16	28	28	...	...	...	...	...	...	...	...	...
Milwaukee	19	20	12	24	...	...	...	...	...	...	...	...	...
Average	18	22	22	24	22	22	20	17	17	16	12	12	9

Source: Arthur Ashe, Jr., *A Hard Road to Glory: A History of the African-American Athlete Since 1946* (New York, 1993), 247.

A Selected Glossary of Baseball Terminology

The game of baseball, as with many kinds of activity, has lended itself to a special language. Much of the terminology has flowed from the rules, objectives, and tools of the game and, if not immediately understandable, can be surmised from the play as it unfolds. Other jargon, however, originated in attitudes, habits, and circumstances encountered in baseball's deep, often localized roots, some so remote as to have become untraceable. Much of this terminology, which on the surface betrayed no linkage to the game's principles and operations, sent the novice spectator searching for translation. The list that follows contains a few examples.

battery The pitcher and catcher of team.

boot Vernacular for failure by a defensive player to play a ball, especially a ground ball, cleanly—an error.

bullpen An area near the playing field where potential relief pitchers "warm up," make practice pitches, preparatory to entering the game.

bunt A batted ball deliberately hit softly, either to catch fielders by surprise or to advance a runner already on base.

can of corn A fly ball hit only modestly well, usually high, easy for outfielders to catch.

collar Failure of a batter to hit safely during the course of a game—going for the collar.

dugout Marked off area where players, coaches, and substitutes remain when not on the playing field—might or might not be beneath level of the playing field.

foot-in-the-bucket Batter who stands with front foot placed near foul line, not pointed toward the pitcher—a stance often regarded as a signal of fear of being struck by pitched ball.

grand slam A home run with the bases full of runners—the ultimate expression of offensive baseball, produces four runs with one play.

hook A conventional "curve" ball by a pitcher—with lefthander, it turns to the right; with righthand pitcher, ball turns to the left.

hot box Base runner trapped between two bases with a fielder on either side—leads to a back-and-forth rundown, usually ending in runner tagged out; occasionally, a fielder's misplay allows runner to return safely to a base.

hot corner Third base, where fielder often must face sharply hit balls.

junk Pitches delivered by pitcher who relies on guile, accuracy, even legal trickery, probably because the pitcher lacks the capacity to utilize speed and overpowering ball movement.

knuckler Knuckleball, a pitched ball usually gripped on fingertips that approaches the batter with no, or very slight, rotation. It can fool the batter by deceptive speed or by strange movements in air currents made possible by lack of spin.

on deck The next batter to come to the plate—waits a turn in a designated, marked out area: the "on-deck circle."

pick off Base runner caught off base by sudden throw of pitcher or catcher and tagged out.

pinch hitter A batter who substitutes for another; replaced batter then is disqualified for the remainder of the game.

pitchout A pitch delivered deliberately wide of the plate in anticipation of attempted steal by base runner—places the catcher in a good position to throw runner out.

rhubarb A major controversy or argument during the game; can lead to a melee—fighting between a few players or entire teams.

rubber arm Possessor of which is a pitcher seemingly immune from fatigue or arm injury—can pitch often and for long periods.

sacrifice A batter who, usually on instruction from the manager, advances a base runner by allowing himself to be put out—usually involves bunting the ball.

screwball A pitch that breaks the opposite way from a curve, or hook; a lefthander's screwball bends to the left, etc.; it is thus a "screwy" curve and requires an unnatural twisting of the arm.

slump A player who experiences a long period without noticeable success—usually a batter who goes many games without getting a safe base hit.

steal A base runner who advances without benefit of batting or fielding developments—a product of speed and timing by runner.

stuff The quality and character of a pitcher's assortment of pitches—"good stuff" usually applies to rapid speed and effective movement of breaking pitches.

twin-killing A double play—the act of rendering two runners, or the batter and a runner, out on the same play.

warmup To prepare a player's arms and body for the game by stretching and throwing—applies especially to practice pitches by a pitcher.

Source: Essentially author's recollection; see also Zander Hollander, *The Encyclopedia of Sports Talk* (New York, 1976), 13–71.

Little League

One of the more remarkable phenomena of sports—and sociology—in the postwar era involved the emergence of Little League baseball. Begun in 1939 in Williamsport, Pennsylvania, the idea did not take off until after the war, expanding beyond Pennsylvania to nationwide in the 1950s. The organization held its first national competition, its World Series, in 1947, welcoming participants from foreign leagues in the early 1950s. By the late 1970s there were some 6,500 leagues; each league had several teams, each team had several—probably 10–15—players. Originally designed for boys no older than 12 (the World Series maintained that classification), the idea later would expand to leagues for younger boys and for young men aged 13–18. Girls began to participate in 1974 after the National Organization for Women filed what would become a sharply divisive lawsuit. Girls continued to make up a minority of players each year thereafter, but most young female athletes chose to participate in a well-structured softball competition. In status and popularity, however, nothing would dethrone the national competition of the 12-years-olds, culminating in the nationally televised World Series each summer in Williamsport.

Within a few years the Little League organization would be able to present a growing list of illustrious alumni. Along with numerous major league players, some of them in the Hall of Fame, are actor Tom Selleck, basketball giant Kareen Abdul-Jabbar, and Vice President Dan Quayle, all supplying testimony to the benefits of growing up in Little League. The development also took shape as an expression of a new society emerging in the heady postwar years—young, vigorous, and upwardly mobile, given to large measures of sameness and imitation, but also to fierce competition. In those formidable years, attention more often than not came to focus on highly excitable parents of the little guys on the field. For those people, noted writer Earl Wilson, a Little League game was "simply a nervous breakdown divided into innings."

Mid-Island (New York) Little Leaguers celebrate national victory in 1964 with a parade in New York City. (National Baseball Hall of Fame Library, Cooperstown, N.Y.)

TABLE 18.23 LITTLE LEAGUE WORLD SERIES CHAMPIONS, 1947–1990

Year	Champion	Runner-up	Score
1947	Williamsport, Pa.	Lock Haven, Pa.	16–7
1948	Lock Haven, Pa.	St. Petersburg, Fla.	6–5
1949	Hammonton, N.J.	Pensacola, Fla.	5–0
1950	Houston, Tex.	Bridgeport, Conn.	2–1
1951	Stamford, Conn.	Austin, Tex.	3–0
1952	Norwalk, Conn.	Monongahela, Pa.	4–3
1953	Birmingham, Ala.	Schenectady, N.Y.	1–0
1954	Schenectady, N.Y.	Colton, Calif.	7–5
1955	Morrisville, Pa.	Merchantville, N.J.	4–3
1956	Roswell, N.M.	Merchantville, N.J.	3–1
1957	Monterrey, Mex.	La Mesa, Calif.	4–0
1958	Monterrey, Mex.	Kankakee, Ill.	10–1
1959	Hamtramck, Mich.	Auburn, Calif.	12–0
1960	Levittown, Pa.	Ft. Worth, Tex.	5–0
1961	El Cajon, Calif.	El Campo, Tex.	4–2
1962	San Jose, Calif.	Kankakee, Ill.	3–0
1963	Granada Hills, Calif.	Stratford, Conn.	2–1
1964	Staten Island, N.Y.	Monterrey, Mex.	4–0
1965	Windsor Locks, Conn.	Stoney Creek, Can.	3–1
1966	Houston, Tex.	W. New York, N.J.	8–2
1967	West Tokyo, Japan	Chicago, Ill.	4–1
1968	Osaka, Japan	Richmond, Va.	1–0
1969	Taipei, Taiwan	Santa Clara, Calif.	5–0
1970	Wayne, N.J.	Campbell, Calif.	2–0
1971	Tainan, Taiwan	Gary, Ind.	12–3
1972	Taipei, Taiwan	Hammond, Ind.	6–0
1973	Tainan City, Taiwan	Tucson, Ariz.	12–0
1974	Kao Hsiung, Taiwan	El Cajon, Calif.	7–2
1975	Lakewood, N.J.	Tampa, Fla.	4–3
1976	Tokyo, Japan	Campbell, Calif.	10–3
1977	Kao Hsiung, Taiwan	El Cajon, Calif.	7–2
1978	Pin-Tung, Taiwan	Danville, Calif.	11–1
1979	Hsien, Taiwan	Campbell, Calif.	2–1
1980	Hua Lian, Taiwan	Tampa, Fla.	4–3
1981	Tai-Chung, Taiwan	Tampa, Fla.	4–2
1982	Kirkland, Wash.	Hsien, Taiwan	6–0
1983	Marietta, Ga.	Barahona, D. Rep.	3–1
1984	Seoul, S. Korea	Altamonte Springs, Fla.	6–2
1985	Seoul, S. Korea	Mexicali, Mex.	7–1
1986	Tainan Park, Taiwan	Tucson, Ariz.	12–0
1987	Hua Lian, Taiwan	Irvine, Calif.	21–1
1988	Tai–Chung, Taiwan	Pearl City, Haw.	10–0
1989	Trumbull, Conn.	Kaohsiung, Taiwan	5–2
1990	Taipei, Taiwan	Shippensburg, Pa.	9–0

Source: Otto Johnson, ed., The Information Please Almanac, Atlas Yearbook, 1995 (New York, 1994), 1001.

Basketball

Basketball underwent massive growth and expansion on virtually all levels in the last half of the 20th century. It became the most universal of the team sports, adaptable to both genders and nearly all age groups. The largest growth and most elaborate organization took place on three levels: high school, college, and the professional ranks. Although basketball retained an identity as a boy's or man's game that rewarded size, speed, strength, and athletic ability, it also provided an agreeable setting for female play, which, although following the same rules, concentrated on different skills.

The game was subjected to continuous tinkering and fine tuning, a process that frequently—but not always—originated on the professional level and then filtered into the lower echelons. A few of the rule changes had a considerable impact. The ban on defensive goal tending was supplemented in 1957 with a rule against offensive goal tending. The dramatic dunk shot, forbidden in college in 1967, was reintroduced in 1976 and became seemingly a permanent and exceptionally popular fixture. Two of the most important changes were designed to speed up the game and promote more scoring—a rule requiring a team to shoot or lose possession of the ball within 24 seconds came to the professional ranks in 1954 (collegians, who seemed to prefer a game with more artistry and deliberation, did not adopt a shot-clock until 1985, and the time limit was 45 seconds); the three-point field goal for specified long shots came to the professionals in 1979 and to college basketball in 1986.

Other changes took place outside the rules. The one-hand "jump" or "set" shot developed gradually in the 1940s and 1950s. Given to a game of movement, the one-hand shot drove into extinction two previous forms of scoring: the artistic but slow-developing two-hand set shot, and the awkward-looking free throw scooped from between the legs. Except for a rare hanger-on to the traditional foul shot, both had vanished by the end of the 1950s. Basketball rapidly became a game of tall men. Pioneer tall players in college and the professionals—Bob Kurland of Oklahoma, Clyde Lovelette of Kansas, George Mikan of De Paul—were outstanding because they were tall. They also were white. By the 1960s all professional teams and many in college had players ranging between 6 feet 7 inches and 7 feet. The good ones could move, catch the ball, jump, possibly even shoot—and they were likely to be black.

Lists of individual leaders in the National Basketball Association (NBA) revealed domination by white players in the first few years of the professional league. Then, starting about 1960, African Americans took over and in the following years produced a full flowering of the black athlete on the hard court. A black starting five became commonplace in most cities of the NBA. When through unusual circumstances the Boston Celtics in the 1980s used and won with three white starting players—Larry Bird, Kevin McHale, and Danny Ainge—sportswriters jocularly referred to the Celtics as "South Africa's team." African-American domination was more gradual and sporadic in college basketball, where factors other than athletic excellence often intervened. But if one surveyed the most successful Division I programs, one likely would find, if not five black starting players, at least three or four.

Both college basketball and the NBA produced a period of dynasty to be followed by a time of balance, or at least periods of close competition. On the university level, domination came in the form of coach John Wooden, who led UCLA to 10 national championships between 1964 and 1975. Wooden's retirement in 1975 was followed by intense competition on the court and in efforts to recruit the most promising high school players. Crowds became larger, as did the buildings constructed to hold them, and CBS in 1990 paid $1 billion for rights to broadcast the

Indiana University was Big 10 Champ and National Champion in 1953. Although the state was not segregated de jure and the university did not refuse to use black players, the team of 1953 was all white. (Media Relations, Indiana University)

John Wooden, the "Wizard of Westwood"—coach of UCLA during its period of absolute and unparalleled dominance of collegiate basketball in the 1960s and 1970s (ASUCLA Photography)

Division I tournament for seven years. No team won the title more than two consecutive years.

Dynasty in the NBA came in the Boston Celtics, a team that won the championship 10 out of 11 years, eight years straight during the period between 1958 and 1969. Competition of big men pitted Bill Russell of Boston against Wilt Chamberlain of Philadelphia/San Francisco. Chamberlain usually had the upper hand, but Russell got the championship rings. The 1970s produced conflicting currents: competition from the ABA, which drove up salaries, new premier performers, such as Kareem Abdul-Jabbar, a titan from one of Wooden's UCLA squads, and (from the ABA) Julius Erving—Doctor J.; there also was adverse publicity about drug use and other misbehavior by the players. The NBA had started to flounder when two truly marquis performers came aboard to give the league not only authority, but also style and respectability. Earvin "Magic" Johnson from Michigan State and Larry Bird of Indiana State, both drafted in 1979, would lead each of their respective teams—the Celtics of Bird, Los Angeles Lakers of Johnson—to four national championships in the 1980s. By the time the Johnson-Bird era had started to recede at the end of the 1980s, there had arrived on the scene one Michael Jordan of the Chicago Bulls, a stylish, intelligent, clean-living young man who also happened to be the best basketball player and arguably the best athlete in American history.

TABLE 18.24 NATIONAL COLLEGIATE MEN'S BASKETBALL CHAMPIONSHIP—NCAA DIVISION I MEN'S BASKETBALL FINAL-FOUR RESULTS, 1946–1990

The first men's national tournament was held in 1939 with eight teams selected from eight geographical regions. At the start a contest largely between major conference champions, the tournament grew in popularity and in numbers—to 16 teams and then 32; in 1977 a system of seeding participants was introduced. In 1978 the number increased to 40, to 48 the following year; in the 1980s the number reached 64—30 conference champions and 34 "at large" selections that would participate in three weeks of national single elimination competition culminating in a "final four" of surviving teams and a national champion—a process that came to be grandly described as "March Madness."

Year	Champion	Score	Runner-up	Third Place	Fourth Place	Champion Coach	Outstanding Player Award	
1946	Oklahoma State	43–40	North Carolina	Ohio State	California	Henry Iba	Bob Kurland	Oklahoma State
1947	Holy Cross	58–47	Oklahoma	Texas	CCNY	Alvin Julian	George Kaftan	Holy Cross
1948	Kentucky	58–42	Baylor	Holy Cross	Kansas State	Aldolph Rupp	Alex Groza	Kentucky
1949	Kentucky	46–36	Oklahoma State	Illinois	Oregon State	Aldolph Rupp	Alex Groza	Kentucky
1950	CCNY	71–68	Bradley	North Carolina State	Baylor	Nat Holman	Irwin Dambrot	CCNY
1951	Kentucky	68–58	Kansas State	Illinois	Oklahoma State	Adolph Rupp	None selected	
1952	Kansas	80–63	St. John's	Illinois	Santa Clara	Forrest Allen	Clyde Lovellette	Kansas
1953	Indiana	69–68	Kansas	Washington	Louisiana State	Branch McCracken	B.H. Born	Kansas
1954	La Salle	92–76	Bradley	Penn State	Southern California	Kenneth Loeffler	Tom Gola	La Salle
1955	San Francisco	77–63	La Salle	Colorado	Iowa	Phil Woolpert	Bill Russell	San Francisco
1956	San Francisco	83–71	Iowa	Temple	Southern Methodist	Phil Woolpert	Hal Lear	Temple
1957	North Carolina	54–53	Kansas	San Francisco	Michigan State	Frank McGuire	Wilt Chamberlain	Kansas
1958	Kentucky	84–72	Seattle	Temple	Kansas State	Adolph Rupp	Elgin Baylor	Seattle
1959	California	71–70	West Virginia	Cincinnati	Louisville	Pete Newell	Jerry West	West Virginia
1960	Ohio State	75–55	California	Cincinnati	New York Univ.	Fred Taylor	Jerry Lucas	Ohio State
1961	Cincinnati	70–65	Ohio State	St. Joseph's (Pa.)	Utah	Edwin Jucker	Jerry Lucas	Ohio State
1962	Cincinnati	71–59	Ohio State	Wake Forest	UCLA	Edwin Jucker	Paul Hogue	Cincinnati
1963	Loyola (Ill.)	60–58	Cincinnati	Duke	Utah	George Ireland	Art Heyman	Duke
1964	UCLA	98–83	Duke	Michigan	Kansas State	John Wooden	Walt Hazzard	UCLA
1965	UCLA	91–80	Michigan	Princeton	Wichita State	John Wooden	Bill Bradley	Princeton
1966	UTEP	72–65	Kentucky	Duke	Utah	Don Haskins	Jerry Chambers	Utah
1967	UCLA	79–64	Dayton	Houston	North Carolina	John Wooden	Lew Alcindor	UCLA
1968	UCLA	78–55	North Carolina	Ohio State	Houston	John Wooden	Lew Alcindor	UCLA
1969	UCLA	92–72	Purdue	Drake	North Carolina	John Wooden	Lew Alcindor	UCLA
1970	UCLA	80–69	Jacksonville	New Mexico State	St. Bonaventure	John Wooden	Sidney Wicks	UCLA
1971	UCLA	68–62	Villanova	Western Kentucky	Kansas	John Wooden	Howard Porter	Villanova
1972	UCLA	81–76	Florida State	North Carolina	Louisville	John Wooden	Bill Walton	UCLA
1973	UCLA	87–66	Memphis State	Indiana	Providence	John Wooden	Bill Walton	UCLA
1974	North Carolina State	76–64	Marquette	UCLA	Kansas	Norm Sloan	David Thompson	North Carolina State
1975	UCLA	92–85	Kentucky	Louisville	Syracuse	John Wooden	Richard Washington	UCLA

Year	Champion	Score	Runner-up	Third Place	Fourth Place	Champion Coach	Outstanding Player Award	
1976	Indiana	86–68	Michigan	UCLA	Rutgers	Bob Knight	Kent Benson	Indiana
1977	Marquette	67–59	North Carolina	UNLV	N. Carolina-Charlotte	Al McGuire	Butch Lee	Marquette
1978	Kentucky	94–88	Duke	Arkansas	Notre Dame	Joe Hall	Jack Givens	Kentucky
1979	Michigan State	75–64	Indiana State	DePaul	Penn	Jud Heathcote	Earvin Johnson	Mighigan State
1980	Louisville	59–54	UCLA	Purdue	Iowa	Denny Crum	Darrell Griffith	Louisville
1981	Indiana	63–50	North Carolina	Virginia	Louisiana State	Bob Knight	Isiah Thomas	Indiana
1982	North Carolina	63–62	Georgetown	Houston	Louisville	Dean Smith	James Worthy	North Carolina
1983	North Carolina State	54–52	Houston	Georgia	Louisville	Jim Valvano	Akeem Olajuwon	Houston
1984	Georgetown	84–75	Houston	Kentucky	Virginia	John Thompson	Patrick Ewing	Georgetown
1985	Villanova	66–64	Georgetown	St. John's	Memphis State	Rollie Massemino	Ed Pinckney	Villanova
1986	Louisville	72–69	Duke	Kansas	Louisiana State	Denny Crum	Pervis Ellison	Louisville
1987	Indiana	74–73	Syracuse	UNLV	Providence	Bob Knight	Keith Smart	Indiana
1988	Kansas	83–79	Oklahoma	Arizona	Duke	Larry Brown	Danny Manning	Kansas
1989	Michigan	80–79	Seton Hall	Illinois	Duke	Steve Fisher	Glen Rice	Michigan
1990	UNLV	103–73	Duke	Georgia Tech	Arkansas	Jerry Tarkanian	Anderson Hunt	UNLV

Source: Wright, *Universal Almanac*, 1991, 592.

TABLE 18.25   NCAA MEN'S DIVISION I SEASON LEADERS, 1948–1990

Scoring Average									
Year	Player and Team	Height	Class	GP	FG	3FG	FT	Points	Average
1948	Murray Wier, Iowa	5–9	Sr	19	152	. . .	95	399	21.0
1949	Tony Lavelli, Yale	6–3	Sr	30	228	. . .	215	671	22.4
1950	Paul Arizin, Villanova	6–3	Sr	29	260	. . .	215	735	25.3
1951	Bill Mlkvy, Temple	6–4	Sr	25	303	. . .	125	731	29.2
1952	Clyde Lovellette, Kansas	6–9	Sr	28	315	. . .	165	795	28.4
1953	Frank Selvy, Furman	6–3	Jr	25	272	. . .	194	738	29.5
1954	Frank Selvy, Furman	6–3	Sr	29	427	. . .	355	1209	41.7
1955	Darrell Floyd, Furman	6–1	Jr	25	344	. . .	209	897	35.9
1956	Darrell Floyd, Furman	6–1	Sr	28	339	. . .	268	946	33.8
1957	Grady Wallace, South Carolina	6–4	Sr	29	336	. . .	234	906	31.2
1958	Oscar Robertson, Cincinnati	6–5	So	28	352	. . .	280	984	35.1
1959	Oscar Robertson, Cincinnati	6–5	Jr	30	331	. . .	316	978	32.6
1960	Oscar Robertson, Cincinnati	6–5	Sr	30	369	. . .	273	1011	33.7
1961	Frank Burgess, Gonzaga	6–1	Sr	26	304	. . .	234	842	32.4
1962	Billy McGill, Utah	6–9	Sr	26	394	. . .	221	1009	38.8
1963	Nick Werkman, Seton Hall	6–3	Jr	22	221	. . .	208	650	29.5
1964	Howard Komives, Bowling Green	6–1	Sr	23	292	. . .	260	844	36.7
1965	Rick Barry, Miami (Fla.)	6–7	Sr	26	340	. . .	293	973	37.4
1966	Dave Schellhase, Purdue	6–4	Sr	24	284	. . .	213	781	32.5
1967	Jim Walker, Providence	6–3	Sr	28	323	. . .	205	851	30.4
1968	Pete Maravich, Louisiana St.	6–5	So	26	432	. . .	274	1138	43.8
1969	Pete Maravich, Louisiana St.	6–5	Jr	26	433	. . .	282	1148	44.2
1970	Pete Maravich, Louisiana St	6–5	Sr	31	522	. . .	337	1381	44.5
1971	Johnny Neumann, Mississippi	6–6	So	23	366	. . .	191	923	40.1
1972	Dwight Lamar, Southwestern Louisiana	6–1	Jr	29	429	. . .	196	1054	36.3
1973	William Averitt, Pepperdine	6–1	Sr	25	352	. . .	144	848	33.9
1974	Larry Fogle, Canisius	6–5	So	25	326	. . .	183	835	33.4
1975	Bob McCurdy, Richmond	6–7	Sr	26	321	. . .	213	855	32.9
1976	Marshall Rodgers, Texas-Pan American	6–2	Sr	25	361	. . .	197	919	36.8
1977	Freeman Williams, Portland St	6–4	Jr	26	417	. . .	176	1010	38.8
1978	Freeman Williams, Portland St	6–4	Sr	27	410	. . .	149	969	35.9
1979	Lawrence Butler, Idaho St	6–3	Sr	27	310	. . .	192	812	30.1
1980	Tony Murphy, Southern-BR	6–3	Sr	29	377	. . .	178	932	32.1
1981	Zam Fredrick, South Carolina	6–2	Sr	27	300	. . .	181	781	28.9
1982	Harry Kelly, Texas Southern	6–7	Jr	29	336	. . .	190	862	29.7
1983	Harry Kelly, Texas Southern	6–7	Sr	29	333	. . .	169	835	28.8
1984	Joe Jakubick, Akron	6–5	Sr	27	304	. . .	206	814	30.1
1985	Xavier McDaniel, Wichita St	6–8	Sr	31	351	. . .	142	844	27.2
1986	Terrance Bailey, Wagner	6–2	Jr	29	321	. . .	212	854	29.4
1987	Kevin Houston, Army	5–11	Sr	29	311	63	268	953	32.9
1988	Hersey Hawkins, Bradley	6–3	Sr	31	377	87	284	1125	36.3
1989	Hank Gathers, Loyola Marymount	6–7	Jr	31	419	0	177	1015	32.7
1990	Bo Kimble, Loyola Marymount	6–5	Sr	32	404	92	231	1131	35.3

Rebounds					
Year	Player and Team	Height	Class	GP	Rebounds	Average
1951	Ernie Beck, Pennsylvania	6–4	So	27	556	20.6
1952	Bill Hannon, Army	6–3	So	17	355	20.9
1953	Ed Conlin, Fordham	6–5	So	26	612	23.5
1954	Art Quimby, Connecticut	6–5	Jr	26	588	22.6
1955	Charlie Slack, Marshall	6–5	Jr	21	538	25.6

(continued)

TABLE 18.25 (continued)

	Rebounds					
Year	Player and Team	Height	Class	GP	Rebounds	Average
1956	Joe Holup, George Washington	6–6	Sr	26	604	.256[a]
1957	Elgin Baylor, Seattle	6–6	Jr	25	508	.235[a]
1958	Alex Ellis, Niagara	6–5	Sr	25	536	.262[a]
1959	Leroy Wright, Pacific	6–8	Jr	26	652	.238[a]
1960	Leroy Wright, Pacific	6–8	Sr	17	380	.234[a]
1961	Jerry Lucas, Ohio St	6–8	Jr	27	470	.198[a]
1962	Jerry Lucas, Ohio St	6–8	Sr	28	499	211[a]
1963	Paul Silas, Creighton	6–7	Sr	27	557	20.6
1964	Bob Pelkington, Xavier (Ohio)	6–7	Sr	26	567	21.8
1965	Toby Kimball, Connecticut	6–8	Sr	23	483	21.0
1966	Jim Ware, Oklahoma City	6–8	Sr	29	607	20.9
1967	Dick Cunningham, Murray St	6–10	Jr	22	479	21.8
1968	Neal Walk, Florida	6–10	Jr	25	494	19.8
1969	Spencer Haywood, Detroit	6–8	So	22	472	21.5
1970	Artis Gilmore, Jacksonville	7–2	Jr	28	621	22.2
1971	Artis Gilmore, Jacksonville	7–2	Sr	26	603	23.2
1972	Kermit Washington, American	6–8	Jr	23	455	19.8
1973	Kermit Washington, American	6–8	Sr	22	439	20.0
1974	Marvin Barnes, Providence	6–9	Sr	32	597	18.7
1975	John Irving, Hofstra	6–9	So	21	323	15.4
1976	Sam Pellom, Buffalo	6–8	So	26	420	16.2
1977	Glenn Mosley, Seton Hall	6–8	Sr	29	473	16.3
1978	Ken Williams, North Texas St	6–7	Sr	28	411	14.7
1979	Monti Davis, Tennessee St	6–7	Jr	26	421	16.2
1980	Larry Smith, Alcorn St	6–8	Sr	26	392	15.1
1981	Darryl Watson, Miss Valley	6–7	Sr	27	379	14.0
1982	LaSalle Thompson, Texas	6–10	Jr	27	365	13.5
1983	Xavier McDaniel, Wichita St	6–7	So	28	403	14.4
1984	Akeem Olajuwon, Houston	7–0	Jr	37	500	13.5
1985	Xavier McDaniel, Wichita St	6–8	Sr	31	460	14.8
1986	David Robinson, Navy	6–11	Jr	35	455	13.0
1987	Jerome Lane, Pittsburgh	6–6	So	33	444	13.5
1988	Kenny Miller, Loyola (Ill.)	6–9	Fr	29	395	13.6
1989	Hank Gathers, Loyola (Calif.)	6–7	Jr	31	426	13.7
1990	Anthony Bonner, St Louis	6–8	Sr	33	456	13.8

[a] From 1956 to 1962, title was based on highest individual recoveries out of total by both teams in all games.
Note: GP = games played; FG = field goals; 3FG = three-point field goal; FT = free throws.
Source: Sports Illustrated 1997 Sports Almanac, 302–04.

TABLE 18.26 CAREER RECORDS IN COLLEGE BASKETBALL

			Points					
Player	Team	Height	Final Year	GP	FG	3FG[a]	FT	Points
Pete Maravich	Louisiana St	6–5	1970	83	1,387	. . .	893	3,667
Freeman Williams	Portland St	6–4	1978	106	1,369	. . .	511	3,249
Lionel Simmons	La Salle	6–7	1990	131	1,244	56	673	3,217
Harry Kelly	Texas Southern	6–7	1983	110	1,234	. . .	598	3,066
Hersey Hawkins	Bradley	6–3	1988	125	1,100	118	690	3,008
Oscar Robertson	Cincinnati	6–5	1960	88	1,052	. . .	869	2,973
Danny Manning	Kansas	6–10	1988	147	1,216	10	509	2,951
Alfredrick Hughes	Loyola (Ill.)	6–5	1985	120	1,226	. . .	462	2,914
Elvin Hayes	Houston	6–8	1968	93	1,215	. . .	454	2,884
Larry Bird	Indiana St	6–9	1979	94	1,154	. . .	542	2,850
Otis Birdsong	Houston	6–4	1977	116	1,176	. . .	480	2,832
Hank Gathers	Southern Cal., Loyola Marymount	6–7	1990	117	1,127	0	469	2,723
Reggie Lewis	Northeastern	6–7	1987	122	1,043	30 (1)	592	2,708
Daren Queenan	Lehigh	6–5	1988	118	1,024	29	626	2,703
Byron Larkin	Xavier (Ohio)	6–3	1988	121	1,022	51	601	2,696
David Robinson	Navy	7–1	1987	127	1,032	1	604	2,669
Wayman Tisdale	Oklahoma	6–9	1985	104	1,077	. . .	507	2,661

Scoring Average							
Player	Team	Final Year	GP	FG	FT	Points	Average
Pete Maravich	Louisiana St	1968	83	1,387	893	3,667	44.2
Austin Carr	Notre Dame	1971	74	1,017	526	2,560	34.6
Oscar Robertson	Cincinnati	1960	88	1,052	869	2,973	33.8
Calvin Murphy	Niagara	1970	77	947	654	2,548	33.1
Dwight Lamar	Southwestern Louisiana	1973	57	768	326	1,862	32.7
Frank Selvy	Furman	1954	78	922	694	2,538	32.5
Rick Mount	Purdue	1970	72	910	503	2,323	32.3
Darrell Floyd	Furman	1956	71	868	545	2,281	32.1
Nick Werkman	Seton Hall	1964	71	812	649	2,273	32.0
Willie Humes	Idaho St	1971	48	565	380	1,510	31.5
William Averitt	Pepperdine	1973	49	615	311	1,541	31.4
Elgin Baylor	Coll of Idaho, Seattle	1958	80	956	588	2,500	31.3
Elvin Hayes	Houston	1968	93	1,215	454	2,884	31.0
Freeman Williams	Portland St	1978	106	1,369	511	3,249	30.7
Larry Bird	Indiana St	1979	94	1,154	542	2,850	30.3

a Listed is the number of three-pointers scored since it became the national rule in 1987; the number in the parentheses is number scored prior to 1987—these counted as three points in the game but counted as two-pointers in the national rankings. The three-pointers in the parentheses are not included in total points.
Note: GP = games played; FG = field goals; 3FG = three-point field goals; FT = free throws.
Source: Sports Illustrated 1997 Sports Almanac, 308–09.

Women's Basketball

Women's basketball developed gradually in high school and college during the postwar era. The teams at the start had six players: three forwards that did the scoring and three guards who protected the basket, and because one set of players did not enter the territory of the other, it was in effect a half-court game for everyone involved. The movement to men's (or boys') rules, to varsity status and popular recognition, received a huge boost in an act of Congress in 1971, of which a section, Title IX, forbade sex discrimination at federally

Bill Walton was one of the very best of a large collection of good players for UCLA during its reign as king of college basketball. (ASUCLA Photography)

Cheryl Miller was a star player at the University of Southern California and a pioneer in the emergence of women's intercollegiate basketball in the 1980s. (USC Sports Information)

supported schools. In theory the sexes were to be treated equally, and in practice movement began toward intercollegiate competition, recruitment, and awarding of scholarships to female athletes.

Women's basketball was recognized at the Olympic games of 1976. The NCAA assumed control of the sport on the college level in the late 1970s, committed to providing women the same structure and status as men. The first female final four tournament, in 1982, was nationally televised. Such established stars as Nancy Lieberman of Old Dominion College and Ann Meyers of UCLA were followed in the 1980s by Cheryl Miller of Southern California,

Clarissa Davis of Texas, and many others. Pat Summitt of Tennessee became the most popular female coach. Many people, including coaching icon John Wooden, formerly of UCLA, saw women's basketball as an appealing antidote to preoccupation in the men's game with size and sheer physical strength. It was refreshing to see guards who were no more than 5 feet 9 inches and forwards at 6 feet 1 inch, and whatever their size, they all had to shoot the ball upward to get it to the basket. With fuller development of the game, however, it appeared that the girls and young women were becoming taller, stronger, and faster.

TABLE 18.27 NCAA WOMEN'S FINAL FOUR, 1982–1990

(Replaced the Association of Intercollegiate Athletics for Women [AIAW] tournament in 1982 as the official playoff for the national championship)

Year	Champion	Head Coach	Score	Runner-up	Third Place	
1982	Louisiana Tech	Sonya Hogg	76–62	Cheyney	Maryland	Tennessee
1983	USC	Linda Sharp	69–67	Louisiana Tech	Georgia	Old Dominion
1984	USC	Linda Sharp	72–61	Tennessee	Cheyney	Louisiana Tech
1985	Old Dominion	Marianne Stanley	70–65	Georgia	NE Louisiana	Western Ky.
1986	Texas	Jody Conradt	97–81	USC	Tennessee	Western Ky.
1987	Tennessee	Pat Summitt	67–44	Louisiana Tech	Long Beach St.	Texas
1988	Louisiana Tech	Leon Barmore	56–54	Auburn	Long Beach St.	Tennessee
1989	Tennessee	Pat Summitt	76–60	Auburn	Louisiana Tech	Maryland
1990	Stanford	Tara VanDerveer	88–81	Auburn	Louisiana Tech	Virginia

Source: 1993 Information Please Sports Almanac, 294.

TABLE 18.28 ANNUAL INDIVIDUAL AWARDS, 1977–1990

The first prize, the Broderick Award, was given to the outstanding woman basketball player, starting in 1977. Since that time three other organizations gave awards to women players. The only person to win all four in the same season was Cheryl Miller of USC in 1985.

Year	Broderick Award[a]	Wade Trophy[b]	Naismith Trophy[c]	Women's Basketball Coaches Association[d]
1977	Lucy Harris, Delta St.*	. . .	. . .	. . .
1978	Anne Meyers, UCLA*	Carol Blazejowski, Montclair St.	. . .	. . .
1979	Nancy Lieberman, Old Dominion*	Nancy Lieberman, Old Dominion	. . .	. . .
1980	Nancy Lieberman, Old Dominion*	Nancy Lieberman, Old Dominion	. . .	. . .
1981	Lynette Woodward, Kansas	Lynette Woodward, Kansas	. . .	. . .
1982	Pam Kelly, La. Tech.	Pam Kelly, La. Tech.	. . .	. . .
1983	Anne Donovan, Old Dominion	LaTaunya Pollard, L. Beach St.	Anne Donovan, Old Dominion	Anne Donovan, Old Dominion
1984	Cheryl Miller, USC*	Janice Lawrence, La. Tech.	Cheryl Miller, USC	Janice Lawrence, La. Tech.
1985	Cheryl Miller, USC	Cheryl Miller, USC	Cheryl Miller, USC	Cheryl Miller, USC
1986	Kamie Ethridge, Texas*	Kamie Ethridge, Texas	Cheryl Miller, USC	Cheryl Miller, USC
1987	Katrina McClain, Georgia	Shelly Pennefather, Villanova	Clarissa Davis, Texas	Katrina McClain, Georgia
1988	Teresa Weatherspoon, La. Tech*	Teresa Weatherspoon, La. Tech.	Sue Wicks, Rutgers	Michelle Edwards, Iowa
1989	Bridgette Gordon, Tennessee	Clarissa Davis, Texas	Clarissa Davis, Texas	Clarissa Davis, Texas
1990	Jennifer Azzi, Stanford	Jennifer Azzi, Stanford	Jennifer Azzi, Stanford	Venus Lacey, La. Tech

[a] Voted on by a national panel of women's collegiate athletic directors and first presented by the late Thomas Broderick, an athletic outfitter, in 1976. Honda has presented the award since 1987. Basketball Player of the Year is one of 10 nominated for Collegiate Woman Athlete of the Year; (*) indicates player also won Athlete of the Year.
[b] Voted on by the National Assn. for Girls and Women in Sports (NAGWS) and awarded for academics and community service as well as player performance. First presented in 1978 in the name of former Delta St. coach Margaret Wade.
[c] Voted on by a panel of coaches, sportwriters and broadcasters and first presented in 1983 by the Atlanta Tip-Off Club in the name of the inventor of basketball, Dr. James Naismith.
[d] Voted on by the WBCA and first presented by Champion athletic outfitters in 1983.
Source: 1993 Information Please Sports Almanac, 295–96.

TABLE 18.29 COACH OF THE YEAR AWARD, 1983–1990

Voted on by the Women's Basketball Coaches Assn. and first presented by Converse athletic outfitters in 1983. **Multiple winner:** Jody Conradt (2).

Year	Player	School
1983	Pat Summitt	Tennessee
1984	Jody Conradt	Texas
1985	Jim Foster	St. Joseph's-Pa.
1986	Jody Conradt	Texas
1987	Theresa Grentz	Rutgers
1988	Vivian Stringer	Iowa
1989	Tara VanDerveer	Stanford
1990	Kay Yow	N.C. State

Source: 1993 Information Please Sports Almanac, 296.

TABLE 18.30 OTHER WOMEN'S CHAMPIONS, 1972–1990

The Association of Intercollegiate Athletics for Women Large College tournament determined the women's national champion for 10 years until supplanted by the NCAA: In 1982, most Division I teams entered the first NCAA tournament rather than the last one staged by the AIAW.

AIAW Finals			
Year	Winner	Score	Loser
1972	Immaculata, Pa.	52–48	West Chester, Pa.
1973	Immaculata, Pa.	59–52	Queens College, NY
1974	Immaculata, Pa.	68–53	Mississippi College
1975	Delta St., Miss.	90–81	Immaculata, Pa.
1976	Delta St., Miss.	69–64	Immaculata, Pa.
1977	Delta St., Miss.	68–55	LSU
1978	UCLA	90–74	Maryland
1979	Old Dominion	75–65	Louisiana Tech
1980	Old Dominion	68–53	Tennessee
1981	Louisiana Tech	79–59	Tennessee
1982	Rutgers	83–77	Texas

NCAA Div. II Finals			
Year	Winner	Score	Loser
1982	Cal Poly Pomona	93–74	Tuskegee, Ala.
1983	Virginia Union	73–60	Cal Poly Pomona
1984	Central Mo.St.	80–73	Virginia Union
1985	Cal Poly Pomona	80–69	Central Mo. St.
1986	Cal Poly Pomona	70–63	North Dakota St.
1987	New Haven, Conn.	77–75	Cal Poly Pomona
1988	Hampton, Va.	65–48	West Texas St.
1989	Delta St., Minn.	88–58	Cal Poly Pomona
1990	Delta St., Minn.	77–43	Bentley, Mass.

NCAA Div. III Finals			
Year	Winner	Score	Loser
1982	Elizabethtown, Pa.	67–66	N.C.-Greensboro
1983	North Central, Ill.	83–71	Elizabethtown, Pa.
1984	Rust College, Miss.	51–49	Elizabethtown, Pa.
1985	Scranton, Pa.	68–59	New Rochelle, N.Y.
1986	Salem St., Mass.	89–85	Bishop, Tex.
1987	WI-Stevens Pt.	81–74	Concordia, Minn.
1988	Concordia, Minn.	65–57	St. John Fisher, N.Y.
1989	Elizabethtown, Pa.	66–65	CS-Stanislaus
1990	Hope, Minn.	65–63	St. John Fisher

NAIA Finals			
Year	Winner	Score	Loser
1981	Kentucky St.	73–67	Texas Southern
1982	S'western Okla.	80–45	Mo. Southern
1983	S'western Okla.	80–68	AL-Huntsville
1984	NC-Asheville	72–70	Portland, Ore.
1985	S'western Okla.	55–54	Saginaw Val., Mich.
1986	Francis Marion, S.C.	75–65	Wayland Baptist, Tex.
1987	S'western Okla.	60–58	North Georgia
1988	Oklahoma City	113–95	Claflin, S.C.
1989	So. Nazarene	98–96	Claflin, S.C.
1990	SW Oklahoma	82–75	AR-Monticello

Source: 1993 Information Please Sports Almanac, 296.

Major NCAA Rule Changes, 1947–1990

1947–48 The clock is stopped on every dead ball the last three minutes of the second half and of every overtime period. This includes every time a goal is scored because the ball is considered dead until put into play again. (This rule was abolished in 1951.)

1948–49 Coaches are allowed to speak to players during a timeout.

1951–52 Games are to be played in four 10-minute quarters. Before this, games were played in two 20-minute halves.

1952–53 Teams can no longer waive free throws in favor of taking the ball out of bounds.

The one-and-one free-throw rule is introduced, although the bonus is used only if the first shot is missed. The rule will be in effect the entire game except the last three minutes, when every foul is two shots.

1954–55 The one-and-one free throw is changed so that the bonus shot is given only if the first shot is made.

Games are changed back to being played in two 20-minute halves.

1955–56 The two-shot penalty in the last three minutes of the game is eliminated. The one-and-one is now in effect the entire game.

1956–57 The free-throw lane is increased from 6 feet to 12 feet. On the lineup for a free throw, the two spaces adjacent to the end line must be occupied by opponents of the free thrower. In the past, one space was marked "H" for a home-team player to occupy, and across the lane the first space was marked "V" for a visiting-team player to stand in.

Grasping the basket is now classified as a technical foul under unsportsmanlike tactics.

1957–58 Offensive goaltending is now banned, as an addition to the original 1945 rule.

One free throw for each common foul is taken for the first six personal fouls by one team in each half, and the one-and-one is used thereafter.

On uniforms, the use of the single digit numbers one and two and any digit greater than five is prohibited.

A ball that passes over the backboard—either front to back or back to front—is considered out of bounds.

1964–65 Coaches must remain seated on the bench except while the clock is stopped or to direct or encourage players on the court. This rule is to help keep coaches from inciting undesirable crowd reactions toward the officials.

1967–68 The dunk is made illegal during the game and pregame warm-up.

1970–71 During a jump ball a nonjumper may not change his position from the time the official is ready to make the toss until after the ball has been touched.

1972–73 The free throw on the first six common fouls each half by a team is eliminated.

Players cannot attempt to create the false impression that they have been fouled in charging-guarding situations or while screening when the contact was only incidental. An official can charge the "actor" with a technical foul for unsportsmanlike conduct if, in the official's opinion, the actor is making a travesty of the game.

Freshmen are eligible to play varsity basketball. This was the result of a change in the NCAA bylaws, not the basketball playing rules.

1973–74 Officials may now penalize players for fouls occurring away from the ball, such as grabbing, holding, and setting illegal screens.

1974–75 During a jump ball, a nonjumper on the restraining circle may move around it after the ball has left the official's hands.

A player charged with a foul is no longer required to raise his hand. (In 1978, however, it was strongly recommended that a player start raising his hand again.)

1976–77 The dunk is made legal again.

1981–82 The jump ball is used only at the beginning of the game and the start of each overtime. An alternating arrow will indicate possession in jump-ball situations during the game.

All fouls charged to bench personnel shall be assessed to the head coach.

1982–83 When the closely guarded five-second count is reached, it is no longer a jump-ball situation. It is a violation, and the ball is awarded to the defensive team out of bounds.

1983–84 Two free throws are taken for each common foul committed within the last two minutes of the second half and the entire overtime period, if the bonus rule is in effect. (This rule was rescinded one month into the season.)

1984–85 The coaching box is introduced, whereby a coach and all bench personnel must remain in the 28-foot-long coaching box unless seeking information from the scorer's table.

1985–86 The 45-second clock is introduced. The team in control of the ball must now shoot for a goal within 45 seconds after it attains team control.

If a shooter is fouled intentionally and the shot is missed, the penalty will be two shots and possession of the ball out of bounds to the team that was fouled.

The head coach may stand throughout the game, while all other bench personnel must remain seated.

1986–87 The three-point field goal is introduced and set at 19 feet 9 inches from the center of the basket.

A coach may leave the confines of the bench at any time without penalty to correct a scorer or timer's mistake. A technical foul is assessed if there is no mistake. (This was changed the next year to a timeout.) Also, a television replay may be used to prevent or rectify a scorer or timer's mistake or a malfunction of the clock.

1987–88 Each intentional personal foul carries a two-shot penalty plus possession of the ball.

1988–89 Any squad member who participates in a fight will be ejected from the game and will be placed on probation. If that player participates in a second fight during the season, he will be suspended for one game. A third fight involving the same person results in suspension for the rest of the season including championship competition.

1990–91 Beginning with the team's 10th personal foul in a half, two free throws are awarded for each common foul, except player-control fouls.

Three free throws are awarded when a shooter is fouled during an unsuccessful three-point try.

The fighting rule is amended. The first time any squad member or bench personnel participates in a fight he will be suspended for the team's next game. If that same person participates in a second fight, he will be suspended for the rest of the season including championship competition.

Source: NCAA Records Book, 1998, 203–04.

TABLE 18.31   EVOLUTION OF THE NATIONAL BASKETBALL ASSOCIATION, 1951–1990

NBA 1951–1952

Final Standings

Eastern Division	W.	L.	PCT.	Western Division	W.	L.	PCT.
Syracuse	40	26	.606	Rochester	41	25	.621
Boston	39	27	.591	Minneapolis	40	26	.606
New York	37	29	.561	Indianapolis	34	32	.515
Philadelphia	33	33	.500	Fort Wayne	29	37	.439
Baltimore	20	46	.303	Milwaukee	17	49	.258

NBA 1967–1968

Final Standings

Eastern Division	W.	L.	PCT.	Western Division	W.	L.	PCT.
Philadelphia	62	20	.756	St. Louis	56	26	.683
Boston	54	28	.659	Los Angeles	52	30	.634
New York	43	39	.524	San Francisco	43	39	.524
Detroit	40	42	.488	Chicago	29	53	.354
Cincinnati	39	43	.476	Seattle	23	59	.280
Baltimore	36	46	.439	San Diego	15	67	.183

NBA 1977–1978

Final Standings

	Eastern Conference								Western Conference						
Atlantic Division				Central Division				Midwest Division				Pacific Division			
	W.	L.	PCT.		W.	L.	PCT.		W.	L.	PCT.		W.	L.	PCT.
Philadelphia	55	27	.671	San Antonio	52	30	.634	Denver	48	34	.585	Portland	58	24	.707
New York	43	39	.524	Washington	44	38	.537	Milwaukee	44	38	.537	Phoenix	49	33	.598
Boston	32	50	.390	Cleveland	43	39	.524	Chicago	40	42	.488	Seattle	47	35	.573
Buffalo	27	55	.329	Atlanta	41	41	.500	Detroit	38	44	.463	Los Angeles	45	37	.549
New Jersey	24	58	.293	New Orleans	39	43	.476	Indiana	31	51	.378	Golden State	43	39	.524
				Houston	28	54	.341	Kansas City	31	51	.378				

NBA 1989–1990

Final Standings

Eastern Conference								Western Conference							
Atlantic Division				Central Division				Midwest Division				Pacific Division			
	W.	L.	PCT.		W.	L.	PCT.		W.	L.	PCT.		W.	L.	PCT.
Philadelphia	53	29	.646	Detroit	59	23	.720	San Antonio	56	26	.683	L.A. Lakers	63	19	.768
Boston	52	30	.634	Chicago	55	27	.671	Utah	55	27	.671	Portland	59	23	.720
New York	45	37	.549	Milwaukee	44	38	.537	Dallas	47	35	.573	Phoenix	54	28	.659
Washington	31	51	.378	Cleveland	42	40	.512	Denver	43	39	.524	Seattle	41	41	.500
Miami	18	64	.220	Indiana	42	40	.512	Houston	41	41	.500	Golden State	37	45	.451
New Jersey	16	65	.207	Atlanta	41	41	.500	Minnesota	22	60	.268	L.A. Clippers	30	52	.366
				Orlando	18	64	.220	Charlotte	19	63	.232	Sacramento	23	59	.280

Source: Alex Sachare, *The Official NBA Basketball Encyclopedia* (New York, 1994), 57, 105, 121, 155.

TABLE 18.32   NATIONAL BASKETBALL ASSOCIATION CHAMPIONS, 1946–1990

The National Basketball Association was originally the Basketball Association of America. It took its current name in 1949 when it merged with the National Basketball League.

Season	Eastern Conference (W-L)	Western Conference (W-L)	Playoff Champions[a]
1946–47	Washington Capitols (49–11)	Chicago Stags (39–22)	Philadelphia Warriors
1947–48	Philadelphia Warriors (27–21)	St. Louis Bombers (29–19)	Baltimore Bullets
1948–49	Washington Capitols (38–22)	Rochester Royals (45–15)	Minneapolis Lakers
1949–50	Syracuse Nationals (51–13)	Indianapolis Olympians (39–25)	Minneapolis Lakers
1950–51	Philadelphia Warriors (40–26)	Minneapolis Lakers (44–24)	Rochester Royals
1951–52	Syracuse Nationals (40–26)	Rochester Royals (41–25)	Minneapolis Lakers
1952–53	New York Knickerbockers (47–23)	Minneapolis Lakers (48–22)	Minneapolis Lakers
1953–54	New York Knickerbockers (44–28)	Minneapolis Lakers (46–26)	Minneapolis Lakers
1954–55	Syracuse Nationals (43–29)	Ft. Wayne Pistons (43–29)	Syracuse Nationals
1955–56	Philadelphia Warriors (45–27)	Ft. Wayne Pistons (37–35)	Philadelphia Warriors
1956–57	Boston Celtics (44–28)	St. Louis Hawks (38–34)	Boston Celtics
1957–58	Boston Celtics (48–23)	St. Louis Hawks (41–31)	St. Louis Hawks
1958–59	Boston Celtics (52–20)	St. Louis Hawks (49–23)	Boston Celtics
1959–60	Boston Celtics (59–16)	St. Louis Hawks (46–29)	Boston Celtics
1960–61	Boston Celtics (57–22)	St. Louis Hawks (51–28)	Boston Celtics
1961–62	Boston Celtics (60–20)	Los Angeles Lakers (54–26)	Boston Celtics
1962–63	Boston Celtics (58–22)	Los Angeles Lakers (53–27)	Boston Celtics
1963–64	Boston Celtics (59–21)	San Francisco Warriors (48–32)	Boston Celtics
1964–65	Boston Celtics (62–18)	Los Angeles Lakers (49–31)	Boston Celtics
1965–66	Philadelphia 76ers (55–25)	Los Angeles Lakers (45–35)	Boston Celtics
1966–67	Philadelphia 76ers (68–13)	San Francisco Warriors (44–37)	Philadelphia 76ers
1967–68	Philadelphia 76ers (62–20)	St. Louis Hawks (56–26)	Boston Celtics
1968–69	Baltimore Bullets (57–25)	Los Angeles Lakers (55–27)	Boston Celtics
1969–70	New York Knickerbockers (60–22)	Atlanta Hawks (48–34)	New York Knicks
1970–71	Baltimore Bullets (42–40)	Milwaukee Bucks (66–16)	Milwaukee Bucks
1971–72	New York Knickerbockers (48–34)	Los Angeles Lakers (69–13)	Los Angeles Lakers
1972–73	New York Knickerbockers (57–25)	Los Angeles Lakers (60–22)	New York Knicks
1973–74	Boston Celtics (56–26)	Milwaukee Bucks (59–23)	Boston Celtics
1974–75	Washington Bullets (60–22)	Golden State Warriors (48–34)	Golden State Warriors
1975–76	Boston Celtics (54–28)	Phoenix Suns (42–40)	Boston Celtics
1976–77	Phildelphia 76ers (50–32)	Portland Trail Blazers (49–33)	Portland Trail Blazers
1977–78	Washington Bullets (44–38)	Seattle Super Sonics (47–35)	Washington Bullets
1978–79	Washington Bullets (54–28)	Seattle Super Sonics (52–30)	Seattle Super Sonics
1979–80	Philadelphia 76ers (59–23)	Los Angeles Lakers (60–22)	Los Angeles Lakers
1980–81	Boston Celtics (62–20)	Phoenix Suns (57–25)	Boston Celtics
1981–82	Boston Celtics (63–19)	Houston Rockets (46–36)	Boston Celtics
1982–83	Philadelphia 76ers (65–17)	Los Angeles Lakers (58–24)	Philadelphia 76ers
1983–84	Boston Celtics (56–26)	Los Angeles Lakers (58–24)	Boston Celtics
1984–85	Boston Celtics (63–19)	Los Angeles Lakers (62–20)	Los Angeles Lakers
1985–86	Boston Celtics (67–15)	Houston Rockets (51–31)	Boston Celtics
1986–87	Boston Celtics (59–23)	Los Angeles Lakers (65–17)	Los Angeles Lakers
1987–88	Detroit Pistons (54–28)	Los Angeles Lakers (62–20)	Los Angeles Lakers
1988–89	Detroit Pistons (63–18)	Los Angeles Lakers (57–25)	Detroit Pistons
1989–90	Detroit Pistons (59–23)	Portland Trail Blazers (59–23)	Detroit Pistons

[a] Playoffs may involve teams other than conference winners.
Source: 1991 Information Please Almanac, 894.

TABLE 18.33 NBA SCORING LEADERS, 1947–1990

Year	Scoring Champion	Pts	Avg
1947	Joe Fulks, Philadelphia[a]	1,389	23.2
1948	Max Zasiofsky, Chicago[a]	1,007	21.0
1949	George Mikan, Minneapolis[a]	1,698	28.3
1950	George Mikan, Minneapolis[a]	1,865	27.4
1951	George Mikan, Minneapolis[a]	1,932	28.4
1952	Paul Arizin, Philadelphia[a]	1,674	25.4
1953	Neil Johnston, Philadelphia[a]	1,564	22.3
1954	Neil Johnston, Philadelphia[a]	1,759	24.4
1955	Neil Johnston, Philadelphia[a]	1,631	22.7
1956	Bob Pettit, St. Louis[a]	1,849	25.7
1957	Paul Arizin, Philadelphia[a]	1,817	25.8
1958	George Yardley, Detroit[a]	2,001	27.8
1959	Bob Pettit, St. Louis[a]	2,105	29.2
1960	Wilt Chamberlain, Philadelphia[b]	2,707	37.9
1961	Wilt Chamberlain, Philadelphia[b]	3,033	38.4
1962	Wilt Chamberlain, Philadelphia[b]	4,029	50.4
1963	Wilt Chamberlain, San Francisco[b]	3,586	44.8
1964	Wilt Chamberlain, San Francisco[b]	2,948	36.5
1965	Wilt Chamberlain, San Francisco, Philadelphia[b]	2,534	34.7
1966	Wilt Chamberlain, Philadelphia[b]	2,649	33.5
1967	Rick Barry, San Francisco[a]	2,775	35.6
1968	Dave Bing, Detroit[b]	2,142	27.1
1969	Elvin Hayes, San Diego[b]	2,327	28.4
1970	Jerry West, Los Angeles[a]	2,309	31.2
1971	Lew Alcindor (Kareem Abdul-Jabbar), Milwaukee[b]	2,596	31.7
1972	Kareem Abdul-Jabbar, Milwaukee[b]	2,822	34.8
1973	Nate Archibald, Kans. City-Omaha[b]	2,719	34.0
1974	Bob McAdoo, Buffalo[b]	2,261	30.6
1975	Bob McAdoo, Buffalo[b]	2,831	34.5
1976	Bob McAdoo, Buffalo[b]	2,427	31.1
1977	Pete Maravich, New Orleans[a]	2,273	31.1
1978	George Gervin, San Antonio[b]	2,232	27.2
1979	George Gervin, San Antonio[b]	2,365	29.6
1980	George Gervin, San Antonio[b]	2,585	33.1
1981	Adrian Dantley, Utah[b]	2,452	30.7
1982	George Gervin, San Antonio[b]	2,551	32.3
1983	Alex English, Denver[b]	2,326	28.4
1984	Adrian Dantley, Utah[b]	2,418	30.6
1985	Bernard King, New York[b]	1,809	32.9
1986	Dominique Wilkins, Atlanta[b]	2,366	30.3
1987	Michael Jordan, Chicago[b]	3,041	37.1
1988	Michael Jordan, Chicago[b]	2,868	35.0
1989	Michael Jordan, Chicago[b]	2,633	32.5
1990	Michael Jordan, Chicago[b]	2,753	33.6

[a] Designates white athlete.
[b] Designates African-American athlete.
Source: Robert Famighetti, *The World Almanac and Book of Facts, 1999* (Mahwah, N.J., 1998), 2351; *African-American Encyclopedia*, 2351.

TABLE 18.34 SELECTED INDIVIDUAL NBA LEADERS, 1946–1990

Assists				Rebounds				Minutes Played			
Year	Player	Team	Record	Year	Player	Team	Record	Year	Player	Team	Record
1946–47	Ernie Calverly	Providence[a]	202	1950–51	Dolph Schayes	Syracuse[a]	1080	1951–52	Paul Arizin	Philadelphia[a]	2939
1947–48	Howie Dallmar	Philadelphia[a]	120	1951–52	Larry Foust	Fort Wayne[a]	880	1952–53	Neil Johnston	Philadelphia[a]	3166
1948–49	Bob Davies	Rochester[a]	321		Mel Hutchins	Milwaukee[a]	880	1953–54	Neil Johnston	Philadelphia[a]	3296
1949–50	Dick McGuire	New York[a]	386	1952–53	George Mikan	Minneapolis[a]	1007	1954–55	Paul Arizin	Philadelphia[a]	2953
1950–51	Andy Phillip	Philadelphia[a]	414	1953–54	Harry Gallatin	New York[a]	1098	1955–56	Slater Martin	Minneapolis[a]	2838
1951–52	Andy Phillip	Philadelphia[a]	539	1954–55	Neil Johnston	Philadelphia[a]	1085	1956–57	Dolph Schayes	Syracuse[a]	2851
1952–53	Bob Cousy	Boston[a]	547	1955–56	Bob Pettit	St. Louis[a]	1164	1957–58	Dolph Schayes	Syracuse[a]	2918
1953–54	Bob Cousy	Boston[a]	578	1956–57	Maurice Stokes	Rochester[b]	1256	1958–59	Bill Russell	Boston[b]	2979
1954–55	Bob Cousy	Boston[a]	557	1957–58	Bill Russell	Boston[b]	1564	1959–60	Wilt Chamberlain	Philadelphia[b]	3338
1955–56	Bob Cousy	Boston[a]	642	1958–59	Bill Russell	Boston[b]	1612		Gene Shue	Detroit[a]	3338
1956–57	Bob Cousy	Boston[a]	478	1959–60	Wilt Chamberlain	Philadelphia[b]	1941	1960–61	Wilt Chamberlain	Philadelphia[b]	3773
1957–58	Bob Cousy	Boston[a]	463	1960–61	Wilt Chamberlain	Philadelphia[b]	2149	1961–62	Wilt Chamberlain	Philadelphia[b]	3882
1958–59	Bob Cousy	Boston[a]	557	1961–62	Wilt Chamberlain	Philadelphia[b]	2052	1962–63	Wilt Chamberlain	San Francisco[b]	3806
1959–60	Bob Cousy	Boston[a]	715	1962–63	Wilt Chamberlain	San Francisco[b]	1946	1963–64	Wilt Chamberlain	San Francisco[b]	3689
1960–61	Oscar Robertson	Cincinnati[b]	690	1963–64	Bill Russell	Boston[b]	1930	1964–65	Bill Russell	Boston[b]	3466
1961–62	Oscar Robertson	Cincinnati[b]	899	1964–65	Bill Russell	Boston[b]	1878	1965–66	Wilt Chamberlain	Philadelphia[b]	3737
1962–63	Guy Rodgers	San Francisco[b]	825	1965–66	Wilt Chamberlain	Philadelphia[b]	1943	1966–67	Wilt Chamberlain	Philadelphia[b]	3682
1963–64	Oscar Robertson	Cincinnati[b]	868	1966–67	Wilt Chamberlain	Philadelphia[b]	1957	1967–68	Wilt Chamberlain	Philadelphia[b]	3836
1964–65	Oscar Robertson	Cincinnati[b]	861	1967–68	Wilt Chamberlain	Philadelphia[b]	1952	1968–69	Elvin Hayes	San Diego[b]	3695
1965–66	Oscar Robertson	Cincinnati[b]	847	1968–69	Wilt Chamberlain	Los Angeles[b]	1712	1969–70	Elvin Hayes	San Diego[b]	3665

Assists					Rebounds					Minutes Played			
Year	Player	Team	Record		Year	Player	Team	Record		Year	Player	Team	Record
1966–67	Guy Rodgers	Chicago[b]	908		1969–70	Elvin Hayes	San Diego[b]	[c]16.9		1970–71	John Havlicek	Boston[a]	3678
1967–68	Wilt Chamberlain	Philadelphia[b]	702		1970–71	Wilt Chamberlain	Los Angeles[b]	18.2		1971–72	John Havlicek	Boston[a]	3698
1968–69	Oscar Robertson	Cincinnati[b]	772		1971–72	Wilt Chamberlain	Los Angeles[b]	19.2		1972–73	Nate Archibald	K.C.-Omaha[b]	3681
1969–70	Lenny Wilkens	Seattle[b]	9.1		1972–73	Wilt Chamberlain	Los Angeles[b]	18.6		1973–74	Elvin Hayes	Capital[b]	3602
1970–71	Norm Van Lier	Cincinnati[b]	10.1		1973–74	Elvin Hayes	Capital[b]	18.1		1974–75	Bob McAdoo	Buffalo[b]	3539
1971–72	Jerry West	Los Angeles[a]	9.7		1974–75	Wes Unseld	Washington[b]	14.8		1975–76	Kareem Abdul-Jabbar	Los Angeles[b]	3379
1972–73	Nate Archibald	KC-Omaha[b]	11.4		1975–76	Kareem Abdul-Jabbar	Los Angeles[b]	16.9		1976–77	Elvin Hayes	Washington[b]	3364
1973–74	Ernie DiGregorio	Buffalo[a]	8.2		1976–77	Bill Walton	Portland[a]	14.4		1977–78	Len Robinson	New Orleans[b]	3638
1974–75	Kevin Porter	Washington[b]	8.0		1977–78	Len Robinson	New Orleans[b]	15.7		1978–79	Moses Malone	Houston[b]	3390
1975–76	Don Watts	Seattle[b]	8.1		1978–79	Moses Malone	Houston[b]	17.6		1979–80	Norm Nixon	Los Angeles[b]	3226
1976–77	Don Buse	Indiana[b]	8.5		1979–80	Swen Nater	San Diego[a]	15.0		1980–81	Adrian Dantley	Utah[b]	3417
1977–78	Kevin Porter	Detroit-N.J.[b]	10.2		1980–81	Moses Malone	Houston[b]	14.8		1981–82	Moses Malone	Houston[b]	3398
1978–79	Kevin Porter	Detroit[b]	13.4		1981–82	Moses Malone	Houston[b]	14.7		1982–83	Isiah Thomas	Detroit[b]	3093
1979–80	Micheal Richardson	New York[b]	10.1		1982–83	Moses Malone	Philadelphia[b]	15.3		1983–84	Jeff Ruland	Washington[b]	3082
1980–81	Kevin Porter	Washington[b]	9.1		1983–84	Moses Malone	Philadelphia[b]	13.4		1984–85	Buck Williams	New Jersey[b]	3182
1981–82	Johnny Moore	San Antonio[b]	9.6		1984–85	Moses Malone	Philadelphia[b]	13.1		1985–86	Maurice Cheeks	Philadelphia[b]	3270
1982–83	Magic Johnson	Los Angeles[b]	10.5		1985–86	Bill Laimbeer	Detroit[a]	13.1		1986–87	Michael Jordan	Chicago[b]	3281
1983–84	Magic Johnson	Los Angeles[b]	13.1		1986–87	Charles Barkley	Philadelphia[b]	14.6		1987–88	Michael Jordan	Chicago[b]	3311
1984–85	Isiah Thomas	Detroit[b]	13.98		1987–88	Michael Cage	L.A. Clippers[b]	13.03		1988–89	Michael Jordan	Chicago[b]	3255
1985–86	Magic Johnson	L.A. Lakers[b]	12.6		1988–89	Hakeem Olajuwon	Houston[b]	13.5		1989–90	Rodney McCray	Sacramento[b]	3238
1986–87	Magic Johnson	L.A. Lakers[b]	12.2		1989–90	Hakeem Olajuwon	Houston[b]	14.0					
1987–88	John Stockton	Utah[a]	13.8										
1988–89	John Stockton	Utah[a]	13.6										
1989–90	John Stockton	Utah[a]	14.5										

[a] Designates white athlete.
[b] Designates African-American athlete.
[c] Based on average, starting in 1969–70.
Source: Sachare, *Official NBA Encyclopedia*, 378; *African-American Encyclopedia, Supplement*, Vol. 8, 2351–52.

TABLE 18.35   NBA CAREER LEADERS[a]

Games		Rebounds		Field Goals Made		Assists		Points	
Player	Record	Player	Record	Player	Record	Player	Record	Player	Record
Kareem Abdul-Jabbar	1,560	Wilt Chamberlain	23,924	Kareem Abdul-Jabbar	15,837	Oscar Robertson	9,887	Kareem Abdul-Jabbar	38,387
Elvin Hayes	1,303	Bill Russell	21,620	Wilt Chamberlain	12,681	Magic Johnson	8.932	Wilt Chamberlain	31,419
John Havlicek	1,270	Kareem Abdul-Jabbar	17,440	Elvin Hayes	10.976	Len Wilkens	7,211	Elvin Hayes	27,313
Paul Silas	1,254	Elvin Hayes	16,279	John Havlicek	10,513	Isiah Thomas	6,985	Oscar Robertson	26,710
Hal Greer	1,122	Moses Malone	14,483	Alex English	10,337	Bob Cousy	6,955	John Havlicek	26,395
Alex English	1,114	Nate Thurmond	14,464	Oscar Robertson	9,508	Guy Rodgers	6,917	Jerry West	25,192
Dennis Johnson	1,100	Walt Bellamy	14.241	Jerry West	9,016	Maurice Cheeks	6,665	Moses Malone	24,868
Robert Parish	1,100	Wes Unseld	13,769	Elgin Baylor	8,693	Nate Archibald	6,476	Alex English	24,850
Moses Malone	1,082	Jerry Lucas	12,942	Moses Malone	8,587	John Lucas	6,454	Elgin Baylor	23,149
Len Wilkens	1,077	Bob Pettit	12,849	Hal Greer	8,504	Norm Nixon	6,386	Adrian Dantley	23,120

[a] Through season of 1989–90.
Source: Wright, *Universal Almanac, 1991*, 598.

TABLE 18.36　NBA MOST VALUABLE PLAYERS, 1955–1990

Year	Name	Team	Points	Average	Rebounds
1955–56	Bob Pettit	St. Louis Hawks	1,849	25.7	1,164
1956–57	Bob Cousy	Boston Celtics	1,319	20.6	309
1957–58	Bill Russell	Boston Celtics	1,142	16.6	1,564
1958–59	Bob Pettit	St. Louis Hawks	2,105	29.2	1,182
1959–60	Wilt Chamberlain	Philadelphia Warriors	2,207	37.6	1,941
1960–61	Bill Russell	Boston Celtics	1,322	16.9	1,868
1961–62	Bill Russell	Boston Celtics	1,436	18.9	1,790
1962–63	Bill Russell	Boston Celtics	1,309	16.8	1,843
1963–64	Oscar Robertson	Cincinnati Royals	2,480	31.4	783
1964–65	Bill Russell	Boston Celtics	1,102	14.1	1,878
1965–66	Wilt Chamberlain	Philadelphia 76ers	2,649	33.5	1,943
1966–67	Wilt Chamberlain	Philadelphia 76ers	1,956	24.1	1,957
1967–68	Wilt Chamberlain	Philadelphia 76ers	1,992	24.3	1,952
1968–69	Wes Unseld	Baltimore Bullets	1,131	13.8	1,491
1969–70	Willis Reed	N.Y. Knicks	1,755	21.7	1,126
1970–71	Kareem Abdul-Jabbar	Milwaukee Bucks	2,596	31.7	1,311
1971–72	Kareem Abdul-Jabbar	Milwaukee Bucks	2,822	34.8	1,346
1972–73	Dave Cowens	Boston Celtics	1,684	20.5	1,329
1973–74	Kareem Abdul-Jabbar	Milwaukee Bucks	2,191	27.0	1,178
1974–75	Bob McAdoo	Buffalo Braves	2,831	34.5	1,155
1975–76	Kareem Abdul-Jabbar	L.A. Lakers	2,275	27.7	1,383
1976–77	Kareem Abdul-Jabbar	L.A. Lakers	2,152	26.2	1,090
1977–78	Bill Walton	Portland Trail Blazers	1,097	18.9	766
1978–79	Moses Malone	Houston Rockets	2,031	24.8	1,444
1979–80	Kareem Abdul-Jabbar	L.A. Lakers	2,034	24.8	886
1980–81	Julius Erving	Philadelphia 76ers	2,014	24.6	657
1981–82	Moses Malone	Houston Rockets	2,520	31.1	1,188
1982–83	Moses Malone	Philadelphia 76ers	1,908	24.5	1,194
1983–84	Larry Bird	Boston Celtics	1,908	24.2	796
1984–85	Larry Bird	Boston Celtics	2,295	28.7	842
1985–86	Larry Bird	Boston Celtics	2,115	25.8	805
1986–87	Magic Johnson	L.A. Lakers	1,909	23.9	504
1987–88	Michael Jordan	Chicago Bulls	2,868	35.0	449
1988–89	Magic Johnson	L.A. Lakers	1,730	22.5	607
1989–90	Magic Johnson	L.A. Lakers	1,765	22.3	525

Note: Named after the first commissioner of the NBA, the Maurice Podoloff Trophy was based on a vote of the players between 1956 and 1980. Beginning in 1981 the selection was made by a panel of basketball writers and broadcasters.
Source: John Wright, *The Universal Almanac, 1995* (New York, 1994), 679.

TABLE 18.37　PROFESSIONAL BASKETBALL DRAFT, ROSTERS, AND COACHES—NUMBER OF BLACK AMERICANS, 1989–1990

Division/Team	1989 NBA Draft		1989–90 Roster		Black Head Coach	Assistant Coaches	
	Number Choices	Number Black American	Number Players	Number Black American		Number	Number Black American
Atlantic							
Boston Celtics	2	1	12	7	. . .	2	0
Miami Heat	3	2	12	8	. . .	2	0
New Jersey Nets	2	2	13	8	. . .	2	1
New York Knicks	1	1	13	11	X	3	0
Philadelphia 76ers	3	3	17	13	. . .	1	1
Washington Bullets	3	2	13	10	X	2	0
Central							
Atlanta Hawks	2	2	13	11	. . .	2	1
Chicago Bulls	3	3	12	9	. . .	3	1
Cleveland Cavaliers	2	2	15	12	X	2	0
Detroit Pistons	1	1	14	11	. . .	2	0
Indianapolis Pacers	2	2	13	8	. . .	2	0
Milwaukee Bucks	1	0	13	6	. . .	3	1
Orlando Magic	2	2	14	9	. . .	2	0
Midwest							
Charlotte Hornets	1	1	13	7	. . .	2	1
Dallas Mavericks	3	2	13	10	. . .	2	0
Denver Nuggets	3	2	13	9	. . .	2	1
Houston Rockets	0	—	16	11	X	3	1
Minneapolis Timberwolves	3	2	14	9	. . .	1	0
San Antonio Spurs	1	1	11	9	. . .	4	2
Utah Jazz	2	2	11	5	. . .	4	0
Pacific							
Golden State Warriors	1	1	12	7	. . .	2	0
Los Angeles Clippers	3	3	11	8	. . .	2	0
Los Angeles Lakers	1	0	11	8	. . .	2	0
Phoenix Suns	4	4	17	11	. . .	3	2
Portland Trailblazers	2	2	15	11	. . .	2	0
Sacramento Kings	1	1	11	8	. . .	1	0
Seattle Supersonics	2	2	11	10	X	2	1
Number	54	46	353	246	5	60	13
Percent	100.0	85.2	100.0	69.7	. . .	100.0	21.7

Source: Carrell P. Horton and Jessie C. Smith, *Statistical Record of Black America* (Detroit, 1990), 617.

American Basketball Association

The American Basketball Association (ABA) developed in the season of 1967–68 as a competitor of the NBA. It began with 10 teams, but the number and locations changed frequently during its nine years of existence. Seeking quick legitimacy, its teams bid lavishly for top draft choices and in so doing drove up the salary for professional players. Ultimate failure probably was preordained, but the ABA left a considerable imprint. It introduced to professional ranks George McGinnis, Julius Erving, Dan Issel, Rick Barry, and David Thompson, some of the best players in the land. It pioneered the three-point shot, the slam-dunk contest in All Star Games, and the red, white, and blue ball. The NBA eventually would adopt two of the three. The end came with a reasonable amount of grace as the four most successful franchises, the Indiana Pacers, Denver Nuggets, New York Nets, and San Antonio Spurs blended into the NBA in 1976–77.

TABLE 18.38 AMERICAN BASKETBALL ASSOCIATION, 1968–1976

ABA Finals					
Year	Winner	Head Coach	Series	Loser	Head Coach
1968	Pittsburgh Pipers	Vince Cazetta	4–3(WLLWLWW)	New Orleans Bucs	Babe McCarthy
1969	Oakland Oaks	Alex Hannum	4–1(WLWWW)	Indiana Pacers	Bob Leonard
1970	Indiana Pacers	Bob Leonard	4–2(WWLWLW)	Los Angeles Stars	Bill Sharman
1971	Utah Stars	Bill Sharman	4–3(WWLLWLW)	Kentucky Colonels	Frank Ramsey
1972	Indiana Pacers	Bob Leonard	4–2(WLWLWW)	New York Nets	Lou Carnesecca
1973	Indiana Pacers	Bob Leonard	4–3(WLLWWLW)	Kentucky Colonels	Joe Mullaney
1974	New York Nets	Kevin Loughery	4–1(WWWLW)	Utah Stars	Joe Mullaney
1975	Kentucky Colonels	Hubie Brown	4–1(WWWLW)	Indiana Pacers	Bob Leonard
1976	New York Nets	Kevin Loughery	4–2(WLWWLW)	Denver Nuggets	Larry Brown

Source: *1993 Information Please Sports Almanac*, 330.

TABLE 18.39 AMERICAN BASKETBALL ASSOCIATION LEADERS, 1968–1976

ABA Leaders									
Most Valuable Player				Scoring Leaders					
Year	Player	Team	Pts	Year	Player	Team	Gm	Avg	Pts
1968	Connie Hawkins	Pittsburgh, C	26.8	1968	Connie Hawkins	Pittsburgh	70	1875	26.8
1969	Mel Daniels	Indiana, C	24.0	1969	Rick Barry	Oakland	35	1190	34.0
1970	Spencer Haywood	Denver, C	30.0	1970	Spencer Haywood	Denver	84	2519	30.0
1971	Mel Daniels	Indiana, C	21.0	1971	Dan Issel	Kentucky	83	2480	29.8
1972	Artis Gilmore	Kentucky, C	23.8	1972	Charlie Scott	Virginia	73	2524	34.6
1973	Billy Cunningham	Carolina, F	24.1	1973	Julius Erving	Virginia	71	2268	31.9
1974	Julius Erving	New York, F	27.4	1974	Julius Erving	N.Y. Nets	84	2299	27.4
1975	George McGinnis	Indiana, F	29.8	1975	George McGinnis	Indiana	79	2353	29.8
	&Julius Erving	New York, F	27.9	1976	Julius Erving	N.Y. Nets	84	2462	29.3
1976	Julius Erving	New York, F	29.3						

Source: *1993 Information Please Sports Almanac*, 330.

Professional Football

Professional football began the postwar period reasonably well established in a 10-team National Football League (NFL) but clearly subordinate in popularity to professional baseball and football as played in college. Expansion came slowly at first, in small spurts and partly by default. Competition from a new league, the All American Football Conference (AAFC), beginning in 1946 did not go far. The AAFC folded in 1949, but out of the ruins came three new teams that would be incorporated into the NFL—the Cleveland Browns and San Francisco Forty-Niners in 1950, and the Baltimore Colts two years later. Needless to say, expansion of the league and of football's popularity had a great deal to do with the emergence of television and proof of its adaptability to the gridiron. The huge audience attracted to televised coverage in 1958 of the championship game between Baltimore and the New York Giants suggested that here was a gold mine for the taking. Television also became involved in the emergence of a rival American Football League in 1960. A contract with NBC helped the infant league survive until the stronger, more popular and prestigious NFL agreed in 1966 to a merger. In 1970 a third national network, ABC, joined NBC and CBS in offering regular television coverage of—and more money for—the reformed NFL. ABC's Monday Night Football quickly became standard prime-time fare.

The league did demand a sort of prenuptial agreement in its marriage with television. Rules determined how coverage would be divided between networks; territory close to the site of a game could be blacked-out unless the game was sold out. The league wisely decided that television revenues would be divided equally among all teams, a move that was crucial to small-market teams, such as Pittsburgh and Green Bay, and to the weaker American Conference in the early years of the merger.

The arrangement did not work flawlessly, but it was profitable and an important ingredient in the league's adding franchises, growing to national dimension. There were 28 teams in 1990. Professional football passed baseball as the leading spectator sport. The postseason meeting of the two conference champions, grandly proclaimed the Super Bowl, came to be treated almost as a national holiday. Pro football took on many characteristics of other team sports. Plentiful money means large profits, soaring salaries, numerous labor disputes, and occasional work stoppage.

Football also paralleled other professional leagues in its treatment of the issue of race. The NFL had been all white before the Second

World War and mostly white during the 1950s. The first black players, Woody Strode and Kenny Washington, joined the Los Angeles Rams about a year before Jackie Robinson played for the Dodgers. But integration came slowly, and the Washington Redskins did not use a black player until 1962. When the door opened, however, it opened widely. To a larger extent than baseball but less than in basketball, professional football became the domain of the black athlete. African Americans dominated the speed and power positions: offensive and defensive backs and the defensive line; they were less well represented as quarterbacks and kickers. By 1990 at least 60 percent of all players were black. The NFL was largely a league of white owners, coaches, and office personnel, and black players.

TABLE 18.40 NATIONAL FOOTBALL LEAGUE CHAMPIONS, 1946–1966

Year	East Winner (W-L-T)	West Winner (W-L-T)	Playoff
1946	New York Giants (7–3–1)	Chicago Bears (8–2–1)	Chicago Bears 24, New York 14
1947	Philadelphia Eagles (8–4–0)	Chicago Cardinals (9–3–0)	Chicago Cardinals 28, Philadelphia 21
1948	Philadelphia Eagles (9–2–1)	Chicago Cardinals (11–1–0)	Philadelphia 7, Chicago Cardinals 0
1949	Philadelphia Eagles (11–1–0)	Los Angeles Rams (8–2–2)	Philadelphia 14, Los Angeles 0
1950	Cleveland Browns (10–2–0)	Los Angeles Rams (9–3–0)	Cleveland 30 Los Angeles 28
1951	Cleveland Browns (11–1–0)	Los Angeles Rams (8–4–0)	Los Angeles 24, Cleveland 17
1952	Cleveland Browns (8–4–0)	Detroit Lions (9–3–0)	Detroit 17, Cleveland 7
1953	Cleveland Browns (11–1–0)	Detroit Lions (10–2–0)	Detroit 17, Celeveland 16
1954	Cleveland Browns (9–3–0)	Detroit Lions (9–2–1)	Cleveland 56, Detroit 10
1955	Cleveland Browns (9–2–1)	Los Angeles Rams (8–3–1)	Cleveland 38, Los Angeles 14
1956	New York Giants (8–3–1)	Chicago Bears (9–2–1)	New York 47, Chicago Bears 7
1957	Cleveland Browns (9–2–1)	Detroit Lions (8–4–0)	Detroit 59, Cleveland 14
1958	New York Giants (9–3–0)	Baltimore Colts (9–3–0)	Baltimore 23, New York 17
1959	New York Giants (10–2–0)	Baltimore Colts (9–3–0)	Baltimore 31, New York 16
1960	Philadelphia Eagles (10–2–0)	Green Bay Packers (8–4–0)	Philadelphia 17, Green Bay 13
1961	New York Giants (10–3–1)	Green Bay Packers (11–3–0)	Green Bay 37, New York 0
1962	New York Giants (12–2–0)	Green Bay Packers (13–1–0)	Green Bay 16, New York 7
1963	New York Giants (11–3–0)	Chicago Bears (11–1–2)	Chicago 14, New York 10
1964	Cleveland Browns (10–3–1)	Baltimore Colts (12–2–0)	Cleveland 27, Baltimore 0
1965	Cleveland Browns (11–3–0)	Green Bay Packers (10–3–1)	Green Bay 23, Cleveland 12
1966	Dallas Cowboys (10–3–1)	Green Bay Packers (12–2–0)	Green Bay 34, Dallas 27

Source: World Almanac, 1992, 882.

TABLE 18.41 EVOLUTION OF THE NATIONAL FOOTBALL LEAGUE, 1946–1990

1946													
AAFC													
Eastern Division						Western Division						Playoffs	
Team	W	L	T	Pct.	PF	PA	Team	W	L	T	Pct.	PF	PA	AAFC championship
New York	10	3	1	.769	270	192	Cleveland	12	2	0	.857	423	137	Cleveland 14 vs. New York 9
Brooklyn	3	10	1	.231	226	339	San Francisco	9	5	0	.643	307	189	
Buffalo	3	10	1	.231	249	370	Los Angeles	7	5	2	.583	305	290	
Miami	3	11	0	.154	167	378	Chicago	5	6	3	.455	263	315	
NFL													
Eastern Division						Western Division						Playoffs	
Team	W	L	T	Pct.	PF	PA	Team	W	L	T	Pct.	PF	PA	NFL championship
N.Y. Giants	7	3	1	.700	236	162	Chicago Bears	8	2	1	.800	289	193	Chicago Bears 24 at N.Y. Giants 14
Philadelphia	6	5	0	.545	231	220	Los Angeles	6	4	1	.600	277	257	
Washington	5	5	1	.500	171	191	Green Bay	6	5	0	.545	148	158	
Pittsburgh	5	5	1	.500	136	117	Chi. Cardinals	6	5	0	.545	260	198	
Boston	2	8	1	.200	189	273	Detroit	1	10	0	.091	142	310	
1966													
AFL													
Eastern Division						Western Division						Playoffs	
Team	W	L	T	Pct.	PF	PA	Team	W	L	T	Pct.	PF	PA	AFL championship
Buffalo	9	4	1	.692	358	255	Kansas City	11	2	1	.846	448	276	Kansas City 31 at Buffalo 7
Boston Patriots	8	4	2	.667	315	283	Oakland	8	5	1	.615	315	288	
N.Y. Jets	6	6	2	.500	322	312	San Diego	7	6	1	.538	335	284	
Houston	3	11	0	.214	335	396	Denver	4	10	0	.286	196	381	
Miami	3	11	0	.214	213	362								

NFL														
Eastern Conference							**Western Conference**							**Playoffs**
Team	W	L	T	Pct.	PF	PA	Team	W	L	T	Pct.	PF	PA	**NFL championship**
Dallas	10	3	1	.769	445	239	Green Bay	12	2	0	.857	335	163	Green Bay 34 at Dallas 27
Cleveland	9	5	0	.643	403	259	Baltimore	9	5	0	.643	314	226	**Super Bowl I**
Philadelphia	9	5	0	.643	326	340	Los Angeles	8	6	0	.571	289	212	Green Bay 35, Kansas City 10,
St. Louis	8	5	1	.615	264	265	San Francisco	6	6	2	.500	320	325	at Los Angeles.
Washington	7	7	0	.500	351	355	Chicago	5	7	2	.417	234	272	
Pittsburgh	5	8	1	.385	316	347	Detroit	4	9	1	.308	206	317	
Atlanta	3	11	0	.214	204	437	Minnesota	4	9	1	.308	292	304	
N.Y. Giants	1	12	1	.077	263	501								

1990														
American Conference							**National Conference**							**Playoffs**
Eastern Division							**Eastern Division**							
Team	W	L	T	Pct.	PF	PA	Team	W	L	T	Pct.	PF	PA	**AFC wild-card playoffs**
Bufallo	13	3	0	.813	428	263	N.Y. Giants	13	3	0	.813	335	211	Miami 17 vs. Kansas City 16
Miami	12	4	0	.750	336	242	Philadelphia	10	6	0	.625	396	299	Cincinnati 41 vs. Houston 14
Indianapolis	7	9	0	.438	281	353	Washington	10	6	0	625	381	301	**AFC divisional playoffs**
N.Y. Jets	6	10	0	.375	.295	345	Dallas	7	9	0	.438	244	308	Buffalo 44 vs. Miami 34
New England	1	15	0	.063	181	446	Phoenix	5	11	0	.313	268	396	L.A. Raiders 20 vs. Cincinnati 10
Central Division							**Central Division**							**AFC championship**
Team	W	L	T	Pct.	PF	PA	Team	W	L	T	Pct.	PF	PA	Buffalo 51 vs. L.A. Raiders 3
Cincinnati	9	7	0	.563	360	352	Chicago	11	5	0	.688	348	280	**NFC wild-card playoffs**
Houston	9	7	0	.563	405	307	Tampa Bay	6	10	0	.375	264	367	Washington 20 at Philadelphia 6
Pittsburgh	9	7	0	563	292	240	Detroit	6	10	0	.375	373	413	Chicago 16 vs. New Orleans 6
Cleveland	3	13	0	.188	228	462	Green Bay	6	10	0	.375	271	347	**NFC divisional playoffs**
							Minnesota	6	10	0	.375	351	326	San Francisco 28 vs. Washington 10
Western Division							**Western Division**							N.Y. Giants 31 vs. Chicago 3
Team	W	L	T	Pct.	PF	PA	Team	W	L	T	Pct.	PF	PA	**NFC championship**
L.A. Raiders	12	4	0	.750	337	268								N.Y. Giants 15 at San Francisco 13
Kansas City	11	5	0	.688	369	257	San Francisco	14	2	0	.875	353	239	**Super Bowl XXV**
Seattle	9	7	0	.563	306	286	New Orleans	8	8	0	.500	274	275	N.Y. Giants 20 vs. Buffalo 19,
San Diego	6	10	0	.375	315	281	L.A. Rams	5	11	0	.313	345	412	at Tampa, Fla.
Denver	5	11	0	.313	331	374	Atlanta	5	11	0	.313	348	365	

Source: The Sporting News, *The Sporting News Pro Football Guide, 1998 Edition* (St. Louis, 1998), 298, 303, 314.

TABLE 18.42   THE SUPER BOWL, 1967–1990

Having merged in 1966, the AFL and NFL became conferences within a single new NFL. Starting in 1967, the conference champions played each other in what became known as the Super Bowl, one of the major sporting days and television spectacles of the year.

Bowl	Date	Winner	Head Coach	Score	Loser	Head Coach	Site
I	1/15/67	GREEN BAY	Vince Lombardi	35–10	Kansas City	Hank Stram	Los Angeles
II	1/14/68	GREEN BAY	Vince Lombardi	33–14	Oakland	John Rauch	Miami
III	1/12/69	NY Jets	Weeb Ewbank	16–7	BALTIMORE	Don Shula	Miami
IV	1/11/70	Kansas City	Hank Stram	23–7	MINNESOTA	Bud Grant	New Orleans
V	1/17/71	Baltimore	Don McCafferty	16–13	DALLAS	Tom Landry	Miami
VI	1/16/72	DALLAS	Tom Landry	24–3	Miami	Don Shula	New Orleans
VII	1/14/73	Miami	Don Shula	14–7	WASHINGTON	George Allen	Los Angeles
VIII	1/13/74	Miami	Don Shula	24–7	MINNESOTA	Bud Grant	Houston
IX	1/12/75	Pittsburgh	Chuck Noll	16–6	MINNESOTA	Bud Grant	New Orleans
X	1/18/76	Pittsburgh	Chuck Noll	21–17	DALLAS	Tom Landry	Miami
XI	1/9/77	Oakland	John Madden	32–14	MINNESOTA	Bud Grant	Pasadena
XII	1/15/78	DALLAS	Tom Landry	27–10	Denver	Red Miller	New Orleans
XIII	1/21/79	Pittsburgh	Chuck Noll	35–31	DALLAS	Tom Landry	Miami
XIV	1/20/80	Pittsburgh	Chuck Noll	31–19	LA RAMS	Ray Malavasi	Pasadena
XV	1/25/81	Oakland	Tom Flores	27–10	PHILADELPHIA	Dick Vermeil	New Orleans
XVI	1/24/82	SAN FRANCISCO	Bill Walsh	26–21	Cincinnati	Forrest Gregg	Pontiac, Mich.
XVII	1/30/83	WASHINGTON	Joe Gibbs	27–17	Miami	Don Shula	Pasadena
XVIII	1/22/84	LA Raiders	Tom Flores	38–9	WASHINGTON	Joe Gibbs	Tampa
XIX	1/20/85	SAN FRANCISCO	Bill Walsh	38–16	Miami	Don Shula	Stanford
XX	1/26/86	CHICAGO	Mike Ditka	46–10	New England	Raymond Berry	New Orleans
XXI	1/25/87	NY GIANTS	Bill Parcells	39–20	Denver	Dan Reeves	Pasadena
XXII	1/31/88	WASHINGTON	Joe Gibbs	42–10	Denver	Dan Reeves	San Diego
XXIII	1/22/89	SAN FRANCISCO	Bill Walsh	20–16	Cincinnati	Sam Wyche	Miami
XXIV	1/28/90	SAN FRANCISCO	George Seifert	55–10	Denver	Dan Reeves	New Orleans

Source: The 2001 ESPN Information Please Sports Almanac *(Boston, 2000), 236.*

TABLE 18.43 NO. 1 DRAFT CHOICES, 1946–1990

Year	Team	Player	Position	School
1946	Boston Yanks	Frank Dancewicz	QB	N. Dame
1947	Chicago Bears	Bob Fenimore	HB	Okla. A&M
1948	Washington	Harry Gilmer	QB	Alabama
1949	Philadelphia	Chuck Bednarik	C	Penn
1950	Detroit	**Leon Hart**	E	Notre Dame
1951	NY Giants	Kyle Rote	HB	SMU
1952	LA Rams	Bill Wade	QB	Vanderbilt
1953	San Francisco	Harry Babcock	E	Georgia
1954	Cleveland	Bobby Garrett	QB	Stanford
1955	Baltimore	George Shaw	QB	Oregon
1956	Pittsburgh	Gary Glick	DB	Colo. A&M
1957	Green Bay	**Paul Hornung**	QB	N. Dame
1958	Chicago Cards	King Hill	QB	Rice
1959	Green Bay	Randy Duncan	QB	Iowa
1960	NFL–LA Rams	**Billy Cannon**	HB	LSU
	AFL–No choice			
1961	NFL–Minnesota	Tommy Mason	HB	Tulane
	AFL–Buffalo	Ken Rice	G	Auburn
1962	NFL–Washington	**Ernie Davis**	HB	Syracuse
	AFL–Oakland	Roman Gabriel	QB	N.C. State
1963	NFL–LA Rams	**Terry Baker**	QB	Oregon St.
	AFL–Kan. City	Buck Buchanan	DT	Grambling
1964	NFL–San Fran	Dave Parks	E	Texas Tech
	AFL–Boston	Jack Concannon	QB	Boston Col.
1965	NFL–NY Giants	Tucker Frederickson	HB	Auburn
	AFL–Houston	Lawrence Elkins	E	Baylor

Year	Team	Player	Position	School
1966	NFL–Atlanta	Tommy Nobis	LB	Texas
	AFL–Miami	Jim Grabowski	FB	Illinois
1967	Baltimore	Bubba Smith	DT	Michigan St.
1968	Minnesota	Ron Yary	T	USC
1969	Buffalo	**O.J. Simpson**	RB	USC
1970	Pittsburgh	Terry Bradshaw	QB	La. Tech
1971	New England	**Jim Plunkett**	QB	Stanford
1972	Buffalo	Walt Patulski	DE	Notre Dame
1973	Houston	John Matuszak	DE	Tampa
1974	Dallas	Ed "Too Tall" Jones	DE	Tenn. St.
1975	Atlanta	Steve Bartkowski	QB	Calif.
1976	Tampa Bay	Lee Roy Selmon	DE	Oklahoma
1977	Tampa Bay	Ricky Bell	RB	USC
1978	Houston	**Earl Campbell**	RB	Texas
1979	Buffalo	Tom Cousineau	LB	Ohio St.
1980	Detroit	**Billy Sims**	RB	Oklahoma
1981	New Orleans	**George Rogers**	RB	S. Carolina
1982	New England	Kenneth Sims	DT	Texas
1983	Baltimore	John Elway	QB	Stanford
1984	New England	Irving Fryar	WR	Nebraska
1985	Buffalo	Bruce Smith	DE	Va. Tech
1986	Tampa Bay	**Bo Jackson**	RB	Auburn
1987	Tampa Bay	**V. Testaverde**	QB	Miami-Fla.
1988	Atlanta	Aundray Bruce	LB	Auburn
1989	Dallas	Troy Aikman	QB	UCLA
1990	Indianapolis	Jeff George	QB	Illinois

Note: Heisman Trophy winners in bold type.
Source: 1993 *Information Please Sports Almanac,* 238–39.

TABLE 18.44 AMERICAN FOOTBALL CONFERENCE LEADERS
(American Football League, 1960–1969)

Passing						Year	Pass-Receiving				
Player	Team	Atts	Com	YG	TD		Player	Team	Ct	YG	TD
Jack Kemp	Los Angeles	406	211	3,018	20	1960	Lionel Taylor	Denver	92	1,235	12
George Blanda	Houston	362	187	3,330	36	1961	Lionel Taylor	Denver	100	1,176	4
Len Dawson	Dallas	310	189	2,759	29	1962	Lionel Taylor	Denver	77	908	4
Tobin Rote	Kansas City	286	170	2,510	20	1963	Lionel Taylor	Denver	78	1,101	10
Len Dawson	Kansas City	354	199	2,879	30	1964	Charley Hennigan	Houston	101	1,546	8
John Hadl	San Diego	348	174	2,798	20	1965	Lionel Taylor	Denver	85	1,131	6
Len Dawson	Kansas City	284	159	2,527	26	1966	Lance Alworth	San Diego	73	1,383	13
Daryle Lamonica	Oakland	425	220	3,228	30	1967	George Sauer	N.Y. Jets	75	1,189	6
Len Dawson	Kansas City	224	131	2,109	17	1968	Lance Alworth	San Diego	68	1,312	10
Greg Cook	Cincinnati	197	106	1,854	15	1969	Lance Alworth	San Diego	64	1,003	8
Daryle Lamonica	Oakland	356	179	2,516	22	1970	Marlin Briscoe	Buffalo	57	1,036	8
Bob Griese	Miami	263	145	2,089	19	1971	Fred Biletnikoff	Oakland	61	929	9
Earl Morrall	Miami	150	83	1,360	11	1972	Fred Biletnikoff	Oakland	58	802	7
Ken Stabler	Oakland	260	163	1,997	14	1973	Fred Willis	Houston	57	371	1
Ken Anderson	Cincinnati	328	213	2,667	18	1974	Lydell Mitchell	Baltimore	72	544	2
Ken Anderson	Cincinnati	377	228	3,169	21	1975	Reggie Rucker	Cleveland	60	770	3
							Lydell Mitchell	Baltimore	60	554	4
Ken Stabler	Oakland	291	194	2,737	27	1976	MacArthur Lane	Kansas City	66	686	1
Bob Griese	Miami	307	180	2,252	22	1977	Lydell Mitchell	Baltimore	71	620	4
Terry Bradshaw	Pittsburgh	368	207	2,915	28	1978	Steve Largent	Seattle	71	1,168	8
Dan Fouts	San Diego	530	332	4,082	24	1979	Joe Washington	Baltimore	82	750	3
Brain Sipe	Cleveland	554	337	4,132	30	1980	Kellen Winslow	San Diego	89	1,290	9
Ken Anderson	Cincinnati	479	300	3,754	29	1981	Kellen Winslow	San Diego	88	1,075	10
Ken Anderson	Cincinnati	309	218	2,495	12	1982	Kellen Winslow	San Diego	54	721	6
Dan Marino	Miami	296	173	2,210	20	1983	Todd Christensen	L.A. Raiders	92	1,247	12
Dan Marino	Miami	564	362	5,084	48	1984	Ozzie Newsome	Cleveland	89	1,001	5
Ken O'Brien	N.Y. Jets	488	297	3,888	25	1985	Lionel James	San Diego	86	1,027	6
Dan Marino	Miami	623	378	4,746	44	1986	Todd Christensen	L.A. Raiders	95	1,153	8
Bernie Kosar	Cleveland	389	241	3,033	22	1987	Al Toon	N.Y. Jets	68	976	5
Boomer Esiason	Cincinnati	388	223	3,572	28	1988	Al Toon	N.Y. Jets	93	1,067	5
Boomer Esiason	Cincinnati	455	258	3,525	28	1989	Andre Reed	Buffalo	88	1,312	9
Jim Kelly	Buffalo	346	219	2,829	24	1990	Haywood Jeffires	Houston	74	1,048	8
							Drew Hill	Houston	74	1,019	5

Scoring						Year	Rushing				
Player	Team	TD	PAT	FG	Points		Player	Team	Yards	Attempts	TD
Gene Mingo	Denver	6	33	18	123	1960	Abner Haynes	Dallas	875	156	9
Gino Cappelletti	Boston	8	48	17	147	1961	Billy Cannon	Houston	948	200	6
Gene Mingo	Denver	4	32	27	137	1962	Cookie Gilchrest	Buffalo	1,096	214	13
Gino Cappelletti	Boston	2	35	22	113	1963	Clem Daniels	Oakland	1,099	215	3
Gino Cappelletti	Boston	7	36	25	155	1964	Cookie Gilchrest	Buffalo	981	230	6
Gino Cappelletti	Boston	9	27	17	132	1965	Paul Lowe	San Diego	1,121	222	7
Gino Cappelletti	Boston	6	35	16	119	1966	Jim Nance	Boston	1,458	299	11
George Blanda	Oakland	0	56	20	116	1967	Jim Nance	Boston	1,216	269	7
Jim Turner	N.Y. Jets	0	43	34	145	1968	Paul Robinson	Cincinnati	1,023	238	8
Jim Turner	N.Y. Jets	0	33	32	129	1969	Dick Post.	San Diego	873	182	6
Jan Stenerud	Kansas City	0	26	30	116	1970	Floyd Little	Denver	901	209	3
Garo Yepremian,	Miami	0	33	28	117	1971	Floyd Little	Denver	1,133	284	6
Bobby Howfield	N.Y. Jets	0	40	27	121	1972	O.J. Simpson	Buffalo	1,251	292	6
Roy Gerela	Pittsburgh	0	36	29	123	1973	O.J. Simpson	Buffalo	2,003	332	12
Roy Gerela	Pittsburgh	0	33	20	93	1974	Otis Amstrong	Denver	1,407	263	9
O.J. Simpson	Buffalo	23	0	0	138	1975	O.J. Simpson	Buffalo	1,817	329	16
Toni Linhart	Baltimore	0	49	20	109	1976	O.J. Simpson	Buffalo	1,503	290	8
Errol Mann	Oakland	0	39	20	99	1977	Mark van Eeghen	Oakland	1,273	324	7
Pat Leahy	N.Y. Jets	0	41	22	107	1978	Earl Campbell	Houston	1,450	302	13
John Smith	New England	0	46	23	115	1979	Earl Campbell	Houston	1,697	368	19
John Smith	New England	0	51	26	129	1980	Earl Campbell	Houston	1,934	373	13
Jim Breech	Cincinnati	0	49	22	115	1981	Earl Campbell	Houston	1,376	361	10
Marcus Allen	L.A. Raiders	14	0	0	84	1982	Freeman McNeil	N.Y. Jets	786	151	6
Gary Anderson	Pittsburgh	0	38	27	119	1983	Curt Warner	Seattle	1,446	335	13
Gary Anderson	Pittsburgh	0	45	24	117	1984	Earnest Jackson	San Diego	1,179	296	8
Gary Anderson	Pittsburgh	0	40	33	139	1985	Marcus Allen	L.A. Raiders	1,759	380	11
Tony Franklin	New England	0	44	32	140	1986	Curt Warner	Seattle	1,481	319	13
Jim Breech	Cincinnati	0	25	24	97	1987	Eric Dickerson	L.A. Rams, Indianapolis	1,288	283	6
Scott Norwood	Buffalo	0	33	32	129	1988	Eric Dickerson	Indianapolis	1,659	388	14
David Treadwell	Denver	0	39	27	120	1989	Christian Okoye	Kansas City	1,480	370	12
Nick Lowery	Kansas City	0	37	34	139	1990	Thurman Thomas	Buffalo	1,297	271	11

Note: Atts = attempts; Com = completions; YG = yards gained; TD = touchdowns; CT = catches; PAT = points after touchdown; FG = field goals.
Source: Robert Famighetti, *The World Almanac and Book of Facts, 1994* (Mahwah, N.J., 1993), 902.

TABLE 18.45   NATIONAL FOOTBALL CONFERENCE LEADERS

(National Football League, 1946–1969)

Rushing, NFL–NFC					
Year	Player	Team	Attempts	Yards	Avg.
1946	Bill Dudley	Pittsburgh	146	604	4.1
1947	Steve Van Buren	Philadelphia	217	1008	4.6
1948	Steve Van Buren	Philadelphia	201	945	4.7
1949	Steve Van Buren	Philadelphia	263	1146	4.4
1950	Marion Motley	Cleveland	140	810	5.8
1951	Eddie Price	New York Giants	271	971	3.6
1952	Dan Towler	Los Angeles	156	894	5.7
1953	Joe Perry	San Francisco	192	1018	5.3
1954	Joe Perry	San Francisco	173	1049	6.1
1955	Alan Ameche	Baltimore	213	961	4.5
1956	Rick Casares	Chicago Bears	234	1126	4.8
1957	Jim Brown	Cleveland	202	942	4.7
1958	Jim Brown	Cleveland	257	1527	5.9
1959	Jim Brown	Cleveland	290	1329	4.6
1960	Jim Brown	Cleveland	215	1257	5.8
1961	Jim Brown	Cleveland	305	1408	4.6
1962	Jim Taylor	Green Bay	272	1474	5.4
1963	Jim Brown	Cleveland	291	1863	6.4
1964	Jim Brown	Cleveland	280	1446	5.1
1965	Jim Brown	Cleveland	289	1544	5.3

Rushing, NFL–NFC					
Year	Player	Team	Attempts	Yards	Avg.
1966	Gale Sayers	Chicago	229	1231	5.4
1967	Leroy Kelly	Cleveland	235	1205	5.1
1968	Leroy Kelly	Cleveland	248	1239	5.0
1969	Gale Sayers	Chicago	236	1032	4.4
1970	Larry Brown	Washington	237	1125	4.7
1971	John Brockington	Green Bay	216	1105	5.1
1972	Larry Brown	Washington	285	1216	4.3
1973	John Brockington	Green Bay	265	1144	4.3
1974	Lawrence McCutcheon	Los Angeles	236	1109	4.7
1975	Jim Otis	St. Louis	269	1076	4.0
1976	Walter Payton	Chicago	311	1390	4.5
1977	Walter Payton	Chicago	339	1852	5.5
1978	Walter Payton	Chicago	333	1395	4.2
1979	Walter Payton	Chicago	369	1610	4.4
1980	Walter Payton	Chicago	317	1460	4.6
1981	George Rogers	New Orleans	378	1674	4.4
1982	Tony Dorsett	Dallas	177	745	4.2
1983	Eric Dickerson	Los Angeles	390	1808	4.6
1984	Eric Dickerson	Los Angeles	379	2105	5.6
1985	Gerald Riggs	Atlanta	397	1719	4.3
1986	Eric Dickerson	Los Angeles	404	1821	4.5
1987	Charles White	Los Angeles	324	1374	4.2
1988	Herschel Walker	Dallas	361	1514	4.2
1989	Barry Sanders	Detroit	280	1470	5.3
1990	Barry Sanders	Detroit	255	1304	5.1

(continued)

TABLE 18.45 (continued)

Scoring, NFL–NFC

Year	Player	Team	TD	FG	PAT	Pts.
1946	Ted Fritsch	Green Bay	10	9	13	100
1947	Pat Harder	Chicago Cards	7	7	39	102
1948	Pat Harder	Chicago Cards	6	7	53	110
1949	Gene Roberts	New York Giants	17	0	0	102
	& Pat Harder	Chicago Cards	8	3	45	102
1950	Doak Walker	Detroit	11	8	38	128
1951	Elroy Hirsch	Los Angeles	17	0	0	102
1952	Gordy Soltau	San Francisco	7	6	34	94
1953	Gordy Soltau	San Francisco	6	10	48	114
1954	Bobby Walston	Philadelphia	11	4	36	114
1955	Doak Walker	Detroit	7	9	27	96
1956	Bobby Layne	Detroit	5	12	33	99
1957	Sam Baker	Washington	1	14	29	77
	& Lou Groza	Cleveland	0	15	32	77
1958	Jim Brown	Cleveland	18	0	0	108
1959	Paul Hornung	Green Bay	7	7	31	94
1960	Paul Hornung	Green Bay	15	15	41	176
1961	Paul Hornung	Green Bay	10	15	41	146
1962	Jim Taylor	Green Bay	19	0	0	114
1963	Don Chandler	New York	0	18	52	106
1964	Lenny Moore	Baltimore	20	0	0	120
1965	Gale Sayers	Chicago	22	0	0	132
1966	Bruce Gossett	Los Angeles	0	28	29	113
1967	Jim Bakken	St. Louis	0	27	36	117
1968	Leroy Kelly	Cleveland	20	0	0	120
1969	Fred Cox	Minnesota	0	26	43	121
1970	Fred Cox	Minnesota	0	30	35	125
1971	Curt Knight	Washington	0	29	27	114
1972	Chester Marcol	Green Bay	0	33	29	128
1973	David Ray	Los Angeles	0	30	40	130
1974	Chester Marcol	Green Bay	0	25	19	94
1975	Chuck Foreman	Minnesota	22	0	0	132
1976	Mark Moseley	Washington	0	22	31	97
1977	Walter Payton	Chicago	16	0	0	96
1978	Frank Corrol	Los Angeles	0	29	31	118
1979	Mark Moseley	Washington	0	25	39	114
1980	Eddie Murray	Detroit	0	27	35	116
1981	Rafael Septien	Dallas	0	27	40	121
	& Eddie Murray	Detroit	0	25	46	121
1982	Wendell Tyler	Los Angeles	13	0	0	78
1983	Mark Moseley	Washington	0	33	62	161
1984	Ray Wersching	San Francisco	0	25	56	131
1985	Kevin Butler	Chicago	0	31	51	144
1986	Kevin Butler	Chicago	0	28	36	120
1987	Jerry Rice	San Francisco	23	0	0	138
1988	Mike Cofer	San Francisco	0	27	40	121
1989	Mike Cofer	San Francisco	0	29	49	136
1990	Chip Lohmiller	Washington	0	30	41	131

Note: TD = touchdowns; FG = field goals; PAT = points after touchdown.
Source: 1993 Information Please Sports Almanac, 230–31.

TABLE 18.46   NATIONAL FOOTBALL CONFERENCE LEADERS, 1946–1990

Passing NFL-NFC

Year	Player	Team	Att	Cmp	Yards	TD
1946	Bob Waterfield	Los Angeles	251	127	1747	18
1947	Sammy Baugh	Washington	354	210	2938	25
1948	Tommy Thompson	Philadelphia	246	141	1965	25
1949	Sammy Baugh	Washington	255	145	1903	18
1950	Norm Van Brocklin	Los Angeles	233	127	2061	18
1951	Bob Waterfield	Los Angeles	176	88	1566	13
1952	Norm Van Brocklin	Los Angeles	205	113	1736	14
1953	Otto Graham	Cleveland	258	167	2722	11
1954	Norm Van Brocklin	Los Angeles	260	139	2637	13
1955	Otto Graham	Cleveland	185	98	1721	15
1956	Ed Brown	Chicago	168	96	1667	11
1957	Tommy O'Connell	Cleveland	110	63	1229	9
1958	Eddie LeBaron	Washington	145	79	1365	11
1959	Charlie Conerly	New York	194	113	1706	14
1960	Milt Plum	Cleveland	250	151	2297	21
1961	Milt Plum	Cleveland	302	177	2416	16
1962	Bart Starr	Green Bay	285	178	2438	12
1963	Y.A. Tittle	New York	367	221	3145	36
1964	Bart Starr	Green Bay	272	163	2144	15
1965	Rudy Bukich	Chicago	312	176	2641	20

Passing NFL-NFC

Year	Player	Team	Att	Cmp	Yards	TD
1966	Bart Starr	Green Bay	251	156	2257	14
1967	Sonny Jurgensen	Washington	508	288	3747	31
1968	Earl Morrall	Baltimore	317	182	2909	26
1969	Sonny Jurgensen	Washington	442	274	3102	22
1970	John Brodie	San Francisco	378	223	2941	24
1971	Roger Staubach	Dallas	211	126	1882	15
1972	Norm Snead	New York	325	196	2307	17
1973	Roger Staubach	Dallas	286	179	2428	23
1974	Sonny Jurgensen	Washington	167	107	1185	11
1975	Fran Tarkenton	Minnesota	425	273	2994	25
1976	James Harris	Los Angeles	158	91	1460	8
1977	Roger Staubach	Dallas	361	210	2620	18
1978	Roger Staubach	Dallas	413	231	3190	25
1979	Roger Staubach	Dallas	461	267	3586	27
1980	Ron Jaworski	Philadelphia	451	257	3529	27
1981	Joe Montana	San Francisco	488	311	3565	19
1982	Joe Theismann	Washington	252	161	2033	13
1983	Steve Bartkowski	Atlanta	432	274	3167	22
1984	Joe Montana	San Francisco	432	279	3630	28
1985	Joe Montana	San Francisco	494	303	3653	27
1986	Tommy Kramer	Minnesota	372	208	3000	24
1987	Joe Montana	San Francisco	398	266	3054	31
1988	Wade Wilson	Minnesota	332	204	2746	15
1989	Don Majkowski	Green Bay	599	353	4318	27
1990	Joe Montana	San Francisco	520	321	3944	26

Receiving NFL-NFC

Year	Player	Team	No	Yards	Avg.	TD
1946	Jim Benton	Los Angeles	63	981	15.6	6
1947	Jim Keane	Chicago Bears	64	910	14.2	10
1948	Tom Fears	Los Angeles	51	698	13.7	4
1949	Tom Fears	Los Angeles	77	1013	13.2	9
1950	Tom Fears	Los Angeles	84	1116	13.3	7
1951	Elroy Hirsch	Los Angeles	66	1495	22.7	17
1952	Mac Speedie	Cleveland	62	911	14.7	5
1953	Pete Pihos	Philadelphia	63	1049	16.7	10
1954	Pete Pihos	Philadelphia	60	872	14.5	10
	& Billy Wilson	San Francisco	60	830	13.8	5
1955	Pete Pihos	Philadelphia	62	864	13.9	7
1956	Billy Wilson	San Francisco	60	889	14.8	5
1957	Billy Wilson	San Francisco	52	757	14.6	6
1958	Raymond Berry	Baltimore	56	794	14.2	9
	& Pete Retzlaff	Philadelphia	56	766	13.7	2
1959	Raymond Berry	Baltimore	66	959	14.5	14
1960	Raymond Berry	Baltimore	74	1298	17.5	10
1961	Red Phillips	Los Angeles	78	1092	14.0	5
1962	Bobby Mitchell	Washington	72	1384	19.2	11
1963	Bobby Joe Conrad	St. Louis	73	967	13.2	10
1964	Johnny Morris	Chicago	93	1200	12.9	10
1965	Dave Parks	San Francisco	80	1344	16.8	12
1966	Charley Taylor	Washington	72	1119	15.5	12
1967	Charley Taylor	Washington	70	990	14.1	9
1968	Clifton McNeil	San Francisco	71	994	14.0	7
1969	Dan Abramowicz	New Orleans	73	1015	13.9	7
1970	Dick Gordon	Chicago	71	1026	14.5	13
1971	Bob Tucker	New York	59	791	13.4	4
1972	Harold Jackson	Philadelphia	62	1048	16.9	4
1973	Harold Carmichael	Philadelphia	67	1116	16.7	9
1974	Charles Young	Philadelphia	63	696	11.0	3
1975	Chuck Foreman	Minnesota	73	691	9.5	9
1976	Drew Pearson	Dallas	58	806	13.9	6
1977	Ahmad Rashad	Minnesota	51	681	13.4	2
1978	Rickey Young	Minnesota	88	704	8.0	5
1979	Ahmad Rashad	Minnesota	80	1156	14.5	9
1980	Earl Cooper	San Francisco	83	567	6.8	4
1981	Dwight Clark	San Francisco	85	1105	13.0	4
1982	Dwight Clark	San Francisco	60	913	12.2	5
1983	Roy Green	St. Louis	78	1227	15.7	14
	Charlie Brown	Washington	78	1225	15.7	8
	& Earnest Gray	New York	78	1139	14.6	5
1984	Art Monk	Washington	106	1372	12.9	7
1985	Roger Craig	San Francisco	92	1016	11.0	6
1986	Jerry Rice	San Francisco	86	1570	18.3	15
1987	J.T. Smith	St. Louis	91	1117	12.3	8
1988	Henry Ellard	Los Angeles	86	1414	16.4	10
1989	Sterling Sharpe	Green Bay	90	1423	15.8	12
1990	Jerry Rice	San Francisco	100	1502	15.0	13

Note: Att = attempts; Cmp = completions; TD = touchdowns; No = number of receptions.
Source: 1993 Information Please Sports Almanc, 228–29.

TABLE 18.47 NFL MOST VALUABLE PLAYER, DEFENSIVE PLAYER OF THE YEAR, AND ROOKIE OF THE YEAR, 1957–1990

The Most Valuable Player is one of many awards given out annually by the Associated Press. The George Halas Trophy is awarded to the outstanding defensive player of the year, as chosen by a panel of sports experts. Rookie of the Year is one of many awards given out annually by *The Sporting News.* Many other organizations give out annual awards honoring the NFL's best players.

Most Valuable Player

Year	Player	Team
1957	Jim Brown	Cleveland
1958	Gino Marchetti	Baltimore Colts
1959	Charley Conerly	N.Y. Giants
1960	Norm Van Brocklin	Philadelphia
	Joe Schmidt	Detroit
1961	Paul Hornung	Green Bay
1962	Jim Taylor	Green Bay
1963	Y.A. Tittle	N.Y. Giants
1964	John Unitas	Baltimore Colts
1965	Jim Brown	Cleveland
1966	Bart Starr	Green Bay
1967	John Unitas	Baltimore Colts
1968	Earl Morrall	Baltimore Colts
1969	Roman Gabriel	L.A. Rams
1970	John Brodie	San Francisco
1971	Alan Page	Minnesota
1972	Larry Brown	Washington
1973	O.J. Simpson	Buffalo
1974	Ken Stabler	Oakland
1975	Fran Tarkenton	Minnesota
1976	Bert Jones	Baltimore
1977	Walter Payton	Chicago
1978	Terry Bradshaw	Pittsburgh
1979	Earl Campbell	Houston
1980	Brian Sipe	Cleveland
1981	Ken Anderson	Cincinnati
1982	Mark Moseley	Washington
1983	Joe Theismann	Washington
1984	Dan Marino	Miami
1985	Marcus Allen	L.A. Raiders
1986	Lawrence Taylor	N.Y. Giants
1987	John Elway	Denver
1988	Boomer Esiason	Cincinnati
1989	Joe Montana	San Francisco
1990	Joe Montana	San Francisco

Defensive Player of the Year

Year	Player	Team
1966	Larry Wilson	St. Louis
1967	Deacon Jones	Los Angeles
1968	Deacon Jones	Los Angeles
1969	Dick Butkus	Chicago
1970	Dick Butkus	Chicago
1971	Carl Eller	Minnesota
1972	Joe Greene	Pittsburgh
1973	Alan Page	Minnesota
1974	Joe Greene	Pittsburgh
1975	Curley Culp	Houston
1976	Jerry Sherk	Cleveland
1977	Harvey Martin	Dallas
1978	Randy Gradishar	Denver
1979	Lee Roy Selmon	Tampa Bay
1980	Lester Hayes	Oakland
1981	Joe Klecko	N.Y. Jets
1982	Mark Gastineau	N.Y. Jets
1983	Jack Lambert	Pittsburgh
1984	Mike Haynes	L.A. Raiders
1985	Howie Long	L.A. Raiders
	Andre Tippett	New England
1986	Lawrence Taylor	N.Y. Giants
1987	Reggie White	Philadelphia
1988	Mike Singletary	Chicago
1989	Tim Harris	Green Bay
1990	Bruce Smith	Buffalo

Rookie of the Year

Year	Player	Team
1964	Charley Taylor	Washington
1965	Gale Sayers	Chicago
1966	Tommy Nobis	Atlanta
1967	Mel Farr	Detroit
1968	Earl McCullouch	Detroit
1969	Calvin Hill	Dallas
1970	(NFC) Bruce Taylor	San Francisco
	(AFC) Dennis Shaw	Buffalo
1971	(NFC) John Brockington	Green Bay
	(AFC) Jim Plunkett	New England
1972	(NFC) Chester Marcol	Green Bay
	(AFC) Franco Harris	Pittsburgh
1973	(NFC) Chuck Foreman	Minnesota
	(AFC) Boobie Clark	Cincinnati
1974	(NFC) Wilbur Jackson	San Francisco
	(AFC) Don Woods	San Diego
1975	(NFC) Steve Bartkowski	Atlanta
	(AFC) Robert Brazile	Houston
1976	(NFC) Sammy White	Minnesota
	(AFC) Mike Haynes	New England
1977	(NFC) Tony Dorsett	Dallas
	(AFC) A. J. Duhe	Miami
1978	(NFC) Al Baker	Detroit
	(AFC) Earl Campbell	Houston
1979	(NFC) Ottis Anderson	St. Louis
	(AFC) Jerry Butler	Buffalo
1980	Billy Sims	Detroit
1981	George Rogers	New Orleans
1982	Marcus Allen	L.A. Raiders
1983	Dan Marino	Miami
1984	Louis Lipps	Pittsburgh
1985	Eddie Brown	Cincinnati
1986	Rueben Mayes	New Orleans
1987	Robert Awalt	St Louis
1988	Keith Jackson	Philadelphia
1989	Barry Sanders	Detroit
1990	Richmond Webb	Miami

Source: Robert Famighetti, *The World Almanac and Book of Facts, 2000* (Mahwah, N.J., 1999), 936.

TABLE 18.48 JIM THORPE TROPHY: MOST VALUABLE PLAYER CHOSEN BY NFL PLAYERS ASSOCIATION, 1955–1992

Year	Player	Team
1955	Harlon Hill	Chicago Bears
1956	Frank Gifford	N.Y. Giants
1957	John Unitas	Baltimore Colts
1958	Jim Brown	Cleveland Browns
1959	Charley Connerly	N.Y. Giants
1960	Norm Van Brocklin	Philadelphia Eagles
1961	Y.A. Tittle	N.Y. Giants
1962	Jim Taylor	Green Bay Packers
1963	Jim Brown	Cleveland Browns
	Y.A. Tittle	N.Y. Giants
1964	Lenny Moore	Baltimore Colts
1965	Jim Brown	Cleveland Browns
1966	Bart Starr	Green Bay Packers
1967	John Unitas	Baltimore Colts
1968	Earl Morrall	Baltimore Colts
1969	Roman Gabriel	Los Angeles Rams
1970	John Brodie	San Francisco 49ers
1971	Bob Griese	Miami Dolphins
1972	Larry Brown	Washington Redskins
1973	O.J. Simpson	Buffalo Bills
1974	Ken Stabler	Oakland Raiders
1975	Fran Tarkenton	Minnesota Vikings
1976	Bert Jones	Baltimore Colts
1977	Walter Payton	Chicago Bears
1978	Earl Campbell	Houston Oilers
1979	Earl Campbell	Houston Oilers

(continued)

TABLE 18.48 (continued)

Year	Player	Team
1980	Earl Campbell	Houston Oilers
1981	Ken Anderson	Cincinnati Bengals
1982	Dan Fouts	San Diego Chargers
1983	Joe Theismann	Washington Redskins
1984	Dan Marino	Miami Dolphins
1985	Walter Payton	Chicago Bears
1986	Phil Simms	N.Y. Giants
1987	Jerry Rice	San Francisco
1988	Roger Craig	San Francisco
1989	Joe Montana	San Francisco
1990	Warren Moon	Houston
1991	Thurman Thomas	Buffalo
1992	Steve Young	San Francisco

Source: World Almanac, 1994, 904.

TABLE 18.49 FIRST AFRICAN AMERICANS ON NATIONAL FOOTBALL LEAGUE TEAMS, 1945–1962

Year	Team	Player	Position
1946	Los Angeles Rams	Kenny Washington	RB
		Woody Strode	E
1948	New York Giants	Emlen Tunnel	DB
	Detroit Lions	Melvin Grooms	RB
		Bob Mann	E
1949	New York Yankees	Sherman Howard	RB
1951	Green Bay Packers	Bob Mann	E
1952	Chicago Bears	Eddie Macon	RB
1952	Chicago Cardinals	Clifton Anderson	E
		Ollie Matson	RB
		Wally Triplett	RB
1952	Philadelphia Eagles	Ralph Goldston	RB
		Donald Stevens	RB
1952	Pittsburgh Steelers	Jack Spinks	G
1953	Baltimore Colts	Melvin Embree	E
		George Taliaferro	RB
		Claude "Buddy" Young	RB
1962	Washington Redskins	Bobby Mitchell	RB
		Ron Hatcher	RB

RB = running back
E = end
G = guard
T = tackle
DB = defensive back
C = center

Source: Arthur Ashe, Jr., A Hard Road to Glory: A History of the African-American Athlete Since 1946 (New York, 1988), 398.

TABLE 18.50 NFL LEADERS IN SELECTED OFFENSIVE CATEGORIES, BY RACE, 1940–1989

Years	Passing		Rushing		Receiving		Field Goals		Punt Returns	
	No. Players	No. Black Americans	No. Players	No. Black Americans	No. Players	No. Black Americans	No. Players	No. Black Americans	No. Players	No. Black Americans
1940–49	10	0	10	0	10	0	14	0	9	0
1950–59	10	0	10	4	10	0	11	0	10	3
1960–69	20	0	20	9	20	9	20	0	20	12
1970–79	10	0	10	10	10	8	12	0	10	4
1980–89	10	0	10	9	10	7	10	0	10	8

Source: Jessie C. Smith and Carrell P. Horton, Statistical Record of Black America (Detroit, 1997), 819–20.

College Football

Expansion of the National Football League did not mean that college football passed into obscurity. The Saturday afternoon game remained part of the college setting and of those distinguishing forces that appeared with the arrival of autumn. In many ways the college game paralleled the professionals. The rules remained basically the same. Both levels adopted the principle of unlimited substitution. Protective wearing equipment, especially for the head, became more sophisticated. The colleges served as a training ground, a minor league, for the NFL. College players enjoyed the excitement and recognition of making the varsity, but at major schools they considered their experience a prelude to being drafted in a high round and a huge salary and new life with the pros.

College football, as with the NFL, took on national dimension, and even with membership in regional conferences, the Division I teams reached into other geographic areas for preconference and postconference competition. Most four-year colleges had football teams, but most of the attention and nearly all the television revenue went to a shifting circle of 100 or so schools from four or five power conferences and a diminishing number of independent competitors. Notre Dame University, for example, an independent that retained more in mystique than athletic dominance, wrestled a television contract from NBC worth $7 million a year. After the regular season came the bowl games—by 1990 there were 19 major ones—and an invitation to a bowl, which meant more money for the school and its conference, was most likely to go to the Big Ten, Big Eight, Pac 10, Southeastern, or other major athletic league.

College teams played nearly as many games as the professionals, and they played them essentially the same way. What they lacked was direct, legal payment of money to the players—but only the players, for other participants were paid; coaches could move interchangeably from one level to the other. The colleges also lacked a superbowl. Unlike the NFL, unlike college baseball and basketball, there was no playoff that produced an unchallenged national champion. The professionals, in fact, already had commandeered the name.

TABLE 18.51   NATIONAL DIVISION I COLLEGE FOOTBALL CHAMPIONS, 1946–1990

Year	Champion	Record	Bowl Game	Head Coach
1946	Notre Dame	8–0–1	No bowl	Frank Leahy
1947	Notre Dame	9–0–0	No bowl	Frank Leahy
	Michigan	10–0–0	Won Rose	Fritz Crisler
1948	Michigan	9–0–0	No bowl	Bennie Oosterbaan
1949	Notre Dame	10–0–0	No bowl	Frank Leahy
1950	Oklahoma	10–1–0	Lost Sugar	Bud Wilkinson
1951	Tennessee	10–1–0	Lost Sugar	Bob Neyland
1952	Michigan St	9–0–0	No bowl	Biggie Munn
1953	Maryland	10–1–0	Lost Orange	Jim Tatum
1954	Ohio St	10–0–0	Won Rose	Woody Hayes
	UCLA (UPI)	9–0–0	No bowl	Red Sanders
1955	Oklahoma	11–0–0	Won Orange	Bud Wilkinson
1956	Oklahoma	10–0–0	No bowl	Bud Wilkinson
1957	Auburn	10–0–0	No bowl	Shug Jordan
	Ohio St (UPI)	9–1–0	Won Rose	Woody Hayes
1958	Louisiana St	11–0–0	Won Sugar	Paul Dietzel
1959	Syracuse	11–0–0	Won Cotton	Ben Schwartzwalder
1960	Minnesota	8–2–0	Lost Rose	Murray Warmath
1961	Alabama	11–0–0	Won Sugar	Bear Bryant
1962	Southern Cal	11–0–0	Won Rose	John McKay
1963	Texas	11–0–0	Won Cotton	Darrell Royal
1964	Alabama	10–1–0	Lost Orange	Bear Bryant
1965	Alabama	9–1–1	Won Orange	Bear Bryant
	Michigan St (UPI)	10–1–0	Lost Rose	Duffy Daugherty
1966	Notre Dame	9–0–1	No bowl	Ara Parseghian
1967	Southern Cal	10–1–0	Won Rose	John McKay
1968	Ohio St	10–0–0	Won Rose	Woody Hayes
1969	Texas	11–0–0	Won Cotton	Darrell Royal
1970	Nebraska	11–0–1	Won Orange	Bob Devaney
	Texas (UPI)	10–1–0	Lost Cotton	Darrell Royal
1971	Nebraska	13–0–0	Won Orange	Bob Devaney
1972	Southern Cal	12–0–0	Won Rose	John McKay
1973	Notre Dame	11–0–0	Won Sugar	Ara Parseghian
	Alabama (UPI)	11–1–0	Lost Sugar	Bear Bryant
1974	Oklahoma	11–0–0	No bowl	Barry Switzer
	Southern Cal (UPI)	10–1–1	Won Rose	John McKay
1975	Oklahoma	11–1–0	Won Orange	Barry Switzer
1976	Pittsburgh	12–0–0	Won Sugar	Johnny Majors
1977	Notre Dame	11–1–0	Won Cotton	Dan Devine
1978	Alabama	11–1–0	Won Sugar	Bear Bryant
	Southern Cal (UPI)	12–1–0	Won Rose	John Robinson
1979	Alabama	12–0–0	Won Sugar	Bear Bryant
1980	Georgia	12–0–0	Won Sugar	Vince Dooley
1981	Clemson	12–0–0	Won Orange	Danny Ford
1982	Penn St	11–1–0	Won Sugar	Joe Paterno
1983	Miami (FL)	11–1–0	Won Orange	Howard Schnellenberger
1984	Brigham Young	13–0–0	Won Holiday	LaVell Edwards
1985	Oklahoma	11–1–0	Won Orange	Barry Switzer
1986	Penn St	12–0–0	Won Fiesta	Joe Paterno
1987	Miami (FL)	12–0–0	Won Orange	Jimmy Johnson
1988	Notre Dame	12–0–0	Won Fiesta	Lou Holtz
1989	Miami (FL)	11–1–0	Won Sugar	Dennis Erickson
1990	Colorado	11–1–1	Won Orange	Bill McCartney
	Georgia Tech (UPI)	11–0–1	Won Citrus	Bobby Ross

Note: Based on vote of Associated Press, 1946–90, and United Press, 1958–90. When the AP vote (of writers) and UPI vote (of coaches) did not agree, both selected teams were listed.
Source: Sports Illustrated 1997 Sports Almanac, 198.

TABLE 18.52 ALL-TIME DIVISION I-A PERCENTAGE LEADERS

(classified as Division I-A for the last 10 years; record includes bowl games; ties computed as half won and half lost)

Team	Years	Won	Lost	Tied	Percentage	Bowl Games		
						Won	Lost	Tied
Notre Dame	102	692	206	40	.759	10	6	0
Michigan	111	712	236	33	.743	10	12	0
Alabama	96	658	233	43	.728	23	17	3
Oklahoma	96	636	230	50	.722	18	10	1
Texas	98	671	257	31	.716	16	16	2
USC	98	613	236	51	.709	22	12	0
Ohio St.	101	633	257	51	.701	11	12	0
Penn St.	104	646	282	41	.688	16	9	2
Nebraska	101	644	284	39	.686	14	15	0
Tennessee	94	609	268	52	.684	17	14	0
Central Michigan	90	464	242	32	.650	3	1	0
Army	101	573	309	50	.642	2	1	0
Louisiana St.	97	561	304	46	.641	11	16	1
Miami (Ohio)	102	530	293	40	.637	5	2	0
Arizona St.	78	426	240	24	.635	9	5	1
Georgia	97	565	322	53	.630	13	13	3
Washington	101	534	303	49	.630	11	7	1
Auburn	98	537	324	45	.618	12	9	2
Florida St.	44	282	172	16	.617	11	7	2
Michigan St.	94	507	308	42	.616	5	5	0
Minnesota	107	547	334	43	.615	2	3	0
Colorado	101	532	340	33	.606	5	10	0
Arkansas	97	536	343	38	.605	9	14	3
UCLA	72	414	268	37	.602	9	7	1

Note: Statistics through the season of 1990.
Source: World Almanac, 1992, 900.

TABLE 18.53 NCAA FOOTBALL—MAJOR BOWL GAMES, 1946–1990

Rose Bowl (Pasadena, Calif.)

Year	Winner	Score	Loser	Score
1946	Alabama	34	Southern Cal.	14
1947	Illinois	45	UCLA	14
1948	Michigan	49	Southern California	0
1949	Northwestern	20	California	14
1950	Ohio State	17	California	14
1951	Michigan	14	California	6
1952	Illinois	40	Stanford	7
1953	Southern California	7	Wisconsin	0
1954	Michigan State	28	UCLA	20
1955	Ohio State	20	Southern Cal	7
1956	Michigan State	17	UCLA	14
1957	Iowa	35	Oregon State	19
1958	Ohio State	10	Oregon	7
1959	Iowa	38	California	12
1960	Washington	44	Wisconsin	8
1961	Washington	17	Minnesota	7
1962	Minnesota	21	UCLA	3
1963	Southern Cal.	42	Wisconsin	37
1964	Illinois	17	Washington	7
1965	Michigan	34	Oregon State	7
1966	UCLA	14	Michigan State	12
1967	Purdue	14	Southern California	13
1968	Southern California	14	Indiana	3
1969	Ohio State	27	Southern Cal.	16
1970	Southern California	10	Michigan	3
1971	Stanford	27	Ohio State	17
1972	Stanford	13	Michigan	12
1973	Southern Cal.	42	Ohio State	17
1974	Ohio State	42	Southern Cal.	21
1975	Southern Cal.	18	Ohio State	17

Rose Bowl (Pasadena, Calif.)

Year	Winner	Score	Loser	Score
1976	UCLA	23	Ohio State	10
1977	Southern California	14	Michigan	6
1978	Washington	27	Michigan	20
1979	Southern Cal.	17	Michigan	10
1980	Southern Cal	17	Ohio State	16
1981	Michigan	23	Washington	6
1982	Washington	28	Iowa	0
1983	UCLA	24	Michigan	14
1984	UCLA	45	Illinois	9
1985	Southern Cal	20	Ohio State	17
1986	UCLA	45	Iowa	28
1987	Arizona State	22	Michigan	15
1988	Michigan St.	20	Southern Cal.	17
1989	Michigan	22	Southern Cal.	14
1990	Southern Cal.	17	Michigan	10

Cotton Bowl (Dallas, Tex.)

Year	Winner	Score	Loser	Score
1946	Texas	40	Missouri	27
1947	Arkansas	0	Louisiana State	0
1948	So. Methodist	13	Penn State	13
1949	Southern Methodist	21	Oregon	13
1950	Rice	27	North Carolina	13
1951	Tennessee	20	Texas	14
1952	Kentucky	20	Texas Christian	7
1953	Texas	16	Tennessee	0
1954	Rice	28	Alabama	0
1955	Georgia Tech	14	Arkansas	6
1956	Mississippi	14	Texas Christian	13
1957	Texas Christian	28	Syracuse	27
1958	Navy	20	Rice	7
1959	Texas Christian	0	Air Force	0
1960	Syracuse	23	Texas	14

Cotton Bowl (Dallas, Tex.)

Year	Winner	Score	Loser	Score
1961	Duke	7	Arkansas	6
1962	Texas	12	Mississippi	7
1963	Louisiana State	13	Texas	0
1964	Texas	28	Navy	6
1965	Arkansas	10	Nebraska	7
1966	Louisiana State	14	Arkansas	7
1967	Georgia	24	Southern Methodist	9
1968	Texas A&M	20	Alabama	16
1969	Texas	36	Tennessee	13
1970	Texas	21	Notre Dame	17
1971	Notre Dame	24	Texas	11
1972	Penn State	30	Texas	6
1973	Texas	17	Alabama	13
1974	Nebraska	19	Texas	3
1975	Penn State	41	Baylor	20
1976	Arkansas	31	Georgia	10
1977	Houston	30	Maryland	21
1978	Notre Dame	38	Texas	10
1979	Notre Dame	35	Houston	34
1980	Houston	17	Nebraska	14
1981	Alabama	30	Baylor	2
1982	Texas	14	Alabama	12
1983	Southern Methodist	7	Pittsburgh	3
1984	Georgia	10	Texas	9
1985	Boston College	45	Houston	28
1986	Texas A&M	36	Auburn	16
1987	Ohio State	28	Texas A&M	12
1988	Texas A&M	35	Notre Dame	10
1989	UCLA	17	Arkansas	3
1990	Tennessee	31	Arkansas	27

Orange Bowl (Miami, Fla.)

Year	Winner	Score	Loser	Score
1946	Miami (Fla)	13	Holy Cross	6
1947	Rice	8	Tennessee	0
1948	Georgia Tech	20	Kansas	14
1949	Texas	41	Georgia	28
1950	Santa Clara	21	Kentucky	13
1951	Clemson	15	Miami (Fla)	14
1952	Georgia Tech	20	Baylor	14
1953	Alabama	61	Syracuse	6
1954	Oklahoma	7	Maryland	0
1955	Duke	34	Nebraska	7
1956	Oklahoma	20	Maryland	6
1957	Colorado	27	Clemson	21
1958	Oklahoma	48	Duke	21
1959	Oklahoma	21	Syracuse	6
1960	Georgia	14	Missouri	0
1961	Missouri	21	Navy	14
1962	Louisiana State	25	Colorado	7
1963	Alabama	17	Oklahoma	0
1964	Nebraska	13	Auburn	7
1965	Texas	21	Alabama	17
1966	Alabama	39	Nebraska	28
1967	Florida	27	Georgia Tech	12
1968	Oklahoma	26	Tennessee	24
1969	Penn State	15	Kansas	14
1970	Penn State	10	Missouri	3
1971	Nebraska	17	Louisiana State	12
1972	Nebraska	38	Alabama	6
1973	Nebraska	40	Notre Dame	6
1974	Penn State	16	Louisiana State	9
1975	Notre Dame	13	Alabama	11
1976	Oklahoma	14	Michigan	6
1977	Ohio State	27	Colorado	10

Orange Bowl (Miami, Fla.)

Year	Winner	Score	Loser	Score
1978	Arkansas	31	Oklahoma	6
1979	Oklahoma	31	Nebraska	21
1980	Oklahoma	24	Florida State	7
1981	Oklahoma	18	Florida State	17
1982	Clemson	22	Nebraska	15
1983	Nebraska	21	Louisiana State	20
1984	Miami (Fla.)	31	Nebraska	30
1985	Washington	28	Oklahoma	17
1986	Oklahoma	25	Penn State	10
1987	Oklahoma	42	Arkansas	8
1988	Miami (Fla.)	20	Oklahoma	14
1989	Miami (Fla.)	23	Nebraska	3
1990	Notre Dame	21	Colorado	6

Sugar Bowl (New Orleans, La.)

Year	Winner	Score	Loser	Score
1946	Oklahoma State	33	St. Mary's	13
1947	Georgia	20	North Carolina	10
1948	Texas	27	Alabama	7
1949	Oklahoma	14	North Carolina	6
1950	Oklahoma	35	Louisiana State	0
1951	Kentucky	13	Oklahoma	7
1952	Maryland	28	Tennessee	13
1953	Georgia Tech	24	Mississippi	7
1954	Georgia Tech	42	West Virginia	19
1955	Navy	21	Mississippi	0
1956	Georgia Tech	7	Pittsburgh	0
1957	Baylor	13	Tennessee	7
1958	Mississippi	39	Texas	7
1959	Louisiana State	7	Clemson	0
1960	Mississippi	21	Louisiana State	0
1961	Mississippi	14	Rice	6
1962	Alabama	10	Arkansas	3
1963	Mississippi	17	Arkansas	13
1964	Alabama	12	Mississippi	7
1965	Louisiana State	13	Syracuse	10
1966	Missouri	20	Florida	18
1967	Alabama	34	Nebraska	7
1968	Louisiana State	20	Wyoming	13
1969	Arkansas	16	Georgia	2
1970	Mississippi	27	Arkansas	22
1971	Tennessee	34	Air Force	13
1972	Oklahoma	40	Auburn	22
1973	Oklahoma	14	Penn State	0
1974	Notre Dame	24	Alabama	23
1975	Nebraska	13	Florida	10
1976	Alabama	13	Penn State	6
1977	Pittsburgh	27	Georgia	3
1978	Alabama	35	Ohio State	6
1979	Alabama	14	Penn State	7
1980	Alabama	24	Arkansas	9
1981	Georgia	17	Notre Dame	10
1982	Pittsburgh	24	Georgia	20
1983	Penn State	27	Georgia	23
1984	Auburn	9	Michigan	7
1985	Nebraska	28	Louisiana State	10
1986	Tennessee	35	Miami (Fla.)	7
1987	Nebraska	30	Louisiana State	15
1988	Syracuse	16	Auburn	16
1989	Florida State	13	Auburn	7
1990	Miami (Fla.)	33	Alabama	25

Source: John W. Wright, *The Universal Almanac, 1995* (New York, 1994), 670.

TABLE 18.54 INDIVIDUAL ACHIEVEMENTS, 1946–1990

Heisman Trophy Winners[a]

Year	Winner	Team	Position
1946	Glenn Davis	Army	HB
1947	John Lujack	Notre Dame	QB
1948	Doak Walker	SMU	HB
1949	Leon Hart	Notre Dame	E
1950	Vic Janowicz	Ohio State	HB
1951	Richard Kazmaier	Princeton	HB
1952	Billy Vessels	Oklahoma	HB
1953	John Lattner	Notre Dame	HB
1954	Alan Ameche	Wisconsin	FB
1955	Howard Cassady	Ohio St.	HB
1956	Paul Hornung	Notre Dame	QB
1957	John Crow	Texas A & M	HB
1958	Pete Dawkins	Army	HB
1959	Billy Cannon	La. State	HB
1960	Joe Bellino	Navy	HB
1961	Ernest Davis	Syracuse	HB
1962	Terry Baker	Oregon State	QB
1963	Roger Staubach	Navy	QB
1964	John Huarte	Notre Dame	QB
1965	Mike Garrett	USC	HB
1966	Steve Spurrier	Florida	QB
1967	Gary Beban	UCLA	QB
1968	O. J. Simpson	USC	RB
1969	Steve Owens	Oklahoma	RB
1970	Jim Plunkett	Stanford	QB
1971	Pat Sullivan	Auburn	QB
1972	Johnny Rodgers	Nebraska	RB-R
1973	John Cappelletti	Penn State	RB
1974	Archie Griffin	Ohio State	RB
1975	Archie Griffin	Ohio State	RB
1976	Tony Dorsett	Pittsburgh	RB
1977	Earl Campbell	Texas	RB
1978	Billy Sims	Oklahoma	RB
1979	Charles White	USC	RB
1980	George Rogers	So Carolina	RB
1981	Marcus Allen	USC	RB
1982	Herschel Walker	Georgia	RB
1983	Mike Rozier	Nebraska	RB
1984	Doug Flutie	Boston College	QB
1985	Bo Jackson	Auburn	RB
1986	Vinny Testaverde	Miami	QB
1987	Tim Brown	Notre Dame	WR
1988	Barry Sanders	Oklahoma St.	RB
1989	Andre Ware	Houston	QB
1990	Ty Detmer	BYU	QB

[a] Awarded annually to the nation's outstanding college football player.
Source: World Almanac, 1992, 900.

Outland Award[b]

Year	Winner	Team	Position
1946	George Connor	Notre Dame	T
1947	Joe Steffy	Army	G
1948	Bill Fischer	Notre Dame	G
1949	Ed Bagdon	Michigan St.	G
1950	Bob Gain	Kentucky	T
1951	Jim Weatherall	Oklahoma	T
1952	Dick Modzelewski	Maryland	T
1953	J. D. Roberts	Oklahoma	G
1954	Bill Brooks	Arkansas	G
1955	Calvin Jones	Iowa	G

Outland Award

Year	Winner	Team	Position
1956	Jim Parker	Ohio State	G
1957	Alex Karras	Iowa	T
1958	Zeke Smith	Auburn	G
1959	Mike McGee	Duke	T
1960	Tom Brown	Minnesota	G
1961	Merlin Olsen	Utah State	T
1962	Bobby Bell	Minnesota	T
1963	Scott Appleton	Texas	T
1964	Steve Delong	Tennessee	T
1965	Tommy Nobis	Texas	G
1966	Loyd Phillips	Arkansas	T
1967	Ron Yary	Southern Cal	T
1968	Bill Stanfill	Georgia	T
1969	Mike Reid	Penn State	DT
1970	Jim Stillwagon	Ohio State	LB
1971	Larry Jacobson	Nebraska	DT
1972	Rich Glover	Nebraska	MG
1973	John Hicks	Ohio State	G
1974	Randy White	Maryland	DE
1975	Lee Roy Selmon	Oklahoma	DT
1976	Ross Browner	Notre Dame	DE
1977	Brad Shearer	Texas	DT
1978	Greg Roberts	Oklahoma	G
1979	Jim Ritcher	No. Carolina St.	C
1980	Mark May	Pittsburgh	OT
1981	Dave Rimington	Nebraska	C
1982	Dave Rimington	Nebraska	C
1983	Dean Steinkuhler	Nebraska	G
1984	Bruce Smith	Virginia Tech	DT
1985	Mike Ruth	Boston College	DT
1986	Jason Buck	BYU	DT
1987	Chad Hennings	Air Force	DT
1988	Tracy Rocker	Auburn	DT
1989	Mohammed Elewonibi	BYU	G
1990	Russell Maryland	Miami (Fla.)	DT

Honoring the outstanding interior lineman, selected by the Football Writers' Association of America.
Source: World Almanac, 1992, 898.

TABLE 18.55 VINCE LOMBARDI AWARD, 1970–1990

Honoring the outstanding lineman, sponsored by the Rotary Club of Houston

Year	Winner	Team	Position
1970	Jim Stillwagon	Ohio State	MG
1971	Walt Patulski	Notre Dame	DE
1972	Rich Glover	Nebraska	MG
1973	John Hicks	Ohio State	OT
1974	Randy White	Maryland	DT
1975	Lee Roy Selmon	Oklahoma	DT
1976	Wilson Whitley	Houston	DT
1977	Ross Browner	Notre Dame	DE
1978	Bruce Clark	Penn State	DT
1979	Brad Budde	USC	G
1980	Hugh Green	Pittsburgh	DE
1981	Kenneth Sims	Texas	DT
1982	Dave Rimington	Nebraska	C
1983	Dean Steinkuhler	Nebraska	G
1984	Tony Degrate	Texas	DT
1985	Tony Casillas	Oklahoma	NG
1986	Cornelius Bennett	Alabama	DE
1987	Chris Spielman	Ohio State	LB
1988	Tracy Rocker	Auburn	DT
1989	Percy Snow	Michigan St.	LB
1990	Chris Zorich	Notre Dame	DL

Source: World Almanac, 1992, 900.

TABLE 18.56 COLLEGE FOOTBALL AWARD WINNERS, BY RACE, 1935–1990

Award/Trophy	Years	Number of Awards	Number Awarded to Black Athletes	Year of First Award to Black Athletes
Heisman Trophy	1935–1990	56	17	1961
Outland Trophy	1946–1990	45	11	1955
Lombardi Award	1970–1990	21	11	1972
Maxwell Award[a]	1937–1990	54	12	1968
Davey O'Brien Award[b]	1981–1990	10	2	1987
Butkus Award[c]	1985–1990	6	3	1988
Jim Thorpe Award[d]	1986–1990	6	6	1986
Doak Walker Award[e]	1990	1	1	1990

[a] Top player award (Maxwell Club).
[b] Top quarterback award.
[c] Top linebacker award.
[d] Top defensive back award.
[e] Top junior or senior running back.
Source: Horton and Smith, *Record of Black America* (1993), 841.

TABLE 18.57 RUSHING, 1946–1990

Individual championship decided on Rushing Yards (1937–1969) and on Yards per Game (since 1970).

Year	Player	Team	Car	Yards
1946	Rudy Mobley	Hardin-Simmons	277	1262
1947	Wilton Davis	Hardin-Simmons	193	1173
1948	Fred Wendt	Texas Mines	184	1570
1949	John Dottley	Ole Miss	208	1312
1950	Wilford White	Arizona St	199	1502
1951	Ollie Matson	San Francisco	245	1566
1952	Howie Waugh	Tulsa	164	1372
1953	J.C. Caroline	Illinois	194	1256
1954	Art Luppino	Arizona	179	1359
1955	Art Luppino	Arizona	209	1313
1956	Jim Crawford	Wyoming	200	1104
1957	Leon Burton	Arizona St	117	1126
1958	Dick Bass	Pacific	205	1361
1959	Pervis Atkins	New Mexico St	130	971
1960	Bob Gaiters	New Mexico St	197	1338
1961	Jim Pilot	New Mexico St	191	1278
1962	Jim Pilot	New Mexico St	208	1247
1963	Dave Casinelli	Memphis St	219	1016
1964	Brian Piccolo	Wake Forest	252	1044
1965	Mike Garrett	USC	267	1440
1966	Ray McDonald	Idaho	259	1329
1967	O.J. Simpson	USC	266	1415
1968	O.J. Simpson	USC	355	1709
1969	Steve Owens	Oklahoma	358	1523

Year	Player	Team	Car	Yards	P/Gm
1970	Ed Marinaro	Cornell	285	1425	158.3
1971	Ed Marinaro	Cornell	356	1881	209.0
1972	Pete Van Valkenburg	BYU	232	1386	138.6
1973	Mark Kellar	Northern Ill	291	1719	156.3
1974	Louie Giammona	Utah St.	329	1534	153.4
1975	Ricky Bell	USC	357	1875	170.5
1976	Tony Dorsett	Pittsburgh	338	1948	177.1
1977	Earl Campbell	Texas	267	1744	158.5
1978	Billy Sims	Oklahoma	231	1762	160.2
1979	Charles White	USC	293	1803	180.3
1980	George Rogers	S. Carolina	297	1781	161.9
1981	Marcus Allen	USC	403	2342	212.9
1982	Ernest Anderson	Okla St	353	1877	170.6
1983	Mike Rozier	Nebraska	275	2148	179.0
1984	Keith Byars	Ohio St	313	1655	150.5
1985	Lorenzo White	Mich St	386	1908	173.5
1986	Paul Palmer	Temple	346	1866	169.6
1987	Ickey Woods	UNLV	259	1658	150.7
1988	Barry Sanders	Okla St.	344	2628	238.9
1989	Anthony Thompson	Ind	358	1793	163.0
1990	Gerald Hudson	Okla St	279	1642	149.3

Note: Car = carries; Yards = rushing yards; P/Gm = yards per game.
Source: 1993 Information Please Sports Almanac, 175.

TABLE 18.58 RECEIVING, 1946–1990

Championship decided on Passes Caught (1973–1969), and on Catches per Game (since 1970).

Year	Player	Team	No	TD	Yds
1946	Neil Armstrong	Okla A&M	32	1	479
1947	Barney Poole	Ole Miss	52	8	513
1948	Red O'Quinn	Wake Forest	39	7	605
1949	Art Weiner	N. Carolina	52	7	762
1950	Gordon Cooper	Denver	46	8	569
1951	Dewey McConnell	Wyoming	47	9	725
1952	Ed Brown	Fordham	57	6	774
1953	John Carson	Georgia	45	4	663
1954	Jim Hanifan	California	44	7	569
1955	Hank Burnine	Missouri	44	2	594
1956	Art Powell	San Jose St	40	5	583
1957	Stuart Vaughan	Utah	53	5	756
1958	Dave Hibbert	Arizona	61	4	606
1959	Chris Burford	Stanford	61	6	756
1960	Hugh Campbell	Wash St	66	10	881
1961	Hugh Campbell	Wash St	53	5	723
1962	Vern Burke	Oregon St	69	10	1007
1963	Lawrence Elkins	Baylor	70	8	873
1964	Howard Twilley	Tulsa	95	13	1178
1965	Howord Twilley	Tulsa	134	16	1779
1966	Glenn Meltzer	Wichita St	91	4	1115
1967	Bob Goodridge	Vanderbilt	79	6	1114
1968	Ron Sellers	Florida St	86	12	1496
1969	Jerry Hendren	Idaho	95	12	1452

Year	Player	Team	No	P/Gm	TD	Yds
1970	Mike Mikolayunas	Davidson	87	8.7	8	1128
1971	Tom Reynolds	S.Diego St	67	6.7	7	1070
1972	Tom Forzani	Utah St	85	7.7	8	1169
1973	Jay Miller	BYU	100	9.1	8	1181
1974	Dwight McDonald	S.Diego St	86	7.8	7	1157
1975	Bob Farnham	Brown	56	6.2	2	701
1976	Billy Ryckman	La. Tech	77	7.0	10	1382
1977	Wayne Tolleson	W. Carolina	73	6.6	7	1101
1978	Dave Petzke	Northern Ill	91	8.3	11	1217
1979	Rick Beasley	Appalach. St	74	6.7	12	1205
1980	Dave Young	Purdue	67	6.1	8	917
1981	Pete Harvey	N. Texas St	57	6.3	3	743
1982	Vincent White	Stanford	68	6.8	8	677
1983	Keith Edwards	Vanderbilt	97	8.8	8	909
1984	David Williams	Illinois	101	9.2	8	1278
1985	Rodney Carter	Purdue	98	8.9	4	1099
1986	Mark Templeton	L. Beach St	99	9.0	2	688
1987	Jason Phillips	Houston	99	9.0	3	875
1988	Jason Phillips	Houston	108	9.8	15	1444
1989	Manny Hazard	Houston	142	12.9	22	1689
1990	Manny Hazard	Houston	78	7.8	9	946

Note: No = number of receptions; TD = touchdowns; Yds = yards; P/Gm = catches per game.
Source: 1993 Information Please Sports Almanac, 177.

TABLE 18.59 PASSING, 1946–1990

Individual championship decided on Completions (1937–1969), on Completions per Game (1970–1978), and on Passing Efficiency rating points (since 1979)

Year	Player	Team	Cmp	Pct	TD	Yds
1946	Travis Tidwell	Auburn	79	.500	5	943
1947	Charlie Conerly	Ole Miss	133	.571	18	1367
1948	Stan Heath	Nev-Reno	126	.568	22	2005
1949	Adrian Burk	Baylor	110	.576	14	1428
1950	Don Heinrich	Washington	134	.606	14	1846
1951	Don Klosterman	Loyola CA	159	.505	9	1843
1952	Don Heinrich	Washington	137	.507	13	1647
1953	Bob Garrett	Stanford	118	.576	17	1637
1954	Paul Larson	California	125	.641	10	1537
1955	George Welsh	Navy	94	.627	8	1319
1956	John Brodie	Stanford	139	.579	12	1633
1957	Ken Ford	H-Simmons	115	.561	14	1254
1958	Buddy Humphrey	Baylor	112	.574	7	1316
1959	Dick Norman	Stanford	152	.578	11	1963
1960	Harold Stephens	H-Simm.	145	.566	3	1254
1961	Chon Gallegos	S. Jose St	117	.594	14	1480
1962	Don Trull	Baylor	125	.546	11	1627
1963	Don Trull	Baylor	174	.565	12	2157
1964	Jerry Rhome	Tulsa	224	.687	32	2870
1965	Bill Anderson	Tulsa	296	.582	30	3464
1966	John Eckman	Wichita St	195	.426	7	2339
1967	Terry Stone	N. Mexico	160	.476	9	1946
1968	Chuck Hixon	SMU	265	.566	21	3103
1969	John Reaves	Florida	222	.561	24	2896

Year	Player	Team	Cmp	P/GM	TD	Yds
1970	Sonny Sixkiller	Wash	186	18.6	15	2303
1971	Brian Sipe	S. Diego St.	196	17.8	17	2532
1972	Don Strock	Va. Tech	228	20.7	16	3243
1973	Jesse Freitas	S. Diego St.	227	20.6	21	2993
1974	Steve Bartkowski	Cal	182	16.5	12	2580
1975	Craig Penrose	S. Diego St.	198	18.0	15	2660
1976	Tommy Kramer	Rice	269	24.5	21	3317
1977	Guy Benjamin	Stanford	208	20.8	19	2521
1978	Stever Dils	Stanford	247	22.5	22	2943

Year	Player	Team	Cmp	TD	Yds	Rating
1979	Turk Schonert	Stanford	148	19	1922	163.0
1980	Jim McMahon	BYU	284	47	4571	176.9
1981	Jim McMahon	BYU	272	30	3555	155.0
1982	Tom Ramsey	UCLA	191	21	2824	153.5
1983	Steve Young	BYU	306	33	3902	168.5
1984	Doug Flutie	BC	233	27	3454	152.9
1985	Jim Harbaugh	Michigan	139	18	1913	163.7
1986	V. Testaverde	Miami-FL	175	26	2557	165.8
1987	Don McPherson	Syracuse	129	22	2341	164.3
1988	Timm Rosenbach	Wash. St.	199	23	2791	162.0
1989	Ty Detmer	BYU	265	32	4560	175.6
1990	Shawn Moore	Virginia	144	21	2262	160.7

Note: Cmp = completions; Pct = percentage of completions; TD = touchdowns; Yds = yards; P/Gm = completions per game.
Source: 1993 Information Please Sports Almanac, 176.

TABLE 18.60 OTHER MEN'S NCAA CHAMPIONS, 1947–1990

Baseball	
Year	**Champion**
1947	California
1948	Southern California
1949	Texas
1950	Texas
1951	Oklahoma
1952	Holy Cross
1953	Michigan
1954	Missouri
1955	Wake Forest
1956	Minnesota
1957	California
1958	Southern California
1959	Oklahoma State
1960	Minnesota
1961	Southern California
1962	Michigan
1963	Southern California
1964	Minnesota
1965	Arizona State
1966	Ohio State
1967	Arizona State
1968	Southern California
1969	Arizona State
1970	Southern California
1971	Southern California
1972	Southern California
1973	Southern California
1974	Southern California
1975	Texas
1976	Arizona
1977	Arizona State
1978	Southern California
1979	California State, Fullerton
1980	Arizona
1981	Arizona State
1982	Miami (Fla.)
1983	Texas
1984	California State, Fullerton
1985	Miami (Fla.)
1986	Arizona
1987	Stanford
1988	Stanford
1989	Wichita State
1990	Georgia

Ice Hockey	
Year	**Champion**
1948	Michigan
1949	Boston College
1950	Colorado College
1951	Michigan
1952	Michigan
1953	Michigan
1954	Rensselaer
1955	Michigan
1956	Michigan
1957	Colorado College
1958	Denver
1959	North Dakota
1960	Denver
1961	Denver
1962	Michigan Tech
1963	North Dakota
1964	Michigan
1965	Michigan Tech

Ice Hockey	
Year	Champion
1966	Michigan State
1967	Cornell
1968	Denver
1969	Denver
1970	Cornell
1971	Boston University
1972	Boston University
1973	Wisconsin
1974	Minnesota
1975	Michigan Tech
1976	Minnesota
1977	Wisconsin
1978	Boston University
1979	Minnesota
1980	North Dakota
1981	Wisconsin
1982	North Dakota
1983	Wisconsin
1984	Bowling Green
1985	Rensselaer
1986	Michigan State
1987	North Dakota
1988	Lake Superior State
1989	Harvard
1990	Wisconsin

Lacrosse	
Year	Champion
1971	Cornell
1972	Virginia
1973	Maryland
1974	Johns Hopkins
1975	Maryland
1976	Cornell
1977	Cornell
1978	Johns Hopkins
1979	Johns Hopkins
1980	Johns Hopkins
1981	North Carolina
1982	North Carolina
1983	Syracuse
1984	Johns Hopkins
1985	Johns Hopkins
1986	North Carolina
1987	Johns Hopkins
1988	Syracuse
1989	Syracuse
1990	Syracuse

Soccer	
Year	Champion
1959	St. Louis
1960	St. Louis
1961	West Chester
1962	St. Louis
1963	St. Louis
1964	Navy
1965	St. Louis
1966	San Francisco
1967	Michigan State
	St. Louis
1968	Maryland
	Michigan State
1969	St. Louis
1970	St. Louis

Soccer	
Year	Champion
1971	Vacated
1972	St. Louis
1973	St. Louis
1974	Howard
1975	San Francisco
1976	San Francisco
1977	Hartwick
1978	Vacated
1979	Southern Illinois Univ. at Edwardsville
1980	San Francisco
1981	Connecticut
1982	Indiana
1983	Indiana
1984	Clemson
1985	UCLA
1986	Duke
1987	Clemson
1988	Indiana
1989	Santa Clara
	Virginia
1990	UCLA

Tennis	
Year	Champion
1946	Southern California
1947	William and Mary
1948	William and Mary
1949	San Francisco
1950	UCLA
1951	Southern California
1952	UCLA
1953	UCLA
1954	UCLA
1955	Southern California
1956	UCLA
1957	Michigan
1958	Southern California
1959	Notre Dame
	Tulane
1960	UCLA
1961	UCLA
1962	Southern California
1963	Southern California
1964	Southern California
1965	UCLA
1966	Southern California
1967	Southern California
1968	Southern California
1969	Southern California
1970	UCLA
1971	UCLA
1972	Trinity (Tex.)
1973	Stanford
1974	Stanford
1975	UCLA
1976	Southern California
	UCLA
1977	Stanford
1978	Stanford
1979	UCLA
1980	Stanford
1981	Stanford
1982	UCLA
1983	Stanford
1984	UCLA
1985	Georgia

(continued)

TABLE 18.60   (continued)

Swimming and Diving	
Year	Champion
1954	Ohio State
1955	Ohio State
	Michigan
1956	Ohio State
1957	Michigan
1958	Michigan
1959	Michigan
1960	Southern California
1961	Michigan
1962	Ohio State
1963	Southern California
1964	Southern California
1965	Southern California
1966	Southern California
1967	Stanford
1968	Indiana
1969	Indiana
1970	Indiana
1971	Indiana
1972	Indiana
1973	Indiana
1974	Southern California
1975	Southern California
1976	Southern California
1977	Southern California
1978	Tennessee
1979	California
1980	California
1981	Texas
1982	UCLA
1983	Florida
1984	Florida
1985	Stanford
1986	Stanford
1987	Stanford
1988	Texas
1989	Texas
1990	Texas

Tennis	
Year	Champion
1986	Stanford
1987	Georgia
1988	Stanford
1989	Stanford
1990	Stanford

Volleyball	
Year	Champion
1970	UCLA
1971	UCLA
1972	UCLA
1973	San Diego State
1974	UCLA
1975	UCLA
1976	UCLA
1977	Southern California
1978	Pepperdine
1979	UCLA
1980	Southern California
1981	UCLA
1982	UCLA
1983	UCLA
1984	UCLA
1985	Pepperdine
1986	Pepperdine
1987	UCLA
1988	Southern California
1989	UCLA
1990	Southern California

Water Polo	
Year	Champion
1969	UCLA
1970	Univ. of California, Irvine
1971	UCLA
1972	UCLA
1973	California
1974	California
1975	California
1976	Stanford
1977	California
1978	Stanford
1979	Univ. of California, Santa Barbara
1980	Stanford
1981	Stanford
1982	Univ. of California, Irvine
1983	California
1984	California
1985	Stanford
1986	Stanford
1987	California
1988	California
1989	California
1990	California

Swimming and Diving	
Year	Champion
1946	Ohio State
1947	Ohio State
1948	Michigan
1949	Ohio State
1950	Ohio State
1951	Yale
1952	Ohio State
1953	Yale

Wrestling	
Year	Champion
1946	Oklahoma State
1947	Cornell College
1948	Oklahoma State
1949	Oklahoma State
1950	Northern Iowa
1951	Oklahoma
1952	Oklahoma
1953	Penn State
1954	Oklahoma State
1955	Oklahoma State
1956	Oklahoma State
1957	Oklahoma
1958	Oklahoma State
1959	Oklahoma State
1960	Oklahoma
1961	Oklahoma State
1962	Oklahoma State
1963	Oklahoma
1964	Oklahoma State
1965	Iowa State
1966	Oklahoma State
1967	Michigan State
1968	Oklahoma State
1969	Iowa State
1970	Iowa State

Wrestling

Year	Champion
1971	Oklahoma State
1972	Iowa State
1973	Iowa State
1974	Oklahoma
1975	Iowa
1976	Iowa
1977	Iowa State
1978	Iowa
1979	Iowa
1980	Iowa
1981	Iowa
1982	Iowa
1983	Iowa
1984	Iowa
1985	Iowa
1986	Iowa
1987	Iowa State
1988	Arizona State
1989	Oklahoma State
1990	Oklahoma State

Cross-Country

Year	Champion
1946	Drake
1947	Penn State
1948	Michigan State
1949	Michigan State
1950	Penn State
1951	Syracuse
1952	Michigan State
1953	Kansas
1954	Oklahoma State
1955	Michigan State
1956	Michigan State
1957	Notre Dame
1958	Michigan State
1959	Michigan State
1960	Houston
1961	Oregon State
1962	San Jose State
1963	San Jose State
1964	Western Michigan
1965	Western Michigan
1966	Villanova
1967	Villanova
1968	Villanova
1969	UTEP
1970	Villanova
1971	Oregon
1972	Tennessee
1973	Oregon
1974	Oregon
1975	UTEP
1976	UTEP
1977	Oregon
1978	UTEP
1979	UTEP
1980	UTEP
1981	UTEP
1982	Wisconsin
1983	Vacated
1984	Arkansas
1985	Wisconsin
1986	Arkansas
1987	Arkansas
1988	Wisconsin

Cross-Country

Year	Champion
1989	Iowa State
1990	Arkansas

Outdoor Track

Year	Champion
1946	Illinois
1947	Illinois
1948	Minnesota
1949	Southern California
1950	Southern California
1951	Southern California
1952	Southern California
1953	Southern California
1954	Southern California
1955	Southern California
1956	UCLA
1957	Villanova
1958	Southern California
1959	Kansas
1960	Kansas
1961	Southern California
1962	Oregon
1963	Southern California
1964	Oregon
1965	Oregon
	Southern California
1966	UCLA
1967	Southern California
1968	Southern California
1969	San Jose State
1970	Brigham Young
	Kansas
1971	UCLA
1972	UCLA
1973	UCLA
1974	Tennessee
1975	UTEP
1976	Southern California
1977	Arizona State
1978	UCLA
	UTEP
1979	UTEP
1980	UTEP
1981	UTEP
1982	UTEP
1983	Southern Methodist
1984	Oregon
1985	Arkansas
1986	Southern Methodist
1987	UCLA
1988	UCLA
1989	Louisiana State
1990	Louisiana State

Indoor Track

Year	Champion
1965	Missouri
1966	Kansas
1967	Southern California
1968	Villanova
1969	Kansas
1970	Kansas
1971	Villanova
1972	Southern California
1973	Manhattan
1974	UTEP

TABLE 18.60 (continued)

Year	Champion
1975	UTEP
1976	UTEP
1977	Washington State
1978	UTEP
1979	Villanova
1980	UTEP
1981	UTEP
1982	UTEP
1983	Southern Methodist
1984	Arkansas
1985	Arkansas
1986	Arkansas
1987	Arkansas
1988	Arkansas
1989	Arkansas
1990	Arkansas

Gymnastics

Year	Champion
1948	Penn State
1949	Temple
1950	Illinois
1951	Florida State
1952	Florida State
1953	Penn State
1954	Penn State
1955	Illinois
1956	Illinois
1957	Penn State
1958	Michigan State
	Illinois
1959	Penn State
1960	Penn State
1961	Penn State
1962	Southern California
1963	Michigan
1964	Southern Illinois
1965	Penn State
1966	Southern Illinois
1967	Southern Illinois
1968	California
1969	Iowa
	Michigan (for trampoline)
1970	Michigan
	Michigan (for trampoline)
1971	Iowa State
1972	Southern Illinois
1973	Iowa State
1974	Iowa State
1975	California
1976	Penn State
1977	Indiana State
	Oklahoma
1978	Oklahoma
1979	Nebraska
1980	Nebraska
1981	Nebraska
1982	Nebraska
1983	Nebraska
1984	UCLA
1985	Ohio State
1986	Arizona State
1987	UCLA
1988	Nebraska
1989	Illinois
1990	Nebraska

Golf

Year	Champion
1946	Stanford
1947	Louisiana State
1948	San Jose State
1949	North Texas
1950	North Texas
1951	North Texas
1952	North Texas
1953	Stanford
1954	Southern Methodist
1955	Louisiana State
1956	Houston
1957	Houston
1958	Houston
1959	Houston
1960	Houston
1961	Purdue
1962	Houston
1963	Oklahoma State
1964	Houston
1965	Houston
1966	Houston
1967	Houston
1968	Florida
1969	Houston
1970	Houston
1971	Texas
1972	Texas
1973	Florida
1974	Wake Forest
1975	Wake Forest
1976	Oklahoma
1977	Houston
1978	Oklahoma State
1979	Ohio State
1980	Oklahoma State
1981	Brigham Young
1982	Houston
1983	Oklahoma State
1984	Houston
1985	Houston
1986	Wake Forest
1987	Oklahoma State
1988	UCLA
1989	Oklahoma
1990	Arizona

Fencing

Year	Champion
1947	New York University
1949	Army
	Rutgers
1950	Navy
1951	Columbia
1952	Columbia
1953	Pennsylvania
1954	Columbia
	New York University
1955	Columbia
1956	Illinois
1957	New York University
1958	Illinois
1959	Navy
1960	New York University
1961	New York University
1962	Navy
1963	Columbia
1964	Princeton
1965	Columbia

Year	Champion
1966	New York University
1967	New York University
1968	Columbia
1969	Pennsylvania
1970	New York University
	Columbia
1971	New York University
1972	Detroit
1973	New York University
1974	New York University
1975	Wayne State
1976	New York University
1977	Notre Dame
1978	Notre Dame
1979	Wayne State
1980	Wayne State
1981	Pennsylvania
1982	Wayne State
1983	Wayne State
1984	Wayne State
1985	Wayne State
1986	Notre Dame
1987	Columbia
1988	Columbia
1989	Columbia

Men's and Women's Rifle

Year	Champion
1980	Tennessee Tech
1981	Tennessee Tech
1982	Tennessee Tech
1983	West Virginia
1984	West Virginia
1985	Murray State
1986	West Virginia
1987	Murray State
1988	West Virginia
1989	West Virginia
1990	West Virginia

Men's and Women's Skiing

Year	Champion
1954	Denver
1955	Denver
1956	Denver
1957	Denver
1958	Dartmouth
1959	Colorado
1960	Colorado
1961	Denver
1962	Denver
1963	Denver
1964	Denver
1965	Denver
1966	Denver
1967	Denver
1968	Wyoming
1969	Denver
1970	Denver
1971	Denver
1972	Colorado
1973	Colorado
1974	Colorado
1975	Colorado
1976	Colorado
	Dartmouth
1977	Colorado
1978	Colorado
1979	Colorado
1980	Vermont
1981	Utah
1982	Colorado
1983	Utah

Year	Champion
1984	Utah
1985	Wyoming
1986	Utah
1987	Utah
1988	Utah
1989	Vermont
1990	Vermont

Men's and Women's Fencing

Year	Champion
1990	Penn State

Source: Universal Almanac, 1991, 593–94.

TABLE 18.61   NCAA WOMEN'S MAJOR SPORTS, 1981–1990

Cross Country	
Year	Champion
1981	Virginia
1982	Virginia
1983	Oregon
1984	Wisconsin
1985	Wisconsin
1986	Texas
1987	Oregon
1988	Kentucky
1989	Villanova
1990	Villanova

Fencing	
Year	Champion
1982	Wayne State
1983	Penn State
1984	Yale
1985	Yale
1986	Pennsylvania
1987	Notre Dame
1988	Wayne State
1989	Wayne State
1990	Wayne State

Field Hockey	
Year	Champion
1981	Connecticut
1982	Old Dominion
1983	Old Dominion
1984	Old Dominion
1985	Connecticut
1986	Iowa
1987	Maryland
1988	Old Dominion
1989	North Carolina
1990	Old Dominion

Golf	
Year	Champion
1982	Tulsa
1983	Texas Christian
1984	Miami (Fla.)
1985	Florida
1986	Florida
1987	San Jose State
1988	Tulsa
1989	San Jose State
1990	Arizona State

(continued)

TABLE 18.61 (continued)

Gymnastics

Year	Champion
1982	Utah
1983	Utah
1984	Utah
1985	Utah
1986	Utah
1987	Georgia
1988	Alabama
1989	Georgia
1990	Utah

Tennis

Year	Champion
1982	Stanford
1983	Southern California
1984	Stanford
1985	Southern California
1986	Stanford
1987	Stanford
1988	Stanford
1989	Stanford
1990	Stanford

Swimming and Diving

Year	Champion
1982	Florida
1983	Stanford
1984	Texas
1985	Texas
1986	Texas
1987	Texas
1988	Texas
1989	Stanford
1990	Texas

Soccer

Year	Champion
1982	North Carolina
1983	North Carolina
1984	North Carolina
1985	George Mason
1986	North Carolina
1987	North Carolina
1988	North Carolina
1989	North Carolina
1990	North Carolina

Softball

Year	Champion
1982	UCLA
1983	Texas A&M
1984	UCLA
1985	UCLA
1986	California State, Fullerton
1987	Texas A&M
1988	UCLA
1989	UCLA
1990	UCLA

Lacrosse

Year	Champion
1982	Massachusetts
1983	Delaware
1984	Temple
1985	New Hampshire
1986	Maryland
1987	Penn State
1988	Temple
1989	Penn State
1990	Harvard

Indoor Track

Year	Champion
1983	Nebraska
1984	Nebraska
1985	Florida State
1986	Texas
1987	Louisiana State
1988	Texas
1989	Louisiana State
1990	Texas

Outdoor Track

Year	Champion
1982	UCLA
1983	UCLA
1984	Florida State
1985	Oregon
1986	Texas
1987	Louisiana State
1988	Louisiana State
1989	Louisiana State
1990	Louisiana State

Volleyball

Year	Champion
1981	Southern California
1982	Hawaii
1983	Hawaii
1984	UCLA
1985	Pacific
1986	Pacific
1987	Hawaii
1988	Texas
1989	Cal State (Long Beach)
1990	UCLA

Source: Universal Almanac, 1999, 595.

Tennis

In the postwar period tennis continued to be perceived as an elitist sport that offered respectable exercise for well-heeled people of middle age. It was a varsity sport in major American colleges, and it remained the most regular and continuing forum for international athletic competition between young ladies and gentlemen of interested nations—mostly European, Commonwealth, and the United States. Tennis underwent several changes in the last part of the 20th century, taking on features that enhanced incentive and popular appeal. Starting in 1968, the major tournaments became Open events, permitting participation by professionals and offering prize money that increased far beyond the inflation rate in any participating nation. The late 1960s also brought the introduction of larger steel, aluminum, or fiberglass rackets that carried a larger punch. Stronger, lighter equipment facilitated adoption of the two-handed backhand stroke, popularized by such top-flight American players as Jimmy Connors and Chris Evert. No less than other major sports, tennis was boosted by the development of television and the revolution in telecommunications. Americans thus could watch the U.S. Open in New York in September, but also follow NBC's "breakfast at Wimbledon" live coverage of the British Open in July. Tennis players, both male and female, became objects of adulation to rival the best in any sport, and the prize money earned marked only the beginning of their wealth.

The 1970s and 1980s brought a proliferation of tournaments, most of them in the United States, funded by corporate sponsors. The most prestigious and rewarding events continued to be the four national tournaments: the Australian Open, French Open, the British—best known as Wimbledon—and the U.S. Open. To win any of them constituted a mark of distinction. To win all four in the same year represented the ultimate accomplishment of the sport: this was the Grand Slam. Five players reached this pinnacle during the years 1946–1990: Maureen Connally, an American, in 1955; Rod Laver, an Australian, in 1962 and 1969; Margaret Court, from Australia, in 1970; and Steffi Graf, of West Germany, in 1988. Martina Navratilova, a recently naturalized American, won the four events consecutively, but over a two-year period, in 1983 and 1984. For all her remarkable accomplishments, Navratilova could not claim a Grand Slam.

TABLE 18.62 MEN'S U.S. OPEN WINNERS AND LOSERS, BY NATIONALITY, 1946–1990

Year	Champion	Runner-Up
1946	Jack Kramer (U.S.)	Tom Brown, Jr. (U.S.)
1947	Jack Kramer (U.S)	Frank Parker (U.S.)
1948	Richard A. Gonzalez (U.S.)	Eric W. Sturgess (South Africa)
1949	Richard A. Gonzalez (U.S.)	Fredrick Schroeder (U.S.)
1950	Arthur Larsen (U.S.)	Herbert Flam (U.S.)
1951	Frank Sedgman (Australia)	E. Victor Seixas, Jr. (U.S.)
1952	Frank Sedgman (Australia)	Gardnar Mulloy (U.S.)
1953	Tony Trabert (U.S.)	E. Victor Seixas, Jr. (U.S.)
1954	E. Victor Seixas, Jr. (U.S.)	Rex Hartwig (Australia)
1955	Tony Trabert (U.S.)	Ken Rosewall (Australia)
1956	Ken Rosewall (Australia)	Lewis Hoad (Australia)
1957	Malcolm J. Anderson (Australia)	Ashley J. Cooper (Australia)
1958	Ashley J. Cooper (Australia)	Malcolm J. Anderson (Australia)
1959	Neale Fraser (Australia)	Alejandro Olmedo (Peru)
1960	Neale Fraser (Australia)	Rod Laver (Australia)
1961	Roy Emerson (Australia)	Rod Laver (Australia)
1962	Rod Laver (Australia)	Roy Emerson (Australia)
1963	Rafael Osuna (Mexico)	Frank Froehling, III (U.S.)
1964	Roy Emerson (Australia)	Fred Stolle (Australia)
1965	Manuel Santana (Spain)	Cliff Drysdale (South Africa)
1966	Fred Stolle (Australia)	John Newcombe (Australia)
1967	John Newcombe (Australia)	Clark Graebner (U.S.)
1968	Arthur Ashe (U.S.)	Tom Okker (Netherlands)
1969	Rod Laver (Australia)	Tony Roche (Australia)
1970	Ken Rosewall (Australia)	Tony Roche (Australia)
1971	Stan Smith (U.S.)	Jan Kodes (Czechoslovakia)
1972	Ilie Nastase (Romania)	Arthur Ashe (U.S.)
1973	John Newcombe (Australia)	Jan Kodes (Czechoslovakia)
1974	Jimmy Connors (U.S.)	Ken Rosewall (Australia)
1975	Manuel Orantes (Spain)	Jimmy Connors (U.S.)
1976	Jimmy Connors (U.S.)	Bjorn Borg (Sweden)
1977	Guillermo Villas (Argentina)	Jimmy Connors (U.S.)
1978	Jimmy Connors (U.S.)	Bjorn Borg (Sweden)
1979	John McEnroe (U.S.)	Vitas Gerulaitis (U.S.)
1980	John McEnroe (U.S.)	Bjorn Borg (Sweden)
1981	John McEnroe (U.S.)	Bjorn Borg (Sweden)
1982	Jimmy Connors (U.S.)	Ivan Lendl (Czechoslovakia)
1983	Jimmy Connors (U.S.)	Ivan Lendl (Czechoslovakia)
1984	John McEnroe (U.S.)	Ivan Lendl (Czechoslovakia)
1985	Ivan Lendl (Czechoslovakia)	John McEnroe (U.S.)
1986	Ivan Lendl (Czechoslovakia)	Miloslav Mecir (Czechoslovakia)
1987	Ivan Lendl (Czechoslovakia)	Mats Wilander (Sweden)
1988	Mats Wilander (Sweden)	Ivan Lendl (Czechoslovakia)
1989	Boris Becker (West Germany)	Ivan Lendl (Czechoslovakia)
1990	Pete Sampras (U.S.)	Andre Agassi (U.S.)

Source: Ronald J. Alsop, *The Wall Street Journal Almanac, 1998* (New York, 1997), 1086.

TABLE 18.63   MEN'S GRAND SLAM CHAMPIONS, 1946–1990

Year	Australian Champion	French Champion	Wimbledon Champion	U.S. Champion
1946	John Bromwich	Marcel Bernard	Yvon Petra	Jack Kramer
1947	Dinny Pails	Joseph Asboth	Jack Kramer	Jack Kramer
1948	Adrian Quist	Frank Parker	Bob Falkenburg	Pancho Gonzales
1949	Frank Sedgman	Frank Parker	Ted Schroeder	Pancho Gonzales
1950	Frank Sedgman	Budge Patty	Budge Patty	Arthur Larsen
1951	Richard Savitt	Jaroslav Drobny	Dick Savitt	Frank Sedgman
1952	Ken McGregor	Jaroslav Drobny	Frank Sedgman	Frank Sedgman
1953	Ken Rosewall	Ken Rosewall	Vic Seixas	Tony Trabert
1954	Mervyn Rose	Tony Trabert	Jaroslav Drobny	E. Victor Seixas Jr.
1955	Ken Rosewall	Tony Trabert	Tony Trabert	Tony Trabert
1956	Lew Hoad	Lew Hoad	Lew Hoad	Ken Rosewall
1957	Ashley Cooper	Sven Davidson	Lew Hoad	Malcolm Anderson
1958	Ashley Cooper	Mervyn Rose	Ashley Cooper	Ashley J. Cooper
1959	Alex Olmedo	Nicola Pietrangeli	Alex Olmedo	Neale Fraser
1960	Rod Laver	Nicola Pietrangeli	Neale Fraser	Neale Fraser
1961	Roy Emerson	Manuel Santana	Rod Laver	Roy Emerson
1962	Rod Laver	Rod Laver	Rod Laver	Rod Laver
1963	Roy Emerson	Roy Emerson	Chuck McKinley	Rafael Osuna
1964	Roy Emerson	Manuel Santana	Roy Emerson	Roy Emerson
1965	Roy Emerson	Fred Stolle	Roy Emerson	Manuel Santana
1966	Roy Emerson	Tony Roche	Manuel Santana	Fred Stolle
1967	Roy Emerson	Roy Emerson	John Newcombe	John Newcombe
1968	Bill Bowrey	Ken Rosewall	Rod Laver	Arthur Ashe
1969	Rod Laver	Rod Laver	Rod Laver	Rod Laver
1970	Arthur Ashe	Jan Kodes	John Newcombe	Ken Rosewall
1971	Ken Rosewall	Jan Kodes	John Newcombe	Stan Smith
1972	Ken Rosewall	Andres Gimeno	Stan Smith	Ilie Nastase
1973	John Newcombe	Ilie Nastase	Jan Kodes	John Newcombe
1974	Jimmy Connors	Bjorn Borg	Jimmy Connors	Jimmy Connors
1975	John Newcombe	Bjorn Borg	Arthur Ashe	Manuel Orantes
1976	Mark Edmondson	Adriano Panatta	Bjorn Borg	Jimmy Connors
1977	Roscoe Tanner	Guillermo Vilas	Bjorn Borg	Guillermo Vilas
	Vitas Gerulaitis			
1978	Guillermo Vilas	Bjorn Borg	Bjorn Borg	Jimmy Connors
1979	Guillermo Vilas	Bjorn Borg	Bjorn Borg	John McEnroe
1980	Brian Teacher	Bjorn Borg	Bjorn Borg	John McEnroe
1981	Johan Kriek	Bjorn Borg	John McEnroe	John McEnroe
1982	Johan Kriek	Mats Wilander	Jimmy Connors	Jimmy Connors
1983	Mats Wilander	Yannick Noah	John McEnroe	Jimmy Connors
1984	Mats Wilander	Ivan Lendl	John McEnroe	John McEnroe
1985	Stefan Edberg	Mats Wilander	Boris Becker	Ivan Lendl
1986	Moved to Jan. 1987	Ivan Lendl	Boris Becker	Ivan Lendl
1987	Stefan Edberg	Ivan Lendl	Pat Cash	Ivan Lendl
1988	Mats Wilander	Mats Wilander	Stefan Edberg	Mats Wilander
1989	Ivan Lendl	Michael Chang	Boris Becker	Boris Becker
1990	Ivan Lendl	Andrés Gomez	Stefan Edberg	Pete Sampras

Source: John W. Wright, *New York Times 1998 Almanac* (New York, 1997), 903–04.

TABLE 18.64   U.S. OPEN WINNERS' PRIZE MONEY, 1968–1990

Year	Singles		Doubles (per team)		
	Men	Women	Men	Women	Mixed
1968	$14,000	$6,000	$4,200	$1,750	—
1969	16,000	6,000	3,000	2,000	$2,000
1970	20,000	7,500	3,000	2,000	2,000
1971	15,000	5,000	2,000	1,000	1,000
1972	25,000	10,000	3,000	2,000	2,000
1973	25,000	25,000	4,000	4,000	2,000
1974	22,500	22,500	4,500	4,500	2,000
1975	25,000	25,000	4,500	4,500	2,000
1976	30,000	30,000	12,000	12,000	6,500
1977	33,000	33,000	13,125	13,125	6,500
1978	38,000	38,000	15,500	15,500	6,500
1979	39,000	39,000	15,750	15,750	7,100

Year	Singles		Doubles (per team)		
	Men	Women	Men	Women	Mixed
1980	46,000	46,000	18,500	18,500	7,100
1981	66,000	66,000	26,400	26,400	9,680
1982	90,000	90,000	36,000	36,000	14,000
1983	120,000	120,000	48,000	48,000	17,000
1984	160,000	160,000	64,000	64,000	17,000
1985	187,500	187,500	65,000	65,000	19,000
1986	210,000	210,000	72,800	72,800	21,800
1987	250,000	250,000	86,667	86,667	26,160
1988	275,000	275,000	95,333	95,333	28,800
1989	300,000	300,000	104,000	104,000	34,000
1990	350,000	350,000	142,861	142,861	42,500

Source: *Wall Street Journal Almanac, 1998,* 1090.

TABLE 18.65   WOMEN'S GRAND SLAM CHAMPIONS, 1946–1990

Year	Australian Champion	French Champion	Wimbledon Champion	U.S. Champion
1946	Nancye Wynne Bolton	Margaret Osborne	Pauline Betz	Pauline Betz
1947	Nancye Wynne Bolton	Patricia Todd	Margaret Osborne	Louise Brough
1948	Nancye Wynne Bolton	Nelly Landry	Louise Brough	Margaret Osborne duPont
1949	Doris Hart	Margaret Osborne duPont	Louise Brough	Margaret Osborne duPont
1950	Louise Brough	Doris Hart	Louise Brough	Margaret Osborne duPont
1951	Nancye Wynne Bolton	Shirley Fry	Doris Hart	Maureen Connolly
1952	Thelma Long	Doris Hart	Maureen Connolly	Maureen Connolly
1953	Maureen Connolly	Maureen Connolly	Maureen Connolly	Maureen Connolly
1954	Thelma Long	Maureen Connolly	Maureen Connolly	Doris Hart
1955	Beryl Penrose	Angela Mortimer	Louise Brough	Doris Hart
1956	Mary Carter	Althea Gibson	Shirley Fry	Shirley Fry
1957	Shirley Fry	Shirley Bloomer	Althea Gibson	Althea Gibson
1958	Angela Mortimer	Zsuzsi Kormoczy	Althea Gibson	Althea Gibson
1959	Mary Carter Reitano	Christine Truman	Maria Bueno	Maria Bueno
1960	Margaret Smith	Darlene Hard	Maria Bueno	Darlene Hard
1961	Margaret Smith	Ann Haydon	Angela Mortimer	Darlene Hard
1962	Margaret Smith	Margaret Smith	Karen Hantze Susman	Margaret Smith
1963	Margaret Smith	Lesley Turner	Margaret Smith	Maria Bueno
1964	Margaret Smith	Margaret Smith	Maria Bueno	Maria Bueno
1965	Margaret Smith	Lesley Turner	Margaret Smith	Margaret Smith
1966	Margaret Smith	Ann Jones	Billie Jean King	Maria Bueno
1967	Nancy Richey	Francoise Durr	Billie Jean King	Billie Jean King
1968	Billie Jean King	Nancy Richey	Billie Jean King	Virginia Wade
1969	Margaret Smith Court	Margaret Smith Court	Ann Jones	Margaret Smith Court
1970	Margaret Smith Court	Margaret Smith Court	Margaret Smith Court	Margaret Smith Court
1971	Margaret Smith Court	Evonne Goolagong	Evonne Goolagong	Billie Jean King
1972	Virginia Wade	Billie Jean King	Billie Jean King	Billie Jean King
1973	Margaret Smith Court	Margaret Smith Court	Billie Jean King	Margaret Smith Court
1974	Evonne Goolagong	Chris Evert	Chris Evert	Billie Jean King
1975	Evonne Goolagong	Chris Evert	Billie Jean King	Chris Evert
1976	Evonne Goolagong Cawley	Sue Barker	Chris Evert	Chris Evert
1977	Kerry Melville Reid			
	Evonne Goolagong Cawley	Mima Jasuovec	Virginia Wade	Chris Evert
1978	Chris O'Neil	Virginia Ruzici	Martina Navratilova	Chris Evert
1979	Barbara Jordan	Chris Evert Lloyd	Martina Navratilova	Tracy Austin
1980	Hana Mandlikova	Chris Evert Lloyd	Evonne Goolagong Cawley	Chris Evert Lloyd
1981	Martina Navratilova	Hana Mandlikova	Chris Evert Lloyd	Tracy Austin
1982	Chris Evert Lloyd	Martina Navratilova	Martina Navratilova	Chris Evert Lloyd
1983	Martina Navratilova	Chris Evert Lloyd	Martina Navratilova	Martina Navratilova
1984	Chris Evert Lloyd	Martina Navratilova	Martina Navratilova	Martina Navratilova
1985	Martina Navratilova	Chris Evert Lloyd	Martina Navratilova	Hana Mandlikova
1986	Moved to Jan. 1987	Chris Evert Lloyd	Martina Navratilova	Martina Navratilova
1987	Hana Mandlikova	Steffi Graf	Martina Navratilova	Martina Navratilova
1988	Steffi Graf	Steffi Graf	Steffi Graf	Steffi Graf
1989	Steffi Graf	Arantxa Sanchez	Steffi Graf	Steffi Graf
1990	Steffi Graf	Monica Seles	Martina Navratilova	Gabriela Sabatini

Source: *New York Times 1998 Almanac,* 904.

Princess of the fans and of professional tennis, Chris Evert appears here with Nancy Reagan. (Courtesy Ronald Reagan Library)

TABLE 18.66 WOMEN'S U.S. OPEN WINNERS AND LOSERS, BY NATIONALITY, 1946–1990

Year	Champion	Country	Runner-Up	Country
1946	Pauline Betz	United States	Patricia Canning	United States
1947	A. Louise Brough	United States	Margaret Osborne	United States
1948	Margaret Osborne duPont	United States	A. Louise Brough	United States
1949	Margaret Osborne duPont	United States	Doris Hart	United States
1950	Margaret Osborne duPont	United States	Doris Hart	United States
1951	Maureen Connolly	United States	Shirley J. Fry	United States
1952	Maureen Connolly	United States	Doris Hart	United States
1953	Maureen Connolly	United States	Doris Hart	United States
1954	Doris Hart	United States	A. Louise Brough	United States
1955	Doris Hart	United States	Patricia Ward	Great Britain
1956	Shirley J. Fry	United States	Althea Gibson	United States
1957	Althea Gibson	United States	A. Louise Brough	United States
1958	Althea Gibson	United States	Darlene R. Hard	United States
1959	Maria Bueno	Brazil	Christine Truman	Great Britain
1960	Darlene R. Hard	United States	Maria Bueno	Brazil
1961	Darlene R. Hard	United States	Ann Haydon	Great Britain
1962	Margaret Smith	Australia	Darlene R. Hard	United States
1963	Maria Bueno	Brazil	Margaret Smith	Australia
1964	Maria Bueno	Brazil	Carole Caldwell Graebner	United States
1965	Margaret Smith	Australia	Billie Jean Moffitt	United States

Year	Champion	Country	Runner-Up	Country
1966	Maria Bueno	Brazil	Nancy Richey	United States
1967	Billie Jean Moffitt King	United States	Ann Haydon Jones	Great Britain
1968	Virginia Wade	Great Britain	Billie Jean King	United States
1969	Margaret Smith Court	Australia	Nancy Richey	United States
1970	Margaret Smith Court	Australia	Rosemary Casals	United States
1971	Billie Jean King	United States	Rosemary Casals	United States
1972	Billie Jean King	United States	Kerry Melville	Australia
1973	Margaret Smith Court	Australia	Evonne Goolagong	Australia
1974	Billie Jean King	United States	Evonne Goolagong	Australia
1975	Chris Evert	United States	Evonne Goolagong	Australia
1976	Chris Evert	United States	Evonne Goolagong	Australia
1977	Chris Evert	United States	Wendy Turnbull	Australia
1978	Chris Evert	United States	Pam Shriver	United States
1979	Tracy Austin	United States	Chris Evert Lloyd	United States
1980	Chris Evert Lloyd	United States	Hana Mandlikova	Czechoslovakia
1981	Tracy Austin	United States	Martina Navratilova	United States
1982	Chris Evert Lloyd	United States	Hana Mandlikova	Czechoslovakia
1983	Martina Navratilova	United States	Chris Evert Lloyd	United States
1984	Martina Navratilova	United States	Chris Evert Lloyd	United States
1985	Hana Mandlikova	Czechoslovakia	Martina Navratilova	United States
1986	Martina Navratilova	United States	Helena Sukova	Czechoslovakia
1987	Martina Navratilova	United States	Steffi Graf	West Germany
1988	Steffi Graf	West Germany	Gabriela Sabatini	Argentina
1989	Steffi Graf	West Germany	Martina Navratilova	United States
1990	Gabriela Sabatini	Argentina	Steffi Graf	West Germany

Source: Wall Street Journal Almanac, 1087–88.

TABLE 18.67 MEN'S TOUR PRIZE MONEY LEADERS, 1968–1990

Year	Player	Prize
1968	Tony Roche	$63,504
1969	Rod Laver	$124,000
1970	Rod Laver	$201,453
1971	Rod Laver	$292,717
1972	Ilie Nastase	$176,000
1973	Ilie Nastase	$228,750
1974	Jimmy Connors	$285,490
1975	Arthur Ashe	$326,750
1976	Raul Ramirez	$484,343
1977	Guillermo Vilas	$766,065
1978	Eddie Dibbs	$575,273
1979	Bjorn Borg	$1,008,742
1980	John McEnroe	$972,369
1981	John McEnroe	$991,000
1982	Ivan Lendl	$2,028,850
1983	Ivan Lendl	$1,747,128
1984	John McEnroe	$2,026,109
1985	Ivan Lendl	$1,971,074
1986	Ivan Lendl	$1,987,537
1987	Ivan Lendl	$2,003,656
1988	Mats Wilander	$1,726,731
1989	Ivan Lendl	$2,344,367
1990	Pete Sampras	$2,900,057

Source: Wall Street Journal Almanac, 1998, 1092–93.

TABLE 18.68 WOMEN'S TOUR PRIZE MONEY LEADERS, 1974–1990

Year	Player	Prize
1974	Chris Evert	$107,485
1975	Chris Evert	$347,227
1976	Chris Evert	$319,565
1977	Chris Evert	$316,045
1978	Chris Evert	$454,486
1979	Martina Navratilova	$618,698
1980	Martina Navratilova	$749,250
1981	Martina Navratilova	$865,437
1982	Martina Navratilova	$1,475,055
1983	Martina Navratilova	$1,456,030
1984	Martina Navratilova	$2,173,556
1985	Martina Navratilova	$1,328,829
1986	Martina Navratilova	$1,905,841
1987	Steffi Graf	$1,063,785
1988	Steffi Graf	$1,378,128
1989	Steffi Graf	$1,963,905
1990	Steffi Graf	$1,921,853

Source: Wall Street Journal Almanac, 1998, 1093.

TABLE 18.69 ANNUAL NUMBER-ONE RANKED TENNIS PLAYERS, 1946–1990

Women

Year	Player
1946	Pauline Betz
1947	Margaret Osborne
1948	Margaret duPont
1949	Margaret duPont
1950	Margaret duPont
1951	Doris Hart
1952	Maureen Connolly
1953	Maureen Connolly
1954	Maureen Connolly
1955	Louise Brough
1956	Shirley Fry
1957	Althea Gibson
1958	Althea Gibson
1959	Maria Bueno
1960	Maria Bueno
1961	Angela Mortimer
1962	Margaret Smith
1963	Margaret Smith
1964	Margaret Smith
1965	Margaret Smith
1966	Billie Jean King
1967	Billie Jean King
1968	Billie Jean King
1969	Margaret Court
1970	Margaret Court
1971	Evonne Goolagong
1972	Billie Jean King
1973	Margaret Court
1974	Billie Jean King
1975	Chris Evert
1976	Chris Evert
1977	Chris Evert
1978	Martina Navratilova
1979	Martina Navratilova
1980	Chris Evert Lloyd
1981	Chris Evert Lloyd
1982	Martina Navratilova
1983	Martina Navratilova
1984	Martina Navratilova
1985	Martina Navratilova
1986	Martina Navratilova
1987	Steffi Graf
1988	Steffi Graf
1989	Steffi Graf
1990	Steffi Graf

Men

Year	Player
1946	Jack Kramer
1947	Jack Kramer
1948	Frank Parker
1949	Pancho Gonzalez
1950	Budge Patty
1951	Frank Sedgman
1952	Frank Sedgman
1953	Tony Trabert
1954	Jaroslav Drobny
1955	Tony Trabert
1956	Lew Hoad
1957	Ashley Cooper
1958	Ashley Cooper
1959	Neale Fraser
1960	Neale Fraser
1961	Rod Laver
1962	Rod Laver
1963	Rafael Osuna
1964	Roy Emerson
1965	Roy Emerson
1966	Manuel Santana
1967	John Newcombe
1968	Rod Laver
1969	Rod Laver
1970	John Newcombe
1971	John Newcombe
1972	Ilie Nastase
1973	Ilie Nastase
1974	Jimmy Connors
1975	Jimmy Connors

(continued)

TABLE 18.69   (continued)

Men	
Year	Player
1976	Jimmy Connors
1977	Jimmy Connors
1978	Jimmy Connors
1979	Bjorn Borg
1980	Bjorn Borg
1981	John McEnroe
1982	John McEnroe
1983	John McEnroe
1984	John McEnroe
1985	Ivan Lendl
1986	Ivan Lendl
1987	Ivan Lendl
1988	Mats Wilander
1989	Ivan Lendl
1990	Stefan Edberg

Note: Rankings by London *Daily Telegraph,* 1946–1972; since then rankings computed by men and women's tours.
Source: 1993 Information Please Sports Almanac, 714–15.

Golf

As befit a society fashioned by growing incomes, increased time for leisure and entertainment, and a penchant for imitating behavior of cultural leaders, the United States took readily to golf in the postwar era. By 1990 some 20 million males and females were chasing the little white ball, and the number of courses had zoomed to 12,000. Virtually all the presidents played and some, notably Dwight Eisenhower and Gerald Ford, made a major point of it. The arrival of golf as a flourishing professional enterprise and a mass-market spectator sport corresponded with placement in virtually every household of a television set. Arnold Palmer, leader—and beneficiary—of the wedding of golf and television, was the best and most popular player of the 1950s and early 1960s. In the 1960s Jack Nicklaus emerged as the competitor and eventual successor to Palmer as the nation's foremost golfer.

By the 1980s the Professional Golf Association (PGA) sanctioned a tournament nearly every week in season, many of them covered on television. Waning of the Nicklaus era left the field open to a body of native competitors that included Tom Watson, John Miller, Curtis Strange, Fred Couples, and many other fine golfers. The PGA tour also had taken on a marked international complexion, with such foreign competitors as Greg Norman, Seve Ballesteros, Nick Faldo, and Bernard Langer. Six of the coveted Masters tournament championships of the 1980s went to golfers from abroad. Women's professional golf also had become a national sport. The purses were smaller, the tournaments less likely to be televised, the heroines slightly slower to catch on, but a female counterpart to the PGA, the LPGA, did evolve. Kathy Whitworth, Nancy Lopez, Beth Daniel, and others did become national sports figures, and by 1990s women's earnings were rapidly catching up.

With all its evenly matched competitors, it might have appeared at the start of the 1990s that professional golf was waiting for a messiah, someone to break free, and some people swore they knew who he was: Still playing in the amateur ranks, a rare black man in a game of whites, a truly exquisite craftsman known as Tiger Woods.

TABLE 18.70   GOLF TOURNAMENT WINNERS, 1946–1990

United States Open Winners	
Year	Winner
1946	Lloyd Mangrum
1947	L. Worsham
1948	Ben Hogan
1949	Cary Middlecoff
1950	Ben Hogan
1951	Ben Hogan
1952	Julius Boros
1953	Ben Hogan
1954	Ed Furgol
1955	Jack Fleck
1956	Cary Middlecoff
1957	Dick Mayer
1958	Tommy Bolt
1959	Billy Casper
1960	Arnold Palmer
1961	Gene Littler
1962	Jack Nicklaus
1963	Julius Boros
1964	Ken Venturi
1965	Gary Player
1966	Billy Casper
1967	Jack Nicklaus
1968	Lee Trevino
1969	Orville Moody
1970	Tony Jacklin
1971	Lee Trevino
1972	Jack Nicklaus
1973	Johnny Miller
1974	Hale Irwin
1975	Lou Graham
1976	Jerry Pate
1977	Hubert Green
1978	Andy North
1979	Hale Irwin
1980	Jack Nicklaus
1981	David Graham
1982	Tom Watson
1983	Larry Nelson
1984	Fuzzy Zoeller
1985	Andy North
1986	Ray Floyd
1987	Scott Simpson
1988	Curtis Strange
1989	Curtis Strange
1990	Hale Irwin
Professional Golfer's Association Championship Winners	
Year	Winner
1946	Ben Hogan
1947	Jim Ferrier
1948	Ben Hogan
1949	Sam Snead
1950	Chandler Harper
1951	Sam Snead
1952	James Turnesa
1953	Walter Burkemo
1954	Melvin Harbert
1955	Doug Ford
1956	Jack Burke
1957	Lionel Hebert
1958	Dow Finsterwald
1959	Bob Rosburg
1960	Jay Hebert

Professional Golfer's Association Championship Winners

Year	Winner
1961	Jerry Barber
1962	Gary Player
1963	Jack Nicklaus
1964	Bob Nichols
1965	Dave Marr
1966	Al Geiberger
1967	Don January
1968	Julius Boros
1969	Ray Floyd
1970	Dave Stockton
1971	Jack Nicklaus
1972	Gary Player
1973	Jack Nicklaus
1974	Lee Trevino
1975	Jack Nicklaus
1976	Dave Stockton
1977	Lanny Wadkins
1978	John Mahaffey
1979	David Graham
1980	Jack Nicklaus
1981	Larry Nelson
1982	Ray Floyd
1983	Hal Sutton
1984	Lee Trevino
1985	Hubert Green
1986	Bob Tway
1987	Larry Nelson
1988	Jeff Sluman
1989	Payne Stewart
1990	Wayne Grady

Masters Golf Tournament Winners

Year	Winner
1946	Herman Keiser
1947	Jimmy Demaret
1948	Claude Harmon
1949	Sam Snead
1950	Jimmy Demaret
1951	Ben Hogan
1952	Sam Snead
1953	Ben Hogan
1954	Sam Snead
1955	Cary Middlecoff
1956	Jack Burke
1957	Doug Ford
1958	Arnold Palmer
1959	Art Wall Jr.
1960	Arnold Palmer
1961	Gray Player
1962	Arnold Palmer
1963	Jack Nicklaus
1964	Arnold Palmer
1965	Jack Nicklaus
1966	Jack Nicklaus
1967	Gay Brewer Jr.
1968	Bob Goalby
1969	George Archer
1970	Billy Casper
1971	Charles Coody
1972	Jack Nicklaus
1973	Tommy Aaron
1974	Gary Player
1975	Jack Nicklaus

Masters Golf Tournament Winners

Year	Winner
1976	Ray Floyd
1977	Tom Watson
1978	Gary Player
1979	Fuzzy Zoeller
1980	Seve Ballesteros
1981	Tom Watson
1982	Craig Stadler
1983	Seve Ballesteros
1984	Ben Crenshaw
1985	Bernhard Langer
1986	Jack Nicklaus
1987	Larry Mize
1988	Sandy Lyle
1989	Nick Faldo
1990	Nick Faldo

British Open Winners

Year	Winner
1946	Sam Snead
1947	Fred Daly
1948	Henry Cotton
1949	Bobby Locke
1950	Bobby Locke
1951	Max Faulkner
1952	Bobby Locke
1953	Ben Hogan
1954	Peter Thomson
1955	Peter Thomson
1956	Peter Thomson
1957	Bobby Locke
1958	Peter Thomson
1959	Gary Player
1960	Kel Nagle
1961	Arnold Palmer
1962	Arnold Palmer
1963	Bob Charles
1964	Tony Lema
1965	Peter Thomson
1966	Jack Nicklaus
1967	Roberto de Vicenzo
1968	Gary Player
1969	Tony Jacklin
1970	Jack Nicklaus
1971	Lee Trevino
1972	Lee Trevino
1973	Tom Weiskopf
1974	Gary Player
1975	Tom Watson
1976	Johnny Miller
1977	Tom Watson
1978	Jack Nicklaus
1979	Seve Ballesteros
1980	Tom Watson
1981	Bill Rogers
1982	Tom Watson
1983	Tom Watson
1984	Seve Ballesteros
1985	Sandy Lyle
1986	Greg Norman
1987	Nick Faldo
1988	Seve Ballesteros
1989	Mark Calcavecchia
1990	Nick Faldo

Source: Robert Famighetti, The World Almanac and Book of Facts, 2000 (Mahwah, N.J., 1999), 923.

TABLE 18.71   PGA LEADING MONEY WINNERS, 1946–1990

Year	Player	Dollars
1946	Ben Hogan	42,556
1947	Jimmy Demaret	27.936
1948	Ben Hogan	36,812
1949	Sam Snead	31,593
1950	Sam Snead	35,758
1951	Lloyd Mangrum	26,088
1952	Jullus Boros	37,032
1953	Lew Worsham	34,002
1954	Bob Toski	65,819
1955	Julius Boros	65,121
1956	Ted Kroll	72,835
1957	Dick Mayer	65,835
1958	Arnold Palmer	42,407
1959	Art Wall Jr	53,167
1960	Arnold Palmer	75,262
1961	Gary Player	64,540
1962	Arnold Palmer	81,448
1963	Arnold Palmer	128,230
1964	Jack Nicklaus	113,284
1965	Jack Nicklaus	140,752
1966	Billy Casper	121,944
1967	Jack Nicklaus	188,988
1968	Billy Casper	205,168
1969	Frank Beard	175,223
1970	Lee Trevino	157,037
1971	Jack Nicklaus	244,490
1972	Jack Nicklaus	320,542
1973	Jack Nicklaus	308,362
1974	Johnny Miller	353,201
1975	Jack Nicklaus	323,149
1976	Jack Nicklaus	266,438
1977	Tom Watson	310,653
1978	Tom Watson	362,429
1979	Tom Watson	462,636
1980	Tom Watson	530,808
1981	Tom Kite	375,699
1982	Craig Stadler	446,462
1983	Hal Sutton	426,668
1984	Tom Watson	476,260
1985	Curtis Strange	542,321
1986	Greg Norman	653,296
1987	Curtis Strange	925,941
1988	Curtis Strange	1,147,644
1989	Tom Kite	1,395,278
1990	Greg Norman	1,165,477

Source: World Almanac, 1992, 912.

TABLE 18.72   MAJOR GOLF CHAMPIONSHIP LEADERS

Player	U.S. Open	British Open	PGA	Masters	U.S. Am.	British Am.	Total
Jack Nicklaus	4	3	5	6	2	0	20
Bobby Jones	4	3	0	0	5	1	13
Walter Hagen	2	4	5	0	0	0	11
Ben Hogan	4	1	2	2	0	0	9
Gary Player	1	3	2	3	0	0	9
John Ball	0	1	0	0	0	8	9
Arnold Palmer	1	2	0	4	1	0	8
Tom Watson	1	5	0	2	0	0	8
Harold Hilton	0	2	0	0	1	4	7
Gene Sarazen	2	1	3	1	0	0	7
Sam Snead	0	1	3	3	0	0	7
Harry Vardon	1	6	0	0	0	0	7
Lee Trevino	2	2	2	0	0	0	6

Note: Tournaments: U.S. Open, British Open, PGA Championship, Masters, U.S. Amateur, and British Amateur. Records reach through year 1990.
Source: 1993 Information Please Sports Almanac, 738.

TABLE 18.73   PGA LEADING CAREER-MONEY WINNERS

Rank	Player	Amount
1.	Tom Kite	$5,867,189
2.	Tom Watson	5,311,598
3.	Curtis Strange	5,195,485
4.	Jack Nicklaus	5,159,964
5.	Ben Crenshaw	4,384,348
6.	Payne Stewart	4,241,323
7.	Lanny Wadkins	4,323,138
8.	Ray Floyd	3,847,674
9.	Greg Norman	3,847,231
10.	Lee Trevino	3,474,916

Note: As of May 20, 1990.
Source: Universal Almanac, 1991, 623.

TABLE 18.74   WOMEN'S PROFESSIONAL GOLF— MAJOR CHAMPIONSHIPS, 1946–1990

U.S. Women's Open	
Year	Player
1946	Patty Berg
1947	Betty Jameson
1948	Babe Zaharias
1949	Louise Suggs
1950	Babe Zaharias
1951	Betsy Rawls
1952	Louise Suggs
1953	Betsy Rawls
1954	Babe Zaharias
1955	Fay Crocker
1956	Kathy Cornelius
1957	Betsy Rawls
1958	Mickey Wright
1959	Mickey Wright
1960	Betsy Rawls
1961	Mickey Wright
1962	Murle Lindstrom
1963	Mary Mills
1964	Mickey Wright
1965	Carol Mann
1966	Sandra Spuzich
1967	Catherine Lacoste
1968	Susie M. Berning
1969	Donna Caponi
1970	Donna Caponi
1971	JoAnne Carner
1972	Susie M. Berning
1973	Susie M. Berning
1974	Sandra Haynie
1975	Sandra Palmer
1976	JoAnne Carner
1977	Hollis Stacy
1978	Hollis Stacy
1979	Jerilyn Britz
1980	Amy Alcott
1981	Pat Bradley
1982	Janet Anderson
1983	Jan Stephenson
1984	Hollis Stacy
1985	Kathy Baker
1986	Jane Geddes
1987	Laura Davies
1988	Liselotte Neumann
1989	Betsy King
1990	Betsy King

LPGA Championship

Year	Player
1955	Beverly Hanson
1956	Marlene Hagge
1957	Louise Suggs
1958	Mickey Wright
1959	Betsy Rawls
1960	Mickey Wright
1961	Mickey Wright
1962	Judy Kimball
1963	Mickey Wright
1964	Mary Mills
1965	Sandra Haynie
1966	Gloria Ehret
1967	Kathy Whitworth
1968	Sandra Post
1969	Betsy Rawls
1970	Shirley Englehorn
1971	Kathy Whitworth
1972	Kathy Ahern
1973	Mary Mills
1974	Sandra Haynie
1975	Kathy Whitworth
1976	Betty Burfeindt
1977	Chako Higuchi
1978	Nancy Lopez
1979	Donna Caponi
1980	Sally Little
1981	Donna Caponi
1982	Jan Stephenson
1983	Patty Sheehan
1984	Patty Sheehan
1985	Nancy Lopez
1986	Pat Bradley
1987	Jane Geddes
1988	Sherri Turner
1989	Nancy Lopez
1990	Beth Daniel

Nabisco Dinah Shore

Year	Player
1972	Jane Blalock
1973	Mickey Wright
1974	JoAnn Prentice
1975	Sandra Palmer
1976	Judy Rankin
1977	Kathy Whitworth

Year	Player
1978	Sandra Post
1979	Sandra Post
1980	Donna Caponi
1981	Nancy Lopez
1982	Sally Little
1983	Amy Alcott
1984	Juli Inkster
1985	Alice Miller
1986	Pat Bradley
1987	Betsy King
1988	Amy Alcott
1989	Juli Inkster
1990	Betsy King

du Maurier Classic

Formerly known as La Canadienne in 1973 and the Peter Jackson Classic from 1974–83, this Canadian stop on the LPGA Tour become the third designated major championship in 1979.

Year	Player
1973	Jocelyne Bourassa
1974	Carole Jo Skala
1975	JoAnne Carner
1976	Donna Caponi
1977	Judy Rankin
1978	JoAnne Carner
1979	Amy Alcott
1980	Pat Bradley
1981	Jan Stephenson
1982	Sandra Haynie
1983	Hollis Stacy
1984	Juli Inkster
1985	Pat Bradley
1986	Pat Bradley
1987	Jody Rosenthal
1988	Sally Little
1989	Tammie Green
1990	Cathy Johnston

Source: 1993 Information Please Sports Almanac, 739–40.

TABLE 18.75   MAJOR GOLF CHAMPIONSHIP LEADERS

Player	U.S. Open	LPGA	duM	Dinah	Title Holders	Western	U.S. Am	Brit Am	Total
Patty Berg	1	0	0	0	7	7	1	0	16
Mickey Wright	4	4	0	0	2	3	0	0	13
Louise Suggs	2	1	0	0	4	4	1	1	13
Babe Zaharias	3	0	0	0	3	4	1	1	12
Betsy Rawls	4	2	0	0	0	2	0	0	8
JoAnne Carner	2	0	0	0	0	0	5	0	7
Kathy Whitworth	0	3	0	0	2	1	0	0	6
Pat Bradley	1	1	3	1	0	0	0	0	6
Juli Inkster	0	0	1	2	0	0	3	0	6
Glenna C. Vare	0	0	0	0	0	0	6	0	6

Note: Tournaments included are U.S. Open, LPGA Championship, du Maurier Classic, Nabisco Dinah Shore, Titleholders (1937–72), Western Open, (1937–67), U.S. Amateur, and British Amateur. Table covers tournaments through 1990.
Source: 1993 Information Please Sports Almanac, 741.

TABLE 18.76 LPGA LEADING MONEY WINNERS, 1954–1990

Year	Player	Dollars	Year	Player	Dollars
1954	Patty Berg	16,011	1973	Kathy Whitworth	82,854
1955	Patty Berg	16,492	1974	JoAnne Carner	87,094
1956	Marlene Hagge	20,235	1975	Sandra Palmer	94,805
1957	Patty Berg	16,272	1976	Judy Rankin	150,734
1958	Beverly Hanson	12,629	1977	Judy Rankin	122,890
1959	Betsy Rawls	26,774	1978	Nancy Lopez	189,813
1960	Louise Suggs	16,892	1979	Nancy Lopez	215,987
1961	Mickey Wright	22,236	1980	Beth Daniel	231,000
1962	Mickey Wright	21,641	1981	Beth Daniel	206,977
1963	Mickey Wright	31,269	1982	JoAnne Carner	310,399
1964	Mickey Wright	29,800	1983	JoAnne Carner	291,404
1965	Kathy Whitworth	28,658	1984	Betsy King	266,771
1966	Kathy Whitworth	33,517	1985	Nancy Lopez	416,472
1967	Kathy Whitworth	32,937	1986	Pat Bradley	492,021
1968	Kathy Whitworth	48,379	1987	Ayako Okamoto	466,034
1969	Carol Mann	49,152	1988	Sherri Turner	347,255
1970	Kathy Whitworth	30,235	1989	Betsy King	654,132
1971	Kathy Whitworth	41,181	1990	Beth Daniel	863,578
1972	Kathy Whitworth	65,063			

Source: World Almanac, 1994, 918.

TABLE 18.77 LPGA LEADING CAREER-MONEY WINNERS

Rank	Player	Dollars
1.	Pat Bradley	3,099,584
2.	Nancy Lopez	2,794,665
3.	Betsy King	2,668,029
4.	Amy Alcott	2,417,197
5.	JoAnne Carner	2,348,956
6.	Beth Daniel	2,272,233
7.	Patty Sheehan	2,265,445
8.	Ayako Okamoto	1,915,779
9.	Jan Stephenson	1,810,792
10.	Kathy Whitworth	1,716,458
11.	Hollis Stacy	1,433,199
12.	Donna Caponi	1,387,920
13.	Jane Blalock	1,290,944
14.	Sandra Palmer	1,277,018
15.	Sally Little	1,272,825

Note: As of May 20, 1990.
Source: Universal Almanac, 1991, 626.

Hockey

For 20 years the National Hockey League (NHL) stood stagnant. In the 1960s it had only six teams: four in large northern cities in the United States and two from Canada's largest metropolitan areas, Montreal and Toronto. To most Americans hockey was a foreign sport: Offside meant being in the opponent's territory, and icing was something that went on cakes. Almost without exception the hockey players were Canadian, and they included some of the best in the history of the game: Maurice Richard of Montreal, Frank Mahovlich of Toronto, Gordie Howe and Ted Lindsay of the Detroit Red Wings, the "Golden Jet" Bobby Hull, "Boom, Boom" Geoffrion, and many others. A period of expansion began in 1968, and it lasted approximately 10 years. First the league doubled its numbers, adding five teams from the United States and one from Canada. In 1972 a new league, the World Hockey Association, came on line and entered into bidding wars with the NHL for the most prized performers. A rivalry of seven years that destroyed some franchises and taxed resources of the others ended in 1979 officially in a merger, but in fact the NHL agreed to absorb the four most solid franchises of the WHA.

After movements and mergers, failures and additions, the league by the 1980s ended up with a very respectable 21 teams located in most regions of the United States and seven cities in Canada. Three major features did much to characterize professional hockey in that decade. First was emergence in the NHL of two semidynasties: the New York Islanders in the first part of the period and the Edmonton Oilers, Wayne Gretzky's team, in the last half. Second was shifting of the personnel base: A majority of players still were Canadian, but absolute domination had become a feature of the past. Improved college programs had brought several Americans into the league, and it became abundantly clear that the Europeans—most strikingly the Russians—had learned to play hockey very well. A few Europeans entered the league in the 1980s and, pending political developments in the Eastern bloc, many others were poised to make the trek West. Finally, a desire to keep pace with rapidly rising salaries in other professional sports in the United States reached the hockey players, prompting the first signals of labor unrest. Hockey might be Canadian but it needed American money—the sort of television payoffs being tendered to the big three team sports in the United States.

TABLE 18.78 TEAMS IN THE NATIONAL HOCKEY LEAGUE, 1946–1990

1945–46	1966–67
Standings	Standings
Team	Team
Montreal Boston Chicago Detroit Toronto New York	Chicago Montreal Toronto New York Detroit Boston

1970–71

Final Standings

East Division

Team	W	L	T	PTS	GF	GA
Boston	57	14	7	121	399	207
New York	49	18	11	109	259	177
Montreal	42	23	13	97	291	216
Toronto	37	33	8	82	248	211
Buffalo	24	39	15	63	217	291
Vancouver	24	46	8	56	229	296
Detroit	22	45	11	55	209	308

West Division

Team	W	L	T	PTS	GF	GA
Chicago	49	20	9	107	277	184
St. Louis	34	25	19	87	223	208
Philadelphia	28	33	17	73	207	225
Minnesota	28	34	16	72	191	223
Los Angeles	25	40	13	63	239	303
Pittsburgh	21	37	20	62	221	240
California	20	53	5	45	199	320

1989–90

Final Standings

Prince of Wales Conference

Adams Division

Team	W	L	T	PTS	GF	GA
Boston	46	25	9	101	289	232
Buffalo	45	27	8	98	286	248
Montreal	41	28	11	93	288	234
Hartford	38	33	9	85	275	268
Quebec	12	61	7	31	240	407

Clarence Campbell Conference					
Patrick Division					
New York R.	36	31	13	85	279	267
New Jersey	37	34	9	83	295	288
Washington	36	38	6	78	284	275
New York I.	31	38	11	73	281	288
Pittsburgh	32	40	8	72	318	359
Philadelphia	30	39	11	71	290	297
Norris Division					
Chicago	41	33	6	88	316	294
St. Louis	37	34	9	83	295	279
Toronto	38	38	4	80	337	358
Minnesota	36	40	4	76	284	291
Detroit	28	38	14	70	288	323
Smythe Division					
Calgary	42	23	15	99	348	265
Edmonton	38	28	14	90	315	283
Winnipeg	37	32	11	85	298	290
Los Angeles	34	39	7	75	338	337
Vancouver	25	41	14	64	245	306

Source: Zander Hollander, *The Complete Encyclopedia of Hockey* (Detroit, 1993), 67, 107, 117, 172).

TABLE 18.79   HOCKEY STANLEY CUP CHAMPIONS, 1946–1990

Year	Winner	Head Coach	Series	Loser	Head Coach
1946	Montreal	Dick Irvin	4–1 (WWWLW)	Boston	Dit Clapper
1947	Toronto	Hap Day	4–2 (LWWWLW)	Montreal	Dick Irvin
1948	Toronto	Hap Day	4–0	Detroit	Tommy Ivan
1949	Toronto	Hap Day	4–0	Detroit	Tommy Ivan
1950	Detroit	Tommy Ivan	4–3 (WLWLLWW)	NY Rangers	Lynn Patrick
1951	Toronto	Joe Primeau	4–1 (WLWWW)	Montreal	Dick Irvin
1952	Detroit	Tommy Ivan	4–0	Montreal	Dick Irvin
1953	Montreal	Dick Irvin	4–1 (WLWWW)	Boston	Lynn Patrick
1954	Detroit	Tommy Ivan	4–3 (WLWWLLW)	Montreal	Dick Irvin
1955	Detroit	Jimmy Skinner	4–3 (WWLLWLW)	Montreal	Dick Irvin
1956	Montreal	Toe Blake	4–1 (WWLWW)	Detroit	Jimmy Skinner
1957	Montreal	Toe Blake	4–1 (WWWLW)	Boston	Milt Schmidt
1958	Montreal	Toe Blake	4–2 (WLWLWW)	Boston	Milt Schmidt
1959	Montreal	Toe Blake	4–1 (WWLWW)	Toronto	Punch Imlach
1960	Montreal	Toe Blake	4–0	Toronto	Punch Imlach
1961	Chicago	Rudy Pilous	4–2 (WLWLWW)	Detroit	Sid Abel
1962	Toronto	Punch Imlach	4–2 (WWLLWW)	Chicago	Rudy Pilous
1963	Toronto	Punch Imlach	4–1 (WWLWW)	Detroit	Sid Abel
1964	Toronto	Punch Imlach	4–3 (WLLWLWW)	Detroit	Sid Abel
1965	Montreal	Toe Blake	4–3 (WWLLWLW)	Chicago	Billy Reay
1966	Montreal	Toe Blake	4–2 (LLWWWW)	Detroit	Sid Abel
1967	Toronto	Punch Imlach	4–2 (LWWLWW)	Montreal	Toe Blake
1968	Montreal	Toe Blake	4–0	St. Louis	Scotty Bowman
1969	Montreal	Claude Ruel	4–0	St. Louis	Scotty Bowman
1970	Boston	Harry Sinden	4–0	St. Louis	Scotty Bowman
1971	Montreal	Al MacNeil	4–3 (LLWWLWW)	Chicago	Billy Reay
1972	Boston	Tom Johnson	4–2 (WWLWLW)	NY Rangers	Emile Francis
1973	Montreal	Scotty Bowman	4–2 (WWLWLW)	Chicago	Billy Reay
1974	Philadelphia	Fred Shero	4–2 (LWWWLW)	Boston	Bep Guidolin
1975	Philadelphia	Fred Shero	4–2 (WWLLWW)	Buffalo	Floyd Smith
1976	Montreal	Scotty Bowman	4–0	Philadelphia	Fred Shero
1977	Montreal	Scotty Bowman	4–0	Boston	Don Cherry
1978	Montreal	Scotty Bowman	4–2 (WWLLWW)	Boston	Don Cherry
1979	Montreal	Scotty Bowman	4–1 (LWWWW)	NY Rangers	Fred Shero
1980	NY Islanders	Al Arbour	4–2 (WLWWLW)	Philadelphia	Pat Quinn
1981	NY Islanders	Al Arbour	4–1 (WWWLW)	Minnesota	Glen Sonmor
1982	NY Islanders	Al Arbour	4–0	Vancouver	Roger Neilson
1983	NY Islanders	Al Arbour	4–0	Edmonton	Glen Sather
1984	Edmonton	Glen Sather	4–1 (WLWWW)	NY Islanders	Al Arbour
1985	Edmonton	Glen Sather	4–1 (LWWWW)	Philadelphia	Mike Keenan
1986	Montreal	Jean Perron	4–1 (LWWWW)	Calgary	Bob Johnson
1987	Edmonton	Glen Sather	4–3 (WWLWLLW)	Philadelphia	Mike Keenan
1988	Edmonton	Glen Sather	4–0	Boston	Terry O'Reilly
1989	Calgary	Terry Crisp	4–2 (WLLWWW)	Montreal	Pat Burns
1990	Edmonton	John Muckler	4–1 (WWLWW)	Boston	Mike Milbury

Source: 1993 Information Please Sports Almanac, 356.

TABLE 18.80 ART ROSS TROPHY, 1945–1990

(leading scorer)

Season	Player	Team	Points
1945–46	Max Bentley	Chicago	61
1946–47	Max Bentley	Chicago	72
1947–48	Elmer Lach	Montreal	61
1948–49	Roy Conacher	Chicago	68
1949–50	Ted Lindsay	Detroit	78
1950–51	Gordie Howe	Detroit	86
1951–52	Gordie Howe	Detroit	86
1952–53	Gordie Howe	Detroit	95
1953–54	Gordie Howe	Detroit	81
1954–55	Bernie Geoffrion	Montreal	75
1955–56	Jean Beliveau	Montreal	88
1956–57	Gordie Howe	Detroit	89
1957–58	Dickie Moore	Montreal	84
1958–59	Dickie Moore	Montreal	96
1959–60	Bobby Hull	Chicago	81
1960–61	Bernie Geoffrion	Montreal	95
1961–62	Bobby Hull	Chicago	84
1962–63	Gordie Howe	Detroit	86
1963–64	Stan Mikita	Chicago	89
1964–65	Stan Mikita	Chicago	87
1965–66	Bobby Hull	Chicago	97
1966–67	Stan Mikita	Chicago	97
1967–68	Stan Mikita	Chicago	87
1968–69	Phil Esposito	Boston	126
1969–70	Bobby Orr	Boston	120
1970–71	Phil Esposito	Boston	152
1971–72	Phil Esposito	Boston	133
1972–73	Phil Esposito	Boston	130
1973–74	Phil Esposito	Boston	145
1974–75	Bobby Orr	Boston	135
1975–76	Guy Lafleur	Montreal	125
1976–77	Guy Lafleur	Montreal	136
1977–78	Guy Lafleur	Montreal	132
1978–79	Bryan Trottier	N.Y. Islanders	134
1979–80	Marcel Dionne	Los Angeles	137
1980–81	Wayne Gretzky	Edmonton	164
1981–82	Wayne Gretzky	Edmonton	212
1982–83	Wayne Gretzky	Edmonton	196
1983–84	Wayne Gretzky	Edmonton	205
1984–85	Wayne Gretzky	Edmonton	208
1985–86	Wayne Gretzky	Edmonton	215
1986–87	Wayne Gretzky	Edmonton	183
1987–88	Mario Lemieux	Pittsburgh	168
1988–89	Mario Lemieux	Pittsburgh	199
1989–90	Wayne Gretzky	Los Angeles	142

Source: Craig Carter, George Puro, Kyle Veltrop, eds., *The Sporting News Complete Hockey Book, 1995–96,* (St. Louis, 1995), 121.

TABLE 18.81 HART MEMORIAL TROPHY, 1945–1990

(most valuable player)

Season	Player	Team
1945–46	Max Bentley	Chicago
1946–47	Maurice Richard	Montreal
1947–48	Buddy O'Connor	N.Y. Rangers
1948–49	Sid Abel	Detroit
1949–50	Chuck Rayner	N.Y. Rangers
1950–51	Milt Schmidt	Boston
1951–52	Gordie Howe	Detroit
1952–53	Gordie Howe	Detroit
1953–54	Al Rollins	Chicago
1954–55	Ted Kennedy	Toronto
1955–56	Jean Beliveau	Montreal
1956–57	Gordie Howe	Detroit
1957–58	Gordie Howe	Detroit
1958–59	Andy Bathgate	N.Y. Rangers
1959–60	Gordie Howe	Detroit

Season	Player	Team
1960–61	Bernie Geoffrion	Montreal
1961–62	Jacques Plante	Montreal
1962–63	Gordie Howe	Detroit
1963–64	Jean Beliveau	Montreal
1964–65	Bobby Hull	Chicago
1965–66	Bobby Hull	Chicago
1966–67	Stan Mikita	Chicago
1967–68	Stan Mikita	Chicago
1968–69	Phil Esposito	Boston
1969–70	Bobby Orr	Boston
1970–71	Bobby Orr	Boston
1971–72	Bobby Orr	Boston
1972–73	Bobby Clarke	Philadelphia
1973–74	Phil Esposito	Boston
1974–75	Bobby Clarke	Philadelphia
1975–76	Bobby Clarke	Philadelphia
1976–77	Guy Lafleur	Montreal
1977–78	Guy Lafleur	Montreal
1978–79	Bryan Trottier	N.Y. Islanders
1979–80	Wayne Gretzky	Edmonton
1980–81	Wayne Gretzky	Edmonton
1981–82	Wayne Gretzky	Edmonton
1982–83	Wayne Gretzky	Edmonton
1983–84	Wayne Gretzky	Edmonton
1984–85	Wayne Gretzky	Edmonton
1985–86	Wayne Gretzky	Edmonton
1986–87	Wayne Gretzky	Edmonton
1987–88	Mario Lemieux	Pittsburgh
1988–89	Wayne Gretzky	Los Angeles
1989–90	Mark Messier	Edmonton

Source: Sporting News Hockey Book, 1995–96, 121–22.

TABLE 18.82 JAMES NORRIS MEMORIAL TROPHY, 1954–1990

(outstanding defenseman)

Year	Player	Team
1954	Red Kelly	Detroit
1955	Doug Harvey	Montreal
1956	Doug Harvey	Montreal
1957	Doug Harvey	Montreal
1958	Doug Harvey	Montreal
1959	Tom Johnson	Montreal
1960	Doug Harvey	Montreal
1961	Doug Harvey	Montreal
1962	Doug Harvey	N.Y. Rangers
1963	Pierre Pilote	Chicago
1964	Pierre Pilote	Chicago
1965	Pierre Pilote	Chicago
1966	Jacques Laperriere	Montreal
1967	Harry Howell	N.Y. Rangers
1968	Bobby Orr	Boston
1969	Bobby Orr	Boston
1970	Bobby Orr	Boston
1971	Bobby Orr	Boston
1972	Bobby Orr	Boston
1973	Bobby Orr	Boston
1974	Bobby Orr	Boston
1975	Bobby Orr	Boston
1976	Denis Potvin	N.Y. Islanders
1977	Larry Robinson	Montreal
1978	Denis Potvin	N.Y. Islanders
1979	Denis Potvin	N.Y. Islanders
1980	Larry Robinson	Montreal
1981	Randy Carlyle	Pittsburgh
1982	Doug Wilson	Chicago
1983	Rod Langway	Washington
1984	Rod Langway	Washington
1985	Paul Coffey	Edmonton
1986	Paul Coffey	Edmonton
1987	Ray Bourque	Boston
1988	Ray Bourque	Boston
1989	Chris Chelios	Montreal
1990	Ray Bourque	Boston

Source: Mark S. Hoffman, *The World Almanac and Book of Facts, 1991* (New York, 1990), 871.

TABLE 18.83 VEZINA TROPHY, 1945–1990

(outstanding goaltender)

Season	Player	Team	GAA
1945–46	Bill Durnan	Montreal	2.60
1946–47	Bill Durnan	Montreal	2.30
1947–48	Turk Broda	Toronto	2.38
1948–49	Bill Durnan	Montreal	2.10
1949–50	Bill Durnan	Montreal	2.20
1950–51	Al Rollins	Toronto	1.75
1951–52	Terry Sawchuk	Detroit	1.98
1952–53	Terry Sawchuk	Detroit	1.94
1953–54	Harry Lumley	Toronto	1.85
1954–55	Terry Sawchuk	Detroit	1.94
1955–56	Jacques Plante	Montreal	1.86
1956–57	Jacques Plante	Montreal	2.02
1957–58	Jacques Plante	Montreal	2.09
1958–59	Jacques Plante	Montreal	2.15
1959–60	Jacques Plante	Montreal	2.54
1960–61	Johnny Bower	Toronto	2.50
1961–62	Jacques Plante	Montreal	2.37
1962–63	Glenn Hall	Chicago	2.51
1963–64	Charlie Hodge	Montreal	2.26
1964–65	Terry Sawchuk	Toronto	2.56
	Johnny Bower	Toronto	2.38
1965–66	Lorne Worsley	Montreal	2.36
	Charlie Hodge	Montreal	2.58
1966–67	Glenn Hall	Chicago	2.38
	Denis DeJordy	Chicago	2.46
1967–68	Lorne Worsley	Montreal	1.98
	Rogatien Vachon	Montreal	2.48
1968–69	Glenn Hall	St. Louis	2.17
	Jacques Plante	St. Louis	1.96
1969–70	Tony Esposito	Chicago	2.17
1970–71	Ed Giacomin	N.Y. Rangers	2.15
	Gilles Villemure	N.Y. Rangers	2.29
1971–72	Tony Esposito	Chicago	1.76
	Gary Smith	Chicago	2.41
1972–73	Ken Dryden	Montreal	2.26
1973–74	Bernie Parent	Philadelphia	1.89
	Tony Esposito	Chicago	2.04
1974–75	Bernie Parent	Philadelphia	2.03
1975–76	Ken Dryden	Montreal	2.03
1976–77	Ken Dryden	Montreal	2.14
	Michel Larocque	Montreal	2.09
1977–78	Ken Dryden	Montreal	2.05
	Michel Larocque	Montreal	2.67
1978–79	Ken Dryden	Montreal	2.30
	Michel Larocque	Montreal	2.84
1979–80	Bob Sauve	Buffalo	2.36
	Don Edwards	Buffalo	2.57
1980–81	Richard Sevigny	Montreal	2.40
	Michel Larocque	Montreal	3.03
	Denis Herron	Montreal	3.50
1981–82	Billy Smith	N.Y. Islanders	2.97
1982–83	Pete Peeters	Boston	2.36
1983–84	Tom Barrasso	Buffalo	2.84
1984–85	Pelle Lindbergh	Philadelphia	3.02
1985–86	John Vanbiesbrouck	N.Y. Rangers	3.32
1986–87	Ron Hextall	Philadelphia	3.00
1987–88	Grant Fuhr	Edmonton	3.43
1988–89	Patrick Roy	Montreal	2.47
1989–90	Patrick Roy	Montreal	2.53

Source: Sporting News Hockey Book, 1995–96, 122.

Boxing

Professional boxing had high points in the decades following the Second World War, but much of the time it was a sport on the defensive. Attitudes varied, of course, but many people found the enterprise controlled by unprincipled operators, laden with corruption, and simply a brutal activity. Long a magnet for aggressive young men from ethnic minority groups, boxing could be viewed as an agent of deliverance or of exploitation. After 1945, origins of the competitors changed; young Irish, Jews, and Italians steadily vanished from the scene. The retirement in 1956 of Rocky Marciano as undefeated heavyweight champion probably marked an end of an era. Boxing thereupon became largely the domain of young black men, and nonblack fighters were likely to be Hispanic, leaving the sport with clear markings of race and class.

For all its perceived or real shortcomings, however, boxing continued to attract an audience. The "gate" might decline on the local circuit, but it remained large for major matches, and a new technological arrangement called closed-circuit television opened new opportunities. Champions or top contenders could demand a "purse" of millions for a few minutes in the ring. The postwar decades also produced some splendid athletes and intense rivalries. There was Tony Zale, Rocky Graziano, and Sugar Ray Robinson in the middleweight classes, and later came Thomas Hearns, Marvin Hagler, Roberto Duran, and Sugar Ray Leonard. The most exciting heavyweight since the retirement of Joe Louis in 1949 was Cassius Marcellus Clay, who, on winning the title in 1964, announced his conversion to Islam and change of name to Muhammad Ali. Ali would fight a long series of matches in the ring, winning most of them; he faced other struggles in the courts, with racism and failing health with determination and courage. Connected to a sport noted for shady deals and spoiled reputations, he became perhaps the most popular sports personality of his era and one of the most respected people in sports.

TABLE 18.84 BOXING CHAMPIONS IN MAJOR CLASSES, 1946–1990

Heavyweights (heavier than 195 lb)	
Year	Fighter
1937–1949	Joe Louis
1949–1951	Ezzard Charles
1951–1952	Joe Walcott
1952–1956	Rocky Marciano
1956–1959	Floyd Patterson
1959–1960	Ingemar Johansson
1960–1962	Floyd Patterson
1962–1964	Sonny Liston
1964–1967	Cassius Clay (Muhammad Ali)
1970–1973	Joe Frazier
1973–1974	George Foreman
1974–1978	Muhammad Ali
1978–1979	Leon Spinks (e), Muhammad Ali
1978	Ken Norton (WBC), Larry Holmes (WBC)
1979	John Tate (WBA)
1980	Mike Weaver (WBA)
1982	Michael Dokes (WBA)
1983	Gerrie Coetzee (WBA)
1984	Tim Witherspoon (WBC); Pinklon Thomas (WBC); Greg Page (WBA)
1985	Tony Tubbs (WBA); Michael Spinks (IBF)
1986	Tim Witherspoon (WBA); Trevor Berbick (WBC); Mike Tyson (WBC); James (Bone-crusher) Smith (WBA)
1987	Mike Tyson (WBA)
1990	James "Buster" Douglas (WBA, WBC, IBF)
1990	Evander Holyfield (WBA, WBC, IBF)

(continued)

TABLE 18.84   (continued)

Light Heavyweights (175–194 lb)

Year	Fighter
1941–1948	Gus Lesnevich, Freddie Mills
1948–1950	Freddie Mills
1950–1952	Joey Maxim
1952–1960	Archie Moore
1961–1962	vacant
1962–1963	Harold Johnson
1963–1965	Willie Pastrano
1965–1966	Jose Torres
1966–1968	Dick Tiger
1968–1974	Bob Foster, John Conteh (WBA)
1975–1977	John Conteh (WBC), Miguel Cuello (WBC), Victor Galindez (WBA)
1978	Mike Rossman (WBA), Mate Parlov (WBC), Marvin Johnson (WBC)
1979	Victor Galindez (WBA), Matthew Saad Muhammad (WBC)
1980	Eddle Mustava Muhammad (WBA)
1981	Michael Spinks (WBA), Dwight Braxton (WBC)
1983	Michael Spinks
1986	Marvin Johnson (WBA); Dennis Andries (WBC)
1987	Thomas Hearns (WBC); Leslie Stewart (WBA); Virgil Hill (WBA); Don Lalonde (WBC)
1988	Ray Leonard (WBC)
1989	Jeff Harding (WBC)
1990	Dennis Andries (WBC)

Middleweights (160–174 lb)

Year	Fighter
1941–1947	Tony Zale
1947–1948	Rocky Graziano
1948	Tony Zale, Marcel Cerdan
1949–1951	Jake LaMotta
1951	Ray Robinson, Randy Turpin, Ray Robinson
1953–1955	Carl (Bobo) Olson
1955–1957	Ray Robinson
1957	Gene Fullmer, Ray Robinson, Carmen Basilio
1958	Ray Robinson
1959	Gene Fullmer (NBA); Ray Robinson (N.Y.)
1960	Gene Fullmer (NBA); Paul Pender (New York and Mass.)
1961	Gene Fullmer (NBA); Terry Downes (New York, Mass., Europe)
1962	Gene Fullmer, Dick Tiger (NBA), Paul Pender (New York and Mass.)

Middleweights (160–174 lb)

Year	Fighter
1963	Dick Tiger (universal)
1963–1965	Joey Giardello
1965–1966	Dick Tiger
1966–1967	Emile Griffith
1967	Nino Benvenuti
1967–1968	Emile Griffith
1968–1970	Nino Benvenuti
1970–1977	Carlos Monzon
1977–1978	Rodrigo Valdez
1978–1979	Hugo Corro
1979–1980	Vito Antuofermo
1980	Alan Minter, Marvin Hagler
1987	Ray Leonard (WBC); Thomas Hearns (WBC); Sumbu Kalambay (WBA)
1988	Iran Barkley (WBC)
1989	Mike McCallum (WBA); Roberto Duran (WBC)
1991	Julian Jackson (WBC)

Welterweights (147–153 lb)

Year	Fighter
1941–1946	Fred Cochrane
1946–1946	Marty Servo; Ray Robinson
1946–1950	Ray Robinson
1951	Johnny Bratton (NBA)
1951–1954	Kid Gavilan

Welterweights (147–153 lb)

Year	Fighter
1954–1955	Johnny Saxton
1955	Tony De Marco, Carmen Basilio
1956	Carmen Basilio, Johnny Saxton, Basilio
1957	Carmen Basilio
1958–1960	Virgil Akins, Don Jordan
1960	Benny Paret
1961	Emile Griffith, Benny Paret
1962	Emile Griffith
1963	Luis Rodriguez, Emile Griffith
1964–1966	Emile Griffith
1966–1969	Curtis Cokes
1969–1970	Jose Napoles, Billy Backus
1971–1975	Jose Napoles
1975–1976	John Stracey (WBC), Angel Espada (WBA)
1976–1979	Carlos Palomino (WBC), Jose Cuevas (WBA)
1979	Wilfredo Benitez (WBC), Sugar Ray Leonard (WBC)
1980	Roberto Duran (WBC), Thomas Hearns (WBA), Sugar Ray Leonard (WBC)
1981–1982	Sugar Ray Leonard
1983	Donald Curry (WBA); Milton McCrory (WBC)
1985	Donald Curry
1986	Lloyd Honeyghan (WBC)
1987	Mark Breland (WBA); Marlon Starling (WBA); Jorge Vaca (WBC)
1988	Tomas Molinares (WBA); Lloyd Honeyghan (WBC)
1989	Marlon Starling (WBC); Mark Breland (WBA)
1990	Maurice Blocker (WBC); Aaron Davis (WBA)

Lightweights (131–135 lb)

Year	Fighter
1945–1951	Ike Williams (NBA: later universal)
1951–1952	James Carter
1952	Lauro Salas, James Carter
1953–1954	James Carter
1954	Paddy De Marco, James Carter
1955	James Carter; Bud Smith
1956	Bud Smith, Joe Brown
1956–1962	Joe Brown
1962–1965	Carlos Ortiz
1965	Ismael Laguna
1965–1968	Carlos Ortiz
1968–1969	Teo Cruz
1969–1970	Mando Ramos
1970	Ismael Laguna, Ken Buchanan (WBA)
1971	Mando Ramos (WBC), Pedro Carrasco (WBC)
1972–1979	Roberto Duran (WBA)
1972	Pedro Carrasco, Mando Ramos, Chango Carmona, Rodolfo Gonzalez (all WBC)
1974–1976	Guts Ishimatsu (WBC)
1976–1977	Esteban De Jesus (WBC)
1979	Jim Watt (WBC), Emesto Espana (WBA)
1980	Hilmer Kenty (WBA)
1981	Alexis Arguello (WBC), Sean O'Grady (WBA), Arturo Frias (WBA)
1982–1984	Ray Mancini (WBA)
1983	Edwin Rosario (WBC)
1984	Livingstone Bramble (WBA); Jose Luis Ramirez (WBC)
1985	Hector (Macho) Camacho (WBC)
1986	Edwin Rosario (WBA); Jose Luis Ramirez (WBC)
1987	Julio Cesar Chavez (WBA)
1989	Edwin Rosario (WBA); Pernell Whitaker (WBC)
1990	Juan Nazario (WBA): Pernell Whitaker (WBC)

Featherweights (126–129 lb)

Year	Fighter
1942–1948	Willie Pep
1948–1949	Sandy Saddler
1949–1950	Willie Pep
1950–1957	Sandy Saddler
1957–1959	Hogan (Kid) Bassey
1959–1963	Davey Moore
1963–1964	Sugar Ramos

Featherweights (126–129 lb)	
Year	Fighter
1964–1967	Vicente Saldivar
1968–1971	Paul Rojas (WBA), Sho Saijo (WBA)
1971	Antonio Gomez (WBA), Kuniald Shibada (WBC)
1972	Ernesto Marcel (WBA), Clemente Sanchez (WBC), Jose Legra (WBC)
1973	Eder Jofre (WBC)
1974	Ruben Olivares (WBA), Alexis Arguelle (WBA), Bobby Chacon (WBC)
1975	Ruben Olivares (WBC), David Kotey (WBC)
1976	Danny Lopez (WBC)
1977	Rafael Ortega (WBA)
1978	Cecilio Lastra (WBA), Eusebio Pedrosa (WBA)
1980	Salvador Sanchez (WBC)
1982	Juan LaPorte (WBC)
1984	Wilfredo Gomez (WBC); Azumah Nelson (WBC)
1985	Barry McGuigan (WBA)
1986	Steve Cruz (WBA)
1987	Antonio Esparragoza (WBA)
1988	Jeff Fenech (WBC)
1990	Marcos Villasana (WBC)

Note: Various sanctioning bodies include the NBA: National Boxing Assn.; WBC: World Boxing Council; WBA: World Boxing Assn.; IBF: International Boxing Federation.
Source: World Almanac, 1992, 871–73.

TABLE 18.85 HISTORY OF WORLD HEAVYWEIGHT CHAMPIONSHIP FIGHTS, 1937–1990

(bouts in which a new champion was crowned)

Date	Where Held	Winner	Weight	Age	Loser	Weight	Age	Rounds
Jun. 22, 1937	Chicago	Joe Louis	197 1/4	23	Jim Braddock	197	31	KO 8
Jun. 22, 1949	Chicago	Ezzard Charles	181 3/4	27	Joe Walcott	195 1/2	35	15
Sep. 27, 1950	New York	Ezzard Charles	184 1/2	29	Joe Louis	218	36	15
Jul. 18, 1951	Pittsburgh	Joe Walcott	194	37	Ezzard Charles	182	30	KO 7
Sep. 23, 1952	Philadelphia	Rocky Marciano	184	29	Joe Walcott	196	38	KO 13
Nov. 30, 1956	Chicago	Floyd Patterson	182 1/4	21	Archie Moore	187 3/4	42	KO 5
Jun. 26, 1959	New York	Ingemar Johansson	196	26	Floyd Patterson	182	24	KO 3
Jun. 20, 1960	New York	Floyd Patterson	190	25	Ingemar Johansson	194 3/4	27	KO 5
Sept. 25, 1962	Chicago	Sonny Liston	214	28	Floyd Patterson	189	27	KO 1
Feb. 25, 1964	Miami Beach, Fla.	Cassius Clay	210	22	Sonny Liston	218	30	KO 7
Mar. 4, 1968	New York	Joe Frazier	204 1/2	24	Buster Mathis	243 1/2	23	KO 11
Apr. 27, 1968	Oakland, Calif.	Jimmy Ellis	197	28	Jerry Quarry	195	22	15
Feb. 16, 1970	New York	Joe Frazier	205	26	Jimmy Ellis	201	29	KO 5
Jan. 22, 1973	Kingston, Jamaica	George Foreman	217 1/2	24	Joe Frazier	214	29	KO 2
Oct. 30, 1974	Kinshasa, Zaire	Muhammad Ali	216 1/2	32	George Foreman	220	26	KO 8
Feb. 15, 1978	Las Vegas, Nev.	Leon Spinks	197	25	Muhammad Ali	224 1/2	36	15
Jun. 9, 1978	Las Vegas, Nev.	Larry Holmes	212	28	Ken Norton	220	32	15
Sept. 15, 1978	New Orleans	Muhammad Ali	221	36	Leon Spinks	201	25	15
Oct. 20, 1979	Pretoria, S. Africa	John Tate	240	24	Gerrie Coetzee	222	24	15
Mar. 31, 1980	Knoxville, Tenn.	Mike Weaver	207 1/2	27	John Tate	232	25	KO 15
Dec. 10, 1982	Las Vegas, Nev.	Michael Dokes	216	24	Mike Weaver	209 1/2	30	KO 1
Sept. 23, 1983	Richfield, Ohio	Gerrie Coetzee	215	28	Michael Dokes	217	25	KO 10
Mar. 9, 1984	Las Vegas, Nev.	Tim Witherspoon	220 1/2	26	Greg Page	239 1/2	25	12
Aug. 31, 1984	Las Vegas, Nev.	Pinklon Thomas	216	26	Tim Witherspoon	217	26	12
Nov. 9, 1984	Las Vegas, Nev.	Larry Holmes	221 1/2	35	James Smith	227	31	KO 12
Dec. 1, 1984	Sun City, S. Africa	Greg Page	236	25	Gerry Coetzee	217	29	KO 8
Apr. 29, 1985	Buffalo, N.Y.	Tony Tubbs	229	26	Greg Page	239 1/2	26	15
Sept. 21, 1985	Las Vegas, Nev.	Michael Spinks	200	29	Larry Holmes	221	35	15
Jan. 17, 1986	Atlanta, Ga.	Tim Witherspoon	227	28	Tony Tubbs	229	27	15
Nov. 23, 1986	Las Vegas, Nev.	Mike Tyson	217	20	Trevor Berbick	220	29	KO 2
Dec. 12, 1986	New York, N.Y.	James Smith	230	33	Tim Witherspoon	218	29	KO 1
Mar. 7, 1987	Las Vegas, Nev.	Mike Tyson	217	20	James Smith	230	33	12
Feb. 10, 1990	Tokyo	James "Buster" Douglas	231 1/2	29	Mike Tyson	220	23	KO 10
Oct. 25, 1990	Las Vegas, Nev.	Evander Holyfield	208	28	James "Buster" Douglas	246	30	KO 3

Note: KO=Knock out; other winners a result of judges' decision.
Source: Information Please Almanac, 1992, 916.

TABLE 18.86 MUHAMMAD ALI'S PROFESSIONAL RECORD

Born Cassius Marcellus Clay, Jr., on January 17, 1942, in Louisville; Amateur record of 100–5; won light-heavyweight gold medal at 1960 Olympic Games; Pro record of 56–50 with 37 KOs in 61 fights.

1960

Date	Opponent	Location	Result
Oct. 29	Tunney Hunsaker	Louisville	Wu 6
Dec. 27	Herb Siler	Miami Beach	TKO 4

1961

Date	Opponent	Location	Result
Jan. 17	Tony Esperti	Miami Beach	TKO 3
Feb. 7	Jim Robinson	Miami Beach	TKO 1
Feb. 21	Donnie Fleeman	Miami Beach	TKO 7
Apr. 19	Lamar Clark	Louisville	KO 2
Jun. 26	Duke Sabedong	Las Vegas	Wu 10
Jul .22	Alonzzo Johnson	Louisville	Wu 10
Oct. 7	Alex Miteff	Louisville	TKO 6
Nov. 29	Willi Besmanoff	Louisville	TKO 7

1962

Date	Opponent	Location	Result
Feb. 10	Sonny Banks	New York	TKO 4
Feb. 28	Don Wamer	Miami Beach	TKO 4
Apr. 23	George Logan	Los Angeles	TKO 4
May 19	Billy Daniels	Los Angeles	TKO 7
Jul. 20	Alejandro Lavorante	Los Angeles	KO 5
Nov. 15	Archie Moore	Los Angeles	KO 4

1963

Date	Opponent	Location	Result
Jan. 24	Charlie Powell	Pittsburgh	KO 3
Mar. 13	Doug Jones	New York	Wu 10
Jun. 18	Henry Cooper	London	TKO 5

1964

Date	Opponent	Location	Result
Feb. 25	Sonny Liston	Miami Beach	TKO 7

(won World Heavyweight title)

After the fight, Clay announces he is a member of the Black Muslim religious sect and has changed his name to Muhammad Ali.

1965

Date	Opponent	Location	Result
May 25	Sonny Liston	Lewiston, Me	KO 1
Nov. 22	Floyd Patterson	Las Vegas	TKO 12

1966

Date	Opponent	Location	Result
Mar. 29	George Chuvaolo	Toronto	Wu 15
May 21	Henry Cooper	London	TKO 6
Aug. 6	Brian London	London	KO 3
Sept. 10	Karl Mildenberger	Franfurt	TKO 12
Nov. 12	Cleveland Williams	Houston	TKO 3

1967

Date	Opponent	Location	Result
Feb. 6	Ernie Terrell	Houston	Wu 15
Mar. 22	Zora Foiley	New York	KO 7
Apr. 28	Refuses induction into U.S. Army and is stripped of world title by WBA and most state commissions the next day.		
June. 20	Found guilty of draft evasion in Houston; fined $10,000 and sentenced to 5 years; remains free pending appeals, but is barred from the ring.		

1968–69 (Inactive)

1970

Date	Opponent	Location	Result
Feb. 3	Announces retirement		
Oct. 26	Jerry Quarry	Atlanta	TKO 3
Dec. 7	Oscar Bonavena	New York	TKO 15

1971

Date	Opponent	Location	Result
Mar. 8	Joe Frazier	New York	Lu 15
	(for World Heavyweight title)		
Jun. 28	U.S. Supreme Court unanimously reverses Ali's 1967 conviction saying he had been drafted improperly.		
Jul. 26	Jimmy Ellis	Houston	TKO 12
	(won vacant NABF Heavyweight title)		
Nov. 17	Buster Mathis	Houston	Wu 12
Dec. 26	Jurgen Blin	Zurich	KO 7

1972

Date	Opponent	Location	Result
Apr. 1	Mac Foster	Tokyo	Wu 15
May 1	George Chuvalo	Vancouver	Wu 12
Jun. 27	Jerry Quarry	Las Vegas	TKO 7
Jul. 19	Al (Blue) Lewis	Dublin, Ire	TKO 11
Sept. 20	Floyd Patterson	New York	TKO 7
Nov. 21	Bob Foster	Stateline, Nev	TKO 8

1973

Date	Opponent	Location	Result
Feb. 14	Joe Bugner	Las Vegas	Wu 12
Mar. 31	Ken Norton	San Diego	Ls 12
	(lost NABF Heavyweight title)		
Sept. 10	Ken Norton	Inglewood, Calif	Ws 12
	(regained NABF Heavyweight title)		
Oct. 20	Rudi Rubbers	Jakarta, Indonesia	Wu 12

1974

Date	Opponent	Location	Result
Jan. 28	Joe Frazier	New York	Wu 12
Oct. 30	George Foreman	Kinshasa, Zaire	KO 8
	(regained World Heavyweight title)		

1975

Date	Opponent	Location	Result
Mar. 24	Chuck Wepner	Cleveland	TKO 15
May 16	Ron Lyle	Las Vegas	TKO 11
Jun. 30	Joe Bugner	Kuala Lumpur, Malaysia	Wu 15
Sept. 30	Joe Frazier	Manila	TKO 14

1976

Date	Opponent	Location	Result
Feb. 20	Jean-Pierre Coopman	San Juan	KO 5
Apr. 30	Jimmy Young	Landover, Md	Wu 15
May 24	Richard Dunn	Munich	TKO 5
Sept. 28	Ken Norton	New York	Wu 15

1977

Date	Opponent	Location	Result
May 16	Alfredo Evangelista	Landover	Wu 15
Sept. 29	Earnie Shavers	New York	Wu 15

1978

Date	Opponent	Location	Result
Feb. 15	Leon Spinks	Las Vegas	Ls 15
	(lost World Heavyweight title)		
Sept. 15	Leon Spinks	New Orleans	Wu 15
	(regained World Heavyweight title)		

1979			
Date			
June 27	Announces retirement		
1980			
Date	Opponent	Location	Result
Oct. 2	Larry Holmes	Las Vegas	TKO by 11
1981			
Date	Opponent	Location	Result
Dec. 11	Trevor Berbick	Nassau	Lu 10

Note: Wu=winner, unanimous decision; TKO=Technical knockout; KO=Knockout; Lu=loser, unanimous decision; Ls=loser, split decision.
Source: 1993 Information please Sports Almanac, 788.

Automobile Racing

Automobile racing came to encompass many types of races and classes of equipment, but as continuing competition and as a spectator sport, most attention in the United States focused on two categories: Indianapolis-type racers and stock cars. Both would be shaped by revolutions in finance and technology. Indy cars came into being for no reason other than competition, specifically in the Indianapolis 500 Race on Memorial Day weekend. Technology concentrated on producing a well-handling ride, a chassis that would stick to the surface when rounding turns at nearly top speed, and of course engines that would run fast. Until the 1960s most Indianapolis cars were roadsters powered by a four-cylinder Offenhauser engine mounted in the front. The early 1960s brought a new design—a V-8 engine mounted in the rear—that would dominate the remainder of the era. Top speeds, which began the period at around 125 mph (pole position speed for

TABLE 18.87 INDIANAPOLIS 500, 1946–1990

First held in 1911, the Indianapolis 500—200 laps of the 2.5-mile Indianapolis Motor Speedway Track (called the Brickyard in honor of its original pavement)—grew to become the most famous auto race in the world. Held on Memorial Day weekend, it annually drew the largest crowd of any sporting event in the world.

Year	Winner	Start Position	Car	Avg MPH	Pole Winner	MPH
1946	George Robson	15	Thorne Engineering Special	114.820	Cliff Bergere	126.471
1947	Mauri Rose	3	Blue Crown Spark Plug Special	116.338	Ted Horn	126.564
1948	Mauri Rose	3	Blue Crown Spark Plug Special	119.814	Rex Mays	130.577
1949	Bill Holland	4	Blue Crown Spark Plug Special	121.327	Duke Nalon	132.939
1950	Johnnie Parsons	5	Wynn's Friction Proofing	124.002	Walt Faulkner	134.343
1951	Lee Wallard	2	Belanger Special	126.244	Duke Nalon	136.498
1952	Troy Ruttman	7	Agajanian Special	128.922	Fred Agabashian	138.010
1953	Bill Vukovich	1	Fuel Injection Special	128.740	Bill Vukovich	138.392
1954	Bill Vukovich	19	Fuel Injection Special	130.840	Jack McGrath	141.033
1955	Bob Sweikert	14	John Zink Special	128.209	Jerry Hoyt	140.045
1956	Pat Flaherty	1	John Zink Special	128.490	Pat Flaherty	145.596
1957	Sam Hanks	13	Belond Exhaust Special	135.601	Pat O'Connor	143.948
1958	Jim Bryan	7	Belond AP Parts Special	133.791	Dick Rathmann	145.974
1959	Rodger Ward	6	Leader Card 500 Roadster	135.857	Johnny Thomson	145.908
1960	Jim Rathmann	2	Ken-Paul Special	138.767	Eddie Sachs	146.592
1961	A. J. Foyt	7	Bowes Seal-Fast Special	139.130	Eddie Sachs	147.481
1962	Rodger Ward	2	Leader Card 500 Roadster	140.293	Parnelli Jones	150.370
1963	Parnelli Jones	1	Agajanian-Willard Special	143.137	Parnelli Jones	151.153
1964	A. J. Foyt	5	Sheraton-Thompson Special	147.350	Jim Clark	158.828
1965	Jim Clark	2	Lotus Ford	150.686	A. J. Foyt	161.233
1966	Graham Hill	15	American Red Ball Special	144.317	Mario Andretti	165.899
1967	A. J. Foyt	4	Sheraton-Thompson Special	151.207	Mario Andretti	168.982
1968	Bobby Unser	3	Rislone Special	152.882	Joe Leonard	171.559
1969	Mario Andretti	2	STP Oil Treatment Special	156.867	A. J. Foyt	170.568
1970	Al Unser	1	Johnny Lightning 500 Special	155.749	Al Unser	170.221
1971	Al Unser	5	Johnny Lightning Special	157.735	Peter Revson	178.696
1972	Mark Donohue	3	Sunoco McLaren	162.962	Bobby Unser	195.940
1973	Gordon Johncock	11	STP Double Oil Filters	159.036	Johnny Rutherford	198.413
1974	Johnny Rutherford	25	McLaren	158.589	A. J. Foyt	191.632
1975	Bobby Unser	3	Jorgensen Eagle	149.213	A. J. Foyt	193.976
1976	Johnny Rutherford	1	Hy-Gain McLaren/Goodyear	148.725	Johnny Rutherford	188.957
1977	A. J. Foyt	4	Gilmore Racing Team	161.331	Tom Sneva	198.884
1978	Al Unser	5	FNCTC Chaparral Lola	161.361	Tom Sneva	202.156
1979	Rick Mears	1	The Gould Charge	158.899	Rick Mears	193.736
1980	Johnny Rutherford	1	Pennzoil Chaparral	142.862	Johnny Rutherford	192.256
1981	Bobby Unser	1	Norton Spirit Penske PC-9B	139.084	Bobby Unser	200.546
1982	Gordon Johncock	5	STP Oil Treatment	162.026	Rick Mears	207.004
1983	Tom Sneva	4	Texaco Star	162.117	Teo Fabi	207.395
1984	Rick Mears	3	Pennzoil Z-7	163.612	Tom Sneva	210.029
1985	Danny Sullivan	8	Miller American Special	152.982	Pancho Carter	212.583
1986	Bobby Rahal	4	Budweiser/Truesports/March	170.722	Rick Mears	216.828
1987	Al Unser	20	Cummins Holset Turbo	162.175	Mario Andretti	215.390
1988	Rick Mears	1	Penske-Chevrolet	144.809	Rick Mears	219.198
1989	Emerson Fittipaldi	3	Penske-Chevrolet	167.581	Rick Mears	223.885
1990	Arie Luyendyk	3	Domino's Pizza Chevrolet	185.981	Emerson Fittipaldi	225.301

Source: Sports Illustrated 1997 Sports Almanac, 507–08.

turning one 2.5-mile lap), went to 150 in 1962, 200 in 1978, and 225 in 1990—a total increase of 100 mph. A small fraternity of Indy car drivers that included such names as Rodger Ward, A. J. Foyt, the Unser family, the Andrettis, and Rick Mears, was well known in the world of sports. Popularity of Indianapolis type, open-wheel racing did not grow in accordance with the advance in technology, but the Indianapolis 500 remained not only the "greatest spectacle in racing" but also the best-attended single sporting event in the world.

The development of stock-car racing or the size of it came as a surprise. Long considered an expression of a coarse, crude, and impoverished southern society, racing in the south moved quickly from ol' boys driving souped-up personal cars to a structured and profitable racing organization called NASCAR (National Association for Stock Car Auto Racing), under the firm hand of a man named Bill France. Growing popularity of the races attracted interest from outsiders, including the automobile manufacturers. The Daytona Speed-

way, a paved, steeply banked, 2.5-mile oval, opened in 1959. Everywhere in the South the tracks were being paved; in the 1970s the circuit expanded to Michigan, Pennsylvania, Maryland, California, and Arizona. Other states were planning new speedways, hoping the "big boys," now called the Winston Cup Series, would come to race. Southern pioneers of stock-car racing—the Pettys, the Allisons, the Yarboroughs, and the Pearsons—were being joined by competent drivers from the North and West. CBS and ESPN took the lead in offering national television coverage of specified races. The stock cars had stolen the show in automobile competition, and evolution of the stock-car race surely was one of the two or three most remarkable developments in sports in the last third of the 20th century.

TABLE 18.88 SPEEDWAY MONEY—THE PAYOUT AT INDY, 1946–1990

Year	Purse	Winner
1946	$115,450	$42,550
1947	137,425	31,450
1948	171,075	42,800
1949	179,050	51,575
1950	201,135	57,458
1951	207,650	63,612
1952	230,100	61,743
1953	246,300	89,496
1954	269,375	74,934
1955	270,400	76,138
1956	282,052	93,819
1957	300,252	103,844
1958	305,217	111,327
1959	338,100	105,805
1960	369,150	110,000
1961	400,000	117,975
1962	426,152	125,015
1963	494,030	148,513
1964	506,575	153,650
1965	628,399	186,621
1966	691,808	156,297
1967	734,634	171,227
1968	712,269	177,523
1969	805,127	205,727
1970	1,000,002	271,697
1971	1,001,604	238,454
1972	1,011,848	218,767
1973	1,006,105	236,022
1974	1,015,686	245,031
1975	1,001,321	214,031
1976	1,037,755	256,121
1977	1,116,807	259,791
1978	1,145,225	290,383
1979	1,271,954	270,401
1980	1,503,225	318,819
1981	1,609,375	299,124
1982	2,067,475	290,609
1983	2,411,450	385,886
1984	2,795,899	434,061
1985	3,271,025	517,662
1986	4,001,450	581,062
1987	4,490,375	526,762
1988	5,025,400	809,853
1989	5,723,725	1,001,604
1990	6,325,803	1,090,940

Source: Wall Street Journal Almanac, 1998, 1105.

TABLE 18.89 RACING AT DAYTONA—THE EARLY YEARS, 1949–1958

(4.1 mile beach/road course)

Year	Winner	Type Car	Laps
1949	Red Byron	Oldsmobile	
1950	Harold Kite	Lincoln	49
1951	Marshall Teague	Hudson	39
1952	Marshall Teague	Hudson	36
1953	Bill Blair	Oldsmobile	39
1954	Lee Petty	Chrysler	39
1955	Tim Flock	Chrysler	39
1956	Tim Flock	'56 Chrysler	39
1957	Cotton Owens	'57 Pontiac	39
1958	Paul Goldsmith	Pontiac	39

Source: Old Cars Publications, Standard Catalogue of American Cars, 1946–1975 (Iola, Wisc., 1976), 782.

TABLE 18.90 DAYTONA 500 WINNERS, 1959–1990

(2.5-mile paved, banked oval)

Year	Driver	Car	Avg. MPH
1959	Lee Petty	Oldsmobile	135.521
1960	Junior Johnson	Chevrolet	124.740
1961	Marvin Panch	Pontiac	149.601
1962	Fireball Roberts	Pontiac	152.529
1963	Tiny Lund	Ford	151.566
1964	Richard Petty	Plymouth	154.334
1965	Fred Lorenzen	Ford	141.539
1966	Richard Petty	Plymouth	160.627
1967	Mario Andretti	Ford	146.926
1968	Cale Yarborough	Mercury	143.251
1969	Lee Roy Yarborough	Ford	160.875
1970	Pete Hamilton	Plymouth	149.601
1971	Richard Petty	Plymouth	144.456
1972	A. J. Foyt	Mercury	161.550
1973	Richard Petty	Dodge	157.205
1974	Richard Petty	Dodge	140.894
1975	Benny Parsons	Chevrolet	153.649
1976	David Pearson	Mercury	152.181
1977	Cale Yarborough	Chevrolet	153.218
1978	Bobby Allison	Ford	159.730
1979	Richard Petty	Oldsmobile	143.977
1980	Buddy Baker	Oldsmobile	177.602
1981	Richard Petty	Buick	169.651
1982	Bobby Allison	Buick	153.991
1983	Cale Yarborough	Pontiac	155.979
1984	Cale Yarborough	Chevrolet	150.994
1985	Bill Elliott	Ford	172.265
1986	Geoff Bodine	Chevrolet	148.124
1987	Bill Elliott	Ford	176.263
1988	Bobby Allison	Buick	137.531
1989	Darrell Waltrip	Chevrolet	148.466
1990	Derrike Cope	Chevrolet	165.761

Source: World Almanac, 1991, 935.

TABLE 18.91   WINSTON CUP NASCAR CHAMPIONS[a], 1949–1990

Year	Driver	Car	Wins	Poles	Winnings ($)
1949	Red Byron	Oldsmobile	2	0	5,800
1950	Bill Rexford	Oldsmobile	1	0	6,175
1951	Herb Thomas	Hudson	7	4	18,200
1952	Tim Flock	Hudson	8	4	20,210
1953	Herb Thomas	Hudson	11	10	27,300
1954	Lee Petty	Dodge	7	3	26,706
1955	Tim Flock	Chrysler	18	19	33,750
1956	Buck Baker	Chrysler	14	12	29,790
1957	Buck Baker	Chevrolet	10	5	24,712
1958	Lee Petty	Olds	7	4	20,600
1959	Lee Petty	Plymouth	10	2	45,570
1960	Rex White	Chevrolet	6	3	45,260
1961	Ned Jarrett	Chevrolet	1	4	27,285
1962	Joe Weatherly	Pontiac	9	6	56,110
1963	Joe Weatherly	Mercury	3	6	58,110
1964	Richard Petty	Plymouth	9	8	98,810
1965	Ned Jarrett	Ford	13	9	77,966
1966	David Pearson	Dodge	14	7	59,205
1967	Richard Petty	Plymouth	27	18	130,275
1968	David Pearson	Ford	16	12	118,824
1969	David Pearson	Ford	11	14	183,700
1970	Bobby Isaac	Dodge	11	13	121,470
1971	Richard Petty	Plymouth	21	9	309,225
1972	Richard Petty	Plymouth	8	3	227,015
1973	Benny Parsons	Chevrolet	1	0	114,345
1974	Richard Petty	Dodge	10	7	299,175
1975	Richard Petty	Dodge	13	3	378,865
1976	Cale Yarborough	Chevrolet	9	2	387,173
1977	Cale Yarborough	Chevrolet	9	3	477,499
1978	Cale Yarborough	Oldsmobile	10	8	530,751
1979	Richard Petty	Chevrolet	5	1	531,292
1980	Dale Earnhardt	Chevrolet	5	0	588,926
1981	Darrell Waltrip	Buick	12	11	693,342
1982	Darrell Waltrip	Buick	12	7	873,118
1983	Bobby Allison	Buick	6	0	828,355
1984	Terry Labonte	Chevrolet	2	2	713,010
1985	Darrell Waltrip	Chevrolet	3	4	1,318,735
1986	Dale Earnhardt	Chevrolet	5	1	1,783,880
1987	Dale Earnhardt	Chevrolet	11	1	2,099,243
1988	Bill Elliott	Ford	6	6	1,574,639
1989	Rusty Wallace	Pontiac	6	4	2,247,950
1990	Dale Earnhardt	Chevrolet	9	4	3,083,056

[a] The ultimate mark of success in the major league of stock-car racing. Scoring is based largely on individual finish in each of the series' races.
Source: *Sports Illustrated 1997 Sports Almanac*, 512.

Horse Racing

While horse racing could never be in the United States the "sport of kings," the racing establishment did play close heed to bloodlines, and it acknowedged a form of aristocracy. The bloodline, of course, existed totally with the horses, and a suggestion of an upper crust pertained to a cast of racing characters that included traders, breeders, trainers, stablehands, and jockeys. The top, the aristocracy, involved the horse or stable owners. Year after year, horse racing attracted an on-site audience far greater than all major league baseball games combined or any other sporting series. People went to the track to experience the thrill of competition in the race—really a series of races—compounded by the fact that spectators probably had a stake in the outcome. Horse racing stood as a familiar outlet for a popular impulse for gambling—a practice that could entail a make-or-break situation with serious amounts of money involved, or it could be passed off as another expression of sporting behavior. Otherwise, the general populace paid at best passing attention to horse racing. Many people might regard the most famous race, the Kentucky Derby, as one of the few national rites of spring, note the name of the winning horse and jockey, and if by chance a horse seemed truly exceptional, the sporting public paid closer attention, and insiders of the sport perhaps identified the makings of a legend, a point of past and future reference for their enterprise. To the extent that any animal fit these characteristics during the years 1946–1990, it would have to be the red stallion that burst on the scene in the early to mid-1970s then retired to a long life of siring new race horses. But none of them would be a match for Secretariat.

TABLE 18.92   TRIPLE CROWN OF HORSE RACING, 1946–1990

Kentucky Derby					Preakness Stakes					Belmont Stakes				
Churchill Downs; 3-year-olds; $1^{1}/_{4}$ miles					Pimlico; 3-year-olds; $1^{3}/_{16}$ miles					Belmont Park; 3-year-olds; $1^{1}/_{2}$ miles				
Year	Winner	Jockey	Wt	Win. Val ($)	Year	Winner	Jockey	Wt	Win. Val ($)	Year	Winner	Jockey	Wt	Win. Val ($)
1946	Assault	W. Mehrtens	126	96,400	1946	Assault	W. Mehrtens	126	96,620	1946	Assault	W. Mehrtens	126	75,400
1947	Jet Pilot	E. Guerin	126	92,160	1947	Faultless	D.Dodson	126	98,005	1947	Phalanx	R. Donoso	126	78,900
1948	Citation	E. Arcaro	126	83,400	1948	Citation	E. Arcaro	126	91,870	1948	Citation	E. Arcaro	126	77,700
1949	Ponde	S. Brooks	126	91,600	1949	Capot	T. Atkinson	126	79,985	1949	Capot	T. Atkinson	126	60,900
1950	Middle-ground	W.Boland	126	92,650	1950	Hill Prince	E. Arcaro	126	56,115	1950	Middle-ground	W. Boland	126	61,350
1951	Count Turf	C. McCreary	126	98,050	1951	Bold	E. Arcaro	126	83,110	1951	Counter point	D. Gorman	126	82,000
1952	Hill Gail	E. Arcaro	126	96,300	1952	Blue Man	C. McCreary	126	86,135	1952	One Count	E. Arcaro	126	82,400
1953	Dark Star	H. Moreno	126	90,050	1953	Native Dancer	E. Guerin	126	65,200	1953	Native Dancer	E. Guerin	126	82,500
1954	Determine	R.Yofk	126	102,050	1954	Hasty Road	J. Adams	126	91,600	1954	High Gun	E. Guerin	126	89,000
1955	Swaps	W. Shoemaker	126	108,400	1955	Nashua	E. Arcaro	126	67,550	1955	Nashua	E. Arcaro	126	83,700
1956	Needles	D. Erb	126	123,450	1956	Fabius	W. Hartack	126	84,250	1956	Needles	D. Erb	126	83,600
1957	Iron Liege	W. Hartack	126	107,950	1957	Bold Ruler	E. Arcaro	126	65,250	1957	Gallant Man	W. Shoemaker	126	77,300
1958	Tim Tam	I. Valenzuela	126	116,400	1958	Tim Tam	I. Valenzuela	126	97,900	1958	Cavan	P. Anderson	126	73,440
1959	Tomy Lee	W. Shoemaker	126	119,650	1959	Royal Orbit	W. Harmatz	126	136,200	1959	Sword Dancer	W. Shoemaker	126	93,525
1960	Venetian Way	W. Hartack	126	114,850	1960	Belly Ache	R. Ussery	126	121,000	1960	Celtic Ash	W. Hartack	126	96,785
1961	Carry Back	J. Sellers	126	120,500	1961	Carry Back	J. Sellers	126	126,200	1961	Sherluck	B. Baeza	126	104,900
1962	Decidedly	W. Hartack	126	119,650	1962	Greek Money	J. Rotz	126	135,800	1962	Jaipur	W. Shoemaker	126	109,550
1963	Chateau-guay	B. Baeza	126	108,900	1963	Candy Spots	W. Shoemaker	126	127,500	1963	Chateauguay	B. Baeza	126	101,700
1964	Northern Dancer	W. Hartack	126	114,300	1964	Northern Dancer	W. Hartack	126	124,200	1964	Quadrangle	M. Ycaza	126	110,850
1965	Lucky Debonair	W. Shoemaker	126	112,000	1965	Tom Rolfe	R. Turcotte	126	128,100	1965	Hail to All	J. Sellers	126	104,150
1966	Kauai King	D. Brumfield	126	120,500	1966	Kauai King	D. Brumfield	126	129,000	1966	Amberoid	W. Boland	126	117,700
1967	Proud Clarion	R. Ussery	126	119,700	1967	Damascus	W. Shoemaker	126	141,500	1967	Damascus	W. Shoemaker	126	104,950
1968	Forward Pass	I. Valenzuela	126	122,600	1968	Forward Pass	I. Valenzuela	126	142,700	1968	Stage Door Johnny	H. Gustines	126	117,700
1969	Majestic Prince	W. Hartack	126	113,200	1969	Majestic Prince	W. Hartack	126	129,500	1969	Arts and Letters	B. Baeza	126	104,050
1970	Dust Com-mander	M. Manga-nello	126	127,800	1970	Personality	E. Belmonte	126	151,300	1970	High Echelon	J. Rotz	126	115,000
1971	Canonero II	G. Avila	126	145,500	1971	Canonero II	G. Avita	126	137,400	1971	Pass Catcher	R. Blum	126	97,710
1972	Riva Ridge	R. Turcotte	126	140,300	1972	Bee Bee Bee	E. Nelson	126	135,300	1972	Riva Ridge	R. Turcotte	126	93,540
1973	Secretariat	R. Turcotte	126	155,050	1973	Secretariat	R. Turcotte	126	129,900	1973	Secretariat	R. Turcotte	126	90,120
1974	Cannonade	A. Cordero, Jr	126	274,000	1974	Little Current	M. Rivera	126	156,000	1974	Little Current	M. Rivera	126	101,970
1975	Foolish Pleasure	J. Vesquez	126	200,600	1975	Master Derby	D. McHargue	126	158,100	1975	Avatar	W. Shoemaker	126	116,160
1976	Bold Forbes	A. Cordero, Jr.	126	165,200	1976	Elocutionist	J. Lively	126	129,700	1976	Bold Forbes	A. Cordero, Jr.	126	117,000
1977	Seattle Slew	J. Cruguet	126	214,700	1977	Seattle Slew	J. Cruguet	126	138,600	1977	Seattle Slew	J. Cruguet	126	109,080
1978	Affirmed	S. Cauthen	126	186,900	1978	Affirmed	S. Cauthen	126	136,200	1978	Affirmed	S. Cauthen	126	110,580
1979	Specta-cular Bid	R. Franklin	126	228,650	1979	Spectacular Bid	R. Franklin	126	165,300	1979	Coastal	R. Hernandez	126	161,400
1980	Genuine Risk	I. Vasquez	121	250,550	1980	Codex	A. Cordero	126	180,600	1980	Temperence Hill	E. Maple	126	176,220
1981	Pleasant Colony	J. Velasquez	126	317,200	1981	Pleasant Colony	J. Velasquez	126	270,800	1981	Summing	G. Martens	126	170,580
1982	Gato del Sol	E. Delahou-ssaye	126	417,600	1982	Aloma's Ruler	J. Kaenel	126	209,900	1982	Conquistador Cielo	L. Pincay, Jr.	126	159,720
1983	Sunny's Halo	E. Delahou-ssaye	126	426,000	1983	Deputed Testamony	D. Miller	126	251,200	1983	Caveat	L. Pincay, Jr.	126	215,100
1984	Swale	L. Pincay, Jr.	126	537,400	1984	Gate Dancer	A. Cordero	126	243,600	1984	Swale	L Pincay, Jr.	126	310,020
1985	Spend a Buck	A. Cordero, Jr.	126	406,800	1985	Tank's Prospect	P. Day	126	423,200	1985	Creme Fraiche	E. Maple	126	307,740
1986	Ferdinand	W. Shoemaker	126	609,400	1986	Snow Chief	A. Solis	126	411,900	1986	Danzig Connection	C. McCarron	126	338,640
1987	Alysheba	C. McCarron	126	618,600	1987	Alysheba	C. McCarron	126	421,100	1987	Bet Twice	C. Perret	126	329,160
1988	Winning Colors	G. Stevens	121	611,200	1988	Risen Star	E. Delahoussaye	126	413,700	1988	Risen Star	E. Delahoussaye	126	303,720
1989	Sunday Silence	P. Valenzuela	126	574,200	1989	Sunday Silence	P. Valenzuela	126	438,230	1989	Easy Goer	P. Day	126	413,520
1990	Unbridled	C. Perret	126	581,000	1990	Summer Squall	P. Day	126	445,900	1990	Go And Go	M. Kinane	126	411,600

Note: Wt = weight; Win. Val ($) = amount of purse ($).
Source: Time Almanac, 2001, 951–53.

TABLE 18.93 HORSE OF THE YEAR, 1946–1990

Year	Horse	Owner	Trainer	Breeder
1946	Assault	King Ranch	Max Hirsch	King Ranch
1947	Armed	Calumet Farm	Jimmy Jones	Calumet Farm
1948	Citation	Calumet Farm	Jimmy Jones	Calumet Farm
1949	Capot	Greentree Stable	John M. Gaver Sr.	Greentree Stable
1950	Hill Prince	C.T. Chenery	Casey Hayes	C.T. Chenery
1951	Counterpoint	C.V. Whitney	Syl Veitch	C.V. Whitney
1952	One Count	Mrs. W.M. Jeffords	O. White	W. M. Jeffords
1953	Tom Fool	Greentree Stable	John M. Gaver Sr.	D.A. Headley
1954	Native Dancer	A.G. Vanderbilt	Bill Winfrey	A.G. Vanderbilt
1955	Nashua	Belair Stud	James Fitzsimmons	Belair Stud
1956	Swaps	Ellsworth-Galbreath	Mesh Tenney	R. Ellsworth
1957	Bold Ruler	Wheatley Stable	James Fitzsimmons	Wheatley Stable
1958	Round Table	Kerr Stables	Willy Molter	Claiborne Farm
1959	Sword Dancer	Brookmeade Stable	Elliott Burch	Brookmeade Stable
1960	Kelso	Bohemia Stable	C. Hanford	Mrs. R.C. duPont
1961	Kelso	Bohemia Stable	C. Hanford	Mrs. R.C. duPont
1962	Kelso	Bohemia Stable	C. Hanford	Mrs. R.C. duPont
1963	Kelso	Bohemia Stable	C. Hanford	Mrs. R.C. duPont
1964	Kelso	Bohemia Stable	C. Hanford	Mrs. R.C. duPont
1965	Roman Brother	Harbor View Stable	Burley Parke	Ocala Stud
1966	Buckpasser	Ogden Phipps	Eddie Neloy	Ogden Phipps
1967	Damascus	Mrs. E.W. Bancroft	Frank Y. Whiteley Jr.	Mrs. E.W. Bancroft
1968	Dr. Fager	Tartan Stable	John A. Nerud	Tartan Farms
1969	Arts and Letters	Rokeby Stable	Elliott Burch	Paul Mellon
1970	Fort Marcy	Rokeby Stable	Elliott Burch	Paul Mellon
1971	Ack Ack	E. E. Fogelson	Charlie Whittingham	H.F. Guggenheim
1972	Secretariat	Meadow Stable	Lucien Laurin	Meadow Stud
1973	Secretariat	Meadow Stable	Lucien Laurin	Meadow Stud
1974	Forego	Lazy F Ranch	Sherrill W. Ward	Lazy F Ranch
1975	Forego	Lazy F Ranch	Sherrill W. Ward	Lazy F Ranch
1976	Forego	Lazy F Ranch	Frank Y. Whiteley Jr.	Lazy F Ranch
1977	Seattle Slew	Karen L. Taylor	Billy Turner Jr.	B.S. Castleman
1978	Affirmed	Harbor View Farm	Laz Barrera	Harbor View Farm
1979	Affirmed	Harbor View Farm	Laz Barrera	Harbor View Farm
1980	Spectacular Bid	Hawksworth Farm	Bud Delp	Mmes. Gilmore and Jason
1981	John Henry	Dotsam Stable	Ron McAnally and Lefty Nickerson	Golden Chance Farm
1982	Conquistador Cielo	H. de Kwiatkowski	Woody Stephens	L.E. Landoli
1983	All Along	Daniel Wildenstein	P.L. Biancone	Dayton
1984	John Henry	Dotsam Stable	Ron McAnally	Golden Chance Farm
1985	Spend a Buck	Hunter Farm	Cam Gambolati	Irish Hill Farm & R.W. Harper
1986	Lady's Secret	Mr. & Mrs. Eugene Klein	D. Wayne Lukas	R.H. Spreen
1987	Ferdinand	Mrs. H.B. Keck	Charlie Whittingham	H.B. Keck
1988	Alysheba	D. & P. Scharbauer	Jack Van Berg	Preston Madden
1989	Sunday Silence	Gaillard, Hancock, & Whittingham	Charlie Whittingham	Oak Cliff Thoroughbreds
1990	Criminal Type	Calumet Farm	D. Wayne Lukas	Calumet Farm

Source: Sports Illustrated 2000 Sports Almanac, 488–89.

TABLE 18.94　TRIPLE CROWN WINNERS

Year	Horse	Jockey	Owner	Trainer
1946	Assault	Warren Mehrtens	King Ranch	Max Hirsch
1948	Citation	Eddie Arcaro	Calumet Farm	Jimmy Jones
1973	Secretariat	Ron Turcotte	Meadow Stable	Lucien Laurin
1977	Seattle Slew	Jean Cruguet	Karen L. Taylor	William H. Turner Jr.
1978	Affirmed	Steve Cauthen	Harbor View Farm	Laz Barrera

Source: Sports Illustrated 2000 Sports Almanac, 488.

TABLE 18.95　TOP MONEY-WINNING JOCKEYS, 1946–1990

Year	Jockey	Amount Won ($)
1946	I. Atkinson	1,036,825
1947	D. Dodson	1,429,949
1948	E. Arcaro	1,686,230
1949	S. Brooks	1,316,817
1950	E. Arcaro	1,410,160
1951	W. Shoemaker	1,329,890
1952	E. Arcaro	1,859,591
1953	W. Shoemaker	1,784,187
1954	W. Shoemaker	1,876,760
1955	E. Arcaro	1,864,796
1956	W. Hartack	2,343,955
1957	W. Hartack	3,060,501
1958	W. Shoemaker	2,961,693
1959	W. Shoemaker	2,843,133
1960	W. Shoemaker	2,123,961
1961	W. Shoemaker	2,690,819
1962	W. Shoemaker	2,916,844
1963	W. Shoemaker	2,526,925
1964	W. Shoemaker	2,649,553
1965	B. Baeza	2,582,702
1966	B. Baeza	2,951,022
1967	B. Baeza	3,088,888
1968	B. Baeza	2,835,108
1969	J. Velasquez	2,542,315
1970	L. Pincay, Jr.	2,626,526
1971	L. Pincay, Jr.	3,784,377
1972	L. Pincay, Jr.	3,225,827
1973	L. Pincay, Jr.	4,093,492
1974	L. Pincay, Jr.	4,251,060
1975	B. Baeza	3,674,398
1976	A. Cordero, Jr.	4,709,500
1977	S. Cauthen	6,151,750
1978	D.G. McHargue	6,188,353
1979	L. Pincay, Jr.	8,183,535
1980	C.J. McCarron	7,666,100
1981	C.J. McCarron	8,397,604
1982	A. Cordero, Jr.	9,702,520
1983	A. Cordero, Jr.	10,116,807
1984	C.J. McCarron	12,038,213
1985	L. Pincay, Jr.	13,415,049
1986	J.A. Santos	11,329,297
1987	J.A. Santos	12,407,355
1988	J.A. Santos	14,877,298
1989	J.A. Santos	13,847,003
1990	G.L. Stevens	13,881,198

Source: Wall Street Journal Almanac, 1998, 1103.

The Most Exciting Sporting Event of the Era

In a quest for the most striking single sporting event of the last half of the 20th century, it is difficult to believe that anything could surpass the victory of the American hockey team against the Soviet Union in the Olympic Games on February 22, 1980. At least, many people in the world of sports reached that conclusion. All the elements favoring a national celebration were present. The game was on home ice, at Lake Placid, New York. It was an upset of the first magnitude, a game that pitted young, inexperienced American college players against the vaunted Soviets, in truth professionals who could hold their own against the very best Canadians in the N.H.L. Only one week before the game the United States had lost to the same Soviet team, 10–3. It was a genuine national victory; there were no losers among the Americans, and it could not have come at a better time. The economy seemingly had gone haywire and with a hostage crisis with Iran that had brought absolute humiliation, the United States was in desperate need of a boost—a reminder of the country's competence and promise, a spark to ignite national pride and the collective spirit.

The Americans won the gold medal, but the 4–3 victory over the Russians, which came in a semifinal game, did not accomplish that deed. In fact, had the Americans not defeated Finland in the final, there would have been no medal of any kind for the United States. It probably would not have mattered. A loss to the Finns could not have erased the magic of the moment or prevented the spontaneous national celebration that erupted or the retrospective thrill years later in a mental recreation of that February evening in 1980.

CHAPTER 19 Crime and Punishment

The national government assumed responsibility for assembling and publishing crime statistics on all levels in the United States. Numerous agencies published many kinds of special reports, but the responsibility for arranging general statistics in a consistent and usable form fell on two agencies, the Federal Bureau of Investigation (FBI), which each year published a volume entitled *Uniform Crime Reports,* and the Bureau of Justice Statistics—as with the FBI, a part of the Department of Justice—which, beginning in 1973, issued an annual publication, *Sourcebook of Criminal Justice Statistics.* The FBI divided the most serious crimes (crime index offenses) into two groups: violent crimes (murder and nonnegligent manslaughter, forcible rape, robbery, and aggravated assault) and crimes of property (arson, burglary, larceny, theft, and motor vehicle theft).

The first generalization about crime in cold war United States during this period was that it increased markedly—in absolute numbers, of course, but also in crime rate, and the numbers went up nearly every year. Between 1960 and 1990 the total crime index decreased

TABLE 19.1 ESTIMATED NUMBER AND RATE OF OFFENSES KNOWN TO POLICE, BY OFFENSE, 1960–1990

Year	Number of Offenses	Total Crime Index	Violent Crime	Property Crime	Murder and Nonnegligent Man-slaughter	Forcible Rape	Robbery	Aggra-vated Assault	Burglary	Larceny —Theft	Motor Vehicle Theft
1960	179,323,175	3,384,200	288,460	3,095,700	9,110	17,190	107,840	154,320	912,100	1,855,400	328,200
1961	182,992,000	3,488,000	289,390	3,198,600	8,740	17,220	106,670	156,760	949,600	1,913,000	336,000
1962	185,771,000	3,752,200	301,510	3,450,700	8,530	17,550	110,860	164,570	994,300	2,089,600	366,800
1963	188,483,000	3,109,500	316,970	3,792,500	8,640	17,650	116,470	174,210	1,086,400	2,297,800	408,300
1964	191,141,000	4,564,000	364,220	4,200,400	9,360	21,420	130,390	203,050	1,213,200	2,514,400	472,800
1965	193,526,000	4,739,400	387,390	4,352,000	9,960	23,410	138,690	215,330	1,282,500	2,572,600	496,900
1966	195,576,000	5,223,500	430,180	4,793,300	11,040	25,820	157,990	235,330	1,410,100	2,822,000	561,200
1967	197,457,000	5,903,400	499,930	5,403,500	12,240	27,620	202,910	257,160	1,632,100	3,111,600	659,800
1968	199,399,000	6,720,200	595,010	6,125,200	13,800	31,670	262,840	286,700	1,858,900	3,482,700	783,600
1969	201,385,000	7,410,900	661,870	6,749,000	14,760	37,170	298,850	311,090	1,981,900	3,888,600	878,500
1970	203,235,298	8,098,000	738,820	7,359,200	16,000	37,990	349,860	334,970	2,205,000	4,225,800	928,400
1971	206,212,000	8,588,200	816,500	7,771,700	17,780	42,260	387,700	368,760	2,399,300	4,424,200	948,200
1972	208,230,000	8,248,800	834,900	7,413,900	18,670	46,850	376,290	393,090	2,375,500	4,151,200	887,200
1973	209,851,000	8,718,100	875,910	7,842,200	19,640	51,400	384,220	420,650	2,565,500	4,347,900	928,800
1974	211,392,000	10,253,400	974,720	9,278,700	20,710	55,400	442,400	456,210	3,039,200	5,262,500	977,100
1975	213,124,000	11,256,600	1,026,280	10,230,300	20,510	56,090	464,970	484,710	3,252,100	5,977,700	1,000,500
1976	214,659,000	11,349,700	1,004,210	10,345,500	18,780	57,080	427,810	500,530	3,108,700	6,270,800	966,000
1977	216,332,000	10,984,500	1,029,580	9,955,000	19,120	63,500	412,610	534,350	3,071,500	5,905,700	977,700
1978	218,059,000	11,209,000	1,085,550	10,123,400	19,560	67,610	426,930	571,460	3,128,300	5,991,000	1,004,100
1979	220,099,000	12,249,500	1,208,030	11,041,500	21,460	76,390	480,700	629,480	3,327,700	6,601,000	1,112,800
1980	225,349,264	13,408,300	1,344,520	12,063,700	23,040	82,990	565,840	672,650	3,795,200	7,136,900	1,131,700
1981	229,146,000	13,423,800	1,361,820	12,061,900	22,520	82,500	592,910	663,900	3,779,700	7,194,400	1,087,800
1982	231,534,000	12,974,400	1,322,390	11,652,000	21,010	78,770	553,130	669,480	3,447,100	7,142,500	1,062,400
1983	233,981,000	12,108,600	1,258,090	10,850,500	19,310	78,920	506,570	653,290	3,129,900	6,712,800	1,007,900
1984	236,158,000	11,881,800	1,273,280	10,608,500	18,960	84,230	485,010	685,350	2,984,400	6,591,900	1,032,200
1985	238,740,000	12,430,000	1,327,440	11,102,600	18,980	87,340	497,870	723,250	3,073,300	6,926,400	1,102,900
1986	241,077,000	13,210,000	1,488,140	11,722,700	20,610	90,430	542,780	834,320	3,241,400	7,257,200	1,224,100
1987	243,400,000	13,508,700	1,484,000	12,024,700	20,100	91,110	517,700	855,090	3,236,200	7,499,900	1,288,700
1988	245,807,000	13,923,100	1,566,220	12,356,900	20,680	92,490	542,970	910,090	3,218,100	7,705,900	1,432,900
1989	248,239,000	14,251,400	1,646,040	12,605,400	21,500	94,500	578,330	951,710	3,168,200	7,872,400	1,564,800
1990	248,709,873	14,475,600	1,820,130	12,655,500	23,440	102,560	639,270	1,054,860	3,073,900	7,945,700	1,635,900
Rate per 100,000 Inhabitants											
1960	N/A	1,887.2	160.9	1,726.3	5.1	9.6	60.1	86.1	508.6	1,034.7	183.0
1961	N/A	1,906.1	158.1	1,747.9	4.8	9.4	58.3	85.7	518.9	1,045.4	183.6
1962	N/A	2,019.8	162.3	1,857.5	4.6	9.4	59.7	88.6	535.2	1,124.8	197.4
1963	N/A	2,180.3	168.2	2,012.1	4.6	9.4	61.8	92.4	576.4	1,219.1	216.6
1964	N/A	2,388.1	190.6	2,197.5	4.9	11.2	68.2	106.2	634.7	1,315.5	247.4
1965	N/A	2,449.0	200.2	2,248.8	5.1	12.1	71.7	111.3	662.7	1,329.3	256.8
1966	N/A	2,670.8	220.0	2,450.9	5.6	13.2	80.8	120.3	721.0	1,442.9	286.9
1967	N/A	2,989.7	253.2	2,736.5	6.2	14.0	102.8	130.2	826.6	1,575.8	334.1
1968	N/A	3,370.2	298.4	3,071.8	6.9	15.9	131.8	143.8	932.3	1,746.6	393.0
1969	N/A	3,680.0	328.7	3,351.3	7.3	18.5	148.4	154.5	984.1	1,930.9	436.2
1970	N/A	3,984.5	363.5	3,621.0	7.9	18.7	172.1	164.8	1,084.9	2,079.3	456.8
1971	N/A	4,164.7	396.0	3,768.8	8.6	20.5	188.0	178.8	1,163.5	2,145.5	459.8
1972	N/A	3,961.4	401.0	3,560.4	22.5	22.5	180.7	188.8	1,140.8	1,993.6	426.1
1973	N/A	4,154.4	417.4	3,737.0	9.4	24.5	183.1	200.5	1,222.5	2,071.9	442.6
1974	N/A	4,850.4	461.1	4,389.3	9.8	26.2	209.3	215.8	1,437.7	2,489.5	462.2
1975	N/A	5,281.7	481.5	4,800.2	9.6	26.3	218.2	227.4	1,525.9	2,804.8	469.4
1976	N/A	5,287.3	467.8	4,819.5	8.8	26.6	199.3	233.2	1,448.2	2,921.3	450.0
1977	N/A	5,077.6	475.9	4,601.7	8.8	29.4	190.7	240.0	1,419.8	2,729.9	451.9
1978	N/A	5,140.3	497.8	4,642.5	9.0	31.0	195.8	262.1	1,434.6	2,747.4	460.5
1979	N/A	5,565.5	548.9	5,016.6	9.7	34.7	218.4	286.0	1,511.9	2,999.1	505.6

TABLE 19.1   (continued)

Year	Number of Offenses	Total Crime Index	Violent Crime	Property Crime	Murder and Nonnegligent Manslaughter	Forcible Rape	Robbery	Aggravated Assault	Burglary	Larceny —Theft	Motor Vehicle Theft
					Rate per 100,000 Inhabitants						
1980	N/A	5,950.0	596.6	5,353.3	10.2	36.8	251.1	298.5	1,684.1	3,167.0	502.2
1981	N/A	5,858.2	594.3	5,263.9	9.8	36.0	258.7	289.7	1,649.5	3,139.7	474.7
1982	N/A	5,603.6	571.1	5,032.5	9.1	34.0	238.9	289.2	1,488.8	3,084.8	458.8
1983	N/A	5,175.0	537.7	4,637.4	8.3	33.7	216.5	279.2	1,337.7	2,868.9	430.8
1984	N/A	5,031.3	539.2	4,492.1	7.9	35.7	205.4	290.2	1,263.7	2,791.3	437.1
1985	N/A	5,206.5	556.0	4,650.5	7.9	36.6	208.5	302.9	1,287.3	2,901.2	462.0
1986	N/A	5,479.9	617.3	4,862.6	8.6	37.5	225.1	346.1	1,344.6	3,010.3	507.8
1987	N/A	5,550.0	609.7	4,940.3	8.3	37.4	212.7	351.3	1,329.6	3,081.3	529.4
1988	N/A	5,664.2	637.2	5,027.1	8.4	37.6	220.9	370.2	1,309.2	3,134.9	582.9
1989	N/A	5,741.0	663.7	5,077.9	8.7	38.1	233.0	383.4	1,276.3	3,171.3	630.4
1990	N/A	5,820.3	731.8	5,088.5	9.4	41.2	257.0	424.1	1,235.9	3,194.8	657.8

Source: Department of Justice, *Sourcebook of Criminal Justice Statistics—1991* (Washington, D.C., 1992), 372.

TABLE 19.2   TOTAL ARRESTS BY RACE, 1970

(6,208 agencies; 1970 population 142,474,000)

Offense Charged	Total Arrests						Percent Distribution				
	Total	White	Black American	Indian	Chinese	Japanese	White	Black American	Indian	Chinese	Japanese
Total	6,257,104	4,373,157	1,688,389	130,981	2,582	3,882	69.9	27.0	2.1	. . .	0.1
Criminal homicide											
Murder and nonnegligent manslaughter	11.847	4,503	7,097	76	6	. . .	38.0	59.9	.6	.1	. . .
Manslaughter by negligence	2,930	2,238	613	25	1	3	76.4	20.9	.9	. . .	.1
Forcible rape	14,419	7,260	6,900	103	5	8	50.4	47.9	.7	. . .	.1
Robbery	74,484	24,770	48,282	545	34	43	33.3	64.8	.7	. . .	.1
Aggravated assault	114,153	59,567	52,323	1,138	67	43	52.2	45.8	1.0	.1	. . .
Burglary—breaking or entering	270,498	174,512	91,305	1,908	102	170	64.5	33.8	.7	. . .	.1
Larceny—theft	590,660	392,769	186,720	4,167	547	753	66.5	31.6	.7	.1	.1
Auto theft	120,082	73,687	43,341	1,205	76	125	61.4	36.1	1.0	.1	.1
Violent crime	214,903	96,100	114,602	1,862	112	94	44.7	53.3	.9	.1	. . .
Property crime	981,240	640,968	321,366	7,280	725	1,048	65.3	32.8	.7	. . .	.1
Subtotal for above offenses	**1,199,073**	**739,306**	**436,581**	**9,167**	**838**	**1,145**	**61.7**	**36.4**	**.8**	**.1**	**.1**
Other assaults	269,716	162,074	102,955	2,018	63	66	60.1	38.2	.7	. . .	. . .
Arson	8,826	6,403	2,295	59	5	7	72.5	26.0	.7	.1	.1
Forgery and counterfeiting	40,145	27,422	12,307	236	27	14	68.3	30.7	.6	.1	. . .
Fraud	75,098	56,180	18,378	308	15	10	74.8	24.5	.4	. . .	. . .
Embezzlement	7,653	5,702	1,904	19	1	4	74.5	24.9	.2	. . .	.1
Stolen property; buying, receiving, possessing	49,028	30,130	18,283	241	29	23	61.5	37.3	.5	.1	. . .
Vandalism	105,518	82,280	21,540	653	43	28	78.0	20.4	.6	. . .	. . .
Weapons; carrying, possessing, etc	96,127	46,040	48,436	463	29	45	47.9	50.4	.5	. . .	. . .
Prostitution and commercialized vice	42,283	14,616	27,210	158	23	22	34.6	64.4	.4	.1	.1
Sex offenses (except forcible rape and prostitution)	46,706	35,705	10,111	247	20	44	76.4	21.6	.5	. . .	.1
Narcotic drug laws	291,600	226,779	61,223	710	167	314	77.8	21.0	.2	.1	.1
Gambling	70,170	20,527	46,550	56	204	470	29.3	66.3	.1	.3	.7
Offenses against family and children	55,940	38,924	16,386	337	4	7	69.6	29.3	.6	. . .	. . .
Driving under the influence	415,024	333,950	69,307	4,872	126	311	80.5	16.7	1.2	. . .	.1
Liquor laws	218,142	190,001	22,812	4,004	44	59	87.1	10.5	1.8	. . .	. . .
Drunkenness	1,496,414	1,101,612	298,826	87,908	246	245	73.6	20.0	5.9	. . .	. . .
Disorderly conduct	572,211	363,998	191,282	7,484	156	132	63.6	33.4	1.3	. . .	. . .
Vagrancy	66,671	47,940	16,630	1,386	22	45	71.9	24.9	2.1	. . .	.1
All other offenses (except traffic)	781,305	564,318	203,339	7,047	342	533	72.2	26.0	.9	. . .	.1
Suspicion	69,142	47,934	20,588	440	63	34	69.3	29.8	.6	.1	. . .
Curfew and loitering law violations	103,955	82,415	18,806	1,188	39	174	79.3	18.1	1.1	. . .	.2
Runaways	176,357	148,901	22,640	1,980	76	150	84.4	12.8	1.1	. . .	.1

Source: F.B.I., *Crime in the United States: Uniform Crime Reports—1970* (Washington, D.C., 1971), 131.

only in 1972, 1977, and 1981–84, and for the general period the crime index multiplied more than three times. The murder rate reached a peak in 1980 at 10.2, exactly double what it had been in 1960. In the 1980s the rate declined slightly, but by 1990 it stood at 9.4 per 100,000 population. Some of the largest increases could be seen in motor-vehicle theft (roughly five times), forcible rape (six times), and aggravated assault (seven times).

Needless to say, criminal offenses as measured by arrests and sentencing to jail or prison were not evenly distributed throughout the population. In sheer numbers the categories most likely to commit

TABLE 19.3 TOTAL ARRESTS, DISTRIBUTION BY RACE, 1990

(10,110 agencies; 1990 population 192,939,000)

Offense Charged	Total Arrests					Percent Distribution				
	Total	White	Black	American Indian or Alaskan Native	Asian or Pacific Islander	Total	White	Black	American Indian or Alaskan Native	Asian or Pacific Islander
Total	11,151,368	7,712,339	3,224,060	122,586	92,383	100.0	69.2	28.9	1.1	.8
Murder and nonnegligent manslaughter	18,190	7,942	9,952	132	164	100.0	43.7	54.7	.7	.9
Forcible rape	30,802	16,973	13,309	249	271	100.0	55.1	43.2	.8	.9
Robbery	135,904	51,229	83,165	482	1,028	100.0	37.7	61.2	.4	.8
Aggravated assault	373,872	223,952	143,540	3,549	2,831	100.0	59.9	38.4	.9	.8
Burglary	338,096	230,310	101,855	3,001	2,930	100.0	68.1	30.1	.9	.9
Larceny—theft	1,231,255	827,860	374,968	13,359	15,068	100.0	67.2	30.5	1.1	1.2
Motor vehicle theft	167,908	99,821	64,526	1,264	2,297	100.0	59.4	38.4	.8	1.4
Arson	14,833	11,154	3,410	162	107	100.0	75.2	23.0	1.1	.7
Violent crime	558,768	300,096	249,966	4,412	4,294	100.0	53.7	44.7	.8	.8
Property crime	1,752,092	1,169,145	544,759	17,786	20,402	100.0	66.7	31.1	1.0	1.2
Crime Index Total	2,310,860	1,469,241	794,725	22,198	24,696	100.0	63.6	34.4	1.0	1.1
Other assaults	795,907	510,552	269,560	9,594	6,201	100.0	64.1	33.9	1.2	.8
Forgery and counterfeiting	73,127	47,330	24,839	434	524	100.0	64.7	34.0	.6	.7
Fraud	273,499	180,671	90,708	1,091	1,029	100.0	66.1	33.2	.4	.4
Embezzlement	11,906	7,900	3,816	53	137	100.0	66.4	32.1	.4	1.2
Stolen property; buying, receiving, possessing	129,698	74,517	53,482	697	1,002	100.0	57.5	41.2	.5	.8
Vandalism	253,273	191,269	57,253	2,520	2,231	100.0	75.5	22.6	1.0	.9
Weapons; carrying, possessing, etc.	174,331	102,228	69,331	878	1,894	100.0	58.6	39.8	.5	1.1
Prostitution and commercialized vice	90,898	54,345	35,398	450	705	100.0	59.8	38.9	.5	.8
Sex offenses (except forcible rape and prostitution)	83,611	65,798	16,271	796	746	100.0	78.7	19.5	1.0	.9
Drug abuse violations	860,016	503,315	349,965	2,935	3,801	100.0	58.5	40.7	.3	.4
Gambling	15,349	7,251	7,294	21	783	100.0	47.2	47.5	.1	5.1
Offenses against family and children	64,606	42,469	19,602	801	1,734	100.0	65.7	30.3	1.2	2.7
Driving under the influence	1,371,236	1,227,221	118,729	15,406	9,880	100.0	89.5	8.7	1.1	.7
Liquor laws	548,292	478,873	52,831	13,478	3,110	100.0	87.3	9.6	2.5	.6
Drunkenness	713,599	566,075	130,226	15,518	1,780	100.0	79.3	18.2	2.2	.2
Disorderly conduct	576,626	379,324	186,671	7,904	2,727	100.0	65.8	32.4	1.4	.5
Vagrancy	30,994	17,617	12,644	620	113	100.0	56.8	40.8	2.0	.4
All other offenses (except traffic)	2,555,503	1,619,001	886,880	24,602	25,020	100.0	63.4	34.7	1.0	1.0
Suspicion	17,746	7,462	10,125	87	72	100.0	42.0	57.1	.5	.4
Curfew and loitering law violations	64,260	50,721	11,379	724	1,436	100.0	78.9	17.7	1.1	2.2
Runaways	136,031	109,159	22,331	1,779	2,762	100.0	80.2	16.4	1.3	2.0

Source: F.B.I., Uniform Crime Reports for the United States—1990 (Washington, D.C., 1991), 192.

crimes were: people under 25, male as opposed to female (by a large margin), white rather than any other color, simply because there were many more white people to commit crimes. To use the year 1987 as an example, in that year people under age 25 were arrested for 57 percent of all index crime offenses; 82 percent of the people arrested (89 percent for violent crimes) were male. Women were most likely to be arrested for theft or larceny. Of all people arrested 69 percent were white, 30 percent were black—a number that was disproportionately high for black people, who made up approximately 12 percent of the population.

Using records of 1970 and 1990 as examples, the highest percentage for blacks was in robbery (61.2 percent of all arrests in 1990) and

TABLE 19.4   NUMBER AND RATE OF PRISONERS IN STATE AND FEDERAL INSTITUTIONS ON DECEMBER 31, BY SEX, 1946–1990

(rate per 100,000 population)

Year	Total	Rate	Males Number	Males Rate	Females Number	Females Rate
1946	140,079	99	134,075	191	6,004	8
1947	151,304	105	144,961	202	6,343	9
1948	155,977	106	149,739	205	6,238	8
1949	163,749	109	157,663	211	6,086	8
1950	166,123	109	160,309	211	5,814	8
1951	165,680	107	159,610	208	6,070	8
1952	168,233	107	161,994	208	6,239	8
1953	173,579	108	166,909	211	6,670	8
1954	182,901	112	175,907	218	6,994	8
1955	185,780	112	178,655	217	7,125	8
1956	189,565	112	182,190	218	7,375	9
1957	195,414	113	188,113	221	7,301	8
1958	205,643	117	198,208	229	7,435	8
1959	208,105	117	200,469	228	7,636	8

Year	Total	Rate	Males Number	Males Rate	Females Number	Females Rate
1960	212,953	117	205,265	230	7,688	8
1961	220,149	119	212,268	234	7,881	8
1962	218,830	117	210,823	229	8,007	8
1963	217,283	114	209,538	225	7,745	8
1964	214,336	111	206,632	219	7,704	8
1965	210,895	108	203,327	213	7,568	8
1966	199,654	102	192,703	201	6,951	7
1967	194,896	98	188,661	195	6,235	6
1968	187,914	94	182,102	187	5,812	6
1969	196,007	97	189,413	192	6,594	6
1970	196,429	96	190,794	191	5,635	5
1971	198,061	95	191,732	189	6,329	6
1972	196,092	93	189,823	185	6,269	6
1973	204,211	96	197,523	191	6,004	6
1974	218,466	102	211,077	202	7,389	7
1975	240,593	111	231,918	220	8,675	8
1976	262,833	120	252,794	238	10,039	9
1977	285,456	129	274,244	255	11,212	10
1978	294,396	132	282,813	261	11,583	10
1979	301,470	133	289,465	264	12,005	10
1980	315,974	138	303,643	274	12,331	11
1981	353,167	153	338,940	302	14,227	12
1982	394,374	170	378,045	336	16,329	14
1983	419,820	179	402,391	352	17,429	14
1984	443,398	188	424,193	. . .	19,205	. . .
1985	480,568	200	458,972	. . .	21,296	. . .
1986	522,084	216	497,540	. . .	24,544	. . .
1987	560,812	228	533,990	. . .	26,822	. . .
1988	603,732	244	573,587	. . .	30,145	. . .
1989	680,907	271	643,643	. . .	37,264	. . .
1990	738,894	292	698,410	. . .	40,484	. . .

Source: Department of Justice, *Sourcebook of Criminal Statistics—1991*, 636.

TABLE 19.5   PERSONS ADMITTED TO STATE AND FEDERAL PRISONS, BY RACE AND SELECTED YEARS, 1946–1986

Year	Number of Admissions to State and Federal Prisons	Percent of State and Federal Prison Admissions Total	White	Black	Other	Number of Admissions to State Prisons	Percent of State Prison Admissions Total	White	Black	Other	Number of Admissions to Federal Prisons	Percent of Federal Prison Admissions Total	White	Black	Other
1946	56,432	100	66	33	1	43,679	100	64	35	1	12,753	100	73	25	2
1947	51,016	100	69	30	1	40,601	100	68	31	1	10,415	100	75	23	2
1948	49,834	100	70	29	1	39,899	100	68	31	1	9,935	100	76	22	2
1949	54,370	100	70	29	1	43,941	100	69	30	1	10,429	100	74	24	2
1950	57,988[a]	100	69	30	1	46,496	100	69	30	1	11,492	100	70	28	2
1960	84,068[a]	100	66	32	2	69,235	100	65	34	1	14,833	100	71	25	4
1964	81,099[a]	100	65	33	2	67,879	100	63	35	2	13,220	100	73	25	2
1970	48,497[a]	100	61	39[b]	. . .	37,437	100	57	43[b]	. . .	11,060	100	73	27[b]	. . .
1974	52,245	100	59	38	3	37,064	100	54	41	5	15,181	100	71	29[b]	. . .
1975	42,351	100	64	35	1	25,796	100	60	38	2	16,555	100	70	30[b]	. . .
1976	69,746	100	61	35	4	51,035	100	58	37	5	18,711	100	71	29[b]	. . .
1977	72,183	100	61	38	1	54,023	100	59	40	1	18,160	100	70	30[b]	. . .
1978	95,502	100	58	41	1	77,017	100	55	44	1	18,485	100	69	31[b]	. . .
1979	94,828	100	60	39	1	79,535	100	58	41	1	15,293	100	73	27[b]	. . .
1980	134,634	100	58	41	1	117,251	100	57	42	1	17,383	100	73	27[b]	. . .
1981	135,611	100	57	42	1	121,211	100	55	44	1	14,400	100	74	26[b]	. . .
1982	131,617	100	55	44	1	114,391	100	53	46	1	17,226	100	75	25[b]	. . .
1983	122,575	100	58	41	1	103,588	100	55	44	1	18,987	100.	76	24[b]	. . .
1984	137,583	100	58	41	1	119,042	100	55	44	1	18,541	100	77	23[b]	. . .
1985	166,743	100	56	43	1	146,862	100	54	45	1	19,881	100	76	24[b]	. . .
1986	183,769	100	55	44	1	167,474	100	53	46	1	16,295	100	77	21	2

[a] No statistics available for 1951–59, 1961–63, 1965–69, 1971–73.
[b] Includes "other" nonwhite races as well as blacks.
Source: Department of Justice, *Sourcebook of Criminal Statistics—1991*, 644.

murder and nonnegligent manslaughter (59.9 percent in 1970). For whites the highest percentages came in vandalism, sex offenses (other than rape or prostitution), and laws dealing with use of alcohol. The government did not do an effective job during much of this period in identifying Hispanic people, but jail statistics of the 1980s suggested that the arrest rate was higher than the proportion of Hispanics in the population. Other racial groups did not leave a distinct mark in criminal statistics (their numbers and rates in most areas were very low, which perhaps was distinctive in itself), but Native Americans did record a disturbing tendency toward drunkenness and liquor-law violations, and Asian Americans revealed a curious inclination for gambling.

If males committed most of the crimes in the United States, males also constituted most of the victims, at least in most categories. With respect to murder and nonnegligent manslaughter victimization, males outnumbered females by a rate of approximately three-to-one for nearly every year. Male victims of aggravated assault surpassed females by two to three times; in simple assault men's numbers also were higher but less strikingly so. The statistics suggested that the people most in danger of violent attack were black males by a considerable margin; next came black females. The safest category was white females. Such a conclusion would be qualified but probably not contradicted by introduction of numbers on forcible rape, the victims of which were overwhelmingly (but not exclusively) female. Of course a rape statistic also could be an assault or a murder statistic. A contention, doubtless true, that many assaults never were reported (by neither female nor male victims) could not be measured.

TABLE 19.6   INMATES IN STATE AND FEDERAL PRISONS, BY STATE AND RACE/ETHNICITY, 1990

Region and Jurisdiction	Total	Asian/Pacific Islander	White Non-Hispanic	Black Non-Hispanic	Hispanic	American Indian/ Alaskan Native
U.S. total	715,649	6,871	274,929	331,880	95,498	6,471
Federal	56,821	461	25,553	15,597	14,346	864
State	658,828	6,410	249,376	316,283	81,152	5,607
Northeast	117,865	270	33,535	57,873	25,705	482
Connecticut	9,577	23	2,571	4,647	2,306	30
Maine	1,503	0	1,439	29	13	22
Massachusetts	8,282	63	4,286	2,367	1,552	14
New Hampshire	1,441	4	1,306	61	67	3
New Jersey	16,721	7	3,673	10,242	2,790	9
New York	56,251	134	9,473	28,473	17,824	383
Pennsylvania	20,822	19	8,541	11,423	824	15
Rhode Island	2,460	20	1,455	653	328	4
Vermont	808	0	791	14	1	2
Midwest	141,726	428	65,857	69,810	4,392	1,239
Illinois	26,712	230	7,993	16,156	2,289	44
Indiana	12,618	8	7,698	4,687	209	16
Iowa	4,522	20	3,466	900	75	61
Kansas	5,500	23	3,301	1,825	268	83
Michigan	31,812	34	12,465	18,711	521	81
Minnesota	3,239	20	1,938	923	95	263
Missouri	14,600	3	7,812	6,708	55	22
Nebraska	2,390	13	1,388	790	108	91
North Dakota	557	1	403	9	12	132
Ohio	31,808	31	14,897	16,476	395	9
South Dakota	1,247	0	909	42	1	295
Wisconsin	6,721	45	3,587	2,583	364	142
South	253,453	506	91,109	146,293	14,359	1,186
Alabama	12,433	19	4,489	7,924	1	0
Arkansas	6,455	0	2,977	3,459	17	2
Delaware	3,449	3	1,268	2,038	138	2
District of Columbia	7,290	12	93	7,012	173	0
Florida	42,306	378	16,004	23,397	2,437	90
Georgia	18,540	4	6,700	11,737	97	2
Kentucky	6,900	1	4,480	2,413	6	0
Louisiana	13,939	2	3,911	9,970	56	0
Maryland	17,057	8	4,291	12,695	60	3
Mississippi	6,852	4	1,824	5,003	14	7
North Carolina	18,346	30	6,819	10,887	163	447
Oklahoma	10,449	7	6,014	3,573	246	609
South Carolina	15,091	2	5,333	9,707	34	15
Tennessee	8,333	2	4,651	3,643	35	2
Texas	49,815	14	15,711	23,266	10,823	1
Virginia	14,649	17	5,227	9,346	54	5
West Virginia	1,549	3	1,317	223	5	1
West	145,784	5,206	58,875	42,307	36,696	2,700
Alaska	2,414	19	1,297	286	53	777
Arizona	13,903	26	7,241	2,228	3,867	541
California	92,604	3,586	28,181	33,542	26,987	308
Colorado	5,593	13	2,717	1,342	1,455	66
Hawaii	2,569	1,350	917	131	167	4
Idaho	1,767	12	1,487	22	186	60
Montana	1,273	0	1,006	21	36	210
Nevada	5,620	65	3,131	1,913	422	89
New Mexico	3,118	10	953	305	1,742	108
Oregon	5,994	21	4,586	840	415	132
Utah	2,799	32	2,020	238	449	60
Washington	7,036	69	4,516	1,388	786	277
Wyoming	1,094	3	823	69	131	68

Source: Susan B. Gall and Timothy L. Gall, *Statistical Record of Asian Americans* (Detroit, 1993), 111–12.

TABLE 19.7 NUMBER AND PERCENT OF HOUSEHOLDS EXPERIENCING CRIME IN PREVIOUS 12 MONTHS, 1975–1990

Crime Victims	1975	1976	1977	1978	1979	1980	1981	1982	1983	1984	1985	1986	1987	1988	1989	1990
Households, total (in thousands)	73,123	74,528	75,904	77,578	78,964	80,622	82,797	85,178	86,146	87,791	88,852	90,014	91,391	92,892	94,553	95,461
Households touched by crime (in thousands)	23,377	23,504	23,741	24,277	24,730	24,222	24,863	24,989	23,621	22,806	22,191	22,201	22,404	22,844	23,221	22,652
Percent of households touched by: Any NCVS crime	32.1	31.5	31.3	31.3	31.3	30.0	30.0	29.3	27.4	26.0	25.0	24.7	24.5	24.6	24.6	23.7
Rape	0.2	0.2	0.2	0.2	0.2	0.2	0.2	0.2	0.1	0.2	0.1	0.1	0.1	0.2	0.1	0.1
Robbery	1.4	1.2	1.2	1.1	1.2	1.2	1.3	1.4	1.1	1.0	0.9	0.9	1.0	0.9	1.0	1.0
Assault	4.5	4.4	4.7	4.6	4.8	4.4	4.7	4.5	4.2	4.1	4.0	3.8	3.8	4.0	3.9	3.8
Personal theft	16.4	16.2	16.3	16.2	15.4	14.2	13.9	13.9	13.0	12.3	11.5	11.2	11.1	11.2	11.2	10.5
Burglary	7.7	7.4	7.2	7.2	7.1	7.0	7.4	6.9	6.1	5.5	5.3	5.3	5.2	5.4	5.0	4.8
Household theft	10.2	10.3	10.2	9.9	10.8	10.4	10.2	9.6	8.9	8.5	8.1	8.0	8.0	7.7	8.0	7.5
Motor vehicle theft	1.8	1.6	1.5	1.7	1.6	1.6	1.6	1.6	1.4	1.4	1.4	1.4	1.5	1.5	1.6	1.9

Source: Department of Justice, *Sourcebook of Criminal Statistics—1991*, 294.

TABLE 19.8 NUMBER AND RATE OF ASSAULT VICTIMS, BY SEX AND RACE, 1973–1990

(rate per 1,000 persons age 12 and older)

	Sex of Victim											
	Male						Female					
	Total		Aggravated		Simple		Total		Aggravated		Simple	
Year	Number	Rate	Number	Rate	Number	Rate	Number	Rate	Number	Rate	Number	Rate
1973	2,697,900	34.3	1,205,400	15.3	1,492,400	19.0	1,389,200	16.2	449,400	5.2	939,900	11.0
1974	2,790,200	34.9	1,285,100	16.1	1,505,200	18.8	1,358,100	15.6	450,300	5.2	907,500	10.4
1975	2,738,600	33.7	1,150,800	14.2	1,587,800	19.6	1,533,200	17.3	480,600	5.4	1,052,700	11.9
1976	2,764,500	33.6	1,185,900	14.4	1,578,700	19.2	1,578,900	17.6	509,300	5.7	1,069,700	11.9
1977	3,128,800	37.5	1,289,700	15.5	1,839,100	22.1	1,535,200	16.9	448,200	4.9	1,087,300	12.0
1978	3,135,600	37.2	1,240,500	14.7	1,895,100	22.5	1,596,000	17.4	467,500	5.1	1,128,600	12.3
1979	3,114,300	36.5	1,272,300	14.9	1,841,800	21.6	1,737,000	18.7	496,300	5.3	1,240,700	13.4
1980	3,099,500	35.2	1,243,700	14.1	1,855,700	21.0	1,647,700	17.1	463,100	4.8	1,184,600	12.3
1981	3,229,600	36.2	1,278,800	14.4	1,950,900	21.9	1,794,200	18.5	516,900	5.3	1,277,200	13.1
1982	3,083,400	34.2	1,229,100	13.6	1,854,300	20.6	1,889,500	19.2	525,000	5.3	1,364,400	13.9
1983	2,900,140	31.8	1,067,520	11.7	1,832,620	20.1	1,699,950	17.1	449,800	4.5	1,250,150	12.6
1984	2,961,500	32.2	1,186,860	12.9	1,774,640	19.3	1,782,980	17.8	540,440	5.4	1,242,540	12.4
1985	2,964,970	31.9	1,131,230	12.2	1,833,740	19.7	1,734,380	17.2	473,950	4.7	1,260,430	12.5
1986	2,710,790	28.8	1,094,480	11.6	1,616,310	17.2	1,665,560	16.3	448,390	4.4	1,217,160	11.9
1987	2,867,400	30.2	1,102,190	11.6	1,765,210	18.6	1,734,250	16.9	485,270	4.7	1,248,980	12.2
1988	2,808,350	29.3	1,153,770	12.0	1,654,580	17.3	1,925,840	18.6	587,610	5.7	1,338,220	12.9
1989	2,837,190	29.3	1,151,120	11.9	1,686,060	17.4	1,796,600	17.2	513,580	4.9	1,283,010	12.3
1990	2,912,550	29.8	1,126,310	11.5	1,786,230	18.3	1,816,250	17.2	474,350	4.5	1,341,890	12.7

	Race of Victim											
	White						Black					
	Total		Aggravated		Simple		Total		Aggravated		Simple	
Year	Number	Rate	Number	Rate	Number	Rate	Number	Rate	Number	Rate	Number	Rate
1973	3,574,100	24.7	1,371,000	9.5	2,203,200	15.2	479,300	27.4	279,600	16.0	199,700	11.4
1974	3,651,300	24.8	1,473,300	10.0	2,178,000	14.8	420,700	23.5	235,000	13.1	185,700	10.4
1975	3,702,400	24.8	1,331,500	8.9	2,370,900	15.9	509,600	27.6	267,200	14.5	242,500	13.1
1976	3,749,300	24.9	1,379,600	9.2	2,369,600	15.7	543,600	28.9	292,900	15.6	250,700	13.3
1977	4,079,800	26.8	1,459,200	9.6	2,620,600	17.2	538,200	27.9	268,100	13.9	270,100	14.0
1978	4,149,500	26.9	1,431,600	9.3	2,717,900	17.6	531,900	27.1	261,500	13.3	270,400	13.8
1979	4,220,100	27.1	1,475,600	9.5	2,744,400	17.6	540,900	27.5	253,300	12.9	387,700	14.6
1980	4,115,900	25.6	1,403,400	8.7	2,712,500	16.9	516,000	25.5	253,400	12.5	262,500	13.0
1981	4,276,800	26.4	1,470,900	9.1	2,805,900	17.3	642,400	31.2	296,800	14.4	345,600	16.8
1982	4,298,700	26.3	1,422,100	8.7	2,876,700	17.6	593,700	28.3	307,700	14.7	286,100	13.6
1983	3,971,830	24.1	1,237,720	7.5	2,734,110	16.6	555,390	26.0	262,280	12.3	293,110	13.7
1984	4,052,600	24.5	1,401,100	8.5	2,651,500	16.0	606,800	27.9	283,900	13.1	322,870	14.9
1985	4,048,110	24.2	1,324,940	7.9	2,723,170	16.3	564,420	25.5	238,250	10.8	326,180	14.8
1986	3,750,940	22.2	1,261,780	7.5	2,489,170	14.8	529,640	23.6	238,570	10.6	291,070	13.0
1987	3,871,460	22.8	1,248,780	7.4	2,622,670	15.4	621,550	27.4	288,920	12.7	332,620	14.6
1988	3,921,600	23.0	1,348,510	7.9	2,573,080	15.1	681,620	29.6	338,160	14.7	343,460	14.9
1989	3,981,210	23.1	1,384,730	8.0	2,596,480	15.1	516,590	22.1	233,770	10.0	282,820	12.1
1990	3,989,480	23.0	1,277,520	7.4	2,711,960	15.7	617,670	26.0	288,850	12.2	328,820	13.9

Source: Department of Justice, *Sourcebook of Criminal Statistics—1992*, 270–71.

TABLE 19.9   AGE-ADJUSTED HOMICIDE RATES, BY RACE AND GENDER, 1946–1990

(rate of offender per 100,000 population)

Year	White Male	White Female	Nonwhite Male	Nonwhite Female	Overall
1946	4.9	1.5	56.4	12.4	6.4
1947	4.7	1.4	53.9	12.1	6.1
1948	4.5	1.5	53.9	11.9	6.0
1949	4.1	1.4	48.9	11.7	5.5
1950	3.9	1.4	49.1	11.5	5.4
1951	3.6	1.4	45.3	11.1	5.0
1952	3.8	1.3	50.4	11.3	5.4
1953	3.6	1.3	46.5	10.2	5.1
1954	3.6	1.4	46.2	10.3	5.1
1955	3.5	1.3	42.6	10.3	4.8
1956	3.5	1.3	43.2	11.3	5.0
1957	3.5	1.4	43.1	10.3	4.9
1958	3.6	1.4	41.6	10.5	4.9
1959	3.8	1.5	42.3	10.7	5.1
1960	3.9	1.5	41.9	11.2	5.2
1961	3.9	1.6	41.5	10.1	5.2
1962	4.1	1.7	44.4	10.3	5.4
1963	4.2	1.6	44.8	10.5	5.5
1964	4.3	1.7	47.1	10.6	5.7
1965	4.8	1.7	50.7	11.7	6.2
1966	4.9	1.9	54.8	12.4	6.7
1967	5.9	2.0	62.7	14.0	7.7
1968	6.5	2.0	68.9	13.6	8.2
1969	6.6	2.1	72.4	13.8	8.6
1970	7.3	2.2	72.8	13.7	9.1
1971	7.9	2.3	81.6	16.0	10.0
1972	8.2	2.4	83.1	14.8	10.3
1973	8.7	2.8	77.1	16.0	10.5
1974	9.3	2.9	77.9	15.5	10.8
1975	9.4	2.9	71.6	14.7	10.5
1976	8.6	2.7	63.3	13.2	9.5
1977	8.8	2.9	60.1	12.5	9.6
1978	9.2	2.9	58.1	12.1	9.6
1979	10.1	3.0	62.9	12.8	10.4
1980	10.9	3.2	61.3	12.2	10.8
1981	10.3	3.1	58.5	11.4	10.4
1982	9.5	3.1	52.2	10.5	9.7
1983	8.4	2.8	45.2	9.8	8.6
1984	8.2	2.9	42.2	9.6	8.4
1985	8.1	2.9	41.4	9.3	8.3
1986	8.4	2.9	46.1	10.2	9.0
1987	7.7	2.9	44.0	10.5	8.6
1988	7.7	2.8	47.4	10.8	9.0
1989	8.1	2.8	49.8	10.7	9.4
1990	8.9	2.8	53.9	10.7	10.2

Source: Adam Dobrin, et al., *Statistical Handbook on Violence in America* (Phoenix, 1996), 22.

TABLE 19.10   MURDER RATE, SELECTED COUNTRIES[a], MID-1970S

(rate per 100,000 population)

Rank	Country	Rate
2.	Bahamas	22.9
6.	Iraq	11.9
11.	United States	9.6
17.	Venezuela	7.2
18.	Netherlands	7.2
27.	West Germany	4.5
31.	Libya	3.8
32.	Egypt	3.5
34.	Sweden	3.4
40.	France	2.7
45.	England & Wales	2.2
47.	Japan	1.7
50.	Zaire	1.2
58.	Spain	0.7
59.	Norway	0.5

[a] From a list of 59 ranked countries, not including communist states. Exact year unidentified. For the U.S. it was 1975.
Source: George Kurian, *The New Book of World Rankings* (New York, 1984), 386.

TABLE 19.11   MURDER RATE, SELECTED COUNTRIES[a], 1988

(rate per 100,000 population)

Rank	Country	Rate
2.	Philippines	42.5
7.	Netherlands	12.3
15.	United States	7.9
20.	Canada	6.3
24.	Sweden	5.7
26.	Italy	5.6
28.	France	4.6
32.	West Germany	4.5
54.	Israel	1.3
63.	Egypt	1.5
64.	Japan	1.5
66.	United Kingdom	1.4
68.	Saudi Arabia	1.2
74.	Norway	0.9
78.	Togo	0.2

[a] From a list of 78 ranked countries, not including communist states.
Source: George Kurian, *The New Book of World Rankings* (New York, 1991), 254–55.

Multiple Murders and Multiple Murderers

Violence, as civil-rights activist H. Rap Brown put it, was as American as cherry pie. Seeking violent means as a way of dealing with, or manifesting, real or perceived problems has not been unique to the United States. However, when it came to murder of multiple victims by one, occasionally more than one, individual for reasons that were at best vague or hypothetical, no nation has surpassed the United States. Suggested explanations abound: General factors likely were grounded in a highly competitive American economic and social system, a focus on the individual rather than the group, easy availability of firearms or other agents of destructive behavior, and a communi-

cation media that stood ready and willing to supply the attention that many a perpetrator otherwise had been unable to obtain.

The American multiple killer came in two forms: the mass murderer who out of anger, frustration, or other emotion killed several people at one time. The mass murderer commonly used a gun or guns, although occasionally one found other means. It was over in a few minutes or hours, the killer often making himself (it was almost always a man) the final victim. The event received national press coverage and except for families of the people involved, almost as suddenly was dropped until the next one came along.

The other type of multiple murderer was the repeat killer, an individual who engaged in homicide one person at a time over a period that differed with the amount of time it took to apprehend the perpetrator. The individual usually established a pattern, received from the press a name appropriate to modus operandi or other peculiarity and seemed to feed on the attention the deeds had attracted. Seeking to find a way to identify or categorize this different type of killer, an FBI agent recalled a type of movie he had watched as a child that told a story one episode at a time, usually weekly. They were called serials. In this fashion a label for the episodic murderer was born. He became known as a *serial killer*. In fact, the serial killer might be male or female of one of several different races, but overwhelmingly the people involved had been white males. The story of a serial killer would build over weeks, months, or in a few cases even years. The murderer's name, not known, of course, until time of apprehension, probably would soon be forgotten. It would be the label—the Boston Strangler, for example, or the Night Stalker—that would live on in infamy. The multiple murderer became a far-too-familiar aspect of American society in the half-century after 1946.

TABLE 19.12 PROMINENT SERIAL KILLERS, 1942–1990

Year	Name	Media Label	Location	Victim Traits	Number of Victims
1942–47	Jake Bird	Tacoma Axe Killer	Tacoma, Wash.	Females	10
1949	Harvey Carigan	Want Ad Killer	Northwest United States	Females	6–100
1957–60	Melvin Rees	Sex Beast	Maryland	Young Females	9
1962–64	Albert DeSalvo	Boston Strangler	Boston, Mass.	Females	13
1965	Posteal Laskey	Cincinnati Strangler	Cincinnati, Ohio	Elderly Females	7
1967–69	John N. Collins	Coed Murderer	Michigan	Coeds	7
1971	Juan Corona	. . .	Yuba City, Calif.	Male Farmers	25
1964–73	Edmund Kemper	Coed Killer	Santa Cruz, Calif.	Coeds	12
1972–78	John Wayne Gacy	Killer Clown	Chicago area, Ill.	Young Males	33
1974–78	Ted Bundy	Ted	Northwest, Florida	Y. Females	19–36
1975–77	Wayne Kearney	Trashbag Murders	California	Males	32
1976–77	David Berkowitz	Son of Sam	New York City, N.Y.	Females	6
1977–78	Carlton Gary	Stocking Strangler	Columbus, Ga.	Elderly Females	7
1977–78	Angelo Buono	Hillside Strangler	Los Angeles, Calif.	Females	10–23
1980	Douglas Clark	Sunset Strip Killer	Hollywood, Calif.	Prostitutes	7–50
1980–81	Wayne Williams	. . .	Atlanta, Ga.	Y. Black Males	2–28
1973–83	Robert Hanson	. . .	Alaska	Prostitutes	17
1985	Richard Ramirez	Night Stalker	Los Angeles, Calif.	Varied	8–15
1987	Richard Angelo	. . .	New York, N.Y.	Hosp. Patients	10–25
1989–90	Danny Rolling	Campus Killer	Florida	Coeds	8

Sources: Eric W. Hickey, *Serial Murderers and Their Victims* (Belmont, Calif., 1997), 133–34; Ronald M. Holmes and James DeBurger, *Serial Murder* (Newbury Park, Calif., 1988), 22.

TABLE 19.13 VICTIMS OF MURDER AND NONNEGLIGENT MANSLAUGHTER, PERCENT DISTRIBUTION BY SEX AND RACE, 1964–1990

Year	Sex of Victim		White	Black	All Other (including race unknown)	Total	Total Number of Murders and Nonnegligent Manslaughters
	Male	Female					
1964	74	26	45	54	1	100	7,990
1965	74	26	45	54	1	100	8,773
1966	74	26	45	54	1	100	9,552
1967	75	25	45	54	1	100	11,114
1968	78	22	45	54	1	100	12,503
1969	78	22	44	55	2	100	13,575
1970	78	22	44	55	1	100	13,649
1971	79	21	44	55	2	100	16,183
1972	78	22	45	53	1	100	15,832
1973	77	23	47	52	1	100	17,123
1974	77	23	48	50	2	100	18,632
1975	76	24	51	47	2	100	18,642
1976	76	24	51	47	2	100	16,605
1977	75	25	52	45	2	100	18,033
1978	76	24	54	44	2	100	18,714
1979	77	23	54	43	2	100	20,591
1980	77	23	53	42	4	100	21,860
1981	77	23	54	44	2	100	20,053
1982	76	24	55	42	2	100	19,485
1983	76	24	55	42	3	100	18,673
1984	75	25	56	41	3	100	16,689
1985	74	26	56	42	3	100	17,545
1986	75	25	53	44	3	100	19,257
1987	74	26	52	45	3	100	17,859
1988	75	25	49	48	3	100	18,269
1989	76	24	48	49	3	100	18,954
1990	78	22	48	49	3	100	20,045

Source: Department of Justice, *Sourcebook of Criminal Statistics—1991*, 402.

TABLE 19.14 PERCENT DISTRIBUTION OF MURDERS AND NONNEGLIGENT MANSLAUGHTERS, BY WEAPON USED, 1964–1990

Year	Type of Weapon Used						Total	Total Number of Murders and Nonnegligent Manslaughters
	Firearm	Cutting or Stabbing Instrument	Blunt Object (club, hammer, etc.)	Personal Weapons (hands, feet, fists, etc.)	Other	Unknown or Not Stated		
1964	55	24	5	10	3	2	100	7,990
1965	57	23	6	10	3	1	100	8,773
1966	59	22	5	9	2	1	100	9,552
1967	63	20	5	9	2	1	100	11,114
1968	65	18	6	8	2	1	100	12,503
1969	65	19	4	8	3	1	100	13,575
1970	66	18	4	8	3	1	100	13,649
1971	66	19	4	8	2	1	100	16,183
1972	66	19	4	8	2	1	100	15,832
1973	66	17	5	8	2	2	100	17,123
1974	67	17	5	8	1	1	100	18,632
1975	65	17	5	9	2	2	100	18,642
1976	64	18	5	8	2	3	100	16,605
1977	62	19	5	8	2	3	100	18,033
1978	64	19	5	8	2	3	100	18,714
1979	63	19	5	8	2	3	100	20,591
1980	62	19	5	8	2	4	100	21,860
1981	62	19	5	7	2	3	100	20,053
1982	60	21	5	8	2	3	100	19,485
1983	58	22	6	9	2	3	100	18,673
1984	59	21	6	8	3	4	100	16,689
1985	59	21	6	8	3	4	100	17,545
1986	59	20	6	9	2	4	100	19,257
1987	59	20	6	8	2	4	100	17,859
1988	61	19	6	8	2	4	100	18,269
1989	62	18	6	7	2	4	100	18,954
1990	64	18	5	7	2	4	100	20,045

Source: Department of Justice, *Sourcebook of Criminal Statistics—1991,* 398.

TABLE 19.15 RISK OF BEING MURDERED, 1985

Group	1 out of:
All Americans	133
All men	84
White men	131
Black men	21
All women	282
White women	369
Black women	104

Source: American Demographics, October, 1987, 10.

Capital Punishment

Capital punishment has had a varied history in the United States, particularly in the postwar period. Although challenged as ghastly and inhumane, an expression of cruel and unusual punishment (thus a violation of the Eighth Amendment to the Constitution), the death penalty was broadly accepted as appropriate punishment for the most grievous crimes (normally deliberately causing death), although at times other offenses—rape, for example—had been deemed equally heinous. As the postwar period began, executions proceeded almost as a matter of course; except for the year 1950 when there were 82, more than 100 executions took place each year between 1946 and 1951. A substantial percentage of persons under the sentence of death

were indeed executed. In 1955 it was nearly 61 percent. Statistics suggested, however, that considerable selectivity went into the practice. The bulk of the executions went on in the southern states, and a large portion of the people executed were black. Between 1946 and 1960, in only three years did the number of whites executed exceed the number of blacks.

In the 1960s and early 1970s the death penalty continued to be assailed in debate and in the courts. Enforcement became such a lengthy and costly process that the states gradually declined to go to the trouble. Only one person was executed in 1967 and in 1968 there were none. In 1972 the Supreme Court ruled that as applied in the case being considered, capital punishment violated the Eighth and Fourteenth Amendments. The Court never ruled that capital punishment was in principle unconstitutional, but the issue had become almost moot. No executions took place between 1968 and 1976.

The moratorium of nearly a decade came to an end in 1977 when Utah executed Gary Gilmore by firing squad. Gilmore wanted no appeals of his sentence. Thereafter, the states, or a few of them, went back into the business of execution. By the mid-1980s a pattern had developed that in one respect differed from and in other ways resembled old practices in the application of capital punishment. The number was much smaller—about 20 a year—than it had been in the 1940s and 1950s. Most states executed no one, whether they had a death penalty statute or not. Once again the southern states took the lead in putting prisoners to death. Of 104 executions between 1977 and 1988, only seven took place outside the South. Between 1977 and 1990, 87 whites and 56 blacks died on death row—a considerable distance, one must say, from the numbers of 1947 when there were 111 blacks and 42 whites, but the number for black people still remained disproportionately high in terms of the percentage of the total U.S. population of that race. The debate went on. Polls showed that a substantial majority supported the principle of the death penalty, but the opposition mounted a challenge on all fronts, adding a reminder that of all the Western democracies, only the United States insisted upon keeping the death penalty.

TABLE 19.16   PERSONS EXECUTED, BY RACE AND OFFENSE, 1946–1990

Year	Total[a]				White[a]				Black[a]			
	Total	Murder	Rape	Other	Total	Murder	Rape	Other	Total	Murder	Rape	Other
1946	131	107	22	2	46	45	0	1	84	61	22	1
1947	153	129	23	1	42	40	2	0	111	89	21	1
1948	119	95	22	2	35	32	1	2	82	61	21	0
1949	119	107	10	2	50	49	0	1	56	10	1	2
1950	82	68	13	1	40	36	4	0	42	32	9	1
1951	105	87	17	1	57	55	2	0	47	31	15	1
1952	83	71	12	0	36	35	1	0	47	36	11	0
1953	62	51	7	4	30	25	1	4	31	25	6	0
1954	81	71	9	1	38	37	1	0	42	33	8	1
1955	76	65	7	4	44	41	1	2	32	24	6	2
1956	65	52	12	1	21	20	0	1	43	31	12	0
1957	65	54	10	1	34	32	2	0	31	22	8	1
1958	49	41	7	1	20	20	0	0	28	20	7	1
1959	49	41	8	0	16	15	1	0	33	26	7	0
1960	56	44	8	4	21	18	0	3	35	26	8	1
1961	42	33	8	1	20	18	1	1	22	15	7	0
1962	47	41	4	2	28	26	2	0	19	15	2	2
1963	21	18	2	1	13	12	0	1	8	6	2	0
1964	15	9	6	0	8	5	3	0	7	4	3	0
1965	7	7	0	0	6	6	0	0	1	1	0	0
1966	1	1	0	0	1	1	0	0	0	0	0	0
1967	2	2	0	0	1	1	0	0	1	1	0	0
1968	0	0	0	0	0	0	0	0	0	0	0	0
1969	0	0	0	0	0	0	0	0	0	0	0	0
1970	0	0	0	0	0	0	0	0	0	0	0	0
1971	0	0	0	0	0	0	0	0	0	0	0	0
1972	0	0	0	0	0	0	0	0	0	0	0	0
1973	0	0	0	0	0	0	0	0	0	0	0	0
1974	0	0	0	0	0	0	0	0	0	0	0	0
1975	0	0	0	0	0	0	0	0	0	0	0	0
1976	0	0	0	0	0	0	0	0	0	0	0	0
1977	1	1	0	0	1	1	0	0	0	0	0	0
1978	0	0	0	0	0	0	0	0	0	0	0	0
1979	2	2	0	0	2	2	0	0	0	0	0	0
1980	0	0	0	0	0	0	0	0	0	0	0	0
1981	1	1	0	0	1	1	0	0	0	0	0	0
1982	2	2	0	0	1	1	0	0	1	1	0	0
1983	5	5	0	0	4	4	0	0	1	1	0	0
1984	21	21	0	0	13	13	0	0	8	8	0	0
1985	18	18	0	0	11	11	0	0	7	7	0	0
1986	18	18	0	0	11	11	0	0	7	7	0	0
1987	25	25	0	0	13	13	0	0	12	12	0	0
1988	11	11	0	0	6	6	0	0	5	5	0	0
1989	16	16	0	0	8	8	0	0	8	8	0	0
1990	23	23	0	0	16	16	0	0	7	7	0	0

[a] Ten persons classified as neither black nor white also were executed.
Source: Department of Justice, *Sourcebook of Criminal Justice Statistics—1997* (Washington, D.C., 1998), 713.

TABLE 19.17   PRISONERS EXECUTED, BY STATE—1930–1988, 1977–1988, AND 1988

System[a]	Number Executed			On Death Row 1988	Method of Execution
	Since 1930	Since 1977	In 1988		
Georgia	379	13	1	91	Electrocution
New York	329	0	No death penalty statute		
Texas	326	29	3	284	Injection
California	292	0	0	299	Gas
North Carolina	266	3	0	80	Injection; gas
Florida	189	19	2	295	Electrocution
Ohio	172	0	0	88	Electrocution
South Carolina	164	2	0	36	Electrocution
Mississippi	157	3	0	48	Injection; gas
Pennsylvania	152	0	0	98	Electrocution
Louisiana	151	18	3	40	Electrocution
Alabama	138	3	0	97	Electrocution
Arkansas	118	0	0	27	Injection
Kentucky	103	0	0	32	Electrocution
Virginia	99	7	1	39	Electrocution
Tennessee	93	0	0	70	Electrocution
Illinois	90	0	0	118	Injection
New Jersey	74	0	0	21	Injection
Maryland	68	0	0	14	Gas
Missouri	62	0	0	68	Gas
Oklahoma	60	0	0	92	Injection
Washington	47	0	0	7	Injection; hanging
Colorado	47	0	0	3	Injection
Indiana	43	2	0	51	Electrocution
West Virginia	40	No death penalty statute			
District of Columbia	40	No death penalty statute			
Arizona	38	0	0	82	Gas
Federal system	33	0	0	0	Method of state of execution
Nevada	31	2	0	44	Injection
Massachusetts	27	0	No death penalty statute		
Connecticut	21	0	0	1	Electrocution
Oregon	19	0	0	15	Injection
Iowa	18	0	No death penalty statute		
Utah	16	3	1	8	Injection; firing squad
Kansas	15	No death penalty statute			
Delaware	12	0	0	7	Injection
New Mexico	8	0	0	2	Injection
Wyoming	7	0	0	2	Injection
Montana	6	0	0	7	Injection; hanging
Nebraska	4	0	0	13	Electrocution
Vermont	4	0	0	0	Electrocution
Idaho	3	0	0	15	Injection; firing squad
South Dakota	1	0	0	0	Injection
New Hampshire	1	0	0	0	Injection
Rhode Island	0	0	No death penalty statute		
North Dakota	0	No death penalty statute			
Michigan	0	No death penalty statute			
Total U.S.	**3,963**	**104**	**11**	**2,124**	

[a] Alaska, Hawaii, Minnesota, and Wisconsin did not have a death penalty statute during these years.
Source: John Wright, *The Universal Almanac 1991* (Kansas City, 1990), 248.

TABLE 19.18 NUMBER OF PEOPLE SENTENCED TO DEATH COMPARED WITH NUMBER EXECUTED, 1953–1990

Year	Number of Persons Under Sentence of Death	Number of Executions	Percentage of Death Sentence Population Executed
1953	131	62	47.3
1954	147	81	55.1
1955	125	76	60.8
1956	146	65	44.5
1957	151	65	43.0
1958	147	49	33.3
1959	164	49	29.9
1960	210	56	26.7
1961	257	42	16.3
1962	267	47	17.6
1963	297	21	7.0
1964	315	15	4.8
1965	331	7	2.1
1966	406	1	0.2
1967	435	2	0.5
1968	517	0	0.0
1969	575	0	0.0
1970	631	0	0.0
1971	642	0	0.0
1972	334	0	0.0
1973	134	0	0.0
1974	244	0	0.0
1975	488	0	0.0
1976	420	0	0.0
1977	423	1	0.2
1978	483	0	0.0
1979	595	2	0.3
1980	697	0	0.0
1981	863	1	0.1
1982	1,073	2	0.2
1983	1,216	5	0.4
1984	1,421	21	1.5
1985	1,589	18	1.1
1986	1,800	18	1.0
1987	1,964	25	1.3
1988	2,111	11	0.5
1989	2,232	16	0.7
1990	2,346	23	0.1

Source: Timothy L. Gall and Daniel M. Lucas, eds., *Statistics on Crime and Punishment* (Detroit, 1996), 180.

TABLE 19.19 DEATH SENTENCES PRONOUNCED UPON FEMALES, 1976–1990

Year	Total Death Sentences	Female Death Sentences	Percentage
1976	234	3	1.3
1977	138	1	0.7
1978	186	4	2.1
1979	154	4	2.6
1980	175	2	1.1
1981	229	3	1.3
1982	269	5	1.8
1983	254	4	1.6
1984	287	8	2.8
1985	271	5	1.8
1986	305	3	1.0
1987	290	5	1.7
1988	295	5	1.7
1989	264	11	4.2
1990	252	7	2.7

Source: Mark Grossman, *Encyclopedia of Capital Punishment* (Santa Barbara, 1998), 269.

TABLE 19.20 FEMALES EXECUTED UNDER CIVIL AUTHORITY, 1946–1990

Year	Total	Offense		Race		Jurisdiction
		Murder	Other	White	Black	
1946	1	1	0	0	1	Pennsylvania
1947	2	2	0	1	1	Calif., South Carol.
1951	1	1	0	1	0	New York
1953	3	1	2	3	0	Ala., 2 federal
1954	2	1	0	1	1	Ohio
1955	1	1	0	1	0	California
1957	1	1	0	1	0	Alabama
1962	1	1	0	1	0	California
1984	1	1	0	1	0	North Carolina
1985–90	0	0	0	0	0	. . .
Totals 1946–90	13	11	2	10	3	. . .

Source: Department of Justice, *Sourcebook of Criminal Statistics—1991*, 714.

TABLE 19.21 PUBLIC OPINION ON THE DEATH PENALTY, 1953–1990

(in percent)

Date	Favor	Oppose	Don't Know
Oct. 1953	68	26	6
Apr. 1956	53	34	13
Sept. 1957	47	34	18
Mar. 1960	53	36	11
Feb. 1965	45	43	12
Jul. 1966	42	47	11
Jun. 1967	54	38	8
Jan. 1969	51	40	9
Oct. 1971	48	41	11
Feb. 1972	51	41	8
Mar. 1972	53	39	8
Nov. 1972	60	30	10
Mar. 1973	60	35	5
Mar. 1974	63	32	5
Mar. 1975	60	33	7
Mar. 1976	66	30	5
Apr. 1976	67	27	7
Mar. 1977	67	26	6
Mar. 1978	66	28	6
Jul. 1979	65	27	8
Mar. 1980	67	27	6
Mar. 1981	66	25	9
Mar. 1982	74	21	6
Jun. 1982	71	20	9
Mar. 1983	73	22	5
Mar. 1984	70	24	6
Jan. 1985	72	20	8
Mar. 1985	76	19	5
Nov. 1985	75	17	8
Jan. 1986	70	22	8
Mar. 1986	71	23	5
Mar. 1987	70	24	6
Mar. 1988	71	22	7
Sept. 1988	79	16	5
Mar. 1989	74	20	6
Mar. 1990	75	19	6

Note: Polls 1953 through February 1972, November 1972, April 1976, January 1981, January 1985, November 1985, and September 1988 are from Gallup surveys; the rest are from General Social Science Survey.
Source: Howard W. Stanley and Richard G. Niemi, *Vital Statistics on American Politics* (Washington, D.C., 1992), 33.

Drugs and the Law

The most common illegal drug in the United States was marijuana. Alcohol, it should be added, although subject to being used illegally, was in fact a legal drug. Proceedings in the district courts suggested that in the 1940s and 1950s, there existed, if not a war, at least a skirmish with breakers of the drug laws. The national courts heard more drug cases each year in the 1950s than in the 1960s at least until the very end of the decade. Nearly all relevant evidence confirmed that illegal drug activity increased substantially at the end of the 1960s and that in the 1970s the numbers took off. After that point the number of arrests declined modestly, although the level of usage remained fairly high. Even though the late 1960s and 1970s were noted for proliferation in kinds of drugs in use, most of the activity continued to be in marijuana, that is, until the mid-1980s when crack cocaine hit the streets. Expansion of the market and the lure of quick, easy, and exceptional profit led to creation of an extensive international mechanism, designed to keep the drug traffic flowing and growing.

TABLE 19.22   DISPOSITION OF DEFENDANTS CHARGED WITH VIOLATION OF DRUG LAWS, U.S. DISTRICT COURTS, 1945–1990

| Year Ending June 30 | Total Defendants | Not Convicted | | Acquitted by | | Convicted and Sentenced | | Convicted by | | | Average Sentence of Imprisonment (in months) | Average Sentence to Probation (in months) |
		Total	Dismissed	Court	Jury	Total	Plea of Guilty or Nolo Contendere	Court	Jury	Total		
1945	1,413	228	197	5	26	1,185	1,062	35	88	861	22.2	. . .
1946	1,687	349	305	13	31	1,338	1,218	37	83	949	18.7	. . .
1947	1,880	210	153	17	40	1,670	1,517	57	96	1,128	19.7	. . .
1948	1,790	308	237	14	57	1,482	1,324	48	110	1,048	18.6	. . .
1949	1,806	208	148	14	46	1,598	1,404	59	135	1,187	18.9	. . .
1950	2,400	264	184	28	52	2,136	1,907	61	168	1,654	21.9	. . .
1951	2,332	304	234	25	45	2,028	1,745	105	178	1,659	27.1	. . .
1952	2,121	252	184	29	39	1,869	1,523	109	237	1,551	35.2	. . .
1953	2,336	333	237	30	66	2,003	1,589	121	293	1,586	38.4	. . .
1954	2,220	310	239	28	43	1,910	1,491	107	312	1,483	41.3	. . .
1955	2,166	363	279	32	52	1,803	1,386	95	322	1,457	43.5	. . .
1956	1,835	314	221	36	57	1,521	1,168	93	260	1,258	45.8	. . .
1957	1,910	256	184	28	44	1,654	1,264	91	299	1,432	66.0	. . .
1958	1,942	301	217	25	59	1,641	1,138	129	374	1,351	69.4	. . .
1959	1,742	364	267	40	57	1,378	1,005	112	261	1,151	74.2	. . .
1960	1,846	340	263	38	39	1,506	1,155	93	258	1,232	72.8	. . .
1961	1,828	313	248	20	45	1,515	1,171	74	270	1,258	74.0	. . .
1962	1,643	240	175	29	36	1,403	1,022	113	268	1,173	70.5	. . .
1963	1,689	283	222	34	27	1,406	1,040	112	254	1,085	70.1	. . .
1964	1,679	271	205	32	34	1,408	1,039	112	257	1,076	63.7	. . .
1965	2,078	323	257	41	25	1,755	1,384	132	239	1,257	60.3	. . .
1966	2,223	349	280	36	33	1,874	1,469	119	286	1,272	61.3	. . .
1967	2,250	428	363	34	31	1,822	1,424	119	279	1,180	62.0	. . .
1968	2,692	563	466	49	48	2,129	1,664	138	327	1,368	64.4	. . .
1969	3,545	836	716	50	70	2,709	2,239	123	347	1,581	63.7	. . .
1970	3,420	959	886	48	45	2,461	2,030	97	334	1,283	64.8	. . .
1971	5,366	2,204	2,080	43	81	3,162	2,682	94	386	1,834	58.5	. . .
1972	6,848	1,600	1,396	52	152	5,248	4,391	228	629	3,050	46.4	. . .
1973	9,983	2,169	1,905	83	181	7,814	6,297	393	1,124	5,097	45.5	. . .
1974	10,989	2,744	2,430	80	234	8,245	6,666	437	1,142	5,125	43.7	. . .
1975	10,901	2,750	2,454	62	234	8,151	6,531	393	1,227	4,887	45.3	. . .
1976	10,762	2,721	2,404	73	244	8,041	6,324	446	1,271	5,039	47.6	. . .
1977	9,741	2,106	1,754	53	299	7,635	5,970	387	1,278	5,223	47.3	. . .
1978	7,860	2,043	1,729	37	277	5,817	4,440	290	1,087	4,119	51.3	38.6
1979	6,609	1,542	1,297	34	211	5,067	3,662	240	1,165	3,641	50.8	37.8
1980	6,343	1,594	1,337	32	225	4,749	3,450	236	1,063	3,479	54.5	38.7
1981	7,008	1,662	1,385	29	248	5,346	3,757	308	1,281	3,856	55.5	36.6
1982	7,981	1,645	1,360	51	234	6,336	4,798	342	1,196	4,586	61.4	34.1
1983	9,164	1,674	1,393	36	245	7,490	5,774	363	1,353	5,449	63.8	33.7
1984	9,191	1,732	1,421	28	283	7,459	5,793	218	1,448	5,756	65.7	43.2
1985	11,208	1,977	1,609	56	312	9,231	7,511	223	1,497	6,914	64.8	36.1
1986	12,934	2,170	1,811	63	296	10,764	8,888	159	1,717	8,152	70.0	38.7
1987	15,130	2,431	2,047	49	335	12,699	10,655	203	1,841	9,907	73.0	39.9
1988	15,750	2,588	2,168	45	375	13,162	11,044	170	1,948	9,983	78.0	33.4
1989	16,834	2,695	2,299	49	347	14,139	11,686	161	2,292	11,626	73.8	32.8
1990	19,271	3,083	2,610	53	420	16,188	13,067	148	2,973	13,838	79.3	32.3

Source: Department of Justice, *Sourcebook of Criminal Statistics—1990*, 494–95.

To meet this challenge, thousands of local officials and successive presidential administrations beginning with Richard Nixon committed themselves to winning the war on drugs. The national government moved to confront the problem from perspective of both supply and demand, although it appeared that the supply side took precedence. The Department of Justice in 1968 created a Bureau of Narcotics and Dangerous Drugs, which in 1975 was changed to the Drug Enforcement Administration (DEA). Congress passed the Controlled Substances Act in 1970 that classified drugs and prescribed penalties for illegal use of them. The government increased drug enforcement personnel, broadened interdiction activity, brought in the military forces, tried to persuade (or to bribe) such governments as Colombia or Mexico into curbing production and movement of marijuana and cocaine. In 1989 the president even sent the army to seize the leader of a foreign nation, General Manuel Noriega of Panama, spiriting him back to the United States for trial on drug charges.

Even though the war on drugs had a part in the program of every national politician and absorbed larger appropriations of national funds, the burden of enforcing the drug laws fell on state and local government. Of 742,687 drug arrests in 1986, only 21, 188 (2.9 percent) were by the national agencies—the FBI or the DEA. The 1980s did produce a decline in use of marijuana and selected other drugs, but traffic in crack cocaine soared. Critics increasingly became convinced that governments should focus less on supply and more on demand—education programs to prevent young people from starting to use drugs and to persuade individuals already involved to stop.

TABLE 19.23 JUVENILE DRUG ARREST RATES, BY RACE, 1965–1990[a]

(rate per 100,000 population)

Year	1965	1970	1975	1980	1985	1990
Marijuana						
White	6.9	181.8	436.1	393.5	284.7	131.0
Black	31.0	100.8	312.8	379.8	378.2	199.5
Other	18.2	163.4	246.5	128.0	160.0	25.5
Heroin/Cocaine						
White	1.3	18.2	14.1	19.4	42.4	68.0
Black	4.0	53.0	36.4	31.0	120.8	766.1
Other	6.8	11.3	21.3	2.8	7.2	6.3
Synthetic Drug						
White	3.7	44.8	14.4	11.6	7.7	7.6
Black	2.8	54.4	7.0	4.9	7.7	12.1
Other	9.9	47.7	8.0	6.0	1.7	1.3

[a] Juvenile in this context meant ages 10–17.
Source: F.B.I., Uniform Crime Reports—1991, 286–87.

TABLE 19.24 ESTIMATED NUMBER OF ADULT ARRESTS FOR DRUG VIOLATIONS REPORTED BY STATE AND LOCAL POLICE, 1981–1990

Year	Sale/Manufacture	Possession	Total
1981	93,143	374,913	468,056
1982	119,309	465,541	584,850
1983	128,948	454,526	583,474
1984	137,218	486,501	623,719
1985	170,307	548,290	718,597
1986	186,414	556,273	742,687
1987	219,176	630,345	849,521
1988	287,858	762,718	1,050,576
1989	404,275	843,488	1,247,763
1990	318,638	689,709	1,008,347
Percent change 1981–90	242.1	84.0	115.4

Source: Department of Justice, Drugs and Crime Facts, 1991 (Rockville, Md., 1992), 8.

TABLE 19.25 PRIOR DRUG USE BY JAIL INMATES, 1983 AND 1989

Type of Drug	Percent of Inmates Who Had Ever Used Drugs	
	1989	1983
Any drug	77.7	76.1
Major drug	55.4	46.2
Cocaine or crack	50.4	38.0
Heroin	18.2	22.4
LSD	18.6	22.3
PCP	13.9	15.6
Methadone	4.8	6.9
Other drug	71.9	74.5
Marijuana	70.7	73.0
Amphetamines	22.1	32.8
Barbiturates	17.2	27.8
Methaqualone	14.7	23.0
T's and blues[a]	11.0	10.9

[a] A combination of amphetamines and barbiturates
Source: Department of Justice, Drugs and Crime Facts, 1991, 8.

TABLE 19.26 COCAINE USE AMONG HIGH SCHOOL SENIORS, 1975–1990

(in percent)

Year	Used Cocaine Within the Last	
	12 Months	30 Days
1975	5.6	1.9
1976	6.0	2.0
1977	7.2	2.9
1978	9.0	3.9
1979	12.0	5.7
1980	12.3	5.2
1981	12.4	5.8
1982	11.5	5.0
1983	11.4	4.9
1984	11.6	5.8
1985	13.1	6.7
1986	12.7	6.2
1987	10.3	4.3
1988	7.9	3.4
1989	6.5	2.8
1990	5.3	1.9

Including the last 30 days.
Source: Department of Justice, Drugs and Crime Facts, 1991, 6.

TABLE 19.27 PERCENT OF HIGH SCHOOL SENIORS REPORTING THAT THEY COULD OBTAIN DRUGS FAIRLY EASILY OR VERY EASILY, 1990

Marijuana	84.4
Amphetamines	59.7
Cocaine powder	49.0
Barbiturates	45.9
Crack	42.4
Tranquilizers	44.7
LSD	40.7
Heroin	31.9
PCP	27.7

Source: Department of Justice, *Drugs and Crime Facts, 1991,* 17.

TABLE 19.28 AGREEMENT WITH STATEMENTS ABOUT MARIJUANA, BY AGE, 1971

Statement	All Adults	Adults by Age (Percent)			
		18 to 25	26 to 34	35 to 49	50 plus
Agree that					
(a) Marijuana makes people want to try stronger things like heroin	70	52	68	76	78
(b) Using marijuana is morally offensive	64	45	59	69	73
(c) It makes people lose their desire to work	59	46	52	63	66
(d) Many crimes are committed by persons who are under the influence of marijuana	56	35	49	59	69
(e) Some people have died from using it	48	35	42	56	51
(f) It is often promoted by people who are enemies of the United States	45	26	37	46	58
(g) It increases enjoyment of things like music and art	45	63	46	42	37
(h) Marijuana helps to relieve some of the tensions of modern life	43	50	47	43	37
(i) While people are smoking marijuana they tend to become more sociable	39	43	45	38	34
(j) Marijuana increases sexual pleasure	24	33	24	19	23
(k) Most people who use marijuana lead a normal life	23	49	29	19	9
Total Number of Adults	2,405	741	659	457	548

Source: Department of Justice, *Sourcebook of Criminal Justice Statistics—1975* (Washington, D.C., 1976), 294.

CHAPTER 20 Selected Documents

This chapter offers a highly selective sample of basic materials that form a backbone of history of the period. The items selected are mostly public documents—speeches, laws, constitutional amendments, and other materials—that reflect and reveal changes in policy, themes, expressions of attitude from the years 1946 to 1990. All the materials included in this unit are crucial to an understanding of this period, but—to remake a point—they stand only as examples. The post–Second World War era was laden with such documents. Some documents appear in full, but most of them, for purposes of space, have had portions deleted. They thus constitute samples of samples.

Amendments to the Constitution (Twenty-Second–Twenty-Seventh)

Amendment to the United States Constitution was designed to be—and was—a difficult process. Between the 1950s and 1980s some 5,400 amendments were proposed, but only five became part of the Constitution and a sixth one was working its way through the ratification process. The five new amendments did not involve public policy; two of them, the 22nd and the 25th, related to the office of the presidency—the term of office and filling of a vacancy. Three amendments pertained to voting: the 23rd allowed residents of Washington, D.C., to vote for the presidency; the 24th banned the poll tax as a prerequisite for voting; the 26th extended suffrage to citizens aged 18 through 20. The 27th amendment, a measure that passed Congress in 1989, pertained to compensation for legislators, an issue that was determined by the legislators themselves. It was not unusual for amendments to originate in swings in opinion caused by exceptional circumstances. The 22nd Amendment followed Franklin Roosevelt's being elected president four times; the 25th was boosted by the vice-presidency being vacant during the presidency of Harry Truman and Lyndon Johnson; the 23rd and 24th carried markings of the Civil Rights movement; and the 26th extended the vote to 18-year-olds at a time when young men of that age were being required to enter military service and perhaps fight and die in Vietnam.

AMENDMENT XXII

(PASSED MARCH 12, 1947; RATIFIED MARCH 1, 1951)

Section 1. No person shall be elected to the office of the President more than twice, and no person who has held the office of President, or acted as President, for more than two years of a term to which some other person was elected President shall be elected to the office of the President more than once. But this Article shall not apply to any person holding the office of President when this Article was proposed by the Congress, and shall not prevent any person who may be holding the office of President, or acting as President, during the term within which this Article becomes operative from holding the office of President or acting as President during the remainder of such term.

Section 2. This Article shall be inoperative unless it shall have been ratified as an amendment to the Constitution by the legislatures of three-fourths of the several States within seven years from the date of its submission to the States by the Congress.

AMENDMENT XXIII

(PASSED JUNE 16, 1960; RATIFIED APRIL 3, 1961)

Section 1. The District constituting the seat of Government of the United States shall appoint in such manner as the Congress may direct:

A number of electors of President and Vice President equal to the whole number of Senators and Representatives in Congress to which the District would be entitled if it were a State, but in no event more than the least populous State; they shall be in addition to those appointed by the States, but they shall be considered, for the purposes of the election of President and Vice President, to be electors appointed by a State; and they shall meet in the District and perform such duties as provided by the twelfth article of amendment.

Section 2. The Congress shall have power to enforce this article by appropriate legislation.

AMENDMENT XXIV

(PASSED AUGUST 27, 1962; RATIFIED JANUARY 23, 1964)

Section 1. The right of citizens of the United States to vote in any primary or other election for President or Vice President, for electors for President or Vice President, or for Senator or Representative in Congress, shall not be denied or abridged by the United States or any State by reason of failure to pay any poll tax or other tax.

Section 2. The Congress shall have power to enforce this article by appropriate legislation.

AMENDMENT XXV

(PASSED JULY 6, 1965; RATIFIED FEBRUARY 11, 1967)

Section 1. In case of the removal of the President from office or of his death or resignation, the Vice President shall become President.

Section 2. Whenever there is a vacancy in the office of the Vice President, the President shall nominate a Vice President who shall take office upon confirmation by a majority vote of both Houses of Congress.

Section 3. Whenever the President transmits to the President pro tempore of the Senate and the Speaker of the House of Representatives his written declaration that he is unable to discharge the powers and duties of his office, and until he transmits to them a written declaration to the contrary, such powers and duties shall be discharged by the Vice President as Acting President.

Section 4. Whenever the Vice President and a majority of either the principal officers of the executive departments or of such other body as Congress may by law provide, transmit to the President pro tempore of the Senate and the Speaker of the House of Representatives their written declaration that the President is unable to discharge the powers and duties of his office, the Vice President shall immediately assume the powers and duties of the office as Acting President.

Thereafter, when the President transmits to the President pro tempore of the Senate and the Speaker of the House of Representatives his written declaration that no inability exists, he shall resume the powers and duties of his office unless the Vice President and a majority of either the principal officers of the executive department or of such other body as Congress may by law provide, transmit within four days to the President pro tempore of the Senate and the Speaker of the House of Representatives their written declaration that the President is unable to discharge the powers and duties of his office. Thereupon Congress shall decide the issue, assembling within forty-eight hours for that purpose if not in session. If the Congress, within twenty-one days after receipt of the latter written declaration, or, if Congress is not in session, within twenty-one days after Congress is required to assemble, determines by two-thirds vote of both houses that the President is unable to discharge the powers and duties of his office, the Vice President shall continue to discharge the same as Acting President; otherwise, the President shall resume the powers and duties of his office.

AMENDMENT XXVI

(PASSED MARCH 23, 1971; RATIFIED JULY 5, 1971)

Section 1. The right of citizens of the United States who are eighteen years of age or older to vote shall not be denied or abridged by the United States or by any State on account of age. *Section 2.* The Congress shall have power to enforce this article by appropriate legislation.

AMENDMENT XXVII

(PASSED SEPTEMBER 25, 1989; NOT YET RATIFIED IN 1990)

No law, varying the compensation for the services of the Senators and Representatives, shall take effect, until an election of Representatives shall have intervened.

Source: John C. Vile, *Encyclopedia of Constitutional Proposed Amendments and Amending Issues, 1789–1995* (Santa Barbara, Calif., 1996), 359–62.

National Security Council Paper Number 68 (NSC–68) April 1950

National Security Council Paper Number 68 represented a review of American foreign policy ordered by President Harry S. Truman at the start of the year 1950, a formative time—needless to say—for dealings of the United States in Europe and Asia. Prepared largely by Paul Nitze, a state department official, the paper constituted one of the most formidable statements of the cold war in terms of the character and scope of the Soviet threat and of the U.S. effort needed to face that challenge. Not all officials agreed with all aspects of the report, and it remained classified for nearly a quarter-century, but NSC–68 was adopted by the Truman administration in summer 1950.

Within the past thirty-five years the world has experienced two global wars of tremendous violence. It has witnessed two revolutions—the Russian and the Chinese—of extreme scope and intensity. It has also seen the collapse of five empires—the Ottoman, the Austro-Hungarian, German, Italian and Japanese—and the drastic decline of two major imperial systems, the British and the French. During the span of one generation, the international distribution of power has been fundamentally altered. For several centuries it had proved impossible for any one nation to gain such preponderant strength that a coalition of other nations could not in time face it with greater strength. The international scene was marked by recurring periods of violence and war, but a system of sovereign and independent states was maintained, over which no state was able to achieve hegemony.

Two complex sets of factors have now basically altered this historical distribution of power. First, the defeat of Germany and Japan and the decline of the British and French Empires have interacted with the development of the United States and the Soviet Union in such a way that power has increasingly gravitated to these two centers. Second, the Soviet Union, unlike previous aspirants to hegemony, is animated by a new fanatic faith, antithetical to our own, and seeks to impose its absolute authority over the rest of the world. Conflict has, therefore, become endemic and is waged, on the part of the Soviet Union, by violent or nonviolent methods in accordance with the dictates of expediency. With the development of increasingly terrifying weapons of mass destruction, every individual faces the ever-present possibility of annihilation should the conflict enter the phase of total war.

On the one hand, the people of the world yearn for relief from the anxiety arising from the risk of atomic war. On the other hand, any substantial further extension of the area under the domination of the Kremlin would raise the possibility that no coalition adequate to confront the Kremlin with greater strength could be assembled. It is in this context that this Republic and its citizens in the ascendancy of their strength stand in their deepest peril. . . .

The fundamental design of those who control the Soviet Union and the international communist movement is to retain and solidify their absolute power, first in the Soviet Union and second in the areas now under their control. In the minds of the Soviet leaders, however, achievement of this design requires the dynamic extension of their authority and the ultimate elimination of any effective opposition to their authority.

The design, therefore, calls for the complete subversion or forcible destruction of the machinery of government and structure of society in the countries of the non-Soviet world and their replacement by an apparatus and structure subservient to and controlled from the Kremlin. To that end Soviet efforts are now directed toward the domination of the Eurasian land mass. The United States, as the principal center of power in the non-Soviet world and the bulwark of opposition to Soviet expansion, is the principal enemy whose integrity and vitality must be subverted or destroyed by one means or another if the Kremlin is to achieve its fundamental design. . . .

The same compulsion which demands total power over all men within the Soviet state without a single exception, demands total power over all Communist Parties and all states under Soviet domination. Thus Stalin has said that the theory and tactics of Leninism as expounded by the Bolshevik party are mandatory for the proletarian parties of all countries. A true internationalist is defined as one who unhesitatingly upholds the position of the Soviet Union and in the satellite states true patriotism is love of the Soviet Union. By the same token the "peace policy" of the Soviet Union, described at a Party Congress as "a more advantageous form of fighting capitalism," is a device to divide and immobilize the non-Communist world, and the peace the Soviet Union seeks is the peace of total conformity to Soviet policy. . . .

The assault on free institutions is worldwide now, and in the context of the present polarization of power a defeat of free institutions anywhere is a defeat everywhere. The shock we sustained in the destruction of Czechoslovakia was not in the measure of Czechoslovakia's material importance to us. In a material sense, her capabilities were already at Soviet disposal. But when the integrity of Czechoslovak institutions was destroyed, it was in the intangible scale of values that we registered a loss more damaging than the material loss we had already suffered. . . .

Our overall policy at the present time may be described as one designed to foster a world environment in which the American system can survive and flourish. It therefore rejects the concept of isolation and affirms the necessity of our positive participation in the world community.

This broad intention embraces two subsidiary policies. One is a policy which we would probably pursue even if there were no Soviet threat. It is a policy of attempting to develop a healthy international community. The other is the policy of "containing" the Soviet system. These two policies are closely interrelated and interact on one another. Nevertheless, the distinction between them is basically valid and contributes to a clearer understanding of what we are trying to do.

The policy of striving to develop a healthy international community is the long-term constructive effort which we are engaged in. It was this policy which gave rise to our vigorous sponsorship of the United Nations. It is of course the principal reason for our long continuing endeavors to create and now develop the Inter-American system. It, as much as containment, underlay our efforts to rehabilitate Western Europe. Most of our international economic activities can likewise be explained in terms of this policy. . . .

As for the policy of "containment", it is one which seeks by all means short of war to (1) block further expansion of Soviet power, (2) expose the falsities of Soviet pretensions, (3) induce a retraction of the Kremlin's control and influence and (4) in general, so foster the seeds of destruction within the Soviet system that the Kremlin is brought at least to the point of modifying its behavior to conform to generally accepted international standards. . . .

It was and continues to be cardinal in this policy that we possess superior overall power in ourselves or in dependable combination with other like-minded nations. One of the most important ingredients of power is military strength. In the concept of "containment," the maintenance of a strong military posture is deemed to be essential for two reasons: (1) as an ultimate guarantee of our national security and (2) as an indispensable backdrop to the conduct of the policy of "containment." Without superior aggregate military strength, in being and readily mobilizable, a policy of "containment"—which is in effect a policy of calculated and gradual coercion—is no more than a policy of bluff.

At the same time, it is essential to the successful conduct of a policy of "containment" that we always leave open the possibility of negotiation with the U.S.S.R. . . .

Our position as the center of power in the free world places a heavy responsibility upon the United States for leadership. We must organize and enlist the energies and resources of the free world in a positive program for peace which will frustrate the Kremlin design for world domination by creating a situation in the free world to which the Kremlin will be compelled to adjust. Without such a cooperative effort, led by the United States, we will have to make gradual withdrawals under pressure until we discover one day that we have sacrificed positions of vital interest.

It is imperative that this trend be reversed by a much more rapid and concerted build-up of the actual strength of both the United States and the other nations of the free world. The analysis shows that this will be costly and will involve significant domestic financial and economic adjustments.

Source: U.S. Department of State, *Foreign Relations of the United States 1950, Vol. I: National Security Affairs; Foreign Economic Policy* (Washington, D.C., 1977), 237–38, 240, 252–53, 290.

Advice to the Working Girl, 1951

The exchange that follows appeared in the advice column of Ruth Millett, a regular offering of the Kalamazoo, Michigan, Gazette. Published in the newspaper's edition of January 4, 1951, the "working woman's" letter and Millett's response suggested what it took for women to get along in the male-dominated workplace of the 1950s, or was it not more broadly, an expression of what it took for women to get along with men?

GIRLS, DON'T HOLD YOUR IQ UP TO MEN — THEY RESENT IT

Writes a working woman: "*When I first started out in my career I got along exceptionally well with my men associates.*

"*After a few years I realized I wasn't on as good terms with the men I worked with as I had once been, and I tried to figure out why.*

"*It finally dawned on me that in the beginning I didn't strive to impress a man with how smart I was. But gradually as I took on more responsibility I became eager to have men respect my brains.*

"*In trying to make them respect my mind I forgot it was even more important to show them how much I respected their opinions and ideas. Since then I've noticed a lot of other career women are making the same mistake. Maybe you could show them how wrong they are.*"

There doesn't need to be much added to that letter. The writer has made her own point.

Once a woman gets to thinking that she has a pretty good mind and wants to be sure every man she meets recognizes the fact, she is well on her way to losing her femininity. She is repelling rather than attracting the men she works with and the men she meets socially.

Men don't really want to admire a woman's brains. If forced to acknowledge that a woman has a goodly supply of them, they'll do so—reluctantly.

That's why it is such a poor idea for a woman to force a man to acknowledge how smart she is.

The best way is to make him think first what a pleasant, charming woman she is. Then when he notices of his own accord that she is far from dumb he'll admit without any reluctance at all: "By George, she's got a pretty good head on her shoulders, too."

Source: Kalamazoo *Gazette*, January 4, 1951, 10.

Supreme Court Case of *Brown v. Board of Education of Topeka, Kansas,* 1954

Racial relations in the southern states for more than a half-century had been based on segregation of blacks from whites, a system sustained by the United States Supreme Court in its doctrine of "separate but equal" handed down in the case of Plessy v. Ferguson of 1896. Subsequent court cases had qualified the Plessy decision—essentially by probing the reality of "equal"—but had allowed the basic decision to stand. In the Brown case of May 1954, the court attacked the Plessy ruling head on: overturned the decision, declared that "separate" conditions never could be "equal," that segregation in southern public schools—and by implication in other areas of society—was unconstitutional. In so doing, the Supreme Court started—or at least gave a solid foundation to—the Civil Rights movement in the South and changes in national racial relations still underway when the century ended. The Brown decision deserved to be ranked in the half-dozen most important rulings by the Supreme Court.

Chief Justice Earl Warren: as appointee of Dwight Eisenhower, wrote the majority opinion:

CHIEF JUSTICE WARREN: These cases come to us from the states of Kansas, South Carolina, Virginia, and Delaware. They are premised on different facts and different local conditions, but a common legal question justifies their consideration together in this consolidated opinion.

In each of the cases, minors of the Negro race, through their legal representatives, seek the aid of the courts in obtaining admission to the public schools of their community on a nonsegregated basis. In each instance, they have been denied admission to schools attended by white children under laws requiring or permitting segregation according to race. This segregation was alleged to deprive the plaintiffs of the equal protection of the laws under the Fourteenth Amendment. In each of the cases other than the Delaware case, a three-judge federal district court denied relief to the plaintiffs on the so-called "separate but equal" doctrine announced by this Court in *Plessy v. Ferguson* (1896).

Under that doctrine, equality of treatment is accorded when the races are provided substantially equal facilities, even though these facilities be separate. . . . The plaintiffs contend that segregated public schools are not "equal" and cannot be made "equal," and that hence they are deprived of the equal protection of the laws. Because of the obvious importance of the question presented, the Court took jurisdiction. . . .

Reargument was largely devoted to the circumstances surrounding the adoption of the Fourteenth Amendment in 1868. It covered exhaustively consideration of the Amendment in Congress, ratification by the states, then existing practices in racial segregation, and the views of proponents and opponents of the Amendment.

This discussion and our own investigation convince us that, although these sources cast some light, it is not enough to resolve the problem with which we are faced. At best, they are inconclusive. The most avid proponents of the post-[Civil] War Amendments undoubtedly intended them to remove all legal distinctions among "all persons born or naturalized in the United States." Their opponents, just as certainly, were antagonistic to both the letter and the spirit of the Amendments and wished them to have the most limited effect. What others in Congress and the state legislatures had in mind cannot be determined with any degree of certainty.

An additional reason for the inconclusive nature of the Amendment's history, with respect to segregated schools, is the status of public education at that time. In the South, the movement toward free common schools, supported by general taxation, had not yet taken hold. Education of white children was largely in the hands of private groups. Education of Negroes was almost nonexistent, and practically all of the race were illiterate. In fact, any education of Negroes was forbidden by law in some states.

Today, in contrast, many Negroes have achieved outstanding success in the arts and sciences as well as in the business and professional world. It is true that public education had already advanced further in the North, but the effect of the amendment on Northern States was generally ignored in the congressional debates. Even in the North, the conditions of public education did not approximate those existing today. The curriculum was usually rudimentary; ungraded schools were common in rural areas; the school term was but three months a year in many states; and compulsory school attendance was virtually unknown. As a consequence, it is not surprising that there should be so little in the history of the Fourteenth Amendment relating to its intended effect on public education.

In the first cases in this Court construing the Fourteenth Amendment, decided shortly after its adoption, the Court interpreted it as proscribing all stateimposed discriminations against the Negro race. The doctrine of "separate but equal" did not make its appearance in this Court until 1896 in the case of *Plessy v. Ferguson,* involving not education but transportation. . . .

In approaching this problem, we cannot turn the clock back. . . . We must consider public education in the light of its full development and its present place in American life throughout the Nation. Only in this way can it be determined if segregation in public schools deprives these plaintiffs of the equal protection of the laws.

Today, education is perhaps the most important function of state and local governments. Compulsory schools attendance laws and the great expenditures for education both demonstrate our recognition of the importance of education to our democratic society. It is required in the performance of our most basic public responsibilities, even service in the armed forces. It is the very foundation of good citizenship. Today it is a principal instrument in awakening the child to cultural values, in prepar-

ing him for later professional training, and in helping him to adjust normally to his environment.

In these days, it is doubtful that any child may reasonably be expected to succeed in life if he is denied the opportunity of an education. Such an opportunity, where the state has undertaken to provide it, is a right which must be made available to all on equal terms.

We come then to the question presented: Does segregation of children in public schools solely on the basis of race, even though the physical facilities and other "tangible" factors may be equal, deprive the children of the minority group of equal educational opportunities? We believe that it does.

In *Sweatt v. Painter,* in finding that a segregated law school for Negroes could not provide them equal educational opportunities, this Court relied in large part on "those qualities which are incapable of objective measurement but which make for greatness in a law school." In *McLaurin v. Oklahoma State Regents,* the Court, in requiring that a Negro admitted to a white graduate school be treated like all other students, again resorted to intangible considerations: ". . . his ability to study, to engage in discussions and exchange views with other students, and, in general, to learn his profession."

Such considerations apply with added force to children in grade and high schools. To separate them from others of similar age and qualifications solely because of their race generates a feeling of inferiority as to their status in the community that may affect their hearts and minds in a way unlikely ever to be undone. The effect of this separation on their educational opportunities was well stated by a finding in the Kansas case by a court which nevertheless felt compelled to rule against the Negro plaintiffs:

"Segregation of white and colored children in public schools has a detrimental effect upon the colored children. The impact is greater when it has the sanction of the law; for the policy of separating the race is usually interpreted as denoting the inferiority of the Negro group. A sense of inferiority affects the motivation of a child to learn. Segregation with the sanction of law, therefore, has a tendency to retard the educational and mental development of Negro children and to deprive them of some of the benefits they would receive in a racially integrated school system."

Whatever may have been the extent of psychological knowledge at the time of *Plessy v. Ferguson,* this finding is amply supported by modern authority. Any language in *Plessy v. Ferguson* contrary to this finding is rejected.

We conclude that in the field of public education the doctrine of "separate but equal" has no place. Separate educational facilities are inherently unequal. Therefore, we hold that the plaintiffs and others similarly situated for whom the actions have been brought are, by reason of the segregation complained of, deprived of the equal protection of the laws guaranteed by the Fourteenth Amendment. . . .

Source: Norman Dorsen, Paul Bender, Burt Neuborne, Sylvia Law, *Political and Civil Rights in the United States, Vol. II, Law School Edition* (Boston, 1979), 67–71.

Origins of the Domino Theory, April 7, 1954

A quest for an explanation of how and why the United States became involved in a devastating war in Vietnam would include the domino theory as one of the early factors. This rationale emerged as President Dwight Eisenhower's explanation of why control of former French Indochina by native communists would be harmful to the United States. The strategy was to make what appeared to be a small issue become very large. The purpose was to justify U.S.

assistance to friendly forces in part of the area that would be called South Vietnam. The theory surfaced as Eisenhower's answer to a question in a news conference of April 7, 1954.

Q. *Robert Richards, Copley Press:* Mr. President, would you mind commenting on the strategic importance of Indochina to the free world? I think there has been, across the country, some lack of understanding on just what it means to us.

The President: You have, of course, both the specific and the general when you talk about such things.

First of all, you have the specific value of a locality in its production of materials that the world needs.

Then you have the possibility that many human beings pass under a dictatorship that is inimical to the free world.

Finally, you have broader considerations that might follow what you would call the "falling domino" principle. You have a row of dominoes set up, you knock over the first one, and what will happen to the last one is the certainty that it will go over very quickly. So you could have a beginning of a disintegration that would have the most profound influences.

Now, with respect to the first one, two of the items from this particular area that the world uses are tin and tungsten. They are very important. There are others, of course, the rubber plantations and so on.

Then with respect to more people passing under this domination, Asia, after all, has already lost some 450 million of its peoples to the Communist dictatorship, and we simply can't afford greater losses.

But when we come to the possible sequence of events, the loss of Indochina, of Burma, of Thailand, of the Peninsula, and Indonesia following, now you begin to talk about areas that not only multiply the disadvantages that you would suffer through loss of materials, sources of materials, but now you are talking about millions and millions and millions of people.

Finally, the geographical position achieved thereby does many things. It turns the so-called island defensive chain of Japan, Formosa, of the Philippines and to the southward: it moves in to threaten Australia and New Zealand.

It takes away, in its economic aspects, that region that Japan must have as a trading area or Japan, in turn, will have only one place in the world to go—that is, towards the Communist areas in order to live.

So, the possible consequences of the loss are just incalculable to the free world.

Source: Public Papers of the Presidents of the United States: Dwight D. Eisenhower, 1954 (Washington, D.C., 1955), 382–83.

John F. Kennedy's Inaugural Address, January 20, 1961

John F. Kennedy's inaugural address in 1961 was perhaps the best of any president in the post–Second World War era. Delivered with excellent timing and rhythm, marked with inspiring phrases, optimism, and grand objectives, it did indeed seem to herald the beginning of a new age for America. Within no more than six or eight years, however, the same words and ideas would have different meaning.

We observe today not a victory of party but a celebration of freedom—symbolizing an end as well as a beginning—signifying renewal as well as change. For I have sworn before you and Almighty God the same solemn oath our forebearers prescribed nearly a century and three-quarters ago.

The world is very different now. For man holds in his mortal hands the power to abolish all forms of human poverty and all forms of human life. And yet the same revolutionary beliefs for which our forebearers fought are still at issue around the globe—the belief that the rights of man come not from the generosity of the state but from the hand of God.

We dare not forget today that we are the heirs of that first revolution. Let the word go forth from this time and place, to friend and foe alike, that the torch has been passed to a new generation of Americans—born in this century, tempered by war, disciplined by a hard and bitter peace, proud of our ancient heritage—and unwilling to witness or permit the slow undoing of those human rights to which this nation has always been committed, and to which we are committed today at home and around the world.

Let every nation know, whether it wishes us well or ill, that we shall pay any price, bear any burden, meet any hardship, support any friend, oppose any foe to assure the survival and the success of liberty.

This much we pledge—and more.

To those old allies whose cultural and spiritual origins we share, we pledge the loyalty of faithful friends. United there is little we cannot do in a host of cooperative ventures. Divided, there is little we can do—for we dare not meet a powerful challenge at odds and split asunder.

To those new states whom we welcome to the ranks of the free, we pledge our word that one form of colonial control shall not have passed away merely to be replaced by a far more iron tyranny. We shall not always expect to find them supporting our view. But we shall always hope to find them strongly supporting their own freedom—and to remember that, in the past, those who foolishly sought power by riding the back of the tiger ended up inside.

To those people in the huts and villages of half the globe struggling to break the bonds of mass misery, we pledge our best efforts to help them help themselves, for whatever period is required—not because the Communists may be doing it, not because we seek their votes, but because it is right. If a free society cannot help the many who are poor, it cannot save the few who are rich.

To our sister republics south of our border, we offer a special pledge—to convert our good words into good deeds—in a new alliance for progress—to assist free men and free governments in casting off the chains of poverty. But this peaceful revolution of hope cannot become the prey of hostile powers. Let all our neighbors know that we shall join with them to oppose aggression or subversion anywhere in the Americas. And let every other power know that this hemisphere intends to remain the master of its own house.

To that world assembly of sovereign states, the United Nations, our last best hope in an age where the instruments of war have far outpaced the instruments of peace, we renew our pledge of support—to prevent it from becoming merely a forum for invective—to strengthen its shield of the new and the weak—and to enlarge the area in which its writ may run.

Finally, to those nations who would make themselves our adversary, we offer not a pledge but a request: that both sides begin anew the quest for peace, before the dark powers of destruction unleashed by science engulf all humanity in planned or accidental self-destruction.

We dare not tempt them with weakness. For only when our arms are sufficient beyond doubt can we be certain beyond doubt that they will never be employed.

But neither can two great and powerful groups of nations take comfort from our present course—both sides overburdened by the cost of modern weapons, both rightly alarmed by the steady spread of the deadly atom, yet both racing to alter that uncertain balance of terror that stays the hand of mankind's final war.

So let us begin anew—remembering on both sides that civility is not a sign of weakness, and sincerity is always subject to proof. Let us never negotiate out of fear. But let us never fear to negotiate.

Let both sides explore what problems unite us instead of belaboring those problems which divide us.

Let both sides, for the first time, formulate serious and precise proposals for the inspection and control of arms—and bring the absolute power to destroy other nations under the absolute control of all nations.

Let both sides seek to invoke the wonders of science instead of its terrors. Together let us explore the stars, conquer the deserts, eradicate disease, tap the ocean depths, and encourage the arts and commerce.

Let both sides unite to heed in all corners of the earth the command of Isaiah—to "undo the heavy burdens . . . [and] let the oppressed go free."

And if a beachhead of cooperation may push back the jungle of suspicion, let both sides join in creating a new endeavor, not a new balance of power, but a new world of law, where the strong are just and the weak secure and the peace preserved.

All this will not be finished in the first one hundred days. Nor will it be finished in the first one thousand days, nor in the life of this administration, nor even perhaps in our lifetime on this planet. But let us begin.

In your hands, my fellow citizens, more than mine, will rest the final success or failure of our course. Since this country was founded, each generation of Americans has been summoned to give testimony to its national loyalty. The graves of young Americans who answered the call to service surround the globe.

Now the trumpet summons us again—not as a call to bear arms, though arms we need —not as a call to battle, though embattled we are—but a call to bear burden of a long twilight struggle, year in and year out, "rejoicing in hope, patient in tribulation"—a struggle against the common enemies of man: tyranny, poverty, disease, and war itself.

Can we forge against these enemies a grand and global alliance, North and South, East and West, that can assure a more fruitful life for all mankind? Will you join in that historic effort?

In the long history of the world, only a few generations have been granted the role of defending freedom in its hour of maximum danger. I do not shrink from this responsibility—I welcome it. I do not believe that any of us would exchange places with any other people or any other generation. The energy, the faith, the devotion which we bring to this endeavor will light our country and all who serve it—and the glow from that fire can truly light the world.

And so, my fellow Americans: ask not what your country can do for you—ask what you can do for your country.

My fellow citizens of the world: ask not what America will do for you, but what together we can do for the freedom of man.

Finally, whether you are citizens of America or citizens of the world, ask of us here the same high standards of strength and sacrifice which we ask of you. With a good conscience our only sure reward, with history the final judge of our deeds, let us go forth to lead the land we love, asking His blessing and His help, but knowing that here on earth God's work must truly be our own.

Source: *Public Papers of the Presidents of the United States: John F. Kennedy, 1961* (Washington, D.C., 1962), 1–3.

The Cuban Missile Crisis: President John F. Kennedy's Report to the Nation, October 22, 1962

President Kennedy's report ended several days of rumor about Soviet military activity in Cuba. The message confirmed the worst suspicions: that the Soviet Union was installing some ninety or so miles from the United States missiles capable of carrying nuclear warheads that had a range of 2,000 miles. Kennedy's explanation of a response was stunning: besides demanding that the missiles be removed, he reported that in the event of a missile striking an American target the United States would retaliate against the USSR; to use the vernacular, Kennedy openly and publicly threatened to "nuke" the Soviets. The issue would be resolved through diplomacy, but the Cuban missile crisis of October 1962 would go down as the most threatening and harrowing public episode of the cold war era.

Good evening, my fellow citizens:

This Government, as promised, has maintained the closest surveillance of the Soviet military buildup on the island of Cuba. Within the past week, unmistakable evidence has established the fact that a series of offensive missile sites is now in preparation on that imprisoned island. The purpose of these bases can be none other than to provide a nuclear strike capability against the Western Hemisphere. . . .

The characteristics of these new missile sites indicate two distinct types of installations. Several of them include medium range ballistic missiles, capable of carrying a nuclear warhead for a distance of more than 1,000 nautical miles. Each of these missiles, in short, is capable of striking Washington, D.C., the Panama Canal, Cape Canaveral, Mexico City, or any other city in the southeastern part of the United States, in Central America, or in the Caribbean area.

Additional sites not yet completed appear to be designed for intermediate range ballistic missiles—capable of traveling more than twice as far—and thus capable of striking most of the major cities in the Western Hemisphere, ranging as far north as Hudson Bay, Canada, and as far south as Lima, Peru. In addition, jet bombers, capable of carrying nuclear weapons, are now being uncrated and assembled in Cuba, while the necessary air bases are being prepared.

This urgent transformation of Cuba into an important strategic base—by the presence of these large, long-range, and clearly offensive weapons of sudden mass destruction—constitutes an explicit threat to the peace and security of all the Americas, in flagrant and deliberate defiance of the Rio Pact of 1947, the traditions of this Nation and hemisphere, the joint resolution of the 87th Congress, the Charter of the United Nations, and my own public warnings to the Soviets on September 4 and 13. This action also contradicts the repeated assurances of Soviet spokesmen, both publicly and privately delivered, that the arms buildup in Cuba would retain its original defensive character, and that the Soviet Union had no need or desire to station strategic missiles on the territory of any other nation. . . .

Only last Thursday, as evidence of this rapid offensive buildup was already in my hand, Soviet Foreign Minister Gromyko told me in my office that he was instructed to make it clear once again, as he said his government had already done, that Soviet assistance to Cuba, and I quote, "pursued solely the purpose of contributing to the defense capabilities of Cuba," that, and I quote him, "training by Soviet specialists of Cuban nationals in handling defensive armaments was by no means offensive, and if it were otherwise," Mr. Gromyko went on, "the Soviet Government would never become involved in rendering such assistance." That statement also was false.

Neither the United States of America nor the world community of nations can tolerate deliberate deception and offensive threats on the part of any nation, large or small. We no longer live in a world where only the actual firing of weapons represents a sufficient challenge to a nation's security to constitute maximum peril. Nuclear weapons are so destructive and ballistic missiles are so swift, that any substantially increased possibility of their use or any sudden change in their deployment may well be regarded as a definite threat to peace. . . .

In that sense, missiles in Cuba add to an already clear and present danger—although it should be noted the nations of Latin America have never previously been subjected to a potential nuclear threat.

But this secret, swift, and extraordinary buildup of Communist missiles—in an area well known to have a special and historical relationship to the United States and the nations of the Western Hemisphere, in violation of Soviet assurances, and in defiance of American and hemispheric policy—this sudden, clandestine decision to station strategic weapons for the first time outside of Soviet soil—is a deliberately provocative and unjustified change in the status quo which cannot be accepted by this country, if our courage and our commitments are ever to be trusted again by either friend or foe. . . .

Our policy has been one of patience and restraint, as befits a peaceful and powerful nation, which leads a worldwide alliance. We have been determined not to be diverted from our central concerns by mere irritants and fanatics. But now further action is required—and it is under way; and these actions may only be the beginning. We will not prematurely or unnecessarily risk the costs of worldwide nuclear war in which even the fruits of victory would be ashes in our mouth—but neither will we shrink from the risk at any time it must be faced.

Acting, therefore, in the defense of our own security and of the entire Western Hemisphere, and under the authority entrusted to me by the Constitution as endorsed by the resolution of the Congress, I have directed that the following *initial* steps be taken immediately:

First: To halt this offensive buildup, a strict quarantine on all offensive military equipment under shipment to Cuba is being initiated. All ships of any kind bound for Cuba from whatever nation or port will, if found to contain cargoes of offensive weapons, be turned back. This quarantine will be extended, if needed, to other types of cargo and carriers. We are not at this time, however, denying the necessities of life as the Soviets attempted to do in their Berlin blockade of 1948.

Second: I have directed the continued and increased close surveillance of Cuba and its military buildup. The foreign ministers of the OAS, in their communique of October 6, rejected secrecy on such matters in this hemisphere. Should these offensive military preparations continue, thus increasing the threat to the hemisphere, further action will be justified. I have directed the Armed Forces to prepare for any eventualities; and I trust that in the interest of both the Cuban people and the Soviet technicians at the sites, the hazards to all concerned of continuing this threat will be recognized.

Third: It shall be the policy of this Nation to regard any nuclear missile launched from Cuba against any nation in the Western Hemisphere as an attack by the Soviet Union on the United States, requiring a full retaliatory response upon the Soviet Union.

Fourth: As a necessary military precaution, I have reinforced our base at Guantanamo, evacuated today the dependents of our personnel there, and ordered additional military units to be on a standby alert basis.

Fifth: We are calling tonight for an immediate meeting of the Organ of Consultation under the Organization of American States, to consider this threat to hemispheric security. . . .

Sixth: Under the Charter of the United Nations, we are asking tonight that an emergency meeting of the Security Council be convoked without delay to take action against this latest Soviet threat to world peace. . . .

Seventh and finally: I call upon Chairman Khrushchev to halt and eliminate this clandestine, reckless, and provocative threat to world peace and to stable relations between our two nations.

I call upon him further to abandon this course of world domination, and to join in an historic effort to end the perilous arms race and to transform the history of man. He has an opportunity now to move the world back from the abyss of destruction—by returning to his government's own words that it had no need to station missiles outside its own territory, and withdrawing these weapons from Cuba—by refraining from any action which will widen or deepen the present crisis—and then by participating in a search for peaceful and permanent solutions.

This Nation is prepared to present its case against the Soviet threat to peace, and our own proposals for a peaceful world, at anytime and in any forum. . . . We have no wish to war with the Soviet Union—for we are a peaceful people who desire to live in peace with all other peoples.

But it is difficult to settle or even discuss these problems in an atmosphere of intimidation. That is why this latest Soviet threat—or any other threat which is made either independently or in response to our actions this week—must and will be met with determination. Any hostile move anywhere in the world against the safety and freedom of peoples to whom we are committed—including in particular the brave people of West Berlin—will be met by whatever action is needed.

Finally, I want to say a few words to the captive people of Cuba, to whom this speech is being directly carried by special radio facilities. I speak to you as a friend, as one who knows of your deep attachment to your fatherland, as one who shares your aspirations for liberty and justice for all. And I have watched and the American people have watched with deep sorrow how your nationalist revolution was betrayed—and how your fatherland fell under foreign domination. Now your leaders are no longer Cuban leaders inspired by Cuban ideals. They are puppets and agents of an international conspiracy which has turned Cuba against your friends and neighbors in the Americas—and turned it into the first Latin American country to become a target for nuclear war—the first Latin American country to have these weapons on its soil.

These new weapons are not in your interest. They contribute nothing to your peace and well-being. They can only undermine it. But this country has no wish to cause you to suffer or to impose any system upon you. We know that your lives and land are being used as pawns by those who deny your freedom.

Many times in the past, the Cuban people have risen to throw out tyrants who destroyed their liberty. And I have no doubt that most Cubans today look forward to the time when they will be truly free—free from foreign domination, free to choose their own leaders, free to select their own system, free to own their own land, free to speak and write and worship without fear or degradation. And then shall Cuba be welcomed back to the society of free nations and to the associations of this hemisphere.

My fellow citizens: let no one doubt that this is a difficult and dangerous effort on which we have set out. No one can foresee precisely what course it will take or what costs or casualties will be incurred. Many months of sacrifice and self-discipline lie ahead—months in which both our patience and our will will be tested—months in which many threats and denunciations will keep us aware of our dangers. But the greatest danger of all would be to do nothing.

The path we have chosen for the present is full of hazards, as all paths are—but it is the one most consistent with our character and courage as a nation and our commitments around the world. The cost of freedom is always high—but Americans have always paid it. And one path we shall never choose, and that is the path of surrender or submission.

Our goal is not the victory of might, but the vindication of right—not peace at the expense of freedom, but both peace *and* freedom, here in this hemisphere, and, we hope, around the world. God willing, that goal will be achieved.

Thank you and good night.

Source: Public Papers of the Presidents of the United States: John F. Kennedy, 1962 Washington, D.C., 1963), 806–09.

Civil Rights Act of 1964

After a decade of reformist activism and determined resistance to change in the postwar South, the Civil Rights Act of 1964 marked the point of culmination of the Civil Rights movement. Designed generally to strike at the bastions of segregation and discrimination in the southern states, the law's major provisions dealt specifically with the right to vote, desegregation of privately owned public facilities and of the public schools, equal employment opportunities, and the national government's intervention on behalf of people whose rights had been violated. Amidst great upheaval in Washington and in the South, having attracted enormous national attention, the measure passed in July 1964.

An Act to enforce the constitutional right to vote, to confer jurisdiction upon the district courts of the United States to provide injunctive relief against discrimination in public accommodations, to authorize the Attorney General to institute suits to protect constitutional rights in public facilities and public education, to extend the Commission on Civil Rights, to prevent discrimination in federally assisted programs, to establish a Commission on Equal Employment Opportunity, and for other purposes.

TITLE I—VOTING RIGHTS

"(2) No person acting under color of law shall—

"(A) in determining whether any individual is qualified under State law or laws to vote in any Federal elections, apply any standard, practice, or procedure different from the standards, practices, or procedures applied under such law to other individuals within the same county, parish, or similar political subdivision who have been found by State officials to be qualified to vote;

"(B) deny the right of any individual to vote in any Federal election because of an error or omission on any record or paper relating to any application, registration, or other act requisite to voting, if such error or omission is not material in determining whether such individual is qualified under State law to vote in such election; or

"(C) employ any literacy as a qualification for voting in any Federal election unless (i) such test is administered to each individual and is conducted wholly in writing, and (ii) a certified copy of the test and of the answers given by the individual is furnished to him within twenty-five days of the submission of his request. . . .

TITLE II—INJUNCTIVE RELIEF AGAINST DISCRIMINATION IN PLACES OF PUBLIC ACCOMMODATION

Sec. 201. (a) All persons shall be entitled to the full and equal enjoyment of the goods, services, facilities, privileges, advantages, and accommodations of any place of public accommodation, as defined in this section, without discrimination or segregation on the ground of race, color, religion, or national origin.

(b) Each of the following establishments which serves the public is a place of public accommodation within the meaning of this title if its operations affect commerce, or if discrimination or segregation by it is supported by State action:

(1) any inn, hotel, motel, or other establishment which provides lodging to transient guests, other than an establishment located within a building which contains not more than five rooms for rent or hire and which is actually occupied by the proprietor of such establishment as his residence;

(2) any restaurant, cafeteria, lunchroom, lunch counter, soda fountain, or other facility principally engaged in selling food for consumption on the premises, including, but not limited to, any such facility located on the premises of any retail establishment; or any gasoline station;

(3) any motion picture house, theater, concert hall, sports arena, stadium or other place of exhibition or entertainment. . . .

(d) Discrimination or segregation by an establishment is supported by State action within the meaning of this title if such discrimination or segregation (1) is carried on under color of any law, statute, ordinance, or regulation; or (2) is carried on under color of any custom or usage required or enforced by officials of the State or political subdivision thereof; or (3) is required by action of the State or political subdivision thereof.

Sec. 202. All persons shall be entitled to be free, at any establishment or place, from discrimination or segregation of any kind on the ground of race, color, religion, or national origin, if such discrimination or segregation is or purports to be required by any law, statute, ordinance, regulation, rule, or order of a State or any agency or political subdivision thereof.

Sec. 206 (a) Whenever the Attorney General has reasonable cause to believe that any person or group of persons is engaged in a pattern or practice of resistance to the full enjoyment of any of the rights secured by this title, and that the pattern or practice is of such a nature and is intended to deny the full exercise of the rights herein described, the Attorney General may bring a civil action in the appropriate district court of the United States. . . .

TITLE IV—DESEGREGATION OF PUBLIC EDUCATION

SUITS BY THE ATTORNEY GENERAL

Sec. 407. (a) Whenever the Attorney General receives a complaint in writing —

(1) signed by a parent or group of parents to the effect that his or their minor children, as members of a class of persons similarly situated, are being deprived by a school board of the equal protection of the laws, or

(2) signed by an individual, or his parent, to the effect that he has been denied admission to or not permitted to continue in attendance at a public college by reason of race, color, religion, or national origin, and the Attorney General believes the complaint is meritorious . . ., the Attorney General is authorized . . . to institute . . . a civil action. . . .

TITLE VI—NONDISCRIMINATION IN FEDERALLY ASSISTED PROGRAMS

Sec. 601. No person in the United States shall, on the ground of race, color, or national origin, be excluded from participation in, be denied the benefits of, or be subjected to discrimination under any program or activity receiving Federal financial assistance. . . .

TITLE VII—EQUAL EMPLOYMENT OPPORTUNITY

DEFINITIONS

Sec. 701. For the purposes of this title —

(a) The term "person" includes one or more individuals, labor unions, partnerships, associations, corporations, legal representatives, mutual companies, joint-stock companies, trusts, unincorporated organizations, trustees, trustees in bankruptcy, or receivers.

(b) The term "employer" means a person engaged in an industry affecting commerce who has twenty-five or more employees for each working day in each of twenty or more calendar weeks in the current or preceding calendar year, and any agent of such a person. . . .

DISCRIMINATION BECAUSE OF RACE, COLOR, RELIGION, SEX, OR NATIONAL ORIGIN

Sec. 703. (a) It shall be an unlawful employment practice for an employer —

(1) to fail or refuse to hire or to discharge any individual, or otherwise to discriminate against any individual with respect to his compensation, terms, conditions, or privileges of employment, because of such individual's race, color, religion, sex, or national origin; or

(2) to limit, segregate, or classify his employees in any way which would deprive or tend to deprive any individual of employment opportunities or otherwise adversely affect his status as an employee, because of such individual's race, color, religion, sex, or national origin.

(b) It shall be an unlawful employment practice for an employment agency to fail or refuse to refer for employment, or otherwise to discriminate against, any individual because of his race, color, religion, sex, or national origin, or to classify or refer for employment any individual on the basis of his race, color, religion, sex, or national origin.

(c) It shall be an unlawful employment practice for a labor organization —

(1) to exclude or to expel from its membership, or otherwise to discriminate against, any individual because of his race, color, religion, sex, or national origin;

(2) to limit, segregate, or classify its membership, or to classify or fail to refuse to refer for employment any individual, in any way which would deprive or tend to deprive any individual of employment opportunities. . . .

Source: United States Code: Congressional and Administration News, 88th Congress— Second Session 1964 (St. Paul, Minn., 1965), 287–319.

Kerner Commission Report on Racial Violence in American Cities, 1968

In the mid-1960s the focus on racial issues in the United States shifted from south to north, as virtually every northern city experienced some form of racial disturbance and several had major race riots. After especially destructive riots in Detroit and Newark in 1967, President Lyndon Johnson appointed a special commission headed by Otto Kerner, governor of Illinois, to investigate the problem. The Kerner Commission's report, in truth a fairly substantial book, appeared in 1968. It described exceptionally complex and deeply rooted problems in the area of race relations, the solution of which would take an enormous national effort.

INTRODUCTION

. . . This is our basic conclusion: Our Nation is moving toward two societies, one black, one white—separate and unequal.

Reaction to last summer's disorders has quickened the movement and deepened the division. Discrimination and segregation have long permeated much of American life; they now threaten the future of every American.

This deepening racial division is not inevitable. The movement apart can be reversed. Choice is still possible. Our principal task is to define that choice and to press for a national resolution.

To pursue our present course will involve the continuing polarization of the American community and, ultimately, the destruction of basic democratic values.

The alternative is not blind repression or capitulation to lawlessness. It is the realization of common opportunities for all within a single society.

This alternative will require a commitment to national action—compassionate, massive, and sustained, backed by the resources of the most powerful and the richest nation on this earth. From every American it will require new attitudes, new understanding, and, above all, new will.

The vital needs of the Nation must be met; hard choices must be made, and, if necessary, new taxes enacted.

Violence cannot build a better society. Disruption and disorder nourish repression, not justice. They strike at the freedom of every citizen. The community cannot—it will not—tolerate coercion and mob rule.

Violence and destruction must be ended—in the streets of the ghetto and in the lives of people.

Segregation and poverty have created in the racial ghetto a destructive environment totally unknown to most white Americans.

What white Americans have never fully understood—but what the Negro can never forget—is that white society is deeply implicated in the ghetto. White institutions created it, white institutions maintain it, and white society condones it. . . .

THE BASIC CAUSES

These factors are complex and interacting; they vary significantly in their effect from city to city and from year to year; and the consequences of one disorder, generating new grievances and new demands, become the causes of the next. Thus was created the "thicket of tension, conflicting evidence, and extreme opinions" cited by the President.

Despite these complexities, certain fundamental matters are clear. Of these, the most fundamental is the racial attitude and behavior of white Americans toward black Americans.

Race prejudice has shaped our history decisively; it now threatens to affect our future.

White racism is essentially responsible for the explosive mixture which has been accumulating in our cities since the end of World War II. Among the ingredients of this mixture are:

■ *Pervasive discrimination and segregation* in employment, education, and housing, which have resulted in the continuing exclusion of great numbers of Negroes from the benefits of economic progress.

■ *Black in-migration and white exodus,* which have produced the massive and growing concentrations of impoverished Negroes in our major cities, creating a growing crisis of deteriorating facilities and services and unmet human needs.

■ *The black ghettos,* where segregation and poverty converge on the young to destroy opportunity and enforce failure. Crime, drug addiction, dependency on welfare, and bitterness and resentment against society in general and white society in particular are the result.

At the same time, most whites and some Negroes outside the ghetto have prospered to a degree unparalleled in the history of civilization. Through television and other media, this affluence has been flaunted before the eyes of the Negro poor and the jobless ghetto youth.

Yet these facts alone cannot be said to have caused the disorders. Recently, other powerful ingredients have begun to catalyze the mixture:

■ *Frustrated hopes* are the residue of the unfulfilled expectations aroused by the great judicial and legislative victories of the civil rights movement and the dramatic struggle for equal rights in the South.

■ *A climate that tends toward approval and encouragement of violence* as a form of protest has been created by white terrorism directed against nonviolent protest; by the open defiance of law and Federal authority by state and local officials resisting desegregation; and by some protest groups engaging in civil disobedience who turn their backs on nonviolence, go beyond the constitutionally protected rights of petition and free assembly, and resort to violence to attempt to compel alteration of laws and policies with which they disagree.

■ *The frustrations of powerlessness* have led some Negroes to the conviction that there is no effective alternative to violence as a means of achieving redress of grievances, and of "moving the system." These frustrations are reflected in alienation and hostility toward the institutions of law and government and the white society which controls them, and in the reach toward racial consciousness and solidarity reflected in the slogan "Black Power."

■ *A new mood* has sprung up among Negroes, particularly among the young, in which self-esteem and enhanced racial pride are replacing apathy and submission to "the system."

■ *The police are not merely a "spark" factor.* To some Negroes police have come to symbolize white power, white racism, and white repression. And the fact is that many police do reflect and express these white attitudes. The atmosphere of hostility and cynicism is reinforced by a widespread belief among Negroes in the existence of police brutality and in a "double standard" of justice and protection—one for Negroes and one for whites. . . .

Recommendations for National Action

INTRODUCTION

No American—white or black—can escape the consequences of the continuing social and economic decay of our major cities.

Only a commitment to national action on an unprecedented scale can shape a future compatible with the historic ideals of American society.

The great productivity of our economy, and a Federal revenue system which is highly responsive to economic growth, can provide the resources.

The major need is to generate new will—the will to tax ourselves to the extent necessary to meet the vital needs of the Nation.

We have set forth goals and proposed strategies to reach those goals. We discuss and recommend programs not to commit each of us to specific parts of such programs, but to illustrate the type and dimension of action needed.

The major goal is the creation of a true union—a single society and a single American identity. Toward that goal, we propose the following objectives for national action:

■ Opening up opportunities to those who are restricted by racial segregation and discrimination, and eliminating all barriers to their choice of jobs, education, and housing.

■ Removing the frustration of powerlessness among the disadvantaged by providing the means for them to deal with the problems that affect their own lives and by increasing the capacity of our public and private institutions to respond to these problems.

■ Increasing communication across racial lines to destroy stereotypes, halt polarization, end distrust and hostility, and create common ground for efforts toward public order and social justice.

We propose these aims to fulfill our pledge of equality and to meet the fundamental needs of a democratic and civilized society—domestic peace and social justice.

. . . The Commission recommends that the Federal Government:

■ Undertake joint efforts with cities and states to consolidate existing manpower programs to avoid fragmentation and duplication.

■ Take immediate action to create 2 million new jobs over the next 3 years—1 million in the public sector and 1 million in the private

sector—to absorb the hard-core unemployed and materially reduce the level of unemployment for all workers, black and white. We propose 250,000 public sector and 300,000 private sector jobs in the first year.

■ Provide on-the-job training by both public and private employers with reimbursement to private employers for the extra costs of training the hard-core unemployed, by contract or by tax credits.

■ Provide tax and other incentives to investment in rural as well as urban poverty areas in order to offer to the rural poor an alternative to migration to urban centers.

■ Take new and vigorous action to remove artificial barriers to employment and promotion, including not only racial discrimination but, in certain cases, arrest records or lack of a high school diploma. Strengthen those agencies such as the Equal Employment Opportunity Commission, charged with eliminating discriminatory practices, and provide full support for Title VI of the 1964 Civil Rights Act allowing Federal grant-in-aid funds to be withheld from activities which discriminate on grounds of color or race. . . .

Source: National Advisory Commission on Civil Disorders, *Report of the National Advisory Commission on Civil Disorders* (Washington, D.C., 1968), 1, 5, 11.

President Lyndon Johnson Explains and Defends American Involvement in Vietnam, April 1965

In the early weeks of 1965 Lyndon Johnson took the first steps in the establishment of an American war in Vietnam. Faced with the fact that the American client in the area, South Vietnam, was losing in its effort to remain a separate entity, Johnson moved to protect the South Vietnamese regime by sending in the first Americans openly identified as combat forces and by start of a bombing campaign of the North, known as Rolling Thunder. At this time when the American role was growing but still being formed, when opposition in the United States was not widespread but beginning to have a voice, Johnson appeared at Johns Hopkins University to offer an explanation of his actions that he would need to repeat many times in the future.

Tonight Americans and Asians are dying for a world where each people may choose its own path to change. This is the principle for which our ancestors fought in the valleys of Pennsylvania. It is a principle for which our sons fight tonight in the jungles of Vietnam.

Vietnam is far away from this quiet campus. We have no territory there, nor do we seek any. The war is dirty and brutal and difficult. And some 400 young men, born into an America that is bursting with opportunity and promise, have ended their lives on Vietnam's steaming soil.

Why must we take this painful road? Why must this nation hazard its ease, its interest, and its power for the sake of a people so far away?

We fight because we must fight if we are to live in a world where every country can shape its own destiny, and only in such a world will our own freedom be finally secure. . . .

The world as it is in Asia is not a serene or peaceful place.

The first reality is that North Vietnam has attacked the independent nation of South Vietnam. Its object is total conquest. Of course, some of the people of South Vietnam are participating in attack on their own government. But trained men and supplies, orders and arms, flow in a constant stream from north to south.

This support is the heartbeat of the war.

And it is a war of unparalleled brutality. Simple farmers are the targets of assassination and kidnapping. Women and children are strangled in the night because their men are loyal to their government. And helpless villages are ravaged by sneak attacks. Large-scale raids are conducted on towns, and terror strikes in the heart of cities.

The confused nature of this conflict cannot mask the fact that it is the new face of an old enemy.

Over this war—and all Asia—is another reality: the deepening shadow of Communist China. The rulers in Hanoi are urged on by Peking. This is a regime that has destroyed freedom in Tibet, attacked India, and has been condemned by the United Nations for aggression in Korea. It is a nation that is helping the forces of violence in almost every continent. The contest in Vietnam is part of a wider pattern of aggressive purposes.

Why are these realities our concern? Why are we in South Vietnam?

We are there because we have a promise to keep. Since 1954 every American president has offered support to the people of South Vietnam. We have helped to build, and we have helped to defend. Thus, over many years, we have made a national pledge to help South Vietnam defend its independence.

And I intend to keep that promise.

To dishonor that pledge, to abandon this small and brave nation to its enemies, and to the terror that must follow, would be an unforgivable wrong.

We are also there to strengthen world order. Around the globe, from Berlin to Thailand, are people whose well-being rests in part on the belief that they can count on us if they are attacked. To leave Vietnam to its fate would shake the confidence of all these people in the value of an American commitment and in the value of America's word. The result would be increased unrest and instability, and even wider war.

We are also there because there are great stakes in the balance. Let no one think for a moment that retreat from Vietnam would bring an end to conflict. The battle would be renewed in one country and then another. The central lesson of our time is that the appetite of aggression is never satisfied. To withdraw from one battlefield means only to prepare for the next. We must say in Southeast Asia—as we did in Europe—in the words of the Bible: "Hitherto shalt thou come, but no further." . . .

Our objective is the independence of South Vietnam and its freedom from attack. We want nothing for ourselves—only that the people of South Vietnam be allowed to guide their own country in their own way. We will do everything necessary to reach that objective, and we will do only what is absolutely necessary.

In recent months attacks on South Vietnam were stepped up. Thus it became necessary for us to increase our response and to make attacks by air. This is not a change of purpose. It is a change in what we believe that purpose requires.

We do this in order to slow down aggression.

We do this to increase the confidence of the brave people of South Vietnam who have bravely borne this brutal battle for so many years with so many casualties.

And we do this to convince the leaders of North Vietnam—and all who seek to share their conquest—of a simple fact:

We will not be defeated.

We will not grow tired.

We will not withdraw, either openly or under the cloak of a meaningless agreement. . . .

We will never be second in the search for . . . a peaceful settlement in Vietnam.

We have stated this position over and over again fifty times and more to friend and foe alike. And we remain ready with this purpose for unconditional discussions.

And until that bright and necessary day of peace we will try to keep conflict from spreading. We have no desire to see thousands die in battle—Asians or Americans. We have no desire to devastate that which the people of North Vietnam have built

with toil and sacrifice. We will use our power with restraint and with all the wisdom that we can command.

But we will use it.

Source: *Public Papers of the Presidents of the United States: Lyndon B. Johnson, 1965* (Washington, D. C., 1966), 394–96.

A Vietnam Veteran Speaks Against the War, 1971

On April 23, 1971, John Kerry appeared before the Senate Foreign Relations Committee to give his impressions about the conflict in Vietnam. A member of Vietnam Veterans Against the War, he described a war much different from the one Lyndon Johnson had defended on many occasions, and during this time of Richard Nixon's program of Vietnamization, he urged that the United States immediately disengage from this disgraceful undertaking. Kerry later would become United States senator from Massachusetts.

I am not here as John Kerry. I am here as one member of the group of 1,000, which is a small representation of a very much larger group of veterans in this country, and were it possible for all of them to sit at this table they would be here and have the same kind of testimony. . . .

I would like to talk to you a little bit about what the result is of the feelings these men carry with them after coming back from Vietnam. The country doesn't know it yet but it has created a monster, a monster in the form of millions of men who have been taught to deal and to trade in violence and who are given the chance to die for the biggest nothing in history; men who have returned with a sense of anger and a sense of betrayal which no one has yet grasped.

As a veteran and one who feels this anger I would like to talk about it. We are angry because we feel we have been used in the worst fashion by the administration of this country.

In 1970 at West Point Vice President Agnew said "some glamorize the criminal misfits of society while our best men die in Asian rice paddies to preserve the freedom which most of those misfits abuse," and this was used as a rallying point for our effort in Vietnam.

But for us, as boys in Asia whom the country was supposed to support, his statement is a terrible distortion from which we can only draw a very deep sense of revulsion, and hence the anger of some of the men who are here in Washington today. It is a distortion because we in no way consider ourselves the best men of this country; because those he calls misfits were standing up for us in a way that nobody else in this country dared to; because so many who have died would have returned to this country to join the misfits in their efforts to ask for an immediate withdrawal from South Vietnam; because so many of those best men have returned as quadruplegics and amputees—and they lie forgotten in Veterans Administration Hospitals in this country which fly the flag which so many have chosen as their own personal symbol—and we cannot consider ourselves America's best men when we are ashamed of and hated for what we were called on to do in Southeast Asia.

In our opinion, and from our experience, there is nothing in South Vietnam which could happen that realistically threatens the United States of America. And to attempt to justify the loss of one American life in Vietnam, Cambodia or Laos by linking such loss to the preservation of freedom, which those misfits supposedly abuse, is to us the height of criminal hypocrisy, and it is that kind of hypocrisy which we feel has torn this country apart. . . .

We found that not only was it a civil war, an effort by a people who had for years been seeking their liberation from any colonial influence whatsoever, but also we found that the Vietnamese whom we had enthusiastically molded after our own

Defoliation mission in the Mekong River delta in South Vietnam (National Archives)

image were hard put to take up the fight against the threat we were supposedly saving them from.

We found most people didn't even know the difference between communism and democracy. They only wanted to work in rice paddies without helicopters strafing them and bombs with napalm burning their villages and tearing their country apart. They wanted everything to do with the war, particularly with this foreign presence of the United States of America, to leave them alone in peace, and they practiced the art of survival by siding with whichever military force was present at a particular time, be it Viet Cong, North Vietnamese or American.

We found also that all too often American men were dying in those rice paddies for want of support from their allies. We saw first hand how monies from American taxes were used for a corrupt dictatorial regime. We saw that many people in this country had a one-sided idea of who was kept free by our flag, and blacks provided the highest percentage of casualties. We saw Vietnam ravaged equally by American bombs and search and destroy missions, as well as by Viet Cong terrorism, and yet we listened while this country tried to blame all of the havoc on the Viet Cong.

We rationalized destroying villages in order to save them. We saw America lose her sense of morality as she accepted very cooly a My Lai and refused to give up the image of American soldiers who hand out chocolate bars and chewing gum.

We learned the meaning of free fire zones, shooting anything that moves, and we watched while America placed a cheapness on the lives of orientals.

We watched the United States falsification of body counts, in fact the glorification of body counts. We listened while month after month we were told the back of the enemy was about to break. . . .

We are here in Washington also to say that the problem of this war is not just a question of war and diplomacy. It is part and parcel of everything that we are trying as human beings to communicate to people in this country—the question of racism, which is rampant in the military, and so many other questions such as the use of weapons; the hypocrisy in our taking umbrage in the Geneva Conventions and using that as justification for a continuation of this war when we are more guilty than any other body of violations of those Geneva Conventions; in the use of free fire zones, harassment interdiction fire, search and destroy missions, the bombings, the torture of prisoners, the killing of prisoners, all accepted policy by many units in South Vietnam. That is what we are trying to say. It is part and parcel of everything. . . .

We wish that a merciful God could wipe away our own memories of that service as easily as this administration has wiped away their memories of us. But all that they have done and all that they can do by this denial is to make more clear than ever our own determination to undertake one last mission—to search out and destroy the last vestige of this barbaric war, to pacify our own hearts, to conquer the hate and the fear that have driven this country these last ten years and more, so when 30 years from now our brothers go down the street without a leg, without an arm, or a face, and small boys ask why, we will be able to say "Vietnam" and not mean a desert, not a filthy obscene memory, but mean instead the place where America finally turned and where soldiers like us helped it in the turning.

Source: Hearings of Senate Committee on Foreign Relations, April 23, 1971, *Congressional Record,* Vol. 117 (Washington, D.C., 1972), 11738–40.

The War Powers Act, 1973

In the wake of the unheroic American departure from Vietnam in 1973, Congress moved to pass what became known as the War Powers Act. The measure was an attempt to resolve a conflict in the Constitution that the war had dramatized (while only Congress can declare war, the president as commander-in-chief can place the armed forces in a war-making situation), but it also represented the most obvious expression of revulsion for the war, at least the American part, now ending and an envisioned guide for policy in the future. The act did not carry the words, but the message was there nonetheless: the Americans will have "no more Vietnams."

CONSULTATION

Sec. 3. The President in every possible instance shall consult with Congress before introducing United States Armed Forces into hostilities or into situations where imminent involvement in hostilities is clearly indicated by the circumstances, and after every such introduction shall consult regularly with the Congress until United States Armed Forces are no longer engaged in hostilities or have been removed from such situations.

REPORTING

Sec. 4. (a) In the absence of a declaration of war, in any case in which United States Armed Forces are introduced —

(1) into hostilities or into situations where imminent involvement in hostilities is clearly indicated by the circumstances;

(2) into the territory, airspace or waters of a foreign nation, while equipped for combat, except for deployments which relate solely to supply, replacement, repair, or training of such forces; or

(3) in numbers which substantially enlarge United States Armed Forces equipped for combat already located in a foreign nation;

the President shall submit within 48 hours to the Speaker of the House of Representatives and to the President pro tempore of the Senate a report, in writing, setting forth —

(A) the circumstances necessitating the introduction of United States Armed Forces;

(B) the constitutional and legislative authority under which such introduction took place; and

(C) the estimated scope and duration of the hostilities or involvement.

(b) The President shall provide such other information as the Congress may request in the fulfillment of its constitutional responsibilities with respect to committing the Nation to war and to the use of United States Armed Forces abroad.

(c) Whenever United States Armed Forces are introduced into hostilities or into any situation described in subsection (a) of this section, the President shall, so long as such armed forces continue to be engaged in such hostilities or situation, report to the Congress periodically on the status of such hostilities or situation as well as on the scope and duration of such hostilities or situation, but in no event shall he report to the Congress less often than once every six months.

CONGRESSIONAL ACTION

(b) Within sixty calendar days after a report is submitted or is required to be submitted pursuant to section 4(a) (1), whichever is earlier, the President shall terminate any use of United States Armed Forces with respect to which such report was submitted (or required to be submitted), unless the Congress (1) has declared war or has enacted a specific authorization for such use of United States Armed Forces, (2) has extended by law such sixty-day period, or (3) is physically unable to meet as a result of an armed attack upon the United States. Such sixty-day period shall be extended for not more than an additional thirty days if the President determines and certifies to the Congress in writing that unavoidable military necessity respecting the safety of United States Armed Forces requires the continued use of such armed forces in the course of bringing about a prompt removal of such forces.

(c) Notwithstanding subsection (b), at any time that United States Armed Forces are engaged in hostilities outside the territory of the United States, its possessions and territories without a declaration of war or specific statutory authorization, such forces shall be removed by the President if the Congress so directs by concurrent resolution.

Source: U.S. Statutes at Large, 1st Session, 93rd Congress, 1973, Vol. 87 (Washington, D.C., 1974), 555–56.

The Women's Movement: Senate Hearings on an Equal Rights Amendment, May 7, 1970

This document contains excerpts of testimony before a United States Senate subcommittee pertaining to passage of an Equal Rights Amendment (ERA) to the Constitution. The amendment would pass both houses of Congress but would fail to receive approval from a sufficient number of state legislatures. Agents of the woman's movement, however, would find other devices to achieve essentially what the amendment had been designed to do. The following testimony by Wilma Scott Heide, chair of the Board of Directors of the National Organization for Women (NOW), thus constitutes an endorsement of the amendment, and also a statement of her perception of the status of women in the United States at the start of the 1970s.

I will testify in favor of the equal rights amendment hopefully so that the next great moment in history—although I think we perhaps should say her story—may be ours.

It is with considerable ambivalence that I do testify today.

All of my social conditioning teaches me to be grateful for the opportunity to speak in a public forum convened by Senators. Yet I am really outraged to even consider gratitude as an appropriate response for a chance to plead for what is the birthright of every male in the United States. My credentials for testifying today were scrutinized; yet perhaps the only relevant credential is that I am a person denied my personhood by law, by legal interpretation, and by practice. This, of course, is not to deny my sex but to affirm my personhood which transcends gender.

To demand to be equal to men under the law is not to state or imply sameness of biology; but biology is not relevant to human equity.

Interestingly, I was asked to quantitatively document especially the educational inequities to women that a ratified equal rights amendment would rectify. And certainly, I can quote statistics if that is necessary, to establish communications. . . .

In 1930, women earned 40 percent of the master's degrees, in 1969, women earned 34 percent of the master's degrees; in

1930, women earned 15 percent of the doctoral degrees, in 1969, women earned only 12 percent of doctoral degrees; in 1930 women formed 30 percent of college faculties and at higher ranks than the mere 22 percent of women on college faculties in 1969.

Significantly, women's participation in the "prestigious" professions reflects this loss of ground: 3 percent of lawyers, 7 percent of physicians, less than 10 percent of scientists and token numbers of executives are women in the United States.

In other countries, propagandized in the United States to be less advanced, actually have women represented in these professions in percentages ranging from 25 to 75 percent. . . .

We must put the need for this amendment precisely in its place and stop trying "to keep women in their place," as decided by someone else.

Its place should be at the top of the congressional agenda for immediate positive action. That top priority is necessary because this society, this Nation is antifemale in its laws, its expressions, its value systems, its language, everything. Ours is an androcentric, that is, male-oriented, male-dominated—culture, however subtle, and never mind the mythology to the contrary.

Any society so structured, biased and value-oriented is unhealthily balanced. It takes enormous individual and national resources to support and sustain the fragile male ego that male supremacy values dictate. The psychological crippling of most girls and women from their inferior legal, political, educational, religious, familial, economic status, will never be cured by consumerism, more sexist Freudian psychotherapy, or one more child.

The fact that some women do not want equal rights is some measure of the depth of their psychological enslavement. . . .

The sex role stereotyped socialization of boys is such that they must exhibit "masculine" traits or be branded sissy or effeminate and pretend to characteristics that presume unchallenged virility. Well, there are no social-psychological traits that are "feminine" or "masculine," whatever that is.

Feminity is often a euphemism for immaturity. Masculinity is often an excuse for brutality. There are only human traits. There are no men's roles or women's roles beyond the biological.

There are no women's interests and men's interests. There are only human interests and human roles. My possession of a uterus does not uniquely qualify me for child care, housework, secretarial work or nursing.

Men's biology does not disqualify them for child care and housework or qualify them for leadership or scientific analysis or any particular courage.

The continuation of sex-stereotyped, sex-caste laws that deny the individuality and humanity of women and men to the distinct mutilation of women is simply intolerable. . . .

This women's liberation, actually human liberation is, I think, the most profound social movement ever. It promises to inject some massive new insights into the bloodstream of our culture, not because women are so different, but because it will bring the life experience of the other half of the population to bear on our common problems and opportunities.

Source: Catharine Stimpson, ed., Women and The "Equal Rights" Amendment: Senate Subcommittee Hearings on the Constitutional Amendment, 91st Congress (New York, 1972), 192–96.

Supreme Court Case of *Roe v. Wade*, 1973

In the case of Roe v. Wade *the Supreme Court invalidated a Texas law, and by implication several other state laws, that had banned virtually all*

forms of abortion. By a 7–2 vote, the Court found the right to abortion absolute in the first trimester of pregnancy, a guarantee provided by a right of privacy implied in 14th Amendment. In effect the Court ruled that an unborn fetus was a part of a woman's body and not a separate being with rights of its own. Rather than settling abortion once and for all, however, the decision set the stage for perhaps the most heated political issue for the rest of the century.

Justice Harry A. Blackmun, an appointee of Richard Nixon, wrote the majority opinion:

We forthwith acknowledge our awareness of the sensitive and emotional nature of the abortion controversy, of the vigorous opposing views, even among physicians, and of the deep and seemingly absolute convictions that the subject inspires. One's philosophy, one's experiences, one's exposure to the raw edges of human existence, one's religious training, one's attitudes toward life and family and their values, and the moral standards one establishes and seeks to observe, are all likely to influence and to color one's thinking and conclusions about abortion. . . .

The Texas statutes that concern us here are Arts. 1191–1194 and 1196 of the State's Penal Code. These make it a crime to "procure an abortion," as therein defined, or to attempt one, except with respect to "an abortion procured or attempted by medical advice for the purpose of saving the life of the mother." Similar statutes are in existence in a majority of the States. . . .

Jane Roe, a single woman who was residing in Dallas County, Texas, instituted this federal action in March 1970 against the District Attorney of the county. She sought a declaratory judgment that the Texas criminal abortion statutes were unconstitutional on their face, and an injunction restraining the defendant from enforcing the statutes.

The principal thrust of appellant's attack on the Texas statutes is that they improperly invade a right, said to be possessed by the pregnant woman, to choose to terminate her pregnancy. Appellant would discover this right in the concept of personal "liberty" embodied in the Fourteenth Amendment's Due Process Clause; or in personal, marital, familial, and sexual privacy said to be protected by the Bill of Rights . . . or among those rights reserved to the people by the Ninth Amendment, . . .

The Constitution does not explicitly mention any right of privacy. In a line of decisions, however, . . . the Court has recognized that a right of personal privacy, or a guarantee of certain areas or zones of privacy, does exist under the Constitution. . . . This right of privacy, whether it be founded in the Fourteenth Amendment's concept of personal liberty and restrictions upon state action, as we feel it is, or, as the District Court determined, in the Ninth Amendment's reservation of rights to the people, is broad enough to encompass a woman's decision whether or not to terminate her pregnancy. . . .

We . . . conclude that the right of personal privacy includes the abortion decision, but that this right is not unqualified and must be considered against important state interest in regulation. . . .

In view of all this, we do not agree that, by adopting one theory of life, Texas may override the rights of the pregnant woman that are at stake. We repeat, however, that the State does have an important and legitimate interest in preserving and protecting the health of the pregnant woman, whether she be a resident of the State or a nonresident who seeks medical consultation and treatment there, and that it has still *another* important and legitimate interest in protecting the potentiality of human life. These interests are separate and distinct. Each grows in substantiality as the woman approaches term and, at a point during pregnancy, each becomes "compelling." . . .

Measured against these standards, Art. 1196 of the Texas Penal Code, in restricting legal abortions to those "procured or attempted by medical advice for the purpose of saving the life of the mother," sweeps too broadly. The statute makes no distinction between abortions performed early in pregnancy and those performed later, and it limits to a single reason, "saving" the mother's life, the legal justification for the procedure. The statute, therefore, cannot survive the constitutional attack made upon it here. . . .

To summarize and to repeat:

1. A state criminal abortion statute of the current Texas type, that excepts from criminality only a *lifesaving* procedure on behalf of the mother, without regard to pregnancy stage and without recognition of the other interests involved, is violative of the Due Process Clause of the Fourteenth Amendment.

(a) For the stage prior to approximately the end of the first trimester, the abortion decision and its effectuation must be left to the medical judgment of the pregnant woman's attending physician.

(b) For the stage subsequent to approximately the end of the first trimester, the State, in promoting its interest in the health of the mother, may, if it chooses, regulate the abortion procedure in ways that are reasonably related to maternal health.

(c) For the stage subsequent to viability, the State in promoting its interest in the potentiality of human life may, if it chooses, regulate, and even proscribe, abortion except where it is necessary, in appropriate medical judgment, for the preservation of the life or health of the mother. . . .

This holding, we feel, is consistent with the relative weights of the respective interests involved, with the lessons and examples of medical and legal history, with the lenity of the common law, and with the demands of the profound problems of the present day. . . .

Source: Eva R. Rubin, *The Abortion Controversy: A Documentary History* (Westport, Conn., 1994), 131–37.

President Reagan Describes the Soviet Union at the Start of His Presidency, 1981, and at the End, 1989

When Ronald Reagan became president, the cold war continued and probably intensified, partly because of Reagan's military policies and his rhetoric. He called the USSR, for example, an evil empire; the attitude prevailed through the first administration. By the time Reagan was prepared to leave office, his tune had changed considerably. He found different Soviet leadership and different objectives. Many forces had fostered the change, but the most important was the emergence of Mikhail Gorbachev as Soviet leader, who set in motion remarkable changes in Soviet policy. Reagan's remarks at the end thus represented a response to new forces he faced. They also constituted a clear signal in January 1989 that the cold war was coming to an end.

REAGAN'S NEWS CONFERENCE, JANUARY 29, 1981

The President. Well, so far détente's been a one-way street that the Soviet Union has used to pursue its own aims. I don't have to think of an answer as to what I think their intentions are; they have repeated it. I know of no leader of the Soviet Union since the revolution, and including the present leader-

The first McDonald's restaurant opens in Moscow, 1990. (Used with permission from McDonald's Corporation)

ship, that has not more than once repeated in the various Communist congresses they hold their determination that their goal must be the promotion of world revolution and a one-world Socialist or Communist state, whichever word you want to use.

Now, as long as they do that and as long as they, at the same time, have openly and publicly declared that the only morality they recognize is what will further their cause, meaning they reserve unto themselves the right to commit any crime, to lie, to cheat, in order to attain that, and that is moral, not immoral, and we operate on a different set of standards, I think when you do business with them, even at a détente, you keep that in mind.

REAGAN'S FAREWELL ADDRESS TO THE NATION, JANUARY 11, 1989

Nothing is less free than pure communism—and yet we have, the past few years, forged a satisfying new closeness with the Soviet Union. I've been asked if this isn't a gamble, and my answer is no because we're basing our actions not on words but deeds. The détente of the 1970's was based not on actions but promises. They'd promise to treat their own people and the people of the world better. But the *gulag* was still the *gulag*, and the state was still expansionist, and they still waged proxy wars in Africa, Asia, and Latin America.

Well, this time, so far, it's different. President Gorbachev has brought about some internal democratic reforms and begun the withdrawal from Afghanistan. He has also freed prisoners whose names I've given him every time we've met. . . .

We must keep up our guard, but we must also continue to work together to lessen and eliminate tension and mistrust. My view is that President Gorbachev is different from previous Soviet leaders. I think he knows some of the things wrong with his society and is trying to fix them. We wish him well. And we'll continue to work to make sure that the Soviet Union that eventually emerges from this process is a less threatening one. What it all boils down to is this: I want the new closeness to continue. And it will, as long as we make it clear that we will continue to act in a certain way as long as they continue to act in a helpful manner. If and when they don't, at first pull your punches. If they persist, pull the plug. It's still trust but verify. It's still play, but cut the cards. It's still watch closely. And don't be afraid to see what you see.

Source: The statement of 1981 is in *Public Papers of the Presidents of the United States: Ronald Reagan, 1981* (Washington D.C., 1982), 57; the second statement is in *Public Papers . . . Reagan, 1988–89, Book II* (Washington, D.C., 1991), 1721.

Selected Bibliography

Publications of the National Government

Bureau of the Census. *Historical Statistics of the United States, Colonial Times to 1970.* Washington, D.C.: U.S. Government Printing Office, 1976.
———. *Martial Status and Living Arrangements: March 1990.* Washington, D.C.: U.S. Government Printing Office, 1991.
———. *Marital Status and Living Arrangements: March 1993.* Washington, D.C.: U.S. Government Printing Office, 1994.
———. *Statistical Abstracts of the United States, annual editions, 1946–1997.* Washington, D.C.: U.S. Government Printing Office, 1946–97.
Bureau of Economic Analysis. *Business Statistics, 1963–91.* Washington, D.C.: U.S. Government Printing Office, 1992.
Bureau of Justice Statistics. *Drug and Crime Facts.* Rockville, Md.: U.S. Government Printing Office, 1990.
Bureau of Labor Statistics. *Employment, Hours and Earnings, United States, 1909–90,* Volume II. Washington, D.C.: U.S. Government Printing Office, 1991.
———. *Handbook of Labor Statistics, 1989.* Washington, D.C.: U.S. Government Printing Office, 1989.
Civil Aeronautics Board. *Handbook of Airline Statistics, 1973 Edition.* Washington, D.C.: Civil Aeronautics Board, 1974.
Council of Economic Advisers. *Economic Report of the President, 1992.* Washington, D.C.: U.S. Government Printing Office, 1992.
Department of Agriculture. *Agricultural Statistics, annual editions, 1946–91.* Washington, D.C.: U.S. Government Printing Office, 1946–91.
Department of Commerce. *U.S. Foreign Trade Highlights, 1990.* Washington, D.C.: U.S. Printing Office, 1991.
Department of Health and Human Services. *Health, United States, annual editions, 1970–92.* Hyattsville, Md.: U.S. Government Printing Office, 1970–92.
———. *Vital Statistics of the United States,* Vol. I. *Natality, 1990.* Hyattsville, Md.: U.S. Government Printing Office, 1994.
Department of Health, Education and Welfare. *100 Years of Marriage and Divorce Statistics, United States, 1867–1967.* Rockville, Md.: U.S. Government Printing Office, 1973.
Department of Justice. *Sourcebook of Criminal Justice Statistics, annual editions, 1973–97.* Washington, D.C.: U.S. Government Printing Office, 1974–98.
———. *Drugs and Crime Facts, 1991.* Rockville, Md.: U.S. Government Printing Office, 1992.
Department of Labor. *CPI Detailed Report Data for January 1990.* Washington, D.C.: U.S. Government Printing Office, 1990.
Department of State. *Foreign Relations of the United States, 1950,* Vol. I: *National Security Affairs; Foreign Economic Policy.* Washington, D.C.: U.S. Government Printing Office, 1977.
Department of Transportation. *Annual Energy Review, annual editions, 1980–91.* Washington, D.C.: U.S. Government Printing Office, 1981–92.
———. *FAA Statistical Handbook of Aviation, annual editions, 1980–91.* Washington, D.C.: U.S. Government Printing Office, 1981–92.
———. *National Transportation Statistics, 1980.* Washington, D.C.: U.S. Government Printing Office, 1980.
Environmental Protection Agency. *Environmental Progress and Challenge: EPA's Update.* Washington, D.C.: U.S. Government Printing Office, 1988.

Federal Bureau of Investigation. *Uniform Crime Reports for the United States, annual editions, 1946–90.* Washington, D.C.: U.S. Government Printing Office, 1947–91.
Federal Deposit Insurance Corporation. *Statistics on Banking: Historical, 1934–1994.* Washington, D.C.: U.S. Government Printing Office, 1995.
National Advisory Commission on Civil Disorders. *Report of the National Advisory Commission on Civil Disorders.* Washington, D.C.: U.S. Government Printing Office, 1968.
National Center for Education Statistics. *Digest of Education Statistics, annual editions, 1980–92.* Washington, D.C.: U.S. Government Printing Office, 1980–92.
———. *120 Years of American Education: A Statistical Portrait.* Washington, D.C.: U.S. Government Printing Office, 1993.
Public Papers of the Presidents of the United States, for the following presidents: *Dwight D. Eisenhower, 1954.* Washington, D.C.: U.S. Government Printing Office, 1955; *John F. Kennedy, 1961.* Washington, D.C.: U.S. Government Printing Office, 1962; *Lyndon B. Johnson, 1965.* Washington, D.C.: U.S. Government Printing Office, 1966; *Ronald W. Reagan, 1981.* Washington, D.C.: U.S. Government Printing Office, 1982; *Ronald W. Reagan, 1988–89.* Washington, D.C.: U.S. Government Printing Office, 1991.

Almanacs, Encyclopedias, and General Reference Works

Aerospace Industries Association of America. *Aerospace Facts and Figures, annual editions, 1964–93.* Washington, D.C.: Aero Publishers, 1964–93.
Aircraft Industries Association of America. *Aviation Facts and Figures, annual editions, 1946–60.* Washington, D.C.: Aero Publishers, 1946–60.
Alsop, Ronald J. *The Wall Street Journal Almanac, 1998.* New York: Ballantine Books, 1997.
American Cancer Society. *Cancer Facts & Figures—1991.* Atlanta, Ga.: American Cancer Society, 1991.
American Council on Education. *The Fact Book on Higher Education: 1997 Edition.* Phoenix: American Council on Education, 1998.
American Hospital Association. *Hospital Statistics, 1994–95 Edition.* Chicago: American Hospital Association, 1994.
Automobile Manufacturers Association. *Automobile Facts and Figures, annual editions 1957–77,* renamed *Motor Vehicle Facts and Figures, 1978–92.* Detroit: Automobile Manufacturers Association, 1957–92.
Bronson, Fred. *Billboard's Hottest 100 Hits.* New York: Billboard Books, 1995.
Brooks, Tim, and Marsh, Earle. *The Complete Directory to Prime Time Network and Cable TV Shows 1946–Present, editions for 1988, 1994, 1995, 1997.* New York: Ballantine Books, 1988, 1994, 1995, 1997.
Brown, Les. *Les Brown's Encyclopedia of Television.* Detroit, Mich.: Gale Research, 1992.
Brunner, Borgna. *Time Almanac 2001 with Information Please.* Boston: Family Education Company, 2000.
Carruth, Gorton. *The Encyclopedia of American Facts and Dates.* New York: HarperCollins, 1997.
Chadwick, Bruce A., and Wheaton, Tim B. *Statistical Handbook on the American Family.* Phoenix: Oryx Press, 1992.
Chronicle of Higher Education. *The Almanac of Higher Education, 1991.* Chicago: University of Chicago Press, 1991.

Congressional Quarterly, Inc. *American Leaders, 1789–1991.* Washington, D.C.: Congressional Quarterly Press, 1994.

———. *Presidential Elections, 1789–1992.* Washington, D.C.: Congressional Quarterly Press, 1995.

Cook, Allan, R. *The New Cancer Sourcebook.* Detroit, Mich.: Omnigraphics, 1996.

Cook, Chris, and Stevenson, John. *The Longman Handbook of the Modern World: International History Since 1945.* New York: Longman, 1998.

Darnay, Arsnen J. *Economic Indicators Handbook.* Detroit, Mich.: Gale Research, 1994.

Dorgan, Charity Anne. *Statistical Record of Health and Medicine.* Detroit, Mich.: Gale Research, 1995.

Douchant, Mike. *Encyclopedia of College Basketball.* Detroit, Mich.: Gale Research, 1994.

Dupuy, Trevor N. *International Military and Defense Dictionary.* New York: Brassey's Publications, 1993.

The ESPN Information Please Sports Almanac. Boston: Hyperion ESPN Books, 2000.

Ferrell, Robert H., and Hoff, Joan. *Dictionary of American History, Supplement, Parts I and II.* New York: Scribner's, 1996.

Franks, Don. *Entertainment Awards: A Music, Cinema, Theatre and Broadcasting Reference, 1928 through 1993.* Jefferson, N.C.: McFarland, 1996.

Gall, Susan B., and Gall, Timothy L. *Statistical Record of Asian Americans.* Detroit, Mich.: Gale Research, 1993.

Gall, Timothy L., and Lucas, Daniel M. *Statistics on Crime and Punishment.* Detroit, Mich.: Gale Research, 1996.

Garraty, John A., and Carnes, Mark C. *American National Biography.* 24 vols. New York: Oxford University Press, 1999.

Garwood, Alfred N. *Black Americans: A Statistical Sourcebook, 1992 edition.* Boulder, Colo.: Numbers and Concepts, 1992.

Gertner, Richard. *1975 International Motion Picture Almanac.* New York: Quigley Publications, 1975.

Grossman, Mark. *Encyclopedia of Capital Punishment.* Santa Barbara, Calif.: ABC–CLIO, 1998.

Heatley, Michael. *The Ultimate Encyclopedia of Rock.* New York: Harper Perennial, 1993.

Hischak, Thomas S. *The Theatregoers Almanac.* Westport, Conn.: Greenwood Press, 1997.

Hollander, Zander. *The Complete Encyclopedia of Hockey.* Detroit, Mich.: Gale Research, 1993.

———. *The Encyclopedia of Sports Talk.* New York: Corwin Books, 1976.

Horton, Carrell P., and Smith, Jessie C. *Statistical Record of Black America, editions of 1990, 1993, 1997.* Detroit, Mich.: Gale Research, 1990, 1993, 1997.

Hoyle, Russ. *Gale Environmental Almanac.* Detroit, Mich.: Gale Research, 1993.

Jacobs, Eva E. *Handbook of Labor Statistics.* Lanham, Md.: Bernan Press, 1997.

Johnson, Otto. *The 1991 Information Please Almanac, Atlas & Yearbook.* Boston: Houghton Mifflin, 1991.

Juliussen, Egil, and Juliussen, Karen. *The Computer Industry Almanac, editions for 1989 and 1993.* New York and Austin, Tex.: Computer Industry Almanac Company, 1988, 1993.

Kingsbury, Paul. *The Encyclopedia of Country Music.* New York: Oxford University Press, 1998.

Kurian, George Thomas. *Datapedia of the United States, 1790–2000: America Year by Year.* Lanham, Md.: Bernan Press, 1994.

Laur, Timothy M., and Llanso, Steven L. *Encyclopedia of Modern U.S. Military Weapons.* New York: Berkley Books, 1995.

Leonard, Thomas. *Day By Day: The Forties.* New York: Facts On File, 1977.

Leonard, Thomas, Crippen, Cynthia, and Aronson, Marc. *Day By Day: The Seventies.* New York: Facts On File, 1988.

Light, Jonathan Fraser. *The Cultural Encyclopedia of Baseball.* Jefferson, N.C.: McFarland, 1997.

Littman, Mark C. *A Statistical Portrait of the U.S., Social Conditions and Trends.* Lanham, Md.: Bernan Press, 1998.

Mabunda, L. Mpho. *The African-American Almanac.* Detroit, Mich.: Gale Research, 1997.

Meltzer, Ellen, and Aronson, Marc. *Day By Day: The Eighties.* New York: Facts On File, 1995.

Merritt, Jeffrey. *Day By Day: The Fifties.* New York: Facts On File, 1979.

Meserole, Mike. *The 1993 Information Please Sports Almanac.* Boston: Houghton Mifflin, 1992.

Michael, Paul. *The American Movies Reference Book: The Sound Era.* Englewood Cliffs, N.J.: Prentice Hall, 1969.

Monush, Barry. *International Motion Picture Almanac, editions for 1991, 1992, 1993.* New York: Quigley Publications, 1991, 1992, 1993.

Morris, Richard R., and Morris, Jeffrey B. *Encyclopedia of American History.* New York: HarperCollins, 1996.

Motor Vehicle Manufacturers Association. *Motor Vehicle Facts and Figures, editions of 1981 and 1991.* Detroit, Mich.: American Automobile Manufacturers Association, 1981, 1991.

National Collegiate Athletic Association. *NCAA Basketball: The Official 1998 Men's College Basketball Records Book.* Overland Park, Kans.: NCAA, 1997.

National Council of Churches of Christ. *Yearbook of American Churches, annual editions, 1946–72.* New York: Round Table Press, 1946–72.

———. *Yearbook of American and Canadian Churches, annual editions, 1973–92.* Nashville: Abingdon Press, 1973–92.

National Safety Council. *Accident Facts, annual editions, 1962–98.* Chicago: National Safety Council, 1962–98.

New York Stock Exchange. *Fact Book, annual editions, 1960–98.* New York: The Exchange, 1960–98.

The New York Public Library African American Desk Reference. New York: Wiley, 1999.

The New York Public Library Book of Chronologies. New York: Prentice Hall, 1990.

The New York Public Library History Desk Reference. New York: Prentice Hall, 1997.

Parker, Thomas, and Nelson, Douglas. *Day By Day: The Sixties.* New York: Facts On File, 1983.

Pendergast, Tom, and Pendergast, Sara. *St. James Encyclopedia of Popular Culture,* 5 vols. Detroit, Mich.: St. James Press, 2000.

Reddy, Marlita A. *Statistical Record of Hispanic Americans.* Detroit, Mich.: Gale Research, 1993.

———. *Statistical Record of Native North Americans.* Detroit, Mich.: Gale Research, 1995.

Sachare, Alex. *The Official NBA Basketball Encyclopedia.* New York: Villard Books, 1994.

Schwartz, Danny, Ryan, Steven, and Wostrock, Fred. *The Encyclopedia of TV Game Shows.* New York: Facts On File, 1995.

Schlesinger, Arthur, M., Jr. *The Almanac of American History.* New York: Barnes and Noble Books, 1993.

Schneider, Stephen H. *Encyclopedia of Climate and Weather.* New York: Oxford University Press, 1996.

Sports Illustrated. *Sports Illustrated 1997 Sports Almanac.* New York: Bishop Books, 1996.

———. *Sports Illustrated 2000 Sports Almanac.* New York: Bishop Books, 1999.

The Sporting News. *The Sporting News Complete Baseball Record Book, 1993 Edition.* St. Louis, Mo.: Sporting News Publishing, 1992.

———. *The Sporting News Complete Hockey Book, 1995–96 edition.* St. Louis, Mo.: Sporting News Publishing, 1995.

———. *The Sporting News Pro Football Guide, 1998 Edition.* St. Louis, Mo.: Sporting News Publishing, 1998.

Taeuber, Cynthia M. *Statistical Handbook on Women in America*. Phoenix: Oryx Press, 1991.

Tax Foundation. *Facts & Figures on Government Finance, editions for 1991, 1993, 1999*. Washington, D.C.: Tax Foundation, 1991, 1993, 1999.

Thorn, John, and Palmer, Pete. *Total Baseball*. New York: Warner Books, 1991.

Tucker, Spence C. *Encyclopedia of the Vietnam War*. 3 vols., Santa Barbara: ABC–CLIO, 1998.

Ward's Communications. *Ward's Automotive Yearbook, 1992*. Detroit, Mich.: Ward's Communications, 1992.

Warren Publishing. *Television & Cable Factbook, 1995*. New York: Warren Publishing, 1995.

Whitburn, Joel. *The Billboard Book of Top 40 Albums*. New York: Billboard Books, 1991.

———. *The Billboard Book of Top 40 Country Hits*. New York: Billboard Books, 1996.

Williams, Jack. *The USA Today Weather Almanac Book*. New York: Vintage Original, 1992.

Wood, Richard. *The Weather Almanac*. Detroit, Mich.: Gale Research, 1996.

The World Almanac and Book of Facts, annual editions, 1969–92. New York: World Almanac Books, 1969–91.

The World Almanac and Book of Facts, 1999. Mahwah, N.J.: World Almanac Books, 1998.

Wright, John. *The Universal Almanac, annual editions, 1990–95*. New York: Andrews and McMeel, 1989–94.

Wright, John. *The New York Times 1998 Almanac*. New York: Penguin Books, 1997.

Zia, Helen, and Gall, Susan B. *Notable Asian Americans*. Detroit, Mich.: Gale Research, 1995.

Specialized Studies

Ambry, Margaret, and Russell, Cheryl. *The Official Guide to the American Marketplace*. Ithaca, N.Y.: New Strategist Publications, 1992.

Ashe, Arthur, Jr. *A Hard Road to Glory: A History of the African-American Athlete Since 1946*. New York: Warner Books, 1993.

American Association of Fund-Raising Counsel. *Giving USA, 1996 edition*. New York: American Association of Fund-Raising Counsel, 1996.

Baskir, Lawrence M., and Strauss, William A. *Chance and Circumstance: The Draft, The War and the Vietnam Generation*. New York: Vintage Books, 1978.

Carson, Rachel. *Silent Spring*. Boston: Houghton Mifflin, 1962.

Christian, Spencer. *Spencer Christian's Weather Book*. New York: Prentice Hall, 1993.

Cole, Barry. *After the Breakup: Assessing the New Post AT&T Divestiture Era*. New York: Columbia University Press, 1991.

Clodfelter, Michael. *Vietnam in Military Statistics 1772–1991*. Jefferson, N.C.: McFarland, 1995.

Cook, David A. *American Cinema in the Shadow of Watergate and Vietnam 1970–1979*. New York: Scribner's, 2000.

Daniels, Roger. *Coming to America: A History of Immigration and Ethnicity in American Life*. New York: HarperCollins, 1990.

Dern, Daniel P. *The Internet Guide for New Users*. New York: McGraw-Hill, 1994.

Douglas, Deborah G. *United States Women in Aviation 1940–1985*. Washington, D.C.: Smithsonian Institution Press, 1990.

DuVall, Nell. *Domestic Technology: A Chronology of Developments*. Boston: G.K. Hall, 1988.

Friedl, Vicki L. *Women in the United States Military, 1901–1995*. Westport, Conn.: Greenwood Press, 1996.

Gross, Lynne S. *Telecommunications: An Introduction to Electronic Media*. Dubuque, Iowa: W.C. Brown, 1988.

Alan Guthmacher Institute. *Sex and America's Teenagers*. New York: Alan Guthmacher Institute, 1994.

Halberstam, David. *The Fifties*. New York: Fawcett-Columbine, 1993.

Kane, Joseph N. *Facts About the Presidents*. New York: H. W. Wilson, 1993.

Krantz, Les. *American Architects*. New York: Facts On File, 1989.

———. *American Artists: An Illustrated Survey of Contemporary Americans*. New York: Facts On File, 1985.

Ludlum, David M. *The American Weather Book*. Boston: Houghton Mifflin, 1982.

Miller, E. Willard and Miller, Ruby M. *Energy and American Society*. Santa Barbara, Calif.: ABC–CLIO, 1993.

Miller, William H. *The Last Transatlantic Liners*. London: Conway Maritime Press, 1985.

———. *Transatlantic Liners 1945–1980*. New York: Dover Publications, 1981.

Old Cars Publications. *Standard Catalogue of American Cars 1946–1975*. Iola, Wis.: Old Cars Publications, 1976.

Osborne, Robert A. *65 Years of the Oscars: The Official History of the Academy Awards*. New York: Abbeville Press, 1994.

Phillips, Kevin. *Boiling Point: Democrats, Republicans and the Decline of the Middle Class*. New York: Random House, 1993.

———. *The Politics of the Rich and Poor*. New York: Random House, 1990.

Polmar, Norman. *The Naval Institute Guide to the Ships and Aircraft of the U.S. Fleet*. Annapolis, Md.: Naval Institute Press, 1993.

Maddocks, Melvin. *The Seafarers: The Great Liners*. Alexandria, Va.: Time-Life Books, 1978.

Prevention Magazine. *Prevention's Giant Book of Health Facts*. Emmaus, Pa.: Rodale Press, 1991.

Norback, Craig T. *Chilton's Complete Book of Automotive Facts*. Radnor, Pa.: Chilton Book Co., 1981.

Prince, Stephen. *A New Pot of Gold: Hollywood Under the Electronic Rainbow 1980–1989*. New York: Charles Scribner's Sons, 2000.

Princeton Religion Research Center. *Religion in America, 1990*. Princeton, N.J.: Princeton University Press, 1990.

Rubin, Eva R. *The Abortion Controversy, A Documentary History*. Westport, Conn.: Greenwood Press, 1994.

Schatz, Thomas. *Boom and Bust: The American Cinema in the 1940s*. New York: Charles Scribner's Sons, 1997.

Schwartz, Bernard. *A History of the Supreme Court*. New York: Oxford University Press, 1993.

Stimpson, Catharine. *Women and the "Equal Rights" Amendment: Senate Subcommittee Hearings on the Constitutional Amendment, 91st Congress*. New York: R.R. Bowker Company, 1972.

Stockholm International Peace Research Institute. *SIPRI Yearbook, 1991: World Armaments and Disarmament*. New York: Humanities Press, 1991.

Summers, Harrison B. *A Thirty Year History of Programs Carried on National Radio Networks in the United States, 1926–1956*. New York: Arno Press, 1971.

Stanley, Harold W., and Niemi, Richard G. *Vital Statistics on American Politics*. Washington, D.C.: Congressional Quarterly Press, 1992.

Wood, Paul, Frascina, Francis, Harris, Jonathan, and Harrison, Charles. *Modernism in Dispute: Art Since the Forties*. New Haven, Conn.: Yale University Press, 1993.

Utter, Glenn H., and Storey, John W. *The Religious Right*. Santa Barbara, Calif.: ABC–CLIO, 1995.

Von Bencke, Matthew J. *The Politics of Space: A History of U.S.—Soviet/Russian Competition and Cooperation in Space*. Boulder, Colo.: Westview Press, 1997.

Zimbalist, Andrew. *Baseball and Billions*. New York: Basic Books, 1992.

APPENDIX: List of Tables

Index

This index is arranged alphabetically letter by letter. Page numbers in *italic* indicate illustrations or captions. Page numbers followed by *t* indicate tables, by *m* indicate maps, by *n* indicate notes, and by **b** indicate biographical profiles.

China (continued)
  immigration 22t, 23t, 24t
  merchant fleets 160t
  nuclear explosions 301t
  as trade partner 94t
  U.S. students from 387t
  weapons exported by 299t
China "White paper" 268
Chinese Americans
  illegitimate births 181t
  population 6t, 15, 15t, 16t
  total arrests 576t–577t
Chinese Civil War 267–268, 270
Chippewa Indians 313
Chisholm, Shirley 58, 243t, 244t
chlordane 425t
chlorine 423t
Choctaw Indians 305, 318
Christian and Missionary Alliance
  224t, 226t
Christian Church (Disciples of
  Christ) 224t, 225t, 226t
Christian Churches and Churches
  of Christ 225t
Christian Congregation 226t
Christianity 222–230, 226t
Christian Methodist Episcopal
  Church 225t
Christian Reformed Church in
  North America 225t
Christian Science Monitor 174t
Christmas, odds of white 44t–46t
chromium 95t
chronic obstructive pulmonary
  diseases, deaths from 197t–198t
Chrysler Building (New York)
  449t
Chrysler Motors Corporation 63,
  64, 74t, 136, 141, 402t
Chryssa 441
Chula Vista, Calif. 329t
Church, Frank 61, 266t, 309
Church, Marguerite S. 243t
Churchill, Winston 48, 314
Churches of Christ 225t
Church of Christ, Scientist 226t
Church of God (Anderson, Ind.)
  224t, 226t
Church of God (Cleveland, Tenn.)
  224t, 225t
Church of God in Christ 225t
Church of God in Christ,
  International 225t
Church of Jesus Christ of Latter-
  day Saints 224t, 225t
Church of the Brethren 224t,
  226t
Church of the Nazarene 224t,
  226t
Church of the Scientology 222
church-related schools 393t
Church's Fried Chicken 437t
CIA. See Central Intelligence
  Agency
Ciba-Geigy Corp. 402t

cigarettes 203, 214, 214t–216t,
  221t
  chronology 56, 60
  high school senior survey on
    220t
Cincinnati, Ohio
  population 327t, 330t
  water transport 159t
  weather and climate 30t, 32t,
    33t, 35t, 46t
Cincinnati Art Museum 443t
Cincinnati Enquirer 173t
Cincinnati-Hamilton metropolitan
  area 8t, 13t, 331t
Cincinnati Redlegs 509
Cincinnati Reds 509
CinemaScope 51
CIO 104. See also AFL-CIO
Cisneros, Henry G. 338
Citicorp Center (New York) 449t
cities and urban areas 326–338.
  See also metropolitan areas;
  suburban areas; specific cities
    air pollution 418
    population 3t, 10t, 11t, 14t
    sexual behavior/attitudes 188t
    in specific states. See specific
      state
    tobacco smoking 215t
    transportation 147t, 157
    women in elective offices 243t
Cities Services 73t
citizens band (CB) radio 62
City Art Museum (St. Louis, Mo.)
  443t
City College of San Francisco
  386t
City Spire (New York) 449t
Civil Aeronautics Board 148
Civiletti, Benjamin R. 235t
Civil Rights Act (1964) 56, 249,
  597–598
  Civil Rights movement 248
  education 374
  and employment 98
  Heart of Atlanta Motel v. United
    States (1964) 252
  United States v. Weber and other
    cases (1979) 252
  voting rights 245
Civil Rights Act (1965) 245, 248
Civil Rights movement 9,
  248–250
  on campuses 379
  chronology 53, 55, 56, 57, 68
  Martin Luther King, Jr.
    345–346b
  Malcolm X 347b
  Thurgood Marshall 347–348
  in Mississippi 314
  in North Carolina 54, 317
  politics and government 231,
    232
  Jackie Robinson 352b
  and school segregation 374

in Tennessee 321
  George C. Wallace 355b
civil service 247t
Claremont McKenna College
  399t
Clark, Barney 64, 204
Clark, Douglas 582t
Clark, Mark W. 269
Clark, Ramsey 234t
Clark, Tom C. 234t, 250
Clark, William P., Jr. 235t, 266t
Clark County, Nev. 332t
Clay, Cassius Marcellus 56, 565.
  See also Ali, Muhammad
Clay, William L. 244t
Clay County, Fla. 332t
Clayton, N.Mex. 45t
Clean Air Act (1963) 417, 418
Clean Air Act (1972) 418, 424t
Clean Water Act (1987) 418, 424t
Cleave, Mary L. 411t
Clements, Earle 240t
clerical workers 127t
Cleveland, Ohio
  population 11t, 327t, 328t,
    330t
  school desegregation 374
  water transport 159t
  weather and climate 30t, 32t,
    33t, 35t, 46t
Cleveland-Akron-Lorain
  metropolitan area 13t, 330t
Cleveland-Akron metropolitan
  area 8t
Cleveland Browns 533
Cleveland metropolitan area
  422t, 423t
Cleveland Museum of Art 443t
Cleveland Plain Dealer 173t
Cleveland Press 173t
Cliburn, Van 53
Clifford, Clark 234t, 266t
Clift, Montgomery 452, 456
clock radios, sales of 169t
closed-circuit television 565
clothes washers and dryers 131t,
  431, 432t, 433, 433t
CNN. See Cable News Network
Coach of the Year Award (women's
  basketball) 526t
Coahuiltec Indians 338
coal 80, 81t–82t, 82t, 83t, 84t
  mining 86
  strip-mining 83, 426
Coast to Coast Total Hardware 76t
Coats, Michael L. 409t
cobalt 95t
Cobb County, Ga. 332t
Coca-Cola 131t, 433
  chronology 62, 65
  largest American businesses
    74t
  as leading market value stock
    79t
  television commercial 478

cocaine 66, 216, 217t, 218t,
  221t, 587, 588
Coelho, Anthony Lee 240t, 244t
Coeur d'Alene Indians 309
coffee 435t
Cohan, George M. 320
Cohen, Wilbur, J. 234t
coke oven emissions 419t
Colby, William E. 267t
Cold Bay, Alaska 44t
cold war 222, 263–264,
  302–303. See also foreign policy
Cole, Nat "King" 49, 57, 214,
  304, 478
Coleman, William T. 235t
collar (baseball term) 519
College of Du Page 385t
College of William and Mary 399t
colleges and universities 378–399
  costs of 388, 389t–392t
  degrees conferred by 388,
    394t–399t
  faculty of 388, 392t–393t
  fields of study 388
  rules of conduct in 383–384
  tuition and fees 130t
college sports 505
  baseball 546t
  basketball 521–522
  champions 546t–551t,
    551t–552t
  cross country 549t, 551t
  fencing 550t–551t, 551t
  field hockey 551t
  football 540–546
  golf 550t, 551t
  gymnastics 550t, 552t
  ice hockey 546t–547t
  indoor track 549t–550t, 552t
  lacrosse 547t, 552t
  outdoor track 549t, 552t
  rifle 551t
  skiing 551t
  soccer 547t, 552t
  softball 552t
  swimming and diving 548t,
    552t
  tennis 547t–548t, 552t
  volleyball 548t, 552t
  water polo 548t
  wrestling 548t–549t
Collier's 172, 495
Collin County, Tex. 332t
Collins, Cardiss R. 243t, 244t
Collins, George W. 244t
Collins, John N. 582t
Collins, Michael 58, 408t
Collins Foods Intl., Inc. 437t
Colombia
  foreign-born U.S. population
    from 27t
  immigration from 22t, 23t
  in Korean War 269t
  population 6t
  Rio Treaty 289m

Hawaii *(continued)*
  prison inmates 579*t*
  transportation
    airplane accident 151;
      import cars 144*t*; rural/
      urban road mileage 147*t*
    U.S. armed forces in 278*t*
Hawaiian Airline 153*t*
Hawaiian Americans 16*t*
Hawaiian Patriot oil spill 87*t*
Hawkins, Augustus F. 244*t*
Hawkins, Paula 242*t*
Hawk missiles 415*t*
Hawley, Steven A. 409*t*, 411*t*
hay 122*t*
Hayes, Charles A. 244*t*
Hayes, Gabby 459
Hays, Will 457
Hayward, Susan 214
hazardous waste 418, 427–429
HBO. *See* Home Box Office
health care 202–221, 203, 207
  and air pollutants 419*t*
  consumer price index 128*t*
  costs of 202–203, 207–210
  diseases 200*t*–202*t*
  expenditures on 208*t*–210*t*,
    259*t*
  federal expenditures for 254*t*
  medical care/providers
    202–207
  Medicare 210–213
  state expenditures for 258*t*
  substance use and abuse
    214–221
health foods 433
health impaired students 361*t*
Health magazine 174*t*
health science degrees awarded
  396*t*–398*t*
hearing aids 431
Hearns, Thomas 565
Hearst, Patricia 61
Hearst newspapers 172
heart diseases 54, 197*t*–198*t*
heart-lung machine 203
heart-lung transplants 206*t*
*Heart of Atlanta Motel v. United
  States* (1964) 252
heart transplants 204, 206*t*
heart valve implants 207*t*
heat index 30*t*
heating, type of 82*t*
heavy metal bands 478
Heckler, Margaret 235*t*, 243*t*
Heimlich maneuver 61
Heisman Trophy 544*t*
Helena, Mont. 45*t*
helicopters, military 280, 294*t*,
  295*t*
Hellman, Lillian 214
Hell's Canyon 309
Helms, Jesse 317
Helms, Richard M. 267*t*
Helmsley, Leona 68

Helsinki Summit 300*t*
Hemingway, Ernest 55, 309
Hendrix, Jimi 324
Henkel KGAA 402*t*
Henry Clay (submarine) 285*t*
Henry County, Ga. 332*t*
Henry L. Stimson (submarine)
  285*t*
Henry M. Jackson (submarine) 286*t*
Henson, Jim 53, 68
hepatitis B 204
Hepburn, Katharine 307
Heptachlor 425*t*
herbicides 424*t*
Hernando County, Fla. 332*t*
heroin 217*t*, 218*t*
Herrington, John S. 235*t*
Hershey, Barbara 452
Hershey, Lewis B. 275
Herter, Christian A. 234*t*, 266*t*
Hewlett-Packard Co. 74*t*, 402*t*
Hialeah, Fla. 328*t*
Hickel, Walter 234*t*, 304
Hicks, Louise Day 243*t*
higher education. *See* colleges and
  universities
High Museum of Art (Atlanta,
  Ga.) 443*t*
high school dropouts 361*t*
high school seniors
  behavior/perception trends in
    220*t*
  and drug use 588*t*–589*t*
Highway Beautification Law
  (1965) 418
highways. *See* roads, streets, and
  highways
Hillary, Edmund 51
Hillenkoetter, Roscoe H. 267*t*
Hill, Lister 240*t*
Hills, Carla A. 235*t*
Hillsboro Light, Fla. 37*t*
Hilmers, David C. 409*t*, 411*t*
Hilo, Hawaii 17*t*
Hinckley, John, Jr. 64
hip-hop 478
hip joints, artificial 207*t*
Hirshhorn, Joseph 57
Hispanic Americans 19, 69
  AIDS cases 200*t*
  in armed forces 278*t*
  birth rates 178
  "born-again" status of 229*t*
  children's living arrangements
    194*t*
  cigarette/drug use by 221*t*
  in Congress 244*t*
  divorce 192*t*
  economy
    below poverty level 114*t*;
    earnings and income
    107; employment of
    women 102*t*; median
    earnings of 109*t*; median
    household income of

110*t*; per capita income
  of 110*t*; poverty 113
education 356
  college completion 395*t*;
  college enrollment
  382*t*; level of
  359*t*–361*t*, 376*t*
family and nonfamily households 194*t*
fertility rates 180*t*
illegitimate births 178, 181*t*
immigration 21
interracial marriages 191*t*
literature by 495
marital status 192*t*
in metropolitan populations
  330*t*–331*t*
population 6, 7*t*–9*t*, 17,
  17*t*–18*t*, 20*m*
as prison inmates 579*t*
sexual behavior and attitudes
  188*t*–189*t*
in sports 506*t*, 507, 507*t*
voting by 246*t*
Hiss, Alger 48
historic preservation 447
history
  pre–cold war. *See specific cities;
    specific states*
  Pulitzer Prize in 502*t*
Hitachi 402*t*
HIV infection, deaths from
  197*t*–198*t*
Hmong Americans 16*t*
Ho, Don 308
Hobby, Oveta Culp 51, 234*t*
Hobby Airport (Texas) 38*t*
hockey 64, 562–565, 574
Hodel, Donald P. 235*t*
Hodges, Luther H. 234*t*
Hodgkin's disease 200*t*
Hodgson, James D. 234*t*
Hoechst A.G. 402*t*
Hoechst Celanese Corp. 402*t*
Hoffa, James 53, 61
Hoffman, Dustin 67
Hoffman, Jeffrey A. 409*t*
Hofmann, Hans 443*t*
hogs and swine 118*t*, 120*t*–121*t*,
  122*t*
Hohokam Indians 337
Holden, William 452
Holiday, Billie 54, 312
Holiday Inns 50, 75*t*
Holiness Churches 226*t*
Holland-America Line 160*t*,
  162
Holliday, Judy 214
Hollings, Ernest 320
Holly, Buddy 54
Holt, Marjorie S. 243*t*
Holtzman, Elizabeth 243*t*
Home & Away 174*t*
Home Box Office (HBO) 60,
  163, 468

home health agencies, Medicare
  and 212*t*
Home Lines 161
Home magazine 174*t*
Home Mechanix 174*t*
home pesticide use 424*t*
homes
  deaths in 199*t*
  electronic equipment in 171*t*
  median sales price 130*t*
home-schooling 357
homicide 197*t*–198*t*
  chronology 57, 64
  crime 575*t*, 581–583,
    581*t*–583*t*, 584*t*
homosexuality 187, 190*t*
  Bowers v. Hardwick (1986) 252
  chronology 61, 62
  defined as mental illness 61
  in literature 495
Honda Motor Co., Ltd. 64, 141,
  402*t*
Honduras 27*t*, 97*t*, 279*t*, 289*m*,
  298*t*, 387*t*
Honest John missiles 415*t*
Honeywell Inc. 402*t*
Hong Kong
  educational comparisons 372*t*
  foreign-born U.S. population
    from 27*t*
  immigration 22*t*, 23*t*, 24*t*
  life expectancy 196*t*
  population 6*t*
  as trade partner 94*t*
  U.S. investments in 97*t*
  U.S. students from 387*t*
Honolulu, Hawaii 17*t*, 30*t*, 32*t*,
  33*t*, 34*t*, 159*t*, 327*t*
Honolulu airport 152*t*
Honolulu metropolitan area 17*t*,
  331*t*
hook (baseball term) 519
Hoover, Herbert 310
Hoover, J. Edgar 60
Hope, Bob 318, 341–342*b*, 466
Hope Diamond 54
Hopewell County, Va. 333*t*
Hopi Indians 304
Hopper, Dennis 311
Hopper, Edward 443*t*
Horizon Air Airline 153*t*
Hormel Meatpacking 105
Hornet (aircraft carrier) 283*t*
horse racing 61, 311, 561–574
hospices, Medicare and 212*t*
hospitals
  federal expenditures for 254*t*
  Medicare spending and 212*t*
  vital statistics and health care
    202, 204*t*–205*t*
    cost of care 207; drug-
      related emergencies 218*t*
hostage crisis, Iran 63, 64, 66,
  236, 296
hot box (baseball term) 519

white Americans (*continued*)
    family and nonfamily households 194*t*
    female householders with families 193*t*
    fertility rates 180*t*
    illegitimate births 178–179, 180*t*, 181*t*
    infant mortality rate 182*t*
    interracial marriage 190, 191*t*
    life expectancy 196*t*
    live births 178*t*
    marital status 192*t*
    medical device implants 207*t*
    persons without health insurance 213*t*
    population 1*t*–2*t*, 3, 6, 6*t*–10*t*
    pregnancy outcomes 186*t*
    in professional sports 506*t*, 507*t*
    religious beliefs 223*t*, 229*t*
    sexual behavior and attitudes 188*t*–189*t*
    southern states voter registration 245*t*–246*t*
    tobacco smoking 215*t*, 216*t*
    voting by 246*t*
white Christmas, odds of 44*t*–46*t*
Whitman, Charles 57
Whitmire, Katherine 335
Whitney Museum of American Art (New York, N.Y.) 443*t*
Whittaker, Charles E. 250
Whitworth, Katy 558
wholesale trade
    earnings in 107*t*, 108*t*
    employment in 99*t*
Wichita, Kans. 30*t*, 32*t*–34*t*, 45*t*, 327*t*
Wichita Eagle 174*t*
Wichita metropolitan area 331*t*
Wiesel, Elie 66
Wiggins, James Russell 266*t*
Wilder, L. Douglas 68, 250
Wilderness Act (1964) 418
Wiley, Alexander 266*t*
William H. Fogg Art Museum (Cambridge, Mass.) 443*t*
Williams, Donald E. 409*t*, 411*t*
Williams, Hank 304, 478
Williams, Tennessee 314
Williams, Vanessa 65
Williams, Wayne 64, 582*t*
Williamsburg Bridge 449*t*
Williams College 399*t*
Williamson County, Tenn. 332*t*
Williamson County, Tex. 332*t*
Williamsport, Pa. 46*t*, 520
Williston, N.Dak. 46*t*
Will Rogers (submarine) 285*t*

Wilmington, Del. 11*t*, 30*t*, 32*t*, 33*t*, 34*t*, 45*t*
Wilmington, N.C. 37*t*, 45*t*
Wilmington News Journal 174*t*
Wilson, Charles E. 234*t*, 266*t*
Wilson, Woodrow (War Message) 177
Wimbledon. *See* British Open
wind-chill 30*t*
wind speed 32*t*–33*t*, 42*t*
wind strength 42*t*
Winecoff Hotel (Atlanta, Ga.) 48
wine coolers 433
Winfrey, Oprah 314
Winn-Dixie 74*t*
Winnebago Indians 324
Winnemucca, Nev. 45*t*
Winslow, Ariz. 44*t*
Winston, Harry 54
Winston Cup Series 570, 571*t*
Winston-Salem, N.C. 45*t*
Wirtz, W. Willard 234*t*
Wisconsin 324–325
    alcoholic purchase age 218*t*
    arts funding 441*t*
    economy
        agricultural output 121*t*; farm income 124*t*; farms 116*t*; Japanese-owned manufacturing plants 96*t*; personal income 111*t*
    education 363*t*, 367*t*
    hazardous waste sites 428*t*, 429*t*
    import cars 144*t*
    population 5*t*
        American Indian 15*t*; Hispanic origin 8*t*, 18*t*; percent increase in 2*m*; by race 8*t*
    prison inmates 579*t*
    rural/urban road mileage 147*t*
    tornadoes 40*t*
Wisconsin Evangelical Lutheran Synod 224*t*, 225*t*
Wm. Preston Lane Jr. Bridge 449*t*
Wolff, Nelson 338
Woman and Bicycle (Willem de Kooning) 441
Woman's Armed Forces Integration Act (1948) 277
Woman's Day 174*t*, 175*t*
Woman's World 174*t*
women. *See* females
Women's Basketball Coaches Association awards 526*t*
women's movement
    abortion rights 184
    Betty Friedan 341*b*
    politics and government 231

Senate Hearings on an Equal Rights Amendment, May 7, 1970 602–603
    and sexual behavior/attitudes 187
Wonder, Stevie 55
wood 82*t*
Wood, Grant 310
Wood, Natalie 64, 452
Wood, Robert C. 234*t*
Wood, Sam 465
Wooden, John 521, *522*, 525, *525*
Woodhouse, Chase G. 243*t*
Woodrow Wilson (submarine) 285*t*
Woodstock music festival 58
Woodward, Bob 236
Woodward, Joanne 308, 452
wool 122*t*
Woolworth 54, 74*t*, 248, *249*
Worcester Art Museum (Mass.) 443*t*
Worcester, Mass. 45*t*
Worcester Telegram & Gazette 174*t*
Worden, Alfred M. 409*t*
word processor 413
Workbasket, The 174*t*
Workbench 174*t*
Working Woman 174*t*
work-related deaths 199*t*
work stoppages (labor) 106*t*
Worldcom 167*t*
World Glory oil spill 87*t*
World Heavyweight Championships 567*t*
World Hockey Association 562
World Series 512*t*
World Series, Little League 520
World Trade Center (New York) 59, 447, 449*t*
Wounded Knee, S.D. 61, 321
Wozniak, Stephen 412, 414
wrestling 548*t*–549*t*
Wright, Frank Lloyd 54, 324, 442, 448*t*
Wright, Jim 239*t*, 240*t*
Wrigley Field (Chicago) 67
Wurster, William 448*t*
Wyandot Indians 318, 335, 337
Wyeth, Andrew 442, 443*t*
Wyoming 325
    alcoholic purchase age 218*t*
    arts funding 441*t*
    economy
        agricultural output 121*t*; farm income 124*t*; farms 116*t*; Japanese-owned manufacturing plants 96*t*; personal income 111*t*; right-to-work laws 105*t*

    education 363*t*, 367*t*
    hazardous waste sites 429*t*
    population 5*t*
        American Indian 15*t*; Hispanic origin 8*t*, 18*t*, 20*m*; percent increase in 2*m*; by race 8*t*
    prisoners executed 585*t*
    prison inmates 579*t*
    rural/urban road mileage 147*t*
Wyoming (submarine) 286*t*

X

Xerox Corp. 74*t*, 402*t*

Y

Yakima, Wash. 46*t*
Yale University 59, 388, 399*t*
Yamasaki, Minoru 448*t*
Yankee 174*t*
Yeager, Chuck 48, 324
Yegorov, Boris B. 408*t*
Yeliseyev, Aleksei S. 408*t*
Yellowstone National Park 325
Yeltsin, Boris 68
Yeutter, Clayton K. 235*t*
YM 174*t*
Yonkers, N.Y. 328*t*
Yo Picasso (Pablo Picasso) 444*t*
Yorktown (aircraft carrier) 283*t*
Yost, Charles W. 266*t*
Young, Andrew 244*t*, 266*t*, 308
Young, Coleman A. 337
Young, John W. 408*t*, 409*t*
Young, Loretta 322
Youngstown, Ohio 46*t*
Youngstown-Warren metropolitan area 331*t*
Yugoslavia
    educational comparisons 371*t*, 372*t*
    immigration 22*t*, 23*t*, 24*t*
    legal abortions 185*t*
    life expectancy 196*t*
    Marshall Plan aid 265*t*
    U.S. students from 387*t*
Yuma, Ariz. 44*t*
yuppies 65

Z

Zaire 24*t*, 298*t*, 581*t*
Zale, Tony 565
Zambia 298*t*
Zantop Airline 153*t*
Zimbabwe 298*t*
Zim Lines 162
zip code system 163